MW01115495

The FIDIC Red Book Contract: An International Clause-by-Clause Commentary

Christopher R. Seppälä

with the assistance of Dimitar Kondev

Incorporating the amendments in the 2022 reprint of the Red Book

Forewords by the former President of FIDIC and Sir Vivian Ramsey

The FIDIC Red Book Contract: An International Clause-by-Clause Commentary

Christopher R. Seppälä

with the assistance of Dimitar Kondev

Incorporating the amendments in the 2022 reprint of the Red Book

Forewords by the former President of FIDIC and Sir Vivian Ramsey

Published by:
Kluwer Law International B.V.
PO Box 316
2400 AH Alphen aan den Rijn
The Netherlands
E-mail: lrs-sales@wolterskluwer.com
Website: www.wolterskluwer.com/en/solutions/kluwerlawinternational

Sold and distributed by:
Wolters Kluwer Legal & Regulatory U.S.
920 Links Avenue
Landisville, PA 17538
United States of America
E-mail: customer.service@wolterskluwer.com

Printed on acid-free paper.

ISBN 978-94-035-2060-5

e-Book: ISBN 978-94-035-2063-6
web-PDF: ISBN 978-94-035-2070-4

Printed in the Netherlands.

Disclaimer

This book presents solely the author's views. It does not purport to present the views of any firm, body or organisation with whom he is, or has been, associated. While the author has exercised reasonable care in preparing it, neither the author nor any firm, body or organisation with which he is, or has been, associated nor the publisher can accept any responsibility for any errors or omissions or their consequences.

--ooOOoo--

To My Family

About the Author

Christopher R. Seppälä is one of the world's leading legal experts on FIDIC contracts who, for more than 30 years, has been Legal/Special Adviser to, or member of, the FIDIC Contracts Committee ('CC'). A former Vice-President Emeritus of the International Court of Arbitration of the ICC, Seppälä currently serves as FIDIC's Observer on that Court and is Dean of the Faculty of Contracts of FIDIC Academy, FIDIC's learning and development body. He has written over 80 articles on various construction or international arbitration topics, many dealing with FIDIC and teaches international construction law at Paris University II (Panthéon-Assas). Ranked as a 'Global Elite Thought Leader' for construction in Europe by *Who's Who Legal,* he is listed as a leading lawyer in international arbitration by *Legal 500 Paris* and *Who's Who Legal.*

For details on Seppälä's experience, see below:

For many years Seppälä has represented or advised international contractors, architects and engineering firms as well as sovereign states or state-owned entities in international arbitrations and has served on, or chaired, numerous international arbitral tribunals.

From 1985 to 1989, as Chairman of an International Bar Association ('IBA') Subcommittee on FIDIC contracts, he assisted FIDIC's CC[1] in the preparation of the fourth edition of the FIDIC Red Book, published in 1987.

In 1988, he founded the international arbitration practice of the Paris office of White & Case, one of the leading practices in the field today in France.

1. Then called Civil Engineering Contracts Committee or 'CECC'.

From 1992 to 2009, he was a member of the CC and served as a member of, and legal adviser to, FIDIC's Update Task Group which prepared the 1999 editions of the Red, Yellow and Silver Books.

In 1999 he received FIDIC's highest award for meritorious service, the Louis Prangey Award.

As Legal Adviser to the CC since 1999, he has advised it on the preparation of the:

- *FIDIC Procurement Procedures Guide* published in 2011;
- 2017 editions of the Red, Yellow and Silver Books;
- *Conditions of Contract for Tunnelling and Underground Works* (the 'Emerald Book') published in 2019;
- *Conditions of Subcontract for Plant and Design-Build* also published in 2019 (being the form of subcontract to go with the 1999 Yellow Book);
- second edition of the *Short Form of Contract* ('Green Book') published in 2021;
- second edition of *The FIDIC Contracts Guide* published in 2022; and
- *Conditions of Contract for Operate, Design, Build and Operate Projects* ('Bronze Book') (forthcoming).

He was a Member of the Working Group which prepared the UNIDROIT Principles of International Commercial Contracts 2016 and Co-Chair of the Committee which produced the 2019 update of the ICC Commission's Report on Construction Industry Arbitrations: Recommended Tools and Techniques for Effective Management.

He was born and schooled in England, is a graduate of Harvard College and Columbia Law School in the U.S.A. and a member of the New York and Paris Bars. He is a Partner of Counsel at White & Case, Paris and serves as an independent arbitrator and mediator in international arbitrations and as an independent expert on international construction contracts.

--ooOOoo--

Table of Contents

--ooOOoo--

List of Appendices

--ooOOoo--

List of Figures

--ooOOoo--

List of Tables

--ooOOoo--

List of Abbreviations and Definitions

In this Commentary, use is made of the defined terms in Clause 1 of the Red Book, 2017, reprinted in 2022 with amendments, ('RB/17'), each word of which generally begins with a capital letter. Use is also made of the following abbreviations or definitions (some of which are provided for in Clause 1).

ABA	American Bar Association, Chicago, IL, USA
ABA For Const L	ABA Forum on Construction Law
ACE	Association of Consulting Engineers, UK
AFNOR	*Association française de normalisation* [French national standards association]
AFNOR form	*Cahier des Clauses Administratives Générales applicable aux travaux de génie civil faisant l'objet de Marchés Privés* [General conditions of contract for civil engineering works for private works contract] NF P 03-002, 3 October 2014 published by *l'Association Française de Normalisation* ('AFNOR'), the French standards association [The main French standard form for non-public/private civil works]
AIA	American Institute of Architects, Washington, DC, USA
ALI	American Law Institute, Philadelphia, PA, USA
Am Rev Int'l Arb	The American Review of International Arbitration, JurisNet, USA
Arb Int'l	Arbitration International, OUP, UK
Art. (art.)	Article

ASA Bull	Bulletin of the Swiss Arbitration Association ('ASA')
Bailey	Julian Bailey, *Construction Law*, 3 vols (3rd edn, London Publishing, UK, 2020)
BGB	*Bürgerliches Gesetzbuch* [German Civil Code]
BLR	Building Law Reports, UK
Cass ch mixte	French Court of Cassation, Mixed Chamber
Cass civ	French Court of Cassation, Civil Chamber
Cass com	French Court of Cassation, Commercial and Financial Chamber
CC	FIDIC Contracts Committee
CE	*See* 'Council of State' below
CECC	FIDIC Civil Engineering Contracts Committee [predecessor of the 'CC']
CIArb	Chartered Institute of Arbitrators, UK
CISG	*United Nations Convention on Contracts for the International Sale of Goods*, 1980
CLInt	Construction Law International, IBA, UK
Coll ICC Arb Awards	*Collection of ICC Arbitration Awards*, Kluwer L Int'l and ICC Services, Paris
Conditions or General Conditions	General Conditions of RB/17
Const L	The Construction Lawyer, ABA Forum on the Construction Industry, ABA, USA
Const LJ	Construction Law Journal, London
COPA	The World Bank's *Conditions of Particular Application* (or *Particular Conditions*) for use with RB/17, issued in 2019
Council of State (*Conseil d'Etat*) or 'CE'	Highest court in the French administrative law system
Court of Cassation (*Cour de Cassation*) or 'Cass.'	Highest court in the French civil law system
DAAB	Dispute Avoidance/Adjudication Board
DAAB Agreement	Dispute Avoidance/Adjudication Board Agreement
DAAB GCs or GCs	General Conditions of DAAB Agreement, which are incorporated by reference into the DAAB Agreement
DAAB Rules	DAAB Procedural Rules, which are attached as an Annex to the DAAB GCs
DAB	Dispute Adjudication Board

D&D Protocol	*Delay and Disruption Protocol*, 2nd edn, 2017, SCL
Demand Guarantee	A guarantee payable on demand and issued normally by a bank
DNP	Defects Notification Period
DRB	Dispute Review Board
EA	Emergency Arbitrator under ICC Arbitration Rules
EIC	European International Contractors, Berlin
Emerald Book	*FIDIC's Conditions of Contract for Underground Works*, 2019
ENAA	Engineering Advancement Association of Japan, Tokyo
EOT	Extension of Time
EU	European Union
FAR	*Federal Acquisition Regulation*, available in Title 48, Code of Federal Regulations ('C.F.R.'), USA
FCEC	Federation of Civil Engineering Contractors, UK
FIDIC	*FIDIC's Fédération Internationale des Ingénieurs Conseils* (International Federation of Consulting Engineers), Geneva, Switzerland
FIDIC Contract, contract or form	A contract based on the Red Book, Yellow Book or Silver Book
fn(s)	Footnote(s)
FPC	Final Payment Certificate
FS	Final Statement
Gold Book or GB/08	*FIDIC's Conditions of Contract for Design, Build and Operate Projects*, 2008
GCs or DAAB GCs	General Conditions of DAAB Agreement
Green Book	*FIDIC's Short Form of Contract*, 1st edn 1999 or 2nd edn, 2021
Guidance	*Guidance for the Preparation of Particular Conditions* of RB/17
HGCRA	*Housing Grants, Construction and Regeneration Act 1996*, as amended, UK
Hudson	Atkin Chambers, *Hudson's Building and Engineering Contracts* (14th edn, Sweet & Maxwell, London, 2020)
IBA	International Bar Association, London
ICC	International Chamber of Commerce, Paris

ICCA	International Council for Commercial Arbitration, The Hague, the Netherlands
ICC Arbitration Rules or 'ICC Rules'	Rules of Arbitration of the International Chamber of Commerce
ICC Court	International Court of Arbitration of the International Chamber of Commerce, Paris
ICC Ct Arb Bull	ICC Court of Arbitration Bulletin, Paris
ICC Disp Resol Bull	ICC Dispute Resolution Bulletin (as from 2015, successor of ICC Ct. Arb. Bull), Paris
ICE	Institution of Civil Engineers, UK
IChemE	Institution of Chemical Engineers, UK
ICLQ	International Comparative Law Quarterly, London
ICLR	The International Construction Law Review, London
ICSID Convention	*Convention on the Settlement of Investment Disputes between States and Nationals of other States*, 1965
ILO	International Labour Organisation, Geneva, Switzerland
ILM	International Legal Materials, American Society of International Law, Washington D.C.
Int'l Bus L	International Business Lawyer, IBA, London
IPC	Interim Payment Certificate
J. Int'l Arb.	Journal of International Arbitration, Kluwer L Int'l, the Netherlands
J. Int'l Disp. Settl.	Journal of International Dispute Settlement, OUP, UK
JV	Joint Venture
Keating	Stephen Furst and the Hon. Sir Vivian Ramsey, *Keating on Construction Contracts* (11th edn, Sweet & Maxwell, London, 2021)
Kluwer L Int'l	Kluwer Law International, the Netherlands
McGill J Disp Resol	McGill Journal of Dispute Resolution
MDB(s)	Multilateral Development Bank(s)
NEC	*New Engineering Contract*, UK, of which there have been several editions, most recently NEC4 (2017)
NOD	Notice of Dissatisfaction
New York Convention	*Convention on the Recognition and Enforcement of Foreign Arbitral Awards*, 1958
Old GCs	General Conditions of Dispute Adjudication Agreement in RB/99

Old Rules	DAB Procedural Rules annexed to the General Conditions of Dispute Adjudication Agreement in RB/99
Orange Book or OB	*FIDIC's Conditions of Contract for Design-Build and Turnkey*, 1st edn (1995)
OUP	Oxford University Press, UK
PAFS	Partially Agreed Final Statement
Para. (para.)	Paragraph
Paris J. Int'l Arb.	The Paris Journal of International Arbitration, France
PECL	*The Principles of European Contract Law 2002, Parts I, II and III*
Pink Book	*FIDIC's Conditions of Contract for Construction MDB (Multilateral Development Bank) Harmonised Edition for Building and Engineering Works Designed by the Employer*, 2010
Rainbow Suite	Red, Yellow and Silver Books, 1999 or 2017
Red Book or RB	*FIDIC's Conditions of Contract for Construction*, 2017 (or any predecessor edition)
RB/57	*FIDIC's Conditions of Contract (International) for Works of Civil Engineering Construction with Forms of Tender and Agreement*, 1st edn (1957)
RB/69	*FIDIC's Conditions of Contract (International) for Works of Civil Engineering Construction with Forms of Tender and Agreement*, 2nd edn (1969)
RB/77	*FIDIC's Conditions of Contract (International) for Works of Civil Engineering Construction with Forms of Tender and Agreement*, 3rd edn (1977)
RB/87	*FIDIC's Conditions of Contract for Works of Civil Engineering Construction*, 4th edn (1987)
RB/99	*FIDIC's Conditions of Contract for Construction for Building and Engineering Works Designed by the Employer*, 1st edn (1999)
RB/17	*FIDIC's Conditions of Contract for Construction for Building and Engineering Works Designed by the Employer*, 2nd edn (2017), reprinted in 2022 with amendments

RDAI/IBLJ	*Revue de Droit des Affaires Internationales* / International Business Law Journal, Paris
Rev. arb.	*Revue de l'arbitrage*, Paris
Rome I Regulation	European Council Regulation no 593/2008 on the law applicable to contractual obligations
S or s (ss)[1]	Section (sections)
Silver Book or SB	*FIDIC's Conditions of Contract for EPC/Turnkey Projects*, 2nd edn (2017), reprinted in 2022 with amendments (or its predecessor edition)
SB/99	*FIDIC's Conditions of Contract for EPC/Turnkey Projects*, 1st edn (1999)
SB/17	*FIDIC's Conditions of Contract for EPC/Turnkey Projects*, 2nd edn (2017), reprinted in 2022 with amendments
SC	Sub-Clause
SCL	Society of Construction Law, UK
So Carolina LR	South Carolina Law Review, USA
Tender dossier	A set of documents which the Employer issues to a tenderer for it to prepare and submit a tender
TOR	Terms of Reference under Article 23 of the ICC Rules of Arbitration
UCC	*Uniform Commercial Code*, USA
UK	United Kingdom
UNCITRAL	United Nations Commission on International Trade Law, Vienna, Austria
UNIDROIT	International Institute for the Unification of Private Law, Rome, Italy
Unif LR	Uniform Law Review, UNIDROIT, OUP, UK
URCB	*Uniform Rules for Contract Bonds*, ICC, 1994, ICC publication no 524
URDG	*Uniform Rules for Demand Guarantees*, ICC, 2010 revision, ICC publication no 758
U Miami ICLR	University of Miami International and Comparative Law Review, USA
US / USA	United States / United States of America
VUWLR	Victoria University of Wellington Law Review, New Zealand

1. In source material referred to (other than RB/17 itself).

White Book	*FIDIC's Client/Consultant Model Services Agreement*, 5th edn, 2017
Wm Mitchell LR	William Mitchell Law Review, USA
World Arb and Med Rev	World Arbitration and Mediation Review, USA
World Bank's COPA or COPA	The World Bank's *Conditions of Particular Application* (or *Particular Conditions*) for use with the General Conditions of RB/17, issued in 2019
YB Comm Arb	*Yearbook Commercial Arbitration*, International Council for International Arbitration ('ICCA'), Kluwer L Int'l, the Netherlands
Yellow Book or YB	*FIDIC's Conditions for Plant and Design-Build*, 2nd edn (2017), reprinted in 2022 with amendments (or any predecessor edition)
YB/63	*FIDIC's Conditions of Contract (International) for Electrical and Mechanical Works (Including Erection on Site) with Forms of Tender and Agreement*, 1st edn (1963)
YB/80	*FIDIC's Conditions of Contract for Electrical and Mechanical Works Including Erection on Site with Forms of Tender and Agreement*, 2nd edn (1980)
YB/87	*FIDIC's Conditions of Contract for Electrical and Mechanical Works Including Erection on Site with Forms of Tender and Agreement*, 3rd edn (1987)
YB/99	*FIDIC's Conditions of Contract for Plant and Design-Build for Electrical and Mechanical Plant, and for Building and Engineering Works, Designed by the Contractor*, 1st edn (1999)
YB/17	*FIDIC's Conditions of Contract for Plant and Design-Build*, 2nd edn (2017), reprinted in 2022 with amendments

--ooOOoo--

Note

The author wishes to thank the International Federation of Consulting Engineers ('FIDIC') for its permission to reproduce its 2022 reprint of the Conditions of Contract for Construction for Building and Engineering Works Designed by the Employer (the 'Red Book'), second edition, 2017 ('RB/17'), in this book. The 2022 reprint incorporates amendments to take account of (1) an errata document issued by FIDIC in 2018[1], (2) a memorandum with additional errata issued by FIDIC in 2019[2] and (3) further amendments issued by FIDIC in 2022 and incorporated in the 2022 reprint of RB/17. All three sets of amendments are available for free download from the FIDIC Bookshop at FIDIC's website at https://fidic.org/.

The author also wishes to thank the International Institute for the Unification of Private Law ('UNIDROIT') for its permission to reproduce extracts from the UNIDROIT Principles of International Commercial Contracts 2016.

--ooOOoo--

1. A two-page errata document for the Red Book was distributed by FIDIC at the FIDIC's Users' Conference in London on 4 and 5 December 2018; https://fidic.org/sites/default/files/bean_files/RED2017_errata_sheet_existing%20stock_fidic.pdf accessed 2 November 2022.
2. http://fidic.org/sites/default/files/bean_files/Memo%20for%20Rainbow%20Suite%202017%2004.06.19.pdf accessed 2 November 2022.

Note

The author wishes to thank the International Federation of Consulting Engineers ("FIDIC") for its permission to reproduce its 2022 reprint of the Conditions of Contract for Construction for Building and Engineering Works Designed by the Employer (the "Red Book"), second edition, 2017 ("RB/17"), in this book. The 2022 reprint incorporates amendments to take account of (1) an errata document issued by FIDIC in 2018[1], (2) a memorandum with additional errata issued by FIDIC in 2019[2] and (3) further amendments issued by FIDIC in 2022 and incorporated in the 2022 reprint of RB/17. All three sets of amendments are available for free download from the FIDIC bookshop at FIDIC's website at https://fidic.org/

The author also wishes to thank the International Institute for the Unification of Private Law ("UNIDROIT") for its permission to reproduce extracts from the UNIDROIT Principles of International Commercial Contracts 2016.

--ooOoo--

1. A two page errata document for the Red Book was distributed by FIDIC at the FIDIC's Users' Conference in London on 4 and 5 December 2018: https://fidic.org/sites/default/files/static_files/RED%2017%20[illegible]%20Book%20[illegible]king.pdf accessed 2 November 2022.
2. https://fidic.org/sites/default/files/static_files/Amendments%20to%20Rainbow%20Suite%202017%20(2019-06-12).pdf accessed 2 November 2022.

Foreword

by William S. Howard, former President of FIDIC

I am honoured to provide this brief 'foreword' to Chris Seppälä's *The FIDIC Red Book Contract: An International Clause-by-Clause Commentary*. The book contains a detailed discussion on the clauses contained in the 2017 Edition of the FIDIC Red Book – 'Conditions of Contract for Construction'. Chris has been very generous with his time to FIDIC over the past 30 years by reviewing and advising FIDIC in matters associated with FIDIC's many Conditions of Contract.

During this time, the challenge to deliver high-quality projects in less time and at lower cost has complicated matters for all entities involved in the delivery of capital projects.

This has made it even more important for Owners/Employers to incorporate in their projects high-quality Conditions of Contract which are fair to all parties. FIDIC is proud of our contribution to addressing this need over many years. In developing our recommended Conditions of Contract, we strive to be fair to all parties by involving many volunteers with various types of expertise in the development, review and production of our documents.

In this regard, Chris Seppälä has done yeoman's work by reviewing and commenting on numerous Conditions of Contract for FIDIC. FIDIC and all parties participating in the delivery of capital projects owe him a debt of gratitude. His latest contribution is this detailed and thoughtful discussion of the FIDIC 2017 Red Book. It reflects his many years of experience in the legal elements of engineering and construction.

Chris' book is a lot more than a commentary on the wording of the Red Book itself, as it provides substantive and detailed discussion and interpretation from an international legal perspective. Chapter II 'Applicable Law' provides expert insight from a common and civil law lawyer with long experience in international construction contract disputes, as he discusses the approach of both systems of law to the many contractual issues which can arise in different parts of the world. Chapter III 'Contract Interpretation' highlights the importance of interpreting a Red Book contract correctly, providing guidance as to how this should be done having regard to the common law, the civil law and the presence of an international arbitration clause in the contract.

While FIDIC cannot endorse the content of this book or Chris' opinions, we can state that it is a very thoughtful and outstanding contribution to the profession, the construction industry and society.

So, thank you very much, Chris, for your effort on behalf of FIDIC and the engineering and construction professions.

Very Truly Yours
William S. Howard
President, FIDIC
(2019-2021)

Foreword

by The Hon. Sir Vivian Ramsey

I have spent much of my working life dealing with projects under the various editions of the FIDIC Red Book. I well recall working with Chris Seppälä in Paris on one of my early cases and debating the meaning and effect of certain clauses. Both then and in our subsequent cases together, I have gained much from Chris' insight, litigation experience and razor-sharp mind. He has for many years, of course, been involved in editions of the Red Book. That combination of abilities and experience means that there is nobody better able to produce a detailed analysis of the 2017 Red Book than he is.

At the start of the book, besides a historical insight into the development of FIDIC forms, there is a section which is unique.[1] Those involved in dealing with international construction contracts under FIDIC forms are only too aware of the common law origins of those standard forms. However, in many cases the governing law of the contract will be a civil law. In such cases the way in which civil law concepts apply to common law words, phrases and concepts can cause difficulties. In a section covering some fifty pages, Chris provides a careful explanation of the differences which can occur when a FIDIC or other construction contract is governed by civil law rather than common law. He considers issues such as adjustments to liquidated damages and requirements for a court order to terminate a contract. These points are unknown to the common law practitioner but essential when civil law applies to a FIDIC form.

1. **Section 4 Common Law and Civil Law Compared** of **Chapter II Applicable Law**.

The frequent temptation in a clause-by-clause commentary on a standard form is merely to set out the text and paraphrase it. This book not only avoids that temptation but instead provides a commentary which practitioners advising on contracts or those dealing with disputes will find essential. First, the commentary identifies changes from the 1999 Red Book. Many are familiar with that version and need an easy way to identify the changes. Second, there is a reference to other related clauses so that the reader does not have to track those down. The third part is the analysis which provides, under a series of headings, a detailed discussion of the contents of the clause. This analysis identifies issues which might arise and then suggests ways in which they may be overcome. It also cross-refers to provisions in other clauses which affect the clause. Fourth, where there is related law, that is cited. The final consideration is headed 'improvements'. This points out issues which might arise on the clauses and ways in which these might be overcome. This is clearly helpful for anyone considering what amendments to make initially. It also provides an insight into how difficulties may arise. Chris is to be commended for breaking the mould of mere commentaries and for providing a full and clear exposition of each provision.

This is therefore much more than a commentary on the 2017 Red Book. It provides helpful guidance on issues which arise on any international construction contract. It also reflects the knowledge and experience of a lifetime dealing with these contracts. Chris is to be congratulated for the dedication and sheer hard work which has gone into this *magnum opus*.

Sir Vivian Ramsey
Former UK High Court Judge in charge of the
Technology and Construction Court
London and Singapore

Usage

While the Red Book 2017 ('RB/17') refers at times to a person as 'he/she', 'his/her', 'him/her' or 'himself/herself', in this commentary reference will always be made to 'it', 'its' or 'itself', as may be appropriate.[1]

--ooOOoo--

1. This is also consistent with The World Bank's *Conditions of Particular Application* for use with RB/17, issued in 2019 ('COPA'), Sub-Clause 1.2. The numbering of footnotes in this book is separate for each of Chapters I, II, III and V, that is, the numbering begins from '1' at the beginning of each of those chapters. However, in the case of Chapter IV, because it is so long, the numbering of footnotes is separate for the commentaries on each of the 21 Clauses making up RB/17; that is, the numbering begins from '1' at the beginning of the commentary on each Clause.

Translations

All translations of the French Civil Code are taken, with sometimes minor revisions, from the English translation of John Cartwright, Bénédicte Fauvarque-Cosson and Simon Whittaker (translation commissioned by the French Ministry of Justice), which is included as an Appendix to John Cartwright and Simon Whittaker (eds), *The Code Napoléon Rewritten: French Contract Law after the 2016 Reforms* (Hart Publishing 2017).

All translations from the Egyptian Civil Code are taken from the well-known English translation of Perrott, Fanner & Sims Marshall, Lawyers, Cairo, Egypt (The New World Publisher, Cairo).

--ooOOoo--

Acknowledgements

This book could not have been written without the help or support of many people.

I would like to thank the Paris office of the law firm of which I am Partner of Counsel (White & Case), especially its arbitration group, for its constant support. I would like first to thank Dr Dimitar Kondev for his assistance at every stage of my work, including preparing initial drafts of several sections of this book. His careful and thoughtful review of multiple drafts of this book and his knowledge of construction law has saved me from many errors, as well as provided me with many valuable insights. Similarly, Zehaan Trivedi has been most helpful at many stages of this work. I also especially appreciate the support of Andrew McDougall KC.

I would like to thank the following colleagues (or former colleagues) on FIDIC's Contracts Committee: Siobhan Fahey (principal drafter of FIDIC Contract Committee's Updates Special Group), Nael Bunni, Vincent Leloup, Christopher Wade and Zoltán Záhonyi. They have been kind enough to answer my numerous questions and/or review and comment upon drafts of certain sections. I would also like to thank Dr Nelson Ogunshakin, FIDIC's CEO, Daduna Kokhreidze, FIDIC's General Counsel, Ieva Liaugaude and Christophe Sisto at the FIDIC Secretariat for their willingness to assist at all times.

I would also like to thank individual lawyers or law professors who are experts in specific fields for commenting upon sections of the book in draft or who have otherwise provided information: Georges Affaki, Lyda Bier, Sylvain Bollée, Paul Cowan, Nora Fung, Sami Houerbi, Anthony Lavers, Jaime Arancibia Mattar, Joseph F. Moore, Sufian Obeidat, Andreas Reiner and Matthew Secomb.

I would like to thank the following who have been especially helpful for their research assistance and/or comments in specific areas: Dolores Bentolila, Samy Markbaoui, Aladin Masri and Poorvi Satija.

I would also like to thank the following who have assisted in multiple ways: Richard Berkeley, Eric Burke-Arevalo, Param Bhalerao, Isobel Blakeway-Phillips, Philippe Boisvert, Piotr Bytnerowicz, Caroline Colbert, Betina Damvergi, Alexandria Davis, Laure Dupain, Polly Efstratiadi, Alexandra Guilbault, Grace Hansen-Gilmour, Adrian Hernandez, Diane Houriez, Julien Huet, Fernando Labombarda, Mounia Larbaoui, Nika Larkimo, Salma Lofty, Arthur Moreau, Fabiana Pardi Otamendi, Vanessa Pitassi, Dan Pront, Yutty Ramen, Devon Robertson, Laoiseach Scullion, Salma Selim, Afolarin Shasore, Henry Spence, Inès Taha, Marianna Troia, Nataliia Tuzheliak, Pauline Weess, Jakub Wolkowicz, and Fernando Zuniga.

I would like to thank Julian Bailey for making available an electronic version of the 3rd edition of his excellent treatise, *Construction Law*, published in 2020, when COVID-19 prevented me from procuring a hard copy.

Last, but by no means least, I would like to thank the following:

(1) Fiona Candy for being available both day and night and on weekends to provide invaluable research assistance.
(2) Gregory Amsellem and Mélanie Badez for procuring legal materials on any manner of subjects which I have needed to consult.
(3) Elodie Baudrier, my personal assistant, who has patiently and good-humouredly typed seemingly endless drafts of this book as well as, when Elodie was not available, Kim Ha and Binta Diop.

All of the above have assisted me in preparing this work and I am extremely grateful to them. But, in addition, I owe many debts to those from whom, well before beginning this book, I learned much. While it is not possible to name and recognise them all, there are three persons I must mention:

(1) The late Dr Aktham El Kholy, Attorney-at-Law, Cairo, Egypt, and former Vice-Dean and Professor, Faculty of Law of the University of Cairo, for his friendship and guidance about arbitration and the legal culture of the Arab Middle East.
(2) Humphrey J. LLoyd (now His Honour Humphrey LLoyd KC), London, for his friendship and advice about construction law and its practice in England.

(3) The late John R. Raben, a senior partner, Sullivan & Cromwell, New York, and an exacting and rigorous taskmaster from whom, as a young lawyer, I learned much.

I have been extremely privileged to have worked in cooperation with, or (in the case of Mr Raben) under the supervision of, three such brilliant and distinguished lawyers.

I am also most grateful to William S. Howard, the former President of FIDIC, and the Hon. Sir Vivian Ramsey, former High Court Judge in charge of the UK Technology and Construction Court, for providing forewords to this work.

I alone am responsible for any errors, omissions or deficiencies which this book may contain.

--ooOOoo--

Chapter I
General Introduction

1 PURPOSE AND STRUCTURE

1.1 Purpose

1.1.1 General Content

This is a commentary on the 2022 reprint with amendments of the latest edition – the second edition published in 2017 – of the most widely used standard form of international construction contract: the *Conditions of Contract for Construction for Building and Engineering*[1] *Works Designed by the Employer* (the 'Red Book', 'RB'), published by the International Federation of Consulting Engineers (known by its French acronym 'FIDIC').[2] The 2022 reprint of the second edition, 2017 ('RB/17') incorporates amendments issued in 2018, 2019 and 2022. This commentary

1. Civil (or non-military) engineering includes:

> most aspects of the design, building and maintenance of the built environment including airports, aqueducts, basements, bridges, canals, car parks, coastal protection, dams, docks, foundations, geotechnics, harbours, hotels, houses, jetties, lighthouses, offices, offshore structures, power stations, railways, reservoirs, river management, roads, sewage treatment, shops, soil mechanics, stadia, structures, traffic, transmission towers, tunnels, warehouses, waste disposal, water supply etc.

David Blockley, *The New Penguin Dictionary of Civil Engineering* (Penguin Books, London, 2005) 84.

2. In French: *Fédération Internationale des Ingénieurs-Conseils*.

also includes references to, where relevant, The World Bank's *Conditions of Particular Application* for use with RB/17 (as it then was), issued in 2019 ('COPA').[3]

After a general introduction to FIDIC, its organisation, FIDIC contracts and RB/17 in **Chapter I ('General Introduction')**, the issue of the law (or rules of law) which may govern, or otherwise apply to, an international construction contract based upon a FIDIC form is discussed in **Chapter II ('Applicable Law')**. **Chapter II** includes (in **Section 4**) an exploration of the major differences in construction law between the common law and civil law countries. The issue of how to interpret a contract based on a FIDIC form under the law of different jurisdictions is discussed in **Chapter III ('Contract Interpretation')**.

The main part of this book is **Chapter IV ('Clause-by-Clause Commentary')** which consists of a commentary on each of the Sub-Clauses (grouped in 21 Clauses) in RB/17. After quoting each Sub-Clause and summarising its content, each Sub-Clause is commented upon in turn.

Other documents making up RB/17 are commented upon in **Chapter V**.

This book is intended to provide practical, as well as legal, guidance to RB/17, from an international perspective, to engineers, other construction professionals and lawyers. To make it easier to understand the subject matter, all legal and technical terms used in the text have been defined, and numerous figures and tables have been included to illustrate steps in contract procedures or provide other information.[4]

This work is designed to provide guidance at all stages of a construction project using RB/17, whether in drafting, negotiating, performing, interpreting or administering such a contract, including dealing with claims or disputes.

While this commentary is limited to RB/17, as many of its provisions are common to FIDIC's *Conditions of Contract for Plant & Design Build* ('Yellow Book' or 'YB/17') and *Conditions of Contract for EPC/Turnkey*

3. These are referred to and/or discussed in footnotes ('fn.(s)') in the commentary.
4. These figures and tables are designed to complement the figures included at the beginning of RB/17 itself. *See* the **Lists of Figures and Tables** at the beginning of this book. Due to the need to encompass the contents of this book in a single volume, there has not been space to include a list of cases, arbitration awards and statutes cited. However, there is a detailed index.

Projects ('Silver Book' or 'SB/17'), also published in 2017, to that extent, this work is relevant to YB/17 and SB/17 as well.

1.1.2 An International Legal Perspective

Like its preceding editions, RB/17 contains a detailed set of General Conditions which, after adaptation (by Particular Conditions) to a specific project, will address most matters that need to be dealt with by an international construction contract. However, regardless of how detailed or comprehensive a standard form may be, it can never provide solutions to the manifold issues to which a project may give rise, or dispense with the occasional need to refer to law (or rules of law).[5]

The law governing the contract[6] is likely to be relevant to such matters as: the validity of provisions for liquidated damages for delay ('Delay Damages' in RB/17), interest (called 'financing charges' in RB/17) and limitations on liability; the rights, if any, of subcontractors; the availability of *force majeure*, hardship, frustration and similar legal doctrines; the feasibility of legally suspending, changing the contents of, or terminating the contract; the regulation of defects liability and limitation periods; and the procedures for the resolution of disputes, as well as how the contract is to be interpreted and understood. For these and other reasons, it is essential, in any clause-by-clause commentary, not just to examine the text of a standard form but also to consider the clauses from a legal perspective.

As RB/17 is for international use, this book will seek to look at this form of contract not only from the point of view of general law and practice in common law countries but also from that in civil law countries (including countries whose codes are inspired by Islamic law) and will refer to relevant international legal principles, practices and international arbitral awards as well.

1.1.3 Common Law and Civil Law

The RB has its origins in England. The earliest editions of the RB were modelled closely on an English standard form of contract conditions.[7]

5. Most especially where the applicable law is mandatory. *See*, e.g., **Section 5 Mandatory Law at the Site** of **Chapter II Applicable Law** below.
6. *See* Sub-Clause 1.4 [*Law and Language*] of RB/17.
7. *See* **Section 3.1 Origin and History** below of **Chapter I General Introduction**.

FIDIC considers the official and authentic texts of its forms of contract to be the versions in the English language. Anglophone engineers continue, very understandably for this reason, to be the principal drafters of the FIDIC forms, and the most informative and useful legal texts and commentaries on the forms have been written by English and Commonwealth lawyers and engineers.

Nevertheless, FIDIC's forms are not intended for use principally in England[8] or the Commonwealth countries but universally. For this reason, FIDIC has sought with each new edition of its forms, to eliminate specifically English legal terminology in favour of language that is neutral and not particular to any legal system.[9] Therefore, this book will, while taking due account of important English and Commonwealth legal material, cite civil law and international legal material as well.

Indeed, as there already exist excellent common law texts and commentaries dealing with the FIDIC forms[10] but relatively little commentary

8. Indeed, they cannot be used in the UK as they are not compliant with the mandatory provisions of the UK's *Housing Grants, Construction and Regeneration Act* 1996, as amended ('HGCRA'), which applies to construction contracts for works within the territorial area of the UK.
9. *See* **Section 3.2 Distinctive Features** of **Chapter I General Introduction**.
10. Albeit none yet on the 2022 reprint of the 2017 Red Book which contains important amendments to the version published in 2017. English law commentaries on the 1999 or 2017 Rainbow Suite include: Ellis Baker and others, *FIDIC Contracts: Law and Practice* (Informa Law, London, 2009), which is being updated; Nicholas Alexander Brown, *FIDIC 2017: A Definitive Guide to Claims and Disputes* (ICE Publishing, London, 2022); Corbett & Co, *FIDIC 2017: A Practical Legal Guide* (Corbett & Co 2020); William Godwin, *International Construction Contracts: A Handbook* (Wiley-Blackwell, Oxford, 2013); and Jeremy Glover and Simon Hughes, *Understanding the FIDIC Red and Yellow Books* (3rd edn, Sweet & Maxwell, London, 2018). Books by engineers include Leo Grutters and Brian Barr, *FIDIC Red, Yellow and Silver Books: A Practical Guide to the 2017 Editions* (Sweet & Maxwell, London, 2018), Kelvin Hughes, *Understanding FIDIC: The Rainbow Suite* (Routledge, Abingdon, Oxford, 2021) and Jakob B Sørensen, *FIDIC Red Book: A Companion to the 2017 Construction Contract* (ICE Publishing, London, 2019) (Mr Sørensen has also written similar books on the Yellow and Silver Books, respectively). An excellent older book by an engineer is Nael G Bunni, *The FIDIC Forms of Contract* (3rd edn, Blackwell Publishing, Oxford, 2005). In addition, helpful English law treatises include: Julian Bailey, *Construction Law*, 3 vols (3rd edn, London Publishing, UK, 2020), Atkin Chambers, *Hudson's Building and Engineering Contracts* (14th edn, Sweet &

from a civil law or continental point of view by comparison,[11] this work will give particular attention to civil law.[12]

1.1.4 *International Construction Law*

An international construction contract is usually expressed to be governed by some national law. The national law that tends in practice to apply to a FIDIC contract is that of the country of the employer where the works are usually being executed, generally a developing country. The law of a developing country will often not address in a clear and understandable way many of the questions to which a complex construction project can give rise. For this reason, it has been argued that there should be a law common to international construction:

> [t]he law applicable to construction contracts has tended to be that of the place of performance, that is, the law of the country where the construction project is located [...]. The lack of a well-developed body of construction law in [developing] countries capable of handling the kinds of disputes that arise in large international projects makes it more desirable that the governing law of international construction contracts be a body of law common to, and understood by, the international construction industry – a sort of *lex constructionis*. Having such a body of law operate within the international construction community would ameliorate the uncertainty that results from subjecting the parties to inadequate national construction law. In turn, greater certainty and predictability would facilitate more participation in international construction projects.[13]

Maxwell, London, 2020) and Stephen Furst and Vivian Ramsey, *Keating on Construction Contracts* (11th edn, Sweet & Maxwell, London, 2021). See also, for standard forms of construction contract used in different countries, Phillip Greenham and the Society of Construction Law Australia (eds), *The International Compendium of Construction Contracts* (De Gruyter, Berlin/Boston, 2021).

11. Exceptions include Axel-Volkmar Jaeger and Götz-Sebastian Hök, *FIDIC-A Guide for Practitioners* (Springer-Verlag, Heidelberg, 2010) and Lukas Klee, *International Construction Contract Law* (2nd edn, Wiley Blackwell, London, 2018).
12. *See*, e.g., **Section 4 Common Law and Civil Law Compared** of **Chapter II Applicable Law** below.
13. Michael Douglas, 'The Lex Mercatoria and the Culture of Transnational Industry' (2006) 13 U Miami ICLR 367, 383-84.
    In this connection, a distinguished English lawyer has urged English construction lawyers to look to international practice:

If there existed a single law common to international construction:

> Contracting parties [could] then have greater confidence when dealing with a party from a different nation, and such uniformity should result in lower costs because there will be no need to spend time arguing about which law should govern the transaction, nor will there be any necessity to spend time and money seeking to discover the relevant rules which prevail in another jurisdiction.[14]

But, while a law common to the international construction industry would have numerous advantages, the reality is that no such distinct body of law yet exists.[15]

1.1.5 International Legal Principles

Nevertheless, while an international law of contract – let alone of construction contracts – may still be a dream,[16] with the increase in recent decades of international trade and investment, a soft law of contract on a worldwide scale has been emerging:

> The law on building and engineering contracts can derive immense benefit from [the] process of international comparison, partly because the practical situation and needs of the parties are much the same in all such contracts, partly because, even outside the Commonwealth, the English language is so often used in international contracts [and partly because of the similarity of the actual forms of contracts used]. I.N. Duncan Wallace, *Hudson's Building and Engineering Contracts* (10th edn, Sweet & Maxwell, London, 1970), vii.

14. Ewan McKendrick, *Contract Law* (14th edn, Red Globe Press, London, 2021) 9 (statement made in relation to the *United Nations Convention on Contracts for the International Sale of Goods*).
15. As recognised by forms of international construction contract, which (like the FIDIC forms) continue to provide that they will be governed by a national law, *see* Sub-Clause 1.4 of RB/17, art. 12.1 of *ENAA Model Form International Contract for Engineering, Procurement and Supply for Plant Construction* (Engineering Advancement Association of Japan, 2013), and art. 5.1 of *ICC Model Turnkey Contract for Major Projects* (ICC Publication no 797 E, 2020).
16. Bruno Zeller, 'The Development of a Global Contract Law. Still a Dream?' in UNIDROIT (ed), *Eppur si Muove: The Age of Uniform Law, Essays in honour of M.J. Bonell* (1st edn, UNIDROIT, Rome, 2016) vol 2, 1179.

> National legislators, when reforming the law of contract, are more and more inspired by what has been done abroad as well as by transnational norms. Gradual convergences occurred, which enabled scholars from around the world to elaborate soft law instruments on a worldwide and European scale. These instruments, in turn, have provided guidance for converging developments of national contract laws.[17]

The best example of such a soft law instrument of worldwide[18] scope is the UNIDROIT Principles of International Commercial Contracts 2016 (the 'UNIDROIT Principles' or 'Principles'), which aim:

> to establish a balanced set of rules designed for use throughout the world irrespective of the legal traditions and the economic and political conditions of the countries in which they are to be applied.[19]

The Principles have influenced the reforms of Chinese (1999),[20] Russian (2015)[21] and French (2016)[22] contract laws. They are not just a model for national legislation but may be chosen by parties as the governing law of a contract.[23] Even if they are not chosen as a governing law, they may be

17. Hugh Beale and others, *Cases, Materials and Text on Contract Law* (3rd edn, Hart Publishing, Oxford, 2019) 3. This same work notes that:

    > [e]ven systems which share little by way of common origin, such as the common law and the French Civil Code, have influenced each other and often produce results that are not too dissimilar.

    Ibid., 5.
18. As distinct from an instrument of regional scope such as *The Principles of European Contract Law, 2002, Parts I, II and III ('PECL')*.
19. *See* International Institute for the Unification of Private Law, *UNIDROIT Principles of International Commercial Contracts* (UNIDROIT, Rome, 2016) xxix. These Principles are discussed in **Section 7 International Legal Principles** of **Chapter II Applicable Law** below.
20. Thomas Kadner Graziano, *Comparative Contract Law: Cases, Materials and Exercises* (Palgrave Macmillan, London, 2009) 5. *See also* **Section 7.4.3 As a Model for National Legislation** of **Chapter II Applicable Law** below.
21. *See* **Section 7.4.3 As a Model for National Legislation** of **Chapter II Applicable Law** below.
22. *Ibid.*
23. *See* **Section 7.4.1 As the 'Governing Law' for a FIDIC Contract** of **Chapter II Applicable Law** below.

used to interpret or supplement a contract's governing law.[24] Some courts have looked to them to provide perspective on national law. Thus, they have been cited by the UK Supreme Court (formerly the House of Lords) in several cases[25] and are also commonly cited in international arbitration awards.[26] They may be considered as an indicator of where contract law is – and should be – heading internationally.[27]

1.1.6 Conclusion for This Commentary

Accordingly, it seems only fitting in this commentary on an international form of construction contract that, in addition to referring, where relevant, to law and practice in common law and civil law countries, attention is given to the UNIDROIT Principles, as well as international practice including international arbitral awards. Like RB/17 itself and complementing it, the Principles establish neutral, fair, harmonised norms for international contracts. They reflect a standard to which the contract laws of all countries should be aspiring, not just the developing countries, and constitute best international contract practice for lawyers much like FIDIC's forms constitute best international practice for engineers.[28]

---

24. *See* **Section 7.4.2 As a Source to Interpret or Supplement the Governing Law** of **Chapter II Applicable Law** below.
25. *Chartbrook Limited v Persimmon Homes Limited and Others* [2009] UKHL 38, 1 AC 1101 [para. 39]; *Cavendish Square Holding BV v Makdessi, Parking Eye Ltd v Beavis* [2015] UKSC 67 [paras 37, 164, 265]; and *Rock Advertising Limited v MWB Business Exchange Centres Limited* [2018] UKSC 24 [paras 13 and 16].
26. *See*, e.g., the international arbitration awards referred to in **Section 7.4 Relevance to a FIDIC Contract** of **Chapter II Applicable Law** below.
27. Similarly, the *Delay and Disruption Protocol*, 2nd edn, 2017 published by the UK's SCL (discussed more fully under **(iii) Analysis** in the commentaries on Sub-Clauses 8.3 [*Programme*] and 8.5 [*Extension of Time for Completion*] below) may be cited as contributing to good international construction contract practice.
28. However, what has been stated about the construction contract forms of the American Institute of Architects ('AIA') applies equally to those of FIDIC:

 > Even if profit is not the principal objective of the association, publishing standardized contracts advances the interests of the association members [...] While forms often are trumpeted as reflecting the best thinking of the entire construction industry, those involved must be realistic enough to recognize that the associations do look after their own members.

Accordingly, when commenting on individual Clauses or Sub-Clauses of RB/17 in **Chapter IV** below, reference will be made to the Principles wherever they appear relevant.[29]

1.2 Structure of Book

This book is organised into five chapters, as follows:

Chapter I, entitled '**General Introduction**', contains a brief description of FIDIC and its activities and an overview of FIDIC's construction contracts. It describes the origin and history of the Red Book, notes distinctive features of FIDIC's construction contracts and describes the way in which they are prepared. The chapter reviews the history of the preparation of the 2017 Rainbow Suite, of which RB/17 is a part, including the documents which comprise RB/17. The chapter then identifies some of the major changes made from the previous 1999 edition of the Red Book ('RB/99'), and describes FIDIC's *Guides* to its construction contracts and its 'Golden Principles'. The chapter concludes with a table listing FIDIC's current forms of construction contract and the translations of the forms which are available or planned.

Chapter II is entitled '**Applicable Law**'. It is ironic that, whereas the Red Book was originally modelled on an English standard form of construction contract and most of the existing (and often excellent) commentary on it is by English and Commonwealth lawyers and engineers, it is not intended for use principally in England[30] or the Commonwealth but in all countries of the world and, in fact, is probably more widely used in civil

---

Justin Sweet, 'Standard Construction Contracts: Some Advice to Construction Lawyers' (no 4, 1989) 40 So Carolina L Rev 823, 825.

29. Art. 1.6 of the Principles (which is similar to art. 2A(1) of the *UNCITRAL Model Law on International Commercial Arbitration 1985 as amended in 2006* (UN Doc A/40/17)) provides that:

> In the interpretation of these Principles, regard is to be had to their international character and to their purposes including the need to promote uniformity in their application [...].

It is hoped, as well, that a commentary such as this will, together with other publications about FIDIC contracts, help to promote greater uniformity in the way FIDIC's forms are understood and interpreted.

30. As previously noted, the Red Book would not actually be HGCRA compliant for use in England.

law countries, such as in the Middle East and Eastern Europe, than in common law countries. Inevitably, this elicits the question of how a standard form of construction contract, derived from practice in a common law country, can operate and be applied successfully in a civil law country. This question itself gives rise to numerous issues which, understandably, have not been fully explored by English and Commonwealth legal commentators. Therefore these matters are examined in some detail in this chapter, notably in Section 4 ('Common Law and Civil Law Compared'). Among the important matters discussed in Section 4 of Chapter II are French and other public contract law theories – as often a contract based on the Red Book is signed with a state or other public body of a civil law country where such theories may apply – most of which have no counterpart in the common law.

Section 5 of this chapter emphasises that, regardless of what nation's law is selected as the governing law, the mandatory law (i.e., law which may not be deviated from) of the Country (i.e. where the site is located) must be respected, and lists the kinds of laws applicable to construction that are often mandatory in nature.[31] Section 6 then considers how to address the difficulty which arises where a contract is governed by the law of a less-developed country that does not provide clear answers to the many legal issues to which the performance of an international construction contract may give rise. Finally, Section 7 examines whether international legal principles, notably, those of UNIDROIT, may or should serve as rules of law to govern a FIDIC contract, or be used to interpret or supplement any governing law chosen by the parties. The chapter concludes in Section 8 with a brief discussion of the relevance of trade usages to an international construction contract.

The wording of every contract may have to be interpreted, and interpretation may be especially important in a contract that frequently gives rise to claims and/or disputes, such as an international construction contract. Accordingly, **Chapter III** entitled '**Contract Interpretation**' describes in Section 4 the approaches of different legal systems or norms to contract interpretation (civil law, common law, and international), and then, in Section 5, identifies and describes matters which must normally be taken into account when interpreting a FIDIC contract. As the potential effect of an international arbitration clause[32] on contract interpretation is

31. For definitions of mandatory law, *see* the fns at the beginning of **Section 5 Mandatory Law at the Site** in **Chapter II Applicable Law** below.
32. Such as is contained in Sub-Clause 21.6 [*Arbitration*] of RB/17.

sometimes overlooked, this subject is given particular attention in Section 5.7. Finally, this chapter concludes in Section 6 with a suggested 'practical approach' to interpreting a FIDIC contract.

Chapter IV entitled **'Clause-by-Clause Commentary'**, which includes a commentary on each of the 168 Sub-Clauses (which are grouped in 21 Clauses) in RB/17, is the main part of the book and by far its longest chapter. Each Sub-Clause is first quoted in full and then summarised in bold text. The Sub-Clause is then examined in detail under up to five headings (to the extent each is relevant to the Sub-Clause) dealing with the following:

(i) main changes in the Sub-Clause compared to the previous 1999 edition;
(ii) other Clauses and Sub-Clauses which are related to the Sub-Clause being commented upon;
(iii) an analysis of the purpose and function of the Sub-Clause being commented upon, including a review of issues to which it gives rise;
(iv) common law, civil law or international legal cases, materials or principles, including arbitral awards, related to the Sub-Clause; and
(v) suggestions, if any, of ways in which the Sub-Clause could be improved, revised or corrected.

Chapter V entitled **'Commentary on Other Documents'** includes a commentary on FIDIC's forms relating to the Dispute Avoidance/Adjudication Board ('DAAB') as well as on miscellaneous documents included in RB/17, such as the Advisory Notes on Building Information Modelling ('BIM'), forms of various securities and, finally, the forms of Letter of Tender, Letter of Acceptance, Contract Agreement and DAAB Agreement.

2 INTRODUCTION TO FIDIC

2.1 What Is FIDIC?

FIDIC is an international federation of national associations of consulting engineers. It was founded in 1913 by three national associations of consulting engineers, namely those of Belgium, France and

Switzerland.[33] About a hundred national associations are members of FIDIC, which is effectively the global representative body for national associations of consulting engineers around the world. FIDIC represents over 1 million consulting engineering professionals and forty thousand firms in more than a hundred countries worldwide.[34]

To the outside world, FIDIC is best known as a publisher of standard forms of conditions of contract for construction suitable for international use. These forms are known to many as 'FIDIC Contracts'. The acronym 'FIDIC' has sometimes erroneously been used simply to designate the Red Book itself without parties having any idea of the term's actual meaning.[35] However, as discussed in Section 2.2 below, preparing and publishing standard forms of contract is only one of FIDIC's multiple activities.

2.2 FIDIC's Organisation and Activities

FIDIC is charged with promoting and implementing the consulting engineering industry's strategic goals on behalf of its national member associations and disseminating information and resources of interest to its members.[36]

FIDIC's organisation consists of a General Assembly, a Board (formerly called the 'Executive Committee'), a Secretariat, Auditor(s) and companies or entities owned by FIDIC.[37] The General Assembly consists of the duly appointed delegates of the Member Associations.[38] The General

33. *See* FIDIC 'History' (*FIDIC*) https://fidic.org/history accessed 2 November 2022. The French origin of the acronym reflects that FIDIC was originally established by representatives from three wholly or partly francophone countries (Belgium, France and Switzerland).
34. *See* FIDIC 'FIDIC Consulting Engineering Professionals in the World' (*FIDIC*) https://www.fidic.org/node/10134 accessed 2 November 2022.
35. *See* John Bowcock, 'The FIDIC Contract Forms: The Present and Future', SCL paper 53, November 1995. Mr Bowcock, a former Chairman of the FIDIC Contracts Committee, states that the RB has perhaps done more than anything else to give FIDIC the international prestige which it enjoys (p. 2 of his paper).
36. *See* FIDIC 'About Us' (*FIDIC*) https://fidic.org/about-us accessed 2 November 2022.
37. International Federation of Consulting Engineers, 'Statutes and By-Laws' (FIDIC 2015) art. 7 (FIDIC's Statutes).
38. *Ibid.*, art. 8.

Assembly elects the members of the Board, determines their number and can give directions to the Board as to future activities of FIDIC.[39] Among its other functions, the General Assembly also elects the President of FIDIC and the Auditor(s), decides on the admission or exclusion of Member Associations and adopts the budget of the federation.[40]

The Board is responsible for the administration and management of FIDIC in all matters not explicitly falling within the competence of the General Assembly.[41] Among its other functions, the Board is empowered to appoint working committees and monitor their activities. As of 2022, FIDIC had nine such committees, one of which is the Contracts Committee ('CC'), which is responsible for preparing FIDIC's standard forms of contract, as discussed in Section 3.3 below.[42]

The FIDIC Secretariat is responsible for the operation of the organisation. The Secretariat has its seat in the World Trade Centre II near Geneva Airport in Switzerland.[43] The Secretariat is managed by a Chief Executive Officer (currently Dr Nelson Ogunshakin CEng, FICE, FREng, OBE) and FIDIC's staff in Geneva consists of about 18 persons (full-time and part-time). FIDIC also has an office in Beijing, China.

3 FIDIC'S CONSTRUCTION CONTRACTS

While engaged in a whole range of professional issues concerning consulting engineers (commonly referred to as 'consultants'), FIDIC is best known for its work in preparing and publishing standard forms of construction contract and agreement forms for consultants, sub-consultants, joint ventures of consultants and consultants' representatives, together with related materials, such as contract guides and standard pre-qualification forms.

39. *Ibid.*, art. 9.
40. *Ibid.*
41. *Ibid.*, art. 12.
42. The other committees deal with matters of interest to professional engineers such as business practice, capacity building, integrity management, risk and quality, sustainable development, adjudicators, trainers and digital transformation. In addition, FIDIC has three Councils which advise FIDIC and its Board on various subjects including diversity and inclusion.
43. Previously, the Secretariat was based in The Hague, the Netherlands, and later in Lausanne, Switzerland.

3.1 Origin and History

3.1.1 *Origins*

The first activity that could be looked upon as the origin of FIDIC's standard forms[44] dates back to 1930 when the 5th International Congress of Consulting Engineers was held in Vienna.[45] The congress was divided

---

44. Standard forms:

> are a by-product of the industrial revolution of the nineteenth century. Just as the production of goods and services was standardized, so were the terms on which goods and services were supplied. Konrad Zweigert and Hein Kötz, *An Introduction to Comparative Law* (3rd edn, OUP, Oxford, 1998) 333.

Standard terms contribute to the rationalisation and development of mass transactions, for they save companies and their customers the cost and trouble of negotiating the terms of each contract individually, or of going to court to have the contract construed and amplified. Standard terms therefore make it easier to forecast the cost of doing business, simplify its procedures, and thus contribute to keeping costs and prices low.
Standard form construction contracts have been in use in domestic construction in England, France and the United States since the 19th century. By 1805, the Barrack Office of the War Department of the English Government had developed a standard form of building contract for providing new barracks for troops and horses. *See* James Nisbet, *Fair and Reasonable: Building Contracts from 1550: A Synopsis* (Stoke Publications, London, 1993) 42. In the 1860s, a standard form of contract for the construction of London's sewers was used by the Metropolitan Board of Works and remained a model for English contracts for more than a century, including the Institution of Civil Engineers' *Conditions of Contract* whose first edition was published in 1945 (Hugh Ferguson and Mike Chrimes, *The Contractors* (ICE Publishing, London, 2014) 9-10) and from which the RB derives – *see* later in **Section 3.1.1**. Each of these forms enshrined the engineer 'in his all-powerful role' (*Ibid.*). France (*Le Directeur général des ponts et chaussées*) issued its first standard conditions of contract (*cahier des clauses et conditions générales*) for public works in 1811 (Circular of July 30, 1811). In the United States, in 1888 the American Institute of Architects and the National Association of Builders co-sponsored the 'first national attempt to create a standard form of construction contract', the so-called Uniform Contract. Philip L Bruner, 'The Historical Emergence of Construction Law' (2007) 34 Wm Mitchell LR 1, 6.

45. Ragnar Widegren, *Consulting Engineers 1913-1988, FIDIC Over 75 Years* (FIDIC, 1988) 76.

into five sections, one being 'Section 4 – To Draw Up Contract Documents for the Achievement of Works as International Standard Documents'. The subject was handed over to a committee for further consideration and a paper on the topic was sent to the Member Associations.[46] However, nothing appears to have become of this initiative until the 1950s after World War II.

The first edition of the Red Book ('RB'), published in 1957, drew heavily on a form of conditions of contract used for civil engineering works in England, namely, the fourth edition of the *Conditions of Contract* of the United Kingdom's Institution of Civil Engineers ('ICE'), which was published in 1955.[47] As one former chairman of the British Association of Consulting Engineers ('ACE') and of the CC has explained:

> The reason for this was that in the years shortly after the Second World War, when a number of international projects were carried out financed by the international financing institutions such as the World Bank, consultants working in many countries used the Institution [of Civil Engineer's] form departing from it only where it was considered essential because of the international character of the work. When FIDIC came to produce the first Red Book it was natural that they should use the work already done as a basis.[48]

The growing need after World War II for a standard form suitable for international projects had resulted in the publication in 1956 by the ACE of the *Overseas (Civil) Conditions of Contract*, also known as the ACE form, which was probably the first international standard form for civil

46. *Ibid.* Unfortunately, it has not been possible to locate this paper.
47. The full name of the standard form was the *General Conditions of Contract and Forms of Tender, Agreement and Bond for Use in Connection with Works of Civil Engineering Construction*. Prompted by a celebrated paper, 'The Conditions of Engineering Contracts' by E J Rimmer, an English civil engineer and barrister, published in the Journal of The Institution of Civil Engineers, no 4, 1938-39, 4, the first edition of the ICE form was published in 1945 by the ICE and the Federation of Civil Engineering Contractors ('FCEC'), which was later known as the Civil Engineering Contractors Association (CECA). Further editions followed in 1950 (2nd edn), issued with the added agreement of the Association of Consulting Engineers, 1951 (3rd edn), 1955 (4th edn), 1973 (5th edn), 1991 (6th edn) and finally in 2001 (7th edn).
48. *See* John Bowcock, 'The FIDIC Contract Forms: The Present and Future', SCL paper 53, November 1995.

engineering works.[49] The ACE form was closely modelled on the *ICE Conditions of Contract*, 4th edition.[50] Accordingly, it contained features that were typical of English Commonwealth and, incidentally, US standard forms, such as the presence of a third party, known as the 'Engineer' (or 'Design Professional' in the US), who acts as a contract administrator and a decision-maker (for claims and/or disputes), as well as a certifier of payments due to the contractor.[51]

3.1.2 Red Book, 1st Edition (1957)

Shortly after the release of the ACE form, the first edition of the RB was published in August 1957 ('RB/57'). It became known as the 'Red Book', owing to its red cover. The full title of the form was *Conditions of Contract (International) for Works of Civil Engineering Construction with Forms of Tender and Agreement*.[52] RB/57 was modelled closely on the ACE form, which, as mentioned, was based on the ICE form, 4th edition. Consequently, the RB reflected contract practices, traditions and legal concepts of the common law system.

This first edition was based on certain fundamental principles that continue to apply today. Thus, the Conditions had as their objective:

> a clear and logical sequence of clauses, the removal of ambiguities, the elimination, so far as possible, of speculative elements *and a fair distribution of the risks inherent in works of civil engineering construction*.[53] (Emphasis added)

---

49. The ACE form was prepared jointly by ACE and the Export Group for the Construction Industries in the UK and was approved by the ICE.
50. For the differences between the ICE form, 4th edn, and the ACE form, *see* Nael Bunni, *The FIDIC Forms of Contract* (3rd edn, Blackwell Publishing, Oxford, 2005) 4-5.
51. For a comparison of the 'Engineer' in the common law system with its counterpart in the civil law system, *see* **Section 4. Common Law and Civil Law Compared – 4.4.1 Contract Administrator (*Maître D'Oeuvre*) *v* Engineer** of **Chapter II Applicable Law** below.
52. The edition was prepared by FIDIC jointly with FIBTP (*Fédération Internationale du Bâtiment et des Travaux Publics*) or the International Federation of Building and Public Works.
53. Explanatory Memorandum contained in RB/57.

The Conditions would, the accompanying Explanatory Memorandum said, 'hold the balance fairly between employers and contractors' and described the basic structure of the Conditions as being that:

> while there were numerous Clauses which would be universally applicable there were some Clauses which must necessarily vary to take account of the circumstances and locality of the Works. The Clauses of universal application have been grouped together and are referred to as Part I-General Conditions [...]
>
> The General Conditions are linked with the Conditions of Particular Application, referred to as Part II [...].
>
> The Clauses in Part II must be specially drafted to suit each particular Contract [...][54]

RB/57, like its successors (through 1987), provided that disputes were initially to be referred to the Engineer for decision and, if not resolved at the level of the Engineer, were to be finally decided in accordance with the 'Rules of Conciliation and Arbitration of the International Chamber of Commerce'.[55]

FIDIC published a second edition of the Red Book in 1969, a third edition in 1977 and a fourth edition in 1987.[56] While the Red Book generally increased in length with each edition, it retained basically the same clause structure and a similar number of clauses – about 70 – as the first edition issued in 1957.[57]

In 1995, FIDIC published the *Conditions of Contact for Design-Build and Turnkey* (the 'Orange Book') which contained important innovations

---

54. *Ibid.*
55. RB/57, Clause 67. In 1963, FIDIC published for the first time a form of standard conditions of contract for electrical and mechanical works suitable for use on contracts between the Employer and the Contractor for the supply and erection of plant and machinery (*Conditions of Contract for Electrical and Mechanical Works* (1st edn, FIDIC, 1963) (the 'Yellow Book' or 'YB'). A second edition of the YB was published in 1980 and a third in 1987, *see Conditions of Contract for Electrical and Mechanical Works* (2nd edn, FIDIC, 1980) and *Conditions of Contract for Electrical and Mechanical Works* (3rd edn, FIDIC 1987).
56. In 1994, FIDIC published *Conditions of Subcontract* for use with RB/87 and, in 2011, *Conditions of Subcontract* for use with RB/99 discussed in **Section 3.1.3** below of **Chapter I**.
57. Apart from the standard forms of contract themselves, FIDIC published 'notes' or guides for each standard form of construction contract and a

that were later to be introduced into the 1999 suite of documents, notably a 20-clause structure and the replacement of the Engineer as a decider of disputes before arbitration by a Dispute Adjudication Board ('DAB').

3.1.3 Red Book, 1st Edition (1999)[58], Rainbow Suite, Gold Book and Pink Book

In 1999, FIDIC's range of forms of construction contract was reorganised into a suite of three contract forms that became known as the 'Rainbow Suite'. This suite consisted of the following:

(1) *Conditions of Contract for Construction* for building and engineering works designed by the Employer (the 'Red Book' or 'RB/99').
(2) *Conditions of Contract for Plant and Design-Build* for electrical and mechanical plant and for building and engineering works designed by the Contractor (the 'Yellow Book' or 'YB/99').
(3) *Conditions of Contract for EPC/Turnkey Projects* ('EPC' being the abbreviation for engineer-procure-construct) (the 'Silver Book' or 'SB/99').[59]

An objective of the Rainbow Suite was to harmonise the contract forms so as to have, wherever possible, a common clause structure, common

---

'Tendering Procedure' document (1st edn, 1982 and 2nd edn 1994) which was updated by the more comprehensive *FIDIC Procurement Procedures Guide* (FIDIC, 2011).

58. *Conditions of Contract for Construction* for building and engineering works designed by the Employer (1st edn, FIDIC 1999) ('RB/99') and is otherwise to be distinguished from the original Red Book (1st edn, FIDIC, 1957) ('RB/57') as explained in **Section 3.1.3**.

59. In addition, FIDIC published in the same year (1999) a *Short Form of Contract* (1st edn, FIDIC, 1999) (the 'Green Book') which was suitable for 'fairly simple or repetitive work or work of short duration' (*see* the 'Foreword' to the Green Book). It did not include an Engineer, although one might be appointed if desired. It was designed to be flexible in terms of the allocation of design work and risk, and to allow the Employer a choice of valuation methods (measurement of the value of the work done versus a lump sum contract price). A second edition of the Green Book was published in 2021. *See* **Table 2 FIDIC's Forms of Contract** below in **Chapter I**.

procedures and a common vocabulary.[60] Each of the Red, Yellow and Silver Books, 1999, therefore featured the same 20-clause structure, with many common clauses or clauses with common wording. This was in marked contrast to previous editions of the Red and Yellow Books: the Red Book, fourth edition (1987), had 72 clauses; the Yellow Book, third edition (1987), had 51 clauses.

The Red, Yellow and Silver Books were also distinguished from each other by who (whether the Employer or the Contractor) was doing the majority of the design work. Before the 1999 editions, the Red and Yellow Books were distinguished from each other by the nature of the work done: the Red Book was for civil engineering work and the Yellow Book was for electrical and mechanical work. However, beginning in 1999, this distinction was dropped and the Red Book was prepared to cover, instead, situations where the majority of the design work was done by the Employer or its consulting engineer, whereas the Yellow Book was prepared to cover design-build projects as well as plant projects where the majority of the design was done by the Contractor.

The Silver Book was a new standard form of contract in 1999. It was issued to respond to market demand from the private sector for a form of contract for turnkey projects which, while allowing the Contractor a correspondingly higher contract price, would provide the Employer with greater certainty of the final price and of timely completion. While traditionally FIDIC's forms had observed the principle of balanced risk sharing between the Employer and the Contractor,[61] the Silver Book avowedly placed more risk on the Contractor than FIDIC's other construction contract forms.[62] At the same time, in an important – but often neglected – Introductory Note to the Silver Book, FIDIC cautioned that it

---

60. Since the previous editions of the Red and Yellow Books (as well as of FIDIC's *Conditions of Contact for Design-Build and Turnkey* or 'Orange Book' or 'OB' published in 1995) had been prepared by separate drafting groups, each with its own preferences, each had a different clause structure and different provisions on matters such as *force majeure*, special risks, limitations on liability, and procedures for seeking an Engineer's decision on disputes. *See* Christopher R Seppälä, 'New Standard Forms of International Construction Contract' (February 2001) Int'l Bus L 60, 61.
61. As stated in **Section 3.1.2** above.
62. Though the Silver Book also differed from the Red and Yellow Books by including some provisions which, arguably, were more protective of the Contractor. For example, under Sub-Clause 3.5, the Contractor could be relieved of having to give effect to a determination of the Employer (who,

was not suitable for use in specified cases, such as where the Contractor could not reasonably be expected to be able to evaluate the risks involved.[63]

The Red Book provided for payment based on the measurement of work done valued at unit rates, whereas the Yellow and Silver Books each provided for payment based on a lump sum price. Each form of contract in the Rainbow Suite had provided, as standard, for a DAB instead of having the Engineer resolve disputes (and, in the Silver Book, the contract administrator was the 'Employer's Representative' rather than the Engineer).

In the simplest terms, the relationship between the three major books in their 2017 editions remains the same as in their 1999 editions: under the Red Book, the Employer takes most of the design responsibility but otherwise risk is shared with the Contractor; under the Yellow Book, the Employer does the conceptual design work, and the Contractor undertakes the final design, but otherwise risk is shared (to some extent as in the Red Book); and under the Silver Book, the Contractor takes on all or almost all of the design work, as well as nearly all risk.

In 2008, FIDIC published *Conditions of Contract for Design, Build and Operate Projects* (the 'Gold Book' or 'GB/08'), which contained a number of innovations that were subsequently introduced into RB/17, YB/17 and SB/17. Under the Gold Book, the Contractor has both a design-build obligation, based on the Yellow Book, and a long-term (20-year) commitment to operate the facility once it has been built.

FIDIC has cooperated with The World Bank and other multilateral development banks ('MDBs')[64] for many years. This resulted in the publication by FIDIC of the *MDB Harmonised Edition* of RB/99 (the 'Pink Book') for use in relation to projects financed by MDBs, the latest version of which was published in 2010. In 2019, The World Bank issued *Conditions of Particular Application* ('COPA') or *Particular Conditions* for

under the Silver Book, replaced the Engineer in this respect) by giving a notice of dissatisfaction to the Employer.

63. 'Introductory Note to First Edition' in SB/99 and in 'Notes' to SB/17.

64. These banks are (or have been): African Development Bank, Asian Development Bank, Black Sea Trade and Development Bank, Caribbean Development Bank, Council of Europe Development Bank, European Bank for Reconstruction and Development, Inter-American Development Bank, International Bank for Reconstruction and Development ('The World Bank'), Islamic Bank for Development Bank and the Nordic Development Fund.

use with the General Conditions of RB/17 and these have effectively replaced the Pink Book.[65]

3.2 Distinctive Features

The following are five distinctive features of FIDIC's forms of construction contract, notably the RB and YB and, in most cases, the SB.

3.2.1 Use of British-English Language

As indicated in **Section 3.1 Origin and History** above, the first three or four editions of the RB derived from and were closely modelled on the United Kingdom's ICE *Conditions of Contract*. Accordingly, they used legal terminology that was typical of British domestic standard forms and – although American-English is influencing international construction contracts[66] – the RB continues today to be written in British-English. To illustrate this (and the varieties of English construction terms being used), certain FIDIC British-English construction terms are shown next to their American-English rough equivalents in Table 1:

Table 1 FIDIC British-English Terms and Their American-English Rough Equivalents

FIDIC British-English	*American-English*
Bill of Quantities	Schedule of Values
Contractor	Contractor / Design-Builder
Contractors' All Risk ('CAR') insurance	Builder's risk insurance[1]
Deeming (provisions), e.g., deemed takeover	Constructive (provisions), e.g., constructive acceptance
Defects Notification Period	Warranty Period
Employer	Owner
Employer's Requirements	[Owner's] Project Criteria
Engineer	Design Professional
Entitled to an EOT	Excusable delay
Entitled to an EOT and Cost	Compensable delay

65. However, some other MDBs are continuing to use the Pink Book.
66. For example., The World Bank's procurement of works' documents tend to be written in American-English.

FIDIC British-English	*American-English*
Interim payment	Progress payment
Invitation to Tender	Request for Bids
Main (Contractor)	Prime (Contractor)
Nominated contractor system	'Prefiled' bids
Programme	Schedule
Provisional Sum	Allowance, Contingency Allowance
Retention (Money)	Retainage
Snag or Snagging List	Punch List
Tender	Bid
Turnover	Revenue
Variation Instruction	Change Order
Variation Payment	Equitable Adjustment
Variation	Change

Source: Author's own work.

Notes

[1] This insurance may be 'all risk' or cover only 'specified perils', John M Mastin and others (eds), *Smith, Currie & Hancock's Common Sense Construction Law: A Practical Guide for the Construction Professional* (6th edn, Wiley, Hoboken, NJ, 2020) 545.

It would be much more difficult to prepare a chart of the British-English rough equivalents of American-English construction terminology as American-English construction terms are more numerous with the result that there are many American-English terms for which there are no simple British-English rough equivalents, e.g., backcharge, cardinal change, constructive acceleration, constructive change, deductive change, design specifications versus performance specifications, fast-track rules, submittals and multi-prime contracting.[67] As a result, a number of American-English terms, often having no simple British-English equivalent, appear gradually to have seeped into British-English, for example: acceleration claim, termination for convenience, turnkey and value engineering.

Beginning with RB/87, FIDIC has endeavoured to simplify the contract language in its contract forms so that it is more understandable to engineers from around the world. Thus, FIDIC eliminated most legal and

67. For a source of American-English construction terms *see* Elizabeth A Patrick and others (eds), *The Annotated Construction Law Glossary* (ABA For Const L, Chicago, IL, 2010).

technical terms that were specifically English or otherwise difficult for engineers from different countries or cultures to understand.[68] Nevertheless, the FIDIC forms continue to retain features typical of standard forms of construction contract in common law countries.

3.2.2 'Independent' Engineer

One such feature is the so-called independent role of the 'Engineer', who acts as contract administrator under an RB (and YB) contract and, until replaced in the 1999 Rainbow Suite by the DAB, had also acted as pre-arbitral decision-maker. This independent role of the Engineer is virtually unknown in civil law countries.[69]

In common law countries, to develop a project, a promoter (who later becomes the 'Employer' when a construction contract is signed) will normally engage a consulting engineer or engineering firm under a consultancy services agreement.[70] Under the terms of this consultancy agreement, the consultant may undertake, among other things, to prepare initial studies, a feasibility report, a project strategy and, assuming the promoter decides to proceed with the project, to prepare documents for the pre-qualification of tenderers and the tender dossier comprising the letter of invitation to tender, instructions to tenderers, conditions of contract, specification, initial drawings and schedules including a bill of

---

68. For example, in the fourth and subsequent editions of the RB, terms or concepts such as 'frustration', 'repudiation' and 'wayleave', which have specific meanings in English law or language, have been replaced by vocabulary which is better understood internationally. Thus: 'Frustration' (Clause 66 of RB/77), 'Release from Performance' (Clause 66 of RB/87), and 'Force Majeure' (Clause 19 of RB/99) have been replaced by 'Exceptional Events' (also a defined term) (Clause 18 in RB/17); the expression 'has repudiated the Contract' (Sub-Clause 63.1 (a) of RB/87) has been replaced by 'plainly demonstrates an intention not to continue performance of the Contractor's obligations under the Contract' (Sub-Clause 15.2.1 (b) of RB/17 – there was similar language in Sub-Clause 15.2(b) of RB/99); and the term 'wayleave' (Sub-Clause 42.3 of RB/87) has been replaced by 'right-of-way' (Sub-Clauses 4.13 of RB/99 and RB/17).
69. *See* **Section 4 Common Law and Civil Law Compared – 4.4.1 Contract Administrator (*Maître D'Oeuvre*) *v* Engineer** in **Chapter II Applicable Law** below.
70. *See*, e.g., FIDIC's *Client/Consultant Model Services Agreement* ('White Book') (5th edn, FIDIC, 2017).

quantities.[71] The consultancy agreement (or a separate agreement) may often require the consultant, once the construction contract is signed, to act as the 'Engineer' under that contract and administer the execution of the Works by the Contractor on behalf of the Employer. In administering a construction contract based on the Red Book, the Engineer is required to act in two capacities: (1) as an agent of the Employer when instructing Variations and supervising and inspecting the construction work on the Employer's behalf[72] and (2) as a person who must act 'neutrally' between the Parties and 'fairly' when determining a Party's matters or Claims as well as 'fairly' when certifying payments under the Contract.[73] It is this second role of the Engineer to act neutrally and/or fairly which is distinctive of FIDIC contracts and virtually unknown in civil law countries.

While in the 19th century British engineers introduced this contracting system into countries of the former British Empire (e.g., Australia, Canada, Hong Kong, India, New Zealand, Nigeria, Pakistan, South Africa) and it was adopted in the USA, it differs from construction contract practices in civil law countries. In civil law countries, the powers of the contract administrator are more attenuated and the authority of the Employer commensurately greater.[74]

---

71. *See* **Section 2.1 Invitation to Tender** in **Chapter IV Clause-by-Clause Commentary** below and the *FIDIC Procurement Procedures Guide* (FIDIC, 2011) 9-41 and 115-124.
72. *See* Sub-Clause 3.2 [*Engineer's Duties and Authority*] of RB/17 providing that, except as otherwise stated in the Conditions, the Engineer 'shall be deemed to act for the Employer' and the commentary on that Sub-Clause in **Chapter IV** below.
73. *See* Sub-Clauses 3.7 [*Agreement or Determination*], 14.6.1 [*The IPC*] and 14.13 [*Issue of FPC*] of RB/17 and the commentaries on those Sub-Clauses in **Chapter IV** below. Earlier editions of the RB required the Engineer to act 'impartially' (Clause 2.6 RB/87) and to make 'fair' determinations (Sub-Clauses 3.5 and 14.6 of the RB/99). Before 1999, the Engineer also had under the RB to decide disputes between the Parties as a condition to arbitration (e.g., in Clause 67 of RB/87). Under RB/99 and RB/17, this role was assumed by a DAB and, in RB/17, a DAAB (Clause 21 of RB/17).
74. *See* **Section 4 – Common Law and Civil Law Compared – 4.4.1 Contract Administrator (*Maître D'Oeuvre*) *v* Engineer** of **Chapter II Applicable Law** below comparing the common law engineer with the civil law contract administrator. *See also* the commentary on Clause 3 [*The Engineer*] in **Chapter IV Clause-by-Clause Commentary** below.

3.2.3 *Balanced Risk Sharing*

Another distinctive feature of most of the FIDIC forms, since the first edition of the RB published in 1957, is their common approach to risk sharing between the Employer and the Contractor. As Christopher Wade, a former Chairman of the FIDIC Contracts Committee, noted when discussing the principles behind the original Rainbow Suite:

> FIDIC's Red and Yellow Books have been recognised for their principles of balanced risk sharing between the employer and the contractor. These risk sharing principles have been beneficial for both parties, the employer signing a contract at a lower price and only having further costs when particular unusual risks actually eventuate, and the contractor avoiding pricing such risks which are hard to evaluate.[75]

The fair and balanced approach to risk allocation has been maintained in RB/17 and YB/17.[76]

FIDIC has stated in its promotional materials that its forms have six characteristics:

- Balanced: Seen as generally fair apportioning of risks, rights and obligations between parties (not Silver Book);
- Accepted: In wide use for international contracting;
- Adaptable: General conditions and particular conditions;
- Supported: Recommended or required by Multilateral Development Bank Standard Bidding Documents;
- Continuity: Long term use, which gives familiarity and a degree of certainty; and
- Proactive: Dispute avoidance and early resolution focused.[77]

3.2.4 *Multiple Clauses for Contingencies*

A fourth feature of FIDIC's forms which has its origin in common law contract practice is that they contain multiple procedures or remedial

75. Christopher Wade, 'FIDIC's Standard Forms of Contract – Principles and Scope of the Four New Books' [2000] ICLR 5, 1.
76. The exception is the *Conditions of Contract for EPC/Turnkey Projects* (2nd edn, FIDIC, 2017) (2017 Silver Book or SB/17), which puts most risk on the Contractor and which should *not* be used in the circumstances listed in the 'Notes' section at the beginning of SB/17.
77. Source: Mr Zoltán Záhonyi, former Chair, FIDIC's CC.

clauses or sub-clauses for dealing with contingencies that may arise under a construction contract as the result of new or unforeseeable events or circumstances that affect the Contractor's and/or Employer's costs and/or the Contractor's time for completion and, indeed, in some cases, the feasibility of completing the Works at all. Examples include clauses or sub-clauses dealing with unforeseeable underground conditions, extreme weather conditions (e.g., tornadoes or hurricanes), natural catastrophes (e.g., earthquakes, volcanoes or epidemics), political events (e.g., war, hostilities, rebellion or terrorism), economic events (e.g., inflation), and changes or suspensions in the Works instructed by the Engineer.

These clauses or sub-clauses allow for the Contract Price and/or Time for Completion to be adjusted to take account of such new events or circumstances, or allow for work to be changed, suspended or, in extreme cases, for the Contract to be terminated. As a general rule, they are designed to ensure that construction can continue without interruption, whenever possible, and for the Contractor to continue to be paid, so far as possible, without resort to courts or arbitration. Typical examples of such provisions in RB/17 are Sub-Clause 1.9 [*Delayed Drawings or Instructions*], Sub-Clause 3.5 [*Engineer's Instructions*], Sub-Clause 3.7 [*Agreement or Determination*], Sub-Clause 4.12 [*Unforeseeable Physical Conditions*], Sub-Clause 8.5 [*Extension of Time for Completion*], Sub-Clause 8.6 [*Delays Caused by Authorities*], Clause 13 [*Variations and Adjustments*], Clause 18 [*Exceptional Events*] and Clause 20 [*Employer's and Contractor's Claims*].

As FIDIC contracts are usually used for works in developing countries where respect for the rule of law is often much weaker than in the developed world,[78] they provide self-contained procedural solutions to address, so far as possible, new and/or unforeseeable (or unforeseen) adverse events and circumstances so as to allow work to continue without the need for recourse to local courts or other legal procedures.

78. Transparency International, a non-profit organisation, maintains an index to measure perceived corruption through opinion surveys of business leaders and others. This index indicates that the developing world is, on average, far more corrupt than the developed world. Corruption Perception Index https://www.transparency.org/en/cpi# accessed 2 November 2022.

3.2.5 *Contract Structure*

Another distinctive feature of the FIDIC forms is their common structure, layout and wording. They consist principally of General Conditions, *Guidance for the Preparation of Particular Conditions*, and certain standard forms, one of which is a one-page form of Contract Agreement which the Parties are expected to sign.

As mentioned above,[79] the General Conditions, which are quite voluminous, comprise Clauses that are considered to be 'universally applicable' but which are subject to modification by Particular Conditions 'to take account of the circumstances and locality of the Works'. This is an advantage as international contractors will usually already be familiar with the General Conditions from prior projects, and therefore need only examine the Particular Conditions in order to ascertain which conditions are new and specific to a project. They are therefore relieved from having to familiarise themselves with a completely new set of contract conditions each time they tender for a new project. Once told that the General Conditions will be those in RB/17, as modified or supplemented by the Particular Conditions, they will know that they have only to study the Particular Conditions.

3.3 How They Are Prepared

As discussed above,[80] the Contracts Committee of FIDIC ('CC') is the committee that is responsible for the preparation of the FIDIC forms. Like members of other FIDIC committees and task groups, the members of the CC generally provide their services voluntarily. The primary functions of the CC include the following:

- Identify and anticipate market needs, strategically position FIDIC and develop FIDIC's approach to contracts.
- Develop and update the FIDIC suite of contracts and related documents.

79. *See* **Section 3.1.2 Red Book, 1st Edition (1957)** above of **Chapter I General Introduction**.
80. *See* **Section 2.2 FIDIC's Organisation and Activities** above of **Chapter I General Introduction**.

- Advocate and guide best practice in FIDIC contracts across the global engineering and construction industry.[81]

In its work the CC is supported by different task groups comprising mainly engineers. These engineers may come from different disciplines, for example, civil engineers for the RB and electrical and mechanical engineers for the YB. Most of these task groups work on the updating of existing contract forms or on developing new ones. However, task groups are also engaged in other matters.

It should be emphasised that the content of FIDIC's forms is determined by engineers drawing on their 'engineering common sense' and not by lawyers.[82] The role of lawyers is generally confined to ensuring that FIDIC's forms, especially clauses having legal content,[83] are satisfactory. At the same time, increasingly, engineers on the CC have some legal qualifications.

In the course of the preparation and revision of FIDIC's forms, FIDIC consults a wide range of organisations and persons.[84] As pointed out by Christopher Wade in 2000 (and no less true today):

> In preparing documents, FIDIC has always consulted widely with those sectors likely to be involved in the use of the documents. Active participation has long been welcomed from the World Bank, and FIDIC today works closely with the European International Contractors (EIC) and ORGALIME, which represents leading mechanical and electrical manufacturers.[85]

As discussed above,[86] FIDIC regularly seeks feedback from The World Bank and other MDBs when preparing new standard forms or updating

81. *See* 'Contracts Committee' (*FIDIC*) www.fidic.org/node/776 accessed 2 November 2022.
82. Christopher Wade, 'FIDIC's Standard Forms of Contract – Principles and Scope of the Four New Books' [2000] ICLR 5, 6.
83. For example, relating to dispute resolution, liquidated damages and limitation of liability.
84. A list of the persons and organisations consulted in the preparation of RB/17 is contained in the 'Acknowledgements' section of that form.
85. Christopher Wade, 'FIDIC's Standard Forms of Contract – Principles and Scope of the Four New Books' [2000] ICLR 5.
86. *See* **Section 3.1.3** above of **Chapter I General Introduction**.

existing ones. FIDIC also cooperates with different contractors' organisations such as European International Contractors ('EIC'), an organisation of European contractors,[87] and the Confederation of International Contractors' Associations ('CICA').[88] Thus, FIDIC regularly invites EIC to comment on drafts of FIDIC's new forms of contract as well as on drafts of new editions of its existing forms.[89]

FIDIC's standard forms of construction contract almost always contain an arbitration clause providing for arbitration under the Rules of Arbitration of the International Chamber of Commerce ('ICC Arbitration Rules'). In addition, the 2017 Red, Yellow and Silver Books provide that challenges to a Dispute Avoidance/Adjudication Board ('DAAB') member will be administered by the ICC International Center for ADR.[90] They also incorporate by reference model forms of security documents published by the ICC.[91]

4 FIDIC RED BOOK (2017) REPRINTED IN 2022 ('RB/17')

4.1 Preparation of RB/17

At the 2008 FIDIC International Users' Conference in London, FIDIC announced that a Task Group had been formed to update the 1999 Rainbow Suite. One purpose of the update was for the Rainbow Suite to incorporate some of the innovations that had been adopted in the Gold Book published in 2008 ('GB/08').[92] That contract form had been prepared for situations where the Contractor was expected to design and

87. *See* European International Contractors (EIC) Federation, 'European International Contractors Mission' https://www.eic-federation.eu/federation/eic-mission accessed 2 November 2022.
88. CICA http://cica.net/ accessed 2 November 2022.
89. However, EIC does not endorse FIDIC's forms. On the contrary, EIC has its own independent views on them, as reflected in EIC Contractor's Guides to the RB, YB and SB, as well as GB/08, which EIC publishes.
90. *See* Rule 11 of the DAAB Procedural Rules ('DAAB Rules').
91. The forms of demand guarantee in the 2017 Rainbow Suite provide that they are subject to the ICC's *Uniform Rules for Demand Guarantees* (ICC Publication no 758, 2010), and the form of surety bond in the same suite provides that it is subject to the ICC's *Uniform Rules for Contract Bonds* (ICC Publication no 524, 1993).
92. That is, the *Conditions of Contract for Design, Build and Operate Projects* (FIDIC 2008) (the 'Gold Book' or 'GB/08').

build a project, and then operate it for a fixed period of time (typically 20 years) before transferring it to the Employer.

FIDIC decided to commence with the revision of the Yellow Book because in terms of content, it is midway between the Red Book and the Silver Book. The terms of reference of the relevant task group required it to take the Gold Book into account and avoid differences in the definitions, approach, structure and wording between the books, unless it was necessary to reflect differences in subject matter between the Red, Yellow and Silver Books. Throughout the drafting process, harmonisation of the procedures in the three books remained an objective, but the new editions were not intended to alter the relationship between the three books as it existed in 1999. The three books remain distinct in their procurement strategy and, accordingly, in the allocation of design responsibility and risk that flows from the choice of that strategy.

Three different task groups worked successively over nine years on the updating: the Initial Update Task Group, the Second Stage Task Group and, finally, the FIDIC Contracts Committee's Updates Special Group.[93] Many individuals and organisations reviewed and commented on drafts of the new books.[94]

A draft of the proposed new Yellow Book was published as a conference edition at the FIDIC Users' Conference in London in December 2016. Definitive editions (called 'second editions') of the new Red, Yellow and Silver Books were published by FIDIC in November 2017.

In 2019, The World Bank adopted the 2017 edition of the Rainbow Suite, as well as other FIDIC forms of contract,[95] for use in projects financed by The World Bank, as appropriate and complemented by the Bank's Conditions of Particular Application ('COPA'). As far as The World Bank is concerned, the 2017 edition of the Red Book, as modified by COPA, replaces the Pink Book.[96]

---

93. *See* 'Acknowledgements' at the beginning of each of the 2017 Red, Yellow and Silver Books.
94. *Ibid.*
95. Notably, the White Book, 2017, the Gold Book, 2008, and the Green Book, 1999.
96. The World Bank has stated that it plans to use the 2017 Rainbow Suite (among other FIDIC forms) in projects financed by the Bank 'as appropriate and complemented by our Conditions of Particular Application (COPA)' according to the statement of Enzo De Laurentiis, Chief Procurement Officer

FIDIC has signed a number of agreements with other multilateral development banks ('MDBs') providing for their use of FIDIC forms of contract.

In 2022, FIDIC published reprints of the 2017 editions of the Red, Yellow and Silver Books incorporating amendments made by FIDIC to these forms in 2018, 2019 and 2022.[97] The 2022 amendments were numerous and included new definitions, in Sub-Clause 1.1, of 'Claim' and 'Dispute' and, in Sub-Clause 3.7 (a), of a 'matter to be agreed or determined'. This book is a commentary upon the 2022 reprint with amendments of the 2017 edition of the Red Book.

4.2 Documents Comprising RB/17

RB/17 comprises three sections:

(1) the General Conditions (107 pages) (and, as an Appendix thereto, the General Conditions of DAAB Agreement ('DAAB GCs') (9 pages) and, as an Annex thereto, DAAB Procedural Rules ('DAAB Rules') (7 pages)), followed by an Index of Sub-Clauses (5 pages);

(2) *Guidance for the Preparation of Particular Conditions*, comprising:
   - Particular Conditions Part A – Contract Data containing Introductory Guidance Notes (1 page) and a Contract Data form (for completion) (5 pages).
   - Particular Conditions Part B – Special Provisions which, after an Introduction (2 pages), contains Notes on the Preparation of Tender Documents (3 pages), detailed Notes on the Preparation of Special Provisions (40 pages), Advisory Notes on Building Information Modelling Systems (3 pages) and, as Annexes A to G, forms of securities (for completion) (10 pages); and

of The World Bank, as reported in a FIDIC Press Release, 'World Bank Signs Five-year Agreement to Use FIDIC Standard Contracts' (14 February 2019).

97. For details, *see* the Note following the List of Abbreviations and Definitions at the beginning of this book. The original 2017 edition of the Red Book should not be used.

(3) forms of Letter of Tender, Letter of Acceptance, Contract Agreement and DAAB Agreement (all for completion) (6 pages in total).[98]

These are designed, once completed and/or adapted by the Employer, for inclusion in a tender dossier for building and engineering works designed by the Employer or its engineering consultant.

4.3 Changes from the Red Book, 1999 ('RB/99')

The changes reflected in RB/17 as compared to RB/99 are very extensive. Almost every Clause or Sub-Clause has been altered in some respect. As these changes are described in detail in the commentary in **Chapter IV** below, no attempt will be made to summarise them here. Instead, this section will note FIDIC's objectives in publishing the 2017 editions and describe the increased length, overall structure and differences in presentation of RB/17 as compared to RB/99. While the fundamental principles and general clause structure of RB/99 have been retained, RB/17 regulates contract administration and claims procedures in much greater detail. Moreover, to some extent,[99] the Engineer has reassumed in RB/17 the role it had in relation to claims in RB/87.[100]

FIDIC has described its objectives in its 2017 contract updates as follows:

> The core aim of the majority of the changes in FIDIC's 2017 contract updates is increased clarity and certainty, to reduce the risk of disagreements regarding the interpretation of contract terms and, as a result, increase the probability of successful projects.

98. FIDIC has published a useful 'Memo to the 2017 Suite' http://fidic.org/sites/default/files/bean_files/Memo%20for%20Rainbow%20Suite%202017%2004.06.19.pdf accessed 2 November 2022.
99. Notably, by Sub-Clause 3.7 [*Agreement or Determination*].
100. Thus, under RB/87, the Engineer had decided not only Contractor's claims but also disputes under Clause 67 before arbitration. While under RB/17 only the DAAB is empowered to decide Disputes (a term which is now defined in RB/17), the Engineer is empowered under Sub-Clause 3.7 – in a much more formal and detailed procedure than in RB/99 – to agree (with the Parties) or determine any matter or Claim (a term now also defined) between the Parties before it can be referred to the DAAB. This is not dissimilar to the role of the Engineer under Clause 67 of RB/87.

> Consistent with the above, FIDIC has improved the contract provisions by making them more prescriptive and introducing step-by-step project management and procedural mechanisms, by setting out exactly what is expected from the Employer, the Contractor and the Engineer during the performance of the Contract.[101]

As mentioned in Section 4.1 above, RB/17 as well as YB/17 and SB/17 incorporate to some extent changes that were introduced in the Gold Book in 2008, the most recent form of construction contract for major works which FIDIC had published.[102] The Gold Book represents in some respects a sort of halfway house between the 1999 contracts and the 2017 contracts.

RB/17 is much longer and more detailed than RB/99. Whereas the General Conditions of RB/99 (excluding the table of contents and appendix) comprised 62 pages, the General Conditions of RB/17 (with the same exclusions) comprises 106 pages. The General Conditions of RB/17 also include more defined terms: 88 compared to 58 in RB/99.

The overall clause structure of the new Red Book is similar to that of RB/99 except that there are now 21 clauses instead of the 20 clauses in RB/99. Moreover, there are differences in the overall presentation of Clauses 17 to 21 of RB/17 compared to RB/99, as follows:

- In RB/17, Clause 17 is entitled '*Care of the Works and Indemnities*' and is to some extent different in content from the same Clause entitled '*Risk and Responsibility*' in RB/99.
- In RB/17, Clause 18 is entitled '*Exceptional Events*' and corresponds (but with a different title) to Clause 19 '*Force Majeure*' in RB/99.
- In RB/17, Clause 19 entitled '*Insurance*' corresponds to Clause 18 entitled '*Insurance*' in RB/99.
- In RB/17, Clause 20 entitled '*Employer's and Contractor's Claims*' corresponds to, but is much more detailed than, Sub-Clause 2.5

101. Paper entitled 'FIDIC Red, Yellow and Silver Books, second edition 2017: a Review of the updated General Conditions of Contract', 1, distributed by FIDIC in November 2017 to speakers (FIDIC International Users' Conference, London, December 2017). A modified version of this paper (omitting, however, the above quotation) is available at https://fidic.org/events/fidic-international-contract-users-conference-london-5-6-december-2017 accessed 2 November 2022.
102. Apart from the Pink Book (representing the views of the MDBs), the last edition of which was published in 2010.

entitled '*Employer's Claims*' and Sub-Clause 20.1 entitled '*Contractor's Claims*', taken together, in RB/99.

- New Clause 21 entitled '*Disputes and Arbitration*' in RB/17 corresponds to Sub-Clauses 20.2 through 20.8 of Clause 20 entitled '*Claims, Disputes and Arbitration*' in RB/99.

The only other change in presentation of note is that, in RB/17, Clause 5 is now entitled '*Subcontracting*' and deals with that subject generally, whereas in RB/99, it was entitled and dealt only with '*Nominated Subcontractors*'.

Along with the 2017 editions of the FIDIC Contract forms, FIDIC has developed much more detailed rules for the dispute board (now called the 'Dispute Avoidance/Adjudication Board' ('DAAB')). These are contained in Clause 21, the DAAB GCs and DAAB Rules.[103] They place greater emphasis on dispute avoidance, address practical problems (e.g., as the result of the refusal of a Party to cooperate in constituting a DAB), and provide a more comprehensive, autonomous code for dispute resolution to minimise the need to resort to remedies outside the contract and international arbitration.

Following the publication of the new Rainbow Suite, some time is likely to elapse before users make significant use of the new forms. Even though the new suite is a great improvement over the 1999 suite, users are habitually reserved – and understandably so – about making use of new, untested editions of forms of contract. Moreover, all will not welcome the greater length and increased procedural complexity of the 2017 forms. Thus, some users who are comfortable with the 1999 forms are likely to continue to use them. A similar trend to continue using older and already familiar FIDIC forms was observed after the release of the 1999 suite. However, that suite eventually gained wide acceptance.

4.4 FIDIC's *Guides*

In addition to the contracts themselves, *The FIDIC Contracts Guide*, first edition (2000), second edition (2022) and the *FIDIC Procurement Procedures Guide* (2011) are valuable sources for explaining the meaning and uses of FIDIC contracts.

103. The DAAB Rules are annexed to the DAAB GCs. The DAAB GCs and DAAB Rules are commented on in **Section 2** of **Chapter V Commentary on Other Documents** below.

4.4.1 The FIDIC Contracts Guide (2022)

The FIDIC Contracts Guide, second edition (2022) comments on the 2017 Red, Yellow, Silver Books, as reprinted in 2022 with amendments, on a clause-by-clause and comparative bases. It refers to each clause, reproducing the three versions of each provision in parallel text, provides commentary on the meaning and function of each, and explains their differences. It also provides a comparison of the main features of each book to enable users to understand which would be best suited for a given project.

As discussed in **Chapter III** below,[104] the legal value of external documents, such as FIDIC's *Guides*, in interpreting a FIDIC form of contract may differ depending on both the applicable law and the forum. In common law jurisdictions, such documents are, theoretically, seen as irrelevant to interpreting contracts under the 'parol evidence rule',[105] as the words of the contract are given primary (if not exclusive) weight when determining the meaning of a contract. In civil law jurisdictions, however, there is no such rule and it is the intention of the parties that determines how the contract should be interpreted.[106] In an international arbitration – and the RB provides for international arbitration[107] making this the most relevant case – arbitrators are unlikely to object to receiving such extrinsic evidence, regardless of what law they are applying.[108]

In fact, *The FIDIC Contracts Guide*, first edition (2000) has played a somewhat special role in influencing the interpretation of these contracts because of its status as a definitive statement from the organisation responsible for publishing them. As such, it has been used as a source for the interpretation of FIDIC contracts by both common law and civil law tribunals. In one Swiss case, for example, the Federal Tribunal (Switzerland's highest court) relied on a passage in the *Guide* to conclude that if a party was being intransigent in constituting a DAB, the other party

104. *See* **Section 5.5 FIDIC's Publications** of **Chapter III Contract Interpretation** below.
105. *See* **Section 4.2 Common Law: State Courts** of **Chapter III Contract Interpretation** below.
106. *See* **Section 4.1 Civil Law: State Courts** in **Chapter III Contract Interpretation** below.
107. *See* Sub-Clause 21.6 [*Arbitration*].
108. *See* **Section 5.7 Effect of an International Arbitration Clause** in **Chapter III Contract Interpretation** below.

could refer a dispute directly to arbitration under Sub-Clause 20.8 of RB/99, without requesting a DAB decision.[109] In an English Technology Court case, the Judge used the *Guide* to clarify the difference between standing and ad hoc DABs, concluding – correctly – that Sub-Clause 20.8 of SB/99 (which is the same in RB/99 and YB/99) was originally intended only for contracts where a standing – not an ad hoc – DAB was provided for.[110]

4.4.2 FIDIC Procurement Procedures Guide (2011)

The early chapters of the *FIDIC Procurement Procedures Guide* provide 'essential guidance on the underlying concepts and philosophy of projects in the broadest sense, to the point where a contract type is chosen'.[111] This *Guide* describes the process of developing a project strategy, including feasibility studies and other preliminary tasks, choosing a contract type, developing tender documents, pre-qualifying tenderers and obtaining tenders. It has separate chapters for obtaining tenders[112] and awarding contracts[113] under the Red Book. The *Guide* is therefore a most useful source of information for the preparatory phase of a project.

4.4.3 FIDIC's 'Golden Principles'

FIDIC's forms of construction contract are widely recognised as providing for a sensible, fair and balanced sharing of risk between the Contractor and the Employer.[114] Accordingly, a contract which is recognised as being a FIDIC contract has a certain commercial value to both the Employer and the Contractor at the tendering stage and during execution of the works.

---

109. *A v B* Swiss Federal Tribunal, Case no 4A_124, Judgment of 7 July 2014 [para. 3.4.3.3].
110. *Peterborough City Council v Enterprise Managed Services Ltd* [2014] EWHC 3193 (TCC) [paras 12, 13 and 33].
111. *FIDIC Procurement Procedures Guide* (FIDIC, 2011) 3.
112. Chapter 11.
113. Chapter 19.
114. *See* **Section 3.2 Distinctive Features** above of **Chapter I General Introduction**. The one exception being the Silver Book, *see* **Section 3.1.3 Red Book 1st Edition (1999), the Rainbow Suite, Gold Book and Pink Book** above of **Chapter I General Introduction**.

However, FIDIC has noted with increasing frequency that parties are making such significant changes to the General Conditions in the Particular Conditions that, though a contract may be presented as a 'FIDIC' contract, it may no longer reflect the principles of fair and balanced risk allocation for which FIDIC contracts (other than the Silver Book[115]) are known and respected. FIDIC sees this sort of practice as misleading to tenderers, the public and others, and as jeopardising the 'FIDIC brand'.

FIDIC therefore appointed a Task Group to determine the 'Golden Principles' or, in other words, the features that a contract must have in order to be considered a genuine FIDIC contract.[116] This led in 2019 to the publication of *The FIDIC Golden Principles* which sets out the Golden Principles, the reasoning behind them and guidance for drafting particular conditions that comply with those Principles.

FIDIC has initially identified five Golden Principles,[117] as follows:

- GP1: Division of Roles – The duties, rights, obligations, roles and responsibilities of all the Contract Participants must be generally as implied in the General Conditions, and appropriate to the requirements of the project.
- GP2: Drafting – The Particular Conditions must be drafted clearly and unambiguously.
- GP3: Risk/Reward – The Particular Conditions must not change the balance of risk/reward allocation provided for in the General Conditions.
- GP4: Time – All time periods specified in the Contract for Contract Participants to perform their obligations must be of reasonable duration.
- GP5: Disputes – Unless there is a conflict with the governing law of the Contract, all formal disputes must be referred to a Dispute Avoidance/Adjudication Board (or a Dispute Adjudication Board,

115. Due to the specific market conditions to which the Silver Book is a response, as explained in the Introductory Note at the beginning of SB/99.
116. The information given here is derived from presentations made by Dr Donald Charrett, the principal drafter of the Task Group, Mr Alfonso Pelosi and Mr Cremona Cotovelea (FIDIC International Contract Users' Conference, London, December 2016).
117. *See The FIDIC Golden Principles* (1st edn, FIDIC, 2019) and the Powerpoints of Mr Husni Madi and Dr Donald Charrett (FIDIC International Contract Users' Conference, London, 5-6 December 2017).

if applicable) for a provisionally binding decision as a condition precedent to arbitration.

Practice over many years has shown that a sensible, balanced risk sharing between the Contractor and the Employer results in the lowest overall total cost for completed projects.[118] Accordingly, consistent with FIDIC's Golden Principles, the MDBs – which are required by their articles of agreement or by-laws to give due attention to considerations of economy[119] – may provide in their procurement guidelines or documents for works that the 'conditions of contract shall provide a balanced allocation of risks and liabilities'.[120]

4.4.4 Proposed Sixth Golden Principle

However, consideration should be given to the adoption of a sixth Golden Principle: where a contract is for international use, it should provide, as a general rule, for *the final settlement of disputes by international commercial arbitration in a neutral venue.*

This Principle is advisable as, in reality, international commercial contracts are usually difficult or impossible to enforce in national courts in the developing world, where FIDIC contracts are usually used – especially against states or other public bodies who often act as the Employer under the Red Book. If a contract cannot be enforced, it has little value. Thus, for a FIDIC contract to be fairly balanced and the parties to be on a 'level playing field', it should provide for international commercial arbitration in a neutral venue unless the national law and arbitration procedures which would otherwise apply provide an equivalent, equally secure solution (as to which, *see* The World Bank's solution below).

This is, indeed, why all of FIDIC's forms of construction contract since the publication of the first edition of the Red Book in 1957 have provided

118. *FIDIC Procurement Procedures Guide* (FIDIC, 2011) 35.
119. *See*, e.g., art. III, s 5(b) of The World Bank's Articles of Agreement requiring it to pay 'due attention to considerations of economy and efficiency' when making loans.
120. *See*, e.g., The World Bank, *Guidelines Procurement of Goods, Works and Non-consulting Services under IBRD Loans and IDA Credits and Grants by World Bank Borrowers* (January 2011, rev July 2014) 2011/01/01 19, s 2.38.

for the final resolution of disputes by international arbitration, generally under the ICC Arbitration Rules.[121]

Therefore, FIDIC should recognise a sixth Golden Principle, especially as there is good precedent for doing so. The World Bank's procurement regulations provide that:

> International commercial arbitration in a neutral venue shall also be required unless the national regulations and arbitration procedures are acceptable to the Bank in terms of equivalence to international commercial arbitration and the venue is neutral [...].[122]

Thus, the Bank requires that its borrowers, who may often be Employers under FIDIC contracts, provide for international commercial arbitration at a neutral venue in their contracts unless they can persuade the Bank that their national regulations provide for a no less fair and efficacious procedure.

4.5 FIDIC's Forms of Contract

Table 2 shows a list of FIDIC's current forms of construction contract and of consultancy agreement.

---

121. FIDIC's forms have deliberately contained no provision for the place of arbitration: (1) so as to limit the risk of a parochial choice, and (2) because, absent a selection of the place by the parties, the International Court of Arbitration of the ICC can be relied upon to choose a suitable, neutral place of arbitration. Jason Fry and others, *The Secretariat's Guide to ICC Arbitration* (ICC, Paris 2012) (ICC Publication 729E), 202-203 (paras 3-685 to 3-687). *See (4) Number of arbitrators, place and language of arbitration* under **(iii) Analysis** of the commentary on Sub-Clause 21.6 [*Arbitration*] below.
122. The only exception to this requirement is where the bidder (i.e., the Contractor) is from the country of The World Bank's borrower (i.e., the Employer). Paragraph 2.25 of Annex IX Contract Conditions in International Competitive Procurement to *The World Bank, Procurement Regulations for IPF (Investment Project Financing) Borrowers, Procurement in Investment Project Financing, Goods, Works, Non-Consulting and Consulting Services* (4th edn, November 2020). This is now reflected in The World Bank's COPA, Sub-Clause 21.6.

Table 2 FIDIC's Forms of Contract

Major Works Suite	*Conditions of Contract for Construction* (second edition, 2017, reprinted in 2022 with amendments) ['Red Book']	The flagship contract. The Employer (or its consulting engineer) does most of the design and the Contractor is paid on a unit price basis. It features a balanced risk allocation.
	Conditions of Contract for Plant and Design-Build (second edition, 2017, reprinted in 2022 with amendments) ['Yellow Book']	The Employer sets the requirements for the finished project ('Employer's Requirements'), and the Contractor does the design and construction and is paid a lump sum. It features a balanced risk allocation.
	Conditions of Contract for EPC/ Turnkey Projects (second edition, 2017, reprinted in 2022 with amendments) ['Silver Book']	The Employer sets the requirements for the finished project ('Employer's Requirements'), and the Contractor does the design and construction and is paid a lump sum. Risk heavily allocated to the Contractor.
	Conditions of Contract for Design, Build and Operate Projects (first edition, 2008) ['Gold Book']	A contract for a greenfield project where the Contractor designs, builds, and then operates the works for a certain period (typically 20 years).
	Conditions of Contract for Operate, Design and Build Projects (forthcoming) ['Bronze Book']	A contract for a brown-field project where the Contractor designs, builds, and then operates the works for a certain period.

	Conditions of Contract for Construction: MDB Harmonised Edition (last version, 2010) ['Pink Book'] replaced in 2019 by The World Bank's *Conditions of Particular Application* ('COPA') for use with the General Conditions of RB/17.	A specific version of the Red Book that is designed for a project funded by The World Bank or other Multilateral Development Bank.
Small Works Form	*Short Form of Contract* (second edition, 2021) ['Green Book']	A short form of contract intended for projects with limited risks and/or where parties prefer simple, straightforward contractual arrangements, without sophisticated contract administration and management. Typically used for low capital value works up to USD 10 million but can be used for larger works. It is suitable for projects that involve both Employer-design and Contractor-design.
Specialist Forms	*Form of Contract for Dredging and Reclamation Works* (second edition, 2016) ['Blue Book']	A specialist contract for dredging and reclamation work.
	Conditions of Contract for Underground Works (1st edition, 2019) ['Emerald Book']	A specialist contract for tunnelling and underground work, which is based on the Yellow Book.

Subcontract Forms	*Conditions of Subcontract for Construction* (second edition, 2011 – the first edition was for the Red Book (1987))	A subcontract for a Red Book (1999) project where the Contractor subcontracts part of the works to a subcontractor.
	Conditions of Subcontract for Plant and Design-Build (first edition, 2019)	A subcontract for a Yellow Book (1999) project where the Contractor subcontracts part of the works to a subcontractor.
Consultancy Forms	*Client / Consultant Model Services Agreement* (fifth edition, 2017) ['White Book']	A model agreement for the purposes of pre-investment and feasibility studies, designs and administration of construction and project management, both for Employer-led design teams and for Contractor-led design and build commissions. Typically, for the services of the Engineer in the case of the Red, Yellow and Blue Books, and Green Book.
	Sub-Consultancy Agreement (second edition, 2017)	A model agreement for situations where an Engineer, other design professional or consultant subcontracts part of the design work or other services.
	Joint Venture (Consortium) Agreement Between Consultants (second edition, 2017)	A model agreement to be entered into by consultants when forming a joint venture or a consortium for a project.

	Model Representative Agreement (first edition, 2013) ['Purple Book']	A model agreement for consultants wishing to enter into a contract with a representative for the provision of representative services.

Source: Author's own work.

4.6 Translations

All of FIDIC's forms have been drafted in the British-English language, and each of the RB/17, YB/17 and SB/17 provides in Notes at the beginning of the form that 'FIDIC considers the official and authentic texts to be the versions in the English language'.

Even so, a number of FIDIC forms have been translated into other languages. For example, the 1999 editions of the FIDIC forms of construction contract for major works, the RB, YB and SB, are available in Arabic, Chinese, French, Polish, Russian, Spanish and other languages.[123]

Similarly, FIDIC has, or plans to have, the 2017 Rainbow Suite (RB/17, YB/17 and SB/17) translated five languages: Arabic, French, Mandarin Chinese, Portuguese and Spanish.

Translations of FIDIC forms of contract are normally made by the national member associations of FIDIC under conditions determined by FIDIC,[124] and are of varying quality. Translations made without FIDIC's authorisation are considered illicit and should not be used.[125]

Given the difficulty – and hence varying quality – of translations, a useful precaution is to require that, in the case of any translation of a FIDIC form into another language, the English text be set out side-by-side in the contract with the translation and to provide where appropriate that, in the event of any discrepancy, the English text shall prevail. Another wise

123. These translations are available for purchase from the FIDIC's website, *see* FIDIC, 'Bookshop' (FIDIC) https://www.fidic.org/bookshop accessed 2 November 2022.

124. *See* FIDIC, 'Copyright' (*FIDIC*, 2015) www.fidic.org/copyright-0 accessed 2 November 2022.

125. *Ibid.*

precaution, even before signing a contract based on a FIDIC form, is to have any translation of a contract retranslated back into English by another translator and then to compare the retranslation with the original FIDIC English text.

--ooOOoo--

CHAPTER II

Applicable Law

1 SCOPE OF CHAPTER

After noting that there are certain general principles of contract law that are of universal application,[1] this chapter describes the importance of selecting a national law or rules of law to govern an international construction contract.[2] This is followed by a general comparison of the common law and civil law legal systems[3] and then, more specifically, by a comparison of the two systems in relation to common issues under international construction contracts.[4] This is followed by an overview of the types of laws that are often mandatory (i.e., which may not be deviated from) in the country of the construction site and therefore which must be complied with.[5]

As international construction takes place largely in the developing world, the law governing an international construction contract will often be that of an undeveloped or developing country and its law may similarly be undeveloped resulting at times in uncertainty about what this law provides. Accordingly, the challenges of this situation and proposals for overcoming them are then described.[6] The chapter concludes by noting the availability today of well-recognised legal principles for international

1. Section 2.
2. Section 3.
3. Section 4.1-4.2.
4. Section 4.3 through 4.6.
5. Section 5.
6. Section 6.

commercial contracts, notably those of UNIDROIT, to serve as a 'governing law' or as a source to interpret or supplement a governing law,[7] as well as of trade usages whose application is provided for by a FIDIC contract.[8]

2 UNIVERSAL PRINCIPLES

Before discussing the importance of the law or rules of law which govern a contract (the 'governing law') and differences between the common law and civil law, it needs to be appreciated that there are some general legal principles of contract law that will apply irrespective of the governing law.

Two principles, in particular, are of such importance and universality that any engineer or other construction professional (as well as a lawyer) should be familiar with them, as they are likely to apply whatever law governs a contract. These principles are:

(1) freedom of contract, that is, the right of parties freely to negotiate, to determine the terms of and to enter into a legally binding agreement[9] subject to limited exceptions, such as their competency and the absence of misconduct, such as fraud or duress, or a violation of public policy; and

(2) the sanctity of contracts (*pacta sunt servanda*), that is, the principle that parties must respect and honour their agreements or, if they do not do so, be liable in damages or to other sanction,[10] subject to very limited exceptions such as – depending on the legal system – *force majeure*, frustration and similar legal doctrines which apply where non-performance is the result of objective factors beyond a party's control.[11]

7. Section 7.
8. Section 8.
9. Thus, art. 1.1 (*Freedom of contract*) of the International Institute for the Unification of Private Law, *UNIDROIT Principles of International Commercial Contracts 2016* (the 'UNIDROIT Principles') provides: 'The parties are free to enter into a contract and to determine its content.'
10. Thus, art. 1.3 (*Binding character of contract*) of the UNIDROIT Principles provides in part: 'A contract validly entered into is binding upon the parties.'
11. *See*, in relation to the foregoing, Donald Charrett, *The Application of Contracts in Engineering and Construction Projects* (Informa Law 2019) 348-349.

To illustrate this second principle, French law refers to contracts as having 'the binding force of law for those who have made them' ('*tiennent lieu de loi à ceux qui les ont faits*').[12]

Another related general principle in both civil law and common law systems is that the great majority of rules or principles of contract law *will only apply if the parties have not agreed otherwise*. In other words, they are 'default rules'. Therefore where the parties' contract regulates the parties' relationship in a detailed and comprehensive way, as will be the case, for example, if it is based on RB/17, the terms of the contract will displace the vast majority of the rules of contract law which might otherwise apply under the relevant governing law. Consequently, in the case of a contract based on RB/17, there should ordinarily be relatively few instances where it would be necessary to look to the governing law.

It follows from these three principles that whatever the governing law, *the terms of the parties' agreement, and how they are to be interpreted, are likely, as a practical matter, to be of the greatest importance in determining their respective rights and obligations*. As one author has correctly put it, referring to the principle of the sanctity of contracts, '[t]his means that the vast majority of construction disputes are fought and won or lost primarily over the wording of the contract (and alleged facts)'.[13] Hence, where a contract is based upon the Red Book, it is essential for a party to have a thorough understanding of that form of contract.

--ooOOoo--

12. French Civil Code, art. 1103. Islamic law (*sharia*) similarly provides for the sanctity of contracts. *See* Tarek Badawy, 'The General Principles of Islamic Law as the Law Governing Investment Disputes in the Middle East' (2012) 29(3), J Int'l Arb, 255, 258-259.
13. Donald Charrett, *The Application of Contracts in Engineering and Construction Projects* (Informa Law, London, 2019) 349, citing Robert Knutson (ed), *FIDIC: An Analysis of International Construction Contracts* (Kluwer L Int'l, IBA, The Hague, the Netherlands, 2005) xiv. Consistent with this, the ICC Rules of Arbitration are said to place the parties' contract at 'centre stage in the resolution of contractual disputes'. Jason Fry and others, *The Secretariat's Guide to ICC Arbitration, A Practical Commentary on the 2012 ICC Rules of Arbitration of the ICC International Court of Arbitration* (ICC, Paris, 2012, ICC Publication no 729 E) 228 (para. 3-777).

3 IMPORTANCE OF THE GOVERNING LAW

As explained above,[14] FIDIC forms contain multiple clauses and sub-clauses for contingencies designed to permit the contract to adjust to take account of new and/or unforeseeable circumstances and ensure that, so far as possible, work will continue without interruption. Where issues arise between the parties, they are to be settled by claims procedures in the contract, thereby limiting the need to resort to law[15] and/or a court or tribunal. However, regardless of how detailed or comprehensive a contract may be, it cannot dispense entirely with the need to refer to law.

As Lord McNair, a former President of the International Court of Justice, has observed:

> It is often said that the parties to a contract make their own law, and it is, of course, true that, subject to the rules of public policy and *ordre public*, the parties are free to agree upon such terms as they may choose. Nevertheless, agreements that are intended to have a legal operation (as opposed to a merely social operation) create legal rights and duties, and *legal rights and duties cannot exist in a vaccum* but must have a place within a legal system which is available for dealing with such questions as the validity, application and interpretation of contracts, and generally, for supplementing their express provisions.[16] (Emphasis added)

3.1 Importance for a FIDIC Contract

In the case of a FIDIC contract, the law which may govern it may perform such varied functions as the following:

(1) Providing rules as to how a contract is to be interpreted. While the Red Book contains some provisions concerning contract

14. *See* **Section 3.2.4 Multiple Clauses for Contingencies** of **Chapter I General Introduction** above.
15. Or 'rules of law', *see* art. 21(1) of the ICC Arbitration Rules which is quoted in part and discussed in **Section 7.1 Introduction** below of **Chapter II Applicable Law**.
16. Lord McNair, 'The General Principles of Law Recognized by Civilised Nations' (1957) 33 BYIL 1, 7.

interpretation,[17] they will be supplemented by provisions on contract interpretation of the governing law.[18]

(2) Determining the validity and/or enforceability of clauses that can give rise to issues under local law, e.g., Sub-Clauses 1.15 [*Limitation of Liability*], Sub-Clause 8.8 [*Delay Damages*], the provision for late payment interest in Sub-Clause 14.8 [*Delayed Payment*] and for time bars in Sub-Clause 20.2 [*Claims for Payment and/or EOT*].

(3) Providing parties with rights and obligations in addition to those in the contract. Thus, Sub-Clauses 15.2 and 16.2 provide that a Party's right to terminate the contract under those Sub-Clauses does not prejudice the Party's rights under the Contract 'or otherwise', such as the Party's right to terminate a contract on the ground of material breach of contract under the governing law. Similarly, while Sub-Clause 10.1 provides for the taking over of the Works and Sub-Clause 11.1 for a Contractor's obligation to remedy defects during a Defects Notification Period ('DNP'), in certain civil law countries these provisions will be complemented by a decennial liability regime under which both the Contractor and the Engineer will remain absolutely liable,[19] possibly jointly and severally, to the Employer for defects which impair the stability of the work which may appear within 10 years after taking over.[20]

(4) Addressing matters not regulated by the contract, such as limitation periods,[21] the scope of recoverable damages, the availability (or not) of a subcontractor's direct claim for payment against

---

17. *See* **Section 5.1.1 Sub-Clauses Dealing with Interpretation** of **Chapter III Contract Interpretation** below and the commentary on Sub-Clause 1.2 [*Interpretation*] in **Chapter IV Clause-by-Clause Commentary** below.
18. *See* **Section 4 Different Approaches to Interpretation** of **Chapter III Contract Interpretation** below.
19. That is, liable without the need for the claimant to prove fault or negligence.
20. For a description of decennial liability, *see* **Section 4 Common Law and Civil Law Compared – 4.4.4 Decennial Liability** of **Chapter II Applicable Law**. On the other hand, under common law, unless there is a specific exclusion, the Contractor remains liable for general damages in respect of defects after the end of the DNP until expiration of the limitation period (the difference with the DNP being that the Contractor is generally not entitled to undertake defect rectification work itself, as it is during the DNP).
21. *See* **Section 4 Common Law and Civil Law Compared – 4.5.3 Limitation Periods** of **Chapter II Applicable Law**.

the Employer[22] and the grounds under which the Engineer may be liable to the Contractor.[23]

In certain places, the Red Book specifically refers to the governing law. For example, Sub-Clause 13.6 allows for adjustment of the Contract Price in the case of a change in Laws, which may include the governing law (if it is the law of the Country), and Sub-Clause 18.6(b) recognises that each Party may, in certain circumstances, seek release under the governing law from having to perform the Contract.

3.2 Choice of the Governing Law

Sub-Clause 1.4 [*Law and Language*] of RB/17 deals directly with the governing law. It provides that the governing law will be the one chosen by the Parties in the document entitled 'Contract Data' and, if not stated therein, the law of the Country,[24] excluding any conflict of law rules. In practice, in most cases, the governing law will be the law of the Country, which is almost always the Employer's law. If the Employer is in the strongest bargaining position, it will impose it on tenderers.[25] In international projects based on a FIDIC form, the Employer or its consultant will prepare the tender documents, of which the Contract Data form is a part. Consequently, the Contract Data will usually refer to the law of the Country as the governing law, and tenderers will usually be expected to bid with little or no possibility to negotiate this issue. Choice of the law of the Country may also be sensible because the mandatory or public policy

22. *See* **Section 4 Common Law and Civil Law Compared – 4.4.3 Subcontractor's Direct Rights** of **Chapter II Applicable Law**.
23. *See* under **(iv) Related Law** of the commentary on Sub-Clause 3.7 [*Agreement or Determination*] below.
24. That is, the law of the country in which the Site (or most of it) is located, where the Permanent Works are to be executed. Sub-Clause 1.1.21 '**Country**'.
25. Philip Britton, 'Choice of Law in Construction Contracts: The View from England' [2002] ICLR 242, 277-78. However, in the case of a private project (e.g., a build-operate-transfer type), the project sponsor, if separate from the employer, or the lenders, may have a determinant role over the governing law (and also over the method of procurement and choice of contract form), *Ibid.*, 277-78.

laws of the country of the Site are likely to apply to the execution of the Works in any event.[26]

There may, however, be cases where the Parties will want to choose as a governing law a law (or rules of law) different from that of any single country. For example, sometimes the Employer is a binational, tri-national or an international entity and/or the Site may be located on the territories of two or more countries. Typical examples are large hydro-electric schemes on rivers at or near national borders or gas pipeline projects crossing the territories of several countries or tunnels between two countries, e.g., the Anglo-French Channel Tunnel. In the case of such projects, the choice of the law of one of the countries where only a part of the Site is located may be unacceptable to the other country or countries involved.[27]

In such cases, the Parties may feel the need to choose a governing law (or rules of law) which favours neither Party,[28] such as the law of a third country or international legal principles such as the UNIDROIT Principles.[29] This may be fairer than choosing the law of the country of one of the Parties as neither of the Parties will then have the advantage of the

---

26. *See* **Section 5 Mandatory Law at the Site** below of **Chapter II Applicable Law**.
27. To address this sort of issue, the contract for the construction of the Anglo-French Channel Tunnel, entered into in 1986 and based partly on RB/77, had contained in Clause 68 the following governing law provision:

    > The construction, validity and performance of the contract shall in all respects be governed by and interpreted in accordance with the principles common to both English law and French law, and in the absence of such common principles by such general principles of international trade law as have been applied by national and international tribunals. Subject in all cases, with respect to the works to be respectively performed in the French and in the English part of the site, to the respective French or English public policy (ordre public) provisions.

    Channel Tunnel Group Ltd v Balfour Beatty Construction Ltd [1993] A.C. 334, 347. As the first edition of the UNIDROIT Principles was not published until 1994, it was not available for possible use when this contract was entered into.
28. *See* the study prepared by the Task Group chaired by Fabio Bortolotti and Franco Silvano Toni di Cigoli, 'Developing Neutral Legal Standards for International Contracts' (ICC Policy and Business Practices, Paris, 2015) 3-4.
29. As regards the UNIDROIT Principles, *see* **Section 7 International Legal Principles** below of **Chapter II Applicable Law**.

application of its own law. In an international construction contract which contains an international arbitration clause (as is true of RB/17), such a choice is generally recognised as valid.[30] The Parties will nevertheless have to comply with any mandatory law that may apply, notably that of the country of the Site.[31]

4 COMMON LAW AND CIVIL LAW COMPARED

Although the Red Book is intended to serve as a standard form of international construction contract it is still based broadly on an English contract form,[32] derived, therefore, from the common law system. As has been noted,[33] most of the texts and commentaries on the FIDIC forms are by lawyers or engineers from England or countries following the English legal tradition. Their texts refer extensively to case law and legal principles from the English common law.

However, as previously mentioned,[34] the Red Book aspires, increasingly, to be a standard form of *international* contract and, somewhat ironically, FIDIC's forms of contact are probably more widely used in civil law countries than common law countries.[35] But despite their wider use in

30. *See*, e.g., English *Arbitration Act 1996*, s 46(1)(b) and French Code of Civil Procedure, art. 1511. In theory, instead of choosing a governing law or rules of law, the Parties might provide that the arbitral tribunal shall have the power of an *amiable compositeur* or to decide *ex aequo et bono*, pursuant to art. 21(3) of the ICC Rules of Arbitration. However, as this power is 'vague and uncertain' it is 'very rare for parties to give an arbitral tribunal [this] power'. Jason Fry and others, *The Secretariat's Guide to ICC Arbitration* (ICC, Paris, 2012, ICC Publication no 729 E) 231 (para. 3-790).
31. *See* **Section 5 Mandatory Law at the Site** below in **Chapter II Applicable Law**.
32. Stephen Furst and Vivian Ramsey, *Keating on Construction Contracts* (11th edn, Sweet & Maxwell, London, 2021) 7 (para. 1-028).
33. **Section 1.1.3 Common Law and Civil Law** of **Chapter I General Introduction** above.
34. *See* **Sections 1.1.2 An International Legal Perspective** and **1.1.3 Common Law and Civil Law** of **Chapter I General Introduction** above.
35. This should not be surprising given that the civil law system is the 'most widespread type of legal system in the world, applied in various forms in approximatively 150 countries', *The CIA World Factbook, 2022-2023* (Skyhorse Publishing, NY, 2022) xix. In addition to most of the Middle East, countries having the civil law system include those in Continental Europe generally, Russia, francophone Africa, Latin America and most of Asia

civil law countries, they have not received the same degree of attention from lawyers and engineers in those countries as they have from lawyers and engineers in common law countries. Whatever may be the reasons for this, a purpose of this book is to help make up for the shortfall in civil law commentary and to address the main issues and problems to which use of the Red Book gives rise under the civil law system, as well as under the common law system and international principles.

There are different legal traditions within the civil law – as within the common law – system as well as significant differences between the laws of different countries within the same legal tradition. Obviously, no attempt can be made to treat all of these differences. Instead, primary attention will be given in this book, within the civil law system, to French law, the most influential law in the civil law world.

The *Code Napoléon* or French Civil Code of 1804 has served as a direct or indirect source of inspiration to, even a template for, countries in Continental Europe,[36] francophone Africa, the Middle East, Latin America, parts of Asia and some parts of North America.[37] French law, including (beginning in the 20th century) its administrative or public law, has served as the basis for, or is mixed with, other legal systems in approximately 50 countries.[38]

---

including China, Japan, Indonesia, Thailand, South Korea and Indo-China. The common law system which refers to the legal system that originated in England and Wales is in force in approximately 80 countries including important commercial countries and financial centres such as the United States (except Louisiana), Canada (except Quebec), Australia, New Zealand, Hong Kong and Singapore, *The CIA World Factbook, 2022-2023* (Skyhorse Publishing, NY, 2022) xix. All these named countries are economically highly developed, each has its own domestic standard forms of construction contract and none, consequently, is an important user of FIDIC's forms of contract. Among common law countries, possibly the biggest users of FIDIC's forms of contract are the anglophone countries of Africa.

36. In Europe, from the French Civil Code were derived the Italian, Spanish, Portuguese, Dutch, Belgian and Romanian Codes. Hans Julius Wolff, *Roman Law: An Historical Introduction* (1st edn 1951 Univ of Oklahoma, Norman, Okla) 4 (fn. 1).
37. Solene Rowan, 'The New French Law of Contract' (2017) 66(4) ICLQ 805, 808.
38. *The CIA World Factbook, 2022-2023* (Skyhorse Publishing, NY, 2022) xix. Illustrative of the importance of French law is its impact in the Arab Middle East. The Egyptian Civil Code of 1948, the most influential civil code in the Arab Middle East and still in effect, was influenced by the French Civil Code

Section 4 will highlight major differences in law between the civil law system, especially the French tradition, and the common law system as regards international construction contracts. Only the broad general legal principles of each of the two legal systems are discussed.[39] Furthermore, *as much attention will be given to traditional (or former) laws of the representative countries of the civil law and common law systems – France and England, respectively – as to their current law, as often the traditional (or former) law of those countries, or remnants of it, continue to apply with little change in the other countries around the world of each system, especially where they are developing countries.*[40]

4.1 Origins of Common Law and Civil Law

While the common law system originated in England and Wales, it was later adopted in the US (except Louisiana), Canada (except Quebec), Australia, India, New Zealand and other former colonies of the British

---

to such an extent that numerous provisions were literally translated from it and the backbone of all Egyptian legal literature is still French legal doctrine and case law [unpublished legal opinion dated 17 June 1989 of the late Dr Aktham El Kholy, former Vice-Dean and Professor in the Faculty of Law, Cairo University (in the author's possession)]. The Egyptian Civil Code was mainly the work of the late Dr Abd al-Razzaq Al Sanhouri, an Egyptian law professor, who also took a substantial part in drafting the Iraqi Civil Code (1951). Nabil Saleh, 'Civil Codes of Arab Countries: the Sanhuri Codes' (1993) 8(2) Arab L Q, 161, 163. The civil codes of Syria (1949) and Libya (1954) are in turn patterned on the Egyptian one [*Ibid.*]. In addition, the Egyptian Civil Code 'has been received by [...] Qatar (1971), Sudan (1971), Somalia (1973), Algeria (1975), Jordan (1976) and Kuwait (1980).' Konrad Zweigert and Hein Kötz, *Introduction to Comparative Law* (3rd rev'd edn, OUP, Oxford, 1998) 111. Egyptian law is described as equally influential in the UAE. *See* Mark Hoyle, *The Arab World's Greatest Jurist – Al Sanhouri* (Mondaq, 25 August 2015). Dr Al Sanhouri's treatise on the Egyptian Civil Code in 11 volumes constitutes the most authoritative commentary on the law of contract in the Arab Middle East and North Africa.

39. For more detailed information, reference should be made to the standard works on the law of contract of each country or legal system, certain of which are referred to in footnotes below in this Section.

40. For example: (1) the *Indian Contracts Act* of 1872 which has only been amended in relatively minor respects; and (2) the Algerian Civil Code which has not been significantly amended since its adoption in 1975 following Algeria's independence, and is still, to this day, close to the French and Egyptian Civil Codes it was modelled after.

Empire. The common law has resulted mainly from judicial decision-making. This has happened based on the principle of stare decisis, that is, that earlier judicial decisions, usually of higher courts, and made in similar cases, should be followed in subsequent cases. Thus, case law has been the primary source of law in the common law system although, increasingly today, the law is based on statutes which judges are expected to interpret and apply.

On the other hand, the development of civil law was much more influenced by Roman Law.[41] In its current form, it is based on the civil and other codes adopted in France at the beginning of the 19th century, following the French Revolution. As the result of Napoleon's conquests, codes based on French law were adopted across much of Continental Europe and thereafter in former colonies of France and elsewhere around the world. The main principles and rules contained in such codes, as well as in statutes, are (in civil law) what constitutes the 'law' (in French: *loi*) together with doctrinal writings (in French: *doctrine*) or the body of writing about law by those learned in it, such as professors of law and informed practitioners. Case law (in French: *jurisprudence*) is not recognised formally as a source of law though, as a practical matter, it is of great importance.

This difference between the two legal systems has contributed to the different ways in which lawyers from each system think about legal problems. As one civil lawyer has put it:

> A civil lawyer usually starts from a legal norm contained in [...] legislation, and by means of deduction makes conclusions regarding the actual case. On the other hand, a lawyer in common law starts with the actual case and compares it with the same or similar issues that have been dealt with by courts in previously decided cases, and from these relevant precedents the binding legal rule is determined by means of induction. A consequence of this fundamental difference between the two systems is that lawyers from civil law countries tend to be more conceptual, while lawyers from common law countries are considered to be more pragmatic.[42]

---

41. Peter Stein, *Roman Law in European History* (Cambridge UP, Cambridge, 1999) 86-88, 104-130.
42. Caslav Pejovic, 'Civil Law and Common Law: Two Different Paths Leading to the Same Goal' (2001) 32 VUWLR 817, 820.

However, due among other things to globalisation, the two systems are to some extent converging. Codes, statutes and regulations play an increasingly important role in the common law system and, as a practical matter, case law appears to have almost as much importance in civil law today as in the common law system, as statutory provisions in the civil law system have, traditionally, at least (by common law standards), been brief, even elliptical.

4.2 Civil Law Generally

4.2.1 Public and Private Law

While the general approach of common law jurisdictions is not to make a formal divide between public law and private law,[43] many civil law countries distinguish between the two. In civil law countries like France, public law regulates the organisation of the State (constitutional law) and the relations between the State – and institutions deriving from it – and private individuals (administrative law).[44] This distinction is based on the notion that relations between those who govern and those who are governed give rise to special problems and call for different regulation than relations between private persons if only because the general public interest and private interests cannot be equated.[45]

Under private law, in civil law countries, the general legislative rules which govern contract law are usually contained in a civil code, which is the fundamental text for private law. Although the French Civil Code contains a number of provisions regulating all contracts generally, it also inherits from Roman law a system of categories of contract, each of which is subject to specific regulation. Among these is the construction contract which is included within the category of the 'contract for the hire

43. For example, in Australia, England and Wales and India. Paul Craig, 'Specific Powers of Public Contractors' in Rozen Noguellou and Ulrich Stelkens (eds), *Comparative Law on Public Contracts* (Bruylant, Brussels, 2010) 173.
44. Barry Nicholas, 'Introduction to the French Law of Contract' in Donald Harris and Denis Tallon (eds), *Contract Law Today Contract Law Today: Anglo-French Comparisons* (OUP, Oxford, 1989) 15.
45. René David and others, *Les Grands Systèmes de Droit Contemporains* (12th edn, Dalloz, Paris, 2016) 69.

of work and skill' ('*contrat de louage d'ouvrage et d'industrie*')[46] and, within this category, is regulated by Articles 1779(3) and 1787 to 1799 of the French Civil Code.[47] But the general provisions on the 'law of obligations', which includes the law of contract, in the French Civil Code still will generally apply to construction contracts, except where they are inconsistent with the provisions specifically regulating construction contracts.

This same scheme or pattern for the regulation of the construction contract – by category and then by general provisions (as in French and Roman law) – *is useful to know about as it is to be found equally in the civil codes of many civil law countries.*[48] *Not only that but also provisions dealing specifically with the construction contract often provide for application of the same or similar legal principles as in French law, e.g., relating to decennial liability and lump sum contracts.*[49]

The general principle in the French Civil Code (as in other civil codes) is that the parties are free to decide on the content of their contracts.[50] Only a relatively small number of provisions of the Civil Code involve public policy and therefore are mandatory and cannot be excluded (these being referred to in French as *lois impératives*).[51] The great majority of rules on

46. The corresponding Latin term is *locatio conductio operis*. *See* Barry Nicholas, *An Introduction to Roman Law* (OUP, Oxford, 1975) 182-83.
47. The same articles of the French Civil Code govern the construction contract today, though they have been amended since the *Code Napoléon* of 1804.
48. Special provisions for building contracts exist in the civil codes or other codifications of, for example, Belgium, Chile, Egypt, Ethiopia, France, Greece, Italy, Japan, Luxembourg, the Netherlands, Poland and Switzerland. Werner Lorenz, 'Chapter 8 Contracts for Work on Goods and Building Contracts', vol VIII Specific Contracts, Konrad Zweigert (chief ed), *International Encyclopedia of Comparative Law* (J.C.B Mohr (Paul Siebeck), Tübingen, 1973), 4.
49. *See* the discussion of these principles in **Section 4.4 Civil Law: Distinctive Features of Construction Law** below in **Chapter II**.
50. French Civil Code, art. 1102 provides as follows: 'Everyone is free to contract or not to contract, to choose the person with whom to contract, and to determine the content and form of the contract, within the limits imposed by legislation. Contractual freedom does not allow derogation from rules which are an expression of public policy.'
51. Barry Nicholas, *The French Law of Contract* (2nd edn, OUP, Oxford, 1992) 33.

contract in French law, as under the common law, are 'default rules';[52] that is, they apply only in the absence of a contrary intention of the parties as expressed by their contract.

As many contracts based on the Red Book are made with states or public or state-owned entities, it is also important to be aware of the distinction in civil law countries between contracts governed by private law, on the one hand, and contracts governed by public or administrative law, on the other hand, as discussed below.

4.2.2 Public and Private Contracts

In many civil law countries which distinguish between public and private law, contracts with public or state-owned bodies may be deemed to be 'administrative contracts', in which event they will be governed by a system of law influenced – more or less strongly – by French administrative or public law. On the other hand, in the civil law system, private law generally governs matters and contracts to which neither the state nor any public entity is a party.

According to French legal thinking, the law relating to administrative contracts is necessarily different from the law relating to contracts between private parties as the law relating to administrative contracts must take into consideration the obligation of the administration to assure the public interest.[53] As a consequence, the private law of contract, applicable to contracts between private parties, which is based on the principle of the equality of the parties, does not apply directly to administrative contracts.[54] Instead, *administrative contracts are governed by administrative law which is based on the principle of the inequality of the parties*. Administrative law endows the public party with special or exceptional powers, *whether provided for in the contract or not*, which are counterbalanced by according rights to compensation to the private party, which are no less special (by private law standards), as discussed below.[55]

---

52. Such default rules are referred to in French as *lois supplétives de volonté* meaning laws that complement the parties' will or intention. *See* **Section 2 Universal Principles** above of **Chapter II**.
53. Rozen Noguellou and Ulrich Stelkens (eds), *Comparative Law on Public Contracts* (Bruylant, Brussels, 2010) 11.
54. *Ibid.*
55. *See* **Section 4.6 Civil Law: Special Public Law Theories** below in **Chapter II**.

The doctrine of the administrative contract has been accepted in many civil law countries, albeit with sometimes important differences.[56] In Europe, it has been accepted in Belgium, Finland, Greece, Portugal and Spain.[57] In Africa, the same is true not only generally of the francophone countries but also of Egypt and, through it, of Algeria, Libya, Sudan and, in the Middle East, Iraq, Kuwait, Lebanon, Qatar, Saudi Arabia, the United Arab Emirates, and Yemen.[58] In Latin America, most countries have incorporated the doctrine into their legal systems: such is the case of Argentina, Brazil, Chile, Colombia, Mexico, Uruguay and Venezuela.[59]

Therefore, in many civil law countries, it will be important for a tendering contractor to know whether a construction contract, for which it is being invited to tender, is an administrative contract and, if so, subject to a separate and distinctive body of law from that applicable to an ordinary (private) contract. While the exact definition of an administrative contract may vary from country to country, in France a contract will be an administrative contract and generally governed by administrative law where:

(1) one of the parties is a public entity, such as the State, a division of the State or a public establishment; and
(2) the contract either provides for the performance of a public service or contains clauses which reserve 'exceptional powers' (*pouvoirs exorbitants*) to the public party which, in the case of a construction contract, would include such powers as those to manage and direct the works, to modify, suspend or terminate

---

56. Héctor A Mairal, 'The Doctrine of the Administrative Contract in International Investment Arbitration' in Borzu Sabahi and others (eds), *A Revolution in the International Rule of Law, Essays in Honor of Don Wallace, Jr.*, ch 32 (Juris Publishing, Huntington, NY, 2014) 417, 419-20. Professor Mairal notes that the doctrine has not been accepted in, among other civil law countries, Germany, Italy and Switzerland, *Ibid.*, 421.
57. *Ibid. See also* Olli Maenpää, 'Finland' in Rozen Noguellou and Ulrich Stelkens (eds), *Comparative Law on Public Contracts* (Bruylant, Brussels, 2010) 657, 661.
58. *See* Héctor A Mairal, 'The Doctrine of the Administrative Contract in International Investment Arbitration' in Borzu Sabahi and others (eds), *A Revolution in the International Rule of Law, Essays in Honor of Don Wallace, Jr.* ch 32 (Juris Publishing, Huntington, NY, 2014) 41920.
59. *Ibid.*

> the contract, if necessary, in the public interest and to sanction the contractor without prior judicial authorisation.[60]

While in France a contract for the execution of public works is considered to be an administrative contract by virtue of a special law,[61] even in the absence of such a law such a contract would normally be considered administrative under case law because it both involves the performance of a public service and accords the public party exceptional powers.[62] In fact, in numerous civil law countries not having a special law, as exists in France, public works contracts are deemed to be administrative contracts.[63] In Arab legal systems, the definition of an administrative contract is similar to the French law definition.[64]

In addition, in France, though not necessarily in other civil law countries, disputes in relation to administrative contracts must be settled in administrative courts, which form a separate court system from the ordinary civil court system.[65] Moreover, French public entities are prohibited from

---

60. André de Laubadère and others, *Traité des contrats administratifs* (2nd edn, LGDJ, Paris, 1983) vol I, 210 (para. 154) – 240 (para. 182); L Neville Brown and others, *French Administrative Law* (5th edn, OUP, Oxford, 1998) 202; and Philippe Malinvaud (ed in chief), *Droit de la Construction* (7th edn, Dalloz Action, Paris, 2018) 1345 (para. 417.471) to 1359 (para. 417.639).
61. *See loi* du 28 *pluviôse* an VII (1800), art. 4.
62. André de Laubadère and others, *Traité des contrats administratifs* (2nd edn, LGDJ, Paris, 1983) vol I, 133 (para. 93).
63. These include Belgium, Spain and most Latin American countries.
64. According to an Arab authority, a contract is administrative if:

    (1) One of its parties is a public authority (administration);
    (2) It has been concluded with the intention of managing or participating in the function of a public service; and
    (3) It contains certain features which are not usually found in private law contracts.

    Adnan Amkhan, 'The Effect of Change in Circumstances in Arab Contract Law' (1994) Arab L Q 258, 271.
65. According to an eminent French legal author, there would have been no separate body of administrative law in France if the ordinary courts had obtained or retained jurisdiction in matters concerning the administrative authorities. Marcel Waline, *Droit Administratif* (1961), para. 45, quoted in Bernard Rudden (ed), *A Source-Book on French Law* (3rd rev'd edn, OUP, Oxford, 1991) 140.

agreeing to arbitration unless, exceptionally, a special permission has been obtained.[66]

By contrast to the French system of having administrative courts separate from the ordinary civil court system, most Latin American countries, except for Colombia,[67] have created an administrative jurisdiction within their ordinary civil court system.

In France and numerous other civil law countries, when a contract is considered to be an administrative contract then, by mandatory law, the public party enjoys 'exceptional powers' (as referred to above) *whether provided for in the contract or not.*[68] At the same time, the law provides the contractor with the right to require that the financial balance of the contract be restored and preserved (called in French: *'le principe d'équation financière'*).[69] According to this principle, to counterbalance the effect of the public party's 'exceptional powers' and protect the contractor, the contractor is accorded rights to compensation which, like the 'exceptional powers', are mandatory law – the contractor enjoys them whether they have been provided for in the contract or not.[70]

---

66. French Civil Code, art. 2060. While the French civil courts have held the prohibition in this art not to apply where a French public entity enters into a contract which implicates international commerce (Cass civ (1) 2 May 1966, *Galakis* JDI 1966, 648, note P Level), the French administrative courts (which have jurisdiction over most disputes with public entities) do not follow this case law and still retain broad competence over any arbitral award rendered against a French public entity. T. confl., 17 May 2010, *Arrêt Inserm* Rev. arb. 2010.275 comm. M. Audit p. 253 and T. confl., 24 April 2017, *SMAC c/ Ryanair*, no C4075, Rec Lebon, Rev arb 2017.883 comm Y Gaudemet. However, there may have been a recent convergence of the civil and administrative courts with respect to the legal regime of review of arbitral awards. *See* Romain Dupeyré & Bruno Richard, 'Two Supreme Courts – One Single Approach to the Review of Arbitral Awards', ICC Disp Resol Bull, 2022 – Issue 1, 27.
67. Colombia has an administrative court system based on the French model headed (as in France) by a Council of State, the highest administrative court, in addition to having, like France, an ordinary civil court system. Articles 228-245 of Colombia's Constitution of 1991 as amended.
68. Philippe Malinvaud (ed in chief), *Droit de la Construction* (7th edn, Dalloz Action, Paris, 2018) 1345 (para. 417.471).
69. L Neville Brown and others *French Administrative Law* (5th edn, OUP, Oxford, 1998) 206.
70. *See*, for discussion of this subject, **Section 4.6 Civil Law: Special Public Law Theories** below in **Chapter II**.

4.2.3 *Domestic and 'International' Contracts*

In France and other civil law countries,[71] there has in recent decades developed the notion that an 'international contract' (*contrat international*) has a specific character and should therefore be subject to more liberal legal rules – designed to be responsive to the specific needs of international commerce – than those applicable to ordinary (domestic) contracts.[72]

There are different views about how an 'international contract' should be defined, whether by reference, for example, to 'legal' factors (such as the nationality of the parties, place where the work is to be made or performed, the language and currency of the contract) or 'economic' factors (such as whether the export of goods, services and payments across national frontiers is involved) or both.[73]

One consequence of being an international contract is that, unlike in the case of a domestic contract, the parties may be free to choose what law, if any, should govern it and, at the same time, exclude – in principle – the provisions of any other law.[74] An international contract may also be

71. For example, Argentina, Brazil, Chile, Panama, Paraguay and Venezuela, *see* Organization of American States (OAS), 'Report by the Inter-American Judicial Committee on the *Guide on the Law Applicable to International Commercial Contracts in the Americas*' (2019) CJI/Doc 577/19, especially 78-92. *See also* for Brazil, R R Almeida, 'O Conceito de Contrato Internacional (The Concept of International Contract)' (2017) 53 (April-June) Revista de Arbitragen e Mediaçao 47.
72. Bernard Audit and Louis d'Avout, *Droit International Privé* (8th edn, LGDJ, Issy-les-Moulineaux, 2018) 854 (para. 1028) fn. 13.
73. M Audit and others, *Droit du Commerce International et des Investissements Etrangers* (3rd edn, LGDJ, Issy-les-Moulineaux, 2019) 36-37. The distinction between what is domestic and what is international is intended to promote French international commercial interests as those interests would be disserved if certain provisions of French law that are mandatory internally would apply internationally. Bernard Audit and Louis d'Avout, *Droit International Privé* (8th edn, LGDJ, Issy-les-Moulineaux, 2018) 854 (para. 1028) fn. 13.
74. M Audit and others, *Droit du Commerce International et des Investissements Etrangers* (3rd edn, LGDJ, 2019) 36-37. Subject to applicable mandatory law, *see* art. 1.4 (*Mandatory rules*) of the UNIDROIT Principles. In the European Union, this same principle is subject to limitation by Council Regulation (EC) 593/2008 on the law applicable to contractual obligations ('Rome I Regulation') [2010] OJ C343/3, art. 3, Freedom of choice, para. 3: '[...] [w]here all

subject to less stringent rules of national public policy than a domestic contract. Thus, in France[75] and other civil law countries,[76] a more liberal legal regime applies to international arbitration (as defined) compared to domestic arbitration. Similarly, following civil law practice, the *UNCITRAL Model Law on International Commercial Arbitration* distinguishes international arbitration (as defined) from domestic arbitration.[77]

As a practical matter, any construction contract between a contractor or a joint venture of contractors from one or several countries and an employer from another country, for work in the employer's country, is likely to be considered an international contract under the French definition. Consequently, depending on applicable law, under this theory - especially as applied by international arbitrators - such a contract should have the benefit of a more liberal legal regime or set of rules (i.e., be subject to fewer, or more limited, public policy constraints) than would a domestic contract.[78]

---

other elements relevant to the situation at the time of the choice are located in a country other than the country whose law has been chosen, the choice of the parties shall not prejudice the application of provisions of the law of that other country which cannot be derogated from by agreement [...]'. While only applicable in the European Community (other than Denmark), this provision may be indicative of law elsewhere.

75. *See* the French Code of Civil Procedure, arts 1504-27 applicable to international arbitration as defined.
76. *See* the Venezuelan Supreme Court case and the arbitration award (involving Turkish law), ICC case 12174 (2003) cited in **Section 7.4 Relevance to a FIDIC Contract – 7.4.2 As a Source to Interpret or Supplement the Governing Law** below of **Chapter II**.
77. *See UNCITRAL Model Law on International Commercial Arbitration*, as amended in 2006, art. 1(3). *See also* the definition in the *United Nations Convention on Contracts for the International Sale of Goods* (adopted 11 April 1980, entered into force 1 January 1988) 1489 UNTS 3 (CISG) art. 1(1) and official comment 1 to the Preamble of the UNIDROIT Principles which assumes that the concept of 'international' contracts '[...] should be given the broadest possible interpretation [...]'.
78. Thus, as one ICC arbitral tribunal has stated when deciding to moderate the application of mandatory domestic law of a Latin American country to a contract based on YB/99:

> [W]hen considering the scope of the mandatory duties to which the [Employer/administrative entity] is subject under the law, one must take into account the fact that the Contract is *an international construction contract* concluded between an autonomous administrative entity and a

4.3 Civil Law: General Rights and Obligations

Section 4.3 through **Section 4.6** discuss principles of civil law which are of special relevance to international construction contracts, as compared and contrasted with their common law counterparts. Except as otherwise indicated below (most notably in **Section 4.6 Civil Law: Special Public Law Theories**), the same or similar principles of civil law will apply whether the contract is a private contract or a public contract.

4.3.1 Duty of Good Faith

Compared to other jurisdictions, 'English law is very much in the minority to the extent that it declines to recognise the existence of a general duty of good faith.'[79] By contrast, the French Civil Code has, since Napoleon, provided that 'contracts must be performed in good faith'.[80] This requires the contractor (or obligor) to perform the contract honestly and completely, whereas it imposes upon the employer (or obligee) an obligation to cooperate with the contractor in order to enable it to perform the contract.[81] Good faith has been defined as:

> the expression of the duty of loyalty by each co-contractor so as not to offend the confidence that gave rise to the contract. The parties must

---

> consortium of international companies, as opposed to *a domestic administrative [...] agreement* concluded between the government of [X] and its constituents. (Emphasis added)

Partial award, ICC case 20910 (2020) (unpublished), para. 689. *See also* **Section 5.7 Effect of an International Arbitration Clause** in **Chapter III Contract Interpretation** below.

79. Ewan McKendrick, *Contract Law* (14th edn, Red Globe Press, London, 2021) 255.
80. Former art. 1134, para. 3 (now art. 1104 and modified by it), which was a sort of corollary to the principle in former art. 1134, para. 1 (now art. 1103), that validly formed contracts constitute the law of the parties. *See also* former art. 1135 (now art. 1194 and slightly modified by it) to the effect that 'contracts oblige the parties [...] to all the consequences which equity, usage or the law give to the obligation, depending on its nature'.
81. Alain Bénabent, *Droit des Obligations* (18th edn, LGDJ, Issy-les-Moulineaux, 2019) 254 (para. 301).

act towards each other with loyalty and honesty, without malice, or fraud.[82]

Provisions requiring contracts to be performed in good faith are to be found in the civil codes or laws of many countries.[83]

Unlike Germany,[84] for many years French courts had made little use of the civil code provision requiring contracts to be performed in good faith. However, since the late 20th century, the French courts have expanded the scope of this duty to include, among other things, performance during pre-contractual negotiations. Reflecting this evolution in case law, the French Civil Code has provided (since 2016) that:

82. Peter Rosher, 'Good Faith in Construction Contracts under French law and Some Comparative Observations with English Law' [2015] ICLR 302, 304. For this author's latest writing on this subject, *see* Peter Rosher, 'Good Faith in Construction Contracts: Comparing French and English Contract Law Approaches' (2020) RDAI/IBLJ, Issue 2, 145. *See*, more recently, Jean-Pierre Harb and others, 'Recent French Construction Law Lessons – Good Faith and Implied Acceptance' [2021] ICLR 376.

83. *See* the civil codes of Algeria (art. 107), Argentina (art. 961), Brazil (art. 422), Chile (art. 1546), Colombia (art. 1603), Egypt (art. 148), Germany (s 242), Iraq (art. 150), Italy (arts 1337, 1366 and 1375), Jordan (art. 202), Lebanon (art. 221, Code of Obligations and Contracts), Libya (art. 148), Mexico (art. 1796), Morocco (art. 231 of Dahir), Panama (art. 1109), Paraguay (art. 372), Peru (art. 1362), Qatar (art. 172), Russia (art. 307(3)), Spain (art. 1258), Switzerland (art. 2), Tunisia (arts 243 and 558 of the Code of Obligations and Contracts), the UAE (art. 246), Ukraine (art. 509(3)), Uruguay (art. 1291) and Venezuela (art. 1.160). *See also* in the United States the *Uniform Commercial Code* (Uniform Law Commission 1952) s 1-203 (UCC) and the *Restatement (Second) of Contracts* (ALI, Philadelphia, PA, 1981) s 205, as well as the UNIDROIT Principles, art. 1.7 (*see also* art. 2.1.15).

84. *See* Barry Nicholas, *The French Law of Contract* (2nd edn, OUP, Oxford, 1992) 153, discussing art. 242 of the German Civil Code upon the basis of which the German courts developed the doctrine of change of circumstances at the time of runaway inflation after World War I. *See also* Marcel Fontaine, '*Cause*, Good Faith and Hardship: Three Issues in the Process of Harmonizing Contract Law' in UNIDROIT (ed), *Eppur si Muove: The Age of Uniform Law, Essays in Honour of M. J. Bonell*, vol 2 (UNIDROIT, Rome, 2016) 1131, 1137.

> Contracts must be negotiated, formed and performed in good faith.[85]

This provision is a matter of public policy (*ordre public*) which means that it cannot, in principle,[86] be modified or excluded by the parties' contract.[87]

Although of more limited scope than in civil law systems, certain common law countries have also recognised the good faith principle. In United States law[88] there is recognised to be an implied duty of 'good faith and fair dealing' that is imposed on each contracting party, which has been described as follows:

> Each party should not only avoid deliberate and willful frustration of the other party's expectations but should also extend a helping hand where to do so would not be unreasonably burdensome. Contracting parties, although not partners in a legal sense, must recognize the interdependence of contractual relationships. This implied duty is generally viewed as applying to all contracts [...].
>
> Some applications of the doctrine are simply recognition of implied terms [...]. But more expansive use of the doctrine emphasizes the unspoken objectives of the contracting parties, the spirit of the contract itself, and the need for elementary fairness.[89]

85. Art. 1104 which replaced old art. 1134, para. 3.
86. This principle is subject to some exceptions: *see* Yves-Marie Laithier, *L'obligation d'exécuter le contrat de bonne foi est-elle susceptible de clause contraire?* (Dalloz, Paris, 2014) 33.
87. Art. 1104, para. 2. *See* also the French Civil Code, art. 1112, requiring that pre-contractual negotiations generally must imperatively satisfy the requirements of good faith.
88. In the United States, s I-304 of the *Uniform Commercial Code* (UCC), which has been enacted by legislation in all 50 States and which applies to commercial contracts, provides that '[e]very contract or duty within [the *UCC*] imposes an obligation of good faith in its performance and enforcement'. Section 205 of the *Restatement (Second) of Contracts* provides for a duty of good faith and fair dealing in the performance and enforcement of contracts, which has been widely followed by courts in the United States.
89. Justin Sweet and Marc M Schneier, *Construction Law for Design Professionals, Construction Managers, and Contractors* (Cengage Learning, Stamford, CT, 2015) 45. The following is a list of 12 implied obligations, many of which are said to derive from the implied duty of 'good faith and fair dealing', which an owner has under United States law:

    (1) The duty to disclose material information to prospective bidders.

In the United States, however, the duty of good faith is not binding during pre-contract negotiations.[90]

The Supreme Court of Canada has recognised 'a general organising principle'[91] to perform contracts in good faith and, as a manifestation of this principle, that 'there is a common law duty which applies to all contracts to act honestly in the performance of contractual obligations'.[92] This duty cannot be excluded by contract.[93]

---

(2) The duty to provide accurate plans and specifications.
(3) The duty to provide accurate site information.
(4) The duty to obtain necessary regulatory approvals, permits, and easements.
(5) The duty to provide access to the work site.
(6) Duties relating to owner-furnished products, materials, or equipment.
(7) The duty to timely review contractor submittals and requests.
(8) The duty not to deny valid requests for time extensions.
(9) The duty to make timely inspections.
(10) The duty to maintain the project site in a reasonably safe condition.
(11) The duty not to hinder, delay, or interfere with the timely completion of work.
(12) The duty to coordinate the work of multiple prime contractors.

Steven Lesser and David Wallach, 'The Twelve Deadly Sins: An Owner's Guide to Avoiding Liability for Implied Obligations During the Construction of a Project' (2008) 28(1) Const L, ABA for Const L, 15. The article contains extensive references to cases in support of each of these 12 implied obligations.

90. E Allan Farnsworth, *Contracts* (4th edn, Aspen, NY, 2004) 490 (para. 7.17).
91. An organising principle 'states in general terms a requirement of justice from which more specific legal doctrines may be derived. An organising principle therefore is not a free-standing rule, but rather a standard that underpins and is manifested in more specific legal doctrines and may be given different weight in different situations [...] It is a standard that helps to understand and develop the law in a coherent and principled way'. *Bhasin v Hrynew* [2014] SCC 71, [2014] 3 SCR 494 [para. 64].
92. *Ibid.* [33]. *See also* Yves-Marie Laithier, 'La consécration par la Cour suprême du Canada d'un principe directeur imposant l'exécution du contrat de bonne foi, Variations sur le droit commun' (Recueil Dalloz 2015) 746.
93. *Bhasin v Hrynew* [2014] SCC 71, [2014] 3 SCR 494 [para. 75]. The case arose out of the termination of a dealership agreement between a financial corporation, Can-Am, and a retail dealer, Bhasin. Can-Am had appointed a competitor of Bhasin, with whom Bhasin had previously refused to merge, to

Similarly, Article 1.7 (*Good faith and fair dealing*) of the UNIDROIT Principles provides that '[e]ach party must act in accordance with good faith and fair dealing in international trade' and that the parties may not exclude or limit this duty (e.g., by contract).[94]

While English law has not any overarching doctrine of good faith,[95] it has 'developed piecemeal solutions in response to demonstrated problems of unfairness'.[96] These include 'implication of terms', which is perhaps the most important such solution as a practical matter, 'unconscionability', 'undue influence', 'economic duress', 'the control of exemption clauses', the requirement of 'utmost fairness' for certain types of contracts (such as insurance, where an insured must reveal facts which an insurer might

---

review Bhasin's confidential business records. When Bhasin objected, Can-Am assured Bhasin that the competitor would be bound to respect confidentiality, which was untrue. Without Bhasin's knowledge, Can-Am then planned for Bhasin to be taken over by its competitor and Can-Am responded equivocally to Bhasin's questions about its plans. As Bhasin refused to allow the competitor to audit its records, Can-Am refused to renew the agreement, Bhasin's sales force was successfully solicited by the competitor and Bhasin suffered other damage. Bhasin brought an action in damages against Can-Am and the competitor for, among other things, breach of an implied contractual duty of good faith and the Canadian Supreme Court upheld Bhasin's claim on this basis. For a more recent Canadian Supreme Court case acknowledging the duty of good faith in contractual performance *see C.M. Callow Inc v Zollinger* [2020] SCC 45.

94. *See also* official comment 2 to art. 1.7 of the UNIDROIT Principles which provides that a typical example of behaviour contrary to the principle of good faith and fair dealing is what in some legal systems is known as 'abuse of rights'. *See also* art. 2.1.15 (*Negotiations in bad faith*) of the UNIDROIT Principles.
95. As has been well pointed out by one English author, good faith can have a spectrum of possible meanings: 'at one end of the spectrum good faith means no more than honesty [...] At the other end of the spectrum good faith may require (a party) [...] to give priority to the best interests of the other party, as in the manner of a fiduciary', quoting from an article by E McKendrick cited in Neil Andrews, 'Good Faith Beneath the Surface: The Ethical Sensitivity of English Contract Law' in UNIDROIT (ed), *Eppur si Muove: The Age of Uniform Law, Essays in Honour of M.J. Bonell* (UNIDROIT, Rome, 2016) vol 2, 953, 956 (fn. 20).
96. *Interfoto Picture Library Ltd v Stiletto Visual Programmes Ltd* [1987] EWCA Civ 6, [1989] QB 433, 439 (Bingham LJ).

regard as material) and other mechanisms.[97] In the construction sphere, the English courts have recognised implied duties of good faith, most notably in *London Borough of Merton v Stanley Leach*.[98] The English High Court found that there were implied duties for the building owner: (1) not to prevent the contractor from carrying out its obligations and (2) to take all reasonable steps to enable the contractor to discharge its obligations.[99]

Accordingly, '[a]t a functional level, the differences between English contract law and civilian contract laws with regard to good faith may [...] be less significant than frequently suggested'.[100] As a practical matter, in the author's experience, English law may often achieve the same result as if it had a doctrine of good faith, though through other means.

The differences between English and French law may be explained by different views of contract law: 'English contract law is premised on

97. Stefan Vogenauer (ed), *Commentary on the UNIDROIT Principles of International Commercial Contracts* (*PICC*) (2nd edn, OUP, Oxford, 2015) 209 (para. 7).
98. (1985) 32 BLR 51 (Ch).
99. *Ibid.*, at 79 and 80. As one English court of first instance has stated:

> there seems [...] to be no difficulty, following the established methodology of English law for the implication of terms in fact, in implying [a duty of good faith] in any ordinary commercial contract based on the presumed intention of the parties.

Yam Seng Pte Ltd v International Trade Corporation Ltd [2013] EWHL III (QB), [2013] BLR 147, 167 [para. 131]. In this case, finding the contract to be a long-term 'relational' contract where there are expectations of loyalty 'not legislated for in the express terms of the contract but [...] implicit in the parties' understanding and necessary to give [the contract] business efficacy' [para. 142], the judge held that the parties were to perform it in good faith [paras 154-230]. Since that 2013 case, the English courts have been prepared to imply a duty of good faith in a number of cases where a relational contract (which, arguably, depending on the facts, might include a construction contract) has been found to exist. *See Alan Bates and others v Post Office Ltd (no 3: Common Issues)* [2019] EWHC 606 (QB), [2019] 3 WLUK 260 which sets out a non-exhaustive list of characteristics of a relational contract [at para. 725] and cites to several cases where a duty of good faith has been found to exist in such contracts [para. 705]. *See also* Rupert Jackson, 'Winners, Losers and a Coda on Good Faith', SCL paper D227 March 2020.
100. Stefan Vogenauer (ed), *Commentary on the UNIDROIT Principles of International Commercial Contracts (PICC)* (2nd edn, OUP, Oxford, 2015) 209 (para. 7).

adversarial self-interested dealing',[101] whereas in French law good faith is 'one of the means used by the legislator and the courts to transfuse morality into the positive law'.[102]

4.3.2 Duty of Disclosure

One area where there remains a very notable difference between the two systems and which is derived, in the French civil law system, from the principle of good faith, is the duty to disclose crucial information when entering into a contract. The French Civil Code provides that:

> The party who knows information which is of decisive importance for the consent of the other [i.e. consent to contract], must inform him of

---

101. Neil Andrews, 'Good Faith Beneath the Surface: The Ethical Sensitivity of English Contract Law' in UNIDROIT (ed), *Eppur si Muove: The Age of Uniform Law, Essays in honour of M.J. Bonell* (UNIDROIT, Rome, 2016) vol 2, 953, 973, quoting Professor R Brownswood, *Contract Law: Themes for the Twenty-first century* (2nd edn, OUP, Oxford, 2006), Chapter 6, at 123 ff. Not all English lawyers, however, *see* English law as premised on adversarial dealing:

> [t]here is sometimes a tendency of English commercial lawyers to view commerce as if it were a kind of Darwinian struggle in which everyone is trying to gain at the expense of those with whom they do business [...] This model of commerce and of contract [...] does not, in my view, correspond to commercial reality [...] [I]t is a mistake to see contracting as an essentially adversarial activity.
>
> Mr Justice Leggatt, 'Contractual duties of good faith', lecture to the Commercial Bar Association, UK, 18 October 2016, 7 (paras 25-26).

102. Citation by Barry Nicholas of Jacques Ghestin in Barry Nicholas, 'The Pre-Contractual Obligation to Disclosure Information – English Report' in Donald Harris and Dennis Tallon (eds), *Contract Law Today: Anglo-French Comparisons* (OUP, Oxford, 1989) 187. In the same vein, Professor Philippe Stoffel-Munck, also (like Professor Ghestin) a respected French professor of contract law, has observed, with apparent disapproval, that if a wrongful termination of contract could be remedied in damages alone rather than by an order requiring performance (the normal remedy for breach of contract under French law, unlike under the common law), the injured promisee would be able 'to atone for a sin with money' (*Cela aboutit ... 'à racheter par de l'argent un péché'*). Philippe Stoffel-Munck, 'Le contrôle a posteriori de la résiliation unilatérale' (Droit & patrimoine 2004, no 126) 70, 75.

> it where the latter, legitimately, does not know the information or relies on the other party.[103]

The parties may not limit or exclude this duty by contract.[104]

The duty to disclose information:

> has been applied to different degrees by French courts depending on the capabilities of the parties. When the contract is concluded between a layman and a professional, the professional will owe a more extensive duty to inform the layman on the different aspects of the product or service.[105]

On the other hand, the position under English law is quite different:

> a party to pre-contractual negotiations is under no duty to disabuse the other of an error concerning the quality, nature or utility of the transaction's subject matter. Lord Hoffmann in the *BCCI* case (2002) said: '[T]here is obviously room in the dealings of the market for legitimately taking advantage of the known ignorance of the other party.' Each party is entitled to remain silent during the negotiations, permitting the other to make miscalculations, unless one of a list of qualifications or exceptions applies [...].[106]

103. French Civil Code, art. 1112-1. The same art provides that 'information of decisive importance' is information which has a 'direct and necessary relationship with the content of the contract or the status of the parties'.
104. French Civil Code, art. 1112-1, fifth paragraph. The same art provides that the duty of disclosure does not apply to 'an assessment of the value' of the services or thing to be supplied (art. 1112-1, second paragraph). As one commentator has put it, it is unnecessary for the seller to tell the buyer that the thing being sold is worth less than its price! Philippe Malaurie and others, *Droit des Obligations* (11th edn, LGDJ, Issy-les-Moulineaux, 2020) 423 (para. 450).
105. Peter Rosher, 'The Potential Impact of French Contract Reform on the Construction Industry' [2016] ICLR 378, 388.
106. Neil Andrews, 'Good Faith Beneath the Surface: The Ethical Sensitivity of English Contract Law' in UNIDROIT (ed) *Eppur si Muove: The Age of Uniform Law, Essays in Honour of M.J. Bonell* (UNIDROIT, Rome, 2016) vol 2, 953, 965. However, the implied duties referred to in *London Borough of Merton v Stanley Leach*, in **Section 4.3.1** above, will come into play once the contract is in being and which do connote a duty of positive assistance.

To similar effect, in a construction context under English law:

> an Employer, in the absence of an actionable misrepresentation or deliberate concealment, or of some express warranty, owes no implied duty to a contractor, whether of disclosure or otherwise, in either contract or tort in regard to the pre-existing state of the site.[107]

On the other hand, the same English authority recognises that the US position is different:

> In the case of US government contracts, [...] the Court of Claims has exceptionally evolved a duty of disclosure by the government where it possesses vital information indispensable to satisfactory performance of the contract, and which the Contractor has no means of ascertaining and would not assume to be the case in the light of the descriptions and wording of the specification.[108]

The same English authority goes on to recognise, however, that:

> [t]he (English) common law position is less important under most standard forms because express terms allocating the risk of problems with the site are extremely common.[109]

In conclusion, given that French law requires a contract be negotiated, formed and performed in good faith, it is:

> very much more difficult for French law than for English to say that 'passive acquiescence of the seller [e.g. an Employer] in the

107. Atkin Chambers, *Hudson's Building and Engineering Contracts* (14th edn, Sweet & Maxwell, London, 2020) 453-454 (para. 3-086).
108. *Ibid.*, citing to *Helene Curtis Industries Inc v US* 312 F 2d 774 (1963). This is referred to in US government contract practice as the 'superior knowledge' principle or doctrine. *See Scott Timber Co v United States*, 692 F 3rd 1365, 1373 (Fed Cir 2012) citing to *Hercules Inc v United States* 24 F 3rd 188, 196 (Fed Cir 1994). Contrary to the implication in Hudson, this doctrine applies in the US also to private contracts, *see Pat J Murphy Inc v Drummond Dolomite Inc* 232 F Supp 509 (ED Wisc 1964) and *Pinkerton and Laws Co Inc v Roadway Exp Inc* 650 F Supp 1138 (ND Ga 1986).
109. Atkin Chambers, *Hudson's Building and Engineering Contracts* (14th edn, Sweet & Maxwell, London, 2020) 455 (para. 3-087). Indeed, consistent with the above, Sub-Clause 4.12 of RB/17 generally allocates the risk of 'Unforeseeable' adverse Site conditions to the Employer.

self-deception of the buyer [e.g. a Contractor]' is a matter of no concern to the law.[110]

4.3.3 Defence of Non-performance (*Exceptio Non Adimpleti Contractus*)

Under French and other civil laws, a contractor enjoys the benefit of the defence of non-performance (*exceptio non adimpleti contractus*),[111] pursuant to which, if one party does not perform a substantial contractual duty,[112] the other party may use this as an excuse not to perform a correlative duty.[113] This right is also recognised by the UNIDROIT Principles.[114] Thus, if the contractor is not being paid amounts which the engineer has certified as due, the contractor may, at some point, suspend work or, in an extreme case, terminate the contract, subject to certain conditions.

Although there exists no equivalent to this remedy in the common law,[115] *it can be a most valuable right for the contractor where, for example, the*

---

110. Barry Nicholas, 'The Pre-contractual Obligation to Disclose Information' in Donald Harris and Denis Tallon (eds), *Contract Law Today: Anglo-French Comparisons* (OUP, Oxford, 1989) 188.
111. Referred to in French as *l'exception d'inexécution*. This is expressly recognised in the French Civil Code, arts 1217, 1219-20. Similar provisions are contained in, among others, the civil codes of Algeria (art. 123), Argentina (art. 1031), Brazil (art. 476), Chile (art. 1552), Colombia (art. 1609), Egypt (art. 161), Libya (art. 163), Qatar (art. 191), Peru (art. 1426), Russia (art. 328(2)), Switzerland (art. 82 of the Code of Obligations), UAE (art. 247), Ukraine (art. 538(3)) and Venezuela (art. 1.168).
112. The breach must be sufficiently serious ('*suffisamment grave*') for this defence to apply – French Civil Code, art. 1219.
113. The contract must be one where the duties of the parties are concurrent. *See* Barry Nicholas, *The French Law of Contract* (2nd edn, OUP, Oxford, 1992) 213. Indeed a party may suspend performance as soon as it becomes evident that the other party will not perform its obligation when it becomes due and when the consequences of this non-performance are sufficiently serious. Notice of this suspension must be given as quickly as possible. *See* French Civil Code, art. 1220.
114. Art. 7.1.3 (*Witholding performance*) of the UNIDROIT Principles quoted under **(iv) Related Law** of the commentary on Sub-Clause 16.1 [*Suspension by Contractor*] below.
115. However, s 112 of HGCRA in the UK confers a statutory right of suspension on a contractor who has not been paid the sums due to it, after it has given a prior notice to the party in default.

employer discontinues making regular monthly payments of certified amounts. Indeed, borrowing from the civil law system, RB/17 provides relief to the Contractor in this case.[116]

However, under the civil law, this remedy is not generally available in the case of public or administrative contracts.[117] The exclusion of this right in that case is justified by the idea that the contractor is a collaborator in the performance of a public service and that such service must not be interrupted except in the case of extreme circumstances, notably *force majeure*.[118] It is also justified on the ground that a contractor is said not to enjoy self-help remedies against the state.[119]

Thus, as an example, the *Implementing Regulations of Governmental Tender and Procurement Law* (the 'IRGTPL') of the Kingdom of Saudi Arabia (whose law has been influenced by French law) provide that:

> A contractor may not refuse to carry out his obligations on grounds that the Government Authority is in default of its obligations.[120]

4.3.4 Notice of Default (*Mise En Demeure*)

In civil law systems, the general principle is that in the case of non-performance of a contract by one party, the other party must put the non-performing party in default by a notice of default.[121] Until the performing party does so, it is presumed to have tacitly accepted that the non-performing party is to be allowed additional time to perform its obligations.[122]

The notice of default may take the form of a letter (normally sent via registered mail with return receipt requested) requiring performance or,

116. *See* Sub-Clause 16.1 [*Suspension by Contractor*].
117. *See* **Section 4.2.2 Public and Private Contracts** above in **Chapter II Applicable Law**. For French law *see* Philippe Malinvaud (ed in chief), *Droit de la Construction* (7th edn, Dalloz Action, Paris, 2018) 1347 (para. 417.496).
118. André de Laubadère and others, *Traité des Contrats Administratifs* (2nd edn, LGDJ, Paris, 1984) vol II, 206-209 (para. 1002).
119. *Ibid*.
120. Art. 49 of IRGTPL, Minister of Finance Decision no 362, 20 *Safar* 1428 H/10 March 2007.
121. In French: *mise en demeure*.
122. Philippe Malaurie and others, *Droit des Obligations* (11th edn, LGDJ, Paris, 2020) 557 (para. 611).

if the contract so provides, may result simply from an obligation falling due.[123] Article 1231 of the French Civil Code provides for the general rule that:[124]

> damages are due only if the debtor has previously been put on notice (*mise en demeure*) to perform its obligation within a reasonable time.[125]

The purpose of this notice is to alert the non-performing party that the other party considers that it is in breach (as it may not necessarily be aware of this) and that, upon expiry of a notice or 'grace' period, the other party may seek an order for specific performance, claim damages (including, under certain civil law systems, interest, which accrues as from the date this notice is received)[126] and/or terminate the contract.[127]

In common law systems, on the other hand, there is no legal requirement for a notice of default, and the general rule is that where one party has failed to perform on time, the other party can sue.[128] However, any contract may require that a notice of default be given to a party in breach.[129]

123. French Civil Code, art. 1344.
124. Other than where non-performance is permanent (*définitive*). For example, where a lease provides that it may not be assigned without the landlord's consent, and the tenant assigns the lease without such consent, a notice would be unnecessary as it would be useless given that the tenant's breach is irreversible. Philippe Malaurie and others, *Droit des Obligations* (11th edn, LGDJ, Issy-les Moulineaux, 2020) 559 (para. 613).
125. For another example to the same effect, *see* the Egyptian Civil Code, art. 218.
126. French Civil Code, arts 1344, 1344-1.
127. Caslav Pejovic, 'Civil Law and Common Law: Two Different Paths Leading to the Same Goal' (2001) 32 VUWLR 817, 826.
128. Cheshire, Fifoot and Furmston, *Law of Contract* (17th edn, OUP, Oxford, 2017) 663 who add that at this moment the period of limitation will begin to run. A failure to take steps to enforce a breach of contract can lead to a waiver of such right to sue.
129. Thus, Sub-Clause 15.1 of RB/17 provides for the Contractor to be given a Notice to Correct and Sub-Clauses 15.2 and 16.2 of RB/17 provide for the giving of a Notice of intention to terminate, in most cases, before the Employer or Contractor, respectively, may terminate the Contract. Similarly, Sub-Clause 16.1 requires the Contractor to give a Notice prior to suspending work.

4.3.5 Contract Termination

While the general rule under the common law is that termination of a contract on the ground of a material default may be effected simply by a notice to that effect, this has not been the traditional rule under French law, and in this area, as elsewhere, traditional French law continues to apply in a number of civil law countries, notably in the Arab Middle East.

Under Article 1184, third paragraph, of the old French (Napoleonic) Civil Code, save in exceptional cases, termination of a bilateral contract (such as a construction contract) for breach had to be ordered by a court, unlike under the common law where a party may simply treat the other party's breach as discharging the contract.[130] The one exceptional case under French law was where the contract contained a clause expressly providing for termination (in French: *une clause résolutoire expresse*).[131] However, the French courts interpreted this exception *very restrictively* and, in the absence of an express provision entitling a party, in defined circumstances, to terminate a contract automatically or *ipso facto* (in French: *de plein droit*), and, preferably, adding expressly 'without obtaining a court judgement', had presumed that, by a contract termination clause, *the*

130. Barry Nicholas, *The French Law of Contract* (2nd edn, OUP, Oxford, 1992) 241-46. Art. 1184 has, since 2016, been replaced by arts 1217 and 1224 et seq. They now permit a party to terminate a contract by a notice in the case of a serious breach (*inexécution suffisamment grave*), as under the common law.

131. This exceptional case (which was not provided for in Art. 1184, third paragraph) resulted from an 1860 French court decision providing that:

> parties are not forbidden, by an express agreement, in the case of a breach of contract, to provide for [in the case of non-performance] the effects of a resolutory condition [i.e. termination clause] which is specific, absolute and operates automatically; there is nothing illegal in such an agreement; it becomes the law for those who have made it; and the courts cannot change it.
>
> (The French original: *'il n'est (...) pas défendu aux parties, par une convention expresse, d'attacher [à l'inexécution du contrat] les effets d'une condition résolutoire, précise, absolue et opérant de plein droit; qu'une pareille convention n'a rien d'illicite; qu'elle tient lieu de loi à ceux qui l'ont faite; que les tribunaux ne peuvent pas la changer'*).
>
> Cass civ, 2 July 1860, D 1860, I, 284-85. *See also* Yves-Marie Laithier, *Etude Comparative des Sanctions de l'Inexécution du Contrat* (LGDJ, Paris, 2007) 227-96.

parties intended no more than a reminder of Article 1184 and not to waive the right to obtain a court judgment ordering discharge of the contract.[132]

As a result of the influence of this old French law, the legal obligation for a party to obtain a court order or judgment[133] to be able to terminate a contract, such as a construction contract, subsists in many civil law countries, such as Egypt, as does the restrictive interpretation of a contract termination clause.[134] Consequently, as the termination provisions in FIDIC contracts had not – due to their common law origin –

132. Philippe Malaurie and others, *Droit des Obligations* (11th edn, LGDJ, Issy-les-Moulineaux, 2020) 507 (para. 545); Barry Nicholas, *The French Law of Contract* (2nd edn, OUP, Oxford, 1992) 244.

133. Or an award of an arbitral tribunal, where the parties have agreed to arbitration.

134. *See* art. 157 of the Egyptian Civil Code requiring a court order to terminate a bilateral contract although art. 158 of the same Code recognises that the parties may agree otherwise. The late Dr Al Sanhouri, the Egyptian legal scholar, has described how a clause providing for termination of a contract for one party's default may be made most effective in excluding the need to refer to a court (translation):

> The strength of this clause can be increased by providing that the contract will be considered as *ipso facto* terminated and this clause can even be strengthened further to provide that the contract will be considered as terminated *ipso facto* without the need to resort to a court judgment. Finally, [the strength of the clause] can reach the peak, and provide that the contract will be considered as terminated *ipso facto* without the need for a judgement nor notice or simply without the need for notice. Al Sanhouri, *Al Wasit in the Explanation of Civil Law*, vol 1, 598-99 ¶ 481.

A court order also seems generally to be required in Algeria (art. 119 of the Civil Code), Iraq (art. 177 of the Civil Code), Jordan (art. 241), Lebanon (art. 241, Code of Obligations and Contracts), Libya (art. 159 of the Libyan Civil Code), Qatar (art. 183 of the Qatari Civil Code) and the United Arab Emirates (*see* art. 267 of the UAE Civil Code). However, as in the case of Egypt, each of these countries appears to accept that the parties may agree otherwise, *see* Algeria (art. 120 of the Civil Code), Iraq (art. 178 of the Civil Code), Lebanese Code of Obligations and Contracts (art. 241), Libyan Civil Code (art. 160), the Qatari Civil Code (art. 184) and UAE Civil Code (art. 271). A 2019 English High Court judgment, *Obrascon Huarte Lain SA v Qatar Foundation for Education, Science and Community Development* [2019] EWHC 2539 (Comm), refused to set aside an arbitral award (on grounds of 'serious irregularity' under s 68(2) (a) of the English

expressly excluded the need for a court judgment (or arbitral award), such a judgment was and is required under the law of those countries.[135]

RB/17 now contains a provision to the effect that, subject to any mandatory requirements of the governing law, termination of the Contract under any Sub-Clause of the Conditions of Contract shall require no action by either Party except as stated in the relevant Sub-Clause.[136] This provision is not as strong as it could – or should – be in terms of excluding the need for a court judgment (or arbitral award). Accordingly, it remains to be seen whether it will be sufficient to relieve a party from having to apply to the DAAB and, if necessary, an arbitral tribunal to terminate a contract under the law of civil law countries.

4.4 Civil Law: Distinctive Features of Construction Law

4.4.1 Contract Administrator (Maître D'Oeuvre) *v Engineer*

The traditional common law (and FIDIC) notion of an 'independent' engineer,[137] that is, of a person who not only may design and administer

Arbitration Act 1996) which found that a contractual provision for termination by notice was effective although it did not expressly state that the contract could be terminated 'automatically, without need for a court judgement' as required by art. 184(1) of Qatari Civil Code. The arbitral tribunal (comprising three English barristers) decided, applying Qatari law, that 'it was sufficient if the contractual provision was sufficiently clear so as to be inconsistent with the requirement of an application to and order of the court' [para. 36]. As indicated in the main text, this legal requirement for a court order no longer exists in French Law, *see* (since 2016) French Civil Code, arts 1217 and 1224 et seq.

135. *See* partial award, ICC case 9202 (1998), ICC Int'l Ct Arb Bull, vol 19, no 2, 2008, 76, 81-85 (commentary in English 42, 46-48) holding, in relation to a contract based on RB/69, which contained a clause giving the Contractor ostensibly the right to terminate the contract (but not that it could do so automatically or *ipso facto*) and which was governed by the law of a civil law country, that for termination by the Contractor to be effective reference to the Engineer under Clause 67 (the equivalent of the reference of a Dispute to the DAAB under Clause 21 of RB/17) and, if necessary, to ICC arbitration was required, and this had not been done with the consequence that the Contractor was held liable for having abandoned the project.
136. *See* Sub-Clause 1.16 [*Contract Termination*] and the commentary thereon in **Chapter IV Clause-by-Clause Commentary** below.
137. *See* **Section 3.2 Distinctive Features – 3.2.2 'Independent' Engineer** of **Chapter I General Introduction** above. It is a misnomer to describe the

a construction contract but also may be required to act fairly and/or impartially between the employer and the contractor in relation to certain matters, is unknown to French and civil law generally.[138]

The role in construction projects in France which corresponds most closely to that of the common law engineer is that of a contract administrator (in French: *maître d'oeuvre*). Like the common law engineer, the civil law contract administrator may design the works, oversee their execution, ensure they are constructed in accordance with the contract and generally assist the employer. However, the civil law contract administrator has no duty to act fairly and/or impartially between his client, the employer, on the one hand, and the contractor, on the other hand.[139]

Engineer as 'independent' as the Engineer is hired and paid by the Employer. Even in England, it is recognised that a professional man in the position of the Engineer: (1) 'can hardly be called independent' (*Beaufort Developments (NI) Ltd v Gilbert-Ash (NI) Ltd* [1999] 1 AC 266, 276 (Lord Hoffmann)), and (2) 'is not, and cannot be regarded as, independent of the employer' *Scheldebouw BV v St James Homes (Grosvenor Dock) Ltd* [2006] BLR 113 [para. 34] (Jackson J).

138. 'In the continental standard conditions of contract for construction work, such as the German VOB or the Swiss SIA norm 118, the engineer or architect hardly figures at all, as in this contractual constellation he acts as the employer's agent and nothing further.' Fritz Nicklisch, 'The Role of the Engineer as Contract Administrator and Quasi-Arbitrator in International Construction and Civil Engineering Projects' [1990] ICLR 322, 323.

139. However, in 1854, the French Government issued a Circular – a 'Circular' is an administrative instruction issued, in this case, by a Minister – setting out how State Engineers should deal with disputes between the Contractor and the State:

> (State) Engineers must consider themselves to be less the defendants of a cause, than as reporters requested to give an impartial opinion on which the judge may safely base his decision. By proceeding this way, (State) Engineers shall meet the Administration's requirements, whose first interest, and also first duty, is to make justice prevail at all times, wherever it may reside. (Emphasis in the original)
>
> ['*M.M. les ingénieurs doivent se considérer moins comme les défenseurs d'une cause que comme des rapporteurs appelés à donner un avis impartial sur lequel le juge puisse baser en toute sécurité sa décision. En se plaçant à ce point de vue, M.M. les ingénieurs répondront aux intentions de l'administration dont le premier intérêt, et aussi le premier devoir, est de faire prévaloir en toute circonstance la justice, de quelque côté qu'elle se*

Under the principal standard form of contract for private (civil engineering) works in France ('AFNOR form'),[140] the contract administrator's authority is much more limited than that of the Engineer under RB/17. For example, under the AFNOR form:

(1) the contractor may not subcontract the work without having obtained the approval of the employer;[141]
(2) while the contract administrator has the authority to issue instructions (in French: *ordres de service*) to the contractor so, to a limited extent, does the employer;[142]
(3) changes to the nature of the works are ordered by the employer, not by the contract administrator;[143]
(4) if new unit prices must be fixed, then they must be agreed between the contractor and the employer;[144]
(5) while the contract administrator verifies the contractor's interim payment applications, its verifications are not binding on the parties;[145]

---

trouve.' Circulaire du Ministre de l'agriculture, du commerce et des travaux publics – Instruction des affaires contentieuses, 27 July 1854].

But the present author has found no more recent instruction on this subject.

140. *Cahier des Clauses Administratives Générales applicable aux travaux de genie civil faisant l'objet de Marchés Privés* (General conditions of contract for civil engineering works for private works contract) NF P 03-002, 3 October 2014 published by *l'Association Française de Normalisation* (AFNOR), the French standards association ('AFNOR form'). While under the form of contract for *public* works in France (*Cahier des Clauses Administratives Générales CCAG. –Travaux, 2014*), the powers of the contract administrator differ somewhat from those under the AFNOR form, they are still much less extensive than those of the Engineer under RB/17.
141. AFNOR form art. 4.6. Under RB/17, the Engineer and not the Employer consents to a proposed subcontractor (Sub-Clause 5.1).
142. AFNOR form arts 3.30 and 15.2. Under RB/17, the Contractor may 'only' take instructions from the Engineer (Sub-Clause 3.5).
143. AFNOR form, arts 11.1.3 and 11.1.4. Under RB/17, the Engineer initiates Variations (Sub-Clause 13.1).
144. AFNOR form art. 9.1.2. Under RB/17, the Engineer fixes new rates and prices (Sub-Clause 12.3).
145. AFNOR form art. 19.3. Under RB/17, the Employer is bound to pay the amount of each Interim Payment Certificate certified by the Engineer (Sub-Clause 14.7).

(6) while the contract administrator examines the draft final statement (in French: *projet de décompte final*) prepared by the contractor, and establishes a draft of the final statement which it submits to the employer, the employer finally decides on its content and notifies the contractor;[146]

(7) the contract administrator has no authority to decide the contractor's or the employer's claims or to rule on disputes;[147] and

(8) while completion of the works (in French: *réception*) is established by minutes of completion drawn up by the contract administrator, completion is decided by the employer who signs the minutes of completion.[148]

Consequently, the contract administrator's authority vis-à-vis the parties is much reduced compared to that of a common law engineer.

As indicated by the above examples, the basic decisions under French private works contracts are taken by and in the name of the employer not the contract administrator.[149] While the employer will ordinarily rely heavily on advice and information from the contract administrator, the employer generally takes the decisions and has final responsibility for them.

There is no absolutely clear line of responsibility between the contract administrator and the contractor or others employed in performing building work (architects, specialist engineers and others) in France. All those engaged in performing such work are perceived as having, in some degree, overlapping responsibilities to the employer and to each other for ensuring that the work is properly done.[150]

146. AFNOR form art. 19.5. Under RB/17, the Engineer decides the content of the Final Statement and issues the Final Payment Certificate which the Employer is required to pay (Sub-Clauses 14.11-14.13) and 14.7.

147. AFNOR form art. 21. Under RB/17, the Engineer has authority to agree or determine any matter or Claim of either Party (Sub-Clause 3.7).

148. AFNOR form art. 17.2.3. Under RB/17, the Engineer issues the Taking-Over Certificate which determines that the Works have been completed in accordance with the Contract (Clause 10).

149. Under a French public works contract, the employer's powers are even greater. *See* **Section 4.2.2 Public and Private Contracts** above of **Chapter II Applicable Law** describing the public employer's exceptional powers under an administrative contract.

150. This is reflected in the principle of decennial liability, originating in Napoleon's Civil Code, providing that:

As a consequence, the contractor may often end up sharing with the contract administrator responsibility for problems of design and construction. Indeed, all those engaged in performing construction work for the employer often end up sharing, in some degree, responsibilities for problems of design and construction.[151]

The overriding objective of French construction law is to protect the interests of the owner, who is perceived as the weaker party, as against 'builder(s)' who are presumed to be experts or specialists in the execution of construction work. This can be seen by the French legal regimes relating to both lump sum contracts and decennial and other post-completion liability discussed below.[152]

4.4.2 Lump Sum Contracts

Since Napoleon, the French Civil Code has contained a specific article, Article 1793, designed to protect the owner against exposure to price increases in relation to a lump sum contract, unless these have been clearly agreed with the owner.[153] This article provides that:

> Every builder of a work is presumed to be liable absolutely to the owner or acquirer of the work for damages for a defect, even if resulting from the ground, which impairs the stability of the work or which, by affecting one of its constituent elements or an element of its equipment, makes it unsuitable for its purpose (Art. 1792 of the French Civil Code).

For the purposes of this provision, a 'builder' ('*constructeur*') is defined to include, among others, an architect, a contractor, a technician or other person bound to the owner by a contract for the hire of work, such as the Engineer under a FIDIC contract (art. 1792-1 of the French Civil Code). If they have a contract with the owner they are all presumed liable for the defect unless, and to the extent that, any 'builder' can prove otherwise (*see* **Section 4.4.4 Decennial Liability** below of **Chapter II Applicable Law**).

151. Christopher R Seppälä, 'The Engineer's Liability to the Contractor: French Law', paper presented to Committee T – International Construction Contracts, Toronto, 1983, IBA, Sect on Bus L.
152. *See* **Section 4.4.2 Lump Sum Contracts** and **Section 4.4.4 Decennial Liability** below in **Chapter II Applicable Law**.
153. The purpose of this art when it was introduced into the original Civil Code in 1804 was (like art. 1792) to protect owners. The concern was that a contractor might induce an owner to enter into a construction contract by proposing a relatively low price and then, once the contract was concluded, propose additional works to which the owner would be unable to object if

> When an architect or contractor has undertaken to construct a building for a lump sum price in accordance with a finalized plan agreed with the owner of the land, he may not ask for any increase in price, either by reason of an increase in the cost of labour or materials, or by reason of changes or additions made in the agreed plan, if these changes or additions have not been authorised in writing and the price agreed with the owner.[154]

As indicated by this article, for it to apply several conditions must be fulfilled. First, the contract has to involve the construction of a building. Second, the building has to be on the owner's property. Third, the contract has to involve a lump sum price, that is, a price which is fixed regardless of the quantities of work executed.[155] Fourth, the parties have to have agreed on a plan or design that defines a scope of works corresponding to the lump sum price. Fifth, although not expressly envisaged by Article 1793, the French courts have interpreted it to require that the agreement on a lump sum price assumes an agreed programme or time schedule.[156]

---

they were necessary (as the contractor, but not the owner, might have foreseen to be the case from the outset). Bernard Boubli, 'Le marché à forfait n'est pas toujours immutable' (*Revue de Droit Immobilier* 2018, no 5) 277-278.

154. In French: *Lorsqu'un architecte ou un entrepreneur s'est chargé de la construction à forfait d'un bâtiment, d'après un plan arrêté et convenu avec le propriétaire du sol, il ne peut demander aucune augmentation de prix, ni sous le prétexte de l'augmentation de la main-d'œuvre ou des matériaux, ni sous celui de changements ou d'augmentations faits sur ce plan, si ces changements ou augmentations n'ont pas été autorisés par écrit, et le prix convenu avec le propriétaire.*
Art. 1793 of the French Civil Code is not mandatory law and therefore the parties can waive its provisions. Christophe Sizaire, comment under Cass civ 3e 19 January 2017 *Construction – Urbanisme* no 3, March 2017, comm 39, 20, citing to Cass civ 3e, 24 May 1972: Bull civ III, no 323.
155. As a Red Book contract is based on unit prices, art. 1793 would ordinarily not apply. However, it could apply: (1) depending upon how precisely the unit prices were calculated and (2), in particular, if part of the price of a contract were lump sum it could be applied to that part. Philippe Malinvaud (ed in chief) *Droit de la Construction* (7th edn, Dalloz Action, Paris, 2018), 1112 (para. 401.42).
156. Jane Jenkins and Dominique Ryder, 'In Search of the Holy Grail (or How to Escape a Lump Sum Price: an Analysis of English and French Law)' [1995] ICLR 240, 250-251, citing to Cass civ (3rd), 27 October 1982, no 1.434.

If these conditions are fulfilled, then the contractor may not ask for an increase in price for changes or additions to the building 'if these changes or additions have not been authorised in writing and the price agreed with the owner'.[157] This prohibition applies even if the additional work is necessary due to conditions not provided for in the contract documents or which were otherwise unforeseeable.[158]

Apart from a written acknowledgement of the owner agreeing to the price, the contractor is denied the right to rely on any other means of proof to make out a case (such as the owner's oral instructions or the owner's knowledge that additional works were being undertaken or the owner's tacit approval) of entitlement to be paid for increases in cost or changes or additions to the works.[159] There are only two exceptions to this prohibition. The first is where the owner ratifies, expressly or tacitly, its agreement to the additional works after they have been done. The second is where the lump sum contract has been totally disrupted by exceptionally large changes required by the owner, or its representative, in the volume and/or nature of the work which had originally been agreed upon. For example, changes having a value exceeding 25% of the original contract price.[160] This second case is referred to in French law as *bouleversement de l'économie du contrat* (literally, the upsetting of the economy of the contract).[161]

This article of the French Civil Code or variations of it (sometimes without requiring a lump sum price) are to be found in the civil codes of many civil law countries.[162]

---

157. Art. 1793 of the French Civil Code.
158. Charles-Edouard Bucher, 'Les travaux supplémentaires nécessaires à la réalisation de l'ouvrage relèvent du forfait' (*Revue de Droit Immobilier* no 6, June 2019) 339.
159. François Llorens, *Contrat d'Entreprise et Marché de Travaux Publics* (LGDJ, Paris, 1981) 386-89.
160. Christophe Sizaire, comment under Cass civ (3rd) 18 April 2019, no 18-18.80 *Construction –Urbanisme*, LexisNexis, no 6 (June 2019), 26, 27; and Cass civ (3rd) 12 June 2002, no 00-14.256.
161. Christophe Sizaire, comment under Cass civ (3rd) 19 January 2017 *Construction – Urbanisme* no 3, March 2017, comm 39, 21. This is analogous to a 'cardinal' change under US law, *see* under (3) *Multiple Variation instructions* under **(iv) Related Law** of the commentary on Sub-Clause 13.1 [*Right to Vary*] below.
162. For example, Algeria (art. 561), Argentina (art. 1264), Brazil (art. 619), Chile (art. 2003), Colombia (art. 2060), Egypt (art. 658), Iraq (art. 877),

4.4.3 Subcontractor's Direct Rights

The law in many civil law countries is, as a matter of public policy, protective of the rights of subcontractors and designed to ensure that, among other things, they will be paid regardless of the contractor's financial difficulty, insolvency or bankruptcy.

In France, subcontractors are protected as a matter of public policy by a special statute from 1975.[163] Under it, a contractor is required to obtain its employer's approval not only of each of its subcontractors but also of the payment terms of the subcontract. The contractor must also, if requested to do so, provide the employer with a copy of each subcontract.[164]

In the case of public works contracts, the subcontractor who has been approved (and the payment terms of whose subcontract has also been approved) by the employer has the right to be paid directly by the employer.[165] In the case of private sector contracts, a subcontractor who has not been paid promptly by its employer has the right under this law to bring a legal action directly against the employer to recover payment.[166] Moreover, in the case of such private sector contracts, the employer is required to have provided the subcontractor with a payment guarantee from an approved financial institution to ensure that the subcontractor will be paid its due.[167]

Jordan (art. 795), Mexico (arts 2617, 2626 and 2627), Panama (art. 1345), Peru (arts 1775 and 1776), Spain (art. 1593) and Venezuela (art. 1638).

163. Law no 75-1334 of 31 December 1975 relating to subcontracting, as amended. In the case of works being constructed in France, this law has been held by French courts to be of a mandatory nature (*loi de police*); that is, it will apply regardless of the law that may govern the subcontract (Cass ch mixte 30 November 2007, Bull civ ch mixte no 12). On the other hand, in the case of works not being performed in France, for the law to apply, a subcontractor must demonstrate the existence of a connecting factor between the works and France given the purpose of the law to protect French subcontractors (*'caractériser l'existence d'un lien de rattachement de l'opération avec la France au regard de l'objectif de protection des sous-traitants'*) – *see* Cass com, 27 April 2011, 09-13.524, and Cass com, 20 April 2017, no 15-16.922.
164. Law no 75-1334 of 31 December 1975, as amended, art. 3.
165. *Ibid.*, art. 6.
166. *Ibid.*, art. 12.
167. *Ibid.*, art. 14. Annex G of RB/17 contains an example form of 'Payment Guarantee by Employer' but it is not designed specifically to satisfy French or any other law.

Under Belgian civil law, a subcontractor has a right of direct legal action against the employer for sums due or payable, interest and penalties.[168] Similarly, under the Algerian, Egyptian, Iraqi, Libyan, Qatari and Spanish Civil Codes, a subcontractor has a right of direct action against the employer for an amount up to that which the employer may owe the contractor when the subcontractor's claim is made.[169] Under the UAE Civil Code, the subcontractor enjoys a right of direct action against the employer only in circumstances where the contractor has made an assignment of a right to payment which it has against the employer to the subcontractor.[170] In such a scenario, the subcontractor is entitled to claim from the employer up to the amount which the employer may owe the contractor.[171]

An issue in relation to the legal right of direct action which may need resolution is: what law determines whether this right is available in any given case? Is this the law governing the main construction contract, the law governing the subcontract (if different) or the law of the country where the works are carried out?[172]

4.4.4 *Decennial Liability*

While FIDIC contracts for major works, including RB/17, require the Contractor to remedy any defect that may appear during either the execution of the Works[173] or the DNP,[174] which is normally a year or two after taking over, they do not address liability for defects appearing much after the DNP. Instead, this matter is left to applicable law.

The French Civil Code addresses this matter by its well-known provisions for 'decennial liability'.[175] Following the precedent of Napoleon's 1804

168. Belgian Civil Code, art. 1798. *See also* M Chao-Duivis, 'Subcontracting in Europe: The Results of a Questionnaire' [2013] ICLR 318-319.
169. Art. 565 of the Algerian, art. 662 of the Egyptian, art. 883 of the Iraqi, art. 661 of the Libyan, art. 702 of the Qatari and art. 1597 of the Spanish Civil Codes.
170. UAE Civil Code, art. 891.
171. *Ibid.*
172. *See* J Florian Pulkowski, 'The Subcontractor's Direct Claim in International Business Law' [2004] ICLR 31, who favours application of the law governing the main construction contract.
173. Sub-Clauses 7.5 and 7.6.
174. Clause 11 [*Defects after Taking Over*].
175. Art. 1792 and the following arts of the French Civil Code.

Civil Code, decennial liability, in one form or another, is provided for, often by mandatory law, in numerous European, Latin American, Middle Eastern and North African countries.[176]

Under the French Civil Code, any builder (*constructeur*) of a work (*ouvrage*) is liable absolutely[177] (*de plein droit*) to the owner for damages for a defect, even if resulting from the ground (*vice du sol*),[178] which impairs the stability (*solidité*) of the work or which, by affecting one of its constituent elements or an element of its equipment, makes it unsuitable for its purpose.[179] For the purposes of this provision, a 'builder' is defined to include, among other persons, an architect, a contractor, a technician

176. For example, Algeria (arts 554 and 556 of the Civil Code), Argentina (arts 1273, 1275 and 1276 of the Civil Code), Colombia (art. 2060 of the Civil Code), Egypt (arts 651 and 653 of the Civil Code), Iraq (art. 870 of the Civil Code), Kuwait (arts 692 and 697 of the Civil Code), Libya (arts 650 and 652 of the Civil Code), Morocco (arts 769 and 772 of the Civil Code ('Dahir')), Qatar (arts 711 and 715 of the Civil Code), Saudi Arabia (art. 76 of the Government Tenders and Procurement Law, Royal Decree no M/58, 4 *Ramadan* 1427H/27 September 2006), Spain (art. 17.1.a of the Construction Act), Tunisia (Law no 94-9 of 31 January 1994), the UAE (arts 880 and 882 of the Civil Code) and Venezuela (art. 1637 of the Civil Code). Other countries reported to have some type of 'decennial' liability include, among others: Angola, Belgium, Cameroon, Chile, Germany (four years), Lebanon (five years), Luxembourg, Malta, Morocco, Portugal and Romania. Amaury Teillard, 'The Start Date for Post-Contractual Liability in French Law in the FIDIC Red and Yellow books' [2014] ICLR 269, 280. The same author states that Italy has adopted an equivalent system of liabilities (*'legge Merloni'*), *ibid.*
177. That is, liable without the need for the claimant to prove fault or negligence.
178. The reference to defects in the ground (*vices du sol*), which has always been part of decennial liability in the French Civil Code, is said to concern in reality design defects resulting from an insufficient ground investigation for which, in principle, the architect or specialist engineer concerned would be responsible. Philippe Malinvaud (ed), *Droit de la Construction* (7th edn, Dalloz Action, Paris, 2018) 1745 (para. 482.72).
179. French Civil Code, art. 1792. The French text (first paragraph) is:

> *Tout constructeur d'un ouvrage est responsable de plein droit, envers le maître ou l'acquéreur de l'ouvrage, des dommages, même résultant d'un vice du sol, qui compromettent la solidité de l'ouvrage ou qui, l'affectant dans l'un de ses éléments constitutifs ou l'un de ses éléments d'équipement, le rendent impropre à sa destination.*

or other person bound to the owner by a contract for the hire of work[180] such as the Contractor or Engineer under a FIDIC contract. Thus, if, after a building work is completed, it suffers damage which impairs the stability of the work or makes it unsuitable for its purpose within 10 years, the Contractor and the Engineer would be presumed to be liable to the owner for the whole damage. Subcontractors who may have worked on the project but who have no contract with the owner are not, by law, subject to this presumption of liability.

The defects giving rise to the damage must not have been visible at the time of completion (in French: *réception des travaux*).[181] Defects which, at the date of completion, would have been visible to a layman do not give rise to a presumption of liability.

A builder can only rebut this presumption if it can prove that the damages resulted from a 'foreign cause' (in French: *cause étrangère*), that is, were attributable to someone else (e.g., faulty maintenance of the building by the owner or bad workmanship by another builder) or due to *force majeure* (as defined in French law).[182]

These provisions are matters of public policy in France and, therefore, cannot be excluded or modified by contract.[183] The same is often the case in other countries where decennial liability applies.[184]

In France, builders are relieved of this presumption of liability 10 years after completion of the works. In order for an owner to be able to benefit from the presumption, the damage must occur, and the owner must bring

180. French Civil Code, art. 1792-1. A contract for the hire of work (*contrat de louage d'ouvrage*) includes a construction contract. *See* **Section 4.2.1 Public and Private Law** above of **Chapter II Applicable Law**.
181. The corresponding date under RB/17 would be the Date of Completion, that is, the date stated in the Taking-Over Certificate issued under Clause 10, *see* Amaury Teillard, 'The Start Date for Post-Contractual Liability in French Law in the FIDIC Red and Yellow Books' [2014] ICLR 269, 278-79 (who, however, refers to RB/99).
182. For *force majeure*, *see* **Section 4.4.7 *Force Majeure* and Hardship** below of **Chapter II Applicable Law**.
183. French Civil Code, art. 1792-5.
184. *See*, e.g., the civil codes of Algeria (art. 556), Egypt (art. 653) and Qatar (art. 715).

legal action, within such ten-year period.[185] The benefit of the presumption is attached to the building or work, not to the person of the original owner. Thus, subsequent owners of the work can, during the ten-year period, benefit from the presumption. This ten-year period is also a period of limitation, with the consequence that no legal action may normally be brought for such damages after this period.[186]

In France and Egypt, builders must take out insurance to cover their warranty obligations for the decennial liability period.[187] At least in France, employers must also take out insurance to cover damages for which builders may be liable under decennial lability.[188]

--ooOOoo--

Under French law, the rights of contractors are also protected by the requirement that an employer provides a contractor with a guarantee of payment.[189] This is also mandatory law.[190]

185. French Civil Code, art. 1792-4-1 and Philippe Malinvaud (ed in chief) *Droit de la Construction* (7th edn, Dalloz Action, Paris, 2018) 1758 (para. 482.201).
186. French Civil Code, art. 1792-4-3.
187. French Insurance Code, art. L242-1 and, according to Michael Grose, *Construction Law in the United Arab Emirates and the Gulf* (Wiley Blackwell, Oxford, 2016) 111, Egyptian Building Law no 119/2008. According to Mr Grose, decennial liability insurance is not mandated pursuant to the civil codes or other laws of the Arabian Gulf region. However, the UAE is reportedly considering introducing mandatory decennial liability insurance.
188. French Insurance Code, art. L242-1. While not provided for in Napoleon's Civil Code of 1804, current French law also provides for: (1) a warranty of good operation (*garantie de bon fonctionnement*) for a minimum of two years for equipment other than that covered by decennial liability, French Civil Code, art. 1792-3; and (2) a perfect completion warranty (*garantie de parfait achèvement*) for the repair of all defects notified to the contractor within one year of completion (*réception*), French Civil Code, art. 1792-6. These warranties are matters of public policy and may not be excluded or limited by contract, French Civil Code, art. 1792-5.
189. Above a specified monetary threshold, French Civil Code, art. 1799-1.
190. Cass Civ (3rd) 1 December 2004, 03-13.949.

4.4.5 Liquidated Damages and Penalties

The meaning of, and differences between, liquidated damages (under the common law), and penalties (*pénalités*) (under civil law), is often a source of confusion.

Generally, clauses dealing with this subject provide for payment of a sum of money agreed in advance in the event of a breach of contract. Thus, under Sub-Clause 8.8 [*Delay Damages*] of RB/17, in the event of delay in completion of the Works for which the Contractor is responsible, the Contractor may be required to pay Delay Damages equal to a percentage of the Contract Price (or some other amount), multiplied by the number of days constituting the delay. As a result, the Employer need not prove its loss on account of the delay and will recover the pre-agreed compensation, Delayed Damages, regardless of its actual loss, if any.

The difference between liquidated damages in common law systems and a penalty in some civil law systems may be said to be that the former purports to define the damage suffered by a party, whereas the latter includes an *in terrorem* (Latin: 'in order to frighten') element intended to induce performance.[191] Sometimes, in civil law systems, a clause will serve both purposes.[192]

The common law and civil law systems approach this subject in quite different ways.

4.4.5.1 Common Law: English Law

Under traditional English common law, if the amount stipulated as liquidated damages is regarded as being a penalty, it is unenforceable and, consequently, the innocent party would be left to prove its actual damages.[193] On the other hand, at least until relatively recently (2015),[194]

191. However, in the case of the United Kingdom, this distinction is now somewhat blurred by the decision of the UK Supreme Court in the *El Makdessi* case discussed in the next Section (*Section 4.4.5.1*).
192. ICC, *Guide to Penalty and Liquidated Damages Clauses* (ICC, Paris, ICC Publication 478/1990) 7.
193. According to English case law, a clause would be penal and thus unenforceable:

    > if the sum stipulated for is extravagant and unconscionable in amount in comparison with the greatest loss that could conceivably be proved to have followed from the breach.

if the amount stipulated as liquidated damages was regarded as a genuine pre-estimate of the damages likely to be suffered, it was enforceable, regardless of the amount of damage actually suffered, if any.[195] The assessment was to be made as of the date of the contract and it was a matter of construction how a clause providing for such a stipulation was to be interpreted.[196]

However, in a 2015 decision, the UK Supreme Court found that this test (in the words of some commentators) 'is not sophisticated enough to identify a penalty in all situations'.[197] Accordingly, the Court advanced a broader test (while not abolishing the pre-estimate of loss test),[198] deciding that the 'true test' of whether a liquidated damages clause is a penalty was:

> whether the impugned provision is a secondary obligation which imposes a detriment on the contract-breaker out of all proportion to any legitimate interest of the innocent party in the enforcement of the primary obligation. The innocent party can have no proper interest in simply punishing the defaulter. His interest is in performance or in some appropriate alternative to performance.[199]

As regards the reference to 'secondary obligation', the court stated that:

> the courts do not review the fairness of men's bargains [that is, their primary obligations] either at law or in equity. The penalty rule

---

Mathias Cheung, 'Shylock's Construction Law: The Brave New Life of Liquidated Damages?' (2017) 33(3) Const LJ 173, 176, citing to *Dunlop Pneumatic Tyre Co Ltd v New Garage & Motor Co Ltd* [1915] A.C. 79, as quoted in Atkin Chambers, *Hudson's Building and Engineering Contracts*, 12th edn with 4th supplement (2014).

194. *See Cavendish Square Holding BV v Talal El Makdessi* [2015] UKSC 67 discussed below.
195. *Dunlop Pneumatic Tyre Co Ltd v New Garage & Motor Co Ltd* [1915] AC 79, [1914] UKHL 1.
196. *Cavendish Square Holding BV v Talal El Makdessi* [2015] UKSC 67 [para. 9].
197. Rupert Reece and others, 'Liquidated Damages – Penalty Clauses – Test in *Dunlop v New Garage* – Whether Amounts Payable Are Extravagant or Unconscionable' (2015) 4 Paris J Int'l Arb 841, 852.
198. *Cavendish Square Holding BV v Talal El Makdessi* [2015] UKSC 67 [para. 22].
199. *Ibid.* [para. 32], judgment of a majority of the judges.

> regulates only the remedies available for breach of a party's primary obligations, not the primary obligations themselves.[200]

Put in a somewhat different way:

> What is necessary in each case is to consider, first, whether any (and if so what) legitimate business interest is served and protected by the clause, and, second, whether, assuming such an interest to exist, the provision made for the interest is nevertheless in the circumstances extravagant, exorbitant or unconscionable.[201]

As one commentator has stated:

> [n]o longer are parties required to justify liquidated damages clauses as a genuine pre-estimate of loss. Instead, they are to focus on the 'legitimate business interest' protected by a clause.[202]

Furthermore, following this 2015 decision, it would appear that clauses that carry a deterrent element can still be enforceable under English law, provided there is a legitimate business interest for them. This was confirmed by Lord Neuberger:

> As we have pointed out, deterrence is not penal if there is a legitimate interest in influencing the conduct of the contracting party which is not satisfied by the mere right to recover damages for breach of contract.[203]

Thus, in a construction contract, to paraphrase another commentator:

> a so-called liquidated damages clause for delay to completion is an (unenforceable) penalty if it imposes a number (£x/day) on the contractor that is out of all proportion to any legitimate interest of the employer/owner/developer in achieving the target completion date.[204]

200. *Ibid.* [para. 13].
201. *Ibid.* [para. 152] (Lord Mance).
202. Mathias Cheung, 'Shylock's Construction Law: The Brave New Life of Liquidated Damages?' (2017) 33(3) Const LJ 173, 181.
203. *Cavendish Square Holding BV v Talal El Makdessi* [2015] UKSC 67 [para. 99].
204. Mathias Cheung, 'Shylock's Construction Law: The Brave New Life of Liquidated Damages?' (2017) 33 (3) Const LJ 173, 183 citing to an article by Hamish Lal, 'A New Test for Penalties' (2015) 46 Building 50-51, 50.

4.4.5.2 Common Law: United States Law

United States law distinguishes between provisions for penalties which are unenforceable and those for liquidated damages which are enforceable. According to a leading US case, the two most important conditions for determining whether a provision is enforceable are that: (1) 'the amount stipulated must be a reasonable one, that is to say, not greatly disproportionate to the presumable loss or injury'; and (2) 'the damages to be anticipated as resulting from the breach must be uncertain in amount or difficult to prove'.[205] The time as of which the forecast of loss must be judged to be reasonable has traditionally been the time when the contract was made, not the time when the breach occurred.[206] However, some courts have assessed whether a provision is reasonable by reference also to the actual, rather than the anticipated, harm caused by the breach, which corresponds to the position in the *Uniform Commercial Code* ('UCC'), 1952 ('an amount which is reasonable in the light of the anticipated *or actual* harm caused by the breach' (emphasis added)),[207] and the *Restatement (Second) of Contracts*, 1981 ('an amount that is reasonable in the light of the anticipated *or actual* loss caused by the breach' (emphasis added)).[208]

While the second numbered condition in the leading US case referred to above is still reiterated in the cases, it has been questioned whether uncertainty or difficulty should be a condition, as opposed to just a factor to be weighed along with others.[209]

4.4.5.3 Civil Law Approach

It is hazardous to generalise about civil law systems, as different systems address the subject of liquidated damages and penalties in different ways. As it is impossible to explore all civil law systems within this book,

205. *Banta v Stamford Motor Co* 92 A 665, 667 (Conn 1914).
206. E Allan Farnsworth, *Contracts* (4th edn, Aspen, NY, 2004) 814 (para. 12.18).
207. UCC 2-718(1).
208. *Restatement (Second) of Contracts* (ALI 1981) s 356 (1). Thus, the provision will be upheld if it is found to be reasonable under either of the two standards.
209. E Allan Farnsworth, *Contracts* (4th edn, Aspen, NY, 2004) 817 (para. 12.18).

the discussion here, as elsewhere, will focus on French law, which has perhaps been the most influential.

Under French law, the clause corresponding to a liquidated damages or penalties clause is commonly referred to as a penal clause (*clause pénale*) and liquidated damages or penalties are, as mentioned earlier, referred to as penalties (*pénalités*). No sanction attaches to the fact that such a clause may be intended to stimulate performance (i.e., have a penal effect), as well as to provide a pre-estimate of the damage likely to result from a breach of contract, as it is recognised that such clauses may legitimately serve both purposes.[210] The words 'penal clause' and 'penalties' which may imply that such a clause is unenforceable in the common law system are, in fact, the normal words used in the civil law system to describe a valid liquidated damages clause and liquidated damages, respectively. *This fundamental difference in the terminology used in the two legal systems goes far to explain the confusion on this subject in international circles.*

The penal clause is regulated by the French Civil Code,[211] according to which a court may, even on its own motion, reduce or increase a penalty which parties have agreed upon if it is found to be 'manifestly excessive or derisory'.[212] This provision is a matter of public policy in France and hence applies notwithstanding any agreement of the parties to the contrary.

210. Alain Bénabent, *Droit des Obligations* (18th edn, LGDJ, Issy-les-Moulineaux, 2019) 346-347 (para. 438).

211. French Civil Code, art. 1231-5.

212. The civil codes of Belgium (art. 1231), Germany (s 343), Italy (art. 1384) and the Swiss Code of Obligations (art. 163) all provide for the possible modification of contractual penalties using tests such as 'manifestly excessive', 'disproportionately high', or 'excessive', *Cavendish Square Holding BV v Talal El Makdessi* [2015] UKSC 67 [para. 265] (Lord Hodge). The civil codes in other civil law countries also authorise a court in similar circumstances to adjust the amount of penalties to which parties may have agreed, for example: Algeria (art. 184), Argentina (art. 794), Brazil (art. 413), Egypt (art. 224), Iraq (art. 170), Qatar (art. 266), Peru (art. 1346), Switzerland (art. 163, Code of Obligations), and the United Arab Emirates (art. 390). In the case of Algeria, Egypt, Iraq, Qatar and the United Arab Emirates, at least, according to the same cited articles, the damages or penalties that may have been payable will not be due if the debtor establishes that the creditor has suffered no loss.

Thus, under French law, a court is given express power to adjust the amount of a penalty upwards or downwards if it is found to be much less than or to greatly exceed the innocent party's real damages. As the language of the relevant Article indicates, this power is to be exercised exceptionally, that is, only in cases where there is a great disparity between the penalty stipulated and the actual damages suffered. Moreover, the court must justify with reasons any decision to reduce the amount of the penalty (no justification is required if the court refuses to do so).[213] The assessment is made at the date of judgment and not, as under the common law, at the date of contract. In addition, unless the parties have agreed otherwise, the innocent party will ordinarily have to have given a notice requiring performance (*mise en demeure*)[214] before it can demand payment of the penalty.[215]

4.4.5.4 Conclusion

Accordingly, there are major differences between the common law and civil law on this subject.[216] While both systems require, at least to some extent, that the pre-agreed sum of damages bears a reasonable relation to the expected or actual damages, they differ notably in the following respects:

(1) under the common law, a court has no power to adjust the amount of the pre-agreed sum, whether up or down, whereas it may often have such power under the civil law;
(2) under the common law, if the pre-agreed sum is found to constitute a penalty, then the corresponding clause is unenforceable,[217] whereas under the civil law, if the amount of the pre-agreed sum is found to be objectionable, the amount may be

213. Philippe Malaurie and others, *Droit des Obligations* (11th edn, LGDJ, Issy-les-Moulineaux, 2020) 573 (para. 629).
214. *See* **Section 4.3.4 Notice of Default *(Mise en Demeure)*** above of **Chapter II Applicable Law**.
215. French Civil Code, art. 1231-5.
216. 'Because of the wide gulf between common law systems and other legal systems, the Vienna Convention [the *United Nations Convention on Contracts for the International Sale of Goods*, 1980] contains no provision on the important subject of stipulated damages.' E Allan Farnsworth, *Contracts* (4th edn, Aspen, NY, 2004) 812, fn. 5 (para. 12.18).
217. A right to recover general damages from an assessment of actual loss applies instead.

adjusted to correspond more closely to the actual damages suffered, and the clause will be saved and continue to apply;

(3) under the common law, the assessment of whether the pre-agreed sum is a penalty is made as of the date of contract, whereas under the civil law, the assessment of whether it is objectionable is made at the date of judgment or award, in light of the actual damages which have been suffered; and

(4) under the civil law, there is a possible requirement of having to give a notice requiring performance before being entitled to payment.

Consistent with the civil law approach, the UNIDROIT Principles and the UNCITRAL *Uniform Rules on Contract Clauses for an Agreed Sum Due upon Failure of Performance* (1983) provide for the adjustment of a stipulated sum which is judged to be 'grossly excessive'[218] or 'substantially disproportionate'.[219] They do not provide, as under the common law, that such stipulated sum ceases to apply and is unenforceable.

4.4.6 Limitations on Damages

4.4.6.1 Conditions for Validity

It is common for international construction contracts in the English language to include a clause limiting and/or excluding liability for 'indirect', 'consequential' or 'special' damage or loss. An example of such a clause is Sub-Clause 1.15 [*Limitation of Liability*] of RB/17.

Generally, in civil law systems, contractual clauses limiting or excluding liability will be valid except in the case of fraud or deceit (in French: *dol*), wilful breach or gross negligence (in French: *faute lourde*, literally, heavy fault).[220] They may also be invalid if they are contrary to major or fundamental obligations of the contract in which they are contained (in French: *la contrariété avec la substance de l'engagement contractuel*), or

218. Art. 7.4.13 (*Agreed payment for non-performance*) of the UNIDROIT Principles.

219. Art. 8 of the UNCITRAL *Uniform Rules on Contract Clauses for an Agreed Sum due upon Failure of Performance* UNGA Res 38/135 (19 December 1983) UN Doc Supp no 38 (A/38/667).

220. Marcel Fontaine and Filip De Ly, *Drafting International Contracts: An Analysis of Contract Clauses* (Martinus Nijhoff, Leiden, the Netherlands, 2009) 384-385.

seek to modify the system of tortious liability or concern liability for personal injuries.[221]

Under the UNIDROIT Principles, such clauses also have qualified validity. A clause limiting or excluding a party's liability for failure in performing a contract will be valid unless 'it would be grossly unfair [...], having regard to the purpose of the contract'.[222]

4.4.6.2 Meaning of Terms: Common Law

Under the common law system, while the interpretation of each clause will depend on its own words and context, the traditional English law view has been that 'consequential' or 'indirect' or 'special' loss approximated to loss within the second 'rule' or 'limb' of the old English case of *Hadley v Baxendale.*[223]

In that case, a mill was idle because the crankshaft of its steam engine was broken. The miller gave the broken shaft to a carrier to take to its manufacturer, so that a duplicate could be made to replace it. When the carriage was delayed, the reopening of the mill was delayed for several days and the miller sued the carrier for loss of profits and other damages for the delayed period. The miller's claim for lost profits was denied and, in denying the claim, the court established two rules.

Under the first rule, the injured party, the miller, could recover damages for loss that 'may fairly and reasonably be considered (as) arising naturally, i.e., according to the usual course of things' from a breach. These damages are commonly referred to as 'direct' or 'general' damages or losses (the first rule of the case). The second rule concerned recovery of damages for loss other than that 'arising naturally', that is, recovery of what has often been referred to in the common law system as 'consequential' or 'indirect' or 'special' damages. Under this second rule,

---

221. *Ibid.*, 385-386.
222. UNIDROIT Principles, art. 7.1.6 (*Exemption clauses*).
223. [1854] EWHC J70 (1854) 156 ER 145. On the other hand, some authorities have recognised that 'consequential damages' can have various other meanings, *see* G H Treitel, *Remedies for Breach of Contract* (OUP, Oxford, 1988) 87-88 (para. 86). Thus, courts in Australia have rejected the view that 'consequential loss' equates with the second limb in *Hadley v Baxendale* and have favoured a much broader interpretation. Andrew Stephenson, 'Consequential Loss' NA-0006 (paper delivered at 8th Int'l SCL Conf, Chicago, IL, 26-28 September 2018) 12.

recovery of such damages could only be made if the loss was 'such as may reasonably be supposed to have been in the contemplation of both parties, at the time they made the contract, as the probable result of the breach of it'. On this basis, the court denied the miller's claim for lost profits as they were not damages that arose 'naturally', that is 'according to the usual course of things' under the first rule and could not have been in the contemplation of the carrier when the contract was made under the second rule.[224]

However, the *Hadley v Baxendale* approach has been criticised in England and a clause excluding or limiting liability for 'consequential' 'indirect' or 'special' damages is no longer necessarily to be interpreted as referring to damages under the second rule. Whether it will be so interpreted will depend upon the facts.[225] Thus, in a more recent case, it was held that these quoted words had a wider meaning than the second rule in *Hadley v Baxendale*.[226]

It would also be wrong to conclude that claims for lost profits of an employer or owner for a delay in construction, for example, are necessarily 'consequential' or 'indirect' damages. Whether they are or not will depend upon the facts of each case. Lost profits may in some cases arise 'naturally', that is 'according to the usual course of things' (the first rule of *Hadley v Baxendale*). Thus, under English law:

> in the case of [construction of] factories, shops, flats and other obviously profit-earning projects, the damages for loss of profit [on account of delay in completion] are likely to arise under the first [...]

---

224. As has been explained:

> for all the carrier knew, the miller might have had a spare crankshaft as a replacement, or the machinery might have been defective in other respects, so that the carrier's delay would have had no effect upon the operation of the mill. Had the miller notified the carrier of all the circumstances, the result would presumably have been different.

E Allan Farnsworth, *Contracts* (4th edn, Aspen, NY, 2004) 793 (para. 12.14).

225. Tony Diamond and Sonja Sreckovic, 'The Interpretation of Consequential Loss in Exclusion Clauses – English Law Perspective' (paper delivered at 8th Int'l SCL Conf. Chicago, IL, September 2018) 9-16.
226. *Star Polaris LLC v HHIC-PHIL INC* [2016] EWHC 2941 (Comm) [paras 39 and 40].

> rule [in *Hadley v Baxendale*], as occurring naturally and in the usual course of things from the breach [...].[227]

Accordingly, where they are considered to arise naturally from the breach, an employer's loss of profits will be recoverable in the face of a clause excluding liability for 'consequential' damages.

In the United States, *Hadley v Baxendale* is still followed.[228] However, '[n]o bright-line' has been created to distinguish direct from consequential damages, the decisions being inconsistent.[229]

4.4.6.3 Meaning of Terms: Civil Law

French law does not rely on the common law dichotomy between 'direct' and 'general' damages, on the one hand, and 'indirect', 'consequential' or 'special' damages, on the other hand.[230] Indeed, under French law, these concepts are not expressly used, or do not have the same meaning as they have in the common law[231] and the situation is likely to be no different in other civil law countries.

While the approach of French law to damages is not radically different from the approach of the common law,[232] the terms 'indirect', 'special' and 'consequential' damages or losses may be given very different meanings under French law from what they have under the common

227. Atkin Chambers, *Hudson's Building and Engineering Contracts* (14th edn, Sweet & Maxwell, London, 2020) 860 (para. 7-039).
228. *Restatement (Second) of Contracts* (ALI, Philadelphia, PA, 1981) s 351.
229. Steven G M Stein, 'Direct vs Consequential Damages in the United States' NA-001 (paper delivered at 8th Int'l SCL Conf, Chicago, IL, 26-28 September 2018) 1.
230. Gregory Odry, 'Exclusion of Consequential Damages: Write What You Mean' [2012] ICLR 142, 162.
231. *Ibid.*, 157.
232. 'In both systems (French and English) the purpose of the award of damages is to compensate [...] the plaintiffs for a loss which he has suffered as a result of the non-performance of the Contract.' Barry Nicholas, *The French Law of Contract* (2nd edn, OUP, Oxford, 1992) 224-25. Under French law, recoverable damages must be 'certain' (not merely possible) and the 'immediate and direct' result of the breach of contract. They are also limited to the damages that were foreseeable at the date of entry into the contract except in the case of fraud, misrepresentation (*l'inexécution dolosive*) or gross negligence, when unforeseeable damages may be recovered. Philippe

law. Therefore, if an agreement is to be governed by French law or that of another civil law system, a limitation on damages clause should be drafted to be made consistent with the civil law concerned, *using its legal vocabulary and not specifically common law terms*.[233]

4.4.7 *Force Majeure* and Hardship

Nothing appears to be more confusing or puzzling to many engineers and some common law lawyers than the term '*force majeure*'.[234] Although RB/99 had contained a clause entitled 'Force Majeure' (Clause 19) and although such a clause had previously been contained in YB/87,[235] it has since been replaced in RB/17 by a clause (Clause 18) entitled 'Exceptional Events', whose effect is the same but whose title is naturally more understandable to a layperson.

However, the meaning of *force majeure* should not be confusing or puzzling once it is appreciated that it can have two distinct meanings: (1) a legal meaning according to the law in civil law countries and (2) a contractual meaning provided for by a clause in a contract.[236]

4.4.7.1 Legal Meaning of Force Majeure

In civil law systems, *force majeure* refers to a legal principle which is to be found in the civil codes or laws of many civil law countries.[237]

Malaurie and others, *Droit des Obligations* (11th edn, LGDJ, Issy-les-Moulineaux, 2020) 548-553 (paras 600-605). *See also* French Civil Code, arts 1231-1 to 1231-4.

233. Gregory Odry, 'Exclusion of Consequential Damages: Write What You Mean' [2012] ICLR 142, 164.

234. Although the term '*force majeure*' has been introduced into English contracts. Stephen Furst and Vivian Ramsey, *Keating on Construction Contracts* (11th edn, Sweet & Maxwell, London, 2021) 804 (para. 21-155).

235. YB/87, Clause 44.

236. It is also, of course, used in this second way – most often in international commerce – in common law countries.

237. For example, in the civil codes of Algeria (art. 127), Argentina (art. 1730), Chile (art. 45), Colombia (art. 64), Egypt (art. 373), Jordan (art. 247), Libya (art. 360), Mexico (art. 2111), Peru (art. 1315), Qatar (art. 187), Russia (art. 401), the UAE (art. 273), Ukraine (art. 617) and Venezuela (art. 1272).

Historically, in French private law, *force majeure* was defined – and continues in many civil law countries to be defined – as comprising a 'classic trilogy':[238]

(1) the event must be external to the parties (*l'extériorité*);
(2) it must be unforeseeable (*l'imprévisibilité*); and
(3) it must be unavoidable and insurmountable (*l'irrésistibilité*).[239]

Thus, the scope allowed to *force majeure* is even narrower than that of the corresponding common law doctrine of frustration.[240] Frustration has been described as occurring where a change of circumstances has so altered the performance of a contract as to render it 'radically different' from what was envisaged by the parties at the time of contracting.[241] However, before the reform of French contract law in 2016, French case law had departed from requiring all three of these elements. Thus, in 2006, the French Court of Cassation[242] found *force majeure* to apply 'where an event was unforeseeable when a contract was made and unavoidable or insurmountable (*irrésistible*) in its performance', without further mention that it was required to be external to the parties (*l'extériorité*).[243]

---

238. In French: *trilogie classique*. For example, in relation to Arab civil codes, *force majeure* is defined by reference to the same three elements. Adnan Amkhan, 'Force Majeure and Impossibility of Performance in Arab Contract Law' (1991) 6 Arab L.Q. 297, 301.
239. *Force majeure* was referred to, although not defined, in the old (pre-2016) French Civil Code, art. 1148.
240. Barry Nicholas, *The French Law of Contract* (2nd edn, OUP, Oxford, 1992) 202.
241. *Davis Contractors Ltd v Fareham Urban District Council* [1956] AC 696. For a fuller discussion of the English law doctrine of frustration and the related US law doctrine of impracticability, *see* under **(iv) Related Law** of the commentary on Sub-Clause 18.6 [*Release from Performance under the Law*] below.
242. France's highest court for civil matters.
243. Alain Bénabent, *Droit des Obligations* (18th edn, LGDJ, Issy-les-Moulineaux, 2019) 292 (para. 349). Thus, an illness affecting a physical person or a strike affecting the personnel of a company or the liquidation of a company preventing the performance of a contract (no such event being 'external' to a party) would not necessarily prevent the party affected from invoking *force majeure*. 294 (para. 352).

In 2016, the French legislature codified this more liberal case law by defining *force majeure* as follows:

> where an event beyond the control of the debtor [i.e. the person having the obligation], which could not reasonably have been foreseen at entry into the contract and whose effects could not be avoided by appropriate measures, prevents the debtor from performing his obligation.[244]

When it occurs and prevents a party from performing its obligations, that party is relieved from having to do so. Thus, it operates much the same way as the doctrines of frustration or impossibility under the common law as they similarly relieve a party from having to perform contract obligations and, like *force majeure*, may in extreme cases permit termination of the contract.

4.4.7.2 Contractual Meaning of Force Majeure

Under French law the rules relating to *force majeure* are not mandatory; hence parties are free to modify them.[245] As *force majeure*, as defined by law (even after the 2016 reform in France) can apply in only a narrow range of circumstances, when negotiating a contract, parties often agree to include a clause which broadens the range of exceptional circumstances which may entitle a party to be relieved, temporarily or permanently, from having to perform a contractual obligation.[246] Sometimes

244. *See* French Civil Code, art. 1218, para. 1, which provides in French as follows: '*Il y a force majeure en matière contractuelle lorsqu'un événement échappant au contrôle du débiteur, qui ne pouvait être raisonnablement prévu lors de la conclusion du contrat et dont les effets ne peuvent être évités par des mesures appropriées, empêche l'exécution de son obligation par le débiteur*'. This definition goes on to provide that if prevention is temporary, performance of the obligation may be suspended and if prevention is permanent the contract is terminated by operation of law.
245. Philippe Malaurie and others, *Droit des Obligations* (11th edn, LGDJ, Issy-les-Moulineaux, 2020) 543 (para. 592).
246. Any specially drafted clause should make clear the relationship between the clause and *force majeure* or frustration as defined in the governing law; i.e., it should clarify whether the definition in the governing law is to be displaced wholly or only partly by the *force majeure* clause. Thus, in one case, the arbitral tribunal found that a specially drafted *force majeure* clause in a contract governed by Libyan law (which provides for the 'classic trilogy' described in *Section 4.4.7.1* above) did not displace the requirement

such a clause may also entitle the party affected to recover its resulting additional costs. It is common to refer to such clause as a '*force majeure* clause', although it will characteristically operate – and is intended to operate – in a much wider range of circumstances than '*force majeure*' as may be defined in the law of a civil law country.[247] *The use of the term 'force majeure' in these two very different cases contributes to the confusion about the meaning of force majeure.*

4.4.7.3 Conclusion Re Force Majeure in Civil Law Countries

Thus, the notion of *force majeure* may refer to *force majeure* as defined in the civil code or other law of a particular civil law country. Alternatively, it may refer to *force majeure* as defined in a clause, known as a *force majeure* clause, in a contract, whether governed by the law of a civil law or common law country.[248] Therefore, it is always necessary to ascertain which use of the term is being employed.

4.4.7.4 Hardship

A significant difference between common law countries and civil law countries is the increasing recognition in civil law countries of the legal principle of hardship in both private and public contracts.

While traditionally the doctrine of hardship (in French: *imprévision*) was not recognised in French private law (though it has been for more than a century in French public law),[249] an article on this subject was introduced into the French Civil Code in 2016 (hence providing for its

---

in Libyan law that performance must be impossible in order for *force majeure* to be constituted. *National Oil Company v Oil Company of Libya* (ICC case 4462 (1985 and 1987) 29 ILM (1990) 565).

247. A law dictionary in the common law world defines a 'force-majeure clause' as follows: 'A contractual provision allocating the risk of loss if performance becomes impossible or impracticable, esp. as a result of an event or effect that the parties could not have anticipated or controlled.' Bryan A Garner (ed in chief), *Black's Law Dictionary* (11th edn, Thomson Reuters, St Paul, MN, 2019). But, in practice, such clauses may be drafted in many different ways.
248. *See*, e.g., *ICC Force Majeure and Hardship Clauses* (ICC, Paris, March 2020).
249. *See* **Section 4.6.2 Hardship (*Imprévision*)** below of **Chapter II Applicable Law**.

application in French private law).[250] The doctrine of hardship in this article – which is to be distinguished from the definition of hardship in French public law – creates a right to renegotiate a contract upon the occurrence of circumstances:

- which were not foreseeable when the contract was made;
- which make performance of the contract excessively onerous for a party; and
- where the risk of such onerous performance was not assumed by that party.

If the other party refuses to negotiate or negotiations fail, a court may, at the request of a party, revise or terminate the contract. As this article is not mandatory law, it may be excluded by contract.

Unlike the position in France until 2016, *the civil codes of many Arab countries have long recognised the principle of hardship in both private and public contracts*. The 1949 Egyptian Civil Code was the first to provide for its application, with the rest of the Arab Civil Codes following suit.[251] Under the Egyptian Civil Code, the doctrine of hardship is defined as follows:

> The contract makes the law of the parties [...]. When, however, as a result of exceptional and unpredictable events of a general character, the performance of the contractual obligation, without becoming impossible, becomes excessively onerous in such way as to threaten the debtor with exorbitant loss, the judge may, according to the circumstances, and after taking into consideration the interests of both parties, reduce to reasonable limits, the obligation that has become excessive [...].[252]

The civil codes of the following 13 Arab countries contain a provision to the same effect:

250. Art. 1195 of the French Civil Code.
251. Adman Amkhan, 'The Effect of Change in Circumstances in Arab Contract Law' (1994) Arab L Q 258, 261.
252. Art. 147 of the Egyptian Civil Code.

Algeria[253]	Bahrain[254]
Egypt[255]	Iraq[256]
Jordan[257]	Kuwait[258]
Libya[259]	Oman[260]
Qatar[261]	Sudan[262]
Syria[263]	United Arab Emirates[264]
Yemen[265]	

No less remarkable than the fact that the principle of hardship applies to both private and public contracts in the above Arab countries is that, in every case, the corresponding civil code article contains a provision similar to that contained in the Egyptian Civil Code: 'Any agreement to the contrary is void.'[266] *Thus the principle of hardship is a mandatory law; that is, it will apply regardless of what, if anything, the relevant contract might provide. Accordingly, the right to invoke hardship, as defined, cannot be excluded or limited by contract under the laws of these countries.*

Numerous other civil law countries also have laws on hardship.[267] In addition, rules on hardship are provided for in Article 6.2 of the UNIDROIT Principles.[268]

253. Art. 107 of the Algerian Civil Code.
254. Art. 130 of the Bahrain Legislative Decree no 19 of 2001 (Civil Code).
255. Art. 147(2) of the Egyptian Civil Code.
256. Art. 146(2) of the Iraqi Civil Code.
257. Art. 205 of the Jordanian Civil Law.
258. Art. 198 of the Kuwaiti Civil Code.
259. Art. 147(2) of the Libyan Civil Code.
260. Art. 159 of the Oman Civil Code.
261. Art. 171(2) of the Qatari Civil Code.
262. Art. 117 of the Sudanese Law of Civil Transactions.
263. Art. 148 of the Syrian Civil Code.
264. Art. 249 of the United Arab Emirates Civil Code.
265. Art. 211 of the Yemen Civil Law.
266. Art. 147(2) of the Egyptian Civil Code.
267. These include Argentina (Civil Code, art. 1091), Brazil (Civil Code, arts 478-80), Chile (*see* Claudio Moraga Klenner, 'Chile' in Rozen Noguellou and Ulrich Stelkens (eds), *Comparative Law on Public Contracts* ((Bruylant, Brussels, 2010) 481-82, para. 4.8 and R Momberg Uribe, 'Teoría de la Imprevisión: La necessidad de su regularisación legal en Chile' (2010) 15 Revista Chilena de Derecho Privado 29-64), Colombia (Commercial Code, art. 868 – claims of hardship are limited to commercial contracts), Finland

The existence of a doctrine of hardship, especially when it is a mandatory law, in numerous civil law countries, is a striking difference with the law in common law countries which has no such doctrine.[269]

4.5 Civil Law: Other Distinctive Features

4.5.1 Interest on Monies Due

The right of an aggrieved party to recover interest from the date at which payment of money is due is widely accepted today in many jurisdictions,[270] including the common law[271] and civil law[272] countries generally. However, civil law countries tend to approach the subject differently from the common law ones. To understand the civil law approach, it is necessary to comment on civil law relating to damages generally.

In common law jurisdictions, the date for the evaluation of damages for breach of contract is generally the date of breach – the date when the cause of action arose – and prejudgment interest on such damages may

---

(Contracts Act, s 36), Italy (Civil Code, arts 1467-69), Peru (Civil Code, arts 1440-46), Poland (Civil Code, art. 357), Portugal (Civil Code, art. 437), the Netherlands (Civil Code, Bk 2, art. 258 (6:258)), Russia (Civil Code, art. 451), Sweden (Contracts Act, s 36), and Switzerland (Code of Obligations, art. 373 – limited to construction contracts). *See* James Otis Rodner, 'Hardship under the UNIDROIT Principles of International Commercial Contracts, Global Reflections on International Law, Commerce and Dispute Resolution' in *Liber Amicorum in Honour of Robert Briner* (ICC Publishing, Paris, 2005) 677, 678.

268. *See* **Section 7.3 UNIDROIT Principles 2016** below of **Chapter II Applicable Law**. *See also ICC Force Majeure and Hardship Clauses* (ICC, Paris, 2020).

269. For analogous common law doctrines, *see* under **(iv) Related Law** of the commentary on Sub-Clause 18.6 [*Release from Performance under the Law*] below.

270. Stefan Vogenauer (ed), *Commentary on the UNIDROIT Principles of International Commercial Contracts (PICC)* (2nd edn, OUP, Oxford, 2015) 1014 (para. 4). *See also* the UNIDROIT Principles art. 7.4.9 (*Interest for failure to pay money*).

271. For English law, *see Sempra Metals Ltd v Inland Revenue Commissioners* [2008] AC 561 and, for US law, *see* the *Restatement of Contracts (Second)* (ALI, Philadelphia, PA, 1981) s 354.

272. *See* below.

be awarded for the period between the date of breach and the date of judgment.[273]

On the other hand, in civil law jurisdictions, the date for the evaluation of damages for breach of contract is generally the date of judgment.[274] Compensation for any loss arising between the date of breach and the date of judgment is determined and taken account of as a component of the total damages fixed by the judge in the judge's discretion.[275] However, the judge's discretion to fix damages generally does not apply in two situations: where the law specifically provides for a measure for the determination of damages, and where the parties have agreed by their contract to fix damages in advance.[276]

The most important example of where French law, and civil law in general, specifically provides a measure for the determination of damages is where the breach is a delay in the payment of a liquidated amount of money, e.g., the amount of a court judgment or arbitral award or an Engineer's Payment Certificate under RB/17. In this situation, damages are, in the ordinary case, limited to interest on the sum due at a legally specified rate or any contractually stipulated rate (which would ordinarily displace the legally specified rate),[277] called 'moratory interest'.[278]

---

273. *McGregor on Damages* (21st edn, Sweet & Maxwell, London, 2021) 653 (para. 19-07) and T J McDonald and O A Tarhuni, 'Compensation for Payment Delays under Libyan Law' [1985-86] 3 ICLR 3, 5.
274. Philippe Malaurie and others, *Droit des Obligations* (11th edn, LGDJ, Issy-les-Moulineaux, 2020) 154 (paras 165-166).
275. Philippe Le Tourneau, *Droit de la Responsabilité et des Contrats Régimes d'Indemnisations* (11th edn, Dalloz Action, Paris, 2018/2019) 1072 (para. 2321.21). While not addressed in the French Civil Code, it is accepted by case law that damages at the date of breach be re-evaluated as of the date of judgment. *See* Cass Com 2 November 1993, Bull Civ I, no 380 and Cass Civ 6 October 1998, Bull Civ, no 275.
276. T J McDonald and O A Tarhuni, 'Compensation for Payment Delays under Libyan Law' [1985-86] 3 ICLR 3, 9.
277. As an example, *see* the provision for financing charges in Sub-Clause 14.8 [*Delayed Payment*] of RB/17.
278. French Civil Code, arts 1231-6 and 1344-1. *See also* Philippe Malaurie and others, *Droit des Obligations* (11th edn, LGDJ, Issy-les-Moulineaux, 2020) 553-554 (para. 606). Prior to 1975, French law provided for different legal rates in the case of civil and commercial obligations. Although this is no longer true in France, different legal rates for civil and commercial obligations continue to apply in some other civil law countries such as Egypt, *see* Egyptian Civil Code, art. 226.

Moratory interest will ordinarily be due as from the date that the creditor has made a 'claim in Court' (Egyptian law)[279] or has given the debtor notification to pay (*mise en demeure*) (French law),[280] unless the parties have agreed otherwise. The creditor is not required to establish that it has suffered any loss.

However, under French and other civil laws there is an exception to this rule. Under French law where the debtor has, by its 'bad faith', caused the creditor 'special damage',[281] the creditor may recover damages in addition to moratory interest.[282] This exception may become important to a contractor, especially where the construction contract provides for no rate of moratory interest and the applicable legal rate is too low to provide adequate compensation.[283]

'Special damage' may include having to borrow money at a higher cost than the rate of moratory interest in order to replace the money which has not been paid, or to compensate for the loss of new business on account of insufficient available capital. *'Bad faith' does not require a showing of an intention to harm the creditor*. It is sufficient for the defaulting party

279. Unless the contract or commercial usage fixes another date, Egyptian Civil Code, art. 226. This art fixes the rate of interest at 4% in civil matters and 5% in commercial matters, subject to what another law might provide. According to art. 227, the parties may agree upon another rate of interest provided that it does not exceed 7%.
280. French Civil Code, art. 1344-1. *See also* **Section 4.3.4 Notice of Default *(Mise en Demeure)*** above of **Chapter II Applicable Law**. There are exceptions, however. Under art. 1551(1) of the Chilean Civil Code, a debtor is generally in default simply when it has not fulfilled an obligation within the stipulated term.
281. In French: '*un préjudice indépendant de ce retard*' (literally, 'a damage independent of this delay').
282. French Civil Code, art. 1231-6. Egyptian Civil Code, art. 231 is to the same effect.
283. *See* Tarek Hamed, Sherif El Haggan and Nabil Yehia, 'Employer's Failure to Make Payment to Contractor – A Study of Construction Contracts under Egyptian Civil Law' [2012] ICLR 406, 415-18, where the Egyptian authors argue that an unpaid contractor should be entitled to recover all financing charges it incurs and not be limited by arts 226 and 227(1) of the Egyptian Civil Code.

'to be aware of the harm he was causing to the creditor by not paying on the due date'.[284]

Under French law, even liquidated amounts denominated in a foreign currency are subject to the above rules. However, in the case of a foreign currency amount, the legal rate of interest which would apply (assuming there is no applicable contractual rate) would normally be that designated by the law of the country applicable to the debt (the *lex monetae*).[285]

None of the above rules is a matter of public policy (in French: *ordre public*). Thus, subject to applicable usury law, parties are free to modify or exclude their application by contract. However, under French law, a contract may not validly provide for interest on overdue interest (i.e., compound interest) unless the interest has been overdue for at least one year.[286]

---

284. French original: *'qu'il ait eu conscience du tort qu'il allait causer au créancier en ne payant pas à l'échéance.'* Philippe Malaurie and others, *Droit des Obligations* (11th edn, LGDJ, Issy-les-Moulineaux, 2020) 555-556 (para. 608).
285. However in a case involving the enforcement of an international arbitral award in France, where the arbitral tribunal had omitted to award post-award interest, the French courts held that this issue is governed by the law applicable to the enforcement procedure, that is, French law. Consequently, they ordered the payment of post-award interest at the rate applicable to judgments as provided for in former art. 1153-1 of the French Civil Code, now art. 1231-7 of the same Code. Cass Civ 30 June 2004, 01-11718, Rev arb 2005.645 note R Libchaber. While not stated in the judgment, it appears from the accompanying note (*see* para. 5) that, to permit application of the rate of interest provided for by the French Civil Code, the amount of the award, which was expressed in US dollars, was converted into euros at the rate prevailing at the date of the French judgment. The French rate of interest was then applied to this euro amount. *See also* Christopher R Seppälä, 'When Post-Award Interest Has Not Been Awarded by an International Arbitration Tribunal May It Be Obtained from State Courts?' (2001) 16(2) Mealey's Int'l Arb Rep, 24.
286. Art. 1343-2 of the French Civil Code, which is mandatory law. Philippe Malaurie and others, *Droit des Obligations* (11th edn, LGDJ, Paris, 2020) 556 (para. 610). In general, the above principles relating to moratory interest are equally applicable to French administrative contracts. André de Laubadère and others, *Traité des Contrats Administratifs* (2nd edn, LGDJ, Paris, 1983) vol I, 786 (para. 783). Egyptian law prohibits compound

Like French law, the UNIDROIT Principles provide for the payment of interest at a stipulated rate for failure to pay money when due[287] (and this rate has been incorporated into Sub-Clause 14.8 [*Delayed Payment*] of RB/17). Moreover, the aggrieved party is entitled to additional damages if that party can demonstrate that the non-payment caused it additional harm.[288] The UNIDROIT Principles (unlike Sub-Clause 14.8 of RB/17) take no stand on compound interest.[289]

4.5.2 *Bankruptcy*

While under Sub-Clause 15.2.1(g) of RB/17 the Employer may terminate the Contract in any case where the Contractor becomes bankrupt or insolvent, under French and other national laws – notwithstanding this provision – a bankruptcy trustee or judge may require the Employer to continue performing the Contract provided the Contractor continues to execute the Works.[290]

4.5.3 *Limitation Periods*

Under the common law, a statute of limitations or limitation period establishes a time limit in which legal proceedings must be brought and

interest '[s]ubject to any commercial rules or practice to the contrary', art. 232 of the Egyptian Civil Code.

287. UNIDROIT Principles, art. 7.4.9 (*Interest for failure to pay money*). Art. 7.4.9(2) provides for the following rate of interest:

> The rate of interest shall be the average bank short-term lending rate to prime borrowers prevailing for the currency of payment at the place for payment, or where no such rate exists at that place, then the same rate in the State of the currency of payment. In the absence of such a rate at either place the rate of interest shall be the appropriate rate fixed by the law of the State of the currency of payment.

288. UNIDROIT Principles, art. 7.4.9(3).
289. The Principles note that compound interest in some national laws 'is subject to rules of public policy limiting compound interest with a view to protecting the non-performing party'. Official comment on art. 7.4.10 of the UNIDROIT Principles.
290. This is the case, for example, under French law (French Commercial Code, art. L622-13) and Argentine law (Santiago Nicholson 'Effectiveness of the FIDIC Contract under Argentine Law' [1992] ICLR 261, 262).

is a matter of procedural law.[291] On the other hand, under French law, it is viewed differently. A limitation period does not establish a time limit for bringing legal proceedings, but instead provides for the extinction of rights by the lapse of time (known as 'extinctive prescription') and is a matter of substantive, not procedural, law.[292]

While both doctrines provide for the loss of a claim or right by the lapse of time,[293] the distinction between the two can be significant. If the law governing a contract is that of a civil law country, it will include (generally, in its law of obligations) rules governing the limitation period. On the other hand, if the law governing a contract is that of a common law country, it will *not* include (in its law of contract) time limits for bringing an action as they will only be in its procedural law.

Where a contract provides for the final resolution of disputes by international arbitration, as is true of the RB/17, this can cause uncertainty as to what limitation period applies.[294] For instance, where a contract is governed by the law of a common law country (the substantive law of which contains no rules on the extinction of rights or time limit for the bringing of proceedings), but the place of arbitration is Paris, France (a country which has no limitation period in its procedural law), which country's limitation period applies? That of the common law country or that of France?

---

291. *See Restatement (Second) Conflicts of Laws*, s 142, comment a (ALI, Philadelphia, PA, 1971) for the United States and *Limitation Act* 1980 for England and Wales.
292. In France, it is provided for in art. 2224 and following arts of the Civil Code. However, the starting date of a limitation period varies from jurisdiction to jurisdiction:

> in some jurisdictions it is the date when the claim accrues while in others it is the date on which the creditor knew, or should have known, of the existence of the claim or, in the case of a sales contract, when the goods were delivered.

Piero Bernardini 'Limitation Periods' in *UNIDROIT Principles: New Developments and Applications* – 2005 Spec Supp ICC Int'l Ct Arb Bull 43.
293. *Ibid.* (Bernardini, 43).
294. Assuming the limitation period applicable to court actions applies to arbitrations. In the US at least, this is not necessarily the case. Lance Currie and Monica Gaudioso, 'Are you SOL in Trying to Enforce a Statute of Limitations in Arbitration' (2020) 22(1) UNDERCONSTRUCTION, ABA for Const L, 4.

Fortunately, the UNIDROIT Principles and a European regulation provide guidance as they indicate that, in such a situation, the law which governs the contract should also govern the limitation of actions. Thus, in the above example, arbitrators sitting in Paris should apply the limitation period of the common law country.[295] Moreover, this was the ruling of a sole arbitrator in an ICC arbitration in Paris involving RB/87 and presenting precisely these facts.[296] The sole arbitrator added that the substantive law of the contract should apply 'particularly since all the construction works, the subject of the Contract, were carried out [in the common law jurisdiction whose governing law applied] for the government of that state'.[297] The arbitrator noted that there was nothing in French law which prevented or inhibited this conclusion.[298]

---

295. The UNIDROIT Principles contain a Chapter 10 entitled 'Limitations Periods' and, thus, treat the limitation of actions as a matter of substantive law governed by those Principles. This is also the solution provided for by Rome I Regulation, art. 12(1)(d), applicable in the European Union. As the result of the English *Foreign Limitation Periods Act 1984*, which applies to arbitrations having their seat in England (*see* English *Arbitration Act 1996*, s 13), this also appears to be the position now under English law. *Chitty on Contracts*, (33rd edn, Sweet & Maxwell, London, 2018) vol 1, 2396-2397 (para. 30-272).

296. Final award, ICC case 16247 (2010), ICC Disp Resol Bull 2016 no 1, 102.

297. *Ibid.*, para. 85.

298. *Ibid.* Under some laws, where a contract provides for the need to satisfy conditions to international arbitration (as is true of RB/17), this can cause uncertainty as to when the limitation period begins. In a partial award, ICC case 19311 (2014), relating to RB/99 and applying Romanian law it was held to begin only when the pre-arbitral conditions had been satisfied and arbitration could commence whereas, in another case, a final award, ICC case 17988 (2014), also involving a FIDIC contract and applying Romanian law, it was held that its beginning was unaffected by the existence of preconditions to arbitration. *See* Gustavo Scheffer da Silveira, *Les Modes de Règlement des Différends Dans Les Contrats Internationaux de Construction* (Bruylant, Brussels, 2019) 260-262 (para. 226). Under English law, in the case of breach of contract, the limitation period begins to run from the date of breach. On the other hand: 'where a contract provides that an ascertainable or ascertained amount is due [as in the case of a certified interim or final payment under RB/17], the obligee's [the Contractor's] cause of action in respect of that amount accrues at the point in time when the amount in question becomes due and payable'. Thus, in the event of an Employer's failure to pay the amount, the limitation period begins at that time. Julian

4.6 Civil Law: Special Public Law Theories

Common law lawyers will expect that any right to adjust a contract price for cost increases or other changed circumstances would have to be provided for in the terms of the contract.[299] The common law is of very limited assistance in changed circumstances.[300] However, in civil law countries following the French administrative law tradition – that is, among others, countries in the Arab Middle East, francophone Africa and most of Latin America – *in the case of an administrative contract (that is, a contract with a state or other public body),*[301] *increases in the contract price may be justified by legal theories that are mandatory law and will apply independent of what, if anything, the contract may provide.* These are the subject of **Section 4.6**.

An important difference between a private law contract and a public law or administrative contract[302] is that, under French law, an administrative contract by definition concerns matters of public interest, and is *based on the principle of the inequality of the parties.* As mentioned above,[303] the public party is endowed, by mandatory law with 'exceptional powers' (*pouvoirs exorbitants*) not generally available to a private employer. These include the power to manage and direct the works, to modify, suspend or terminate a contract in the public interest, and to sanction the contractor, whether these powers are provided for in the contract or not.[304] In France, the public party also has the privilege of *exécution*

Bailey, *Construction Law* (3rd edn, London Publishing, UK, 2020), vol 3, 2142-2144 (paras 26.42-26.44).

299. In common law countries, a court has generally no power to vary the terms of a contract.

300. Apart from the doctrines of impracticability (in the United States) and frustration (in England and Wales, and the United States). Paul Craig 'Specific Powers of Public Contractors' and Paul Craig and Martin Trybus 'England and Wales' in Rozen Noguellou and Ulrich Stelkens (eds), *Comparative Law on Public Contracts* (Bruylant, Brussels, 2010) 173, 191-92, 339 and 353.

301. *See* the definition in **Section 4.2.2 Public and Private Contracts** above of **Chapter II Applicable Law**.

302. Discussed in **Section 4.2.2 Public and Private Contracts** above of **Chapter II Applicable Law**.

303. *See* **Section 4.2.2 Public and Private Contracts** above of **Chapter II Applicable Law**.

304. André de Laubadère and others, *Traité des contrats administratifs* (2nd edn, LGDJ, Paris, 1983) vol I, 210 (para. 154) – 239-240 (para. 182) and

d'office; that is, it can act on its own initiative, and take directly whatever steps it considers necessary unilaterally in the public interest to enforce or supervise the contract, without any need to request the support of a court, i.e., without prior judicial authorisation.[305] Judicial control of administrative action takes place only after the fact. Consequently, as one authority has stated '[t]he administration is never the plaintiff'.[306]

To counterbalance these 'exceptional powers' which the public employer enjoys under an administrative contract, and thereby restore and maintain the 'economic balance' of the contract (*l'équilibre financier*), French administrative (or public) law provides the contractor by mandatory law with exceptional rights to compensation independent of the contract. Without these rights, the economic balance of the contract would be upset and thus potentially cause, under this theory, interruption of a public service – a result absolutely to be avoided as contrary to the public interest.[307]

Philippe Malinvaud (ed in chief), *Droit de la Construction* (7th edn Dalloz Action, Paris, 2018) 1345 (para. 417.471) to 1359 (para. 417.639).

305. Barry Nicholas, *The French Law of Contract* (2nd edn, OUP, Oxford, 1992) 27.

306. *Ibid*. According to French legal doctrine (known as *privilège du préalable*), members of the public receiving orders or instructions from a public authority must conform to them. Such orders or instructions are presumed to be legally valid so long as they have not been withdrawn or abrogated by the administration or been suspended or set aside by a court. If they are later set aside, the affected person's remedy is in damages. Council of State (CE) 27 February 1903, no 97.217, *Olivier and Zimmermann* S 1905.3.17.

307. According to Rozen Noguellou and Ulrich Stelkens (eds), *Comparative Law on Public Contracts* (Bruylant, Brussels, 2010), the principle that the economic or financial balance of an administrative contract should be maintained is accepted in, among other countries, Belgium 412, Brazil 444, Colombia 531-33, France 691, Spain 580 and Tunisia 989-990. This is also true in Argentina (Hector A Mairal, 'Government Contracts under Argentine Law: A Comparative Law Overview' (2002) 26 Fordham Int'l L J 1716, 1738), Egypt (Ali El Shalakany, 'The Application of the FIDIC Civil Engineering Conditions of Contract in a Civil Code System Country' [1989] ICLR 266, 270) and, given the important influence of Egyptian law in the Arab Middle East, probably in other Arab countries. On the other hand, as has been noted (partial award, ICC case 20910 (2020) (unpublished), para. 714), a FIDIC contract includes provisions that aim at rebalancing the financial conditions in the case of extraordinary and/or unforeseen events, for example – in the case of RB/17 – in Sub-Clause 4.12 [*Unforeseeable*

The exceptional rights to compensation or other relief to which the contractor may, in such circumstances, be entitled under French law include those described in Sections 4.6.1 through 4.6.6 below. Significantly, *a contractor enjoys similar rights, with significant variations, in numerous other civil law countries following the French administrative law tradition.*[308]

4.6.1 Unforeseeable Physical Difficulties (Sujétions Imprévues)

According to this theory (in French: *sujétions imprévues*), if the contractor encounters difficulties of a physical nature that are absolutely abnormal and which could not reasonably have been foreseen when it concluded the contract and which make performance more onerous (costly), then those conditions – typically, site conditions – entitle the contractor to be fully compensated by an increase in the contract price.[309] However, the contractor's compensation may be reduced if and to the extent that the contractor had been itself at fault by, for example, having failed properly to examine the site.[310]

The amount to which the contractor is entitled would normally be calculated by reference to the prices in the bill of quantities or on the basis of new prices if the existing prices were inappropriate or could not

---

Physical Conditions], Clause 13 [*Variations and Adjustments*] and Sub-Clause 18.4 [*Consequences of an Exceptional Event*]. The availability of these provisions may offset, though not necessarily exclude, the need and right to maintain the economic balance of an administrative contract.

308. *See* **Section 4.2.2 Public and Private Contracts** above of **Chapter II Applicable Law**.

309. André de Laubadère and others, *Traité des Contrats Administratifs* (2nd edn, LGDJ, Paris, 1984) vol II, 499 (para. 1276); Yves Gaudemet, *Traité de droit administratif* (15th edn, LGDJ, Paris, 2014) vol II, 607 (para. 1102). These difficulties relate generally to soil or climatic conditions. Philippe Malinvaud (ed in chief), *Droit de la Construction* (7th edn, Dalloz Action, Paris, 2018) 1340 (para. 417.425). Interestingly, this doctrine is echoed in Recital 109 of Directive 2014/24 EU of the European Parliament and of the Council of 26 February 2014 on public procurement, which provides a definition of unforeseeable circumstances which may justify modification of a procurement contract.

310. André de Laubadère and others, *Traité des Contrats Administratifs* (2nd edn, LGDJ, Paris, 1984) vol II, 513 (para. 1289); Yves Gaudemet, *Traité de droit administratif* (15th edn, LGDJ, Issy-les-Moulineaux, 2014) vol II, 608 (para. 1105).

be applied.[311] Where the unforeseeable physical difficulty has caused the contractor to be in delay, then this theory will, like Sub-Clause 4.12 [*Unforeseeable Physical Conditions*] of RB/17, relieve the contractor of liability for liquidated damages for delay.[312]

Thus, this theory is more favourable to the contractor than Sub-Clause 4.12 as, under this theory, the contractor is compensated based on the contract prices, entitling it to recover profit, whereas under Sub-Clause 4.12 the Contractor would only be entitled to recover its costs and/or obtain an extension of time.[313]

This theory is mandatory law and will apply regardless of whether there is a provision on this subject in the contract or not.[314] The only practical consequence of a clause seeking to place the risk of unforeseeable physical difficulties on the contractor is that it may cause a tribunal to be more demanding before it will recognise an unforeseeable adverse physical difficulty under this theory.[315]

In the case of a lump sum contract,[316] this theory will only apply where the unforeseeable condition or circumstance results in what French law refers to as the upsetting of the economy of the contract (*bouleversement de l'économie du contrat*)[317] or was due to the fault of the public party.[318]

---

311. André de Laubadère and others, *Traité des Contrats Administratifs* (2nd edn, LGDJ, Paris, 1984) vol II, 513 (para. 1289); Laurent Richer and François Lichère, *Droit des contrats administratifs* (11th edn, LGDJ, Issy-les-Moulineaux, 2019) 264 (para. 551).
312. André de Laubadère and others, *Traité des Contrats Administratifs* (2nd edn, LGDJ, Paris, 1984) vol II, 512 (para. 1288).
313. *See* the commentary on Sub-Clause 4.12 [*Unforseeable Physical Conditions*] in **Chapter IV Clause-by-Clause Commentary** below.
314. André de Laubadère and others, *Traité des Contrats Administratifs* (2nd edn, LGDJ, Paris, 1984) vol II, 503 (para. 1278); Marcel Waline, 'L'évolution récente des rapports de l'Etat avec ses cocontractants' (Revue du Droit Public 1951) 5, 27.
315. André de Laubadère and others, *Traité des Contrats Administratifs* (2nd edn, LGDJ, Paris, 1984) vol II, 504 (para. 1278); Yves Gaudemet, *Traité de droit administratif* (15th edn, LGDJ, Issy-les-Moulineaux, 2014) vol II, 607 (para. 1103).
316. *See* **Section 4.4.2 Lump Sum Contracts** above of **Chapter II Applicable Law**.
317. André de Laubadère and others, *Traité des Contrats Administratifs* (2nd edn, LGDJ, Paris, 1984) vol II, 510-11 (para. 1285-5); Yves Gaudemet, *Traité de droit administratif* (15th edn, LGDJ, Paris, 2014) vol II, 608 (para.

The upsetting of the economy of the contract will be evaluated by comparing the importance of the additional expenses incurred by the unforeseen event with the 'importance of the contract'.[319]

Apart from France and Belgium,[320] this theory is recognised to apply to public law or administrative contracts in, among others, Argentina,[321] Chile,[322] Egypt[323] and (within certain limits) Peru.[324]

It may also apply in the case of private law contracts for the construction of buildings on a lump sum basis in Chile[325] and Colombia.[326]

4.6.2 *Hardship* (Imprévision)

According to this theory (in French: *imprévision*),[327] when unforeseeable circumstances for which the contractor is not responsible arise and upset

1104); Laurent Richer and François Lichère, *Droit des Contrats Administratifs* (11th edn, LGDJ, Issy-les-Moulineaux, 2019) 264-265 (para. 552).

318. Philippe Malinvaud (ed in chief), *Droit de la Construction* (7th edn, Dalloz Action, Paris, 2018) 1341 (para. 417.428).
319. André de Laubadère and others, *Traité des Contrats Administratifs* (2nd edn, LGDJ, Paris, 1984) vol II, 510-11 (para. 1285-5). For more details about upsetting the economy of the contract, *see* **Section 4.6.2, Hardship (*Imprévision*)** below of **Chapter II Applicable Law**.
320. Maurice André-Flamme, *Traité Théorique et Pratique des Marchés Publics* (Emile Bruylant, Brussels, 1969) vol I, 58-59 (para. 24).
321. Hector A Mairal, 'Government Contracts under Argentine Law: A Comparative Law Overview' (2002) 26 Fordham Int'l L J 1716, 1738-39.
322. Claudio Moraga Klenner in Rozen Noguellou and Ulrich Stelkens (eds), 'Chile' in *Comparative Law on Public Contracts* (Bruylant, Brussels, 2010) 465, 478-479, para. 4.5.
323. Ali El Shalakany, 'The Application of the FIDIC Civil Engineering Conditions of Contract in a Civil Code System Country, A Comparison of Legal Concepts and Solutions' [1989] ICLR 266, 270-72.
324. Peruvian Legislative Decree no 1341 of 2017 which modified Public Procurement Law no 30225 of 2014, art. 34.
325. Chilean Civil Code, art. 2003(2).
326. Colombian Civil Code, art. 2060(2).
327. As explained under *Section 4.4.7.4 Hardship* above, the new definition of hardship in French private law (art. 1195 of the Civil Code) is to be distinguished from its traditional definition in French public law, discussed in **Section 4.6.2**, which has had a wide influence on both private and public laws in civil law countries.

the economy of a contract, without rendering its performance impossible, and cause substantial loss to the contractor then, while the contractor remains strictly bound to perform the contract, it has the right to require that the public body share in the loss so as to enable the contractor to overcome the difficulty.[328] The purpose of the indemnity is to assist the contractor in overcoming an exceptional, temporary difficulty so as to allow the contract to be performed without – or with minimal – interruption.[329]

---

328. André de Laubadère and others, *Traité des Contrats Administratifs* (2nd edn, LGDJ, Paris, 1984) vol II, 560 (para. 1332). This theory derives from case law of the French Council of State (the highest court in the administrative court system), notably the celebrated *Gaz de Bordeaux* case (CE 30 March 2016, Recueil Lebon 125).

329. Yves Gaudemet, *Manuel de droit administratif* (23rd edn, LGDJ, Issy-les-Moulineaux, 2020) 429 (para. 925). The existence of this theory of hardship (*imprévision*) in French administrative or public law was for many years a major difference with French civil law where no such theory was recognised, as illustrated by the well-known *Canal de Craponne* case (Cass civ 6 March 1876). In that case, in 1567, Adam de Craponne had constructed a canal and formally undertaken to maintain it against receipt of payment of a certain sum from nearby residents. As time went by, this sum became derisory and out of all proportion to the cost of maintaining the canal so, in the 1870s, the heirs of Adam de Craponne sued for an increase, but the *Cour de Cassation* held in 1876 that:

> it is no part of the function of courts, however equitable it may seem to them, to modify the parties' agreements in the light of changing times and circumstances or to substitute new terms in the place of those freely accepted by the parties.

However, as the result of a reform in 2016, as stated in *Section 4.4.7.4 Hardship* above, French civil law is now closer to French administrative law in this respect, *see* French Civil Code, art. 1195, first paragraph, providing that:

> If a change of circumstances that was unforeseeable at the time of the conclusion of the contract renders performance excessively onerous for a party who had not accepted the risk of such a change, that party may ask the other contracting party to renegotiate the contract. The first party must continue to perform his obligations during renegotiation.

In the case of a refusal to negotiate or a failure of renegotiations, a court may, at the request of a party, revise or terminate the contract. *See Section 4.4.7.4 Hardship* above of **Chapter II Applicable Law**.

The event which gives rise to the application of this theory must normally be of an economic nature[330] or one having economic consequences.[331]

For the economy of a contract to have been upset, there must have been 'a profound and abnormal disturbance' of the contract.[332] Assessment of whether the economy of a contract has been upset is determined on a case-by-case basis – there are no established thresholds.[333] As an example, in one case relief was available when extra-contractual costs had reached 7% of the initial amount of the contract price.[334] On the other hand, in another case, an increase in cost representing 10% of the contract price was considered to be insufficient to give rise to an upsetting of the economy of a contract.[335] The particular facts in each case will be determinative.

The contractor must bear a part of the extra costs which have been incurred as a result of the relevant event.[336] However, in France at least, generally 80% to 90% of the loss will be borne by the public body, sometimes a little more, sometimes a little less.[337]

This theory is mandatory law. Accordingly, any clause purporting to exclude its application is invalid as contrary to public policy because this

---

330. André de Laubadère and others, *Traité des Contrats Administratifs* (2nd edn, LGDJ, Paris, 1984) vol II, 578 (para. 1345).
331. Yves Gaudemet, *Traité de droit administratif* (16th edn, LGDJ, Issy-les-Moulineaux, 2001) vol I, 714-715 (para. 1491); Laurent Richer and François Lichère, *Droit des Contrats Administratifs* (11th edn, LGDJ, Issy-les-Moulineaux, 2019) 267 (para. 556).
332. André de Laubadère and others, *Traité des Contrats Administratifs* (2nd edn, LGDJ, Paris, 1984) vol II, 597 (para. 1361).
333. Fédération Nationale des Travaux Publics, Avis du Comité Juridique, Possibilités d'adaptation des marchés à l'évolution des prix des matières premières et des fournitures, October 2021, 6.
334. Société Altagna, Admin. Ct of App Marseille, 17 January 2008, n° 05MA00493.
335. Société Balas Mahey, Admin. Ct of App Paris, 10 July 2015, n° 12PA04253.
336. André de Laubadère and others, *Traité des Contrats Administratifs* (2nd edn, LGDJ, Paris, 1984) vol II, 622-23 (para. 1393); Yves Gaudemet, *Traité de droit administratif* (16th edn, LGDJ, Issy-les-Moulineaux, 2001) vol I, 715 (para. 1492).
337. André de Laubadère and others, *Traité des Contrats Administratifs* (2nd edn, LGDJ, Paris, 1984) vol II, 623 (para. 1394).

theory is designed to ensure in the public interest the continuation of a public service.[338]

As a practical matter, a contractor may be protected against economic hardship if a contract contains a price adjustment formula, such as is an option in Sub-Clause 13.7 [*Adjustments for Changes in Cost*] of RB/17.[339] However, if such a formula fails to protect the contractor sufficiently, it might still be entitled to relief under this legal doctrine.[340] Furthermore, as this doctrine is based on equity,[341] should the employer be the one to endure hardship, the employer might, arguably, be entitled to relief against the contractor under this theory.[342]

A simplified comparison of this theory of hardship (*imprévision*) with act of the prince (*fait du prince*) described below, or the theory of unforeseeable physical difficulties (*sujétions imprévues*) described above, is as follows: economic events give rise to this theory of hardship; natural phenomena give rise to the theory of unforeseeable physical difficulties; and actions of a state or a public body, at least where it is the other contracting party, give rise to the theory of the act of the prince.

In a number of civil law countries, notably in the Arab Middle East (as explained in Section 4.4.7.4 above), the theory of hardship (as defined in their respective civil codes) applies to private contracts, not just public or administrative contracts, and (as in France) is mandatory law and cannot be excluded by contract.[343]

338. *Ibid.*, 600 (para. 1364-1); Yves Gaudemet, *Traité de droit administratif* (16th edn, LGDJ, Issy-les-Moulineaux, 2001) vol I, 713 (paras 1489-1490).
339. Sub-Clause 13.7 describes such a formula(ae) as Schedule(s) of cost indexation.
340. Philippe Malinvaud (ed in chief), *Droit de la Construction* (7th edn, Dalloz Action, Paris, 2018) 1343 (para. 417.447).
341. André de Laubadère and others, *Traité des Contrats Administratifs* (2nd edn, LGDJ, Paris, 1984) vol II, 608-10 (para. 1376).
342. Legal opinion, September 1986, of Professor Maurice-André Flamme, Brussels, Belgium, provided to the author.
343. *See* specifically *Section 4.4.7.4 Hardship* above of **Chapter II Applicable Law**.

4.6.3 *Act of the Prince* (Fait Du Prince)

This theory (in French: *fait du prince*) has been defined in different ways at different times.[344] However, it is now defined in French law as any measure or action taken by a public body in its public role - and not in its capacity as a contracting party[345] - which was unforeseeable when the contract was signed and which makes performance by the contractor more difficult or onerous.[346] In these circumstances, the public body must compensate the contractor for the damages that it has suffered as well as - possibly - for any profits of which it has been deprived.[347]

The damages must be attributable to the legal person which signed the contract and no one else.[348] Thus, if the contract was signed by one minister but is affected by a measure or action of another minister then,

344. *See*, e.g., André de Laubadère and others, *Traité des Contrats Administratifs* (2nd edn, LGDJ, Paris, 1984) vol II, 516-18 (paras 1292-1293); Yves Gaudemet, *Traité de droit administratif* (16th edn, LGDJ, Issy-les-Moulineaux, 2001) vol I, 710-11 (paras 1485-1486); Laurent Richer and François Lichère, *Droit des Contrats Administratifs* (11th edn, LGDJ, Issy-les-Moulineaux, 2019) 285 (para. 604).

345. Philippe Malinvaud (ed in chief), *Droit de la Construction* (7th edn, Dalloz Action, Paris, 2018) 1344 (para. 417.452). Examples might include measures taken by a State in its sovereign capacity such as the adoption of tax laws, labour legislation or construction work undertaken by a public body unrelated to the contract. *Ibid.*

346. Yves Gaudemet, *Traité de droit administratif* (16th edn, LGDJ, Issy-les-Moulineaux, 2001) vol I, 709 (para. 1482) and 710-711 (para. 1485); Laurent Richer and François Lichère, *Droit des Contrats Administratifs* (11th edn, LGDJ, Issy-les-Moulineaux, 2019) 284-285 (paras 603 and 606).

347. André de Laubadère and others, *Traité des Contrats Administratifs* (2nd edn, LGDJ, Paris, 1984) vol II, 556 (para. 1327); Yves Gaudemet, *Traité de droit administratif* (16th edn, LGDJ, Issy-les-Moulineaux, 2001) vol I, 712 (para. 1487). If the contract is terminated as the result of war or hostilities then, according to Messrs. de Laubadère and others, the contractor is not entitled to lost profits as termination is said in that case to be justified in 'the public interest'. André de Laubadère and others, *Traité des Contrats Administratifs* (2nd edn, LGDJ, Paris, 1984) vol II, 556-57 (para. 1328).

348. André de Laubadère and others, *Traité des Contrats Administratifs* (2nd edn, LGDJ, Paris, 1984) vol II, 523-524 (para. 1300); Yves Gaudemet, *Traité de droit administratif* (16th edn, LGDJ, Issy-les-Moulineaux, 2001) vol I, 711 (para. 1486); Laurent Richer and François Lichère, *Droit des Contrats Administratifs* (11th edn, LGDJ, Issy-les-Moulineaux, 2019) 285 (para. 605).

at least under French law, the doctrine applies as all ministries of the French State are considered to be part of the same legal person.[349] On the other hand, if the measure or action was taken by a public legal entity that was legally separate from the public entity that was the contracting party, the doctrine will not apply but the contractor may be able to invoke the doctrine of hardship (*imprévision*) against its contracting party instead,[350] assuming the conditions for its application can be fulfilled.[351]

It is also necessary to distinguish between measures or decisions taken by a public body against a party individually and laws, decrees or regulations having general application to the public. Any individual measure or decision taken by the public body which signed the contract, which affects either its terms or the conditions for its performance, such as a unilateral modification of the contract, may entitle the contractor to compensation under this theory.[352] On the other hand, it is much less clear whether the public body will have liability for general measures, such as those affecting a whole class of persons (e.g., increased general taxes or customs duties where the public body concerned is the state), as the requirement for a contractor to comply with them is considered to be among the normal risks of performing any contract.[353]

The normal remedy for an act of the prince is damages.[354] However, if the public body's action has made performance of the contract impossible, the contractor could be excused from performing the contract. If the action made performance of the contract more onerous, though not impossible, this might relieve the contractor of liability for any liquidated damages for delay it might otherwise incur. Finally, if the measure would cause the contractor difficulties above a certain threshold, the contractor might be entitled to request termination of the contract.[355]

349. André de Laubadère and others, *Traité des Contrats Administratifs* (2nd edn, LGDJ, Paris, 1983) vol II, 525, fn. 8 (para. 1302).
350. *See* **Subsection 4.6.2 Hardship (*Imprévision*)** above of **Chapter II Applicable Law**.
351. André de Laubadère and others, *Traité des Contrats Administratifs* (2nd edn, LGDJ, Paris, 1984) vol II, 524 (para. 1301).
352. *Ibid.*, 543 (para. 1315).
353. *Ibid.*, 528-42 (paras 1304-1314); Yves Gaudemet, *Traité de droit administratif* (16th edn, LGDJ, Issy-les-Moulineaux, 2001) vol I, 711 (para. 1486).
354. Philippe Malinvaud (ed in chief), *Droit de la Construction* (7th edn, Dalloz Action, Paris, 2018) 1344 (para. 417.454).
355. André de Laubadère and others, *Traité des Contrats Administratifs* (2nd edn, LGDJ, Paris, 1984) vol II, 552 (para. 1324).

As a state is, like any other contracting party, normally liable for its own actions or inactions and as the allocation of the risk of act of the prince and its consequences is often, in any event, dealt with today by a contract provision, this theory has lost much of its practical application.[356] In the case of RB/17, provisions such as Sub-Clause 8.6 [*Delays Caused by Authorities*] and Clause 13.6 [*Adjustments for Changes in Laws*], as well as the principle of breach of contract, provide the Contractor with remedies which might otherwise be provided for by this theory.

Under French law, a contractor may not generally waive in advance its entitlement to an indemnity on account of damages caused by an act of the prince.[357]

4.6.4 'Necessary' or 'Indispensable' Work

While, in the case of a lump sum contract, a contractor is bound to perform the work it has agreed to do for the lump sum price,[358] nevertheless, in certain circumstances, it may be entitled to additional payment for work it has undertaken on its own initiative (i.e., without an instruction from the employer), where it is found to have been 'necessary' or 'indispensable'.[359]

The supplementary work must be necessary or indispensable to ensure the good execution of the contracted work including respect for construction norms.[360] For example, this may be the case where the defective work of contractor A has obliged contractor B to perform work not foreseen by contractor B's contract in order for the work of contractor B

356. *Ibid.*, 534-35 (para. 1310).

357. *Ibid.*, 557-58 (para. 1330). But a contractor could waive its right to an indemnity for the consequences of a particular act the public body might take or agree to conditions for its payment or manner of payment, *Ibid.*

358. *See* **Section 4.4.2 Lump Sum Contracts** above in **Chapter II Applicable Law**.

359. André de Laubadère and others, *Traité des Contrats Administratifs* (2nd edn, LGDJ, Paris, 1983) vol II, 265-70 (paras 1068-1071 and specifically 1070); Laurent Richer and François Lichère, *Droit des Contrats Administratifs* (11th edn, LGDJ, Issy-les-Moulineaux, 2019) 225-226 (para. 462) and 265 (para. 553).

360. André de Laubadère and others, *Traité des Contrats Administratifs* (2nd edn, LGDJ, Paris, 1984) vol II, 267 (para. 1070) and Philippe Malinvaud (ed in chief), *Droit de la Construction* (7th edn, Dalloz Action, Paris, 2018) 1305 (para. 417.23).

to be complete. Where this is the case, contractor B is entitled to be fully compensated for the cost of the additional work by reference to prices in the bill of quantities and prices (in its contract) for analogous works.[361]

This theory is justified on the basis of the implicit intention of the parties.[362] As the additional works are indispensable to enable the contract to be performed, they must – so the theory goes – have been encompassed by the common intention of the parties, at least implicitly. Therefore, though not covered by the contract price initially agreed upon, they must be paid for.[363]

Supplementary work that is merely useful but not necessary or indispensable does not give a right to compensation. Thus, in one case, a contractor had to perform works on a town's country roads on a lump sum basis. The contract provided that any change orders had to be in writing. The contractor performed work on parts of these roads that were not provided for in the contract in addition to performing the contract works. The French Council of State held that though the additional works done may have been useful to the local community, they were not necessary for the performance of works included in the contract. Consequently, the contractor's claim for compensation was denied.[364]

4.6.5 Force Majeure

Under French administrative law, *force majeure* continues to be defined in the same way as under French private law prior to the reform of the French Civil Code in 2016.[365] Thus, *force majeure* comprises the 'classic trilogy': (1) the event must be external to the parties (*l'extériorité*), (2) it

361. André de Laubadère and others, *Traité des Contrats Administratifs* (2nd edn, LGDJ, Paris, 1984) vol II 267 (para. 1070).
362. André de Laubadère and others, *Traité des Contrats Administratifs* (2nd edn, LGDJ, Paris, 1984) vol II, 268 (para. 1070).
363. *Ibid.*
364. CE 17 October 1975, no 93704, *Cne Canari*, AJDA 1975, 233, chron Franc et Boyon.
365. André de Laubadère and others, *Traité des Contrats Administratifs* (2nd edn, LGDJ, Paris, 1983) vol I, 726-36 (para. 729); Yves Gaudemet, *Traité de droit administratif* (16th edn, LGDJ, Issy-les-Moulineaux, 2001) vol I, 709-10 (paras 1483-1484); Laurent Richer and François Lichère, *Droit des Contrats Administratifs* (11th edn, LGDJ, Issy-les-Moulineaux, 2019) 280 (para. 587).

must be unforeseeable (*l'imprévisibilité*), and (3) it must be unavoidable and insurmountable (*l'irrésistibilité*).[366]

However, unlike the situation applicable to private contracts in France, in the case of an administrative contract, a contractor may recover the damages it has suffered directly as a result of *force majeure*.[367]

4.6.6 Termination for Convenience

As in the case of state or other public contracts in most countries, under French law a public body may terminate an administrative contract in certain circumstances for its own convenience. To do so, the public body must be able to demonstrate that the termination is in the public interest (*pour motif d'intérêt général*),[368] and must pay the contractor, among other things, the profit it would have earned on the work which remained uncompleted.[369] The French administration enjoys this power of termination whether it is provided for in the contract or not,[370] as it is one of the 'exceptional powers' enjoyed by the administration in the case of an

366. *See Section 4.4.7.1 Legal Meaning of Force Majeure* above of **Chapter II Applicable Law**.
367. Philippe Malinvaud (ed in chief), *Droit de la Construction* (7th edn, Dalloz Action, Paris, 2018) 1344 (para. 417.465).
368. CE 2 February 1987, no 81131, *Société TV6*, Rec 29. In this case, the French State had ordered the termination of a concession contract with a television company on the basis that there existed a draft law for reform of the television industry. The Council of State held this termination to be invalid as until the relevant law had been promulgated as a law it was not certain that the reform would take place and thus that the termination would be justified in the public interest.
369. CE 15 April 1959, *Ville de Puteaux c Schwab*, req no 35200, Lebon 236; André de Laubadère and others, *Traité des Contrats Administratifs* (2nd edn, LGDJ, Paris, 1984) vol II, 886-87 (para. 1640). Thus, this manner of termination is not especially favourable to a French public body. *See also* Philippe Malinvaud (ed in chief), *Droit de la Construction* (7th edn, Dalloz Action, Paris, 2018) 1349 (para. 417.514). By contrast, a contractor is denied the right to recover anticipated profits on work not done in the case of termination for convenience under, for example, a United States government contract. Joshua Schwartz, 'United States of America' in Rozen Noguellou and Ulrich Stelkens (eds), *Comparative Law on Public Contracts* (Bruylant, Brussels 2010) 641.
370. André de Laubadère and others, *Traité des Contrats Administratifs* (2nd edn, LGDJ, Paris, 1984) vol II, 658-71 (paras 1425-1433).

administrative contract.[371] In the case of RB/17, the Employer has the right to terminate the Contract for its convenience under Sub-Clauses 15.5 to 15.7 and must, similarly, pay the Contractor the profit it would have earned on the work which remained uncompleted.

5 MANDATORY LAW AT THE SITE

As mentioned above, while it is not usual to do so, parties may want to choose a law (or rules of law) to govern their construction contract which is different from the law of the country where the site is located.[372] By choosing such a law (or rules), however, parties may not derogate, by contract or otherwise, from those provisions of the law of the country of the site which are mandatory in nature.[373]

Laws of a mandatory nature of the country of the site will apply regardless of the law chosen by the parties and will thus prevail over any conflicting provision contained in the law they have chosen.[374] Therefore, parties selecting a law to govern their contract which differs from

---

371. *Ibid.*, 667 (para. 1433). *See* the beginning of **Section 4.6** above.

372. *See* **Section 3 Importance of the Governing Law** of **Chapter II Applicable Law.**

373. According to Pierre Mayer, 'Mandatory Rules of Law in International Arbitration' (1986) 2(4) Arb Int'l 274-275:

> A mandatory rule (*loi de police* in French) is an imperative provision of law which must be applied to an international relationship irrespective of the law that governs the relationship.

Art. 9 of Rome I Regulation, which is generally directly applicable in the EU, is to the same effect, describing mandatory law ('[o]verriding mandatory provisions'), as follows:

> 1. Overriding mandatory provisions are provisions the respect for which is regarded as crucial by a country for safeguarding its public interests, such as its political, social or economic organisation, to such an extent that they are applicable to any situation falling within their scope, irrespective of the law otherwise applicable to the contract under this Regulation.
> 2. Nothing in this Regulation shall restrict the application of the overriding mandatory provisions of the law of the forum.

374. It is striking how different things were in the 19th century, as can be seen from the report of a 1872 English Court of Appeal case (still cited in *Hudson*) involving claims by an English contractor related to its construction of a railway in Brazil financed by the Brazilian Government. It was apparently

the law of the country of the site should inform themselves about all mandatory laws at the site that may bear on the execution of the project.[375]

It is for each state or country to determine which provisions of its own law have a mandatory nature. In some cases, the mandatory nature of a provision may be explicitly stated in legislation.[376] In other cases, national courts may have decided that a certain provision has such a character.[377] In still other cases, there will be no indication in legislation or case law as to the mandatory nature of a law. In all three instances, it will be up to the arbitrators under a FIDIC contract (and, ultimately, possibly national courts) to decide whether an invoked provision of law is mandatory and must be taken into account in a given case.

It would be beyond the scope of this book to embark on a detailed overview of the mandatory provisions in different countries or jurisdictions relevant to construction works. Instead, the list below provides an overview of the kinds of legal provisions relevant to construction that are often mandatory and will thus apply regardless of the law governing the contract.

---

so obvious to the English court what national law it was to apply (English law) that it saw no need to discuss the issue of applicable law. Brazilian law is not mentioned and the decision would read no differently had the railway been built in England. *See Sharpe v São Paulo Railway Company* (1873) LR 8, Ch App 597.

375. Sub-Clause 1.13 [*Compliance with Laws*] of RB/17 implicitly acknowledges this by providing that the Contractor 'shall [...] comply with all applicable Laws'. '**Laws**' is defined very broadly in Sub-Clause 1.1.49 of RB/17.
376. *See*, for example, the UK HGCRA, s 104(7).
377. For example, in the case of works being constructed in France, Law No 75-1334 of 31 December 1975 relating to subcontracting has been held by French courts to be of a mandatory nature (*loi de police*); that is, it will apply regardless of the law that may govern the subcontract (Cass ch mixte 30 November 2007 Bull Civ Ch Mixte no 12). On the other hand, in the case of works not being performed in France, French courts have ruled that, for the law to apply, a subcontractor must demonstrate the existence of a connecting factor between the works and France given the purpose of the law to protect French subcontractors ('*caractériser l'existence d'un lien de rattachement de l'opération avec la France au regard de l'objectif de protection des sous-traitants*'). *See* Cass com 27 April 2011, 09-13524 and Cass com 20 April 2017, 15-16.922.

1. **Public procurement laws.** The procurement of public works contracts is usually regulated by local public laws of a mandatory nature. Generally, these determine or regulate how public works are to be procured (the requirement for publicity, the necessity and conditions for an invitation to tender and the possibility, if any, of negotiation) and may also decide the content of contract conditions including any need to use local suppliers or subcontractors, the governing law and dispute resolution.[378]

   In the case of projects in civil law countries, it is of special importance to determine if a construction contract is an 'administrative contract' (because, e.g., it has been concluded with the State or a public body) as, if this is the case, the contract may be subject not just to a public procurement law but to a mandatory legal regime of administrative law, as in, for example, France[379] or Egypt.[380]
2. **Decennial liability**. In many civil law countries, the contractor, the engineer and others in contract with the employer will be absolutely liable to the employer, possibly jointly and severally, for a defect which impairs the stability of a work and appears within 10 years after taking over. The decennial liability regime in some jurisdictions (e.g., France)[381] is complemented by a requirement that persons subject to this regime obtain mandatory insurance.[382]
3. **Laws concerning zoning and land use.** These laws usually must be complied with before commencement of construction works. They may require a change of designation of the land if its status does not allow for the contemplated development (e.g., in case of agricultural lands), procedures for approval

---

378. *See* Dr Götz-Sebastian Hök, 'Relationship Between FIDIC Conditions and Public Procurement Law – Reliability of Tender Documents' [2009] ICLR 23, 24-31.
379. *See* **Sections 4.2.1 Public and Private Law** and **4.2.2 Public and Private Contracts** above of **Chapter II Applicable Law**.
380. *Ibid.*
381. However, it is not certain (though probable) that decennial liability constitutes an 'overriding mandatory provision' (*loi de police*) within the meaning of Rome I Regulation, art. 9.6. In other words, it is uncertain whether such regime would prevail where the construction contract is governed by another law than French law.
382. *See* **Section 4.4.4 Decennial Liability** above of **Chapter II Applicable Law**.

and/or amendment of zoning plans, land use, special permits, etc., Sub-Clause 1.13 [*Compliance with Laws*] of RB/17 addresses this issue.

4. **Laws regarding construction and operation**. These laws concern matters such as design, construction and/or building norms and standards which must be observed, the procedure for approval of the designs for the contemplated construction, the issuance of construction documents (such as building or construction permits, etc.) and, where appropriate, construction and/or operating permits, by competent state authorities. These regulations may be very detailed in sensitive industries, such as the nuclear industry. Sub-Clause 1.13 [*Compliance with Laws*] of RB/17 addresses this issue.
5. **Environmental laws**. The country of the site will usually have detailed laws and regulations concerning environmental aspects of a construction project (e.g., the necessity to carry out ecological and environmental impact assessments and the treatment of hazardous materials and waste), including possibly international treaties or conventions,[383] which the contractor must comply with. Sub-Clauses 4.18 [*Protection of the Environment*] and 4.22 [*Contractor's Operations on Site*] of RB/17 address these issues.
6. **Labour and social legislation**. These laws regulate matters, such as health and safety at work, working hours, official holidays, rates of wages and conditions of employment. Sub-Clauses 6.2 [*Rates of Wages and Conditions of Labour*], 6.4 [*Labour Laws*], 6.5 [*Working Hours*] and 6.7 [*Health and Safety of Personnel*] in RB/17 explicitly stipulate that the Contractor must comply with such laws or local practices. Foreign contractors may be required to employ a minimum percentage of local nationals.
7. **Laws concerning acquisition and transfer of title over real estate and immovables.** The acquisition and transfer of title over real estate and immovables are usually governed by the law of the country where these assets are located.[384] Sub-Clause 7.7 [*Ownership of Plant and Materials*] of RB/17 deals with the time for the passing of ownership over Plant and Materials (which are to become part of the Permanent Works)

383. For example, the Paris Agreement of 2015 relating to climate change.
384. For example, in the European Union *see* Rome I Regulation, art. 4.1(c).

to the Employer and stipulates that the regime in that Sub-Clause will apply to the extent consistent with the mandatory Laws of the Country.

8. **Tax laws and customs duties**. Foreign contractors and their staff will be liable (unless exempted) for domestic income and other taxes, customs duties and governmental impositions generally in the country where the works are carried out.[385] Furthermore, they may be subject to certain tax-related obligations, such as to have an address in the territory of the country where the works are carried out, where tax authorities may serve relevant notices.
9. **Foreign exchange / currency restrictions**. In some countries, the local currency is not freely convertible or transferable and may be subject to exchange control or other restrictions unless an approval has been obtained. These are important as, upon the conclusion of a construction contract, and having no further work in a country, a foreign contractor paid partly in local currency as foreseen in Sub-Clause 14.15 [*Currencies of Payment*] of RB/17 is likely to want to repatriate its earnings, after conversion of local currency amounts into its own currency.
10. **Registration / licensing requirements**. Some countries require that construction works be carried out by legal entities which are registered or approved in those countries,[386] or may subject foreign contractors to licensing requirements.[387] Generally, foreign contractors should obtain such a registration or licence prior to commencement of construction works. Similarly, the performance of architectural or engineering services in a country may require a special local permit or licence.[388]
11. **Subcontracting laws**. Some (mostly civil law) countries have legislation protective of subcontractors and which guarantee,

385. *See*, e.g., sub-para. (b) of both Sub-Clause 1.13 [*Compliance with Laws*] and Sub-Clause 14.1 [*The Contract Price*].
386. This is the situation, for example, in Lithuania and Latvia. *See* Dalia Foigt and others 'Construction Law: An Overview of Recent Developments in the Baltics' [2008] ICLR 134, 136-139.
387. This is, for example, the case in Russia. *See* Ilya Nikiforov, 'Using FIDIC Contracts in Eastern Europe' [2000] ICLR 539, 547.
388. As is the case of architects in France and engineers in the United States. *See* under **(iii) Analysis** of the commentary on Sub-Clause 3.1 [*The Engineer*] below.

subject to certain conditions, that a subcontractor will be paid notwithstanding the bankruptcy or insolvency of the contractor.[389]

12. **Immigration laws.** Foreign workers working in the country of the site will likely have to comply with local immigration laws, including requirements for visas and work permits.
13. **Criminal laws, including tort law.** Criminal law, such as laws against bribery or corruption, use of illicit drugs or regulating traffic, always has a mandatory character and will generally apply in the territory of the country where the crime is committed. Local law is likely to apply to a tort or civil wrong such as defamation or as may arise from a traffic accident. In addition to Sub-Clause 1.13 [*Compliance with Laws*] of RB/17 requiring the Parties to comply with all applicable Laws, Sub-Clause 6.11 [*Disorderly Conduct*] requires the Contractor to prevent any unlawful or disorderly conduct by the Contractor's Personnel.

The above list is not exhaustive. Generally, any contractor or construction professional proposing to undertake work in a foreign country should obtain local legal advice as to all provisions of law or regulations that may have a mandatory character.[390]

389. For example, the French law on subcontracting provides in private sector contracts, among other things, a subcontractor with a right to take legal action directly against an employer if the contractor does not pay sums due under a subcontract. Law No 75-1334 of 31 December 1975 relating to subcontracting, as amended, art. 12. *See* **Section 4.4.3 Subcontractor's Direct Rights** above of **Chapter II Applicable Law**.

390. For example, the HGCRA applicable in England, Wales, Scotland and Northern Ireland explicitly states that it will apply to construction operations in those places whether or not the law there is the applicable law in relation to the construction contract concerned (s 104(7)). This act entitles a party to a construction contract to refer a dispute to statutory adjudication under a procedure described in the act which right cannot be waived by a contractual stipulation (*see* s 108). The procedure provides for, among other things, the appointment of an adjudicator within 7 days of the giving of a notice of a party's intention to refer a dispute to adjudication and a 28-day period for an adjudicator to reach a decision.

6 CHALLENGES OF A LESS-DEVELOPED LAW

An international construction contract often relates to a project in a developing country for an employer residing in that country (the contractor being usually from a developed country). The employer will normally require – especially where it is a state or other public body – that the contract be governed by the law of its country, which is also logical as the site will usually be located there. But typically therein lies a problem, because often the law of that country, and particularly its law of contract or obligations (which will apply to the contract), will also be developing, and often not provide answers to all the legal issues to which a complex construction project may give rise. Its legislature and courts may never have had to address them. As a construction specialist has aptly put it: 'the frequent problem for construction arbitrators is the dearth of precedent in most developing countries'.[391]

How might parties negotiating an international construction contract arrange to overcome this problem? How, when confronted with resolving a dispute under the law of a developing country, might the DAAB or international arbitrators do so?

There are at least two solutions:

(1) have regard to legal principles or court precedent from an appropriate developed system of law to complement and fill in 'gaps' in the governing law; and/or
(2) have regard to legal principles relating to international commercial contracts such as the UNIDROIT Principles to interpret or supplement the governing law.[392]

391. Charles Molineaux, 'Moving Toward a Construction Lex Mercatoria – A Lex Constructionis' (1997) 1(1) J Int'l Arb 55, 60.
392. To avoid the application of a less-developed law, another solution would be for parties to provide that any arbitral tribunal called upon to decide a dispute should have the power of an *amiable compositeur* or to decide *ex aequo et bono*, pursuant to art. 21(3) of the ICC Rules of Arbitration. However, as this power is 'vague and uncertain' it is 'very rare for parties to give an arbitral tribunal [this] power'. Jason Fry and others, *The Secretariat's Guide to ICC Arbitration* (ICC, Paris, 2012, ICC Publication no 729 E) 231 (para. 3-790).

The solution in (2) above is discussed below in Section 7 of **Chapter II**.[393] Thus, the discussion here will focus on solution (1) above.

In the case of an international construction contract being executed in the developing world and governed by local law, how then should one fill an apparent 'gap' in the governing law? In such a situation, a party may be well advised, in addition to investigating such relevant legal principles of the governing law as may exist (even if at a high level of generality),[394] as these must be respected, to search for relevant legal principles and/or court precedent in the law of an appropriate developed country.[395] A developed country which could be appropriate would include one from whose law the governing law derives, or a country which is part of the same legal system or family of law as that of the governing law.[396] Thus:

393. Notably in **Section 7.4.2 As a Source to Interpret or Supplement the Governing Law**.
394. Such as, most obviously, the duty under civil law systems to perform contracts in good faith. *See* **Section 4.3.1 Duty of Good Faith** above of **Chapter II Applicable Law**.
395. As national courts may do, *See* Jan Smits, 'Comparative Law and its Influence on National Legal Systems' in Mathias Reimann and Reinhard Zimmermann (eds), *The Oxford Handbook of Comparative Law* (2nd edn, OUP, Oxford, 2019) 502, 518 who states:

    > courts look elsewhere for inspiration in cases where there is either no domestic rule or the domestic rule is unclear, because they think that this will save time and money or will provide prestige [...] courts are particularly keen to refer to foreign law when they have to deal with a controversial new issue. It is likely that the more controversial or novel an issue is, the more the court feels obliged to convince its audience of the correctness of its decision. To convince outside observers that its decision is correct, the court can seek support in legal systems where a similar issue has been decided before. Thus, courts can use references to foreign law strategically to improve the acceptance of their decisions by the legal community of their own country.

    For the willingness of the US Supreme Court, for example, to look at foreign or international legal rules, *see* Stephen Breyer, *The Court and the World: American Law and the New Global Realities* (Knopf, NY, 2015) 236-46.
396. For an example of the use of this technique in an ICC construction case, *see* Christopher R Seppälä, 'The Development of a Case Law in Construction Disputes Relating to FIDIC Contracts' in Emmanuel Gaillard and Yas Banifatemi (eds), *Precedent in International Arbitration* (Juris Publishing,

(1) if the governing law is that of a civil law country, and its legal system has historic links to France, as is true of Egypt and other countries in the Arab Middle East, Latin America and francophone Africa, one may want to look to French civil and/or administrative law for more detail;
(2) if the governing law is that of a common law country, and its legal system has historic links to England, as is true of countries of the former British Empire, such as Canada, India, Nigeria or Pakistan, one may want to look to the English (or, sometimes United States[397]) law of contract and to its construction law for more detail;
(3) if the governing law is that of Greece one might look to German law for more detail as the Greek Civil Code '[i]n content [...] relies predominantly on the German Civil Code'[398] and German law is more developed; and
(4) if the governing law is that of Turkey, one may want to look to Swiss law as the Turkish Civil Code and Code of Obligations are based closely on the corresponding Swiss Codes and Swiss law is more developed than Turkish law.[399]

There are many such examples of relationships – sometimes very close – between the law of a less-developed country and the law of a developed country. Where relevant, they should be identified and investigated.

Provided the solution offered by the foreign law is compatible with such principles of the governing law as may exist and can be justified as indicating, at least arguably, how a court of the country of the governing law would likely decide the question if it were submitted to it, then a court decision on similar facts, or a relevant legal principle, from a developed system of law, may provide a better reasoned and more convincing means of filing a gap than an attempt to do so by resorting to

Huntington, NY, 2008) 67, 74-77. *See also* Emmanuel Gaillard, 'Du Bon Usage du Droit Comparé dans l'Arbitrage International' (2005) (2) Rev Arb 375.

397. For example, by comparison to US law, there is little or nothing in English law on the duties of an employer to coordinate multiple construction contracts on a single site, or on value engineering clauses.
398. Konrad Zweigert and Hein Kötz, *Introduction to Comparative Law* (3rd rev'd edn, OUP, Oxford, 1998) 155-56.
399. *Ibid.*, 178-79.

the general principles of the governing law in isolation and then attempting to reason from there. In short, there is no reason 'to re-invent the wheel', given the possibility to refer to and apply by analogy the wealth of analysis and wisdom available from the related law of developed countries.

As every construction lawyer knows, the same or similar issues arise repeatedly in construction disputes such as: late possession of the site, adverse site conditions, the scope of variations, delay and disruption issues, hardship and the interpretation of 'pay when paid' clauses in subcontracts. When these issues arise under the law of a less-developed country, they are fundamentally no different from the same issues which have been addressed numerous times by the courts or legislatures in countries with developed legal systems. Therefore when there is no clear answer under the law of a developing country, a sensible solution will often be to look to the analysis and solutions provided for by the law of a relevant developed country.[400]

Under this proposal, international arbitrators, who are the final judges under a FIDIC contract, would not be asked to disregard the governing local law.[401] On the contrary, they would be expected to apply the foreign legal principle only to the extent that it is consistent and compatible with the governing local law. Given the multinational composition of most international arbitral tribunals, international arbitrators are generally willing – and qualified – to apply this sort of comparative law methodology as it may help them to decide a dispute in accordance with the governing law better than it might be done otherwise.[402]

400. For an article related to this subject, *see* Paul Cowan and John Bellhouse, 'Common Law "Time at Large" Arguments in a Civil Law Context' (2007) 23 Const L J 592.

401. As an English judge did in *Petroleum Dev (Trucial Coast) Ltd and the Sheikh of Abu Dhabi*, Award of 28 August 1951 (1952) 1 ICLQ 247. In that case, Lord Asquith disregarded the law of Abu Dhabi, which was referred to in the contract, as not sufficiently sophisticated to provide a solution to the relevant dispute and applied instead English law insofar as it reflected universal legal principles. *See* Emmanuel Gaillard and John Savage (eds), *Fouchard Gaillard Goldman on International Commercial Arbitration* (Kluwer L Int'l, the Netherlands, 1999) 842-44.

402. Christopher R Seppälä, 'The Development of a Case Law in Construction Disputes Relating to FIDIC Contracts' in Emmanuel Gaillard and Yas Banifatemi (eds), *Precedent in International Arbitration* (Juris Publishing, Huntington, NY, 2008) 67; Emmanuel Gaillard, 'Du Bon Usage du Droit

In conclusion, parties should make use of the resources of comparative law when dealing with an underdeveloped governing law.[403] To the extent that the foreign law is consistent and compatible with the governing law and provides sound analysis, an international arbitral tribunal should welcome it.[404]

7 INTERNATIONAL LEGAL PRINCIPLES

7.1 Introduction

Parties are not necessarily bound to choose a national substantive law to govern their contractual relationship. Where their contract contains an international arbitration clause, as in the case of a FIDIC contract, they may instead choose a more amorphous body of law such as general principles of law or *lex mercatoria* to govern their contract. This is recognised by model international arbitration laws, modern arbitration legislation and rules governing international commercial arbitration, all of which envisage that international commercial contracts may be governed by 'rules of law' and not merely the national law of a given country.

Thus, the *UNCITRAL Model Law on International Commercial Arbitration of 1985, as amended in 2006,* which is the basis of many national arbitration laws,[405] provides in Article 28(1) that:

Comparé dans l'Arbitrage International' (2005) Rev Arb, 375 and *see* **Sections 5.6 Other Sources** and **5.7 Effect of an International Arbitration Clause** of **Chapter III Contract Interpretation** below where this point is further discussed.

403. The problem, as a practical matter, may be not merely that the law is developing but that what law may exist is poorly reported or difficult to access. *See* Sub-Clause 2.2 [*Assistance*] of RB/17, providing that the Employer should, if requested by the Contractor, promptly provide reasonable assistance to the Contractor so as to allow it to obtain copies of the laws of the Country which are relevant to the contract but 'are not readily available'.
404. *See also* **Section 5.7 Effect of an International Arbitration Clause** of **Chapter III Contract Interpretation** below.
405. Over a hundred jurisdictions have adopted arbitration laws based on the UNCITRAL Model Law. *See* https://uncitral.un.org/sites/uncitral.un.org/files/media-documents/uncitral/en/19-09955_e_ebook.pdf accessed 2 November 2022.

> The arbitral tribunal shall decide the dispute in accordance which such *rules of law* as are chosen by the parties as applicable to the substance of the dispute [...]. (Emphasis added)

Similarly, French law provides that arbitrators shall decide disputes according to the 'rules of law' chosen by the parties.[406] The English *Arbitration Act* is to similar effect providing that parties may agree that a contract be governed in accordance with 'such other considerations as are agreed by them'.[407]

The ICC Arbitration Rules, referred to in Sub-Clause 21.6 [*Arbitration*] of RB/17, provide that the 'parties shall be free to agree upon the *rules of law* to be applied by the arbitral tribunal to the merits of the dispute'[408] (emphasis added).

Accordingly, parties to a contract based on RB/17 are free to provide that their contract shall be governed by rules of law or criteria that they consider appropriate instead of by a national law. They may even authorise arbitrators to act as *amiables compositeurs* or decide *ex aequo et bono* (i.e., in equity),[409] though this is rarely done in practice.

Thus, parties to a FIDIC contract may elect for it to be governed, or be interpreted or supplemented, by international legal principles. For this reason and because of a FIDIC form's international nature, consideration of the UNIDROIT Principles, discussed in the next Section, is appropriate.

---

406. French Code of Civil Procedure, art. 1511.
407. English *Arbitration Act* 1996, s 46(1)(b).
408. ICC Arbitration Rules, art. 21(1). To the same effect are the UNCITRAL Arbitration Rules 2010: 'The arbitral tribunal shall apply the *rules of law* designated by the parties [...].', UNCITRAL Arbitration Rules (2010), art. 35(1) (emphasis added). The term 'rules of law' encompasses 'an almost limitless range of options', such as transnational commercial law, the UNIDROIT Principles and even 'tailor-made concoctions of applicable legal principles'. Jason Fry and others, *The Secretariat's Guide to Arbitration* (ICC, Paris, 2012, ICC Publication no 729E) 222-223 (paras 3-761 to 3-762).
409. ICC Arbitration Rules, art. 21(3).

7.2 UNIDROIT Principles

The UNIDROIT[410] Principles of International Commercial Contracts of 2016 (the 'UNIDROIT Principles' or 'Principles')[411] are an 'elaboration of an international restatement of general principles of contract law'.[412] The objective of the Principles is:

> to establish a balanced set of rules designed for use throughout the world irrespective of the legal traditions and the economic and political conditions of the countries in which they are to be applied.[413]

Though for the most part reflecting concepts found in many, though not all, legal systems, the Principles also embody what are perceived to be the best solutions, even if still not yet ones that are generally adopted, since they are intended to serve both as a model law for legislators and as a guide for contracts between individual parties.

---

410. The International Institute for the Unification of Private Law ('UNIDROIT') was founded as an auxiliary organ of the League of Nations in Rome in 1926. Following the demise of the League, it was re-established in 1940 as an independent intergovernmental organisation on the basis of a multilateral agreement, the UNIDROIT statute (Stefan Vogenauer (ed), *Commentary on the UNIDROIT Principles of International Commercial Contracts (PICC)* (2nd edn, OUP, Oxford, 2015) 7 (para. 14)). UNIDROIT has 63 Member States including all major trading nations. Its purpose is to examine ways of harmonising and coordinating private, particularly commercial, law at a global level and it formulates uniform law instruments, principles and rules to this end.
411. Another respected set of principles is *The Principles of European Contract Law* 2002 ('PECL'). However, the PECL appear less relevant to the Red Book for two reasons. First, while the Principles aim at the global level, the PECL are directed at Member States of the European Union. Second, while the Principles are directed to business-to-business transactions, the PECL are also directed to business-to-consumer transactions, which are irrelevant to FIDIC contracts and for which party autonomy is more restricted. *See* Klaus Peter Berger, *The Creeping Codification of the New Lex Mercatoria* (2nd edn, Kluwer L Int'l, the Netherlands, 2010) 11-12.
412. Stefan Vogenauer (ed), *Commentary on the UNIDROIT Principles of International Commercial Contracts (PICC)* (2nd edn, OUP, Oxford, 2015) 1 (para. 1).
413. Introduction to the 1994 Edition, UNIDROIT Principles.

While the Principles do not deal specifically with international construction contracts but rather with international commercial contracts generally, nevertheless, as explained below, they are well suited to complement a comprehensive international construction contract like RB/17.

7.3 UNIDROIT Principles 2016

The Principles 2016 is the latest edition of the Principles.[414] They cover all stages in the life of a commercial contract: formation, content, performance, validity, interpretation, termination and limitation periods.

The Principles were originally inspired by the *Restatements* of law published by the American Law Institute ('ALI') in the United States which are designed to harmonise selected fields of law in that country. Like the US *Restatement (Second) of Contracts* (1981), the UNIDROIT Principles are composed of black letter rules ('Articles') – there are 211 such rules divided into 11 chapters – each of which is accompanied by comments and, where appropriate, by factual illustrations intended to explain the reasons for the black letter rule and the different ways in which it may operate in practice.[415]

The Principles have been prepared by experts from both civil and common law systems to reflect best international contract practice. During the drafting process, preference was given to solutions generally accepted at the international level (referred to as the 'common core' approach) except where there was found to be no generally accepted rule at the international level in which case the 'better rule' under international contract practice was selected (referred to as the 'better rule'

414. Earlier editions were issued in 1994, 2004 and 2010. An IBA publication regarding the Principles is: *Perspectives in Practice of the UNIDROIT Principles 2016 (Views of the IBA Working Group on the practice of the UNIDROIT Principles 2016)*, published in 2019. This work contains reports on the application of the Principles in 28 different countries as well as a collection of over 250 summaries of court and arbitration cases where the Principles were referred to or relied upon. It is available at https://www.ibanet.org/MediaHandler?id=D266F2AF-3E0B-4DC0-AFCE-662E5D49BB7E accessed 2 November 2022 and has been published in hardcover by the International Law Institute, Washington DC, USA, https://www.ili.org/publications/catalogue.html accessed 2 November 2022.

415. Michael Joachim Bonell, 'The Law Governing International Commercial Contracts and the Actual Role of the UNIDROIT Principles' (2018) 23 Unif L Rev 15, 21.

approach).[416] The Principles are available in English, French and Spanish, which are three of the official languages of UNIDROIT.[417]

Examples of civil law additions to the Principles unknown, traditionally, to the common law include the following:

- general obligation to act in good faith (Article 1.7);
- lack of a consideration requirement (Article 3.1.2); and
- rules on contract interpretation (Chapter 4).

Examples of common law additions to the Principles unknown, traditionally, to the civil law include the following:

- termination for non-performance by mere notice (Article 7.3.2);
- formation of a contract without *cause* (Article 3.1.2); and
- order of performance (Article 6.1.4).

Additions believed to address the special needs of international business include the following:

- hardship and the right of the disadvantaged party to request renegotiation of a contract (Article 6.2.1–6.2.3); and
- exclusion of liability for *force majeure* events (Article 7.1.7).

The Principles provide that they are to be interpreted and supplemented as follows:

(1) In the interpretation of these Principles, regard is to be had to their international character and to their purposes including the need to promote uniformity in their application.

(2) Issues within the scope of these Principles but not expressly settled by them are as far as possible to be settled in accordance with their underlying general principles.[418]

416. *Ibid.*, 22.

417. The other two official languages of UNIDROIT are German and Italian. Translations into Chinese, Korean, Romanian and Russian, non-official languages of UNIDROIT, have also been published. Other translations into non-official languages of UNIDROIT are said to be in preparation.

418. Art. 1.6 (*Interpretation and supplementation of the Principles*) of the Principles.

At the same time, application of the Principles will be restricted by the mandatory rules of any national or other law which may be relevant.[419]

7.4 Relevance to a FIDIC Contract

While the Principles have multiple potential uses,[420] they may be relevant to FIDIC contracts in broadly four ways:

(1) they may be chosen or applied as the 'governing law' for a FIDIC contract;
(2) if a FIDIC contract already provides for a governing law, they may be used to interpret or supplement that law;
(3) they may serve as a model for national legislation; and
(4) more controversially, they may serve as trade usages.

Each of these ways of resorting to the Principles is examined further below.

7.4.1 As the 'Governing Law' for a FIDIC Contract

Though they appear not often to have been chosen as the 'governing law',[421] there is no good reason why the Principles cannot serve satisfactorily as the governing law (or, more accurately, 'rules of law') for a

419. *See* art. 1.4 (*Mandatory rules*) of the Principles.
420. According to the Preamble of the Principles, they:

(1) must be applied where the parties have chosen them as a governing law;
(2) may be applied where the parties have agreed that their contract be governed by general principles of law, the *lex mercatoria* or the like;
(3) may be applied where the parties have not chosen a governing law;
(4) may be used to interpret or supplement international uniform law instruments;
(5) may be used to interpret or supplement domestic law; and
(6) may serve as a model for national and international legislators.

More controversially (and not in the Preamble), they may be used as trade usages.

421. 26 arbitral awards have been reported of where an arbitral tribunal applied the UNIDROIT Principles as rules of law to govern a contract. UNILEX database, 'Principles applicable if expressly chosen by the parties in

FIDIC contract. A FIDIC contract deals comprehensively with most of the issues that are likely to arise on an international construction project. Consequently, as others have noted, it should not matter that the Principles do not deal specifically with international construction projects.[422]

While the Principles only contain general principles, they are accompanied by official comments and illustrations and have, as well, been the subject of doctrinal commentary[423] and published case law (*see* the following paragraphs below). Thus, they may be more up-to-date and relevant to an international project, and just as comprehensive, as the law of a developing country which might otherwise apply. Furthermore, where an issue is not dealt with expressly by the Principles, they provide for a useful method of supplying a term.[424] A further attraction is their drafting style:

---

disputes before arbitral tribunal', http://www.unilex.info/principles/cases/article/102/issue/1941#issue_1941 accessed 2 November 2022.

422. Donald Charrett, 'The Use of the UNIDROIT Principles in International Construction Contracts' [2013] 30 ICLR 507, 523 and International Chamber of Commerce Policy and Business Practice, 'Developing Neutral Legal Standards for International Contracts' https://iccwbo.org/content/uploads/sites/3/2017/01/Developing-Neutral-Legal-Standards-Int-Contracts.pdf accessed 2 November 2022.

423. For two commentaries *see* Stefan Vogenauer (ed), *Commentary on the UNIDROIT Principles of International Commercial Contracts (PICC)* (2nd edn, OUP, Oxford, 2015) and Eckart J Brödermann, *UNIDROIT Principles of International Commercial Contracts, An Article-by-Article Commentary* (Kluwer L Int'l, the Netherlands, 2018).

424. Thus art. 4.8 (*Supplying an omitted term*) provides as follows:

(1) Where the parties to a contract have not agreed with respect to a term which is important for a determination of their rights and duties, a term which is appropriate in the circumstances shall be supplied.
(2) In determining what is an appropriate term regard shall be had, among other factors, to:
  (a) the intention of the parties;
  (b) the nature and purpose of the contract;
  (c) good faith and fair dealing;
  (d) reasonableness.

Furthermore, issues not settled by the Principles should be settled: 'as far as possible … in accordance with their underlying general principles'. Art. 1.6(2) (*Interpretation and supplementation of the Principles*).

> The language is concise and straight forward so as to facilitate comprehension also by non-lawyers and deliberately avoids terminology peculiar to any given legal system, thereby creating a legal *lingua franca* to be used and uniformly understood throughout the world.[425]

A decision by parties to have their contract governed by the Principles will, as indicated above,[426] generally be recognised by arbitral tribunals[427] and their awards upheld by national courts.[428]

The following are two examples of use of the Principles by arbitral tribunals:

Example 1: Contract termination

In a 2006 case before a Mexican arbitral institution, a Mexican grower of vegetables had entered into a contract to supply the same on an exclusive basis to a Californian distributor. The contract contained an arbitration clause, and specified that any dispute should be governed by the Principles. The distributor claimed that the grower failed to supply the promised vegetables, and had breached the exclusivity clause, whereas the grower claimed that heavy rainstorms (caused by the weather pattern El Niño) had ruined its crops. The distributor sought termination of the contract and damages. The arbitral tribunal upheld the use of the Principles, noting that this was in accordance with Article 1445 of the Mexican Commercial Code which provides that disputes were to be governed by the 'rules of law' chosen by the parties.[429] The tribunal then

425. Michael Joachim Bonell, 'The Law Governing International Commercial Contracts and the Actual Role of the UNIDROIT Principles' (2018) 23 Unif L Rev, 15, 22.
426. *See* **Section 7.1 Introduction** above of **Chapter II Applicable Law**.
427. Stefan Vogenauer (ed), *Commentary on the UNIDROIT Principles of International Commercial Contracts (PICC)* (2nd edn, OUP, Oxford, 2015) 116-117 (para. 9) (at least where the law of the place of arbitration allows parties to resort to 'rules of law').
428. French courts, among others, have confirmed that where the parties are in dispute about the governing law for a commercial contract, international arbitrators may select the Principles as the governing law. Ct of App Paris (1st Ch), 25 February 2020, no 17/18001 (*Prakash Steelage Limited v Uzuc SA*). For a commentary on this decision, *see* Christopher R Seppälä and another, 'Correspondent's Report: France', [2021] ICLR 121.
429. The party names of this award are unknown, but excerpts of the award and an English abstract are available here www.unilex.info/case.cfm?pid = 2& do = case&id = 1149&step = Abstract accessed 2 November 2022.

upheld termination of the contract by the distributor under Article 7.3.1 (*Right to terminate the contract*) of the Principles, and the award of damages under Article 7.4.2 (*Full compensation*) of the Principles.

Example 2: Multiple contracts

An ICC arbitration in Holland in 1995 involved nine related contracts for the supply of military equipment by a British company to the Iranian government which were cancelled by one or other of the parties after the Islamic Revolution. While the parties had provided for ICC arbitration, they had not chosen a domestic law to govern their contracts, but some had specified that any disputes should be settled by 'natural justice', 'laws of natural justice' or 'rules of natural justice'. The arbitral tribunal decided (by a majority) that the contracts should be governed by the Principles, finding that 'general rules and principles enjoying wide international consensus, applicable to international contractual obligations and relevant to the Contracts, are primarily reflected by the principles of' UNIDROIT. The arbitral tribunal also noted the 'high quality and neutrality' of the Principles, and their relationship to the Vienna Convention on the International Sale of Goods. Appeals to a Dutch Court and the Dutch Supreme Court were unsuccessful.[430]

--ooOOoo--

As, in the interpretation of the Principles, regard is to be had to 'the need to promote uniformity in their application',[431] previous decisions of courts or tribunals referring to the Principles will have precedential value.

430. First partial award, ICC case 7110 www.unilex.info/case.cfm?pid = 2&do = case&id = 713&step = FullText accessed 2 November 2022. *BAE Systems v Ministry of Defence and Support for Armed Forces of the Islamic Republic of Iran*, Supreme Court of the Netherlands, Case no 14/00945 www.unilex.info/case.cfm?pid = 2&do = case&id = 1924&step = Abstract accessed 2 November 2022.

431. Art. 1.6 (*Interpretation and supplementation of the Principles*) of the Principles.

7.4.2 *As a Source to Interpret or Supplement the Governing Law*

The Principles may have their greatest value when used in interpreting or supplementing the governing law which the parties have chosen. Moreover, it is in performing this function that the Principles appear to have been used the most in practice.[432]

A Red Book contract will normally have been entered into following an invitation to tender procedure where the Employer, or its consultant, will have drafted the conditions of contract, including the governing law clause, which will usually provide that the law of the country of the Employer will apply as the governing law.[433] But, as explained above,[434] the legal system of the Employer's country may be rudimentary and not provide answers to all of the legal questions to which a complex construction project may give rise.[435] In these circumstances, it may be appropriate to resort to the Principles as a source to interpret or supplement the governing law.

In a number of reported cases, an arbitral tribunal has explicitly stated that the applicable law was underdeveloped, or had a gap, or even, in the case of a more developed law, that the law was 'unsettled', and has consequently resorted to the Principles. The remainder of Section 7.4.2 provides examples of where the Principles have been used to interpret or supplement a governing law.

1) Russia

In an international arbitration in Russia in 2009, a sales contract between a Russian and a Chinese company had been terminated and the Russian

432. Of more than five-hundred reported uses of the Principles by courts or arbitral tribunals, the Principles were used to interpret domestic law in 213 cases. UNILEX database, 'Principles as means for interpreting and supplementing applicable domestic law', http://www.unilex.info/principles/cases/article/102/issue/1941#issue_1941 accessed 2 November 2022.
433. *See* **Section 2 Context of a Red Book Contract** of **Chapter IV Clause-by-Clause Commentary** below.
434. *See* **Section 6 Challenges of a Less-Developed Law** above of **Chapter II Applicable Law**.
435. Indeed, this may be true of highly developed systems like those of England and Switzerland. *See* the quotations from Sir Roy Goode on English law and Ingeborg Schwenzer on Swiss law in Michael Joachim Bonell, 'The Law Governing International Commercial Contracts and the Actual Role of the UNIDROIT Principles' (2018) 23 Unif L Rev 15, 16-17.

buyer sought the return of its advance payment. The arbitral tribunal found that there was 'no specific regulation' in the governing law, the law of the Russian Federation, addressing the issue, and they therefore relied on Article 7.4.8 (*Mitigation of harm*) of the Principles and, specifically, on what the tribunal describes as the 'duty to mitigate the harm caused by the non-performance and the right to reimbursement of the expenses reasonably incurred', to justify return of the advance payment.[436]

2) New Zealand

New Zealand has a relatively developed legal system but a small economy. In an ad hoc arbitration in Auckland in 1995, where the contract was governed by New Zealand law, there was a dispute as to whether post-contractual conduct of the parties was admissible as evidence for resolving ambiguities in the contract. The arbitral tribunal found that the law of New Zealand was 'in a somewhat unsettled state' on the point. The tribunal, which was inclined to accept the evidence of post-contractual conduct, sought support for this inclination at an international level, and referred to Chapter 4, Interpretation, of the Principles.[437] While the published details do not elucidate the final outcome, the tribunal stated of the Principles that:

> there could be no more definitive contemporary international statement governing the interpretation of contractual terms than in the UNIDROIT Principles.[438]

3) Other countries

There are also numerous cases where an arbitral tribunal or a court has relied on the Principles to complement a relatively stark legislative or regulatory landscape. For example, in an Uruguayan court case in 2014, an owner had sought to terminate a construction contract and claim damages because of the contractor's defective work. The Uruguayan court awarded not just actual damages but also foreseeable damages,

436. The full details of this award are not currently available, but there is an abstract on the UNILEX website www.unilex.info/case.cfm?pid = 2&do = case&id = 1552&step = Abstract accessed 2 November 2022.
437. In the interpretation of a contract, art. 4.3(c) of the Principles expressly authorises regard to 'the conduct of the parties subsequent to the conclusion of the contract'.
438. The full details of this award are not currently available, but there is an abstract on the UNILEX website www.unilex.info/case.cfm?pid = 2&do = case&id = 628&step = Abstract accessed 2 November 2022.

relying on both Uruguayan law and Article 7.4.4 (*Foreseeability of harm*) of the Principles.[439]

In a Paraguayan court case in 2014, a government institution had adjudicated the sale of land at a certain price to a certain individual and then later reversed its decision and established a new and higher price for the land. Upon suit by the individual, the Paraguayan appellate court found that the institution's action was contrary to good faith and Article 1.8 (*Inconsistent behaviour*) of the Principles. While the Principles were not binding on the parties:

> they constitute widely recognised principles in international commercial law that propose uniform solutions and that as such they can be used to interpret or supplement domestic law [...].[440]

In 1997, the Venezuelan Supreme Court found that a contract, albeit between two Venezuelan companies (one a subsidiary of a US company), was 'international' – for the purposes of determining whether a clause providing for arbitration in New York under the ICC Arbitration Rules was valid – relying on, among other things, the Principles which provide that '[...] the concept of "international" contracts should be given the broadest possible interpretation [...]'.[441]

--ooOOoo--

What is interesting in the above cases is the reliance on the Principles to shore up a legal finding, or to refine and clarify the applicable law.

---

439. The full details of this award are not currently available, but there is an abstract on the UNILEX website http://www.unilex.info/case.cfm?pid=2&do=case&id=1991&step=Abstract accessed 2 November 2022.
440. The full details of this award are not currently available, but there is an abstract on the UNILEX website www.unilex.info/case.cfm?pid=2&do=case&id=1866&step=FullText accessed 2 November 2022.
441. Official comment 1 to the Preamble to the Principles. *Bottling Companies v Pepsi Cola Panamericana*, Supreme Court of Venezuela www.unilex.info/case.cfm?pid=2&do=case&id=643&step=Abstract accessed 6 November 2022. Similarly, in 2003 an ICC tribunal placed reliance on the same provision of the Principles to conclude that certain arbitral proceedings (the applicable law being Turkish) were of an international nature. ICC case 12174 (2003) www.unilex.info/case.cfm?pid=2&do=case&id=1406&step=Abstract accessed 6 November 2022.

As the Principles may serve, among other things, as the 'governing law'[442] of a FIDIC contract, or as a source to interpret or supplement a domestic law that may govern such a contract, they are referred to regularly in the clause-by-clause commentary below.[443]

7.4.3 As a Model for National Legislation

The Principles have served as a model for national legislation in numerous countries where FIDIC contracts are used.[444] These include the transition economies of Eastern Europe (Russian Federation, Lithuania, Latvia and Estonia) and the People's Republic of China, both being regions or countries which had not dealt with free-market contracts for decades and had therefore needed to adopt new civil codes or laws to regulate them.[445] They also include Western and other countries as varied as Argentina, France, Germany, Japan and Spain which have recently updated their laws on contracts.[446] Thus, the Principles have a continuing influence on the development of contract law around the world.

Consequently, when a FIDIC contract is governed by the domestic law of a country whose legislation has been influenced by the Principles, there

442. Or 'rules of law', *see* art. 21(1) of the ICC Arbitration Rules which is quoted in part and discussed in **Section 7.1 Introduction** above of **Chapter II Applicable Law.**
443. **Chapter IV Clause-by-Clause Commentary** below.
444. The Principles are said to have two advantages as models for legislation:

> One is that much comparative work has already gone into such instruments, so that they are likely to be a good repository of rules which have stood the test of time [...], and hence a good indicator of where things might be heading internationally. The other consideration is [...] [b]y looking to supra-national instruments, a national legislator can avoid the sensitive political issue and potential embarrassment of appearing to copy a neighbouring state's law.
>
> Birke Häcker, 'A German Lawyer Looks at the Reform of French Contract Law' in John Cartwright and Simon Whittaker (eds), *Code Napoléon Rewritten: French Contract Law after the 2016 Reforms* (Hart, Oxford, 2017) 387, 393.

445. José Angelo Estrella Faria, 'The Influence of the UNIDROIT Principles of International Commercial Contracts on National Laws' in UNIDROIT (ed), *Eppur si Muove: The Age of Uniform Law, Essays in honour of M.J. Bonell* (UNIDROIT, Rome, 2016) 1318, 1322-32.
446. *Ibid.*, 1332-48.

may naturally be similarities between that law and what the Principles provide. Thus, the hardship provisions in the Russian Civil Code[447] are almost literally taken from Section 6.2 of the Principles dealing with hardship,[448] and the 2016 reform of French contract law in this area has been strongly influenced by the Principles.[449] This is another reason for the frequent references to the Principles in the clause-by-clause commentary in **Chapter IV** below.

7.4.4 As Trade Usages

A further, though more controversial, use of the Principles, is to serve as trade usages.[450] As FIDIC contracts provide for ICC arbitration and as the ICC Arbitration Rules require an arbitral tribunal to 'take account of [...] any relevant trade usages',[451] it may be argued that the Principles apply already to a FIDIC contract as trade usages and thus complement whatever domestic law may be provided for as the governing law.

However, the acceptance of the Principles as 'trade usages' is mixed. In an ICC arbitration from 2003, concerning the manufacture of trucks in Mexico, the contract was governed by Mexican law, and one of the parties sought to rely on the Principles as 'international trade usages'. The arbitral tribunal found that the Principles 'do not reflect trade usages', but can be used to interpret domestic law.[452] And yet in the same

447. Russian Civil Code, art. 451.
448. Stefan Vogenauer (ed), *Commentary on the UNIDROIT Principles of International Commercial Contracts (PICC)* (2nd edn, OUP, Oxford, 2015) 809, fn. 7 (para. 3).
449. Bénédicte Fauvarque-Cosson, 'The UNIDROIT Principles and French Reform of Contract Law' in UNIDROIT (ed), *Eppur si Muove: The Age of Uniform Law, Essays in honour of M.J. Bonell* (UNIDROIT, Rome, 2016) 1350, 1355-1364.
450. Roy Goode and others, *Transnational Commercial Law* (2nd edn, OUP, Oxford, 2015) 478-479 (para. 16.38) and Michael Joachim Bonell, 'The Law Governing International Commercial Contracts and the Actual Role of the UNIDROIT Principles' (2018) 23 Unif L Rev 15, 34. Gary Born states that such usage is 'ill-considered'. Gary Born, *International Commercial Arbitration* (3rd edn, Kluwer L Int'l, the Netherlands, 2021) vol II, 2986 (s 19.07).
451. ICC Arbitration Rules, art. 21(2).
452. *See* **Section 7.4.2 As a Source to Interpret or Supplement the Governing Law** above of **Chapter II Applicable Law.** ICC case 11256 http://www.unilex.info/case.cfm?pid = 2&do = case&id = 1423&step = FullText accessed 6 November 2022.

year in another ICC arbitration, where there was no domestic law agreed upon and the contract involved activities in four different countries, the arbitral tribunal found that the Principles could be treated as trade usages since they were (translation from French): 'a codification of trade usages and an expression of the general principles of contract law'.[453] Similarly, in a number of Russian arbitrations, the tribunal has relied on the Principles as internationally recognised trade usages.[454]

But, in an ICC arbitration in 1998, where the contract provided for the application of Italian law, the tribunal (in rejecting a claim of hardship and gross disparity based on the Principles) refused to apply the Principles as trade usages (or *lex mercatoria*), finding that:

> although the Unidroit Principles constitute a set of rules theoretically appropriate to prefigure the future *lex mercatoria* should they be brought into line with international commercial practice, at present there is no necessary connection between the individual Principles and the rules of the *lex mercatoria*, so that recourse to the Principles is not purely and simply the same as recourse to an actually existing international commercial usage [...].[455]

---

453. ICC case 11265 www.unilex.info/case.cfm?pid=2&do=case&id=1416&step=FullText accessed 6 November 2022.
454. International Commercial Arbitration Court of the Chamber of Commerce and Industry of the Russian Federation (ICAC of the CCI of the Russian Federation), Case 229/1996, Award of 5 June 1997. The full details of this award are available on the Pace database of the CISG and International Commercial Law https://iicl.law.pace.edu/cisg/case/5-june-1997-tribunal-international-commercial-arbitration-russian-federation-chamber and the UNILEX database www.unilex.info/case.cfm?id=669 accessed 6 November 2022; ICAC at the CCI of the Russian Federation, Case 302/1997, Award of 27 July 1999. The full details of this award are not currently available, but an abstract is on the UNILEX website www.unilex.info/case.cfm?id=671 accessed 6 November 2022; ICAC at the CCI of the Russian Federation, Case no 217/2001, Award of 6 November 2002. The full details of this award are not currently available, but an abstract is on the UNILEX website http://www.unilex.info/case.cfm?id=856 accessed 6 November 2022.
455. ICC case 9029, www.unilex.info/case.cfm?pid=2&do=case&id=660&step=FullText accessed 6 November 2022. To the same effect, *see* ICC case 8873 (1997) 4 Journal de Droit International 1017.

But, in another ICC case from 1999, concerning a dispute over a trademark, the Principles were stated to be an 'accurate representation, although incomplete, of the usages of international trade.'[456]

Tribunals appear to be more inclined to accept the Principles as trade usages in cases where the domestic law that would otherwise apply is not already adapted to a free-market market economy or is less developed (e.g., the law in some countries of Eastern Europe, Russia and Latin America)[457] than where the law is adapted to such an economy or developed.

7.5 Conclusion

As explained above, the Principles may serve as the 'governing law' for a comprehensive construction contract such as a FIDIC contract. Where a FIDIC contract is governed by a less-developed domestic law, the Principles may be useful as a resource to fill in gaps or to assist in the interpretation of the domestic law. Indeed, this is where they may be most useful as, while the law of a less-developed country will still apply, the Principles are available to supplement it or assist in its interpretation.[458] In addition to serving as a model for legislation, though more

456. ICC case 9479, www.unilex.info/case.cfm?pid = 2&do = case&id = 680& step = FullText accessed 6 November 2022.
457. For example, in one case the contract did not contain a choice of law clause and the parties authorised the arbitral tribunal to act as *amiables compositeurs.* Notwithstanding the fact that both parties based their claims on specific provisions of Argentinean law, the arbitral tribunal applied the Principles. It held that the Principles 'constituted usages of international trade reflecting the solutions of different legal systems and of international contract practice, and as such, according to art. 28(4) of the new UNCITRAL Model Law on International Commercial Arbitration (which, like art. 21 of the ICC Arbitration Rules, requires a tribunal to "take account of" trade usages), they should prevail over any domestic law'. *See* arbitral award, ad hoc arbitration, Buenos Aires, dated 10 December 1997 http://www.unilex.info/case.cfm?id = 646 accessed 6 November 2022.
458. UNIDROIT has published '*Model Clauses for the Use of the UNIDROIT Principles of International Commercial Contracts*' dealing, among other things, with where the Principles are chosen as governing rules of law or to supplement or assist in the interpretation of a governing law. These are available on the website of UNIDROIT https://www.unidroit.org/instruments/commercial-contracts/upicc-model-clauses/ accessed 6 November 2022 and in hard copy from UNIDROIT in Rome.

controversially, the Principles may be qualified as trade usages and be resorted to on that basis.

8 TRADE USAGES

As noted above,[459] Article 21(2) of the ICC Arbitration Rules provides that, in addition to taking account of the contract: '[t]he arbitral tribunal shall take account of [...] any relevant trade usages'.

The use of the words 'take account of' implies that the arbitrators have the discretion to apply trade usages and are not obliged to do so in all cases, e.g., in cases where the application of the usage will result in an unjust outcome.[460] Many national arbitration laws also require arbitrators to take account of trade usages.[461]

Article 1.9 (*Usages and practices*) of the Principles describes, in two numbered paragraphs, three types of usages and practices that can apply to an international commercial contract (the references to 'type' in square brackets below are the present author's):

> (1) The parties are bound by any usage to which they have agreed [type one] and by any practices which they have established between themselves [type two].

459. **Section 7.4 Relevance to a FIDIC Contract – 7.4.4 As Trade Usages**, of **Chapter II Applicable Law.**
460. Tolga Ayoglu, 'Application of Trade Usages in International Institutional Arbitration – Some Reflections' (2012) 30 ASA Bull 539, 545.
461. Art. 28(4) of the *UNCITRAL Model Law on International Commercial Arbitration* on which numerous arbitration laws are based requires arbitral tribunals, when deciding disputes, to 'take into account the usages of trade applicable to the transaction'. *See also* art. 1511 of the French Code of Civil Procedure to the same effect. A significant exception is England, as the English *Arbitration Act* 1996 does not require arbitrators to take trade usages into account. England rejected this, *see* DAC Report on the Arbitration Bill (February 1996) (para. 222):

> on the grounds that developed legal systems already took such considerations into account in fashioning and applying rules of commercial law.
>
> Gary Born, *International Commercial Arbitration* (3rd edn, Kluwer L Int'l, the Netherlands, 2021) vol II, 2984 (s 19.07).

(2) The parties are bound by a usage that is widely known to and regularly observed in international trade by parties in the particular trade concerned except where the application of such a usage would be unreasonable [type three].[462]

In general, a party that invokes a certain trade usage or a practice bears the burden of proving that such a usage or practice exists.[463]

8.1 Usage Agreed to (Type One)

As indicated above, type one refers to usages agreed by the parties. Such an agreement can be either explicit (e.g., by reference to them in the parties' contract) or implicit.[464] Some examples of explicitly agreed trade usages are to be found in the RB/17. For instance, Sub-Clause 4.10 [*Use of Site Data*] stipulates that the Contractor, subject to certain qualifications, shall be deemed to have satisfied itself before submitting the Tender as to all matters relevant to the execution of the Works, including, among others, the 'labour practices of the Country' where the Works are carried out; Sub-Clause 7.1 [*Manner of Execution*] states that the Contractor shall execute the Works 'in accordance with recognised good practice'; and Sub-Clause 19.2.6 [*Other Insurances Required by Laws and by Local Practice*] refers to insurances which are 'required by local practice (if any)'.

8.2 Practices Between the Parties (Type Two)

Type two refers to practices which the parties have established between themselves when, for example, performing the contract. This is sometimes referred to as 'course of dealings' or 'course of performance'. As opposed to the usages addressed in paragraph (2) of Article 1.9, such practices are restricted to a commercial relationship established between the parties and without them being widely observed in a particular

462. Art. 1.9 of the Principles deals with usages and practices in general. There are other articles in the Principles which address the role of usages in specific circumstances (*see*, for example, arts 2.1.6(3) and 4.3(f)).
463. Stefan Vogenauer (ed), *Commentary on the UNIDROIT Principles of International Commercial Contracts (PICC)* (2nd edn, OUP, Oxford, 2015) 240 (para. 23).
464. Stefan Vogenauer (ed), *Commentary on the UNIDROIT Principles of International Commercial Contracts (PICC)* (2nd edn, OUP, Oxford, 2015) 235-236 (para. 10).

trade.[465] It is only required that the parties have observed them in the past. Hence, the parties should have had some previous business contact of a similar kind.[466] However, the parties' behaviour on the occasion of only one previous transaction will normally not amount to an established practice.[467] A decisive test as to whether parties are bound by any such practice is, according to the Principles, whether a point has been reached where 'both parties may reasonably expect that the practice represents a common understanding' by which they are bound.[468] In this case, such practices amount to an implied agreement that has been added to the provisions of the contract.[469]

Examples of practices that parties may have established between themselves might be: (1) if for many months an employer has been paying a contractor based on the amount in its payment application without waiting for the engineer to certify that account, then, at some point, the contractor may be entitled to claim that a usage exists that the contractor should be paid based on its payment application without having to wait for the engineer's certificate; or (2) if the engineer or the employer has been regularly settling the contractor's claims without regard to the notice provisions or other procedures applicable to claims in the contract, then, at some point, the engineer or the employer may be precluded from insisting upon compliance with those provisions as a condition to settling the contractor's claims.[470]

465. Stefan Vogenauer (ed), *Commentary on the UNIDROIT Principles of International Commercial Contracts (PICC)* (2nd edn, OUP, Oxford, 2015) 234 (para. 7).
466. *Ibid.*
467. Official comment 2 to art. 1.9 of the Principles.
468. Stefan Vogenauer (ed), *Commentary on the UNIDROIT Principles of International Commercial Contracts (PICC)* (2nd edn, OUP, Oxford, 2015) 235 (para. 7). Art. 1.8 (*Inconsistent behaviour*) of the Principles may also become relevant.
469. *See* Lauro Gama, Jr 'Usages and Implied Obligations under the UNIDROIT Principles of International Commercial Contracts', in Fabien Gélinas (ed), *Trade Usages and Implied Terms in the Age of Arbitration* (OUP, Oxford, 2016) 145, 159.
470. However, in the case of RB/17, the last paragraph of Sub-Clause 3.2 [*Engineer's Duties and Authority*] of RB/17 is designed to prevent such an inference or conclusion from being drawn from the actions or inactions of the Engineer, the Engineer's Representative or any assistant.

8.3 International Trade Usages (Type Three)

Type three deals with a wider category of usages observed in international trade. These usages are binding if they meet the following three requirements:

(1) they must be widely known by parties in the particular trade (e.g., international construction);
(2) they must be regularly observed in international trade by parties in the particular trade; and
(3) the application of the usage should not be unreasonable in the particular case.

The reference to 'international trade' in the article excludes resort to usages of purely local or national origin.[471] Usages of a purely local or national origin may be applicable only in exceptional circumstances.[472] As an example of an exceptional circumstance, it may be maintained that an international contractor who has participated in the execution of numerous construction projects in a particular country over many years should be bound by the usages established in that country that are relevant to the local construction industry. Thus, if in accordance with local custom, the international contractor rather than the employer has consistently obtained a certain construction-related permit in that country and the contract is silent on the question as to which party should obtain the permit, the responsibility for it would most likely be placed on the international contractor.

The criterion that the usage should be widely known to the parties in the particular trade introduces an objective standard. It does not require knowledge of the usage on the part of the actual parties bound by that usage.[473] It would be sufficient if a significant majority of the persons engaged in the particular trade have such knowledge.[474]

--ooOOoo--

471. Official comment 4 to art. 1.9 (*Usages and Practices*) of the Principles.
472. *Ibid.*
473. Stefan Vogenauer (ed), *Commentary on the UNIDROIT Principles of International Commercial Contracts (PICC)* (2nd edn, OUP, Oxford, 2015) 237 (para. 16).
474. *Ibid.* The contention that the Principles may serve as trade usages remains controversial, *see* **Section 7.4.4 As Trade Usages** above of **Chapter II Applicable Law**.

Whether and to what extent international standard forms of contract may themselves constitute trade usages and bind parties has been considered in several ICC cases. In ICC case 8873 of 1997, the tribunal held that the principles contained in the FIDIC or ENAA ('Engineering Advancement Association of Japan') standard forms of construction contract did not satisfy the requirements to become trade usages as: (i) it was not proven that these principles were applied in the construction industry in the absence of an express agreement of the parties, and (ii) the solutions provided by these forms were not found to have been applied in practice with a sufficient degree of uniformity.[475] On the other hand, in ICC case 14392 of 2009 the arbitral tribunal held that although the FIDIC conditions:

> were not applicable per se, they could nonetheless provide an *indication* of the type of contract entered into by the parties since they are universally regarded as usages of the international construction industry. (Emphasis in the original)[476]

In the latter case, the tribunal stated that priority must be given to the actual wording of the parties' agreement, and that reference to international trade usages is justified only when they:

> *confirm the terms of that agreement or may help to interpret unclear or ambiguous clauses as well as when lacunae have to be filled* provided that this is compatible with the applicable law [Portuguese law in this case].[477]

In the case of conflict between usages and practices, on the one hand, and the express provisions of the contract, on the other hand, the latter should normally prevail.[478] However, this may not be the case where

475. Final award, ICC case 8873 (1997) commented on in Christopher R Seppälä, 'International Construction Contract Disputes: Commentary on ICC Awards Dealing with the FIDIC International Conditions of Contract' (1998) 9(2) ICC Int'l Ct Arb Bull, 32, 45. *See also* the extract of this award, extracts 61-62.

476. Cited in Emmanuel Jolivet, Giacomo Marchisio and Fabien Gélinas, 'Trade Usages in ICC Arbitration' in Fabien Gélinas (ed), *Trade Usages and Implied Terms in the Age of Arbitration* (OUP, Oxford, 2016) 211, 220.

477. *Ibid.*

478. Stefan Vogenauer (ed), *Commentary on the UNIDROIT Principles of International Commercial Contracts (PICC)* (2nd edn, OUP, Oxford, 2015) 239-240 (para. 21). *See also* Michael Grose, *Construction Law in the United*

parties' continuous disregard of contractual provisions results in the establishment of practices between the parties which prevail over explicit contract terms (*see* **Section 8.2** above and the examples of practices established between the parties).

There may also be a conflict between trade usages and the law governing the contract. For example, trade usages may prescribe a higher standard for the quality of materials to form part of the works than the one prescribed by the governing law. Some arbitrators have applied trade usages to extend or modify the chosen governing law.[479] However, the prevailing view seems to be that arbitrators may not apply trade usages in a way that takes precedence over the governing law.[480] This view is certainly correct when provisions of the governing law have a mandatory character but not necessarily otherwise, e.g., where trade usages provide for a minimum quality standard higher than that of the governing law.

--ooOOoo--

Arab Emirates and the Gulf (Wiley Blackwell, Oxford, 2016) 38, fn. 16, referring to a decision of the Dubai Court of Cassation (Dubai Cassation no 138/1994 dated 13 November 1994) in which the court reversed a decision of the lower court by which a subcontractor's liability for delay damages was capped at 10% of the contract price in accordance with a common local practice. The Court of Cassation held that resort to local practice was inappropriate as the delay damages clause contained no cap.

479. Emmanuel Gaillard and John Savage (eds), *Fouchard Gaillard Goldman on International Arbitration* (Kluwer L Int'l, the Netherlands, 1999) 844-45 (para. 1513).

480. Gary Born, *International Commercial Arbitration* (3rd edn, Kluwer L Int'l, the Netherlands, 2021) vol II, 2986 (s 19.07); final award, ICC case 13954, YB Comm Arb, XXXV-2010, 218, 234. *See also* Emmanuel Gaillard and John Savage (eds), *Fouchard Gaillard Goldman on International Arbitration* (Kluwer L Int'l, the Netherlands, 1999) 846 (para. 1514).

Chapter III

Contract Interpretation

1 SCOPE OF CHAPTER

This chapter notes the special character of a FIDIC contract[1] and the frequent practical need to interpret it.[2] The chapter then compares the different approaches of state courts in civil law countries to contract interpretation with those in common law countries and describes the rules of contract interpretation in the UNIDROIT Principles, concluding with a list of widely accepted principles.[3] It then describes the particular considerations which need to be taken into account in interpreting a FIDIC contract, including the effect on such interpretation of an international arbitration clause,[4] and concludes with a practical approach to interpreting such a contract.[5]

2 CHARACTER OF A FIDIC CONTRACT

When interpreting a FIDIC contract, it is necessary to bear its particular character in mind. FIDIC contracts are drafted mainly by engineers for their practical use. As Christopher Wade, a former Chairman of FIDIC's Contracts Committee, has noted:

1. **Section 2.**
2. **Section 3.**
3. **Section 4.**
4. **Section 5.**
5. **Section 6.**

> [I]t should be emphasised that the contents of the FIDIC documents are essentially determined by engineers drawing on their extensive experience in contract management and on many diverse projects – in other words their 'engineering common sense'. Lawyers have performed an important role in ensuring legal consistency, but the topics covered and the principles involved are determined by engineers, and the Books are to be considered primarily *as handbooks for the management of the execution of engineering projects according to the best modern standards and practice.*[6] (Emphasis added)

As FIDIC contracts are for practical day-to-day use by engineers, they are intentionally drafted – by engineers – in a language that an engineer can understand without having to consult a lawyer. The industry-specific nature of the contract therefore needs to be borne in mind.

For example, in the course of certain litigation in Singapore relating to RB/99, the courts had initially set aside an ICC arbitral award enforcing a binding and not final decision of a DAB providing for a payment to the contractor,[7] based on their interpretation of the somewhat unclear wording of the dispute resolution clause (Clause 20) of RB/99.

However, when this issue was presented to the Singapore courts a second time, they grasped the 'engineering common sense' of the DAB in a FIDIC contract, and, contrary to their earlier ruling,[8] enforced the binding decision recognising – as they had not done initially – that this 'serves the

6. Christopher Wade, 'FIDIC's Standard Forms of Contract – Principles and Scope of the Four New Books' [2000] ICLR 5, 6.
7. *PT Perusahaan Gas Negara (Persero) TBK v CRW Joint Operation (Indonesia)* [2011] SGCA 33 ('Persero I'). In this case, the DAB had issued a decision awarding a sum of money to the Contractor. The Employer then issued a notice of dissatisfaction with that decision. Consequently, the decision was binding but not final and binding on the parties. But the Employer refused to pay it. The Contractor then began an ICC arbitration to enforce the decision by an arbitral award. The arbitral tribunal, by a majority, enforced the decision – given that it was temporarily binding, at least, on the parties – while at the same time recognising that the Employer had the right to have the DAB's decision reviewed on its merits and, if appropriate, overturned. The arbitral tribunal's award was set aside by the Singapore courts. *See* Christopher R Seppälä, 'How Not to Interpret the FIDIC Disputes Clause: The Singapore Court of Appeal Judgement in Persero' [2012] ICLR 4.
8. And to the great credit of the Singapore courts.

financial objective of safeguarding cash flow in the building and construction industry, especially that of the contractor, who is usually the receiving party'.[9]

Thus, appreciating and giving due weight to the particular commercial / engineering logic of a construction contract - such as the fundamental need to satisfy the contractor's reasonable cash flow requirements if it can be expected to continue to work without interruption - are important to bear in mind in contract interpretation.

3 IMPORTANCE OF INTERPRETATION

Construction contracts often give rise to difficult issues of interpretation because, among other things, of the following:

---

9. *PT Perusahaan Gas Negara (Persero) TBK v CRW Joint Operation (Indonesia)* (CA) [2015] SGCA 30 [para. 71] ('Persero II'). Under a FIDIC contract, whether RB/99 or RB/17, whereas the Employer provides the financing (*see* Sub-Clause 2.4), the Contractor is expected to construct the Works and, in exchange for regular interim payments, to do so without interruption (*see* Sub-Clause 8.1, second paragraph). Disputes are decided, at least on a provisional basis, by a DAAB (formerly a DAB) so as, among other things, to preserve the Contractor's cash flow and allow execution of the Works to continue uninterruptedly. The DAAB's decisions are binding on the Parties. If the DAAB decides a Contractor's claim against the Contractor, whether rightly or wrongly, the Contractor must continue working as the Contractor, like the Employer, takes the risk of a wrong decision and may refer the matter to ICC arbitration for correction. But if the DAAB decides in favour of the Contractor, whether rightly or wrongly, but the Employer does not pay the Contractor, then this may be a material breach of contract by the Employer. Unless promptly rectified, it may entitle the Contractor to suspend work (*see* Sub-Clause 16.1) or force it to finance the execution of the Works contrary to the basic assumption of the contract that this is for the Employer to do. *See* Christopher R Seppälä, 'The Second *Persero* Case before the Singapore Court of Appeal' (2015) 10 (4), C L Int, 19. To similar effect, *see* the following statement of the United States Supreme Court:

> As is usually the case with building contracts, it evidently was in the contemplation of the parties that *the contractor could not be expected to finance the operation to completion without receiving the stipulated payments on account as the work progressed.* In such cases a substantial compliance as to advance payments is a condition precedent to the contractor's obligation to proceed. *Guerini Stone Co v P.J. Carlin Constr. Co.* 248 U.S. 334, 345 (1919). [Emphasis added]

(i) They usually comprise a 'documentary bricolage'[10] – multiple documents of a different nature (drawings, specifications, schedules, conditions of contract, bills of quantities, etc.) – often drawn up by different people, each of which may address the same or similar subjects but do so in dissimilar ways.

(ii) They have both a technical and legal content, and just as lawyers may have difficulty understanding what is technical, so engineers may have difficulty understanding what is legal; yet each is often expected to work with – and even prepare – documentation having content of the other.

(iii) Whatever their profession, those who negotiate and prepare the contract may have little previous familiarity with FIDIC forms and how to modify or supplement them.

(iv) Those preparing or drafting the contract may have an English or Commonwealth background, and be employing common law principles and practices, whereas the law governing the contract may be that of a civil law country.

(v) While the language of the contract may often be English, those who prepare and negotiate the contract may lack fluency in English.

(vi) By whomever the contract is prepared, in the case of public works projects at least, qualified lawyers are often insufficiently involved at the drafting and negotiation stage.

As FIDIC forms are mainly for practical, day-to-day use on projects by engineers, how an engineer interprets a contract is of the greatest practical importance. The better and more even-handedly that they interpret contracts, the greater the chances that their instructions, determinations and actions will be accepted without referral to DAAB procedures and/or arbitration.

Below is a list of some commonly encountered scenarios requiring contract interpretation:

(i) There is a discrepancy between two or more documents that form part of the contract (e.g., the specification and the drawings) or within the same document (e.g., the specification).

10. Julian Bailey, *Construction Law* (3rd edn, London Publishing, UK, 2020) vol 1, 166 (para. 3.59).

(ii) There is a disagreement as to whether the employer or the contractor is responsible for obtaining a certain permit, licence and/or approval for the design and/or construction of the works.

(iii) The engineer has issued an instruction necessary for the execution of the works which the contractor argues amounts to a variation, entitling it to an EOT and/or additional payment.

(iv) The contractor claims additional payment and/or an EOT due to Unforeseeable (as defined in the Red Book) adverse physical conditions at the site, and the question arises as to what extent these were Unforeseeable.

(v) The contractor requests the issuance of a taking-over certificate, and a question arises as to whether the contractor has achieved a sufficient degree of completion to be entitled to one.

In cases such as this, the engineer may be called upon to interpret the contract. How should the engineer do this? What weight must the engineer give to the language of the contract as opposed to the general purpose of the provision concerned? Apart from the contract documents themselves, what other documents or evidence, if any, may the engineer consider (e.g., minutes of meetings or documents from contract negotiations) when interpreting a FIDIC contract? These and other questions will also be of concern to the DAAB, and later to international arbitrators and judges should they be required to interpret the contract.

Relatively little appears to have been written about interpreting specifically a construction contract. Clearly, how such a contract is to be interpreted should – as in the case of any contract – be decided, initially, by reference to the terms and wording of the contract itself. A careful, common-sense reading of the provision in dispute in the context of the contract as a whole – as contracts should be interpreted as a whole[11] – may be sufficient to resolve the issue.[12] Engineers experienced in dealing with contract documentation can often do this as well, if not better (as they know construction, and often construction documentation, better) than lawyers. However, if a scrupulous reading of the contract is

11. *See*, e.g., art. 4.4 (*Reference to contract or statement as a whole*) of the UNIDROIT Principles quoted in **Section 4.4 Widely Accepted Principles** below of **Chapter III Contract Interpretation**.

12. Reference to publications related to FIDIC contracts might also be made. *See* **Subsection 5.5 FIDIC's Publications** below of **Chapter III Contract Interpretation**.

insufficient, then it may be necessary to refer to the rules of contract interpretation provided for by the law (or rules of laws) which governs the contract.

Therefore, discussed below (in **Sections 4.1** and **4.2**) are the rules of contract interpretation of State courts of the two major legal systems (civil law and common law). Thereafter, consideration will be given to contract interpretation by reference to international principles (**Sections 4.3** and **4.4** below) and the special factors to be taken into account when interpreting a FIDIC contract (**Section 5** below), including the effect of an international arbitration clause (**Section 5.7** below). Finally, a practical method of interpreting a FIDIC contract is proposed (**Section 6** below).

4 DIFFERENT APPROACHES TO INTERPRETATION

Every country's system of law has rules or principles providing for how contracts governed by that country's law are to be interpreted. Accordingly, how a FIDIC contract is to be interpreted will, subject to what is stated below, be determined by the rules or principles on contract interpretation provided for by the law (or rules of law) which, according to Sub-Clause 1.4 [*Law and Language*], governs the contract.

Common law and civil law jurisdictions approach the matter of contract interpretation differently.[13] The next two sections examine the main differences in contract interpretation *as applied by State courts* in the two legal systems. This does not mean, however, that there are no differences in the rules of contract interpretation between countries in each of those systems. They most definitely do exist and, where relevant, some of these differences are pointed out, but it is not possible to do more within the confines of this book.

While the discussion in **Sections 4.1** and **4.2** describes the approach taken *by State courts*, FIDIC contracts provide for the final resolution of disputes *by international arbitration*, and as explained in **Section 5.7** below, international arbitrators may not apply a national law in the same way as a state court of that law would do. As explained in **Section 5.7** below, international arbitrators tend to do things differently. Therefore, what is stated in **Sections 4.1** and **4.2** below is qualified by **Section 5.7** below as concerns the interpretation of a FIDIC contract.

13. *See* **Section 4 Common Law and Civil Law Compared** of **Chapter II Applicable Law** above.

4.1 Civil Law: State Courts

Courts in civil law countries generally follow a subjective approach to contract interpretation. Under this approach, one should seek to discover the common or real intention of the contracting parties, that is, what the parties actually had in mind when they concluded the contract. If the parties' common intentions are established, those intentions should be given preference over the literal meaning of the interpreted contractual clause. For example:

The first paragraph of Article 1188 of the French Civil Code provides that:

> A contract is to be interpreted according to the common intention of the parties rather than stopping at the literal meaning of its terms.

Article 18 of the Swiss Federal Code of Obligations provides that:

> it is necessary to seek the real and common intention of the parties, instead of relying on the incorrect expressions or terms that they may have used in error, or with the aim of dissimulating the real nature of the contract.[14]

Similarly, under Section 133 of the German BGB:

> When a declaration of intent is interpreted, it is necessary to ascertain the true intention rather than adhering to the literal meaning of the declaration.[15]

In order to determine the parties' common intention, one may look at any evidence that may be of assistance, including the parties' pre-contractual negotiations, subjective declarations of intent and the conduct of the parties after the conclusion of the contract.[16]

This approach can be exemplified by ICC case 17146 of 2013.[17] The case concerned a contract for the construction of a pipeline in an Eastern

---

14. Unofficial translation.
15. Unofficial translation. BGB is the German acronym of the German Civil Code (in German: *Bürgerliches Gesetzbuch*).
16. *See*, e.g., for Swiss law, Shona Frame and Sam Moss, 'UK v Swiss Law on Contract Interpretation: Which Approach Is Best Suited to International Construction Contracts?' (2015) 3(10) C L Int 9, 11.
17. Final award, ICC case 17146 (2013), ICC Disp Resol Bull, Issue 1 (2015) 114-25.

European country, and the governing law was the law of the same country (a civil law country). An ICC tribunal was constituted. There was no designation of the arbitral institution that had to administer the case under the executed contractual documents and the employer challenged the jurisdiction of the ICC tribunal on this ground. The tribunal confirmed its jurisdiction by taking into account drafts exchanged between the parties during the negotiation of the contract that revealed the parties' common intention to submit disputes to arbitration under the ICC Rules.[18]

Although the civil law approach gives primacy to the parties' common intentions, the interpretation of a contract will start with the terms of the contract which are seen as a strong indicator of their intentions.[19] Furthermore, the application of the subjective approach of contract interpretation in civil law countries is usually balanced against other factors having an objective character. For example, since the reform of French contract law in 2016,[20] the French Civil Code has provided that if the parties' common intention cannot be ascertained from the available evidence, the contract will be interpreted as having the meaning which a reasonable person in the same situation would have given it.[21] Reference to the standard of a reasonable person – an objective standard – brings French law closer to the common law.[22]

The French Civil Code identifies several factors that are to be taken into account to determine the parties' common intention. First, all terms of a

18. The drafts contained the sentence: 'Insert rules of arbitration if different from those of the International Chamber of Commerce', *see* para. 446 (page 122).
19. This is implicit from art. 1188, first paragraph, of the French Civil Code: 'A contract is to be interpreted according to the common intention of the parties *rather than stopping at the literal meaning of its terms*.' (Emphasis added) This provision assumes that interpretation begins with 'the literal meaning of [the contract's] terms'. Moreover, art. 1192 of the same code provides that '[c]lear and unambiguous terms are not subject to interpretation'. However, as discussed later in this **Section**, this latter principle is no longer accepted in Germany or Switzerland.
20. Even before the reform in 2016, the French Civil Code contained guides to contract interpretation in nine articles (arts 1156-64) which added an element of objectivity to the process. Certain of these were not retained in the new Code as a result of the reform whereas others have been added, *see* new arts 1188-1192 of the French Civil Code.
21. Art. 1188 of the French Civil Code, second paragraph.
22. *See* **Section 4.2 Common Law: State Courts** immediately below.

contract are to be interpreted in relation to each other, giving to each the meaning that respects the consistency of the contract as a whole.[23] Where, according to the parties' common intention, several contracts contribute to one and the same operation, they are to be interpreted by reference to this operation.[24] In case of ambiguity, a bespoke contract is to be interpreted against the creditor and in favour of the debtor, and an adhesion contract is to be interpreted against the person who put it forward.[25] Where a contract term is capable of bearing two meanings, the one which gives it some effect is to be preferred to the one which makes it produce no effect.[26]

In some civil law countries, such as France, Egypt and most countries in the Arabian Gulf, the wording of the contract may have a decisive role. Thus, pursuant to the French doctrine of clear and precise terms (*la doctrine des termes clairs et précis*)[27] if a clause is clear and unambiguous, it is not subject to interpretation.[28] Consequently, a sufficiently clear clause should be respected and there is no reason to interpret it with a view to identifying whether the parties meant something different from what has been expressed. As a clear and unambiguous clause is such a strong indication of the parties' intention, it may not be undermined by reference to other factors that will necessarily be less strong.[29] However,

23. French Civil Code, art. 1189, para. 1.
24. French Civil Code, art. 1189, para. 2.
25. French Civil Code, art. 1190.
26. French Civil Code, art. 1191.
27. Pursuant to the French Civil Code, art. 1192: 'Clear and unambiguous terms are not subject to interpretation as doing so risks their distortion.' For a more detailed discussion of the doctrine, *see* Hugh Beale and others, *Cases, Materials and Text on Contract Law* (3rd edn, Hart Publishing, Oxford, 2019) 731-43.
28. The same doctrine applies in Egypt. Pursuant to art. 150(1) of the Egyptian Civil Code: 'When the wording of a contract is clear, it cannot be deviated from in order to ascertain by interpretation the intention of the parties.' As to the position of the doctrine and its application in the Arabian Gulf countries, *see* Michael Grose, *Construction Law in the United Arab Emirates and the Gulf* (Wiley Blackwell, Oxford, 2016) 36-38. The doctrine applies in Panama (art. 1132, Civil Code).
29. *See*, for example, Cass civ 14 December 1942, D 1944, 112. In this case, a contract for the supply of fish clearly provided that the quantities to be sold would depend on the quantities caught as determined by an industry federation. Consequently, the seller could not be liable in damages for

this doctrine does not have universal application in civil law countries and it is no longer applied in Germany[30] or Switzerland.[31]

4.2 Common Law: State Courts

The rules of contract interpretation applied by courts in the common law world are more complex than those in civil law countries. In general, common law jurisdictions follow an objective method of contract interpretation that gives primary weight to the text of the contract. The focus is not on the subjective intentions of the parties, but on their objective expression, i.e., on the words actually used by the parties. The principal position in common law countries, which generally follow the so-called parol evidence rule (discussed in **Section 4.2.2** below), is that extrinsic evidence is not admissible to interpret a written contract. There are however numerous exceptions to this rule.

4.2.1 English Law

The approach to contract interpretation under English law is stated by Lord Hoffmann in the leading English House of Lords case of *Investors Compensation Scheme v West Bromwich Building Society*:

> Interpretation is the ascertainment of the meaning which the document would convey to a reasonable person having all the background knowledge which would reasonably have been available to the parties in the situation in which they were at the time of the contract.[32]

---

reducing the quantity of fish to be sold by 50% when it was observing a decision of this federation as clearly required by the contract.

30. In Germany, the doctrine (known as '*Eindeutigkeitsregel*') was applied until the 1980s when the Supreme Court decided that it should not be followed any longer (*see* Hugh Beale and others, *Cases, Materials and Text on Contract Law* (3rd edn, Hart Publishing, Oxford, 2019) 737).
31. In Switzerland, the doctrine was applied until the beginning of the 2000s, when the Swiss Supreme Court decided to abandon it. *See* Hugh Beale and others, *Cases, Materials and Text on Contract Law* (3rd edn, Hart Publishing, Oxford, 2019) 737 (footnote 28) and Sam Moss, 'Swiss Law vs English Law on Contract Interpretation: Is Swiss Law Better Suited to the Realities of International Construction Contracts' [2015] ICLR 470, 477.
32. *Investors Compensation Scheme v West Bromwich Building Society* [1998] 1 WLR 896, 912. In *Bank of Credit & Commerce International SA v ALI* [2001] 1 AC 25, Lord Hoffmann marginally adjusted what he said by clarifying that

In other words, the guiding criterion is not what the parties had in mind when they signed the contract (subjective element), but how a reasonable commercial person with the same background knowledge as the parties would have understood the text of the agreement (objective element). As stated in *Chartbrook Limited v Persimmon Homes*, 'the document should, so far as possible, speak for itself'.[33] The language of the contract is of paramount importance.[34] Words in ordinary usage are given their usual meaning, and technical words their technical meaning, unless the context suggests otherwise.[35]

The extent to which one looks to the text or to the context to ascertain the objective meaning of the language in an agreement will vary according to the circumstances.[36] The text may be given more weight in well-drafted agreements, whereas the 'factual matrix' of the case may be given more weight in less well-drafted ones.[37] Because of the need sometimes for negotiators to compromise, even well-drafted agreements may contain unclear provisions for whose interpretation it may be helpful to consider their factual matrix.[38]

If there is an ambiguity in a certain clause so that there are two possible interpretations, the court is entitled to prefer the interpretation that is consistent with business common sense and reject the other one.[39] However, business common sense may be relevant to the interpretation only to the extent that it would or could have been perceived by the parties at the time the contract was made.[40] Consequently, there is no ground to depart from the language of the contract if the contract has worked out badly, or even disastrously, for one of the parties due to

---

the background knowledge that a reasonable person must have must be relevant: 'I meant anything which a reasonable man would have regarded as *relevant*' [para. 39].

33. *Chartbrook Limited v Persimmon Homes Limited and Others* [2009] UKHL 38, 1 AC 1101 [para. 36].
34. *Arnold v Britton* [2015] UKSC 36, 2 WLR 1593 [para. 17].
35. Atkin Chambers, *Hudson's Building and Engineering Contracts* (14th edn, Sweet & Maxwell, London, 2020) 31 (para. 1-031).
36. *Wood v Capita Insurance Services Ltd* [2017] UKSC 24 [para. 13].
37. *Ibid.*
38. *Ibid.*
39. *Rainy Sky v Kookmin Bank* [2011] UKSC 50, [2011] 1 WLR 2900 [paras 14-30].
40. *Arnold v Britton* [2015] UKSC 36, 2 WLR 1593 [para. 19].

events following its execution.[41] This approach can be illustrated by the UK Supreme Court decision of *Arnold v Britton*, where the court dealt with several 99-year lease agreements executed in the 1970s containing a service charge provision that provided for an annual payment of GBP 90 for the first year subject to a 10% annual increase on a compound basis for each subsequent year. The consequences of the provision were 'plainly unattractive, indeed alarming' to lessees from a commercial perspective, as they would have allowed the lessors to charge an exorbitant amount of service charge at the end of the lease period, which would be in sharp disparity with the current annual inflation rates in England.[42] Nevertheless, the clause was upheld by the court as the wording of the clause was clear.[43] It was pointed out that the service charge provision was not devoid of business common sense at the time when the agreements were entered into as the inflation rates then were higher. According to the court, the notion of commercial common sense could not be applied retrospectively, and therefore there was no sufficient ground to depart from the plain meaning of the words.[44]

41. *Ibid.* [19] and *Wood v Capita Insurance Services Ltd* [2017] UK SC 24 [para. 41].
42. Under the clause, the lessors would have been entitled to charge service charges of over GBP 550,000 per annum at the end of the lease period. Furthermore, the 10% annual increase envisaged in the contracts was in sharp contrast to the current annual inflation rate in England, which in the previous 15 years had hardly ever been above 4% and had constantly been falling almost to the point of turning negative, *see Arnold v Britton* [2015] UKSC 36, 2 WLR 1593 [para. 30].
43. There was a dissenting judgment by Lord Carnwath, who said that the clause in question produced 'commercial nonsense' and that the court should have done its utmost to find a way to substitute a more likely alternative. *See Arnold v Britton* [2015] UKSC 36, 2 WLR 1593 [paras 115 and 158] (Lord Carnwath).
44. *Ibid.* [19]. The English courts applied the *Arnold v Britton* rule to a construction context in *Balfour Beatty v Grove Developments* [2016] EWCA Civ 990, [2017] BLR 1. In that case, the Court of Appeal found that '[c]ommercial common sense can only come to the rescue of a contracting party if it is clear in all the circumstances what the parties intended, or would have intended, to happen in the circumstances which subsequently arose' [para. 42]. In that case, the contractor had appealed against a decision that it had no entitlement to interim payments after the contractual date for practical completion. The appeal was dismissed because it was not clear on what dates and by what valuation method the parties would have intended interim payments to continue beyond that contractual date.

The interpretation of individual contract clauses may be revised on the basis of the rule that one must look at the contract as a whole and divine its overall purpose.[45] Consequently, words or whole provisions that are inconsistent with the main purpose of the contract may be rejected.[46]

4.2.2 Parol Evidence Rule

A corollary of the objective approach followed in England and other common law jurisdictions is the so-called parol evidence rule.[47] Pursuant to this rule, a party to a written contract is not permitted to adduce evidence that is extraneous to that contract to show that the contractual terms have a different meaning from the one recorded.[48] Thus, the parol evidence rule excludes as inadmissible a wide range of extrinsic evidence, such as any evidence of pre-contractual negotiations, declarations of subjective intent, parties' conduct and so forth.[49] Evidence from the professional body that produced the standard form used by the parties as to that body's understanding or intent as to the meaning of a particular term or clause in the standard form will also be inadmissible.[50] Earlier editions of the same standard form used by the parties are equally inadmissible.[51]

As mentioned above, there are many exceptions to the parol evidence rule, only some of which will be referred to here. First, extrinsic evidence is admissible to consider the relevant background surrounding the contract. This background (often referred to in England as 'the matrix of facts' or the 'commercial context') 'includes absolutely anything which would have affected the way in which the language of the document

45. Atkin Chambers, *Hudson's Building and Engineering Contracts* (14th edn, Sweet & Maxwell, London, 2020) 36 (para. 1-037).
46. *Glynn v Margetson & Co* [1893] AC 351, 357. *See* Isabel Hitching, 'Recent Developments in Interpretation of Contracts: A Picture of Consistency and Clarity?', SCL paper 223, April 2020.
47. Also referred to as the 'exclusionary rule'. *See Chartbrook Limited v Persimmon Homes Limited and Others* [2009] UKHL 38, 1 AC 1101 [para. 32].
48. Julian Bailey, *Construction Law* (3rd edn, London Publishing, UK, 2020) vol 1, 236-37 (para. 3-191).
49. *Chartbrook Limited v Persimmon Homes Limited and Others* [2009] UKHL 38, 1 AC 1101 [paras 41 and 42].
50. Julian Bailey, *Construction Law* (3rd edn, London Publishing, UK, 2020) vol 1, 239 (para. 3.194). *See also National Coal Board v Leonard & Partners* [1985] 31 BLR 117.
51. *Blackpool Borough Council v F Parkinson Ltd* [1991] 58 BLR 85, 103.

would have been understood by a reasonable man'.[52] The background of the contract can be considered even if there is no apparent ambiguity in the written document.[53] It should, however, be emphasised that it is only the background that is known or reasonably available to both parties at contract signature which is relevant to interpretation.[54] Therefore, a fact or circumstance that is known to one of the parties alone may not be taken into account. A prior contract that is followed by a further contract could form part of the admissible background in the interpretation of the latter contract if the first contract was not intended to be superseded by the second.[55] Thus, for example, if an employer hires a contractor to lay down the foundations of a building and later on decides to hire that same contractor to construct the building, the first contract can be considered in the interpretation of the second one. The parties' pre-contractual negotiations and declarations of subjective intent remain inadmissible when considering the relevant background,[56] but the precise boundaries of this exclusionary rule remain somewhat unclear.[57] Post-contract conduct is also inadmissible as an aid to interpretation.[58]

52. *Investors Compensation Scheme Ltd v West Bromwich Building Society* [1998] 1 WLR 896, 913. But 'absolutely anything' was later qualified by Lord Hoffmann in *Bank of Credit & Commerce International SA v ALI* [2001] 1 AC 25. *See* fn. 32 above of **Chapter III Contract Interpretation.**
53. *Chartbrook Limited v Persimmon Homes Limited and Others* [2009] UKHL 38, 1 AC 1101 [para. 37].
54. *Arnold v Britton* [2015] UKSC 36, 2 WLR 1593 [para. 21].
55. Atkin Chambers, *Hudson's Building and Engineering Contracts* (14th edn, Sweet & Maxwell, London, 2020) 34-35 (para. 1-035). *See also HIH Casualty & General Insurance Ltd v New Hampshire Insurance* [2001] 2 LLoyd's Rep 161, [2001] EWCA Civ 735 [para. 83].
56. *Investors Compensation Scheme Ltd v West Bromwich Building Society* [1998] 1 WLR 896, 913. But 'absolutely anything' was later qualified by Lord Hoffmann in *Bank of Credit & Commerce International SA v ALI* [2001] 1 AC 25. *See* fn. 32 above of **Chapter III Contract Interpretation.**
57. For example, in *Chartbrook Limited v Persimmon Homes Limited and Others* [2009] UKHL 38, 1 AC 1101 [paras 33 and 42], the court found that evidence of pre-contractual negotiations could be used to establish a fact relevant to the background known by the parties.
58. Atkin Chambers, *Hudson's Building and Engineering Contracts* (14th edn, Sweet & Maxwell, London, 2020) 34 (para. 1-035).

Second, there are a number of other exceptions that allow the introduction of extrinsic evidence.[59]

---

59. Those that are probably most relevant to the construction sector are the following:
    (i) Extrinsic evidence is admissible to determine whether a contract has actually been formed, i.e., whether the essential elements are present. *Chitty on Contracts* (33rd edn, Sweet & Maxwell, London, 2018) vol 1, 1085 (para. 13-119).
    (ii) Evidence of pre-contractual negotiations may be admissible in cases where the meaning of certain words in a contract is unclear if they can shed light on their true meaning. *Partenreederei MS Karen Oltmann v Scarsdale Shipping co* [1976] 2 LLoyd's Rep 708 [para. 712] (*The Karen Oltmann*). In this case, the court had to determine the meaning of the word 'after' in the phrase 'after 12 months' trading'. After looking at earlier telex exchanges the court decided that the phrase meant on the expiry of 12 months and not at any time after 12 months. However, Lord Hoffmann and the House of Lords in *Chartbrook Limited v Persimmon Homes Limited and Others* [2009] UKHL 38, 1 AC 1101 [para. 47] stated that this decision was not legitimate:

    > On its facts, *The Karen Oltmann* was in my opinion an illegitimate extension of the 'private dictionary' principle which, taken to its logical conclusion, would destroy the exclusionary rule and any practical advantages which it may have.

    The 'private dictionary' principle provides that evidence may be adduced that parties 'habitually used words in an unconventional sense in order to support an argument that words in a contract should bear a similar unconventional meaning' [para. 45].
    (iii) Subsequent conduct of the parties may be considered to determine the parties' original intentions in cases where the construction contract was made partly in writing and partly orally. Julian Bailey, *Construction Law* (3rd edn, London Publishing, UK, 2020) vol 1, 240-241 (para. 3.197).
    (iv) Extrinsic evidence is admissible if it takes the form of another contract entered into as part of the same 'single transaction'. For example, *Bailey*, referring to case law in Singapore, states that a main contract may be read together with a contemporaneously executed contract between the employer and a design professional concerning the same project. *Ibid.*, 242. *See also Sunny Metal & Engineering Pte Ltd v Ng Khim Ming Eric* [2007] 3 SLR(R) 782 [para. 30].
    (v) Evidence is admissible to show that a word used in a contract is used in accordance with a special custom or usage which is notorious to everyone in the trade or locality applicable to the contract, provided

4.2.3 *United States Law*

Broadly speaking, the rules of contract interpretation in the United States also follow an objective method of contract interpretation that gives primary weight to the text of the contract. Therefore, the rules of contract interpretation in the United States are similar to those of English law, described above. There are however some notable differences. First, there has been case law suggesting that in certain instances US courts are prepared to give effect to the subjective meaning shared by both parties

---

that it is not inconsistent with the express or necessarily implied terms of the contract. Stephen Furst and Vivian Ramsey, *Keating on Construction Contracts* (11th edn, Sweet & Maxwell, London, 2021) 51-52 (para. 3-023). For example, in *Symonds v Lloyd* (1859) 6 CB (NS) 691, the term 'reduced brickwork' was interpreted to mean brickwork nine inches thick.

(vi) Extrinsic evidence is admissible if it is alleged that a liquidated damages clause in a contract operates as a penalty and is thus under English law unenforceable, and the question arises as to whether the amount required by the clause to be paid actually constitutes a penalty. *See* Julian Bailey, *Construction Law* (3rd edn, London Publishing, UK, 2020) vol 1, 242 (para. 3.197). *See also Azimut-Benetti Spa v Healey* [2010] 132 Con LR 113 [117], and *Multiplex Construction Pty Ltd v Abgarus Pty Ltd* [1992] 33 NSWLR 504 [paras 507-513].

(vii) Extrinsic evidence is admissible in a claim under English law for rectification (in the United States, the rectification of contracts is known as 'reformation of contracts'), i.e., a party's claim for rectifying words in a contract that have been mistakenly used by the parties. Even though rectification is conceptually different from interpretation, the line to be drawn between these two mechanisms is not always straightforward. Atkin Chambers, *Hudson's Building and Engineering Contracts* (14th edn, Sweet & Maxwell, London, 2020) 37 (para. 1-039). Rectification should be distinguished from cases where there is an obvious error in the contract. In the latter case, an English court will usually interpret the contract as if the error had been corrected in order to give effect to the intentions of the parties. *See* Julian Bailey, *Construction Law* (3rd edn, London Publishing, UK, 2020) vol 1, 235 (para. 3.188). *See also Liberty Mercian Ltd v Dean & Dyball Construction Ltd* [2008] EWHC 2617 (TCC) [paras 19-21]. Thus, for example, when the contract lists various dates 'of' completion and it is clear that they were meant to be dates 'for' completion, the court will interpret the contract as if the latter had been written into the text.

in preference to an objective meaning.[60] The *Restatement (Second) of Contracts* adopts this approach.[61]

Another difference concerns the breadth of the context within which words should be read.[62] As mentioned above, in England extrinsic evidence is in principle admissible to determine the commercial context, i.e., the relevant background existing at the time when the parties entered into the contract. This contextual approach may be employed even if there is no apparent ambiguity on the face of the document.[63] On the other hand, in the United States, if the words used by the parties have a plain meaning, extrinsic evidence is not normally admissible in any circumstances – not even to show that there is an ambiguity behind the otherwise plain wording of the text.[64] This is known as the 'plain meaning' rule. In order to determine whether the rule applies, the judge should first make a preliminary determination on whether the agreement in question is sufficiently clear or ambiguous. The prevailing view is that in that determination the judge should normally look solely to the writing.[65] Extrinsic evidence may be admitted in the interpretation

---

60. E Allan Farnsworth, *Contracts* (4th edn, Aspen, NY, 2004) 445-448 (para. 7.9). *See also Berke Moore Co v Phoenix Bridge Co* 98 A2d 150, 156 (NH 1953), *Sprucewood Investment Corporation v Alaska Housing Finance Corporation*, 33 P3d 1156, 1163-1164 (Alaska 2001), and *Sunbury Textile Mills v Commissioner*, 585 F2d 1190, 1198-1199 (3d Cir 1978).
61. *See* s 201(1) of the *Restatement (Second) of Contracts* (ALI, Philadelphia, PA, 1981) that states: 'Where the parties have attached the same meaning to a promise or agreement or a term thereof, it is interpreted in accordance with that meaning.'
62. Joshua Karton, *The Culture of International Arbitration and the Evolution of Contract Law* (OUP, Oxford, 2013) 200-201.
63. However, such evidence will not cause the court to depart from the clear meaning of a provision. For example, while the relevant background of annual inflation rates was admissible in *Arnold v Britton* (*see* at [30]), the court still found that the natural meaning of the service charge clause was not to be departed from.
64. Justin Sweet and Marc M Schneier, *Legal Aspects of Architecture, Engineering and the Construction Process* (9th edn, Cengage Learning, Stamford, CT, 2013) 484.
65. *See* Joseph M Perillo, *Contracts* (7th edn, West Publishing, St Paul, MN, 2014) 136-137 (s 3.10), who states that the (US) courts divide on the question of whether extrinsic evidence is admissible to show that a term of the written agreement is ambiguous. Farnsworth states that evidence of

process only if the contract is ambiguous.[66] Although the plain meaning rule is not universally applied in the United States,[67] it is still followed in the great majority of states.[68] An exception to the plain meaning rule in certain States is that, even if the wording of the contract is unambiguous, evidence of industry custom and usages may be adduced to show that a term has a specialised meaning different from its ordinary meaning.[69] For example, if the parties have used a term which has a clear ordinary

surrounding circumstances, as distinguished from evidence of prior negotiations, should be admitted at the first stage to determine whether the meaning is ambiguous as opposed to 'plain'. He describes two different views (the 'restrictive' and the 'liberal' one) as to what types of extrinsic evidence may be considered for the purposes of such a preliminary determination. Under the restrictive view, the determination of whether language is ambiguous is made on the basis of the language itself in light of the surrounding circumstances but without regard to prior negotiations. Under the liberal view, evidence of prior negotiations is admissible for purposes of determining whether the language is ambiguous. E Allan Farnsworth, *Contracts* (4th edn, Aspen, NY, 2004) 461-469 (para. 7.12).

66. Justin Sweet and others, *Construction Law for Design Professionals, Construction Managers, and Contractors* (Cengage Learning, Stamford, CT, 2015) 46. *See also TEG-Paradigm Environmental Inc v United States*, 465 F3d 1329 (2006).
67. *See* Joseph M Perillo, *Contracts* (7th edn, West Publishing, St Paul, MN, 2014) 139-142 (s 3.11-3.12) who refers, among other things, to rules of contract interpretation proposed by Messrs. Williston and Corbin, highly respected US contract law scholars, both of whom reject the application of the plain meaning rule. *See also*, for example, *TEG-Paradigm Environmental Inc v United States*, 465 F3d 1329 (2006), where the court considered a pre-bid conference call in order to confirm its interpretation of the otherwise plain meaning of the terms of the contract. Moreover, the *Restatement (Second) of Contracts* allows the admission of extrinsic evidence – for example, s 214 states that evidence of prior or contemporaneous agreements and negotiations are admissible in evidence to establish, among other things, the meaning of the writing.
68. E Allan Farnsworth, *Contracts* (4th edn, Aspen, NY, 2004) 463 (para. 7.12). *See also* Justin Sweet and Marc Schneier, *Legal Aspects of Architecture, Engineering and the Construction Process* (9th edn, Cengage Learning, Stamford, CT, 2013) 485.
69. John M Mastin and others (eds), *Smith, Currie & Hancock's Common Sense Construction Law: A Practical Guide for the Construction Professional* (6th edn, Wiley, Hoboken, NJ, 2020) 17.

meaning, industry custom may be used to show that the term is susceptible to two meanings and the parties have used it as having a meaning that complies with industry custom.[70]

Another difference between England and the United States concerns the type of extrinsic evidence that may be admitted. As mentioned above, pre-contractual negotiations and post-contract conduct of the parties are largely inadmissible in English courts; they may in principle not be considered even as part of the factual background surrounding the contract. Such evidence may only be adduced in situations falling within one of the specific exceptions to the parol evidence rule referred to above. On the other hand, US courts will likely be prepared to consider this type of extraneous evidence whenever there is an ambiguity in the contract terms, in order to ascertain the true intention of the parties.[71] Therefore, when it comes to interpretation of ambiguous contract terms, the approach in the United States resembles to some extent the civil law approach.

4.3 International Approach: UNIDROIT Principles

The UNIDROIT Principles 2016, which have been prepared by experts from both civil law and common law systems,[72] may be stated to reflect best practice as far as the law of international commercial contracts is concerned. They are widely relied upon by arbitral tribunals.[73]

70. *TEG-Paradigm Environmental Inc v United States*, 465 F3d 1329 (2006).
71. *See* E Allan Farnsworth, *Contracts* (4th edn, Aspen, NY, 2004) 461-462 (para. 7.12); John M Mastin and others (eds), *Smith, Currie, and Hancock's Common Sense Construction Law: A Practical Guide for the Construction Professional* (6th edn, Wiley, Hoboken, NJ, 2020) 15-16; Justin Sweet and Marc Schneier, *Legal Aspects of Architecture, Engineering and the Construction Process* (9th edn, Cengage Learning, Stamford, CT, 2013) 475. *See also EnerQuest Oil & Gas LLC v Plains Exploration & Production Co*, 981 F Supp 2d 575 (WD Tex 2013); *Hickman v Kralicek Realty and Constr Co*, 129 SW3d 317 (Ark App 2003); E Allan Farnsworth, 'The Interpretation of International Contracts and the Use of Preambles' (2002) RDAI/IBLJ no 3/4, 271.
72. *See* **Section 7.2 UNIDROIT Principles** of **Chapter II Applicable Law** above.
73. Juan Eduardo Figueroa Valdés, 'The Use of the UNIDROIT Principles by Arbitrators in International Construction Projects' (2015) 10(1) C L Int 24, 27.

Pursuant to Article 4.1 (*Intention of the parties*) of the Principles:

(1) A contract shall be interpreted according to the common intention of the parties.
(2) If such an intention cannot be established, the contract shall be interpreted according to the meaning that reasonable persons of the same kind as the parties would give to it in the same circumstances.

Thus, as a starting point in paragraph (1), the Principles adopt a subjective approach to contract interpretation that is similar to the civil law approach (described in **Section 4.1** above). According to paragraph (2), only if the parties' common intention cannot be established may the interpreter rely on the objective method of contract interpretation, that is, on how a reasonable third person of the same kind as the parties would have understood the terms of the contract. Under the UNIDROIT Principles, in order to establish what the parties' common intention is or, if such intention cannot be established, how a reasonable person would have understood the contract regard is to be had to all relevant circumstances, including those in Article 4.3 (*Relevant circumstances*). Pursuant to that Article, all circumstances include:

(a) preliminary negotiations between the parties;
(b) practices which the parties have established between themselves;
(c) the conduct of the parties subsequent to the conclusion of the contract;
(d) the nature and purpose of the contract;
(e) the meaning commonly given to terms and expressions in the trade concerned;
(f) usages.

The above list is not exhaustive and thus there may be other circumstances which should be considered.[74] This method of contract interpretation resembles the civil law approach and, most particularly, the French approach.[75]

74. *See* official comments 1 and 2 to art. 4.3 of the Principles.
75. Discussed in **Section 4.1 Civil Law: State Courts** above of **Chapter III Contract Interpretation**.

However, the UNIDROIT Principles provide that the method of interpretation under Article 4.1 of the Principles may not always be appropriate in the context of contracts based on 'standard terms', that is, contract provisions 'prepared in advance for general and repeated use by one party and which are actually used without negotiation with the other party'.[76] This would be relevant, for example, to standard conditions of contract based on a FIDIC form, used regularly by a ministry of public works in invitations to tender, and which a tenderer is to accept on a 'take it or leave it basis'. In these circumstances, the Principles indicate that the subjective test in paragraph (1) and the 'reasonableness' test in paragraph (2) of Article 4.1 may be inappropriate, and that these standard terms should instead be interpreted:

> primarily in accordance with the reasonable expectations of their average users irrespective of the actual understanding which either of the parties to the contract concerned, or reasonable persons of the same kind as the parties, might have had.[77]

This would provide an opening for resort to published commentaries or interpretations of the relevant conditions to the extent they represent the reasonable expectations of average users.

4.4 Widely Accepted Principles

The UNIDROIT Principles provide for a number of principles of contract interpretation that derive from, and are common to, the common law and civil law systems. They may therefore be considered to be broadly applicable to FIDIC contracts, subject to the relevant governing law.

Thus, Article 4.4 (*Reference to contract or statement as a whole*) of the Principles provides that: '[t]erms and expressions shall be interpreted in the light of the whole contract or statement in which they appear'.

Article 4.5 (*All terms to be given effect*) of the Principles stipulates another widely accepted principle of contract interpretation: '[c]ontracts terms shall be interpreted so as to give effect to all the terms rather than to deprive some of them of effect'.

Article 4.5 comes into play only if the terms in question remain unclear, notwithstanding the application of the basic rules of interpretation in

76. Art. 2.1.19 (*Contracting under standard terms*), para. (2) of the Principles.
77. Official comment 4 to art. 4.1 of the Principles.

Article 4.1 and 4.3 discussed above.[78] It recognises that when parties draft a contract they normally intend that each of its provisions has a certain meaning and effect.

The Principles also provide for the *contra proferentem* rule in Article 4.6 (*Contra proferentem rule*):

> If contract terms supplied by one party are unclear, an interpretation against that party is preferred.

This rule allows an ambiguous provision in a contract to be construed against the party that prepared or put forward the contract and is widely recognised in both civil law and common law countries.[79] Contractual provisions to which the rule is typically applied include limitation of liability clauses, liquidated damages clauses and indemnity provisions.[80]

Article 4.7 (*Linguistic discrepancies*) of the Principles deals with linguistic discrepancies in the interpreted document:

> Where a contract is drawn up in two or more language versions which are equally authoritative there is, in case of discrepancy between the

78. *See* official comment to art. 4.5 of the Principles.
79. Pursuant to art. 1190 of the French Civil Code:

    > In case of ambiguity, a bespoke contract is interpreted against the creditor and in favour of the debtor, and a standard form contract is interpreted against the person who put it forward.

    Pursuant to art. 151 of the Egyptian Civil Code:

    > (1) A doubt shall be resolved in favour of the obligor/debtor;
    > (2) Nevertheless it shall not be permissible to construe ambiguous words in contracts of adhesion in a manner detrimental to the interests of the adhering party.

    Similar provisions exist in countries of the Arabian Gulf (*see*, e.g., art. 266 of the UAE Civil Code). For the English common law position, *see Persimmon Homes Ltd v Ove Arup & Partners Ltd* [2017] EWCA Civ 373 where it was stated, in relation to an exemption clause, that the *contra proferentem* rule has 'a very limited role' [para. 52] in commercial contracts negotiated between parties of equal bargaining power and that such rule is more relevant to indemnity clauses than exemption clauses [para. 56].
80. Julian Bailey, *Construction Law* (3rd edn, London Publishing, UK, 2020) vol 1, 227 (para. 3.169). The application of this rule in the context of a FIDIC contract is addressed in **Section 5.3** below.

versions, a preference for the interpretation according to a version in which the contract was originally drawn up.

International construction contracts are often drafted in two or more language versions. If they have been well prepared the parties will explicitly stipulate which language version shall prevail,[81] in which case there would be no need to apply Article 4.7. This article will only apply in the relatively rare cases where the different language versions are specified as equally authoritative, or if the contract in question does not address which language version shall prevail.[82]

5 INTERPRETING A FIDIC CONTRACT

Interpreting a FIDIC contract has its own particular features. First, the FIDIC forms, like the Red Book, contain specific provisions concerning contract interpretation, and therefore these are discussed first (**Section 5.1**). In addition, the following matters may be relevant in interpreting a FIDIC contract and are discussed below:

- the language of the contract (**Section 5.2**);
- the potential application of the *contra proferentem* rule (**Section 5.3**);
- deletions from the FIDIC's general conditions (**Section 5.4**);
- FIDIC's publications (**Section 5.5**);
- foreign case law, treatises and comparative law generally (**Section 5.6**); and
- the international arbitration clause in the FIDIC forms (**Section 5.7**).

5.1 Specific Contract Provisions

5.1.1 Sub-Clauses Dealing with Interpretation

By far the most important consideration in interpreting a FIDIC contract will be the terms of the particular contract which incorporates the FIDIC form. The FIDIC forms themselves provide extensive guidance as to how they are to be interpreted. While the relevant Sub-Clauses dealing with

81. As foreseen by Sub-Clause 1.4 [*Law and Language*] and the form of Contract Data of RB/17.
82. *See* **Section 5.2 Relevance of Language** below of **Chapter III Contract Interpretation**.

interpretation will be discussed in detail in the Clause-by-Clause commentary (**Chapter IV** below) the following are perhaps the main provisions dealing with interpretation in RB/17:

Sub-Clause 1.1 [*Definitions*] contains nearly ninety defined terms. There are also defined terms in the General Conditions that are not in Sub-Clause 1.1 (e.g. in Sub-Clauses 4.12, 5.2.1, 17.3, 20.2.3 and 20.2.4).

Sub-Clause 1.2 [*Interpretation*] describes how certain terms are to be interpreted and notes that marginal words and other headings are not to be taken into consideration in the interpretation of the Conditions.

Sub-Clause 1.3 [*Notices and Other Communications*] describes how Notices and communications are to be made and when they are deemed to have been received.

Sub-Clause 1.4 [*Law and Language*] provides for the law[83] of the country that shall govern the contract and, where versions of the Contract are in different languages, which language version shall prevail.

Sub-Clause 1.5 [*Priority of Documents*] provides that the documents forming the Contract are to be mutually explanatory of one another and that, for purposes of interpretation, the priority of the documents forming the Contract shall be in accordance with the sequence prescribed in the Sub-Clause. This Sub-Clause further provides that if an ambiguity or discrepancy is found in a document, the Engineer shall issue any necessary clarification or instruction, whether at the request of a Party or at the Engineer's own initiative. Thus, it is the duty of the Engineer, in the first instance, to interpret the documents forming the Contract and to rectify any ambiguity or discrepancy, if necessary by a clarification or an instruction.

Sub-Clause 3.5 [*Engineer's Instructions*] provides the Engineer with authority to issue instructions. It further provides that the Contractor shall comply with the instructions given by the Engineer. Thus, at least in the first instance, the Contractor is bound by the interpretation of the Contract made by the Engineer under this Sub-Clause and, should it be questioned, by a determination of the Engineer under Sub-Clause 3.7 [*Agreement or Determination*].

83. As previously mentioned (*see* **Section 7.1 Introduction** of **Chapter II Applicable Law** above), Sub-Clause 21.6 [*Arbitration*] incorporates by references the ICC Rules of Arbitration which provides for the application of 'rules of law' (art. 21(1)), a broader concept than 'law' provided for in Sub-Clause 1.4.

5.1.2 Absence of Entire Agreement Clause

What a FIDIC contract does *not say* about how it should be interpreted may be just as significant as what it does provide on the subject. As an example, the FIDIC forms contain no 'entire agreement' clause as is often found in commercial contracts in common law countries. Such a clause typically stipulates that the concluded contract is the entire agreement between the parties and supersedes all prior negotiations, representations or agreements, whether written or oral, on the same subject matter.[84] The purpose of such a clause is to isolate the contract from any and all elements that are external to it. Consequently, an entire agreement clause aims to exclude evidence such as that relating to the Contractor's tender, pre-contractual negotiations, trade usages or prior dealings between the parties, which may be submitted in order to contradict or supplement the agreement in writing.[85] It is debatable, however, whether such a clause will also have the effect of excluding extrinsic evidence for the purposes of interpretation of ambiguous wording in the contract.[86] The answer will ultimately depend on the wording of the clause. The more likely view with regard to entire agreement clauses containing the typical wording described above is that extrinsic evidence may still be used as a means of interpreting the wording of the contract.[87] This is also the position of the UNIDROIT Principles.[88]

The absence of an entire agreement clause from the FIDIC forms of construction contract indicates that a party is not prevented from resorting to extrinsic evidence in order to contradict or supplement such a contract.

---

84. In the United States, these types of clauses are known as 'merger' or 'integration' clauses.

85. For an English case on this subject, *see Rock Advertising Limited v MWB Business Exchange Centres Limited* [2018] UKSC 24 [para. 14].

86. *See* on that point Marcel Fontaine and Filip De Ly, *Drafting International Contracts, An Analysis of Contract Clauses* (Martinus Nijhoff, Leiden, the Netherlands, 2009) 131, 134-145.

87. *Ibid.*

88. Pursuant to art. 2.1.17 (*Merger clauses*) of the UNIDROIT Principles:

> A contract in writing which contains a clause indicating that the writing completely embodies the terms on which the parties have agreed cannot be contradicted or supplemented by evidence of prior statements or agreements. *However, such statements or agreements may be used to interpret the writing.* (Emphasis added)

5.1.3 Absence of Reciprocal Non-waiver Clause

Subject to Sub-Clause 3.2 [*Engineer's Duties and Authority*], RB/17 also contains no general, reciprocal non-waiver clause, that is, a clause providing that a failure by a Party to insist upon strict compliance with any term of the Conditions will not be deemed to be a waiver by that Party of such term. Such a clause may be useful in protecting a Party against losing its contractual rights where it has not required strict adherence with the Conditions by the other Party.

However, the last paragraph of Sub-Clause 3.2 of RB/17 provides generally that no act (or failure to act) of the Engineer, the Engineer's Representative or any assistant, shall relieve the Contractor of any obligation under or in connection with the Contract. Thus, the Employer is protected from losing its rights by an act or failure to act by the Engineer or those assisting it.

5.1.4 Absence of Exclusive Remedy Clause

The FIDIC forms contain no provision providing that the remedies therein are exclusive of rights at law.[89] On the contrary, they provide explicitly in several places that the rights in the contract do not preclude rights at law. For example, Sub-Clause 15.2 of RB/17 provides that:

> Termination of the Contract under this Clause *shall not prejudice any other rights of the Employer* under the Contract *or otherwise*. (Emphasis added)

The phrase 'or otherwise' refers to rights at law.[90]

A similar clause is contained in Sub-Clause 16.2 dealing with the Contractor's right to terminate the contract. The lack of an 'exclusive remedies' clause indicates that a Party is free to resort to remedies other than those provided for in the Contract, namely, those that are available under the law governing the Contract. As a practical matter, this means

89. On the other hand, Sub-Clause 42.4 of YB/87 had provided that the contractual remedies provided thereunder shall be the exclusive remedies available to the parties, except in cases of gross misconduct (as defined in YB/87).
90. *Guide to the Use of FIDIC Conditions of Contract for Works of Civil Engineering Construction, Fourth Edition* (FIDIC 1989) 119 (commenting on Sub-Clause 53.1 [*Notice of Claim*] in RB/87).

that whenever a Party wishes to ascertain its rights in a given situation (e.g., whether it has a right to claim against the other Party or to terminate the Contract), it should not necessarily confine itself to analysis of the Contract, but consider seeking advice about the law governing the Contract.[91]

5.2 Relevance of Language

As stated earlier,[92] all the FIDIC forms have been drafted in English and RB/17 provides in Notes at the beginning of the form that 'FIDIC considers the official and authentic texts to be the versions in the English language'.[93] Thus, any translations from English may not necessarily reflect faithfully the original English text.

As has been explained earlier,[94] a Red Book contract will normally, as a practical matter, be governed by the law of the Employer's country, and that law will normally be expressed in its language. Therefore to ensure consistency with the governing law, it may be sensible for the Employer's language also to serve as the ruling language of the Contract. If the Contractor is from a country using another language, it will often be prudent for it to have the Contract in the Employer's language translated into the Contractor's language rather than rely on the FIDIC conditions in the English language.

Translation of a construction contract into another language is a very difficult exercise. In the case of a FIDIC form, translation should be done by persons who are fluent in both English and the language into which the contract is to be translated and who, at the same time, have an excellent knowledge of the vocabularies of both engineering and law in

91. The Conditions could be more informative and helpful to users in this respect by providing explicitly that the duties, obligations, rights and remedies provided for by the Contract are in addition to, and not a limitation on, the duties, obligations, rights and remedies otherwise available at law. *See*, for example, s 13.3.1 of American Institute of Architects (AIA) Document A201- 2017 *General Conditions of the Contract for Construction*.
92. *See* **Section 4.6 Translations** of **Chapter I General Introduction** above.
93. Naturally, however, if parties have translated a FIDIC form into another language and signed a contract which is in this translation, they will be bound by their translation and not by the English language text of the FIDIC form.
94. *See* **Section 3 Importance of the Governing Law** of **Chapter II Applicable Law** above.

the two languages.[95] This is a very demanding combination of skills that, as a practical matter, would likely require a small team of qualified people for it to be done properly. As few are inclined – or able – to make this level of effort, translations are usually of poor quality.[96]

The work of the translator is further complicated by the fact that, as the FIDIC's forms are written in English, they are inclined to use legal terms and concepts that are rooted in English law and practice, and which may be unknown or have no exact equivalent in the civil law world and civil law vocabulary (although FIDIC strives to avoid this). Consequently, these terms and concepts may be difficult or impossible to translate correctly. For example, the term 'Delay Damages' in Sub-Clause 8.8, which is based on the common law concept of liquidated damages, is often translated in some civil law countries as a 'penalty', which may be the corresponding legal concept (e.g., under French law), but a liquidated damages clause may be considered invalid and unenforceable under the common law if the amount stated is a 'penalty'.[97] Furthermore, whereas one of the functions of a liquidated damages clause in common law jurisdictions is to cap the liability of the party liable for such damages, the amount of a penalty in French law may be increased where it is manifestly derisory.[98] There are also other common law concepts in FIDIC forms, such as 'fitness of purpose', 'provisional sums' or 'nominated subcontractors', which remain largely unknown in the civil law world and are consequently difficult to translate.

95. Since the FIDIC documents use British-English language, for the purposes of translation of these documents British-English dictionaries (such as the *Concise Oxford English Dictionary* and the *Dictionary of Construction, Surveying & Civil Engineering* (1st edn, OUP, Oxford, 2012)) will likely be of more assistance than US dictionaries when trying to arrive at the equivalent term, if any, in the language into which the contract is translated.
96. Consequently, it is advisable to take precautions as described in **Section 4.6 Translations** of **Chapter I General Introduction** above.
97. *See* **Section 4 Common Law and Civil Law Compared – 4.4.5 Liquidated Damages and Penalties** of **Chapter II Applicable Law** above and the commentary on **Sub-Clause 8.8 [*Delay Damages*]** in **Chapter IV. Clause-by-Clause Commentary** below.
98. French Civil Code, art. 1231-5, second paragraph. *See also* **Section 4 Common Law and Civil Law Compared – 4.4.5 Liquidated Damages and Penalties** of **Chapter II Applicable Law** above.

5.3 *Contra Proferentem*

As mentioned in **Section 4.4** above, the *contra proferentem* rule allows an ambiguous provision in a contract to be construed against the party that prepared or put forward the contract. The main rationale for this rule is that the party in a weaker bargaining position should have the benefit of the interpretation that is more favourable to it on the basis that the stronger party could always have removed the ambiguity with clearer words.[99] Consequently, there seems to be little ground to apply the rule if the parties have thoroughly negotiated their contract and have incorporated amendments that reflect the positions of both parties. However, in international projects it is common that the Employer, or its consultant, will prepare the tender documents of which a FIDIC form – such as RB/17 – is a part. In these cases, a tenderer may be expected to bid for the project on a more or less 'take-it-or-leave-it' basis with very limited – or no – possibility to renegotiate the terms of the proposed conditions. In these circumstances, when RB/17 is incorporated in invitation to tender documents and is found to contain an ambiguity, should it be interpreted against the Employer?

Before answering this query, an initial question is whether there is a place for application of the *contra proferentem* rule to contracts based on standard industry forms, which are drafted not by the parties but by independent professional bodies or institutions such as FIDIC. In principle, the answer will depend on the governing law. For example, the French Civil Code explicitly stipulates that a standard form to which a party has adhered with no negotiation of individual terms, and whose general conditions are determined in advance by one of the parties, may be interpreted against the person who put it forward.[100] It seems debatable, however, whether a FIDIC form can be qualified as an adhesion

99. Julian Bailey, *Construction Law* (3rd edn, London Publishing, UK, 2020) vol 1, 226-227 (para. 3.168).

100. French Civil Code, art. 1190 provides as follows: '[i]n case of ambiguity, a bespoke contract is interpreted against the creditor and in favour of the debtor, and a standard form contract is interpreted against the person who put it forward'.
Under art. 1110, a standard form contract (*contrat d'adhésion*) is defined as 'one whose general conditions are determined in advance by one of the parties without negotiation'.

contract in the sense given to it in the French Civil Code.[101] In Switzerland, at least, it is unlikely that such a rule will be applied in cases where both parties work in the construction industry and are familiar with the standard form concerned.[102] In England, *Keating* states that in principle the rule should not be applied to standard forms drafted by professional bodies.[103] The position remains unclear in the United States.[104] There are some US court decisions where domestic standard forms have been interpreted against the party that proposed them. For example, in *John L. Mattingly Constr. Co., Inc. v Hartford Underwriters Ins. Co.*,[105] the court found that the *contra proferentem* rule extends to the party 'who proposed the form contract used in the present case, among the various AIA [American Institute of Architects] forms that may have been available'. A similar position has been followed in other US cases.[106] On the other hand, there is US case law suggesting that the rule should not be applied to construction contracts based on standard forms in cases where the contractors are sophisticated business people.[107]

---

101. *See* Peter Rosher 'The Potential Impact of French Contract Law Reform on the Construction Industry' [2016] ICLR 378, 385-86.
102. Sam Moss, 'Swiss Law vs English Law on Contract Interpretation: Is Swiss Law Better Suited to the Realities of International Commercial Contracts?' [2015] ICLR 470, 480.
103. Stephen Furst and Vivian Ramsey, *Keating on Construction Contracts* (11th edn, Sweet & Maxwell, London, 2021) 61 (para. 3-050). *See also* the *Persimmon Homes* case referred to in fn. 79 above in **Chapter III** finding that the *contra proferentem* rule has very little application in construing commercial contracts negotiated between parties of equal bargaining power.
104. Justin Sweet and Marc Schneier, *Legal Aspects of Architecture, Engineering and the Construction Process* (9th edn, Cengage Learning, Stamford, CT, 2013) 491-493.
105. 415 Md 313, 999 A2d 1066, 1078 (2010). The form at issue in this case was a form of performance bond issued by the American Institute Architects ('AIA') whose standard forms are widely used in the United States.
106. *See Durand Associates Inc v Guardian Investment Co* [1971] 186 Neb 349, 183 NW 2d 246, where an AIA standard form was construed against the engineer that supplied it despite the fact that the owners were experienced business people. In *Osolo School Buildings Inc v Thorleif Larsen and Son of Indiana Inc* 473 NE 2d 643 (Ind App 1985), an AIA standard form was interpreted against the owner.
107. *Robinhorne Constr Corp v Snyder* [1969] 113 Ill App 2d 288, 251 NE 2d 641, aff'd, 47 Ill 2d 349 (1970) 265 NE.2d 670.

In practice, unless they have been changed very significantly, the *contra proferentem* rule is unlikely to apply to the RB or the YB. First, these forms are prepared by an independent professional body of engineers (FIDIC).[108] Second, as is well known, they are based on principles of balanced risk sharing between the Employer and the Contractor. Third, the rule can be applied only if there is an ambiguity in the form's terms. Therefore, the rule cannot be invoked to defeat the application of clear contractual provisions that shift most contractual risk to one of the parties. Fourth, it is accepted that the rule can be applied only as a last resort, that is, in case of an ambiguity that cannot be resolved by using all other methods of contract interpretation.[109] Finally, parties often elect or accept the use of the FIDIC forms because they are familiar with them and they represent good practice. From that perspective, there seems to be little ground to argue that the standard of interpretation of these documents should differ depending on the party who proposed the use of the particular FIDIC form.

---

108. The remarks of Lord Pearson in *Tersons Ltd v Stevenage Development Corporation* in relation to the English ICE Conditions (upon which the FIDIC Conditions were originally based) are relevant in this regard:

> The General Conditions are not a partisan document or an 'imposed standard contract' as that phrase is sometimes used. It was not drawn upon by one party in its own interest and imposed on the other party. It is a general form, evidently in common use, and prepared and revised jointly by several representative bodies including the Federation of Civil Engineering Contractors. It would naturally be incorporated in a contract of this kind, and should have the same meaning whether one party or the other happens to have made the first mention of it in negotiations.

Tersons Ltd v Stevenage Development Corporation [1963] 5 BLR 54, 78-79 (Pearson LJ).
While Lord Pearson was describing the English ICE Conditions, his remarks might apply equally to the RB and YB. Although they have not been prepared 'jointly by several representative bodies', like the ICE Conditions, they have been prepared by a federation of consulting engineers (i.e., by neither employers nor contractors) and seek to take account of the interest of employers and contractors in a balanced way.

109. *See* Julian Bailey, *Construction Law* (3rd edn, London Publishing, UK, 2020) vol 1, 227-228 (para. 3.169). *See also* Stephen Furst and Vivian Ramsey, *Keating on Construction Contracts* (11th edn, Sweet & Maxwell, London, 2021) 60 (para. 3-048); Joseph M Perillo, *Contracts* (7th edn, West Publishing, St Paul, MN, 2014) 145 (s 3.13).

5.4 Effect of Deletions

The question may arise as to whether clauses which have been deleted from the text of the General Conditions of the Red Book may be taken into account in interpretation. Thus, the Parties may have amended Sub-Clause 2.5 [*Employer's Claims*] in RB/99. This Sub-Clause deals with the procedure for Employer's claims, including the Employer's right to set off[110] amounts it believes it is owed against sums due to the Contractor. Assume that, in the amended Sub-Clause, the words 'set off' are deleted for the purpose of excluding the Employer's right of set-off, which also happens to be a right available under the governing law. If one were to consider the amended Sub-Clause alone, without the deletion displayed, the Sub-Clause could still be interpreted to permit the Employer's right to set off because of its broad wording and the availability of set-off under the governing law.[111] However, by comparing the amended Sub-Clause with Sub-Clause 2.5 of the General Conditions, from which the Parties have departed, one may readily infer that the Parties' intention was to exclude such right from the scope of the provision as well as the legal right to set off.

The answer to the question whether deletions or replacements can be taken into account when interpreting a construction contract will depend, once again, on the governing law. If the governing law is that of a civil law jurisdiction, these deletions may generally be taken into account to ascertain the parties' common intentions as under civil law one may look at any evidence that may be of assistance in interpreting a contract.[112] In common law jurisdictions, however, the position is far from

110. 'Set off' refers to a debtor's rights to reduce the amount of a debt by any sum the creditor owes the debtor. Bryan A Garner (ed in chief), *Black's Law Dictionary* (11th edn, Thomson Reuters, St Paul, MN, 2019).

111. The last sentence of Sub-Clause 2.5 from the RB/99 provides that:

> The Employer shall only be entitled to ~~set off against or~~ make any deduction from an amount certified in a Payment Certificate, or to otherwise claim against the Contractor, in accordance with this Sub-Clause (strike-through added).

The strike-through aims to illustrate how the clause would have looked like without the deleted words.

112. *See* **Section 4.1 Civil Law: State Courts** of **Chapter III Contract Interpretation.**

clear.[113] In England, for example, there is conflicting case law on the subject.[114] However, *Keating* suggests that the better view is that deletions can be considered in construing ambiguous clauses if the deleted words could throw light on the meaning of the retained words.[115]

5.5 FIDIC's Publications

As indicated above,[116] for many years FIDIC has published *Guides* or *Notes* commenting on its forms of construction contract or similar instruments. These have included *The FIDIC Contracts Guides* (2000 and 2022) and the *FIDIC Procurement Procedures Guide* (2011).[117] Furthermore, some of the FIDIC forms of construction contract may contain, or be supplemented by, errata by which errors in FIDIC forms are corrected.[118] A question may arise as to whether these documents and errata can be taken into account when interpreting construction contracts based on the FIDIC forms.

113. Stephen Furst and Vivian Ramsey, *Keating on Construction Contracts* (11th edn, Sweet & Maxwell, London, 2021) 47-48 (paras 3-011 to 3-014).
114. *Ibid.*
115. *Ibid.*, 48-49, 3-013. This view finds support in the English case of *J Murphy & Sons Ltd v Beckton Energy Ltd*, [2016] EWHC 607 (TCC) where the court, when interpreting a bespoke liquidated damages clause under a contract based on YB/99, looked at the wording of the clause as contained in YB/99 in the course of its interpretation of the amended clause. More particularly, the court noted that the parties had deleted reference to the employer's claim procedure (Sub-Clause 2.5) in Sub-Clause 8.7 [*Delay Damages*] of YB/99, which, together with other evidence, led the court to conclude that payment of delay damages under amended Sub-Clause 8.7 was not subject to the employer's claims procedure that required, among other things, an engineer's determination under Sub-Clause 3.5. *See also* Atkin Chambers, *Hudson's Building and Engineering Contracts* (14th edn, Sweet & Maxwell, London, 2020) 38-40 (paras 1-040 to 1-041).
116. **Section 4.4 FIDIC's *Guides*** of **Chapter I General Introduction**.
117. In 2013, FIDIC also issued *FIDIC's Guidance Memorandum to Users of the 1999 Conditions of Contract*. This document concerned the enforcement of a binding and not final decision of a DAB.
118. For example, the reprints of the RB/99, YB/99 and SB/99 contain a list of errata towards the end of these books. For amendments and errata relating to the 2017 contracts, *see* the Note following the List of Abbreviations and Definitions at the beginning of this book.

In civil law countries, one would normally have the discretion to look at any extrinsic evidence when interpreting contractual clauses, and therefore the FIDIC's *Guides* and similar documents are likely to be considered admissible in litigation or arbitration in those countries.[119] It is uncertain, however, whether these documents can be given much weight in ascertaining the subjective common intentions of the parties. They reflect the intention of the professional body (FIDIC) that published the respective standard form, which may not necessarily reflect the parties' actual intention when entering into their particular contract, especially where the parties have departed from the general conditions by introducing bespoke clauses, as they will ordinarily have done. FIDIC's own publications may have more weight in cases where FIDIC's forms have been little changed and/or the parties' subjective intentions cannot be ascertained as in these cases interpretation will have to be based on objective criteria.

In England, the position of the courts has traditionally been reserved as regards the admissibility of such kind of evidence. *Keating* has stated that such documents are unlikely to be admissible (in English courts) in the interpretation process.[120] *Bailey* has described the position as 'uncertain' by pointing at court decisions taking divergent approaches.[121] The position of United States courts is not much different. One authority has stated, when referring to the commentaries of the American Institute of Architects ('AIA') on its standard forms of construction contract, that this kind of evidence is 'untrustworthy at best' and that '[i]t is probably best for courts to ignore this evidence'.[122]

In practice, however, courts and arbitral tribunals in both common law and civil law countries have considered FIDIC's *Guides* and similar documents when interpreting contracts based on FIDIC's forms. For

119. *See* **Section 4.1 Civil Law: State Courts** of **Chapter III Contract Interpretation.**
120. Stephen Furst and Vivian Ramsey, *Keating on Construction Contracts* (11th edn, Sweet & Maxwell, London, 2021) 49, para. 3-015 citing *T.F.W Printers Ltd v Interserve Project Services Ltd* [2006] EWCA Civ 875 [24]. But *Keating* states that the position is different if the practice or guidance notes are bound into and form part of the contract documents. *Ibid.*
121. Julian Bailey, *Construction Law* (3rd edn, London Publishing, UK, 2020) vol 1, 233-234 (para. 3.185).
122. Justin Sweet and Marc Schneier, *Legal Aspects of Architecture, Engineering and the Construction Process* (9th edn, Cengage Learning, Stamford, CT, 2013) 493.

example, in the *Persero II* case,[123] the Singapore Court of Appeal found support for its interpretation of Clause 20 of RB/99 in *FIDIC's Guidance Memorandum to Users of the 1999 Conditions of Contract* as well as in the drafting history of that clause. The Swiss Federal Supreme Court referred to *The FIDIC Contracts Guide* when interpreting Sub-Clause 20.8 of RB/99.[124] The Court relied on a passage in that *Guide* to conclude that if a party is being intransigent in constituting a DAB, the other party may be able to refer a dispute directly to arbitration under Sub-Clause 20.8, without requesting a DAB decision.[125] In the English *Peterborough* case, *The FIDIC Contracts Guide* was relied upon by the judge to clarify the difference between standing and ad hoc DABs, concluding – correctly – that Sub-Clause 20.8 of SB/99 was originally intended only for where a contract provides for a standing DAB, as is provided for in RB/99, but not in SB/99 or YB/99 providing for ad hoc DABs.[126]

Therefore, notwithstanding the contrary views of commentators described above, the reality is that courts and arbitrators from both civil law and common law countries are, in practice, taking these documents into account in interpreting FIDIC contracts.

5.6 Other Sources

5.6.1 FIDIC's Forms

Whenever a judge or an arbitrator is faced with an issue under a FIDIC contract with which he or she is unfamiliar, or is uncertain how to approach a particular problem or to deal with a particular argument, if neither the relevant contract nor the governing law provides an answer, he or she may want to consider other FIDIC forms of contract or foreign case law if it deals with, or illuminates, the same issue, problem or argument.[127] As regards other FIDIC forms, judges and arbitrators have rightly shown a willingness to consider them when they deal with similar

---

123. *PT Perusahaan Gas Negara (Persero) TBK v CRW Joint Operation (Indonesia)* (CA) [2015] SGCA 30.
124. Swiss Federal Supreme Court, Case no 4A_124/2014 (7 July 2014).
125. *Ibid.*, para. 3.4.3.3.
126. *Peterborough City Council v Entreprise Managed Services Ltd* (2014) EWHC 3193 (TLC) [paras 12-13 and 33]. *See* Christopher R Seppälä, 'The Arbitration Clause in FIDIC Contracts for Major Works' [2005] ICLR, 4, 13 (fn. 21).
127. As regards foreign case law, *see* **Section 6 Challenges of a Less-Developed Law** in **Chapter II Applicable Law** above.

subject matter.[128] Thus, the Swiss Federal Supreme Court used the definitions of 'shall' and 'may' in the Gold Book in interpreting Sub-Clause 20.2 of RB/99 since RB/99 did not provide for such definitions.[129] In another case (and as mentioned above), an English court concluded that removal of the reference to Sub-Clause 2.5 [*Employer's Claims*] from Sub-Clause 8.7, entitled 'Delay Damages and Bonus', from a contract based upon YB/99, whereas Sub-Clause 2.5 is referred to in Sub-Clause 8.7 [*Delay Damages*] of YB/99, indicated that the Employer would be entitled to recover Delay Damages under Sub-Clause 8.7 *without an agreement or determination of the engineer under Sub-Clauses 2.5* and 3.5 (to which Sub-Clause 2.5 refers).[130] In yet another case, referred to in the previous section, an English Judge noted that Sub-Clause 20.8 of SB/99 is 'in the same form in all three FIDIC Books', before concluding that that Sub-Clause 'probably applies only in cases where the contract provides for a standing DAB, rather than the procedure of appointing an ad hoc DAB after a dispute has arisen'.[131]

5.6.2 Comparative Law and ICC Awards

In the case of a FIDIC contract, in addition to commentaries on FIDIC's forms, it may sometimes be helpful to refer to English and other common law precedents and treatises, such as *Bailey*, *Hudson* or *Keating* because of the common law origin of the FIDIC forms. These precedents and treatises are valuable for an understanding of the legal principles and practices underlying FIDIC contracts (e.g., the role of the Engineer as an intermediary between the parties or the procedure for the Engineer to instruct Variations) and the intention of the language of these contracts. More generally, law and practice in countries with a developed system of

---

128. Thus, RB/17, YB/17 and SB/17 are part of the same 'family' of contracts (the 'Rainbow Suite') and share common characteristics, including a common approach to risk allocation and a similar vocabulary. See the glossary 'FIDICTerms' at: https://fidic.org/other-resources/fidic-terms-glossary accessed at 14 November 2022 comprising terms and definitions commonly used in FIDIC standard forms of contract (especially under the category 'Contracts and Agreements') and other publications.
129. Swiss Federal Supreme Court, Case no 4A_124 (7 July 2014), para. 3.4.3.1.
130. *J. Murphy & Sons Ltd v Beckton Energy Ltd* [2016] EWHC (TCC) 607 [para. 48].
131. *Peterborough City Council v Entreprise Managed Services Ltd* (2014) EWHC 3193 (TLC) [para. 33]. *See* Christopher R Seppälä, 'The Arbitration Clause in FIDIC Contracts for Major Works' [2005] ICLR, 4, 13 (fn. 21).

law can be used to fill 'gaps' in the governing law of a developing country, as has previously been explained.[132]

By virtue of their multinational composition and international character, international arbitration tribunals are well qualified, and usually open, to looking to comparative law for solutions. The reasoning and experience of a developed system of law can either help confirm a tentative conclusion they may have reached under the governing law or can point them in the right direction if the governing law does not yield a clear conclusion. Published arbitral awards dealing with FIDIC contracts may also be persuasive, notably those issued under the auspices of the ICC International Court of Arbitration,[133] and there is evident value in FIDIC forms being interpreted in a correct and uniform manner.

5.6.3 *Examples of ICC Cases*

Two examples from ICC cases may illustrate how an arbitral tribunal can use foreign case law to fill 'gaps' in the applicable governing law.[134] The first case involved a contract based on RB/69 and concerned a project to

132. *See* **Section 6 Challenges of a Less-Developed Law** of **Chapter II Applicable Law** above where this matter is addressed.

133. For commentaries on ICC awards dealing with the FIDIC Contracts *see* the following articles by the present author: 'International Construction Contract Disputes: Commentary on ICC Awards Dealing with the FIDIC International Conditions of Contract' in (1998) 9(2) ICC Ct Arb Bull 32; 'International Construction Contract Disputes: Second Commentary on ICC Awards Dealing Primarily with FIDIC Contracts' (2008) 19(2) ICC Ct Arb Bull 41; 'International Construction Contract Disputes: Third Commentary on ICC Awards Dealing Primarily with FIDIC Contracts' (2012) 23(2) ICC Ct Arb Bull 23; 'International Construction Contract Disputes: Fourth Commentary on ICC Awards Dealing Primarily with FIDIC Contracts' (2013) 24 ICC Ct Arb Bull 49; and 'Commentary on Recent ICC Arbitral Awards dealing with Dispute Adjudication Boards under FIDIC Contracts' in (2015) 1 ICC Disp Resol Bull 21.

134. This and other examples concerning the use of comparative law as an aid in interpreting construction contracts are discussed in Christopher R Seppälä, 'The Development of a Case Law in Construction Disputes Relating to FIDIC Contracts' in Emmanuel Gaillard and Yas Banifatemi (eds), *Precedent in International Arbitration* (Juris Publishing, Huntington, NY, 2017) 73-82. The examples given in the next two paragraphs are discussed in some more detail in the above-mentioned paper.

build a town consisting of housing units and related utilities and infrastructure in an Arab country. The governing law was the law of that same country. The employer had let the works for a housing programme out to three different contractors under three separate main construction contracts commonly known, in the United States (where such practice is common), as 'multi-prime' construction contracts. One contract was for building the housing units, the second contract was for the 'primary' utilities' networks (trunk mains or lines for fresh water, waste water, electricity, telecommunications and roads) leading from the municipal utilities' networks to the site of the planned town, where the 'secondary' utilities networks began, and the third contract was for the 'secondary' and 'tertiary' utilities networks, which led from the 'primary' utilities networks directly to and into the housing units.[135]

While all of the contracts related to work for the same building programme, *none addressed the issue of who was to coordinate the performance of the work under the three different contracts*. As a result, the performance of one contract ended up interfering with the performance of another (especially after one of the contractors went bankrupt and ceased work) and the execution of the works became chaotic causing the different contractors substantial damages. In arbitration therefore the question was, in the absence of a contractual provision on the subject, *who, if anyone, was responsible for coordinating the work of the various contractors?*

Neither the contract based on RB/69[136] nor the governing law clearly addressed this issue. The governing law provided only that a party must perform a contract in good faith but contained no guidance as to how this duty applied to the issue in question. The law relating to multi-prime construction contracts, though not much developed in Europe (e.g., in England and France), was and is highly developed in the United States where in such circumstances the employer (or owner) is held to have an

135. The 'primary' utilities are the main – and largest – diameter trunk pipelines for the utilities (e.g., fresh water, waste water, electricity, telecommunications, etc.) and originate at the local municipality or other off-site location; the 'secondary' utilities are the intermediate – and medium-size in diameter – pipelines leading from the 'primary' utilities to the 'tertiary' utilities; and the 'tertiary' utilities – the smallest pipelines in diameter – lead from the 'secondary' utilities directly to and into the housing units.

136. RB/17 does not address this kind of issue either.

implied affirmative duty to coordinate work under the various contracts.[137] The contractor directed the arbitral tribunal's attention to this US case law as indicating how the duty of a party to perform a contract in good faith under the governing law should be interpreted in a multi-prime contract context. The tribunal adopted the solution from this case law and referred to it in its award.[138]

The second case concerned the construction of a road in francophone Africa. The subcontract, which was governed by local law, contained a 'pay-when-paid' clause providing that the subcontractor would only be paid if and when, or as and when, the contractor was paid by the employer. The employer had effectively gone bankrupt, leaving money unpaid to the contractor who, in turn, had not paid the subcontractor, and the question arose as to how to interpret the 'pay-when-paid' clause in the subcontract. The contractor argued that it was relieved of its obligation to pay the subcontractor as that clause created a condition precedent to its obligation to pay the subcontractor, namely, that the employer pays the contractor and, as the contractor had not been paid, it had no obligation to pay the subcontractor. On the other hand, the subcontractor argued that the clause regulated the time for payment only, which, if correct, would have meant that it did not create a condition precedent and therefore did not relieve the contractor from having ultimately to pay the subcontractor what was unpaid.

As there was no guidance as to how to interpret the clause in the governing law and little relevant law in France and Belgium (from whose law the governing law of the African state concerned derived), both parties cited to the wealth of US case law interpreting such clauses (and which explores virtually all possible interpretations of the contract

137. For an excellent though not recent article on this subject, *see* John B Tieder, *The Duty to Schedule and Co-ordinate on Multi-Prime Contractor Projects – The United States Experience* [1985-86] 3 ICLR 97.

138. Final award, ICC cases 3790/3902/4050/4051/4054 (joined cases) (1984). This award is described both in the author's paper 'The Development of a Case Law in Construction Disputes Relating to FIDIC Contracts' in Yas Banifatemi (ed) and Emmanuel Gaillard (gen ed) *Precedent in International Arbitration* (1st edn Juris Publishing, Huntington, NY, 2008) 67, 73-77 and in Abdul Hamid Ahdab, *Arbitration with the Arab Countries* (1st edn, Kluwer Law, the Netherlands, 1990) 896-909 (Subject no 3) and 920- 922 (Subject no 6). The final award is available on Jus Mundi.

language commonly used).[139] While the dispute was ultimately settled before an award, the arbitral tribunal would have been expected to take account of such case law, to the extent consistent with the governing law, when rendering its award.[140]

5.7 Effect of an International Arbitration Clause

As in the past, FIDIC forms of contract issued in 2017 provide for the final resolution of disputes by international arbitration under the ICC Arbitration Rules.[141] Accordingly, international arbitrators are the final interpreters of a FIDIC contract. Therefore, in order to determine how such a contract is to be interpreted, it is necessary to examine how it is likely to be interpreted by an international arbitral tribunal – the final forum for the resolution of disputes under a FIDIC contract.

As discussed earlier,[142] each national law contains rules dealing with the interpretation of contracts and arbitrators will generally (as they are required to do) interpret contracts by reference to that law as well as, in an appropriate case, relevant trade usages.[143] However, they will not necessarily interpret contracts or apply the governing law as they would be interpreted or applied by a national court. This is because arbitrators have greater freedom to decide a case in light of its particular facts, the parties' contract and the international nature of the transaction, and they normally are expected to exercise that freedom for the following reasons, among others:

---

139. *See* the brief discussion of 'pay when paid' clauses in subcontracts in the present author's 'International Construction Contract Disputes-Commentary on ICC Award Dealing with the FIDIC International Conditions of Contract' [1999] 16 ICLR 339, 353.
140. ICC case 6158.
141. Sub-Clause 21.6 [*Arbitration*].
142. *See* **Section 4 Different Approaches to Interpretation** above of **Chapter III Contract Interpretation**.
143. Pursuant to art. 21 of the ICC Arbitration Rules:

> 1. The parties shall be free to agree upon the rules of law to be applied by the arbitral tribunal to the merits of the dispute. In the absence of any such agreement, the arbitral tribunal shall apply the rules of law which it determines to be appropriate.
> 2. The arbitral tribunal shall take account of the provisions of the contract, if any, between the parties and of any relevant trade usages [...].

(1) Unlike court judges who are appointed by, and serve, a state, arbitrators are nominated or appointed by the parties or their delegate (commonly, an arbitral institution) and the source of their power is the agreement of the parties and not a state.[144]

(2) The arbitrators' main mission is settle a dispute between the parties,[145] unlike a judge whose duty is to settle disputes between anyone within his/her jurisdiction, and they 'give more weight to what they regard as fairness in commercial relations, rather than to a strict consideration of the law'.[146]

(3) Arbitration awards in commercial cases are normally not published (arbitrators in such cases have no responsibility to contribute to the development of the law),[147] unlike court judgments which normally are public and have precedential value, at least in common law jurisdictions.[148]

(4) Arbitrators enjoy wide discretion to admit evidence and tend to admit all evidence submitted, while retaining the power to decide what weight, if any, to give to such evidence. Most arbitration laws, as well as many arbitration rules, recognise such discretion.[149] This discretion seems to apply regardless of the law governing the contract. Even common law lawyers

---

144. As a distinguished French scholar has put it, 'arbitrators do not have a forum', Berthold Goldman, 'Les conflits de lois dans l'arbitrage international de droit privé' (1963) vol 109 The Hague Academy of International Law, Collected Courses, 347, 374 quoted in Emmanuel Gaillard, *Legal Theory of International Arbitration* (Nijhoff, the Netherlands, 2010) 1. *See also* Georgios Petrochilos, *Procedural Law in International Arbitration* (OUP, Oxford, 2004) 170, s 5.08 ('It is from the agreement of the parties that the arbitrators draw their jurisdiction').
145. Julian Lew and others, *Comparative International Commercial Arbitration* (Kluwer, The Hague, 2003) 279 (para. 12-12).
146. René David, *Arbitration in International Trade* (1985) quoted in W Laurence Craig, 'The Arbitrator's Mission and the Application of Law in International Commercial Arbitration' (2010) 21 Am Rev Int'l Arb 243, 245.
147. The position is different in investment arbitration where a tribunal may consider itself bound to contribute to the 'harmonious development of investment law'. *Austrian Airlines v Slovak Republic*, UNCITRAL, Award of 9 October 2009, para. 84.
148. Commercial arbitration is confidential or, at least, private. Julian Lew and others, *Comparative International Commercial Arbitration* (Kluwer, The Hague, 2003) 283 (para. 12-20) and art. 26(3) of the ICC Arbitration Rules.
149. For example, art. 19(2) of the *UNCITRAL Model Law on International Commercial Arbitration* provides that:

recognise that the parol evidence rule[150] and strict rules of evidence, otherwise applicable in common law countries, need not apply in arbitration.[151]

(5) Most modern arbitration laws[152] and rules[153] require arbitrator(s) to decide on the basis of the contract between the parties. On this basis, arbitrators have often given precedence to the contract over the law or have even resolved a dispute without referring to the law.[154]

> [t]he power conferred upon the arbitral tribunal includes the power to determine the admissibility, relevance, materiality and weight of any evidence.

S 34(2) (f) of the English *Arbitration Act 1996* follows art. 19(2) of the *Model Law*. In a similar vein, the IBA Rules on the Taking of Evidence in International Arbitration 2010, which are widely referred to in international arbitration practice, provide in art. 9(1) that:

> The Arbitral Tribunal shall determine the admissibility, relevance, materiality and weight of evidence.

150. *See* **Section 4.2.2 Parol Evidence Rule** above of **Chapter III Contract Interpretation**.
151. *See* David St John Sutton and others, *Russell on Arbitration* (24th edn, Sweet & Maxwell, London, 2015) 161, para. 4-082, who state (as regards English law) that: 'Difficult doctrines like the parol evidence or hearsay rules need not concern an arbitral tribunal, unless, exceptionally, it is decided to apply strict rules of evidence in the arbitration.' However, the admission of any such evidence should not change the actual interpretation of the clause itself by reference to the applicable English law principles. *See also* Justin Sweet and Marc Schneier, *Legal Aspects of Architecture, Engineering and the Construction Process* (9th edn, Cengage Learning, Stamford, CT, 2013) 485 who state (as regards the United States) that 'The plain meaning rule applies only to litigation. An arbitrator can examine extrinsic evidence, if she chooses, without first finding the language was not plain on its face.' *See also* Joshua Karton, *The Culture of International Arbitration and the Evolution of Contract Law* (OUP, Oxford, 2013) 214, 219, 225, 232.
152. *See* art. 28(4) of the *UNCITRAL Model Law on International Commercial Arbitration*.
153. *See* art. 21(2) of the ICC Arbitration Rules.
154. *See* Jason Fry and others, *The Secretariat's Guide to ICC Arbitration, A Practical Commentary on the 2012 ICC Rules of Arbitration of the ICC International Court of Arbitration* (ICC, Paris, 2012, ICC Publication no 729

(6) Given the international nature of disputes submitted to arbitration and that one or more of the arbitrators is likely to be applying a law other than his or her own, they are likely to be more open to supplementing their reasoning by reference to comparative law, international principles[155] and international arbitration case law than a state court judge.[156]

E) 228 (para. 3-777) where the authors comment on art. 21(2) of the ICC Arbitration Rules providing:

> The arbitral tribunal shall take account of the provisions of the contract, if any, between the parties and of any relevant trade usages.

According to the authors, this article:

> requires the arbitral tribunal to place the parties' contract, if any, centre stage in the resolution of contractual disputes. This provision is a further reflection of the importance of the parties' agreements in international arbitration, where contractual terms are often considered to have greater importance than legal requirements and technicalities. In some instances, an ICC arbitral tribunal may render its award simply by applying the terms of the contract to its factual findings, without needing to refer to the law governing the merits.

155. Thus, an official comment to the Preamble to the UNIDROIT Principles provides:

> In applying a particular domestic law, courts and arbitral tribunals may be faced with doubts as to the proper solution to be adopted under that law, either because different alternatives are available or because there seem to be no specific solutions at all. Especially where the dispute relates to an international commercial contract, it may be advisable to resort to the Principles as a source of inspiration. By so doing the domestic law in question would be interpreted and supplemented in accordance with internationally accepted standards and/or the special needs of cross-border trade relationships.
>
> Official comment 6 to the Preamble to the Principles.

156. *See* Gabrielle Kaufmann-Kohler, 'The Transnationalization of National Contract Law by the International Arbitrator' in Marcello Kohen and Dolores Bentolila, *Mélanges en l'honneur du Professeur Jean-Michel Jacquet* (LexisNexis, Paris, 2013) 107, 119:

> in some cases, the arbitrators consider that the multinational nature of the transaction which gives rise to the dispute is incompatible with the

(7) Arbitrators will be less inclined to give weight to a national law to the extent it has been developed specifically for domestic use or if in an international context the national law concerned otherwise appears to clash with commercial sense.[157]

(8) With limited exceptions,[158] under national arbitration laws, arbitral awards cannot be set aside because of misinterpretation of a contract or generally on account of errors of fact or law and international enforcement cannot be denied on these grounds under the New York Convention relating to the enforcement of foreign arbitral awards.[159]

For these reasons, among others, international arbitrators have greater freedom to do justice in the individual case, which may accord most with

---

application of a single national law and therefore choose to apply transnational law (footnote referring to ICC cases omitted).

157. Thus, ICC arbitral tribunals have sometimes refused to apply national laws to international contracts. *See*, for example, ICC case 5514 (1990) *Coll of ICC Arb Awards 1991-1995* (ICC, Paris / Kluwer, the Netherlands, 1997) 459 (where the tribunal refused to enforce a provision prohibiting compound interest) and ICC case 1717 (1972) *Coll of ICC Arb Awards 1974-1985* (ICC, Paris / Kluwer, the Netherlands, 1998) 191 (where the tribunal refused to enforce a provision prohibiting gold clauses). *See also* Julian Lew and others, *Comparative International Commercial Arbitration* (Kluwer L Int'l, the Netherlands, 2003) 444, paras 18-22, who state that international tribunals need to take account of the fact that they are dealing with an international transaction and therefore '[...] should interpret national law rules to reflect international practice and to give effect to the parties intentions. Many arbitrators are from jurisdictions different to the applicable law and may have difficulty interpreting the law in accordance with that legal system itself. Although the applicable substantive law should be interpreted in its context tribunals have employed international standards in interpreting domestic or uniform law'.

158. *See* Laurent Lévy and Fabrice Robert-Tissot, 'Interprétation Arbitrale' (2013) 4 Rev Arb 882, 882-83, para. 51.

159. Under the New York Convention, the incorrect application of substantive law, part of which are the rules of contract interpretation, is not a ground to deny the recognition or enforcement of an arbitral award. *See* Guiditta Cordero-Moss, 'International Arbitration and Commercial Contract Interpretation: Contract Wording, Common Law, Civil Law and Transnational Law' in Ulf Maunsbach and others (eds), *Essays in Honour of Michael Bogdan* (Juristförlaget, Sweden, 2013) 43.

the expectations of the parties, and are less inclined to give weight to the strict application of law.[160] Thus, a Canadian academic who, having examined 73 international arbitral awards, concludes as follows:

> When one looks at what these tribunals have *done* – as opposed to what they have *said* – it appears that *they see their primary interpretative task as discerning the true common intention of the parties*, and will restrict themselves to objective interpretation only when the applicable law is that of a common law jurisdiction (and even then, not always). *They tend to see the written contract as the best evidence of the parties intent*; accordingly, they usually begin by examining the natural and ordinary meaning of the contractual terms in dispute, and (if such a meaning is determinable) may not allow extrinsic evidence of the parties' intentions to overtake it. However, *they do not prohibit parties from introducing whatever extrinsic evidence the parties may think relevant, including direct evidence of subjective intent and evidence of subsequent conduct*. In general, these tribunals seem to have disregarded extrinsic evidence only in those cases where they were able to reach a linguistically plausible and commercially reasonable interpretation based on the words of the contract alone.
>
> *One might therefore conclude that a civil law perspective on contract interpretation predominates in [international commercial arbitration].*[161] (Emphasis added)

The tendency of arbitrators, described above, has evident implications for parties. As arbitral tribunals tend to admit all materials that may help to reveal the subjective understandings of the parties, even where the applicable law is a common law, parties to a FIDIC contract should take pains to retain copies of all contemporaneous memoranda, notes, correspondence and documents from the beginning of their involvement in a construction project. Internal memoranda, notes, personal diaries and documents may later be used to evidence a party's subjective intention at the time of contracting (for whatever value they may be found to have) and enhance the credibility of corresponding witness evidence.

---

160. Nigel Blackaby and others, *Redfern and Hunter on International Arbitration* (6th edn, OUP, Oxford, 2015) 155, 581-600 (paras 10.34-10.88). It should be stressed that this is the case notwithstanding that the arbitrators will not have been given the power of an *amiable compositeur* or to decide *ex aequo et bono* pursuant to art. 21(3) of the ICC Rules of Arbitration.

161. Joshua Karton, *The Arbitral Role in Contractual Interpretation* (Queen's University Legal Research Paper no 2015-012) (March 2015) 6(1) J Int'l Disp Settl 11.

6 A PRACTICAL APPROACH

In light of the above, how then should engineers, members of DAABs, arbitrators and others interpret a contract based on the FIDIC conditions?

6.1 FIDIC's View

The traditional view of FIDIC has been that the Engineer should not get into legalities. Thus, FIDIC's 'Notes on Documents for Civil Engineering Contracts', 1977, stated:

> The Engineer's task is to interpret the contract as written and not to determine the legal rights of either party.[162]

RB/87 envisaged that whenever the Engineer was required to exercise his discretion, including when giving his decision, opinion or consent:

> he shall exercise such discretion impartially within the terms of the Contract and having regard to all the circumstances.[163]

RB/99 and YB/99 envisaged that the Engineer:

> shall make a fair determination in accordance with the Contract, taking due regard of all relevant circumstances.[164]

Similarly RB/17 provides in Sub-Clause 3.7 [*Agreement or Determination*] that the Engineer must act 'neutrally' between the Parties and make a 'fair' determination of a matter or Claim in accordance with the Contract and relevant circumstances.[165]

6.2 How the Engineer and DAAB Should Approach Interpretation

When appropriate, the Engineer and members of DAABs should not limit themselves to applying the contract as written but, if the necessary resources are available to them, take advice as to the rules of contract

162. *Notes on Documents for Engineering Contracts* (FIDIC 1979) 16.
163. Sub-Clause 2.6 of the RB/87.
164. Sub-Clause 3.5 of RB/99 and YB/99.
165. *See* **Sub-Clause 3.7 [*Agreement or Determination*]** and the commentary thereon in **Chapter IV Clause-by-Clause Commentary** below. Similarly, pursuant to Clause 14.6.1 [*Issue of IPC*], the Engineer is required 'fairly' to certify payments.

interpretation prescribed by the law governing the contract.[166] This means that, broadly speaking, they should have regard to either the subjective approach to contract interpretation (if the contract is governed by the law of a civil law country) or the objective approach (if the contract is governed by the law of a common law country).[167]

However, as discussed in **Section 5.7** above, international arbitrators are the final interpreters of a FIDIC contract. Thus, the Engineer and members of DAABs should, subject to the resources available to them, be interpreting a FIDIC contract, ideally, in the same manner in which a future ICC arbitral tribunal could be expected to do so. The better the Engineer or a DAAB can anticipate how such a tribunal would decide a dispute the more acceptable its decision is likely to be to the Parties.

As shown in **Section 5.7** above, arbitral tribunals tend to admit any evidence submitted by the parties and then decide what weight, if any, to give to it. Not being bound by rules of evidence, the Engineer and DAAB members should similarly be open to receive virtually any type of evidence[168] or argument that the parties submit.[169] There is no ground for them to exclude extrinsic evidence, such as of pre-contractual negotiations and the parties' post-contract conduct. As has previously been mentioned,[170] FIDIC contracts are often concluded by persons from different cultural, commercial and/or legal backgrounds, who have a less than perfect English. In such a setting, in the case of an English language contract, reliance on the broadest range of evidence is advisable or necessary if the Engineer and DAAB members are to be sure to understand and give effect to the parties' intentions and communications.[171]

---

166. Sub-Clause 21.1 [*Constitution of the DAAB*] envisages the possibility that the DAAB may consult an expert.
167. *See* **Sections 4.1 Civil Law: State Courts** and **4.2 Common Law: State Courts** above of **Chapter III Contract Interpretation**.
168. Excluding only documents generally regarded as privileged or confidential such as those relating to settlement negotiations. In this connection, the DAAB, by analogy to an arbitral tribunal, should have regard to art. 9 (*Admissibility and Assessment of Evidence*) of the IBA Rules on the Taking of Evidence in International Arbitration 2020, specifically arts 9.2(b), 9.3 and 9.4.
169. Under the DAAB Rules - Rule 8 - the DAAB has broad power to establish the procedure to be applied.
170. **Section 3 Importance of Interpretation** of **Chapter III Contract Interpretation.**
171. A Swiss author notes that:

Thus, when the meaning of a contractual provision is unclear, the Engineer and DAAB members, respectively, should review all the relevant circumstances as listed in Article 4.3 (*Relevant circumstances*) of the Principles[172] and determine from an examination of the documents, and after hearing the Parties, the real intention of the Parties in the case at hand. Moreover, it may also be appropriate for them to consider, to the extent practicable, FIDIC's *Guides* or other publications, foreign court decisions, international arbitral awards and legal commentaries that have relevance to the question of interpretation and are not inconsistent with the governing law. Where relevant to the question at hand, particular attention should often be given to examining the tender and other documents preceding the conclusion of the contract, regardless of the extent (if any) to which these documents constitute part of the contract, as they may help explain how the contract has come to be written in the way it is.

6.3 Interpretation of International Construction Contracts

Unlike many other types of commercial contract, international construction contracts based on the Red Book are not drawn up in a day or a month. Instead, as the nature of their contents indicates,[173] they are built up in stages over an invitation to tender process that may involve a pre-qualification procedure, an invitation to tender accompanied by a tender dossier, possibly one or more series of amendments to the tender

> according to the Swiss Supreme Court's jurisprudence, a more careful analysis of the other circumstances surrounding a contract is necessary if a party is foreign, or if the party's declaration of intent is made in a foreign language.

Sam Moss 'Swiss Law versus English Law on Contract interpretation: Is Swiss Law Better Suited to the Realities of International Construction Contracts?' [2015] ICLR 470, 478 citing to Swiss Federal Tribunal case 129 III 702 [para. 2.4.1]. The same author continues:

> [t]herefore, even the 'objective' interpretation of international construction contracts would, under Swiss law, take into account the parties different linguistic, cultural and legal backgrounds.

Ibid.

172. *See* **Section 4.3 International Approach: UNIDROIT Principles** above of **Chapter III Contract Interpretation**.
173. *See* the list of them in Sub-Clause 1.5 [*Priority of Documents*].

dossier, the submission of a Letter of Tender, possibly negotiations whose results may be recorded in minutes of meetings, the sending of a Letter of Acceptance, possibly more negotiations that are recorded somewhere, and, finally, often a Contract Agreement.[174] In the case of large projects, this process may extend over months or even years during which the parties' contract, which may include hundreds, thousands or even tens of thousands of pages, is incrementally built up. Thus, the ultimate 'agreement of the parties' may in fact be the cumulative result of multiple provisional mini-agreements on individual matters made at different meetings and at different times, possibly by different representatives of the parties, but all of which become effective on the date of the parties' final agreement – that is, the Letter of Acceptance and/or Contract Agreement. As it will have been built up in increments over time, when an issue of interpretation arises, each stage of that process may have to be reconstituted and examined in its context if the meaning of the contract on the particular point at issue is to be determined. Consequently, it is often necessary to go back to a stage in the formation of the contract (e.g., the minutes of a particular meeting or exchange of correspondence) when something was first provisionally agreed, subject to the parties' final agreement, and examine the circumstances of that stage to find out exactly what was agreed and was later included in, or incorporated by reference into, the Letter of Acceptance and/or the Contract Agreement.

When difficult issues of interpretation arise, such contracts may therefore not be understood, or be fully comprehensible, from an examination of the contract on its face only or (put another way) by reference to the 'four corners of the agreement'. Instead, to determine their meaning, one may need to seek out the parties' subjective intentions by an examination of the history of the preparation of the contract. If, from this history, a persuasive case can be made out of what the parties' subjective common intentions were, this is likely to be powerful evidence before an arbitral tribunal of the true meaning of the contract, regardless of the legal rules of contract interpretation that may apply. No international arbitrator is likely to want to go against what the actual common subjective intentions of the parties can be shown to have been.

At the same time, there may be cases where such common subjective intentions cannot be ascertained. This may, for example, be the case as regards provisions in the general conditions which have been neither

174. The words with initial capital letters are defined terms in RB/17.

discussed during the contract negotiations nor amended in the particular conditions. In these cases, it may be more appropriate to revert to a more objective approach to interpretation (i.e., how a reasonable person with the parties' knowledge and in the same circumstances would have understood the clause in question).[175] In such cases, it may be necessary to rely upon FIDIC's *Guides* or other publications commenting on FIDIC forms of contract, foreign case law, international arbitral awards and well-known legal treatises dealing with the interpretation of the relevant provisions.

6.4 Conclusion

The method of interpretation described in **Section 6** is appropriate because, as stated above, the final judges of the contract will be international arbitrators who will, as mentioned above, normally admit all evidence regardless of the source, reserving for themselves the right to decide what weight, if any, to give to the evidence submitted. Those initially called upon to decide issues of interpretation under the contract – the Engineer and the DAAB – should therefore endeavour, albeit with their more limited resources, to decide such issues in the same way that any future arbitral tribunal is likely to decide them, as this is most likely to avoid need for further proceedings.

To permit a contract to be interpreted properly in this way, the parties will have had to retain from the outset all project records, including, in particular, all tender and other documents relating to the pre-contractual period so that these are available to be examined when an issue of contract interpretation arises. All pre-contractual documents from the pre-qualification stage, as well as post-contract documents, should be carefully kept until the Final Payment Certificate has been paid and no further claims can be anticipated. A prudent Party should keep them still longer, until expiry of the applicable limitation period.[176]

--ooOOoo--

175. *See* para. (2) of art. 4.1 (*Intention of the parties*) of the Principles quoted in **Section 4.3 International Approach: UNIDROIT Principles** above of **Chapter III Contract Interpretation.**
176. *See* **Section 4.5.3 Limitation Periods** of **Chapter II Applicable Law** above. Care should also be taken to maintain contact with all staff involved in a project so that they can be available to be interviewed and/or serve as witnesses to the extent necessary.

Chapter IV

Clause-by-Clause Commentary

1 SCOPE OF CHAPTER

This chapter begins by describing the context or circumstances in which a contract based on RB/17 will normally be entered into; namely, it will be the result of an invitation to tender procedure.[1] This is followed by a description of the way in which this Clause-by-Clause commentary is organised and structured.[2] This is, in turn, followed by the Clause-by-Clause commentary itself which is, in fact, a Sub-Clause-by-Sub-Clause commentary on the 168 Sub-Clauses (21 Clauses) comprising RB/17. In this commentary, each of the Sub-Clauses, beginning with Sub-Clause 1.1 of Clause 1 and continuing through Sub-Clause 21.8 of Clause 21, is discussed in turn under four or five standard headings as described below. This Sub-Clause-by-Sub-Clause commentary[3] constitutes the main part of this book.

2 CONTEXT OF A RED BOOK CONTRACT

2.1 Invitation to Tender

Once a prospective Employer[4] has identified a project which it wishes executed, be it, for example, a highway, a bridge or an airport, and once

1. **Section 2**.
2. **Section 3**.
3. **Section 4**.
4. Strictly, the promoter of a project is not the 'Employer' until after a construction contract has been signed.

feasibility and other preparatory studies for it have been completed, the Employer will need to develop a procurement strategy and determine the type of construction contract to be used. Assuming that the Employer decides to proceed with a Red Book-type contract, then a specification and design drawings for the project will, among other things, need to be prepared.

A contract based on RB/17 assumes that it will have been entered into following an invitation to tender procedure. However, before the Employer can invite tenders it (or its consultant) must have prepared:

(1) a list of qualified contractors whom it would like to invite to tender; and
(2) a set of invitation to tender documents (the 'tender dossier' as described below).

The Employer may want to ensure that the tenderers to be invited will have the necessary skill, experience and resources, to execute the works. In that case, before inviting tenders, it may require potentially interested contractors to participate in a pre-qualification process in order to establish a list of contractors qualified to tender.[5]

The tender dossier, which will be prepared by the Employer, or a consultant on the Employer's behalf, will normally comprise the following documents:

- Letter of invitation to tender;
- Instructions to tenderers;
- Forms of Letter of Tender, Letter of Acceptance and annexed memoranda, if any;
- Conditions of Contract: General and Particular, including a Contract Data form and Special Provisions;
- Technical information, including the data referred to in Sub-Clause 2.5 [*Site Data and Items of Reference*] of the General Conditions;
- Specification;
- Drawings;
- Bill of Quantities with method of measurement and payment procedure;
- Schedules from the Employer;

5. *See FIDIC Procurement Procedures Guide* (FIDIC, 2011) 97-105.

- Other schedules for completion by tenderers, if any;
- Required forms of Contract Agreement, securities and guarantees; and
- JV Undertaking (if the tenderer is a joint venture).[6]

The tender dossier contains all the documentation necessary for a Contract to be concluded other than those terms which the Employer expressly requests the tenderer to supply. Most notably, these terms are the tenderer's proposed prices and certain other matters which are left for tenderers to complete, such as in spaces next to Sub-Clauses in the Contract Data form (*see* above) or in relation to certain Sub-Clauses.[7]

Most or all of the documents in the tender dossier will normally form part of the eventual construction contract other than the letter of invitation to tender and the instructions to tenderers.[8]

The tender dossier will usually require any tender to conform to the instructions to tenderers and to be unqualified.[9] The objective of the Employer is to secure an offer by way of reply from each tenderer which, ideally, leaves nothing for further agreement, so that it will be capable of immediate acceptance by the Employer thereby creating a legally binding contract.[10] Thus, the tender dossier will provide that a tender will be

6. *Guidance for the Preparation of Particular Conditions* included in RB/17, 10. An excellent general description of what each of the documents comprising the tender dossier should contain is in the *FIDIC Procurement Procedures Guide* (FIDIC, 2011) 115-121.
7. The tenderer may be required to provide information on matters referred to in the following Sub-Clauses:

   - Sub-Clause 4.3 [*Contractor's Representative*].
   - Sub-Clause 6.12 [*Key Personnel*].
   - Sub-Clause 19 [*Insurance*].

   Guidance for the Preparation of Particular Conditions, 12.
8. *FIDIC Procurement Procedures Guide* (FIDIC, 2011) 115.
9. Thus, the Introductory Guidance Notes to the Contract Data form provide that '[e]xcept where indicated "Tenderer to Complete" tenderers shall not amend the Contract Data as provided by the Employer' *Guidance for the Preparation of Particular Conditions*, 2.
10. Atkin Chambers, *Hudson's Building and Engineering Contracts* (14th edn, Sweet & Maxwell, London, 2020) 360 (para. 3-005) and form of Letter of Acceptance included in RB/17.

rejected unless it is substantially responsive and that the Employer is not bound to award a contract to any tenderer.[11]

2.2 Tender Period

When determining the tender period, the Employer is advised to ensure that adequate time is allowed for tenderers to prepare their tenders, taking into account the size, complexity and location of the project.[12]

After receipt of the tender dossier and during the tender period, tenderers are expected to obtain, to the extent practicable (taking account of cost and time), all necessary information as to risks, contingencies and other circumstances which may be relevant to their tender.[13] The Employer will normally arrange for a formal visit to the Site[14] and tenderers are expected, among other things, to inspect and examine it and its surroundings.[15] If tenderers have queries for the Employer during the tender period, these are usually handled either by correspondence or by a tenderers' conference. Explanations of, or revisions, additions or deletions to, the tender dossier by the Employer during the tender period may be the subject of addenda notified to all tenderers.[16]

Tenderers will be assumed to have calculated their tender prices by reference to the information available 28 days before the latest date for submission of tenders[17] (the 'Base Date' as defined in RB/17).[18]

2.3 Submission of Tenders

Tenderers will normally be required to accompany their tenders with a guarantee or bond securing their obligation to keep their tenders open for a designated period.[19] The period of validity of the security should be equal to the period of validity of the tender plus the time allowed for the successful tenderer to provide the Performance Security required by the

11. *FIDIC Procurement Procedures Guide* (FIDIC, 2011) 116-117.
12. *Ibid.*, 116.
13. *See* Sub-Clause 4.10 [*Use of Site Data*].
14. *FIDIC Procurement Procedures Guide* (FIDIC, 2011), 122.
15. Sub-Clause 4.10 [*Use of Site Data*].
16. *FIDIC Procurement Procedures Guide* (FIDIC, 2011) 123.
17. *See* the definition of '**Unforeseeable**' in Sub-Clause 1.1.85.
18. *See* the definition of '**Base Date**' in Sub-Clause 1.1.4.
19. *See* the form of tender security included as Annex B in RB/17.

General Conditions of the eventual Contract[20] between the Contractor and the Employer.[21]

After tenders have been submitted and the Employer has selected the most advantageous tender, sometimes – while not respecting strictly the principles of international competitive bidding – a period of negotiation may ensue.[22] This may result from proposals, qualifications or other reservations in a tender or requests from the Employer to a tenderer to clarify its tender. Once all issues have been clarified and negotiations concluded, the Employer should, ideally, prepare a memorandum recording the details of all matters which have been clarified and agreed (sometimes called a 'memorandum of understanding').[23] This memorandum is signed by the successful tenderer and the Employer and then attached to the Letter of Acceptance which the Employer signs and sends to the tenderer.[24] Assuming that there are no further matters requiring the tenderer's agreement, upon the tenderer's (future Contractor's) receipt of the Letter of Acceptance, there should be a legally binding contract between the Employer and the Contractor.

If the Employer does not take the approach of preparing a memorandum and is unwilling to accept the proposals, qualifications or other reservations in a tender (which it otherwise judges to be the most favourable tender), it may reply by a 'Letter of Acceptance' rejecting such reservations in which case this letter will amount legally to a counter-offer. This might require the 'Letter of Acceptance' to be formally accepted by the relevant tenderer for a legally binding contract to be created. The Employer's counter-offer may sometimes be followed by a further counter-offer from the tenderer, and it may sometimes become quite

20. *See* Sub-Clause 4.2 [*Performance Security*] of the General Conditions.
21. *FIDIC Procurement Procedures Guide* (FIDIC, 2011) 117-118.
22. The World Bank recognises that negotiations may take place under certain conditions in relation to international competitive procurement for projects which it finances, *see* ss 6.34-6.36 of *The World Bank Procurement Regulations for IPF Borrowers – Procurement in Investment Project Financing – Goods, Works, Non-Consulting and Consulting Services* (4th edn, November 2020).
23. Ideally, the memorandum should include agreement on members of the Dispute Avoidance/Adjudication Board ('DAAB'). *See Guidance for the Preparation of Particular Conditions*, 47.
24. *See FIDIC Procurement Procedures Guide* (FIDIC, 2011) 183-184, and the form of Letter of Acceptance included in RB/17.

complicated to determine, as a legal matter, when the Parties entered into a legally binding agreement.[25]

2.4 Contract Agreement

To avoid this kind of legal uncertainty, as well as for other reasons, RB/17 provides that, once the Parties have agreed on all terms of their contract – and even if the Contractor has received a Letter of Acceptance – they should enter into a Contract Agreement[26] which incorporates all those terms and sets them out clearly and comprehensively. Whenever this occurs, the Contract, as a whole, will take effect if this has not occurred upon the Contractor's receipt of the Letter of Acceptance. Thus, the Clauses of the General Conditions commented on hereafter should be taken to be legally operative from that date, at the latest.

3 ORGANISATION OF COMMENTARY

In the commentary below, the various Sub-Clauses of the General Conditions of RB/17[27] are commented upon sequentially.[28] At the

25. Where it is not immediately possible for the Employer to award the contract and issue a Letter of Acceptance, the Employer may wish to advise the tenderer submitting the most favourable tender of the Employer's intention to award it the contract by issuing a letter of intent. If the Employer should wish the tenderer to commence work in anticipation of the issue of a Letter of Acceptance, the Employer and the tenderer should agree on a separate pre-contract work agreement, instead of a letter of intent. *See* the *FIDIC Procurement Procedures Guide* (FIDIC, 2011) 184 for a description of provisions such an agreement should contain.
26. Unless the Parties agree otherwise. *See* Sub-Clause 1.6 [*Contract Agreement*].
27. The text reproduces the 2022 reprint of RB/17 and thus takes account of: (1) an errata document issued by FIDIC in 2018, http://fidic.org/sites/default/files/bean_files/RED2017_errata_sheet_existing%20stock_fidic.pdf accessed 6 November 2022, (2) a memorandum with additional errata issued by FIDIC in 2019 http://fidic.org/sites/default/files/bean_files/Memo%20for%20Rainbow%20Suite%202017%2004.06.19.pdf accessed 6 November 2022 and (3) further amendments incorporated by FIDIC in the 2022 reprint of RB/17. All three sets of amendments are available for free download from the FIDIC Bookshop at FIDIC's website at fidic.org. *See* Christopher R Seppälä, 'Welcome Amendments to FIDIC's 2017 Contracts', https://www.i-law.com/ilaw/doc/view.htm?id=432162, to be published in the ICLR in 2023.
28. The General Conditions of RB/17 are divided principally into Clauses and Sub-Clauses in which there are also sometimes lettered or numbered

beginning of the commentary on each Clause, there is a brief description, in a few sentences, of what it contains. Thereafter, each Sub-Clause is generally commented on separately. In the commentary on each Sub-Clause, following quotation of the reproduced text of the Sub-Clause (or group of Sub-Clauses) from RB/17, its content is summarised **in bold text** followed by a commentary under up to **five bold text** headings (to the extent each appears relevant to the Sub-Clause), as follows:

(i) **Main Changes from RB/99**: This describes the main changes from RB/99 and refers occasionally to other relevant history of the Sub-Clause.

(ii) **Related Clauses / Sub-Clauses**: While not an exhaustive listing of related provisions, this identifies the principal related Clauses or Sub-Clauses, if any, in the General Conditions (omitting, however, terms defined in Clause 1 [*General Provisions*], as they are readily identifiable by having initial capital letters) and (in a few cases) the General Conditions of the DAAB Agreement.

(iii) **Analysis**: This will, where appropriate, review the purpose and function of the Sub-Clause and the key issues raised by it including those to which, in previous editions of the RB, YB or SB (as their content is similar), a provision like it has given rise in practice to a dispute, occasionally referring to legal cases or arbitral awards.

(iv) **Related Law**: This refers to common law, civil law, international arbitral awards and legal principles (specifically, the

sub-paragraphs. The Clauses and Sub-Clauses often contain multiple paragraphs. However, as the paragraphs are not numbered or their length always identifiable, it can be difficult to refer to them in a practical way. Indeed, when a paragraph extends from the bottom of one page to the next page it is sometimes unclear, when a sentence ends at the bottom of the page, whether the text on the next page is part of the same paragraph or, if it begins with a new sentence, whether it is the beginning of a new paragraph. Accordingly, in this commentary, individual paragraphs have been identified as well as possible in the circumstances. In future editions, referencing and cross-referencing would be easier and more practical if every paragraph and sub-paragraph were consecutively numbered and if each paragraph or sub-paragraph contained merely one idea or requirement. This would also make each paragraph and sub-paragraph shorter as well as easier to read and refer to.

UNIDROIT Principles), if any, which are relevant to the provision (other than those already discussed under **(iii) Analysis** above), as well as to legal and contract practice in various jurisdictions, without any pretence to being exhaustive.

(v) **Improvements**: This indicates suggested improvements, revisions or corrections, if any, to the Sub-Clause, which users may wish to take into account when drafting the Particular Conditions and/or which FIDIC may wish to consider when preparing a new edition of the Red Book.

In the commentary, the terms defined in Clause 1 of the General Conditions (e.g., 'Contractor', 'Employer' and 'Works') are used throughout. They are readily identifiable by having, like nearly all terms defined in Clause 1, initial capital letters. For the meaning of abbreviations commonly used, *see* the ***List of Abbreviations and Definitions*** at the beginning of this book.

This commentary includes in footnotes reference to, and/or discussion of, the most relevant provisions – for general users – of The World Bank's Particular Conditions ('COPA') for use with RB/17 which were issued in 2019.[29]

--ooOOoo--

4 CLAUSE-BY-CLAUSE COMMENTARY

There is contained below a Clause-by-Clause commentary on the General Conditions of RB/17 beginning with **Clause 1. General Provisions**.

29. The COPA consists of Part A – Contract Data; Part B – Special Provisions; Part C – Bank's Policy: Corrupt and Fraudulent Practices; Part D – Environmental and Social (ES) Reporting Metrics for Progress Reports; and Part E – Sexual Exploitation and Abuse (SEA) and/or Sexual Harassment Performance Declaration for Subcontractors. There is no reference in this commentary below to provisions of the COPA related to The World Bank's role as lender and limited discussion of its detailed provisions concerning staff and labour, principally modifications to Clause 6, and environmental and social conditions, these all being special concerns of the Bank and not necessarily of general users of RB/17.

1 General Provisions

1.1 Definitions

(1) Their purpose

Sub-Clause 1.1 defines a number of words and expressions. These defined terms are a sort of verbal shorthand for describing various persons, matters or things referred to in the General Conditions and more generally in the Contract. Their use avoids the need to repeat, perhaps many times over, a longer series of words. For example, use of the defined term 'Contract' obviates the need to have to refer to its exact title, date and (possibly) number, and use of the defined term 'Contractor' obviates the need to have to refer to the full name of the company, or companies in a joint venture, constituting the Contractor. Defined terms also permit the same person, matter or thing to be referred to in the same way consistently throughout the Contract making it clear when a particular person, matter or thing is meant.[1]

(2) A common language (lingua franca)

In addition, the defined terms provide a vocabulary or set of words and expressions which the Parties and the Engineer can and should be employing – though RB/17 does not generally require this[2] – in their day-to-day communications. To avoid misunderstandings and disputes, all Notices (as defined) and other communications, whether oral or written, between the Parties or with the Engineer (and later with the DAAB and arbitrators, if any) should use consistently the defined terms

1. For a case where a failure to define the term 'main contract' in an agreement may have ended up costing the contractor over GBP 1 million pounds *see Almacantar (Centre Point) Ltd v Sir Robert McAlpine Ltd* [2018] EWHC 232 (TCC).
2. However, the documents making up the Contract in RB/17 are increasingly (compared to RB/99) *being defined by reference to how they are 'entitled'*, making the use of the correct title for a document that is to make up the Contract essential. *See*, e.g., Sub-Clauses 1.1.5 '**Bill of Quantities**', 1.1.72 '**Schedule of Payments**' and 1.1.76 '**Specification**'. If a document does not bear the correct title, as provided for in **Section 1.1 Definitions**, it may not be considered to be part of the Contract.

and refrain from different terminology.[3] The defined terms should, in effect, be incorporated into the language for communications referred to in Sub-Clause 1.4.[4]

As the Contract is for international use, definitions may also be helpful as they provide a *lingua franca* or common language for the Parties and the Engineer to use in their communications. Otherwise, Parties from different countries with different languages and cultures may find themselves resorting to different words or terms for the same thing or the same term or word for different things, leading to misunderstandings and disputes.[5]

(3) Knowledge of the definitions is necessary

Thus, the Employer, the Contractor and the Engineer need each to be very familiar with the defined terms and their use in the Contract. As a

3. A case involving YB/99 provides an example of a dispute resulting from failure to use the vocabulary of the contract. The tribunal had to consider whether the Employer's claim for delay damages had previously been settled by an agreement providing 'All claims formulated until the date of this [settlement agreement] are deemed by the Parties as fully settled'. The Employer argued that the expression 'formulation of a claim' was intended to mean 'substantiation of a claim' so as to exclude the Employer's claim from the scope of the settlement agreement. The Contractor, on the other hand, argued that 'formulation of a claim' had to mean 'notification of a claim' and that the Employer's claim had been notified before that agreement and therefore was settled by it. As 'formulation of a claim' is not an expression used in FIDIC conditions, the tribunal had to engage in a lengthy analysis before arriving at the conclusion that the Employer's claim, which was notified before the settlement agreement, was formulated before that agreement and was therefore settled by that agreement. This dispute could have been avoided had the Parties restricted themselves, as much as possible, to the vocabulary and defined terms in the FIDIC form concerned. Final award, ICC case 19346 (2014) ICC Disp Resol Bull, 2015, Issue 1, 142-146 (commentary 34).
4. If the language for communications is different from the ruling language (*see* Sub-Clause 1.4 [*Law and Language*]) of the Contract, then reliance must be placed on a carefully prepared translation from the ruling language, ideally agreed between the Parties. *See* **Section 5.2 Relevance of Language** of **Chapter III Contract Interpretation** above which discusses translation of the FIDIC forms.
5. To illustrate how easily this problem can arise, even within the English language, *see* the comparison of British-English construction terms with their 'rough equivalent' American-English terms in **Table 1** in **Section 3.2.1 Use of British-English Language** of **Chapter I General Introduction** above.

matter of good practice, they should apply them exclusively – always, with their initial capital letters where they are capitalised – when performing the Contract. Absent any indication to the contrary, it will tend to be assumed that whenever the defined terms are used with their initial capital letters in any Notice or other communication during performance of the Contract they will have the meanings assigned to them by Sub-Clause 1.1. This is, moreover, how the defined terms are used in this commentary.[6]

Commentary

(i) Main Changes from RB/99: The organisation, number and importance or significance of the definitions have changed. Sub-Clause 1.1 in RB/99 contained 58 definitions grouped under six subject matter headings, as follows:

1.1.1 The Contract
1.1.2 Parties and Persons
1.1.3 Dates, Tests, Periods and Completion
1.1.4 Money and Payments
1.1.5 Works and Goods
1.1.6 Other Definitions

On the other hand, in RB/17, there are 88 definitions not grouped under headings, but listed alphabetically.[7] Alternatives have also been added in the definitions. For example, the abbreviation 'EOT' has been added as an alternative to Extension of Time, 'DNP' as an alternative to Defects Notification Period, 'IPC' as an alternative to Interim Payment Certificate, and 'NOD' as an alternative to Notice of Dissatisfaction.

6. FIDIC has published a glossary of 'FIDIC Terms' at https://fidic.org/other-resources/fidic-terms-glossary accessed at 14 November 2022 comprising terms and definitions commonly used in FIDIC's standard forms of contract (especially under the FIDIC Terms' category 'Contracts and Agreements') and other publications. The descriptions or definitions in this glossary are not intended to replace the definitions in a FIDIC form of contract but only to indicate the overall principle involved. A Glossary of Terminology used in the construction industry is contained in *The FIDIC Contracts Guide* (2nd edn, FIDIC, 2022) 611.

7. Accordingly, 30 new definitions have been added. For example, there are new definitions of '**Claim**', '**Date of Completion**', '**Delay Damages**', '**Dispute**', '**Extension of Time**', '**Notice**', '**Notice of Dissatisfaction**'.

Unlike RB/99 which limited the application of defined terms to the General and Particular Conditions, Sub-Clause 1.1 in RB/17 states that the definitions apply to the 'Contract',[8] which is defined in Sub-Clause 1.1.10. The Contract comprises not only the Conditions but also the Contract Agreement, Letter of Acceptance, Letter of Tender, addenda and the JV Undertaking, if any, as well as technical documents such as the Specifications, Drawings and Schedules. *Consequently, all persons engaged in the preparation of the documents making up the Contract need to be alerted to the wide application of the definitions.*

(ii) Analysis: The defined terms in Sub-Clause 1.1 (except for the definitions of 'day', 'month' and 'year') are set forth with initial capital letters. Accordingly, whenever users of RB/17 come across a term or expression with initial capital letters in the Contract, they should check Sub-Clause 1.1 for its meaning. This meaning will apply 'except where the context requires otherwise'.[9]

As in RB/99, a number of 'definitions' are not strictly definitions; that is, they do not state the exact meaning of a word or expression but, instead, cross-refer to Sub-Clauses where the meaning of the relevant term is defined or described.[10]

Sub-Clause 1.1 also does not include all definitions used. A number of Clauses or Sub-Clauses provide for additional definitions for the purposes of those Clauses or Sub-Clauses; e.g., Sub-Clause 2.5 provides for a definition of 'items of reference', Sub-Clause 4.12 provides for a definition of 'physical conditions' and Sub-Clause 5.2.1 provides for a definition of 'nominated Subcontractor'. As can be seen, those definitions do not have initial capital letters (other than Subcontractor which is itself a defined term).

In general, changes to the definitions in Sub-Clause 1.1 should be avoided.[11] However, in some circumstances, it may be desirable to amend a definition for a particular construction project.[12] If new definitions are introduced into Sub-Clause 1.1, care needs to be taken to ensure that the numbering and placement of the new definitions are consistent with the numbering and alphabetical ordering in that Sub-Clause.

8. Sub-Clause 1.1 [*Definitions*] first sentence.
9. *Ibid.*
10. For example, Sub-Clauses 1.1.13 '**Contract Price**', 1.1.37 '**Exceptional Event**' and 1.1.41 '**Final Statement**'.
11. *Guidance for the Preparation of Particular Conditions*, 14.
12. *Ibid.*

The following are comments on the individual definitions in Sub-Clause 1.1 [*Definitions*].

> In the Contract the following words and expressions shall have the meanings stated, except where the context requires otherwise

1.1.1 'Accepted Contract Amount'

> 1.1.1 "**Accepted Contract Amount**" means the amount accepted in the Letter of Acceptance for the execution of the Works in accordance with the Contract.

The Accepted Contract Amount is the amount which, upon entry into the Contract, the Parties have agreed that the Employer should pay the Contractor for the execution of the Works. It is set forth in the Letter of Tender, which the Employer accepts by the Letter of Acceptance and/or in the Contract Agreement. The Accepted Contract Amount, which is a fixed amount,[13] is to be contrasted with the Contract Price which is variable and the actual amount to be paid to the Contractor after adjustments on account of Claims, Variations, changes in Cost, etc.[14]

1.1.2 'Advance Payment Certificate'

> 1.1.2 "**Advance Payment Certificate**" means a Payment Certificate issued by the Engineer for advance payment under Sub-Clause 14.2.2 [*Advance Payment Certificate*].

---

13. Sub-Clause 14.2.3(a) implies that it includes Provisional Sums as it refers to the Accepted Contract Amount 'less Provisional Sums'. This is confirmed by the form of the Letter of Acceptance reproduced in **Appendix 3** hereto.
14. The Accepted Contract Amount is useful to the Employer in establishing the budget for a project as it represents the amount which the Employer is committed initially to pay for the project, before adjustments for future events such as Claims, Variations and changes in Cost, which, if necessary (for budgetary purposes), may be estimated collectively as corresponding to some percentage of the Accepted Contract Amount. The General Conditions make use of the 'Accepted Contract Amount' in, for example: Sub-Clause 1.15 [*Limitation of Liability*], Sub-Clause 2.4 [*Employer's Financial Arrangements*], third paragraph, Sub-Clause 4.2 [*Performance Security*] and Sub-Clause 5.1 [*Subcontractors*].

This newly defined term refers to the Payment Certificate issued by the Engineer under Sub-Clause 14.2.2 [*Advance Payment Certificate*] for the advance payment. As provision for an Advance Payment Certificate helps clarify how, when and under what conditions, the advance payment is to be made, this is a welcome new addition.[15]

1.1.3 'Advance Payment Guarantee'

> 1.1.3 "**Advance Payment Guarantee**" means the guarantee under Sub-Clause 14.2.1 [*Advance Payment Guarantee*].

This guarantee is provided by the Contractor to the Employer, with a copy to the Engineer, to secure the repayment to the Employer of the advance payment or the remaining unamortised portion of it.[16]

1.1.4 'Base Date'

> 1.1.4 "**Base Date**" means the date 28 days before the latest date for submission of the Tender.

In the context of an international tendering procedure (which RB/17 assumes),[17] the Base Date is the date as of which the Contractor is taken to have calculated the rates and prices in its Tender. It assumes that the Contractor will have had the time and opportunity by then to take account of all information relevant to the preparation of its Tender.[18]

As in RB/99, the Base Date is defined as the date 28 days before the latest date for submission of the Tender. In a number of Sub-Clauses matters are linked to the Base Date.[19]

15. *See* the commentary on Sub-Clause 14.2 [*Advance Payment*] below.
16. An example form of advance payment guarantee is included as Annex E in RB/17.
17. *See* **Section 2 Context of a Red Book Contract** above of **Chapter IV**.
18. If the Employer makes significant data/information available to tenderers 28 days or less before the due date for the submission of tenders, the Employer should consider extending the Base Date. *Guidance for the Preparation of Particular Conditions,* 14.
19. For example: the definition of '**Unforeseeable**' in Sub-Clause 1.1.85 is linked to the Base Date, as are Sub-Clauses 2.5 [*Site Data and Items of Reference*], 4.15 [*Access Route*] and 13.6 [*Adjustments for Changes in Laws*].

1.1.5 'Bill of Quantities'

> 1.1.5 "**Bill of Quantities**" means the document entitled bill of quantities (if any) included in the Schedules.

The Bill of Quantities is prepared by the Employer's advisers on the basis of the Drawings and Specification, and is included in the tender dossier. It will typically break down the entire project into its constituent trades and processes and contain estimated quantities of different items of work necessary for the execution of the Works.[20] Tenderers are required to price the individual items in the Bill of Quantities which are then grossed up to produce a total contract sum.[21] After the Contract is entered into, the Bill of Quantities is for valuing work, including Variations.[22]

The Bill of Quantities is used as a basis for assessing interim payments pursuant to Sub-Clause 14.6.1 and for producing a final remeasurement

20. For an excellent discussion of the nature of the bill of quantities, *see* I.N. Duncan Wallace, *The ICE Conditions of Contract Fifth Edition, A Commentary*, Appendix A: *The Use of Bills of Quantities in Civil Engineering and Building Contracts* (Sweet & Maxwell, London, 1978), 305-316.
21. *Ibid.*, 307.
22. *See* the commentaries on Sub-Clauses 12.3 [*Valuation of the Works*] and 13.3 [*Variation Procedure*] below. FIDIC explains that:

> The bill of quantities should comprise brief identifying descriptions and estimated quantities of work comprised in the execution of the works. The employer may choose to divide the bill of quantities into work groups or otherwise to facilitate comparison of tenders, as well as to facilitate the making of interim payments during the progress of the works. However, the bill of quantities should be formed in such a way as to ensure that tenderers fill in rates and prices that cover, without duplication or omission, for the total work to be carried out as well as for all other obligations of the contractor under the contract. The preamble to the bill of quantities should describe the measurement procedures adopted for its preparation and to be used in measuring work done, which may be a published standard method or the employer's own.
>
> *FIDIC Procurement Procedures Guide* (FIDIC, 2011) 121.

or recalculation of the Contract Price pursuant to Clause 12. The method of measurement of the Works should be stated in the Contract Data or elsewhere.[23]

Note from the definition that, as mentioned earlier,[24] for a document to be considered to be the 'Bill of Quantities' included in the Schedules (and, thus, in the Contract), *it must be entitled 'Bill of Quantities'* (or '*bill of quantities*'). *The same need to use correct titles* applies to other documents that make up the Contract; e.g., *see* the definitions of '**Contract Data**' and '**Daywork Schedule**' commented on below.

1.1.6 'Claim'

> 1.1.6 "**Claim**" means a request or assertion by one Party to the other Party (excluding a matter to be agreed or determined under sub-paragraph (a) of Sub-Clause 3.7 [*Agreement or Determination*]), for an entitlement or relief under any Clause of these Conditions or otherwise in connection with, or arising out of, the Contract or the execution of the Works.

This is the first definition of a claim in a FIDIC form. According to this definition, the word 'Claim' covers not only a 'request or assertion' by one Party to the other arising 'under any Clause' of the Conditions (i.e., a Contractor's claim for additional payment and/or an EOT or an Employer's claim for payment and/or extension of the DNP) but also (because of the words 'or otherwise in connection with, or arising out of, the Contract or the execution of the Works') a claim relating to the Contract or the Works arising under applicable law, whether in contract or tort.[25]

23. According to Sub-Clause 12.2 [*Method of Measurement*], the method of measurement of the Works shall be as stated in the Contract Data or, if not so stated, that which shall be in accordance with the Bill of Quantities or other applicable Schedule(s).
24. *See* fn. 2 above in this commentary on **Clause 1**.
25. *See* for more details the author's letter to the Editors of the ICLR published in [2011] ICLR on the unnumbered page after page 133. 'Tort' is a common law term meaning a civil wrong, other than a breach of contract, for which a remedy may be obtained usually in the form of damages. Bryan A Garner (ed in chief), *Black's Law Dictionary* (11th edn, Thomson Reuters, St Paul, MN,

While this definition is very broad, as the result of FIDIC's amendments issued in 2022,[26] it expressly excludes a 'matter to be agreed or determined' as defined in sub-paragraph (a) of Sub-Clause 3.7. A 'matter to be agreed or determined' is the subject of a separate procedure under the Conditions from that applicable to a 'Claim'.[27] A Claim is also to be distinguished from a Dispute which is separately defined.[28]

Claims, whether of the Employer or the Contractor, are subject to detailed regulation in Clause 20 [*Employer's and Contractor's Claims*].[29] The term 'claim' with a small 'c' is also used in the General Conditions and, in that case, unless defined for purposes of use in a specific sub-clause,[30] it has its ordinary meaning in the English language, e.g., a 'claim under the Performance Security' as provided for in Sub-Clause 4.2.2.

1.1.7 'Commencement Date'

> 1.1.7 "**Commencement Date**" means the date as stated in the Engineer's Notice issued under Sub-Clause 8.1 [*Commencement of Works*].

Sub-Clause 8.1 [*Commencement of Works*] specifies that the Engineer's Notice of the Commencement Date must be given not less than 14 days before the Commencement Date and that, unless stated otherwise in the Particular Conditions, the Commencement Date shall be within 42 days after the Contractor receives the Letter of Acceptance.[31]

2019). Examples of tort are libel, defamation or any culpable or unlawful conduct resulting in harm to another.

26. *See* the Note following the List of Abbreviations and Definitions at the beginning of this book.
27. *See* Sub-Clause 3.7, second paragraph.
28. A '**Dispute**' is defined in Sub-Clause 1.1.29.
29. *See* the commentary on Clause 20 below which also includes in **Tables 5** and **6** lists of Employer's and Contractor's Claims.
30. As in the case of a 'third party claim' alleging infringement under Sub-Clause 17.3 [*Intellectual and Industrial Property Rights*].
31. *See* the commentary on Sub-Clause 8.1 [*Commencement of Works*] below.

The Commencement Date marks the beginning of the Time for Completion as defined in Sub-Clause 1.1.84. Many of the Contractor's obligations are therefore linked to the Commencement Date.[32]

1.1.8 'Compliance Verification System'

> 1.1.8 "**Compliance Verification System**" means the compliance verification system to be prepared and implemented by the Contractor for the Works in accordance with Sub-Clause 4.9.2 [*Compliance Verification System*].

This is a project management tool which the Contractor must prepare and implement to demonstrate that the design, if any, Materials, Employer-Supplied Materials, if any, Plant, work and workmanship comply with the Contract.[33]

1.1.9 'Conditions of Contract' or 'these Conditions'

> 1.1.9 "**Conditions of Contract**" or "**these Conditions**" means these General Conditions and the Particular Conditions.

Together with the Letter of Acceptance, Contract Agreement, if any, and JV Undertaking, if any, the Conditions of Contract comprise, roughly speaking, the 'legal' as distinct from the 'technical' portion of the Contract.[34] The Conditions of Contract consist of the General Conditions, containing the Conditions of Contract as published by FIDIC (*see* Sub-

---

32. *See*, for example, Sub-Clauses 4.3 [*Contractor's Representative*], 4.8 [*Health and Safety Obligations*], 4.9 [*Quality Management and Compliance Verification Systems*], 6.8 [*Contractor's Superintendence*], 14.1 [*The Contract Price*], 14.4 [*Schedule of Payments*] and 17.1 [*Responsibility for Care of the Works*]. *See also* **Figures 5 Sequence of Events Before the Commencement Date ('CD')** at the end of the commentary on Clause 4 and **7 Sequence of Initial Events After the Commencement Date ('CD')** at the end of the commentary on Sub-Clause 8.2 below.
33. *See* the commentary on Sub-Clause 4.9 [*Quality Management and Compliance Verification Systems*] below.
34. Strictly, the entire Contract is 'legal' as it establishes the legal rights and obligations of the Parties.

Clause 1.1.43), as modified by the Particular Conditions consisting of a Part A, Contract Data and a Part B, Special Provisions consisting of amendments or additions to the General Conditions. The 'technical' portion of the Contract comprises the Specification, the Drawings and the Schedules.

1.1.10 'Contract'

> 1.1.10 "**Contract**" means the Contract Agreement, the Letter of Acceptance, the Letter of Tender, any addenda referred to in the Contract Agreement, these Conditions, the Specification, the Drawings, the Schedules, the JV Undertaking (if applicable) and the further documents (if any) which are listed in the Contract Agreement or in the Letter of Acceptance.

The 'Contract' comprises the numerous documents described in this definition. These documents are now, in RB/17, defined for the first time as including: (1) 'any addenda referred to in the Contract Agreement'[35] and (2) the 'JV Undertaking (if applicable)'.[36]

This definition, as it may have been amended by the Particular Conditions, is likely to speak as of the date of issuance of the tender dossier, when the Conditions of Contract are issued. When the Contract comes into force (upon the Contractor's receipt of the Letter of Acceptance and/or the Parties' signature of a Contract Agreement), the documents described in this Sub-Clause as making up the Contract may be superseded by those which actually do so (reflecting changes resulting from post-tender negotiations, if any, or other events) as they may be listed in the Contract Agreement[37] and/or the Letter of Acceptance.[38]

---

35. *See* Sub-Clause 1.1.50 **'Letter of Acceptance'** (which expression can mean, according to Sub-Clause 1.1.50, the Contract Agreement) which refers to the possible existence of 'annexed memoranda comprising agreements between and signed by both Parties'.
36. *See* the commentary below on Sub-Clause 1.1.47 **'JV Undertaking'**.
37. *See* Clause 2 of the form of Contract Agreement in RB/17.
38. Sub-Clause 1.1.10 does not exclude the possibility that there could be other documents contradicting or supplementing the documents described as making up the Contract. In this connection, *see* **Section 5.1.2 Absence of Entire Agreement Clause** in **Chapter III Contract Interpretation** above.

The priority of the documents comprising the Contract is addressed in Sub-Clause 1.5 [*Priority of Documents*].

1.1.11 'Contract Agreement'

> 1.1.11 "**Contract Agreement**" means the agreement entered into by both Parties in accordance with Sub-Clause 1.6 [*Contract Agreement*].

While Sub-Clause 1.6 [*Contract Agreement*] provides that the Parties shall sign a Contract Agreement after the Contractor receives the Letter of Acceptance, that Sub-Clause also envisages that they may 'agree otherwise'. They may do so as the Contractor's Letter of Tender and the Employer's Letter of Acceptance, taken together, may be sufficient (upon the Contractor's receipt of the Letter of Acceptance, if not earlier) to create a legally binding contract between the Parties,[39] making more paperwork to this end unnecessary. However, if there have been post-tender negotiations or discussions, they may have resulted in additional agreements or understandings between the Parties which they wish to record.[40] For these reasons and/or because of the requirements of local law, the Parties often enter into a Contract Agreement.[41]

1.1.12 'Contract Data'

> 1.1.12 "**Contract Data**" means the pages, entitled contract data which constitute Part A of the Particular Conditions.

The 'Appendix to Tender' in RB/99 has been replaced by a form entitled 'Contract Data' which, instead of being appended to the Letter of Tender as in RB/99, constitutes Part A of the Particular Conditions in RB/17. Numerous Sub-Clauses of the General Conditions refer to data or information which needs to be inserted in the Contract Data – many more than in the case of the Appendix to Tender. This information comprises key terms which are specific to the project, such as the Employer's and

39. In the form of the Letter of Acceptance in RB/17, the Employer acknowledges that it 'creates a binding Contract' between the Parties.
40. RB/17 includes a form of Contract Agreement.
41. *See* the commentary on Sub-Clause 1.6 [*Contract Agreement*] below.

Engineer's name and address, the durations of the Time for Completion and the Defects Notification Period, the governing law, the ruling language, the amount of the Performance Security, the amount of Delay Damages and the currencies for payment of the Contract Price.

Most of this information will have been completed by the Employer or a consultant, when preparing the tender dossier,[42] but some items will be left for completion by tenderers.[43] If the Employer should fail to provide information required for inclusion in the Contract Data, either the fallback provisions to be found in some of the Sub-Clauses in the General Conditions will apply or essential information may be missing from the Contract.[44]

The provisions of the Contract Data (Particular Conditions – Part A) take precedence over the Special Provisions (Particular Conditions – Part B).[45]

1.1.13 'Contract Price'

> 1.1.13 **"Contract Price"** means the price defined in Sub-Clause 14.1 [*The Contract Price*].

This definition refers to the price defined in Sub-Clause 14.1 [*The Contract Price*] which is the value of the Works, as evaluated by the Engineer, subject to any adjustments, additions and/or deductions in accordance with the Contract. Thus, the Contract Price is the actual price ultimately to be paid to the Contractor under the Contract. For the difference between the Contract Price and the Accepted Contract Amount, *see* the commentary on Sub-Clause 1.1.1 above.

1.1.14 'Contractor'

> 1.1.14 **"Contractor"** means the person(s) named as contractor in the Letter of

42. The Employer should insert 'Not Applicable' in the space next to any Sub-Clause which the Employer does not wish to use. *Guidance for the Preparation of Particular Conditions*, 2.
43. The Employer should insert 'Tenderer to Complete' in the space next to any Sub-Clause in the Contract Data which tenderers are to complete. *Guidance for the Preparation of Particular Conditions*, 2.
44. *Guidance for the Preparation of Particular Conditions*, 2.
45. Sub-Clause 1.5 [*Priority of Documents*].

Tender accepted by the Employer and the legal successors in title of such person(s).

The Contractor will have been the signatory of the Letter of Tender accepted by the Employer. In any Contract it is essential that each Party is clearly and fully identified. Accordingly, the full name of the Contractor should be stated together with, it is suggested, its legal nature (e.g., whether it is a company or some other type of person), its place of incorporation or where it has its seat (if it is a company) and its nationality (regardless of its legal nature).[46] If the Contractor comprises more than one person (e.g., constitutes a Joint Venture, as defined),[47] this information should, it is suggested, be provided for each person.[48] With regard to Joint Ventures, additional requirements apply.[49]

The expression 'legal successors in title' in RB/17 appears to be a misnomer, at least in the case of the definitions of the 'Contractor' and the 'Subcontractor'.[50] What appears to be intended by this expression, at least in the case of the Contractor and Subcontractor, is simply 'legal successor', that is, the person who succeeds by operation of law to the rights and obligations of its predecessor, the original person designated as the 'Contractor' or 'Subcontractor'.[51]

46. It is necessary to provide all this information from a legal standpoint as otherwise a company or other legal person is not fully identified. For example, two companies may have exactly the same name if they have been formed in different jurisdictions but not if they have been formed in the same jurisdiction.
47. Sub-Clause 1.1.46 '**Joint Venture**' or '**JV**'.
48. Accordingly, the form of the Letter of Tender included in RB/17 should be revised to allow for the inclusion of this information. If the Employer requires the Contractor or a member of a Joint Venture constituting the Contractor to provide a parent company guarantee, Annex A in RB/17 provides for such a form.
49. *See* the commentaries on Sub-Clause 1.1.46, 1.1.47 and 1.14 below.
50. *See* Sub-Clause 1.1.78 '**Subcontractor**'. 'Legal successor in title' has no established, fixed meaning in the common law. But as the Employer would often own the land upon which the Works would be executed, it might have been thought that 'Employer' should include subsequent persons acquiring title to the land or 'legal successors in title' to the land on which the Works were executed.
51. The national law which will decide the issue of exactly who that successor is will be determined under whatever conflict of laws rules apply. Conflict of laws rules refer to the legal principles relied on to determine preliminary

1.1.15 'Contractor's Documents'

> 1.1.15 "**Contractor's Documents**" means the documents prepared by the Contractor as described in Sub-Clause 4.4 [*Contractor's Documents*], including calculations, digital files, computer programs and other software, drawings, manuals, models, specifications and other documents of a technical nature.

The definition of Contractor's Documents in RB/99 referred broadly to certain documents and to 'other documents of a technical nature (if any) supplied by the Contractor under the Contract'.[52] The new definition refers to documents 'prepared by the Contractor as described in Sub-Clause 4.4 [*Contractor's Documents*]' and is then followed by a similar list of documents of a technical nature as contained in RB/99, plus 'digital files' and 'specifications'. Pursuant to Sub-Clause 4.4, Contractor's Documents are stated to comprise those:

(a) stated in the Specification;
(b) required to satisfy all permits, permissions, licences and other regulatory approvals which are the Contractor's responsibility under Sub-Clause 1.13 [*Compliance with Laws*];
(c) described in Sub-Clauses 4.4.2 [*As-Built Records*] and 4.4.3 [*Operation and Maintenance Manuals*], where applicable; and
(d) required under sub-paragraph (a) of Sub-Clause 4.1 which refers to documents for any part of the Permanent Works to be

issues of applicable law where more than one jurisdiction is involved in a dispute. *See* Bryan A Garner (ed in chief), *Black's Law Dictionary* (11th edn, Thomson Reuters, St Paul, MN, 2019). Under common law conflict of laws rules, where the Contractor or Subcontractor is a corporation, this is likely to be the law of the jurisdiction where it is incorporated (Dicey, Morris and Collins, *The Conflict of Laws* (15th edn, Sweet & Maxwell, London, 2012), vol 2, 1533 (para. 30-011)), and, where either is a natural person, this is likely to be law of the jurisdiction where the person is domiciled (or has his/her permanent home) (Dicey, Morris and Collins, *The Conflict of Laws* (15th edn, Sweet & Maxwell, London, 2012), vol 2, 1414 (para. 27R-010)).

52. Sub-Clause 1.1.6.1 of RB/99.

designed by the Contractor (and any other documents necessary to complete and implement the design and to instruct the Contractor's Personnel).[53]

The definition of Contractor's Documents is extremely broad as it covers not merely normal deliverables, such as drawings, records or manuals, but also documents used in their preparation, such as 'calculations, digital files, computer programs and other software' as well as 'models'.[54] Certain Contractor's Documents must be submitted to the Engineer for Review.[55]

The Contractor's Documents are to be distinguished from the documents which make up the Contract referred to in the definition of the 'Contract' in Sub-Clause 1.1.10, in Sub-Clause 1.5 [*Priority of Documents*] as well as in Article 2 of the form of Contract Agreement.

1.1.16 'Contractor's Equipment'

1.1.16 "**Contractor's Equipment**" means all apparatus, equipment, machinery, construction plant, vehicles and other items required by the Contractor for the execution of the Works. Contractor's Equipment excludes Temporary Works, Plant, Materials and any other things intended to form or forming part of the Permanent Works.

Contractor's Equipment forms part of 'Goods'[56] and refers to the equipment or other items required by the Contractor[57] for the execution of the Works. But it excludes Temporary Works and anything which is to form part of the Permanent Works. The reference to 'construction plant' in the

53. *See* sub-para. (a) of Sub-Clause 4.1 [*Contractor's General Obligations*].
54. This could raise issues for a Contractor concerned about protecting intellectual property owned or in its possession when it enters into the Contract.
55. For further details, *see* the commentary on Sub-Clause 4.4 below.
56. Defined in Sub-Clause 1.1.44.
57. Including its Subcontractors.

definition should be distinguished from 'Plant' defined in Sub-Clause 1.1.65. Whereas 'construction plant' is plant or equipment required by the Contractor for the execution of the Works, 'Plant' is the apparatus or equipment that is to form part of the Permanent Works.

1.1.17 'Contractor's Personnel'

> 1.1.17 "**Contractor's Personnel**" means the Contractor's Representative and all personnel whom the Contractor utilises on Site or other places where the Works are being carried out, including the staff, labour and other employees of the Contractor and of each Subcontractor; and any other personnel assisting the Contractor in the execution of the Works.

Whereas the RB/99 definition referred to 'all personnel whom the Contractor utilises on Site',[58] the new definition covers in addition personnel the Contractor utilises in 'other places where the Works are being carried out'.[59] The Contractor's Personnel comprise not only the Contractor's Representative (Sub-Clause 1.1.18), Key Personnel (Sub-Clause 1.1.48) and the Contractor's and Subcontractor's other employees but also (as in RB/99) 'any other personnel assisting the Contractor in the execution of the Works'.[60]

1.1.18 'Contractor's Representative'

> 1.1.18 "**Contractor's Representative**" means the natural person named by the Contractor in the Contract or appointed by the Contractor under Sub-Clause 4.3 [*Contractor's Representative*], who acts on behalf of the Contractor.

58. Sub-Clause 1.1.2.7 of RB/99.
59. Such as the 'additional areas' referred to in the first paragraph of Sub-Clause 4.22 [*Contractor's Operations on Site*].
60. *See also* Sub-Clause 6.9 [*Contractor's Personnel*].

The new definition specifies (unlike RB/99)[61] that the Contractor's Representative must be a 'natural' person, that is, not a legal entity.[62]

1.1.19 'Cost'

> 1.1.19 "**Cost**" means all expenditure reasonably incurred (or to be incurred) by the Contractor in performing the Contract, whether on or off the Site, including taxes, overheads and similar charges, but does not include profit. Where the Contractor is entitled under a Sub-Clause of these Conditions to payment of Cost, it shall be added to the Contract Price.

The definition of 'Cost' refers to expenditure by the Contractor, not the Employer. Cost encompasses both actual costs (i.e., expenditure which has been incurred) and estimated costs (i.e., expenditure 'to be incurred') and must have been 'reasonably incurred'. Cost includes expenditure whether on or off the Site to the extent that it is incurred (or to be incurred) 'in performing the Contract'.[63] Examples of references to Cost are in Sub-Clauses entitling the Contractor to claim additional payment.[64] Profit is explicitly excluded from the definition of Cost.

'Cost' includes 'taxes, overheads and similar charges'. The corresponding definition in RB/99 did not refer to taxes.[65] Thus, for example, VAT paid for Materials will be covered by the new definition of Cost.

61. Sub-Clause 1.1.2.5 of RB/99.
62. *See* the commentary on Sub-Clause 4.3 [*Contractor's Representative*] below.
63. In construction accounting, the terms 'direct costs' and 'indirect costs' are often used. While they are not defined in RB/17, generally speaking, direct costs are costs directly associated with the performance of the Works on the Site (e.g., costs of Materials, Plant and salaries of personnel on the Site), whereas indirect costs are primarily 'off-site' costs that are not directly attributable to a particular project (e.g., salaries of staff who are not on Site and head office rent). *See* Julian Bailey, *Construction Law* (3rd edn, London Publishing, UK, 2020) vol 2, 1027-1032 (paras 11.139-11.150).
64. *See* **Table 6 Contractor's Claims for Time and/or Money** at the end of the commentary on Clause 20 below.
65. *See* Sub-Clause 1.1.4.3 of RB/99.

'[O]verheads' can be of two types: site overheads and head office overheads.[66] Site overheads costs (sometimes also referred to as 'preliminaries') are specific to the project and comprise items of necessary cost that do not usually become part of the Permanent Works. Examples are site supervision, scaffolding, costs for a construction trailer and temporary utilities on Site. Head office overheads (sometimes also referred to as 'off-site overheads'), on the other hand, are indirect costs that are related to the running of the Contractor's business in general and are not specific to a project. These include, for example, a portion of the following: salaries of head office executives, costs of head office supplies and utilities and head office insurance premiums.[67]

'Cost' to which the Contractor is entitled under any Sub-Clause is to be added to the Contract Price.[68]

1.1.20 'Cost Plus Profit'

> 1.1.20 **"Cost Plus Profit"** means Cost plus the applicable percentage for profit stated in the Contract Data (if not stated, five percent (5%)). Such percentage shall only be added to Cost, and Cost Plus Profit shall only be added to the Contract Price, where the Contractor is entitled under a Sub-Clause of these Conditions to payment of Cost Plus Profit.

This newly defined term refers to a percentage of profit to be stated in the Contract Data and to a default rate of 5% in the event that nothing is

66. *See* Stephen Furst and Vivian Ramsey, *Keating on Construction Contracts* (11th edn, Sweet & Maxwell, London, 2021) 303-304 (paras 9-049 to 9-053).
67. Calculation of claims for loss of overheads is a complex exercise and different formulae have been suggested for this purpose. The best known are the Hudson, Eichleay and Emden formulae. *See* Julian Bailey, *Construction Law* (3rd edn, London Publishing, UK, 2020) vol 2, 1032-1035 (paras 11.152-11.158).
68. *See* Sub-Clause 14.1(a).

stated. In the individual Sub-Clauses entitling the Contractor to recover Cost and profit, RB/99 had referred to 'reasonable profit, which shall be included in the Contract Price'.[69]

Under individual Clauses or Sub-Clauses of RB/17, the Contractor is entitled to recover either Cost or Cost Plus Profit.[70] Cost Plus Profit (as distinct from Cost) is used:

> where the Employer is typically blameworthy [...] but not in circumstances which are not the fault of either Party [...].[71]

1.1.21 'Country'

> 1.1.21 "**Country**" means the country in which the Site (or most of it) is located, where the Permanent Works are to be executed.

In the case of cross-border projects, unless most of the Site is located in just one country, this definition would need to be revised.[72] Typical cross-border projects are hydroelectric schemes on a river between two or more countries, or bridges, gas pipeline projects or tunnels crossing the borders of several countries, or certain maritime projects.

1.1.22 'DAAB' or 'Dispute Avoidance/Adjudication Board'

> 1.1.22 "**DAAB**" or "**Dispute Avoidance/Adjudication Board**" means the sole member or three members (as the case may be) so named in the Contract, or

69. *See*, for example, Sub-Clause 2.1 and Sub-Clause 4.7 of RB/99. FIDIC had specified that the amount of profit may depend on the circumstances and suggested specifying profit as 5% of Cost. *The FIDIC Contracts Guide* (1st edn, FIDIC 2000) 54.
70. *See* **Table 6 Contractor's Claims for Time and/or Money** at the end of the commentary on Clause 20 below.
71. *The FIDIC Contracts Guide* (2nd edn, FIDIC, 2022) 18. Like 'Cost', 'Cost Plus Profit' is added to the Contract Price. Sub-Clause 14.1(a).
72. In such cases, Sub-Clause 1.1.21 may be amended as follows: 'Country means either xxxxx or yyyyyy depending on the location to which the reference will apply.' *Guidance for the Preparation of Particular Conditions*, 14.

appointed under Sub-Clause 21.1 [*Constitution of the DAAB*] or Sub-Clause 21.2 [*Failure to Appoint DAAB Member(s)*].

Generally, Disputes between the Parties must be referred to the DAAB for decision before they may be referred to arbitration pursuant to Sub-Clause 21.6 [*Arbitration*]. Whereas RB/99 had referred to a 'DAB' or 'Dispute Adjudication Board', RB/17 refers to a 'DAAB' or 'Dispute Avoidance/Adjudication Board', as it puts greater emphasis on its dispute avoidance function, as reflected in Sub-Clause 21.3 [*Avoidance of Disputes*].[73] The DAAB in RB/17 remains, as in RB/99, a standing board appointed at the start of the Contract.[74]

1.1.23 'DAAB Agreement'

1.1.23 "**DAAB Agreement**" means the agreement signed or deemed to have been signed by both Parties and the sole member or each of the three members (as the case may be) of the DAAB in accordance with Sub-Clause 21.1 [*Constitution of the DAAB*] or Sub-Clause 21.2 [*Failure to Appoint DAAB Member(s)*], incorporating by reference the General Conditions of DAAB Agreement contained in the Appendix to these General Conditions with such amendments as are agreed.

This newly defined term refers to the agreement required to be signed (or deemed to be signed) among the Employer, the Contractor and each member of the DAAB (or, if there is only one member, the sole member) in order to constitute the DAAB. The DAAB Agreement incorporates by reference the General Conditions of DAAB Agreement ('DAAB GCs') to

73. *See* the commentary on Sub-Clause 21.3 [*Avoidance of Disputes*] below.
74. The ad hoc DAB that was provided for in the General Conditions of YB/99 and SB/99 has also been replaced in the General Conditions of YB/17 and SB/17 by a standing DAAB. *See* the commentary on Sub-Clauses 21.1 to 21.4 below which also describes how the DAAB differs from the DAB. *See* also **Section 2** of **Chapter V Commentary on Other Documents** below.

which are annexed the DAAB Procedural Rules ('DAAB Rules'), both being together an Appendix to the General Conditions.[75]

1.1.24 'Date of Completion'

> 1.1.24 **"Date of Completion"** means the date stated in the Taking-Over Certificate issued by the Engineer under Sub-Clause 10.1 [*Taking Over the Works and Sections*] or the first paragraph of Sub-Clause 10.2 [*Taking Over Parts*]; or, if the last paragraph of Sub-Clause 10.1 [*Taking Over the Works and Sections*] applies, the date on which the Works or Section are deemed to have been completed in accordance with the Contract; or, if the second paragraph of Sub-Clause 10.2 [*Taking Over Parts*] or Sub-Clause 10.3 [*Interference with Tests on Completion*] applies, the date on which the Works or Section or Part are deemed to have been taken over by the Employer.

This is a newly defined term which may refer to the date of completion of the Works or of a Section, or a Part, of the Works. Therefore, in the case of any reference to the Date of Completion, it is necessary to determine to what it relates. The Date of Completion of the Works or a Section may be: (i) the date stated in the Taking-Over Certificate issued by the Engineer under the fourth paragraph of Sub-Clause 10.1 [*Taking Over the Works and Sections*] or the first paragraph of Sub-Clause 10.2 [*Taking Over Parts*], (ii) the date when the Works or a Section are deemed to have been completed under the last paragraph of Sub-Clause 10.1, or (iii) the date when the Works or a Section is deemed to have been taken over by the Employer under Sub-Clause 10.3 [*Interference with Tests on Completion*]. The Date of Completion of a Part will be the date when that Part shall be deemed to have been taken over by the Employer under the second paragraph of Sub-Clause 10.2 [*Taking Over Parts*]. However, the first sentence of Sub-Clause 10.2 provides also that '[t]he Engineer may, at the sole discretion of the Employer, issue a Taking-Over Certificate for any part of the Permanent Works'. In this case, the Date of Completion for

75. A form of DAAB Agreement is also included in RB/17.

that Part is – as stated in Sub-Clause 1.1.24 – the date stated in the Taking-Over Certificate issued under that provision.

The Date of Completion of the Works, a Section or a Part, as the case may be, has important contractual consequences.[76]

1.1.25 'day'

> 1.1.25 "**day**" means a calendar day.

As in RB/99, whenever the Contract refers to a 'day', this means a (working or non-working) calendar day, that is, from midnight to midnight.[77] Nothing is said about the relevant time zone that applies, which would therefore be for resolution by the governing law.

Time periods specified in days 'commence on the beginning of the day following the date of the act which constitutes the starting point'.[78]

1.1.26 'Daywork Schedule'

> 1.1.26 "**Daywork Schedule**" means the document entitled daywork schedule (if any) included in the Contract, showing the amounts and manner of payments to be made to the Contractor for labour, materials and equipment used for daywork under Sub-Clause 13.5 [*Daywork*].

Compared to RB/99,[79] the definition is expanded to describe the contents of a Daywork Schedule. If no Daywork Schedule is included in the Contract, Sub-Clause 13.5 [*Daywork*] states that it does not apply.

---

76. For example, it marks the beginning of the DNP for the Works, Section or Part (*see* the commentary on Sub-Clause 1.1.27 below). For other consequences, *see* under **(iii) Analysis** of the commentary on Sub-Clause 10.1 below.
77. *See* the commentary on Sub-Clause 1.3 [*Notices and Other Communications*] below.
78. *The FIDIC Contracts Guide* (2nd edn, FIDIC, 2022) 21.
79. Sub-Clause 1.1.1.10 of RB/99.

1.1.27 'Defects Notification Period' or 'DNP'

> 1.1.27 **"Defects Notification Period"** or **"DNP"** means the period for notifying defects and/or damage in the Works or a Section or a Part (as the case may be) under Sub-Clause 11.1 [*Completion of Outstanding Work and Remedying Defects*], as stated in the Contract Data (if not stated, one year), and as may be extended under Sub-Clause 11.3 [*Extension of Defects Notification Period*]. This period is calculated from the Date of Completion of the Works or Section or Part.

The Defects Notification Period or DNP is the period beginning at the Date of Completion[80] during which the Contractor is required to complete any outstanding work and (and is entitled to) remedy any defects or damage in the Works notified to it. Unlike the RB/99 definition,[81] Sub-Clause 1.1.27 refers to a DNP not only in respect of the Works or a Section but also in respect of a Part. Furthermore, the new definition specifies that the DNP will be of one year's duration if nothing is stated in the Contract Data.[82] The RB/99 definition stated that the DNP is calculated from the date of completion of the Works or a Section 'as certified under Sub-Clause 10.1 [*Taking Over of the Works and Sections*]'. Hence, the DNP was to be calculated from the date of issuance of a Taking-Over Certificate. Under the new definition the period runs from the relevant Date of Completion[83] and thus includes where the Works, a Section or a Part are deemed to have been completed whether or not a Taking-Over Certificate has been issued.[84]

80. Defined in Sub-Clause 1.1.24.
81. Sub-Clause 1.1.3.7 of RB/99.
82. Sub-Clause 1.1.3.7 of RB/99 referred to a period to be stated in the Appendix to Tender without providing for a default period. The Appendix to Tender had referred to a period of '365 days' which the Parties were free to amend.
83. *See* the commentary on Sub-Clause 1.1.24 above.
84. For further details concerning the DNP, *see* the commentaries on Sub-Clauses 11.1 [*Completion of Outstanding Work and Remedying Defects*] and 11.3 [*Extension of Defects Notification Period*] below.

1.1.28 'Delay Damages'

1.1.28 "**Delay Damages**" means the damages for which the Contractor shall be liable under Sub-Clause 8.8 [*Delay Damages*] for failure to comply with Sub-Clause 8.2 [*Time for Completion*].

This is a newly defined term in RB/17 and refers to the fixed amount of damages per day of delay (up to a maximum)[85] for which the Contractor is liable, pursuant to Sub-Clause 8.8, if it should fail to complete the Works or a Section within the relevant Time for Completion.[86]

1.1.29 'Dispute'

1.1.29 "**Dispute**" means any situation where:

(a) one Party has made a Claim, or there has been a matter to be agreed or determined under sub-paragraph (a) of Sub-Clause 3.7 [*Agreement or Determination*];

(b) the Engineer's determination under Sub-Clause 3.7.2 [*Engineer's Determination*] was a rejection (in whole or in part) of:

  (i) the Claim (or there was a deemed rejection under sub-paragraph (i) of Sub-Clause 3.7.3 [*Time limits*]); or

  (ii) a Party's assertion(s) in respect of the matter

as the case may be; and

(c) either Party has given a NOD under Sub-Clause 3.7.5 [*Dissatisfaction with Engineer's determination*].

85. *See* the form of Contract Data in RB/17.

86. For the different treatment of liquidated damages such as Delay Damages, in civil law and common law countries, *see* **Section 4 Common Law and Civil Law Compared – 4.4.5 Liquidated Damages and Penalties** of **Chapter II Applicable Law** above. *See also* the commentary on Sub-Clause 8.8 [*Delay Damages*] below.

GB/08 was the first form of FIDIC contract to contain a definition of 'Dispute'.[87] That definition corresponded closely to the definition in English case law.[88] Under the GB/08 definition, a Dispute is essentially 'any situation' where '(a) one Party makes a claim against the other Party, (b) the other Party rejects the claim in whole or in part, and (c) the first Party does not acquiesce'. The original definition of Dispute in RB/17 was similar to that in GB/08. In both cases, the existence of a Dispute is to be inferred from the existence of a particular controversy or difference between the Parties and whether one exists or not depends upon the particular facts.

The new definition introduced by the 2022 reprint of the 2017 Rainbow Suite is very different. Instead of a Dispute to be inferred from facts, it requires the satisfaction of three conditions:

(1) one Party must have made a Claim, or there must be a matter to be agreed or determined as defined in Sub-Clause 3.7 (a);[89]
(2) the Engineer must have rejected, in whole or in part, the Claim (or there must have been a deemed rejection under sub-paragraph (i) in the last paragraph of Sub-Clause 3.7.3) or a Party's assertion in respect of the matter; and
(3) either Party must have given a NOD under Sub-Clause 3.7.5 with respect to the Engineer's determination of rejection or (in the case of a Claim) deemed rejection.

Under the new, narrow and, one may say, artificial definition, no matter how fierce or great a difference or controversy between the Parties may

87. Sub-Clause 1.1.31 of GB/08.
88. For a good description of the English law background to the meaning of 'dispute' as a condition to arbitration (and now of the definition of a 'Dispute' in RB/17) *see* Julian Bailey, *Construction Law* (3rd edn, London Publishing, UK, 2020) vol 3, 2025-2027 (paras 25.93-25.97) and two English cases, *Monmouthshire C.C. v Costelloe & Kemple Ltd.* (1965) 5 BLR 83 and *AMEC Civil Engineering Ltd v Secretary of State for Transport* [2005] EWCA Civ 291, [2005] 1 W.L.R. 2339, which describes the *Monmouthshire* case as 'now middle-aged' at 2346 [para. 25].
89. Such a matter could concern, for example, the following: an Engineer's measurement of the Works under Sub-Clause 12.1 [*Works to Be Measured*], an Engineer's determination of a new rate or price under Sub-Clause 12.3 [*Valuation of the Works*] or an Engineer's determination of an EOT and/or adjustment of the Contract Price in case of Variations under Sub-Clause 13.3 [*Variation Procedure*]. *See* **Table 3 Matters to be Agreed or Determined by the Engineer** in the commentary on Sub-Clause 3.7 below.

be, with limited exceptions,[90] it will only give rise to a Dispute if the above three conditions are satisfied. The effect - and the intention - here is to reinforce the Engineer's role at the center of contract administration (as FIDIC had been concerned that the Engineer had sometimes been bypassed in referrals to the DAB under RB/99). Thus, where it is the Employer rather than the Engineer who has rejected the Contractor's Claim – as can sometimes happen in practice – then this literally will not satisfy the condition in sub-paragraph (b) of this Sub-Clause. There must be a rejection or deemed rejection, of the Claim, in whole or in part, by the Engineer, as well as the giving of a NOD by one of the Parties. Thus, Dispute with a capital 'D' has a very distinctive meaning.[91]

While the new definition acknowledges that, if the Engineer does not give a determination on a Claim within the relevant time-limit under Sub-Clause 3.7.3, the Claim is deemed to have been rejected by the Engineer, as provided for in sub-paragraph (i) in the last paragraph of Sub-Clause 3.7.3, it does not address where the Engineer fails to determine a matter (as distinct from a Claim), within the relevant time-limit, as in that case sub-paragraph (ii) in the last paragraph of Sub-Clause 3.7.3 provides that the matter is deemed to be a Dispute which may be referred by either Party to the DAAB for its decision under Sub-Clause 21.4. Thus, the procedure for a matter to become a Dispute is less onerous than that for a Claim to do so.

In addition, although not referred to in Sub-Clause 1.1.29, because of the narrowness of the definition (requiring, as it does, the giving of a NOD) a Dispute is deemed to have arisen in the three additional cases provided for in sub-paragraphs (a), (b) and (c) of Sub-Clause 21.4 [*Obtaining the DAAB's Decision*] (failure of the Engineer to issue, or the Employer to pay, a Payment Certificate; failure of the Contractor to receive financing charges when due; and in cases involving possible or actual termination of the Contract).

90. *See* sub-paragraph (ii) in the last paragraph of Sub-Clause 3.7.3 and those provided for in sub-paragraphs (a), (b) and (c) of Sub-Clause 21.4 below.
91. This definition is not much more complicated than that of 'Dispute' in the ICC's Dispute Board Rules (2015): 'any Disagreement (as defined) that is formally referred to a Dispute Board (as defined) for a Conclusion (as defined) under the terms of the Contract (as defined) and pursuant to Article 18 of the Rules.' Art. 2(iv).

The need for a 'Dispute' is important as only a difference, disagreement or controversy between the Parties that becomes a Dispute (as defined) may be referred to the DAAB for decision and, if necessary to international arbitration.[92]

1.1.30 'Drawings'

> 1.1.30 "**Drawings**" means the drawings of the Works included in the Contract, and any additional and modified drawings issued by (or on behalf of) the Employer in accordance with the Contract.

This definition is almost identical to the RB/99 definition.[93] It refers to both drawings included in the Contract when the Contract was entered into and additional or modified drawings that may be issued by (or on behalf of) the Employer thereafter in accordance with the Contract.[94] Together with the Specification, the Drawings form the primary technical requirements that the Contractor needs for the execution of the Permanent Works.

1.1.31 'Employer'

> 1.1.31 "**Employer**" means the person named as the employer in the Contract Data and the legal successors in title to this person.

As stated in relation to the definition of '**Contractor**' in Sub-Clause 1.1.14, in any contract it is essential that each Party is clearly and fully identified. Accordingly, the full name of the Employer should be stated together with, it is suggested, its legal nature (e.g., whether it is a company or some other type of person), its place of incorporation or where it has its seat (if it is a company) and its nationality (regardless of its legal nature).

Where the Employer is a state, government, ministry, public entity or some other public body or instrumentality, its precise legal nature under

92. *See* Sub-Clause 21.4 [*Obtaining DAAB's Decision*], first paragraph.
93. *See* Sub-Clause 1.1.1.6 of RB/99.
94. Sub-Clause 1.9 [*Delayed Drawings or Instructions*] envisages that the Engineer may be issuing drawings during the execution of the Works.

its national law should be described.[95] *In particular, it should be stated expressly whether or not the Employer is legally part of the state according to the law of the state concerned.*

Among other things, the Contractor will wish to ascertain that the Employer has the resources to fund the project,[96] which it can only do if it has identified the legal nature of the Employer. Thus, a sovereign state, being backed by the state's treasury, will have the financial resources of the state at its disposal, whereas an entity that is legally separate from the state, such as a state enterprise, will not and may have only very limited financial resources. Consequently, a failure sufficiently to identify the legal nature of the state party acting as the Employer may lead to unexpected difficulties for the Contractor later.[97]

---

95. How state bodies or instrumentalities are described and legally classified in one country (e.g., whether a ministry is a separate legal entity from the State) has no relevance in another. The Employer's national law must be investigated in each case.
96. Sub-Clause 2.4 [*Employer's Financial Arrangements*] requires the Employer to describe in the Contract Data the arrangements it has made to finance its obligations under the Contract.
97. Some of these difficulties have been described by authoritative commentators as follows: 'A state may decide that for certain activities it will create an enterprise possessing separate personality and enjoying the normal legal consequences of that form. But when the state itself, through its senior officials, is engaged in the negotiation of the contract and is required to give various consents or permissions for the transaction to proceed, the identity of the state party may be obscured. If difficulties arise, the foreign investor may be surprised to find that the host state and the signatory state enterprise stress their legal independence. In many arbitrations, a state joined as a party has objected to proceedings instituted against it because the contract containing the agreement to refer disputes to arbitration was signed by a subservient separate legal entity. States in such a position may object to jurisdiction on the ground of an alleged incapacity or the invalidity of the arbitration agreement. A review of published ICSID awards [*see (7) ICSID investment arbitration* under **(iii) Analysis** of the commentary on Sub-Clause 21.6 [*Arbitration*] below] reveals that in around half, the state party raises some preliminary objection to jurisdiction on grounds such as these.' James Crawford and Anthony Sinclair, 'The UNIDROIT Principles and Their Application to State Contracts', ICC Int'l Ct Arb Bull, Spec Supp. *UNIDROIT Principles of International Commercial Contracts: Reflections on Their Use in International Arbitration* (2002), 57, 60. Under the state's internal law, the necessary funds may also need to have been appropriated and/or budgeted for the project concerned. Thus, the United States Constitution provides that:

If the Employer comprises more than one person (e.g., constitutes a Joint Venture as defined),[98] the information required by the Contract Data (name and address and, it is suggested, its legal nature, place of incorporation if it is a company, and nationality) should be provided for each person comprising the Employer, while also making clear which person is empowered to represent the Employer.[99]

1.1.32 'Employer's Equipment'

> 1.1.32 "**Employer's Equipment**" means the apparatus, equipment, machinery, construction plant and/or vehicles (if any) to be made available by the Employer for the use of the Contractor under Sub-Clause 2.6 [*Employer-Supplied Materials and Employer's Equipment*]; but does not include Plant which has not been taken over under Clause 10 [*Employer's Taking Over*].

This definition refers to any apparatus, equipment, machinery construction plant and/or vehicles which are to be made available by the Employer for the Contractor's use under Sub-Clause 2.6 [*Employer-Supplied Materials and Employer's Equipment*], which envisages that Employer's Equipment (as defined) for this purpose should be listed in the Specification.

It is usually preferable to let the Contractor select its equipment and make the necessary arrangements directly with manufacturers and suppliers. But the Employer may provide, for example, any Employer's cranes (or other Employer equipment) which are permanently allocated to the Site and/or:

'No money shall be drawn from the Treasury, but in Consequence of Appropriations made by Law.' Art. 1(9). Where this is the case, a Contractor may want to assure itself that the necessary funds have been appropriated and/or are budgeted.

98. Sub-Clause 1.1.46 '**Joint Venture**' or '**JV**'.
99. As regards 'legal successors in title', *see* the commentary on Sub-Clause 1.1.14 '**Contractor**' above.

> any plant and/or materials which will take so long to procure that the Works would be completed sooner if they are ordered before the Parties enter into the Contract [...].[100]

This refers to 'long lead items',[101] such as certain equipment to be ordered even before a contract is awarded in order for it to be available in accordance with the desired time programme. In this case, the Employer will usually need to order it itself.[102]

1.1.33 'Employer's Personnel'

> 1.1.33 "**Employer's Personnel**" means the Engineer, the Engineer's Representative (if appointed), the assistants described in Sub-Clause 3.4 [*Delegation by the Engineer*] and all other staff, labour and other employees of the Engineer and of the Employer engaged in fulfilling the Employer's obligations under the Contract; and any other personnel identified as Employer's Personnel, by a Notice from the Employer or the Engineer to the Contractor.

This definition is very broad. It comprises the Engineer's Representative (if appointed), assistants described in Sub-Clause 3.4 and any other employees of the Engineer 'and'[103] of the Employer 'engaged in fulfilling

100. *The FIDIC Contracts Guide* (2nd edn, FIDIC, 2022) 117.
101. A 'long lead item' is one whose purchase and delivery time is so long that it can impact the construction programme, e.g., specially fabricated components that must be made to order and thus may take considerable time to manufacture and supply.
102. The wording 'but does not include Plant which has not been taken over under Clause 10 [*Employer's Taking Over*]' at the end of the definition (and which was also in RB/99) presumably refers to the risk that there could be confusion between Employer's Equipment and Plant supplied by the Contractor which has not yet been taken over. If the Employer's Equipment for the Contractor's use is listed in the Specification (as contemplated by Sub-Clause 2.6), this risk should be obviated.
103. Presumably, the word 'and' here should be 'or' as it is not required that 'staff, labour and other employees' be employees of both the Engineer and the Employer simultaneously.

the Employer's obligations under the Contract', words which were not in the corresponding definition in RB/99.[104] The definition is also open-ended as it includes:

> any other personnel identified as Employer's Personnel, by a Notice from the Employer or the Engineer to the Contractor.

However, it includes neither the Employer itself[105] nor the Employer's other contractors on the Site working under different contracts,[106] unless they are identified as Employer's Personnel by a Notice from the Employer or the Engineer to the Contractor.

1.1.34 'Employer-Supplied Materials'

> 1.1.34 "**Employer-Supplied Materials**" means the materials (if any) to be supplied by the Employer to the Contractor under Sub-Clause 2.6 [*Employer-Supplied Materials and Employer's Equipment*].

This newly defined term refers, according to Sub-Clause 2.6, to Materials supplied by the Employer and listed in the Specification for the Contractor's use in the execution of the Works.

1.1.35 'Engineer'

> 1.1.35 "**Engineer**" means the person named in the Contract Data appointed by the Employer to act as the Engineer for the purposes of the Contract, or any replacement appointed under Sub-Clause 3.6 [*Replacement of the Engineer*].

104. *See* Sub-Clause 1.1.2.6 of RB/99.
105. The Employer is not referred to in Sub-Clause 1.1.33 and the Conditions refer to the Employer as being distinct from the Employer's Personnel in Sub-Clauses 7.6(i), 8.5(e), 17.4 and 19.2.5.
106. *See* Sub-Clause 2.3 of RB/99 and RB/17 which, by referring to 'Employer's Personnel and the Employer's other contractors' on the Site, implies that the Employer's other contractors are not normally covered by the definition.

The Engineer, who may be a legal entity or a natural person,[107] is appointed by the Employer and is part of the Employer's Personnel.[108] The name and address of the Engineer, and if it is a legal entity, it is suggested, its legal nature and nationality as well, should be given in the Contract Data. As indicated by the definition, the Employer may replace the Engineer subject to compliance with Sub-Clause 3.6 [*Replacement of the Engineer*].[109]

1.1.36 'Engineer's Representative'

> 1.1.36 "**Engineer's Representative**" means the natural person who may be appointed by the Engineer under Sub-Clause 3.3 [*Engineer's Representative*].

Although a newly defined term in RB/17, the Engineer's Representative was not unknown in previous RB editions.[110] In RB/99, Sub-Clause 3.2 [*Delegation by Engineer*] referred to a 'resident engineer' or other assistants who performed a very similar role to that of the Engineer's Representative. The Engineer in RB/17 has discretion over whether to appoint an Engineer's Representative.[111] The Engineer's Representative, who must be a natural person, is like the Engineer part of the Employer's Personnel.[112]

1.1.37 'Exceptional Event'

> 1.1.37 "**Exceptional Event**" means an exceptional event or circumstance as defined in Sub-Clause 18.1 [*Exceptional Events*].

107. *See* the commentary on Sub-Clause 3.1 [*The Engineer*] below.
108. *See* Sub-Clause 1.1.33 '**Employer's Personnel**' above.
109. For a discussion of the role of the Engineer, *see* **Section 3.2 Distinctive Features – 3.2.2 'Independent' Engineer** of **Chapter I General Introduction** above as well as the commentary on Clause 3 [*The Engineer*] below.
110. The term 'Engineer's Representative' was used in RB/87 (*see* Sub-Clause 2.2 of that form) but dropped for some reason in RB/99.
111. Sub-Clause 3.3, first paragraph.
112. *See* the commentary on Sub-Clause 3.3 [*The Engineer's Representative*] below.

RB/99 had referred to 'Force Majeure' instead of 'Exceptional Event'.[113] The term 'Force Majeure' was believed to have caused confusion as *force majeure* is also a legal concept under the national laws of many civil law countries where it has a different meaning from that provided for in FIDIC's forms.[114] In order to avoid this confusion, GB/08 had replaced 'Force Majeure' with 'Exceptional Event'[115] and the same term is now used in Clause 18 of RB/17 for events or circumstances previously described as Force Majeure.[116]

1.1.38 'Extension of Time' or 'EOT'

1.1.38 "**Extension of Time**" or "**EOT**" means an extension of the Time for Completion under Sub-Clause 8.5 [*Extension of Time for Completion*].

This is a newly defined term. In each Sub-Clause giving the Contractor an entitlement to an extension of the Time for Completion, RB/99 had referred to 'an extension of time for any such delay, if completion is or will be delayed, under Sub-Clause 8.4 [*Extension of Time for Completion*]'.[117] To avoid such repetition, RB/17 simply refers to the defined terms Extension of Time or EOT.[118]

1.1.39 'FIDIC'

1.1.39 "**FIDIC**" means the Fédération Internationale des Ingénieurs-Conseils, the International Federation of Consulting Engineers.

FIDIC is the author and publisher of RB/17.

113. *See* Sub-Clause 19.1 [*Definition of Force Majeure*] of RB/99.
114. *See* the *FIDIC DBO Guide* (1st edn, FIDIC, 2011) 14. *See also* **Section 4 Common Law and Civil Law Compared – 4.4.7 *Force Majeure* and Hardship** of **Chapter II Applicable Law** above.
115. *See* the *FIDIC DBO Guide* (1st edn, FIDIC, 2011) 14.
116. *See* the commentary on Clause 18 [*Exceptional Events*] below.
117. *See*, for example, Sub-Clause 1.9 and Sub-Clause 2.1 of RB/99.
118. *See* the commentary on Sub-Clause 8.5 [*Extension of Time for Completion*] below.

1.1.40 'Final Payment Certificate' or 'FPC'

> 1.1.40 **"Final Payment Certificate"** or **"FPC"** means the payment certificate issued by the Engineer under Sub-Clause 14.13 [*Issue of FPC*].

This is normally the last Payment Certificate issued by the Engineer to the Employer (with a copy to the Contractor) under the Conditions, *see* Sub-Clause 14.13 [*Issue of FPC*].[119]

1.1.41 'Final Statement'

> 1.1.41 **"Final Statement"** means the Statement defined in Sub-Clause 14.11.2 [*Agreed Final Statement*].

After the issue of the Performance Certificate, the Contractor must submit a draft final Statement to the Engineer.[120] Assuming that Statement is agreed with the Engineer, the Contractor must submit to the Engineer the final Statement as agreed, which is defined as the 'Final Statement'.[121] If there are amounts in the draft final Statement that cannot be agreed with the Engineer, the Contractor must prepare and submit to the Engineer a Partially Agreed Final Statement.[122]

1.1.42 'Foreign Currency'

> 1.1.42 **"Foreign Currency"** means a currency in which part (or all) of the Contract Price is payable, but not the Local Currency.

The Local Currency is defined in Sub-Clause 1.1.52 as the currency of the Country.[123]

---

119. *See* **Figure 10 Sequence of Final Payment Events** after the commentary on Sub-Clause 14.10 below.
120. Under Sub-Clause 14.11.1 [Draft Final Statement].
121. Sub-Clause 14.11.2 [Agreed Final Statement]. *See* the commentary on Sub-Clause 14.11 [*Final Statement*] and **Figure 10 Sequence of Final Payment Events** after the commentary on Sub-Clause 14.10 below.
122. *Ibid.*
123. *See* the commentary on Sub-Clause 14.15 [*Currencies of Payment*] below.

1.1.43 'General Conditions'

> 1.1.43 "**General Conditions**" means this document entitled "General Conditions", as published by FIDIC.

This term refers to the *unamended* Conditions of Contract of RB/17 published by FIDIC. It is to be distinguished from 'Conditions of Contract' or 'these Conditions' which refer to the General Conditions as amended by the Particular Conditions.[124]

1.1.44 'Goods'

> 1.1.44 "**Goods**" means Contractor's Equipment, Materials, Plant and Temporary Works, or any of them as appropriate.

This definition covers both things which become part of the Permanent Works (Plant and Materials) and things required by the Contractor on Site which do not become part of the Permanent Works (Contractor's Equipment and Temporary Works), or any of them as appropriate.

1.1.45 'Interim Payment Certificate' or 'IPC'

> 1.1.45 "**Interim Payment Certificate**" or "**IPC**" means a Payment Certificate issued by the Engineer for an interim payment under Sub-Clause 14.6 [*Issue of IPC*].

The Contractor is paid the Contract Price following the issue by the Engineer to the Employer of Payment Certificates,[125] whether Interim, Final[126] or other, except for amounts due pursuant to the decision of the DAAB[127] or international arbitration.[128]

124. *See* Sub-Clause 1.1.9.
125. Sub-Clause 1.1.61.
126. Sub-Clause 1.1.40.
127. *See* Sub-Clause 21.4.3, penultimate paragraph.
128. *See* Sub-Clause 21.6 and art. 35(6) of the ICC Arbitration Rules.

1.1.46 'Joint Venture' or 'JV'

> 1.1.46 "**Joint Venture**" or "**JV**" means a joint venture, association, consortium or other unincorporated grouping of two or more persons, whether in the form of a partnership or otherwise.

This is a newly defined term. Construction projects may require expertise and/or resources beyond the capacity of a single construction company, or the local law or practice of the Country (as defined)[129] may require or favour the participation of a local construction company. For these and other reasons, the Contractor (as defined)[130] may take the form of a joint venture, association, consortium or other unincorporated grouping of two or more companies or other persons.

A joint venture of contractors is normally unincorporated, that is, it is not a separate legal entity,[131] as this definition recognises.[132] Thus, though the term 'Contractor' in the Conditions is singular, in the case of a JV, it will refer to two or more legal entities or other persons. This means that, subject to applicable law, those entities or persons will have to act together and in agreement in order for the Contractor to be able to act unless, as they usually do, they appoint a leader of the JV who is authorised to act for them and in their place and name.[133]

1.1.47 'JV Undertaking'

> 1.1.47 "**JV Undertaking**" means the letter provided to the Employer as part of the Tender setting out the legal undertaking between the two or more persons constituting the Contractor as a JV. This letter shall be signed by all the persons

129. Sub-Clause 1.1.21.
130. Sub-Clause 1.1.14.
131. However, sometimes the tender dossier or local law may require, or a Contractor may find it advantageous to constitute (e.g., for local tax or other reasons), a local company. If so, this definition will need amendment.
132. The term 'Joint Venture' or 'JV' is used in the Conditions only connection with the Contractor although it could apply equally to the Employer.
133. *See* Sub-Clauses 1.1.47 and 1.14 commented upon below.

who are members of the JV, shall be addressed to the Employer and shall include:

(a) each such member's undertaking to be jointly and severally liable to the Employer for the performance of the Contractor's obligations under the Contract;
(b) identification and authorisation of the leader of the JV; and
(c) identification of the separate scope or part of the Works (if any) to be carried out by each member of the JV.

This is a new document in the Red Book. The JV Undertaking is a letter to the Employer which is to be provided by each tenderer which is in the form of a JV. It is to be provided as part of the Tender and to set out those terms of the JV agreement to which the members of the JV are a party which will be of interest to the Employer.[134] It must be signed by each member and include: each member's undertaking to be jointly and severally liable to the Employer for the performance of the Contractor's obligations under the Contract; identify and give authority to the leader of the JV who will represent the JV in its relations with the Employer; and describe the separate scope of the Works (if any) to be carried out by each member.[135] Once the Contract is signed, neither the identity of the leader nor the scope of the Works of each member may be altered without the Employer's prior consent.[136]

134. The Contractor is not required to disclose to the Employer the contract creating the JV.
135. The authority of the leader and the joint and several liability of the JV members is discussed further in the commentary on Sub-Clause 1.14 [*Joint and Several Liability*] below.
136. Each member's scope may not be altered without consent as the Contractor may have been pre-qualified on the basis that each member would be performing a designated task appropriate to its skills and/or experience. *See also* Sub-Clause 1.14 [*Joint and Several Liability*]. As to 'consent', *see* Sub-Clauses 1.2(g) [*Interpretation*] and 1.3 [*Notices and Other Communications*].

1.1.48 'Key Personnel'

> 1.1.48 **"Key Personnel"** means the positions (if any) of the Contractor's Personnel, other than the Contractor's Representative, that are stated in the Specification.

This is a newly defined term in RB/17. When inviting tenderers, the Employer may want to be informed of the names, qualifications and experience of those senior personnel whom a tenderer proposes should manage the execution of the Works or occupy other important positions. This personnel is referred to as 'Key Personnel'. For example, if the Employer requires the Contractor to have a Quality Manager employed on the Site, such position should be stated in the Specification as being one of the positions of Key Personnel.[137] Accordingly, the instructions to tenderers may require a tenderer to provide information, including a curriculum vitae, for the person proposed to occupy this position.

Sub-Clause 6.12 [*Key Personnel*] assumes that the names of the natural persons to be appointed to these positions will have been specified in the Tender, so as to permit the Employer and its consultants to evaluate their suitability.[138]

1.1.49 'Laws'

> 1.1.49 **"Laws"** means all national (or state or provincial) legislation, statutes, acts, decrees, rules, ordinances, orders, treaties, international law and other laws, and regulations and by-laws of any legally constituted public authority.

The definition covers not just all national (or state) laws of various kinds as in RB/99[139] but also now 'provincial' laws including specifically 'acts,

137. *See* the *Guidance for the Preparation of Particular Conditions*, 24.
138. After entry into the Contract, the Contractor may not revoke or replace any Key Personnel without the Engineer's consent. *See* Sub-Clause 6.12 and the commentary thereon below.
139. *See* Sub-Clause 1.1.6.5 of RB/99.

decrees, rules […] orders, treaties, international law'.[140] The Contractor and the Employer are required by Sub-Clause 1.13 [*Compliance with Laws*] to comply with all applicable Laws.[141] These include not just Laws of the Country (the country of the Site) but also Laws applicable to the Contractor or the Employer in any other country (including international law)[142] where they may be performing the Contract.[143]

While the definition of 'Laws' has been broadened, nevertheless, some kind of prescriptive rule, order or norm is still, as a minimum, required.

1.1.50 'Letter of Acceptance'

> 1.1.50 "**Letter of Acceptance**" means the letter of formal acceptance, signed by the Employer, of the Letter of Tender, including any annexed memoranda comprising agreements between and signed by both Parties. If there is no such letter of acceptance, the expression "Letter of Acceptance" means the Contract Agreement and the date of issuing or receiving the Letter of Acceptance means the date of signing the Contract Agreement.

By the Letter of Acceptance, the Employer formally accepts the Contractor's Letter of Tender stating the Contractor's offer to the Employer for the execution of the Works. The amount of the Contractor's offer

140. The World Bank's COPA does not accept this expanded definition, preferring that in RB/99. Sub-Clause 1.1.49, COPA. Even this expanded definition does not include case law.
141. *See* the commentaries on Sub-Clauses 1.13 [*Compliance with Laws*] and 1.4 [*Law and Language*] below.
142. Some countries, like England, have a dualist legal system under which international law or an international treaty has legal force at the domestic level only after it has been implemented by a national statute. James Crawford, *Brownlie's Principles of Public International Law* (9th edn, OUP, Oxford, 2019) 59-60. But other jurisdictions adopt a monist stance, that is, postulate that national and international law form one single legal order and therefore may have effect at the domestic level more or less immediately.
143. *See* **Chapter II Applicable Law** above.

accepted by the Letter of Acceptance is the Accepted Contract Amount.[144] Upon the Contractor's receipt of the Letter of Acceptance (if not earlier), a binding contract is created between the Parties.[145] The Letter of Acceptance will be the contractual document which, in case of conflict, will have the highest priority unless the Parties sign a Contract Agreement.[146] Various matters are linked to the Contractor's receipt of the Letter of Acceptance.[147]

The definition also refers to 'any annexed memoranda comprising agreements between and signed by both Parties' which may form part of the Letter of Acceptance. Such memoranda may include:

- a breakdown of the Accepted Contract Amount, which may differ from the sum stated in the Letter of Tender by reason of arithmetic errors and/or so as to define which alternative option is being accepted; and/or
- the outcome of any post-tender negotiations and/or clarifications of the Tender, although [according to FIDIC] [...] it is [...] unfair for the Employer to have asked or permitted the tenderer to change the substance or value of the Tender [...].[148]

As a practical matter, a Letter of Acceptance may take many forms (beyond what RB/17 provides) and be of varying length. In some cases, it may amount legally to a counter-offer to the Tender with the consequence that, unless it is accepted by the tenderer, no binding contract is entered into by the Parties. It is partly to clear up the ambiguities and uncertainties to which such post-tender exchanges may give rise, that it

144. *See* Sub-Clause 1.1.1 '**Accepted Contract Amount**' above.
145. The Employer acknowledges that a 'binding Contract' has been created in the form of the Letter of Acceptance in RB/17.
146. *See* Sub-Clause 1.5 [*Priority of Documents*].
147. For example, *see* Sub-Clauses 1.6 [*Contract Agreement*], 4.2 [*Performance Security*], 8.1 [*Commencement of the Works*] and 21.1 [*Constitution of the DAAB*].
148. *The FIDIC Contracts Guide* (2nd edn, FIDIC, 2022) 43. The annexed memoranda may also comprise any agreement between the Parties as regards the terms of insurance to be provided under Clause 19 [*Insurance*]. *See* the first paragraph of Sub-Clause 19.1 [*General Requirements*] and the commentary on that Sub-Clause below.

is foreseen that the Parties enter into a Contract Agreement, unless they agree otherwise,[149] establishing definitively that a Contract has been entered into and its key terms.

1.1.51 'Letter of Tender'

> 1.1.51 "**Letter of Tender**" means the letter of tender, signed by the Contractor, stating the Contractor's offer to the Employer for the execution of the Works.

The Letter of Tender, which is usually a short one-page document, is the Contractor's signed offer to the Employer for the execution of the Works.[150] By the Letter, the Contractor confirms that it has examined the tender dossier, offers to execute the Works for a stated sum and currency, and agrees to keep its offer open for acceptance until a specified date. The example form of Letter contained in RB/17 stipulates that unless and until a Contract Agreement is executed, the Letter together with the Employer's written acceptance (the Letter of Acceptance[151]) will constitute a binding agreement between the Employer and the Contractor. The Letter is usually accompanied by tender security securing the Contractor's obligation to keep its offer open for acceptance until the specified date.[152] According to the General Conditions, the Letter of Tender is the document with the third highest priority after the Contract Agreement, if any, and the Letter of Acceptance.[153]

1.1.52 'Local Currency'

> 1.1.52 "**Local Currency**" means the currency of the Country.

149. *See* Sub-Clause 1.6 [*Contract Agreement*].
150. *See* the form of Letter of Tender in RB/17. It is to be distinguished from the '**Tender**' (Sub-Clause 1.1.81) which comprises both the Letter of Tender and the other documents submitted with it which are included in the Contract.
151. Sub-Clause 1.1.50.
152. RB/17 contains an example form of Tender Security (Annex B).
153. Sub-Clause 1.5 [*Priority of Documents*].

This is to be distinguished from Foreign Currency defined in Sub-Clause 1.1.42. If the Local Currency is not the currency of the Country, this needs to be specified in the Particular Conditions.[154]

1.1.53 'Materials'

> 1.1.53 "**Materials**" means things of all kinds (other than Plant), whether on the Site or otherwise allocated to the Contract and intended to form or forming part of the Permanent Works, including the supply-only materials (if any) to be supplied by the Contractor under the Contract.

While 'Materials' refers to all things (other than Plant) intended to form part of the Permanent Works, 'supply-only materials' refers to materials supplied by the Contractor under the Contract but which are not intended to form part of the Permanent Works.

1.1.54 'month'

> 1.1.54 "**month**" is a calendar month (according to the Gregorian calendar).

This is a newly defined term in RB/17.

1.1.55 'No-objection'

> 1.1.55 "**No-objection**" means that the Engineer has no objection to the Contractor's Documents, or other documents submitted by the Contractor under these Conditions, and such Contractor's Documents or other documents may be used for the Works.

This is a newly defined term which is used in relation to numerous different documents, such as Contractor's Documents pursuant to Sub-

154. *See* the commentary on Sub-Clause 14.15 [*Currencies of Payment*] below.

Clause 4.4,[155] which the Contractor must submit to the Engineer for Review or which the Engineer may decide in its discretion to Review.

When submitted for Review, the Engineer may give either a Notice of No-objection (if it has no objection to the document) or a Notice stating the extent to which the document does not comply with the Contract. Failure of the Engineer to give either Notice within the specified period will ordinarily mean that the Engineer is deemed to have given a Notice of No-objection.[156] A Notice of No-objection given (or deemed to be given) does not relieve the Contractor from any duty, obligation or responsibility under the Contract.[157]

1.1.56 'Notice'

> 1.1.56 "**Notice**" means a written communication identified as a Notice and issued in accordance with Sub-Clause 1.3 [*Notices and Other Communications*].

A Notice, which is a newly defined term in RB/17, is a formal 'written communication identified as a Notice' issued by a Party or the Engineer in accordance with Sub-Clause 1.3 [*Notices and Other Communications*].[158] Thus, a failure by a Party or the Engineer to identify a communication as a Notice and/or to issue it in accordance with all of the requirements in Sub-Clause 1.3 may give rise to a question as to whether it is a valid Notice. While every case will depend upon its facts, it is suggested that a common sense approach should be taken and that if a communication satisfies substantially all of the requirements for a Notice, and especially if the recipient is not (or should not be) prejudiced by any non-compliance, then this should be a basis for considering it to be a valid Notice.[159]

155. For other examples, *see* Sub-Clauses 7.5 [*Defects and Rejection*], 8.3 [*Programme*] and 9.1 [*Contractor's Obligations*].
156. *See*, for example, the sixth paragraph of Sub-Clause 4.4.1 and the third paragraph of Sub-Clause 8.3.
157. *See* last paragraph of Sub-Clause 3.2 [*Engineer's Duties and Authority*].
158. The requirement for a Notice to be identified as a Notice is also specified in sub-para. (b) of Sub-Clause 1.3 [*Notices and Other Communications*]. *See* the commentary on that Sub-Clause below.
159. *See* item (2) under **(v) Improvements** of the commentary on Sub-Clause 1.3 [*Notices and Other Communications*] below.

While there is no requirement for a Notice to refer to the provision(s) of the Contract to which it relates, it will be good practice for the Parties and the Engineer always to do so.

1.1.57 'Notice of Dissatisfaction' or 'NOD'

> 1.1.57 "**Notice of Dissatisfaction**" or "**NOD**" means the Notice one Party may give to the other Party if it is dissatisfied, either with an Engineer's determination under Sub-Clause 3.7 [*Agreement or Determination*] or with a DAAB's decision under Sub-Clause 21.4 [*Obtaining DAAB's Decision*].

This is a newly defined term in RB/17. A NOD is to be distinguished from a (normal) Notice.[160] The timely giving of a NOD may be essential to prevent an Engineer's determination under Sub-Clause 3.7 [*Agreement or Determination*] or a DAAB's decision under Sub-Clause 21.4 [*Obtaining DAAB's Decision*] from becoming 'final and binding' upon the Parties, thereby time barring further consideration of a matter to be agreed or determined, or a Claim or Dispute.

1.1.58 'Part'

> 1.1.58 "**Part**" means a part of the Works or part of a Section (as the case may be) which is taken over by the Employer under the first paragraph, or used by the Employer and deemed to have been taken over under the second paragraph, of Sub-Clause 10.2 [*Taking-Over Parts*].

The definition of 'Part' refers to a part of the Works or a Section (as the case may be) which is taken over, or deemed to have been taken over, by the Employer under Sub-Clause 10.2 [*Taking-Over Parts*] before a Taking-Over Certificate for the corresponding Works or Section has been issued.

160. *See* the second and last paragraphs of Sub-Clause 1.3 which distinguish between the two. On the other hand, the first paragraph of that Sub-Clause expressly includes a NOD within the meaning of a Notice.

1.1.59 'Particular Conditions'

1.1.59 "**Particular Conditions**" means the document entitled particular conditions of contract included in the Contract, which consists of Part A - Contract Data and Part B – Special Provisions.

Part A – Contract Data of the Particular Conditions has been commented on in relation to the definition of Contract Data above.[161] Part B – Special Provisions comprise principally options for amendments or additions to the General Conditions which may be used by the Employer or its consultant. If used, they 'will always over-rule and supersede the equivalent provisions in the General Conditions'.[162] This is consistent with the UNIDROIT Principles:

> In case of conflict between a standard term and a term which is not standard the latter prevails.[163]

1.1.60 'Party' and 'Parties'

1.1.60 "**Party**" means the Employer or the Contractor, as the context requires. "**Parties**" means both the Employer and the Contractor.

The Parties are to be distinguished from the Engineer who, although having an important role under the Contract,[164] is not a Party to it. Where the Contractor is a JV, the Contractor 'Party' may consist of several persons.[165]

161. Sub-Clause 1.1.12 '**Contract Data**'.
162. *Guidance for the Preparation of Particular Conditions*, 9. To the same effect, *see* Sub-Clause 1.5 [*Priority of Documents*].
163. Art. 2.1.21 (*Conflict between standard terms and non-standard terms*) of the UNIDROIT Principles.
164. *See* Clause 3 [*The Engineer*], and the commentary below on that Clause.
165. Though less usual, the same may be true of the Employer.

1.1.61 'Payment Certificate'

> 1.1.61 **"Payment Certificate"** means a payment certificate issued by the Engineer under Clause 14 [*Contract Price and Payment*].

These words refer to an Advance Payment Certificate issued under Sub-Clause 14.2.2 [*Advance Payment Certificate*], an Interim Payment Certificate (or IPC) issued under Sub-Clause 14.6 [*Issue of IPC*] or a Final Payment Certificate (or FPC) issued under Sub-Clause 14.13 [*Issue of FPC*].

1.1.62 'Performance Certificate'

> 1.1.62 **"Performance Certificate"** means the certificate issued by the Engineer (or deemed to be issued) under Sub-Clause 11.9 [*Performance Certificate*].

The Performance Certificate issued (or deemed to be issued) by the Engineer under Sub-Clause 11.9 [*Performance Certificate*] is a particularly important document as it establishes that the Contractor has essentially completed its obligations under the Contract. Only the Performance Certificate is 'deemed to constitute acceptance of the Works'.[166]

1.1.63 'Performance Security'

> 1.1.63 **"Performance Security"** means the security under Sub-Clause 4.2 [*Performance Security*].

The Performance Security to be provided by the Contractor under Sub-Clause 4.2 [*Performance Security*] secures the Contractor's 'proper performance of the Contract'.[167] It may take the form of a guarantee

166. *See* the commentary on Sub-Clause 11.9 [*Performance Certificate*] as well as **Figure 10 Sequence of Final Payment Events** at the end of the commentary on Sub-Clause 14.10 below. *The FIDIC Contracts Guide* (2nd edn, FIDIC, 2022) 334 contains a sample form of a Performance Certificate and states that it may be in the form of a letter.
167. *See* the first paragraph of Sub-Clause 4.2.

payable on demand issued by a bank or of a surety bond issued by an insurance company or an affiliate of an insurance company, in the amount and currencies stated in the Contract Data. RB/17 contains example forms of both types of securities.[168]

1.1.64 *'Permanent Works'*

> 1.1.64 **"Permanent Works"** means the works of a permanent nature which are to be executed by the Contractor under the Contract.

Permanent Works are to be distinguished from Temporary Works defined in Sub-Clause 1.1.80. The Permanent Works are generally described in the Drawings and Specification.

1.1.65 *'Plant'*

> 1.1.65 **"Plant"** means the apparatus, equipment, machinery and vehicles (including any components) whether on the Site or otherwise allocated to the Contract and intended to form or forming part of the Permanent Works.

'Plant' is to be distinguished from 'construction plant' required by the Contractor for the execution of the Works and which forms part of the 'Contractor's Equipment'.[169]

1.1.66 *'Programme'*

> 1.1.66 **"Programme"** means a detailed time programme prepared and submitted by the Contractor to which the Engineer has given (or is deemed to have given) a Notice of No-objection under Sub-Clause 8.3 [*Programme*].

168. *See* the *Guidance for the Preparation of Particular Conditions*, 59-62 (Annexes C and D). For a fuller discussion of Performance Security, *see* the commentary on Sub-Clause 4.2 [*Performance Security*] below.
169. Defined in Sub-Clause 1.1.16 above.

This is a newly defined term in RB/17. The definition only covers a detailed time programme for the execution of the Works to which the Engineer has given (or is deemed to have given) a Notice of No-objection under Sub-Clause 8.3 [*Programme*]. An initial and/or revised programmes submitted by the Contractor under Sub-Clause 8.3 which have not yet been the subject of a Notice of No-objection are excluded from the definition.

A detailed time programme should include all the information listed in sub-paragraphs (a) to (k) of Sub-Clause 8.3 and otherwise comply with that Sub-Clause and the Specification.[170]

1.1.67 'Provisional Sum'

> 1.1.67 "**Provisional Sum**" means a sum (if any) which is specified in the Contract by the Employer as a provisional sum, for the execution of any part of the Works or for the supply of Plant, Materials or services under Sub-Clause 13.4 [*Provisional Sums*].

This definition is similar to the corresponding definition in RB/99 and almost identical with the definition in GB/08.[171] With regard to the GB/08 definition, FIDIC has stated that:

> Provisional Sums may be included in the Contract by the Employer for various reasons. Either he may wish to provide a sum of money for the execution of additional work or the provision of additional services, or he may wish to provide a sum of money for the purchase of a particular item of equipment where he has not finally decided on all the details. It is he, the Employer, who decides how many Provisional Sums he wishes to include and their purpose, and it is he who puts a price against each one. The Contractor includes the items and the sums in his tender, but they are only used to the extent ordered by the Employer through his Representative [who under GB/08 performs the role of the Engineer under RB/17].[172]

170. *See* the commentary on Sub-Clause 8.3 [*Programme*] below.
171. Sub-Clause 1.1.4.10 of RB/99 and Sub-Clause 1.1.63 of GB/08.
172. *FIDIC DBO Contract Guide* (FIDIC, 2011) 17. *See also* the commentary on Sub-Clause 13.4 [*Provisional Sums*] below.

Provisional sums are used to pay nominated Subcontractors, among others.[173]

1.1.68 *'QM System'*

> 1.1.68 **"QM System"** means the Contractor's quality management system (as may be updated and/or revised from time to time) in accordance with Sub-Clause 4.9.1 [*Quality Management System*].

The QM System is a project management tool designed to help the Contractor to demonstrate to the Engineer that the Contractor is complying with the Contract.[174]

1.1.69 *'Retention Money'*

> 1.1.69 **"Retention Money"** means the accumulated retention moneys which the Employer retains under Sub-Clause 14.3 *[Application for Interim Payment]* and pays under Sub-Clause 14.9 [*Release of Retention Money*].

Retention Money is money deducted for retention in Statements of the Contractor under Sub-Clause 14.3 until the amount of retention reaches the limit stated in the Contract Data. The amount to be retained from each IPC is calculated by applying the percentage of retention stated in the Contract Data (commonly 5% to 10% of the Accepted Contract Amount) to the estimated contract value of the executed Works (and certain other amounts) until the amount so retained reaches the limit of Retention Money.[175] Typically, the first half of the Retention Money is released to

173. *See* Sub-Clauses 5.2.3 and 13.4. If their use is instructed by the Engineer, the Contract Price is adjusted accordingly. Sub-Clause 13.4 [*Provisional Sums*]. Provisional sums are included in the Accepted Contract Amount. *See* the discussion of Sub-Clause 1.1.1 above.
174. *See* the commentary on Sub-Clause 4.9 [*Quality Management and Compliance Verification Systems*] below.
175. Sub-paragraph (iii) of Sub-Clause 14.3.

the Contractor after the issue of the Taking-Over Certificate for the Works and the second half after the expiry of the latest of the expiry dates of the DNPs.[176]

In practice, the Contractor may prefer to substitute a Retention Money Guarantee in the form of a demand guarantee[177] for Retention Money and generally Employers will agree to this.[178]

The Conditions do not specify the purpose of Retention Money. However, the example form of Retention Money Guarantee annexed to RB/17, which may be issued in lieu of Retention Money, provides that it is payable only after the 'Beneficiary' (the Employer) has submitted, among other things, a written statement that the Contractor 'has failed to carry out his/her obligation(s) to rectify the following defect(s) for which he/she is responsible under the Contract'. This implies that the sole purpose of Retention Money is to provide security to ensure that the Contractor will rectify defects in the Works. If so, this could have been expressed more clearly.[179]

1.1.70 'Review'

> 1.1.70 "**Review**" means examination and consideration by the Engineer of a Contractor's submission in order to assess whether (and to what extent) it complies with the Contract and/or with the Contractor's obligations under or in connection with the Contract.

This is a newly defined term. Numerous Sub-Clauses provide that the Contractor must submit specified documents to the Engineer 'for Re-

176. *See* the commentary on Sub-Clause 14.9 [*Release of Retention Money*] and sub-para. (viii) of Sub-Clause 14.3 [*Application for Interim Payment*].
177. *See* the commentary on Sub-Clause 4.2 [*Performance Security*] below regarding demand guarantees.
178. An example form of a Retention Money Guarantee is contained as Annex F in RB/17.
179. In the meantime, as stated in the commentary on Sub-Clause 14.9 below, Retention Money appears to be available to the Employer as security against any breaches of the Contractor.

view',[180] meaning examination by the Engineer, 'as a skilled professional',[181] in order to assess whether they comply with the Contract.[182] If so, the Engineer issues a Notice of No-objection.[183]

1.1.71 'Schedules'

> 1.1.71 "**Schedules**" means the document(s) entitled schedules prepared by the Employer and completed by the Contractor, as attached to the Letter of Tender and included in the Contract. Such document(s) may include data, lists and schedules of payments and/or rates and prices, and guarantees.

The Schedules are prepared by the Employer or a consultant, on the Employer's behalf, included in the tender dossier and, where required, are to be completed by tenderers.[184] While they are to be 'attached to the Letter of Tender', possibly by an oversight, the form of Letter of Tender in RB/17 does not refer to them. The Schedules include the Bill of Quantities, if any,[185] and may include other data, lists and schedules of payments and/or rates and prices, and guarantees. Once completed they are included in the Contract.[186]

---

180. *See*, for example, Sub-Clause 4.1 (a), the fourth paragraph of Sub-Clause 4.4.1 and the second and third paragraphs of Sub-Clause 8.3.
181. Sub-Clause 3.2 [*Engineer's Duties and Authority*].
182. Sub-Clause 1.3 [*Notices and Other Communications*] requires that a 'communication', which term is stated to include a 'Review', should be made in writing and that it should be identified as such and include a reference to the provision of the Contract pursuant to which it is made. It makes little sense to apply Sub-Clause 1.3 to a 'Review' in this way as a Review, as defined, refers to 'examination and consideration by the Engineer' of a Contractor's submission and not to any form of 'communication'. While Sub-Clause 1.3 might logically be made to apply to a Notice communicating the results of a Review, it should not purport to apply to other matters such as the process by which the Engineer arrives at those results.
183. *See* Sub-Clause 1.1.55 '**No-objection**'.
184. *FIDIC Procurement Procedures Guide* (FIDIC, 2011) 121.
185. *See* the definition of the '**Bill of Quantities**' in Sub-Clause 1.1.5 above.
186. *See* the definition of '**Contract**' in Sub-Clause 1.1.10 above.

1.1.72 'Schedule of Payments'

> 1.1.72 "**Schedule of Payments**" means the document(s) entitled schedule of payments (if any) in the Schedules showing the amounts and manner of payments to be made to the Contractor.

This is a newly defined term. A Schedule of Payments may or may not be included in the Contract.[187] If none is included, the Contractor must submit, periodically, non-binding estimates of the payments which the Contractor expects to become due, as provided for in the last paragraph of Sub-Clause 14.4 [*Schedule of Payments*].

1.1.73 'Section'

> 1.1.73 "**Section**" means a part of the Works specified in the Contract Data as a Section (if any).

If the Employer requires the taking over of the Works in stages, they should be defined as Sections[188] in the Contract Data.[189] It is advisable to define them geographically with precision, so that the extent of each Party's responsibility after taking over of a Section is clear.[190]

Each Section may be the subject of a separate Time for Completion,[191] a separate Taking-Over Certificate[192] and a separate DNP.[193] Delay Damages may also be agreed for each Section.[194]

187. Sub-Clause 14.4 [*Schedule of Payments*], first paragraph.
188. *The FIDIC Contracts Guide* (2nd edn, FIDIC, 2022) 64.
189. The information concerning Sections should be inserted in the table at the end of the Contract Data form.
190. *The FIDIC Contracts Guide* (2nd edn, FIDIC, 2022) 64.
191. Sub-Clause 8.2.
192. Sub-Clause 10.1.
193. Sub-Clauses 1.1.27 and 11.3.
194. Sub-Clauses 8.8 and 8.2.

A Section should be distinguished from a Part of either the Works or a Section.[195] A Part is the subject of a separate Taking-Over Certificate[196] and a separate DNP.[197] However, it is not the subject of a separate Time for Completion or Delay Damages.

1.1.74 'Site'

> 1.1.74 "**Site**" means the places where the Permanent Works are to be executed and to which Plant and Materials are to be delivered, and any other places specified in the Contract as forming part of the Site.

The Site, which may comprise one or multiple locations, whether on land or at sea, should be clearly specified in the Drawings and/or Specification. The working areas obtained by the Contractor referred to in the first paragraph of Sub-Clause 4.22 [*Contractor's Operations on Site*] do not constitute part of the Site and the Employer has no responsibility for them.[198]

1.1.75 'Special Provisions'

> 1.1.75 "**Special Provisions**" means the document (if any), entitled special provisions which constitutes Part B of the Particular Conditions.

See the commentary on Sub-Clause 1.1.59 '**Particular Conditions**' above.

1.1.76 'Specification'

> 1.1.76 "**Specification**" means the document entitled specification included in the Contract, and any additions and modifications

195. *See* the commentary on Sub-Clause 1.1.58 above.
196. Sub-Clause 10.2, second paragraph.
197. Sub-Clauses 1.1.27 and 11.3.
198. *The FIDIC Contracts Guide* (2nd edn, FIDIC, 2022) 209. However, The World Bank's COPA defines the Site as 'including storage and working area'. Sub-Clause 1.1.74, COPA.

to the specification in accordance with the Contract. Such document specifies the Works.

The Specification (its initial text) is prepared by the Employer or its consultant and included in the tender dossier. Together with the Drawings, it specifies the scope of the Contractor's work:

> The specification document is where the employer specifies his precise requirements for all matters not covered by the conditions of contract or shown on the drawings. It is here that he gives all details and descriptions of the materials, plant and equipment, workmanship and other matters required for or relevant to the construction of the works, and (if necessary) a time programme showing the work sequence, phases and completion dates.[199]

In numerous places, the General Conditions refer to information to be given in the Specification[200] included in the Contract.[201]

1.1.77 'Statement'

1.1.77 "**Statement**" means a statement submitted by the Contractor as part of an appli-

199. *See FIDIC Procurement Procedures Guide* (FIDIC, 2011) 119. This *Guide* also contains on page 120 a table setting out the '[t]ypical specification items'.
200. For a list of Sub-Clauses which make reference to matters stated in the Specification and/or Drawings, *see Guidance for Preparation of Particular Conditions*, 10-11.
201. In the United States and, increasingly, internationally, it is the practice to distinguish between 'design specifications' and 'performance specifications', as follows:

> **Design specifications** state precise measurements, tolerances, materials, construction methods, sequences, quality control, inspection requirements, and other information. They tell the contractor in detail the material it must furnish and how to perform the work.
>
> **Performance specifications** state the performance characteristics required; for example, the pump will deliver fifty units per minute, a heating system will heat to 70° F within a designated time, or a wall will resist flames for a designated period. As long as performance requirements are met, how that result is achieved is up to the contractor [...].
>
> Justin Sweet and others, *Construction Law for Design Professionals, Construction Managers, and Contractors* (Cengage Learning, Stamford, CT, 2015) 283-84.

> cation for a Payment Certificate under Sub-Clause 14.2.1 [*Advance Payment Guarantee*] (if applicable), Sub-Clause 14.3 [*Application for Interim Payment*], Sub-Clause 14.10 [*Statement at Completion*] or Sub-Clause 14.11 [*Final Statement*].

The Contractor's application for payment under Clause 14 [*Contract Price and Payments*] takes the form of a 'Statement'. Each of the four Sub-Clauses of Clause 14 referred to in Sub-Clause 1.1.77 describes what the relevant Statement must provide.[202] However, Sub-Clause 14.11 [*Final Statement*], in fact, describes three kinds of Statement: a draft Final Statement, a Partially Agreed Final Statement and a Final Statement (also sometimes referred to as a 'final Statement as agreed').[203]

1.1.78 'Subcontractor'

> 1.1.78 "**Subcontractor**" means any person named in the Contract as a subcontractor, or any person appointed by the Contractor as a subcontractor or designer, for a part of the Works; and the legal successors in title to each of these persons.

A 'Subcontractor' is stated to mean any person named in the Contract as a subcontractor, or any person appointed by the Contractor as a subcontractor or designer for the Works.[204] A Subcontractor named in the Contract may include a 'nominated Subcontractor', that is, a Subcontractor who has been named as such in the Specification or whom the

202. Any Statement must also, like other communications, comply with Sub-Clause 1.3 [*Notices and Other Communications*]. More particularly, sub-para. (b) of Sub-Clause 1.3 requires that it be identified as a Statement and includes a reference to the provision(s) of the Contract under which it is issued where appropriate.
203. Sub-Clause 14.11.2 [Agreed Final Statement]. Only Sub-Clause 15.6 appears to allow the Engineer to issue a Payment Certificate without the Contractor first submitting a Statement.
204. As a designer performs services just like any other subcontractor, there should have been no need for a specific reference to 'designer'. This term may have been added because, although a designer is a provider of services, it may not be perceived as a subcontractor in the UK.

Engineer under Sub-Clause 13.4 [*Provisional Sums*] instructs the Contractor to employ as a Subcontractor.[205]

1.1.79 'Taking-Over Certificate'

1.1.79 "**Taking-Over Certificate**" means a certificate issued (or deemed to be issued) by the Engineer in accordance with Clause 10 [*Employer's Taking Over*].

The new definition refers not only to cases where a Taking-Over Certificate is issued but also (unlike in RB/99)[206] to where it is deemed to be issued. A Taking-Over Certificate may be issued (or be deemed to be issued) by the Engineer for the Works, a Section or a Part, as the case may be.[207] The Taking-Over Certificate states the date that the relevant Works, Section or Part have been completed (called the 'Date of Completion'[208]) in accordance with the Contract, including the passing of Tests on Completion, except for any minor outstanding work and defects (as listed in the Taking-Over Certificate) as described in Sub-Clause 10.1.

1.1.80 'Temporary Works'

1.1.80 "**Temporary Works**" means all temporary works of every kind (other than Contractor's Equipment) required on Site for the execution of the Works.

Temporary Works are to be distinguished from Permanent Works defined in Sub-Clause 1.1.64.

205. Sub-Clause 5.2.1 [Definition of 'nominated Subcontractor']. As regards 'legal successors in title', *see* the commentary on Sub-Clause 1.1.14 '**Contractor**' above. More generally on the Subcontractor *see* the commentary on Clause 5 [*Subcontracting*] below.
206. Sub-Clause 1.1.3.5 of RB/99.
207. *See* the commentaries on Sub-Clauses 10.1 [*Taking Over the Works and Sections*] and 10.2 [*Taking Over Parts*] below.
208. Sub-Clause 1.1.24 '**Date of Completion**'.

1.1.81 'Tender'

> 1.1.81 "**Tender**" means the Letter of Tender, the JV Undertaking (if applicable), and all other documents which the Contractor submitted with the Letter of Tender, as included in the Contract.

This definition refers to the package of documents which the Contractor submits with the Letter of Tender and which are 'as included in the Contract'. These last quoted words are important as some of the documents which the Contractor may have submitted with its Letter of Tender (such as those containing reservations, qualifications or alternative proposals) may have been excluded from the Contract. The JV Undertaking, a new document in RB/17, is now (if the tenderer is a JV) made part of the Tender.

1.1.82 'Tests after Completion'

> 1.1.82 "**Tests after Completion**" means the tests (if any) which are stated in the Specification and which are carried out in accordance with the Special Provisions after the Works or a Section (as the case may be) are taken over under Clause 10 [*Employer's Taking Over*].

Tests after Completion are uncommon in a project designed by the Employer and are therefore not provided for in the General Conditions of RB/17. The Employer may, however, wish to carry out these tests if the Contractor has designed part of the Permanent Works.[209] In this case, a description of them should be included in the Specification.[210]

1.1.83 'Tests on Completion'

> 1.1.83 "**Tests on Completion**" means the tests which are specified in the Contract or

209. *Guidance for the Preparation of Particular Conditions*, 14.
210. *Ibid.* Consideration should also be given to including provisions in the Special Provisions based on those in Clause 12 [*Tests after Completion*] of YB/17. *Ibid.*, 15.

> agreed by both Parties or instructed as a Variation, and which are carried out under Clause 9 [*Tests on Completion*] before the Works or a Section (as the case may be) are taken over under Clause 10 [*Employer's Taking Over*].

The successful passing of these tests is ordinarily a condition to the issue of a Taking-Over Certificate.[211]

1.1.84 'Time for Completion'

> 1.1.84 "**Time for Completion**" means the time for completing the Works or a Section (as the case may be) under Sub-Clause 8.2 [*Time for Completion*], as stated in the Contract Data as may be extended under Sub-Clause 8.5 [*Extension of Time for Completion*], calculated from the Commencement Date.

The Time for Completion under Sub-Clause 8.2 refers to the time for completing the Works or a Section (but not to a Part). The Time for Completion of the Works begins on the Commencement Date[212] and ends on the Date of Completion.[213] Failure to complete the Works or a Section by the relevant Date for Completion, as it may be extended pursuant to Sub-Clause 8.5, will entitle the Employer to Delay Damages pursuant to Sub-Clause 8.8 [*Delay Damages*].[214]

1.1.85 'Unforeseeable'

> 1.1.85 "**Unforeseeable**" means not reasonably foreseeable by an experienced contractor by the Base Date.

---

211. *See* the commentary on Clause 9 [*Tests on Completion*] and **Figure 9 Steps in Tests on Completion** at the end of the commentary on Sub-Clause 9.1 below.
212. Sub-Clause 1.1.7 **'Commencement Date'**.
213. Sub-Clause 1.1.24 **'Date of Completion'**.
214. *See* the commentaries on Sub-Clauses 8.2 [*Time for Completion*] and 8.8 [*Delay Damages*] below.

Whereas RB/99 defined 'Unforeseeable' as 'not reasonably foreseeable by an experienced contractor by the date for submission of the Tender',[215] RB/17 refers to what was 'not reasonably foreseeable by an experienced contractor by the Base Date', that is, the 'date 28 days before the latest date for submission of the Tender'.[216] 'Experienced contractor', it is suggested, means a contractor who is 'experienced in the type of Works being executed'.[217]

Assessment of Unforeseeability by reference to the Base Date is understandable as 28 days before the latest date for submission of the Tender is estimated (by FIDIC) to be the date – for a complex project as an RB project is likely to be – as of which the Contractor will have calculated its rates and prices so as to include them in the Tender. A consequence of this will be that whatever the Contractor may learn later from its investigations, if any, or indeed from the Employer or otherwise, between the Base Date and entry into the Contract, is to be disregarded.

While criticised from time to time, the 'not reasonably foreseeable by an experienced contractor' test has been essentially unchanged since the first edition of the RB in 1957. It provides a rough, objective yardstick for determining whether a Contractor who has encountered, for example, adverse physical conditions underground should be entitled to relief pursuant to Sub-Clause 4.12 [*Unforeseeable Physical Conditions*].

FIDIC has defined whether an operation of forces of nature (e.g., earthquakes, tornados and extreme weather) is Unforeseeable as follows:

> The question whether a natural event is Unforeseeable may be resolved by reference to the duration of the Time for Completion of the Works and to the statistical frequency of the event, based upon historic records. For example, if the Time for Completion is three years, an experienced contractor might be expected to foresee an event which occurs (on average) once in every six years, but an event

215. Sub-Clause 1.1.6.8 of RB/99.
216. Sub-Clause 1.1.4 '**Base Date**'.
217. *FIDIC DBO Contract Guide* (FIDIC, 2011) 19 (the commentary on Sub-Clause 1.1.80). In RB/17, the new defined term 'Unforeseeable' is referred to in, for example, Sub-Clause 4.6 [*Co-operation*], Sub-Clause 4.12 [*Unforeseeable Physical Conditions*], Sub-Clause 8.5 [*Extension of Time for Completion*], Sub-Clause 8.6 [*Delays Caused by Authorities*], Sub-Clause 13.1 [*Right to Vary*] and Sub-Clause 17.2 [*Liability for Care of the Works*]. The definition is most often used in relation to Contractor's entitlements for Cost and/or EOT.

which occurs only once in every ten years might be regarded as Unforeseeable.[218]

An alternative to the Unforeseeability test would be to refer to whether:

an experienced contractor would have judged at the Contract Date [or Base Date] [the adverse physical conditions encountered] to have such a small chance of occurring that it would have been unreasonable to have allowed for them.[219]

This corresponds better to how a tenderer is likely actually to make this evaluation.[220]

1.1.86 'Variation'

1.1.86 "**Variation**" means any change to the Works, which is instructed as a variation under Clause 13 [*Variations and Adjustments*].

The definition is the same as in RB/99[221] except that the provision that any Variation is 'approved' has been removed. The definition of a Variation as 'any change to the Works' instructed under Clause 13 [*Variations and Adjustments*] may be too narrow as Works are defined as the Permanent Works and the Temporary Works.[222] The definition should, among other things, cover the Contractor's methods of working especially as Sub-Clause 8.7 [*Rate of Progress*] recognises that 'revised methods' of working (such as 'acceleration measures') resulting from an Engineer's instruction are to be treated as a Variation.[223]

218. *The FIDIC Contracts Guide* (1st edn, FIDIC 2000) 274-75 and, to similar effect (2nd edn, FIDIC, 2022) 195.
219. *NEC4 Engineering and Construction Contract* of the UK Institution of Civil Engineers, June 2017, Clause 60.1 (12).
220. Use of the term 'Unforeseeable' to distinguish certain work as being beyond the scope and nature of the Works provided for in the Contract and which therefore entitles the Contractor to object to its being instructed as a Variation, pursuant to Sub-Clause 13.1 (a), is more questionable. *See* the commentary on Sub-Clause 13.1 [*Right to Vary*] below.
221. Sub-Clause 1.1.6.9 of RB/99.
222. *See* Sub-Clause 1.1.87 '**Works**'.
223. *See* the commentary on Sub-Clause 8.7 below.

The description of what a Variation may include in Sub-Clause 13.1, fifth paragraph, is much broader. Consequently, this definition should be broadened so that it clearly incorporates the matters referred to in that paragraph.

1.1.87 'Works'

> 1.1.87 **"Works"** mean the Permanent Works and the Temporary Works, or either of them as appropriate.

See the discussion of 'Permanent Works' and 'Temporary Works' above.

1.1.88 'year'

> 1.1.88 **"year"** means 365 days.

While a 'year' is any period of 365 days and not the calendar year from 1 January to 31 December, a month, on the other hand, is defined as a calendar month according to the Gregorian calendar[224] and a day as a calendar day.[225]

(iii) Improvements

(1) As indicated above, a number of 'definitions' are not definitions in the true sense,[226] but rather cross-references to Sub-Clauses where the meaning of the term is defined or described, e.g., 1.1.13 '**Contract Price**', 1.1.37 '**Exceptional Event**' and 1.1.41 '**Final Statement**'. It would be more useful for the definitions to be, so far as practicable, statements of the meanings of the word or expression concerned.

(2) While the number of defined terms has increased – a positive development in this long document – some key terms still remain undefined. Two of considerable practical importance are

224. Sub-Clause 1.1.54 '**month**'.
225. Sub-Clause 1.1.25 '**day**'.
226. The dictionary defines a 'definition' as 'a formal statement of the exact meaning of a word'. *Concise Oxford English Dictionary* (10th edn, rev'd, OUP, Oxford, 2002).

'completion' and 'defect', which are used extensively in RB/17.[227] Definitions of these could usefully be included in any new edition of the RB.[228]

(3) Whether in the Conditions or in a future FIDIC guide to the Conditions, users should be strongly encouraged to make use of the defined terms in the Conditions in all Notices and other communications relating to the Contract, to the exclusion of other terminology.[229]

(4) A number of comments or suggestions for improvement have also been made in relation to the individual definitions commented on above and are not repeated here.

--ooOOoo--

1.2 Interpretation

In the Contract, except where the context requires otherwise:

(a) words indicating one gender include all genders; and "he", "his" and "himself" shall be read as "he/she", "his/her" and "himself/herself" respectively;

227. For example, in the case of 'completion' Clauses 9 [*Tests on Completion*] and 10 [*Employer's Taking Over*] and, in the case of 'defect', Sub-Clauses 1.8 [*Care and Supply of Documents*], 7.5 [*Defects and Rejection*] and Clause 11 [*Defects after Taking Over*].

228. Definitions of both these terms are contained in the *NEC4 Engineering and Construction Contract*, June 2017, Core Clauses 1. General 11.2(2) and (6), and the *ICC Model Turnkey Contract for Major Projects* (ICC Publication no 797 E 2020) art. 1, 1.1., and 'Defect' is defined as well in the *International Form of Contract – lump sum contracts* (1st edn, UK Institution of Chemical Engineers (IChemE) 2007) Sub-Clause 1.1. '[D]efective' is defined in art. 1.02 of the *Standard General Conditions of the Contract between Owner and Design-Builder* prepared by the Engineers Joint Contract Documents Committee (EJCDC) Washington DC, USA, 2016. 'Substantial Completion' is defined in The American Institute of Architects' *General Conditions of the Contract for Construction* (AIA document, A201-2017), s 9.8.1.

229. In this connection, *see* the beginning of this commentary on Sub-Clause 1.1.

(b) words indicating the singular also include the plural and words indicating the plural also include the singular;
(c) provisions including the word "agree", "agreed" or "agreement" require the agreement to be recorded in writing;
(d) "written" or "in writing" means hand-written, type-written, printed or electronically made, and resulting in a permanent record;
(e) "may" means that the Party or person referred to has the choice of whether to act or not in the matter referred to;
(f) "shall" means that the Party or person referred to has an obligation under the Contract to perform the duty referred to;
(g) "consent" means that the Employer, the Contractor or the Engineer (as the case may be) agrees to or gives permission for, the requested matter;
(h) "including", "include" and "includes" shall be interpreted as not being limited to, or qualified by, the stated items that follow;
(i) words indicating persons or parties shall be interpreted as referring to natural and legal persons (including corporations and other legal entities); and
(j) "execute the Works" or "execution of the Works" means the construction and completion of the Works and the remedying of any defects (and shall be deemed to include design to the extent, if any, specified in the Contract).

In any list in these Conditions, where the second-last item of the list is followed by "and" or "or" or "and/or" then all of the list items going before this item shall also be read as if they are followed by "and" or "or" or "and/or" (as the case may be).

The marginal words and other headings shall not be taken into consideration in the interpretation of these Conditions.

This Sub-Clause specifies how in the Contract, except where the context requires otherwise, words indicating a person's gender (e.g., he/she) and the singular or the plural are to be interpreted. In

addition, except where the context requires otherwise, it provides how words such as 'agree', 'in writing', 'may', 'shall', 'consent', 'including', 'persons or parties' and 'execution of the Works', are to be interpreted. Marginal words and other headings are not to be taken into consideration in the interpretation of the Conditions.

Commentary

(i) Main Changes from RB/99: The first paragraph of Sub-Clause 1.2 of RB/99 contained only four sub-paragraphs, corresponding more or less to sub-paragraphs (a) to (d) in Sub-Clause 1.2 of RB/17. However, new sub-paragraphs have been added to deal with how terms such as 'may', 'shall', 'consent', 'including', and how words indicating persons or parties and 'execute the Works' or 'execution of the Works', should be construed. In addition, a new paragraph has been added stipulating how the words 'and', 'or' and 'and/or' should be interpreted if used in the second-last item in a list of items.

(ii) Related Clauses / Sub-Clauses: 1.1 [*Definitions*], 1.3 [*Notices and Other Communications*] and 1.4 [*Law and Language*].[230]

(iii) Analysis: The interpretation rules in Sub-Clause 1.2 apply not just to the Conditions but also to all of the documents, technical or other, comprising the Contract.[231] They are not unvarying rules, however, as they only apply 'except where the context requires otherwise'. Therefore, a different interpretation applies if required by the context.

Sub-paragraph (c) deals with the interpretation of the words 'agree', 'agreed' or 'agreement' and requires such agreement to be recorded in writing. *The FIDIC Contracts Guide* (2000) had stated with regard to the identical sub-paragraph in RB/99 that an 'agreement' does not need to be subject to Sub-Clause 1.3 [*Communications*].[232] This is no longer true as the first paragraph of Sub-Clause 1.3 [*Notices and Other Communications*] of RB/17 explicitly refers to an 'agreement' as a type of communication which is subject to Sub-Clause 1.3 (and repeats that it must be 'in writing').

Sub-paragraph (d) states that the term 'written' or 'in writing' means handwritten, type-written, printed or electronically made, and resulting

230. Sub-Clause 1.2 is relevant to the entire Contract. These are no more than several of the most important related Sub-Clauses of the Conditions.
231. *See* the commentary on Sub-Clause 1.1.10 **'Contract'**.
232. *The FIDIC Contracts Guide* (1st edn, FIDIC, 2000) 58.

in a permanent record. Emails are likely to satisfy the requirement to be 'in writing' as they can result in a permanent record (e.g., if they are saved in an electronic database or printed out). However, in order to avoid any disagreement as to whether emails are a valid form of communication, the Parties should agree on a method of electronic transmission in the Contract Data as noted in Sub-Clause 1.3(a)(ii), and on the electronic addresses to which communications should be sent.

Sub-paragraphs (e) and (f), dealing with the interpretation of the words 'may' and 'shall', are a welcome development. They clarify that 'may' refers to a Party's or a person's option to act and 'shall' refers to an obligation to perform the duty referred to.

Sub-paragraph (g) explains that 'consent' means that a Party or the Engineer 'agrees to or gives permission for, the requested matter'. The *Guidance* notes that, in keeping with the dictionary,[233] 'consent' does not mean 'approve' or 'approval' which, under some legal systems, may be interpreted as accepting or acceptance that the requested matter is wholly satisfactory with the result that the requesting party may no longer have any – or have only reduced – responsibility or liability for it.[234]

Sub-paragraph (j) clarifies that 'execute the Works' and 'execution of the Works' comprise the construction and completion of the Works and remedying defects as well as design (if the Contract specifies that the Contractor shall design some part of the Works). Thus, 'execution of the Works' is used as a generic term replacing the lengthy references in RB/99 to execution and completion of the Works and the remedying of any defects.[235]

(iv) Related Law: The interpretation rules in Sub-Clause 1.2 are not the only ones that will apply. Practically, every country's system of law has rules providing how contracts are to be interpreted. Therefore, the rules on contract interpretation of the law governing the Contract under Sub-Clause 1.4 [*Law and Language*] will complement the rules in Sub-Clause 1.2.[236]

233. Consent is defined as 'give permission' (core sense) and 'agree to do something' (subsense) in the *Concise Oxford English Dictionary* (10th edn, rev'd, OUP, Oxford, 2002).
234. *Guidance for the Preparation of Particular Conditions*, 15.
235. *See* e.g., Sub-Clause 4.1 of RB/99, first paragraph.
236. Common law and civil law countries approach the matter of contract interpretation differently as discussed in **Chapter III Contract Interpreta-**

(v) Improvements:

(1) Numerous Sub-Clauses use the term 'at the sole discretion of' a Party,[237] 'at the Employer's sole discretion',[238] 'at the sole discretion of the Employer',[239] or 'at [the DAAB's] sole discretion'.[240] A law dictionary defines 'sole discretion' as meaning: '[a]n individual's power to make decisions without anyone else's advice or consent'.[241] If this is the intended meaning,[242] it would be better if this were clearly explained rather than left to inference.

(2) While FIDIC has stated that time periods specified in days 'commence on the beginning of the day following the date of the act which constitutes the starting-point',[243] this important point should be in the General Conditions and not just in the Guide. But it does not entirely resolve the ambiguity about time periods. When referring to time periods stated in days, RB/17 often refers to terms, such as 'before', 'after', 'within', 'not less than', 'not more than' and 'not later than'. Difficulties may arise in practice with regard to computation of these time periods. For example, if a Party or the Engineer has to do something under the Contract 'within 7 days' after a certain event or circumstance,[244] would the seventh day of the period be considered to be 'within' the seven-day period or only the sixth day?[245]

---

tion, above which also discusses interpreting a FIDIC contract specifically (*see* **Section 5 Interpreting a FIDIC Contract**).

237. For example, Sub-Clauses 1.7(a) and 13.2.
238. For example, Sub-Clauses 5.2.4, 7.6 and 11.4.
239. For example, Sub-Clause 10.2.
240. For example, Rule 8.6 of the DAAB Rules.
241. Bryan A. Garner (ed in chief) *Black's Law Dictionary* 11th edition, Thomson Reuters, St Paul, MN, 2019).
242. If this is the intended meaning, it would indicate, for example, that the 'not be unreasonably withheld or delayed' language applicable to the giving of a Notice in the penultimate paragraph of Sub-Clause 1.3 will not apply.
243. *The FIDIC Contracts Guide* (2nd edn FIDIC, 2022) 21.
244. For example, as in the last paragraph of Sub-Clause 3.4 [*Delegation by the Engineer*].
245. A related issue is how to address Parties in different time zones. Which time zone applies? The UNIDROIT Principles address this issue, *see* art. 1.12 (*Computation of time set by parties*), though its solution does not seem appropriate or sufficient for a FIDIC contract.

In order to avoid uncertainty, Parties may consider adding an additional sub-paragraph in Sub-Clause 1.2 stating not only that the day when the respective event or circumstance has occurred or will occur is not to be taken into account in the calculation of the time period (as FIDIC has specified), but that, in such a case, the last day of the time period will be deemed included in such period.[246]

(3) As gender-neutral wording has already been introduced into RB/17, consideration should be given to deleting sub-paragraph (a) of Sub-Clause 1.2. In addition, the references to 'he/she', 'his/her' and/or 'himself/herself' should be replaced by 'it', 'its' and 'itself', which are more modern and concise (and consistent with the usage both in The World Bank's COPA and this commentary on RB/17).

--ooOOoo--

1.3 Notices and Other Communications

Wherever these Conditions provide for the giving of a Notice (including a Notice of Dissatisfaction) or the issuing, providing, sending, submitting or transmitting of another type of communication (including acceptance, acknowledgement, advising, agreement, approval, certificate, Claim, consent, decision, determination, disagreement, discharge, instruction, No-objection, record(s) of meeting, permission, proposal, record, reply, report, request, Review, Statement, statement, submission or any

246. Another possibility is to have regard to the position taken in art. 3 d. and e. of the *ICC Uniform Rules for Demand Guarantees*, 2010, revision ('URDG') (discussed in relation to Sub-Clause 4.2 [*Performance Security*] below) which provide as follows:

d. When used with a date or dates to determine the start, end or duration of any period, the terms:
   i. 'from', 'to', 'until', 'till' and 'between' include; and
   ii. 'before' and ' 'after' exclude,
   the date or dates mentioned.

e. The term 'within', when used in connection with a period after a given date or event, excludes that date or the date of that event but includes the last date of that period.

other similar type of communication), the Notice or other communication shall be in writing and:

(a) shall be:
   (i) a paper-original signed by the Contractor's Representative, the Engineer, or the authorised representative of the Employer (as the case may be); or
   (ii) an electronic original generated from any of the systems of electronic transmission stated in the Contract Data (if not stated, system(s) acceptable to the Engineer), where the electronic original is transmitted by the electronic address uniquely assigned to each of such authorised representatives,

   or both, as stated in these Conditions; and
(b) if it is a Notice, it shall be identified as a Notice. If it is another form of communication, it shall be identified as such and include reference to the provision(s) of the Contract under which it is issued where appropriate;
(c) delivered by hand (against receipt), or sent by mail or courier (against receipt), or transmitted using any of the systems of electronic transmission under sub-paragraph (a)(ii) above; and
(d) delivered, sent or transmitted to the address for the recipient's communications as stated in the Contract Data. However, if the recipient gives a Notice of another address, all Notices and other communications shall be delivered accordingly after the sender receives such Notice.

Where these Conditions state that a Notice or NOD or other communication is to be delivered, given, issued, provided, sent, submitted or transmitted, it shall have effect when it is received (or deemed to have been received) at the recipient's current address under sub-paragraph (d) above. An electronically transmitted Notice or other communication is deemed to have been received on the day after transmission, provided no non-delivery notification was received by the sender.

All Notices, and all other types of communication as referred to above, shall not be unreasonably withheld or delayed.

When a Notice or NOD or certificate is issued by a Party or the Engineer, the paper and/or electronic original shall be sent to the intended recipient and a copy shall be sent to the Engineer or the other Party, as the case may be. All other communications shall be copied to the Parties and/or the Engineer as stated under these Conditions or elsewhere in the Contract.

Wherever these Conditions provide for the giving of a Notice or another type of communication (including, among other things, agreement, approval, certificate, Claim, consent, decision, determination, instruction, Review, Statement 'or any other similar type of communication'), such communication must be in writing, and in the form of: (i) a paper-original signed by an authorised person; or (ii) an electronic original generated from any of the systems of electronic transmission stated in the Contract Data (if not stated, system(s) acceptable to the Engineer); or (iii) both, as stated in these Conditions. A Notice must be identified as such. If it is another form of communication, it must be identified as such and include a reference to the provision(s) of the Contract under which it is issued where appropriate. A Notice or other communication must be delivered by hand (against receipt), or sent by mail or courier (against receipt) or by electronic means as in (ii) above.

A Notice or other communication shall have effect when received (or deemed to have been received) at the recipient's current address. If transmitted electronically, it is deemed to have been received on the day after transmission provided that no non-delivery notification was received by the sender.

Notices and other communications must not be unreasonably withheld or delayed.

A Notice or certificate issued by a Party or the Engineer shall be sent to the intended recipient with a copy to the Engineer or the other Party, as the case may be. All other communications shall be copied to the Parties and/or the Engineer as stated in the Contract.

Commentary

(i) Main Changes from RB/99:

(1) Sub-Clause 1.3 in RB/99 identified six types of communication ('approvals, certificates, consents, determinations, notices and requests') to which it applied. The new Sub-Clause contains a greatly expanded list of types of communication.

(2) The new Sub-Clause also deals for the first time with:

(a) whether a Notice or other communication in a paper form must be a paper-original;

(b) who should sign a Notice or communication in paper form;

(c) when a Notice or communication is deemed to have been received and/or take effect;

(d) whether a Notice or other form of communication should be identified as such; and

(e) whether it should refer to the provision(s) of the Contract under which it is issued.

(3) GB/08 had introduced, for the first time in a FIDIC contract, a definition of a 'Notice' as well as a requirement for it and other forms of communication to be identified as such and include a reference to the Clause under which it is issued.[247] RB/17 has kept the requirement for a Notice or other form of communication to be identified as such, but dispensed with the requirement, in the case of a Notice, that it includes a reference to the provision(s) of the Contract under which it is issued.

(ii) Related Clauses / Sub-Clauses: 1.4 [*Law and Language*], 4.3 [*Contractor's Representative*] and 4.9.1 [*Quality Management System*].[248]

---

247. Sub-Clauses 1.1.56 '**Notice**' and 1.3 [*Notices and Other Communications*] of GB/08.

248. These are mainly the Sub-Clauses which contain an explicit reference to Sub-Clause 1.3. However, Sub-Clause 1.3 has a much broader scope of application as it applies to the many references to communications that are issued, sent or submitted under the Conditions. Notices in relation to the DAAB Agreement are the subject of separate procedures, *see* Sub-Clause 1.8 (1.7) '**Notification**' of the DAAB GCs. *See also* under *(1) New 'Notification' provision* under **(iii) Analysis** in **Section 2.2 General Conditions of DAAB Agreement ('GCs')** of **Chapter V Commentary On Other Documents** below.

(iii) Analysis:

(1) Requirements for Notices and communications

Compared to RB/99, the new Sub-Clause contains a greatly expanded list of types of communication. Some of the items may seem surprising as they do not constitute communications in the common sense of the term; that is, a means of sending or receiving information. For example, 'agreement', 'disagreement', 'No-Objection', 'record(s) of meeting', 'record' or 'Review'[249] do not fall within the common meaning of a communication as none is a means of sending or receiving information. Consequently, it may make little sense to say, as in the third paragraph, that they 'shall not be unreasonably withheld or delayed'.

After stating that a Notice or other communication 'shall be in writing', sub-paragraph (a) provides that it shall be a paper-original or an electronic original or both as stated in the Conditions.[250] If it is a paper-original, it must be signed by the authorised person specified in item (i) of sub-paragraph (a). If it is an electronic original, it must be generated from any of the systems of electronic transmission in the Contract Data. If no such system has been stated, it must be acceptable to the Engineer.

Sub-paragraph (b) requires that each Notice be identified as a Notice. When it comes to other forms of communication, there is a further requirement for it to refer to the provision(s) of the Contract under which it is issued. However, this requirement does not apply to Notices[251] as, according to FIDIC, the consequences of failing to serve a valid Notice are potentially severe (e.g.: application of the deeming provisions if served late; or the time bar of a Claim).[252] In FIDIC's view, by requiring that a

249. *See* Sub-Clause 1.1.70 above which defines '**Review**' as the 'examination and consideration by the Engineer' of a Contractor's submission.
250. What if the Conditions require both a paper-original and an electronic original but, for example, the Contractor submits a Notice of Claim pursuant to Sub-Clause 20.2.1 in the form of an email only within the relevant 28-day time period? Would this satisfy Sub-Clause 20.2.1? For an English case suggesting that it might (although unrelated to a FIDIC contract and holding that the email was not a valid notice under the relevant contract), *see Jawaby Property Investment Limited v The Interiors Group Limited* and *Andrew Stephan George Black* [2016] EWHC 557 (TCC) [paras 60-69].
251. Although it had so applied in Sub-Clause 1.3(a) of GB/08.
252. Presentation of Ms. Siobhan Fahey at the FIDIC International Contract Users' Conference in London on 3 and 4 December 2018. However, in some cases a Notice must state that it is given under a particular Sub-Clause, e.g.,

Notice be identified as a Notice, it should be sufficiently recognisable and nothing more should be necessary.

Sub-paragraph (c) allows the Party or the Engineer giving the Notice or sending the communication to decide upon the method of transmission, namely, whether by hand, mail, courier or electronically. If the Notice or communication is to be sent by hand, mail or courier – electronic communications are not mentioned[253] – the delivery should be done against receipt.[254]

Sub-paragraph (d) deals with the addresses for recipients' communications. It is obviously important that such addresses of the Parties and the Engineer are stated in the Contract Data (as this sub-paragraph provides) and are updated as appropriate by Notices.

As 'day' is defined in Sub-Clause 1.1.25 to mean any (working or non-working) calendar day from midnight to midnight,[255] a Notice or other type of communication may therefore – subject to applicable law – validly be sent or received on any day of the year, without restriction as to the time of day.[256]

Any Notice or other communication should be in the language of communications[257] stated in the Contract Data using, it is recommended, the defined terms in the Conditions, which provide a sort of *lingua franca* (common language) for communications.[258]

Sub-Clauses 15.2.1, 15.5, 16.1 and 16.2.1 relating to termination of the Contract by either the Employer or the Contractor.

253. As an electronic communication may also be subject to a receipt it is not clear why a receipt for them is not also explicitly required.
254. This eliminates a gap in RB/99 (Sub-Clause 1.3) which required delivery against receipt only with regard to a communication delivered by hand but not with regard to one sent by mail or courier.
255. *See The FIDIC Contracts Guide* (2nd edn, FIDIC 2022) 21.
256. For another approach to the question of when notices or other communications are deemed to have been received, *see* art. 63.3 of the *ICC Model Turnkey Contract for Major Projects* (ICC Publication no 797 E 2020) (providing that communications are deemed received on 'Business Days'). *See also* art. 1.12 (*Computation of time set by parties*) of the UNIDROIT Principles.
257. *See* Sub-Clause 1.4 [*Law and Language*].
258. *See* under *(2) A common language* (*lingua franca*) at the beginning of the commentary on Sub-Clause 1.1 [*Definitions*] above in **Chapter IV**.

Only the Contractor's Representative – not a delegate – has authority to give or receive Notices and other communications on behalf of the Contractor.[259]

(2) When Notices and communications have effect

The second paragraph, which has no analogue in RB/99, is important. It states that where:

> a Notice or NOD or other communication is to be delivered, given, issued, provided, sent, submitted or transmitted, it shall have effect when it is received (or deemed to have been received).

at the recipient's current address for communications stated in the Contract Data. In case of a Notice or communication in a paper form, the return receipt will show when such Notice or communication has become effective. An electronically transmitted Notice or communication is deemed to have been received *on the day after transmission*, provided that no non-delivery notification was received by the sender.[260] *Important: this means that an email sent only on the last day of a notification period will be sent too late.*

A practical approach should be taken to the formal requirements applicable to Notices and other communications in the first two paragraphs of this sub-clause: if it can be established that a Notice or communication has indeed been received and the notified Party (including the Engineer) has not been prejudiced, it should not be fatal that one or more of the formal requirements have not been respected. All of the facts and circumstances, including the purpose of the Notice, should be considered.[261]

The same Notice may, if properly prepared and given, satisfy the requirements of different Sub-Clauses.[262] A separate Notice is not necessary for each Sub-Clause requiring a Notice, so long as the single Notice document satisfies the Notice requirements of each relevant Sub-Clause.

259. Sub-Clause 4.3(a).
260. Sub-Clause 1.3, second paragraph.
261. *See also* Atkin Chambers, *Hudson's Building and Engineering Contracts* (14th edn, Sweet & Maxwell, London, 2020) 951-953 (paras 8-050 to 8-051, especially 8-051).
262. *The FIDIC Contracts Guide* (2nd edn, FIDIC, 2022) 193.

(3) *'Shall not be unreasonably withheld or delayed'*

The third paragraph specifies that all Notices and other types of communication 'shall not be unreasonably withheld or delayed', which is important where a sub-clause requires that some action be taken by reference to some communication, but does not specify a time period within which this should be done. A Party or the Engineer who is required to act should do so within a reasonable period of time; otherwise a Party may be in breach of this provision. What is a reasonable period is a question of fact and will depend on the particular circumstances of the case.[263]

Whereas the third paragraph applies to all types of communication, as defined in Sub-Clause 1.3, the corresponding paragraph in RB/99 applied to '[a]pprovals, certificates, consents and determinations' only; that is, to matters which could be expected to be communicated by a particular time. The paragraph in RB/99 did not apply, understandably, to the other two types of communication identified in RB/99 (namely 'notices' and 'requests') as there was not necessarily an expectation that they be communicated by a particular time.

As the new Sub-Clause makes no such distinction, it may be unclear when some of the 'communications' should 'not be unreasonably withheld or delayed'. While it may be understandable that an approval, certificate, consent or determination, for example, not be 'unreasonably withheld or delayed', these words make less sense in relation to, for example, an agreement, Notice or request, as these things may not have to be communicated by any particular time, or at all.

While the position is not clear, presumably where the Conditions refer to a communication being at 'the sole discretion' of a Party or person (an expression which is undefined),[264] this requirement would not apply.

---

263. While 'reasonableness' has not been defined in the Conditions, it has been defined elsewhere:

> reasonableness is to be judged by what persons acting in good faith and in the same situation as the parties would consider to be reasonable. In particular, in assessing what is reasonable the nature and purpose of the contract, the circumstances of the case, and the usages and practices of the trades or professions involved should be taken into account.
>
> Art. 1:302 of *The Principles of European Contract Law*, 2002.

264. *See* item (1) under **(v) Improvements** of the commentary on Sub-Clause 1.2 [*Interpretation*] above in **Chapter IV**.

(4) Sending of copies

The last paragraph specifies to whom copies of a 'Notice or NOD or certificate' should be sent, specifying that the paper and/or electronic original (whatever method of communication the Parties have agreed upon) shall be sent or copied to the Engineer and the other Party so that all three (each Party and the Engineer) are kept aware, on a current basis, of those communications under the Contract. All other communications are to be copied to the Parties and/or the Engineer as provided in the Contract.[265]

(iv) Related Law: Like other Sub-Clauses, Sub-Clause 1.3 is subject to the governing law,[266] and certain countries or jurisdictions (e.g., the European Union[267]) have adopted legislation concerning electronic signatures, providing that such signatures have the same weight as physical counterparts.

(v) Improvements:

(1) As stated under **(iii) Analysis** above, Sub-Clause 1.3 identifies as a communication numerous matters that do not typically constitute a communication, that is, something that is sent or received. This issue should be addressed.

(2) Similar to GB/08,[268] a Notice could benefit from a reference to the provision(s) of the Contract under which it is issued. Concern about the risk that a Notice might be invalidated because of a failure in a Notice to refer to such provision(s) may be overcome by adding a provision to the following effect: even if a Notice fails to comply with all of the requirements of Sub-Clause 1.3, it would still be deemed valid if, in light of its content, means

265. '[R]elevant Notices' and 'relevant communications' between the Parties and/or with the Engineer should be provided to the DAAB. Rule 4.3 (f) and (g), DAAB Rules.

266. *See* the commentary on Sub-Clause 1.4 [*Law and Language*] below.

267. Since 1 July 2016, electronic signatures in the European Union are governed by the Electronic Identification and Trust Services (eIDAS) Regulation (Regulation no 910/2014) of 23 July 2014, known as the eIDAS Regulation. This regulation is directly applicable in all EU Member States. It aims to enable secure and seamless electronic interaction between businesses, citizens and public authorities.

268. Sub-Clause 1.3(a) of GB/08. The *ICC Model Turnkey Contract for Major Projects* (ICC Publication no 797 E 2020) is to the same effect. *See* art. 63.4(f) of this form.

of transmission and other relevant circumstances, the intended recipient could reasonably have been expected to have been informed of its content, especially if it were not prejudiced by the non-compliance. By requiring that a Notice include a reference to the provision(s) of the Contract under which it is issued, a recipient would be alerted to its relevance and, even should users neglect to include such reference at times, as is to be expected, this would not be fatal if a provision such as that described above were added.

(3) As they can easily be obtained, receipts should be explicitly required for electronic communications.

(4) Given the global nature of construction and the increased number of time bars in RB/17, it could be useful to include an explicit provision as to when Notices and other communications will be deemed to have been delivered and take effect when the Parties and/or the Engineer are residing in different time zones.[269] Thus, the Sub-Clause could deal with the issue of where a Notice which is timely and thus valid in one time zone (e.g., England), but may be delivered late and thus be invalid in another (e.g., China).

--ooOOoo--

1.4 Law and Language

The Contract shall be governed by the law of the country (or other jurisdiction) stated in the Contract Data (if not stated, the law of the Country), excluding any conflict of law rules.

The ruling language of the Contract shall be that stated in the Contract Data (if not stated, the language of these Conditions). If there are versions of any part of the Contract which are written in more than one language, the version which is in the ruling language shall prevail.

The language for communications shall be that stated in the Contract Data. If no language is stated

269. *See*, e.g., art. 63.3 of the *ICC Model Turnkey Contract for Major Projects* (ICC Publication no 797 E 2020).

there, the language for communications shall be the ruling language of the Contract.

The governing law shall be the law of the jurisdiction stated in the Contract Data or, if not stated there, the law of the Country, excluding any conflict of law rules.

The ruling language shall be the language stated in the Contract Data or, if not stated there, the language of these Conditions. If any part of the Contract is written in more than one language, the version in the ruling language shall prevail.

The language of communications shall be that stated in the Contract Data or, if not stated there, the ruling language.

Commentary

(i) Main Changes from RB/99:

(1) Unlike RB/99, the Sub-Clause provides that if no governing law is stated in the Contract Data (formerly the 'Appendix to Tender'), the law of the Country (i.e., the country in which the Site, or most of it, is located) shall govern.
(2) Unlike RB/99, the Sub-Clause expressly excludes any conflict of law rules of the applicable governing law.
(3) Whereas RB/99 provided that, where the language for communications was not stated in the Contract (the Appendix to Tender), the language for communications would be that in which the Contract (or most of it) was written, the new Sub-Clause specifies that where such language is not stated in the Contract Data, it will be the ruling language of the Contract.

(ii) Related Clauses / Sub-Clauses: 1.13 [*Compliance with Laws*], 3.1 [The *Engineer*], 3.4 [*Delegation by the Engineer*], 4.1 [*Contractor's General Obligations*], 4.3 [*Contractor's Representative*], 4.4 [*Contractor's Documents*], 6.4 [*Labour Laws*], 6.8 [*Contractor's Superintendence*], 6.12 [*Key Personnel*], 13.6 [*Adjustments for Changes in Laws*], 18.6 [*Release from Performance under the Law*], 21.2 [*Failure to Appoint DAAB Member(s)*] and 21.6 [*Arbitration*]. Rule 4.1 of the DAAB Rules and Article 6 of the example form of DAAB Agreement.

(iii) Analysis:

(1) The governing law[270]

The Sub-Clause provides that the Contract shall be governed by the law of the country (or other jurisdiction[271]) stated in the Contract Data (or, if not stated, the law of the Country), excluding any conflict of law rules.[272]

The purpose of the exclusion is to make clear that only the substantive law[273] of the country concerned – not its conflict of law rules which are also a part of its law – will apply. Otherwise, the conflict of law rules of the law of the country which is to apply might (under the legal doctrine known as renvoi[274]) provide that the law to be applied to a particular matter is the law of some other country.[275]

The Sub-Clause assumes that the Contract will be governed by a national law of some kind. As the tender dossier is prepared by, or on behalf of, the Employer, it will usually specify that the governing law is the law of

---

270. *See* **Sections 3 Importance of the Governing Law** and **5 Mandatory Law at the Site** of **Chapter II Applicable Law** above.
271. The reference to 'other jurisdiction' is to take account of countries with a federal system of government, like Australia, Canada and the United States, where the applicable law may be that of a state, province or other territory within the country.
272. Conflict of laws rules refer to the legal principles relied on to determine preliminary issues of applicable law where more than one jurisdiction is involved in a dispute. *See* Bryan A Garner (ed in chief), *Black's Law Dictionary* (11th edn, Thomson Reuters, St Paul, MN, 2019).
273. Substantive law refers to the part of the law (of a country or other jurisdiction) that creates, defines and regulates the rights, duties and powers of parties. It is to be contrasted with procedural law which are rules that prescribe the steps for having a right or duty judicially enforced, as opposed to the law that defines the specific rights or duties themselves that are comprised by substantive law. *See* Bryan A Garner (ed in chief), *Black's Law Dictionary* (11th edn, Thomson Reuters, St Paul, MN, 2019).
274. Renvoi (from French 'sending back') is the legal doctrine under which a court, in resorting to foreign law, adopts as well the foreign law's conflicts of laws principles, which may in turn refer the court back to the law of the forum. Bryan A Garner (ed in chief), *Black's Law Dictionary* (11th edn, Thomson Reuters, St Paul, MN, 2019).
275. This exclusion is provided for, for example, in the European Union by art. 20 of Rome I Regulation and elsewhere by, among others, art. 17 of the *Inter-American Convention on the Law Applicable to International Contracts 1994* and s 46(2) of the English *Arbitration Act 1996*.

the Employer's country where the Site, or part of it, will usually be located. There may be little or no possibility for a tenderer to renegotiate this issue.[276] Indeed, where the Employer is a State or other public body, it may be mandatory, under the law of the State concerned, that its law (and language) apply.[277]

If the law to be applied is that of a less-developed legal system, it may not sufficiently address the issues that arise under a complex construction contract or do so consistent with internationally accepted standards.[278] In these circumstances, the Parties may wish to add in the Contract Data that the national law selected will be interpreted and supplemented in accordance with internationally accepted principles and rules as contained in the *UNIDROIT Principles of International Commercial Contracts* 2016.[279] To achieve this, the Contract Data should provide:

> The Contract shall be governed by the law of [State X] interpreted and supplemented by the UNIDROIT Principles of International Commercial Contracts (2016).[280]

The governing law is not the only legal norm by which the Parties are bound. Pursuant to Sub-Clause 4.1(f), the Contractor must comply with the 'technical standards' stated in the Specification, as well as with

---

276. *See* **Section 2.1 Invitation to Tender** above in **Chapter IV Clause-by-Clause Commentary**.
277. *See* **Section 5 Mandatory Law at the Site** of **Chapter II Applicable Law** above.
278. *See* **Section 6 Challenges of a Less-Developed Law** of **Chapter II Applicable Law** above on this subject.
279. For a description of the UNIDROIT Principles, *see* **Section 7 International Legal Principles** of **Chapter II Applicable Law** above.
280. This is based on Model Clause 4(a) of the *Model Clauses for the Use of the UNIDROIT Principles of International Commercial Contracts*, UNIDROIT, Rome, 2013, 20. The Parties could also select the Principles to govern the Contract instead of a national law. While this is not recognised by Sub-Clause 1.4, it is recognised by art. 21(1) of the ICC Rules of Arbitration which are incorporated into the Contract by Sub-Clause 21.6 of the General Conditions. Art. 21(1) of the ICC Rules of Arbitration provides for the application of 'rules of law' which would encompass international principles such as the UNIDROIT Principles.

applicable Laws generally.[281] In addition, pursuant to Sub-Clause 21.6 [*Arbitration*] and Article 21 of the ICC Arbitration Rules, the Parties are bound by any relevant trade usages.[282]

(2) The ruling language

The paragraph in the new Sub-Clause relating to the ruling language is only relevant if there are different versions of the Contract, or of parts of it, in different languages.[283] In principle, it is desirable for the ruling language, and the language of the country whose law will govern the Contract, to be the same as it is often difficult to translate accurately legal concepts from one language (the language of the governing law) to another. But, even so, it is not uncommon for the language of the law governing a contract to be different from the language of the Contract.[284]

The Engineer is required to be fluent in the ruling language of the Contract.[285] In addition, unless otherwise agreed by the Parties, any arbitration under the Contract must be conducted in the ruling language of the Contract.[286]

The choice of a ruling language other than English (the language of the official and authentic text of the RB[287]) may cause difficulties as translating a construction contract into another language is a very challenging

281. Sub-Clause 1.13 [*Compliance with Laws*]. Local law may, where it is mandatory, override the technical standards in the Specification. *See* **Section 5 Mandatory Law at the Site** of **Chapter II Applicable Law** above.
282. *See also* **Section 8 Trade Usages** of **Chapter II Applicable Law** above. As discussed in that section, observance of specified trade usages is expressly required by Sub-Clauses 4.10 [*Use of Site Data*], 7.1 [*Manner of Execution*] and 19.2.6 [*Other Insurances Required by Laws and by Local Practice*].
283. For where a state entity argued – unsuccessfully – that a contract (based on a FIDIC form) was void because it was in a foreign language, *see* partial award, ICC case 9202 (1998), ICC Int'l Ct Arb Bull, vol 19/no 2, 2008, 79-81 (commentary 42, 45-46).
284. In this case, the Parties may be well advised to agree on a translation of the Contract into the language of the law governing the Contract.
285. *See* Sub-Clause 3.1(b) [*The Engineer*].
286. *See* Sub-Clause 21.6(c) [*Arbitration*].
287. *See* the last sentence of the 'Notes' at the beginning of RB/17, before the sequence charts and the Table of Contents.

exercise.[288] If there are versions of any part of the Contract in more than one language, then in case of discrepancies, the version written in the ruling language will prevail. However, sometimes certain parts of the Contract are written in one language only and other parts are written in a different language. Such situations should be avoided and the Parties should ensure, where possible, that all the documents comprising the Contract are written or translated into the ruling language of the Contract from the outset.[289]

(3) The language for communications

The language for communications must be stated in the Contract Data, or, if no such language is stated there, it will be the ruling language of the Contract.[290] Assistants to whom the Engineer may delegate authority under Sub-Clause 3.4, the Contractor's Representative and any person to whom the Contractor's Representative may delegate authority under Sub-Clause 4.3 and Key Personnel under Sub-Clause 6.12 are all required to be fluent in the language for communications. Persons providing superintendence for the Contractor under Sub-Clause 6.8 are also required to be fluent in the language for communications or, at least, to have adequate knowledge of that language. Therefore, the Parties should consider amending the foregoing Sub-Clauses if any of those persons may not have sufficient knowledge of the language of communications.[291]

The language for communications will apply to communications not just between the Parties and/or with the Engineer but also with the DAAB, unless the Parties and the DAAB agree jointly otherwise.[292]

(iv) Related Law: A discussion of the main differences between civil law and common law system as they may relate to RB/17 is contained in **Section 4 Common Law and Civil Law Compared** of **Chapter II Applicable Law** above.

288. *See* **Section 5.2 Relevance of Language** of **Chapter III Contract Interpretation**, above.
289. *Ibid.*
290. Sub-Clause 1.4, third paragraph.
291. *Guidance for the Preparation of Particular Conditions*, 20-23, 29-30.
292. Rule 4.1, DAAB Rules.

(v) Improvements: As stated in relation to Sub-Clause 1.1 [*Definitions*] above, the Parties and the Engineer should be strongly encouraged, if not required, to use the defined terms in the Conditions in their communications.

--ooOOoo--

1.5 Priority of Documents

The documents forming the Contract are to be taken as mutually explanatory of one another. If there is any conflict, ambiguity or discrepancy in the documents, the priority of the documents shall be in accordance with the following sequence:

(a) the Contract Agreement;
(b) the Letter of Acceptance;
(c) the Letter of Tender;
(d) the Particular Conditions Part A – Contract Data;
(e) the Particular Conditions Part B – Special Provisions;
(f) these General Conditions;
(g) the Specification;
(h) the Drawings;
(i) the Schedules;
(j) the JV Undertaking (if the Contractor is a JV); and
(k) any other documents forming part of the Contract.

If a Party finds a conflict, ambiguity or discrepancy in the documents, that Party shall promptly give a Notice to the Engineer, describing the conflict, ambiguity or discrepancy. After receiving such Notice, or if the Engineer finds a conflict, ambiguity or discrepancy in the documents, the Engineer shall issue the necessary clarification or instruction.

The documents forming the Contract are to be taken as mutually explanatory of one another. In case of a conflict, ambiguity or discrepancy, the priority of the documents shall be in accordance with the sequence given in the Sub-Clause.

If a Party finds a conflict, ambiguity or discrepancy in the documents, it must promptly give a Notice to the Engineer who must issue the

necessary clarification or instruction. The Engineer must also do so of its own volition if it finds such a conflict, ambiguity or discrepancy.

Commentary

(i) Main Changes from RB/99:

(1) The Appendix Tender, which was appended to the Letter of Tender in RB/99, has been replaced by the Contract Data, which is contained in a new Part A of the Particular Conditions of RB/17.
(2) The rest of the Particular Conditions are contained in a new Part B – Special Provisions of RB/17.
(3) The JV Undertaking (if the Contractor is a JV) is a new document in RB/17.[293]
(4) RB/99 had stipulated that the Engineer should issue any necessary clarification or instruction '[if] an ambiguity or discrepancy is found in the documents', without specifying who was to make the finding. The second paragraph now requires the Parties, if either finds a conflict, ambiguity or discrepancy in the Contract documents, promptly to give the Engineer a Notice describing it. Similarly, if the Engineer finds a conflict, ambiguity or discrepancy in them, it must issue the necessary clarification or instruction.

(ii) Related Clauses / Sub-Clauses: 1.2 [*Interpretation*], 1.3 [*Notices and Other Communications*], 1.4 [*Law and Language*], 1.6 [*Contract Agreement*], 1.8 [*Care and Supply of Documents*] and 3.5 [*Engineer's Instructions*].

(iii) Analysis:

(1) Normal order of priority

As shown by Sub-Clause 1.1.10 '**Contract**', the Contract comprises numerous, often (in practice) quite voluminous, documents some of which overlap and describe the same subject matter but in different ways, e.g., the Drawings and Specification. The first sentence of Sub-Clause 1.5, stating that the documents forming the Contract are to be taken 'as mutually explanatory of one another', means that they are all to be given effect and reconciled as though they are complementary, as this

293. *See* the commentary on Sub-Clause 1.1.47 '**JV Undertaking**' above.

is the presumed intention of the Parties. However, it is not unusual for a conflict, ambiguity or discrepancy to appear and for it to be necessary to determine which document should prevail. In such a case, the document which is higher on the list in this Sub-Clause does so.

The order or priority of documents will only come into play if there is an actual conflict, ambiguity or discrepancy in the documents. The starting point is, as mentioned in the opening sentence of this Sub-Clause, that the documents forming the Contract are to be taken as mutually explanatory of one another. Therefore, there should be no ground to invoke the list or order of priority if potentially conflicting documents can be reconciled so as to reach a consistent interpretation of the Contract across the several documents comprising it.[294]

The Contract Agreement has the highest priority, followed by the Letter of Acceptance and the Letter of Tender. This is logical as, assuming a Contract Agreement is signed, it is likely to be the last document prepared and signed by the Parties and as such, may contain changes from the Contractor's Letter of Tender or even the Letter of Acceptance (e.g., if the Letter of Acceptance contained a counter-offer).[295] The Particular Conditions – first, the Contract Data and then the Special Provisions – have a higher priority over, and complete (in the case of the Contract Data) or amend (indeed, are intended to complete or amend), the General Conditions. Their higher priority reflects the legal principle that documents prepared for a specific transaction should prevail over generic documents, as the former are likely better to reflect the intention of the parties.[296] The list then refers to certain technical or quasi-technical documents, such as the Specification, the Drawings and the Schedules. The JV Undertaking (if any), a unilateral document of, and signed by, the Contractor, is logically near the bottom of the list followed by 'any other documents forming part of the Contract'.[297]

294. Julian Bailey, *Construction Law* (3rd edn, London Publishing, UK, 2020) vol 1, 232-233 (paras 3.182-83).

295. This may be the case if the Letter of Acceptance does not conform with the Tender and/or proposes new conditions requiring agreement by the Contractor.

296. The Particular Conditions 'will always over-rule and supersede the equivalent provisions in the General Conditions'. *Guidance for the Preparation of Particular Conditions*, 9.

297. This provision is quite open-ended. In this connection, *see* **Section 5.1.2 Absence of Entire Agreement Clause** of **Chapter III Contract Interpretation** above.

(2) Exceptions to normal order of priority

Notwithstanding the order of priority in Sub-Clause 1.5, there may be cases where a document with a lower priority according to the list prevails over a document with a higher priority if this is stated in the higher priority document. For example, on numerous occasions, the General Conditions contain wording such as 'unless otherwise stated in the Contract' and 'unless otherwise stated in the Specification'.[298] In a case such as this, if a lower priority Contract document, such as the Specification, contains a provision which is inconsistent with the General Conditions, it is the wording in the lower priority document (the Specification) which will prevail over the General Conditions.

It might also be maintained that a document with a lower priority should prevail over a document with a higher priority which it contradicts where it can be demonstrated that, during the tender and/or negotiation process, the lower priority document was finalised and agreed upon by the Parties after the higher priority document was agreed upon (and the Parties had neglected to overcome the contradiction by modifying the higher priority document). In those circumstances, it could be argued that the lower priority document represented the Parties' real final intentions,[299] and should therefore prevail over a standard clause like Sub-Clause 1.5 which merely sets forth a general rule of priority but is always subject to the particular facts of a case.

A document listed in Sub-Clause 1.5 may comprise several documents, for example, the Specification. If there is a conflict, ambiguity or discrepancy within the documents comprising the Specification, the list of the priority of documents in Sub-Clause 1.5 is of no assistance. In those cases, the Parties should consider amending sub-paragraph (g) of Sub-Clause 1.5 to add an additional order of precedence for the documents comprising the Specification.[300]

298. *See*, for example, Sub-Clauses 1.8, first paragraph, 1.13, first paragraph, and 4.11, second paragraph.

299. *See* **Sections 5.7 Effect of an International Arbitration Clause** and **6 A Practical Approach** of **Chapter III Contract Interpretation** above.

300. *Guidance for Preparation of Particular Conditions*, 15. If the Parties fail to address this matter in the Contract, any ambiguity or discrepancy within a document listed in Sub-Clause 1.5 would be resolved under the rules of contract interpretation provided for by the governing law (*see* **Chapter III Contract Interpretation**, above).

The *Guidance* contains alternative wording which the Parties may use if no order of priority is to be prescribed.[301]

(3) Conflict, ambiguity or discrepancy

The last paragraph requires each Party promptly to give Notice to the Engineer of a conflict, ambiguity or discrepancy in the Contract documents and the Engineer is then required to issue the necessary clarification or instruction. Similarly, if the Engineer finds a conflict, ambiguity or discrepancy in them, it must issue the same. When doing so, the Engineer should act neutrally and fairly.[302]

A similar obligation on each Party (and the Engineer) to draw attention to problems with documents (and not just documents forming the Contract, as in the case of Sub-Clause 1.5) is to be found in the last paragraph of Sub-Clause 1.8 [*Care and Supply of Documents*].[303]

--ooOOoo--

1.6 Contract Agreement

> The Parties shall sign a Contract Agreement within 35 days after the Contractor receives the Letter of Acceptance, unless they agree otherwise. The Contract Agreement shall be based on the form annexed to the Particular Conditions. The costs of stamp duties and similar charges (if any) imposed by law in connection with entry into the Contract Agreement shall be borne by the Employer.
>
> If the Contractor comprises a JV, the authorised representative of each member of the JV shall sign the Contract Agreement.

Unless agreed otherwise, the Parties must sign a Contract Agreement based on the form annexed to the Particular Conditions within 35 days after the Contractor receives the Letter of Acceptance. If the

301. *Guidance for Preparation of Particular Conditions*, 15.
302. For the reasons given in *(2) When exercising discretion the Engineer must act fairly* under **(iii) Analysis** of the commentary on Sub-Clause 3.2 [*Engineer's Duties and Authority*] below.
303. *See also* Sub-Clause 8.4 [*Advance Warning*] and, more generally, 4.6 [*Co-operation*], and the respective commentaries thereon below.

Contractor is a JV, an authorised representative of each member of the JV must sign the Contract Agreement.

The costs of stamp duties and similar charges (if any) imposed by law in connection with the entry into the Contract Agreement shall be borne by the Employer.

Commentary

(i) Main Changes from RB/99: Under the Sub-Clause, unless agreed otherwise, the Parties must now sign a Contract Agreement within 35 days after the Contractor receives the Letter of Acceptance, whereas in RB/99 it was 28 days. The provision for where the Contractor comprises a JV is also new.

(ii) Related Clauses / Sub-Clauses: 1.5 [*Priority of Documents*], 1.10 [*Employer's Use of Contractor's Documents*], 1.14 [*Joint and Several Liability*], 8.1 [*Commencement of Works*] and 16.2.1 [*Termination by Contractor – Notice*].

(iii) Analysis:

(1) Desirability of a Contract Agreement

A legally binding contract between the Parties should normally come into effect once the Contractor has received the Letter of Acceptance from the Employer (if not earlier).[304] However, the Contractor's actual Letter of Tender and/or the Employer's actual Letter of Acceptance, if any, may contain further conditions or terms which the other Party must accept and which therefore prevent a legally binding contract from coming into effect when the Letter of Acceptance, if any, is signed and delivered.[305] Moreover, in some countries the signing of a Contract Agreement may be necessary or advisable for legal reasons. Even when this is not the case, the signing of a Contract Agreement may serve to clarify what the Parties have agreed to, especially where there have been lengthy and/or detailed post-tender negotiations. In such a case, the Contract Agreement can

304. This is foreseen by the forms of the Letter of Tender and Letter of Acceptance contained in RB/17.

305. Indeed, sometimes due to offers and counter-offers exchanged between the Parties it may be difficult to determine when – if at all – the Parties have entered into a legally binding contract. *See* Atkin Chambers, *Hudson's Building and Engineering Contracts* (14th edn, Sweet & Maxwell, London, 2020) 369-370 (para. 3-015).

serve to confirm the results of those negotiations, including such matters as the Accepted Contract Amount and the Time for Completion, as they may have been adjusted.[306]

(2) Where the Contractor is a JV

If the Contractor comprises a JV, then, as a JV (as defined[307]) is not a separate legal entity, the authorised representative of each member of the JV is required to sign the Contract Agreement. A construction contract based on the RB is likely to be a substantial undertaking and, pursuant to Sub-Clause 1.14 [*Joint and Several Liability*], each member of the JV will be jointly and severally liable to the Employer for the Contractor's obligations.[308] Given the importance of such a liability, it is understandable that each member should sign the Contract Agreement.

(iv) Related Law: As indicated above, whether a Contract Agreement is necessary – it is generally desirable – may be determined by the law governing the Contract.

(v) Improvements: It may be desirable to clarify what type of failure by the Employer under Sub-Clause 1.6 will entitle the Contractor to give a Notice of its intention to terminate the Contract under Sub-Clause 16.2.1(g)(i). The current text of 16.2.1(g)(i) indicates that it could be either a failure to sign the Contract Agreement or a failure to pay stamp duties and similar charges. However, a failure to pay stamp duties and similar charges appears to be much less serious (it might be remedied by the other Party) than a failure to sign the Contract Agreement. Therefore is it really sensible that either failure may justify the giving of such a Notice?

--ooOOoo--

1.7 Assignment

Neither Party shall assign the whole or any part of the Contract or any benefit or interest in or under the Contract. However, either Party:

306. *Ibid. See* **Figure 5 Sequence of Events Before the Commencement Date ('CD')** at the end of the commentary on Clause 4 below.
307. *See* Sub-Clause 1.1.46 **'Joint Venture'**.
308. *See* the commentary on Sub-Clause 1.14 below.

(a) may assign the whole or any part of the Contract with the prior agreement of the other Party, at the sole discretion of such other Party; and
(b) may, as security in favour of a bank or financial institution, assign the Party's right to any moneys due, or to become due, under the Contract without the prior agreement of the other Party.

Neither Party may assign the whole or any part of the Contract or any benefit or interest in it without the prior agreement of the other Party, at its sole discretion, except that either Party may assign its right to moneys due, or to become due, under the Contract, as a security in favour of a bank or financial institution.

Commentary

(i) Main Changes from RB/99: The Sub-Clause makes clear that the agreement of the other Party is unnecessary for an assignment of a Party's right to moneys due, or to become due, in favour of a bank or financial institution. Sub-Clause 1.7 of RB/99 was less clear on this matter.

(ii) Related Clauses / Sub-Clauses: 1.2 [*Interpretation*], 1.3 [*Notices and Other Communications*], 5 [*Subcontracting*], 15.2.1 [*Termination for Contractor's Default – Notice*], 15.2.3 [*Termination for Contractor's Default – After Termination*] and 16.2.1 [*Termination by Contractor – Notice*].

(iii) Analysis: The Sub-Clause provides that, as a general rule, neither Party shall assign the whole or any part of the Contract without the prior agreement of the other Party which must be in writing.[309] It may only do so 'at the sole discretion' of the other Party, meaning (it would appear) that the other Party has complete freedom whether to agree or not.[310] Where the proposed assignment is to be made by the Contractor, the Employer may object as the:

309. Sub-paragraph (c) of Sub-Clause 1.2 [*Interpretation*] and Sub-Clause 1.3 [*Notices and Other Communications*].

310. The 'not be unreasonably withheld' language in the penultimate paragraph of Sub-Clause 1.3 might not therefore apply. *See* item (1) under **(v) Improvements** of the commentary on Sub-Clause 1.2 [*Interpretation*] above.

> Employer will typically [...] have taken account of the Contractor's reputation and experience when deciding to enter into the Contract, [...]. Having done so, the Employer may well be reluctant [...] to agree to any assignment under this [Sub-Clause 1.7].[311]

As an assignment refers to the transfer of the whole or part of the Contract to a third party,[312] leading possibly to the complete discharge of the assigning Party from the Contract,[313] it is understandably severely restricted. The exception for the assignment of moneys as security in favour of a bank or financial institution is principally for the benefit of the Contractor as the recipient of the Contract Price. Such assignment is a common way to secure bank financing.

Any assignment without the other Party's written agreement may be an irremediable breach of the Contract, entitling the aggrieved Party to terminate the Contract immediately pursuant to Sub-Clause 15.2.1(f) (unauthorised assignment by the Contractor) or Sub-Clause 16.2.1g(ii) (unauthorised assignment by the Employer), as the case may be.[314]

311. *The FIDIC Contracts Guide* (2nd edn, FIDIC 2022) 89. The Contractor may have comparable concerns about a proposed assignment by the Employer.
312. Assignment can have different meanings under different laws. Under English law, 'assignment' refers to the transfer of an existing right under a contract from one party to the other and it is said to be inaccurate to speak of a party being able to 'assign the contract' to another party (as Sub-Clause 1.7 does). Julian Bailey, *Construction Law* (3rd edn, London Publishing, UK, 2020) vol 3, 1554-1555, fn. 151 (paras 20.57-20.59). Similarly, US law distinguishes the 'assignment of rights' from the 'delegation of performance of duties' but, however, recognises that 'assignment of a contract' is sometimes used to refer to a transaction in which both rights are assigned and duties are delegated. E Allan Farnsworth, *Contracts* (4th edn, Aspen, N Y, 2004), 680, fn. 4 (para. 11.1) 'Assignment of a contract' is also recognised by the UNIDROIT Principles as involving the transfer by agreement from one person (the 'assignor') to another person (the 'assignee') of the assignor's 'rights and obligations arising out of a contract' with another person. UNIDROIT Principles, art. 9.3.1 (*Definitions*).
313. *See*, for example, art. 9.3.5 (*Discharge of the assignor*) of the UNIDROIT Principles.
314. Sub-Clause 1.7 does not prevent the Contractor from subcontracting the execution of parts of the works, subject to Sub-Clause 5.1 [*Subcontractors*], and/or from assigning to its insurers or banks or other sources of financing. *The FIDIC Contracts Guide* (1st edn, FIDIC, 2000) 64 and, to similar effect (2nd edn, FIDIC, 2022) 89.

(iv) Related Law: The law governing the Contract will almost certainly contain rules dealing with assignment of contractual rights and/or obligations.[315] The Parties should be wary of mandatory provisions in the governing law, especially local public procurement law, if applicable, which may override the provisions of Sub-Clause 1.7.[316] Chapter 9 of the UNIDROIT Principles addresses in detail 'Assignment of Rights, Transfer of Obligations, Assignment of Contracts' which may assist where they can apply or be useful.

(v) Improvements: While this Sub-Clause effectively restricts assignment, if there is a change in the ownership or control of a Party, or if a Party transfers all or substantially all of its assets or business to a third person, this can be as prejudicial to the other Party as an assignment of the whole or any part of the Contract, *yet it is not regulated by RB/17*. For example, the ownership or control of a Party may pass to a competitor of the other Party, or to a hostile or undesirable group, or the transfer of assets or business of a Party may limit its ability to perform the Contract, e.g., if the Contractor transfers its qualified personnel and/or assets and/or business to another company. While a change in ownership or control of a Party may be beyond that Party's ability to prevent, it can, nevertheless, be made a ground for the other Party to terminate the Contract under Clauses 15 and/or 16 if this change occurs without the other Party's consent. The risk that such a right of termination may be exercised may be enough to discourage such a change or transfer.

--ooOOoo--

1.8 Care and Supply of Documents

> The Specification and Drawings shall be in the custody and care of the Employer. Unless otherwise stated in the Contract, two copies of the Contract and of each subsequent Drawing shall be supplied to the Contractor, who may make or request further copies at the cost of the Contractor.

315. For the position under the common law, *see* Julian Bailey, *Construction Law* (3rd edn, London Publishing, UK, 2020) vol 3, 1554-1566 (paras 20.57-20.80) and Atkin Chambers, *Hudson's Building and Engineering Contracts* (14th edn, Sweet & Maxwell, London, 2020) 1003-1045 (paras 9-001 to 9-052).
316. *See* **Section 5 Mandatory Law at the Site** of **Chapter II Applicable Law** above.

Each of the Contractor's Documents shall be in the custody and care of the Contractor, unless and until submitted to the Engineer. The Contractor shall supply to the Engineer one paper-original, one electronic copy (in the form as stated in the Specification or, if not stated, a form acceptable to the Engineer) and additional paper copies (if any) as stated in the Contract Data of each of the Contractor's Documents.

The Contractor shall keep at all times, on the Site, a copy of:

(a) the Contract;
(b) the records under Sub-Clause 6.10 [*Contractor's Records*] and Sub-Clause 20.2.3 [*Contemporary records*];
(c) the publications (if any) named in the Specification;
(d) the Contractor's Documents;
(e) the Drawings; and
(f) Variations, Notices and other communications given under the Contract.

The Employer's Personnel shall have right of access to all these documents during all normal working hours, or as otherwise agreed with the Contractor.

If a Party (or the Engineer) becomes aware of an error or defect (whether of a technical nature or otherwise) in a document which was prepared for use in the execution of the Works, the Party (or the Engineer) shall promptly give a Notice of such error or defect to the other Party (or to the Parties).

The Specification and Drawings shall be in the custody and care of the Employer. The Contractor's Documents shall be in the custody and care of the Contractor until submitted to the Engineer. The Contractor must supply to the Engineer copies of the Contractor's Documents as provided for in the Sub-Clause and the Contract Data.

The Contractor shall keep on the Site a copy of: the Contract, records under Sub-Clauses 6.10 and 20.2.3, any publications named in the Specification, the Contractor's Documents, the Drawings, Variations, Notices and other communications under the Contract. The Employer's Personnel shall have the right of access to these documents.

If a Party (or the Engineer) becomes aware of an error or defect in a document that Party (or the Engineer) shall promptly give a Notice to the other Party (or the Parties).

Commentary

(i) Main Changes from RB/99:

(1) Whereas Sub-Clause 1.8 of RB/99 provided that the Contractor's Documents shall be in the custody and care of the Contractor 'unless and until taken over by the Employer', under the new Sub-Clause they must be in its custody and care 'unless and until submitted to the Engineer'.

(2) The description of the documents which the Contractor must keep on the Site has been expanded to include the Contractor's records under Sub-Clause 6.10 [*Contractor's Records*] and contemporary records under Sub-Clause 20.2.3 [*Contemporary Records*].

(3) Unlike RB/99 where the Employer's Personnel had right of access to these documents 'at all reasonable times', now such right of access is 'during all normal working hours, or as otherwise agreed with the Contractor'.

(4) Whereas under RB/99 'a Party' was to give prompt notice of an error or defect of a technical nature of which it became aware in a document prepared for the execution of the Works, now each Party and the Engineer must promptly give a Notice to this effect and do so whether the error or defect is of a technical nature or otherwise.

(ii) Related Clauses / Sub-Clauses: 1.3 [*Notices and Other Communications*], 1.5 [*Priority of Documents*], 1.10 [*Employer's Use of Contractor's Documents*], 1.11 [*Contractor's Use of Employer's Documents*], 4.4 [*Contractor's Documents*], 4.6 [*Co-operation*], 6.5 [*Working Hours*], 6.10 [*Contractor's Records*], 8.4 [*Advance Warning*], 17.1 [*Responsibility for Care of the Works*] and 20.2.3 [*Contemporary Records*].

(iii) Analysis:

(1) Custody and care of documents

Sub-Clause 1.8 specifies the Party that is responsible for the custody and care of different documents related to the Contract. Thus, the Employer is responsible for the Specification and the Drawings, which the Employer or its consultant will have prepared or (in the case of the Drawings) may be continuing to prepare,[317] and the Contractor is responsible for the custody and care of the Contractor's Documents,[318] which it will be preparing and handing over under the Contract.[319]

The Contractor's Documents must be in the custody and care of the Contractor 'unless and until submitted to the Engineer'.[320] This appears to provide for a clear point of time when the Contractor's Documents will cease to be in the Contractor's custody and care. However, if so, it appears to be contradicted by Sub-Clause 17.1 [*Responsibility for Care of the Works*] providing that the Contractor shall have full responsibility for the care of the Contractor's Documents 'from the Commencement Date until the issue (or deemed issue) of the Taking-Over Certificate for the Works'.[321]

(2) Error or defect in documents

The last paragraph of the Sub-Clause obliges each Party (and the Engineer) to give a prompt Notice to the other Party (or the Parties) should it discover any error or defect of whatever nature in a document prepared for use in the execution of the Works. Such a document might have been prepared by a Party, the Engineer or a third party. This duty to notify (similar to the duty to notify any conflict, ambiguity or discrepancy in a Contract document in the last paragraph of Sub-Clause 1.5) reflects the idea that, while the Party which prepared the document is in principle responsible for its content, the other Party (and the Engineer) has an obligation to cooperate in minimising the consequences of any mistake in it which may have been made.[322] Thus, if the Contractor becomes aware of an error or a defect in the Specification or a Drawing, it should notify the Engineer of this promptly. Should the Contractor fail to do so and later on make a Claim related to this error or defect, the amount of the

317. Sub-Clause 1.11 [*Contractor's Use of Employer's Documents*] provides that the Employer retains the copyright and other intellectual property rights in the Specification and Drawings.
318. *See* the commentary on Sub-Clause 1.1.15 '**Contractor's Documents**' above.
319. Sub-Clause 1.10 [*Employer's Use of Contractor's Documents*] provides that the Contractor retains the copyright and other intellectual property rights in the Contractor's Documents.
320. Sub-Clause 1.8, second paragraph.
321. Sub-Clause 17.1, first paragraph.
322. Brian Barr and Leo Grutters, *FIDIC Users' Guide* (3rd edn, ICE Publishing, London, 2014) 100.

Contractor's Claim may be reduced or even rejected entirely if this failure has 'prevented or prejudiced proper investigation' of the Claim by the Engineer.[323]

The duty of each Party (and of the Engineer) to notify the other Party (or Parties) of an error or defect of which it is aware is reinforced by Sub-Clause 8.4 [*Advance Warning*] which obliges each Party to advise the other Party and the Engineer (and the Engineer to advise the Parties) in advance of any known or probable adverse future events or circumstances.[324]

(iv) Related Law: The law governing the Contract may similarly require each Party to warn the other Party if it becomes aware of matters that may negatively affect the project.[325] Thus, in the US, an implied duty of good faith and fair dealing is deemed to exist which requires each party to warn the other party when the latter is proceeding in a way that will cause failure.[326] Under US law, a contractor who knows that the employer's design is not compatible with the soil conditions should express its concerns to the employer. If the contractor notifies the employer of errors in the employer's documents, it will not be liable for the defects that result from these documents and is entitled to be paid for what it has done.[327] On the other hand, if the contractor does not notify the owner of obvious errors, it may not be able to escape liability by arguing at a later stage that it has strictly followed the owner's documents.[328]

(v) Improvements: The apparent contradiction (*see* under item **(iii) Analysis** above) between this Sub-Clause and Sub-Clause 17.1 as regards the duration of the Contractor's responsibility for the care of the Contractor's Documents needs to be resolved.

--ooOOoo--

323. *See*, in this connection, the last paragraph of Sub-Clause 20.2.7.
324. *See* Sub-Clause 8.4 [*Advance Warning*] and the commentary thereon below. *See also*, more generally, Sub-Clause 4.6 [*Co-operation*].
325. For the position under common law and civil law on this subject *see* under **(iv) Related Law** of the commentary on Sub-Clause 8.4 [*Advance Warning*] below.
326. Justin Sweet and others, *Construction Law for Design Professionals, Construction Managers, and Contractors* (Cengage Learning, Stamford, CT, 2015) 322-323.
327. *Ibid.*
328. *Ibid.*

1.9 Delayed Drawings or Instructions

The Contractor shall give a Notice to the Engineer whenever the Works are likely to be delayed or disrupted if any necessary drawing or instruction is not issued to the Contractor within a particular time, which shall be reasonable. The Notice shall include details of the necessary drawing or instruction, details of why and by when it should be issued, and details of the nature and amount of the delay or disruption likely to be suffered if it is late.

If the Contractor suffers delay and/or incurs Cost as a result of a failure of the Engineer to issue the notified drawing or instruction within a time which is reasonable and is specified in the Notice with supporting details, the Contractor shall be entitled subject to Sub-Clause 20.2 [*Claims for Payment and/or EOT*] to EOT and/or payment of such Cost Plus Profit.

However, if and to the extent that the Engineer's failure was caused by any error or delay by the Contractor, including an error in, or delay in the submission of, any of the Contractor's Documents, the Contractor shall not be entitled to such EOT and/or Cost Plus Profit.

The Contractor must give a Notice to the Engineer with details whenever the Works are likely to be delayed or disrupted if a necessary drawing or instruction is not issued to the Contractor within a reasonable time specified in the Notice.

If the Contractor suffers delay and/or incurs Cost as a result of the Engineer's failure to issue the notified drawing or instruction within the reasonable time specified in the Notice, the Contractor shall be entitled, subject to Sub-Clause 20.2, to an EOT and/or Cost Plus Profit if, and to the extent that, the Engineer's failure was not caused by the Contractor.

Commentary

(i) Main Changes from RB/99: The Sub-Clause is similar to Sub-Clause 1.9 in RB/99 except that RB/99 required the Contractor to give a 'further notice' to the Engineer before the Contractor could make a claim subject to Sub-Clause 20.1 [*Contractor's Claims*] which created uncertainty as to the number of notices required to be given for a claim under Sub-Clause 1.9.[329] The requirement for a further notice has been deleted. The term 'Notice' has also been defined for the first time in RB/17.[330]

(ii) Related Clauses / Sub-Clauses: 1.3 [*Notices and Other Communications*], 3.5 [*Engineer's Instructions*], 4.4 [*Contractor's Documents*], 4.20 [*Progress Reports*], 8.3 [*Programme*], 8.4 [*Advance Warning*] and 20.2 [*Claims for Payment and/or EOT*].

(iii) Analysis:

(1) Contractor's required Notice

The Engineer is expected to administer the Contract so as to anticipate, based on the Programme and the Contractor's progress, the Contractor's need for drawings or instructions, and to issue them when required.[331] However, Sub-Clause 1.9 foresees the possibility that the Engineer may delay or fail to issue a necessary drawing or instruction when required. It provides that the Contractor is to give a Notice[332] to the Engineer 'whenever the Works are likely to be delayed or disrupted' if a necessary drawing or instruction is not issued by a particular reasonable time.

The Contractor should give this Notice whenever there is significant risk that the lack of timely receipt of a drawing or instruction may result in delay or disruption. The Notice should include the details prescribed in the first paragraph so that the Engineer may identify the required drawing or instruction, and is forewarned of the delay or disruption which may ensue should it be issued late. The Notice should be given sufficiently in advance to allow the Engineer a reasonable time within

329. Sub-Clause 1.9 first paragraph, had required a 'notice' and the second paragraph had required a 'further notice'. Sub-Clause 20.1, first paragraph, of RB/99 then appeared to require a third notice, as the last paragraph of Sub-Clause 20.1 provided that '[t]he requirements of this Sub-Clause [Sub-Clause 20.1] are in addition to those of any other Sub-Clause which may apply to a claim'.
330. Sub-Clause 1.1.56 '**Notice**'.
331. That is, without a Notice under this sub-clause. *The FIDIC Contracts Guide* (2nd edn, FIDIC, 2022) 91.
332. Which must comply with Sub-Clause 1.3.

which to prepare and issue the drawing or instruction. What is reasonable will depend on the circumstances of the case.[333]

While Sub-Clause 1.9 does not itself indicate how the Engineer should respond to the Contractor's Notice, the Engineer 'should immediately acknowledge its receipt, comment on the extent if any to which it does not include the details specified [in the Sub-Clause], and indicate the actions which he/she intends to take'.[334] The Engineer's response should be copied to the Employer.[335]

(2) Related Sub-Clause 8.4 [Advance Warning]

The need for a timely drawing or instruction may also constitute 'known or probable future events or circumstances' that may adversely affect the performance of the Works under Sub-Clause 8.4 [*Advance Warning*] of which each Party is required to advise the other Party and the Engineer.[336] Therefore, the Contractor may wish to formulate its Notice so that it complies with both Sub-Clauses 1.9 and 8.4 and state that it is made in respect of both of them.[337] A Notice given under those Sub-Clauses should also be included in the Contractor's Progress Reports under sub-paragraph (h) of Sub-Clause 4.20 [*Progress Reports*].

(3) Contractor's entitlement

If the Contractor suffers delay and/or incurs Cost because of the Engineer's failure to issue the notified drawing or instruction within a time period 'which is reasonable and is specified in the Notice with supporting details', the Contractor is entitled, subject to Sub-Clause 20.2, to an EOT and/or Cost Plus Profit. As the Contractor's entitlement is dependent on the elapse of the 'reasonable' time period specified in the Contractor's Notice, the giving of that Notice and the elapse of such period, as well as

333. For a definition of reasonableness *see* the definition in fn. 263 above of this commentary on **Clause 1**.
334. *The FIDIC Contracts Guide* (2nd edn, FIDIC, 2022) 91.
335. Sub-Clause 1.3, last paragraph.
336. *See* the commentary on Sub-Clause 8.4 below.
337. *The FIDIC Contracts Guide* (2nd edn, FIDIC, 2022) 193, acknowledges that 'one notice' may satisfy the requirements of different Sub-Clauses. But to achieve this a Party needs to make it clear in that communication that it constitutes both Notices and ensure that the specific requirements for each Notice are complied with in that communication.

compliance with Sub-Clause 20.2 (requiring a second Notice), are pre-conditions to the Contractor's Claim.[338]

(iv) Related Law: Under both civil and common law systems, a Contractor may have a legal duty to notify the Engineer about the lack of a necessary drawing or instruction, independent of what is provided for in Sub-Clause 1.9.[339]

--ooOOoo--

1.10 Employer's Use of Contractor's Documents

As between the Parties, the Contractor shall retain the copyright and other intellectual property rights in the Contractor's Documents (and other design documents, if any, made by (or on behalf of) the Contractor).

The Contractor shall be deemed (by signing the Contract Agreement) to give to the Employer a non-terminable transferable non-exclusive royalty-free licence to copy, use and communicate the Contractor's Documents (and such other design documents, if any), including making and using modifications of them. This licence shall:

(a) apply throughout the actual or intended operational life (whichever is longer) of the relevant parts of the Works;

(b) entitle any person in proper possession of the relevant part of the Works to copy, use and communicate the Contractor's Documents (and

338. *The reference to Sub-Clause 20.2 – here and in numerous other sub-clauses – means, among other things, that the Contractor will be required to give a further Notice, that is, a Notice of Claim under Sub-Clause 20.2.1 [Notice of Claim], within 28 days of the event or circumstance giving rise to the claim or be time-barred. See* the commentary on Sub-Clause 20.2 below. The Contractor is entitled to claim Cost Plus Profit as the Engineer is part of the Employer's Personnel and therefore the Employer is considered responsible for the Engineer's failure. *See* the commentary on Sub-Clause 1.1.20 '**Cost Plus Profit**' above.

339. *See* **Section 4 Common Law and Civil Law Compared – 4.3.1 Duty of Good Faith** and **4.3.2 Duty of Disclosure** of **Chapter II Applicable Law** above and the commentary on Sub-Clause 8.4 [*Advance Warning*] below.

such other design documents, if any) for the purposes of completing, operating, maintaining, altering, adjusting, repairing and demolishing the Works;

(c) in the case of Contractor's Documents (and such other design documents, if any) which are in the form of electronic or digital files, computer programs and other software, permit their use on any computer on the Site and/or at the locations of the Employer and the Engineer and/or at other places as envisaged by the Contract; and

(d) in the event of termination of the Contract:

(i) under Sub-Clause 15.2 [*Termination for Contractor's Default*], entitle the Employer to copy, use and communicate the Contractor's Documents (and other design documents made by or for the Contractor, if any); or

(ii) under Sub-Clause 15.5 [*Termination for Employer's Convenience*], Sub-Clause 16.2 [*Termination by Contractor*] or Sub-Clause 18.5 [*Optional Termination*], entitle the Employer to copy, use and communicate the Contractor's Documents for which the Contractor has received payment

for the purpose of completing the Works and/or arranging for any other entities to do so.

The Contractor's Documents (and other design documents, if any, made by (or on behalf of) the Contractor) shall not, without the Contractor's prior consent, be used, copied or communicated to a third party by (or on behalf of) the Employer for purposes other than those permitted under this Sub-Clause.

The Contractor shall retain the copyright and other intellectual property rights in the Contractor's Documents. By signing the Contract Agreement, the Contractor gives to the Employer a non-terminable transferable non-exclusive royalty-free licence to copy, use and communicate the Contractor's Documents, including modifying them, as specified in sub-paragraphs (a) to (d) of the Sub-Clause. The use by, or copying or communication of Contractor's

Documents to, a third party by (or on behalf of) the Employer for purposes other than those permitted by this Sub-Clause requires Contractor's prior consent.

Commentary

(i) Main Changes from RB/99: The Sub-Clause is very similar to Sub-Clause 1.10 in RB/99 except that an additional sub-paragraph (d) has been added which clarifies the Employer's position in relation to its licence of Contractor's Documents from the Contractor in the case of different grounds for termination of the Contract.

(ii) Related Clauses / Sub-Clauses: 1.2 [*Interpretation*], 1.3 [*Notices and Other Communications*], 1.6 [*Contract Agreement*], 1.11 [*Contractor's Use of Employer's Documents*], 4.1 [*Contractor's General Obligations*], 4.4 [*Contractor's Documents*], 15 [*Termination by Employer*], 16 [*Suspension and Termination by the Contractor*], 17.3 [*Intellectual and Industrial Property Rights*], 17.6 [*Shared Indemnities*] and 18.5 [*Optional Termination*].

(iii) Analysis:

(1) Contractor's licence to Employer

Sub-Clause 1.10 stipulates that the Contractor retains the copyright[340] and other intellectual property[341] rights in the Contractor's Documents and other design documents, if any, made by the Contractor.[342] At the same time, by signing the Contract Agreement the Contractor is deemed to have granted to the Employer a licence to copy, use and communicate the Contractor's Documents (and design documents, if any), including making and using modifications of them. Such licence is non-terminable (i.e., the Contractor may not revoke it), transferable (i.e., the Employer

340. 'Copyright' is a legal term which may be defined broadly as 'the right to make copies of a given work […] and to stop others from making copies without one's permission'. Paul Goldstein, *Copyright's Highway* (rev'd edn, Stanford UP, Stanford, CA, 2003) 1.

341. 'Intellectual property' is another legal term and comprises 'primarily trademark, copyright, and patent rights, but also includes trade-secret rights, publicity rights, moral rights and rights against unfair competition'. Bryan A Garner (ed in chief), *Black's Law Dictionary* (11th edn, Thomson Reuters, St Paul, MN, 2019).

342. *See* the fifth paragraph of Sub-Clause 4.1 [*Contractor's General Obligations*] regarding the possible design of part(s) of the Permanent Works by the Contractor.

may transfer it to third parties), non-exclusive (i.e., the Contractor retains the right to use the Contractor's Documents and to license others to use them) and royalty-free (i.e., is made without charge, beyond the Contract Price). The licence applies throughout the actual or intended (whichever is longer) operational life of the relevant parts of the Works. The licence entitles not only the Employer but also 'any person in proper possession of the relevant part of the Works' to copy, use and communicate the Contractor's Documents for the purposes specified in sub-paragraph (b) of the Sub-Clause. Such other person may include, for example, the owner of the constructed facility to whom the Employer may have transferred title, a lessee to whom the facility has been leased or any contractor hired by the Employer to alter, repair or demolish the Works.

The licence under Sub-Clause 1.10 applies to the Contractor's Documents, which are broadly defined[343] (and other design documents of the Contractor, if any), but not to other documents of the Contractor.

The licence is granted for the purposes of 'completing, operating, maintaining, altering, adjusting, repairing and demolishing the Works'[344] only. Otherwise the Contractor's prior consent is required:

> Unless the Contractor gives his/her consent in advance [...], the Employer is not entitled to use the Contractor's Documents or other design documents prepared by the Contractor for the provision of similar works on the Site or elsewhere. In particular, if a further stage or expansion of the Works is executed, the Contractor's Documents or other design documents may be used as records of construction in order to determine the details of the existing facilities, but are not permitted to be used as working drawings for the construction of identical facilities.[345]

The Contractor's consent must be in writing, may not be unreasonably withheld or delayed and must otherwise comply with Sub-Clause 1.3. The Contractor may reasonably withhold consent if the Employer does not agree to generally accepted conditions in the industry for secrecy and/or restrictions on use of the Contractor's Documents.[346]

343. *See* the commentary on Sub-Clause 1.1.15 **'Contractor's Documents'** above.
344. Sub-paragraph (b) of Sub-Clause 1.10.
345. *The FIDIC Contracts Guide* (2nd edn, FIDIC, 2022) 97.
346. *Ibid.*

(2) Employer's rights on Contract termination

The new sub-paragraph (d), entitling the Employer to use the Contractor's Documents under certain conditions in the case of termination of the Contract, is welcome, as RB/99 was silent on the matter. Upon termination of the Contract, the Works may be incomplete and the question may arise whether the Contractor's Documents may be used by the Employer and/or other contractors hired by it for the purposes of their completion. According to sub-paragraph (d), the conditions for being entitled to do so will depend on the grounds for termination. If the Contract has been terminated due to the Contractor's default under Sub-Clause 15.2, the Employer will be entitled to use the Contractor's Documents (and other design documents of the Contractor, if any) without the need for further payment on this account. On the other hand, if the Contract is terminated under Sub-Clauses 15.5, 16.2 or 18.5, that is, without the Contractor having been at fault, the Employer is only entitled to copy, use and communicate the Contractor's Documents (and presumably any other design documents the Contractor has made for the Works, though these are not mentioned) for which the Contractor has received payment. Consequently, the Parties would then need to discuss and agree upon the price and payment terms.

(iv) Related Law: Virtually every country has adopted law(s) which deal with copyright and other intellectual property rights in respect of creative works, including, among other things, designs.[347] Broadly speaking, the holder of a copyright has the exclusive right to copy, use, communicate and sell the designs or other intellectual property concerned and to license others to do so on terms to be agreed. Applicable copyright laws should always be consulted, especially as they may contain mandatory provisions which must therefore be complied with.

--ooOOoo--

1.11 Contractor's Use of Employer's Documents

As between the Parties, the Employer shall retain the copyright and other intellectual property rights in the Specification and Drawings and other documents made by (or on behalf of) the Employer. The Con-

347. *See* the commentary on Sub-Clause 17.3 [*Intellectual and Industrial Property Rights*] below.

tractor may, at the Contractor's cost, copy, use and communicate these documents for the purposes of the Contract.

These documents (in whole or in part) shall not, without the Employer's prior consent, be copied, used or communicated to a third party by the Contractor, except as necessary for the purposes of the Contract.

The Employer shall retain the copyright and other intellectual property rights in the Specification, Drawings and other documents made by or on behalf of the Employer. The Contractor may, as its cost, copy, use and communicate these documents for the purposes of the Contract. The use of these documents for any other purposes requires Employer's prior consent.

Commentary

(i) Main Changes from RB/99: The Sub-Clause is almost identical to that in RB/99 except that it has been broken into two paragraphs and the words ('in whole or in part') have been inserted in the last sentence.

(ii) Related Clauses / Sub-Clauses: 1.2 [*Interpretation*], 1.3 [*Notices and Other Communications*], 1.10 [*Employer's Use of Contractor's Documents*], 17.3 [*Intellectual and Industrial Property Rights*] and 17.6 [*Shared Indemnities*].

(iii) Analysis: Sub-Clause 1.11 dealing with the Contractor's use of Employer's documents is the counterpart of Sub-Clause 1.10 dealing with the Employer's use of the Contractor's Documents. The Employer retains the copyright and other intellectual property rights in the documents which have been prepared by or on the Employer's behalf and the Contractor may, at its cost, copy, use and communicate these documents for the purposes of the Contract. As with Sub-Clause 1.10 in the case of the Contractor's Documents, any other use of the Employer's documents would require the Employer's prior consent which must be given in writing, may not be unreasonably withheld or delayed and must otherwise comply with Sub-Clause 1.3.

(iv) Related Law: *See* under **(iv) Related Law** of the commentary on Sub-Clause 1.10 above.

--ooOOoo--

1.12 Confidentiality

The Contractor shall disclose all such confidential and other information as the Engineer may reasonably require in order to verify the Contractor's compliance with the Contract.

The Contractor shall treat all documents forming the Contract as confidential, except to the extent necessary to carry out the Contractor's obligations under the Contract. The Contractor shall not publish, permit to be published, or disclose any particulars of the Contract in any trade or technical paper or elsewhere without the Employer's prior consent.

The Employer and the Engineer shall treat all information provided by the Contractor and marked "confidential", as confidential. The Employer shall not disclose or permit to be disclosed any such information to third parties, except as may be necessary when exercising the Employer's rights under Sub-Clause 15.2 [*Termination for Contractor's Default*].

A Party's obligation of confidentiality under this Sub-Clause shall not apply where the information:

(a) was already in that Party's possession without an obligation of confidentiality before receipt from the other Party;
(b) becomes generally available to the public through no breach of these Conditions; or
(c) is lawfully obtained by the Party from a third party which is not bound by an obligation of confidentiality.

The Contractor shall disclose such confidential and other information as the Engineer may reasonably require in order to verify the Contractor's compliance with the Contract.

The Contractor shall treat all documents forming the Contract as confidential, except to the extent necessary to carry out its contractual obligations, and shall not disclose any particulars of the Contract without the Employer's consent. The Employer and the Engineer

shall treat all information provided by the Contractor and marked 'confidential' as confidential except as necessary under Sub-Clause 15.2.

A Party's confidentiality obligation does not apply in the cases specified in sub-paragraphs (a) to (c) of this Sub-Clause.

Commentary

(i) Main Changes from RB/99: The second, third and fourth paragraphs are new compared to RB/99. However, the second and much of the third paragraph were already in GB/08.[348]

(ii) Related Clauses / Sub-Clauses: 1.2 [*Interpretation*], 1.3 [*Notices and Other Communications*], 15.2 [*Termination for Contractor's Default*], 21.5 [*Amicable Settlement*] and, in addition, 7 [*Confidentiality*] and 10 [*Resignation and Termination*] of the DAAB GCs.

(iii) Analysis:

(1) The Contractor's disclosure obligations

The first paragraph requires the Contractor to disclose confidential and other information which 'the Engineer may reasonably require' in order to verify the Contractor's compliance with the Contract. Therefore the Engineer should be prepared to provide reasons to justify a request for information under this Sub-Clause.

There may be certain processes or design criteria which the Contractor or its Subcontractors consider involve trade secrets or otherwise wish to keep confidential.[349] In that case, when providing such information to the Employer and the Engineer, the Contractor should take the usual precautions to protect their proprietary nature by, among other things, marking the information as 'confidential', thereby obliging the Employer and the Engineer under the third paragraph to keep such information confidential.[350]

348. *See* Sub-Clause 1.13 [*Confidential Details*] of GB/08.
349. *The FIDIC Contracts Guide* (2nd edn, FIDIC, 2022) 99.
350. Confidential information entitled to legal protection is 'information that (i) is capable of identification with specificity, and not merely in global terms; (ii) has the necessary quality of confidence about it (e.g. it is not publicly available information); and (iii) was communicated in circumstances importing an obligation of confidence, that is, where it is clear that the person who communicated the information did not intend for the recipient

If the Contractor wants to avoid disclosing confidential information which it might otherwise have to provide under this Sub-Clause, then it should include a provision to this effect in a document with a higher priority than the General Conditions (e.g., in the Letter of Tender or the Particular Conditions).

(2) The Parties' respective confidentiality obligations

The Parties' respective confidentiality obligations are not reciprocal. Under the second paragraph, the Contractor agrees to treat all documents forming the Contract as confidential and not to publish or disclose particulars of the Contract in a trade or technical paper or elsewhere without the Employer's prior consent.[351] On the other hand, under the third paragraph, the Employer and the Engineer undertake to treat information provided by the Contractor as confidential only if it is marked as 'confidential'.[352]

The confidentiality obligation of the Contractor applies only to documents 'forming the Contract'. The Contractor is not required to treat as confidential other documents in relation to the project, such as general project information or Notices or other forms of communication exchanged between the Parties that are not part of the Contract.[353] *This may surprise Employers who may consider such information to be equally sensitive and private*. Therefore, Employers who want to prevent the disclosure of such information to third parties should insert a provision to that effect in the Particular Conditions. Confidentiality provisions con-

to use it generally or communicate it to others [...] [a] rough-and-ready test of whether [confidential information] should be regarded as confidential is whether the information could be sold to an interested person. If so, it may well be confidential'. Julian Bailey, *Construction Law* (3rd edn, London Publishing, UK, 2020) vol 3, 1393-1394 (paras 16.32-16.34).

351. Such consent must be in writing, may not be unreasonably delayed or withheld and must otherwise comply with Sub-Clause 1.3.
352. Arguably, this should include, among other things, a settlement offer that is so marked and that is made under Sub-Clause 21.5 [*Amicable Settlement*].
353. The confidentiality obligations imposed upon DAAB members are significantly more onerous. DAAB members are required to treat the DAAB's Activities (as defined) and generally all documents provided under the Contract as confidential (*see* Sub-Clause 7.1 of the DAAB GCs) whereas the Contractor has no similarly extensive obligation of confidentiality.

cerning both the construction contract and other information exchanged between the parties in relation to the contract can be found in other international standard forms.[354]

Furthermore, the Contractor's confidentiality obligation is stated to apply 'except to the extent necessary to carry out the Contractor's obligations under the Contract'.[355] In carrying out its obligations, the Contractor will often be engaging Subcontractors and/or suppliers to which it will have to disclose some of the documents comprising the Contract or information contained therein so that they can perform their contractual obligations. Such disclosure should fall within this exception and therefore not involve a breach of the Contractor's confidentiality obligation.

(3) Exceptions to Parties' confidentiality obligations

There is an exception to the Employer's obligation not to disclose (or permit the disclosure of) confidential information to third parties in the case of the Employer's termination of the Contract for the Contractor's default under Sub-Clause 15.2 [*Termination for Contractor's Default*]. This exception would allow the Employer, for example, to communicate any confidential information of the Contractor that is necessary for the execution of the Works to any new Contractor whom the Employer engages to complete the Works.[356]

The last paragraph of the Sub-Clause contains three exceptions to the Party's obligations of confidentiality which are standard in confidentiality clauses.[357]

(iv) Related Law: At common law, a duty of confidentiality may be implied in certain cases even if there is no confidentiality provision in a

354. *See*, for example, GC 16 of the *ENAA Model Form International Contract for Process Plant Construction*, Engineering Advancement Association of Japan, Tokyo, 2010, art. 57 of the *ICC Model Turnkey Contract for Major Projects* (ICC Publication no 797 E 2020) and Clause 20 of the *International Form of Contract – lump sum contracts* (1st edn, IChemE, 2007).
355. Second paragraph of Sub-Clause 1.12.
356. There is no reciprocal exception in cases where the Contractor terminates the Contract for Employer's default under Sub-Clause 16.2 [*Termination by Contractor*] as a Contractor should then no longer have any need to use information relating to the Contract.
357. They are sometimes referred to as the 'three classic [...] exceptions'. *See* Marcel Fontaine and Filip De Ly, *Drafting International Contracts: An Analysis of Contract Clauses* (Martinus Nijhoff, Leiden, the Netherlands, 2009) 248.

contract.[358] The UNIDROIT Principles provide for a pre-contractual duty of confidentiality[359] but otherwise do not deal with the subject.

(v) Improvements:

(1) It should be indicated whether each Party's obligation of confidentiality should survive completion of the Works and/or termination of the Contract and, if so, for how long.[360]
(2) In some cases at least, it might be stipulated that the Contractor's and/or each Party's duty of confidentiality applies to both the Contract and any other documents or information provided to the other Party in relation to the Contract whether marked 'confidential' or not.
(3) The obligation of the Employer and the Engineer to treat information provided by the Contractor as confidential under the third paragraph should be extended to the Employer's Personnel, as such information is likely to be disclosed to them.[361] As

358. Julian Bailey, *Construction Law* (3rd edn, London Publishing, UK, 2020) vol 1, 185 (para. 3.93) and vol 3, 1393-1397 (paras 16.32-16.40).
359. Art. 2.1.16 (*Duty of confidentiality*) of the UNIDROIT Principles provides as follows:

> Where information is given as confidential by one party in the course of negotiations, the other party is under a duty not to disclose that information or to use it improperly for its own purposes, whether or not a contract is subsequently concluded. Where appropriate, the remedy for breach of that duty may include compensation based on the benefit received by the other party.

360. *See* GC 16.5 of the *ENAA Model Form International Contract for Process Plant Construction*, Engineering Advancement Association of Japan, Tokyo, 2010 which provides that GC 16 relating to confidential information shall survive termination for whatever reason, without giving a time limit. Art. 57.4 of *ICC Model Turnkey Contract for Major Projects* (ICC Publication no 797 E 2020) stipulates that the confidentiality obligation under that Article shall continue for a period of four years after Final Acceptance (as defined). Clause 20.5 of the *International Form of Contract – lump sum contracts* (1st edn, IChemE, 2007) states that the confidentiality clause shall survive and remain in full force for a period of 10 years following the issue of the last Final Certificate (as defined). Too long a period might contravene laws prohibiting restrictive trade practices.
361. As noted by Leo Grutters and Brian Barr, *FIDIC Red, Yellow and Silver Books, A Practical Guide to the 2017 Editions* (Sweet & Maxwell, London, 2018), 72.

only the Employer is a Party to the Contract (not the Engineer or the Employer's Personnel), the Contract should provide that the Employer shall be responsible for ensuring that the Employer's Personnel (which includes the Engineer) comply with their confidentiality obligations, just as the Employer is responsible for ensuring that the Employer's Personnel and others cooperate and perform other obligations pursuant to Sub-Clause 2.3 [*Employer's Personnel and Other Contractors*].

--ooOOoo--

1.13 Compliance with Laws

The Contractor and the Employer shall, in performing the Contract, comply with all applicable Laws. Unless otherwise stated in the Specification:

(a) the Employer shall have obtained (or shall obtain) the planning, zoning or building permit or similar permits, permissions, licences and/or approvals for the Permanent Works, and any other permits, permissions, licences and/or approvals described in the Specification as having been (or being) obtained by the Employer. The Employer shall indemnify and hold the Contractor harmless against and from the consequences of any delay or failure to do so, unless the failure is caused by the Contractor's failure to comply with sub-paragraph (c) below;

(b) the Contractor shall give all notices, pay all taxes, duties and fees, and obtain all other permits, permissions, licences and/or approvals, as required by the Laws in relation to the execution of the Works. The Contractor shall indemnify and hold the Employer harmless against and from the consequences of any failure to do so unless the failure is caused by the Employer's failure to comply with Sub-Clause 2.2 [*Assistance*];

(c) within the time(s) stated in the Specification the Contractor shall provide such assistance and all documentation, as described in the Specification or otherwise reasonably required by the Employer, so as to allow the Employer to obtain any permit, permission, licence or approval under sub-paragraph (a) above; and

(d) the Contractor shall comply with all permits, permissions, licences and/or approvals obtained by the Employer under sub-paragraph (a) above.

If, having complied with sub-paragraph (c) above, the Contractor suffers delay and/or incurs Cost as a result of the Employer's delay or failure to obtain any permit, permission, licence or approval under sub-paragraph (a) above, the Contractor shall be entitled subject to Sub-Clause 20.2 [*Claims for Payment and/or EOT*] to EOT and/or payment of such Cost Plus Profit.

If the Employer incurs additional costs as a result of the Contractor's failure to comply with:

(i) sub-paragraph (c) above; or
(ii) sub-paragraph (b) or (d) above, provided that the Employer shall have complied with Sub-Clause 2.2 [*Assistance*],

the Employer shall be entitled subject to Sub-Clause 20.2 [*Claims for Payment and/or EOT*] to payment of these costs by the Contractor.

Both Parties must, in performing the Contract, comply with applicable Laws. Unless otherwise stated in the Specification:

(a) the Employer must have obtained (or must obtain) the planning, zoning or building permit or similar permits, permissions, licences and/or approvals for the Permanent Works, and/or as described in the Specification;
(b) the Contractor must give all notices, pay all taxes, duties and fees and obtain all other permits, permissions, licences and/or approvals as required by the Laws;
(c) within the time(s) stated in the Specification, the Contractor must provide assistance and documentation as described therein or as reasonably required by the Employer so as to allow it to comply with sub-paragraph (a) above; and

(d) Contractor must comply will all permits, permissions, licences and/or approvals obtained under sub-paragraph (a) above.

The Employer must indemnify the Contractor against any failure by the Employer under sub-paragraph (a) above and the Contractor must indemnify the Employer against any failure by the Contractor under sub-paragraph (b) above.

If having provided the assistance and documentation under sub-paragraph (c) above, the Contractor suffers delay and/or incurs Cost as a result of the Employer's delay or failure to obtain any permit, permission, licence or approval under sub-paragraph (a) above, the Contractor will be entitled, subject to Sub-Clause 20.2, to an EOT and/or Cost Plus Profit.

If the Employer incurs additional costs as a result of Contractor's failure to comply with sub-paragraphs (b), (c) or (d) above (in the case of sub-paragraphs (b) or (d), provided that the Employer has complied with Sub-Clause 2.2), the Employer will be entitled, subject to Sub-Clause 20.2, to payment of these costs.

Commentary

(i) Main Changes from RB/99:

(1) Both Parties must comply with all applicable Laws, and not only the Contractor as under Sub-Clause 1.13 of RB/99.

(2) Sub-paragraphs (a) to (d) of the first paragraph apply '[u]nless otherwise stated in the Specification', whereas sub-paragraphs (a) and (b) of Sub-Clause 1.13 of RB/99 apply '[u]nless otherwise stated in the Particular Conditions'.

(3) There is an exception – not in RB/99 – to each Party's obligation to indemnify the other Party under sub-paragraphs (a) and (b) in cases where the other Party has failed to provide required assistance.

(4) Sub-paragraphs (c) and (d) of the first paragraph are new.

(5) The last two paragraphs, specifying each Party's entitlement to claim in case of the other Party's failure to comply with the Sub-Clause, are also new.

(ii) Related Clauses / Sub-Clauses: 1.2 [*Interpretation*], 1.3 [*Notices and Other Communications*], 1.4 [*Law and Language*], 2.2 [*Assistance*], 4.4.1 [*Contractor's Documents – Preparation and Review*], 4.6 [*Co-operation*], 4.8 [*Health and Safety Obligations*], 4.10 [*Use of Site Data*], 4.18 [*Protection of the Environment*], 6.4 [*Labour Laws*], 8.6 [*Delays Caused by Authorities*], 13.6 [*Adjustments for Changes in Laws*], 14.1 [*The Contract Price*], 19.2 [*Insurance to Be Provided by the Contractor*], 20.2 [*Claims for Payment and/or EOT*] and 21.6 [*Arbitration*].

(iii) Analysis:

(1) Scope of applicable Laws

The first paragraph of the Sub-Clause provides that both Parties must, in performing the Contract, comply with all applicable Laws,[362] that is:

> all national (or state or provincial) legislation, statutes, acts, decrees, rules, ordinances, orders, treaties, international law and other laws, and regulations and by-laws of any legally constituted public authority.[363]

that are applicable when performing the Contract. While the Laws most likely to apply will be those of the Country (i.e., where the Permanent Works are to be executed), the expression 'all applicable Laws' in the first paragraph covers Laws anywhere. Thus, the Employer and the Contractor must each comply with the Laws of every country (whether it be their own country or others, such as from where the Contractor is procuring equipment or materials, or engaging labour) that are applicable where it performs the Contract.

Such Laws may deal with such wide-ranging matters as, procurement and tendering for projects, building and/or operation permits, licences or approvals, environmental matters, labour regulations (including health and safety requirements), subcontracting, protection of antiquities and fossils, liquidated damages, taking over or acceptance of the Works, decennial liability, taxation, customs duties, limitations of liability and

362. In addition, the Contractor must require the Contractor's Personnel to obey all applicable Laws, Sub-Clause 6.4 [*Labour Laws*], second paragraph.
363. *See* the definition of '**Laws**' in Sub-Clause 1.1.49 and the commentary thereon above.

the Contractor's right to suspend work or terminate the Contract.[364] Some of these Laws will have a mandatory character.[365]

(2) Parties' compliance with applicable Laws

Before inviting tenders, the Employer can be expected to have investigated the laws and regulations which will apply to the project. It can therefore be expected to have taken whatever preparatory steps were necessary regarding such matters as land use and ownership, building regulations and environmental issues, and to have determined what permits, permissions, licences and/or approvals are required for the execution of the Permanent Works. Indeed, as the Site will normally be located in the Employer's country, the Employer may already be very familiar with such requirements.

Consequently, the Contractor can normally be expected to rely on the Employer to have planned the execution of the Permanent Works in accordance with local law, and that all necessary permits, permissions, licences and/or approvals which the Employer is required to obtain either have been obtained or will be obtainable when required. This may be important to enable the Contractor to take possession of the Site and commence work.[366]

On the other hand, the Contractor will often be a foreign company or joint venture of partly or wholly foreign companies with little or no experience of working in the Country. While the Contractor is deemed by the Conditions to have investigated and familiarised itself with the Laws and procedures of the Country before tendering,[367] it will have had limited time to do so during the tender period. Accordingly, obtaining[368] and

364. *FIDIC Procurement Procedures Guide* (FIDIC, 2011) 14.

365. *See* **Section 5 Mandatory Law at the Site** of **Chapter II Applicable Law** above. In addition, pursuant to Sub-Clause 21.6 [*Arbitration*] which incorporates by reference the ICC Rules of Arbitration, an arbitral tribunal must take account of any relevant trade usages, implying that, in performing the Contract, Parties should be doing so as well. Art. 21(2) of the ICC Rules of Arbitration.

366. Pursuant to Sub-Clause 8.1 [*Commencement of Works*].

367. Sub-paragraph (d) of Sub-Clause 4.10 [*Use of Site Data*].

368. *See*, e.g., Sub-Clause 2.2 [*Assistance*] which only applies once the Contract has been entered into.

complying with the Laws of the Country will often be more challenging for the Contractor than the Employer.[369]

At the same time, it is reasonable for the Employer to expect the Contractor to comply with the laws of the Employer's country as, should the Contractor not do so (e.g., fail to pay local taxes or customs duties or to obtain all necessary permits, permissions, licences and/or approvals), this could be embarrassing and/or a source of liability for the Employer, who may be responsible to local authorities for the Contractor's conduct and/or compliance with local law.

Consequently, this Sub-Clause provides, in sub-paragraph (a), that the Employer shall indemnify the Contractor against the consequences of any delay or failure to obtain permits, permissions, licences or approvals for which the Employer is responsible (unless caused by a Contractor failure), and in sub-paragraph (b), that the Contractor must indemnify the Employer against the consequences of any failure on the Contractor's part to comply with Laws in relation to the execution of the Works (unless caused by an Employer failure).

(3) Parties' Claims

Under the second paragraph, the Contractor is entitled, subject to Sub-Clause 20.2, to an EOT and/or Cost Plus Profit if the Contractor suffers delay and/or incurs Cost as a result of the Employer's delay or failure to obtain a permit, permission, licence or approval under sub-paragraph (a). The Contractor's entitlement is conditioned on the Contractor having provided assistance and documentation to the Employer, as required under sub-paragraph (c).

Similarly, under the last paragraph, if the Employer incurs additional costs as a result of the Contractor's failure to comply with sub-paragraphs (b), (c) or (d), the Employer will be entitled, subject to Sub-Clause 20.2, to payment of these costs. The Employer's entitlement in the case of the Contractor's failure to comply with sub-paragraphs (b) or (d) is conditioned on the Employer having provided assistance to the Contractor, as required under Sub-Clause 2.2 [*Assistance*].

(iv) Related Law: The division of responsibility for obtaining permits, permissions, licences and/or approvals provided for in the Sub-Clause is

369. Ideally, all permits, permissions, licences and/or approvals to be obtained by the Contractor should be set forth in the Specification and/or the Contract.

broadly consistent with the division of responsibility for obtaining public permissions provided for by Article 6.1.14 (*Application for public permission*) of the UNIDROIT Principles which provides that:

> Where the law of a State requires a public permission affecting the validity of the contract or its performance and neither that law nor the circumstances indicate otherwise
> (a) if only one party has its place of business in that State, that party shall take the measures necessary to obtain the permission;
> (b) in any other case the party whose performance requires permission shall take the necessary measures.

Under Article 6.1.15 (*Procedure in applying for permission*) of the Principles, the party that is required to apply for the permission should do so 'without undue delay and shall bear any expenses incurred'. That party is also obliged whenever appropriate to give to the other party 'notice of the grant or refusal of such permission without undue delay'. Other articles of the Principles that may be of interest include Article 6.1.16 (*Permission neither granted nor refused*) and Article 6.1.17 (*Permission refused*).

Pursuant to Article 5.1.3 (*Co-operation between the parties*) of the UNIDROIT Principles, '[e]ach party shall co-operate with the other party when such co-operation may reasonably be expected for the performance of that party's obligations.' This article is consistent with sub-paragraph (c) of Sub-Clause 1.13 and Sub-Clause 2.2 which require each Party reasonably to assist the other, as well as Sub-Clause 4.6 [*Co-operation*] providing for the Contractor's cooperation.

(v) Improvements: The Contractor's obligation under sub-paragraph (d) to comply with all permits, permissions, etc., obtained by the Employer should be limited to those of which the Contractor may reasonably be aware, as it cannot necessarily be expected to know them all.

--ooOOoo--

1.14 Joint and Several Liability

If the Contractor is a Joint Venture:

(a) the members of the JV shall be jointly and severally liable to the Employer for the performance of the Contractor's obligations under the Contract;

(b) the JV leader shall have authority to bind the Contractor and each member of the JV; and

(c) neither the members nor (if known) the scope and parts of the Works to be carried out by each member nor the legal status of the JV shall be altered without the prior consent of the Employer (but such consent shall not relieve the altered JV from any liability under sub-paragraph (a) above).

If the Contractor is a Joint Venture, its members shall be jointly and severally liable to the Employer for the performance of the Contractor's obligations and the JV leader shall have authority to bind the Contractor and each member of the JV. Neither the members, the scope and parts of the Works to be carried out by each member nor the legal status of the JV shall be altered without the Employer's prior consent.

Commentary

(i) Main Changes from RB/99: The Sub-Clause is essentially unchanged except that it has been added to sub-paragraph (c) that the scope and parts of the Works to be carried out by each member shall not be altered without the Employer's prior consent.

(ii) Related Clauses / Sub-Clauses: 1.2 [*Interpretation*], 1.3 [*Notices and Other Communications*], 1.5 [*Priority of Documents*], 1.6 [*Contract Agreement*], 4.9.1 [*Quality Management and Compliance Verification Systems – Quality Management System*] and 15.2.1 [*Termination for Contractor's Default – Notice*].

(iii) Analysis:

(1) The Contractor as a Joint Venture

This Sub-Clause should be read together with the definitions of a 'JV' in Sub-Clause 1.1.46 and of a 'JV Undertaking' in Sub-Clause 1.1.47.[370]

As projects become larger and more complex, it is increasingly common for the Contractor to take the form of a joint venture (or 'JV') of two or

370. *See* the commentaries on Sub-Clauses 1.1.46 '**Joint Venture**' and 1.1.47 '**JV Undertaking**' above.

more companies. Each such company may be able to contribute different skills or expertise and/or greater financial and other resources than a single company.[371]

As a general rule, the JV will be a contractual joint venture, that is, an unincorporated grouping of companies[372] as distinct from a joint venture incorporated as a company and thus constituting a separate legal entity from its members. Accordingly, a JV is defined in Sub-Clause 1.1.46 as a contractual joint venture and this is the kind of JV which is assumed to constitute the 'Contractor' in Sub-Clause 1.14. *The Contractor is not required to disclose the contract creating the JV to the Employer.*

(2) Joint and several liability

Sub-paragraph (a) provides that the JV members shall be 'jointly and severally' liable to the Employer for the performance of the Contractor's obligations. This legal expression means that if any member should default or be otherwise unable to perform the Contractor's obligations, the other members or member (if there is only one other member) shall be responsible to the Employer for performing them. Thus, if all the other member(s) were to default, then the one remaining non-defaulting member would have to perform the entire Contract.[373]

371. Where a construction company is a subsidiary within a group of companies, the only security for the performance by the subsidiary of its obligations is the subsidiary's assets. No reliance can be placed, as a legal matter, on the assets of the group of companies of which it is a part. Therefore, in such a case, an Employer should consider requiring a parent company guarantee from a company within the group having the assets necessary to ensure full performance of the construction contract. An example form of guarantee is contained in Annex A – example form of parent company guarantee of RB/17. The text of this form of guarantee, as in the case of any guarantee, needs to be reviewed against (and almost certainly revised in light of) the law governing the guarantee, which may not be the same as the law governing the Contract.

372. Typically, under the common law a form of partnership and under French law a *société en participation*. *See* art. 1871 and following of the French Civil Code.

373. Art. 11.1.3 (*Obligee's rights against joint and several obligors*), UNIDROIT Principles. The member performing the contract would then normally have a right of contribution or indemnity from the other members in proportion to their shares in the JV. Art. 11.1.10 (*Extent of contributory claim*), UNIDROIT Principles.

Sub-paragraph (a) reiterates the joint and several undertaking which the JV members will have already made to the Employer in the JV Undertaking submitted at the tender stage.[374] Joint and several liability of the JV members is advantageous to the Employer – indeed, it normally insists upon it – but it entails much more risk for a member than 'several' liability, that is, where each is responsible only for its respective share or portion of the Works.[375]

(3) JV leader and changes to JV

By providing in sub-paragraph (b) that the JV leader shall have the authority to bind the Contractor and each JV member, the Employer is relieved from having to deal with each member of the JV in order to be able to deal with the Contractor. Instead, it can just deal with the JV leader, who should be identified and appropriately authorised in the JV Undertaking at the tender stage.[376]

Pursuant to sub-paragraph (c), any changes in the JV, including changes in the JV members, the scope and parts of the Works to be carried out by each member (which information should be disclosed in the JV Undertaking at tender stage) and the legal status of the JV (e.g., its incorporation as a company, if any), require the Employer's consent. Such consent must be in writing, should not be unreasonably withheld or delayed, and otherwise must comply with Sub-Clause 1.3.

374. The JV Undertaking is not identified (as it probably should be, where the tenderer is a JV) in the form of Letter of Tender included in RB/17 but it is 'part of the Tender' (*see* Sub-Clause 1.1.47) and thus will have been submitted to the Employer.

375. In the case of joint and several liability, while a member may be obliged to perform the obligations of other members where they default, it is usually (as mentioned in fn. 373 above) entitled thereafter to seek contribution from the defaulting member(s). But seeking contribution will be to no avail if they are insolvent. Consequently, a prospective tenderer will be reluctant to enter into a JV where it anticipates that, if things go wrong, it will, because of its greater resources, be the 'last man standing', i.e., will be left to bear the entire cost. Therefore, before entering into a JV, a prospective tenderer will want to satisfy itself as to the competence and financial condition of the other members. As a practical matter, joint and several liability may only provide an acceptable level of risk where all members are roughly of similar financial strength.

376. *See* Sub-Clause 1.1.47 '**JV Undertaking**'.

(iv) Related Law: The law governing the contract creating the JV and governing the JV Undertaking is likely, as a practical matter, to be the law of the country of at least one of the members of the JV, perhaps the leader of the JV. The General Conditions do not regulate this matter. However, the JV and the JV Undertaking must comply with Sub-Clauses 1.14 and 1.1.47 as interpreted by the law governing the Contract provided for in Sub-Clause 1.4. There may be no inconsistencies.[377]

(v) Improvements:

(1) The Conditions do not address where the Employer is constituted as a JV, although this is not uncommon. Accordingly, similar provisions should be introduced to deal with that situation. For example, the need for a JV leader who has the authority to bind the JV members is desirable whichever Party is constituted as a JV.[378]

(2) The form of Letter of Tender in RB/17 should include reference to a JV Undertaking (*see* Sub-Clause 1.1.47) where the tenderer is a JV. This reference may be similar to that contained in the form of Contract Agreement included in RB/17.

--ooOOoo--

1.15 Limitation of Liability

Neither Party shall be liable to the other Party for loss of use of any Works, loss of profit, loss of any contract or for any indirect or consequential loss or damage which may be suffered by the other Party in connection with the Contract, other than under:

(a) Sub-Clause 8.8 [*Delay Damages*];
(b) sub-paragraph (c) of Sub-Clause 13.3.1 [*Variation by Instruction*];

377. International legal principles relating to joint and several obligations are to be found in Chapter 11 [*Plurality of Obligors and Obligees*], UNIDROIT Principles.

378. For an example of a provision addressing where either the employer or the contractor is constituted as a JV, *see* art. 60 [*Joint and several liability*] of the *ICC Model Turnkey Contract for Major Projects* (ICC Publication no 797 E 2020).

(c) Sub-Clause 15.7 [*Payment after Termination for Employer's Convenience*];
(d) Sub-Clause 16.4 [*Payment after Termination by Contractor*];
(e) Sub-Clause 17.3 [*Intellectual and Industrial Property Rights*];
(f) the first paragraph of Sub-Clause 17.4 [*Indemnities by Contractor*]; and
(g) Sub-Clause 17.5 [*Indemnities by Employer*].

The total liability of the Contractor to the Employer under or in connection with the Contract, other than under:

(i) Sub-Clause 2.6 [*Employer-Supplied Materials and Employer's Equipment*];
(ii) Sub-Clause 4.19 [*Temporary Utilities*];
(iii) Sub-Clause 17.3 [*Intellectual and Industrial Property Rights*]; and
(iv) the first paragraph of Sub-Clause 17.4 [*Indemnities by Contractor*],

shall not exceed the sum stated in the Contract Data or (if a sum is not so stated) the Accepted Contract Amount.

This Sub-Clause shall not limit liability in any case of fraud, gross negligence, deliberate default or reckless misconduct by the defaulting Party.

Neither Party shall be liable to the other Party for loss of use of any Works, loss of profit, loss of any contract or for any indirect or consequential loss or damage other than under the provisions listed in sub-paragraphs (a) through (g) of Sub-Clause 1.15.

The total liability of the Contractor to the Employer in connection with the Contract, other than under Sub-Clauses listed in items (i) through (iv) of Sub-Clause 1.15, shall not exceed the sum stated in the Contract Data or (if no sum is stated there) the Accepted Contract Amount.

This Sub-Clause shall not limit liability in case of fraud, gross negligence, deliberate default or reckless misconduct by the defaulting Party.

Commentary

(i) Main Changes from RB/99:

(1) This Sub-Clause replaces Sub-Clause 17.6 [*Limitation of Liability*] in RB/99.[379]

(2) In relation to the exclusion from liability of each Party in the first paragraph, the exceptions to the exclusion have been expanded to include Sub-Clause 8.8 [*Delay Damages*], sub-paragraph (c) of Sub-Clause 13.3.1 [*Variation by Instruction*], Sub-Clause 15.7 [*Payment after Termination for Employer's Convenience*][380] and Sub-Clause 17.3 [*Intellectual and Industrial Property Rights*].

(3) In the second paragraph, the exclusion from the Contractor's total liability to the Employer (i.e., the Contractor's 'cap' on liability) does not apply to the second paragraph of Sub-Clause 17.4 [*Indemnities by Contractor*] dealing with the Contractor's obligation to indemnify for errors of design. On the other hand, the first paragraph of Sub-Clause 17.1 [*Indemnities*] of RB/99, which included the Contractor's obligation to indemnify for its design, was excluded from the Contractor's total liability 'cap' under Sub-Clause 17.6 [*Limitation of Liability*] of RB/99.

(4) '[G]ross negligence' by the defaulting Party has been added in the last paragraph as a case where the limitations on liability provided for by the Sub-Clause will not apply.

---

379. Prior to RB/99, the Red Book had contained no limitation on the Contractor's (or the Employer's) liability. It appears to have been introduced in RB/99: (1) because it was increasingly recognised that the Contractor might be engaged in design (*see* Sub-Clause 4.1 [*Contractor's General Obligations*] of RB/99) and (2) in the interest of harmonising RB/99 with YB/99 (and SB/99), harmonisation across these Books being one of the goals of the 1999 editions ('[w]henever possible, similar wording is used in all three new Books in the equivalent sub-clauses'. Peter Booen, 'The Three Major New FIDIC Books' [2000] ICLR 24, 29). The Yellow Book, which is for Works designed by the Contractor, had always provided for a limitation on the Contractor's liability, *see*, e.g., Clause 15.6 of YB/63.

380. The correct reference should have been to Sub-Clause 15.6 [*Valuation after Termination for Employer's Convenience*] which addresses loss of profit in sub-para. (b). Sub-Clause 15.7 refers to payment to the Contractor of an amount certified under Sub-Clause 15.6.

(ii) Related Clauses / Sub-Clauses: 1.2 [*Interpretation*], 2.6 [*Employer-Supplied Materials and Employer's Equipment*], 4.19 [*Temporary Utilities*], 8.8 [*Delay Damages*], 11.10 [*Unfulfilled Obligations*], 13.3.1 [*Variation by Instruction*], 14.14 [*Cessation of Employer's Liability*], 15.7 [*Payment after Termination for Employer's Convenience*], 16.4 [*Payment after Termination by Contractor*], 17.3 [*Intellectual and Industrial Property Rights*], 17.4 [*Indemnities by Contractor*] and 17.5 [*Indemnities by Employer*].

(iii) Analysis: While this Sub-Clause limits the liability of each Party to the other, it is probably of particular importance to the Contractor because, as the Party executing the Works, it might otherwise be exposed to especially large losses or damages. Like the corresponding Sub-Clause in RB/99, its purpose is:

> to maintain a balance between the differing objectives of the Parties, each of whom will wish to minimise his/her own liability while being entitled to receive full compensation for default by the other Party.[381]

(1) First paragraph: exclusion from liability

What is meant by providing in the first paragraph that neither Party shall be liable to the other 'for loss of use of any Works, loss of profit, loss of any contract or for any indirect or consequential loss or damage'? While terms like these are familiar ones in clauses excluding liability in contracts governed by common law systems, certain of them make much less sense in civil law systems. Loss of use of any Works, loss of profit and loss of any contract should not present any difficulty under either legal system. Thus, if the Contractor is late in delivering, for example, housing units, the Employer will be deprived of being able to occupy them itself or lease them to others ('loss of use'). If the Contractor is late in delivering a manufacturing facility or plant, the Employer will be deprived of being able to sell the output of the plant, e.g., widgets ('loss of profit and loss of any contract').[382] Similarly, if the Employer wrongfully terminates a Contract early, it will be depriving the Contractor of the profit it might have earned on the uncompleted work had it been able to complete the Contract ('loss of profit').

381. *The FIDIC Contracts Guide* (2nd edn, FIDIC 2022) 104.
382. In this and the previous case, the liability of the Contractor may already be limited by the second paragraph of Sub-Clause 8.8 [*Delay Damages*] providing that Delay Damages shall be the 'only' damages due for a failure to comply with the Time for Completion other than under Sub-Clause 15.2.

The difficulty in comparative law arises with respect to 'any indirect or consequential loss or damage'. In common law jurisdictions, these words have often been interpreted as referring to damages under the second rule in the well-known 19th century English case, *Hadley v Baxendale*, that is, damages other than those 'arising naturally i.e. according to the usual course of things' from a breach of contract.[383] However, these terms or concepts are not expressly used or do not have the same meaning under the civil law as they have – or often have had – under the common law.[384] Therefore in the case of a contract governed by the law of a civil law system, this Sub-Clause should be reconsidered and changed in the Particular Conditions so as to replace the common law terminology with appropriate wording of the applicable civil law system.

(2) First paragraph: exceptions to exclusion from liability

The exceptions to the exclusion from liability in the first paragraph all appear to relate to Sub-Clauses that allow either explicitly or implicitly for the recovery of lost profits or which provide for indemnities. The provisions that allow explicitly for recovery of loss of profit are sub-paragraph (c) of Sub-Clause 13.3.1, Sub-Clause 15.7 (in relation to Sub-Clause 15.6) and Sub-Clause 16.4. The reference to Sub-Clause 8.8[385] appears to have been included as when Parties agree the amount of Delay Damages, they may be expected to have taken into account the likely

383. *See* **Section 4 Common Law and Civil Law Compared – 4.4.6 Limitations on Damages** of **Chapter II Applicable Law** above, where the two rules in the case are explained. As stated there, the second rule will no longer necessarily apply in England and is rejected by *McGregor on Damages* (21st edn, Sweet & Maxwell, London, 2021) 30-34 (paras 3-013 to 3-018). As explained in **Section 4.4.6**, 'consequential damages' may have various meanings depending on a case's factual background.
384. **Section 4 Common Law and Civil Law Compared – 4.4.6 Limitations on Damages** of **Chapter II Applicable Law** above.
385. The second paragraph of Sub-Clause 8.8 provides that Delay Damages shall be the 'only' damages due from the Contractor for failure to complete the Works on time 'other than in the event of termination under Sub-Clause 15.2 [*Termination for Contractor's Default*]'. Consequently, recovery of 'any losses and damages suffered by the Employer' (Sub-Clause 15.4(b)) is allowed where the Employer terminates the Contract for the Contractor's default.

value of loss of use, loss of profits and other damages referred to that the Employer may suffer from the Contractor's failure to complete on time.[386]

The exceptions for the Sub-Clauses providing for indemnities, namely, Sub-Clauses 17.3, 17.4 (first paragraph) and 17.5, appear intended to ensure that the indemnified party is fully compensated for its loss whatever may be its cause. This seems fair, as in the situations envisaged by those Sub-Clauses, the indemnified party will have had no responsibility for the cause of the loss.[387]

Only the first paragraph of Sub-Clause 17.4 has been listed as an exception to the exclusion of each Party from liability. This means that the second paragraph, which provides for the Contractor's obligation to indemnify the Employer against any errors in the Contractor's design that result in the Works not being fit for the purpose, is still subject to the general exclusion from liability for loss of use, loss of profit, loss of any contract or for any indirect and consequential loss or damage.[388]

---

386. On the other hand if, for example, the Employer were to terminate the Contract on account of the Contractor's default pursuant to:
    (a) sub-paragraph (b) of Sub-Clause 9.4 [*Failure to Pass Tests on Completion*] and sub-para. (d) of Sub-Clause 11.4 [*Failure to Remedy Defects*];
    (b) the same sub-para. (d) of Sub-Clause 11.4 alone; or
    (c) Sub-Clause 15.2 [*Termination for Contractor's Default*] (the counterpart of Clause 16 referred to above entitling the Contractor to terminate the Contract for the Employer's default),

    the exclusion from liability in the first paragraph would apply. Consequently, the Contractor would not be liable for 'loss of use of any Works, loss of profit, loss of any contract or for any indirect or consequential loss or damage' (if any) of the Employer unless the Employer could establish fraud, gross negligence, deliberate fault or reckless misconduct by the Contractor. This results from the risk allocation provided for by the first and last paragraphs of Sub-Clause 1.15.
387. Shared liability is addressed in Sub-Clause 17.6 [*Shared Indemnities*].
388. Other Sub-Clauses limiting liability are: Sub-Clause 8.8 [*Delay Damages*], which limits the Contractor's liability for delay to Delay Damages; Sub-Clause 11.10 [*Unfulfilled Obligations*], which limits the Contractor's liability for defects or damage in Plant occurring more than two years after expiry of the DNP for the Plant; and Sub-Clause 14.14 [*Cessation of Employer's Liability*], which limits the Employer's liability after issue and payment of the Final Statement or Partially Agreed Final Statement. As in the case of Sub-Clause 1.15, these limits contain an exception for fraud, gross negligence, deliberate default or reckless misconduct.

(3) *Second paragraph: liability cap*

The second paragraph places a cap on the total liability of the Contractor to the Employer under or in connection with the Contract. This, of course, refers to liability beyond the Contractor's obligation (which might also be interpreted as being a liability) to execute the Works in accordance with the Contract.[389] While there is no similar limitation on the Employer's liability to the Contractor, the Employer's liability will generally cease following: (i) the submission of the Contractor's discharge;[390] (ii) the Employer's payment of the Final Payment Certificate; and (iii) return to the Contractor of the Performance Security.[391]

The cap on the Contractor's liability to the Employer should be agreed by the Parties and stated in the Contract Data. If no amount is stated there, the Contractor's liability will be restricted to the Accepted Contract Amount, which is a fixed amount unaffected by changes in the Contract Price.[392] This limitation of liability does not apply in respect of obligations under Sub-Clauses 2.6, 4.19, 17.3 and the first paragraph of 17.4.

The exceptions for Sub-Clauses 2.6 and 4.19 are readily understandable as they relate to materials, equipment and temporary utilities purchased from the Employer. As the Contractor would have to bear their cost anyway, there is no reason that their cost should be less when they are supplied by the Employer. Thus, they are excluded from the cap on the Contractor's liability. The exception for Sub-Clauses 17.3 and the first paragraph of 17.4 is justified on the grounds that, in these cases, the Contractor is indemnifying the Employer against the claims of third parties on account of matters for which the Contractor is responsible; i.e., these are claims for which the Employer should not have been liable in the first place. Consequently, they are properly excluded from the cap on the Contractor's liability.

---

389. Thus, when Sub-Clause 1.15 uses the terms 'liable' or 'liability', they mean liability as may arise from a breach of contract or tort (or wrong) of some kind rather than liability as may arise from having to perform a contractual obligation.
390. Subject to any qualifications or reservations which it may contain, *see* Sub-Clause 14.12 [*Discharge*], and the Employer's liability under its indemnification obligations. This also assumes no fraud, gross negligence, deliberate default or reckless misconduct on the part of the Employer.
391. Unless the Contractor has made a Claim under Sub-Clause 20.2 in respect of amount(s) under the FPC within 56 days of receiving it. *See* Sub-Clause 14.14 [*Cessation of Employer's Liability*].
392. *See* Sub-Clause 1.1.1 '**Accepted Contract Amount**'.

(4) Third paragraph: fraud, etc., exception

The last paragraph states that this Sub-Clause shall not limit liability in any case of 'fraud, gross negligence, deliberate default or reckless misconduct by the defaulting Party'.[393] This merely gives expression to an exception to limitation on liability which is recognised by most legal systems. Under the common law and civil law, a party can generally not limit its liability for acts that involve fraud, gross negligence or deliberate default.[394]

Compared to RB/99, the phrase 'gross negligence' has been added to the list.[395] While 'gross negligence' is not an accepted term in English law, it is a familiar legal concept distinct from negligence under the civil law and US law. Under French law, gross negligence is equivalent to *faute lourde* (literally, heavy fault) and in civil law generally it is equivalent to the Latin (Roman law) expression *lata culpa*.[396] Arab civil codes[397] refer to gross negligence as does US law.[398] The term 'gross negligence' is also

393. The same paragraph, or similar language, is to be found in Sub-Clauses 8.8 [*Delay Damages*], 11.10 [*Unfulfilled Obligations*] and 14.14 [*Cessation of Employer's Liability*].
394. Marcel Fontaine and Filip De Ly, *Drafting International Contracts: An Analysis of Contract Clauses* (Martinus Nijhoff, Leiden, the Netherlands, 2009) 362-63 ad 382-88.
395. YB/87 had instead provided for, and contained a definition of, 'Gross Misconduct', *see* Sub-Clause 1.1.20 and Clause 42 of that form.
396. *See* the definition of *lata culpa* in Bryan A Garner (ed in chief), *Black's Law Dictionary* (11th edn, Thomson Reuters, St Paul, MN, 2019).
397. *See* art. 217(2) of the Egyptian Civil Code and art. 220(2) of the Libyan Civil Code where, as in the case of Sub-Clause 1.15, a party may not limit its liability for gross negligence.
398. The principal US law dictionary which is also used in England defines gross negligence as '[a] lack of even slight diligence or care' and '[a] conscious, voluntary act or omission in reckless disregard of a legal duty and of the consequences to another party'. This dictionary adds:

> As it originally appeared, this was very great negligence, or the want of even slight or scant care. It has been described as a failure to exercise even that care which a careless person would use [...] [It] is still true that most courts consider that 'gross negligence' falls short of a reckless disregard of the consequences, and differs from ordinary negligence only in degree, and not in kind.

Bryan A Garner (ed in chief), *Black's Law Dictionary* (11th edn, Thomson Reuters, St Paul, MN, 2019) (citing W Page Keeton et al, *Prosser and Keeton*

used in other international standard forms of construction contract.[399] This is not to suggest, however, that the term has the same meaning wherever it is used.

Helpfully, the *Guidance* proposes a definition of gross negligence, which Parties may adopt, as follows:

> any act or omission of a party which is contrary to the most elementary rules of diligence which a conscientious employer or contractor would have observed in similar circumstances, and/or which show serious reckless disregard for the consequences of such an act or omission. It involves materially more want of care than mere inadvertence or simple negligence.[400]

(iv) Related Law: Limitation of liability clauses, such as Sub-Clause 1.15, are recognised and upheld in both civil law and common law jurisdictions, at least where they are reasonable.[401] However such clauses may be overridden and invalidated by applicable mandatory law. Thus, in some civil law countries, it is mandatory law that a contractor will be absolutely liable (i.e., without proof of fault) to its employer for damages which affect the stability of a work (which it has constructed) for 10 years after completion.[402]

---

on the Law of Torts (5th edn 1984) (para. 34 at 211-12)). For a discussion of gross negligence in English law, *see* James Pickavance and James Bowling, 'Exclusions from Immunity: Gross Negligence and Wilful Misconduct', a paper presented to the SCL in 2017 (Paper D207, October 2017).

399. *See* the *General Conditions for the Supply and Installation of Mechanical, Electrical and Electronic Products*, January 2014, known as ORGALIME SI 94, published by ORGALIME – The European Engineering Industries Association Brussels – https://www.orgalim.eu/sites/default/files/attachment/Pages_from_SI14-EN_sample.pdf accessed 6 November 2022. 'Gross Negligence' is defined in Clause 2. Definitions as:

> an act or omission implying either a failure to pay due regard to serious consequences, which a conscientious contracting party would normally foresee as likely to ensue, or a deliberate disregard of the consequences of such an act or omission.

See also Clause 71.

400. *Guidance for the Preparation of Particular Conditions*, 15.
401. *See* the discussion in **Section 4 Common Law and Civil Law Compared – 4.4.6 Limitations on Damages** of **Chapter II Applicable Law**, above.
402. *See* **Section 4 Common Law and Civil Law Compared – 4.4.4 Decennial Liability** of **Chapter II Applicable Law** above. *See also* the commentary on Sub-Clause 11.10 [*Unfulfilled Obligations*] below.

The UNIDROIT Principles recognise clauses limiting liability as valid under certain conditions:

> [a] clause which limits or excludes one party's liability for non-performance [...] may not be invoked if it would be grossly unfair to do so, having regard to the purpose of the contract.[403]

An example of where such a clause limiting liability may not be invoked, under this provision, would be where the term is 'inherently unfair and its application would lead to an evident imbalance between the performances of the parties' or 'where the non-performance is the result of grossly negligent conduct'.[404]

(v) Improvements: There should be included in the General Conditions the definition of 'gross negligence' which is presently in the *Guidance* so as to eliminate uncertainty as to its meaning when included in a Contract.

--ooOOoo--

1.16 Contract Termination[405]

> Subject to any mandatory requirements under the governing law of the Contract, termination of the Contract under any Sub-Clause of these Conditions shall require no action of whatsoever kind by either Party other than as stated in the Sub-Clause.

Subject to any mandatory requirements under the governing law, termination of the Contract under any Sub-Clause requires no action other than that stated in the Sub-Clause.

---

403. Art. 7.1.6 (*Exemption clauses*) of the UNIDROIT Principles.
404. Official comment 5 to art. 7.1.6 (*Exemption clauses*) of the Principles. This official comment includes two illustrations.
405. Unlike Sub-Clause 1.16 of RB/17, Sub-Clause 1.16 of FIDIC's new Conditions of Contract for Underground Works 2019 (the 'Emerald Book') provides for the Contractor to complete and maintain a Contract Risk Register (as defined) and to prepare and maintain a Contract Risk Management Plan (as defined) to manage and control the risks identified in the Contract Risk Register. Sub-Clause 1.16 [*Contract Termination*] of RB/17 is provided for in Sub-Clause 1.17 of the Emerald Book.

Commentary

(i) Main Changes from RB/99: This is a new Sub-Clause with no analogue in the previous editions of RB.

(ii) Related Clauses / Sub-Clauses: 11.4 [*Failure to Remedy Defects*], 15 [*Termination by Employer*], 16 [*Suspension and Termination by Contractor*], 18.5 [*Optional Termination*] and 18.6 [*Release from Performance under the Law*].

(iii) Analysis: This provision has been introduced into the Conditions as the law in some civil law countries whose law is based on old French law, such as in the Arab Middle East, may require a party to obtain an order from a court (or arbitral tribunal) in order to be able to terminate a contract without the other party's consent. In such countries, termination of a contract without a court order will be possible only where the contract entitles a party, in defined circumstances, to terminate the contract automatically or *ipso facto* (in French: *de plein droit*) and, preferably, adding 'without obtaining a court judgement or order'.[406]

This legal requirement for a court order to terminate a contract in some civil law countries has been a source of difficulty under FIDIC contracts as their provisions for termination of a contract *merely upon notice* where, for example, the other Party is alleged to be in default – as permitted in common law countries – have been held to be insufficient to dispense with the need for a court order.[407]

The purpose of Sub-Clause 1.16 is to make clear that, subject to any mandatory requirements of the governing law, the only actions required for the termination of the Contract under the Sub-Clauses of the Conditions providing for termination are those contained in the relevant Sub-Clause, and that no further actions, such as the obtaining of a court order, are required.[408]

---

406. *See* **Section 4 Common Law and Civil Law Compared – 4.3.5 Contract Termination** of **Chapter II Applicable Law**, above.
407. *See*, e.g., the partial award, ICC case 9202 (1969) ('Issue 3'), ICC Int'l Ct Arb Bull, vol 19, no 2-2008, 76, 81-85 (commentary 42, 46-48) where an ICC arbitral tribunal held the termination provisions of RB/69 to be insufficient to dispense with the need for a court order under the law of the civil law country concerned.
408. This is also consistent with modern practice as reflected in art. 3.1.2 (*Validity of mere agreement*) of the UNIDROIT Principles providing that '[a]

It remains to be seen whether this Sub-Clause goes far enough and is sufficiently explicit to relieve a Party from having to apply to a court (or arbitral tribunal) for an order to be able to terminate a Contract governed by the law of such civil law countries.

(iv) Related Law: *See* the discussion of this issue in **Section 4 Common Law and Civil Law Compared – 4.3.5 Contract Termination** of **Chapter II Applicable Law** above. A commentator in the Arabian Gulf notes that the issue of whether termination of a contract requires a court order:

> is especially acute in the United Arab Emirates and Oman by virtue of a prohibition on termination of an innominate contract [that is, a contract not classifiable under any particular name] other than by mutual consent, by court order or by law.[409]

He concludes that 'the risks associated with termination can be mitigated by including in a contractual termination mechanism an explicit waiver of any requirement for a court order and generally reflecting the wording of the relevant provisions of the civil codes'.[410]

(v) Improvements: To increase the chances that this Sub-Clause will have the desired effect, it would be highly desirable for it to state explicitly that, to terminate the Contract under any Sub-Clause providing for termination, *no order from a court or arbitral tribunal shall be required*. As long as there is any doubt about this Sub-Clause's adequacy and sufficiency (as there may be in some civil law countries, as described under **(iii) Analysis** above), prudent users will apply for a court (or arbitral) order to avoid the risk that they will be found to have terminated the Contract wrongfully.

--ooOOoo--

contract is concluded, modified or *terminated* by the mere agreement of the parties, without any further requirement' (emphasis added).

409. Citing to the UAE Civil Code, art. 267, and the Oman Civil Code, art. 167, as well as the Qatar Civil Code, art. 184, which allows the parties to agree to an 'automatic' termination as long as this is recorded expressly. Michael Grose, *Construction Law in the United Arab Emirates and the Gulf* (Wiley Blackwell, Oxford, 2016), 185.

410. Michael Grose, *Construction Law in the United Arab Emirates and the Gulf* (1st edn, Wiley Blackwell, Oxford, 2016) 187.

Figure 1 Key Contract Dates

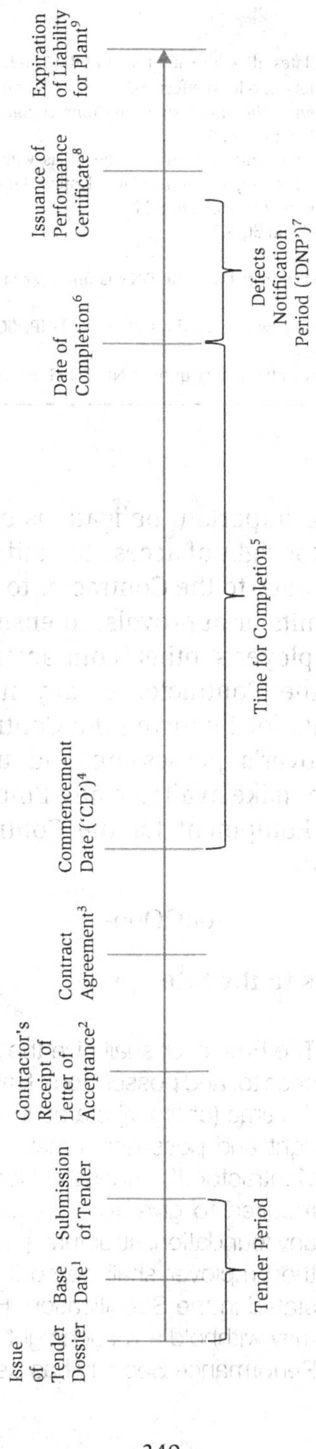

Issue of Tender Dossier

Base Date[1]

Submission of Tender

Tender Period

Contractor's Receipt of Letter of Acceptance[2]

Contract Agreement[3]

Commencement Date ('CD')[4]

Time for Completion[5]

Date of Completion[6]

Defects Notification Period ('DNP')[7]

Issuance of Performance Certificate[8]

Expiration of Liability for Plant[9]

Source: Author's own work.

Figure 1 Key Contract Dates

Notes SC = Sub-Clause

1. This date is 28 days before the latest date for submission of the Tender. SC 1.1.4 'Base Date'.
2. The Contract now normally enters into legal effect. SC 1.1.50 'Letter of Acceptance'.
3. Unless the Parties agree otherwise, they must sign the Contract Agreement within 35 days after the Contractor receives the Letter of Acceptance. SC 1.6.
4. Unless otherwise stated in the Particular Conditions, the CD is within 42 days after the Contractor receives the Letter of Acceptance. The Engineer must give a Notice stating the CD not less than 14 days before the CD. SC 1.1.7 'Commencement Date' and SC 8.1.
5. SC 1.1.84 'Time for Completion' and SC 8.2.
6. SC 1.1.24 'Date of Completion'.
7. Unless otherwise stated in the Contract Data, the DNP is one year, as it may be extended. SC 1.1.27 'Defects Notification Period'.
8. This certificate is normally issued within 28 days after the DNP. SC 11.9 and 1.1.62 'Performance Certificate'.
9. This period is normally two years after expiry of the DNP. SC 11.10 and 1.1.65 'Plant'.

2 THE EMPLOYER

This Clause provides for important obligations of the Employer including: to give the Contractor right of access to, and possession of, the Site; to give reasonable assistance to the Contractor to allow it to obtain Laws of the Country and permits or approvals; to ensure that the Employer's Personnel and the Employer's other contractors cooperate with the Contractor; to advise the Contractor of any material change in the Employer's arrangements for financing the Contract; to make available Site data in the Employer's possession and items of reference (as defined); and, finally, to make available any Employer-Supplied Materials and/or Employer's Equipment for the Contractor's use which are listed in the Specification.

--ooOOoo--

2.1 Right of Access to the Site

The Employer shall give the Contractor right of access to, and possession of, all parts of the Site within the time (or times) stated in the Contract Data. The right and possession may not be exclusive to the Contractor. If, under the Contract, the Employer is required to give (to the Contractor) possession of any foundation, structure, plant or means of access, the Employer shall do so in the time and manner stated in the Specification. However, the Employer may withhold any such right or possession until the Performance Security has been received.

If no such time is stated in the Contract Data, the Employer shall give the Contractor right of access to, and possession of, those parts of the Site within such times as may be required to enable the Contractor to proceed in accordance with the Programme or, if there is no Programme at that time, the initial programme submitted under Sub-Clause 8.3 [*Programme*].

If the Contractor suffers delay and/or incurs Cost as a result of a failure by the Employer to give any such right or possession within such time, the Contractor shall be entitled subject to Sub-Clause 20.2 [*Claims for Payment and/or EOT*] to EOT and/or payment of such Cost Plus Profit.

However, if and to the extent that the Employer's failure was caused by any error or delay by the Contractor, including an error in, or delay in the submission of, any of the applicable Contractor's Documents, the Contractor shall not be entitled to such EOT and/or Cost Plus Profit.

The Employer shall give the Contractor right of access to, and possession of, all parts of the Site within the time or times stated in the Contract Data. The right and possession may not be exclusive to the Contractor. If, under the Contract, the Employer is required to give possession of any foundation, structure, plant or means of access, the Employer shall do so in the time and manner stated in the Specification.

If no such time is stated in the Contract Data, the Employer shall give the Contractor right of access to, and possession of, those parts of the Site within such times as may be required to enable the Contractor to proceed in accordance with the Programme.

If the Contractor suffers delay and/or incurs Cost as a result of failure by the Employer to give such right or possession, the Contractor shall be entitled, subject to Sub-Clause 20.2, to EOT and/or payment of such Cost plus Profit.

Commentary

(i) Main Changes from RB/99:

(1) The Employer must give the Contractor right of access to, and possession of, all parts of the Site within the time or times stated in the Contract Data instead of as stated in the Appendix to Tender as provided for in Sub-Clause 2.1 of RB/99.

(2) Whereas the Appendix to Tender in RB/99 had shown the time for access as being a fixed number of days after the Commencement Date, in the Contract Data in RB/17 the time for access is shown as a fixed number of days after the Contractor receives the Letter of Acceptance or, if the Contractor is to be given access to different parts of the Site at different times, the times when the Contractor is to be given access to them.

(3) Whereas RB/99 had provided that, if no time was stated in the Appendix to Tender, the Employer would give the Contractor right of access as might be required to enable the Contractor to proceed with its programme, RB/17 provides that, where no such time is stated in the Contract Data, the Employer shall give the Contractor right of access within such times as may be required to enable it to proceed with the Programme (as defined) or, if there is none, the initial programme submitted under Sub-Clause 8.3.

(ii) Related Clauses / Sub-Clauses: 2.5 [*Site Data and Items of Reference*], 4.2 [*Performance Security*], 4.4 [*Contractor's Documents*], 4.10 [*Use of Site Data*], 4.13 [*Rights of Way and Facilities*], 4.15 [*Access Route*], 8.3 [*Programme*], 16.2 [*Termination by Contractor*] and 20.2 [*Claims for Payment and/or EOT*].

(iii) Analysis:

(1) The Employer's obligation

The Employer is required to give the Contractor the 'right' (i.e., the legal right) of access to, as well as possession of, the Site. It is not required to provide 'means of access' or physical access unless this is specified in the

Contract.[1] Accordingly, to obtain physical access, the Contractor may be obliged, by its own means, to build an access road or airport, where the Site is a remote area of land, or to provide access by ship or helicopter where the Site is at sea.[2] Similarly, the Employer is not responsible for preparing the Site by the construction of, for example, a concrete foundation for the installation of gas turbines or other structures or plant unless this is provided for by the Specification.[3]

Once the Contractor has gained physical access then, in the case of a new project, it is entitled to 'undisturbed' or 'quiet' possession of the Site from the Employer.[4] However, the extent to which the Employer may be bound, if at all, to protect the Contractor from interferences by third parties with the Contractor's possession will depend upon the terms of the contract[5] and the governing law.

(2) Contractor not necessarily entitled to whole Site

The Employer is not necessarily required to give right of access and possession immediately of the whole Site.[6] Instead, it must give right of access and possession of 'all parts of the Site within the time (or times) stated in the Contract Data'[7] implying that the Contractor may receive different parts of the Site at different times.[8]

1. The Contractor is deemed to have satisfied itself about 'requirements for access' (Sub-Clause 4.10(e)) and as to the 'suitability and availability of the access routes to the Site' (Sub-Clause 4.15) at the tender stage.
2. For example, in the latter case, involves the laying of underwater piping on the seabed.
3. *See* Sub-Clause 2.1, first paragraph. Pursuant to this paragraph, the Employer may withhold right of access or possession until it has received the Performance Security.
4. Under English law, Atkin Chambers, *Hudson's Building and Engineering Contracts* (14th edn, Sweet & Maxwell, London, 2020) 455-458 (paras 3-088 to 3-089).
5. *See*, e.g., Sub-Clause 2.3 requiring the Employer to ensure that the Employer's Personnel and the Employer's other contractors, if any, on or near the Site cooperate with the Contractor; but *see also* Sub-Clause 4.21 making the Contractor responsible for the security of the Site.
6. *See* the commentary on Sub-Clause 1.1.74 **'Site'**, above.
7. Sub-Clause 2.1, first paragraph.
8. This is confirmed by the form of Contract Data which envisages that the Contractor may, depending upon the Employer's election, be given access to different parts of the Site at different times.

For example, if the Contract involved the construction of a 100-kilometre-long toll road, it could be sufficient to give the Contractor access to the first 10 kilometres[9] and then, as the Contractor progresses, in 10-kilometre segments thereafter. If no time (or times) is (are) stated in the Contract Data (because, e.g., the Parties have neglected to insert this information), the Employer is required to give right of access to the Contractor to enable it to proceed in accordance with either:

(1) the Programme, which is a newly defined term in RB/17 meaning a time programme of the Contractor to which the Engineer has given, or is deemed to have given, a Notice of No-objection under Sub-Clause 8.3;[10] or
(2) if there is no Programme, the initial programme which the Contractor has submitted under Sub-Clause 8.3 [*Programme*].[11]

Consequently, if the Engineer has not given a Notice of No-objection to the Contractor's initial programme, the Employer must give right of access to the Contractor on the date or dates stipulated by the Contractor in that programme, whether the Engineer should later object to it or not.

(3) Contractor's right not necessarily exclusive

The Contractor's right and possession of either parts of, or the whole, Site 'may not be exclusive'.[12] Other contractors of the Employer, as well as other third parties (such as public authorities or private utilities), may have to work on or near the Site at the same time. Thus, a housing contractor engaged to build housing units on a greenfield site[13] may be required to allow for the contractor or contractors installing utilities (fresh water and waste water piping, electrical wiring and telecommunications facilities) to work on the site concurrently – indeed, their programmes may need to dovetail with the programme of the contract for the housing units. In this case, information about the planned activities

9. *FIDIC DBO Contract Guide* (FIDIC, 2011) 26.
10. Sub-Clause 1.1.66 '**Programme**'.
11. Sub-Clause 8.3 (b) expressly provides that any programme submitted by the Contractor under that Sub-Clause must state the date or dates that each part of the Site is to be given to the Contractor, as stated in the Contract Data or, if none is stated, 'the dates the Contractor requires the Employer to give right of access to and possession of (each part of) the Site'.
12. Sub-Clause 2.1, first paragraph.
13. Denoting a previously undeveloped site.

of the utility contractor(s) should have been set forth in the invitation to tender documents for the housing contract[14] so as to allow tenderers for that contract to take account and plan for their presence on the site in their tenders.[15]

(4) Delayed access and possession

It is vital that the Employer, who will usually, but not always, be the owner of the Site, give the Contractor right of access and possession on time, as stated in the Contract Data (or the Programme or initial programme), as otherwise the project may be in critical delay, with possibly serious consequences.

If the Employer is late in doing so and the Contractor suffers critical delay and/or incurs Cost, then, as provided in the third paragraph, the Contractor will be entitled, subject to Sub-Clause 20.2, to an EOT and/or payment of such Cost plus Profit.[16] Where the Employer is very late in giving right of access or possession of the Site (or parts of it), this may be a material breach of the Contract entitling the Contractor to give a Notice of intention to terminate the Contract[17] and claim damages.

(iv) Related Law: Under the common law, a contractor who occupies a site to perform work under a construction contract is in the position of a holder of a licence or a licensee.[18]

(v) Improvements: Unlike the FIDIC forms, some standard forms of construction contract authorise the Contractor to request the Employer to

14. In this connection:

> [t]he work to be carried out by [other parties having access to the Site] should be described in the tender documents [...], so that tenderers may anticipate the consequences.
>
> *The FIDIC Contracts Guide* (2nd edn, FIDIC, 2022) 108.

15. *See* Sub-Clause 4.6 [*Co-operation*] and the commentary on this Sub-Clause below.
16. The Contractor is entitled to Cost Plus Profit in this case, as the Employer's delay amounts to a breach of the Contract.
17. Under Sub-Clause 16.2.1(e). *See also* Sub-Clause 16.2.1(f).
18. Julian Bailey, *Construction Law* (3rd edn, London Publishing, UK, 2020) vol 2, 700 (para. 8.12). In this context, a 'licence' is an authority to enter on and be on land, which would otherwise be a trespass or prohibited, David M Walker, *The Oxford Companion to Law* (Clarendon Press, Oxford, 1980) 769.

supply information about its legal right, title or other interest in the Site.[19] Unless this information is provided in the tender dossier, this seems reasonable. At a minimum, tenderers should be warned if there is any issue or dispute about the Employer's legal right to the Site and/or ability to give the Contractor full possession.

--ooOOoo--

2.2 Assistance

If requested by the Contractor, the Employer shall promptly provide reasonable assistance to the Contractor so as to allow the Contractor to obtain:

(a) copies of the Laws of the Country which are relevant to the Contract but are not readily available; and
(b) any permits, permissions, licences or approvals required by the Laws of the Country (including information required to be submitted by the Contractor in order to obtain such permits, permissions, licences or approvals):
   (i) which the Contractor is required to obtain under Sub-Clause 1.13 [*Compliance with Laws*];
   (ii) for the delivery of Goods, including clearance through customs; and
   (iii) for the export of Contractor's Equipment when it is removed from the Site.

If requested by the Contractor, the Employer shall promptly provide reasonable assistance to the Contractor so as to allow it to obtain: (a) copies of the Laws of the Country which are not readily available and (b) any permits, permissions, licences or approvals which the Contractor is required to obtain by such Laws.

19. *See* the US form Engineers Joint Contract Documents Committee, *Standard General Conditions of the Construction Contract* (EJCDC) Document D-700 (2016), art. 5.01 B, which provides that this is to allow the contractor, among other things, to file a mechanic's or construction lien against the land.

Commentary

(i) Main Changes from RB/99: This Sub-Clause is essentially the same as Sub-Clause 2.2 in RB/99 (where it was entitled 'Permits, Licences or Approvals'), except that:

(1) in relation to the Employer's assistance the parenthetical '(where he is in a position to do so)' has been deleted;
(2) the Employer is now required to provide reasonable assistance to the Contractor 'promptly';
(3) the Employer is now required to assist the Contractor 'so as to allow the Contractor to obtain' copies of the Laws of the Country instead of (as in RB/99) the Employer having itself to obtain the Laws for the Contractor;
(4) 'permissions' have now been added to 'permits, licences or approvals' in sub-paragraph (b); and
(5) in addition to assisting the Contractor to obtain permits, permissions, licences or approvals, the Employer is now required to assist the Contractor to obtain 'information required to be submitted by the Contractor in order to obtain such permits, permissions, licences or approvals'.

(ii) Related Clauses / Sub-Clauses: 1.3 [*Notices and Other Communications*], 1.4 [*Law and Language*], 1.13 [*Compliance with Laws*], 2.3 [*Employer's Personnel and Other Contractors*], 4.16 [*Transport of Goods*] and 4.17 [*Contractor's Equipment*].

(iii) Analysis: In developing countries where the Red Book is commonly used, the public administration and/or legal system may neither be advanced nor efficient. Consequently, the Contractor may have difficulty procuring copies of its Laws, as well as information about permits, permissions, licences and/or approvals (including information about how to apply for them).[20] In some countries, even with the assistance of a local lawyer, it can be difficult to obtain copies of local Laws.

An Employer from the Country, especially a public body, should be in a position to help. Therefore, the Employer is required promptly to provide 'reasonable assistance' in this respect to the Contractor, when requested

20. *See* **Section 6 Challenges of a Less-Developed Law** of **Chapter II Applicable Law** above. *See also* Sub-Clause 1.13(b).

to do so,[21] but does not guarantee that its assistance will be effective. Consequently, assuming the Employer has made a reasonable effort to assist the Contractor,[22] it has no liability in the probably unlikely event that its help should be unavailing.

(iv) Related Law: Consistent with Sub-Clause 2.2, the UNIDROIT Principles provide for a general duty of cooperation between parties to a contract: '[e]ach party shall cooperate with the other party when such co-operation may reasonably be expected for the performance of that party's obligations'.[23]

--ooOOoo--

2.3 Employer's Personnel and Other Contractors

The Employer shall be responsible for ensuring that the Employer's Personnel and the Employer's other contractors (if any) on or near the Site:

(a) co-operate with the Contractor's efforts under Sub-Clause 4.6 [*Co-operation*]; and
(b) comply with the same obligations which the Contractor is required to comply with under sub-paragraphs (a) to (e) of Sub-Clause 4.8 [*Health and Safety Obligations*] and under Sub-Clause 4.18 [*Protection of the Environment*].

The Contractor may require the Employer to remove (or cause to be removed) any person of the Employer's Personnel or of the Employer's other contractors (if any) who is found, based on reasonable evidence, to have engaged in corrupt, fraudulent, collusive or coercive practice.

21. *See* Sub-Clause 1.3 [*Notices and Other Communications*] for the form such a 'request'.
22. '[I]t would not be reasonable for the Contractor to expect the Employer's assistance to extend to anything which the Contractor can do himself/herself [...].' *The FIDIC Contracts Guide* (2nd edn, FIDIC, 2022) 110.
23. Art. 5.1.3 (*Co-operation between the parties*) of the UNIDROIT Principles. *See also* Sub-Clauses 2.3 [*Employer's Personnel and Other Contractors*] and 4.6 [*Co-operation*] of RB/17.

The Employer shall be responsible for ensuring that the Employer's Personnel and the Employer's other contractors (if any): (a) cooperate with the Contractor's efforts under Sub-Clause 4.6 and (b) comply with the same obligations as the Contractor is required to comply with under Sub-Clauses 4.8 and 4.18.

The Contractor may require the Employer to remove any of the Employer's Personnel or of its other contractors who have engaged in corrupt practice.

<u>Commentary</u>

(i) Main Changes from RB/99:

(1) The Employer is now responsible for ensuring compliance by the Employer's Personnel and the Employer's other contractors 'near' the Site, and not only 'on' the Site as in Sub-Clause 2.3 of RB/99.

(2) The Employer's Personnel and the Employer's other contractors must comply with 'the same obligations' relating to health, safety and protection of the environment as those with which the Contractor must comply (and not merely 'take actions similar to those which the Contractor is required to take' in relation to these matters as in RB/99).

(3) The Contractor may require the Employer to remove any of the Employer's Personnel or of its other contractors (if any) that is found to have engaged in corrupt or fraudulent practice, which is a new provision.

(ii) Related Clauses / Sub-Clauses: 3.8 [*Meetings*], 4.6 [*Co-operation*], 4.8 [*Health and Safety Obligations*], 4.18 [*Protection of the Environment*] and 16.2 [*Termination by Contractor*].

(iii) Analysis: This Sub-Clause places a duty on the Employer to ensure, among other things, that the Employer's Personnel and the Employer's other contractors (if any) on or near the Site cooperate with the Contractor. This is the counterpart of a reciprocal duty of the Contractor under Sub-Clause 4.6 to cooperate with the Employer's Personnel, other contractors of the Employer, public authorities and private utilities employed on or near the Site. Such mutual cooperation is essential for the proper execution of any construction contract.

The Employer is further required to ensure that the Employer's Personnel and the Employer's other contractors comply with the same obligations in relation to health, safety and protection of the environment[24] as the Contractor, as it would be self-defeating to require the Contractor comply with them and not insist on their equal observance by others within the Employer's control on or near the Site.

The new right of the Contractor to require the Employer to remove any of the Employer's Personnel or any person of the Employer's other contractors found, based on reasonable evidence, to have engaged in corrupt or fraudulent practice reflects FIDIC's dedication to fighting corruption.[25] The evidence must be sufficient to convince a reasonable Employer.

(iv) Related Law: Sub-Clauses 2.3 and 4.6 are consistent with the general duty of cooperation between the parties provided for by the UNIDROIT Principles:

> Each party shall cooperate with the other party when such co-operation may reasonably be expected for the performance of that party's obligations.[26]

(v) Improvements: Often, the Contractor may be merely one of a number of contractors of the Employer working together on or near the Site; e.g., in the case of a hydroelectric project, there may be separate contractors for the civil works (e.g., the dam, tunnels and building works), mechanical works (e.g., the turbines and gates) and electrical works (e.g., the electrical generator), respectively.[27] In this case, it needs to be made clear both in the general project programme and during the execution of the Works on Site (where adjustments may need to be made to fit actual circumstances), who, whether it be the Employer or a consultant of the Employer or a contractor, will be responsible for the overall coordination of these different activities to ensure that they are executed in a harmonious way and that each does not interfere unduly with another. *RB/17 does not address this issue – that is, the issue of who has the power and duty of coordinating performance under multiple construction contracts – either in this Sub-Clause or in Sub-Clause 4.6 [Co-operation].*

24. Provided for in sub-paras (a) to (e) of Sub-Clause 4.8 and Sub-Clause 4.18.
25. *See* the commentary on Sub-Clauses 15.2.1(h) and 16.2.1(j) below, which contain similar wording, and where difficulties with it are discussed.
26. Art. 5.1.3 [*Co-operation between the parties*].
27. Indeed, the Employer may itself be directly performing work on or near the Site with its own staff and labour, as well.

As the Employer is in contract with each contractor, the Employer is in a position to carry out such coordination itself or, if it prefers, to delegate it, for example, to its engineering consultant. *Allocation of the power and duty of coordination needs to be provided for expressly in the relevant contracts.*[28] Otherwise, it will be unclear, where there are several contractors of the Employer working at similar times on or near the same Site, who has this responsibility.[29]

--ooOOoo--

28. For an example of such a provision *see* art. 6.1 *Owner's Right to Perform Construction and to Award Separate Contracts* of American Institute of Architects ('AIA') Document A201-2017 *General Conditions of the Contract for Construction* which provides as follows:

> **§6.1.1** The term 'Separate Contractor(s)' shall mean other contractors retained by the Owner under separate agreements. The Owner reserves the right to perform construction or operations related to the Project with the Owner's own forces, and with Separate Contractors retained under Conditions of the Contract substantially similar to those of this Contract, including those provisions of the Conditions of the Contract related to insurance and waiver of subrogation.
> **§6.1.2** When separate contracts are awarded for different portions of the Project or other construction or operations on the site, the term 'Contractor' in the Contract Documents in each case shall mean the Contractor who executes each separate Owner-Contractor Agreement.
> **§6.1.3** The Owner shall provide for coordination of the activities of the Owner's own forces and of each Separate Contractor with the Work of the Contractor, who shall cooperate with them. The Contractor shall participate with any Separate Contractors and the Owner in reviewing their construction schedules. The Contractor shall make any revisions of its construction schedule deemed necessary after a joint review and mutual agreement. The construction schedules shall then constitute the schedules to be used by the Contractor, Separate Contractors, and the Owner until subsequently revised.
> **§6.1.4** Unless otherwise provided in the Contract Documents, when the Owner performs construction or operations related to the Project with the Owner's own forces or with Separate Contractors, the Owner or its Separate Contractors shall have the same obligations and rights that the Contractor has under the Conditions of the Contract, including, without excluding others, those stated in Article 3, this Article 6 and Articles 10, 11 and 12.

29. *See* under **(iv) Related Law** of the commentary on Sub-Clause 4.6 [*Co-operation*] below.

2.4 Employer's Financial Arrangements

The Employer's arrangements for financing the Employer's obligations under the Contract shall be detailed in the Contract Data.

If the Employer intends to make any material change (affecting the Employer's ability to pay the part of the Contract Price remaining to be paid at that time as estimated by the Engineer) to these financial arrangements, or has to do so because of changes in the Employer's financial situation, the Employer shall immediately give a Notice to the Contractor with detailed supporting particulars.

If the Contractor:

(a) receives an instruction to execute a Variation with a price greater than ten percent (10%) of the Accepted Contract Amount, or the accumulated total of Variations exceeds thirty percent (30%) of the Accepted Contract Amount;
(b) does not receive payment in accordance with Sub-Clause 14.7 [*Payment*]; or
(c) becomes aware of a material change in the Employer's financial arrangements of which the Contractor has not received a Notice under this Sub-Clause,

the Contractor may request and the Employer shall, within 28 days after receiving this request, provide reasonable evidence that financial arrangements have been made and are being maintained which will enable the Employer to pay the part of the Contract Price remaining to be paid at that time (as estimated by the Engineer).

The Employer's arrangements for financing its contractual obligations shall be detailed in the Contract Data. If the Employer intends to make any material change (affecting its ability to pay the Contract Price) to these financial arrangements, or has to do so because of changes in its financial situation, the Employer shall immediately give a Notice with particulars to the Contractor.

If the Contractor: (a) receives either an instruction to execute a Variation, or an accumulated total of Variations, exceeding specified values; (b) does not receive payment in accordance with Sub-Clause 14.7; or (c) becomes aware of a material change in the Employer's financial arrangements of which it has not received a Notice, the Contractor may request, and the Employer must – within 28 days – provide, reasonable evidence that financial arrangements are being maintained to enable the Employer to pay the remaining Contract Price.

Commentary

(i) Main Changes from RB/99: Compared to Sub-Clause 2.4 of RB/99, but consistent with Sub-Clause 2.4 [*Employer's Financial Arrangements*] of GB/08, the Contractor's rights are reinforced:

(1) the Employer must now detail its arrangements for financing the Contract in the Contract Data;
(2) whereas Sub-Clause 2.4 of RB/99 required the Employer to give notice to the Contractor if it intended to make any material change to its financial arrangements for paying the Contract Price, the Employer is now required, instead, to give a Notice to the Contractor 'immediately' if it either intends to make any material change '(affecting the Employer's ability to pay the part of the Contract Price remaining to be paid [...])' or has to do so 'because of changes in the Employer's financial situation'; and
(3) whereas, under RB/99, the Contractor could make a request for reasonable evidence of the Employer's financial arrangements at any time, now the Contractor may only do so in the specific cases of sub-paragraphs (a), (b) and (c) listed in the third paragraph.

(ii) Related Clauses / Sub-Clauses: 1.3 [*Notices and Other Communications*], 13 [*Variations and Adjustments*], 14 [*Contract Price and Payment*], 16.1 [*Suspension by Contractor*] and 16.2 [*Termination by Contractor*].

(iii) Analysis:

(1) Employer's financial arrangements to be detailed in Contract Data

Sub-Clause 2.4 of RB/99 had provided, for the first time in the RB, an obligation on the Employer to submit to the Contractor, upon its request, reasonable evidence that financial arrangements had been made to pay the Contract Price. The Employer had no obligation to do so at the tender stage, though in 2011, FIDIC had recommended this.[30]

However, consistent with GB/08, the Employer is now required to detail its arrangements for financing the Contract in the Contract Data,[31] which would initially be included in the tender dossier. This is a positive change, as it allows the Contractor, at the tender stage, to satisfy itself that the Employer has sufficient funding to pay the Contract Price.[32]

As in the case of RB/99, if the Employer intends to make any material change to its financial arrangements, it must give a Notice to the Contractor, but the description of when it must do so is more detailed in the new Sub-Clause.

(2) Reasonable evidence of the Employer's financial arrangements

As stated above,[33] the circumstances in which the Contractor may request reasonable evidence that the Employer is maintaining the necessary financial arrangements are more limited than in RB/99.

What amounts to 'reasonable evidence' may be assessed by reference to how the Employer's arrangements for financing its contractual obligations were detailed in the Contract Data. If the Employer should want to change those arrangements in a material way, it would be reasonable to expect it to provide comparable details of changes in those arrangements (and supporting evidence, as appropriate).

Such evidence might include allocations to the project and their amounts in a state's official annual budget, loan documentation, guarantees from shareholders of the Employer or others and 'comfort' letters from banks. Thus:

> [I]f funding is being provided as a bank loan, or a loan or grant from an international financing institution (such as one of the bilateral or multilateral development banks) it may be possible to provide [...] copies of the written loan or grant agreement from the Employer's

30. 'Tenderer(s) should be informed of the source(s) of finance, their amount and related conditions for the proposed Works.' *FIDIC Procurement Procedures Guide* (FIDIC, 2011) 117.
31. *See* item **(i) Main Changes from RB/99** above.
32. If the Contractor should require further assurance in this respect, the Contractor may, as provided for as an option in RB/17, ask the Employer to supply a payment guarantee from a bank, *see* Annex G example form of payment guarantee by Employer included in RB/17.
33. *See* **(i) Main Changes from RB/99**.

> bank or funding agency [...]. Or, if funding is coming from a national or governmental source, an officially authorised formal letter confirming the arrangements and the availability of funds should be provided [...].[34]

In the obverse situation, an Employer may wish similarly to be notified by a Contractor of adverse changes in the Contractor's financial situation. For a clause on this subject, *see* Sub-Clause 4.25 [*Changes in the Contractor's Financial Situation*] of GB/08.

(3) Sanctions for failure to comply

If the Employer fails to comply with Sub-Clause 2.4, the Contractor may, after giving not less than 21 days' Notice, suspend, or reduce the rate of, work under Sub-Clause 16.1 [*Suspension by Contractor*] and, if the failure continues, may ultimately give a Notice to terminate the Contract under Sub-Clause 16.2 [*Termination by Contractor*].[35]

(iv) Related Law: The UK's Privy Council,[36] when interpreting the corresponding provision of RB/99, has confirmed that an Employer cannot simply rely on its wealth, or on general assurances, to avoid complying with a request from a Contractor under Sub-Clause 2.4. As stated by this court, this Sub-Clause:

> required more than showing that 'the employer is able to pay', let alone that it was enthusiastic about the project [...] what was required was evidence of 'positive steps' on the part of the employer which showed that 'financial arrangements' had been made to pay sums due under the Agreement.[37]

In that case, the public Employer concerned had failed to confirm, as the Contractor had requested, that the government's cabinet had approved

34. *The FIDIC Contracts Guide* (2nd edn, FIDIC, 2022) 113.
35. After giving a Notice of intention to terminate which goes unremedied and without prejudice to any other rights which the Contractor may have. Sub-Clause 16.2, first sentence.
36. The Privy Council or, more accurately, the Judicial Committee of the Privy Council, is a UK tribunal which, among other things, hears appeals from the highest courts of the Commonwealth countries.
37. *NH International (Caribbean) Ltd v National Insurance Property Development Company Ltd (Trinidad and Tobago)* [2015] UKPC 37 [para. 22].

the funds which the arbitrator found to be necessary for the Contractor to be paid. For this reason, the Contractor was held to be justified in terminating the contract pursuant to Clause 16 of RB/99.

The UNIDROIT Principles refer to an analogous situation to that in Sub-Clause 2.4:

> A party who reasonably believes that there will be a fundamental non-performance by the other party may demand adequate assurance of due performance and may meanwhile withhold its own performance. Where this assurance is not provided within a reasonable time the party demanding it may terminate the contract.[38]

(v) Improvements: The Contractor's right to request reasonable evidence that financial arrangements have been made to enable the Employer to pay the Contract Price could be broadened to cover *financial arrangements to enable the Employer to perform its contractual obligations to the Contractor*, as the Contractor needs to be assured about them too, e.g., (1) if the Employer is not the owner of the Site, the Employer's financial arrangements for leasing or otherwise securing its availability and (2) the Employer's obligation to supply any promised Materials or Employer's Equipment.

--ooOOoo--

2.5 Site Data and Items of Reference

The Employer shall have made available to the Contractor for information, before the Base Date, all relevant data in the Employer's possession on the topography of the Site and on sub-surface, hydrological, climatic and environmental conditions at the Site. The Employer shall promptly make available to the Contractor all such data which comes into the Employer's possession after the Base Date.

The original survey control points, lines and levels of reference (the "items of reference" in these

38. Art. 7.3.4 (*Adequate assurance of due performance*) of the UNIDROIT Principles.

> Conditions) shall be specified on the Drawings and/or in the Specification or issued to the Contractor by a Notice from the Engineer.

The Employer shall have made available to the Contractor before the Base Date all relevant data in the Employer's possession on the topography, subsurface, hydrological, climatic and environmental conditions at the Site and, after the Base Date, shall make available all such data as comes into the Employer's possession.

The original survey control points, lines and levels of reference shall be specified on the Drawings and/or in the Specification or in a Notice from the Engineer.

Commentary

(i) Main Changes from RB/99:

(1) Sub-Clause 2.5 of RB/99 dealt with another subject, Employer's Claims, which is now addressed in Sub-Clause 20.1 [*Claims*];
(2) the first paragraph of Sub-Clause 2.5 of RB/17 is similar to the first two sentences of Sub-Clause 4.10 of RB/99 except that data on both the topography[39] and climatic conditions at the Site have been added;
(3) the last sentence of the first paragraph of Sub-Clause 4.10 of RB/99, providing that '(t)he Contractor shall be responsible for interpreting all such data', is now essentially the first sentence of Sub-Clause 4.10 of RB/17; and
(4) the second paragraph of Sub-Clause 2.5 is derived, in part, from the first sentence of Sub-Clause 4.7 of the RB/99.[40]

(ii) Related Clauses / Sub-Clauses: 1.3 [*Notices and Other Communications*], 1.9 [*Delayed Drawings or Instructions*], 4.7 [*Setting Out*], 4.10 [*Use of Site Data*], 4.11 [*Sufficiency of the Accepted Contract Amount*], 4.12 [*Unforeseeable Physical Conditions*], 4.18 [*Protection of the Environment*] and 8.5 [*Extension of Time for Completion*].

---

39. *See* the definition of topography under the heading *(3) The Site data and items of reference to be made available* under **(iii) Analysis** below.
40. But *see also* the first sentence of Sub-Clause 4.7 of RB/17.

(iii) Analysis:

(1) The Employer's Site information

When a project is being prepared, and before inviting tenders, the Employer should have a strong interest in having a comprehensive site exploration programme carried out.[41] The more factual information tenderers receive about subsurface, geotechnical and other conditions at the Site, the less they will need to make their own investigations or include contingencies or allowances for the unknown in their tenders, thereby allowing for lower tender prices. Studies have shown that a contractor's claims for differing site conditions can be reduced significantly if comprehensive site investigation information is provided at the tender stage.[42] Comprehensive information from the Employer will also mean that tenders can be made on the same or similar basis, thereby making it easier for the Employer and its engineering consultant to compare and evaluate tenders.[43]

For many projects, the Employer will have carried out studies concerning feasibility (to verify the likelihood of the project being economically advantageous and otherwise viable) and various subsurface, hydrological and environmental investigations.[44]

---

41. An effective site investigation has been estimated as usually costing 1% to 2% of the overall construction cost. Site Investigation Steering Group, *Effective Site Investigation* (ICE Publishing, London, 2013) 11. A site investigation of subsurface conditions typically involves the following steps:

    - preliminary activities such as: desk studies, selection of techniques and, planning;
    - field work such as: hydrographical surveys, geophysical survey and, in-situ geological and geotechnical work;
    - laboratory testing; and
    - interpretation and reporting.

    David Kinlan, *Adverse Physical Conditions & The Experienced Contractor* (Delft Academic Press, Delft, the Netherlands, 2014) 11-12.
42. William W Edgerton (ed), *Recommended Contract Practices for Underground Construction* (US) Society for Mining, Metallurgy and Exploration (SME), ProQuest Ebook Central (2008) 13-14 and David Kinlan, *Adverse Physical Conditions & The Experienced Contractor* (Delft Academic Press, Delft, the Netherlands, 2014) 5.
43. *FIDIC Procurement Procedures Guide* (FIDIC, 2011) 47.
44. *Ibid.*

(2) The Employer's obligation to make available Site data and items of reference

Sub-Clause 2.5 provides that the Employer must make available to the Contractor before the Base Date, that is, 28 days before the latest date for the submission of the Tender, all 'relevant'[45] data in its possession about the Site,[46] and must make available to it any such data that may later come into its possession.[47] Any limitations on the data provided or doubts about its reliability should also be disclosed. *'Data' refers to factual information and not interpretative reports.*[48] Thus, the Employer is under no obligation to provide tenderers with interpretative reports or opinions about factual information, although it may sometimes do so together with factual information.

(3) The Site data and items of reference to be made available

The expression 'all relevant data' in the Employer's possession would include both data which it had obtained from investigations for the Works and data obtained by others, including publicly available data which is in the Employer's possession.[49]

45. This requires the Employer to decide on what data is 'relevant'. As the Contractor may have a different - and more knowledgeable - view on this subject, it may want to amend this provision, where it is in a position to do so.
46. The Site is broadly defined as the 'places where the Permanent Works are to be executed and to which Plant and Materials are to be delivered, and any other places specified in the Contract as forming part of the Site'. *See* the commentary on Sub-Clause 1.1.74 '**Site**' above.
47. As the Contractor will have based its Tender price on the information available to it by the Base Date (*see* Sub-Clauses 4.10 and 4.11), any data provided by the Employer thereafter may, in suitable circumstances, entitle the Contractor to claim an EOT and/or its additional Cost.
48. Data is defined as 'facts and statistics used for reference or analysis'. *Concise Oxford English Dictionary* (10th edn, rev'd, OUP, Oxford, 2002). Although the line between factual and interpreted data is not always clear, for a description of the typical content of factual and interpretative reports, respectively, *see* Appendix K of *Effective Site Investigation* prepared by the Site Investigation Steering Group (ICE publishing, London, 2013). Note that bore logs are regarded as interpreted data and not as factual data, *see* David Kinlan, *Adverse Physical Conditions and the Experienced Contractor* (Delft Academic Press, Delft, the Netherlands, 2014) 25-27.
49. *The FIDIC Contracts Guide* (2nd edn, FIDIC, 2022) 115.

Data as to:

(i) 'topography of the Site' is information '(r)elating to the surface characteristics of the ground, particularly mapping both natural and artificial surface features, such as mountains, rivers, roads, and railways';[50]
(ii) 'sub-surface' conditions are the conditions below the surface, including those within a body of water and those below the riverbed or seabed;
(iii) 'hydrological' conditions mean the flows of water, including those in rivers and the underwater currents in open seas; and
(iv) 'environmental' conditions include such matters as the (known or suspected) presence of pollutants.[51]

The subsurface site information supplied in the tender documents may comprise: (a) geophysical data, (b) bore logs or vibrocore logs, and (c) laboratory test results.[52]

'Make available' means either supplying such information directly to tenderers or indicating where it can be examined or obtained (whether at the Employer's premises, the Site or elsewhere), for example:

> the information [...] may be too bulky to distribute or it may be available at a central point (e.g. borehole cores) or it may only be available on film or tape or in reference volumes such as hydrological and meteorological records.[53]

While the Employer is required to make all relevant data available by the Base Date, as a practical matter, it should already have been made available before tenderers inspect the Site,[54] when it is most useful to them. The Employer must also make available such data as comes into its possession after the Base Date until the end of the Contract.

50. Christopher A Gorse and others, *A Dictionary of Construction, Surveying & Civil Engineering* (OUP, Oxford, 2012) 449.
51. *The FIDIC Contracts Guide* (2nd edn, FIDIC, 2022) 115.
52. David Kinlan, *Adverse Physical Conditions & The Experienced Contractor* (Delft Academic Press, Delft, the Netherlands, 2014) 18.
53. *Guide to the Use of FIDIC Conditions of Contract for Works of Civil Engineering Construction* (4th edn, FIDIC, 1989) 60.
54. Pursuant to Sub-Clause 4.10 [*Use of Site Data*].

The Employer must also provide the items of reference (as defined in the second paragraph of Sub-Clause 2.5) to the Contractor to enable it to set out the Works on the Site.[55]

(4) Meaning of 'for information'

According to this Sub-Clause, Site information is provided, usually in the tender dossier, 'for information' and will therefore not normally become part of the Contract unless a specific exception is made, e.g., sometimes, in the case of a geotechnical report. By providing Site information 'for information', whether included in the Contract or not, the Employer will not usually be taken under English law, at least, to have 'warranted' the accuracy of it;[56] that is, it will not have promised that the information is true with the consequence that, if it were not, the Employer would be liable in damages to the Contractor. Accordingly, tenderers may not rely on the Employer for the truth of this information but must verify it by their own means.[57]

On the other hand, after providing that the Contractor is deemed to have satisfied itself as to the Accepted Contract Amount, Sub-Clause 4.11 provides that the 'Contractor shall be deemed to [...] have based the Accepted Contract Amount on the data [provided by the Employer]', which arguably provides the Contractor with a basis to claim if the data

---

55. The Contractor is required to verify the accuracy of the items of reference and any errors in them are to be dealt with as provided in Sub-Clause 4.7 [*Setting Out*].
56. *Co-operative Insurance Society Ltd v Henry Boot Scotland Ltd* [2002] EWHC 1270 (TCC) (2003), 19 Const L J no 2 109. This case notes that the fact that a ground investigation report is referred to in contract drawings does not have the effect of incorporating the report into the contract or of making it a 'Contract Document', *see* para. 49 of this judgment. *See also* Julian Bailey, *Construction Law* (3rd edn, London Publishing, UK, 2020) vol 1, 327-328 (para. 4-166) ('An owner will not usually be taken to warrant the accuracy of information provided to the contractor').
57. *See* final award, ICC case 10619 (2002) where it was stated of a 'Materials Report' contained in invitation for tender documents (comprising RB/87) and provided 'for information only' that:

> that statement should have been an incentive for bidders to carefully verify by their own means the reliability of the relevant information. ICC Int'l Ct Arb Bull, vol 19 (2008), no 2, 85, 90-91 (commentary 52, 56-57).

is wrong.[58] Moreover, any data provided by the Employer may be taken into account, together with other relevant information the Contractor is deemed to have inspected and examined (*see* Sub-Clause 4.10), in determining whether the Contractor has encountered 'Unforeseeable' physical conditions at the Site entitling it to relief under Sub-Clause 4.12.[59]

(5) Disclaimers and qualifications

Some Employers will go further and expressly disclaim responsibility for the Site data which they may have supplied by providing, for example, that 'the Employer waives any responsibility or liability for the accuracy or sufficiency of the Site data in the tender documents'.[60]

While such 'disclaimer' or 'no reliance' clauses may, in some common law jurisdictions, be effective,[61] they may face difficulty under US law.[62] Under US law, disclaimers with respect to *interpretations and opinions* drawn from subsurface data may be upheld (as equally competent

58. *See* the commentary on Sub-Clause 4.11 [*Sufficiency of the Accepted Contract Amount*] below.
59. *See* final award, ICC case 5597 (1990), ICC Int'l Ct Arb Bull, vol 2 (1991), no 1, 19, where an erroneous description of site conditions in the Contract was found to support a claim under RB/77 for unforeseeable adverse site conditions.
60. This subject is discussed with reference to Australian cases in David Kinlan, *Adverse Physical Conditions & The Experienced Contractor* (Delft Academic Press, Delft, the Netherlands, 2014) 36-39.
61. Julian Bailey, *Construction Law* (3rd edn, London Publishing, UK, 2020) vol 1, 329 -331 (paras 4.169-172).
62. According to one source, disclaimers are unenforceable in US Federal Government construction contracts:

> The rationale is that bidders have no realistic opportunity to investigate subsurface conditions and must rely on the government's representations. The government owns the property and has the time and resources to become informed regarding its characteristics. The contractor is responsible only for information that can be gleaned during a reasonable pre-bid inspection of the surface.
>
> Bruce Jervis, 'Project Owners Disclaim Their Own Subsurface Information' (13 January 2017) 6(2) Construction Pro Network.

professionals may differ on the subject), whereas disclaimers of *subsurface data itself* (which tenderers may have difficulty verifying) may be much harder to justify.[63]

While RB/17 contains no express disclaimer, a Contractor's ability to rely on data received from the Employer is qualified by:

(1) Sub-Clause 4.10 [*Use of Site Data*] providing, among other things, that the Contractor shall be responsible for interpreting all data referred to in Sub-Clause 2.5 and, to the extent practicable, for carrying out its own inspections and examinations of the Site and elsewhere in preparing its Tender; and

(2) Sub-Clause 4.11 [*Sufficiency of the Accepted Contract Amount*] providing that the Contractor shall be deemed, among other things, to have based the Accepted Contract Amount on the various matters, including the data, referred to in Sub-Clause 4.10, and its interpretations, and that this Amount shall be deemed to cover generally all of the Contractor's obligations under the Contract and all things necessary to execute the Works, subject, however, to Sub-Clause 4.12 [*Unforeseeable Physical Conditions*] and as otherwise stated in the Contract.

(6) ICC case upholding the Employer's liability

Nevertheless, where an Employer provides tenderers with a technical document which is specified to be 'for information only', the Employer will not necessarily escape liability should it prove to be inaccurate. Thus, in the case of a road project based on RB/87, the Employer had provided tenderers with a 'Materials Report' which proved to be erroneous. In upholding the Contractor's claim for an EOT and extra costs, the tribunal stated:

> one cannot expect from a bidder, within the short period of time left for him to prepare his bid, to investigate on matters of local resources of materials over (sic) the Employer's findings which are deemed to result from lengthy prior queries in subsoil and are supported by graphs, diagrams, samples and other probatory materials; a bidder is justifiably required to interpret the data made available to him; he is not required to expedite new thorough investigations which the

63. Philip L Bruner and Patrick J O'Connor, Jr, *Bruner and O'Connor on Construction Law* (Thomson Reuters, St Paul, MN, 2017) vol 4A, 711-715 (s 14:34).

> Employer says in good faith to have carefully carried on presumably for months if not years, in the interest of the Works. Interpreting data is one thing; undertaking new investigations in a region plus or minus close to a road of about 180 kms to check whether the required materials exist or not as described in quantity and quality, at the locations identified by the Employer, is not a thing which can reasonably be said to pertain to a bidder.[64]

(iv) Related Law: Under the traditional common law rule, the Contractor will bear the risk of unforeseen subsurface conditions.[65] Under English law, 'an owner will be under no general obligation [...] to make available to the contractor information in its possession (including as to site conditions) that may be helpful to the contractor in performing its work or pricing its tender'.[66] Thus, the affirmative obligation on the Employer in Sub-Clause 2.5 to disclose information in the Employer's possession regarding Site conditions imposes a duty on it going beyond English common law.[67]

On the other hand, the position under US and civil law is different. Under US law, the well-settled general rule is that:

> where the owner possesses special knowledge, not shared by the contractor, which is vital to the performance of the contract, the owner has an affirmative duty to disclose such knowledge. He cannot remain silent, with impunity.[68]

64. *See* final award, ICC case 10619 (2002), ICC Int'l Ct Arb Bull, vol 19 (2008), no. 2, 85, 90-91 (para. 73) (commentary 52, 56-57). RB/87 included in Sub-Clause 11.1 [*Inspection of Site*] the following language: 'The Contractor shall be deemed to have based his Tender on the data made available by the Employer and/or his own inspection and examination, [...]' which is not dissimilar to the language in Sub-Clause 4.11 of RB/17 (mentioned earlier): 'The Contractor shall be deemed to [...] have based the Accepted Contract Amount on the data [from the Employer] [...].'
65. Philip L Bruner and Patrick J O'Connor, Jr, *Bruner and O'Connor on Construction Law* (Thomson Reuters, St Paul, MN, 2017) vol 4A, 653-662 (s 14:24). S/W, 123 and Julian Bailey, *Construction Law* (3rd edn, London Publishing, UK, 2020) vol 1, 327-329 (paras 4.165-4.168).
66. Julian Bailey, *Construction Law* (3rd edn, London Publishing, UK, 2020) vol 1, 328 (para. 4-166).
67. *Ibid.*, 328, fn. 528 (para. 4-166).
68. Philip L Bruner and Patrick J O'Connor, Jr, *Bruner and O'Connor on Construction Law* (Thomson Reuters, St Paul, MN, 2017) vol 4A, 738-9

The employer's duty to disclose may be violated where *either* the employer:

> fails to disclose facts material to the contractor's performance known or accessible only to the owner, knowing that those facts are not known to or reasonably discoverable by the contractor,

or 'actively conceals discovery of material facts from the contractor'.[69] On the other hand, to the extent that non-disclosed information:

> is readily available to the contractor from other sources, any inference of prejudice to the contractor as a result of the nondisclosure is negated.[70]

The position under the civil law, as illustrated by French law, is also different from the English common law position. As mentioned in **Chapter II Applicable Law** above, as a development of the principle of good faith, the French Civil Code provides that:

> The party who knows information which is of decisive importance for the consent [that is, the decision to contract] of the other party, must inform that party of it where the latter legitimately does not know the information or trusts the informed party.[71]

(s 14:41). In the US, this rule is sometimes referred to as the 'superior knowledge' doctrine.

69. Philip L Bruner and Patrick J O'Connor, Jr, *Bruner and O'Connor on Construction Law* (Thomson Reuters, St Paul, MN, 2017) vol 4A, 739 (s 14.41). These principles apply to private and public works contracts alike. For private contracts, *see* Steven G M Stein, *Construction Law*, LexisNexis, vol 2, 5-89-94 (s 5.03[2][d]) and especially *Anderson v Golden* 569 F Supp 122 (S.D. Ga 1982). For public works contracts *see* the aforementioned section of *Bruner and O'Connor on Construction Law*.
70. Philip L Bruner and Patrick J O'Connor, Jr, *Bruner and O'Connor on Construction Law* (Thomson Reuters, St Paul, MN, 2017) vol 4A, 739 (s 14.41).
71. French Civil Code, art. 1112-1. This same provision adds that this duty to inform 'does not apply to an assessment of the value of the act of performance'. *See* **Section 4 Common Law and Civil Law Compared – 4.3.2 Duty of Disclosure** of **Chapter II Applicable Law** above, especially fn. 104.

Information of 'decisive importance' is defined as information that:

> has a direct and necessary relationship with the content of the contract or the status of the parties.[72]

--ooOOoo--

2.6 Employer-Supplied Materials and Employer's Equipment

> If Employer-Supplied Materials and/or Employer's Equipment are listed in the Specification for the Contractor's use in the execution of the Works, the Employer shall make such materials and/or equipment available to the Contractor in accordance with the details, times, arrangements, rates and prices stated in the Specification.
>
> The Contractor shall be responsible for each item of Employer's Equipment while any of the Contractor's Personnel is operating it, driving it, directing it, using it, or in control of it.

If Employer-Supplied Materials and/or Employer's Equipment are listed in the Specification for the Contractor's use, the Employer shall make such materials and/or equipment available to the Contractor in accordance with the Specification.

The Contractor shall be responsible for each item of Employer's Equipment while the Contractor's Personnel are using it.

<u>Commentary</u>

(i) Main Changes from RB/99:

(1) This Sub-Clause corresponds, as regards Employer's Equipment, to the first paragraph of Sub-Clause 4.20 [*Employer's Equipment and Free-Issue Material*] in RB/99.

(2) As regards the details and other information about Employer-Supplied Materials, this Sub-Clause basically refers to the Specification, whereas the third and fourth paragraphs of Sub-Clause 4.20 of RB/99 had provided more information about them (referring to them as 'free issue materials').

72. *Ibid.*

(3) Sub-Clause 4.20 of RB/99 had foreseen that the Employer would supply materials (but not Employer's Equipment) free of charge to the Contractor, whereas the new Sub-Clause foresees that, like Employer's Equipment, materials would be paid for.

(ii) Related Clauses / Sub-Clauses: 1.15 [*Limitation of Liability*], 4.9.2 [*Compliance Verification System*], 4.19 [*Temporary Utilities*], 7.1 [*Manner of Execution*], 7.2 [*Samples*], 8.5 [*Extension of Time for Completion*] and 14.3 [*Application for Interim Payment*].

(iii) Analysis: This Sub-Clause envisages that the Employer may agree to supply to the Contractor for use in the execution of the Works:

(1) Materials; and
(2) Employer's Equipment, which includes all types of apparatus and equipment excluding Plant which has not been taken over by the Employer.[73]

Complete details of such Materials and Employer's Equipment, including rates and prices, are to be included in the Specification.[74]

While FIDIC acknowledges that it is usually preferable to let the Contractor select and procure its own equipment and materials, nevertheless, the Employer may elect otherwise and accept the risk of doing so in, for example, the case of an Employer's cranes (or its other equipment) which are permanently allocated to the Site and/or any plant and/or materials which will take so long to procure that the Works would be completed sooner if they are ordered before the Parties enter into the Contract.[75]

Another example is where an item of Equipment represents a major cost, e.g., a large tunnel boring machine valued at USD 10 million or more. In such a case, to relieve the Contractor's cash flow, an Employer might purchase the machine itself and make it available to the Contractor for

73. *See* Sub-Clause 1.1.32 '**Employer's Equipment**'. This is in addition to temporary utilities which the Employer may provide the Contractor pursuant to Sub-Clause 4.19 [*Temporary Utilities*].
74. Any amount due from the Contractor for such Materials and Employer's Equipment would be a deduction in the Contractor's Statement(s) pursuant to Sub-Clause 14.3 (vi).
75. *The FIDIC Contracts Guide* (2nd edn, FIDIC, 2022) 117.

the purposes of the Contract. A further example is where it would be economical for the Employer to purchase Materials in bulk and then to resell or otherwise supply them to the Contractor.

(iv) Improvements: Sub-Clause 14.3(ix) provides for the Employer to be paid for the Contractor's use of the Employer's utilities by deductions from the Contractor's Statements without the need for the Employer to comply with Sub-Clause 20.2. It seems anomalous that the same procedure does not apply to Employer-Supplied Materials and Employer-Supplied Equipment for which the Contractor may be required to pay the Employer.

--ooOOoo--

3 The Engineer

This Clause provides for the appointment of the Engineer, its duties and authority, the instructions which it may issue to the Contractor and how the Employer may replace the Engineer. It provides for how the Engineer may appoint an Engineer's Representative and assistants, as well as for how the Engineer is to proceed 'to agree or determine' any matter (as defined) or Claim between the Parties. Finally, it provides that the Engineer or the Contractor's Representative may require the other to attend a management meeting.

--ooOOoo--

3.1 The Engineer

The Employer shall appoint the Engineer, who shall carry out the duties assigned to the Engineer in the Contract.

The Engineer shall be vested with all the authority necessary to act as the Engineer under the Contract.

If the Engineer is a legal entity, a natural person employed by the Engineer shall be appointed and authorised to act on behalf of the Engineer under the Contract.

The Engineer (or, if a legal entity, the natural person appointed to act on its behalf) shall be:

(a) a professional engineer having suitable qualifications, experience and competence to act as the Engineer under the Contract; and
(b) fluent in the ruling language defined in Sub-Clause 1.4 [*Law and Language*],

Where the Engineer is a legal entity, the Engineer shall give a Notice to the Parties of the natural person (or any replacement) appointed and authorised to act on its behalf. The authority shall not take effect until this Notice has been received by both Parties. The Engineer shall similarly give a Notice of any revocation of such authority.

The Employer shall appoint the Engineer who shall carry out the duties assigned to it in the Contract. The Engineer or, if a legal entity, a natural person appointed to act on its behalf, shall be a qualified professional engineer fluent in the ruling language defined in Sub-Clause 1.4. Where the Engineer is a legal entity, the Engineer shall give a Notice to the Parties of the natural person authorised to act on its behalf.

Commentary

(i) Main Changes from RB/99:

(1) Sub-Clauses 3.1 and 3.2 of RB/17 effectively replace Sub-Clause 3.1 in RB/99.
(2) While the first sentence of Sub-Clause 3.1 in RB/17 is basically the same as in RB/99, the rest of Sub-Clause 3.1, dealing principally with where the Engineer is a legal entity, was not addressed in RB/99 and is new.

(ii) Related Clauses / Sub-Clauses: 1.3 [*Notices and Other Communications*], 1.4 [*Law and Language*], 2 [*The Employer*], 3 [*The Engineer*], 12 [*Measurement and Valuation*], 13 [*Variations and Adjustments*] and 20.2 [*Claims for Payment and/or EOT*].[1]

1. As the Engineer features throughout the Conditions, this is only a partial selection of related Clauses and Sub-Clauses.

(iii) Analysis:

(1) The need for, and person of, the Engineer

The first sentence of the Sub-Clause provides that the Employer shall appoint the Engineer. While the Sub-Clause specifies no time by which the Employer should do so, the name and address of the Engineer are required to be stated in the Contract Data[2] which would normally be sent out as part of the tender dossier.[3] Accordingly, the Conditions envisage that the Engineer will normally have been appointed by the date of the invitation to tender. Given the Engineer's important role under the Conditions, this seems only appropriate as the identity of the Engineer will be a relevant consideration for tenderers when calculating their tender prices.

In view of the numerous duties assigned to the Engineer by the Conditions,[4] an RB contract cannot be performed without the Engineer.[5] Together with the Contractor, the Engineer is essential to the execution of works under an RB contract.

Thus, at the date of tender, in most cases, there will already exist a contract between the Employer and the Engineer[6] pursuant to which, in addition to possibly having agreed to prepare initial studies and design the Works, the Engineer agrees, on behalf of the Employer, to administer the execution of the Works under the Contract by the Contractor.

The person appointed as Engineer has traditionally been an independent consulting engineer who, as a professional, has in common law countries been either a natural person or a partnership and not a corporation or other legal entity. However, increasingly today, engineering firms may be

2. *See* Sub-Clause 1.1.35 '**Engineer**' and the form of Contract Data included in RB/17.
3. *FIDIC Procurement Procedures Guide* (FIDIC, 2011) 115 (which refers to the 'appendix to tender' the old name for 'Contract Data').
4. For example, in inspecting and supervising the Contractor's work under Clause 7, in certifying payments to the Contractor under Clause 14 and in determining matters or Claims between the Parties under Sub-Clause 3.7.
5. *See* final award, ICC case 10892 (2002), ICC Int'l Ct Arb Bull, vol 19/no 2, 2008, 91-93 (commentary 57-59) (after finding that a contract based on RB/87 was unworkable without an Engineer, it was held that the Contractor had tacitly accepted the Employer as the Engineer).
6. *See* FIDIC's standard form of contract between the Employer and the Engineer entitled 'Client/Consultant Model Services Agreement' (5th edn, 2017), also referred to as the 'White Book'.

corporations and the new Sub-Clause 3.1 recognises that the Engineer may be a legal entity (e.g., a corporation) and makes provision for who will act on its behalf.

In some cases, the Engineer will be a natural person who is a member of the staff of the Employer. Thus, where the Employer is a state-owned body, it is not uncommon for it to appoint one of its own employees as the Engineer.[7] While feasible, this may not, however, be in the interests of an Employer, as the appointment of an *independent* consulting engineer as the Engineer is likely to attract lower tender prices.

(2) Duties of the Engineer

This Sub-Clause further requires that the Engineer carries out the duties assigned to the Engineer in the Contract. These duties include principally the following:

(1) possibly, to design the Works (if the Engineer is the designer), for example, as indicated by Sub-Clauses 1.1.30, 1.9 and 13.1;
(2) to administer the Contract and control the proper and timely execution of the Works, as indicated by Sub-Clause 3.5 and Clauses 7, 8, 9, 10, 11 and 15;
(3) to value the Works and/or certify both payments and the status of the execution of the Works under Clauses 10, 11, 12, 13, 14 and 15; and
(4) to agree or determine matters or Claims of either Party under Sub-Clause 3.7 and Clause 20.[8]

An advantage of the Engineer also being the designer[9] is that this may better ensure that the Works are executed consistently with the design. This may also be less costly as the designer will already be familiar with the project. For these reasons, Bill Howard, FIDIC's former President, says that:

7. Indeed, this has also been the practice of local authorities in England. *See* J.B. Wikeley *Municipal Engineering Law and Administration* (CR Books 1964) 28-29.
8. It is implicit that the Employer is responsible for ensuring that the Engineer carries out these duties. This is even explicit in the case of Sub-Clause 21.4.3, fourth paragraph: 'The Employer shall be responsible for the Engineer's compliance with the DAAB decision.'
9. As FIDIC recommends, *see Guidance for the Preparation of Particular Conditions*, 20.

> Employers/Owners are well advised to give strong consideration to utilizing the designer as the Engineer if the Employer/Owner is satisfied with the designer's services and if the designer has the required qualifications to serve as the Engineer.[10]

On the other hand, where a new person has been appointed as the Engineer, that person can cast a fresh eye on the design and perhaps spot issues which the former consultant may have overlooked or not disclosed. Where the Engineer has been the designer, it may be more reluctant to acknowledge design errors, and less inclined to treat claims from the Contractor on this subject fairly to the extent that they may expose the Engineer to liability to the Employer.[11]

(3) Qualifications of the Engineer

In order to be qualified to act, the Engineer[12] is required, among other things, to be 'a professional engineer', that is, an engineer who carries out professional duties analogous to those of an architect under a building contract, as the term 'engineer' alone in English can refer also to a contractor carrying out construction works.[13] But, even in the common law world, the term 'professional engineer' may have widely different meanings. Thus, English law does not require registration or qualification before a person can practice as an engineer or term itself an 'engineer'.[14] In France, while an architect who is licensed (by the *Ordre des Architectes*) is required for a building project and while the title of

10. Interview of William S Howard, then President of FIDIC, 22 October 2019.
11. However, to this objection, Bill Howard replies that:

> in consciously doing so, an Engineer would be damaging their reputation and, in some cases, violating the code of ethics of the profession, exposing himself/herself to negligence claims/litigation and would likely be only delaying and/or increasing the economic consequences his/her action. While it is not unusual for the Employer to appoint a person other than the designer as the Engineer, doing so can actually add to the complexity of the project and increase the possibility of disputes. In addition, including a DAAB in the project would arguably minimize the potential reluctance of the designer in the role of the Engineer to fail to acknowledge designer error. In the end, the highest probability for a successful project occurs when all parties act with integrity and within the standards of their profession.

Interview of William S Howard, then President of FIDIC, 22 October 2019.

12. Or, if a legal entity, the natural person appointed to act on its behalf.
13. Stephen Furst and Vivian Ramsey, *Keating on Construction Contracts* (11th edn, Sweet & Maxwell, London, 2021) 428-429 (paras 14-012-14-013).
14. *Ibid.*

engineer (*ingénieur*) is protected (an engineering degree from a school of engineering approved by the French State is required), there is otherwise no legal requirement that, to perform the functions of a FIDIC Engineer (the equivalent of a *maître d'oeuvre* in France),[15] one needs to hold a licence.[16] On the other hand, in the United States, practically all States require engineers to be licensed in order to practise engineering.[17] Thus, the absence of a more precise description of 'professional engineer' in Sub-Clause 3.1 may simply result from the lack of an international consensus on what qualifications are required.

Accordingly, should the original Engineer (who, as mentioned above, would normally already be named in the Contract Data, and therefore whose qualifications would already be known and accepted) need to be replaced, the Parties may want to detail in the Particular Conditions what they intend by the requirement that the Engineer has 'suitable qualifications, experience and competence to act'[18] under the Contract.

The Engineer must be fluent in the ruling language of the Contract defined in Sub-Clause 1.4 but, like the Engineer's Representative,[19] is not required (as are, however, assistants to the Engineer pursuant to Sub-Clause 3.4) to be fluent in the language for communications stated in the Contract Data.

(iv) Related Law: The duties of the Engineer under RB/17 are discussed in the commentary on Sub-Clause 3.2 [*Engineer's Duties and Authority*] below. The Engineer is, for most (if not all) purposes, the agent of the Employer.[20]

---

15. *See* **Section 4 Common Law and Civil Law Compared – 4.4.1 Contract Administrator (*Maître D'Oeuvre*) *v* Engineer** of **Chapter II Applicable Law** above.
16. The author is grateful to Mr Vincent Leloup, Exequatur, Nantes, France, for this information.
17. A Elizabeth Patrick and others (eds), *The Annotated Construction Law Glossary* (ABA Publishing, ABA, Chicago, IL, 2010). According to the same source, the requirements for obtaining an engineering licence in most States include minimum age, formal education and type of degree, years of experience, recommendations, proof of good moral character, passing an examination, and paying a fee.
18. Sub-Clause 3.1, para. (a).
19. *See* Sub-Clause 3.3 [*The Engineer's Representative*].
20. For international legal principles on the subject of agency *see* Chapter 2: Formation and Authority of Agents of the UNIDROIT Principles, which contains detailed rules relating to the formation and authority of agents.

(v) Improvements: To an international user, the role of the Engineer under an RB contract may be difficult to grasp as no single clause or sub-clause sets out what the powers and duties of this central figure in the Contract are.[21] As the Engineer has radically different powers (e.g., to instruct Variations by itself and to decide on claims between the Contractor and the Employer) from those, for example, of a civil law contract administrator, this is most unsatisfactory in an international standard form of contract. Accordingly, the Conditions should include a clause or sub-clause describing the overall general role of the Engineer, thereby relieving users of having to glean its role from the many sub-clauses which refer to the Engineer.[22]

--ooOOoo--

3.2 Engineer's Duties and Authority

Except as otherwise stated in these Conditions, whenever carrying out duties or exercising authority, specified in or implied by the Contract, the Engineer shall act as a skilled professional and shall be deemed to act for the Employer.

The Engineer shall have no authority to amend the Contract or, except as otherwise stated in these Conditions, to relieve either Party of any duty, obligation or responsibility under or in connection with the Contract.

The Engineer may exercise the authority attributable to the Engineer as specified in or necessarily to be implied from the Contract. If the Engineer is required

21. The absence of any such clause is a carry-over from the English conditions of contract upon which the RB was originally based, namely, the Conditions of Contract of the United Kingdom's Institution of Civil Engineers, *see* **Section 3.1.1** of **Chapter 1 General Introduction** above. They contained no such clause presumably because English parties would have been already familiar with the Engineer's role and therefore it called for no explanation or description.
22. *See* **Section 4 Common Law and Civil Law Compared – 4.4.1 Contract Administrator (*Maître D'Oeuvre*) *v* Engineer** of **Chapter II Applicable Law** above.

to obtain the consent of the Employer before exercising a specified authority, the requirements shall be as stated in the Particular Conditions. There shall be no requirement for the Engineer to obtain the Employer's consent before the Engineer exercises his/her authority under Sub-Clause 3.7 [*Agreement or Determination*]. The Employer shall not impose further constraints on the Engineer's authority.

However, whenever the Engineer exercises a specified authority for which the Employer's consent is required, then (for the purposes of the Contract) such consent shall be deemed to have been given.

Any acceptance, agreement, approval, check, certificate, comment, consent, disapproval, examination, inspection, instruction, Notice, No-objection, record(s) of meeting, permission, proposal, record, reply, report, request, Review, test, valuation, or similar act (including the absence of any such act) by the Engineer, the Engineer's Representative or any assistant shall not relieve the Contractor from any duty, obligation or responsibility the Contractor has under or in connection with the Contract.

Except as otherwise stated in the Conditions, the Engineer shall act as a skilled professional and shall be deemed to act for the Employer. The Engineer shall have no authority to amend the Contract or, except as stated in these Conditions, to relieve either Party of any obligation in connection with the Contract.

The Engineer may exercise the authority attributable to it in the Contract. If the Engineer is required to obtain the consent of the Employer before exercising a specified authority, the requirements shall be as stated in the Particular Conditions, but there shall be no requirement for the Engineer to obtain the Employer's consent before acting under Sub-Clause 3.7. Whenever the Engineer exercises a specified authority, for the purposes of the Contract, any required consent shall be deemed to have been given. Any action or inaction by the Engineer shall not relieve the Contractor of any of its obligations.

Commentary

(i) Main Changes from RB/99:

The new Sub-Clause 3.2 is somewhat similar to Sub-Clause 3.1 of RB/99:

(1) the first two paragraphs are derived from sub-paragraphs (a) and (b) of the fifth paragraph of Sub-Clause 3.1 of RB/99;
(2) the first sentence states for the first time that the Engineer 'shall act as a skilled professional';
(3) the third paragraph states for the first time that the Engineer shall not be required to obtain the Employer's consent before the Engineer acts under Sub-Clause 3.7 (in RB/99 this was not stated in relation to Sub-Clause 3.5, the predecessor of Sub-Clause 3.7 in RB/17);
(4) the statement at the end of the third paragraph that the 'Employer shall not impose further constraints on the Engineer's authority' is now unqualified whereas Sub-Clause 3.1 of RB/99 had added 'except as agreed with the Contractor';
(5) the last paragraph contains a much more detailed description than Sub-Clause 3.1(c) of RB/99 of the actions (or inactions) of the Engineer which may not be construed as relieving the Contractor from any contractual duty or obligation and also now expressly includes in the description the actions (or inactions) of the Engineer's Representative or any assistant; and
(6) the last paragraph is no longer qualified (as was the corresponding language in Sub-Clause 3.1(c) of RB/99) by the important words '[e]xcept as otherwise stated in these Conditions'.

(ii) Related Clauses / Sub-Clauses: 1.3 [*Notices and Other Communications*], 2 [*The Employer*], 3 [*The Engineer*], 12 [*Measurement and Valuation*], 13 [*Variations and Adjustments*], 14.6 [*Issue of IPC*], 14.13 [*Issue of FPC*] and 20.2 [*Claims for Payment and/or EOT*].[23]

23. As the Engineer features throughout the Conditions, this is only a partial selection of related Clauses and Sub-Clauses.

(iii) Analysis:

(1) The Engineer's dual role[24]

The first paragraph states that, except as otherwise stated in the Conditions, whenever carrying out duties or exercising authority under the Contract, the Engineer 'shall act as a skilled professional and shall be deemed to act for the Employer'. As regards acting as a 'skilled professional', under the common law, this means that the Engineer shall act in accordance with the standard of reasonable skill and care generally required of a construction professional (i.e., without negligence).[25] The *Guidance* further notes that the Engineer should have due regard to both FIDIC's Code of Ethics for consulting engineers and the duty to prevent corruption and bribery as described in specified FIDIC publications.[26]

The statement that, except as otherwise stated in the Conditions, the Engineer is 'deemed to act for the Employer' may be somewhat confusing as the Engineer has a contract only with the Employer and therefore is necessarily always acting for the Employer, at least in the broad sense of that expression. What this statement and the exception are implying, or

24. For a comparison of the role of the Engineer under the RB with that of a contract administrator in a civil law country *see* **Section 4 Common Law and Civil Law Compared – 4.4.1 Contract Administrator (*Maître D'Oeuvre*) *v* Engineer** of **Chapter II Applicable Law** above.
25. This has been described as follows:

> a professional man should command the corpus of knowledge which forms part of the professional equipment of the ordinary member of his profession. He should not lag behind other ordinarily assiduous and intelligent members of his profession in knowledge of new advances, discoveries and developments in his field. He should have such awareness as an ordinarily competent practitioner would have of the deficiencies in his knowledge and the limitations on his skill. He should be alert to the hazards and risks inherent in any professional task he undertakes to the extent that other ordinarily competent members of the profession would be alert. He must bring to any professional task he undertakes no less expertise, skill and care than other ordinarily competent members of his profession would bring, but need bring no more. The standard is that of the reasonable average. The law does not require of a professional man that he be a paragon, combining the qualities of polymath and prophet. Bingham LJ in *Eckersley v Binnie & Partners* 1988 WL 624028, [1988] 18 Con. L.R., 80.

This is consistent with the required standard of care in Sub-Clause 3.3.1 of the FIDIC's Client/Consultant Model Services Agreement (5th edn, 2017) ('White Book').

26. *Guidance for the Preparation of Particular Conditions*, 20.

drawing attention to, is that, in accordance with traditional English construction contract practice, the Engineer has under the RB two distinct roles.[27] First, the Engineer acts for the Employer in supervising the work carried out by the Contractor, ensuring that the Contractor complies with the terms of the Contract, instructing Variations and verifying, through inspection and testing procedures under Clauses 7 and 9, that the work executed complies with the Specification. In these cases, the Engineer is 'deemed to act' for the Employer and therefore, in effect, as the Employer.

Second, there are other cases under the Conditions where the Engineer is required to act fairly or impartially[28] in its relations with the Parties, by certifying, determining or exercising discretion in the discharge of its professional duties. An obvious case is Sub-Clause 3.7 pursuant to which the Engineer is required, with respect to any matter or Claim referred to it by a Party, to act 'neutrally between the Parties',[29] consulting with them in an endeavour to reach agreement and, failing an agreement, to make a 'fair' determination of the matter or Claim. Similarly, under Sub-Clauses 14.6 and 14.13, the Engineer is required to make 'fair' assessments of amounts due to the Contractor in Payment Certificates.[30]

---

27. *See* the quotation from the English case *Sutcliffe v Thachrah*, [1974] A.C. 727 (1974), under **(iv) Related Law** below.
28. As a practical matter, there is no difference between the meaning of 'fairly' and 'impartially'. The dictionary gives as its first definition of 'fairly': 'with justice'. Its definition of 'impartial' is: 'treating all rivals or disputants equally'. *Concise Oxford English Dictionary* (10th edn, rev'd, OUP, Oxford, 2002).
29. The dictionary gives as its first definition of 'neutral' the following: 'impartial', 'belonging to an impartial state or group' and 'unbiased'. Thus, there is no practical difference between the meaning of 'neural' and the words 'fairly' and 'impartially'. *Concise Oxford English Dictionary* (10th edn, rev'd, OUP, Oxford, 2002).
30. This dual role of the Engineer is recognised in FIDIC's *Client/Consultant Model Services Agreement* (5th edn, 2017) ('White Book') in the following terms:

    > When acting as the engineer [...] the Consultant shall have the authority to act on behalf of the Client to the extent provided for in the Works Contract [...] If the Consultant is authorised under the Works Contract to certify, determine or exercise discretion in the discharge of its duties then the Consultant shall act fairly as go-between [*sic*] the Client and the contractor, exercising independent professional judgement and using reasonable skill, care and diligence (Sub-Clause 3.9.3).

These Sub-Clauses (3.7, 14.6 and 14.13), at least, appear to be what is intended by the words '[e]xcept as otherwise stated in these Conditions', as they expressly require Engineer to act 'neutrally' or 'fairly'. Indeed, these are the only provisions of the Conditions which explicitly require the Engineer to act in this way.

(2) When exercising discretion the Engineer must act fairly

Even though the Engineer is not explicitly required to act neutrally and fairly in relation to other provisions of the Conditions, where the Engineer is required to exercise discretion,[31] *as a practical matter, the Engineer is required to act neutrally and fairly.*

This is the case because, if the Contractor is dissatisfied with any action or inaction of the Engineer (whether, e.g., in assessing whether an item of Plant, Materials, design or workmanship is defective under Sub-Clause 7.5 [*Defects and Rejection*] or should be repaired or remedied under Sub-Clause 7.6 [*Remedial Work*] or when requested to issue a Taking-Over Certificate under Sub-Clause 10.1 [*Taking Over the Works and Sections*] or deciding to issue the Performance Certificate under Sub-Clause 11.9 [*Performance Certificate*]), it can always refer this action or inaction back to the Engineer as a Claim under Sub-Clause 3.7, pursuant to which the Engineer is expressly required to act 'neutrally' between the Parties and to make a 'fair' determination.

If the Engineer fails to make a neutral and fair determination, the Contractor (or, indeed, the Employer, if it considers it has been treated unfairly) may, if dissatisfied (and having expressed dissatisfaction by giving a NOD), refer the issue as a Dispute to the DAAB which, acting 'fairly and impartially between the Parties',[32] may:

> open up, review and revise any certificate, decision, determination, instruction, opinion or valuation of (or acceptance, agreement, approval, consent, disapproval, No-objection, permission, or similar act by) the Engineer that is relevant to the Dispute.[33]

31. Exercise discretion refers to exercise of 'the freedom to decide what should be done in a particular situation' (*Concise Oxford English Dictionary* (10th edn, rev'd, OUP, Oxford, 2002)). This is to be distinguished from where the Engineer acts for the Employer and solely in the Employer's interest, e.g., when instructing a Variation.
32. Rule 6.2 of the DAAB Rules.
33. Rule 5.1(k) of the DAAB Rules. While not expressly stated, this must exclude a final and binding determination of the Engineer under Sub-Clause 3.7.5

Accordingly, if the Engineer has not interpreted and applied the Contract correctly, the Engineer's action can be revised by the DAAB.[34] If the Contractor (or the Employer) is dissatisfied with the DAAB's decision, it may (having expressed dissatisfaction), in turn, refer the Dispute to arbitration. The arbitrator(s), who is (are) required to be impartial and independent of the Parties,[35] has, like the DAAB, full power to open up, review and revise any action of the Engineer, other than a final and binding determination, as well as any decision of the DAAB, other than a final and binding decision.[36] In making its award, the arbitrator(s) is (are) required to apply the governing law, take account of the Contract and any relevant trade usages.[37]

Thus, whenever the Contractor (or the Employer) is dissatisfied with an action or inaction of the Engineer under the Conditions, it can refer the issue (as a Claim) back to the Engineer for a 'neutral' and 'fair' determination, failing which (having given a NOD) it can refer the resulting Dispute to the DAAB and, finally, the arbitrator(s), who is (are) the final interpreter(s) of the Contract. *Consequently, to avoid having the Engineer's discretionary actions revised, the Engineer is always required, in effect, in the case of those actions, to act fairly, neutrally and in a manner consistent with the Contract.*

---

which the arbitrator(s) is, as well, precluded from opening up, reviewing and revising under Sub-Clause 21.6.

34. In an English case, counsel for the project manager (in the position of the Engineer) had argued that as the decisions of the project manager were 'not determinative' and could be referred to adjudication, the 'existence of these procedures has the effect of excluding any implied term that the project manager would act impartially'. The judge (Jackson J) gave this argument short shrift:

> This submission has surprising consequences. If (a) the project manager assesses sums due partially and in a manner which favours the employer, but (b) the adjudicator assesses those sums impartially and without favouring either party, then this is likely to lead to successive, expensive and time-consuming adjudications. I do not see how that arrangement could make commercial sense. *Costain v Bechtel Ltd.* [2005] EWHC 1018 (TCC), 2005 WL 3027218 [para 47].

35. Art. 11.1 of the ICC Rules of Arbitration.
36. Sub-Clause 21.6, second paragraph.
37. Art. 21 of the ICC Rules of Arbitration. *See also* the commentary on Sub-Clause 21.6 [*Arbitration*] below.

(3) Limits on the Engineer's authority

The Engineer, when purporting to act in its first role described above (i.e., 'for the Employer'),[38] is bound to act within the limits of its authority under its contract with the Employer and the Conditions. If the Engineer is required to obtain the Employer's consent with respect to any matter (e.g., instructing a Variation having a value above a certain amount pursuant to Sub-Clause 13.3),[39] this must be stated in the Particular Conditions,[40] so that the Contractor will know the position. However, there must be no requirement for the Engineer to obtain the Employer's consent before the Engineer acts under Sub-Clause 3.7, pursuant to which the Engineer is to act 'neutrally between the Parties' and make 'fair' determinations.[41]

Moreover, new Sub-Clause 3.2 contains the unqualified statement that, except as stated in the Particular Conditions, the Employer 'shall not impose further constraints on the Engineer's authority'.[42] RB/99 had stated that the Employer undertakes not to impose further constraints 'except as agreed with the Contractor'.[43] The new Sub-Clause no longer recognises that the Contractor might agree to further constraints.

As has long been the case under the RB,[44] the Contractor does not need to enquire whether the Engineer has the authority from the Employer to

38. Sub-Clause 3.2, first paragraph.
39. The World Bank's COPA requires the Engineer to obtain the consent in writing of the Employer before taking any action under Sub-Clauses 13.1 [*Right to Vary*] and 13.2 [*Value Engineering*] except that the Engineer may act under Sub-Clause 13.1 in an emergency situation or if the Variation would increase the Accepted Contract Amount by less than the percentage specified in the Contract Data. Sub-Clause 3.2, COPA.
40. FIDIC notes that the Employer's consent:

    [m]ust allow the Engineer to exercise its duties within the time limits required under the Contract, as any delay may entitle the Contractor to EOT and/or recover the additional costs he/she incurs for any delay caused by the Engineer waiting for the Employer's written consent.

    The FIDIC Contracts Guide (2nd edn, FIDIC, 2022) 123.

41. Sub-Clause 3.2, third paragraph.
42. *Ibid.*
43. Sub-Clause 3.1, third paragraph, RB/99.
44. *See* Sub-Clause 2.1 (b) of RB/87 providing that 'any requisite approval [of the Employer] shall be deemed to have been given by the Employer for any such authority exercised by the Engineer'.

take any action as Sub-Clause 3.2, fourth paragraph, states expressly that whenever the Engineer exercises an authority for which the Employer's consent is required 'such consent shall be deemed to have been given'.

(4) Contractor not relieved by Engineer's action (or inaction)

The last paragraph of Sub-Clause 3.2 makes clear that the Contractor cannot rely on any action, or failure to act, of the Engineer, the Engineer's Representative or any assistant, to excuse a failure of the Contractor to respect the Contract. Thus, for example, a Notice of No-objection, Taking-Over Certificate or Performance Certificate issued by the Engineer cannot relieve the Contractor of its obligations should it have failed to fulfil them.[45] Given the increased role of the Engineer in contract administration, including determining the Contractor's Claims, under RB/17 (as compared to RB/99) and the Contractor's interest to invoke – where it can – any concession by the Engineer to justify its position, this paragraph provides important protection to the Employer.

(iv) Related Law: Sub-Clause 3.2 gives effect to the long-standing English practice, incorporated into the RB, that the Engineer has two different roles to perform. As stated in an English case about an architect, which applies equally to an engineer:

> It has often been said, I think rightly, that the architect has two different types of function to perform. In many matters he is bound to act on his client's instructions, whether he agrees with them or not; but in many other matters requiring professional skill he must form and act on his own opinion.
>
> Many matters may arise in the course of the execution of a building contract where a decision has to be made which will affect the amount of money which the contractor gets. Under the R.I.B.A. [Royal Institute of British Architects] contract many such decisions have to be made by the architect and the parties agree to accept his decisions. For example, he decides whether the contractor should be reimbursed for loss under clause 11 (variation), clause 24 (disturbance) or clause 34 (antiquities); whether he should be allowed extra time (clause 23); or when work ought reasonably to have been completed (clause 22). And, perhaps most important, he has to decide whether work is defective. These decisions will be reflected in the amounts contained in certificates issued by the architect.

45. This is consistent with the second paragraph of Sub-Clause 21.6 [*Arbitration*] providing that the arbitrators have full power to open up, review and revise any certificate or opinion of the Engineer.

The building owner and the contractor make their contract on the understanding that in all such matters the architect will act in a fair and unbiased manner and it must therefore be implicit in the owner's contract with the architect that he shall not only exercise due care and skill but also reach such decisions fairly, holding the balance between his client and the contractor.[46]

(v) Improvements:

(1) For the benefit of international users, at least outside the Commonwealth, FIDIC should make explicit in the Conditions or *Guidance*: (a) when the Engineer is expected to act as the Employer's agent 'for the Employer' and (b) when it is to exercise discretion and, in effect, to act neutrally and fairly. The relevant Clauses or Sub-Clauses should be identified in each case so that international users are left in no doubt about this matter.

(2) Sub-Clause 3.2 could be supplemented to provide that the duties and authority of the Engineer may not be changed without the Contractor's consent which shall not be unreasonably withheld.[47]

(3) The last paragraph of Sub-Clause 3.2 might usefully be broadened to extend beyond the Engineer, the Engineer's Representative or any assistant to refer to the Employer's Personnel as, for example, the Employer's Personnel (and not merely the Engineer) may be inspecting the Contractor's work pursuant to Sub-Clause 7.3 [*Inspection*]. As Clause 3 relates to the Engineer, this might be done, for example, in Clause 2 relating to the Employer.

--ooOOoo--

46. *Sutcliffe v Thachrah* (per Lord Reid), [1974] A.C. 727, 737. In that case the House of Lords held that, when issuing interim certificates, an architect did not act as an arbitrator or quasi-arbitrator, was under a duty to act fairly in making its valuation and was liable in an action in negligence brought by the building owner. By contrast, under US law an architect or engineer *may* have immunity in those circumstances. Philip Bruner and Patrick O'Connor, *Bruner & O'Connor on Construction Law* (Thomson Reuters, St Paul, MN, 2016) vol 5, 769 (s 17.82).

47. *See* for such a provision s 4.1.2 of American Institution of Architects (AIA) Document A 201-2017 *General Conditions of the Contract for Construction*.

3.3 The Engineer's Representative

The Engineer may appoint an Engineer's Representative and delegate to him/her in accordance with Sub-Clause 3.4 [*Delegation by the Engineer*] the authority necessary to act on the Engineer's behalf at the Site, except to replace the Engineer's Representative.

The Engineer's Representative (if appointed) shall comply with sub-paragraphs (a) and (b) of Sub-Clause 3.1 [*The Engineer*] and shall be based at the Site for the whole time that the Works are being executed at the Site. If the Engineer's Representative is to be temporarily absent from the Site during the execution of the Works, an equivalently qualified, experienced and competent replacement shall be appointed by the Engineer, and the Contractor shall be given a Notice of such replacement.

3.4 Delegation by the Engineer

The Engineer may from time to time assign duties and delegate authority to assistants, and may also revoke such assignment or delegation, by giving a Notice to the Parties, describing the assigned duties and the delegated authority of each assistant. The assignment, delegation or revocation shall not take effect until this Notice has been received by both Parties. However, the Engineer shall not delegate the authority to:

(a) act under Sub-Clause 3.7 [*Agreement or Determination*]; and/or
(b) issue a Notice to Correct under Sub-Clause 15.1 [*Notice to Correct*].

Assistants shall be suitably qualified natural persons, who are experienced and competent to carry out these duties and exercise this authority, and who are fluent in the language for communications defined in Sub-Clause 1.4 [*Law and Language*].

Each assistant, to whom duties have been assigned or authority has been delegated, shall only be authorised to issue instructions to the Contractor to the extent defined by the Engineer's Notice of delegation under this Sub-Clause. Any act by an assistant, in accordance with the Engineer's Notice of delegation, shall have the same effect as though the act had been an act of the Engineer. However, if the Contractor questions any instruction or Notice given by an assistant, the Contractor may by giving a Notice refer the matter to the Engineer. The Engineer shall be deemed to have confirmed the assistant's instruction or Notice if the Engineer does not respond within 7 days after receiving the Contractor's Notice, by giving a Notice reversing or varying the assistant's instruction or Notice (as the case may be).

The Engineer may appoint an Engineer's Representative and delegate to it the authority to act on the Engineer's behalf at the Site. The Engineer's Representative shall comply with Sub-Clause 3.1 (a) and (b) and be the whole time at the Site.

The Engineer may also from time to time delegate authority to assistants, but not authority to act under Sub-Clause 3.7 and/or issue a Notice to Correct under Sub-Clause 15.1.

Assistants shall be suitably qualified natural persons who are fluent in the language for communications defined in Sub-Clause 1.4. Each assistant shall only be authorised to issue instructions to the extent defined by the Engineer's Notice of delegation. Any act by an assistant, in accordance with the Engineer's Notice of delegation, shall have the same effect as though it had been an act of the Engineer. The Contractor may question any instruction or Notice given by an assistant by referring the matter to the Engineer.

Commentary

(i) Main Changes from RB/99:

(1) Reflecting the increased role of the Engineer under RB/17, the Engineer's Representative has been reintroduced by the inclusion of an entirely new Sub-Clause dealing with it, Sub-Clause 3.3 [*Engineer's Representative*].[48]

48. Sub-Clause 3.3 [*Engineer's Representative*] had no counterpart in RB/99, although provision had been made for an Engineer's Representative in all

(2) New Sub-Clause 3.4 [*Delegation by the Engineer*] corresponds to Sub-Clause 3.2 in RB/99 with the following significant changes:
   (a) the description of who assistants may include, which was contained in Sub-Clause 3.2 of RB/99, has been omitted, but a helpful description of them is now contained in the *Guidance*;[49]
   (b) the qualification 'unless otherwise agreed by both Parties' has been removed from the provision that the Engineer shall not delegate the authority to act under Sub-Clause 3.7 (the successor to Sub-Clause 3.5 in RB/99);
   (c) the Engineer may not delegate authority to issue a Notice to Correct under Sub-Clause 15.1 to the Engineer's Representative or an assistant, which is new; and
   (d) if, by a Notice to the Engineer, the Contractor questions any instruction or Notice given by an assistant, the Engineer shall be deemed to have confirmed the instruction or Notice if the Engineer does not respond by a Notice within 7 days, which is new.

(ii) Related Clauses / Sub-Clauses: 1.3 [*Notices and Other Communications*], 1.4 [*Law and Language*], 3 [*The Engineer*] and 15.1 [*Notice to Correct*].

(iii) Analysis:

(1) Appointment of Engineer's Representative (Sub-Clause 3.3)

It appears from the first sentence of Sub-Clause 3.3 that Sub-Clause 3.4 relating to delegation by the Engineer to assistants applies equally to delegation by the Engineer to the Engineer's Representative (just as under RB/99[50] a resident engineer was considered as an assistant to whom the Engineer could delegate duties). Thus, the appointment of an Engineer's Representative should be notified to the Parties in the same way as delegation of authority to assistants is notified to them under

---

previous editions of the RB. RB/99 had referred in its Sub-Clause 3.2 [*Delegation by the Engineer*] to a 'resident engineer'. Under RB/17, the Engineer's Representative is to carry out delegated duties in such a way that the Contractor's Representative (provided for in Sub-Clause 4.3) has a known individual counterpart with which to interact in respect of the day-to-day contract administration on the Site.

49. *Guidance for the Preparation of Particular Conditions*, 20.

50. *See* Sub-Clause 3.2 [*Delegation by the Engineer*] of RB/99.

Sub-Clause 3.4.[51] Similarly, the restrictions in Sub-Clause 3.4 on what matters the Engineer may delegate to assistants apply equally to delegation to the Engineer's Representative.

The second paragraph of Sub-Clause 3.3 makes clear that the Engineer's Representative, who must have the basic qualifications of the Engineer,[52] is expected, like a resident engineer, to be based at the Site for the whole time that the Works are being executed there. Therefore, where the Site is in a remote location and communications with it are difficult, the Engineer may wish to delegate more authority than usual to the Engineer's Representative and to assistants, pursuant to Sub-Clause 3.4.

(2) Delegation by the Engineer (Sub-Clause 3.4)

The Engineer may not delegate the authority to 'act under Sub-Clause 3.7 [*Agreement or Determination*]'.[53] It is understandable that the Engineer may not delegate its authority to determine a matter or Claim under Sub-Clause 3.7 as this directly affects the Parties' rights. But was it really appropriate – or intended – that the Engineer not delegate its authority to consult with the Parties in an endeavour to reach agreement, as is also provided for by Sub-Clause 3.7? Is this not something that the Engineer should be delegating to assistants on the Site? What is the objection to such delegation?

While under sub-paragraphs (a) and (b) the Engineer may not delegate authority to act under Sub-Clause 3.7 or to issue a Notice to Correct under Sub-Clause 15.1, there is no restriction on the Engineer's power to delegate authority to certify payments to the Contractor under Sub-Clause 14.6 [*Issue of IPC*] or 14.13 [*Issue of FPC*] or issue a Taking-Over Certificate or Performance Certificate under Sub-Clauses 10.1 and 11.9, respectively. It is not clear what is the justification for the distinction between these various important duties.

The provision in the last paragraph of Sub-Clause 3.4 to the effect that where, by a Notice to the Engineer, the Contractor questions any instruction or Notice given by an assistant (including the Engineer's Representative), the Engineer shall be deemed to have confirmed the

51. However, The World Bank's COPA requires the Engineer to obtain the consent of the Employer before appointing or replacing an Engineer's Representative. Sub-Clause 3.3, COPA.
52. Be a professional engineer and fluent in the ruling language. Sub-paragraphs (a) and (b) of Sub-Clause 3.1.
53. Sub-paragraph (a) of Sub-Clause 3.4.

instruction or Notice if the Engineer does not respond by a Notice within 7 days, is a welcome addition. Where there has been no action by the Engineer, it makes the contractual position clear.

(3) Typical Engineer's set-up

A **Typical Engineer's Set-Up for Construction Supervision** is contained below in **Figure 2**. In this figure, the Engineer, who is empowered to take the critical decisions on the project (e.g., to act under Sub-Clause 3.7 and to issue Notices to Correct under Sub-Clause 15.1) will not necessarily be based full-time on the Site, whereas the Engineer's Representative (the 'Senior Resident Engineer' in the **figure**) is required to be there full-time.

Figure 2 Typical Engineer's Set-Up for Construction Supervision[54]

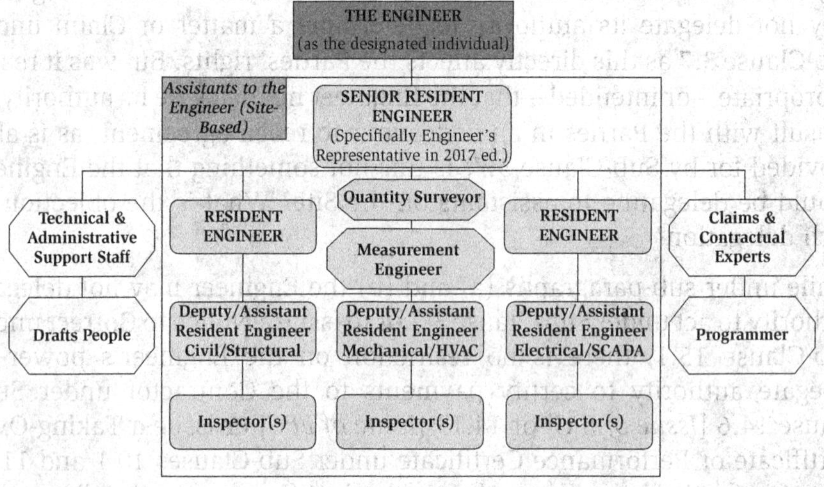

(iv) Improvements:

(1) It is suggested that, for the reasons given under **(iii) Analysis** above, sub-paragraph (a) of Sub-Clause 3.4 be revised to read: '(a) make a determination under Sub-Clause 3.7 [*Agreement or Determination*]; and/or'.

54. The author is grateful to Mr Simon R Worley, chartered civil engineer, for having provided this figure. Note, however, that, contrary to what is indicated by it, there is no explicit requirement in Sub-Clause 3.4 of RB/17 for an assistant to be Site-based though, of course, an assistant might be.

(2) Sub-Clause 3.3 provides that the Engineer may delegate authority to the Engineer's Representative 'in accordance with Sub-Clause 3.4', which relates to delegation by the Engineer of authority to assistants. It is unclear from this provision how much therefore of Sub-Clause 3.4 applies to the Engineer's Representative. Among other things, must the Engineer's Representative, like any assistant, be fluent in the language for communications? Must the Engineer's Representative have the qualifications of an assistant?

(3) As another commentator has noted,[55] while Sub-Clause 3.4, last paragraph, provides that any 'act' of an assistant has the same effect as though it were an 'act' of the Engineer, it says nothing about an 'absence' to act[56] of an assistant and whether this would have the same effect as inaction by the Engineer. It may be important to know this given that inaction by the Engineer, especially under these new Conditions, can have important consequences.[57]

--ooOOoo--

3.5 Engineer's Instructions

The Engineer may issue to the Contractor (at any time) instructions which may be necessary for the execution of the Works, all in accordance with the Contract. The Contractor shall only take instructions from the Engineer, or from the Engineer's Representative (if appointed) or an assistant to whom the appropriate authority to give instruction has been delegated under Sub-Clause 3.4 [*Delegation by the Engineer*].

55. Jakob B Sørensen, *FIDIC Red Book: A Companion to the 2017 Construction Contract* (ICE Publishing, London, 2019) 58.
56. By contrast, Sub-Clause 3.2, last paragraph, addresses an 'absence' to act by the Engineer.
57. For example, an omission by an assistant to react to the Contractor's application for a Taking-Over Certificate under Sub-Clause 10.1 [*Taking Over the Works and Sections*] within 28 days may have the effect that the Taking-Over Certificate is deemed issued.

Subject to the following provisions of this Sub-Clause, the Contractor shall comply with the instructions given by the Engineer or the Engineer's Representative (if appointed) or delegated assistant, on any matter related to the Contract.

If an instruction states that it constitutes a Variation, Sub-Clause 13.3.1 [*Variation by Instruction*] shall apply.

If not so stated, and the Contractor considers that the instruction:

(a) constitutes a Variation (or involves work that is already part of an existing Variation); or
(b) does not comply with applicable Laws or will reduce the safety of the Works or is technically impossible

the Contractor shall immediately, and before commencing any work related to the instruction, give a Notice to the Engineer with reasons. If the Engineer does not respond within 7 days after receiving this Notice, by giving a Notice confirming, reversing or varying the instruction, the Engineer shall be deemed to have revoked the instruction. Otherwise the Contractor shall comply with and be bound by the terms of the Engineer's response.

The Engineer may issue instructions to the Contractor for the execution of the Works. The Contractor shall only take instructions from the Engineer or the Employer's Representative or an authorised assistant and, subject to this Sub-Clause, shall comply with instructions given by them.

If an instruction does not state that it constitutes a Variation and the Contractor considers that it:

(a) constitutes a Variation, or
(b) does not comply with applicable Laws, will reduce the safety of the Works or is technically impossible,

the Contractor shall immediately, and before commencing work related to the instruction, give a Notice to the Engineer with reasons.

If the Engineer does not respond within 7 days, the Engineer shall be deemed to have revoked the instruction.

Commentary

(i) Main Changes from RB/99:

(1) The first paragraph of Sub-Clause 3.5, which needs to be read together with Sub-Clause 1.2(j) defining 'execution of the Works' and Sub-Clause 1.3 [*Notices and Other Communications*] relating to 'instruction', is similar to the first paragraph of Sub-Clause 3.3 [*Instructions of the Engineer*] of RB/99, except that it refers only to instructions and no longer to 'additional or modified Drawings'.

(2) The last paragraph of Sub-Clause 3.5, which contains elements from the corresponding Sub-Clause (Sub-Clause 3.3, last paragraph) of GB/08, is entirely new and replaces the last paragraph of Sub-Clause 3.3 of RB/99 describing how a Contractor's written confirmation of an oral instruction from the Engineer or a delegated assistant could be deemed a written instruction of the Engineer.

(3) The provision for written confirmation of an oral instruction contained in Sub-Clause 3.3, last paragraph, of RB/99 has been omitted from the General Conditions and is now an alternative clause in the *Guidance*.[58]

(ii) Related Clauses / Sub-Clauses: 1.2 [*Interpretation*], 1.3 [*Notices and Other Communications*], 1.13 [*Compliance with Laws*], 3.1 [*The Engineer*], 3.4 [*Delegation by the Engineer*], 4.1 [*Contractor's General Obligations*], 4.3 [*Contractor's Representative*], 4.8 [*Health and Safety Obligations*], 8.4 [*Advance Warning*], 13 [*Variations and Adjustments*], 17.1 [*Responsibility for Care of the Works*] and 18.6 [*Release from Performance under the Law*].

(iii) Analysis:

(1) The Engineer's instructions

Sub-Clause 3.5 is of great practical importance as it describes the principal means by which the Engineer directs the Contractor to carry out the Works in accordance with the Contract. The Engineer does so by

58. *Guidance for the Preparation of Particular Conditions*, 21.

issuing 'instructions' to the Contractor, an instruction being 'a direction or order'.[59] Thus, for a communication to be interpreted as an instruction, words of command are necessary.

Instructions must be issued to the Contractor in writing and otherwise comply with Sub-Clause 1.3, which provides that an instruction 'shall be identified as such and include reference to the provision(s) of the Contract under which it is issued where appropriate'.[60] Thus, it should be identifiable as an instruction and include reference to its contractual basis where appropriate.

The new third paragraph provides that if an instruction states that it constitutes a Variation, Sub-Clause 13.3.1 [*Variation by Instruction*] applies. This paragraph requires the Engineer to acknowledge that an instruction is a Variation whenever the Engineer believes it to be one[61] as otherwise the inference is that the instruction is not a Variation as far as the Engineer is concerned.

(2) Only the Engineer or its delegate may issue an instruction

Sub-Clause 3.5 provides, among other things, that:

> [t]he Contractor shall *only* take instructions from the Engineer, or from the Engineer's Representative (if appointed) or an [duly authorised] assistant [...] (emphasis added).

Accordingly, by signing the Contract, the Employer acknowledges, implicitly, that it may not itself give instructions to the Contractor but may only do so through (and with the cooperation of) the Engineer or someone duly authorised by the Engineer.

(3) The Contractor's duty to comply with instructions

On the Contractor's side, only the Contractor's Representative has authority to receive instructions from the Engineer[62] and, when it does so, the Contractor must comply with them, with very limited exceptions. If the Contractor should fail to do so, the Engineer may require the Contractor to remedy this failure by a Notice to Correct under Sub-Clause

59. *Concise Oxford English Dictionary* (10th edn, rev'd, OUP, Oxford, 2002).
60. Sub-Clause 1.3(b). Under Sub-Clause 1.3, first paragraph, an instruction is stated to be 'another type of communication'.
61. By giving a Notice describing the required change and any requirements for the recording of Costs, Sub-Clause 13.3.1, first paragraph.
62. Sub-Clause 4.3 [*Contractor's Representative*], penultimate paragraph.

15.1 and, ultimately, by termination of the Contract under Sub-Clause 15.2.1(a)(i), assuming the Contractor's failure to comply with the Notice to Correct amounts to a material breach of the Contract, and Sub-Clause 15.2.2.[63]

The Contractor may be excused, at least temporarily, from complying with an instruction, where it considers that the instruction:

(1) although not stated to constitute a Variation, constitutes one (or involves work that is already part of an existing Variation);
(2) does not comply with applicable Laws, such as to protect the environment;
(3) will reduce the safety of the Works; or
(4) is technically impossible.

In each of the four cases, the Contractor must immediately, and before commencing any work related to the instruction, give a Notice[64] to the Engineer with reasons, that is, explaining and justifying its view that the instruction constitutes a Variation (or involves work that is part of an existing Variation), does not comply with applicable Laws, will reduce the safety of the Works or is technically impossible. If the Contractor maintains that the instruction does not comply with applicable Laws, it should be prepared to produce the relevant laws and/or a reasoned legal opinion supporting its position. In the latter two cases, it should be prepared to produce the reasoned opinion of either an in-house[65] or, possibly, independent expert to justify its position.

If the Engineer does not respond otherwise within 7 days, the Engineer is deemed to have revoked the instruction. Otherwise, the Contractor must 'comply with and be bound by the terms of the Engineer's response'.

While this is what this Sub-Clause provides, the Engineer may, of course, be in error. If the issue is over whether an instruction is a Variation, the Contractor must nevertheless comply with the Engineer's response.[66] But

63. Failure by the Contractor to comply with a Notice to Correct within 42 days will also entitle the Employer to claim under the Performance Security. Sub-Clause 4.2.2(c).
64. The Notice must comply with Sub-Clause 1.3 [*Notices and Other Communications*].
65. For example, the Contractor's health and safety officer appointed under Sub-Clause 6.7.
66. The Contractor could then assert a Claim under Sub-Clause 20.1.

not necessarily if the instruction might violate applicable Laws,[67] and/or reduce the safety of the Works,[68] or is technically impossible.[69] In these situations, the Contractor may be justified, even obliged, to warn the Engineer[70] and refuse to comply with the Engineer's instruction.[71] *See* **(iv) Related Law** below.

(4) Instruction (allegedly) not constituting a Variation

This is the first time that the RB has explicitly addressed the very common situation of where the Engineer issues an instruction not purporting to be a Variation but which the Contractor considers to be one. This is a welcome, not to say overdue,[72] development, which is likely to reduce significantly disputes over whether an Engineer's instruction constitutes a Variation.

The parenthetical language in sub-paragraph (a) '(or involves work that is already part of an existing Variation)' is designed to alert the Engineer that the Contractor considers the work concerned will be performed at the rates applicable to an existing Variation or at least one that the Contractor maintains to be an existing Variation.

---

67. *See* Sub-Clause 1.13 [*Compliance with Laws*].
68. *See* Sub-Clause 4.8 [*Health and Safety Obligations*].
69. *See* Sub-Clause 18.6 [*Release from Performance under the Law*].
70. *See* Sub-Clause 8.4 [*Advance Warning*] and the commentary thereon below.
71. The Contractor could then assert a Claim under Sub-Clause 20.1 or, if the matter is urgent, request an interim or conservatory measure from the DAAB pursuant to Rule 5.1(j) of the DAAB Rules or an Emergency Arbitrator under art. 29 of the ICC Rules of Arbitration or applicable law.
72. More than 20 years ago, I N Duncan Wallace (the then Editor of *Hudson*) remarked on the surprising absence of such a provision in standard form construction contracts:

    > The unreality of draftsmanship requiring open recognition of the owner's liability by the A/E [Architect/Engineer] at the time of the instruction, [...], lies in the fact that such draftsmanship totally fails to deal with probably the commonest of all confrontational situations on a construction site – namely the A/E's desire to have work carried out which he considers to be covered by the contractor's original completion and pricing obligations, in the face of the Contractor's contention that the requirement constitutes a variation and so entitles him to extra payment. I N Duncan Wallace, *Construction Contracts: Principles and Policies in Tort and Contract*, vol 2 (Sweet & Maxwell 1996) 471 (para 25-07).

(iv) Related Law: Both English and French law may (quite independent of Sub-Clause 3.5) justify a Contractor in refusing to comply with instructions in circumstances such as those described in sub-paragraph (b) of this Sub-Clause.

Thus, in an English case involving a main construction contract and subcontract, it had been agreed by the parties that the subcontractor had to follow the employer's instructions. The employer's in-house engineer overruled the subcontractor's design for building supports and instructed the adoption of temporary supports which the subcontractor had recognised at the time to be inadequate and which it had informed the contractor were inadequate. But the subcontractor nevertheless complied with the employer's instruction.

The inadequate temporary supports later failed and a room collapsed with potentially fatal consequences to workmen. In a suit brought by the contractor (which had previously settled the employer's claim for damages), the subcontractor was held liable for having breached its duty to warn the employer and the contractor that the supports instructed by the employer were unsafe (though its liability in damages was reduced due to the contractor's contributory negligence).

In finding the subcontractor liable, the judge stated that, given the 'serious' safety risk involved, it was not enough for the subcontractor simply to have informed the contractor of the inadequacy of the employer's solution. Instead:

> [the subcontractor] should [...] have pressed its objections [...] [and] been progressively more formal and insistent if [its objections were] not met – for example by being put in writing if oral presentations were ignored, by going to successively higher levels of management in [the contractor] and [the employer] if lower levels did not respond – and they could have been accompanied by the threat or actuality of report to regulatory authorities. The crucial question is whether [the subcontractor] could and should, in the last resort, have refused to continue to work if the safety of workmen was at risk [...] I am clear that it could and should have done so.[73]

Similarly, under French law, if a contractor receives instructions or drawings from or on behalf of an employer relating to, for example,

73. *Plant Construction Ltd v Clive Adams Associates* (TCC) [2000] BLR, 205 [paras 17 and 18]. While appealed, the Court of Appeal did not disturb this finding [2000] BLR 137.

foundations, processes or other technical issues which it believes are defective or inadequate, it must clearly express its objections if it is to be relieved of liability.[74] Where appropriate, it should refuse to proceed.[75]

Where safety issues are concerned, the Contractor may be required by local law to report the matter to the competent health and safety authorities.

--ooOOoo--

3.6 Replacement of the Engineer

> If the Employer intends to replace the Engineer, the Employer shall, not less than 42 days before the intended date of replacement, give a Notice to the Contractor of the name, address and relevant experience of the intended replacement Engineer.
>
> If the Contractor does not respond within 14 days after receiving this Notice, by giving a Notice stating an objection to such replacement with reasons, the Contractor shall be deemed to have accepted the replacement.
>
> The Employer shall not replace the Engineer with a person (whether a legal entity or a natural person) against whom the Contractor has raised reasonable objection by a Notice under this Sub-Clause.
>
> If the Engineer is unable to act as a result of death, illness, disability or resignation (or, in the case of a legal entity, the Engineer becomes unable or unwilling to carry out any of its duties, other than for a cause attributable to the Employer) the Employer shall be entitled to immediately appoint a replacement by giving a Notice to the Contractor with reasons and the name, address and relevant experience of the replacement. This appointment shall be treated as a temporary appointment until this replacement is accepted by the Contractor, or another replacement is appointed, under this Sub-Clause.

74. Philippe Malinvaud (ed in chief), *Droit de la Construction* (7th edn, Dalloz Action, Paris, 2018) 1135 (paras 402.51-402.61). *See also* the commentary on Sub-Clause 8.4 [*Absence Warning*] below.
75. *Ibid.*

If the Employer intends to replace the Engineer, the Employer shall give not less than 42 days' Notice to the Contractor of the intended replacement. If the Contractor does not respond within 14 days by a Notice stating an objection with reasons, the Contractor shall be deemed to have accepted the replacement. The Employer shall not replace the Engineer with a person against whom the Contractor has raised reasonable objection by a Notice.

If the Engineer is unable to act as the result of death, illness, disability or resignation, the Employer shall be entitled to immediately appoint a replacement. This appointment shall be treated as a temporary appointment until the replacement is accepted by the Contractor.

(i) Main Changes from RB/99:

(1) The first and third paragraphs of Sub-Clause 3.6 correspond closely to Sub-Clause 3.4 in RB/99.
(2) The second paragraph of Sub-Clause 3.6 dealing with where the Contractor does not respond within 14 days to a Notice from the Employer who intends to replace the Engineer, and the fourth paragraph, dealing with where the Engineer is unable to act, are new.

(ii) Related Clauses / Sub-Clauses: 1.3 [*Notices and Other Communications*] and 3.1 [*The Engineer*].

(iii) Analysis: Given the Engineer's wide authority and discretionary powers,[76] the question of whether and, if so, by whom the Employer may replace the Engineer has always been a highly sensitive one between Employers and Contractors. Under the earliest editions of the RB, the Employer was apparently free to replace the Engineer at will.[77] However, this gave rise to problems, notably where the Employer sought to replace an independent consulting engineer as the Engineer by an engineer who was part of the Employer's own staff and, thus, not separate from, or likely to behave independently of, the Employer.[78] In a subsequent edition of the RB, FIDIC decided that the Employer could not replace the

76. Notably, in agreeing or determining matters or Claims under Sub-Clause 3.7, in issuing certificates under Sub-Clauses 10.1 and 11.9 and in certifying payment under Sub-Clauses 14.6 and 14.13.
77. Notably, RB/57, RB/69 and RB/77. *See* Clause 1 (1) (c) of those forms.
78. *See*, for example, the discussion of ICC case 4416 (1985) under **(iv) Related Law** below.

Engineer without an amendment to the contract.[79] But this restriction was, in turn, found to be too harsh and inflexible. Consequently, beginning with RB/99, FIDIC adopted the present compromise solution whereby the Engineer may not be replaced by a person against whom the Contractor raises reasonable objection.

When preparing to tender, tenderers may be expected to attach considerable weight to the technical competence, reputation and degree of independence (from the Employer) of the Engineer.[80] Accordingly, as the Contractor could be prejudiced if the Employer should later replace the Engineer by a person of radically inferior qualifications, the Contractor is given the right to prevent the Employer from appointing a replacement to whom the Contractor reasonably objects.

What would suffice as a 'reasonable objection' to a proposed replacement would depend upon the circumstances, including:

> the representations originally made by the Employer to tenderers as regards the identity of the Engineer and his/her experience and managerial/technical skills, as compared to the replacement Engineer's experience and competence in respect of the duties and authority necessary to administer the Contract and supervise the full scope of the Contractor's execution of the Works.[81]

Thus, for example, this sub-clause should allow the Contractor to prevent the Employer from replacing an independent consulting engineer by a member of the Employer's own staff.

(iv) Related Law: ICC case 4416 (1985) involved RB/69 or RB/77 which (like the English ICE Conditions of Contract from which they were derived) authorised the Employer (in this case, an African state corporation) freely to replace, apparently, the firm originally appointed as the Engineer (a European engineering firm).[82] The Employer had replaced the original Engineer – an independent engineering firm – by the Employer's 'own Supervisory Staff'. Thereafter, the Contractor presented claims for additional payment to the Employer, which the Employer rejected as the Contractor had not complied with Clause 52(5) requiring particulars of such claims to be sent to the Engineer's Representative

79. *See* Sub-Clause 1.1 (a) (iv) of RB/87.
80. The Engineer's name and address are required to be stated in the Contract Data which would be included in the tender dossier.
81. *The FIDIC Contracts Guide* (2nd edn, FIDIC, 2022) 131.
82. *See* Clause 1(1)(c) of RB/69 and RB/77.

every month, failing which they were (according to the Employer) time-barred. While not disputing the Employer's right to replace the original Engineer, the tribunal of three arbitrators – all lawyers – found that, by unilaterally replacing an independent Engineer by its own staff, the Employer had 'frustrated' the provisions of the contract which, the tribunal found, presupposed the presence of an independent Engineer. Consequently, they refused to interpret Clause 52(5) as barring the Contractor's claims.[83]

In an English case, it has been held that, in the case of a (non-FIDIC) contract allowing the employer to replace a 'construction manager' (who, like the Engineer, under RB/17, had a dual 'agency function' and 'decision-making function'),[84] the employer could not validly replace an independent construction manager by the employer itself. The court reasoned that:

> The whole structure of the contract is built upon the premise that the employer and the construction manager are separate entities. Endless anomalies arise if the employer and the construction manager become one and the same. For example, under clause 1.6 the employer issues certificates to himself. Under clause 21 the scheme for dispute resolution becomes distorted.[85]

It was noted that it 'is unrealistic to envisage the employer challenging his own decisions by any form of legal proceedings'.[86]

(v) Improvements:

(1) As the original Engineer is required to have, among other things, 'suitable qualifications, experience and competence to act' (sub-paragraph (a) of Sub-Clause 3.1), so, if the Employer intends to replace the Engineer, the Employer should provide the Contractor with the same information as to the intended replacement,

83. Interim award, ICC case 4416 (1985), Sigvard Jarvin and others (eds), *Coll of ICC Arb Awards*, 1986-1990 (ICC, Paris / Kluwer, the Netherlands, 1994) 460 (English text) and Sigvard Jarvin and others (eds), *Coll of ICC Arb Awards* 1974-1985 (ICC, Paris / Kluwer, the Netherlands, 1988) 542 (French text).

84. *See (1) The Engineer's dual role* under **(iii) Analysis** in the commentary on Sub-Clause 3.2 [*Engineer's Duties and Authority*] above.

85. *Scheldebouw BV v St James Homes (Grosvenor Dock) Ltd* (TCC) [2006] BLR 113, 127 [para. 45].

86. *Ibid.*, 127 [para. 44].

and not merely 'relevant experience' of the intended replacement Engineer, as provided for in the first paragraph of Sub-Clause 3.6.

(2) It has correctly been pointed out that, in the fourth paragraph, the reference to 'other than for a cause attributable to the Employer' is only contained in the parenthesis that deals with the situation where the Engineer is a legal entity and, therefore, literally does not apply where the Engineer is a natural person.[87] However, plainly, if the Engineer is a natural person and is unable to act as a result of a cause attributable to the Employer, this should also not entitle the Employer immediately to appoint a replacement. Thus, it is suggested, this needs to be rectified.

--ooOOoo--

3.7 Agreement or Determination

When carrying out his/her duties under this Sub-Clause, the Engineer shall act neutrally between the Parties and shall not be deemed to act for the Employer.

Whenever these Conditions provide that the Engineer shall proceed under this Sub-Clause 3.7 to agree or determine either:

(a) any matter, as provided for in Sub-Clauses 4.7.3, 10.2, 11.2, 12.1, 12.3, 13.3.1, 13.5, 14.4, 14.5, 14.6.3, 15.3, 15.6 and 18.5, identifying in the same Sub-Clause the date of commencement of the corresponding time limit for agreement under Sub-Clause 3.7.3 [*Time limits*], or

(b) any Claim,

the following procedure shall apply:

3.7.1 Consultation to reach agreement

The Engineer shall consult with both Parties jointly and/or separately, and shall encourage discussion between the Parties in an endeavour to reach agree-

87. Jeremy Glover and Simon Hughes, *Understanding the FIDIC Red and Yellow Books* (3rd edn, Sweet & Maxwell, London, 2018) 64.

ment. The Engineer shall commence such consultation promptly to allow adequate time to comply with the time limit for agreement under Sub-Clause 3.7.3 [*Time limits*]. Unless otherwise proposed by the Engineer and agreed by both Parties, the Engineer shall provide both Parties with a record of the consultation.

If agreement is achieved, within the time limit for agreement under Sub-Clause 3.7.3 [*Time limits*], the Engineer shall give a Notice to both Parties of the agreement, which agreement shall be signed by both Parties. This Notice shall state that it is a "Notice of the Parties' Agreement" and shall include a copy of the agreement.

If:

(a) no agreement is achieved within the time limit for agreement under Sub-Clause 3.7.3 [*Time limits*]; or

(b) both Parties advise the Engineer that no agreement can be achieved within this time limit

whichever is the earlier, the Engineer shall give a Notice to the Parties accordingly and shall immediately proceed as specified under Sub-Clause 3.7.2 [*Engineer's Determination*].

3.7.2 Engineer's Determination

The Engineer shall make a fair determination of the matter or Claim, in accordance with the Contract, taking due regard of all relevant circumstances.

Within the time limit for determination under Sub-Clause 3.7.3 [*Time limits*], the Engineer shall give a Notice to both Parties of his/her determination. This Notice shall state that it is a "Notice of the Engineer's Determination", and shall describe the determination in detail with reasons and detailed supporting particulars.

3.7.3 Time limits

The Engineer shall give the Notice of agreement, if agreement is achieved, within 42 days or within such other time limit as may be proposed by the Engineer and agreed by both Parties (the "time limit for agreement" in these Conditions), after:

(a) in the case of a matter to be agreed or determined under sub-paragraph (a) of Sub-Clause 3.7 [*Agreement or Determination*], the date of commencement of the time limit for agreement as stated in the applicable Sub-Clause of these Conditions;
(b) in the case of a Claim under sub-paragraph (c) of Sub-Clause 20.1 [*Claims*], the date the Engineer receives a Notice under Sub-Clause 20.1 from the claiming Party; or
(c) in the case of a Claim under sub-paragraph (a) or (b) of Sub-Clause 20.1 [*Claims*], the date the Engineer receives:

 (i) a fully detailed Claim under Sub-Clause 20.2.4 [*Fully Detailed Claim*]; or
 (ii) in the case of a Claim under Sub-Clause 20.2.6 [*Claims of continuing effect*], an interim or final fully detailed Claim (as the case may be).

The Engineer shall give the Notice of his/her determination within 42 days or within such other time limit as may be proposed by the Engineer and agreed by both Parties (the "time limit for determination" in these Conditions), after the date corresponding to his/her obligation to proceed under the last paragraph of Sub-Clause 3.7.1 [*Consultation to reach agreement*].

If the Engineer does not give the Notice of determination within the relevant time limit:

(i) in the case of a Claim, the Engineer shall be deemed to have given a determination rejecting the Claim; or
(ii) in the case of a matter to be agreed or determined under sub-paragraph (a) of Sub-Clause 3.7 [*Agreement or Determination*], the matter shall be deemed to be a Dispute which may be referred by either Party to the DAAB for its decision under Sub-Clause 21.4 [*Obtaining DAAB's Decision*] without the need for a NOD

(and Sub-Clause 3.7.5 [*Dissatisfaction with Engineer's determination*] and sub-paragraph (a) of Sub-Clause 21.4.1 [*Reference of a Dispute to the DAAB*] shall not apply).

3.7.4 Effect of the agreement or determination

Each agreement or determination shall be binding on both Parties (and shall be complied with by the Engineer) unless and until corrected under this Sub-Clause or, in the case of a determination, it is revised under Clause 21 [*Disputes and Arbitration*].

If an agreement or determination concerns the payment of an amount from one Party to the other Party, the Contractor shall include such an amount in the next Statement and the Engineer shall include such amount in the Payment Certificate that follows that Statement.

If, within 14 days after giving or receiving the Engineer's Notice of agreement or determination, any error of a typographical or clerical or arithmetical nature is found:

(a) by the Engineer: then he/she shall immediately advise the Parties accordingly; or
(b) by a Party: then that Party shall give a Notice to the Engineer, stating that it is given under this Sub-Clause 3.7.4 and clearly identifying the error. If the Engineer does not agree there was an error, he/she shall immediately advise the Parties accordingly.

The Engineer shall within 7 days of finding the error, or receiving a Notice under sub-paragraph (b) above (as the case may be), give a Notice to both Parties of the corrected agreement or determination. Thereafter, the corrected agreement or determination shall be treated as the agreement or determination for the purpose of these Conditions.

3.7.5 Dissatisfaction with Engineer's determination

If either Party is dissatisfied with a determination of the Engineer:

(a) the dissatisfied Party may give a NOD to the other Party, with a copy to the Engineer;
(b) this NOD shall state that it is a "Notice of Dissatisfaction with the Engineer's Determination" and shall set out the reason(s) for dissatisfaction;
(c) this NOD shall be given within 28 days after receiving the Engineer's Notice of the determination under Sub-Clause 3.7.2 [*Engineer's Determination*] or, if applicable, his/her Notice of the corrected determination under Sub-Clause 3.7.4 [*Effect of the agreement or determination*] (or, in the case of a deemed determination rejecting the Claim, within 28 days after the time limit for determination under Sub-Clause 3.7.3 [*Time limits*] has expired); and
(d) thereafter, either Party may proceed under Sub-Clause 21.4 [*Obtaining DAAB's Decision*].

If no NOD is given by either Party within the period of 28 days stated in sub-paragraph (c) above, the determination of the Engineer shall be deemed to have been accepted by both Parties and shall be final and binding on them.

If the dissatisfied Party is dissatisfied with only part(s) of the Engineer's determination:

(i) this part(s) shall be clearly identified in the NOD;
(ii) this part(s), and any other parts of the determination that are affected by such part(s) or rely on such part(s) for completeness, shall be deemed to be severable from the remainder of the determination; and
(iii) the remainder of the determination shall become final and binding on both Parties as if the NOD had not been given.

In the event that a Party fails to comply with an agreement of the Parties under this Sub-Clause 3.7 or a final and binding determination of the Engineer, the other Party may, without prejudice to any other rights it may have, refer the failure itself directly to arbitration under Sub-Clause 21.6 [*Arbitration*] in which case the first and the third paragraphs of Sub-Clause 21.7 [*Failure to Comply with DAAB's*

Decision] shall apply to such reference in the same manner as these paragraphs apply to a final and binding decision of the DAAB.

Whenever the Conditions provide that the Engineer shall proceed under this Sub-Clause to agree or determine any matter (as defined) or Claim, the procedure in this Sub-Clause applies. When carrying out duties under this Sub-Clause, the Engineer shall act 'neutrally' between the Parties and shall not be deemed to act for the Employer. The Engineer is required first to consult with both Parties (about the matter or Claim) in an endeavour to reach agreement within 42 days.[88] If no agreement is achieved, or both Parties advise the Engineer that no agreement can be achieved within this period, the Engineer shall make a 'fair' determination within a further period of 42 days, taking due regard of all relevant circumstances.[89] If either Party is dissatisfied with an Engineer's determination, it may give a Notice of Dissatisfaction ('NOD') to the other Party, with a copy to the Engineer, within 28 days after receiving the Engineer's Notice of the determination.[90] Thereafter either Party may proceed under Sub-Clause 21.4 to obtain a decision of the DAAB.[91] An Engineer's determination will become final and binding on the Parties if no NOD has been given within this 28-day period.[92] If a Party fails to comply with an agreement or a final and binding Engineer's determination, the other Party may, without prejudice to its rights, refer the failure directly to arbitration under Sub-Clause 21.6.[93]

Commentary

(i) Main Changes from RB/99:

(1) Compared to the corresponding Sub-Clause in RB/99, that is Sub-Clause 3.5 (two short paragraphs), Sub-Clause 3.7 (almost three pages) is much more detailed and elaborate. Unlike former Sub-Clause 3.5, which dealt with how the Engineer should proceed to agree or determine any matter (which was unde-

88. Sub-Clauses 3.7.1 and 3.7.3.
89. Sub-Clauses 3.7.1, 3.7.2 and 3.7.3.
90. Sub-Clause 3.7.5.
91. *Ibid.*
92. *Ibid.*
93. *Ibid.*

fined), Sub-Clause 3.7 provides for a detailed step-by-step procedure for dealing with a Party's 'matter' (now, as a result of amendments in 2022, defined in sub-paragraph (a)) or 'Claim' (now defined in Sub-Clause 1.1.6), together with strict time limits for each step and severe sanctions for failing to comply with them. Whereas Sub-Clause 3.5 had provided that the Engineer consult with each Party in an endeavour to reach agreement, Sub-Clause 3.7 provides that the Engineer shall consult with both Parties 'jointly and/or separately' to this end.

(2) Sub-Clause 3.5 of RB/99 had provided in embryo for the agreement/determination procedure which is set out in Sub-Clause 3.7. Under Sub-Clause 3.5, if no agreement was achieved, the Engineer was required to make 'a fair determination in accordance with the Contract, taking due regard of all relevant circumstances'.[94] On the other hand, Sub-Clause 3.7 provides that when carrying out its duties under this Sub-Clause 'the Engineer shall act *neutrally* between the Parties and shall not be deemed to act for the Employer'. (Emphasis added) The reference to 'neutrally' is new in FIDIC forms.[95] Sub-Clause 3.7

94. As to this provision, FIDIC had stated that the Engineer 'should carry out this duty in a professional manner [...]'. *The FIDIC Contracts Guide* (1st edn, FIDIC, 2000) 89. This is repeated in the 2nd edn of the Guide (2022) at 139 ('entirely professional manner').

95. Instead, under earlier editions of the RB, the Engineer had been expected to act 'fairly and impartially' in certain cases (e.g., when certifying payment or deciding disputes). *See* FIDIC's commentary on RB/77: *Notes on Documents for Civil Engineering Contracts* (FIDIC, 1977) 16. In RB/87, the Engineer had been required under Sub-Clause 2.6 [*Engineer to Act Impartially*] to exercise his discretion 'impartially' when 'giving his decision, opinion or consent', when 'expressing his satisfaction or approval', when 'determining value', or when 'otherwise taking action which may affect the rights and obligations of the Employer or the Contractor'. According to FIDIC's *Guide to the Use of FIDIC Conditions of Contract for Works of Civil Engineering Construction Fourth Edition* (FIDIC, 1989), which was FIDIC's commentary on RB/87, '[b]ehaving impartially implies being prepared to listen to and consider the views of both the Employer and the Contractor and then to make a determination based upon the facts', 48. There appears to be no practical difference between acting impartially (defined in *Concise Oxford English Dictionary* (10th edn, rev'd, OUP, Oxford, 2002) as 'treating all rivals or disputants equally') and, under the new Sub-Clause, acting neutrally (defined in the same dictionary as being 'impartial') and being fair (defined in the same dictionary as 'treating people equally').

further provides that the Engineer shall make a '*fair*' determination of the matter or Claim.[96] The Notice of any determination must contain 'reasons and detailed supporting particulars', not only 'supporting particulars' as under Sub-Clause 3.5.

(3) In Sub-Clause 3.7 the Engineer is, to some extent, reassuming the power which it had under Clause 67 of RB/87 (and gave up to the DAB in RB/99), to render a pre-arbitral decision on a dispute between the Parties. As in the case of Clause 67, the Engineer's determination is interim binding and becomes final and binding if neither Party expresses dissatisfaction with it within a specific time limit. Unlike Sub-Clause 3.5 of RB/99, Sub-Clause 3.7 introduces specific time limits within which the Engineer is to act, and each Party is now required to serve a NOD if dissatisfied with the Engineer's determination, thereby preventing it from becoming final and binding. The giving of a NOD by a Party within the required time limit is a condition to enable either Party to refer the resulting Dispute to the DAAB.

(4) Sub-Clause 3.7 for the first time deals with the situation where a Party is dissatisfied with only part(s) of the Engineer's determination.[97]

(5) Whereas the RB/99 was silent on the question of enforcement of a Parties' agreement and/or an Engineer's determination, Sub-Clause 3.7 now explicitly provides that, where a Party fails to comply with an agreement or an Engineer's final and binding determination, the other Party may, without prejudice to its rights, refer the failure directly to arbitration.[98]

(6) Another novelty is that Sub-Clause 3.7 addresses situations where the Engineer's determination contains errors of a typographical, clerical or arithmetical nature, providing a procedure for their correction.[99]

(ii) Related Clauses / Sub-Clauses: Two types of related Sub-Clauses should be distinguished. The first group encompasses those which merely refer to Sub-Clause 3.7 but do not specifically require the Engineer

96. Sub-Clause 3.7.2 and *see* prior footnote. The term 'fairly' is also used of the Engineer's actions in Sub-Clauses 14.6.1(a) [*The IPC*] and 14.13 [*Issue of FPC*].
97. Sub-Clause 3.7.5, penultimate paragraph.
98. Sub-Clause 3.7.5, last paragraph.
99. Sub-Clause 3.7.4, third and fourth paragraphs.

'to agree or determine any matter or Claim' pursuant to Sub-Clause 3.7, second paragraph. In other words, the Engineer's duty to act 'neutrally' (Sub-Clause 3.7, first paragraph) is not directly applicable to the subject matter of the Sub-Clause concerned.

These Sub-Clauses are the following: 3.2 [*Engineer's Duties and Authority*], 3.4 [*Delegation by the Engineer*], 4.2 [*Performance Security*], 8.5 [*Extension of Time for Completion*], 14.3 [*Application for Interim Payment*], 14.6 [*Issue of IPC*], 14.13 [*Issue of FPC*], 15.2 [*Termination for Contractor's Default*], 16.1 [*Suspension by Contractor*], 16.2.1 [*Notice*], 21.3 [*Avoidance of Disputes*], 21.4 [*Obtaining DAAB's Decision*] and 21.6 [*Arbitration*].

The second group covers those Sub-Clauses which not only refer to Sub-Clause 3.7 but also specifically provide that the Engineer shall proceed under Sub-Clause 3.7 'to agree or determine any matter or Claim' or provide that Sub-Clause 3.7 'shall apply'. In these cases, the Engineer is required to act 'neutrally' between the Parties. This second group comprises the following Sub-Clauses: 4.7.3 [*Agreement or Determination of Rectification Measures, Delay and/or Cost*], 10.2 [*Taking Over Parts*], 11.2 [*Cost of Remedying Defects*], 12.1 [*Works to Be Measured*], 12.3 [*Valuation of the Works*], 13.3.1 [*Variation by Instruction*], 13.5 [*Daywork*], 14.4 [*Schedule of Payments*], 14.5 [*Plant and Materials Intended for the Works*], 14.6.3 [*Correction or Modification*], 15.3 [*Valuation after Termination for Contractor's Default*], 15.6 [*Valuation after Termination for Employer's Convenience*], 18.5 [*Optional Termination*], 20.1 [*Claims*], 20.2.5 [*Agreement or Determination of the Claim*] and 20.2.6 [*Claims of Continuing Effect*].

In addition, Sub-Clauses 1.2 [*Interpretation*] and 1.3 [*Notices and Other Communications*] will generally be applicable.[100]

(iii) Analysis:

(1) Purpose of Sub-Clause

Sub-Clause 3.7 provides for a procedure whereby the Engineer assists the Parties to resolve any matter (as defined in sub-paragraph (a)) or Claim that may arise between them relating to the Contract and the execution of the Works. The Engineer does this, first, by consulting with the Parties

100. Sub-Clause 1.3 expressly applies to a 'Notice (including a Notice of Dissatisfaction)', an 'agreement', a 'determination' and a 'record'.

jointly and/or separately and encouraging them to reach an agreement and, second, failing agreement, by making a determination on the matter or Claim.[101]

While Sub-Clause 1.1 [*Definitions*] contains a definition of 'Claim', it contains no definition of a 'matter to be agreed or determined'. Instead, as the result of FIDIC's amendments in 2022,[102] such a matter is defined in sub-paragraph (a) of Sub-Clause 3.7 by reference to the thirteen sub-clauses described in **Table 3 Matters to be Agreed or Determined by the Engineer**.

Table 3 Matters to Be Agreed or Determined by the Engineer

Sub-Clause of RB/17	*Heading*	*The Matter*	*Originating Action*	*Consequence*
4.7.3	Setting Out	- '*whether or not there is an error in the items of reference*' - '*whether or not* [...] *an experienced contractor exercising due care would have discovered such an error* [...]'; and - '*what measures (if any) the Contractor is required to take to rectify the error*'	Notice by the Contractor to the Engineer '*If the Contractor finds an error in any items of reference,* [...]'	'[...] *the Engineer shall proceed under Sub-Clause 3.7 [Agreement or Determination] to agree or determine*' the matter

101. *See* **Figure 3 Timeline for Agreeing/Determining Claim or Matter** below in this commentary on Sub-Clause 3.7 and **Figure 4 Agreement/Determination Procedure** at the end of this commentary on Sub-Clause 3.7.
102. *See* the Note following the List of Abbreviations and Definitions at the beginning of this book.

Sub-Clause of RB/17	*Heading*	*The Matter*	*Originating Action*	*Consequence*
10.2	Taking Over Parts	Reduction in Delay Damages	Notice by the Contractor to the Engineer *'if the Employer does use any part of the Works before the Taking-Over Certificate is issued* [...]'	*'The Engineer shall proceed under Sub-Clause 3.7 [Agreement or Determination] to agree or determine'* the matter
11.2	Cost of Remedying Defects	The cause of a defect	Notice by the Contractor to the Engineer *'If the Contractor considers that the work is attributable to any other cause* [...]'	'[...] *the Engineer shall proceed under Sub-Clause 3.7 [Agreement or Determination] to agree or determine'* the matter
12.1	Works to Be Measured	Measurement of the Works	Notice by the Contractor to the Engineer '[...] *setting out the reasons why the Contractor considers the measurement on Site or records are inaccurate'*	'[...] *the Engineer shall:- proceed under Sub-Clause 3.7 [Agreement or Determination] to agree or determine'* the matter

Sub-Clause of RB/17	*Heading*	*The Matter*	*Originating Action*	*Consequence*
12.3	Valuation of the Works	The appropriate rate or price	Notice by the Contractor to the Engineer '*If, for any item of work, the Engineer and the Contractor are unable to agree the appropriate rate or price* [...] *setting out the reasons why the Contractor disagrees*'	'[...] *the Engineer shall:- proceed under Sub-Clause 3.7 [Agreement or Determination] to agree or determine*' the matter
13.3.1	Variation by Instruction	EOT and/or adjustment to the Contract Price as a result of the Variation	Submission by the Contractor to the Engineer of '*detailed particulars* [...]'	'*The Engineer shall then proceed under Sub-Clause 3.7 [Agreement or Determination] to agree or determine*' the matter
13.5	Daywork	Resources used in executing daywork	The Engineer disagrees with, or finds to be incorrect, the Contractor's statement of resources for daywork	'[...] *the Engineer shall proceed under Sub-Clause 3.7 [Agreement or Determination] to agree or determine*' the matter
14.4	Schedule of Payments	Revised instalments for payment	The Engineer finds that '*actual progress is* [...] *differ[ent] from that on which the Schedule of Payments was based* [...]'	'[...] *the Engineer may proceed under Sub-Clause 3.7 [Agreement or Determination] to agree or determine*' the matter

Sub-Clause of RB/17	*Heading*	*The Matter*	*Originating Action*	*Consequence*
14.5	Plant and Materials Intended for the Works	Amount to be added for Plant and Materials when shipped/ delivered	The Contractor includes amount(s) to be added in a Statement and conditions in sub-paragraphs (a) and either (b) or (c) are fulfilled	'*The Engineer shall proceed under Sub-Clause 3.7 [Agreement or Determination] to agree or determine*' the matter
14.6.3	Issue of IPC – Correction or Modific-ation	Amounts not certified by the Engineer in previous IPCs	Notice by the Contractor to the Engineer '*to the extent that: (a) the Contractor is not satisfied that this next Payment Certificate includes the identified amounts;* [...]'	'[...] *refer this matter to the Engineer and Sub-Clause 3.7 [Agreement or Determination] shall apply*'
15.3	Valuation after Ter-mination for Contra-ctor's Default	The value of the Permanent Works and any other sums due to the Contractor	'[...]. *termination of the Contract under Sub-Clause 15.2 [Termination for Contractor's Default]*'	'[...] *the Engineer shall proceed under Sub-Clause 3.7 [Agreement or Determination] to agree or determine*' the matter
15.6	Valuation after Ter-mination for Employer's Conveni-ence	The value of work done and the amount of any loss of profit or other losses and damages suffered by the Contractor	Submission by the Contractor to the Engineer of '*detailed supporting particulars*'	'*The Engineer shall then proceed under Sub-Clause 3.7 [Agreement or Determination] to agree or determine the matters*'

Sub-Clause of RB/17	*Heading*	*The Matter*	*Originating Action*	*Consequence*
18.5	Optional Termination	The value of the work done	Submission by the Contractor to the Engineer of '*detailed supporting particulars*'	'*The Engineer shall then proceed under Sub-Clause 3.7 [Agreement or Determination] to agree or determine*' the matter

Source: *The FIDIC Contracts Guide* (2nd edn, FIDIC, 2022) 133.

Sub-Clause 3.5 of RB/99, which provided for how the Engineer should agree or determine any matter (which was undefined), led the Engineer to have to deal not only with claims but also with subjects that did not involve – or necessarily involve – claims such as the valuation of normal work done (under Sub-Clause 12.3), the revision of instalments in a Schedule of Payments (Sub-Clause 14.4) the correction of IPCs (under Sub-Clause 14.6) or the valuation of work at termination (under Clause 15). In Sub-Clause 3.7 of RB/17, these and other subjects are referred to as 'matters to be agreed or determined' and are identified comprehensively by their sub-clause number in sub-paragraph (a) of this sub-clause (and listed in Table 3 above). The reason for the creation of this separate category of 'matters to be agreed or determined' was that it was felt to be unjustified and inappropriate, in those cases, to require the Contractor to comply with the Claims procedure (as might otherwise apply, given the broad definition of Claim), especially as it had become more burdensome in RB/17 compared to RB/99. Accordingly, a simplified procedure applies to 'matters to be agreed or determined' as discussed below and in the commentary on Clause 20.

When proceeding under Sub-Clause 3.7, the Engineer is required to act 'neutrally' between the Parties and 'shall not be deemed to act for the Employer'. According to the *Guidance*,[103] by these statements it is intended that 'the Engineer treats both Parties even-handedly, in a fair-minded and unbiased manner'.[104]

103. *Guidance for the Preparation of Particular Conditions*, 21.
104. There seems to be no clear-cut difference between 'impartially' (used in RB/87, *see* fn. 95 in relation to item (2) under **(i) Main Changes from RB/99** in the commentary on this Sub-Clause above) and 'neutrally'. According to the dictionary, 'neutral' means 'impartial' or 'unbiased'. *Concise Oxford English Dictionary* (10th edn, rev'd, OUP, Oxford, 2002).

As indicated above,[105] the Engineer was relieved of the obligation which it had (under Clause 67 of RB/87) to decide disputes before arbitration when the DAB replaced the Engineer as a decider of disputes in RB/99. This change was made, in part, because it was believed to be unrealistic in an international construction contract to expect the Engineer to decide disputes 'impartially'[106] and, if necessary, against its own client, the Employer, and sometimes even against its own direct interest, such as where it was the designer and a design issue was in dispute. It remains to be seen whether, in its newly enhanced role of determining Claims or matters under this Sub-Clause (where the Parties cannot agree), the Engineer will be any more effective.

As mentioned above, failing an agreement, the Engineer is required to make a determination in respect of a matter or Claim between the Parties. This procedure is illustrated in **Figure 3 Timeline for Agreeing/Determining Claim or Matter**.

--ooOOoo--

105. *See* item (3) under **(i) Main Changes from RB/99** of this commentary on Sub-Clause 3.7.
106. As it was required to do under Sub-Clause 2.6 of RB/87.

Figure 3 Timeline for Agreeing/Determining Claim or Matter[1]

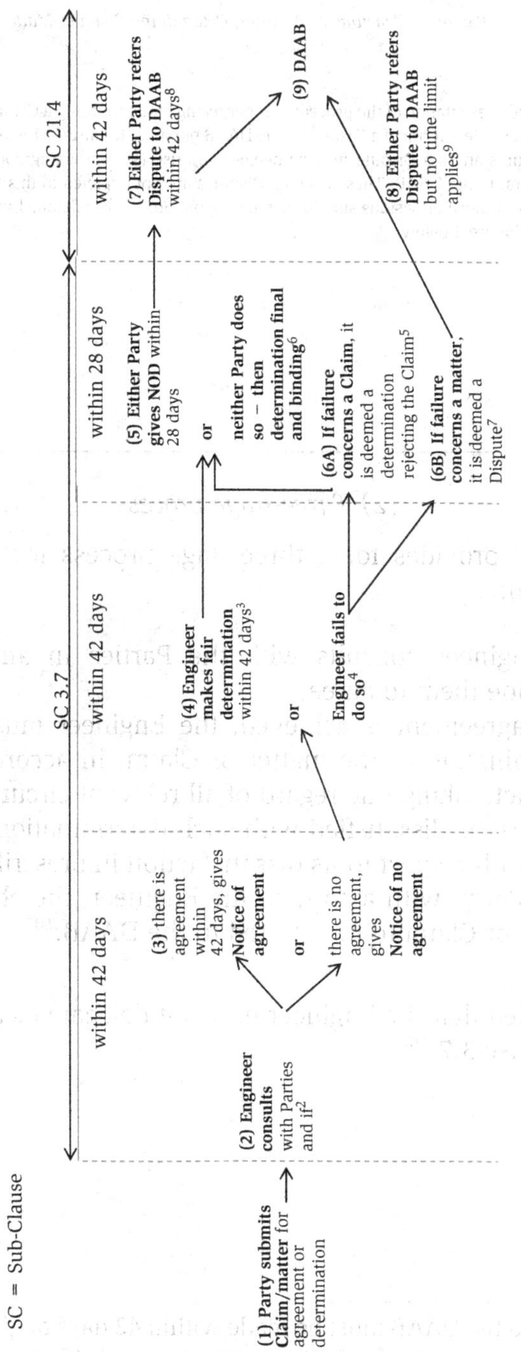

Source: Author's own work.

Figure 3 Timeline for Agreeing/Determining Claim or Matter

Notes

1. This is a simplified presentation of the procedure for agreeing or determining a Claim or matter under SC 3.7, leading to the possible referral of a Dispute to the DAAB pursuant to the SC 21.4. SC 21.4 also provides that in certain circumstances a Dispute may be deemed to arise (*see* sub-paragraphs (a), (b) and (c)), allowing for a referral to the DAAB. These deemed Disputes are not depicted in this figure.
Only the actual text of those provisions should be relied upon. For a more detailed visual presentation of this procedure, *see* Figure 4 below.
2. SC 3.7.1.
3. SC 3.7.3.
4. *Ibid.*
5. *Ibid.*
6. SC 3.7.5.
7. SC 3.7.3.
8. SC 21.4.
9. SC 3.7.3

(2) Three-stage process

Sub-Clause 3.7 provides for a three-stage process for dealing with a matter or Claim:

(1) the Engineer consults with the Parties in an endeavour to persuade them to agree;
(2) if no agreement is achieved, the Engineer must make 'a fair determination of the matter or Claim, in accordance with the Contract, taking due regard of all relevant circumstances'; and
(3) if a Party is dissatisfied with such determination, it may give a NOD with respect to its dissatisfaction in prescribed form to the other Party, with a copy to the Engineer, thereby enabling the matter or Claim to be referred to the DAAB.[107]

It will be recalled that the Engineer may not delegate its authority to act under Sub-Clause 3.7.[108]

107. Reference to the DAAB must be made within 42 days of giving or receiving (as the case may be) a NOD, pursuant to Sub-Clause 21.4 [*Obtaining DAAB's Decision*].
108. Sub-Clause 3.4(a). *See also* the commentary on Sub-Clause 3.4 above.

(3) <u>First stage</u>: Engineer's consultation with the Parties to reach an agreement[109]

The first stage requires the Engineer to consult with both Parties and encourage discussion between them in an endeavour to persuade them to reach an agreement.[110] The Engineer has the discretion to consult the Parties jointly and/or separately. Unlike RB/99 which did not provide for a time limit for reaching agreement, under RB/17, the Parties should endeavour to reach an agreement within 42 days or such other time limit as may be proposed by the Engineer and agreed by the Parties.[111] The Engineer is required to commence such consultation 'promptly' in order to allow the Parties adequate time to comply with this time limit.[112] The time limit commences to run:

(1) in the case of a matter (which is not a Claim), on the date stated in the applicable Sub-Clause of the Conditions, the relevant Sub-Clauses being 4.7, 10.2, 11.2, 12.1, 12.3, 13.3.1, 13.5, 14.4, 14.5, 14.6.3, 15.3, 15.6 and 18.5,[113] each of which specifies a date for the commencement of the time limit;
(2) in the case of either an Employer's Claim for additional payment (or reduction in the Contract Price) and/or extension of the DNP or a Contractor's Claim for additional payment and/or an EOT, on the date when the Engineer receives a fully detailed Claim under Sub-Clause 20.2.4 or an interim or final fully detailed Claim, as the case may be, under Sub-Clause 20.2.6;[114] and

---

109. Sub-Clauses 3.7.1, 3.7.3 and 3.7.4.
110. Sub-Clause 3.7.1.
111. Sub-Clause 3.7.3.
112. Sub-Clause 3.7.1.
113. *See* Sub-Clause 3.7.3(a) and, specifically, **Table 3 Matters to be Agreed or Determined by the Engineer**.
114. Sub-Clause 3.7.3(c). In the case of sub-para. (c)(ii), it is not entirely clear when the calculation is made, whether from the date when the Engineer receives an interim fully detailed Claim or from when it receives a final fully detailed Claim or whether both may apply. However, FIDIC indicates elsewhere that it is 'only after the claiming Party has submitted the final fully detailed Claim that the Engineer ... becomes obliged to proceed under RB2017 3.7'. *The FIDIC Contracts Guide* (2nd edn, 2022) 517. Meanwhile, as regards interim Claims, FIDIC notes that the Engineer has under Sub-Clause 20.2.7 the obligation to include in each IPC 'such amounts for any Claim as have been reasonably substantiated as due to the claiming Party

(3) in the case of any other Claim, on the date when the Engineer receives a Notice of such Claim under Sub-Clause 20.1, third paragraph, from the claiming Party.[115]

The Engineer is to play a facilitator role between the Parties to help them reach their agreement.[116] In this connection, FIDIC 'strongly recommend[s] that the Engineer and the Parties actively engage with each other … in the procedure, so that the Parties themselves remain in control of the decision-making in order to avoid it escalating into something that must be formally determined by the Engineer'.[117] Among other things, the Engineer could be expected to invite the Parties to a meeting (*see* Sub-Clause 3.8) so that each can better understand the other's views and the Engineer can assist the Parties to resolve them. The requirement that the Engineer must normally provide both Parties with a record of the consultation[118] confirms that the Engineer and the Parties must actively engage with each other.

If agreement is achieved, the Engineer is required to give both Parties a Notice (stating it is a 'Notice of the Parties' Agreement') of the agreement within the time limit, together with a copy of the agreement that the Parties are expected to have signed.[119]

Each agreement is binding on the Parties – and must be complied with by the Engineer – though it is subject to possible correction under Sub-Clause 3.7.4.[120]

[…] rather than the claiming Party having to wait until the effects of the event/circumstance have ended […]' Ibid.

115. Sub-Clause 3.7.3(b).
116. *The FIDIC Contracts Guide* (2nd edn, FIDIC, 2022) 138.
117. *Ibid.*
118. Sub-Clause 3.7.1, first paragraph. The record must comply with Sub-Clause 1.3 [*Notices and Other Communications*].
119. Sub-Clauses 3.7.1, second paragraph, and 3.7.3.
120. Sub-Clause 3.7.4, first, third and fourth paragraphs.

(4) Second stage: Engineer's determination[121]

If:

(a) no agreement is achieved 'within' the relevant 42-day time limit for agreement;[122] or
(b) both Parties advise the Engineer that no agreement can be achieved within this time limit,

whichever is the earlier, the Engineer shall immediately proceed with the second stage,[123] that is, making a 'fair'[124] determination. In this case, the Engineer must give a Notice to the Parties that no agreement has been, or can be, achieved within the relevant time limit for agreement and must then 'immediately' proceed to make a fair determination of the matter or Claim 'in accordance with the Contract, taking due regard of all relevant circumstances'.[125]

(a) Engineer's determination

The Engineer must give a Notice of its determination 'within' 42 days[126] or within such other time limit as may be proposed by the Engineer and agreed by both Parties after the date of its obligation to proceed to make

121. Sub-Clauses 3.7.2, 3.7.3 and 3.7.4.
122. A '**day**' is defined as a calendar day. Sub-Clause 1.1.25. The term 'within' in relation to a time period in days is susceptible to different meanings as explained in item (2) under **(v) Improvements** in the commentary on Sub-Clause 1.2 [*Interpretation*] above.
123. Sub-Clause 3.7.1, third paragraph. The requirement in sub-para. (b) seems odd. If one of the Parties is unwilling to agree, then agreement is unlikely and there seems to be no reason to wait for both to advise the Engineer that they cannot agree. Therefore, sub-para. (b) of Sub-Clause 3.7.1 might be amended in the Particular Conditions to provide that a Notice from either Party to the Engineer that no agreement can be reached will suffice so that the Engineer may then proceed to make a determination.
124. For a discussion of the Engineer's duty to act in a 'fair' manner, *see* (1) under the heading *(2) When exercising discretion the Engineer must act fairly* under **(iii) Analysis** of the commentary on Sub-Clause 3.2 [*Engineer's Duties and Authority*] above, and (2) under item (2) under **(i) Main Changes from RB/99** of this commentary on Sub-Clause 3.7.
125. Sub-Clauses 3.7.1, third paragraph, and 3.7.2.
126. The term 'within' in relation to a time period in days is susceptible to different meanings as explained in item (2) under **(v) Improvements** in the commentary on Sub-Clause 1.2 [*Interpretation*] above.

a determination (described above).[127] The Notice must state that it is a 'Notice of the Engineer's Determination' and describe the determination in detail 'with reasons and detailed supporting particulars'.[128]

(b) Errors in Engineer's determination

Sub-Clause 3.7.4 also addresses where the Engineer's agreement or determination is believed to contain an error of a typographical, clerical or arithmetical nature, and provides a procedure for its correction. The provisions that regulate this procedure are clear and do not call for particular comment.[129]

(c) Effect of an agreement and of the Engineer's determination

Each agreement of the Parties or determination of the Engineer (whether or not a NOD has been served in respect of it) is 'binding' on both Parties[130] and must, as well, be complied with by the Engineer, subject to possible correction under Sub-Clause 3.7.4 and/or revision by the DAAB, an amicable settlement or arbitration under Clause 21.[131] If the agreement or determination concerns a payment to be made by one Party to the other, the Contractor should include this amount in its next Statement and the Engineer should include the amount in its next Payment Certificate following that Statement.[132]

* * *

When aggregating the two main time periods under Sub-Clause 3.7.3, that is, the 42-day period for a Parties' agreement and, failing their agreement, the 42-day period for an Engineer's determination, it can be seen that it may take up to 84 days before the Engineer is obliged to make

127. Sub-Clause 3.7.3, second paragraph.
128. Sub-Clause 3.7.2, second paragraph.
129. The ICC Arbitration Rules contain an analogous provision as regards an error in an arbitral award. *See* art. 36 of those Rules. Thus, in the absence of experience with this new provision, practice under those Rules may be looked to.
130. This means that it must be respected by them.
131. Sub-Clause 3.7.4, first paragraph.
132. Sub-Clause 3.7.4, second paragraph. The Employer is not entitled to refuse to make a payment on the ground that it has served a NOD with respect to a determination by the Engineer providing for a payment to the Contractor.

a determination.[133] This period may in some cases be too long or too short. It mirrors the preceding 84-day period allowed to a claiming Party to submit a fully detailed Claim to the Engineer.[134]

(5) Third stage: NOD with Engineer's determination, if any[135]

(a) Where Engineer makes a determination

If a Party is dissatisfied with an Engineer's determination, it may – and must if it wishes to pursue the matter or Claim – give a NOD to the other Party with a copy to the Engineer 'within' 28 days[136] after receiving the Engineer's Notice of the determination or, if applicable, the Engineer's Notice of a corrected determination.[137] A NOD must comply with Sub-Clause 1.3 [*Notices and Other Communications*], explicitly state that it is a 'Notice of Dissatisfaction with the Engineer's Determination' and set out the reason(s) for dissatisfaction.[138] Thereafter, either Party may refer the matter or Claim as a Dispute to the DAAB.[139]

If no NOD is given by either Party within the relevant 28-day period, the determination of the Engineer is deemed to have been accepted by the Parties and to be 'final and binding' on them.[140] This means that it is not just 'binding' (as under the *Second Stage* above) but also no longer subject to legal recourse.[141] *Thus, it is critical if a Party wishes to preserve*

133. This period may be even longer if the Engineer has proposed this and the Parties have so agreed. Sub-Clause 3.7.3. *See* **Figure 3 Timeline for Agreeing/Determining Claim or Matter** above.
134. Sub-Clause 20.2.4.
135. Sub-Clauses 3.7.2-3.7.5.
136. A '**day**' is defined as a calendar day. Sub-Clause 1.1.25. The term 'within' in relation to a time period in days is susceptible to different meanings as explained in item (2) under **(v) Improvements** in the commentary on Sub-Clause 1.2 [*Interpretation*] above.
137. Sub-Clause 3.7.5, first paragraph.
138. Sub-Clause 3.7.5, sub-para. (b).
139. Pursuant to Sub-Clause 21.4.1 [*Obtaining DAAB's Decision – Reference of a Dispute to the DAAB*].
140. Sub-Clause 3.7.5, second paragraph.
141. For further details of the situation under English law, *see* Clive Freedman and James Farrell, *Kendall on Expert Determination* (5th edn, Sweet & Maxwell, London, 2015) 164-166. There is no provision for disapplying this time bar, as is the case under Sub-Clause 20.2.5 [Agreement or determination of the Claim].

its rights in relation to a matter or Claim determined by the Engineer, that it gives a NOD in the required form and manner within the relevant 28-day time limit.

If a Party is dissatisfied with only part(s) of the Engineer's determination, then those parts must be clearly identified in the NOD and the remainder of the determination that is unaffected by such parts, and is not relied upon by them, will become final and binding as if no NOD had been given as to it.[142]

(b) Where Engineer fails to make a determination

In practice, it may happen that a Party has referred a matter or a Claim to the Engineer but the Engineer has failed to give a Notice of its determination within the relevant 42-day time limit (as it may have been extended by agreement with the Parties). This may be due to various reasons, such as the complexity of the matter or Claim and/or the voluminous documentation accompanying it[143] or a simple failure of the Engineer to perform its duty. Whatever the reason, the procedure which a Party must observe in order to protect its rights is different depending upon whether the Engineer has failed to determine a *Claim* or a *matter*.

(i) The failure relates to a Claim

The Engineer's failure to give a Notice of determination of a *Claim* within the relevant time limit is deemed to be a rejection of the Claim.[144] The claiming Party must then make sure that it serves a NOD in respect of this deemed rejection of the Claim within 28 days after the date on which the time limit for the determination (or, if applicable, the Engineer's corrected determination) has expired if it wishes to preserve its right to refer that Claim, as a Dispute, to the DAAB under Sub-Clause 21.4.[145] The NOD must comply with Sub-Clause 1.3, explicitly state that it is a 'Notice of Dissatisfaction with the Engineer's Determination' and set out the reason(s) for dissatisfaction.[146] Thereafter, either Party may refer the Claim

142. Sub-Clause 3.7.5, third paragraph.
143. In these cases, the Engineer should normally have proposed an extension of time for the Parties' agreement. Their agreement may not be unreasonably withheld or delayed. *See* Sub-Clause 1.3.
144. Sub-Clause 3.7.3, last paragraph.
145. Sub-Clause 3.7.5(c).
146. Sub-Clause 3.7.5 (b).

as a Dispute to the DAAB.[147] *Failure by a Party within such period of 28 days to give a NOD in respect of the Engineer's deemed determination rejecting the Claim will result in the deemed determination becoming final and binding.*[148]

Thus, the Contractor, for example, would make a serious mistake to assume that a failure by the Engineer to determine a Claim of the Contractor within the required time would relieve the Contractor from having to give a NOD. *If the Contractor were to neglect to do so within the relevant 28 day period, it would be deemed to have accepted the deemed rejection of its Claim by the Engineer and would lose its rights as to the Claim concerned.*[149]

Furthermore, unless the claiming Party decides to abandon its Claim at this point, *it must refer it as a Dispute to the DAAB within 42 days of giving or receiving, as the case may be, a NOD, as otherwise the NOD will be deemed to have lapsed and no longer be valid – again leading to the loss of rights.*[150] The reference to the DAAB must be done in compliance with certain formalities.[151]

(ii) The failure relates to a matter

The procedure is simpler if the Engineer fails to make a determination of a *matter*, as defined in sub-paragraph (a) of Sub-Clause 3.7, within the relevant time limit, normally 42 days. In this case, the matter will be deemed to be a Dispute which may be referred by either Party to the DAAB for its decision under Sub-Clause 21.4 without the need for a NOD.[152] The 42-day time limit in sub-paragraph (a) of Sub-Clause 21.4.1 will not apply in this case which means that there would be no

147. Pursuant to Sub-Clause 21.4.1 [*Obtaining DAAB's Decision-Reference of a Dispute to the DAAB*].
148. Sub-Clause 3.7.5, second paragraph. There is no provision for disapplying this time bar.
149. Sub-Clause 3.7.5(c) and 3.7.5, second paragraph.
150. Sub-Clause 21.4.1(a). As each Party may have given a NOD, it is not clear what 'such NOD' in Sub-Clause 21.4.1 (a) would refer to where both Parties have given a NOD. A Party should be entitled to refer a Dispute to the DAAB, it is suggested, so long as it does so within 42 days of the latest NOD to be given in relation to that Dispute irrespective of who gave it.
151. *Ibid.*, and Sub-Clause 1.3 [*Notices and Other Communications*].
152. Sub-Clause 3.7.3, item (ii).

contractual time limit by which the Dispute has to be referred to the DAAB.[153] However, reference to the DAAB must be done in compliance with certain formalities.[154]

(6) Enforcement of an agreement or final and binding determination

The last paragraph of Sub-Clause 3.7.5 deals with the important question of enforcement of the Parties' agreement (reached under Sub-Clause 3.7.1) or of a final and binding determination of the Engineer, if one Party fails to comply with such an agreement or determination. It allows for their enforcement directly by arbitration in the same way in which a DAAB decision, whether binding or final and binding, may be enforced,[155] that is, by referral of the Party's failure itself directly to arbitration without the need to refer such failure first, as a Dispute, to a DAAB, pursuant to Sub-Clause 21.4, or to amicable settlement, pursuant to Sub-Clause 21.5.[156] Such enforcement is without prejudice to any other rights which a Party may have,[157] such as the right to claim damages or late payment interest (financing charges).[158]

(iv) Related Law:

(1) Assuming an agreement between a consulting engineer and the Employer requires the consulting engineer to perform the functions of the Engineer under RB/17, the consulting engineer will, naturally, be liable to the Employer for any breach of those obligations.[159] On the other hand, may the Contractor claim damages against the Engineer – with whom it has no contract – if the Contractor should be dissatisfied, for example, with certificates or determinations of the Engineer? In an English case, the Contractor sought to do so,[160] but its claim was dismissed on the ground that its contract with the Employer contained an

153. *Ibid*.
154. *See* Sub-Clause 21.4.1 and Sub-Clause 1.3 [*Notices and Other Communications*].
155. Sub-Clause 21.7, first paragraph.
156. *See* the commentary on Sub-Clause 21.7 below.
157. Sub-Clause 3.7.5, last paragraph.
158. *See* Sub-Clause 14.8 [*Delayed Payment*].
159. *See* Sub-Clause 3.9 of the FIDIC White Book (5th edn, 2017) and *Sutcliffe v Thachrah* (1974) AC 727 referred to in fn. 46 above of this commentary on **Clause 3**.
160. The contract was based on RB/69.

arbitration clause[161] – that is, it provided an effective remedy (against the Employer) for the Contractor's claims of dissatisfaction with the Engineer's actions – and the availability of that remedy was found to exclude the creation of any direct duty (in tort) of the Engineer to the Contractor that could entitle the Contractor to sue the Engineer.[162] As RB/17 also contains an arbitration clause (Clause 21), the position should be no different under it but may be so where a contract contains no such clause or otherwise provides an inadequate remedy for the Contractor.[163]

(2) If the Engineer makes a determination having previously met separately with the Parties to see if they could reach an agreement, the either binding or final and binding nature of the Engineer's determination might be subject to challenge on the same basis as a decision of the DAAB might be challenged as discussed under **(iv) Related Law** of the commentary on Sub-Clause 21.3 [*Avoidance of Disputes*] below.

(v) Improvements: As discussed in footnote 123 under heading *(4) Second stage: Engineer's Determination* in **(iii) Analysis** above, the requirement in Sub-Clause 3.7.1(b) that both Parties advise the Engineer that no agreement has been achieved might be reconsidered – it should be sufficient if one Party were to do so which should speed things up.

Figure 4 Agreement/Determination Procedure outlines the agreement / determination procedure in Sub-Clause 3.7.

161. Clause 67 of RB/69.
162. *Pacific Associates Inc v Baxter* (1990) 44 BLR 33.
163. Anthony Lavers, 'An Officer of the Contract? The Delicate Position of the Contract Administrator', SCL paper 224, 1 May 2020, 19. Should the Contractor assert a claim against the Engineer then, assuming the Engineer's contract with the Employer is based upon the FIDIC White Book (5th edn, 2017), the Engineer would be entitled, insofar as applicable law permits, to be indemnified by the Employer against such claim. Sub-Clause 3.9.4 of the White Book.

Figure 4 Agreement/Determination Procedure[1]

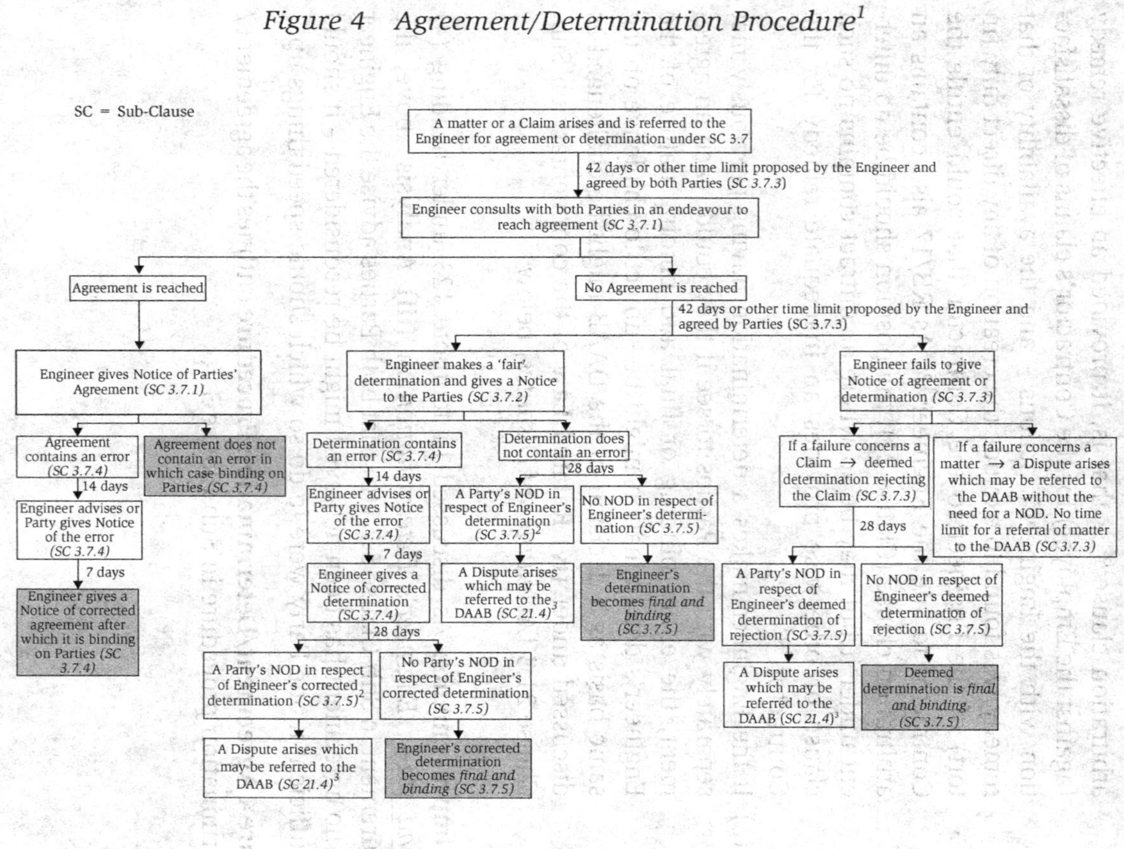

Source: Author's own work.

Figure 4 Agreement/Determination Procedure

Notes

1. This figure presents a simplified version of SCs 3.7 and 21.4 for illustrative purposes. Only the actual text of those SCs should be relied upon. Where a box is shaded, it shows an agreement or determination which is final and binding.
2. A Party may give a NOD with respect to only part(s) of the Engineer's determination (SC 3.7.5). This is not shown here.
3. Pursuant to SC 21.4.1(a), with certain exceptions, reference of a Dispute to the DAAB must be made within 42 days of giving or receiving (as the case may be) a NOD under SC 3.7.5. Otherwise, such NOD is deemed to have lapsed and no longer be valid.

--ooOOoo--

3.8 Meetings

The Engineer or the Contractor's Representative may require the other to attend a management meeting to discuss arrangements for future work and/or other matters in connection with execution of the Works.

The Employer's other contractors, the personnel of legally constituted public authorities and/or private utility companies, and/or Subcontractors may attend any such meeting, if requested by the Engineer or the Contractor's Representative.

The Engineer shall keep a record of each management meeting and supply copies of the record to those attending and to the Employer. At any such meeting, and in the record, responsibilities for any actions to be taken shall be in accordance with the Contract.

The Engineer or the Contractor's Representative may require the other to attend a management meeting. The Employer's other contractors, the personnel of legally constituted public authorities and/or private utilities and/or Subcontractors may attend if requested. The Engineer shall keep a record of each meeting and supply copies to those attending and the Employer.

Commentary

(i) Main Changes from RB/99: This Sub-Clause is entirely new in RB/17.[164]

(ii) Related Clauses / Sub-Clauses: 1.3 [*Notices and Other Communications*], 2.3 [*Employer's Personnel and Other Contractors*], 3.1 [*The Engineer*], 3.2 [*Engineer's Duties and Authority*], 3.3 [*Engineer's Representative*], 4.3 [*Contractor's Representative*], 4.6 [*Co-operation*] and 8.4 [*Advance Warning*].

(iii) Analysis: This new Sub-Clause acknowledges the reality – perhaps insufficiently recognised in earlier editions – that different types of management meetings attended by the Engineer, the Contractor's Representative and others concerned with work at or near the Site are a normal feature of project management under an RB contract. Therefore it is now specified how the Engineer or the Contractor's Representative may require them to take place, who may attend them, if requested by the Engineer or the Contractor's Representative to do so, how responsibilities for actions decided at such meetings are to be recorded and who is to keep the relevant records and supply copies to those attending and to the Employer.[165] Such meetings may be weekly at the Site, monthly progress meetings or sometimes quarterly meetings with high-level stakeholders, whether at the Site or elsewhere.

The occasion for a management meeting may, for example, be where one of the Parties had advised the other and the Engineer, or the Engineer had advised the Parties, of a known or probable future adverse event or circumstance, pursuant to Sub-Clause 8.4 [*Advance Warning*].[166]

The Sub-Clause provides that the Engineer or the Contractor's Representative may 'require' the other to attend a management meeting. Thus, attendance at such a meeting required by the other is mandatory. While

164. However, RB/99 had included an example clause on this subject in its *Guidance for the Preparation of Particular Conditions*, 5-6.
165. Any record of such a meeting must comply with Sub-Clause 1.3 [*Notices and Other Communications*]. Pursuant to the last paragraph of Sub-Clause 3.2 [*Engineer's Duties and Authority*], no record of a meeting may relieve the Contractor from any duty, obligation or responsibility under the Contract.
166. Thus, it may be a first informal step before invoking the claims procedure provided for by Sub-Clause 20.1 [*Claims*].

no sanction for non-compliance is specified,[167] it would ordinarily be imprudent and unprofessional for the Engineer or the Contractor's Representative to disregard a requirement from the other to attend a management meeting. Ideally, the record of each meeting should be signed at least by the Engineer.

--ooOOoo--

4 The Contractor

This Clause provides for the Contractor's general obligations in relation to execution of the Works including, among other things: the provision of a Performance Security; the appointment of the Contractor's Representative; the manner for providing Contractor's Documents; provisions for training, cooperation and setting out; health and safety obligations; and implementation of quality management systems. Sub-Clause 4.12 provides that if the Contractor encounters Unforeseeable adverse physical conditions, it may be entitled to an EOT and/or payment of Cost. Clause 4 also deals with the Contractor's obligations for access routes to the Site, transport of Goods, protection of the environment and others matters.

--ooOOoo--

4.1 Contractor's General Obligations

The Contractor shall execute the Works in accordance with the Contract. The Contractor undertakes that the execution of the Works and the completed Works will be in accordance with the documents forming the Contract, as altered or modified by Variations.

The Contractor shall provide the Plant (and spare parts, if any) and Contractor's Documents specified in the Contract, and all Contractor's Personnel, Goods, consumables and other things and services, whether of a temporary or permanent nature, required to fulfil the Contractor's obligations under the Contract.

167. But see for the Parties' duty to cooperate with each other Sub-Clauses 2.3 and 4.6.

The Contractor shall be responsible for the adequacy, stability and safety of all the Contractor's operations and activities, of all methods of construction and of all the Temporary Works. Except to the extent specified in the Contract, the Contractor:

(i) shall be responsible for all Contractor's Documents, Temporary Works, and such design of each item of Plant and Materials as is required for the item to be in accordance with the Contract; and
(ii) shall not otherwise be responsible for the design or specification of the Permanent Works.

The Contractor shall, whenever required by the Engineer, submit details of the arrangements and methods which the Contractor proposes to adopt for the execution of the Works. No significant alteration to these arrangements and methods shall be made without this alteration having been submitted to the Engineer.

If the Contract specifies that the Contractor shall design any part of the Permanent Works, then unless otherwise stated in the Particular Conditions:

(a) the Contractor shall prepare, and submit to the Engineer for Review, the Contractor's Documents for this part (and any other documents necessary to complete and implement the design during the execution of the Works and to instruct the Contractor's Personnel);
(b) these Contractor's Documents shall be in accordance with the Specification and Drawings and shall include additional information required by the Engineer to add to the Drawings for co-ordination of each Party's designs. If the Engineer instructs that further Contractor's Documents are reasonably required to demonstrate that the Contractor's design complies with the Contract, the Contractor shall prepare and submit them promptly to the Engineer at the Contractor's cost;
(c) construction of this part shall not commence until a Notice of No-objection is given (or is deemed to have been given) by the Engineer

under sub-paragraph (i) of Sub-Clause 4.4.1 [*Preparation and Review*] for all the Contractor's Documents which are relevant to its design, and construction of such part shall be in accordance with these Contractor's Documents;

(d) the Contractor may modify any design or Contractor's Documents which have previously been submitted for Review, by giving a Notice to the Engineer with reasons. If the Contractor has commenced construction of the part of the Works to which such design or Contractor's Documents are relevant, work on this part shall be suspended, the provisions of Sub-Clause 4.4.1 [*Preparation and Review*] shall apply as if the Engineer had given a Notice in respect of the Contractor's Documents under sub-paragraph (ii) of Sub-Clause 4.4.1, and work shall not resume until a Notice of No-objection is given (or is deemed to have been given) by the Engineer for the revised documents;

(e) the Contractor shall be responsible for this part and it shall, when the Works are completed, be fit for such purpose(s) for which the part is intended as are specified in the Contract (or, where no purpose(s) are so defined and described, fit for their ordinary purpose(s));

(f) in addition to the Contractor's undertaking above, the Contractor undertakes that the design and the Contractor's Documents for this part will comply with the technical standards stated in the Specification and Laws (in force when the Works are taken over under Clause 10 [*Employer's Taking Over*]) and in accordance with the documents forming the Contract, as altered or modified by Variations;

(g) if Sub-Clause 4.4.2 [*As-Built Records*] and/or Sub-Clause 4.4.3 [*Operation and Maintenance Manuals*] apply, the Contractor shall submit to the Engineer the Contractor's Documents for this part in accordance with such Sub-Clause(s) and in sufficient detail for the Employer to operate, maintain, dismantle, reassemble, adjust and repair this part; and

(h) if Sub-Clause 4.5 [*Training*] applies, the Contractor shall carry out training of the Employer's Personnel in the operation and maintenance of this part.

The Contractor must execute the Works in accordance with the Contract and provide the Plant, Contractor's Documents and other things and services required to fulfil its obligations. The Contractor is responsible for the adequacy, stability and safety of all its operations, methods of construction and Temporary Works. Except as specified in the Contract, the Contractor is responsible for all Contractor's Documents, Temporary Works, and such design of Plant and Materials as is required by the Contract.

Whenever the Engineer so requires, the Contractor must submit details of the arrangements and methods which it proposes to adopt for the execution of the Works, and the Contractor may make no significant alteration to these without submitting them to the Engineer.

If the Contract specifies that the Contractor shall design any part of the Permanent Works, then unless otherwise stated in the Particular Conditions:

(a) the Contractor must submit to the Engineer for Review the Contractor's Documents for this part, which shall be in accordance with the Specification and Drawings;
(b) construction of this part must not commence until a Notice of No-objection has been given by the Engineer for all Contractor's Documents relevant to its design;
(c) the Contractor may modify any design or Contractor's Documents which have previously been submitted for Review by giving a Notice to the Engineer with reasons;
(d) the Contractor is responsible for ensuring that, when completed, this part is fit for such purpose(s) for which it is intended as specified in the Contract or, where no purposes are defined, then for their ordinary purposes, and that the design and Contractor's Documents for this part comply with the technical standards stated in the Specification and Laws in force when the Works are taken over under Clause 10 and in accordance with the Contract; and

(e) if Sub-Clauses 4.4.2 and/or 4.4.3 and/or Sub-Clause 4.5 apply to this part, then the Contractor shall comply with them.

Commentary

(i) Main Changes from RB/99: This Sub-Clause is similar to Sub-Clause 4.1 of RB/99, except that:

(1) the second paragraph now refers in parenthesis to 'spare parts, if any' and the third paragraph to the Contractor's 'activities';
(2) in sub-paragraph (a) the text in parenthesis is new;
(3) the second sentence of sub-paragraph (b) is new;
(4) sub-paragraphs (c), (d), (f) and (h) are new and sub-paragraph (g) is partly new; and
(5) sub-paragraph (e) now provides (complementing former sub-paragraph (c)) that where no purpose(s) for the part (of the Permanent Works to be designed by the Contractor) is (are) defined or prescribed, it shall, when the Works are completed, be 'fit for their ordinary purpose(s)'.

(ii) Related Clauses / Sub-Clauses: 1.3 [*Notices and Other Communications*], 1.4 [*Law and Language*], 1.5 [*Priority of Documents*], 4 [*The Contractor*], 6.9 [*Contractor's Personnel*], 8.7 [*Rate of Progress*], 10 [*Employer's Taking Over*], 13.2 [*Value Engineering*], 15.2.3 [*Termination for Contractor's Default – After Termination*], 17.4 [*Indemnities by Contractor*] and 19.2.3 [*Insurance to Be Provided by the Contractor – Liability for Breach of Professional Duty*].

(iii) Analysis:

(1) Construction obligations

This Sub-Clause provides for the Contractor's overall obligations under the Contract, including where the Contractor is responsible for the design of part of the Permanent Works. The Contractor is required to execute the Works 'in accordance with the [...] Contract' (first paragraph) and to provide the Plant, spare parts, if any, and Contractor's Documents specified in the Contract (second paragraph). The Contractor must also provide all 'Contractor's Personnel, Goods, consumables and other things and services, whether of a temporary or permanent nature, required to fulfil the Contractor's obligations under the Contract' (second paragraph). Thus, the Contractor must provide all the things and services required to fulfil its obligations under the Contract, whether or not these are specified in the Contract.

As is normal in this type of contract, the Contractor is responsible for all of its methods of construction and Temporary Works (third paragraph). The Contractor, who may have been required to submit a tender programme and method statement as part of its Tender,[1] must submit details of its proposed 'arrangements and methods' whenever required by the Engineer, and thereafter they may not be altered significantly without being further submitted to the Engineer.[2]

The Engineer can be expected to object to the Contractor's proposed arrangements and methods if the Engineer believes that they will not enable the Contractor to comply with the Contract.

(2) Design obligations

RB/17 contains an entirely new Sub-Clause, Sub-Clause 4.4 [*Contractor's Documents*], dealing in Sub-Clause 4.4.1 [*Preparation and Review*] with where a part of the Works is to be designed by the Contractor. Reflecting increased attention to the Contractor's role as designer as compared to RB/99, the last paragraph of the present Sub-Clause, concerned with where the Contractor is to design a part of the Permanent Works, has been expanded from four sub-paragraphs in RB/99 to eight in RB/17.

The Specification should clearly describe the extent to which the Contractor is required to design a part of the Permanent Works so that there is no doubt about where the Employer's obligation ends and the Contractor's obligation begins. Thus, for example:

> Notes on the Drawings may be too brief to specify [the extent of the Contractor's design obligations] with sufficient clarity, and may be overlooked [...].[3]

In addition, the Specification should stipulate the criteria and procedures applicable to the part of the Works to be designed by the Contractor, and how such part is to be accepted by the Employer.[4]

1. *FIDIC Procurement Procedures Guide* (FIDIC, 2011) 122. As to reporting the Contractor's methods, *see also* Sub-Clause 8.3 (k)(ii).
2. Sub-Clause 4.1, fourth paragraph.
3. *The FIDIC Contracts Guide* (2nd edn, FIDIC, 2022) 152.
4. *Ibid.*, 97.

In the last paragraph of this Sub-Clause, the eight sub-paragraphs (a) to (h) contain general provisions dealing with the preparation and submission of Contractor's Documents for any part of the Works designed by the Contractor and with the Contractor's construction and completion of this part. Among other things, the Contractor's Documents must comply with the technical standards stated in the Specification and Laws (as defined) not merely when they were prepared and originally submitted but also possibly years later, when the Works are taken over under Clause 10.[5]

(3) Fitness for purpose obligations

Of particular importance, sub-paragraph (e) provides that the part of the Works designed by the Contractor must be 'fit for such purpose(s) for which the part is intended', as specified in the Contract. Furthermore – and this is a new provision – where no purpose(s) for the part is (are) described in the Contract, the part must be 'fit for their ordinary purpose(s)'.

Under the common law, there is nothing unusual in these 'fit for purpose(s)' provisions. Under the common law, where the Contractor is responsible only for construction (and not design) of a work under a construction contract, it will be liable to use materials of satisfactory quality, to do the work with care and skill, and the workmanship and materials must be reasonably fit the purpose for which they are required.[6] It will be liable to the Employer only for fault or negligence on its part.

On the other hand, where a Contractor undertakes both the design and the construction of a work, the Contractor will have a higher duty, namely – if no purpose for the work is specified in the relevant contract – to produce a work which will be suitable for its normal or ordinary purpose.[7] If the work is not suitable for such purpose, the Contractor will

5. Though changes in such standards or Laws after the Base Date may entitle the Contractor to a Variation, *see*, e.g., Sub-Clause 13.6 [*Adjustments for Changes in Laws*].
6. Atkin Chambers, *Hudson's Building and Engineering Contracts* (14th edn, Sweet & Maxwell, London, 2020) 388-395 (paras 3-033 to 3-039).
7. Thus, if a contractor is engaged to design and construct the roof of a house, and the roof leaks when it rains then, as the ordinary purpose of a roof is to protect against rain, the roof will not be fit for its purpose and the contractor will be responsible without the employer having to prove that the contractor was at fault in the manner in which it had designed or constructed the roof. Similarly, if a contractor is engaged to design and build a house, together with

be liable to the Employer without any need for the Employer to prove fault or negligence on the Contractor's part.[8] Similarly, if the Employer should specify in the Contract the purpose which the work to be designed and constructed by the Contractor is to achieve, the Contractor's responsibility will be to achieve that purpose and, if it fails to do so, it will be liable to the Employer without proof of fault or negligence.

Accordingly, if the purpose is to be specified in the Contract, the Employer should define it carefully. For example, if failure of the Contractor-designed part has the potential to undermine the successful operation or use not only of that part but also of the entire project, then to ensure that the Contractor will have heightened responsibility in that case, this needs to be made clear in the purpose provision.[9]

As a practical matter, Contractors tend to prefer the purpose of the part of the Works they are to design to be specified in the Contract, rather than to be left unstated, as then the extent of their responsibility will be clear and limited to what is expressly stated.

---

its foundations, and the house collapses because the subsoil subsided, the contractor will be responsible for the collapse of the house as the contractor is liable to produce a stable structure as the result of its work. Atkin Chambers, *Hudson's Building and Engineering Contracts* (14th edn, Sweet & Maxwell, London, 2020) 417 (para. 3-053) citing *Mansal Pty Ltd v Brokenshire*, unreported, Supreme Court of Western Australia, 3 December 1982.

8. For an English case finding the works concerned, wind turbine foundations, not to be fit for purpose, *see MT Højgaard A/S v E.ON Climate & Renewables UK Robin Rigg East Ltd and another* [2017] UKSC 59 [2017] BLR 477. In that case, the contractor was required by the relevant contract both to provide foundations having a 20-year design life and to comply with a specified design which (as it emerged after completion) would prevent that design life from being achieved. Notwithstanding this contradiction in the contract, the contractor was held by the UK Supreme Court to be bound by its more rigorous fitness for purpose obligation, the design life requirement. While each case turns on its facts, courts are generally inclined, the UK Supreme Court stated, to give full effect to the requirement that the item produced complies with its fitness for purpose obligation on the ground that the contractor can be expected to take the risk that the design is not in fact capable of achieving its purpose [para. 44].

9. Atkin Chambers, *Hudson's Building and Engineering Contracts* (14th edn, Sweet & Maxwell, London, 2020) 423 (para. 3-057).

(4) Contractor's indemnity for design

Pursuant to Sub-Clause 17.4, second paragraph, the Contractor agrees to indemnify the Employer against 'all acts, errors or omissions' in carrying out its design obligations that result in the Works (or Section or Part or major item of Plant, if any), when completed, not being fit for the purpose(s) for which they are intended.[10] Pursuant to Sub-Clause 1.15, the Contractor's liability for loss of profit, indirect or consequential loss on account of this indemnity is excluded, and its liability is, as well, subject to the total liability limit provided for by that Sub-Clause.

(iv) Related Law:

(1) Under French law and law in numerous European, Latin American, Middle Eastern and North African countries, the Contractor (and others in contract with the Employer) may have, by mandatory law, decennial liability (liability for 10 years) in one form or another for defects impairing the stability of a work which appear after completion.[11]

(2) The 'fitness for purpose' obligation under the common law corresponds to a type of obligation which is referred to in the civil law system as an obligation to guarantee a specific result (in French: *obligation de résultat*) as distinguished from an obligation to use best efforts or 'reasonable skill and care' under the common law (in French: *obligation de moyens*).[12] This distinction is recognised in the UNIDROIT Principles as follows:

> Article 5.1.4 (*Duty to achieve a specific result. Duty of best efforts*)
>
> (1) To the extent that an obligation of a party involves a duty to achieve a specific result, that party is bound to achieve that result.
>
> (2) To the extent that an obligation of a party involves a duty of best efforts in the performance of an activity, that party is

10. *See* the commentary on Sub-Clause 17.4 [*Indemnities by Contractor*] below.
11. *See* **Section 4 Common Law and Civil Law Compared – 4.4.4 Decennial Liability** of **Chapter II Applicable Law** above.
12. *See* Stefan Vogenauer (ed), *Commentary on the UNIDROIT Principles of International Commercial Contracts (PICC)* (2nd edn, OUP, Oxford, 2015) 626 (para. 1). For more details, *see* Ulrich Helm and others, 'Fitness for Purpose v Reasonable Skill and Care: How Do English Principles Regarding Standards of Care Fit in Civil Law Jurisdictions?' [2021] ICLR 39.

bound to make such efforts as would be made by a reasonable person of the same kind in the same circumstances.

(3) The approach taken by Sub-Clause 4.1(e) to the Contractor's fitness for purpose obligation is similar to that taken by the *United Nations Convention on Contracts for the International Sale of Goods*. This provides that, unless the parties have agreed otherwise, goods do not conform with a contract unless they:
   (a) are fit for the purposes for which goods of the same description would ordinarily be used;
   (b) are fit for any particular purpose expressly or impliedly made known to the seller at the time of the conclusion of the contract, except where the circumstances show that the buyer did not rely, or that it was unreasonable for him to rely, on the seller's skill and judgement [...].[13]

(v) Improvements:

Sub-Clause 4.1 (d) provides that 'the Contractor may modify any design or Contractor's Documents which have previously been submitted for Review' merely 'by giving a Notice to the Engineer with reasons'. This is because the requirement in the following sentence that the work shall not resume until a Notice of No-objection is given by the Engineer for the revised documents literally only applies '[i]f the Contractor has commenced construction of the part of the Works to which such design or Contractor's Documents are relevant'. If the Contractor wishes to modify any design or Contractor's Documents which have previously been submitted for Review *but has not yet commenced construction*, the requirement does not apply. This is clearly not the intention. The provisions of Sub-Clause 4.4.1 [*Preparation and Review*] should apply to the modified design or Contractor's Documents (not merely the requirement to give 'a Notice to the Engineer with reasons', as indicated by the first sentence of Sub-Clause 4.1 (d)). Therefore the language should be corrected.

--ooOOoo--

13. Art. 35(2) of the *United Nations Convention on Contracts for the International Sale of Goods* ('CISG').

4.2 Performance Security

The Contractor shall obtain (at the Contractor's cost) a Performance Security to secure the Contractor's proper performance of the Contract, in the amount and currencies stated in the Contract Data. If no amount is stated in the Contract Data, this Sub-Clause shall not apply.

4.2.1 Contractor's obligations

The Contractor shall deliver the Performance Security to the Employer, with a copy to the Engineer, within 28 days after receiving the Letter of Acceptance. The Performance Security shall be issued by an entity and from within a country (or other jurisdiction) to which the Employer gives consent and shall be in the form annexed to the Particular Conditions, or in another form agreed by the Employer (but such consent and/or agreement shall not relieve the Contractor from any obligation under this Sub-Clause).

The Contractor shall ensure that the Performance Security remains valid and enforceable until the issue of the Performance Certificate and the Contractor has complied with Sub-Clause 11.11 [*Clearance of Site*]. If the terms of the Performance Security specify an expiry date, and the Contractor has not become entitled to receive the Performance Certificate by the date 28 days before the expiry date, the Contractor shall extend the validity of the Performance Security until the issue of the Performance Certificate and the Contractor has complied with Sub-Clause 11.11 [*Clearance of Site*].

Whenever Variations and/or adjustments under Clause 13 [*Variations and Adjustments*] result in an accumulative increase or decrease of the Contract Price in one currency by more than twenty percent (20%) of the Accepted Contract Amount in that currency:

(a) in the case of such an increase, at the Employer's request the Contractor shall promptly increase the amount of the Performance Security in that currency by a percentage equal to the accumulative increase. If the Contractor incurs Cost as a result of this Employer's request, Sub-Clause 13.3.1 [*Variation by Instruction*] shall apply as if the increase had been instructed by the Engineer; or

(b) in the case of such a decrease, subject to the Employer's prior consent the Contractor may decrease the amount of the Performance Security in that currency by a percentage equal to the accumulative decrease.

4.2.2 Claims under the Performance Security

The Employer shall not make a claim under the Performance Security, except for amounts to which the Employer is entitled under the Contract in the event of:

(a) failure by the Contractor to extend the validity of the Performance Security, as described in this Sub-Clause, in which event the Employer may claim the full amount (or, in the case of previous reduction(s), the full remaining amount) of the Performance Security;
(b) failure by the Contractor to pay the Employer an amount due, as agreed or determined under Sub-Clause 3.7 [*Agreement or Determination*] or agreed or decided under Clause 21 [*Disputes and Arbitration*], within 42 days after the date of the agreement or determination or decision or arbitral award (as the case may be);
(c) failure by the Contractor to remedy a default stated in a Notice given under Sub-Clause 15.1 [*Notice to Correct*] within 42 days or other time (if any) stated in the Notice;
(d) circumstances which entitle the Employer to terminate the Contract under Sub-Clause 15.2 [*Termination for Contractor's Default*], irrespective of whether a Notice of termination has been given; or
(e) if under Sub-Clause 11.5 [*Remedying of Defective Work off Site*] the Contractor removes any defective or damaged Plant from the Site, failure by the Contractor to repair such Plant, return it to the Site, reinstall it and retest it by the date of

expiry of the relevant duration stated in the Contractor's Notice (or other date agreed by the Employer).

The Employer shall indemnify and hold the Contractor harmless against and from all damages, losses and expenses (including legal fees and expenses) resulting from a claim under the Performance Security to the extent that the Employer was not entitled to make the claim.

Any amount which is received by the Employer under the Performance Security shall be taken into account:

(i) in the Final Payment Certificate under Sub-Clause 14.13 [*Issue of FPC*]; or
(ii) if the Contract is terminated, in payment due to the Contractor under Sub-Clause 15.4 [*Payment after Termination for Contractor's Default*], Sub-Clause 15.7 [*Payment after Termination for Employer's Convenience*], Sub-Clause 16.4 [*Payment after Termination by Contractor*], Sub-Clause 18.5 [*Optional Termination*], or Sub-Clause 18.6 [*Release from Performance under the Law*] (as the case may be).

4.2.3 Return of the Performance Security

The Employer shall return the Performance Security to the Contractor:

(a) within 21 days after the issue of the Performance Certificate and the Contractor has complied with Sub-Clause 11.11 [*Clearance of Site*]; or
(b) promptly after the date of termination if the Contract is terminated in accordance with Sub-Clause 15.5 [*Termination for Employer's Convenience*], Sub-Clause 16.2 [*Termination by Contractor*], Sub-Clause 18.5 [*Optional Termination*] or Sub-Clause 18.6 [*Release from Performance under the Law*].

The Contractor shall obtain a Performance Security in the amount and currencies stated in the Contract Data to secure its proper performance of the Contract. If no amount is stated, then this Sub-Clause does not apply.

The Contractor shall deliver the Performance Security to the Employer with a copy to the Engineer, within 28 days after receiving the Letter of Acceptance. The Performance Security must be issued by an entity and from within a country to which the Employer has consented, and in the form annexed to the Particular Conditions or in another form agreed by the Employer. The Performance Security must remain valid and enforceable until the issue of the Performance Certificate and the Contractor's compliance with Sub-Clause 11.11. If the Performance Security specifies an expiry date and the Contractor has not become entitled to receive the Performance Certificate by 28 days before the expiry date, the Contractor shall extend the Performance Security. The Performance Security may be increased, at the Employer's request, or decreased, subject to the Employer's prior consent, in case of any accumulative increase or decrease, respectively, of the Contract Price in one currency by more than 20% of the Accepted Contract Amount in that currency.

The Employer may not make a claim under the Peformance Security except for amounts to which it is entitled as described in sub-paragraphs (a) to (e) of Sub-Clause 4.2.2.

Any amount that has been received by the Employer under the Performance Security shall be taken into account in the Final Payment Certificate or in payments due to the Contractor where the Contract has been terminated prematurely.

The Employer must return the Performance Security to the Contractor within 21 days after the issue of the Performance Certificate and the Contractor's compliance with Sub-Clause 11.11 or promptly after the termination of the Contract other than for the Contractor's default.

Commentary

(i) Main Changes from RB/99: Since the first edition of the RB in 1957,[14] the Contractor has been required to provide the Employer with a performance security from an insurance company or a bank to secure its due performance of the Contract. Since the 1970s, especially in the

14. *See* Clause 10 of RB/57.

Middle East, employers have been requiring that this security takes the form of a bond or guarantee payable on demand. Such an instrument is commonly known as an 'on-demand' bond or guarantee or simply as a 'demand guarantee(s)'. As it is payable on demand and does not require an Employer to show that the Contractor is in default, it is liable to abuse by an unscrupulous Employer. To curb such abuse, the corresponding provision of RB/87 had stipulated that:

> [p]rior to making a claim under the performance security the Employer shall, in every case, notify the Contractor stating the nature of the default in respect of which the claim is to be made.[15]

Sub-Clause 4.2 of RB/99 ceased to provide for such an advance warning but instead, to protect the Contractor, provided that the Employer must not make a claim under the performance security except for amounts to which the Employer was entitled under any of the four grounds listed in sub-paragraphs (a) to (d), which correspond roughly to sub-paragraphs (a) to (d) in Sub-Clause 4.2 of RB/17. RB/99 also included as annexes thereto (as does RB/17) example forms of both a surety bond and an on-demand guarantee that could serve as the performance security.

Sub-Clause 4.2 has been expanded and restructured in RB/17:

(1) It now includes five (instead of four) grounds under which the Employer may make a claim under the Performance Security,[16] and allows for an increase or decrease of the amount of the security in the event that Variations and/or adjustments under Clause 13 result in an accumulative increase or decrease of the Contract Price in a particular currency beyond a stated threshold.

(2) There is new wording to the effect that any amount received by the Employer pursuant to a claim under the Performance Security is to be taken into account in the Final Payment Certificate or, in the case of termination under specified Sub-Clauses of the Contract, in the payment due after termination.

15. Sub-Clause 10.3 of RB/87. FIDIC stated it then to be normal practice that, when the Contractor is notified of any default, it is given an opportunity to remedy it before a claim under the security is made. *See* FIDIC's *Guide to the Use of FIDIC Conditions of Contract for Works of Civil Engineering Construction* (4th edn, FIDIC, 1989) 58.
16. The new ground is in sub-para. (e) of Sub-Clause 4.2.2.

(3) The proposed form of demand guarantee attached as Annex C is new and based on the *Uniform Rules for Demand Guarantees* issued in 2010 ('URDG'), ICC publication no. 758, whereas in RB/99 it was based on an earlier edition of the URDG, ICC publication no. 458.

(4) In the last paragraph, provision is made for the return of the Performance Security after termination of the Contract other than for the Contractor's default, which is new.

(ii) Related Clauses / Sub-Clauses: 1.3 [*Notices and Other Communications*], 2.1 [*Right of Access to the Site*], 3.7 [*Agreement or Determination*], 11.5 [*Remedying Defective Work Off Site*], 11.11 [*Clearance of Site*], 13 [*Variations and Adjustments*], 14.2.2 [*Advance Payment – Advance Payment Certificate*], 14.6 [*Issue of IPC*], 14.13 [*Issue of FPC*], 15 [*Termination by Employer*], 16.2 [*Termination by Contractor*], 16.4 [*Payment after Termination by Contractor*], 18.5 [*Optional Termination*], 18.6 [*Release from Performance under the Law*] and 21 [*Disputes and Arbitration*].

(iii) Analysis:

(1) The requirement for Performance Security

The principal security which a Contractor must provide to an Employer to ensure the Contractor's good performance of a construction contract has traditionally been, in both the common law and civil law worlds,[17] a performance security of some kind. Sub-Clause 4.2 reflects this long-standing practice. The form of performance security acceptable to the Employer should (and usually will) be included in the tender documents.[18]

The Contractor is required to obtain a Performance Security (as defined in the Contract) in the amount and currencies stated in the Contract Data. If no amount is stated there, which would be highly unusual, Sub-Clause 4.2 will not apply.

While no percentage is indicated or suggested in RB/17, where the Performance Security takes the form of a demand guarantee (discussed

17. In French law, it is referred to as '*une garantie de bonne fin de travaux*' and normally takes the form of a guarantee issued by a bank. Jacques Montmerle and others, *Passation et Exécution des Marchés Privés de Travaux* (5th edn, Le Moniteur, Paris, 2006) 376-77 (para. 1006).

18. *Guidance for the Preparation of Particular Conditions*, 22.

below) it will usually be for 10% or 15% of the Accepted Contract Amount, that is, of the amount of the Contractor's tender price accepted by the Employer in the Letter of Acceptance.[19] The currencies and proportions of those currencies of the Performance Security will correspond, typically, to the currencies and proportions in which the Accepted Contract Amount is expressed.

Pursuant to Sub-Clause 4.2.1, the Contractor is required to deliver the Performance Security to the Employer, with a copy to the Engineer, within 28 days after receiving the Letter of Acceptance, that is, within 28 days after the Contract will ordinarily have entered into legal effect.[20] This will normally be before work formally begins, as the Commencement Date need only be within 42 days after the Contractor receives the Letter of Acceptance.[21] Indeed, the Employer may withhold right of access to, and possession of, the Site, until it has received the Performance Security.[22] Furthermore, no amount may be certified or paid to the Contractor until the Employer has received the Performance Security.[23] The Performance Security must remain valid and enforceable until the issue of the Performance Certificate[24] and the Contractor has complied

19. The World Bank's COPA, by contrast, provides for the issue of both an Environmental and Social ('ES') Performance Security (to secure the Contractor's ES obligations under the Contract) and a Performance Security and stipulates that the total of these securities (to be in the form of a demand guarantee or guarantees) 'shall normally not exceed 10% of the Accepted Contract Amount'. Sub-Clause 4.2, Contract Data, COPA.
20. It should also be within the period of validity of any tender security which the Contractor may have provided. *FIDIC Procurement Procedures Guide* (FIDIC, 2011) 118. Although not mentioned here – surprisingly – the Contractor should also be expected by the same date to submit the insurance policies required by Sub-Clause 19.2 [*Insurance to be provided by the Contractor*] as these must be in place before the Contractor commences work on Site. *See* the *FIDIC Procurement Procedures Guide* (FIDIC, 2011) 36.
21. *See* Sub-Clause 8.1 [*Commencement of Works*]. *See also* **Figure 5 Sequence of Events Before the Commencement Date ('CD')** at the end of this commentary on Clause 4.
22. Sub-Clause 2.1 [*Right of Access to the Site*].
23. Sub-Clause 14.6 [*Issue of IPC*].
24. What if the Employer should call a performance security after it should, rightfully, have been allowed to expire? In a case involving a modified form of FIDIC contract, an English court issued an interim injunction (pending arbitration) against an Employer, preventing it from calling performance security in the form of demand guarantees which, under the relevant

with Sub-Clause 11.11 [*Clearance of Site*],[25] that is, until the Contractor has performed essentially all of its obligations under the Contract.

If the Contractor should fail to comply with Sub-Clause 4.2, then this may entitle the Employer to terminate the Contract for the Contractor's default, pursuant to Sub-Clause 15.2.1 (e).

(2) Performance Security in the form of a demand guarantee

Pursuant to Sub-Clause 4.2.1, the Performance Security must be in the form annexed to the Particular Conditions, or in another form agreed by the Employer. As a practical matter, in international contracting outside Latin America (which may be influenced by use of the surety bond in the United States), the Employer will normally insist that the Performance Security is in the form of a guarantee payable on demand issued by a bank. Furthermore, as a practical matter, the Employer will normally require that the bank (or branch of, perhaps, an international bank) which issues the guarantee is located in the Employer's country, so as to facilitate suit against it by the Employer, and is otherwise an entity satisfactory to the Employer. To enable this bank (or branch) to issue the guarantee, the Contractor will normally have previously arranged for a bank in the Contractor's country, usually the Contractor's normal bank, to issue a counter-guarantee of the obligations to be undertaken by the bank (or branch) in the Employer's country that will issue the demand guarantee. The counter-guarantee will effectively 'mirror' the obligations in the demand guarantee. The Contractor will, in turn, agree to indemnify the counter-guaranteeing bank for any amount which it may be required to pay out.

Attached as Annex C in RB/17 is an example form of demand guarantee, which can be provided as Performance Security. It is based upon, and

contract, were due to expire on the issue of taking-over certificates, where there was a 'strong case' that the Employer was in breach of contract in having failed to issue the taking-over certificates. *Doosan Babcock v Commercializadora de Equipos y Materiales Mabe Limitada* [2013] EWHC 3010 (TCC).

25. Sub-Clause 4.2.1, second paragraph. Under some forms of contract – but not RB/17 – the amount of performance security may be reduced at taking over and/or to be replaced by other security during the defects notification or other guarantee period. *See*, e.g., the *ENNA Model Form International Contract for Process Plant Construction*, 2010 edn, GC 13.3.2, providing for a 50% reduction of the amount of the performance bond upon 'Acceptance' of the 'Plant'.

incorporates by reference, the *Uniform Rules for Demand Guarantees*, 2010 revision ('URDG'),[26] which are modern rules for demand guarantees, and are considered to be fair to each party involved. As they are incorporated by reference into the form of the guarantee, their legal effect is the same as if they were written out in full in the guarantee itself and therefore they should be read carefully.[27]

The form of demand guarantee at Annex C, as is true of most such guarantees, contains an expiration date, which it is suggested be 70 days after the expected expiry of the DNP for the Works. On the other hand, construction projects are often delayed. Accordingly, Sub-Clause 4.2.1 provides that if the Contractor has not become entitled to receive the Performance Certificate (which is to be issued shortly after expiry of the DNP) by the date 28 days before such expiration date, the Contractor must extend the validity of the Performance Security until the issue of the Performance Certificate and the Contractor has complied with Sub-Clause 11.11 [*Clearance of Site*]. If the Contractor should fail to do so, then, pursuant to Sub-Clause 4.2.2(a), the Employer is entitled to demand payment of the full amount, or full remaining amount, of the Performance Security. The Employer's demand must be accompanied by a written statement 'indicating in what respect the [Contractor] is in breach of its obligations under the Contract'.[28]

Sub-Clause 4.2.1 also provides that the amount of the Performance Security may be adjusted where the Contract Price is increased or decreased by Variations and/or adjustments under Clause 13. Under this provision, if Variations and/or adjustments under Clause 13 result in an accumulative increase or decrease of the Contract Price in one currency by more than 20% of the Accepted Contract Amount in that currency, the amount of the Performance Security in the relevant currency may be increased, at the Employer's request, 'by a percentage equal to the accumulative increase' or decreased, subject to the Employer's prior consent, 'by a percentage equal to the accumulative decrease'.

26. Published by the International Chamber of Commerce as ICC publication no 758.
27. For an authoritative commentary on the URDG, *see* Georges Affaki and Roy Goode, *Guide to ICC Uniform Rules for Demand Guarantees URDG 758* (ICC publication no 702E, Paris, 2011). *See also International Standard Demand Guarantee Practice for URDG 758 (ISDGP)* (ICC Publication 814E, Paris, 2021).
28. *See* the form of demand guarantee contained as Annex C in RB/17 and art. 15a of the URDG.

(3) Claims under Performance Security in the form of a demand guarantee

While Sub-Clause 4.2.2 provides that the Employer shall not make a claim under the Performance Security, except for amounts to which the Employer is entitled under the Contract in the case of any of five events or grounds (described in sub-paragraphs (a) through (e)),[29] the form of demand guarantee in Annex C does not refer to any restrictions on the Employer's ability to call the guarantee except for the requirement for a written statement of the breach, as described above. The written statement should, it is suggested, refer expressly to one or more of the five grounds listed in Sub-Clause 4.2.2, identifying the ground or grounds relied upon, although the form itself does not formally require this. The guaranteeing bank must then inform the Contractor, assuming that it is the 'instructing party' or, where applicable, the counter-guarantor (i.e., whoever gave the instructions to issue the guarantee and who may be the 'Applicant'), 'without delay' of such demand.[30] The Contractor or whoever is the instructing party may, if it considers the demand to be unjustified, seek to take protective action.[31]

While it would be a breach of the Contract by the Employer to call the guarantee on other than the five grounds (or for amounts that exceed what the Employer may be entitled to on those grounds), as the demand guarantee is a separate legal agreement from the Contract,[32] the guaranteeing bank is not bound by the restrictions in Sub-Clause 4.2.2. Consequently, if the guaranteeing bank should receive a written demand from the Employer to pay and a written statement specifying the respect in which the Contractor is in breach of the Contract, then – regardless of whether it is one of those five grounds or other grounds – the guaranteeing bank will be obliged to pay on the basis of this demand. This is

29. The World Bank's COPA requires that the first paragraph of Sub-Clause 4.2.2 be replaced by: 'The Employer shall not make a claim under the Performance Security, except for amounts for which the Employer is entitled under the Contract' which gives the Employer a wider right to call the Performance Security.
30. *See* art. 16 of the URDG.
31. This might include by way of an application to the DAAB, which has the power to decide on 'interim or conservatory measures' (*see* Rule 5.1(j) of the DAAB Rules), or to an Emergency Arbitrator (*see* art. 29 of the ICC Arbitration Rules) or to an ICC arbitral tribunal (*see* art. 28 of the ICC Arbitration Rules), or to a national court.
32. *See* art. 5 of the URDG.

because the guaranteeing bank's only obligation is to conform with the terms of the demand guarantee, that is, to pay on the basis of the Employer's written demand and written statement. If these documents conform on their face to the terms of the demand guarantee, the bank must pay. The guaranteeing bank has no obligation to investigate whether the respect in which the Contractor is said to be in breach is true or not.[33] The guaranteeing bank has five business days following presentation of a demand to examine it and determine whether it is a complying demand.[34] If and when the guaranteeing bank finds that the demand is complying, it must make payment.[35]

While requiring the Employer's written statement to specify one of the grounds listed in Sub-Clause 4.2.2 would not necessarily improve the Contractor's position as regards the guaranteeing bank (as the bank would have no obligation to investigate its accuracy), it would compel the Employer, in its relationship with the Contractor, to justify its action on one of the identified grounds as, if it were demonstrably baseless then, in England at least: 'there is in principle no reason why the beneficiary [i.e. the Employer] should not be injuncted from making the call'.[36]

Thus, if the Contractor should foresee that the Employer would make a call on a demand guarantee which could not be justified under Sub-Clause 4.2.2, the Contractor could take pre-emptive action by applying – subject to applicable law – for interim injunctive or similar relief against

33. *See* art. 19 of the URDG.
34. Art. 20a of the URDG.
35. Art. 20b of the URDG.
36. Atkin Chambers, *Hudson's Building and Engineering Contracts* (14th edn, Sweet & Maxwell, London, 2020) 1163 (para. 10-085). *See also Doosan Babcock Ltd v Comercializadora de Equipos y Materiales Mabe Limitada* [2013] EWHC 3010 (TCC). Even if the statement did not expressly identify one of the grounds listed in Sub-Clause 4.2.2, the Contractor could still require the Employer to justify its call on one of those grounds. However, it would be easier if the Employer were required to specify a ground in its written statement to the guaranteeing bank. For a review of common law cases involving circumstances where a call would be a violation of an express agreement between the beneficiary (e.g., the Employer) and the applicant (e.g., the Contractor), *see* Michael Valo and Markus Rotterdam, 'Beyond Fraud: Rethinking the Autonomy of Letters of Credit in Canada' [2020] ICLR 72.

the Employer from the DAAB, if it should be in place[37] or, from an Emergency Arbitrator[38] or an arbitral tribunal (if constituted[39]) or a competent national court. Alternatively, relying on Sub-Clause 4.2.2 and in the case of clear or manifest fraud (*see* under **(iv) Related Law** below), the Contractor could seek such relief against the guaranteeing bank from a court of the country of the guaranteeing bank[40] and/or against any counter-guaranteeing bank from a court of the country where such bank is located.

---

37. A DAAB has authority to decide on interim or conservatory measures. *See* Rule 5.1 (j) of the DAAB Rules.
38. *See* art. 29 of the ICC Arbitration Rules.
39. *See* art. 28 of the ICC Arbitration Rules.
40. Where the guaranteeing entity is a branch of an international bank, the Contractor could seek injunctive relief against the bank in the court of any country where the bank (assuming it is, as one would expect, the same legal entity as the branch) is located and which would accept jurisdiction. Thus if, for example, the guaranteeing entity were the branch in Cairo, Egypt, of an international bank having also a branch in the United States and if the relevant US court would accept jurisdiction and be more welcoming to the Contractor's action than an Egyptian court might be, the Contractor could proceed before the US court. If the Contractor were to obtain a temporary restraining order or a preliminary injunction against the bank from a US court, this would be binding on the bank wherever it had branches, including in Egypt. The author was involved in just such a case. In that case, the US court issued a temporary restraining order which was binding on the bank (including, naturally, its Cairo, Egypt, branch) subject to the condition that the contractor places funds equal to the amount of the guarantee in escrow under the US court's supervision. As a consequence, when the Egyptian beneficiary called on the Cairo branch to pay the guarantee, the branch could (and did) justify refusing to pay by reference to the US court order, failure to comply with which could subject the bank to criminal penalties. This solution was a positive outcome for the contractor who was concerned that if the funds were paid out in Egypt they would be irrecoverable, as a practical matter, whatever the merits.
However, there is a well-established legal doctrine in certain jurisdictions and in international law to the effect that a branch of a bank in one country is to be treated for certain purposes, including for interim measures or the enforcement of a foreign judgment or arbitral award, as being a separate legal entity from the bank's head office in another country. *See*, e.g., Resolution no 3/2012 entitled '*Principles of Jurisdiction over Foreign Bank Branches in the Matter of Extraterritorial Attachment and Turnover*' of the Committee on International Monetary Law of the 75th Conference of the International Law Association held in Sofia, Bulgaria, 26 to 30 August 2012

Thus, the restrictions in Sub-Clause 4.2.2, while not binding on the guaranteeing bank or any counter-guaranteeing bank, may nevertheless, in an appropriate case, be relied upon by the Contractor to prevent or delay a call on the guarantee by the Employer or, in an appropriate case, to prevent or delay a guaranteeing bank or a counter-guaranteeing bank (a guaranteeing bank may, in practice, be hesitant to pay if it is unsure of being reimbursed by its counter-guaranteeing bank) from paying under its guarantee or counter-guarantee, respectively. The Employer is also expressly required by Sub-Clause 4.2.2 to indemnify the Contractor for any damages which it might suffer as the result of an unjustified claim under the Performance Security.

Nevertheless, as the Contractor is exposed to the risk that any guarantee payable on demand will be called and paid out without justification,[41] it must always take this into account when calculating its tender price.[42]

When making a claim under the Performance Security, the Employer should be complying with other relevant provisions of the Conditions – as they naturally continue to apply – including the possible need for a Notice of Claim under Sub-Clause 20.2.1.

(4) Performance Security in the form of a surety bond

Attached as Annex D in RB/17 is an example form of surety bond, which some Employers might be prepared to accept as Performance Security. This form is based upon, and incorporates by reference, the *Uniform Rules for Contract Bonds* ('URCB'), published as document no. 524 by the

---

and the English case, *Societe Eram Shipping Co Ltd. v Hong Kong and Shanghai Banking Corp Ltd* [2003] UKHL 30, [2004] 1 AC 260. Application of this doctrine (referred to as the 'separate entity rule') may sometimes prevent a contractor from obtaining an injunction from courts in one country where a bank has a branch or its head office so as to stop payment by the bank of a demand guarantee issued and payable by a branch in another country. Thus, whether the separate entity rule might apply needs to be investigated in each case.

41. While its attraction may be limited, insurance against the improper call of a demand guarantee may be available. *See* Nicholas Brown and Ang Wee Jian, 'Bond Call Insurance: Is It Worth the Candle' [2018] ICLR 364.
42. *See Edward Owen Engineering v Barclays Bank International and Umma Bank* (CA 1977), 6 BLR 4,10, where Lord Denning stated that an unconditional demand guarantee 'bears the colour of a discount on the [contract] price of 10 per cent or 5 per cent or as the case may be'.

International Chamber of Commerce,[43] which are modern and internationally accepted rules for such instruments.

In certain common law countries, it is customary for the Contractor to be required to provide performance security in the form of a surety bond. Unlike a demand guarantee, a surety bond is only payable upon the actual default of the Contractor, and not upon a simple demand. The surety bond is an accessory to the Contract or a secondary obligation in relation to the primary obligation represented by the Contract. On the other hand, a demand guarantee is the primary obligation of the bank which issues it and (like a surety bond) a separate contract from the Contract. Whereas a demand guarantee is a banking instrument normally issued by a bank, a surety bond is an insurance instrument normally issued by an insurance company or by a company (sometimes known as a 'surety company') affiliated to an insurance company.

Under the form attached as Annex D, the surety (the 'Guarantor') undertakes that, upon any 'Default'[44] of the Contractor (the 'Principal') or upon the occurrence of any of the events and circumstances listed in Sub-Clause 15.2.1 entitling the Employer to terminate the Contract for the Contractor's default, the surety will 'satisfy and discharge the damages' that the Employer sustains due to such default, events or circumstances up to the 'Bond Amount'.[45] A Default is deemed to be established upon issue of a certificate of a Default by a third party (which may include, among others, 'an independent architect or engineer') if the bond so provides and such certificate is served upon the surety.[46]

43. For more information about this form *see* Javier Camacho de los Ríos, 'The New ICC Regulations on Contract Bonds', 30(1) The Int'l Lawyer, ABA (Spring 1996), 1.
44. Art. 2 of the URCB defines 'Default' as '[a]ny breach, default or failure to perform any Contractual Obligation [as defined] which shall give rise to a claim for performance, damages, compensation or other financial remedy by the Beneficiary [the Employer]'. The URCB defines 'Contractual Obligation' as '[a]ny duty, obligation or requirement imposed by a clause, paragraph, section, term, condition, provision or stipulation contained in or forming part of a Contract or tender'.
45. There are several fns to the form, one of which provides the Guarantor with the option, in lieu of paying damages, of performing the Contractor's obligations under the Contract.
46. Art. 7(j) of the URCB. The form of bond attached as Annex D in RB/17 does not provide for this but could, naturally, be amended to do so.

The amount of a surety bond (corresponding to the cover provided to the Employer) will usually be higher – from 30% of the value of the contract upwards[47] – than the amount of a demand guarantee, and may equal the Accepted Contract Amount. As in the case of the form of demand guarantee (Annex C), a call on the surety bond is not expressed in the form of surety bond (Annex D) to be restricted to the five events listed in Sub-Clause 4.2.2 of the Conditions, but a surety can (unlike a guaranteeing bank under a demand guarantee) be expected to examine Sub-Clause 4.2.2 as part of its obligation to satisfy itself whether there has been a 'Default' under the Contract and will not pay on the bond unless either it is satisfied that one or more of these events entitling the Employer to claim under the Performance Security has occurred, or it is ordered to do so by a competent tribunal.

As a surety bond may only be called upon actual proof of default of the Contractor – to the satisfaction of the surety or a competent tribunal – the surety bond obviously presents much less risk for the Contractor than a demand guarantee. However, as indicated above, use of the surety bond appears to be generally limited to the common law countries, which have a corresponding law of suretyship. Surety bonds appear to be little used in civil law countries or internationally outside Latin America.

(5) Return of the Performance Security

Sub-Clause 4.2.3 provides that the Employer must return the Performance Security to the Contractor, within 21 days after issue of the Performance Certificate and the Contractor's compliance with Sub-Clause 11.11 [*Clearance of Site*], or promptly after termination of the Contract other than for the Contractor's default.[48] The obligation to do so is necessary as, at least where it takes the form of a demand guarantee, it may be called upon demand until its expiration date, and the Contractor will be liable for the related premiums until then.

(iv) Related Law: The forms of Performance Security in Annexes C and D of the Conditions contain a governing law provision. A bank issuing a demand guarantee will normally require that this law be that of the location of the branch or office of the bank that issues the guarantee and this is, in fact, what the URDG provides, unless the demand guarantee

47. Javier Camacho de los Ríos, 'The New ICC Regulations on Contract Bonds', 30(1) The Int'l Lawyer, ABA (Spring 1996), 1, 20.
48. Under Sub-Clause 15.2 [*Termination for Contractor's Default*].

provides otherwise.[49] The law chosen will be important as in the case of a demand guarantee it will determine, among other things, the circumstances in which a guaranteeing bank is justified in refusing to honour a demand to pay such a guarantee. Whether under the common law or under civil law, where a demand guarantee has been called in accordance with its terms, the bank must ordinarily pay.[50] Under English law, the only ground that can justify a refusal to pay, apart from a discrepancy in the demand, is fraud, that is, where the Employer 'knows that there is no right to payment, but expressly or impliedly represents his claim to be valid, provided that this [that is, that the Employer has no right to payment] is known to the issuing bank at the time of paying or passing on the demand [...]'.[51] Australia and Singapore take a broader approach as to when a demand may be restrained.[52] In Singapore, fraud and unconscionability are the two bases upon which a demand on a bank guarantee may be restrained.[53]

Under French law, a bank is only justified in refusing such a demand in the case of manifestly abusive or fraudulent conduct,[54] apart from a discrepancy in the demand, including late presentation. Thus, a call was held in France to be manifestly fraudulent where the employer had failed

49. Art. 34 of URDG.
50. *See* art. 20 of URDG.
51. Atkin Chambers, *Hudson's Building and Engineering Contracts* (14th edn, Sweet & Maxwell, London, 2020) 1159 (para. 10-080) citing *Edward Owen Engineering Ltd. v Barclays Bank International Ltd and Umma Bank* (CA 1977) 6 BLR 4, *United City Merchants (Investments) and Glass Fibres and Equipment Ltd v Royal Bank of Canada* [1983] A.C. 168 and *Bolivinter Oil S.A. v Chase Manhattan Bank* [1984] I W.L.R. 392, CA.
52. Julian Bailey, *Construction Law* (3rd edn, London Publishing, UK, 2020) vol 2, 1090 (para. 12.70).
53. *Ibid.* Julian Bailey gives several examples of unconscionability such as 'where the beneficiary of a bond makes an "astronomical and grossly inflated" claim for damages as a pretext for calling on a bond' and 'where the conduct of the beneficiary of the bond brought about the circumstances that would otherwise justify a demand being made'. Julian Bailey, *Construction Law* (3rd edn, London Publishing, UK, 2020) vol 2, 1092-1093 (para. 12.73). *See also* Atkin Chambers, *Hudson's Building and Engineering Contracts* (14th edn, Sweet & Maxwell, London, 2020) 1162-1163 (para. 10-084).
54. In French: *fraude manifeste*. *See* French Civil Code, art. 2321.

to pay certificates for amounts due to a contractor which the employer had itself approved and invoices of the contractor which the employer had not contested.[55]

(v) Improvements:

(1) It should be made clear that the Contractor's obligation under Sub-Clause 4.2 to provide a Performance Security is a continuing obligation to ensure that the Performance Security remains valid, enforceable and effective for its full amount until the issue of the Performance Certificate and the Contractor's fulfilment of its Sub-Clause 11.11 obligations. As it is a continuing obligation, if the original Performance Security should prove deficient for any reason, the Contractor should have to provide additional and/or substitute security to make up for the shortfall. This appears to be the intention, but it is not stated explicitly.

(2) Sub-Clause 4.2.2 provides that the Employer may not make a claim under the Performance Security except for amounts to which the Employer 'is entitled under the Contract' in the event of the five grounds listed, (a) to (e). This language may enable the Contractor to argue that, where the Performance Security takes the form of a demand guarantee, the Employer must first prove its entitlement to the relevant amounts before it can call the guarantee (much as a default must be proved under a surety bond).[56] As this would contradict the normal intention of a

55. Cass com, 10 June 1986 (no 84-17.769). In such a situation, the result under English law may be similar, *see* Eveleigh LJ in *Potton Homes Ltd v Coleman Contractors (Overseas) Ltd* (CA 1984) 28 BLR 19. For a more recent French case denying that a call was manifestly fraudulent or abusive *see* Ct of App Paris, 19 May 2017 (no 17/05850) (*Salini Impregilo v Société Générale*). Italian law appears to be little different from French law. *See* Giuseppe Broccoli and Lauren Adams, 'On-demand Bonds: A Review of Italian and English Decisions on Fraudulent or Abusive Calling' [2015] ICLR 103.

56. Support for this argument may be found in *Pearson Bridge (N.S.W.) Ltd v State Rail Authority of New South Wales* (1982) 1 A.C.L.R. 81, cited in Atkin Chambers, *Hudson's Building and Engineering Contracts* (14th edn, Sweet & Maxwell, London, 2020) 1166-1167 (para. 10-087). Moreover, an ICC award has held that the identical language in Sub-Clause 4.2 of RB/99 required that entitlement has been established under the contract, that is, pursuant to Sub-Clause 2.5 and either an agreement of the Parties or a determination of the Engineer under Sub-Clause 3.5 of RB/99. The tribunal stated that entitlement in Sub-Clause 4.2 'must mean an entitlement for the time being

demand guarantee,[57] to foreclose such an argument, it would be better if Sub-Clause 4.2.2 were drafted so as to provide that, where the Performance Security takes the form of a demand guarantee, the Employer has simply to assert a bona fide claim for amounts under the Contract on any of the five listed grounds, without any need to prove its 'entitlement' to such amounts.[58]

(3) The form of demand guarantee annexed to the Conditions as Annex C should provide that any demand be accompanied by a written statement not merely 'indicating in what respect the Applicant is in breach' – as at present – but specifying that one or more of the five events listed in Sub-Clause 4.2.2 has occurred and describing such event. This is justified as without the occurrence of such a specified event or events, the Employer has no right to call the demand guarantee. The surety bond annexed to the Conditions as Annex D should be to the same effect.

(4) In Sub-Clause 4.2.1, the words '(but such consent and/or agreement shall not relieve the Contractor from any obligation under this Sub-Clause)' in the first paragraph can safely be omitted as they add nothing to this Sub-Clause. Where the Employer's consent to the entity (or its country) issuing the Performance

(that is to say, at the time when the demand is made), even though that entitlement might subsequently be revised by a decision of the DB or an award by the arbitral tribunal [...]'. Partial award in ICC arbitration (June 2018) described in the PowerPoints of Gerlando Butera, Addleshaw Goddard, London, presented at the *FIDIC International Contract Users' Conference* in London, 4 and 5 December 2018. In this connection, *see* the English case *A and B* 2017 EWHC 2055 (QB), 31 March 2017.

57. As stated by one authority:

> insofar as a construction contract may make clear provision for the furnishing of an unconditional guarantee as security for due performance, the normal interpretation [...] will be that, in response to the stipulated demand, an unqualified transfer of the sums in question is intended, provided only that there is a bona fide dispute or claim on the secured party's part, and any further investigation of its merits or extent is not usually intended by the contract.
>
> Atkin Chambers, *Hudson's Building and Engineering Contracts* (14th edn, Sweet & Maxwell, London, 2020) 1164 (para. 10-085).

58. *See* Julian Bailey, *Construction Law* (3rd edn, London Publishing, UK, 2020) vol 2, 1094-1097 (para. 12.74) which addresses this issue.

Security is expressly required by the Contract, as is the case here, the giving of such consent should not relieve the Contractor from any contractual obligation.

(5) An alternative to a guarantee payable without any condition except for the Employer's demand would be a guarantee providing as a condition that the Employer presents a decision of the DAAB, or an Engineer's determination under Sub-Clause 3.7, in the Employer's favour for the amount demanded.[59] While this would be fairer to the Contractor, Employers have been generally disinclined to accept any such conditions.

--ooOOoo--

4.3 Contractor's Representative

The Contractor shall appoint the Contractor's Representative and shall give him/her all authority necessary to act on the Contractor's behalf under the Contract, except to replace the Contractor's Representative.

The Contractor's Representative shall be qualified, experienced and competent in the main engineering discipline applicable to the Works and fluent in the language for communications defined in Sub-Clause 1.4 [*Law and Language*].

Unless the Contractor's Representative is named in the Contract, the Contractor shall, before the Commencement Date, submit to the Engineer for consent the name and particulars of the person the Contractor proposes to appoint as Contractor's Representative. If consent is withheld or subsequently revoked, or if the appointed person fails to act as Contractor's Representative, the Contractor shall similarly submit the name and particulars of another suitable replacement for such appointment. If the Engineer does not respond within 28 days after

59. The condition of a decision of a 'Combined Dispute Board', as qualifying to the right to call a performance security, is provided for in the *ICC Model Turnkey Contract for Major Projects* (ICC Publication no 659 E 2007) art. 11.1, but not in the 2020 edition of this form (ICC Publication 797E).

receiving this submission, by giving a Notice to the Contractor objecting to the proposed person or replacement, the Engineer shall be deemed to have given his/her consent.

The Contractor shall not, without the Engineer's prior consent, revoke the appointment of the Contractor's Representative or appoint a replacement (unless the Contractor's Representative is unable to act as a result of death, illness, disability or resignation, in which case his/her appointment shall be deemed to have been revoked with immediate effect and the appointment of a replacement shall be treated as a temporary appointment until the Engineer gives his/her consent to this replacement, or another replacement is appointed, under this Sub-Clause).

The whole time of the Contractor's Representative shall be given to directing the Contractor's performance of the Contract. The Contractor's Representative shall act for and on behalf of the Contractor at all times during the performance of the Contract, including issuing and receiving all Notices and other communications under Sub-Clause 1.3 [*Notices and Other Communications*] and for receiving instructions under Sub-Clause 3.5 [*Engineer's Instructions*].

The Contractor's Representative shall be based at the Site for the whole time that the Works are being executed at the Site. If the Contractor's Representative is to be temporarily absent from the Site during the execution of the Works, a suitable replacement shall be temporarily appointed, subject to the Engineer's prior consent.

The Contractor's Representative may delegate any powers, functions and authority except:

(a) the authority to issue and receive Notices and other communications under Sub-Clause 1.3 [*Notices and Other Communications*]; and
(b) the authority to receive instructions under Sub-Clause 3.5 [*Engineer's Instructions*]),

to any suitably competent and experienced person and may at any time revoke the delegation. Any delegation or revocation shall not take effect until the Engineer has received a Notice from the Contractor's Representative, naming the person, specifying the powers, functions and authority being delegated or revoked, and stating the timing of the delegation or revocation.

All these persons shall be fluent in the language for communications defined in Sub-Clause 1.4 [*Law and Language*].

The Contractor shall appoint the Contractor's Representative and give it all authority to act on its behalf except to replace itself. The Contractor's Representative must be qualified, experienced and competent in the main engineering discipline of the Works and fluent in the language for communications.

Unless named in the Contract, the Contractor must submit the name and particulars of the person it proposes for this role to the Engineer for consent before the Commencement Date, and the Engineer must respond within 28 days. If the Engineer does not do so, the Engineer is deemed to have consented.

The Contractor shall not revoke the appointment or appoint a replacement without the Engineer's consent unless the representative is unable to act due to death, illness, disability or resignation, in which case its appointment is deemed to have been revoked, and the appointment of a replacement will be treated as a temporary appointment, until the Engineer consents to this replacement.

The Contractor's Representative must be based at the Site during the whole time that the Works are being executed, and its entire time must be given to directing the Contractor's performance of the Contract. While the Contractor's Representative may generally delegate its authority, it may not do so to issue and receive Notices and other communications, or to receive instructions from the Engineer. Any delegation or revocation shall not be effective until the Engineer has been notified. Any delegate must be fluent in the language for communications.

Commentary

(i) Main Changes from RB/99:

(1) The provision in the first paragraph that the Contractor's Representative may not replace itself is new.
(2) The second paragraph providing for the qualifications of the Contractor's Representative is new.
(3) The provision in the third paragraph that if the Engineer does not respond within 28 days after submission of the name and particulars of a person proposed to act as Contractor's Representative, the Engineer shall be deemed to have given its consent is new.
(4) The fourth paragraph, providing more detail where the Contractor's Representative is unable to act as a result of death, illness, disability or resignation, is new.
(5) The provision in the fifth paragraph that the Contractor's Representative acts for and on behalf of the Contractor at all times is new.
(6) The provision in the sixth paragraph that the Contractor's Representative shall be based at the Site for the whole time that the Works are being executed at the Site is new.
(7) While under RB/99 the Contractor's Representative's power to delegate was unlimited so long as the Engineer was notified beforehand, the Contractor's Representative may no longer delegate authority either to issue and receive Notices and other communications under Sub-Clause 1.3 or to receive instructions from the Engineer under Sub-Clause 3.5.

(ii) Related Clauses / Sub-Clauses: 1.2 [*Interpretation*], 1.3 [*Notices and Other Communications*], 1.4 [*Law and Language*], 3.3 [*The Engineer's Representative*], 3.5 [*Engineer's Instructions*], 3.8 [*Meetings*], 6.8 [*Contractor's Superintendance*], 6.9 [*Contractor's Personnel*], 6.12 [*Key Personnel*], 12.1 [*Works to Be Measured*] and 14.6 [*Issue of IPC*].

(iii) Analysis:

(1) The Contractor's Representative's qualifications

Once work commences, the Contractor's Representative (sometimes referred to by the Contractor internally as 'Project Manager'[60]) becomes

60. Or by another title.

the most important member of the Contractor's staff executing the Works, as the Contractor's Representative is directly responsible to the Employer and the Engineer for the Contractor's performance of the Contract. The Contractor's Representative has 'all' authority necessary to act on the Contractor's behalf under the Contract, except to replace the Contractor's Representative itself.

Given its important role, the Contractor's Representative is required to be competent 'in the main engineering discipline applicable to the Works', that is, 'the engineering discipline of the Works which is of highest value proportionate to the value of the Works'.[61] If it is desired to stipulate the particular engineering discipline in which it should be qualified, the *Guidance* provides drafting advice in this regard.[62] The Contractor's Representative must also be fluent in the language for communications,[63] and if the Contractor's Representative or its delegates should have other language skills, the *Guidance* provides drafting advice.[64]

The Contractor's Representative also needs to be competent in contract administration, including in the drafting of Notices, letters, and claims, and be experienced in claims procedures generally. While the Contractor's Representative may be advised or assisted by persons competent in these areas, authority for issuing and receiving Notices and other communications under the Sub-Clause 1.3 (including for receiving instructions under Sub-Clause 3.5) is now a non-delegable one of the Contractor's Representative.[65] This means they must be issued or received by and in the name of the Contractor's Representative – and no one else – if they are to be communications of, with, or to, the Contractor.

(2) The Engineer's consent

The natural person to be appointed as the Contractor's Representative must have been consented to by the Engineer,[66] which consent may not be unreasonably withheld or delayed.[67] Either the Contractor's Representative must have been named in the Contract or the name and other particulars of the person proposed must have been submitted to the

61. *Guidance for the Preparation of Particular Conditions*, 22-23.
62. *Ibid.*
63. *See* Sub-Clause 1.4 [*Law and Language*].
64. *Guidance for the Preparation of Particular Conditions*, 22-23.
65. Sub-Clause 4.3, seventh paragraph.
66. Sub-Clause 4.3, third paragraph and, for the meaning of 'consent', *see* Sub-Clause 1.2(g).
67. Sub-Clause 1.3, third paragraph.

Engineer for consent before the Commencement Date.[68] Similarly, the Engineer must consent to any revocation or replacement of the Contractor's Representative.[69] No amount may be certified or paid to the Contractor until the Contractor has appointed the Contractor's Representative.[70]

An excellent addition – here and similarly elsewhere – is the provision to the effect that if the Engineer does not respond within 28 days after receiving a request to consent to a proposed person to act as the Contractor's Representative, or to replace one, the Engineer shall be deemed to have given its consent.[71]

(3) Required presence at Site

Under the new Sub-Clause, as under its predecessor, the Contractor's Representative must give its whole time to direction of the Contractor's performance of the Contract. However, what is now explicit is that the Contractor's Representative 'shall be based at the Site for the whole time that the Works are being executed at the Site'.[72] Given the development of modern communications systems, among other things, there has been a tendency for Contractor's Representatives to become 'arm-chair generals' and to direct the performance of major construction contracts from the home office, sometimes a continent away, or elsewhere other than the Site. Though temporary absences are permitted (in which case a suitable replacement must be temporarily appointed and consented to by the Engineer), acting in this way is clearly now unacceptable.

--ooOOoo--

Thus, the new Sub-Clause, overall, places greater non-delegable responsibility on the Contractor's Representative.

--ooOOoo--

68. *Ibid. See also* **Figure 5 Sequence of Events Before the Commencement Date ('CD')** at the end of the commentary on this Clause 4 below.
69. Sub-Clause 4.3, fourth paragraph.
70. Sub-Clause 14.6.
71. Sub-Clause 4.3, third paragraph.
72. Sub-Clause 4.3, sixth paragraph.

4.4 Contractor's Documents

4.4.1 Preparation and Review

The Contractor's Documents shall comprise the documents:

(a) stated in the Specification;

(b) required to satisfy all permits, permissions, licences and other regulatory approvals which are the Contractor's responsibility under Sub-Clause 1.13 [*Compliance with Laws*];

(c) described in Sub-Clause 4.4.2 [*As-Built Records*] and Sub-Clause 4.4.3 [*Operation and Maintenance Manuals*], where applicable; and

(d) required under sub-paragraph (a) of Sub-Clause 4.1 [*Contractor's General Obligations*], where applicable.

Unless otherwise stated in the Specification, the Contractor's Documents shall be written in the language for communications defined in Sub-Clause 1.4 [*Law and Language*].

The Contractor shall prepare all Contractor's Documents and the Employer's Personnel shall have the right to inspect the preparation of all these documents, wherever they are being prepared.

If the Specification or these Conditions specify that a Contractor's Document is to be submitted to the Engineer for Review, it shall be submitted accordingly, together with a Notice from the Contractor stating that the Contractor's Document is ready for Review and that it complies with the Contract.

The Engineer shall, within 21 days after receiving the Contractor's Document and this Notice from the Contractor, give a Notice to the Contractor:

(i) of No-objection (which may include comments concerning minor matters which will not substantially affect the Works); or

(ii) that the Contractor's Document fails (to the extent stated) to comply with the Contract, with reasons.

If the Engineer gives no Notice within this period of 21 days, the Engineer shall be deemed to have given a Notice of No-objection to the Contractor's Document.

After receiving a Notice under sub-paragraph (ii), above, the Contractor shall revise the Contractor's Document and resubmit it to the Engineer for Review in accordance with this Sub-Clause and the period of 21 days for Review shall be calculated from the date that the Engineer receives it.

4.4.2 As-Built Records

If no as-built records to be prepared by the Contractor are stated in the Specification, this Sub-Clause shall not apply.

The Contractor shall prepare, and keep up-to-date, a complete set of "as-built" records of the execution of the Works, showing the exact as-built locations, sizes and details of the work as executed by the Contractor. The format, referencing system, system of electronic storage and other relevant details of the as-built records shall be as stated in the Specification (if not stated, as acceptable to the Engineer). These records shall be kept on the Site and shall be used exclusively for the purposes of this Sub-Clause.

The as-built records shall be submitted to the Engineer for Review, and the Works shall not be considered to be completed for the purposes of taking-over under Sub-Clause 10.1 [*Taking Over the Works and Sections*] until the Engineer has given (or is deemed to have given) a Notice of No-objection under sub-paragraph (i) of Sub-Clause 4.4.1 [*Preparation and Review*].

The number of copies of as-built records to be submitted by the Contractor under this Sub-Clause shall be as required under Sub-Clause 1.8 [*Care and Supply of Documents*].

4.4.3 Operation and Maintenance Manuals

If no operation and maintenance manuals to be prepared by the Contractor are stated in the Specification, this Sub-Clause shall not apply.

> The Contractor shall prepare, and keep up-to-date, the operation and maintenance manuals in the format and other relevant details as stated in the Specification.
>
> The operation and maintenance manuals shall be submitted to the Engineer for Review, and the Works shall not be considered to be completed for the purposes of taking-over under Sub-Clause 10.1 [*Taking Over the Works and Sections*] until the Engineer has given (or is deemed to have given) a Notice of No-objection under sub-paragraph (i) of Sub-Clause 4.4.1 [*Preparation and Review*].

The Contractor's Documents comprise: those stated in the Specification; those required to satisfy all permits and other approvals which are the Contractor's responsibility; as-built records and operation and maintenance manuals; and documents implementing the Contractor's design of part of the Works. They are to be in the language for communications defined in Sub-Clause 1.4 unless otherwise stated in the Specification.

The Contractor shall prepare the Contractor's Documents and the Employer's Personnel may inspect their preparation. If the Specification or the Conditions specify that a Contractor's Document is to be submitted to the Engineer for Review, then the Contractor must do so together with a Notice stating that it is ready for Review and complies with the Contract. Thereafter, within 21 days, the Engineer shall give a Notice to the Contractor either of No-objection or that the document fails to comply with the Contract, with reasons. If the Engineer gives neither Notice within 21 days, the Engineer is deemed to have given a Notice of No-objection. If the Engineer notifies the Contractor of a non-compliance, then the Contractor must revise and resubmit the document for Review and the 21-day Review period will begin again.

Unless the Specification does not provide for them, the Contractor shall prepare, keep up-to-date and submit to the Engineer as-built records and operation and maintenance manuals for Review. The Works are not considered complete until the Engineer has given a Notice of No-objection for them.

(i) Main Changes from RB/99:

(1) This Sub-Clause is entirely new.
(2) Sub-Clause 4.4.1 is based on Sub-Clause 5.2 in each of YB/99 and GB/08, whereas Sub-Clauses 4.4.2 and 4.4.3 correspond to Sub-Clauses 5.6 and 5.7, respectively, of YB/99 and Sub-Clauses 5.5 and 5.6, respectively, of GB/08.
(3) Whereas YB/99 and GB/08 provided that the Engineer or Employer's Representative might have to 'approve' or 'consent' to a Contractor's Document, implying an endorsement of it by the Engineer or the Employer, this language has been replaced by a Notice of No-objection from the Engineer.

(ii) Related Clauses / Sub-Clauses: 1.2 [*Interpretation*], 1.3 [*Notices and Other Communications*], 1.4 [*Law and Language*], 1.8 [*Care and Supply of Documents*], 1.10 [*Employer's Use of Contractor's Documents*], 1.13 [*Compliance with Laws*], 3.7 [*Agreement or Determination*], 4.1 [*Contractor's General Obligations*], 4.9 [*Quality Management and Compliance Verification Systems*], 4.20 [*Progress Reports*], 9.1 [*Contractor's Obligations*], 10.1 [*Taking Over the Works and Sections*], 11.1 [*Completion of Outstanding Work and Remedying Defects*], 11.2 [*Cost of Remedying Defects*], 11.9 [*Performance Certificate*] and 14.3 [*Application for Interim Payment*].[73]

(iii) Analysis:

(1) Preparation of Contractor's Documents

Like the last paragraph of Sub-Clause 4.1,[74] this entirely new Sub-Clause in RB/17 relating to Contractor's Documents[75] assumes that the Contractor will have a larger role in the design of the Permanent Works than was foreseen by RB/99. After stating what Contractor's Documents comprise, Sub-Clause 4.4.1 describes the procedure for their preparation, submission and Review (as defined, as explained below) by the Engineer. It complements sub-paragraphs (a) through (h) of Sub-Clause 4.1 dealing with where the Contractor designs a part of the Permanent Works. Sub-Clauses 4.4.2 dealing with as-built records and 4.4.3 dealing with

73. As Contractor's Documents are referred to throughout the Conditions, this is only a partial selection of related Clauses and Sub-Clauses.
74. *See* the commentary on this Sub-Clause above.
75. *See* the commentary on Sub-Clause 1.1.15 '**Contractor's Documents**', above.

operation and training manuals complement sub-paragraph (g) of Sub-Clause 4.1, dealing with those subjects.

The Contractor's Documents are stated to comprise: those stated in the Specification, or required to satisfy all permits and approvals which are the Contractor's responsibility (those described in sub-paragraph (b) of Sub-Clause 1.13), as-built records, operation and maintenance manuals and documents to implement the Contractor's design of part of the Permanent Works and to instruct the Contractor's Personnel. They include, but are not limited to:[76] 'calculations, digital files, computer programs and other software, drawings, manuals, models, specifications and other documents of a technical nature'.[77]

Thus, they include not merely normal deliverables, such as drawings or manuals, but also documents used in the preparation of deliverables, such as calculations, digital files, computer programs, other software as well as models.[78]

The Sub-Clause provides that the Contractor's Documents shall, unless otherwise specified, be written in the language for communications defined in Sub-Clause 1.4 and that the Employer's Personnel (defined to include the Engineer and the Engineer's Representative) shall have a right to inspect them 'wherever they are being prepared'.[79] No indication is given of when inspections may take place[80] or how often they may occur.

76. *See* Sub-Clause 1.2(h).
77. *See* Sub-Clause 1.1.15. However, Contractor's Documents do not include all documents prepared by the Contractor pursuant to the Contract. Thus, records prepared by the Contractor pursuant to Sub-Clause 6.10 and contemporary records maintained by the Contractor pursuant to Sub-Clause 20.2.3 are not comprehended by Contractor's Documents.
78. This could raise issues for a Contractor concerned about protecting intellectual property owned or in its possession when it enters into the Contract.
79. Sub-Clause 4.4.1, second and third paragraphs.
80. Compare Sub-Clause 20.2.3 [*Employer's and Contractor's Claims-Contemporary Records*] providing for inspections by the Engineer of the Contractor's records 'during normal business hours' or as otherwise agreed by the Contractor.

(2) Review by the Engineer

The Sub-Clause then sets out the procedure for the Review by the Engineer of those Contractor's Documents required to be submitted for Review, according to either the Specification or the Conditions.[81] Review means:

> examination and consideration by the Engineer of a Contractor's submission in order to assess whether (and to what extent) it complies with the Contract and/or with the Contractor's obligations under or in connection with the Contract.[82]

The purposes of this pre-construction Review are to:

(1) permit the Engineer to verify that Contractor's Documents comply with the Contract; and
(2) give the earliest opportunity to the Employer to consider whether the proposed works are what the Employer actually requires, or whether it wishes to initiate a Variation.[83]

Under the Review procedure, the first step is for the Contractor to review its own document to ascertain that it is ready for Review and complies with the Contract. Having done this and satisfied itself that this is the case, the Contractor must then submit it to the Engineer with a Notice to this effect, which is reasonable as the Engineer should not have to commence a Review without the Contractor's prior assurance that the document complies with the Contract.

The Engineer is then required, within 21 days after receiving the Contractor's Document and such Notice, to give a Notice to the Contractor either of No-objection (which may include comments concerning minor matters) or that the Contractor's Document fails (to the extent stated) to comply with the Contract, with reasons. If the Engineer does not respond within 21 days, it is deemed to have given a Notice of No-objection.[84]

While not expressly stated in this Sub-Clause, the implication is that the Contractor may not proceed to use a Contractor's Document that is subject to Review by the Engineer until that document has received a

81. As all Contractor's Documents are not usually required to be submitted to the Engineer for Review.
82. *See* Sub-Clause 1.1.70 and the commentary on this Sub-Clause above.
83. *See The FIDIC Contracts Guide* (2nd edn, FIDIC, 2022) 224.
84. Sub-Clause 4.4.1, sixth paragraph.

Notice of No-objection. This is expressly stated in Sub-Clause 4.1(c) in relation to all the Contractor's Documents which are relevant to design.

(3) The Engineer does not 'approve' or 'consent'

As noted above,[85] unlike the review procedure provided for in Sub-Clause 5.2 of the YB/99 (and of the Employer's Representative under the GB/08), the Engineer is not required to 'approve' or 'consent' to the Contractor's Document, implying their endorsement by the Engineer. The Engineer merely ascertains whether the Contractor's Document fails, to any extent, to comply with the Contract.[86] On the other hand, where a Contractor's Document needs to satisfy some legal or regulatory standard independent of the Contract (e.g., building regulations), approval or consent by the Engineer may be required as a matter of law, in which case it needs to be provided for in the Particular Conditions.

(4) As-built records and operation and maintenance manuals

Where the Contractor is designing a part of the Works, the Specification may provide that the Contractor supply the Engineer or the Employer with as-built records for such part as and when it is completed. Sub-Clause 4.4.2 requires that, like other Contractor's Documents, they be submitted to the Engineer for Review, enabling the Engineer to verify that they comply with the Contract. Similarly, the Specification may provide that the Contractor provides operation and maintenance manuals in which case, pursuant to Sub-Clause 4.4.3, they are also subject to Review by the Engineer. In the meantime, the Employer is prevented (to some extent) by Sub-Clauses 2.1 and 10.2 from using any part of the Works before it is the subject of a Taking-Over Certificate.

The Contractor must submit the as-built records and operation and maintenance manuals to the Engineer as a condition to carrying out the Tests on Completion, pursuant to Sub-Clause 9.1. Subject to some exceptions, it is a condition of taking over of the Works (or a Section or part of the Works, as may be appropriate) that the Engineer will have given (or is deemed to have given) a Notice of No-objection as to the

85. Under **(i) Main Changes from RB/99**.

86. This may avoid the potential liability of the Engineer (and possibly the Employer) for errors in the Contractor's design, *see* Atkin Chambers, *Hudson's Building and Engineering Contracts* (14th edn, Sweet & Maxwell, London, 2020) 426 (para. 3-062).

as-built records submitted under Sub-Clause 4.4.2 and the operation and maintenance manuals submitted under Sub-Clause 4.4.3.[87]

(iv) Improvements: While the procedure for the Engineer's Review of a Contractor's Document envisages that it may have been objected to once by the Engineer, it does not address the not uncommon situation where a Contractor's Document has repeatedly to be resubmitted to the Engineer and is repeatedly objected to by the Engineer. Presumably, the same procedure should apply repeatedly, but it would be much clearer if this were stated explicitly.

--ooOOoo--

4.5 Training

If no training of employees of the Employer (and/or other identified personnel) by the Contractor is stated in the Specification, this Sub-Clause shall not apply.

The Contractor shall carry out training of the Employer's employees (and/or other personnel identified in the Specification) in the operation and maintenance of the Works, and any other aspect of the Works, to the extent stated in the Specification. The timing of the training shall be as stated in the Specification (if not stated, as acceptable to the Employer). The Contractor shall provide qualified and experienced training staff, training facilities and all training materials as necessary and/or as stated in the Specification.

If the Specification specifies training which is to be carried out before taking over, the Works shall not be considered to be completed for the purposes of taking over under Sub-Clause 10.1 [*Taking Over the Works and Sections*] until this training has been completed in accordance with the Specification.

If the Specification so requires, the Contractor will train the Employer's employees (and/or other identified personnel) in the operation, maintenance and other specified aspects of the Works, by providing

87. Sub-Clause 10.1 [*Taking Over the Works and Sections*].

qualified training staff, training facilities and training materials as necessary and/or as stated in the Specification.

If the training is to be carried out before taking over, the Works will not be considered completed for the purposes of taking over under Sub-Clause 10.1 until the training has been completed.

Commentary

(i) Main Changes from RB/99: This Sub-Clause, which had no counterpart in RB/99, is based upon Sub-Clause 5.5 of YB/99 and Sub-Clause 10.5 of GB/08 but is somewhat more detailed than both.

(ii) Related Clauses / Sub-Clauses: 4.1 [*Contractor's General Obligations*], 8.3 [*Programme*], 10.1 [*Taking Over the Works and Sections*] and 11.2 [*Cost of Remedying Defects*].

(iii) Analysis: The Employer will be responsible for operating and maintaining the Works after taking over, yet it may not have employees who are qualified to do so. If it does not, then the training of its employees will be necessary. This is often the case where the Works include Plant that comprises new or innovative technology.[88] If training is desired, it must be provided for in the Specification.

If the training is intended to enable the employees to attain a specified level of competence, then this should be stated in the Specification together with the expected qualifications and experience of both those who are to provide and those expected to undertake the training. Otherwise, the Contractor can be expected to provide training competently and in accordance with 'recognised' good practice[89] of whatever amount and duration is stated in the Specification, but without necessarily any assurance or expectation of the result. As has been justly stated:

> The Parties must agree where the division of responsibility lies between the process of teaching and the process of learning as it is not always clear how much responsibility the Contractor can carry as to how much the Employer's Personnel will actually learn.[90]

88. *Guidance for the Preparation of Particular Conditions*, 23.
89. As required by Sub-Clause 7.1 [*Manner of Execution*].
90. *FIDIC DBO Contract Guide* (FIDIC, 2011) 71.

The time(s) for training should be indicated in the Contractor's initial programme (and subsequent Programme) submitted pursuant to Sub-Clause 8.3.[91]

Where training is provided for in the Specification, the Works will not be considered completed for the purposes of taking over under Sub-Clause 10.1 until this training has been completed.[92] Thus, its completion is a condition to the taking over of the Works[93] and (where applicable) of any Section of the Works.[94]

--ooOOoo--

4.6 Co-operation

The Contractor shall, as stated in the Specification or as instructed by the Engineer, co-operate with and allow appropriate opportunities for carrying out work by:

(a) the Employer's Personnel;
(b) any other contractors employed by the Employer; and
(c) the personnel of any legally constituted public authorities and private utility companies,

who may be employed in the carrying out, on or near the Site, of any work not included in the Contract. Such appropriate opportunities may include the use of Contractor's Equipment, Temporary Works, access arrangements which are the responsibility of the Contractor, and/or other of the Contractor's facilities or services on the Site.

The Contractor shall be responsible for the Contractor's construction activities on the Site, and shall use all reasonable endeavours to co-ordinate these activities with those of other contractors to the extent (if any) stated in the Specification or as instructed by the Engineer.

91. Sub-Clause 8.3(g).
92. Sub-Clause 4.5, third paragraph.
93. *See* Sub-Clause 10.1(d).
94. *See* Sub-Clause 10.1, second and third paragraphs.

> If the Contractor suffers delay and/or incurs Cost as a result of an instruction under this Sub-Clause, to the extent (if any) that co-operation, allowance of opportunities and co-ordination was Unforeseeable having regard to that stated in the Specification, the Contractor shall be entitled subject to Sub-Clause 20.2 [*Claims for Payment and/or EOT*] to EOT and/or payment of such Cost Plus Profit.

As stated in the Specification or instructed by the Engineer, the Contractor must cooperate with, and allow opportunities for carrying out work by, the following persons who may be employed on or near the Site on work not included in the Contract: the Employer's Personnel, any other contractors of the Employer and personnel of public authorities or private utility companies. This may include allowing them the opportunity to use Contractor's Equipment, Temporary Works, access arrangements of the Contractor and/or other Contractor's facilities or services on the Site.

In case the Contractor suffers delay and/or incurs Cost as a result of an instruction requiring cooperation that was Unforeseeable from the Specification then, subject to Sub-Clause 20.2, the Contractor is entitled to an EOT and/or payment of such Cost Plus Profit.

__Commentary__

(i) Main Changes from RB/99:

(1) A Sub-Clause entitled 'Co-operation', such as the present, was first introduced into the RB by Sub-Clause 4.6 in RB/99.[95] However, despite its heading (and headings are to be disregarded),[96] the body of that Sub-Clause did not use the word 'co-operation'. The new Sub-Clause thus, for the first time, foresees that the Specification or an instruction of the Engineer will require the Contractor to 'co-operate' with the Employer's Personnel, the Employer's other contractors, public authorities and private utilities – private utilities were not mentioned in

95. RB/87 had contained Sub-Clauses 31.1 [*Opportunities for Other Contractors*] and 31.2 [*Facilities for Other Contractors*] which performed, to some extent, the same function.

96. *See* Sub-Clause 1.2 [*Interpretation*] in both RB/99 and RB/17.

RB/99 – and do so in addition to allowing them appropriate opportunities for carrying out their work.

(2) The second paragraph, requiring the Contractor to 'use all reasonable endeavours to co-ordinate these activities with those of other contractors' to the extent, if any, stated in the Specification or as instructed by the Engineer is also new but similar to the third paragraph of Sub-Clause 4.6 of YB/99 and GB/08.

(3) The last paragraph, giving the Contractor a general right to claim if, as a result of an instruction of the Engineer, 'co-operation, allowance of opportunities and coordination was Unforeseeable' having regard to the Specification, is also new.[97] In RB/99, the Sub-Clause had provided instead that if and to the extent an instruction of the Engineer (requiring the Contractor to allow opportunities to others) caused the Contractor 'Unforeseeable Cost', this would constitute a Variation.

(4) The last paragraph of Sub-Clause 4.6 of RB/99 (providing that if the Employer is required under the Contract to give the Contractor possession of any foundation, structure, plant or means of access in accordance with Contractor's Documents, the Contractor shall submit them in the time and manner as stated in the Specification) has been omitted and the subject is to some extent covered in the first paragraph of Sub-Clause 2.1.

(ii) Related Clauses / Sub-Clauses: 2.1 [*Right of Access to the Site*], 2.3 [*Employer's Personnel and Other Contractors*], 3.5 [*Engineer's Instructions*], 3.8 [*Meetings*], 8.5 [*Extension of Time for Completion*], 8.6 [*Delays Caused by Authorities*], 15.5 [*Termination for Employer's Convenience*] and 20.2 [*Claims for Payment and/or EOT*].

97. In the second and last paragraphs it would be better to use the term 'co-operate' in place of 'coordinate' as 'coordinate' may imply that a contractor has a power of control which it may not have. One contractor of an employer may not have power to control another contractor of the same employer. It can cooperate with another contractor but it may not have the power to coordinate (or control) it. On the other hand, an employer (or its delegate) has the power to coordinate (or control) the employer's contractors.

(iii) Analysis:

(1) Requirement for coöperation

As has been well stated:

> [t]here are countless examples of where an owner and a contractor may be required to cooperate with each other to secure the performance of the contract, or to refrain from acting in such a way as to prevent the other party from performing its obligations.[98]

In larger projects, there may be multiple contractors of the employer working under separate contracts on or near the site at the same time. For example, on a greenfield site for a housing project, there may at the same time be a contractor constructing housing, a contractor installing sewerage and fresh water piping, a contractor building roads, a contractor installing telecommunications facilities and a contractor responsible for connecting all these utilities to housing units and installing them in those units. Their work may often be interdependent; e.g., the commencement of work by the contractor constructing the housing may depend upon completion of roads by the contractor building them, as otherwise the housing contractor will be unable to reach the housing site. On the other hand, the contractor responsible for installing utility networks (e.g., sewerage and fresh water piping) in the housing units may not be able to begin its work until the contractor responsible for building the same networks that connect the local municipal networks to the housing units has completed its work and the housing contractor has completed building the housing units. Consequently, it will be important that the contractors' respective time programmes are compatible and integrated with one another, are adhered to in practice and that the contractors cooperate in the performance of their respective scopes of work, e.g., in the event that one contractor needs to cross the site, or use the facilities (e.g., roads), of another contractor.[99] Otherwise, if they are allowed to act independently and each solely in its own interest, they may disrupt each other and disorganise the execution of the Works.

98. Julian Bailey, *Construction Law* (3rd edn, London Publishing, UK, 2020) vol 1, 210-212 (para. 3.142). Mr Bailey lists numerous examples.

99. If the Contractor is critically delayed by one of the Employer's other contractors on the Site (or by the Employer or the Employer's Personnel), it will be entitled to an EOT. *See* sub-para. (e) of Sub-Clause 8.5 [*Extension of Time for Completion*].

(2) Related Sub-Clauses

Two other Sub-Clauses are directly relevant to the Contractor's duty of cooperation. Sub-Clause 2.1 expressly provides that, while the Employer shall give right of access to and possession of the Site to the Contractor, '[t]he right and possession may not be exclusive to the Contractor'. Thus, if the Specification provides for the presence of others on or near the Site, the Contractor must have made allowance for them in its tender programme and its tender price. On the other hand, the Employer has an obligation to reciprocate and cooperate with the Contractor. Thus, Sub-Clause 2.3(a) requires the Employer to ensure that the Employer's Personnel and the Employer's other contractors, if any, on or near the Site 'co-operate with the Contractor's efforts under the Sub-Clause 4.6'.[100]

(3) Importance of the Specification

As a practical matter, at the time of tender, the Specification should describe both the scope of work to be performed by the Contractor and how it may relate to work of other contractors of the Employer or of other persons (including the Employer itself) that may be going on at the same time at or near the Contractor's Site. Often the Contractor's scope is merely a part – sometimes but a small part – of a much larger construction project. In that case, the Specification should describe the larger project and how the Contractor's work may relate to, and be integrated with, the work of other contractors of the Employer, as well as the activities of public authorities and private utilities, to the extent known.[101] The Contractor must take careful account of all these things when tendering.

(4) Claim right

This Sub-Clause provides that if the Contractor suffers delay and/or Costs as a result of an instruction of the Engineer under this Sub-Clause then, to the extent, if any, that the cooperation, allowance of opportunities and coordination was Unforeseeable having regard to the Specification, the Contractor is entitled, subject to Sub-Clause 20.2, to an EOT and/or payment of such Cost Plus Profit. The term 'Unforeseeable' is defined to mean 'not reasonably foreseeable by an experienced contractor by the

100. Numerous other Sub-Clauses require the Parties to cooperate on particular matters, e.g., 1.5 [*Priority of Documents*], last paragraph, 1.8 [*Care and Supply of Documents*], last paragraph, and 8.4 [*Advance Warning*].
101. *See FIDIC Procurement Procedures Guide* (FIDIC, 2011) 119-120.

Base Date'.[102] Subject to what is stated below under **(v) Improvements**, this claim provision seems entirely justified and appropriate.

(iv) Related Law: While under the strict terms of this Sub-Clause, the Contractor has a duty to cooperate with the Employer only as stated in the Specification or as instructed by the Engineer, where the Contract is governed by the law of a civil law country, at least, both the Contractor and the Employer are likely to have an obligation to cooperate with each other as a matter of law. As explained in **Chapter II Applicable Law** above, where parties have entered into a contract governed by the law of a civil law country (or even of some common law countries), they will have a duty to perform the contract in good faith, which will include a duty to cooperate with the other.[103] The duty to perform a contract in good faith is a matter of public policy (*ordre public*) under French law.[104]

Similarly, Article 1.7 (*Good faith and fair dealing*) of the UNIDROIT Principles provides not only that '[e]ach party must act in accordance with good faith and fair dealing in international trade' but also (like French law) that this duty is mandatory and therefore '[t]he parties may not limit or exclude this duty' (e.g., by contract). Furthermore, Article 5.1.3 (*Co-operation between the parties*) of these Principles provides that: '[e]ach party shall cooperate with the other party when such co-operation may reasonably be expected for the performance of that party's obligations'.

In its first official comment on this article, UNIDROIT states:

> A contract is not merely a meeting point for conflicting interests but must also, to a certain extent, be viewed as a common project in which each party must cooperate. This view is clearly related to the principle of good faith and fair dealing (see Article 1.7) which permeates the law of contract,
>
> [...]
>
> The duty of co-operation must of course be confined within certain limits, i.e. it only exists to the extent that co-operation may reasonably be expected to enable the other party to perform, without upsetting the allocation of duties in the contract. Within these limits each party may be under a duty not only to refrain from hindering the other party

102. Sub-Clause 1.1.85.

103. *See* **Section 4 Common Law and Civil Law Compared – 4.3.1 Duty of Good Faith** of **Chapter II Applicable Law** above.

104. *Ibid.*

> from performing its obligation(s), *but also to take affirmative steps to enable the other party's performance.*[105] (Emphasis added)

Of particular relevance to RB/17, the second official comment on this article provides that:

> contracts involving performance of a complex nature may especially need co-operation throughout the life of the contract in order for the transaction to work, although always within the limit of reasonable expectations. Thus, by way of example, in a contract for the construction of industrial works the employer may be required to prevent interferences in the contractor's work by other contractors it employs to carry out other works at the site.[106]

Similarly:

> American jurisprudence implies in all contracts and upon all parties the obligation to cooperate with each other in the performance of the contract and not to delay, hinder or interfere with the performance of other parties.[107]

---

105. UNIDROIT Principles, official comment 1 to art. 5.1.3 (*Co-operation between the parties*).
106. UNIDROIT Principles, official comment 2 to art. 5.1.3 (*Co-operation between the parties*). This comment then provides two illustrations relevant to construction contracts:

    4. Contractor A is awarded by B, a Governmental Agency in country X, a contract to build a 3000 house complex in country X. Since it is a greenfield project, electricity and water also have to be brought in, and the respective works have to be executed in a certain sequence so as not to conflict with each other. B awards the electrical contracts to local contractors, but then completely fails to coordinate their work with A's work with the result that A repeatedly has to interrupt its work thereby causing A considerable loss. B is liable for this loss since, in the circumstances, it should have actively coordinated the work of the local contractors so that A's work would not be interrupted in such manner.
    5. Company A, situated in country X, and Company B, situated in country Y, enter into a joint venture agreement for participation in a public bidding procedure in country X. The contract is finally awarded to a third party. The procedure was manifestly improper, but B refuses to provide A with information necessary to appeal the award before the competent authority, thereby hindering A from pursuing the appeal. By its refusal, B has breached its general duty of co-operation to A under the joint venture agreement.

107. Philip L Bruner and Patrick J O'Connor, Jr, *Bruner & O'Connor on Construction Law* (Thomson Reuters, St Paul, MN, 2002) vol 3, 705-6 (s 9:99).

US law is especially developed and instructive as to the duties of the Employer where it has engaged a number of contractors under separate contracts to work at the same time on or near the same site (a 'multi-prime contractor project', in US parlance).[108] There are at least two international arbitral awards dealing with this subject under civil law.[109]

(v) Improvements:

(1) The Contractor should be required to cooperate not merely with the Employer's Personnel and other contractors of the Employer, as required by this Sub-Clause, but also with the Employer itself (as the Employer is not encompassed by the definition of the

108. According to one US authority: 'When an owner elects to execute a project with multiple prime contractors, many jurisdictions [in the US] recognise a duty on the part of the owner to coordinate the work activities of the separate prime contractors. Thus, the owner may be responsible to one prime contractor for delays caused by another. Even where the owner attempts to shift this duty to coordinate to one of the prime contractors, the owner still may be liable for delays if the lead contractor is not also given the power to enforce its coordination responsibilities' (citations omitted). John M Mastin and others (eds), *Smith, Currie, and Hancock's Common Sense Construction Law: A Practical Guide for the Construction Professional* (6th edn, Wiley, Hoboken, NJ, 2020) 319. *See especially Broadway Maintenance Corporation v Rutgers, State University* 90 N.J. 253, 447 A. 2nd 906 [1982] and John B Tieder, 'The Duty to Schedule and Co-ordinate on Multi-Prime Contractor Projects – The United States Experience' [1985-86] 3 ICLR 97.

109. *See* (1) the final award, ICC cases 3790 / 3902 / 4050 / 4051 / 4054 (joined cases) (1984), cited in Abdul Hamid El-Ahdab, *Arbitration with the Arab Countries* (Kluwer, the Netherlands, 1990), 896 (subject no 3) and 920 (subject no 6) (the full award is available on Jus Mundi); and (2) *J.V. of American and EU Dredging Companies v. Red Sea Public Authority (RSPA), final award, CRCICA case No. 281/2002, 28 June 2004* in Mohie-Eldin Alam-Eldin (ed.), *Arbitral Awards of the Cairo Regional Centre for International Commercial Arbitration IV* (Kluwer L. Int'l, the Netherlands, 2014) 185, especially 253-265.
See also Christopher R Seppälä, 'The Development of Case Law in Construction Disputes Relating to FIDIC Contracts' [2009] ICLR 105, 109-111. English law appears to be less developed in this area. *See*, for example, Julian Bailey, *Construction Law* (3rd edn, London Publishing, UK, 2020) vol I, 208-213 (paras 3.140-3.144) and Atkin Chambers, *Hudson's Building and Engineering Contracts* (14th edn, Sweet & Maxwell, London, 2020) 448-452 (paras 3-079 to 3-082).

Employer's Personnel). This would make this Sub-Clause more reciprocal with Sub-Clause 2.3 [*Employer's Personnel and Other Contractors*] requiring the Employer to ensure cooperation with the Contractor. This would also ensure respect for the Employer's rights under, for example, Sub-Clause 13.6 [*Adjustments for Changes in Laws*], entitling the Employer to a reduction in the Contract Price where there has been a decrease in the Contractor's Cost as the result of a change in Laws which, as a practical matter, the Employer may only be able to demonstrate with the Contractor's cooperation.

(2) The final paragraph of this Sub-Clause is unduly restrictive as it should be unnecessary for there to have been an instruction from the Engineer under this Sub-Clause in order for the Contractor to be entitled to relief. The Contractor may encounter Unforeseeable matters of the kind described in this final paragraph independently of any instruction from the Engineer, e.g., interference by the personnel of any legally constituted public authorities or private utility companies. If the Contractor should encounter any such Unforeseeable matters and provided that it was not itself at fault, then, subject to Sub-Clause 20.2, the Contractor should be entitled to relief, whether there had been an instruction from the Engineer or not.
Accordingly, given the wording of this Sub-Clause, it will be prudent for a Contractor, should it encounter the Unforeseeable matters described in this Sub-Clause, which cause it damage and have not resulted from an instruction by the Engineer, to request and obtain, if possible, such an instruction so that it will be entitled to claim in accordance with this Sub-Clause's wording.

--ooOOoo--

4.7 Setting Out

The Contractor shall set out the Works in relation to the items of reference under Sub-Clause 2.5 [*Site Data and Items of Reference*].

4.7.1 Accuracy

The Contractor shall:

(a) verify the accuracy of all these items of reference before they are used for the Works;
(b) promptly deliver the results of each verification to the Engineer;
(c) rectify any error in the positions, levels, dimensions or alignment of the Works; and
(d) be responsible for the correct positioning of all parts of the Works.

4.7.2 Errors

If the Contractor finds an error in any items of reference, the Contractor shall give a Notice to the Engineer describing it:

(a) within the period stated in the Contract Data (if not stated, 28 days) calculated from the Commencement Date, if the items of reference are specified on the Drawings and/or in the Specification; or
(b) as soon as practicable after receiving the items of reference, if they are issued by the Engineer under Sub-Clause 2.5 [*Site Data and Items of Reference*].

4.7.3 Agreement or Determination of rectification measures, delay and/or Cost

After receiving a Notice from the Contractor under Sub-Clause 4.7.2 [*Errors*], the Engineer shall proceed under Sub-Clause 3.7 [*Agreement or Determination*] to agree or determine:

(a) whether or not there is an error in the items of reference;
(b) whether or not (taking account of cost and time) an experienced contractor exercising due care would have discovered such an error
    - when examining the Site, the Drawings and the Specification before submitting the Tender; or
    - when examining the items of reference within the period stated in sub-paragraph (a) of Sub-

Clause 4.7.2, if the items of reference are specified on the Drawings and/or in the Specification; and

(c) what measures (if any) the Contractor is required to take to rectify the error

(and, for the purpose of Sub-Clause 3.7.3 [*Time limits*], the date the Engineer receives the Contractor's Notice under Sub-Clause 4.7.2 [*Errors*] shall be the date of commencement of the time limit for agreement under Sub-Clause 3.7.3).

If it is agreed or determined, under sub-paragraphs (a) and (b) above, that there is an error in the items of reference that an experienced contractor would not have discovered:

(i) Sub-Clause 13.3.1 [*Variation by Instruction*] shall apply to the measures that the Contractor is required to take (if any); and
(ii) if there are no such measures, and therefore no Variation, but the Contractor suffers delay and/or incurs Cost as a result of the error, the Contractor shall be entitled subject to Sub-Clause 20.2 [*Claims for Payment and/or EOT*] to EOT and/or payment of such Cost Plus Profit.

The Contractor must set out the Works in relation to the 'items of reference' under Sub-Clause 2.5. The Contractor must verify their accuracy before use and promptly deliver the results to the Engineer, rectify any errors in the positions of the Works and correctly position the Works. The Contractor must give a Notice to the Engineer of any error in any items of reference: (a) within the period stated in the Contract Data (if not stated, 28 days) from the Commencement Date if they are specified on the Drawings and/or in the Specification; or (b) as soon as practicable if they are issued by the Engineer under Sub-Clause 2.5.

After receiving such Notice, the Engineer must proceed under Sub-Clause 3.7 to agree or determine: (a) if there is an error in the items of reference; (b) whether an experienced contractor would have discovered such error at an earlier stage (as defined); and (c) what measures (if any) the Contractor is required to take to rectify the error. If an

experienced contractor would not have discovered the error at such earlier stage, then Sub-Clause 13.3.1 shall apply to any measures the Contractor is required to take and, if there are no such measures and therefore no Variation, but the Contractor suffers delay and/or incurs Cost then, it shall be entitled subject to Clause 20.2, to EOT and/or payment of Cost Plus Profit.

(i) Main Changes from RB/99:

(1) This Sub-Clause is more structured and more detailed than Sub-Clause 4.7 in RB/99 and GB/08.
(2) The obligation of the Employer (or the Engineer) to provide the Contractor with items of reference, which was contained in the first sentence of Sub-Clause 4.7 of RB/99, is now dealt with in Sub-Clause 2.5 of RB/17.
(3) Both Sub-Clauses 4.7.1 and 4.7.2 are largely new.
(4) In Sub-Clause 4.7.3, the Sub-Clause 3.7 procedure for agreeing or determining matters or Claims has replaced the Sub-Clause 3.5 procedure in RB/99 and the method of ascertaining whether an experienced contractor could have discovered and reported the error at an earlier stage is now more detailed.
(5) In the last paragraph of Sub-Clause 4.7.3, the Contractor is now entitled to relief as a Variation, which is new.

(ii) Related Clauses / Sub-Clauses: 1.3 [*Notices and Other Communications*], 2.5 [*Site Data and Items of Reference*], 3.7 [*Agreement or Determination*], 4.10 [*Use of Site Data*], 8.5 [*Extension of Time for Completion*], 13.3.1 [*Variation by Instruction*] and 20.2 [*Claims for Payment and/or EOT*].

(iii) Analysis:

(1) Definition of items of reference

This Sub-Clause needs to be read together with Sub-Clause 2.5 dealing with the Site data and 'items of reference', which the Employer should make available to the Contractor. Sub-Clause 2.5, second paragraph, defines 'items of reference' as 'original survey control points, lines and levels of reference'. These are specified on the Drawings and/or in the Specification, or are issued to the Contractor by a Notice from the Engineer.[110]

110. Sub-Clause 2.5, second paragraph.

(2) Contractor's duty to notify errors

Under Sub-Clause 4.7.1, the Contractor is required to verify the accuracy of these items of reference before they are used for the Works.

Under Sub-Clause 4.7.2, if the Contractor finds an error in any items of reference, the Contractor must give a Notice to the Engineer describing it either within a specified period from the Commencement Date, as stated in the Contract Data, if the items of reference are specified on the Drawings[111] and/or in the Specification (sub-paragraph (a)), or 'as soon as practicable after receiving the items of reference', if they are issued by the Engineer under Sub-Clause 2.5 (sub-paragraph (b)).

(3) If the Contractor finds an error

Assuming there is an error in the items of reference, Sub-Clause 4.7.3 then provides that, after receiving a Notice to this effect from the Contractor, the Engineer shall proceed under Sub-Clause 3.7 to agree or determine, among other things, whether (taking account of cost and time) an experienced contractor would have discovered such an error either:

- when examining the Site, the Drawings and the Specification before submitting the Tender; or
- when examining the items of reference within the period stated in sub-paragraph (a) of Sub-Clause 4.7.2 if the items of reference are specified on the Drawings and/or in the Specification.

The last paragraph of Sub-Clause 4.7.3 provides that, if it is agreed or determined that an experienced contractor 'would not have discovered the error', the Contractor would be entitled to a Variation in respect of any measures that it is required to take. If there are no such measures but it has suffered delay and/or incurred Costs it will be entitled subject to Sub-Clause 20.2 to an EOT and/or payment of such Cost Plus Profit.

(4) Difficulties with Sub-Clause

The intention appears to be that if there is an error in the items of reference of which the Contractor has given a Notice, the Contractor will only be entitled to relief, whether by way of a Variation or otherwise, if

111. Sub-Clause 4.7.2 appears in this case to be referring to Drawings included in the Contract. But 'Drawings' is defined in Sub-Clause 1.1.30 to include 'additional and modified drawings' issued on behalf of the Employer as well, making it unclear how Sub-Clause 4.7.2 is to be interpreted.

the Contractor had discovered the error within the time that (taking account of cost and time) an experienced contractor would have done so (and, although this is not mentioned, given Notice of it to the Engineer).

However, there are several matters that are obscure, as follows:

(1) Sub-Clause 4.7.2 (a) provides that the Contractor shall give a Notice to the Engineer if it finds an error in any items of reference within a period stated in the Contract Data (if not stated, 28 days) calculated from the Commencement Date if they are 'specified on the Drawings' and/or in the Specification. But, according to the definition of Drawings (Sub-Clause 1.1.30), they comprise not only drawings included in the Contract but any additional and modified drawings issued by or on behalf of the Employer. Thus, errors in items of reference contained in additional and modified drawings issued after such period (and not under Sub-Clause 2.5, referred to in Sub-Clause 4.7.2 (b)) are not addressed.

(2) Sub-Clause 4.7.3 (b) provides that, after receiving Notice of an error under Sub-Clause 4.7.2, the Engineer must under Sub-Clause 3.7 agree or determine whether an experienced contractor would have discovered it, according to the first bullet point, 'when examining the Site, the Drawings and the Specification before submitting the Tender', it being suggested that, in that case, the Contractor should have given Notice of it at that time. But, under the Letter of Tender of RB/17, unlike the Letter of Tender of YB/17, the Contractor has no obligation to give a Notice of such errors. By contrast, the Letter of Tender of YB/17 provides that: '[w]e have examined, understood and checked these [the proposed Contract documents] and have ascertained that they contain no errors or other defects'.

(3) In the case of Sub-Clause 4.7.3 (b), second bullet point, as in the case mentioned in comment (1) above, the issue of errors in items of reference in Drawings issued after the period stated in Sub-Clause 4.7.2 (a) is not addressed.

(4) The last paragraph of Sub-Clause 4.7.3 refers to where it is agreed or determined under sub-paragraphs (a) and (b) of Sub-Clause 4.7.3 that there is an error in the items of reference that an experienced contractor 'would not have discovered' without making clear what time is being referred to, whether before or after the submission of the Tender.

Accordingly, it is questionable whether the Sub-Clause can achieve its apparent intention.

(iv) Improvements: The four points listed under *(4) Difficulties with Sub-Clause* under **(iii) Analysis** above need to be addressed.

--ooOOoo--

4.8 Health and Safety Obligations

The Contractor shall:

(a) comply with all applicable health and safety regulations and Laws;
(b) comply with all applicable health and safety obligations specified in the Contract;
(c) comply with all directives issued by the Contractor's health and safety officer (appointed under Sub-Clause 6.7 [*Health and Safety of Personnel*]);
(d) take care of the health and safety of all persons entitled to be on the Site and other places (if any) where the Works are being executed;
(e) keep the Site, Works (and the other places (if any) where the Works are being executed) clear of unnecessary obstruction so as to avoid danger to these persons;
(f) provide fencing, lighting, safe access, guarding and watching of:
   (i) the Works, until the Works are taken over under Clause 10 [*Employer's Taking Over*]; and
   (ii) any part of the Works where the Contractor is executing outstanding works or remedying any defects during the DNP; and
(g) provide any Temporary Works (including roadways, footways, guards and fences) which may be necessary, because of the execution of the Works, for the use and protection of the public and of owners and occupiers of adjacent land and property.

Within 21 days of the Commencement Date and before commencing any construction on the Site, the Contractor shall submit to the Engineer for information a health and safety manual which has been specifically prepared for the Works, the Site and other places (if any) where the Contractor intends to execute the Works. This manual shall be in addition to any other similar document required under applicable health and safety regulations and Laws.

The health and safety manual shall set out all the health and safety requirements:

(i) stated in the Specification;
(ii) that comply with all the Contractor's health and safety obligations under the Contract; and
(iii) that are necessary to effect and maintain a healthy and safe working environment for all persons entitled to be on the Site and other places (if any) where the Works are being executed.

This manual shall be revised as necessary by the Contractor or the Contractor's health and safety officer, or at the reasonable request of the Engineer. Each revision of the manual shall be submitted promptly to the Engineer.

In addition to the reporting requirement of sub-paragraph (g) of Sub-Clause 4.20 [*Progress Reports*], the Contractor shall submit to the Engineer details of any accident as soon as practicable after its occurrence and, in the case of an accident causing serious injury or death, shall inform the Engineer immediately.

The Contractor shall, as stated in the Specification and as the Engineer may reasonably require, maintain records and make reports (in compliance with the applicable health and safety regulations and Laws) concerning the health and safety of persons and any damage to property.

The Contractor shall comply with all applicable health and safety regulations, Laws and obligations in the Contract, including the directives of its health and safety officer. The Contractor shall keep the Site and Works clear of unnecessary obstruction; provide fencing, lighting, safe access, guarding and watching of the Works until taking

over; and provide any Temporary Works, as necessary. Within 21 days of the Commencement Date and before commencing construction, the Contractor must submit to the Engineer a health and safety manual for the Works, which is in addition to any similar document that may be required under applicable health and safety regulations and Laws. The manual must set out all health and safety requirements, as defined, and be revised by the Contractor as necessary. Each revision must be submitted to the Engineer. In case of any accident, the Contractor must submit the details to the Engineer as soon as practicable and do so immediately in case of serious injury or death. As required by the Specification and/or the Engineer, the Contractor must maintain records and make reports concerning the health and safety of persons and any damage to property.

Commentary

(i) Main Changes from RB/99:

(1) This Sub-Clause is more than twice the length of that in RB/99 and GB/08.
(2) Sub-paragraphs (b), (c), (e) and (f)(ii) are entirely new as are all of the paragraphs after the first paragraph.
(3) The last two paragraphs effectively replace the last paragraph of Sub-Clause 6.7 of RB/99.

(ii) Related Clauses / Sub-Clauses: 1.3 [*Notices and Other Communications*], 1.13 [*Compliance with Laws*], 2.3 [*Employer's Personnel and Other Contractors*], 3.5 [*Engineer's Instructions*], 4.18 [*Protection of the Environment*], 4.20 [*Progress Reports*], 6.4 [*Labour Laws*], 6.7 [*Health and Safety of Personnel*], 6.8 [*Contractor's Superintendance*], 10 [*Employer's Taking Over*] and 13.1 [*Right to Vary*].

(iii) Analysis:

(1) Purpose of Sub-Clause

Under any international construction contract, work will be dangerous and/or present health risks, especially heavy construction (e.g., bridges, dams and tunnelling works). Other risks may arise from disease such as malaria, cholera, epidemics or pandemics and/or the security situation in the country where the works are being carried out.

Sub-Clause 4.8, which should be read together with Sub-Clause 6.7 [*Health and Safety of Personnel*], provides for the Contractor's health and safety obligations. These are generally self-explanatory and, except in the case of sub-paragraph (c), call for no special comment. Sub-paragraph (c) is noteworthy as – given safety's paramount importance – it requires the Contractor to comply with all directives of the Contractor's own health and safety officer. Essentially, this entitles this individual to police the health and safety behaviour of the Contractor, its own employer, as well as others as described below.

(2) The Contractor's health and safety obligations

In the first paragraph of the Sub-Clause, the health and safety obligations of the Contractor listed in sub-paragraphs (a) through (e) apply equally to the Employer's Personnel and the Employer's other contractors on or near the Site, pursuant to Sub-Clause 2.3(b). On the other hand, the Contractor's obligations in sub-paragraphs (f) and (g) complement its responsibility for the care of the Works under Sub-Clauses 4.1, third paragraph, and 17.1.

The importance of all these obligations is underlined by the fact that the Contractor may object to the instruction of a Variation if it will adversely affect its ability to comply with this Sub-Clause.[112]

Within 21 days of the Commencement Date and before commencing work on Site, the Contractor is required to submit to the Engineer 'for information'[113] a health and safety manual for the Works complying with Sub-Clause 4.8. The manual must be revised 'as necessary'. In addition, the Contractor must submit to the Engineer details of any accident as soon as practicable[114] and maintain records and make reports concerning health and safety.

If the Contractor is sharing occupation of the Site with others, it may be appropriate for the Sub-Clause to be amended to specify exactly what health and safety obligations are to be fulfilled by the Contractor, by others and/or by the Employer, respectively.[115] In this way, the obligations of each Party or person concerned are clear.[116]

112. Sub-paragraph (c) of Sub-Clause 13.1 [*Right to Vary*]. The Contractor may similarly object to any instruction of the Engineer which may reduce the safety of the Works. Sub-Clause 3.5(b).
113. Thus, it is not subject to Review or consent by the Engineer.
114. '[I]mmediately' in the case of serious injury or death. Sub-Clause 4.8, penultimate paragraph.
115. *See* the *Guidance for the Preparation of Particular Conditions*, 24.
116. *Ibid.*

(3) Protection of the Site

Where the Site is located in a dangerous or insecure environment, the Contractor's responsibility for guarding and watching over the Site may be a heavy one. Special armed guards to protect personnel and the Works so as to keep them safe may be needed.

(iv) Related Law: Every country where Works are carried out will have Laws dealing with health and safety issues which will often be of a mandatory nature. Among other things, the Safety and Health in Construction Convention, 1988 (No. 167), of the International Labour Organisation ('ILO'), which has been ratified by more than 30 countries, deals with a number of the matters addressed in this Sub-Clause.[117]

--ooOOoo--

4.9 Quality Management and Compliance Verification Systems

4.9.1 Quality Management System

The Contractor shall prepare and implement a QM System to demonstrate compliance with the requirements of the Contract. The QM System shall be specifically prepared for the Works and submitted to the Engineer within 28 days of the Commencement Date. Thereafter, whenever the QM System is updated or revised, a copy shall promptly be submitted to the Engineer.

The QM System shall be in accordance with the details stated in the Specification (if any) and shall include the Contractor's procedures:

(a) to ensure that all Notices and other communications under Sub-Clause 1.3 [*Notices and Other Communications*], Contractor's Documents, as-built records (if applicable), operation and maintenance manuals (if applicable), and con-

117. *ILO Convention no 167* (Safety and Health in Construction Convention, 1988), https://www.ilo.org/dyn/normlex/en/f?p=NORMLEXPUB:12100:0::NO::P12100_INSTRUMENT_ID:312312 accessed 6 November 2022. Transnational corporations should also be attentive to Chapter VI dealing with the environment of the *Guidelines for Multinational Enterprises*, 2011, of the Organisation for Economic Cooperation and Development ('OECD') as this also covers health issues.

temporary records can be traced, with full certainty, to the Works, Goods, work, workmanship or test to which they relate;

(b) to ensure proper co-ordination and management of interfaces between the stages of execution of the Works, and between Subcontractors; and

(c) for the submission of Contractor's Documents to the Engineer for Review.

The Engineer may Review the QM System and may give a Notice to the Contractor stating the extent to which it does not comply with the Contract. Within 14 days after receiving this Notice, the Contractor shall revise the QM System to rectify such non-compliance. If the Engineer does not give such a Notice within 21 days of the date of submission of the QM System, the Engineer shall be deemed to have given a Notice of No-objection.

The Engineer may, at any time, give a Notice to the Contractor stating the extent to which the Contractor is failing to correctly implement the QM System to the Contractor's activities under the Contract. After receiving this Notice, the Contractor shall immediately remedy such failure.

The Contractor shall carry out internal audits of the QM System regularly, and at least once every 6 months. The Contractor shall submit to the Engineer a report listing the results of each internal audit within 7 days of completion. Each report shall include, where appropriate, the proposed measures to improve and/or rectify the QM System and/or its implementation.

If the Contractor is required by the Contractor's quality assurance certification to be subject to external audit, the Contractor shall immediately give a Notice to the Engineer describing any failing(s) identified in any external audit. If the Contractor is a JV, this obligation shall apply to each member of the JV.

4.9.2 Compliance Verification System

The Contractor shall prepare and implement a Compliance Verification System to demonstrate that the design (if any), Materials, Employer-Supplied Materials (if any), Plant, work and workmanship comply in all respects with the Contract.

The Compliance Verification System shall be in accordance with the details stated in the Specification (if any) and shall include a method for reporting the results of all inspections and tests carried out by the Contractor. In the event that any inspection or test identifies a non-compliance with the Contract, Sub-Clause 7.5 [*Defects and Rejection*] shall apply.

The Contractor shall prepare and submit to the Engineer a complete set of compliance verification documentation for the Works or Section (as the case may be), fully compiled and collated in the manner described in the Specification or, if not so described, in a manner acceptable to the Engineer.

4.9.3 General provision

Compliance with the QM System and/or Compliance Verification System shall not relieve the Contractor from any duty, obligation or responsibility under or in connection with the Contract.

The Contractor must submit to the Engineer a QM System for the Works to demonstrate its compliance with the Contract. The QM System must comply with the Specification and include the Contractor's procedures: (a) to ensure that all Notices and other documents can be traced to the matters to which they relate; (b) to ensure coordination and management of interfaces between stages of the Works; and (c) for the submission of Contractor's Documents to the Engineer for Review.

The Engineer may Review the QM System. If the Engineer has not given a Notice of any non-compliance to the Contractor within 21 days of receipt, the Engineer is deemed to have given a Notice of No-objection. If the Engineer has given a Notice of non-compliance within 21 days, the Contractor must rectify the non-compliance within 14 days.

The Contractor must also carry out internal audits of the QM System at least once every 6 months and submit the results to the Engineer within 7 days of completion.

The Contractor must implement a Compliance Verification System in accordance with the Specification to demonstrate that its work complies with the Contract. The Contractor must submit a complete set of compliance verification documentation for the Works (or Section) to the Engineer, in accordance with the Specification or otherwise as acceptable to the Engineer.

(i) Main Changes from RB/99:

(1) This Sub-Clause is more than three times as long as Sub-Clauses 4.9 [*Quality Assurance*] in RB/99 and GB/08.
(2) Sub-Clause 4.9.1 provides for a detailed Quality Management System, as opposed to the briefly described (first paragraph of Sub-Clause 4.9) 'quality assurance system' provided for in RB/99.
(3) Sub-Clause 4.9.2 provides for a Compliance Verification System which had no counterpart in RB/99.

(ii) Related Clauses / Sub-Clauses: 1.3 [*Notices and Other Communications*], 3.2 [*Engineer's Duties and Authority*], 4.1 [*Contractor's General Obligations*], 4.20 [*Progress Reports*], 7.4 [*Testing by the Contractor*], 7.5 [*Defects and Rejection*] and 14.5 [*Plant and Materials Intended for the Works*].

(iii) Analysis:

(1) Increased attention to quality

Since RB/99 was published, FIDIC has been especially concerned about quality issues:

> Quality of Construction or rather, the lack of quality, is increasingly being identified by consulting engineers as a serious concern worldwide. A lack of sustainability as well as potential health and safety problems in completed projects, an increase in the number of disputes and a failure to provide value for money in completed contracts are obvious outcomes of the lack of Quality of Construction.[118]

By quality of construction, FIDIC means quality which 'meets or exceeds the requirements of the employer, as specified in the contract documents,

118. *Improving the Quality of Construction, A Guide for Actions* (FIDIC 2004) Preface, http://fidic.org/books/improving-quality-construction-2004 accessed 6 November 2022.

while complying with law, codes, standards and regulatory policy that apply to the contract for construction'.[119]

(2) The QM System and Compliance Verification System

Accordingly, to complement the responsibility for quality of the Contractor and the Engineer, the Sub-Clause requires the Contractor to prepare and implement, for the first time, a Quality Management System ('QM System') specifically for the Works, in accordance with the Specification. A QM System has been defined as:

> a set of formalised or documented procedures or processes, documentation and resource requirements etc. covering the Contractor's execution of the work under the Contract. The purpose of a QM System is primarily to document best practices and lessons learnt from previous projects and to correct processes that might increase the risk of errors.[120]

The QM System is subject to possible Review by the Engineer.[121]

In addition, the Contractor is required to prepare and implement, also for the first time, a Compliance Verification System, in accordance with the Specification. The Compliance Verification System is designed to: 'demonstrate that the design (if any), Materials, Employer-Supplied Materials (if any), Plant, work and workmanship comply in all respects with the Contract'.[122]

If the Employer requires the Contractor to have a Quality Manager employed on the Site, such position should be stated in the Specification as one of the positions of Key Personnel.[123]

---

119. *Ibid.*, s 2.3.
120. Jakob B Sørensen, *FIDIC Red Book: A Companion to the 2017 Construction Contract* (1st edn, ICE Publishing, London, 2019) 71-72.
121. Sub-Clause 4.9.1, third paragraph.
122. Sub-Clause 4.9.2, first paragraph. While this System must be submitted to the Engineer, it is not subject to the Engineer's Review.
123. *See* Sub-Clause 6.12 [*Key Personnel*] and *Guidance for the Preparation of Particular Conditions*, 24. In this connection, FIDIC recommends that the Contractor and the Engineer have due regard to the FIDIC publication Improving the Quality of Construction – a Guide for Actions, 2004 http://fidic.org/books/improving-quality-construction-2004 accessed 6 November 2022.

(3) Sanctions for failure to implement

If the Contractor should fail to implement the QM System correctly, the Engineer may give the Contractor a Notice, pursuant to Sub-Clause 4.9.1, to remedy such failure. Similarly, in relation to the Compliance Verification System, if any inspection or test identifies a non-compliance with the Contract, Sub-Clause 7.5 [*Defect and Rejection*] applies. Ultimately, the Engineer may issue a Notice to Correct under Sub-Clause 15.1 and, if this is not complied with, claim under the Performance Security and/or possibly give a Notice of intention to terminate the Contract under Sub-Clause 15.2 [*Termination for Contractor's Default*].

As the QM System and Compliance Verification System are merely a check (possibly also required by regulatory authorities) to assure or ascertain that the Contractor is complying with the Contract, compliance with them does not relieve the Contractor of any of its contractual obligations.[124]

(iv) Related Law: Article 5.1.6 (*Determination of quality of performance*) of the UNIDROIT Principles provides that:

> Where the quality of performance is neither fixed by, nor determinable from, the contract a party is bound to render a performance of a quality that is reasonable and not less than average in the circumstances.[125]

--ooOOoo--

4.10 Use of Site Data

> The Contractor shall be responsible for interpreting all data referred to under Sub-Clause 2.5 [*Site Data and Items of Reference*].

124. Sub-Clause 4.9.3. Similarly, the last paragraph of Sub-Clause 3.2 [*Engineer's Duties and Authority*] provides that no action (or inaction) of the Engineer shall relieve the Contractor of any contractual obligation.
125. According to official comment 2 to art. 5.1.6 of the Principles, the additional reference to reasonableness: 'is intended to prevent a party from claiming that it has performed adequately if it has rendered an "average" performance in a market where the average quality is most unsatisfactory and is intended to give the judge or arbitrator an opportunity to raise those insufficient standards'.

> To the extent which was practicable (taking account of cost and time), the Contractor shall be deemed to have obtained all necessary information as to risks, contingencies and other circumstances which may influence or affect the Tender or Works. To the same extent, the Contractor shall be deemed to have inspected and examined the Site, access to the Site, its surroundings, the above data and other available information, and to have been satisfied before submitting the Tender as to all matters relevant to the execution of the Works, including:
>
> (a) the form and nature of the Site, including sub-surface conditions;
> (b) the hydrological and climatic conditions, and the effects of climatic conditions at the Site;
> (c) the extent and nature of the work and Goods necessary for the execution of the Works;
> (d) the Laws, procedures and labour practices of the Country; and
> (e) the Contractor's requirements for access, accommodation, facilities, personnel, power, transport, water and any other utilities or services.

The Contractor is responsible for interpreting all data referred to under Sub-Clause 2.5. To the extent practicable (taking account of cost and time), the Contractor is deemed to have obtained all necessary information as to risks and contingencies which may influence the Tender or Works. To the same extent, the Contractor is deemed to have examined the Site, access to the Site, its surroundings, the above data and other available information, and to have been satisfied before the Tender as to all matters relating to execution of the Works.

Commentary

(i) Main Changes from RB/99: This Sub-Clause is virtually identical to Sub-Clause 4.10 in RB/99. However, the first two sentences of Sub-Clause 4.10 in RB/99, dealing with the Site data which the Employer makes available to the Contractor, have been transferred (with minor changes) to, and are now at the beginning of, Sub-Clause 2.5, which deals generally with Site data and items of reference provided by the Employer, either before or after the Base Date.

(ii) Related Clauses / Sub-Clauses: 2.1 [*Right of Access to the Site*], 2.2 [*Assistance*], 2.5 [*Site Data and Items of Reference*], 4.11 [*Sufficiency of the Accepted Contract Amount*], 4.12 [*Unforeseeable Physical Conditions*] and 8.5 [*Extension of Time for Completion*].

(iii) Analysis:

(1) The Contractor's obligation to interpret Site data

Pursuant to Sub-Clause 2.5, the Employer shall have made available to the Contractor for information before the Base Date - normally it would do so in the tender dossier - all relevant data in the Employer's possession relating to the Site. 'Data' will normally be factual information about conditions at the Site.[126]

The Site data is to be made available at least 28 days before the latest date for submission of tenders[127] so as to allow tenderers time in which to take it into account when finalising their tenders. The Employer must also make available to the Contractor all such data which later comes into the Employer's possession.[128]

While the Contractor has no responsibility for verifying, it is expressly made responsible for interpreting, all data provided by the Employer.[129]

(2) The Contractor's obligation to obtain, inspect and examine

In addition, the Contractor is expected to have inspected and examined the form and nature of the Site, including subsurface conditions, access to the Site[130] and its surroundings and to have satisfied itself as to climatic conditions (e.g., by studying historical records from public sources), the extent and nature of the work and Goods necessary for its execution (e.g., the availability of local quarries), the Laws, procedures and labour practices of the Country (e.g., by consulting local laws and lawyers) and generally, the Contractor's requirements for access to the Site (including transportation), accommodation, facilities, and any utilities or services

126. Data is defined as 'facts and statistics used for reference or analysis'. *Concise Oxford English Dictionary* (10th edn, rev'd, OUP, Oxford, 2002).
127. *See* the commentary on Sub-Clause 1.1.4 '**Base Date**' above.
128. *See* the commentary on Sub-Clause 2.5 above.
129. Sub-Clause 4.10, first sentence.
130. While the Employer is responsible for providing legal access, the Contractor is responsible for obtaining physical access, to the Site. *See* the commentary on Sub-Clause 2.1 [*Right of Access to the Site*].

(e.g., for fresh and waste water, electricity and telecommunications).[131] Accordingly, the Contractor should have obtained all this information as well as information as to risks, contingencies and other circumstances which may bear on its tender.

A tenderer (the Contractor) is required to have made these investigations '[t]o the extent which was practicable (taking account of cost and time)'.[132] As the tender period may be of no more than several months' duration and as a tenderer has no assurance of obtaining the contract, there is an obvious practical limit on the investigations that a tenderer can be expected to have carried out and on the cost that it can be expected to have incurred.[133]

(3) The Contractor's right to claim

A Contractor will need to demonstrate that it has complied with Sub-Clause 4.10 in order to be able to claim, for example, for an Unforeseeable adverse physical condition under Sub-Clause 4.12. To make such a claim, it would need to show not only that it had properly interpreted the data coming from the Employer but also that it had inspected and examined the Site and carried out all other investigations and research described in this Sub-Clause '[t]o the extent which was practicable (taking account of cost and time)'.

---

131. Including their potential availability from the Employer, *see* Sub-Clause 4.19 [*Temporary Utilities*].
132. Sub-Clause 4.10, second paragraph.
133. As was stated in relation to the corresponding clause (Clause 11) of RB/87 for a road contract:

> one cannot expect from a bidder, within the short period of time left for him to prepare his bid, to investigate on matters of local resources of materials over (sic) the Employer's findings which are deemed to result from lengthy prior queries in subsoil and are supported by graphs, diagrams, samples and other probatory materials; a bidder is justifiably required to interpret the data made available to him; he is not required to expedite new thorough investigations which the Employer says in good faith to have carefully carried on presumably for months if not years, in the interest of the Works. Interpreting data is one thing; undertaking new investigations in a region plus or minus close to a road of about 180 kms to check whether the required materials exist or not as described in quantity and quality, at the locations identified by the Employer, is not a thing which can reasonably be said to pertain to a bidder.

Final award, ICC case 10619 (2002), ICC Int'l Ct Arb Bull, vol 19 (2008), no 2, 85, 90-91 (commentary 52, 56-57).

Thus, a Contractor should conserve records of its pre-tender studies and investigations carefully so as to be able to demonstrate, if necessary, that it had made all practicable '(taking account of cost and time)' inspections and examinations. The Contractor needs to be able to prove that, notwithstanding its proper interpretation of the data coming from the Employer and its investigations, to the extent practicable, of all relevant matters, including those listed in Sub-Clause 4.10, the adverse physical condition was not reasonably foreseeable by an experienced contractor by the Base Date.[134] Only then may the Contractor be entitled to claim under Sub-Clause 4.12.

--ooOOoo--

4.11 Sufficiency of the Accepted Contract Amount

The Contractor shall be deemed to:

(a) have satisfied himself/herself as to the correctness and sufficiency of the Accepted Contract Amount; and

(b) have based the Accepted Contract Amount on the data, interpretations, necessary information, inspections, examinations and satisfaction as to all relevant matters described in Sub-Clause 4.10 [*Use of Site Data*].

Unless otherwise stated in the Contract, the Accepted Contract Amount shall be deemed to cover all the Contractor's obligations under the Contract and all things necessary for the proper execution of the Works in accordance with the Contract.

The Contractor shall be deemed to have satisfied itself as to the correctness and sufficiency of the Accepted Contract Amount, and to have based it on the data and information in Sub-Clause 4.10. Unless otherwise stated in the Contract, it is deemed to cover all of the Contractor's obligations.

134. For the definition of '**Unforeseeable**', *see* Sub-Clause 1.1.85.

Commentary

(i) Main Changes from RB/99: The new Sub-Clause does not expressly state (as did RB/99) that the Accepted Contract Amount covers all the Contractor's obligations under the Contract '(including those under Provisional Sums, if any)'.[135]

(ii) Related Clauses / Sub-Clauses: 2.5 [*Site Data and Items of Reference*], 4.1 [*Contractor's General Obligations*], 4.10 [*Use of Site Data*], 4.12 [*Unforeseeable Physical Conditions*] and 13.7 [*Adjustments for Changes in Cost*].

(iii) Analysis: The Accepted Contract Amount is defined as the amount accepted in the Letter of Acceptance by the Employer for the execution of the Works in accordance with the Contract[136] and is thus a fixed and unchanging sum, unlike the Contract Price which varies with the value of work executed and is subject to adjustment as provided for by Sub-Clause 14.1.[137] Sub-Clause 4.11 provides that, unless otherwise stated in the Contract, the Accepted Contract Amount is deemed to cover all of the Contractor's obligations under the Contract.

Sub-paragraph (a) of Sub-Clause 4.11 provides that the Contractor shall be deemed to have satisfied itself as to the correctness and sufficiency of the Accepted Contract Amount. This is designed to foreclose it from later claiming, for example, that there was a mathematical or calculation error in its Tender price or that it had overlooked to price for, or had mistakenly under-priced, an item of work, risk or contingency.

Sub-paragraph (b) provides that the Contractor shall be deemed to have based the Accepted Contract Amount on the data, interpretations, other information and inspections and satisfaction as to all relevant matters described in Sub-Clause 4.10. By this, the Contractor acknowledges that it has taken account of all information as to the risks, contingencies and other circumstances described in that Sub-Clause, making it difficult for it later to claim that there was a risk or contingency which it had overlooked or neglected.

---

135. On the other hand, Sub-Clause 14.2.3(a) implies that the Accepted Contract Amount includes Provisional Sums. *See* the reference there to the Accepted Contract Amount 'less Provisional Sums'.
136. Sub-Clause 1.1.1 '**Accepted Contract Amount**'.
137. *See* the commentary on Sub-Clause 1.1.1 '**Accepted Contract Amount**', above.

On the other hand, sub-paragraph (b) is not unhelpful to the Contractor in that it provides that the Contractor has based its Tender price on, among other things, the 'data' provided by the Employer, albeit subject to interpretation by the Contractor. Thus, if the Employer's data should prove to be inaccurate, then – provided that the Contractor had not misinterpreted it – the Contractor may argue that, as the Accepted Contract Amount is deemed to have been based on that false data, it should no longer apply, and the Contractor should be entitled to relief.[138]

--ooOOoo--

4.12 Unforeseeable Physical Conditions

In this Sub-Clause, "physical conditions" means natural physical conditions and physical obstructions (natural or man-made) and pollutants, which the Contractor encounters at the Site during execution of the Works, including sub-surface and hydrological conditions but excluding climatic conditions at the Site and the effects of those climatic conditions.

If the Contractor encounters physical conditions which the Contractor considers to have been Unforeseeable and that will have an adverse effect on the progress and/or increase the Cost of the execution of the Works, the following procedure shall apply:

138. *See* Julian Bailey, *Construction Law* (3rd edn, London Publishing, UK, 2020) vol 1, 327 (para. 4-164) providing that:

> [a] representation made during the course of tendering [...] does not, in general, have any contractual effect, unless the representation is promissory in nature [...] *A representation will be promissory where it constitutes an express term of the contract.* (Emphasis added)

Arguably, as the Contractor is deemed to have based its price on, among other things, the data made available by the Employer under Sub-Clause 2.5, Sub-Clause 4.11(b) amounts to a representation by the Employer that such data is accurate.

4.12.1 Contractor's Notice

After discovery of such physical conditions, the Contractor shall give a Notice to the Engineer, which shall:

(a) be given as soon as practicable and in good time to give the Engineer opportunity to inspect and investigate the physical conditions promptly and before they are disturbed;
(b) describe the physical conditions, so that they can be inspected and/or investigated promptly by the Engineer;
(c) set out the reasons why the Contractor considers the physical conditions to be Unforeseeable; and
(d) describe the manner in which the physical conditions will have an adverse effect on the progress and/or increase the Cost of the execution of the Works.

4.12.2 Engineer's inspection and investigation

The Engineer shall inspect and investigate the physical conditions within 7 days, or a longer period agreed with the Contractor, after receiving the Contractor's Notice.

The Contractor shall continue execution of the Works, using such proper and reasonable measures as are appropriate for the physical conditions and to enable the Engineer to inspect and investigate them.

4.12.3 Engineer's instructions

The Contractor shall comply with any instructions which the Engineer may give for dealing with the physical conditions and, if such an instruction constitutes a Variation, Sub-Clause 13.3.1 [*Variation by Instruction*] shall apply.

4.12.4 Delay and/or Cost

If and to the extent that the Contractor suffers delay and/or incurs Cost due to these physical conditions, having complied with Sub-Clauses 4.12.1 to 4.12.3 above, the Contractor shall be entitled subject to Sub-Clause 20.2 [*Claims for Payment and/or EOT*] to EOT and/or payment of such Cost.

4.12.5 Agreement or Determination of Delay and/or Cost

The agreement or determination, under Sub-Clause 20.2.5 [*Agreement or determination of the Claim*], of any Claim under Sub-Clause 4.12.4 [*Delay and/or Cost*] shall include consideration of whether and (if so) to what extent the physical conditions were Unforeseeable.

The Engineer may also review whether other physical conditions in similar parts of the Works (if any) were more favourable than could reasonably have been foreseen by the Base Date. If and to the extent that these more favourable conditions were encountered, the Engineer may take account of the reductions in Cost which were due to these conditions in calculating the additional Cost to be agreed or determined under this Sub-Clause 4.12.5. However, the net effect of all additions and reductions under this Sub-Clause 4.12.5 shall not result in a net reduction in the Contract Price.

The Engineer may take account of any evidence of the physical conditions foreseen by the Contractor by the Base Date, which the Contractor may include in the supporting particulars for the Claim under Sub-Clause 20.2.4 [*Fully detailed Claim*], but shall not be bound by any such evidence.

If the Contractor encounters Unforeseeable adverse 'physical conditions' (as defined) at the Site, the Contractor must give a Notice (as described) to the Engineer as soon as practicable. The Engineer must then inspect the physical conditions within 7 days, during which time the Contractor must continue with the Works and comply with any instructions which the Engineer may give. If the Contractor suffers delay and/or incurs Cost, having complied with this Sub-Clause, the Contractor is entitled, subject to Sub-Clause 20.2, to an EOT and/or such Cost.

The agreement or determination, under Sub-Clause 20.2.5, of any Claim under this Sub-Clause must include consideration of whether and to what extent the physical conditions were Unforeseeable. However, if physical conditions encountered in similar parts of the Works (if any) were more favourable than could reasonably have

been foreseen by the Base Date, the Engineer may take account of the reductions in Cost due to these conditions in calculating the additional Cost to be agreed or determined. The Engineer may also take account of evidence of the physical conditions foreseen by the Contractor by the Base Date.

(i) Main Changes from RB/99: Since RB/57, the RB has contained a provision allocating the risk of unforeseeable adverse physical conditions of one kind or another[139] to the Employer. However, the provision has, with each edition, progressively become more detailed and elaborate. This is again true of the present Sub-Clause in RB/17 compared to RB/99.

This Sub-Clause contains the following changes compared to RB/99:

(1) It is now better and more clearly structured with five sub-sub-clauses, 4.12.1 through 4.12.5.
(2) The definition of 'physical conditions' expressly includes 'physical obstructions (natural or man-made)', whereas previously it referred to 'man-made and other physical obstructions'.
(3) It now excludes not just climatic conditions at the Site but also the 'effects of those climatic conditions'.
(4) The Notice required of the Contractor is more detailed and must satisfy sub-paragraphs: (a), (b), (c) and (d) of Sub-Clause 4.12.1.
(5) The Engineer is required to inspect and investigate the physical conditions within 7 days, or longer if agreed with the Contractor, after receiving the Contractor's Notice.[140]
(6) The Contractor is required to have complied with Sub-Clauses 4.12.1 to 4.12.3, in order to be entitled to an EOT and/or payment of Cost.[141]
(7) The new procedure for agreeing or determining claims under Sub-Clause 20.2.5 must be complied with.
(8) While the former Sub-Clause provided that the Engineer might take account of any evidence of the physical conditions foreseen by the Contractor when submitting the Tender, which may be made available by the Contractor, the new Sub-Clause provides that the Engineer may take account of such evidence foreseen by the Contractor 'by the Base Date, which the Contractor may

139. Referred to in Clause 12 of RB/57 through RB/77 as 'physical conditions or artificial obstructions which […] could not have been reasonably foreseen by an experienced contractor'.
140. Sub-Clause 4.12.2.
141. Sub-Clause 4.12.4.

include in the supporting particulars for the Claim under Sub-Clause 20.2.4'.[142] As in the case of the former Sub-Clause, the Engineer is not bound by such evidence.

(ii) Related Clauses / Sub-Clauses: 1.3 [*Notices and Other Communications*], 2.5 [*Site Data and Items of Reference*], 3.7 [*Agreement or Determination*], 4.10 [*Use of Site Data*], 4.11 [*Sufficiency of Accepted Contract Amount*], 4.23 [*Archaeological and Geological Findings*], 7.3 [*Inspection*], 8.5 [*Extension of Time for Completion*], 13.3.1 [*Variation by Instruction*], 18 [*Exceptional Events*] and 20.2 [*Claims for Payment and/or EOT*].

(iii) Analysis:

(1) The Employer's assumption of underground risk (among others)

In principle, under the common law, a Contractor is responsible for overcoming any unforeseeable adverse physical conditions which it may encounter at the Site, and is not entitled to claim additional payment or an extension of time on this account unless the Contract contains a specific provision to this effect.[143] This principle is reflected in the immediately preceding Sub-Clause, Sub-Clause 4.11 [*Sufficiency of the Accepted Contract Amount*]. Under the common law, this obligation of the Contractor is deemed to be part of its generally unqualified duty to complete the Works.[144]

However, under numerous standard forms of construction contract, the Employer will generally bear the risk of unforeseeable adverse physical conditions at the Site.[145] The rationale for this is that the Employer will

142. Sub-Clause 4.12.5, last paragraph.

143. *Stees v Leonard*, 20 Minn 494 (1874) (refusing to excuse a contractor after its partly completed building had, for a second time, collapsed due to being built on quick sand); *Bottoms v The City of York* (1892), A Hudson, *Building Contracts* vol 2 (2nd edn 1895) 147 (refusing to excuse a contractor because of the unforeseen adverse nature of soil); and *Re Nuttall and Lynton and Barnstaple Ry* (1899) 82 L.T.17 (refusing railway contractor's claim under a lump sum contract for unforeseeable quantities of excavation). *See also* Atkin Chambers, *Hudson's Building and Engineering Contracts* (14th edn, Sweet & Maxwell, London, 2020) 436-443 (paras 3-070 to 3-072).

144. *Stees v Leonard*, 20 Minn 494 (1874).

145. For example, in the UK, the *Institution of Civil Engineers (ICE) Conditions of Contract* (Clause 12) (7th edn, 1999) *NEC4 Engineering and Construction Contract*, June 2017, published by the ICE, Clauses 60.1(12) and (13), and, in the United States, the *American Institute of Architects ('AIA') Document*

normally be familiar with the Site (which it will either own or of which it will have possession); will have chosen it for the Works and will normally have had ample opportunity to investigate it; and, based on its investigations and perhaps experience of other projects in the area, is likely to know generally what to expect from conditions there. On the other hand, tenderers will normally have no prior knowledge of the Site, will have had to prepare their tenders within a limited tender period and, as they will have had no assurance of obtaining the contract, can only be expected to devote limited cost and time to exploring and examining site conditions before submitting their tenders. Therefore the Employer is generally considered to be the appropriate party to bear the risk of the adequacy of the Site for the Works to be constructed.[146]

The advantage of such a contractual provision for the Employer is that, in theory at least, it will only pay for unforeseeable adverse physical conditions which the Contractor actually encounters and avoid paying the Contractor a contingency allowance for unforeseeable adverse conditions that never eventuate. Sub-Clause 4.12, which should be read together with Sub-Clauses 1.1.85, 2.5, 4.10 and 4.11, gives effect to this widely accepted policy in the construction industry.

(2) Six conditions to claim

To assert a claim under this Sub-Clause, the Contractor must satisfy six conditions. It must demonstrate that: (1) it has encountered physical conditions (as defined), (2) which were Unforeseeable, and (3) which adversely affect the progress and/or increase the Cost of the execution of the Works. If so, the Contractor is required: (4) to give a Notice containing specified information to the Engineer, (5) continue the execution of the Works using such proper and reasonable measures as are appropriate for the physical conditions encountered and to enable the Engineer to inspect and investigate them, and (6) give a Notice of Claim under Sub-Clause 20.2.1 and otherwise comply with Sub-Clause 20.2. As

---

A201-2017 (s 3.7.4 Concealed or Unknown Conditions) and *Federal Acquisition Regulation ('FAR')* s 52.236-2 in Title 48 of the US Code of Federal Regulations (C.F.R.).

146. David Kinlan, *Adverse Physical Conditions & the Experienced Contractor* (1st edn, Delft Academic Press, Delft, the Netherlands, 2014) 7-8. As an alternative to providing, as does Sub-Clause 4.12, that the Employer bears the risk of Unforeseeable adverse physical conditions, the Parties might agree that such risk be shared between them. *Guidance for the Preparation of Particular Conditions*, 24, contains an example provision on this subject.

in the case of the Contract generally, the Contractor is required to comply with any instruction which the Engineer may give[147] and, if such instruction should constitute a Variation, Sub-Clause 13.3.1 will apply.

Each of these six conditions is reviewed below:

(1) Physical conditions are defined to mean natural physical conditions, physical obstructions (natural or man-made) and pollutants,[148] which the Contractor encounters at the Site,[149] including subsurface and hydrological conditions but excluding climatic conditions at the Site and the effects of those climatic conditions.[150] Physical conditions as defined could include anything from unforeseeable hard rock or underground piping or ordnance (munitions) to unforeseeable water levels when constructing a lake or pond.[151] However, climatic conditions at the

147. Sub-Clause 3.5 [*Engineer's Instructions*].
148. In FIDIC's Conditions of Contract for Underground Works 2019 (the 'Emerald Book') there is added in Sub-Clause 4.12 [*Unforeseeable Physical Conditions*] after the word 'pollutants' the words 'and reactions of the ground to Excavation'. Excavation is a defined term in the Emerald Book.
149. Thus, a Contractor's claim under Clause 12 of RB/77 for an unforeseeable physical condition at the source for roading materials for incorporation into the works (as opposed to such a condition at the site itself) was denied. Partial award, ICC case 11499 (2002), ICC Int'l Ct Arb Bull, vol 19, no 2, 2008, 97-101 (commentary 48-51).
150. The Contractor is expected by Sub-Clause 4.10 (b) to have satisfied itself about these before submitting the Tender.
151. In an English case, the term 'physical condition' in Clause 12 of the English ICE Conditions, 5th edn, was held to apply to where the contractor had encountered soil which behaved in an unforeseeable manner when stress was applied to it; i.e., the term was recognised to apply to transient and not just intransient or permanent conditions. *Humber Oil Terminals Trustee v Harbour and General Works* (C.A. 1991) 59 BLR 1. The English court (at least in that case) 'tended to give a generous interpretation to the expression "physical condition"'. Atkin Chambers, *Hudson's Building and Engineering Contracts* (14th edn, Sweet & Maxwell, London, 2020), 678-679 (para. 5-066). A leading US treatise lists the site conditions 'most frequently generating controversy between owners and contractors' as follows:

    (1) Soil-bearing capacity (*see* the *Humber Oil* case above).
    (2) Soil composition, classification, and 'toughness'.
    (3) Rock strength, elevation, and quantity.
    (4) Groundwater elevation, flow, and quantity.

Site as well as their effects are excluded because, based on historical, statistical records (e.g., regarding the frequency and intensity of rainfall), they should be foreseeable and therefore capable of being taken into account by an experienced contractor.[152]

(2) Unforeseeable is defined in Sub-Clause 1.1.85[153] to mean not reasonably foreseeable by an experienced contractor by the Base Date, that is, the date 28 days before the latest date for submission of the Tender.[154] Thus, unforeseeability is assessed by reference to what an experienced contractor should have known by that date based on the Site data supplied by the Employer,[155] the Contractor's interpretation of such data and the investigations of the Site and its surroundings which it is deemed to have

---

(5) Soil moisture content, and swelling and shrinkage characteristics.
(6) Unsuitable fill.
(7) Buried man-made obstructions.
(8) Topographic survey inaccuracies regarding site elevation, site drainage and estimated quantities of excavation and fill.
(9) Surface water resulting from excessive rains, hurricanes, or high rivers.
(10) High tides and heavy currents.
(11) Permafrost.
(12) Environmental problems, e.g., hazardous wastes and sedimentation conditions, etc.

Philip L Bruner and Patrick J O'Connor, Jr, *Bruner & O'Connor on Construction Law* (Thomson Reuters, St Paul, MN, 2009) vol 4A, 585-586 (s 14:3). Although no FIDIC contract may have been involved in these cases, there is no reason why most, if not all, of the site conditions described could not, in an appropriate case, give rise to a claim under Sub-Clause 4.12 other than if they were climatic conditions at the Site or the effects of those climatic conditions.

152. But, in the case of adverse climate conditions at the Site which are Unforeseeable, the Contractor may be able to claim an extension of time pursuant to Sub-Clause 8.5 (c).
153. *See* the commentary on Sub-Clause 1.1.85 '**Unforeseeable**', above.
154. *See* Sub-Clause 1.1.4 '**Base Date**'. The Unforeseeable condition could also constitute an Exceptional Event under Clause 18 [*Exceptional Events*], allowing for relief under that Sub-Clause.
155. *See* Sub-Clause 2.5.

undertaken during the Tender period.[156] The test is an objective one. It is based upon what an experienced contractor should or should not have foreseen. In answering this question, it will therefore be relevant to know, among other things, whether other tendering contractors priced for whatever eventuality may be at issue.[157]

(3) Physical conditions have an adverse effect on the progress and/or increase the Cost of the execution of the Works because, for example, they delay or disrupt the Contractor's work and/or require additional excavation, tunnelling or exploratory work.[158] If they impact the Contractor's critical path, then the Contractor may be entitled to an extension of time under Sub-Clause 8.5 [*Extension of Time for Completion*].

(4) The Contractor must give a Notice to the Engineer as soon as practicable. The Notice must fulfil four requirements: (1) be given in good time to allow the Engineer the opportunity to inspect the physical conditions before they are disturbed, (2) describe the physical conditions, (3) set out why they are Unforeseeable, and (4) describe the manner in which they will have an adverse effect on the progress and/or increase the Cost of the execution of the Works.[159]

156. *See* Sub-Clause 4.10. In an English case relating to YB/99, the Contractor had been provided, at the tender stage, with the results of the Employer's estimate of the volume of contaminated ground. Based on this, the Contractor had assumed that it could be dealt with at limited cost. When the volume of contaminated material exceeded the Employer's estimate, the Contractor claimed that the excess constituted an unforeseeable ground condition under Sub-Clause 4.12. Denying the claim, the Court of Appeal held that, under the FIDIC Conditions, the Contractor should have made its own assessment of the ground conditions and could not simply accept the Employer's assessment and claim that that was all that was forseeable. *Obrascon Huarte Lain SA v HM Attorney General for Gibraltar* [2015] EWCA Civ 712 (paras 83-100).
157. Atkin Chambers, *Hudson's Building and Engineering Contracts* (14th edn, Sweet & Maxwell, London, 2020) 679 (para. 5-066).
158. Sub-Clause 13.1 (v) recognises that additional work comprising 'boreholes and other testing and exploratory work' may constitute a Variation if the other requirements for a Variation are met.
159. The Notice must also comply with Sub-Clause 1.3 [*Notices and Other Communications*].

(5) The Contractor must continue with the execution of the Works using such proper and reasonable measures as are appropriate for the physical conditions and to enable the Engineer to inspect and investigate them. Where the physical conditions are, in fact, Unforeseeable, any instruction that the Engineer might give to deal with them may constitute a Variation to which Sub-Clause 13.3.1 would apply.

(6) The Contractor must give a Notice of Claim to the Engineer within 28 days – *or be time-barred*, as provided for in Sub-Clause 20.2.1. The Contractor may combine this Notice with the Notice referred to in (4) above in which case the Contractor should make this expressly clear in its Notice and the Notice must satisfy the requirements of both Sub-Clauses 4.12.1 and 20.2.1.[160] Thereafter the Contractor must otherwise comply with Sub-Clause 20.2.[161]

(3) The Engineer's review

If the Contractor can satisfy these conditions and demonstrate a right to claim, the Sub-Clause further provides that the Engineer may review whether other physical conditions in similar parts of the Works, if any (there may be none), are more favourable than could reasonably have been foreseen, and if so, may take account of the ensuing reductions in Cost when calculating the additional Cost to be accorded the Contractor.[162] This limits the chance that the Contractor would enjoy a windfall.

A simple example would be the case of tunnelling work. Some parts of the tunnel may be unforeseeably difficult and costly to excavate (e.g., excavation through hard rock, such as granite), whereas others may be unforeseeably easy and inexpensive to excavate (e.g., excavation through soft rock, such as grey chalk or chalk marl encountered in

160. *The FIDIC Contracts Guide* (2nd edn, FIDIC, 2022) 193 acknowledges that the same Notice may, if properly prepared and given, satisfy the requirements of different Sub-Clauses.

161. *See* the commentary on Sub-Clause 20.2 [*Claims for Payment and/or EOT*] below.

162. More favourable physical conditions may also allow the Contractor to work more quickly. However, this Sub-Clause does not authorise the Engineer to require the Contractor to accelerate. But *see* Sub-Clause 8.7 [*Rate of Progress*].

construction of the Anglo-French Channel Tunnel).[163] However, the net effect of all additions and reductions must not result in a net reduction in the Contract Price.

This last provision, which was introduced for the first time in the 1999 Rainbow Suite, is a reasonable one so long as the Engineer acts fairly (as the Engineer is expressly required to do when making a determination under Sub-Clause 3.7.2). In this connection, for its own protection, the Contractor will be well advised, when preparing its tender and before the Base Date, to make a detailed record of the physical conditions which the Contractor expects to encounter at the Site, as this may serve as a sort of baseline for application of this Sub-Clause.

The last paragraph of this Sub-Clause provides helpfully that, when considering a claim from the Contractor, the Engineer may take account of any such record which the Contractor may have prepared pre-tender, though the Engineer is not bound by such evidence. Even if the Engineer should disregard it, the Contractor would, nevertheless, be able to use it to support its position in settlement negotiations, before the DAAB and in arbitration.[164]

(iv) Related Law:

(1) Contractual v legal remedies

The general position in common law countries in relation to contractor's claims for unforeseeable adverse physical conditions has been described at the beginning of the previous **(iii) Analysis** section. As the Conditions may (by Sub-Clauses 4.12 and 8.5 as well as Clause 18) expressly entitle the Contractor to relief where it encounters Unforeseeable adverse

163. '[S]oft enough to cut with ease, but strong enough to stand without support'. Drew Fetherston, *The Chunnel: The Amazing Story of the Undersea Crossing of the English Channel* (Times Books, New York, 1997) 33.

164. Facts justifying a claim under Sub-Clause 4.12 (and 8.5) might also justify a claim for an Exceptional Event under Clause 18 entitling a Contractor to claim an EOT and, possibly, Cost, under that Clause and, in extreme circumstances, release from the Contract under Sub-Clause 18.6. For a case where submerged explosives at the sea-bottom of a port (the importance and quantity of which was beyond what the parties had foreseen) were held to constitute *force majeure* (the equivalent of an Exceptional Event under Clause 18) under a dredging contract based on a FIDIC form, *see* award, ICC case 2763 (1980) (English translation of original in French) Sigvard Jarvin and Yves Derains (eds), *Coll of ICC Arb Awards 1974-1985* (ICC, Paris / Kluwer, the Netherlands, 1988) 157.

physical conditions, it will normally be in the Contractor's interest to invoke these remedies in preference to any available at law.

Nonetheless, there may be circumstances where it will be justified to invoke remedies at law as well or in the alternative.[165] Under the common law, these remedies would include the doctrines of frustration, impossibility and, in the United States, impracticability.[166] Under the civil law, these remedies would include the legal doctrines of force majeure and hardship (*imprévision*)[167] and, in the case of public works contracts and most relevant, the theory of unforeseeable physical conditions (*sujétions imprévues*) *which is even more favourable to the Contractor than Sub-Clause 4.12.*[168]

Relief might also be available, pursuant to the UNIDROIT Principles,[169] where they may apply.[170]

(2) Work done in accordance with Engineer's plan

Where work is required to be done in accordance with the plans and specifications of the Engineer, which prove deficient and have to be changed, causing the Contractor delay and expense, English and US law differ on whether the Contractor is entitled to relief from the Employer. Under English law, the Contractor has no claim as the Employer does not impliedly warrant the Engineer's plans and specifications.[171] On the other hand, under US law, where the plans and specifications direct the Contractor as to the precise manner of performance (i.e., they are what US law refers to as 'design specifications', as opposed to 'performance specifications' which merely prescribe the final result to be achieved),

165. For example, when much is at stake and/or when the Parties are before a DAAB or in international arbitration.
166. *See* under **(iv) Related Law** of the commentary below on Sub-Clause 18.6 [*Release from Performance under the Law*].
167. Both doctrines are discussed in **Section 4 Common Law and Civil Law Compared – 4.4.7 *Force Majeure* and Hardship** of **Chapter II Applicable Law** above.
168. Discussed in **Section 4 Common Law and Civil Law Compared – 4.6.1 Unforseeable Physical Difficulties** (*Sujétions Imprévues*) of **Chapter II Applicable Law** above.
169. *See* **Section 7 International Legal Principles**, **Chapter II Applicable Law**, above discussing these Principles.
170. *See* for hardship arts 6.2.1-6.2.3 of the Principles, and for *force majeure*, art. 7.1.7.
171. *Thorn v London Corporation*, 3 App Cas. 1040, 1876.

under the *Spearin* doctrine,[172] the Employer impliedly warrants that the plans and specifications are suitable for construction of the structure in question and, accordingly, the Contractor may claim against the Employer where they are found to be defective.[173]

(v) Improvements:

(1) NEC 4 contract has two innovations compared to this Sub-Clause which Parties may want to adopt: (1) it provides, as a 'compensation event', for where the Contractor encounters physical conditions which an experienced contractor would have judged at the Contract Date to have 'such a small chance of occurring that it would have been unreasonable to have allowed for them' (Clause 60.1(12)), which seems better than the Unforeseeable test in Sub-Clause 4.12, as it corresponds more closely to the way a tenderer is likely to assess and price for such a risk;[174] and (2) it provides for an Early Warning Register to register early warning matters which are either listed as such in the Contract Data or notified as early warning matters by the Project Manager or the Contractor (Clause 11.2(8)).[175]

(2) Where a project involves significant subsurface works, it would be desirable to go beyond what is stated in the last paragraph of Sub-Clause 4.12.5[176] and provide for the preparation and use of a 'Geotechnical Baseline Report' ('GBR').[177] A GBR is a set of site parameters or baselines included in a construction contract

172. Based on the United States Supreme Court case, *United States v Spearin*, 248 US 132 (1918).

173. J Bailey and S.A. Hess, 'Delay Damages and Site Conditions: Contrasts in US and English Law' (2015) 35(3) Const L, ABA for Const L, 6, 15-20. The Contractor's claim is for misrepresentation. Justin Sweet and Marc M Schneier, *Construction Law for Design Professionals, Construction Managers, and Contractors* (Cengage Learning, Stamford, CT, 2015) 326.

174. *See* the commentary on Sub-Clause 1.1.85 '**Unforeseeable**', above.

175. FIDIC's *Conditions of Contract for Underground Works* 2019 (the 'Emerald Book') provides in Sub-Clause 1.16 for a Contract Risk Register which appears to perform this function. *See also* Sub-Clause 8.4 [*Advance Warning*] of RB/17.

176. Providing that the Engineer may take account of any evidence of the physical conditions foreseen by the Contractor by the Base Date.

177. *Guidance for the Particular Conditions* in relation to Sub-Clause 4.12 refers to this as a 'Baseline Report', 24. For more details on this subject, *see* FIDIC's Emerald Book.

which sets out the parties' mutual understanding of the conditions expected to be encountered during subsurface construction. The actual conditions subsequently encountered can then be measured against these baselines to determine whether, and to what extent, they differ from what was expected and, if so, whether, and to what extent, the contractor may claim for unforeseeable adverse physical conditions.[178] Risks associated with conditions consistent with or less adverse than the baselines are allocated to the contractor, whereas those more adverse than the baselines are borne by the employer.[179]

--ooOOoo--

4.13 Rights of Way and Facilities

> The Contractor shall bear all costs and charges for special and/or temporary rights-of-way which may be required for the purposes of the Works, including those for access to the Site.
>
> The Contractor shall also obtain, at the Contractor's risk and cost, any additional facilities outside the Site which may be required for the purposes of the Works.

The Contractor shall bear all costs for special and/or temporary rights of way which may be required for the purposes of the Works, as well as for any additional facilities outside the Site that the Contractor may require.

---

178. This procedure is more fully described in *Recommended Contract Practices for Underground Construction*, edited by William W Edgerton and published by the (US) Society for Mining, Metallurgy and Exploration Inc (SME) ProQuest Ebook Central (2008), 19, and in David Kinlan, *Adverse Physical Conditions & the Experienced Contractor* (Delft Academic Press, Delft, the Netherlands, 2014) 101-105.
179. A GBR may also have other objectives. *See* ASCE (American Society of Civil Engineers), *Geotechnical Baseline Reports for Construction: Suggested Guidelines* (Randall J Essex ed) (Reston, VA 2007) 5.

Commentary

(i) Main Changes from RB/99: This Sub-Clause is essentially unchanged from RB/99 and GB/08, except that it is now presented in two paragraphs instead of in one.

(ii) Related Clauses / Sub-Clauses: 1.13 [*Compliance with Laws*], 2.1 [*Right of Access to the Site*], 2.2 [*Assistance*], 4.10 [*Use of Site Data*], 4.15 [*Access Route*] and 4.22 [*Contractor's Operations on Site*].

(iii) Analysis: While the Contractor is expected to have determined at the time of tender its requirements for access to the Site,[180] and to have satisfied itself then as to the suitability and availability of access routes,[181] this Sub-Clause deals with the possible need of the Contractor for additional or special rights of way.[182] These may be to access the Site or to the Contractor's camp or workshop area, outside the defined area of the Site.[183] In these cases, the Contractor is fully responsible for obtaining all permissions and paying all costs associated with such rights of way and access.[184]

Similarly, the Contractor must bear the risk and cost of obtaining any additional facilities outside the Site which it may require. These may be located on the 'additional areas which may be obtained by the Contractor' referred to in the first sentence of Sub-Clause 4.22 [*Contractor's Operations on Site*].

--ooOOoo--

4.14 Avoidance of Interference

The Contractor shall not interfere unnecessarily or improperly with:

180. *See* Sub-Clause 4.10 [*Use of Site Data*] above.
181. *See* Sub-Clause 4.15 [*Access Route*] below.
182. Right of way is 'the legal right to pass along a specific route through property belonging to another' or a 'thoroughfare subject to such a right'. *Concise Oxford English Dictionary* (10th edn, rev'd, OUP, Oxford, 2002).
183. *FIDIC DBO Contract Guide* (FIDIC, 2011) 40.
184. *Ibid.*

(a) the convenience of the public; or
(b) the access to and use and occupation of all roads and footpaths, irrespective of whether they are public or in the possession of the Employer or of others.

The Contractor shall indemnify and hold the Employer harmless against and from all damages, losses and expenses (including legal fees and expenses) resulting from any such unnecessary or improper interference.

The Contractor must not interfere unnecessarily or improperly with the convenience of the public or with the access and use of roads and footpaths. The Contractor must indemnify the Employer against all damages resulting from any such interference.

Commentary

(i) Main Changes from RB/99: This Sub-Clause is unchanged from RB/99.

(ii) Related Clauses / Sub-Clauses: 1.13 [*Compliance with Laws*], 1.15 [*Limitation of Liability*], 4.6 [*Co-operation*], 4.15 [*Access Route*], 4.22 [*Contractor's Operations on Site*], 17.4 [*Indemnities by Contractor*] and 17.5 [*Indemnities by Employer*].

(iii) Analysis: Understandably, when executing the Works, the Contractor should not interfere 'unnecessarily or improperly' with the convenience of the public or with access to or use of public or private roads and footpaths. Consequently, pursuant to this Sub-Clause, the Contractor must indemnify the Employer in respect of claims from third parties or other expenses resulting from any such interference.[185]

However, the Contractor's liability is not unlimited in this respect.[186] Moreover, pursuant to Sub-Clause 17.5(b), the Employer is required to indemnify the Contractor against third-party claims in respect of 'damage

185. This indemnity overlaps with that provided for by the first paragraph of Sub-Clause 17.4 [*Indemnities by Contractor*]. However, while the Contractor's indemnity under the first paragraph of Sub-Clause 17.4 is excluded from the liability limits in Sub-Clause 1.15 [*Limitation of Liability*], the Contractor's indemnity under Sub-Clause 4.14 is not so excluded.
186. *See* Sub-Clause 1.15 [*Limitation of Liability*].

to or loss of any property real or personal (other than the Works)' to the extent such damage or loss arises out of any event described in sub-paragraphs (a) to (f) of Sub-Clause 17.2 [*Liability for Care of the Works*]. These include, among others, 'interference, whether temporary or permanent, with any right of way [...] (other than resulting from the Contractor's method of construction) which is the unavoidable result of the execution of the Works in accordance with the Contract'. Thus, the Employer bears the risk if the interference is the unavoidable result of the Contractor's performance of the Contract.

Although the second paragraph of Sub-Clause 4.14 does not stipulate that a claim in relation to the Contractor's indemnity is subject to Sub-Clause 20.2 [*Claims for Payment and/or EOT*], it would certainly seem very arguable (as the Employer would be seeking an 'additional payment' from the Contractor under a 'Clause of these Conditions') that Sub-Clause 20.2 should apply.[187] Accordingly, prudence would suggest compliance with Sub-Clause 20.2.

--ooOOoo--

4.15 Access Route

The Contractor shall be deemed to have been satisfied, at the Base Date, as to the suitability and availability of the access routes to the Site. The Contractor shall take all necessary measures to prevent any road or bridge from being damaged by the Contractor's traffic or by the Contractor's Personnel. These measures shall include the proper use of appropriate vehicles (conforming to legal load and width limits (if any) and any other restrictions) and routes.

Except as otherwise stated in these Conditions:

(a) the Contractor shall (as between the Parties) be responsible for repair of any damage caused to, and any maintenance which may be required for the Contractor's use of, access routes;

(b) the Contractor shall provide all necessary signs or directions along access routes, and shall ob-

187. *See* the commentary on Sub-Clause 20.2 [*Claims for Payment and/or EOT*] below.

tain any permissions or permits which may be required from the relevant authorities, for the Contractor's use of routes, signs and directions;

(c) the Employer shall not be responsible for any third party claims which may arise from the Contractor's use or otherwise of any access route;

(d) the Employer does not guarantee the suitability or availability of particular access routes; and

(e) all Costs due to non-suitability or non-availability, for the use required by the Contractor, of access routes shall be borne by the Contractor.

To the extent that non-suitability or non-availability of an access route arises as a result of changes to that access route by the Employer or a third party after the Base Date and as a result the Contractor suffers delay and/or incurs Cost, the Contractor shall be entitled subject to Sub-Clause 20.2 [*Claims for Payment and/or EOT*] to EOT and/or payment of such Cost.

The Contractor is deemed to have been satisfied, at the Base Date, about the suitability and availability of the access routes to the Site. The Contractor must take all necessary measures not to damage any road or bridge.

Except as stated in the Conditions, the Contractor is responsible for any damage caused to, and any maintenance required for, access routes and for providing all necessary signs or directions. The Employer does not guarantee the suitability or availability of any access routes, all Costs of which shall be borne by the Contractor.

To the extent that the non-suitability or non-availability of an access route arises due to changes made by the Employer or a third party after the Base Date, causing the Contractor delay and/or Cost then subject to Clause 20.2, the Contractor will be entitled to an EOT and/or payment of such Cost.

Commentary

(i) Main Changes from RB/99:

(1) There have been minor changes in the wording in the first two paragraphs: for example, reference to the Base Date has been

added in the first sentence; 'take all necessary measures' has been substituted for 'use reasonable efforts' in the second sentence; 'permits' has been added in sub-paragraph (b); and 'third party claims' has been substituted for 'claims' in sub-paragraph (c).

(2) The third paragraph, providing the Contractor with a right to claim where the non-suitability or non-availability of an access route arises from changes by the Employer or a third party after the Base Date, is entirely new.

(ii) Related Clauses / Sub-Clauses: 1.13 [*Compliance with Laws*], 2.1 [*Right of Access to the Site*], 2.2 [*Assistance*], 2.5 [*Site Data and Items of Reference*], 4.10 [*Use of Site Data*], 4.13 [*Rights of Way and Facilities*], 4.14 [*Avoidance of Interference*], 6.9 [*Contractor's Personnel*], 17.4 [*Indemnities by Contractor*] and 20.2 [*Claims for Payment and/or EOT*].

(iii) Analysis: Under Sub-Clause 2.1, the Employer is required to give the Contractor 'right' of access (i.e., the legal right of access) to the Site such that 'the Contractor is entitled to go onto the Site'.[188] This might include the legal right to traverse land belonging to third parties. On the other hand, the practical difficulties in actually getting to and from the Site are for the Contractor to solve.[189] Before submitting its Tender, the Contractor is expected to have inspected and examined access to the Site, and to have satisfied itself as to 'the Contractor's requirements for access'.[190]

Sub-Clause 4.15 reemphasises this point as it provides that the Contractor shall be deemed to have satisfied itself, at the Base Date, as to the suitability (e.g., for the transport of Plant and equipment) and availability (e.g., that the Contractor can reach the Site with them) of the access routes to the Site, and that the Contractor is responsible for overcoming any practical difficulties in using and maintaining them. Among other things, the Contractor will be responsible for reinforcing bridges or upgrading roads should this be necessary.

FIDIC has explained the meaning of 'route', as follows:

> The word 'route' indicates something which can be represented as a line on a map, typically overland, without implying that a road to the

188. *The FIDIC Contracts Guide* (2nd edn, FIDIC, 2022) 199.
189. *Ibid.*
190. Sub-Clause 4.10(e), including costs and charges for special rights of way for access to the Site. Sub-Clause 4.13.

> Site exists. It is only assumed that there is a route by which access would be physically practicable […] [The practical difficulties of getting to the Site are for the Contractor and do not preclude] the possibility of [the Contractor] constructing a road along the route […].[191]

The final paragraph of the Sub-Clause, providing that, to the extent that non-suitability or non-availability of an access route arises from changes by the Employer or a third party after the Base Date, the Contractor is entitled, subject to Sub-Clause 20.2, to claim if it suffers delay, and/or incurs Cost, is a welcome new provision. Access routes may traverse the property of the Employer, or of third parties whose actions the Contractor cannot control. Consequently, the Contractor should be entitled to relief where those actions cause it delay and/or Cost.

The Sub-Clause assumes access to the Site by land. Where access by air (e.g., a Site in jungle or desert) or sea (e.g., for the laying of an underwater pipeline) is necessary, analogous considerations will apply.

(iv) Related Law: Local laws will likely regulate access routes to the Site such as permitted traffic, legal load and width limits, if any, for vehicles, and permitted signs or directions along such routes, and must be complied with.[192]

(v) Improvements: The last paragraph provides that to the extent that non-suitability or non-availability of an access route arises as a result of changes to that route by the Employer or a third party after the Base Date, the Contractor has a right to claim if, as a result, it suffers delay and/or incurs Cost. However, the Contractor is not entitled to Profit. Should the Contractor not be entitled to Profit as well, at least where the Employer is responsible for the change?[193]

--ooOOoo--

191. *The FIDIC Contracts Guide* (2nd edn, FIDIC 2022) 199.
192. *See* Sub-Clause 1.13 [*Compliance with Laws*].
193. As the Contractor is entitled to Profit in other cases where the Employer is blameworthy. *See* the commentary on Sub-Clause 1.1.20 '**Cost Plus Profit**' above.

4.16 Transport of Goods

The Contractor shall:

(a) give a Notice to the Engineer not less than 21 days before the date on which any Plant, or a major item of other Goods (as stated in the Specification), will be delivered to the Site;
(b) be responsible for packing, loading, transporting, receiving, unloading, storing and protecting all Goods and other things required for the Works;
(c) be responsible for customs clearance, permits, fees and charges related to the import, transport and handling of all Goods, including all obligations necessary for their delivery to the Site; and
(d) indemnify and hold the Employer harmless against and from all damages, losses and expenses (including legal fees and expenses) resulting from the import, transport and handling of all Goods, and shall negotiate and pay all third party claims arising from their import, transport and handling.

The Contractor must give a Notice to the Engineer not less than 21 days before the date on which any Plant or a major item of other Goods will be delivered to the Site. The Contractor is responsible for transporting and delivering all Goods to the Site, including customs clearance, and shall indemnify the Employer against damages resulting therefrom, as well as all third-party claims.

Commentary

(i) Main Changes from RB/99:

(1) This Sub-Clause is no longer qualified at the outset by '[u]nless otherwise stated in the Particular Conditions'.
(2) Sub-paragraph (c) relating to responsibility for customs clearance and related matters is new.

(ii) Related Clauses / Sub-Clauses: 1.3 [*Notices and Other Communications*], 1.13 [*Compliance with Laws*], 2.2 [*Assistance*], 4.1 [*Contractor's General Obligations*], 4.13 [*Rights of Way and Facilities*], 4.15 [*Access*

Route], 4.17 [*Contractor's Equipment*], 4.20 [*Progress Reports*], 17.4 [*Indemnities by Contractor*], 17.5 [*Indemnities by Employer*] and 19.2.2 [*Insurance to Be Provided by the Contractor – Goods*].

(iii) Analysis: Under Sub-Clause 4.1, second paragraph, the Contractor is responsible for providing all Goods, defined as 'Contractor's Equipment, Materials, Plant and Temporary Works',[194] for the Works. Under Sub-Clause 4.16, the Contractor is responsible for delivering all Goods to the Site.

The Contractor must give not less than 21 days' Notice to the Engineer before any Plant or a major item of other Goods (as stated in the Specification) is delivered to the Site. The Engineer and/or the Employer may need such advance Notice so as to enable them to prepare to receive and store or position these items.[195]

Similarly, each monthly progress report of the Contractor must include, for each 'main item of Plant and Materials', the actual or expected dates of its shipment and arrival at the Site.[196] Where Contractor's Equipment comes from abroad, it may be imported under a temporary import licence requiring its export upon completion of the Works.

The Contractor's indemnity provided for in sub-paragraph (d)[197] is qualified by the Employer's obligation to indemnify the Contractor against third-party claims pursuant to Sub-Clause 17.5(b).

(iv) Related Law: Every country is likely to have tariff laws and/or customs duties or charges and/or import restrictions. Among other things, these may allow for a temporary import regime, whereby a foreign Contractor may import Contractor's Equipment and/or other things into the Country duty-free for a specific project provided, among

194. Sub-Clause 1.1.44 '**Goods**'.
195. In some cases, the Engineer's permission may be required before the delivery of Goods to the Site. *Guidance for the Particular Conditions*, 24, contains an example provision on this subject.
196. Sub-Clause 4.20 (c) (iv).
197. This indemnity overlaps with that provided for by the first paragraph of Sub-Clause 17.4 [*Indemnities by Contractor*] but, unlike that indemnity, is not excluded from the liability limits in Sub-Clause 1.15 [*Limitation of Liability*]. For the possible need to comply with Sub-Clause 20.2 [*Claims for Payment and for EOT*] with respect to this indemnity, *see* under **(iii) Analysis** of the commentary on Sub-Clause 4.14 [*Avoidance of Interference*] above, as the same reasoning applies.

other things, that such things are re-exported within a specific time limit and/or upon the completion of the project.

--ooOOoo--

4.17 Contractor's Equipment

The Contractor shall be responsible for all Contractor's Equipment. When brought on to the Site, Contractor's Equipment shall be deemed to be exclusively intended for the execution of the Works. The Contractor shall not remove from the Site any major items of Contractor's Equipment without the Engineer's consent. However, consent shall not be required for vehicles transporting Goods or Contractor's Personnel off Site.

In addition to any Notice given under Sub-Clause 4.16 [*Transport of Goods*], the Contractor shall give a Notice to the Engineer of the date on which any major item of Contractor's Equipment has been delivered to the Site. This Notice shall be given within 7 days of the delivery date, shall identify whether the item of Contractor's Equipment is owned by the Contractor or a Subcontractor or another person and, if rented or leased, shall identify the rental or leasing entity.

The Contractor is responsible for all Contractor's Equipment which, when brought on to the Site, is deemed to be exclusively for the Works. Major items of Contractor's Equipment cannot be removed from the Site without the Engineer's consent. In the case of the delivery of any major item of Contractor's Equipment to the Site, the Contractor must give the Engineer Notice of the delivery within 7 days of the delivery date and provide particulars of its ownership or rental.

Commentary

(i) Main Changes from RB/99: This Sub-Clause is unchanged from RB/99, except for the second paragraph, which requires the Contractor to give Notice to the Engineer of the date of delivery of any major item of Contractor's Equipment to the Site and requiring it to include particulars regarding the ownership or rental of such equipment. This paragraph is entirely new.

(ii) Related Clauses / Sub-Clauses: 1.3 [*Notices and Other Communications*], 2.2 [*Assistance*], 4.1 [*Contractor's General Obligations*], 4.16 [*Transport of Goods*], 4.22 [*Contractor's Operations on Site*], 6.10 [*Contractor's Records*], 8.3 [*Programme*], 11.11 [*Clearance of Site*] and 15.2 [*Termination for Contractor's Default*].

(iii) Analysis: Under this Sub-Clause, the Contractor is responsible for all Contractor's Equipment[198] which, when brought on to the Site, is deemed to be exclusively for the execution of the Works and cannot be used elsewhere. Major items of Contractor's Equipment, presumably as defined in the Specification,[199] cannot be removed without the Engineer's consent, which may not be unreasonably withheld or delayed.[200]

As Contractor's Equipment may serve the Employer as additional security[201] that the Contractor will perform its obligations,[202] it is understandable that major items may not be removed without the Engineer's consent. In addition, in the event of termination of the Contract for the Contractor's default, pursuant to Sub-Clause 15.2, the Employer is entitled to use the Contractor's Equipment and other Goods to complete the Works.[203] By Sub-Clause 4.17, the Contractor is required to give Notice to the Engineer of the date on which any major item of Contractor's Equipment has been delivered to the Site, and to provide details as to its ownership or rental (as, if not owned by the Contractor, it may not be available as security to the Employer).

If the Employer does not require the Contractor to provide all the Contractor's Equipment necessary for the completion of the Works, the

198. *See* the commentary on the definition in Sub-Clause 1.1.16 '**Contractor's Equipment**', above.
199. *See* Sub-Clause 4.16(a) which refers to a major item of Goods other than Plant being 'stated in the Specification'.
200. Sub-Clause 1.3 [*Notices and Other Communications*].
201. Additional to Performance Security, Retention Money and any unpaid IPCs.
202. Contractor's Equipment, such as dredging equipment, tower cranes and tunnel boring machines, may have a high value.
203. *See* Sub-Clauses 15.2.3 and 15.2.4 giving the Employer the right also to sell the Contractor's Equipment and Temporary Works (if permitted by applicable Laws) should the Contractor have failed to pay an amount due.

Employer's obligations in this respect should be stated in the Specification, as foreseen by Sub-Clause 2.6 [*Employer-Supplied Materials and Employer's Equipment*].[204]

If vesting of the Contractor's Equipment with the Employer[205] is required and consistent with applicable law, the *Guidance*[206] contains an example provision on this subject.

--ooOOoo--

4.18 Protection of the Environment

The Contractor shall take all necessary measures to:

(a) protect the environment (both on and off the Site);
(b) comply with the environmental impact statement for the Works (if any); and
(c) limit damage and nuisance to people and property resulting from pollution, noise and other results of the Contractor's operations and/or activities.

The Contractor shall ensure that emissions, surface discharges, effluent and any other pollutants from the Contractor's activities shall exceed neither the values indicated in the Specification, nor those prescribed by applicable Laws.

The Contractor must take all necessary measures to protect the environment (both on- and off-Site), comply with any applicable environmental impact statement, limit damage and nuisance to people and property and ensure any pollutants used comply with the Contract.

204. For example, to assist the Contractor to finance execution of the Works, the Employer might itself purchase expensive equipment, such as tunnel boring machines, and make them available to the Contractor for the execution of the Works.
205. That is, essentially, transferring ownership of Contractor's Equipment to the Employer.
206. *Guidance for the Preparation of the Particular Conditions*, 25.

Commentary

(i) Main Changes from RB/99:

(1) This Sub-Clause now refers in the first sentence to 'all necessary measures', instead of 'all reasonable steps' as in RB/99, to perform what is stated in sub-paragraphs (a), (b) and (c).
(2) Sub-paragraph (b) has been added requiring compliance with the environmental impact statement for the Works, if any.

(ii) Related Clauses / Sub-Clauses: 1.13 [*Compliance with Laws*], 2.3 [*Employer's Personnel and Other Contractors*], 2.5 [*Site Data and Items of Reference*], 4.8 [*Health and Safety Obligations*], 4.12 [*Unforeseeable Physical Conditions*], 4.20 [*Progress Reports*], 6.9 [*Contractor's Personnel*], 13.1 [*Right to Vary*] and 17.4 [*Indemnities by Contractor*].

(iii) Analysis:

(1) Interpretation of Sub-Clause

While this Sub-Clause is drafted very broadly (providing that the 'Contractor shall take all necessary measures to [...] protect the environment (both on and off the Site)', etc.), it should presumably be interpreted more narrowly as meaning that *in performing the Contract* the Contractor shall take all necessary measures to do the things provided for by this Sub-Clause. While no one can question the importance of protecting the environment,[207] the purpose of the Conditions is more limited and therefore, it is suggested that this Sub-Clause should be understood in this more restricted way.[208]

207. The 'environment' is defined in a dictionary as being either 'the surroundings or conditions in which a person, animal or plant lives or operates' or as 'the natural world, especially as affected by human activity'. *Concise Oxford English Dictionary* (10th edn, rev'd, 2002). Environmental law may encompass, among others, human rights. Philippe Sands and Jacqueline Peel, *Principles of International Environmental Law* (4th edn, Cambridge UP, UK, 2018) 16-17, 811-838.

208. The Contractor may object to the instruction of a Variation if it will adversely affect its ability to comply with this Sub-Clause. *See* sub-para. (c) of Sub-Clause 13.1 [*Right to Vary*]. FIDIC's *Project Sustainability Management Applications Manual*, 2nd edition, 2013, notes that, while the Employer and its consulting engineer are primary drivers of sustainability in the initial stages of project development, 'the contractor takes over that role

(2) Environmental impact assessment

As virtually all projects have some impact on the environment, at least in their immediate locality, in developing the project pre-Tender, the Employer will almost certainly have undertaken environmental studies,[209] including an environmental impact assessment ('EIA').[210] An EIA is now required for virtually all projects of a significant size, and most funding institutions make such a report compulsory.[211] The Contractor is required to comply with any EIA for the Works.[212]

(3) Other Obligations

More generally by this Sub-Clause, the Contractor must 'take all necessary measures' to limit damage and nuisance to the environment on and off the Site,[213] and must remove from the Site any person who persists in conduct prejudicial to the protection of the environment.[214]

---

during construction and makes numerous choices that affect the short-term sustainability of the site – material selection and delivery, energy and water use and site discharge, emissions of dust and noise and light pollution, community health and safety and relationships to name but a few', 12.

209. *FIDIC Procurement Procedures Guide* (FIDIC, 2011) 17. *See also* FIDIC's *Project Sustainability Management – Applications Manual* (2nd edn, 2013).

210. An EIA:

> will catalogue the expected effects of the project on the environment, including the sociological effects on the local population and the anticipated effects on flora and fauna as well as on the surrounding countryside, rivers and so on. The report should identify all effects, whether positive or negative.
>
> *FIDIC Procurement Procedures Guide* (FIDIC, 2011) 17.

211. *Ibid. See* under **(iv) Related Law** below of this commentary on Sub-Clause 4.18. The World Bank's COPA eliminates sub-para. (b) requiring compliance with an EIA from Sub-Clause 4.18 as an EIA is already provided for by The World Bank's Operational Policy ('OP') 4.01 and Bank Procedures ('BP') 4.01. The COPA adds a paragraph to this Sub-Clause providing that if the Contractor causes environmental damage, on or off the Site, the Contractor must remedy the same at its cost and by taking appropriate actions as agreed with the Engineer.

212. Sub-Clause 4.18(b).

213. Sub-Clause 4.18(c).

214. Sub-Clause 6.9(d) [*Contractor's Personnel*].

The last paragraph of this Sub-Clause applies only to pollutants arising from the Contractor's activities and not to the operation of the Works after taking-over[215] (as this is out of the Contractor's control).

For its part, the Employer is responsible for ensuring that the Employer's Personnel and the Employer's other contractors on or near the Site comply with the same obligations with which the Contractor is required to comply under this Sub-Clause.[216]

(iv) Related Law: At least one international award deals with a provision very similar to Sub-Clause 4.18 of RB/99.[217]

An EIA is now required by the domestic law of many countries.[218] In addition, the *Rio Declaration* resulting from the *United Nations Conference on Environment and Development* in Rio de Janeiro, 1992, confirmed that EIAs are required by general international law, particularly in respect of environmentally harmful activities which may have transboundary consequences.[219]

A recent English court decision vividly illustrates how the law relating to the environment may impact construction projects. Although overturned on appeal by the Supreme Court,[220] the Court of Appeal had found that Heathrow Airport's plans to build a third runway were illegal because the

215. *The FIDIC Contracts Guide* (2nd edn, FIDIC, 2022) 203. The Contractor may be entitled to relief under Sub-Clause 4.12 [*Unforeseeable Physical Conditions*] where 'pollutants' constitute Unforeseeable adverse physical conditions.
216. Sub-Clause 2.3(b).
217. *J.V. of American and EU Dredging Companies v. Red Sea Public Authority (RSPA), final award, CRCICA case No. 281/2002, 28 June 2004* in Mohie-Eldin Alam-Eldin (ed.), *Arbitral Awards of the Cairo Regional Centre for International Commercial Arbitration IV* (Kluwer L. Int'l, the Netherlands, 2014) 185, especially 286-296.
218. More than 150 countries are reported as having a domestic environmental impact assessment law. David Hunter and others, *International Environmental Law and Policy* (5th edn, 2015, Foundation Press, St Paul, MN) 498.
219. *See* Principle 17 of the *Rio Declaration on Environment and Development*, 1992, and Philippe Sands and Jacqueline Peel, *Principles of International Environmental Law* (4th edn, Cambridge, UP, UK, 2018,) 658. Transnational corporations should also be complying with Chapter VI entitled 'Environment' of the *Guidelines for Multinational Enterprises*, 2011, Organisation for Economic Cooperation and Development ('OECD'). Chapter IV of the *Guidelines* is entitled 'Human Rights'.
220. *R (Friends of the Earth) v Heathrow Airport* [2020] UKSC 52.

British Government had failed to consider its climate change obligations under the Paris Agreement of 2015.[221]

(v) Improvements: The first sentence of this Sub-Clause should be revised to begin: '*In performing the Contract*, the Contractor shall take all necessary measures to [...]' (emphasis added).

--ooOOoo--

4.19 Temporary Utilities

The Contractor shall, except as stated below, be responsible for the provision of all temporary utilities, including electricity, gas, telecommunications, water and any other services the Contractor may require for the execution of the Works.

The following provisions of this Sub-Clause shall only apply if, as stated in the Specification, the Employer is to provide utilities for the Contractor's use. The Contractor shall be entitled to use, for the purposes of the Works, the utilities on the Site for which details and prices are given in the Specification. The Contractor shall, at the Contractor's risk and cost, provide any apparatus necessary for the Contractor's use of these services and for measuring the quantities consumed. The apparatus provided for measuring quantities consumed shall be subject to the Engineer's consent. The quantities consumed (if any) during each period of payment stated in the Contract Data (if not stated, each month) shall be measured by the Contractor, and the amount to be paid by the Contractor for such quantities (at the prices stated in the Specification) shall be included in the relevant Statement.

Generally, the Contractor is responsible for the provision of all temporary utilities, including electricity, gas, telecommunications, water, and other services that it may require for the execution of the Works. However, if, according to the Specification, the Employer is to

221. *R (Friends of the Earth) v Secretary of State for Transport and Others* [2020] EWCA Civ 214.

provide utilities for the Contractor's use, then the Contractor may use those on the Site for which details and prices are given in the Specification.

Commentary

(i) Main Changes from RB/99:

(1) The new Sub-Clause is similar to Sub-Clause 4.19 in RB/99, but is now headed 'Temporary Utilities', whereas the former Sub-Clause was headed 'Electricity, Water and Gas'.
(2) It is now provided that any apparatus provided by the Contractor for measuring quantities of any services consumed shall be subject to the Engineer's consent.
(3) Whereas previously the Employer was to be paid for any services provided pursuant to the Employer's claim procedure (former Sub-Clause 2.5) and the Engineer's determination procedure (former Sub-Clause 3.5), this has been replaced by requiring that the Employer be paid by way of deductions in the Contractor's Statements pursuant to Sub-Clause 14.3(ix).

(ii) Related Clauses / Sub-Clauses: 1.2 [*Interpretation*], 1.15 [*Limitation of Liability*], 4.10 [*Use of Site Data*], 7.4 [*Testing by the Contractor*] and 14.3 [*Application for Interim Payment*].

(iii) Analysis: At least where the Employer owns the Site, it may be able to make available the basic utilities and services which the Contractor requires for the execution of the Works. If the Employer does so, both paragraphs of this Sub-Clause will apply and the Employer will include details and prices in the Specification.

The Contractor is responsible for providing any apparatus necessary for measuring the quantities consumed, which is subject to the Engineer's consent.[222] Payment for the Contractor's use of utilities provided by the Employer is to be made by way of deductions in the Contractor's Statements.[223]

222. Consent may not be unreasonably withheld. Sub-Clause 1.3, third paragraph.
223. *See* Sub-Clause 14.3(ix).

On the other hand, in the case of a greenfield Site or a Site not owned by the Employer, the Contractor will often have to make its own arrangements for the provision of utilities and services.[224]

--ooOOoo--

4.20 Progress Reports

Monthly progress reports, in the format stated in the Specification (if not stated, in a format acceptable to the Engineer) shall be prepared by the Contractor and submitted to the Engineer. Each progress report shall be submitted in one paper-original, one electronic copy and additional paper copies (if any) as stated in the Contract Data. The first report shall cover the period up to the end of the first month following the Commencement Date. Reports shall be submitted monthly thereafter, each within 7 days after the last day of the month to which it relates.

Reporting shall continue until the Date of Completion of the Works or, if outstanding work is listed in the Taking-Over Certificate, the date on which such outstanding work is completed. Unless otherwise stated in the Specification, each progress report shall include:

(a) charts, diagrams and detailed descriptions of progress, including each stage of (design by the Contractor, if any) Contractor's Documents, procurement, manufacture, delivery to Site, construction, erection and testing;
(b) photographs and/or video recordings showing the status of manufacture and of progress on and off the Site;
(c) for the manufacture of each main item of Plant and Materials, the name of the manufacturer, manufacture location, percentage progress, and the actual or expected dates of:

 (i) commencement of manufacture,
 (ii) Contractor's inspections,
 (iii) tests, and
 (iv) shipment and arrival at the Site;

224. *See* Sub-Clause 4.10(e).

(d) the details described in Sub-Clause 6.10 [*Contractor's Records*];
(e) copies of quality management documents, inspection reports, test results, and compliance verification documentation (including certificates of Materials);
(f) a list of Variations, and any Notices given (by either Party) under Sub-Clause 20.2.1 [*Notice of Claim*];
(g) health and safety statistics, including details of any hazardous incidents and activities relating to environmental aspects and public relations; and
(h) comparisons of actual and planned progress, with details of any events or circumstances which may adversely affect the completion of the Works in accordance with the Programme and the Time for Completion, and the measures being (or to be) adopted to overcome delays.

However, nothing stated in any progress report shall constitute a Notice under a Sub-Clause of these Conditions.

The Contractor must submit monthly progress reports to the Engineer in the format stated in the Specification (or, if not stated, acceptable to the Engineer). The first report shall cover up to the end of the first month following the Commencement Date and reporting shall continue until the Date of Completion of the Works or, if outstanding work is listed in the Taking-Over Certificate, until such work is completed. Unless stated otherwise in the Specification, each report must include the details specified in sub-paragraphs (a) to (h) of this Sub-Clause and be submitted within 7 days after the last day of the previous month to which it relates. Nothing stated in a progress report will constitute a Notice under the Conditions.

Commentary

(i) Main Changes from RB/99:[225]

(1) Compared to the first paragraph of Sub-Clause 4.21 of RB/99, there are more details about the format of reports which now must be as stated in the Specification or, if not stated there, be in a format acceptable to the Engineer.
(2) The description of the contents of reports in sub-paragraphs (a) to (h) is now qualified by the statement '[u]nless otherwise stated in the Specification'.
(3) In sub-paragraph (a), 'diagrams' have been added and information about the work of each nominated Subcontractor is no longer required.
(4) Sub-paragraph (b) now provides that reports shall include video recordings of the status of work on and off the Site.
(5) Sub-paragraph (e) now calls for inspection reports and compliance verification documentation.[226]
(6) Sub-paragraph (f) now calls for a list of Variations.
(7) Sub-paragraph (g) now calls for health, as well as safety, statistics.
(8) The final paragraph provides that nothing in any progress report shall constitute a Notice under the Conditions, which is also new.

(ii) Related Clauses / Sub-Clauses: 1.3 [*Notices and Other Communications*], 1.9 [*Delayed Drawings or Instructions*], 4.8 [*Health and Safety Obligations*], 4.9 [*Quality Management and Compliance Verification System*], 6.10 [*Contractor's Records*], 8.4 [*Advance Warning*], 13 [*Variations and Adjustments*], 14.3 [*Application for Interim Payment*], 11.1 [*Completion of Outstanding Works and Remedying Defects*], 14.7 [*Payment*] and 20 [*Employer's and Contractor's Claims*].

225. Sub-Clause 4.20 of RB/99 relating to Employer's Equipment and free-issue materials is dealt with in Sub-Clause 2.6 [*Employer-Supplied Materials and Employer's Equipment*] of RB/17.
226. *See* Sub-Clause 4.9.2 [*Compliance Verification System*].

(iii) Analysis:

(1) Nature of progress reports

The principal means by which the Contractor keeps the Engineer informed about the progress of the Works is through the submission of monthly progress reports containing specified information and enclosing documents, as provided for by this Sub-Clause. These reports are now required to include more information about the quality of work done (e.g., inspection reports and compliance verification documentation), which is designed to bring any issues of non-conformance to a head in good time and before the Works are complete.[227]

Among other things, progress reports must include details of any events or circumstances 'which may adversely affect the completion of the Works' in accordance with the Programme.[228] These may include, for example, details of those reported in Notices or other communications given by the Contractor under Sub-Clauses 1.9 [*Delayed Drawings or Instructions*], 8.4 [*Advance Warning*] or 20.2.1 [*Notice of Claim*].[229] Reporting must continue until the Date of Completion of the Works or, if outstanding work is listed in the Taking-Over Certificate, until such outstanding work is completed. If the Works are suspended, whatever the reason, the Contractor must continue to submit progress reports.

(2) Monthly progress reports are conditions for payments

Monthly payments to the Contractor pursuant to Sub-Clause 14.7 are conditioned on the Contractor's submission of monthly progress reports. The Contractor's Statement to the Engineer (as part of an application for a Payment Certificate) must be submitted together with 'supporting documents' which include 'the relevant report on progress in accordance

227. Atkin Chambers, *Hudson's Building and Engineering Contracts* (14th edn, Sweet & Maxwell, London, 2020) 578 (para. 4-083). The World Bank's COPA: (1) provides for replacing sub-para. (g) of Sub-Clause 4.20 relating to health and safety statistics by the detailed and rigorous Environmental and Social (ES) metrics set out in Part D of COPA and (2) requires the Contractor to inform the Engineer immediately of any allegation or incident which is likely to have a significant adverse effect on the environment, the affected communities, the public or the personnel of the Parties. Sub-Clause 4.20, COPA.
228. Sub-paragraph (h) of Sub-Clause 4.20.
229. Progress reports may serve as 'contemporary records' under Sub-Clause 20.2.3 [*Contemporary Records*].

with Sub-Clause 4.20'.[230] The period for paying the Contractor's Statement under Sub-Clause 14.7(b)(i) does not commence until the Engineer has received the 'Statement with these supporting documents'.[231]

(3) Progress reports are not Notices of Claims

In practice, Contractors have often sought to rely on statements in monthly progress reports (and other communications of various kinds), as giving notice of claims. The last paragraph of the new Sub-Clause now prohibits this practice, as it provides that nothing stated in any progress report shall constitute a Notice under the Conditions. This is consistent with the more formal procedure for the notification of Claims provided for in Clause 20.

(iv) Improvements: *See* under **(v) Improvements** of the commentary on Sub-Clause 8.4 [*Advance Warning*] below.

--ooOOoo--

4.21 Security of the Site

The Contractor shall be responsible for the security of the Site, and:

(a) for keeping unauthorised persons off the Site; and

(b) authorised persons shall be limited to the Contractor's Personnel, the Employer's Personnel, and to any other personnel identified as authorised personnel (including the Employer's other contractors on the Site), by a Notice from the Employer or the Engineer to the Contractor.

The Contractor is responsible for the security of the Site and must keep unauthorised persons off the Site. Authorised persons are limited to the Contractor's Personnel, the Employer's Personnel and others identified as such by a Notice from the Employer or the Engineer to the Contractor.

230. Sub-Clause 14.3 (c).
231. *The FIDIC Contracts Guide* (2nd edn, FIDIC, 2022) 207.

Commentary

(i) Main Changes from RB/99:

(1) The words '[u]nless otherwise stated in the Particular Conditions' at the beginning of Sub-Clause 4.22 [*Security of the Site*] of RB/99 have been eliminated.
(2) The phrase '[t]he Contractor shall be responsible for the security of the Site' replaces part of former sub-paragraph (a) of Sub-Clause 4.22 of RB/99.
(3) In sub-paragraph (b), the Employer or the Engineer may, by a Notice to the Contractor, identify as authorised personnel (allowing access to the Site) 'any other personnel' and therefore 'authorised persons' is no longer limited (as under RB/99) to the Contractor's Personnel, the Employer's Personnel and authorised personnel of the Employer's other contractors on the Site.

(ii) Related Clauses / Sub-Clauses: 1.3 [*Notices and Other Communications*], 2.3 [*Employer's Personnel and Other Contractors*], 4.6 [*Co-operation*], 4.8 [*Health and Safety Obligations*], 6.9 [*Contractor's Personnel*], 6.11 [*Disorderly Conduct*], and 17.1 [*Responsibility for Care of the Works*].

(iii) Analysis: The Contractor is responsible for the security of the Site from the date that it takes possession, pursuant to Sub-Clause 2.1 [*Right of Access to the Site*], until issue of the Taking-Over Certificate for the Works, when responsibility passes to the Employer.[232]

The Contractor is no longer responsible for just keeping unauthorised persons off the Site (as in Sub-Clause 4.22 of RB/99), but is now plainly responsible for the security of the Site generally, implying that it must protect and ensure the safety of all persons and property on the Site.[233] This obligation for security will be especially important in countries or areas where political unrest, disturbances and/or theft are common. In

232. If a Taking-Over Certificate is issued (or is deemed to be issued) for any Section or Part of the Works, responsibility for the security of the Section or Part passes then to the Employer, Sub-Clause 17.1 [*Responsibility for Care of the Works*].
233. The World Bank's COPA goes further and requires the Contractor to submit for the Engineer's No-objection a security management plan. Sub-Clause 4.21, COPA.

such cases, the Contractor may need to engage a security firm or special guards to protect people and property on the Site.

This Sub-Clause should be read together with Sub-Clause 4.8 [*Health and Safety Obligations*], especially Sub-Clause 4.8(d), (e), (f) and (g), requiring the Contractor to take care of the health and safety of all persons on the Site and other places, if any, where the Works are being executed, and generally to guard and watch over the Site.[234]

At the same time, the Contractor itself is not unrestricted in whom it may bring on to the Site. It may only bring Contractor's Personnel on to the Site, defined as the Contractor's Representative and all personnel whom the Contractor utilises on the Site and 'any other personnel assisting the Contractor in the execution of the Works'.[235] Others must be authorised by a Notice from the Employer or the Engineer.[236]

If the Contractor is sharing occupation of the Site with others (including the Employer), it may be appropriate to amend the Conditions to provide for the Contractor to share responsibility for security with those others.[237]

(iv) Improvements: In the third line of sub-paragraph (b), the reference to 'authorised personnel' should be changed to 'authorised persons' in order to be consistent with usage in the rest of the Sub-Clause.

--ooOOoo--

4.22 Contractor's Operations on Site

> The Contractor shall confine the Contractor's operations to the Site, and to any additional areas which may be obtained by the Contractor and acknowledged by the Engineer as working areas. The Contractor shall take all necessary precautions to keep Contractor's Equipment and Contractor's Personnel within the Site and these additional areas, and to keep them off adjacent land.

234. *See also* Sub-Clause 6.11 [*Disorderly Conduct*] requiring the Contractor 'to preserve peace and protection of persons and property on and near the Site'.
235. Sub-Clause 1.1.17 '**Contractor's Personnel**'.
236. Sub-Clause 4.21(b).
237. *See Guidance for the Preparation of Particular Conditions*, 25.

At all times, the Contractor shall keep the Site free from all unnecessary obstruction, and shall properly store or remove from the Site any Contractor's Equipment (subject to Sub-Clause 4.17 [*Contractor's Equipment*]) and/or surplus materials. The Contractor shall promptly clear away and remove from the Site any wreckage, rubbish, hazardous waste and Temporary Works which are no longer required.

Promptly after the issue of a Taking-Over Certificate, the Contractor shall clear away and remove, from that part of the Site and Works to which the Taking-Over Certificate refers, all Contractor's Equipment, surplus material, wreckage, rubbish, hazardous waste and Temporary Works. The Contractor shall leave that part of the Site and the Works in a clean and safe condition. However, the Contractor may retain at locations on the Site agreed with the Engineer, during the DNP, such Goods as are required for the Contractor to fulfil obligations under the Contract.

The Contractor must confine its operations to the Site, and to additional areas acknowledged by the Engineer as working areas. It must also keep the Site free from unnecessary obstruction. Subject to Clause 4.17, the Contractor must store or remove any Contractor's Equipment and/or surplus material from the Site, as well as any wreckage, rubbish, hazardous waste and Temporary Works which are no longer required. Promptly after the issue of a Taking-Over Certificate, the Contractor must clear away and remove all Contractor's Equipment, surplus material, wreckage, rubbish, hazardous waste and Temporary Works from that part of the Site to which the Taking-Over Certificate refers. However, the Contractor may retain at the Site during the DNP such Goods as are required to fulfil its contractual obligations.

Commentary

(i) Main Changes from RB/99:

(1) In the first paragraph, whereas Sub-Clause 4.23 of RB/99 had required that any additional areas obtained by the Contractor

had to be 'agreed by the Engineer as working areas', it is now sufficient if they are 'acknowledged by the Engineer as working areas'.

(2) In the second paragraph, whereas RB/99 had required the Contractor to keep the Site free from all unnecessary obstruction '[d]uring the execution of the Works', the Contractor is now required to do so '[a]t all times', as well as to 'properly' store or 'remove from the Site' (not merely 'dispose of') any Contractor's Equipment, subject to Sub-Clause 4.17, and/or surplus materials.

(3) Also in the second paragraph, the Contractor must 'promptly' clear away and remove from the Site any wreckage and rubbish, and this now expressly includes 'hazardous waste'.

(4) In the third paragraph, there are further new references to 'promptly' and 'hazardous waste'.

(5) It is now specified in the last sentence that, as regards Goods required to fulfil the Contractor's obligations during the DNP, they are to be retained 'at locations on the Site agreed with the Engineer', and not merely retained by the Contractor on the Site.

(ii) Related Clauses / Sub-Clauses: 1.3 [*Notices and Other Communications*], 4.8 [*Health and Safety Obligations*], 4.14 [*Avoidance of Interference*], 4.17 [*Contractor's Equipment*], 4.18 [*Protection of the Environment*], 6.9 [*Contractor's Personnel*], 10 [*Employer's Taking Over*], 11.1 [*Completion of Outstanding Work and Remedying Defects*], 11.7 [*Right of Access*], 11.11 [*Clearance of Site*] and 17.4 [*Indemnities by Contractor*].

(iii) Analysis: As stated in the first paragraph, the Contractor is required to confine its 'operations' (which must therefore be taken to exclude, e.g., head office work and off-Site manufacture) to the Site and to any additional areas 'acknowledged' by the Engineer as working areas.[238] Requiring the Contractor to confine the location of its operations in this

238. These might include areas from which the Contractor obtains natural Materials or disposes of material from demolitions and excavations. *See* Sub-Clause 7.8 [*Royalties*]. They might also include the Contractor's camp or workshop area. An 'acknowledgment' is a type of 'communication' which must be 'in writing' and otherwise satisfy the conditions of Sub-Clause 1.3. Among other things, it may not 'be unreasonably withheld or delayed'.

way facilitates their inspection by the Employer's Personnel and minimises the risk of claims from adjacent landowners.[239]

The Sub-Clause should be read in conjunction with: Sub-Clause 4.14, requiring the Contractor to avoid interfering unnecessarily with the convenience of the public; Sub-Clause 4.18, requiring the Contractor to limit damage and nuisance to people and property from the results of the Contractor's activities; and Sub-Clause 11.11, requiring the Contractor to leave the Site in a clean and safe condition after issue of the Performance Certificate.

As in the case of Sub-Clause 4.21, if the Contractor is sharing occupation of the Site with others, it may be appropriate to amend the Conditions to provide for the Contractor to share with them its responsibilities under the second and third paragraphs.[240]

(iv) Improvements: This Sub-Clause could define what is meant by 'hazardous waste', which it refers to twice. A US form of construction contract defines 'Hazardous Material' as:

> any substance or material identified now or in the future as hazardous under Laws [defined as US laws and regulations], or any other substance or material that may be considered hazardous or otherwise subject to statutory or regulatory requirement governing handling, disposal, or cleanup.[241]

--ooOOoo--

239. *The FIDIC Contracts Guide* (2nd edn, FIDIC, 2022) 209.
240. *See Guidance for the Preparation of Particular Conditions*, 26.
241. *ConsensusDocs 200, Standard Agreement and General Conditions between Owner and Constructor [Lump Sum Price]*, 2014, art. 3.13.1 https://www.consensusdocs.org/contract_category/general-contracting/ accessed 10 November 2022. The United States *Solid Waste Disposal Act* ('SWDA') contains the following more comprehensive definition:

> The term 'hazardous waste' means a solid waste, or combination of solid wastes, which because of its quantity, concentration, or physical, chemical, or infectious characteristics may—
> (A) cause, or significantly contribute to an increase in mortality or an increase in serious irreversible, or incapacitating reversible, illness; or
> (B) pose a substantial present or potential hazard to human health or the environment when improperly treated, stored, transported, or disposed of, or otherwise managed.

4.23 Archaeological and Geological Findings

All fossils, coins, articles of value or antiquity, and structures and other remains or items of geological or archaeological interest found on the Site shall be placed under the care and authority of the Employer. The Contractor shall take all reasonable precautions to prevent Contractor's Personnel or other persons from removing or damaging any of these findings.

The Contractor shall, as soon as practicable after discovery of any such finding, give a Notice to the Engineer in good time to give the Engineer opportunity to promptly inspect and/or investigate the finding before it is disturbed. This Notice shall describe the finding and the Engineer shall issue instructions for dealing with it.

If the Contractor suffers delay and/or incurs Cost from complying with the Engineer's instructions, the Contractor shall be entitled subject to Sub-Clause 20.2 [*Claims for Payment and/or EOT*] to EOT and/or payment of such Cost.

All items of geological or archaeological interest found on the Site shall be placed under the care of the Employer. The Contractor must, as soon as practicable, give Notice to the Engineer of any such finding. This Notice must describe the finding, and the Engineer must issue instructions for dealing with it. If the Contractor suffers delay or incurs Cost from complying with the Engineer's instructions, the Contractor shall, subject to Sub-Clause 20.2, be entitled to an EOT and/or payment of such Cost.

S 1004 (5) of the *Solid Waste Disposal Act*, 42 USC 6901-6992k, which consists of Title II of Public Law 89-272, 1965, and amendments. For different international law approaches to the definition of hazardous or dangerous substances, *see* Philippe Sands and Jacqueline Peel, *Principles of International Environmental Law* (4th edn, Cambridge, UP, UK, 2018), 610-613.

Commentary

(i) Main Changes from RB/99:

(1) The title of Sub-Clause 4.24 of RB/99 has been changed from 'Fossils' to 'Archaeological and Geological Findings' in Sub-Clause 4.23.
(2) Whereas in RB/99 the Contractor was required, upon discovery of a finding, 'promptly' to give notice to the Engineer, the Contractor is now required to do so 'as soon as practicable' and 'in good time' to allow the Engineer to inspect it before it is disturbed.
(3) The Contractor's Notice of the finding must now 'describe the finding'.
(4) Having received a Notice of a finding from the Contractor, the Engineer is required 'to promptly inspect and/or investigate the finding before it is disturbed', whereas nothing was said before about what the Engineer was expected to do (other than, as in the new Sub-Clause, issue instructions).
(5) As elsewhere in RB/17, the Contractor is required to comply with the claims procedure in Sub-Clause 20.2 (instead of that in RB/99).

(ii) Related Clauses / Sub-Clauses: 1.3 [*Notices and Other Communications*], 3.5 [*Engineer's Instructions*], 3.7 [*Agreement or Determination*], 4.10 [*Use of Site Data*], 6.9 [*Contractor's Personnel*], 8.5 [*Extension of Time for Completion*], 8.9 [*Employer's Suspension*] and 20.2 [*Claims for Payment and/or EOT*].

(iii) Analysis: While all fossils and other antiquities may by law be the property of the State concerned,[242] they are required by this Sub-Clause to be placed initially under the authority of the Employer, who may in turn, where required, contact the relevant State officials. When this happens, the execution of the Works may need to be suspended, in whole or in part, as the area concerned may need to remain undisturbed while investigated by State authorities, causing possible delay and Cost to the Contractor. Assuming the Contractor has given the Engineer a Notice of

242. *FIDIC DBO Guide* (1st edn, FIDIC, 2011) 45.

the situation in good time, this Sub-Clause entitles the Contractor to relief in this situation subject to Sub-Clause 20.2.[243]

The Contractor's right to claim under this Sub-Clause is not conditioned on the finding having been Unforeseeable. However, the Contractor is treated in much the same way as if it had encountered an Unforeseeable adverse physical condition, as the Contractor is entitled to an EOT and to payment of its Cost just as it would be pursuant to Sub-Clause 4.12 [*Unforeseeable Physical Conditions*].[244]

(iv) Improvements: In the second paragraph, the requirement that the Contractor gives a Notice to the Engineer 'in good time' is redundant, as the same sentence provides that the Contractor shall do so 'as soon as practicable after discovery of a finding'.

--ooOOoo--

243. *This requires the Contractor to give an additional notice, a Notice of Claim, within 28 days or be time barred.* Sub-Clause 20.2.1.
244. The World Bank's COPA contains a new Sub-Clause 4.24 (immediately following Sub-Clause 4.23) requiring the Contractor to have a Code of Conduct for the Contractor's Personnel, which is also referred to in the Bank's revision of Sub-Clause 6.9 [*Contractor's Personnel*].

Figure 5 Sequence of Events Before the Commencement Date ('CD')[1]

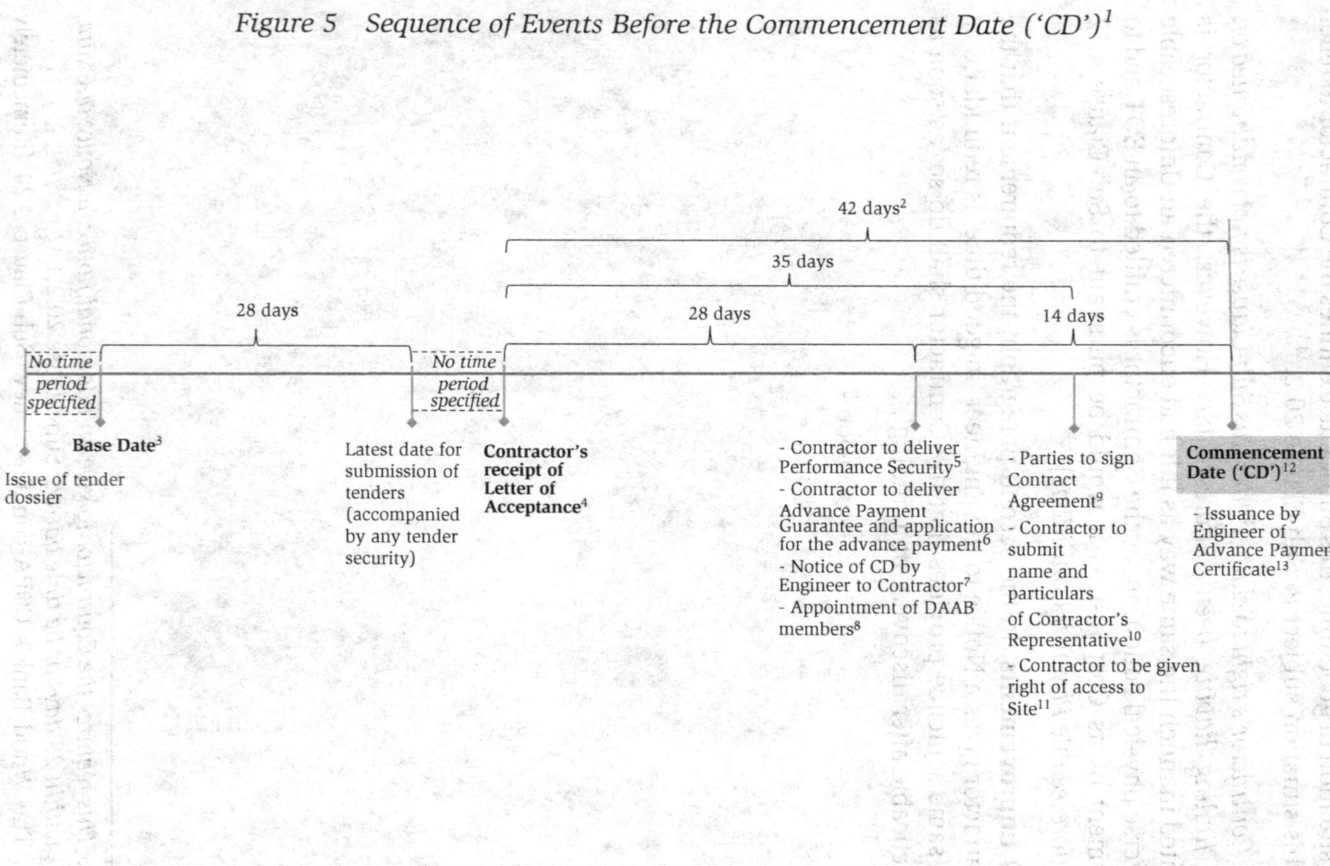

Source: Author's own work.

Figure 5 Sequence of Events Before the Commencement Date ('CD')

Notes SC = Sub-Clause

1. This figure is a simplified presentation of the events before the CD. Only the text of the Sub-Clauses ('SC(s)') referred to should be relied upon.
2. SC 8.1. The CD must be within 42 days after the Contractor receives the Letter of Acceptance unless the Parties agree otherwise in the Particular Conditions.
3. SC 1.1.4. The Base Date is 28 days before the latest date for submission of the Tender.
4. SC 19.1 and 21.1 Before the Letter of Acceptance is issued, the Parties should: (1)agree on the insurances for which the Contractor is responsible and (2) ideally, agree on the members of the DAAB. Upon receipt by the Contractor of the Letter of Acceptance, the Contract ordinarily enters into effect. *See* the last paragraph of the form of the Letter of Acceptance included in RB/17.
5. SC 4.2.1. The Contractor must deliver the Performance Security to the Employer, with a copy to the Engineer, within 28 days after receiving the Letter of Acceptance. The Performance Security should be delivered within the period of validity of any tender security which the Contractor may have provided. By about the same date, the Contractor should also have submitted the insurances required by SC 19.2.
6. The exact date for the delivery of these documents is not specified in SC 14.2.
7. SC 8.1. The Notice should be given not less than 14 days before the CD.
8. SC 21.1. This appointment must be made within 28 days after the Contractor receives the Letter of Acceptance, if no other period is stated in the Contract Data.
9. SC 1.6. The Contract Agreement must be signed within 35 days after the Contractor receives the Letter of Acceptance, unless the Parties agree otherwise.
10. SC 4.3. Unless the Contractor's Representative is named in the Contract, these must be submitted to the Engineer 'before' the CD.
11. SC 2.1 The Contractor must be given right of access to, and possession of, the Site within the time (or times) stated in the Contract Data.
12. SC 8.1. The Contractor must commence execution of the Works on, or as soon as reasonably practicable after, the CD.
13. SC 14.2.2. Assuming the Employer or the Engineer has received the Performance Security and the Advance Payment Guarantee and the Contractor has applied for the advance payment. *See* notes 5 and 6 above. According to Sub-Clause 14.7, the Employer must pay the amount certified in an Advance Payment Certificate within the period stated in the Contract Data (if not stated, 21 days) after the Employer receives that Certificate.

--ooOOoo--

5 SUBCONTRACTING

This Clause deals with the conditions under which the Contractor may subcontract works and with the Contractor's responsibility for the work of its Subcontractors. The Clause defines a 'nominated Subcontractor' and describes the grounds under which the Contractor may reasonably object to a nominated Subcontractor and the related indemnity the Employer may provide. The Clause also provides for the procedure for payments to nominated Subcontractors, and the right of the Engineer, before issuing a Payment Certificate including an amount payable to a nominated Subcontractor, to request reasonable evidence that the nominated Subcontractor has received all amounts due to it. Failing the presentation of such evidence, the Employer may pay the nominated Subcontractor directly.

--ooOOoo--

5.1 Subcontractors[1]

The Contractor shall not subcontract:

(a) works with a total accumulated value greater than the percentage of the Accepted Contract Amount stated in the Contract Data (if not stated, the whole of the Works); or

(b) any part of the Works for which subcontracting is not permitted as stated in the Contract Data.

The Contractor shall be responsible for the work of all Subcontractors, for managing and co-ordinating all the Subcontractors' works, and for the acts or defaults of any Subcontractor, any Subcontractor's agents or employees, as if they were the acts or defaults of the Contractor.

The Contractor shall obtain the Engineer's prior consent to all proposed Subcontractors, except:

(i) suppliers of Materials; or

(ii) a subcontract for which the Subcontractor is named in the Contract.

Where the Contractor is required to obtain the Engineer's consent to a proposed Subcontractor, the Contractor shall submit to the Engineer the name, address, detailed particulars and relevant experience of such a Subcontractor and the work intended to be subcontracted and further information which the Engineer may reasonably require. If the Engineer does not respond within 14 days after receiving this submission (or further information if requested), by giving a Notice objecting to the proposed Subcontractor, the Engineer shall be deemed to have given his/her consent.

1. *See* the commentary on Sub-Clause 1.1.78 '**Subcontractor**', above.

The Contractor shall give a Notice to the Engineer not less than 28 days before the intended date of the commencement of each Subcontractor's work, and of the commencement of such work on the Site.

The Contractor shall not subcontract: (a) works with a total accumulated value greater than the percentage of the Accepted Contract Amount stated in the Contract Data (if not stated, the whole of the Works) or (b) any part of the Works for which subcontracting is not permitted in the Contract Data. The Contractor is responsible for the work of all Subcontractors. The Contractor must obtain the prior consent of the Engineer to proposed Subcontractors, except suppliers of Materials or a Subcontractor named in the Contract. If the Engineer does not give Notice of its objection within 14 days, the Engineer is deemed to have consented. The Contractor must give a Notice to the Engineer not less than 28 days before the intended date of commencement of each Subcontractor's work, and of the commencement of such work on Site.

Commentary

(i) Main Changes from RB/99:

(1) In RB/99, the subject of 'Subcontractors' was dealt with in Sub-Clause 4.4, the 'Assignment of Benefit of Subcontract' was dealt with in Sub-Clause 4.5 and only 'Nominated Subcontractors' was dealt with in Clause 5. In RB/17, both Subcontractors and nominated Subcontractors are dealt with together in Clause 5 and the 'Assignment of Benefit of Subcontract' provision (applicable where a Subcontractor's obligations extend beyond the expiry date of the relevant DNP) is no longer in the General Conditions.[2]

(2) In Sub-Clause 4.4 of RB/99, the Contractor was only prevented from subcontracting 'the whole' of the Works and thus was free to subcontract nearly all of the Works as well as any part of it, subject to the Engineer's consent. However, in new Sub-Clause 5.1, the Contractor is prevented instead from subcontracting: (a)

2. However, an example provision dealing with assignment of the benefit of a subcontract, where a Subcontractor's obligations extend beyond the expiry date of the DNP relating to the Subcontractor's work, is contained in the *Guidance for the Preparation of Particular Conditions*, 28-29.

works with a total accumulated value greater than the percentage stated in the Contract Data (or, if none is stated, the whole of the Works) or (b) any part of the Works for which subcontracting is not permitted by the Contract Data.

(3) The third paragraph dealing with obtaining the Engineer's consent to proposed Subcontractors is new, although the Engineer's consent had similarly been required by RB/99.

(4) The last paragraph, dealing with the commencement of each Subcontractor's work, is new.[3]

(ii) Related Clauses / Sub-Clauses: 1.2 [*Interpretation*], 1.3 [*Notices and Other Communications*], 1.7 [*Assignment*], 3.8 [*Meetings*], 4.9.1 [*Quality Management System*], 4.17 [*Contractor's Equipment*], 13.4 [*Provisional Sums*], 15.2 [*Termination for Contractor's Default*], 18.1 [*Exceptional Events*] and 19.2.5 [*Insurance to Be Provided by the Contractor – Injury to Employees*].

(iii) Analysis:

(1) Definition of Subcontractor

Under Sub-Clause 1.1.78, a '**Subcontractor**' is defined to mean:

> any person named in the Contract as a subcontractor, or any person appointed by the Contractor as a subcontractor or designer, for a part of the Works; and the legal successors in title to each of these persons.[4]

A person 'named in the Contract' as a subcontractor[5] refers to a subcontractor named by the Contractor in, for example, its Tender which is subsequently included in the Contract. It is to be distinguished from a 'nominated Subcontractor' which refers to a Subcontractor nominated as such in the Specification (and thus by the Employer) or whom the

3. The definition of '**Subcontractor**' in Sub-Clause 1.1.78 has been amended to include any person 'appointed by the Contractor as a subcontractor' instead of, as in Sub-Clause 1.1.2.8 of RB/99, 'appointed as a subcontractor', and now includes a 'designer, for part of the Works'. FIDIC has published forms of conditions of subcontract for use with RB/87 in 1994, with RB/99 in 2011 and with YB/99 in 2019. FIDIC is planning to publish forms of conditions of subcontract for use with the 2017 Rainbow Suite.
4. As to 'legal successors in title', *see* the commentary in relation Sub-Clause 1.1.14 '**Contractor**' above.
5. Sub-Clause 5.1, third paragraph, (ii).

Engineer, under Sub-Clause 13.4 [*Provisional Sums*], instructs the Contractor to employ as a Subcontractor.[6] A further feature of the above definition of Subcontractor is that no distinction is made between, on the one hand, a subcontractor in the strict sense, that is, like a contractor, a person who is principally providing services, and, on the other hand, a subsupplier, that is, a person who is principally providing goods or materials. Both are treated in RB/17 as Subcontractors[7] (and as being part of the 'Contractor's Personnel').[8]

(2) Restrictions on subcontracting

Based apparently on feedback from users,[9] this Sub-Clause now provides that the Contractor shall not subcontract works with a total accumulated value greater than the percentage of the Accepted Contract Amount stated in the Contract Data. If nothing is stated, then the Contractor may not, as was provided in RB/99,[10] subcontract the whole of the Works. In addition, the Contractor may not subcontract any part of the Works for which subcontracting is not permitted as stated in the Contract Data.[11]

These potential restrictions, although largely new, are understandable as the Employer may have awarded the Contract to the Contractor based on its particular competence, resources or experience. In such cases, the Employer may not want more than a limited amount of work, nor certain type(s) of work, to be delegated by the Contractor to someone else nor to have to justify that the withholding of its consent was 'reasonable', as it would have to do if the matter were subject to the Employer's consent and Sub-Clause 1.3 applied.

If the Contractor subcontracts the whole, or any part, of the Works in breach of Sub-Clause 5.1, then, as the breach may be irremediable, the Employer is entitled under Sub-Clause 15.2 to terminate the Contract with immediate effect.[12]

---

6. *See* Sub-Clause 5.2.1.
7. It is unclear why it was felt necessary to add 'a designer' to the definition as a designer is merely another performer of services like a normal subcontractor. *See* the commentary on Sub-Clause 1.1.78 '**Subcontractor**' above.
8. Sub-Clause 1.1.17 '**Contractor's Personnel**'.
9. FIDIC's undated note entitled 'FIDIC Red, Yellow and Silver Books, second edition, 2017: a Review of the updated General Conditions of Contract', 6, issued in connection with the publication of the new forms in December 2017.
10. Sub-Clause 4.4 of the RB/99.
11. Sub-Clause 5.1, first paragraph.
12. *See* Sub-Clauses 15.2.1(f) and 15.2.2.

Pursuant to the third paragraph, the Contractor must obtain the Engineer's prior consent to all proposed Subcontractors, except suppliers of Materials or a Subcontractor who is named in the Contract. The third paragraph now elaborates on the procedure for obtaining such consent. As provided in Sub-Clause 1.3, any consent may 'not be unreasonably withheld or delayed'. The paragraph adds a 'deeming' provision – as is standard in RB/17 – that if the Engineer does not object to the Contractor's submission within 14 days, the Engineer is deemed to have given its consent.

(3) Other provisions

The Contractor is further stated to be responsible, as is usual, for the work of all Subcontractors (who include nominated Subcontractors),[13] including their acts and defaults, and for managing and coordinating all the Subcontractors' work.[14]

(iv) Related Law:

(1) Protection of subcontractors

In many countries the rights of subcontractors, especially their right to payment, are protected by either statute or case law against potential abuse by contractors, who are usually the stronger party. The statutory rights of subcontractors in some civil law countries to be paid directly by, or to be entitled to take legal action directly against, an employer have been described elsewhere.[15]

13. *See* Sub-Clause 1.1.78 '**Subcontractor**' and Sub-Clause 5.2.1.
14. Sub-Clause 5.1, second paragraph. The *Guidance* contains a number of example provisions which may be used to modify or add to the Sub-Clause, including provisions: (1) encouraging the Contractor to employ local contractors and (2) requiring that all of the Contractor's subcontracts should provide for their assignment to the Employer in the event that the Employer terminates the Contract pursuant to Sub-Clause 15.2 [*Termination for Contractor's Default*] or in the event that a Subcontractor's obligations continue after expiry of the DNP. *Guidance for the Preparation of Particular Conditions*, 28-29. It is surprising that the provisions referred to in (2) of the preceding sentence are not in the General Conditions, as they were in Sub-Clause 4.4(d) of RB/99.
15. *See* **Section 4 Common Law and Civil Law Compared – 4.4.3 Subcontractor's Direct Rights**, **Chapter II Applicable Law**, above.

(2) Pay-when-paid clauses, etc.

In common law countries, 'pay-when-paid' and 'pay-if-paid' clauses in construction contracts, by which a contractor seeks to transfer the risk of a delay in payment or non-payment by an employer onto a subcontractor, have been the subject of regulation by statute and/or restrictive interpretation by courts.

Thus, in the UK,[16] such provisions may generally only be effective if the contractor has not received payment for the subcontract works due to the employer's insolvency.[17] In other cases, literal application of pay-when-paid provisions is seen in the UK as likely to give rise to unfairness, where the reason for the non-payment by the contractor is unconnected with the performance of the subcontractor.[18] In particular, a contractor will be prevented from relying on such a clause if the reason for non-payment is its own breach of contract or default.[19]

In the United States, in some States, such clauses are invalid by legislation.[20] In other States, where the matter has been left to the courts to decide, their general tendency has been to refuse to interpret such a clause as transferring the risk of the employer's non-payment from the contractor to the subcontractor unless the clause made it clear that payment by the employer to the contractor was a 'condition precedent' – ideally, the clause should use those two quoted words – to the obligation

16. S 113(1) of the UK *Housing Grants, Construction and Regeneration Act 1996* ('HGCRA').
17. Legislative prohibitions of such clauses apply also in Australia and Singapore. Julian Bailey, *Construction Law* (3rd edn, London Publishing, UK, 2020) vol 2, 595-596 (para. 6.314). Furthermore, the *International Form of Contract – lump sum contracts* (1st edn, IChemE, 2007) prohibits any provision in a subcontract that makes payment to the subcontractor dependent upon receipt of payment by the contractor under the main contract. *See* Sub-Clause 9.6.
18. Atkin Chambers, *Hudson's Building and Engineering Contracts* (14th edn, Sweet & Maxwell, London, 2020) 1058 (para. 9-071).
19. *Ibid.*
20. This is the case in New York. *See* Robert A Rubin and Jeffrey R Cruz, 'Contingent Payment Clauses' Violate New York's Mechanic's Lien Law' [1997] ICLR 245 and *West-Fair Electrical Contractors and L.J. Coppola, Inc v The Aetna Casualty & Surety Company and Gilbane Building Company*, 87 NY 2d 148, 638 NYS 2d 394 [1995].

of the contractor to pay the subcontractor (and did not merely permit postponement of the time for payment by the contractor to the subcontractor).[21]

Such clauses appear to be generally valid in civil law countries[22] subject to local legislation providing, for example, the subcontractor with the right by mandatory law to be paid directly by, or to be entitled to take legal action directly against, the employer for sums not paid by the contractor, which may negate the effect of such clauses.[23]

(v) Improvements:

(1) This Sub-Clause should be revised to provide that all subcontracts include a provision which entitles the Employer to require the subcontract to be assigned to the Employer if: (a) Sub-Clause 15.2 [*Termination for Contractor's Default*] applies, as such assignment to the Employer is envisaged by Sub-Clause 15.2.3(a)(i); and (b) a Subcontractor's obligations continue after expiry of the DNP.[24]

(2) As there appears to be an international consensus that subcontractors, as a class, require protection, FIDIC might consider

21. *Thomas J. Dyer Co v Bishop Int'l Engineering Co*, 303 F.2d 655 (6th Cir. 1962), regarded as the leading case, and Justin Sweet and Marc M Schneier, *Legal Aspects of Architecture, Engineering and the Construction Process* (9th edn, Cengage Learning, Stamford, CT, 2013) 657. The reasons given for this general tendency of courts in the US have included that: (1) the contractor is in contract with the employer and therefore has had the opportunity to evaluate the employer's financial position and negotiate its contract accordingly; (2) to the extent a subcontract has been drafted or imposed by the contractor, in the case of an ambiguity, it should be interpreted against the contractor, *contra proferentem*; (3) according to the legal principle against forfeitures, in a case of doubt, an interpretation is to be preferred that will reduce the risk that a party will lose its rights (*see* s 227, *Restatement (Second) of Contracts*, ALI, Philadelphia, PA, 1981); and (4) the subcontract works may represent only a small portion of the contract works.

22. M.A.B. Chao-Duivis, '*Subcontracting in Europe: The Results of a Questionnaire*' [2013] ICLR 318, 323-5. For an ICC award in relation to a FIDIC main contract which contains an interesting analysis of such clauses in a related subcontract under Swiss law, *see* the final award, ICC case 6230 (1990), in YB Com Arb, vol XVII-1992, 164.

23. *See* **Section 4 Common Law and Civil Law Compared – 4.4.3 Subcontractor's Direct Rights, Chapter II Applicable Law**, above.

24. Examples of such provisions are contained in the *Guidance for the Preparation of Particular Conditions*, 28-29, and inclusion of the former provision

including in the RB a prohibition on the Contractor engaging a Subcontractor under a subcontract that makes payment to the Subcontractor dependent upon the Contractor's receipt of payment under the main RB contract.[25]

--ooOOoo--

5.2 Nominated Subcontractors

5.2.1 Definition of "nominated Subcontractor"

> In this Sub-Clause, "nominated Subcontractor" means a Subcontractor named as such in the Specification or whom the Engineer, under Sub-Clause 13.4 [*Provisional Sums*], instructs the Contractor to employ as a Subcontractor.

5.2.2 Objection to Nomination

> The Contractor shall not be under any obligation to employ a nominated Subcontractor whom the Engineer instructs and against whom the Contractor raises reasonable objection by giving a Notice to the Engineer, with detailed supporting particulars, no later than 14 days after receiving the Engineer's instruction. An objection shall be deemed reasonable if it arises from (among other things) any of the following matters, unless the Employer agrees to indemnify the Contractor against and from the consequences of the matter:
>
> (a) there are reasons to believe that the nominated Subcontractor does not have sufficient competence, resources or financial strength;
>
> (b) the subcontract does not specify that the nominated Subcontractor shall indemnify the Contractor against and from any negligence or misuse of Goods by the nominated Subcontractor, the nominated Subcontractor's agents and employees; or

(the provision referred to in (a)) is expressly required by The World Bank's COPA.

25. As is provided for in the UK's IChemE form referred to in fn. 17 above.

(c) the subcontract does not specify that, for the subcontracted work (including design, if any), the nominated Subcontractor shall:

(i) undertake to the Contractor such obligations and liabilities as will enable the Contractor to discharge the Contractor's corresponding obligations and liabilities under the Contract, and

(ii) indemnify the Contractor against and from all obligations and liabilities arising under or in connection with the Contract and from the consequences of any failure by the Subcontractor to perform these obligations or to fulfil these liabilities.

5.2.3 Payments to nominated Subcontractors

The Contractor shall pay to the nominated Subcontractor the amounts due in accordance with the subcontract. These amounts plus other charges shall be included in the Contract Price in accordance with sub-paragraph (b) of Sub-Clause 13.4 [*Provisional Sums*], except as stated in Sub-Clause 5.2.4 [*Evidence of Payments*].

5.2.4 Evidence of Payments

Before issuing a Payment Certificate which includes an amount payable to a nominated Subcontractor, the Engineer may request the Contractor to supply reasonable evidence that the nominated Subcontractor has received all amounts due in accordance with the previous Payment Certificates, less applicable deductions for retention or otherwise. Unless the Contractor:

(a) submits this reasonable evidence to the Engineer, or

(b) (i) satisfies the Engineer in writing that the Contractor is reasonably entitled to withhold or refuse to pay these amounts, and

(ii) submits to the Engineer reasonable evidence that the nominated Subcontractor has been notified of the Contractor's entitlement, then the Employer may (at the Employer's sole discretion) pay, directly to the nominated Subcontractor, part or all of such amounts previously certified (less applicable deductions) as are due to the nominated Subcontractor and for which the Contractor has failed to submit the evidence described in sub-paragraphs (a) or (b) above.

Thereafter, the Engineer shall give a Notice to the Contractor stating the amount paid directly to the nominated Subcontractor by the Employer and, in the next IPC after this Notice, shall include this amount as a deduction under sub-paragraph (b) of Sub-Clause 14.6.1 [*The IPC*].

A 'nominated Subcontractor' means a Subcontractor named as such in the Specification or whom the Engineer, under Sub-Clause 13.4, instructs the Contractor to employ as a Subcontractor. The Contractor shall be under no obligation to employ a nominated Subcontractor against whom the Contractor raises reasonable objection by giving a Notice to the Engineer, with detailed particulars, within 14 days after receiving the Engineer's instruction. An objection is deemed reasonable if it arises from, among others, any of the matters described in (a), (b) and (c) of Sub-Clause 5.2.2 unless the Employer agrees to indemnify the Contractor against the matter.

The Contractor shall pay the nominated Subcontractor the amounts due in accordance with the subcontract, and these amounts plus other charges are to be included in the Contract Price in accordance with Sub-Clause 13.4(b), except as stated in Sub-Clause 5.2.4. Before issuing a Payment Certificate which includes an amount payable to a nominated Subcontractor, the Engineer may ask the Contractor to supply reasonable evidence that the nominated Subcontractor has received all amounts due under previous Payment Certificates, failing which, the Employer may, at its sole discretion, pay the amounts previously certified due directly to the nominated Subcontractor. The Engineer shall give a Notice to the Contractor of such direct payment, and include it as a deduction in the next IPC.

Commentary

(i) Main Changes from RB/99:

(1) Under Sub-Clause 5.2.1, a nominated Subcontractor now means, among other things, a Subcontractor named as such in the Specification, whereas under Sub-Clause 5.1 of RB/99 it meant a Subcontractor stated 'in the Contract' as being a nominated Subcontractor.

(2) Under Sub-Clause 5.2.1, a nominated Subcontractor also now means a Subcontractor whom the Engineer, under Sub-Clause 13.4 [*Provisional Sums*], instructs the Contractor to employ as a Subcontractor, whereas Sub-Clause 5.1 of RB/99 had provided that the Engineer's instruction to employ a Subcontractor would be made under Clause 13 [*Variations and Adjustments*].

(3) Under Sub-Clause 5.2.2, any objection by the Contractor to a nominated Subcontractor must now be made no later than 14 days after receiving the Engineer's instruction, whereas under RB/99 it had to be made 'as soon as practicable'.

(4) The last paragraph of Sub-Clause 5.2.4, which is new, provides that the Engineer shall give a Notice to the Contractor of the amount which the Employer has paid directly to a nominated Subcontractor, and then include such amount as a deduction in the next IPC under Sub-Clause 14.6.1(b). Sub-Clause 5.4 of RB 99 had required simply that the Contractor repays to the Employer the amount which the nominated Subcontractor was paid directly by the Employer – without indicating how the Contractor was to know this amount.

(ii) Related Clauses / Sub-Clauses: 1.2 [*Interpretation*], 1.3 [*Notices and Other Communications*], 3.5 [*Engineer's Instructions*], 5.1 [*Subcontractors*], 8.3 [*Programme*], 13.4 [*Provisional Sums*], 13.5 [*Daywork*] and 14.6.1 [*Issue of IPC – The IPC*].

(iii) Analysis:

(1) Nominated subcontracting not widespread

As FIDIC rightly pointed out in relation to the corresponding provisions of RB 99, this Sub-Clause includes provisions which 'should only be invoked with a degree of caution', as the Contractor should be given reasonable freedom to decide, subject to the Engineer's consent, what parts of the Works it may subcontract, and to whom.[26] The purposes accomplished by nominated subcontracting may be achieved in other ways than by use of a nominated Subcontractor, such as by requiring in the Specification either that certain items of Plant or Materials be sourced from a particular manufacturer, or that certain parts of the Works be undertaken only by a person from a list of acceptable potential subcontractors[27] (e.g., in the case of elevators for a proposed building, that the Subcontractor be selected from a list of elevator manufacturers previously approved by the Employer). Moreover, nominated subcontracting is not widespread outside the English common law world and the Arabian Gulf and the law relating to this practice may be scarce or non-existent elsewhere. Absent its recognition by applicable law, the legal consequences of resorting to it would be unpredictable.

(2) Definition of nominated Subcontractor

As provided in Sub-Clause 5.2.1, a nominated Subcontractor means a Subcontractor named as such in the Specification,[28] or whom the Engineer, under Sub-Clause 13.4 [*Provisional Sums*], instructs the Contractor to employ as a Subcontractor. Thus, this Sub-Clause should be read together with Sub-Clause 13.4 as, in the case of an Engineer's instruction, there needs to be a Provisional Sum in the Contract for payment to the nominated Subcontractor.

An Employer can thus, subject to Sub-Clause 5.2.2 (discussed below), require the Contractor to engage a particular subcontractor, either in the Specification or later after the Contract is signed, by an instruction from the Engineer.[29] At the same time, that 'nominated Subcontractor' is a

26. *The FIDIC Contracts Guide* (1st edn, FIDIC, 2000) 132.
27. *Ibid.*
28. FIDIC recommends this procedure over subsequent nomination by the Engineer. *See* the *Guidance for the Preparation of the Particular Conditions*, 29.
29. It appears to be the intention that the Engineer may instruct the Contractor to employ an entirely new subcontractor, that is, one that is neither named in the Specification or elsewhere in the Contract (otherwise Sub-Clause 5.2.2 giving the Contractor a right to object to such nomination would seem unnecessary). However, ambiguity is created by Sub-Clause 5.2.1 which states that a 'nominated Subcontractor' means 'a *Subcontractor* [...] whom the Engineer [...] instructs' (emphasis added). A '**Subcontractor**' is defined in Sub-Clause 1.1.78 as either a person named in the Contract as a subcontractor or any person appointed by the Contractor as a subcontractor. In view of this definition, a nominated Subcontractor must be a person either named

Subcontractor under Sub-Clause 5.1, meaning that the Contractor is responsible for its work, including its acts and defaults, and for managing and coordinating its work with that of the work of other Subcontractors.

(3) Objection to nomination

However, pursuant to Sub-Clause 5.2.2, the Contractor is not obliged to employ a nominated Subcontractor whom the Engineer instructs, against whom the Contractor raises 'reasonable objection' by a Notice to the Engineer, with detailed supporting particulars, no later than 14 days after receiving the instruction. An objection is deemed to be reasonable if it arises from '(among other things)' any of the three grounds listed in sub-paragraphs (a), (b) and (c) of Sub-Clause 5.2.2 'unless the Employer agrees to indemnify the Contractor against and from the consequences of the matter'. Thus, the Employer can, arguably at least, by agreeing to provide an indemnity, force the Contractor to employ any Subcontractor of the Employer's choice,[30] regardless of the nature, possibly,[31] of the Contractor's objection, whether it be one of the grounds listed in those sub-paragraphs or otherwise.[32]

If the Employer should be able in this way to force the Contractor – over its objection – to employ as a Subcontractor, for example, a competitor of the Contractor to whom the Contractor objects or someone whom the Contractor has reason to believe is dishonest or corrupt, then it goes too far. Much better – and simpler – was Sub-Clause 59.2 of RB/87 which gave the Contractor a general right to refuse to employ any nominated Subcontractor to whom it 'may raise reasonable objection'. The Employer should not be entitled (as it arguably is under this Sub-Clause) to override the Contractor's objection by providing an indemnity. As FIDIC's *Guide* to RB/87 had noted: '(i)t is important to ensure that the Contractor approves of the Subcontractor and is prepared to collaborate' with it.[33]

in the Contract as a subcontractor or a person appointed by the Contractor as a subcontractor in order to become a nominated Subcontractor.

30. This is indicated by *The FIDIC Contracts Guide* (2nd edn, FIDIC, 2022) 170. However, *see* the preceding fn. 29.
31. The Clause is unclear on this point.
32. Sub-Clause 5.2 of RB/99 was to similar effect. Any disagreement concerning an objection may give rise to a Claim under Sub-Clause 20.1(c).
33. *Guide to the Use of FIDIC Conditions of Contract for Works of Civil Engineering Construction, fourth edition* (FIDIC, 1989) 131.

If the Contractor fails to give such a Notice of objection within 14 days, the Contractor may, implicitly, be bound to employ the Subcontractor according to the Engineer's instructions under Sub-Clause 13.4.[34]

(4) Payment to nominated Subcontractor

The Contractor must pay the nominated Subcontractor the amounts due in accordance with the subcontract.[35] The Contractor is entitled to be paid by the Employer the actual amounts paid (or due to be paid) to the nominated Subcontractor, plus a sum for overhead charges and profit, and these will be included in the Contract Price.[36] However, pursuant to Sub-Clause 5.2.4, before issuing a Payment Certificate, including an amount payable to a nominated Subcontractor, the Engineer may request the Contractor to supply 'reasonable evidence' that the nominated Subcontractor has received all amounts due in accordance with previous Payment Certificates. While 'reasonable evidence' is not defined, it is evidence sufficient to convince a reasonable Engineer/Employer that the nominated Subcontractor was already paid what was due to it or, if not fully paid, that the reasons for non-payment were justified.

Unless the Contractor can show the Engineer, in this way, that the nominated Subcontractor has received all amounts to which it is entitled, or satisfies the Engineer that the Contractor is reasonably entitled to withhold or refuse to pay amounts of which the Subcontractor has been notified, the Employer may, at its sole discretion,[37] pay the nominated Subcontractor directly part or all of the certified amounts which the Subcontractor has not received. Those amounts will be deducted from future IPCs pursuant to Sub-Clause 14.6.1(b). The Engineer must give a Notice to the Contractor of the amounts which the Employer has paid directly.[38]

(iv) Related Law: In a case before the Iran-US Claims Tribunal, a nominated subcontractor under the RB/57 or RB/69 forms[39] was held to be entitled to payment directly by the Employer on the basis of unjust

34. Work to be undertaken by any nominated Subcontractor must be identified in the Contractor's programme. Sub-Clause 8.3(c).
35. Sub-Clause 5.2.3.
36. Sub-Clause 13.4(b).
37. *See* item (1) under **(v) Improvements** of the commentary on Sub-Clause 1.2 [*Interpretation*] above.
38. Sub-Clause 5.2.4.
39. It is unclear which applied. However, as a practical matter, it makes no difference as the two editions are practically identical.

enrichment for monies due to the nominated subcontractor which had not been paid by the Contractor. In arriving at this decision, the tribunal placed emphasis on Clause 59(2) of the relevant FIDIC form which, like Sub-Clause 5.2.4 of RB/17, would allow the Employer to deduct sums paid directly to a nominated subcontractor from any moneys due by the Employer to the Contractor. Consequently, the tribunal found that the Employer would not run the risk of double liability.[40]

While the practice of nominated subcontracting originated in England, it is now 'very rarely employed in practice' there.[41] However, it does continue to be used in countries of the former British Empire (e.g., Ireland, Singapore and South Africa) as well as in the United Arab Emirates.[42] The practice does not seem to be widely used in either the United States[43] or Continental Europe apart from the Netherlands.[44]

Given the complex legal issues to which nominated subcontracting can give rise (as, while nominating the Subcontractor, the Employer still generally requires the Contractor to be responsible for it), it should only be resorted to in cases where it cannot be avoided, and where the relevant governing law recognises this practice.

(v) Improvements:

(1) Assuming that – despite its declining use – FIDIC continues to retain a Sub-Clause dealing with nominated Subcontractors then, for the reasons given under **(iii) Analysis** above, this Sub-Clause should be revised to provide that the Contractor has an unqualified right to refuse to employ a nominated Subcon-

---

40. *Schlegel Corporation v National Iranian Copper Industries Company*, IUST Case no 834 (295-834-2), 27 March 1987, YB Com Arb – vol XIII – 1988, 367.
41. Stephen Furst and Vivian Ramsey, *Keating on Construction Contracts* (11th edn, Sweet & Maxwell, London, 2021) 411 (para. 13-058). For example, it is not provided for in the English NEC4 engineering and construction contract (2017).
42. Based on the author's experience and *see also* Aymen Masadeh, 'Vicarious Performance and Privity in Construction Contracts' [2014] ICLR 108.
43. The US version used in some public contracts is called 'prefiled' bids. Justin Sweet and Marc M Schneier, *Legal Aspects of Architecture, Engineering and the Construction Process* (9th edn, Cengage Learning, Stamford, CT, 2013) 655.
44. M.A.B. Chao-Duivis, *Subcontracting in Europe: The Results of a Questionnaire* [2013] ICLR 318, 321-322.

tractor to whom it may raise reasonable objection (as was the case in Sub-Clause 59.2 of RB/87).

(2) Nevertheless, if Sub-Clause 5.2.2 is retained, its wording should be revised, as it is ambiguous as to whether the right of the Employer to override any reasonable objection of the Contractor to a proposed nominated Subcontractor, by the giving of an indemnity, applies only to the objections listed in sub-paragraphs (a), (b) and (c) of that Sub-Clause, or to any reasonable objection made by the Contractor. As explained under *(3) Objection to nomination* under **(iii) Analysis** above, the Employer's right – if it should exist at all – should apply only to the objections listed in those three sub-paragraphs. What is necessary, in any event, is that the position be made clear in the Conditions, one way or the other.

--ooOOoo--

6 Staff and Labour

This Clause provides that, except as stated in the Specification, the Contractor shall make arrangements for the engagement of all the Contractor's Personnel, as well as for their payment, working hours, accommodation, health, safety, welfare and superintendence. The Clause requires the Contractor to submit records of labour and other resources being used with its progress reports. It requires the Contractor to prevent disorderly conduct among its personnel. In addition, it restricts either Party from recruiting personnel from the other and authorises the Engineer to request the removal of Contractor's Personnel in certain cases. Finally, the Clause deals with the conditions for the appointment and replacement of Key Personnel.[1]

--ooOOoo--

1. The World Bank's COPA requires many changes and additions (more than 6 pages) to Clause 6, which are too extensive to describe or comment on here. It also requires the Contractor to have a Code of Conduct for Contractor's Personnel. *See* Sub-Clause 4.24, COPA.

6.1 Engagement of Staff and Labour

> Except as otherwise stated in the Specification, the Contractor shall make arrangements for the engagement of all Contractor's Personnel, and for their payment, accommodation, feeding, transport and welfare.

Except as stated in the Specification, the Contractor must engage all Contractor's Personnel and is responsible for them and their welfare.

Commentary

(i) Main Changes from RB/99:

(1) Whereas Sub-Clause 6.1 of RB/99 referred to the engagement of 'all staff and labour, local or otherwise', the same Sub-Clause of RB/17 refers to the engagement of 'all Contractor's Personnel'.

(2) Unlike Sub-Clause 6.1 in RB/99, the new Sub-Clause explicitly requires the Contractor to make arrangements for the 'welfare' of the Contractor's Personnel.

(ii) Related Clauses / Sub-Clauses: 4.1 [*Contractor's General Obligations*], 4.3 [*Contractor's Representative*], 4.19 [*Temporary Utilities*], 5 [*Subcontracting*] and 6 [*Staff and Labour*].

(iii) Analysis:

(1) Contractor's general obligation

Under Sub-Clause 4.1 [*Contractor's General Obligations*], the Contractor has the obligation to provide all 'Contractor's Personnel' who are defined as:

> the Contractor's Representative and all personnel whom the Contractor utilises on Site or other places where the Works are being carried out, including the staff, labour and other employees of the Contractor and of each Subcontractor; and any other personnel assisting the Contractor in the execution of the Works.[2]

2. Sub-Clause 1.1.17 '**Contractor's Personnel**'.

Sub-Clause 6.1 elaborates on this obligation, by providing that '[e]xcept as otherwise stated in the Specification' the Contractor shall engage 'all Contractor's Personnel' and provide 'for their payment, accommodation, feeding, transport and welfare'.

Thus, the Contractor must provide full support and accommodation for all Contractor's Personnel, except for any facilities which the Employer has agreed in the Specification to provide. For example, the Employer may agree to provide accommodation and/or transport for the Contractor's staff to and from the Site.[3] However, if nothing is stated in the Specification,[4] the Contractor must provide accommodation and transport, wherever the Site is located, and generally all things necessary to support the Contractor's Personnel.

As a practical matter, the Contractor's first task, when arriving at a greenfield Site in the Country, may be to build a camp or other accommodation, together with related living facilities, for the Contractor's Personnel and possibly the Employer's Personnel as well – notably the Engineer and its staff where they are expatriates.[5] This building project can amount to a sort of dress rehearsal for the main construction project to follow.

The Contractor's general obligation to engage and be responsible for the Contractor's Personnel in Sub-Clause 6.1 is particularised in Sub-Clauses 6.2 to 6.11 commented on below.

(2) Example Clauses and policies

The *Guidance* contains example Sub-Clauses that may be adopted to take account of particular circumstances and the locality of the Site.[6]

---

3. *See also* under Sub-Clause 6.6 [*Facilities for Staff and Labour*] in the *Guidance for the Preparation of Particular Conditions*, 29. Another example is Sub-Clause 4.19 [*Temporary Utilities*] pursuant to which the Employer might provide temporary utilities for the Contractor's use.
4. In this respect, the Specification will have a higher priority than the General Conditions, although under Sub-Clause 1.5 [*Priority of Documents*] the General Conditions normally have priority over the Specification.
5. *See* the last sentence of Sub-Clause 6.6 [*Facilities for Staff and Labour*].
6. *Guidance for the Preparation of Particular Conditions*, 30-32. These deal with matters such as foreign personnel, food and water supply, measures against insect and pest nuisance, alcohol and drugs, arms and ammunition, festivals and religious customs, funeral arrangements, forced and/or child labour, employment records of workers, workers' organisations, non-discrimination and equal opportunity. Local Laws may deal with many of these matters.

Some major international contractors have adopted worldwide policies for their operations abroad due to the need to comply with international legislation and/or best practices.[7] Adherence to such policies may result in the application of standards concerning health, safety and welfare which are higher and more costly to implement than those required by local Laws.[8] While desirable in themselves, this may naturally give a cost advantage to local or regional contractors not following such policies, who have to comply with local Laws only.

(iv) Related Law: *See* the Labour Clauses (Public Contracts) Convention, 1949 (No. 94) of the International Labour Organisation ('ILO'), containing clauses for the protection of workers in contracts (including expressly construction contracts) to which at least one of the parties is a public authority. This Convention has been ratified by more than 60 countries. *See* **(iv) Related Law** in the commentary below on Sub-Clause 6.4 [*Labour Laws*].

--ooOOoo--

6.2 Rates of Wages and Conditions of Labour

> The Contractor shall pay rates of wages, and observe conditions of labour, which comply with all applicable Laws and are not lower than those established for the trade or industry where the work is carried out.
>
> If no established rates or conditions are applicable, the Contractor shall pay rates of wages and observe conditions which are not lower than the general level of wages and conditions observed locally by employers whose trade or industry is similar to that of the Contractor.

The Contractor must pay rates of wages and observe labour conditions which comply with applicable Laws and are not lower than those for where the work is carried out.

---

7. *See* 'Time for Change: Construction in the GCC Reaches a Tipping Point' (DLA Piper, 2018) 24, 37.
8. *Ibid*.

Commentary

(i) Main Changes from RB/99: The Sub-Clause is identical to Sub-Clause 6.2 of RB/99 except for the addition in the first paragraph that the Contractor must pay rates of wages and observe labour conditions 'which comply with all applicable Laws'.

(ii) Related Clauses / Sub-Clauses: 1.13 [*Compliance with Laws*], 2.2 [*Assistance*], 6.1 [*Engagement of Staff and Labour*], 6.4 [*Labour Laws*], 6.5 [*Working Hours*] and 6.7 [*Health and Safety of Personnel*].

(iii) Analysis: The spirit of sub-clauses like this which are customary in international construction contracts[9] is that the Contractor is expected to be 'a good employer of his/her labour force'.[10]

The first paragraph provides that the Contractor must pay rates of wages and observe conditions of labour which comply with 'all applicable Laws', reiterating the Contractor's obligation in Sub-Clause 1.13 [*Compliance with Laws*]. The latter part of the same paragraph indicates that the applicable Laws of principal concern are those 'where the work is carried out', which may be the country where the Site is located or the work done, e.g., where Plant is manufactured in the Contractor's country. Where the Contractor's Personnel comprises expatriate staff or where employment contracts for Contractor's Personnel are governed by the law of the Contractor's country, then the law of the Contractor's country or possibly a third country could apply.

The first paragraph of the Sub-Clause also states that the rates of wages and labour conditions must not be lower than those established for the local trade or industry, or, if no established rates or conditions are applicable (second paragraph), then the general level of wages and conditions observed locally by employers whose trade or industry is similar to that of the Contractor. It is not explicitly stated how such rates of wages and conditions should be 'established', whether, for example, by a law or by some general agreement between representatives of labour and employers (e.g., a collective bargaining agreement). Also, in the

9. *See*, e.g., Sub-Clause 28.1-28.3 of the *International Form of Contract – lump sum contracts* (1st edn, IChemE, 2007).
10. *The FIDIC Contracts Guide* (2nd edn, FIDIC, 2022) 240.

second paragraph, the concepts of 'general level of wages and conditions' and 'similar' trade or industry are broad terms and lack precise meaning.[11]

The intention of this Sub-Clause appears to be, as this is a standard form of contract and individual situations will vary, to lay down general principles of how the Contractor should be paying and treating its staff and labour with regard to practice in the country or countries where the work is being carried out. More precise rules, taking account of local laws and conditions, need then to be elaborated by the Employer in the Particular Conditions included in the tender dossier. Absent more precision, during the tender period, a tenderer should request the Employer to explain how this Sub-Clause is to be interpreted and applied in practice so as to avoid disputes later.[12]

(iv) Related Law: Most countries have adopted labour legislation – which is mandatory law[13] – to deal with matters such as minimum wages, working time, health, safety and similar issues, making this Sub-Clause in those cases perhaps superfluous. There are also international legal instruments in the field, such as numerous Conventions and Recommendations adopted by the ILO.[14] For example, the ILO has adopted Convention No. 182, which calls for the prohibition and

11. However, these broad rules are similar to those contained in art. 2 of the ILO's *Labour Clauses (Public Contracts) Convention*, 1949 (no 94). Accordingly, the greater detail provided for by that Convention may be helpful in interpreting these rules.
12. *See* Leo Grutters & Brian Barr, *FIDIC Red, Yellow and Silver Books, A Practical Guide to the 2017 Editions* (Sweet & Maxwell, London, 2018) 140, who make the same point.
13. *See* **Section 5 Mandatory Law at the Site** of **Chapter II Applicable Law** above.
14. There are almost two hundred ILO Conventions and the same number of Recommendations dealing with a wide range of labour issues. For more information about the Conventions and Recommendations adopted by the International Labour Organization, *see* https://www.ilo.org/global/standards/introduction-to-international-labour-standards/conventions-and-recommendations/lang--en/index.htm accessed 10 November 2022.

elimination of certain forms of child labour,[15] and ILO Convention No. 94 mentioned previously.[16]

(v) Improvements: The *Guidance for the Preparation of Particular Conditions* should provide expressly that, when preparing the tender dossier, the Employer should consider elaborating in the Particular Conditions what its intentions and requirements are in relation to this Sub-Clause, taking account of the Laws and conditions in the Country, as well as applicable international (ILO) standards.

--ooOOOoo--

6.3 Recruitment of Persons

> The Contractor shall not recruit, or attempt to recruit, staff and labour from amongst the Employer's Personnel.
>
> Neither the Employer nor the Engineer shall recruit, or attempt to recruit, staff and labour from amongst the Contractor's Personnel.

Neither Party will recruit, or attempt to recruit, staff and labour from the other Party, nor the Engineer from the Contractor.

Commentary

(i) Main Changes from RB/99: Whereas under RB/99 the prohibition only applied to the Contractor, now the Employer and the Engineer are similarly forbidden from recruiting, or attempting to recruit, staff and labour from among the Contractor's Personnel.

(ii) Related Clauses / Sub-Clauses: 6.1 [*Engagement of Staff and Labour*], 6.9 [*Contractor's Personnel*] and 15.2 [*Termination for Contractor's Default*].

15. *ILO Convention no 182 (Convention concerning the Prohibition and Immediate Action for the Elimination of the Worst Forms of Child Labour)*, available at https://www.ilo.org/dyn/normlex/en/f?p=NORMLEXPUB:12100:0::NO::P12100_ILO_CODE:C182 accessed 10 November 2022. The Convention entered into force on 19 November 2000. It has been ratified by at least 182 out of 187 ILO Member States.
16. *See* under **(iv) Related Law** in the commentary on Sub-Clause 6.1 above.

(iii) Analysis:

(1) The Sub-Clause's prohibitions

In RB/99, when providing that the Contractor must not recruit from the Employer's Personnel, a particular concern of FIDIC was that this could undermine the Employer's activities either on the project or elsewhere.[17] Accordingly, RB/99 had only prohibited the Contractor from recruiting from the Employer's Personnel and not the Employer from recruiting from the Contractor's Personnel. However, FIDIC had recognised that such recruitment could take place with the other Party's prior agreement.[18]

The new Sub-Clause prohibits the Employer and the Engineer from recruiting from the Contractor's Personnel as well, which is reasonable and fair.

The Employer's employees may have local knowledge that is valuable to the Contractor,[19] while those of the Contractor may have experience and/or expertise that would be useful to the Employer, whether in the operation of the Works or otherwise. Therefore, each Party may have an incentive to hire personnel from the other Party.

At the same time, during the execution of the Works, the Employer and its representative, the Engineer, on the one hand, and the Contractor, on the other hand, have an evident conflict of interest. Among other things, the Engineer will be evaluating the Contractor's work and approving its payment applications. For this reason, and for reasons of confidentiality, the hiring by the Contractor from the Employer's Personnel, as well as vice versa, can present delicate issues. Note that even an 'attempt to recruit' would be a breach of contract. Moreover, an attempt by the Contractor to do so from, for example, the Engineer's staff might constitute a 'corrupt' practice under Sub-Clauses 6.9(e) and 15.2.1(h).[20]

The Engineer may, under Sub-Clause 6.9(f), require the removal from the Contractor's employ of any person recruited in breach of Sub-Clause 6.3.

---

17. *See The FIDIC Contracts Guide* (1st edn, FIDIC, 2000) 151.
18. *Ibid.*
19. Brian Barr and Leo Grutters, *FIDIC Users' Guide: A Practical Guide to the Red, Yellow, MDB Harmonised and Subcontract Books* (3rd edn, ICE Publishing, London, 2014) 154.
20. The same may apply to an attempt to recruit a member of the Employer's staff.

(2) Practical solution

If the Contractor or the Employer (including the Engineer) is interested in recruiting a member of the staff of the other Party, the practical solution is for the Contractor or the Employer, before approaching the relevant employee, to obtain the other Party's written consent to do so.[21] Unless the other Party's prior consent has been obtained, the Contractor or the Employer may have breached Sub-Clause 6.3.[22]

(iv) Related Law: This Sub-Clause may require amendment in light of local labour Laws.[23]

(v) Improvements:

(1) The Sub-Clause should provide explicitly that the Contractor and Employer will ensure compliance with the Sub-Clause by the Contractor's Personnel and Employer's Personnel, respectively.
(2) There could also be introduced a reciprocal power (similar to Sub-Clause 6.9(f) referred to under **(iii) Analysis** above) for the Engineer to require the removal of a person recruited by the Employer in breach of this Sub-Clause.

--ooOOoo--

6.4 Labour Laws

The Contractor shall comply with all the relevant labour Laws applicable to the Contractor's Personnel, including Laws relating to their employment (including wages and working hours), health, safety, welfare, immigration and emigration, and shall allow them all their legal rights.

The Contractor shall require the Contractor's Personnel to obey all applicable Laws, including those concerning health and safety at work.

21. If the Engineer is the one interested in recruiting, it would be prudent for it to obtain both Parties' prior written consent.
22. Assuming the Sub-Clause is legal under applicable law.
23. *See Guidance for the Preparation of Particular Conditions*, 29.

The Contractor must comply with all labour Laws applicable to the Contractor's Personnel and require the Contractor's Personnel to obey all applicable Laws.

Commentary

(i) Main Changes from RB/99:

(1) In the first paragraph, the parenthetical '(including wages and working hours)' has been inserted.
(2) Whereas Sub-Clause 6.4 of RB/99 had provided in the second paragraph that the Contractor requires its 'employees' to obey all applicable Laws, including those concerning 'safety' at work, the new Sub-Clause provides that the Contractor requires the 'Contractor's Personnel' to obey all applicable Laws, including those concerning 'health and safety' at work.

(ii) Related Clauses / Sub-Clauses: 1.13 [*Compliance with Laws*], 4.8 [*Health and Safety Obligations*], 6.2 [*Rates of Wages and Conditions of Labour*] and 6.7 [*Health and Safety of Personnel*].

(iii) Analysis: This Sub-Clause complements Sub-Clause 1.13 [*Compliance with Laws*], under which the Contractor is required to comply with all applicable Laws, and Sub-Clause 6.2 which requires the Contractor to pay rates of wages, and observe labour conditions, which comply with all applicable Laws.

(1) Contractor to comply with all labour Laws

The first paragraph requires the Contractor to comply with all labour Laws applicable to the Contractor's Personnel.[24] As the term 'Laws' is broadly defined to include legal norms of any country,[25] applicable labour Laws may be either the local labour Laws applicable in the Country or the labour Laws of a third country, whether of the Contractor or otherwise. In addition, as the term 'Laws' is defined to include 'international law' and 'treaties', it will include, for example, the Conventions of the ILO to the extent that these may apply.

24. 'Contractor's Personnel' is defined broadly to cover not only Contractor's staff but also staff and employees of each Subcontractor, as well as any other personnel assisting the Contractor in the execution of the Works. *See* Sub-Clause 1.1.17 **'Contractor's Personnel'**.
25. Sub-Clause 1.1.49 **'Laws'**.

The first paragraph also contains a non-exhaustive list of matters that may be the subject matter of these Laws, such as terms of employment, health, safety, welfare, immigration and emigration. Consequently, if the Contractor brings expatriate staff into the Country, it is responsible for ensuring that visas and work permits are issued to them.[26]

The Site may be located in a country whose social legislation does not afford the Contractor's expatriate employees the same degree of legal protection and benefits as they would enjoy in the country of the Contractor or their other country of origin. In those cases, the Contractor may engage them under employment contracts governed by the law of the Contractor's country. Even so, it must ensure that the terms of those contracts do not contravene local labour Laws, which are often of a mandatory nature and will thus necessarily (regardless of what an employment contract may provide) apply to anyone working in the Country. Some local Laws may contain mandatory requirements that foreign contractors use local labour.[27]

(2) Contractor to require compliance of Contractor's Personnel

Under the second paragraph, the Contractor must require the Contractor's Personnel to obey all applicable Laws, including those concerning health and safety. Unlike the first paragraph, this second paragraph is not limited to labour Laws. Therefore, the Contractor must require the Contractor's Personnel, which (as mentioned above) includes subcontractors, to obey all Laws applicable to them regardless of their subject matter.[28] While the Employer may have difficulties in proving the extent

26. Some standard forms contain explicit provisions concerning employment of expatriate staff. *See*, for example, Sub-Clause 28.6 of the *International Form of Contract – lump sum contracts* (1st edn, IChemE, 2007). The Contractor's obligations with regard to health and safety matters are dealt with in more detail in Sub-Clause 4.8 [*Health and Safety Obligations*] and Sub-Clause 6.7 [*Health and Safety of Personnel*]. *See* the commentaries on Sub-Clauses 4.8 and 6.7.
27. *See* **Section 5 Mandatory Law at the Site** of **Chapter II Applicable Law** above.
28. The heading of the Sub-Clause is 'Labour Laws' but, pursuant to Sub-Clause 1.2 [*Interpretation*], headings must not be taken into consideration in the interpretation of the Conditions.

of its loss resulting from the Contractor's non-compliance with Sub-Clause 6.4, it may, nevertheless, refer to it when resisting claims from the Contractor.[29]

(iv) Related Law: Prior to tender, a Contractor should have carefully investigated the 'Laws [...] and labour practices' of the Country,[30] certain of which are likely to be mandatory,[31] including those relating to health and safety. In addition, ILO Conventions deal with a wide range of labour matters such as wages, working time, migrant workers and occupational and safety issues, not to mention forced and child labour. Attention should be given to whether these Conventions have been ratified and are in effect in the States concerned. Whether or not ILO Conventions apply, ILO Recommendations should be looked to.

(v) Improvements: This Sub-Clause could be more explicit about the Contractor's obligations for ensuring that foreign workers and expatriate staff are in compliance with applicable Laws by providing something as follows:

> Foreign workers including expatriate staff employed by the Contractor and all relevant Subcontractors must be in possession of valid work permits, appropriate medical clearances, immigration and tax clearances and any permission that may be required for them to work at the Site or any other location where any part of the Works is being carried out [...] The Project Manager [the Engineer] shall have the right to require the Contractor to provide formal evidence that any foreign worker is in possession of the required documents and permissions prior to the worker being engaged upon the Works.[32]

--ooOOoo--

29. *The FIDIC Contracts Guide* (2nd edn, FIDIC, 2022) 241. '[R]iot, commotion or disorder' or 'strike or lockout' by the Contractor's Personnel are excluded from being Exceptional Events in Sub-Clause 18.1 [*Exceptional Events*], sub-paragraphs (c) and (d).
30. *See* Sub-Clause 4.10 (d).
31. *See* **Section 5 Mandatory Law at the Site** of **Chapter II Applicable Law** above.
32. Taken from Sub-Clause 28.6 of the *International Form of Contract – lump sum contracts* (1st edn, IChemE, 2007).

6.5 Working Hours

> No work shall be carried out on the Site on locally recognised days of rest, or outside the normal working hours stated in the Contract Data, unless:
>
> (a) otherwise stated in the Contract;
> (b) the Engineer gives consent; or
> (c) the work is unavoidable or necessary for the protection of life or property or for the safety of the Works, in which case the Contractor shall immediately give a Notice to the Engineer with reasons and describing the work required.

No work may be carried out on the Site on locally recognised days of rest, or outside the normal working hours stated in the Contract Data, unless: (a) otherwise stated in the Contract, (b) the Engineer consents, or (c) the work is unavoidable or necessary for the protection of life or property or for the safety of the Works.

Commentary

(i) Main Changes from RB/99: Whereas sub-paragraph (c) of Sub-Clause 6.5 of RB/99 had provided that where work on locally recognised days of rest or outside normal working hours was unavoidable or necessary for other reasons, the Contractor 'shall immediately advise the Engineer', the new Sub-Clause provides that the Contractor 'shall immediately give a Notice to the Engineer with reasons and describing the work required'.

(ii) Related Clauses / Sub-Clauses: 1.2 [*Interpretation*], 1.3 [*Notices and Other Communications*], 1.8 [*Care and Supply of Documents*], 1.13 [*Compliance with Laws*], 4.10 [*Use of Site Data*], 6.2 [*Rates of Wages and Conditions of Labour*], 6.4 [*Labour Laws*], 6.10 [*Contractor's Records*], 7.3 [*Inspection*], 8.3 [*Programme*], 8.7 [*Rate of Progress*] and 20.2.3 [*Contemporary Records*].

(iii) Analysis:

(1) Normal working hours

When preparing the tender dossier, the Employer may wish to specify the normal working hours on the Site in the Contract Data where provision for it is made. This may be especially desirable in the case of work on an existing operational facility.[33] Alternatively, the Employer may leave the Contract Data blank in this respect in the tender dossier and instead invite tenderers to complete it.

If the Employer does not specify the Contractor's working hours in the Contract Data, the Employer's Personnel may wish to know the Contractor's working hours on the Site in advance, so that they can plan and manage their activities accordingly.[34]

In practice, the normal working hours referred to in this Sub-Clause will apply principally or solely to local workers and staff and not to expatriate staff. Expatriate staff may work uninterruptedly for weeks or months without regard to normal working hours or locally recognised days of rest out of a preference to take their rest days on their trips to their home country.

(2) No work on days of rest

The prohibition of work on locally recognised days of rest applies only to work carried out 'on the Site' and thus will not apply to work carried out at other places where work or related activities are performed.[35] If the Parties want to extend this prohibition to all work carried out in the Country, they should state so explicitly in the Particular Conditions.

The provision for locally recognised days of rest is to respect the rights and/or religious traditions of local workers, which may be specified in local Laws or result from local custom or tradition. A tenderer is expected to have taken them into account when preparing its tender,[36] and the Contractor is required to allow for them in its initial and revised programmes.[37]

(3) Exceptions

Work on days of rest or outside normal working hours may be necessary for various reasons, e.g., large concrete pours which cannot be stopped, closing a river when building a dam and continuous testing of Plant. Such work may also become necessary because of an Engineer's instruction to the Contractor under Sub-Clause 8.7 to expedite progress. Therefore, the

33. *The FIDIC Contracts Guide* (2nd edn, FIDIC, 2022) 241.
34. *Ibid.*
35. For example 'additional areas' under Sub-Clause 4.22 [*Contractor's Operations on Site*] or the home office.
36. *See* Sub-Clause 4.10(d).
37. *See* Sub-Clause 8.3(h).

general prohibition of work outside normal working hours or days of rest is qualified by three exceptions: (a) the Contract states otherwise, (b) the Engineer gives its consent, or (c) the work is unavoidable or necessary for the protection of life or property or for the safety of the Works.

If it is known at the tender stage that some activities need to be carried out outside normal working hours, it is advisable to specify these activities in the Specification or the Contract Data. In this case, the Engineer's consent will not be required and the exception in sub-paragraph (a) will apply.[38]

What would constitute unavoidable or necessary work under sub-paragraph (c) will depend on the particular circumstances. If the Contractor considers that circumstances have arisen which require the carrying out of such work outside normal working hours or on days of rest, it must immediately give a Notice to the Engineer, with reasons, and describe the required work. The Engineer's consent is not required in this case – indeed, there may be no time for it – and the Contractor may proceed with the work.[39]

(iv) Related Law: Local labour laws will usually contain provisions dealing with working hours and may restrict the number of such hours per day or week or month. These laws will usually be mandatory in nature.[40] International legal instruments may also apply. For example, within the European Union, the Working Time Directive lays down minimum safety and health requirements for the organisation of working time and stipulates that the maximum weekly average working time (including overtime) must not exceed 48 hours.[41] There are at least seven ILO Conventions dealing with working time.[42]

---

38. Work outside normal working hours is also possible with the Engineer's consent under sub-para. (b), which must not be unreasonably withheld or delayed and must otherwise comply with Sub-Clause 1.3 [*Notices and Other Communications*].
39. A disagreement over whether the work in question has met the criteria in sub-para. (c) may give rise to a Claim under Sub-Clause 20.1(c).
40. *See* **Section 5 Mandatory Law at the Site** of **Chapter II Applicable Law** above.
41. Directive 2003/88/EC of the European Parliament and of the Council of 4 November 2003 concerning certain aspects of the organisation of working time. *See*, in particular, art. 6.
42. These are Convention Nos 1, 14, 30, 47,132, 171 and 175.

(v) Improvements: It might be considered whether the prohibition of work on locally recognised days of rest should apply to work carried out in areas within the Country which are not part of the Site.

--ooOOoo--

6.6 Facilities for Staff and Labour

> Except as otherwise stated in the Specification, the Contractor shall provide and maintain all necessary accommodation and welfare facilities for the Contractor's Personnel.
>
> If such accommodation and facilities are to be located on the Site, except where the Employer has given the Contractor prior permission, they shall be located within the areas identified in the Contract. If any such accommodation or facilities are found elsewhere within the Site, the Contractor shall immediately remove them at the Contractor's risk and cost. The Contractor shall also provide facilities for the Employer's Personnel as stated in the Specification.

Except as stated in the Specification, the Contractor must provide and maintain all necessary accommodation and welfare facilities for the Contractor's Personnel. If these are on the Site, they must be located within areas identified in the Contract. The Contractor must remove at its own risk and cost any facilities found elsewhere within the Site. The Contractor must also provide facilities for the Employer's Personnel as stated in the Specification.

Commentary

(i) Main Changes from RB/99:

(1) The second sentence of the first paragraph of Sub-Clause 6.6 of RB/99 providing that the Contractor shall provide facilities for the Employer's Personnel is now the last sentence of the new Sub-Clause.

(2) The second paragraph of the new Sub-Clause (except for the last sentence) is new.

(3) The second paragraph of Sub-Clause 6.6 of RB/99, providing that the Contractor shall not permit the maintenance of living quarters within the Permanent Works, has been deleted.

(ii) Related Clauses / Sub-Clauses: 4.1 [*Contractor's General Obligations*], 6.1 [*Engagement of Staff and Labour*] and 17.4 [*Indemnities by Contractor*].

(iii) Analysis:

This Sub-Clause complements Sub-Clause 6.1, which sets out the Contractor's general obligation to make arrangements for the Contractor's Personnel, including their accommodation and welfare.[43]

(1) Contractor's obligation to provide accommodation and welfare facilities

Under this Sub-Clause, the Contractor must provide and maintain 'all necessary'[44] accommodation and welfare facilities for the Contractor's Personnel, unless otherwise stated in the Specification. Consequently, if the Employer plans to make any facilities and/or accommodation available for the Contractor's use (e.g., office accommodation), it should so state, with relevant details, in the Specification included in the tender dossier.[45]

When tendering, the Contractor will need to decide for itself what 'accommodation and welfare facilities' are 'necessary' for the 'Contractor's Personnel'. Contractors from different countries and cultures will have different views on the subject, and each is free to decide for itself what may be 'necessary' in light of the composition of its staff and labour practices as well as those in the Country. However, what is clear from the first paragraph is that, unless the Specification states otherwise, the Contractor will be responsible for providing and maintaining all necessary accommodation and welfare facilities for the Contractor's Personnel and cannot claim on this account against the Employer.

---

43. *See* the commentary on Sub-Clause 6.1 above.
44. *See* the discussion of these words in the commentary on Sub-Clause 6.11 below. The same words are used also in Sub-Clauses 6.7 and 6.8.
45. *See* the *Guidance for the Preparation of Particular Conditions*, 29, 45-46. The *Guidance* also contains a suggested additional Sub-Clause, pursuant to which the Contractor takes full responsibility for the care of these facilities and/or accommodation from the date of use until the date of their return to the Employer.

(2) Location of accommodation and facilities

The second paragraph provides that, if accommodation and facilities are to be located on the Site, they must be located within areas identified in the Contract, unless the Employer has given permission otherwise. For example, the Contractor's Personnel cannot normally maintain living quarters within structures forming part of the Permanent Works. The Contractor must immediately remove at its own risk and cost any accommodation and/or facilities within the Site placed outside areas identified in the Contract or the areas for which the Employer has given permission.[46]

(3) Facilities, if any, for Employer's Personnel

According to the last sentence of the second paragraph, the Contractor must provide facilities for the Employer's Personnel as stated in the Specification. The Employer's Personnel is defined to include the Engineer and employees of the Engineer and of the Employer and any other personnel identified as Employer's Personnel by a Notice from the Employer or the Engineer to the Contractor.[47] It is quite common for the Contractor to have to provide facilities at least for the Engineer and its employees where both the Contractor and the Engineer are expatriates. On the other hand, the Employer, who will usually be from the Country, normally has no need for the Contractor to supply them, unless the Site is in a remote area.

(iv) Related Law: Local Laws may contain provisions regarding the type and level of accommodation and/or welfare facilities the Contractor is required to provide to its staff.

--ooOOoo--

46. The Employer's 'permission' is subject to Sub-Clause 1.3 [*Notices and Other Communications*] and must not be unreasonably withheld or delayed.
47. *See* Sub-Clause 1.1.33 '**Employer's Personnel**'. As the definition of the Employer's Personnel may include anyone identified by a Notice to the Contractor, and as such a provision must – like all Contract provisions – be interpreted reasonably, the Contractor might be entitled at some point to claim Cost and/or EOT if the Employer and/or the Engineer gives a Notice defining additional persons as Employer's Personnel after the Base Date. *See* Leo Grutters and Brian Barr, *FIDIC Red Yellow and Silver Books: A Practical Guide to the 2017 Editions* (Sweet & Maxwell, London, 2018) 143.

6.7 Health and Safety of Personnel

In addition to the requirements of Sub-Clause 4.8 [*Health and Safety Obligations*], the Contractor shall at all times take all necessary precautions to maintain the health and safety of the Contractor's Personnel. In collaboration with local health authorities, the Contractor shall ensure that:

(a) medical staff, first aid facilities, sick bay, ambulance services and any other medical services stated in the Specification are available at all times at the Site and at any accommodation for Contractor's and Employer's Personnel; and

(b) suitable arrangements are made for all necessary welfare and hygiene requirements and for the prevention of epidemics.

The Contractor shall appoint a health and safety officer at the Site, responsible for maintaining health, safety and protection against accidents. This officer shall:

(i) be qualified, experienced and competent for this responsibility; and

(ii) have the authority to issue directives for the purpose of maintaining the health and safety of all personnel authorised to enter and/or work on the Site and to take protective measures to prevent accidents.

Throughout the execution of the Works, the Contractor shall provide whatever is required by this person to exercise this responsibility and authority.

The Contractor must take all necessary precautions to maintain the health and safety of the Contractor's Personnel. The Contractor must ensure, in collaboration with local authorities, that medical staff and services stated in the Specification are available at all times at the Site and at any accommodation for Contractor's and Employer's Personnel and that suitable arrangements are made for welfare, hygiene and the prevention of epidemics.

The Contractor must appoint a health and safety officer at the Site who is responsible for maintaining health, safety and protection against accidents and authorised to issue directives and/or to take protective measures.

Commentary

(i) Main Changes from RB/99:

(1) It is now explicitly stated in the first paragraph that this Sub-Clause applies in addition to the requirements under Sub-Clause 4.8 [*Health and Safety Obligations*].

(2) The Contractor's obligation in the first paragraph of Sub-Clause 6.7 of RB/99 to take 'all reasonable precautions' to maintain health and safety has been replaced by an obligation to take 'all necessary precautions'.

(3) In addition to the medical staff, services and related facilities that the Contractor was required to provide under RB/99, according to sub-paragraph (a) of the new Sub-Clause, the Contractor must also ensure the availability of 'any other medical services stated in the Specification'.

(4) In the second paragraph of Sub-Clause 6.7 of RB/99, the 'accident prevention officer' at the Site has been replaced by a 'health and safety officer'; this person must be 'qualified, experienced and competent for this responsibility' and this person's responsibility includes maintaining the 'health' and not just 'safety' and protection against accidents of the personnel, as was the case in RB/99; and this person must have authority to issue 'directives for the purpose of maintaining the health and safety of all personnel' on the Site which, pursuant to Sub-Clause 4.8(c), the Contractor must itself now comply with.

(5) The last paragraph of Sub-Clause 6.7 of RB/99 has been deleted and replaced by the last two paragraphs in Sub-Clause 4.8 of RB/17.

(ii) Related Clauses / Sub-Clauses: 1.13 [*Compliance with Laws*], 4.8 [*Health and Safety Obligations*], 4.20 [*Progress Reports*], 6.1 [*Engagement of Staff and Labour*], 6.4 [*Labour Laws*], 6.6 [*Facilities for Staff and Labour*], 6.8 [*Contractor's Superintendence*], 6.9 [*Contractor's Personnel*] and 13.1 [*Right to Vary*].

(iii) Analysis:

(1) Dangers of international construction

A construction site can be a hazardous place where the risk of injury or death (e.g., from falling from a height, being struck by a falling object, falling in a manhole, or suffering a landslide or tunnel collapse) is ever-present. This may be especially the case in developing countries.[48]

Moreover, many international civil engineering projects are undertaken in places where the staff on a site may be more exposed to, or affected by, disease, epidemic, harsh working conditions, local violence or political instability.[49] This Sub-Clause, together with Sub-Clause 4.8 [*Health and Safety Obligations*][50] with which it should be read, is intended to ensure the protection of the health and safety of the Contractor's Personnel.

(2) Contractor's health and safety obligations

The first sentence of the Sub-Clause provides that, in addition to the requirements of Sub-Clause 4.8, the Contractor shall 'take all *necessary* precautions to maintain' (emphasis added) the health and safety of the

48. For example, in a 2015 publication it was reported that: '[s]ince 2012, almost 900 worker deaths were reported in Qatari infrastructure construction projects. The International Trade Union Confederation stated that if the conditions did not get any better, at least 4,000 construction workers fatality (sic) are expected by the time the World Cup kicks off [in 2022]'. Ahmed Senouci, Ibrahim Al-Abbadi and Neil Eldin, 'Safety Improvement on Building Construction Sites in Qatar' (2015) 123 Procedia Engineering 504-509 available at https://www.sciencedirect.com/science/article/pii/S1877705815032038 accessed 10 November 2022. By 2021, more than 6,500 migrant workers were reported to have died in Qatar since it won the right to host the World Cup in December 2010. *The Guardian*, 23 February 2021.
49. However, working conditions today are generally much safer, thankfully, than the extremely harsh conditions of the past. For example: (1) in the unsuccessful French attempt to build the Panama Canal in the 1880s, over five thousand French people and over twenty-five thousand people in all died, primarily from malaria and yellow fever (Bernard G Dennis (ed), *Engineering the Panama Canal: A Centennial Retrospective* (American Society of Civil Engineers, Reston, Virginia, 2014) 31-32); and (2) in the construction of the 600-mile Mombasa to Nairobi railway in Kenya around 1900, over one hundred workers were killed by lions alone (Charles Miller, *The Lunatic Express* (Head of Zeus, London 2016), xviii).
50. *See* the commentary on Sub-Clause 4.8 above.

Contractor's Personnel, which is a more stringent standard than to take 'all *reasonable* precautions to maintain' (emphasis added) in RB/99.[51]

The next sentence then provides that '[i]n collaboration with local health authorities, the Contractor shall ensure' that the services described in sub-paragraphs (a) and (b) will be available to Contractor's and Employer's Personnel. Sub-paragraph (a) specifies particular medical services and facilities which the Contractor is to provide, adding that they are to include any other medical services stated in the Specification. Sub-paragraph (b) then provides that the Contractor must ensure that suitable arrangements are made for all necessary welfare and hygiene requirements and for the prevention of epidemics (e.g., adequate supply of drinking water, sufficient number of sanitary premises, measures against insect infestation). What is suitable will likely depend on the type of works carried out, the number of personnel engaged and the location of the Site (e.g., in certain countries the risk of epidemics may be significantly higher than in others).[52]

As mentioned above, the provision of the services described in sub-paragraphs (a) and (b) is to be done in collaboration with local health authorities. Thus, if the local health authorities can provide a satisfactory nearby hospital, it should be unnecessary for the Contractor to do so, as it is not required to duplicate services available locally. On the other hand, if there are no local health authorities or they are inadequate to permit the Contractor to fulfil its obligation in the first sentence to 'at all times take all necessary precautions to maintain the health and safety of the Contractor's Personnel', then the Contractor must make up the shortfall, which could mean providing a fully equipped hospital.[53]

(3) Health and safety officer

The Contractor is also required to appoint a 'health and safety officer' at the Site who is responsible for 'maintaining health, safety and protection

51. It implies that the Contractor will take the measures that are sufficient to maintain health and safety, making the Contractor almost a guarantor towards the Employer of the health and safety of the Contractor's Personnel.
52. If an 'epidemic' causes Unforeseeable (as defined) shortages in the availability of personnel or Goods that delay or will delay completion of the Works, the Contractor may be able to claim, subject to Sub-Clause 20.2, an EOT. *See* Sub-Clause 8.5(d).
53. *The FIDIC Contracts Guide* (2nd edn, FIDIC, 2022) 244.

against accidents'.[54] This officer must be 'qualified, experienced and competent', the precise meaning of which should be clarified in the Specification. The officer is authorised to issue 'directives' (these being 'official or authoritative instruction[s]'[55]) concerning health and safety matters for the protection of all personnel who may enter on the Site (including the Employer's Personnel) and the Contractor itself is required to comply with them.[56] The officer is authorised to revise, as necessary, the health and safety manual for the Works which the Contractor will have submitted to the Engineer before commencing construction.[57] The Contractor is also required to provide this officer with 'whatever is required' by this person to exercise its authority.[58] As the actions of the officer may impact the day-to-day execution of the Works, it is recommended that all involved, including all Site personnel, the Engineer and its staff, are duly informed about the authority and identity of this officer.[59]

(4) Reporting health statistics

As part of its progress reports under Sub-Clause 4.20 [*Progress Reports*], the Contractor is also obliged to report health and safety statistics, including details of any hazardous incidents and activities.[60] In addition, the Contractor must submit to the Engineer details of any accident that has occurred, as well as maintain records and make reports concerning the health and safety of persons and any damage to property.[61]

(iv) Related Law: Local laws will usually contain detailed provisions of a mandatory nature concerning health and safety matters.[62] Among other things, the Safety and Health in Construction Convention, 1988 (No. 167), of the International Labour Organisation ('ILO'), which has been

54. This officer falls within the definition of **Contractor's Personnel**. *See* Sub-Clause 1.1.17.
55. *Concise Oxford English Dictionary* (10th edn, rev'd, OUP, Oxford, 2002).
56. *See* Sub-Clause 4.8(c).
57. *See* Sub-Clause 4.8, third from last paragraph.
58. Sub-Clause 6.7, last paragraph.
59. Leo Grutters and Brian Barr, *FIDIC Red Yellow and Silver Books: A Practical Guide to the 2017 Editions* (Sweet & Maxwell, London, 2018) 144.
60. *See* Sub-Clause 4.20(g).
61. *See* Sub-Clause 4.8 [*Health and Safety Obligations*], last two paragraphs.
62. *See* **Section 5 Mandatory Law at the Site** of **Chapter II Applicable Law** above.

ratified by more than 30 countries, regulates a number of the matters addressed in this Sub-Clause.

--ooOOoo--

6.8 Contractor's Superintendence

From the Commencement Date until the issue of the Performance Certificate, the Contractor shall provide all necessary superintendence to plan, arrange, direct, manage, inspect, test and monitor the execution of the Works.

Superintendence shall be given by a sufficient number of persons:

(a) who are fluent in or have adequate knowledge of the language for communications (defined in Sub-Clause 1.4 [*Law and Language*]); and

(b) who have adequate knowledge of the operations to be carried out (including the methods and techniques required, the hazards likely to be encountered and methods of preventing accidents),

for the satisfactory and safe execution of the Works.

From the Commencement Date until the issue of the Performance Certificate, the Contractor must provide all necessary superintendence for the execution of the Works. The superintendence must be given by a sufficient number of persons who have the knowledge required by sub-paragraphs (a) and (b).

Commentary

(i) Main Changes from RB/99:

(1) Unlike Sub-Clause 6.8 of RB/99, which envisaged that the Contractor must provide necessary superintendence '[t]hroughout the execution of the Works, and as long thereafter as is necessary to fulfil the Contractor's obligations', the new Sub-Clause provides that such superintendence must be provided '[f]rom the Commencement Date until the issue of the Performance Certificate'.

(2) The Contractor has an additional obligation to 'monitor the execution of the Works'.

(3) Whereas RB/99 had provided that superintendents be persons 'having adequate knowledge of the language for communications', sub-paragraph (a) of the new Sub-Clause requires that they 'are fluent in or have adequate knowledge of the language for communications'.

(ii) Related Clauses / Sub-Clauses: 1.4 [*Law and Language*], 4.1 [*Contractor's General Obligations*], 4.3 [*Contractor's Representative*], 6.7 [*Health and Safety Personnel*], 6.9 [*Contractor's Personnel*], 6.12 [*Key Personnel*], 8.1 [*Commencement of Works*] and 11.9 [*Performance Certificate*].

(iii) Analysis:

(1) The meaning of superintendence

Under this Sub-Clause, which may usefully be read together with Sub-Clause 4.3 [*Contractor's Representative*], the Contractor must provide 'all necessary superintendence'[63] of the execution of the Works from the Commencement Date until issue of the Performance Certificate. The necessary superintendence is 'to plan, arrange, direct, manage, inspect, test and monitor the execution of the Works'. This superintendence must be given by 'a sufficient number of persons' having the qualifications in sub-paragraphs (a) and (b).

As in the case of Sub-Clause 6.2, the intention here, as this is a standard form of contract and individual situations will vary, is to lay down general principles of how the Contractor should be conducting itself in supervising the execution of the Works. The Contractor should be the best judge, in the first instance, of what degree of superintendence of its staff is 'necessary' and of how many persons will be 'sufficient' to provide it as no one will know the Contractor's workforce or work methods better. If the Contractor executes the Works satisfactorily, no question is likely to arise as to whether it has provided the 'necessary superintendence' and done so with a 'sufficient number of persons'.

63. The verb 'superintend' means to 'act as superintendent of' and the noun 'superintendent' means 'a person who supervises or is in charge of an organisation, department, etc.', *Concise Oxford English Dictionary* (10th edn, rev'd, OUP, Oxford, 2002).

On the other hand, for example, if issues of quality with its work arise or it is unable to adhere to its Programme or the Contractor's Personnel engage in dangerous or improper work practices, then the Engineer may require the Contractor to justify that it has provided 'all necessary superintendence' and done so with 'a sufficient number of persons'. The Engineer may then, if necessary, instruct the Contractor to change its work practices and/or submit a revised programme to expedite progress.[64]

(2) The required knowledge of superintendents

The superintending staff are to be 'fluent in or have adequate knowledge of the language for communications' in Sub-Clause 1.4 [*Law and Language*][65] and to have 'adequate knowledge' of the operations to be carried out including the methods and techniques required and methods of preventing accidents. This does not mean that the superintendents should have necessarily carried out the same operations before, but they must have sufficient knowledge to permit satisfactory and safe execution of the Works.

--ooOOoo--

6.9 Contractor's Personnel

The Contractor's Personnel (including Key Personnel, if any) shall be appropriately qualified, skilled, experienced and competent in their respective trades or occupations.

The Engineer may require the Contractor to remove (or cause to be removed) any person employed on the Site or Works, including the Contractor's Representative and Key Personnel (if any), who:

(a) persists in any misconduct or lack of care;
(b) carries out duties incompetently or negligently;
(c) fails to comply with any provision of the Contract;

64. For example, under Sub-Clause 3.5 [*Engineer's Instructions*], or Sub-Clause 8.7 [*Rate of Progress*].
65. The *Guidance* contains suggested amendments to the Sub-Clause for where the superintending staff have insufficient knowledge of the language for communications or if fluency in a particular language is required. *Guidance for the Preparation of Particular Conditions*, 29-30.

(d) persists in any conduct which is prejudicial to safety, health, or the protection of the environment;
(e) is found, based on reasonable evidence, to have engaged in corrupt, fraudulent, collusive or coercive practice; or
(f) has been recruited from the Employer's Personnel in breach of Sub-Clause 6.3 [*Recruitment of Persons*].

If appropriate, the Contractor shall then promptly appoint (or cause to be appointed) a suitable replacement. In the case of replacement of the Contractor's Representative, Sub-Clause 4.3 [*Contractor's Representative*] shall apply. In the case of replacement of Key Personnel (if any), Sub-Clause 6.12 [*Key Personnel*] shall apply.

The Contractor's Personnel must be appropriately qualified, skilled, experienced and competent in their respective trades or occupations. The Engineer may require the Contractor to remove any person on the Site in the cases in sub-paragraphs (a) to (f). If appropriate, the Contractor must appoint a suitable replacement.

Commentary

(i) Main Changes from RB/99:

(1) In the first paragraph, it is now specified that Contractor's Personnel includes Key Personnel, if any.
(2) The list of grounds that entitle the Engineer to require the removal of any person on the Site has been expanded to include engagement in corrupt or similar practices (sub-paragraph (e)) and recruitment from Employer's Personnel in breach of Sub-Clause 6.3 [*Recruitment of Persons*] (sub-paragraph (f)).
(3) The last two sentences of the Sub-Clause are new.

(ii) Related Clauses / Sub-Clauses: 4.1 [*Contractor's General Obligations*], 4.3 [*Contractor's Representative*], 4.18 [*Protection of the Environment*], 6.1 [*Engagement of Staff and Labour*], 6.3 [*Recruitment of Persons*], 6.4 [*Labour Laws*], 6.8 [*Contractor's Superintendence*], 6.11 [*Disorderly Conduct*], 6.12 [*Key Personnel*] and 15.2 [*Termination for Contractor's Default*].

(iii) Analysis: Understandably, this Sub-Clause requires that the Contractor's Personnel, who are broadly defined,[66] shall be appropriately qualified and otherwise competent in their respective trades or occupations.[67]

(1) Grounds for removal

The Engineer may require the removal of 'any person employed on the Site or Works, including the Contractor's Representative and Key Personnel (if any)' upon any of the grounds specified in sub-paragraphs (a) to (f).[68] This would include an employee of a Subcontractor, whether nominated or not, as Subcontractors are included within the definition of Contractor's Personnel.[69] While the list of grounds is broad, it is also exhaustive – the Engineer may not require the removal of Contractor's Personnel on grounds different from those specified. All grounds, except possibly for sub-paragraph (f), presuppose some form of default or misbehaviour by the person in question, such as, persistence in misconduct or lack of care, carrying out of duties incompetently or negligently, failure to comply with a Contract provision and persistent conduct prejudicial to health and safety.

Sub-paragraph (e) authorises the Engineer to require the removal of a person who 'is found, based on reasonable evidence, to have engaged in corrupt, fraudulent, collusive or coercive practice'. This gives rise to the following questions: (i) who is to find that the person has engaged in such practices (e.g., the Employer, the Engineer, the DAAB, a competent court, public prosecutor(s) or other entities and/or persons); (ii) what would constitute 'reasonable evidence'; and (iii) what would constitute 'corrupt, fraudulent, collusive or coercive practice'? Unfortunately, the Conditions do not answer these questions.[70] A finding that the Contractor has engaged in corrupt or similar practices – and not merely a person among the Contractor's Personnel – may also entitle the Employer to terminate the Contract with immediate effect under Sub-Clause 15.2 [*Termination for Contractor's Default*].[71]

66. *See* Sub-Clause 1.1.17 **'Contractor's Personnel'**.
67. Sub-Clause 6.9, first paragraph.
68. Sub-Clause 6.9, second paragraph.
69. *See* Sub-Clause 1.1.78 **'Subcontractor'**.
70. *See* the commentary on Sub-Clause 15.2.1(h) below which includes similar language.
71. *See* Sub-Clauses 15.2.1(h) and 15.2.2.

Sub-paragraph (f) allows the Engineer to require the removal of a person recruited from the Employer's Personnel in breach of Sub-Clause 6.3, but not a person recruited from the Contractor's Personnel, although this would also be a breach of Sub-Clause 6.3.

(2) The Engineer must act reasonably

While the Sub-Clause does not require the Engineer to state its reasons for such a removal, the Engineer must act reasonably and be able to justify its action, if necessary, on one of the grounds in sub-paragraphs (a) through (f).[72] Assuming the Engineer requires the removal by an instruction under Sub-Clause 3.5 [*Engineer's Instructions*], the Contractor must comply.[73] If the Contractor disagrees, it may assert a Claim under Sub-Clause 20.1(c) and be entitled to compensation if it can demonstrate that the request for removal was unfounded.[74] However, it would be preferable for the Parties to agree on the removal of a person so that action by the Engineer would be a last resort.[75]

The last paragraph deals with the appointment of a suitable replacement, if a replacement is 'appropriate'. The criterion of appropriateness is an objective one; that is, it depends on whether there is a real need in the particular circumstances and not solely on the Contractor's subjective or personal view of whether a replacement is necessary.

--ooOOoo--

72. An unreasonable and unfounded removal may entitle the Contractor to compensation. *The FIDIC Contracts Guide* (2nd edn, FIDIC, 2022) 247.
73. *See* Sub-Clause 3.5 ('[...] the Contractor shall comply with the instructions given by the Engineer [...]').
74. *The FIDIC Contracts Guide* (2nd edn, FIDIC, 2022) 247. Unlike Sub-Clause 6.9, the notice of the contract administrator requiring the removal of a person from the Contractor's Personnel is stated in some standard forms to be final, conclusive, binding, and not capable of being revised in arbitration or other proceedings. *See* Sub-Clause 28.4 of the *International Form of Contract – lump sum contracts* (1st edn, IChemE, 2007). While RB/17 does not provide for this remedy in this case, it does, by contrast, provide that in the case of an appointment of a DAAB member by an appointing official, pursuant to Sub-Clause 21.2, the appointment shall be 'final and conclusive'.
75. *The FIDIC Contracts Guide* (2nd edn, FIDIC, 2022) 247.

(iv) Improvements:

(1) For the reasons given under **(iii) Analysis** above, the ground for removal for corrupt and similar practices in sub-paragraph (e) gives rise to many questions that should be clarified.

(2) In the cases described in sub-paragraphs (a) through (f), it should be clarified whether removal of the person concerned is the sole remedy of the Employer or is without prejudice to any other rights which the Employer may have.

--ooOOoo--

6.10 Contractor's Records

Unless otherwise proposed by the Contractor and agreed by the Engineer, in each progress report under Sub-Clause 4.20 [*Progress Reports*], the Contractor shall include records of:

(a) occupations and actual working hours of each class of Contractor's Personnel;
(b) the type and actual working hours of each of the Contractor's Equipment;
(c) the types of Temporary Works used;
(d) the types of Plant installed in the Permanent Works; and
(e) the quantities and types of Materials used

for each work activity shown in the Programme, at each work location and for each day of work.

Unless the Engineer agrees otherwise, each progress report under Sub-Clause 4.20 must include records of the matters specified in sub-paragraphs (a) to (e) for each work activity shown in the Programme, at each work location and for each day of work.

Commentary

(i) Main Changes from RB/99:

(1) Whereas Sub-Clause 6.10 of RB/99 treated the submission of the Contractor's records to the Engineer as a separate obligation of the Contractor from its obligation to report under Sub-Clause

4.21 [*Progress Reports*] of RB/99, the new Sub-Clause provides that, unless otherwise agreed by the Engineer, the Contractor's records are to be submitted as part of its progress reports under Sub-Clause 4.20 [*Progress Reports*].

(2) The scope of the Contractor's records has been significantly expanded to include:

(i) not merely the number of each class of Contractor's Personnel but the occupations and actual working hours of each such class;

(ii) not merely the number of each type of Contractor's Equipment on the Site but the actual working hours of each of the Contractor's Equipment; and

(iii) information about types of Temporary Works and Plant installed as well as quantities and types of Materials.[76]

(3) Unlike RB/99, the new Sub-Clause states that the records should include the relevant information for each work activity in the Programme, at each work location and for each day of work.

(ii) Related Clauses / Sub-Clauses: 1.2 [*Interpretation*], 1.3 [*Notices and Other Communications*], 1.8 [*Care and Supply of Documents*], 4.17 [*Contractor's Equipment*], 4.20 [*Progress Reports*], 6.9 [*Contractor's Personnel*], 8.3 [*Programme*], 13.5 [*Daywork*], 14.5 [*Plant and Materials Intended for the Works*], 20.2.3 [*Claims for Payment and/or EOT – Contemporary Records*] and 20.2.4 [*Claims for Payment and/or EOT – Fully Detailed Claim*].

(iii) Analysis:

(1) The importance of records

This Sub-Clause is of great importance as the Contractor must prepare, keep, maintain and, at the proper time, submit specified records if it is to get paid and otherwise assert its rights, whether for additional payment, EOT or otherwise under the Contract. Among other things, it must keep contemporary records under Sub-Clause 20.2.3 [*Contemporary Records*] necessary to substantiate its Claims.[77] If the Contractor fails to do so, a

76. For this reason, the title of the Sub-Clause has been changed from 'Records of Contractor's Personnel and Equipment' to 'Contractor's Records'.

77. Under Sub-Clause 20.2.3, 'contemporary records' are defined as records 'prepared or generated at the same time, or immediately after, the event or circumstance giving rise to the Claim' which corresponds to the one in the *Falkland Islands* case discussed in the commentary on Sub-Clause 20.2.3

Claim may be reduced or rejected if the 'failure has prevented or prejudiced proper investigation of the Claim by the Engineer'.[78] The Contractor's records may also be required for the evaluation of Variations.[79]

(2) Requirement to submit records with progress reports

Under this Sub-Clause, specific records relating to the Contractor's Personnel, Contractor's Equipment and work must be submitted as part of the Contractor's monthly progress reports under Sub-Clause 4.20 [*Progress Reports*].[80] Therefore, this Sub-Clause should be read together with Sub-Clause 4.20, which deals with the format and content of these reports which, among other things, must accompany the Contractor's applications for interim payment under Sub-Clause 14.3.[81]

The records in this Sub-Clause must contain the information listed in sub-paragraphs (a) to (e), such as the occupations and actual working hours of the Contractor's Personnel, the types and actual working hours of the Contractor's Equipment, the types of Temporary Works and Plant installed and the quantity and types of Materials used. This list is non-exhaustive.[82] Therefore, the Contractor should discuss and agree with the Engineer on an exhaustive list as early as possible in order to avoid later disagreements about the range and scope of the records to be submitted.[83] The Contractor's records must be detailed enough to reflect the above information with regard to each work activity in the Programme, at each work location (which may be on- or off-Site) and for each day of work.

[*Contemporary Records*] below. There is, however, no requirement in Sub-Clause 6.10 that the records should comprise contemporary records only.

78. *See* Sub-Clause 20.2.7 [*General requirements*], last paragraph, and the commentary on it below.
79. *See* Sub-Clause 13.3 [*Variation Procedure*] and *The FIDIC Contracts Guide* (2nd edn, FIDIC, 2022) 248.
80. *See* the commentary on Sub-Clause 4.20 above.
81. *See* sub-para. (c) of Sub-Clause 14.3 [*Application for Interim Payment*].
82. *See* paragraph (h) of Sub-Clause 1.2 [*Interpretation*].
83. Leo Grutters and Brian Barr, *FIDIC Red Yellow and Silver Books: A Practical Guide to the 2017 Editions* (Sweet & Maxwell, London, 2018) 147.

(3) Inspection by Employer's Personnel

The Contractor must keep a copy of these records at all times on the Site and the Employer's Personnel has a right of access to them during normal business hours or otherwise as agreed with the Contractor.[84]

(iv) Improvements:

(1) The list of records in this Sub-Clause could be supplemented by records of the names of the Subcontractors on the Site and the nature of their work.

(2) Details of the form which records should take could be provided,[85] such as that they include the contract title and any contract identification number, identify the topic to be covered and use as vocabulary the defined terms in the Conditions.

--ooOOoo--

6.11 Disorderly Conduct

> The Contractor shall at all times take all necessary precautions to prevent any unlawful, riotous or disorderly conduct by or amongst the Contractor's Personnel, and to preserve peace and protection of persons and property on and near the Site.

The Contractor shall at all times take all necessary precautions to prevent disorderly conduct among the Contractor's Personnel, and protect persons and property on or near the Site.

Commentary

(i) Main Changes from RB/99: Unlike Sub-Clause 6.11 of RB/99, which required the Contractor to take 'all reasonable precautions' to prevent disorderly conduct, the new Sub-Clause requires that the Contractor take 'all necessary precautions'.

(ii) Related Clauses / Sub-Clauses: 1.13 [*Compliance with Laws*], 4 [*The Contractor*], 6.4 [*Labour Laws*], 6.8 [*Contractor's Superintendence*], 6.9

84. Sub-paragraph (b) of Sub-Clause 1.8 [*Care and Supply of Documents*].
85. Beyond what is provided for a 'record' in Sub-Clause 1.3.

[*Contractor's Personnel*], 17.4 [*Indemnities by Contractor*], 18.1 [*Exceptional Events*] and 19.2.4 [*Insurance to Be provided by the Contractor – Injury to Persons and Damage to Property*].

(iii) Analysis:

(1) Purpose of Sub-Clause

The Contractor's Personnel on or near the Site may comprise hundreds or thousands of persons, possibly of mixed nationalities and cultures, speaking different languages and coming from different countries. Having engaged the Contractor and perhaps assisted in bringing it to the Country, the Employer may have legal responsibility for the conduct of the Contractor's Personnel in the Country. Consequently, for this and other reasons, the Contractor is required to agree with the Employer to prevent their misconduct. This means that, as between the Employer and the Contractor, the Contractor is responsible for their behaviour.

(2) The Contractor's responsibility under Sub-Clause

Under this Sub-Clause, the Contractor agrees to take 'all *necessary* precautions to prevent' (emphasis added) any unlawful, riotous or disorderly conduct by or among the Contractor's Personnel as well as to preserve peace and protection of persons and property on or near the Site. Compared to RB/99, which required the Contractor to take merely 'all *reasonable* precautions to prevent' (emphasis added) such misconduct, the new Sub-Clause imposes a more stringent obligation. If any misconduct should occur, the Employer may claim that the Contractor has evidently not taken 'all *necessary* precautions' as, had it done so, the misconduct would have been prevented. Previously the Contractor could have maintained that it had taken all precautions that were 'reasonable' and did not assure against misconduct occurring.[86]

Breach of this Sub-Clause may, depending on the circumstances, result in claims against the Contractor under, among others, Sub-Clauses, 4.14 [*Avoidance of Interference*] and 17.4 [*Indemnities by Contractor*]. In addition, disorderly conduct by a person among the Contractor's Personnel may result in that person's removal from the Site under Sub-Clause

86. In Clause 6 [*Staff and Labour*], the 'all necessary' formulation of words is also to be found in Sub-Clauses 6.6 ('all necessary accommodation'), 6.7 ('all necessary precautions') and 6.8 ('all necessary superintendence').

6.9 [*Contractor's Personnel*] and is excluded from being an Exceptional Event under Sub-Clause 18.1 [*Exceptional Events*].[87]

(iv) Related Law: Disorderly conduct among the Contractor's Personnel may also result in tort and possible criminal liability for the Contractor and/or the Employer under applicable Laws if it causes injury to persons and/or damages property.[88]

--ooOOOoo--

6.12 Key Personnel

If no Key Personnel are stated in the Specification this Sub-Clause shall not apply.

The Contractor shall appoint the natural persons named in the Tender to the positions of Key Personnel. If not so named, or if an appointed person fails to act in the relevant position of Key Personnel, the Contractor shall submit to the Engineer for consent the name and particulars of another person the Contractor proposes to appoint to such position. If consent is withheld or subsequently revoked, the Contractor shall similarly submit the name and particulars of a suitable replacement for such position.

If the Engineer does not respond within 14 days after receiving any such submission, by giving a Notice stating his/her objection to the appointment of such person (or replacement) with reasons, the Engineer shall be deemed to have given his/her consent.

The Contractor shall not, without the Engineer's prior consent, revoke the appointment of any of the Key Personnel or appoint a replacement (unless the person is unable to act as a result of death, illness, disability or resignation, in which case the appointment shall be deemed to have been revoked with immediate effect and the appointment of a replacement shall be treated as a temporary appointment

87. *See* Sub-Clause 18.1(c).
88. The applicable law is likely to be the law of the country where the tort or criminal act occurred. *See* **Section 5 Mandatory Law at the Site** of **Chapter II Applicable Law** above.

until the Engineer gives his/her consent to this replacement, or another replacement is appointed, under this Sub-Clause).

All Key Personnel shall be based at the Site (or, where Works are being executed off the Site, at the location of the Works) for the whole time that the Works are being executed. If any of the Key Personnel is to be temporarily absent during execution of the Works, a suitable replacement shall be temporarily appointed, subject to the Engineer's prior consent.

All Key Personnel shall be fluent in the language for communications defined in Sub-Clause 1.4 [*Law and Language*].

This Sub-Clause does not apply if no Key Personnel are stated in the Specification. The Contractor shall appoint the natural persons named in the Tender as Key Personnel and obtain the Engineer's consent for the appointment of any other person as a Key Personnel. The Engineer is deemed to have consented if it does not respond within 14 days.

The Contractor shall not, without the Engineer's consent, revoke the appointment of any Key Personnel or appoint a replacement, unless the person is unable to act, in which case the appointment will be deemed revoked and a replacement will be treated as temporary until the Engineer gives its consent.

All Key Personnel shall be based at the Site. If any Key Personnel is to be temporarily absent, a suitable replacement shall be temporarily appointed, subject to the Engineer's prior consent. All Key Personnel must be fluent in the language for communications.

Commentary

(i) Main Changes from RB/99: This is an entirely new Sub-Clause in RB/17. No such provision was contained in either RB/99 or GB/08.

(ii) Related Clauses / Sub-Clauses: 1.2 [*Interpretation*], 1.3 [*Notices and Other Communications*], 1.4 [*Law and Language*], 4.3 [*Contractor's Representative*], 4.9.1 [*Quality Management System*] and 6.9 [*Contractor's Personnel*].

(iii) Analysis:

(1) Purpose of Sub-Clause

Key Personnel are defined as the positions, if any, 'of the Contractor's Personnel, other than the Contractor's Representative, that are specified in the Specification'.[89] Where the Employer believes that supervisory staff having particular knowledge or experience are necessary to execute the Works, it may require in the Specification that tenderers propose supervisors having these qualifications, that is, Key Personnel. If the Employer requires the Contractor to have a Quality Manager employed on the Site, such position should be stated in the Specification as a Key Personnel position.[90]

(2) Appointment and revocation of Key Personnel

Assuming the Specification provides positions for Key Personnel, a tenderer (the future Contractor) is obliged to appoint to those positions the natural persons proposed for them in its Tender. As a precaution, when preparing the Tender, a tenderer may wish to name an alternative individual in case a preferred person becomes unavailable during the tender period. As the Employer will already have agreed to those named in the Tender when entering into the Contract, the Engineer's later consent should not be required.

If the Contractor intends to appoint to a Key Personnel position a person who is not so named or to replace an appointed person who fails to act, the Contractor must submit the name and particulars of this person to the Engineer for its consent.[91] If the Engineer objects to the appointment, it must provide reasons,[92] and will be deemed to have consented if it fails to respond within 14 days.[93]

The fourth paragraph deals with the revocation of the appointment of any of the Key Personnel or the appointment of a replacement, and makes

89. *See* Sub-Clause 1.1.48 '**Key Personnel**'. The Contractor's Representative is excluded from the definition of Key Personnel as Sub-Clause 4.3 [*Contractor's Representative*] contains detailed (albeit similar) provisions regulating its position.
90. *See Guidance for the Preparation of Particular Conditions*, 24.
91. Sub-Clause 6.12, second paragraph. This submission must comply with Sub-Clause 1.3 [*Notices and Other Communications*] and the Engineer's consent may not be unreasonably withheld or delayed.
92. Sub-Clause 6.12, third paragraph.
93. *Ibid.*

these subject to the Engineer's prior consent. Much of the wording is similar to the second paragraph but, unlike the second paragraph, the fourth paragraph allows for a temporary appointment of a replacement if the appointed person is unable to act due to death, illness, disability or resignation. The replacement's appointment will cease to be temporary once the Engineer consents to it, or another replacement is appointed under this Sub-Clause.

(3) Requirement for Key Personnel to be at Site

All Key Personnel are required to be based at the Site (or other off the Site locations where Works are being executed) 'for the whole time that the Works are being executed'.[94] The 'execution of the Works' covers not only the construction and completion of the Works but also the remedying of any defects, including during the DNP.[95] Temporary absences during these periods are possible provided that a suitable replacement has been temporarily appointed subject to the Engineer's prior consent.

(iv) Related Law:

A contract otherwise based on YB/99 had provided that the contractor 'shall employ key personnel as proposed in the Tender [...] and shall retain them for the entire duration of the Contract' subject to monetary penalties if this obligation was breached. An exemption applied where replacement was necessary 'for [...] reasons beyond the Contractor's control (e.g. resignation, illness, death, etc.)'. The contractor submitted statements from several key personnel to the effect that due to 'personal and family reasons' – 'without making any further remarks' – they had all to be replaced. The arbitral tribunal found that 'this general and impersonal wording does not meet the requirements' of the exemption and that the contractor's reasons 'must be objective and must be proved in substance so that they can be checked by the Employer and the Engineer'. Accordingly, the monetary penalties applied. Final award, ICC case 23492 (2022) (unpublished).

(v) Improvements:

(1) What is missing from the Sub-Clause is a requirement that the Contractor shall use all reasonable endeavours, at least, to ensure that Key Personnel remain employed in their designated positions for so long as the Works require.

94. Sub-Clause 6.12, fifth paragraph.
95. Under sub-para. (j) of Sub-Clause 1.2 [*Interpretation*].

(2) The requirement that all Key Personnel be based on the Site (or at an off-Site location where the Works are being executed) for the whole time that the Works are being executed may be too onerous, given that, as a result of modern communications, it is not uncommon today that key staff are able to operate from the Contractor's home office, provided they visit the Site regularly. Also, whether Key Personnel need to be based permanently at the Site may depend upon their particular qualifications and skills.

--ooOOoo--

7 Plant, Materials and Workmanship

This Clause provides for: the manner in which the Contractor is to execute the Works; the obligation of the Contractor to submit samples of Materials to the Engineer; the inspection of the Contractor's work by the Employer's Personnel; and its testing by the Contractor in the presence of the Engineer. It further provides procedures for dealing with defects in Plant, Materials, Contractor's design or workmanship which arise during the execution of the Works; when ownership of Plant and Materials is transferred from the Contractor to the Employer; and the Contractor's obligation to pay royalties for natural Materials obtained outside the Site and for the disposal of material from demolitions and excavations.

--ooOOoo--

7.1 Manner of Execution

The Contractor shall carry out the manufacture, supply, installation, testing and commissioning and/or repair of Plant, the production, manufacture, supply and testing of Materials, and all other operations and activities during the execution of the Works:

(a) in the manner (if any) specified in the Contract;
(b) in a proper workmanlike and careful manner, in accordance with recognised good practice; and
(c) with properly equipped facilities and non-hazardous Materials, except as otherwise specified in the Contract.

The Contractor must carry out the manufacture, installation and/or repair of Plant, the production and supply of Materials, and all other operations, in the manner specified in the Contract, in a proper workmanlike manner, in accordance with good practice, and with properly equipped facilities and non-hazardous Materials.

Commentary

(i) Main Changes from RB/99:

(1) Whereas Sub-Clause 7.1 of RB/99 simply required the Contractor to carry out the 'manufacture' of Plant in the manner specified in the Contract and properly, the new Sub-Clause requires the Contractor to carry out the 'manufacture, supply, installation, testing and commissioning and/or repair of Plant' in the manner specified in the Contract and properly.

(2) Whereas Sub-Clause 7.1 of RB/99 had required the Contractor to carry out the 'production and manufacture of Materials' in the manner specified in the Contract and properly, the new Sub-Clause requires it to carry out the 'production, manufacture, supply and testing' of them in the manner specified in the Contract and properly as well as 'all other operations and activities during the execution of the Works' (instead of, as in RB/99, 'all other execution of the Works').

(ii) Related Clauses / Sub-Clauses: 4.1 [*Contractor's General Obligations*], 4.9 [*Quality Management and Compliance Verification System*], 7 [*Plant, Materials and Workmanship*], 9 [*Tests on Completion*], 11.4 [*Failure to Remedy Defects*] and 13.2 [*Value Engineering*].

(iii) Analysis:

Like Clause 6 [*Staff and Labour*], Clause 7 elaborates on the Contractor's obligation under Sub-Clause 4.1 to execute the Works in accordance with the Contract but, in this case, in relation to Plant, Materials and workmanship. Under Sub-Clause 7.1, the Contractor must carry out the manufacture and supply of Plant, the production and supply of Materials and all other operations in the manner prescribed in sub-paragraphs (a), (b) and (c).

(1) Manner of working

Sub-paragraph (a) provides that the Contractor shall execute the Works 'in the manner (if any) specified in the Contract'. As a practical matter, the Contract documents, notably the Drawings and Specification, will normally describe in detail the Materials to be used, the Plant which is to form part of the Permanent Works, the requirements for Temporary Works and Contractor's Equipment.[1]

According to sub-paragraph (b), the Contractor must execute the Works 'in a proper workmanlike and careful manner, in accordance with recognised good practice'. This language corresponds to the normal standard of workmanship in construction contracts in common law countries.[2] While the exact meaning of sub-paragraph (b) may vary with the law governing the Contract (*see* under **(iv) Related Law** below) and applicable 'recognised good practice',[3] essentially, it means that the work will be done free of defects.

The Contract may call for a higher standard. If, for example, the workmanship is to be 'the best of its kind', this obligation would not be discharged by average workmanship but only if the 'best' workmanship is brought to bear.[4]

(2) Non-hazardous Materials

Sub-paragraph (c) stipulates that the Contractor must execute the Works 'with properly equipped facilities and non-hazardous Materials, except as otherwise specified in the Contract'. Consequently, the use of hazard-

1. *FIDIC Procurement Procedures Guide* (FIDIC, 2011) 120.
2. Thus, under English law, there is an implied condition in all construction contracts (i.e., it is a condition which will apply even if not expressly stated in the Contract) that work 'will be carried out carefully and skilfully or [...] in a good and workmanlike manner', Atkin Chambers, *Hudson's Building and Engineering Contracts* (14th edn, Sweet & Maxwell, London, 2020) 394 (para. 3-039). Similarly, under US law, there is implied by law into a construction contract 'the warranty of good and workmanlike construction in accordance with customary trade standards'. John M Mastin and others (eds), *Smith, Currie, and Hancock's Common Sense Construction Law: A Practical Guide for the Construction Professional* (6th edn, Wiley, Hoboken, NJ, 2020) 357.
3. *See*, as regards the Contractor's design obligations, sub-para. (f) of Sub-Clause 4.1 [*Contractor's General Obligations*] requiring compliance with applicable technical standards and **Section 8 Trade Usages** of **Chapter II Applicable Law** above.
4. Julian Bailey, *Construction Law* (3rd edn, London Publishing, UK, 2020) vol 1, 169-170 (para. 3.66).

ous Materials (such as asbestos, lead paint and contaminated soil) is prohibited except as provided in the Contract.[5]

'Materials' is defined broadly as:

> things of all kinds (other than Plant) [...] intended to form or forming part of the Permanent Works, including the supply-only materials (if any) to be supplied by the Contractor under the Contract.[6]

Though not defined in the Contract, hazardous materials may be defined as '[m]aterials or substances that, despite reasonable precautions, present a risk of bodily injury or death'.[7]

Once the Materials form part of the Permanent Works, they must not be hazardous thereafter 'during their working life or during any subsequent procedures for their demolition and disposal'.[8] The requirement that the Materials be non-hazardous does not imply that the processes used for manufacturing the Materials must be non-hazardous[9] or that the construction methods used by the Contractor should not involve any hazards.

If a tenderer wishes to use hazardous Materials in the execution of the Works, it should so state in its Tender and ensure that its proposal is

5. The Engineer is not empowered to relax this provision. *See also* Sub-Clause 3.2 [*Engineer's Duties and Authority*], last paragraph.
6. *See* Sub-Clause 1.1.53 '**Materials**'. For a definition of 'Hazardous Materials' contained in another form of construction contract, *see* under **(v) Improvements** of this commentary on Sub-Clause 7.1.
7. Elizabeth Patrick and others (eds), *The Annotated Construction Law Glossary* (ABA Publishing, Chicago, IL, 2010) 91. The United States *Solid Waste Disposal Act* ('SWDA') defines hazardous waste as follows:

   > The term 'hazardous waste' means a solid waste, or combination of solid wastes, which because of its quantity, concentration, or physical, chemical, or infectious characteristics may
   > (A) cause, or significantly contribute to an increase in mortality or an increase in serious irreversible, or incapacitating reversible, illness; or
   > (B) pose a substantial present or potential hazard to human health or the environment when improperly treated, stored, transported, or disposed of, or otherwise managed.

   S 1004(5) of the *Solid Waste Disposal Act*, 42 USC 6901-6992k, which consists of Title II of Public Law 89-272, 1965, and amendments.
8. *The FIDIC Contracts Guide* (2nd edn, FIDIC, 2022) 253.
9. *Ibid*, 252.

incorporated into the Contract. In this way, the Contractor can overcome the general prohibition in Sub-Clause 7.1(c),[10] as their use would then be authorised by the Employer.[11]

If, during the execution of the Works, the Contractor wants to use Materials that do not comply with Sub-Clause 7.1, it may propose their use under Sub-Clause 13.2 [*Value Engineering*] by drawing the Engineer's attention to the hazards, as well as the perceived overriding benefits,[12] of their use.[13]

(3) Sanctions

If the Engineer believes that the Contractor is not executing the Works in compliance with this Sub-Clause, it has powers to deal with this under Sub-Clauses 7.5 [*Defects and Rejection*] and 7.6 [*Remedial Work*].

(iv) Related Law: In many civil law jurisdictions, local laws will require that the Contractor carries out the work in accordance with good construction practice.[14] In common law jurisdictions, in the absence of a specific provision as to the adequacy or quality of the materials to be supplied and/or used by the contractor or its workmanship, the law will usually imply terms into the contract that the materials should be of 'satisfactory' or of 'merchantable' quality and that work will be carried out 'carefully and skilfully'.[15]

10. *Ibid*, 253.
11. *See* Sub-Clause 7.1(c) and in particular the wording 'except as otherwise specified in the Contract', as well as Sub-Clause 7.1(a).
12. Under Sub-Clause 13.2 [*Value Engineering*], the Contractor may only make such a proposal if it would bring some benefit to the Employer. *See* the commentary on Sub-Clause 13.2 below.
13. *The FIDIC Contracts Guide* (2nd edn, FIDIC, 2022) 253.
14. Thus, under French law, a contractor must perform work in accordance with the '*règles de l'art*', defined as 'the ordinary skills the employer can expect from professionals in their field of activity' ('*le savoir-faire habituel que le maître d'ouvrage peut attendre des professionnels considérés, dans leur champ d'activité*'), even where the work is done gratuitously for a friend. Philippe Malinvaud (ed in chief), *Droit de la Construction* (7th edn., Dalloz Action, 2018) 1131 (para. 402.31).
15. *See* Julian Bailey, *Construction Law* (3rd edn, London Publishing, UK, 2020) vol 1, 172 (para. 3.71), 188 (para. 3.102) and 200-202 (paras 3.123-3.125), and Atkin Chambers, *Hudson's Building and Engineering Contracts* (14th edn, Sweet & Maxwell, London, 2020) 391-395 (paras 3-038-039).

Similarly, according to the UNIDROIT Principles, where the quality of performance is not fixed by, or determinable from, the contract, a party is bound to render a performance of 'a quality that is reasonable and not less than average in the circumstances'.[16] The reference to 'reasonable' is:

> intended to prevent a party from claiming that it has performed adequately if it has rendered an 'average' performance in a market where the average quality is most unsatisfactory and is intended to give the judge or arbitrator an opportunity to raise those insufficient standards.[17]

This principle is relevant in a country where local performance or quality may be of a lower standard than the performance or quality expected under a FIDIC contract.

Local law also often defines and regulates hazardous materials, their disposal and use.

(v) Improvements:

(1) This Sub-Clause could usefully define what is meant by 'non-hazardous Materials'. By way of illustration, a US form defines 'Hazardous Material' as:

> any substance or material identified now or in the future as hazardous under Laws [defined as US laws and regulations], or any other substance or material that may be considered hazardous or otherwise subject to statutory or regulatory requirement governing handling, disposal, or cleanup.[18]

---

16. UNIDROIT Principles, art. 5.1.6 (*Determination of quality of performance*).
17. UNIDROIT Principles, official comment 2 on art. 5.1.6. This Comment is accompanied by the following illustration:

    > A company based in country X organises a banquet to celebrate its 50th anniversary. Since the cuisine in country X is mediocre, the company orders the meal from a renowned restaurant in Paris. In these circumstances the quality of the food provided must not be less than the average standards of the Parisian restaurant. It would clearly not be sufficient simply to meet the average standards of country X.

    As regards the UNIDROIT Principles, *see* **Section 7 International Legal Principles** of **Chapter II Applicable Law** above.
18. *ConsensusDocs 200, Standard Agreement and General Conditions between Owner and Constructor [Lump Sum Price]*, 2014, art. 3.13.1. For more

(2) Unlike some other forms, the Sub-Clause does not specify that Plant or Materials should be 'new' and of 'good' or 'suitable' quality.[19] Therefore Parties may wish to consider introducing an explicit requirement to this effect.

--ooOOoo--

7.2 Samples

The Contractor shall submit the following samples of Materials, and relevant information, to the Engineer for consent prior to using the Materials in or for the Works:

(a) manufacturer's standard samples of Materials and samples specified in the Contract, all at the Contractor's cost, and

(b) additional samples instructed by the Engineer as a Variation.

Each sample shall be labelled as to origin and intended use in the Works.

The Contractor must submit samples of Materials and relevant information to the Engineer for consent prior to use. Each sample must be labelled as to origin and intended use.

---

information about ConsensusDocs *see* www.consensusdocs.org accessed 10 November 2022. The definition of hazardous waste contained in the US *Solid Waste Disposal Act* has been provided in an earlier fn. 7 in this commentary on Sub-Clause 7.1.

19. Thus, the US Federal Acquisition Regulation ('FAR'), which governs US Federal Government procurement, provides that materials employed are to be 'new and of the most suitable grade for the purpose intended' unless the contract provides otherwise, s 52.236.5 Material and Workmanship. *See also* art. 3.8 of *ConsensusDocs 200, Standard Agreement and General Conditions between Owner and Constructor (Lump Sum Price)* ('new unless otherwise specified, of good quality') and s 3.5.1 of the US AIA Document A201-2017, *General Conditions of the Contract for Construction* ('of good quality and new unless the Contract Documents [...] permit otherwise').

Commentary

(i) Main Changes from RB/99: This Sub-Clause is identical to Sub-Clause 7.2 of RB/99.

(ii) Related Clauses / Sub-Clauses: 1.2 [*Interpretation*], 1.3 [*Notices and Other Communications*], 3.5 [*Engineer's Instructions*], 7.1 [*Manner of Execution*] and 13 [*Variations and Adjustments*].

(iii) Analysis: As the Engineer needs to be satisfied that the Materials that the Contractor is supplying are in accordance with the Contract,[20] this Sub-Clause requires the Contractor to submit samples of Materials and 'relevant information' to the Engineer for consent[21] prior to their use. 'Materials' are broadly defined as 'things of all kinds (other than Plant), whether on the Site or otherwise allocated to the Contract and intended to form or forming part of the Permanent Works [...]'.[22] '[R]elevant information' includes, among other things, details relevant to the use of the Materials and to their maintenance requirements.[23]

The Engineer's consent must be in writing and may not be unreasonably withheld or delayed.[24] If the Engineer decides to reject a certain sample, it should therefore be prepared to justify such rejection, e.g., by reference to relevant test results.

As the variety of Materials to be used may be vast and might, for example, include samples of 50 different sizes of screws that are used to fit a suspended ceiling, the Parties may wish to limit the range of samples subject to this Sub-Clause to a defined list of standard samples of Materials, which is part of the Contract.[25]

--ooOOoo--

20. As required by Sub-Clauses 4.1 [*Contractor's General Obligations*] and 7.1 [*Manner of Execution*].
21. *See* sub-para. (g) of Sub-Clause 1.2 [*Interpretation*].
22. Sub-Clause 1.1.53 '**Materials**'.
23. *The FIDIC Contracts Guide* (2nd edn, FIDIC, 2022) 254. Samples 'specified in the Contract' will usually mean in the Specification or the Contractor's Tender.
24. And must comply with the other requirements under Sub-Clause 1.3 [*Notices and Other Communications*]. *See* the commentary on Sub-Clause 1.3 above.
25. Leo Grutters and Brian Barr, *FIDIC Red, Yellow and Silver Books: A Practical Guide to the 2017 Editions* (Sweet & Maxwell, London, 2018) 150-151.

7.3 Inspection

The Employer's Personnel shall, during all the normal working hours stated in the Contract Data and at all other reasonable times:

(a) have full access to all parts of the Site and to all places from which natural Materials are being obtained;
(b) during production, manufacture and construction (at the Site and elsewhere), be entitled to:

   (i) examine, inspect, measure and test (to the extent stated in the Specification) the Materials, Plant and workmanship,
   (ii) check the progress of manufacture of Plant and production and manufacture of Materials, and
   (iii) make records (including photographs and/or video recordings); and

(c) carry out other duties and inspections, as specified in these Conditions and the Specification.

The Contractor shall give the Employer's Personnel full opportunity to carry out these activities, including providing safe access, facilities, permissions and safety equipment.

The Contractor shall give a Notice to the Engineer whenever any Materials, Plant or work is ready for inspection, and before it is to be covered up, put out of sight, or packaged for storage or transport. The Employer's Personnel shall then either carry out the examination, inspection, measurement or testing without unreasonable delay, or the Engineer shall promptly give a Notice to the Contractor that the Employer's Personnel do not require to do so. If the Engineer gives no such Notice and/or the Employer's Personnel do not attend at the time stated in the Contractor's Notice (or such time as may be agreed with the Contractor), the Contractor may proceed with covering up, putting out of sight or packaging for storage or transport.

If the Contractor fails to give a Notice in accordance with this Sub-Clause, the Contractor shall, if and when required by the Engineer, uncover the work and thereafter reinstate and make good, all at the Contractor's risk and cost.

The Employer's Personnel shall, during reasonable times: (a) have full access to the Site and places from which natural Materials are obtained; (b) be entitled to examine and test (to the extent stated in the Specification) the Materials, Plant and workmanship, check the progress of manufacture of Plant and production of Materials, and make records; and (c) carry out other duties and inspections as specified in the Contract.

The Contractor shall give a Notice to the Engineer when any work is ready for inspection and before it is to be covered up. The Employer's Personnel shall then examine or test it without unreasonable delay, or the Engineer shall give a Notice that they do not require to do so. If the Engineer gives no such Notice and/or the Employer's Personnel fail to attend the inspection, the Contractor may proceed with covering up.

If the Contractor fails to give a Notice under this Sub-Clause, the Contractor must, if required by the Engineer, uncover the work and reinstate it at its risk and cost.

Commentary

(i) Main Changes from RB/99:

(1) Whereas in Sub-Clause 7.3 of RB/99 the Employer's Personnel had the right to inspect, as specified in the Sub-Clause, 'at all reasonable times', the new Sub-Clause provides that they may do so 'during all the normal working hours stated in the Contract Data and at all other reasonable times'.

(2) Sub-paragraph (b) of the new Sub-Clause stipulates, for the first time, that the Employer's Personnel's right during production, manufacture and construction (at the Site and elsewhere) to examine, inspect, measure and test the Materials, Plant and workmanship is limited by the parenthetical '(to the extent stated in the Specification)'.

(3) The Employer's Personnel's rights during production, manufacture and construction explicitly include, under sub-paragraph (b), to 'make records (including photographs and/or video recordings)', whereas this was not stated in RB/99.

(4) Sub-paragraph (c) of the new Sub-Clause, which entitles the Employer's Personnel to carry out 'other duties and inspections, as specified in these Conditions and the Specification', is new.[26]
(5) Whereas in the third paragraph of Sub-Clause 7.3 of RB/99, the Engineer was to carry out the examination, inspection, measurement or testing, under the same paragraph of the new Sub-Clause, this is to be done by the Employer's Personnel.
(6) The new Sub-Clause, third paragraph, stipulates that the Contractor may proceed with covering up, putting out of sight or packaging for storage and transport if the Engineer gives no Notice that the Employer's Personnel do not require to undertake examination, inspection, measurement or testing and/or if the Employer's Personnel fail to attend it at the time specified in the Contractor's Notice; there was no such provision in RB/99.

(ii) Related Clauses / Sub-Clauses: 1.3 [*Notices and Other Communications*], 3.2 [*Engineer's Duty and Authority*], 4.9.2 [*Compliance Verification System*], 4.12 [*Unforeseeable Physical Conditions*], 4.20 [*Progress Reports*], 6.5 [*Working Hours*], 7.1 [*Manner of Execution*], 7.5 [*Defects and Rejection*], 7.6 [*Remedial Work*], 8.3 [*Programme*], 14.5 [*Plant and Materials Intended for the Works*] and 20.1 [*Claims*].

(iii) Analysis:

(1) Purpose

Like the Contractor's obligation to submit samples under Sub-Clause 7.2 [*Samples*], the Employer's Personnel's broad rights of inspection under this Sub-Clause are designed to enable them to verify that the Contractor is executing the Works in accordance with the Contract.[27]

(2) General requirements

This Sub-Clause authorises the Employer's Personnel – not merely the Engineer who is included within Employer's Personnel[28] – to have full access to the Site and to all places from which natural Materials are obtained, to ascertain that Materials, Plant and workmanship are in accordance with the Contract.

26. A somewhat similar provision was contained in sub-para. (c) Sub-Clause 7.3 [*Inspection*] of GB/08.
27. *See* Sub-Clauses 4.1 [*Contractor's General Obligations*] and 7.1 [*Manner of Execution*].
28. Sub-Clause 1.1.33 **'Employer's Personnel'**.

During production, manufacture and construction (at the Site and elsewhere, which may be in the Contractor's or a Subcontractor's country), the Employer's Personnel are entitled to examine, inspect, measure and test '(to the extent stated in the Specification)' the Materials, Plant and workmanship, to check the progress of manufacture of Plant and production and manufacture of Materials and to make records of various kinds. Consequently, the Contractor must provide access to all places where Plant is manufactured or Materials produced or from where they are obtained (such as factories, quarries, plants, and storage warehouses), as well as to all places where the Permanent Works are to be executed and to which Plant and Materials are to be delivered,[29] and to any other places specified in the Contract as forming part of the Site. This right of access and the Employer's Personnel's related entitlements to examine and inspect may be exercised during normal working hours on the Site stated in the Contract Data[30] and otherwise 'at all other reasonable times'. In order to avoid future disagreements, the Parties may wish to clarify the meaning of this latter phrase in the Special Provisions.

Under sub-paragraph (b)(i), the Employer's Personnel are entitled to examine, inspect, measure and test '(to the extent stated in the Specification)'[31] the Materials, Plant and workmanship. What would be the consequences if the Specification does not state anything on the subject? Would that mean that the Employer's Personnel would have unlimited power to carry out such activities or no such power at all? In order to avoid potential disagreements, the Parties should be sure to clarify this matter in the Specification.

(3) Tests under Sub-Clause 7.3

The tests referred to in Sub-Clause 7.3 should be distinguished from the tests referred to in Sub-Clause 7.4 [*Testing by the Contractor*] and Clause 9 [*Tests on Completion*].[32] Sub-Clause 7.3 refers to testing by the Employer's Personnel, whereas Sub-Clause 7.4 and Clause 9 refer to tests to be carried out by the Contractor.

29. *See* the commentary on Sub-Clause 1.1.74 '**Site**' above.
30. *See* Sub-Clause 6.5 [*Working Hours*] and the Contract Data.
31. As drafted, it is unclear whether this restrictive wording applies to 'test' alone or also to 'examine, inspect, measure' as well. *See* Jakob B Sørensen, *FIDIC Red Book: A Companion to the 2017 Construction Contract* (1st edn, ICE Publishing, London, 2019) 92.
32. *The FIDIC Contracts Guide* (2nd edn, FIDIC, 2022) 256.

FIDIC notes that as the Contractor is obliged to give the Employer's Personnel 'full opportunity' to carry out inspection activities:

> tenderers must make appropriate allowance for providing access and facilities for the inspections and testing that are mentioned in the Contract. However, this Sub-Clause assumes that no significant Cost will be incurred by the Contractor. If it is anticipated that the Employer's Personnel will carry out inspections or testing for which the Contractor will be required to provide special access arrangements or any apparatus, equipment, instruments, materials, etc., then this requirement and the necessary details must be specified in the Specification [...] in order that tenderers can make the appropriate allowance for providing them [...] That said, if such a requirement is not specified, it may be instructed as a Variation by the Engineer [...][33]

Consequently, the extent of the right of the Employer's Personnel to test should be described in the Specification.

(4) Other rights of Employer's Personnel

In addition to the above-mentioned examinations, inspections, measurements and tests, the Employer's Personnel is entitled to check the progress of manufacture of Plant and the production and manufacture of Materials – whether at the Site or elsewhere – and make records, including photographs and/or video recordings.[34] The Employer's Personnel may also carry out other duties and inspections if specified in the Conditions and the Specification.[35]

Any inspection, test or similar act (or failure to act) by the Engineer, the Engineer's Representative or any assistant would not relieve the Contractor of any obligation or responsibility under the Contract.[36]

---

33. *Ibid.*
34. Sub-Clause 7.3(b)(ii)-(iii).
35. Sub-Clause 7.3(c). To facilitate, among other things, examinations and inspections by the Employer's Personnel, the Contractor is obliged to submit monthly progress reports to the Engineer, including photographs and/or video recordings showing the status of manufacture and progress on and off the Site, and information relating to the manufacture of 'each main item of Plant and Materials', including the name of the manufacturer, the manufacture location, percentage progress and the actual or expected dates of commencement of manufacture, Contractor's inspections, tests and shipment and arrival at Site, as well as other information relating to Materials. Sub-Clause 4.20 (b)-(e).
36. Sub-Clause 3.2 [*Engineer's Duties and Authority*], last paragraph.

(5) Contractor's Notice and related obligations of the Engineer

Under the third paragraph, the Contractor is required to give a Notice to the Engineer whenever any Materials, Plant or Work is ready for inspection and before it is covered up, put out of sight or packaged. The Notice may contain the Contractor's proposal for a time for the Employer's Personnel to attend in order to carry out an inspection. If the Contractor proceeds with the covering up or packaging of the work without giving such a Notice then, if and when required by the Engineer, it must uncover or unpack the same work, at its own risk and cost, whether or not the work in question turns out to be in accordance with the Contract.[37]

Having received the Contractor's Notice, if the Employer's Personnel want to carry out any inspection and testing, they must do so 'without unreasonable delay'.[38] If they do not, the Contractor may proceed with the covering up, putting out of sight or packaging.

(iv) Related Law: Inspection must be reasonable in extent and amount. As a US authority has stated:

> Inspection in the absence of specified requirements must meet a standard of 'reasonableness'. [...] Where inspection is conducted unreasonably or enforces requirements in excess of those reasonably required by the specifications, the issues of 'hypertechnical inspection' and 'constructive change' are raised.[39]

In US parlance, 'hyper-technical inspection' refers to the use of inspection standards more stringent than those specified in the contract or that are otherwise unreasonable.[40] When such standards are applied, they give rise to a constructive change or (in FIDIC terms) a Variation.[41]

37. Sub-Clause 7.3 last paragraph.
38. Sub-Clause 7.3, third paragraph. While the Employer's Personnel are authorised to carry out inspections, the Contractor is only required to take instruction from the Engineer or the Engineer's delegate. *See* Sub-Clause 3.5, first paragraph.
39. Philip Bruner and Patrick O'Connor, *Bruner and O'Connor on Construction Law* (Thomson Reuters, St Paul, MN, 2016) vol 4A, 468 (s 13:36).
40. *Ibid.*, vol 4A, 476 (s 13:39).
41. *Ibid.*

In an ICC case based on a FIDIC form,[42] the Engineer was found to have been overly nitpicking in examining building works, and to have required an excessive number of inspections, delaying the issue of certificates of completion. Finding that the Employer was responsible for the conduct of the Engineer, the tribunal held the Employer liable for breach of Contract and the Contractor's damages. In the same case, the tribunal found the Engineer to have insisted on a level of painting work which exceeded the standard of quality required by applicable building standards, holding the Employer similarly liable.[43]

Under RB/17, the Contractor's remedy, apart from breach of contract, would be to claim that the Engineer's unreasonable inspecting or testing requirements amount to the instruction of a Variation unacknowledged by the Engineer. In this case, the Contractor should 'immediately, and before commencing any work related to the instruction', give a Notice to the Engineer with reasons as provided for by the last paragraph of Sub-Clause 3.5 [*Engineer's Instructions*].[44]

(v) Improvements: The third paragraph of Sub-Clause 7.3 states that the Contractor may proceed to cover up, put out of sight or package Materials, Plant or work if: (i) the Engineer *has not given* a Notice that the Employer's Personnel do not require to carry out an examination, inspection, measurement or testing, and/or (ii) the Employer's Personnel do not attend at the time stated in the Contractor's Notice (or such time as may be agreed with the Contractor). This paragraph should be supplemented to provide that, as one would expect, the Contractor is also entitled to proceed with covering up, putting out of sight or packaging of work in cases where the Engineer *has given* a Notice that the Employer's Personnel do not require the carrying out of an examination, inspection, measurement or testing.

--ooOOoo--

42. RB/69.
43. Final award, ICC cases 3790 / 3902 / 4050 / 4051 / 4054 (joined cases) (1984), reported in Abdul Hamid El-Ahdab, *Arbitration with the Arab Countries* (Kluwer Law and Taxation, the Netherlands) (1990) 892-895 (Subject no 2 Procedure for provisional completion and the problems of the finishing standard of the works and of determination of applicable norms). The full award is available on Jus Mundi.
44. *See* the commentary on Sub-Clause 3.5 above.

7.4 Testing by the Contractor

This Sub-Clause shall apply to all tests specified in the Contract, other than the Tests after Completion (if any).

The Contractor shall provide all apparatus, assistance, documents and other information, temporary supplies of electricity and water, equipment, fuel, consumables, instruments, labour, materials, and suitably qualified, experienced and competent staff, as are necessary to carry out the specified tests efficiently and properly. All apparatus, equipment and instruments shall be calibrated in accordance with the standards stated in the Specification or defined by applicable Laws and, if requested by the Engineer, the Contractor shall submit calibration certificates before carrying out testing.

The Contractor shall give a Notice to the Engineer, stating the time and place for the specified testing of any Plant, Materials and other parts of the Works. This Notice shall be given in reasonable time, having regard to the location of the testing, for the Employer's Personnel to attend.

The Engineer may, under Clause 13 [*Variations and Adjustments*], vary the location or timing or details of specified tests, or instruct the Contractor to carry out additional tests. If these varied or additional tests show that the tested Plant, Materials or workmanship is not in accordance with the Contract, the Cost and any delay incurred in carrying out this Variation shall be borne by the Contractor.

The Engineer shall give a Notice to the Contractor of not less than 72 hours of his/her intention to attend the tests. If the Engineer does not attend at the time and place stated in the Contractor's Notice under this Sub-Clause, the Contractor may proceed with the tests, unless otherwise instructed by the Engineer. These tests shall then be deemed to have been made in the Engineer's presence. If the Contractor suffers delay and/or incurs Cost from complying with any such instruction or as a result of a delay for which the Employer is responsible, the Contractor shall be entitled subject to Sub-Clause 20.2 [*Claims for Payment and/or EOT*] to EOT and/or payment of Cost Plus Profit.

If the Contractor causes any delay to specified tests (including varied or additional tests) and such delay causes the Employer to incur costs, the Employer shall be entitled subject to Sub-Clause 20.2 [*Claims for Payment and/or EOT*] to payment of these costs by the Contractor.

The Contractor shall promptly forward to the Engineer duly certified reports of the tests. When the specified tests have been passed, the Engineer shall endorse the Contractor's test certificate, or issue a test certificate to the Contractor, to that effect. If the Engineer has not attended the tests, he/she shall be deemed to have accepted the readings as accurate.

Sub-Clause 7.5 [*Defects and Rejection*] shall apply in the event that any Plant, Materials and other parts of the Works fails to pass a specified test.

This Sub-Clause applies to all tests specified in the Contract, except for Tests after Completion (if any).

The Contractor must provide all facilities and qualified staff as are necessary to carry out the specified tests. The Contractor must give a Notice to the Engineer in reasonable time stating the time and place for the testing. The Engineer may, under Clause 13, vary the location, timing or details of the tests, or instruct the Contractor to carry out additional tests and, if these varied or additional tests show that the tested work is not in accordance with the Contract, the Cost and delay incurred will be borne by the Contractor.

The Engineer must give a Notice to the Contractor of no less than 72 hours of its intention to attend the tests. If the Engineer does not attend, the Contractor may proceed with the tests, unless instructed otherwise, and they will be deemed to have been made in the Engineer's presence. If the Contractor suffers delay and/or incurs Cost as a result of any instruction of the Engineer or a delay for which the Employer is responsible, then, subject to Sub-Clause 20.2, the

Contractor will be entitled to an EOT and/or payment of Cost Plus Profit. If the Employer has incurred cost as a result of the Contractor's delay, the Employer will be entitled, subject to Sub-Clause 20.2, to payment of these costs.

The Contractor must forward to the Engineer certified reports of the tests. When the tests have been passed, the Engineer shall either endorse the Contractor's test certificate or issue a test certificate to the Contractor. Sub-Clause 7.5 will apply in case of failure to pass a specified test.

Commentary

(i) Main Changes from RB/99:

(1) The second sentence of the second paragraph requiring that all apparatus, equipment and instruments be calibrated in accordance with standards stated in the Specification or defined by applicable Laws and that the Contractor, if requested by the Engineer, submit calibration certificates before carrying out the tests is new in RB/17.

(2) The new Sub-Clause no longer requires (like the second paragraph of Sub-Clause 7.4 of RB/99) that the Contractor agrees with the Engineer on the time and place for testing but instead requires (in the third paragraph) that the Contractor gives a Notice to the Engineer stating the time and place of the tests, which must be given in reasonable time, having regard to the location of testing, in order to enable the Employer's Personnel to attend. It is then left to the Engineer to respond as provided in the fourth and fifth paragraphs.

(3) Whereas under Sub-Clause 7.4 of RB/99, the Engineer had to give the Contractor not less than 24 hours' notice of its intention to attend the tests, the Engineer must now, under the fifth paragraph, give a Notice of not less than 72 hours of its intention to do so.

(4) The sixth paragraph, entitling the Employer to claim for its costs as a result of Contractor's delay to specified tests, is new.

(5) The last paragraph, stating that Sub-Clause 7.5 will apply in the case of a failure to pass a specified test, is also new.

(ii) Related Clauses / Sub-Clauses: 1.3 [*Notices and Other Communications*], 4.9.2 [*Compliance Verification System*], 4.20 [*Progress Reports*],

7.1 [*Manner of Execution*], 7.5 [*Defects and Rejection*], 7.6 [*Remedial Work*], 8.3 [*Programme*], 9 [*Tests on Completion*], 10.3 [*Interference with Tests on Completion*], 11.5 [*Remedying of Defective Work Off Site*], 11.6 [*Further Tests after Remedying Defects*], 13 [*Variations and Adjustments*], 14.5 [*Plant and Materials Intended for the Works*] and 20.2 [*Claims for Payment and/or EOT*].

(iii) Analysis:

(1) General requirements

Unlike Sub-Clause 7.3 [*Inspection*] that relates, among other things, to testing (to the extent stated in the Specification) by the Employer's Personnel, this Sub-Clause relates to all tests by the Contractor specified in the Contract including notably Tests on Completion provided for in Clause 9 but excluding Tests *after* Completion, if any.[45] Tests by the Contractor may take place at many different stages of production, manufacture and construction and may be critical in verifying that Plant, Materials and workmanship comply with the Contract. They may also take place upon completion and before the Employer's takeover of the Works (i.e., the Tests on Completion).[46] Any tests which the Engineer instructs the Contractor to do which are not provided for in the Contract should be instructed as Variations under Clause 13.[47]

Under the second paragraph, the Contractor must, naturally enough, provide all apparatus and other facilities and suitably qualified staff to carry out the tests specified in the Contract.

(2) Contractor's Notice of tests

Under the third paragraph, the Contractor must give a Notice to the Engineer of the time and place for the specified testing.[48] There is no requirement that the Engineer should 'agree' with the time and location

45. Tests *after* Completion, as are provided for in detail by Clause 12 of YB/17 and SB/17 but not by RB/17, will require different procedures as, when these tests are carried out, the Works will already have been taken over and be under the control of the Employer.
46. The sequence and timing of tests must be provided for in the Contractor's programmes. Sub-Clause 8.3(e).
47. Sub-Clause 7.4, fourth paragraph.
48. Such a Notice must comply with the requirements of Sub-Clause 1.3. *See* the commentary on Sub-Clause 1.3 above.

of the testing proposed (as was the case in Sub-Clause 7.4 of RB/99). However, the Notice must be given a reasonable time in advance of the proposed tests, having regard to the location of the testing, to enable the Employer's Personnel to attend the tests.

While 'reasonable time' is not defined, the Engineer, pursuant to the fifth paragraph, must give a Notice to the Contractor of not less than 72 hours of its intention to attend the tests. Thus, for the time to be reasonable, it must, at a minimum, be given sufficiently in advance to allow the Engineer the time to provide such notice.

(3) Engineer's Variation of the tests

Under the fourth paragraph, the Engineer is authorised to vary the location, timing or details of specified tests, or instruct the Contractor to carry out additional tests, subject to the Variation procedure in Clause 13, which presupposes the issuance of an Engineer's instruction.[49] Consequently, if the Contractor suffers delay and/or incurs Cost from complying with any such instruction, it will be entitled to an EOT and/or adjustment of the Contract Price without having to comply with the claims' procedure under Sub-Clause 20.2.[50] However, if the varied or additional tests demonstrate non-compliance with the Contract, such Cost and/or delay will be borne by the Contractor.[51]

(4) Engineer's attendance at the tests

Under the fifth paragraph, if the Engineer intends to attend the tests, it must (as mentioned above) give a Notice to the Contractor of not less than 72 hours before their commencement. It is not clear why such a long period is required, given that RB/99 had only required the Engineer to give the Contractor 24 hours' notice of its intention to attend.[52] Concerns have been expressed that 72 hours may be too long in civil engineering

49. Sub-Clause 13.3. In this connection, Sub-Clause 13.1(v) states that a Variation may include any additional work or services necessary for the Permanent Works, including 'any associated Tests on Completion [...] and other testing'.
50. *See* Sub-Clause 7.4, fourth paragraph, which refers to Clause 13 and, thus, to Sub-Clause 13.3.1, last paragraph, providing that compliance with Sub-Clause 20.2 is not required.
51. Sub-Clause 7.4, fourth paragraph.
52. Sub-Clause 7.4, fourth paragraph, of RB/99.

projects.[53] If the Engineer does not attend at the time and place stated in the Contractor's Notice, the Contractor is allowed to proceed with the tests 'unless otherwise instructed by the Engineer', and they will be deemed to be carried out in the Engineer's presence.[54]

(5) Parties' remedies in case of test delays

The last sentence of the fifth paragraph states that if the Contractor suffers delay and/or incurs Cost from complying with 'any such instruction' by the Engineer, or as a result of a delay for which the Employer is responsible, the Contractor will be entitled to an EOT and/or Cost Plus Profit subject to compliance with Sub-Clause 20.2. *This wording is ambiguous*. The phrase 'any such instruction' seems to refer to the Engineer's instruction in the same paragraph whereby the Engineer has instructed the Contractor not to proceed with the tests in the Engineer's absence. However, if the Engineer's instruction changes the location, timing or details of the tests specified in the Contractor's Notice or instructs the carrying out of additional tests, such an instruction would likely amount to a Variation under the fourth paragraph of Sub-Clause 7.4 for which, as already mentioned, compliance with the claims' procedure under Sub-Clause 20.2 is not normally required. *Therefore, it is unclear – notwithstanding the reference to Sub-Clause 20.2 – whether the claims' procedure should apply to instructions concerning these matters*.[55]

Moreover, if the tests concerned are the Tests on Completion, and the Engineer's instruction prevents the Contractor from carrying them out for more than 14 days, then Sub-Clause 10.3 [*Interference with Tests on Completion*] will apply.

Sub-Clause 7.4 also envisages, in the sixth paragraph, that the Employer may recover from the Contractor, subject to the claims' procedure under

53. Leo Grutters and Brian Barr, *FIDIC Red, Yellow and Silver Books: A Practical Guide to the 2017 Editions* (Sweet & Maxwell, London, 2018) 154.
54. Sub-Clause 7.4, fifth paragraph.
55. Specifically, how is an instruction under the fourth paragraph (for which compliance with the claims procedure is not required) to be distinguished, in practical terms, from an instruction under the fifth paragraph (for which compliance with the claims procedure is required) given that both may vary the location, timing or details of tests? The Parties may wish to clarify this matter in the Special Provisions.

Sub-Clause 20.2,[56] any costs which the Employer may have incurred as a result of the Contractor's delay to specified tests.

(6) Test results

The penultimate paragraph provides for the proper recording of tests. The Contractor must promptly forward to the Engineer duly certified reports[57] of the tests it has conducted under the Sub-Clause. When the tests have been passed, the Engineer must either endorse the Contractor's test certificate or issue a separate test certificate to the Contractor to that effect.[58] If the Engineer has not attended the tests (of which it has been given a Notice), the Engineer is deemed by the Sub-Clause to have 'accepted' the readings as accurate.[59]

The penultimate paragraph should be read together with Sub-Clause 4.9.2 [*Compliance Verification System*] which requires the Contractor to prepare and implement a Compliance Verification System that includes a method for reporting the results of all tests which the Contractor carries out.

56. Requiring the Employer, among other things, to give a Notice of Claim under Sub-Clause 20.2.1 within 28 days of the event or circumstance giving rise to the Claim *or be time barred*.
57. The term 'certified report' of the results of the tests is not defined. However, both a 'certificate' and a 'report' must comply with Sub-Clause 1.3 [*Notices and Other Communications*]. Moreover, more generally, a certificate has been defined as:

> the expression in a definite form of the exercise of the opinion of the certifier in relation to some matter provided for by the terms of the contract.

Atkin Chambers, *Hudson's Building and Engineering Contracts* (14th edn, Sweet & Maxwell, London, 2020) 484 (para. 4-001). Thus, one would expect the Contractor to have to attest, in a document entitled 'Certificate', to the truth or accuracy of the report containing the test results.
58. In either case, the Engineer's certificate will not be conclusive as to the performance of the asset tested. According to the first paragraph of Sub-Clause 7.6, a test certificate will not prevent the Engineer from instructing remedial work (described there as being '(i)n addition to' a test certificate), which is consistent with Sub-Clause 3.2, last paragraph, providing that a 'certificate' or 'similar act' of the Engineer does not relieve the Contractor of its contractual obligations.
59. Under Sub-Clause 3.2, last paragraph, an 'acceptance' by the Engineer does not relieve the Contractor of its contractual obligations.

The last paragraph clarifies that Sub-Clause 7.5 [*Defects and Rejection*] will apply if any Plant, Materials and other parts of the Works fail to pass a specified test.[60] Under Sub-Clause 7.5, the Engineer may by a Notice require the Contractor to submit a proposal for necessary remedial work and, if it fails to do so or to carry out proposed remedial work to which the Engineer has given a Notice of No-objection, the Engineer will have the further remedies provided for in that Sub-Clause.[61]

(iv) Related Law: A practical question which can sometimes arise, and which is not addressed in the Conditions (and perhaps cannot be), is: how much testing by the Contractor may the Employer or the Engineer insist upon? In common law countries, depending on the circumstances, a term may be implied into the contract that the level of testing is to be both reasonable and necessary, and therefore not disproportionate in the circumstances.[62]

(v) Improvements: As discussed under *(5) Parties' remedies in case of test delays* in **(iii) Analysis** above, it should be clarified when compliance with the claims' procedure under Sub-Clause 20.2 is required in relation to the Engineer's instructions under the fourth and fifth paragraphs of this Sub-Clause.

--ooOOoo--

7.5 Defects and Rejection

If, as a result of an examination, inspection, measurement or testing, any Plant, Materials, Contractor's design (if any) or workmanship is found to be defective or otherwise not in accordance with the Contract, the Engineer shall give a Notice to the Contractor describing the item of Plant, Materials, design or workmanship that has been found to be defective. The Contractor shall then promptly prepare and submit a proposal for necessary remedial work.

60. This is consistent with Sub-Clause 4.9.2 which contains similar wording. Sub-Clause 4.9.2 [*Compliance Verification System*], second paragraph.
61. *See* the commentary on Sub-Clause 7.5 below.
62. *See* Julian Bailey, *Construction Law* (3rd edn, London Publishing, UK, 2020) vol 2, 1282 (para. 14.12). *See also* the discussion under **(iv) Related Law** of the commentary on Sub-Clause 7.3 above.

The Engineer may Review this proposal, and may give a Notice to the Contractor stating the extent to which the proposed work, if carried out, would not result in the Plant, Materials, Contractor's design (if any) or workmanship complying with the Contract. After receiving such a Notice the Contractor shall promptly submit a revised proposal to the Engineer. If the Engineer gives no such Notice within 14 days after receiving the Contractor's proposal (or revised proposal), the Engineer shall be deemed to have given a Notice of No-objection.

If the Contractor fails to promptly submit a proposal (or revised proposal) for remedial work, or fails to carry out the proposed remedial work to which the Engineer has given (or is deemed to have given) a Notice of No-objection, the Engineer may:

(a) instruct the Contractor under sub-paragraph (a) and/or (b) of Sub-Clause 7.6 [*Remedial Work*]; or
(b) reject the Plant, Materials, Contractor's design (if any) or workmanship by giving a Notice to the Contractor, with reasons, in which case sub-paragraph (a) of Sub-Clause 11.4 [*Failure to Remedy Defects*] shall apply.

After remedying defects in any Plant, Materials, design (if any) or workmanship, if the Engineer requires any such items to be retested, the tests shall be repeated in accordance with Sub-Clause 7.4 [*Testing by the Contractor*] at the Contractor's risk and cost. If the rejection and retesting cause the Employer to incur additional costs, the Employer shall be entitled subject to Sub-Clause 20.2 [*Claims for Payment and/or EOT*] to payment of these costs by the Contractor.

If, as a result of an inspection, any Plant, Materials, Contractor's design or workmanship is found to be defective, the Engineer shall give a Notice to the Contractor describing the defect. The Contractor shall then submit a proposal to remedy it.

The Engineer may Review this proposal and state, by a Notice, the extent to which it would not result in compliance with the Contract.

The Contractor must then submit a revised proposal. If the Engineer gives no such Notice within 14 days, the Engineer shall be deemed to have given a Notice of No-objection.

If the Contractor fails to submit a proposal (or a revised one), or to carry out the proposed remedial work for which the Engineer has given a Notice of No-objection, the Engineer may either: (i) instruct the Contractor to repair or remedy the defect pursuant to sub-paragraph (a) and/or (b) of Sub-Clause 7.6 or (ii) reject the work by a Notice, with reasons, in which case sub-paragraph (a) of Sub-Clause 11.4 will apply.

After remedying any defect, if the Engineer so requires, the relevant items must be retested in accordance with Sub-Clause 7.4 at the Contractor's risk and cost. If the rejection and retesting cause the Employer to incur additional costs, it will be entitled to recover them subject to Sub-Clause 20.2.

Commentary

(i) Main Changes from RB/99:

(1) The new Sub-Clause 7.5 refers not only to Plant, Materials or workmanship found to be defective (as did Sub-Clause 7.5 of RB/99) but also to the Contractor's design (if any), with the consequence that the Engineer now has the remedies provided in this Sub-Clause if the Contractor's design is found to be not in accordance with the Contract.

(2) Sub-Clause 7.5 of RB/99 had provided that, in cases where any Plant, Materials or workmanship was found to be defective, the Engineer might reject the defective item, by giving a notice with reasons. Thereafter, the Contractor had to promptly make good the defect and ensure that the rejected item complied with the Contract. The first and second paragraphs of the new Sub-Clause prescribe a more detailed procedure, comprising: the giving by the Engineer of a Notice of defective work; the submission by the Contractor of a proposal for remedial work; the Engineer's right to Review the same; and, if the Engineer should give no Notice (of objection) within 14 days, a Notice of No-objection is deemed to have been given.

(3) Whereas the former Sub-Clause simply provided that the Engineer might reject the defective work, which the Contractor had then to make good, the new Sub-Clause provides that where the

Contractor has failed to submit a proposal (or revised proposal) – as described in (2) above – or fails to carry out proposed remedial work to which the Engineer has given (or is deemed to have given) a Notice of No-objection, the Engineer has the remedies specified in sub-paragraph (a) or (b) of the third paragraph.

(4) The last paragraph of the new Sub-Clause dealing with retesting is more detailed than in RB/99.

(ii) Related Clauses / Sub-Clauses: 1.3 [*Notices and Other Communications*], 4.9.2 [*Compliance Verification System*], 7.4 [*Testing by the Contractor*], 7.6 [*Remedial Work*], 8.3 [*Programme*], 9.3 [*Retesting*], 9.4 [*Failure to Pass Tests on Completion*], 10.1 [*Taking Over the Works and Sections*], 10.2 [*Taking Over Parts*], 11 [*Defects after Taking Over*], 14.6.2 [*Issue of IPC-Withholding (amounts in) an IPC*], 15.2 [*Termination for Contractor's Default*], 17.2 [*Liability for Care of the Works*] and 20.2 [*Claims for Payment and/or EOT*].

(iii) Analysis:

(1) Context of Sub-Clause 7.5

Sub-Clause 7.3 [*Inspection*] provides that during production, manufacture and construction at the Site or elsewhere, the Employer's Personnel are entitled to examine, inspect, measure and test the Materials, Plant and workmanship. If, as a result of these activities, or testing by the Contractor under Sub-Clause 7.4 or otherwise, any Plant, Materials, Contractor's design, if any, or workmanship is found to be defective or otherwise not in accordance with the Contract, Sub-Clause 7.5 prescribes the procedure which is to apply.[63]

(2) Engineer's Notice of a defect

Under Sub-Clause 7.5, the Engineer must give a Notice to the Contractor 'describing the item of Plant, Materials, design or workmanship that has

63. *See* **Figure 6 Remedying Defects during Execution of the Works** at the end of this commentary on Sub-Clause 7.5.

been found to be defective'.[64] Although the Notice does not need to contain reasons,[65] the Engineer should be prepared to justify its position.

There is also no need for the Engineer to identify the cause of the defect,[66] which is often contentious and may be hard to determine. Moreover, the Engineer should usually refrain from prescribing a method for rectifying it, at least in the first instance, as this should be the Contractor's responsibility.[67]

Surprisingly, the Conditions contain no definition of 'defect'. But it can generally be taken to mean work which fails to comply with the requirements of the Contract – this is implied by the first sentence of this Sub-Clause ('defective or otherwise not in accordance with the Contract') – and so is a breach of contract.[68] Thus, work that does not comply with the Drawings or the Specification or other provisions of the Contract, including applicable Laws (e.g., building regulations) with which the Contractor must comply,[69] or technical standards,[70] may be treated as defective.[71]

If the Contractor disagrees that the work is defective, the Contractor's remedy is to assert a Claim under Sub-Clauses 20.1(c) and 3.7 and, if the matter is not settled by an agreement or a determination of the Engineer under Sub-Clause 3.7, the Contractor may (having given a NOD with respect to the Engineer's determination) proceed under Sub-Clause 3.7.5 and refer the matter to the DAAB pursuant to Sub-Clause 21.4 [*Obtaining DAAB's Decisions*].

64. The same sentence also refers to 'or otherwise not in accordance with the Contract', which appears to mean the same thing as defective, as noted below in this commentary. Like other Notices, this Notice must comply with Sub-Clause 1.3 [*Notices and Other Communications*].
65. Sub-Clause 7.5 of RB/99 had required that the Engineer's notice of rejection be given 'with reasons'.
66. *The FIDIC Contracts Guide* (2nd edn, FIDIC, 2022) 261.
67. *Ibid.*
68. Atkin Chambers, *Hudson's Building and Engineering Contracts* (14th edn, Sweet & Maxwell, London, 2020) 572 (para. 4-075).
69. *See* Sub-Clause 1.13 [*Compliance with Laws*].
70. *See*, for example, sub-para. (f) of Sub-Clause 4.1 [*Contractor's General Obligations*].
71. '[F]air wear and tear' during the Defects Notification Period is excepted. *See* Sub-Clause 11.1, first paragraph, and the commentary on that Sub-Clause.

(3) Contractor's proposal for remedial work

After the Contractor receives the Engineer's Notice of a defect, it must 'promptly' prepare and submit a proposal for necessary remedial work to the Engineer for Review. This new requirement to submit a proposal before proceeding to make good the defect allows the Engineer to evaluate whether the proposal will achieve the desired result. This is important as the defect may be caused simply by the Contractor's failure to use proper work methods.

If the Engineer undertakes a Review – it is not required to do so[72] – the Engineer must give either a Notice of No-objection or a Notice stating the extent to which the proposed remedial work, if carried out, would not result in the work complying with the Contract. In the latter case, the Contractor must 'promptly' submit a revised proposal to the Engineer and – though it is not stated – must, it is suggested, continue to do so repeatedly, if necessary, until it receives, or is deemed to have received, a Notice of No-objection.[73]

(4) Remedies upon Contractor's failure

If the Contractor fails promptly to submit a proposal (or revised proposal) for remedial work, or to carry out proposed remedial work to which the Engineer has given (or is deemed to have given) a Notice of No-objection, the Engineer may either:

(a) instruct the Contractor to repair, remedy, remove, replace and/or re-execute the defective work under sub-paragraphs (a) and/or (b) of Sub-Clause 7.6 [*Remedial Work*]; or
(b) reject the defective work by a Notice, with reasons, in which case the Employer may carry out the work itself or have others do so, at the Contractor's cost, pursuant to sub-paragraph (a) of Sub-Clause 11.4 [*Failure to Remedy Defects*].[74]

72. Note the word 'may' in Sub-Clause 7.5, second paragraph and Sub-Clause 1.2(e).
73. Sub-paragraph (f) of Sub-Clause 8.3 [*Programme*] requires that any revised programme includes the sequence and timing of the remedial work to which the Engineer has given a Notice of No-objection including, it is suggested, a deemed Notice of No-objection. A Notice of No-objection of the Engineer will not relieve the Contractor of any contractual obligation (Sub-Clause 3.2, last paragraph).
74. Sub-Clause 7.5, third paragraph. However, in Sub-Clause 11.4 there is a condition to the application of sub-para. (a), namely, that the Employer will

According to Sub-Clause 15.2.1(d), if 'without reasonable excuse' the Contractor fails to comply with:

(1) an Engineer's instruction under Sub-Clause 7.6,[75] or
(2) a Notice of rejection given by the Engineer under Sub-Clause 7.5,

within 28 days after receiving it, the Employer would be entitled to give the Contractor a Notice of its intention to terminate the Contract. Unless the Contractor remedies the matter described in the Notice within 14 days of receiving it, the Employer may[76] give a second Notice to the Contractor immediately terminating the Contract pursuant to Sub-Clause 15.2.2, without prejudice to the Employer's other rights.[77]

In this connection, it would seem safer for an Employer to rely on a failure by the Contractor to comply with an Engineer's instruction under Sub-Clause 7.6 rather than on a Notice of rejection by the Engineer under Sub-Clause 7.5. A Notice of rejection under Sub-Clause 7.5(b) leads to the application of Sub-Clause 11.4(a) entitling the Employer to carry out the work itself or have it carried out by others at the Contractor's cost. As the initiative is then with the Employer and there is nothing for the Contractor to do, it is unclear what Sub-Clause 15.2.1(d) means when it refers to where the Contractor 'fails to comply with a Notice of rejection given by the Engineer under Sub-Clause 7.5'. For this reason, assuming an Employer has the choice, it would be safer for it to rely on a failure by the Contractor to comply with an Engineer's instruction under Sub-Clause 7.6.

In parallel with the remedies under Sub-Clause 7.5, the Engineer might be able to withhold amounts in IPCs, pursuant to Sub-Clause 14.6.2, and

have given a specified Notice to the Contractor under the first paragraph of Sub-Clause 11.4. It is not clear whether it is to apply or not. As this Notice is not referred to, possibly Sub-Clause 7.5(b) is to be construed as though this Notice, which would normally under Sub-Clause 11.4 be issued during the DNP, is not required.

75. Arguably, 'without reasonable excuse' only applies to a Notice of rejection under Sub-Clause 7.5.
76. Possibly, after first giving a Notice to Correct under Sub-Clause 15.1 which goes unremedied, though this is not required.
77. *See* Sub-Clause 1.16 [*Contract Termination*] and the commentary on it above.

the Employer claim under the Performance Security, pursuant to Sub-Clause 4.2.2(d),[78] and on Retention Money accumulated under Sub-Clause 14.3(iii).[79]

(5) Retesting

Under the last paragraph of this Sub-Clause, after remedying the defects, the Engineer may require retesting of the remedied work which must be carried out in compliance with Sub-Clause 7.4 at the Contractor's risk and cost. The Employer may then recover, subject to Sub-Clause 20.2, the additional costs, if any, which it may have incurred as a result of the rejection and retesting.

(iv) Related Law:

(1) ICC case

In an ICC case based on a FIDIC form,[80] the Contractor had fabricated reinforced concrete panels near the site for use in a housing project. After their fabrication, the panels were found to contain hairline cracks[81] and the Employer instructed the Engineer to reject these panels, which the Engineer accordingly did. The Contractor argued that hairline cracks are inherent in reinforced concrete (as is the case), that the width of the cracks was within the tolerances permitted by applicable technical standards and that, therefore, rejection of the panels was unjustified. The arbitral tribunal upheld the Contractor's position, finding that the Employer's instruction combined with the Engineer's rejection of panels, was a Variation order for which the Contractor was entitled to compensation.[82]

78. And possibly (c).
79. Or claim on any retention money guarantee given in lieu of retention money. *See Guidance for the Preparation of Particular Conditions*, 42, relating to Sub-Clause 14.9 and Annex F of RB/17 containing an example form of retention money guarantee.
80. RB/69.
81. *Bulles* in French.
82. Final award, ICC cases 3790 / 3902 / 4050 / 4051 / 4054 (joined cases) (1984), reported in Abdul Hamid El-Ahdab, *Arbitration with the Arab Countries* (Kluwer Law and Taxation, the Netherlands, 1990) 892-895 (Subject 2: Procedure for provisional completion and the problems of the finishing standard of the works and of the determination of applicable norms). The full award is available on Jus Mundi.

(2) UNIDROIT Principles

Sub-Clause 7.5 and the following Sub-Clause 7.6 are generally consistent with the UNIDROIT Principles. Pursuant to Article 7.1.1 (*Non-performance defined*) of the Principles, defective performance by a party (i.e., the Contractor) will be considered as non-performance, which may allow certain remedies to the aggrieved party (i.e., the Employer).

Under Article 7.2.2 (*Performance of non-monetary obligation*), the aggrieved Party may insist on performance by the other party (i.e., the Contractor) if the latter does not perform a non-monetary obligation, subject to certain exceptions. Thus, for example (as exceptions), the Employer may not insist on performance by the Contractor if it has become impossible in law and/or in fact[83] or where performance is unreasonably burdensome or expensive or the Employer may reasonably obtain performance from another source.[84] This last exception is broadly consistent with Sub-Clause 7.5(b) which entitles the Engineer to reject defective work in which case the work may be carried out by the Employer or others. A further exception, not reflected expressly in RB/17, is that performance may not be requested if it is not required within a reasonable period of time after the aggrieved party has – or ought to have – become aware of the non-performance.[85] Article 7.2.3 (*Repair and replacement of defective performance*) of the Principles then states that the right to performance includes in appropriate cases the right to require 'repair, replacement, or other cure of defective performance', which is consistent with the remedies in Sub-Clause 7.6 [*Remedial Work*], next commented upon.

(v) Improvements:

(1) A definition of the term 'defect' should be provided in the Conditions as this matter can often be the subject of dispute.[86]
(2) It should be clarified what is meant by the Contractor's failure 'to comply with a Notice of rejection given by the Engineer under

83. Art. 7.2.2(a) of the UNIDROIT Principles. For example, performance might have become impossible if the Contractor had to build a second floor on a building that was completely demolished as a result of an earthquake.
84. Art. 7.2.2 (b) and (c) of the UNIDROIT Principles. *See also* official comment 3 on art. 7.2.2 of the UNIDROIT Principles.
85. Art. 7.2.2(e) of the UNIDROIT Principles.
86. *See* item (2) of **(iii) Improvements** at the end of the commentary on Sub-Clause 1.1 [*Definitions*] above where this point is developed.

Sub-Clause 7.5', which is referred to in Sub-Clause 15.2.1(d). Unlike Sub-Clause 7.5 of RB/99, which required the Contractor promptly to make good the defect, a Notice of rejection under Sub-Clause 7.5 of RB/17 leads to the application of sub-paragraph (a) of Sub-Clause 11.4, providing for the work to be carried out by the Employer or others, and imposes no obligation on the Contractor 'to comply with a Notice of rejection' of the Engineer.

--ooOOoo--

Figure 6 Remedying Defects During Execution of the Works[1]

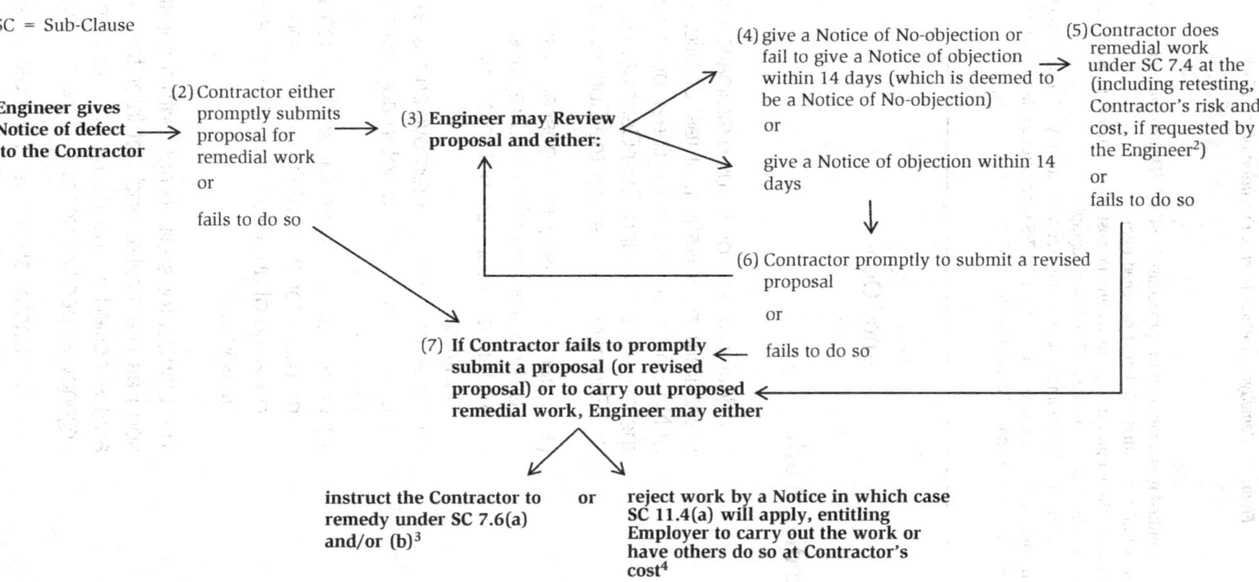
SC = Sub-Clause
(1) Engineer gives Notice of defect to the Contractor
(2) Contractor either promptly submits proposal for remedial work
or
fails to do so
(3) Engineer may Review proposal and either:
(4) give a Notice of No-objection or fail to give a Notice of objection within 14 days (which is deemed to be a Notice of No-objection)
or
give a Notice of objection within 14 days
(5) Contractor does remedial work under SC 7.4 at the (including retesting, Contractor's risk and cost, if requested by the Engineer[2])
or
fails to do so
(6) Contractor promptly to submit a revised proposal
or
fails to do so
(7) If Contractor fails to promptly submit a proposal (or revised proposal) or to carry out proposed remedial work, Engineer may either
instruct the Contractor to remedy under SC 7.6(a) and/or (b)[3]
or
reject work by a Notice in which case SC 11.4(a) will apply, entitling Employer to carry out the work or have others do so at Contractor's cost[4]

Source: Author's own work.

Figure 6 Remedying Defects During Execution of the Works

Notes

1. This figure is a simplified presentation of the procedure in SC 7.5 [*Defects and Rejection*] for illustrative purposes. Only the actual text of that SC should be relied upon.
2. If the retesting causes the Employer to incur additional cost, then, subject to SC 20.2, it is entitled to recover the same from the Contractor. *See* SC 7.5, last paragraph.
3. Pursuant to SC 15.2.1(d), a failure 'without reasonable excuse' to comply with an Engineer's instruction under SC 7.6 or an Engineer's Notice of rejection under SC 7.5 may, after 28 days, entitle the Employer to give a Notice of intention to terminate the Contract to the Contractor.
4. *Ibid.*

--ooOOoo--

7.6 Remedial Work

In addition to any previous examination, inspection, measurement or testing, or test certificate or Notice of No-objection by the Engineer, at any time before the issue of the Taking-Over Certificate for the Works the Engineer may instruct the Contractor to:

(a) repair or remedy (if necessary, off the Site), or remove from the Site and replace any Plant or Materials which are not in accordance with the Contract;
(b) repair or remedy, or remove and re-execute, any other work which is not in accordance with the Contract; and
(c) carry out any remedial work which is urgently required for the safety of the Works, whether because of an accident, unforeseeable event or otherwise.

The Contractor shall comply with the instruction as soon as practicable and not later than the time (if any) specified in the instruction, or immediately if urgency is specified under sub-paragraph (c) above.

The Contractor shall bear the cost of all remedial work required under this Sub-Clause, except to the extent that any work under sub-paragraph (c) above is attributable to:

(i) any act by the Employer or the Employer's Personnel. If the Contractor suffers delay and/or incurs Cost in carrying out such work, the Contractor shall be entitled subject to Sub-Clause 20.2 [*Claims for Payment and/or EOT*] to EOT and/or payment of such Cost Plus Profit; or

(ii) an Exceptional Event, in which case Sub-Clause 18.4 [*Consequences of an Exceptional Event*] shall apply.

If the Contractor fails to comply with the Engineer's instruction, the Employer may (at the Employer's sole discretion) employ and pay other persons to carry out the work. Except to the extent that the Contractor would have been entitled to payment for work under this Sub-Clause, the Employer shall be entitled subject to Sub-Clause 20.2 [*Claims for Payment and/or EOT*] to payment by the Contractor of all costs arising from this failure. This entitlement shall be without prejudice to any other rights the Employer may have, under the Contract or otherwise.

In addition to any previous examination, testing, test certificate or Notice of No-objection by the Engineer, the Engineer may instruct the Contractor to undertake the remedial work stated in sub-paragraphs (a) to (c) of the Sub-Clause before the issue of the Taking-Over Certificate for the Works.

The Contractor must comply with the Engineer's instruction not later than the time (if any) specified in the instruction, or immediately in case of remedial works urgently required for safety.

The cost of remedial work will be borne by the Contractor, except to the extent of urgently required work for safety attributable to: (i) an act by the Employer or the Employer's Personnel, or (ii) an Exceptional Event. In the case of item (i), the Contractor shall be entitled, subject to Sub-Clause 20.2, to an EOT and/or Cost Plus Profit. In the case of item (ii), Sub-Clause 18.4 shall apply.

If the Contractor fails to comply with the Engineer's instruction, the Employer may employ other persons to carry out the remedial work. The Employer will be entitled, subject to Sub-Clause 20.2 and without

prejudice to its rights, to payment of all costs arising from this failure, except to the extent the Contractor would have been entitled to payment under this Sub-Clause.

Commentary

(i) Main Changes from RB/99:

(1) Whereas Sub-Clause 7.6 of RB/99 stated that the Engineer might give an instruction under the Sub-Clause '[n]otwithstanding any previous test or certification', the new Sub-Clause stipulates that the Engineer's power to give an instruction applies '[i]n addition to any previous examination, inspection, measurement or testing, or test certificate or Notice of No-objection by the Engineer'.

(2) Whereas, under the new Sub-Clause, the Engineer may give an instruction for remedial work 'at any time before the issue of the Taking-Over Certificate for the Works', there was no similar provision in Sub-Clause 7.6 of RB/99.

(3) The Engineer's instructions under the new Sub-Clause provide for a wider range of relief than RB/99: sub-paragraphs (a) and (b) state that the Engineer's instruction may concern not only the removal and replacement of Plant or Materials, or removal and re-execution of any other work, not in accordance with the Contract (as was the case in RB/99), but also – and first of all – the 'repair or remedy' of such Plant, Materials and/or any other work.

(4) Whereas, under sub-paragraph (c) of Sub-Clause 7.6 of RB/99, the Engineer was authorised to give an instruction to the Contractor to execute 'any work' urgently required for the safety of the Works, under the new sub-paragraph, the Engineer is authorised instead to give an instruction to carry out 'any remedial work' which is urgently required for the safety of the Works.

(5) Whereas Sub-Clause 7.6 of RB/99 provided that the Contractor had to comply with the Engineer's instruction 'within a reasonable time, which shall be the time (if any) specified in the instruction', the new Sub-Clause states that the Contractor must do so 'as soon as practicable and not later than the time (if any) specified in the instruction'.

(6) The third paragraph of the new Sub-Clause, dealing with allocation of the cost of all remedial work between the Parties, is new.

(7) The last sentence of the Sub-Clause, stating that the Employer's entitlement to payment as a result of Contractor's failure to

comply with an Engineer's instruction will be without prejudice to the Employer's other rights, is also new.

(ii) Related Clauses / Sub-Clauses: 1.3 [*Notices and Other Communications*], 3.5 [*Engineer's Instructions*], 7.4 [*Testing by the Contractor*], 7.5 [*Defects and Rejection*], 8.3 [*Programme*], 10.1 [*Taking Over the Works and Sections*], 11.1 [*Completion of Outstanding Work and Remedying Defects*], 14.6.2 [*Withholding (amounts in) an IPC*], 15.2 [*Termination for Contractor's Default*], 18.4 [*Consequences of an Exceptional Event*] and 20.2 [*Claims for Payment and/or EOT*].

(iii) Analysis:

(1) Purpose of Sub-Clause

Whereas Sub-Clause 7.5 deals with where, as a result of any examination, inspection, measurement or testing (mainly under Sub-Clauses 7.3 or 7.4), the Engineer finds the Contractor's work to be defective, Sub-Clause 7.6 deals with where, independent of – and notwithstanding – any such previous examination, etc., including a test certificate[87] or Notice of No-objection[88] by the Engineer, the Engineer finds defective work 'before the issue of the Taking-Over Certificate for the Works'.[89] This Sub-Clause complements and reinforces the powers of the Engineer for dealing with defective work under Sub-Clause 7.5.

Under Sub-Clause 7.6, the Engineer may instruct the Contractor to: (a) repair or remedy (if necessary, off the Site), or remove from the Site and replace, Plant or Materials not in accordance with the Contract;[90] (b) repair or remedy, or remove and re-execute, any other work not in accordance with the Contract; and (c) carry out any remedial work urgently required for the safety of the Works.[91]

87. For example, under Sub-Clause 7.4, seventh paragraph.
88. For example, under Sub-Clause 7.5, second paragraph.
89. *See* the discussion below under *(2) Timing of Engineer's instructions* below.
90. If the Contractor desires to remove any Plant from the Site to remedy a defect during the DNP then, pursuant to Sub-Clause 11.5 [*Remedying of Defective Work off Site*], the Contractor must obtain the Employer's consent and, as a condition to this consent, the Employer may require the Contractor to increase the amount of the Performance Security. The possible need for the Contractor to increase the amount of the Performance Security is not mentioned in Sub-Clause 7.6.
91. The Engineer's instruction must comply with Sub-Clause 1.3 [*Notices and Other Communications*]. *See* the commentary on Sub-Clause 1.3 above.

As 'repair or remedy' should normally be less drastic than 'remove from the Site and replace' or 'remove and re-execute', normally the Engineer should be expected to instruct the less drastic remedy in the first instance, where it might be sufficient.[92]

(2) Timing of Engineer's instructions

The first paragraph provides that the Engineer is authorised to issue instructions 'at any time before the issue of the Taking-Over Certificate *for the Works*' (emphasis added). This indicates that no account is taken of where a separate Taking-Over Certificate has been issued for Sections or Parts of the Works or of where Sections or Parts are deemed to be complete. It thus appears, based on this wording, that the Engineer may issue instructions under Sub-Clause 7.6 with regard to any part of the Works, including Sections or Parts that have already been taken over by a separate Taking-Over Certificate, until a Taking-Over Certificate is issued for the whole of the Works.

(3) Compliance with Engineer's instructions

The second paragraph of the Sub-Clause requires the Contractor to comply with the Engineer's instruction 'as soon as practicable and not later than the time (if any) specified in the instruction'.[93] While more stringent than in RB/99, which required that the Contractor comply 'within a reasonable time', the new wording is appropriate, as work which the Engineer perceives to be defective should be rectified promptly. Complying with the Engineer's instruction is also likely to be the least expensive solution, whatever may be the cause, as the Contractor is on the Site, ready and able to perform. The Contractor must comply immediately if remedial work is urgently required for safety reasons. If immediate compliance is required, this should be specified in the instruction.

---

92. This is commanded by the legal principle of 'mitigation of damages' (i.e., making reasonable efforts to make damages less severe). Art. 7.4.8 (*Mitigation of harm*), para. 1, of the UNIDROIT Principles provides:

> The non-performing party [the Contractor] is not liable for harm suffered by the aggrieved party [the Employer] to the extent that the harm could have been reduced by the latter party's taking reasonable steps.

This principle is recognised, albeit in another context, in RB/17, *see* Sub-Clause 18.3 [*Duty to Minimise Delay*].

93. The sequence and timing of the remedial work must be included in the Contractor's Programme. Sub-Clause 8.3(f).

(4) Costs of remedial works

The third paragraph of the Sub-Clause provides that if the Engineer's instruction concerns the type of remedial works under sub-paragraphs (a) and (b) discussed above,[94] these costs shall be borne by the Contractor. While the Contractor may disagree that its work is not in accordance with the Contract, whether it does so or not, it must comply with the Engineer's instruction 'as soon as practicable [...], or immediately if urgency is specified [...]'.[95] If the Contractor believes that the Engineer's instruction amounts to the instruction of a Variation, then, pursuant to the last paragraph of Sub-Clause 3.5, the Contractor should immediately, before commencing any work related to the instruction, give a Notice to the Engineer to this effect with reasons. The Engineer would then have the opportunity to confirm, reverse or vary the instruction, should it wish to do so, and the Contractor would be bound by the Engineer's response. If the Engineer does not respond within 7 days, it is deemed to have revoked the instruction.[96]

As regards the Engineer's instruction under sub-paragraph (c) above (i.e., to carry out remedial works urgently required for the safety of the Works), the Contractor is bound also to comply. It must also bear the related costs unless the remedial work is attributable to: (i) the Employer or the Employer's Personnel or (ii) possibly, an Exceptional Event. In the case of (i), the Contractor will be entitled, subject to Sub-Clause 20.2, to claim an EOT and/or Cost Plus Profit. In the case of (ii), the Contractor will be entitled, again subject to Sub-Clause 20.2 and provided that the Contractor has given a Notice of the Exceptional Event under Sub-Clause 18.2, to an EOT and, in some cases, Cost (but not Cost Plus Profit).[97]

(5) Remedies upon Contractor's failure to comply with an Engineer's instruction

Under the last paragraph of the Sub-Clause, the Employer is entitled, at its sole discretion,[98] to employ and pay other persons to carry out the remedial work if the Contractor fails to comply with the Engineer's

94. Under *(1) Purpose of Sub-Clause*. Sub-paragraph (c) is discussed below.
95. Sub-Clause 7.6, second paragraph.
96. Sub-Clause 3.5 [*Engineer's Instructions*].
97. *See* the commentary on Sub-Clause 18.4 [*Consequences of an Exceptional Event*] below.
98. *See* item (1) of **(v) Improvements** of the commentary on Sub-Clause 1.2 [*Interpretation*] above.

instruction.[99] The Employer is also entitled, subject to Sub-Clause 20.2, to payment of all costs arising from such Contractor's failure, except to the extent that the Contractor would have been entitled to payment under the Sub-Clause.

The Employer's entitlement to payment is without prejudice to any other rights the Employer may have under the Contract or otherwise. Such other rights would include the Employer's rights under Sub-Clauses 15.1 [*Notice to Correct*] and 15.2 [*Termination for Contractor's Default*], the Engineer's right to withhold amounts in IPCs, and the Employer's right to claim on the Performance Security and retention money, described in the commentary on Sub-Clause 7.5 above[100] as available in case of a failure to comply with sub-paragraphs (a) and/or (b) of Sub-Clause 7.6 (referred to in Sub-Clause 7.5).[101]

(iv) Related Law: *See* the discussion above of the UNIDROIT Principles under **(iv) Related Law** in the commentary on Sub-Clause 7.5 above.

(v) Improvements: In light of the comments made under **(iii) Analysis** above, the following changes should be considered:

(1) The opening wording of the Sub-Clause ('[i]n addition to any previous examination [...]') should be clarified in order to avoid an argument that the Sub-Clause only applies to items of work that the Engineer has previously examined, inspected, measured or tested. In particular, the phrase '[i]n addition to' may be replaced by '[n]otwithstanding any' (the wording used in RB/99), which seems more appropriate.

(2) The Sub-Clause provides that the Engineer may only issue instructions for remedial work 'before the issue of a Taking-Over Certificate for the Works', i.e., before the commencement of the DNP. However, Sub-Clause 11.1 [*Completion of Outstanding Work and Remedying Defects*] allows, by way of a cross-reference to Sub-Clause 7.5, which in turn cross-refers in its third

99. But if the matter is contentious and if, as a result of the remedial work, evidence will be destroyed, the Employer should consider giving the Contractor advance warning of its intentions. *See* Nelson A.F. Mixon, 'My Building Is Evidence? The Line Between Repairs and Spoliation of Evidence' (2019) 21(1) UNDERCONSTRUCTION, ABA for Const L, 1.

100. *See* under *(4) Remedies upon Contractor's failure* under **(iii) Analysis** of the commentary on Sub-Clause 7.5 above.

101. *See also* the commentaries on Sub-Clauses 15.1 and 15.2 below.

paragraph to Sub-Clause 7.6, for the application of Sub-Clause 7.6 with regard to defects or damage occurring during the DNP,[102] which appears contradictory and should be clarified.

(3) It is unclear why the exception to the general rule in the third paragraph that the Contractor bears the cost of all remedial work applies only to the type of instruction 'under sub-paragraph (c) above' and not to those under sub-paragraphs (a) and (b) as well. It would be sensible if the same exception were to apply to the instructions under sub-paragraphs (a) and (b) as the Contractor should not be expected to bear the cost of *any* remedial work attributable to the Employer or the Employer's Personnel, or for which the Contractor is entitled to relief because of an Exceptional Event.

--ooOOoo--

7.7 Ownership of Plant and Materials

Each item of Plant and Materials shall, to the extent consistent with the mandatory requirements of the Laws of the Country, become the property of the Employer at whichever is the earlier of the following times, free from liens and other encumbrances:

(a) when it is delivered to the Site;
(b) when the Contractor is paid the value of the Plant and Materials under Sub-Clause 8.11 [*Payment for Plant and Materials after Employer's Suspension*]; or

102. Pursuant to Sub-Clause 11.1(iii), the second, third and fourth paragraphs of Sub-Clause 7.5 will apply with regard to the Contractor's proposal for remedial work concerning defects or damage occurring during the DNP and the consequences of any failure of the Contractor to submit such a proposal or to undertake the proposed remedial work. Sub-Clause 7.5, third paragraph, cross-refers to the application of Sub-Clause 7.6, sub-paras (a) and/or (b), that is, to the Engineer's authority to issue instructions for the repair, remedy, removal, replacement and/or re-execution of defective items of work (as the case may be) as a possible remedy in case of such Contractor's failures. Consequently, the Engineer seems authorised to issue instructions under Sub-Clause 7.6 concerning defects or damage occurring during the DNP.

(c) when the Contractor is paid the amount determined for the Plant and Materials under Sub-Clause 14.5 [*Plant and Materials intended for the Works*].

Each item of Plant and Materials will, to the extent consistent with the mandatory Laws of the Country, become the Employer's property, free from liens and encumbrances, when: (a) delivered to the Site, (b) the Contractor is paid its value under Sub-Clause 8.11, or (c) the Contractor is paid the amount determined for it under Sub-Clause 14.5, whichever is earlier.

Commentary

(i) Main Changes from RB/99:

(1) Whereas, under Sub-Clause 7.7 of RB/99, the provisions relating to the transfer of property in Plant and Materials to the Employer applied to the extent consistent with 'the Laws of the Country', the new Sub-Clause provides that they apply to the extent consistent with 'the mandatory requirements' of these Laws.
(2) Whereas under RB/99 the transfer of property in Plant and Materials would pass to the Employer when the Contractor was 'entitled to payment' for them in case of an Employer's suspension,[103] under the new Sub-Clause this occurs when the Contractor is actually 'paid' for them in such case.[104]
(3) Sub-paragraph (c) of the new Sub-Clause introduces a third alternative for the transfer of ownership over Plant and Materials when Sub-Clause 14.5 applies, which is new.

(ii) Related Clauses / Sub-Clauses: 1.13 [*Compliance with Laws*], 3.7 [*Agreement or Determination*], 8.11 [*Payment for Plant and Materials after Employer's Suspension*], 14.3 [*Application for Interim Payment*], 14.5 [*Plant and Materials Intended for the Works*], 14.7 [*Payment*], 17.1 [*Responsibility for Care of the Works*] and 17.2 [*Liability for Care of the Works*].

(iii) Analysis: The Sub-Clause identifies the point in time at which the Employer will acquire unencumbered (i.e., free from liens and encum-

103. *See* Sub-Clause 8.10 of RB/99.
104. *See* Sub-Clause 8.11 of RB/17.

brances[105]) ownership of Plant and Materials supplied by the Contractor which are not yet incorporated into the Permanent Works. This may be important in case, for example, during the execution of the Works, the Contractor (or the Employer) becomes bankrupt or insolvent and its assets need to be ascertained.

The Sub-Clause identifies the following times when ownership of Plant and Materials may pass to the Employer, free from any liens and encumbrances:

(1) when delivered to the Site;
(2) when the Contractor is paid their value under Sub-Clause 8.11 [*Payment for Plant and Materials after Employer's Suspension*], which enables the Contractor, under certain conditions, to be paid for Plant and Materials which, due to the Employer's suspension of the Works, have not yet been delivered to the Site;[106] or
(3) when the Contractor is paid the amount determined by the Engineer pursuant to Sub-Clause 3.7 [*Agreement or Determination*] for Plant and Materials under Sub-Clause 14.5 [*Plant and Materials Intended for the Works*], which enables the Contractor to receive an advance for Plant and Materials which have been shipped or delivered to the Site, subject to certain conditions.[107]

The ownership will pass to the Employer at whichever is the earlier of the above-mentioned times, subject to the mandatory Laws of the Country.[108]

---

105. A 'lien' is a legal right or interest that a creditor has in another's property, lasting usually until a debt or duty that it secures is satisfied. An 'encumbrance' is a claim or liability that is attached to property or some other right and that may lessen its value, such as a lien or mortgage; it is any property right that is not an ownership interest. Bryan A Garner (ed in chief), *Black's Law Dictionary* (11th edn, Thomson Reuters, St Paul, MN, 2019).
106. *See* the commentary on Sub-Clause 8.11 below.
107. *See* the commentary on Sub-Clause 14.5 below.
108. The Sub-Clause requires that the time of transfer of ownership or title be 'consistent with the mandatory requirements of the Laws of the Country'. *See* **Section 5 Mandatory Law at the Site** of **Chapter II Applicable Law** above. The *Guidance* contains an example provision which may be adopted if the Contractor is to provide high-value items of Plant and/or Materials under the Contract. This provision contains certain restrictions on the

The transfer of ownership over Plant and Materials does not mean that the Contractor will cease to be responsible for the risk of their loss or damage. Under Sub-Clause 17.1 [*Responsibility for Care of the Works*], the Contractor remains fully responsible, subject to the exceptions in Sub-Clause 17.2 [*Liability for Care of the Works*], for the care of the Works and Goods (which include Plant and Materials) from the Commencement Date until the issue of the Taking-Over Certificate for the Works or for any Section or Part thereof, as the case may be.

The provisions regarding the transfer of property in Sub-Clause 7.7 may conflict, potentially, with the Contractor's subcontracts and/or supply agreements should they provide, for example, that property in Plant and/or Materials will only pass to the Contractor once the respective Subcontractor and/or supplier has been paid.[109] If so, those agreements will need to be amended.

The Contractor's Equipment and Temporary Works do not become the property of the Employer or subject to its disposition except, in certain circumstances, in the case of termination of the Contract for the Contractor's default.[110]

(iv) Related Law: Laws in some countries grant lien rights to contractors, subcontractors or suppliers who have contributed to the improvement of real property – such as building works – but who have not been paid.[111] Such lien rights will attach to the Employer's improved property and are

removal from the Site of such Plant and/or Materials that have become Employer's property. *Guidance for Preparation of Particular Conditions*, 32-33. This provision could be supplemented by one entitling the Employer to require the Contractor to increase the amount of the Performance Security by the replacement cost of any Plant removed, as permitted in the circumstances provided for in Sub-Clause 11.5 [*Remedying of Defective Work off Site*], third paragraph. The *Guidance* also contains an example sub-clause for where a contract is being financed by an institution whose rules or policies restrict the use of its funds. *Guidance for Preparation of Particular Conditions*, 33.

109. *The FIDIC Contracts Guide* (2nd edn, FIDIC, 2022) 266.
110. *See* the commentary on Sub-Clause 15.2.4 [*Termination for Contractor's Default – Completion of the Works*] below.
111. In the US and Canada, these security rights are known as 'mechanic's liens'. *See* Justin Sweet and others, *Construction Law for Design Professionals, Construction Managers, and Contractors* (Cengage Learning, Stamford, CT, 2015) 418-422.

usually mandatory in nature. Consequently, those security interests will be unaffected by the rights granted to the Employer by Sub-Clause 7.7.

Laws concerning bankruptcy and similar proceedings, which are usually mandatory in nature, may also affect the passing of property in Plant and Materials, e.g., in a case where a Contractor who is in possession of Plant and Materials to be incorporated into the Permanent Works files for bankruptcy.[112]

(v) Improvements: A requirement could be added in RB/17 that the Contractor inserts provisions in its subcontracts and supply contracts that ensure that it is able to comply with the transfer of property provided for by this Sub-Clause.

--ooOOoo--

7.8 Royalties

Unless otherwise stated in the Specification, the Contractor shall pay all royalties, rents and other payments for:

(a) natural Materials obtained from outside the Site, and
(b) the disposal of material from demolitions and excavations and of other surplus material (whether natural or man-made), except to the extent that disposal areas within the Site are stated in the Specification.

Unless otherwise stated in the Specification, the Contractor must pay all royalties, rents and other payments for: (a) natural Materials obtained from outside the Site and (b) the disposal of surplus material, except to the extent disposal areas within the Site are stated in the Specification.

<u>**Commentary**</u>

(i) Main Changes from RB/99: The Sub-Clause is almost identical to the corresponding Sub-Clause 7.8 [*Royalties*] in RB/99.

112. For US law, *see* John M Mastin and others (eds), *Smith, Currie, and Hancock's Common Sense Construction Law: A Practical Guide for the Construction Professional* (6th edn, Wiley, Hoboken, NJ, 2020) 610-613.

(ii) Related Clauses / Sub-Clauses: 2.1 [*Right of Access to the Site*], 4.1 [*Contractor's General Obligations*], 4.22 [*Contractor's Operations on Site*] and 11.1 [*Clearance of Site*].

(iii) Analysis: As the Contractor must provide all Goods, which are defined to include Materials, required to fulfil its contractual obligations,[113] it is understandable that, unless stated otherwise in the Specification, the Contractor should pay all royalties, rents and other payments for natural Materials obtained from outside the Site, as provided for by this Sub-Clause. Similarly, in light of the Contractor's obligations to keep the Site at all times clear of surplus materials,[114] it is normal for it to be responsible for off-Site disposal of excavation, demolition and other surplus materials (whether natural or man-made). Therefore the Contractor will be responsible for making all necessary arrangements with owners and/or occupiers of quarries, borrow areas and spoil tips outside the Site for the procurement of Materials as well as for disposal activities.[115]

On the other hand, the Contractor will usually have no obligation to pay any royalties, rents and other payments for obtaining natural Materials from the Site and/or for disposal of surplus material to specified areas within the Site stated in the Specification.[116] Indeed, this may be implied from the wording of Sub-Clause 7.8 and the Contractor's right to possession of the Site under Sub-Clause 2.1 [*Right of Access to the Site*].

If the Employer foresees that a substantial amount of material may need to be disposed of, it may want to specify the areas where surplus material is to be placed. If so, the Employer should make clear whether these areas would be part of the Site or 'additional areas' acknowledged by the

113. Sub-Clause 4.1 [*Contractor's General Obligations*].
114. Sub-Clauses 4.22 [*Contractor's Operations on Site*] and 11.11 [*Clearance of Site*].
115. *The FIDIC Contracts Guide* (2nd edn, FIDIC, 2022) 267. The *Guide* also notes that the owners and/occupiers of these areas may, in certain cases, be ready to pay the Contractor for the benefit of being able to use the disposed surplus materials and the Contractor is generally allowed to retain such payments.
116. *The FIDIC Contracts Guide* (2nd edn, FIDIC, 2022) states that the Contractor would typically be entitled to use, without payment, the earth, rock and other natural Materials on the Site for any earthworks which may be necessary for the Works. Similarly, the Contractor would not expect to pay the Employer for the disposal of materials at specified areas within the Site. *The FIDIC Contracts Guide* (2nd edn, FIDIC, 2022) 266-267.

Engineer as working areas, as referred to in Sub-Clause 4.22 [*Contractor's Operations on Site*], which are not part of the Site, or elsewhere.

--ooOOoo--

8 Commencement, Delays and Suspension

This Clause relates to matters of time, including when Works commence, the Time for Completion, the Contractor's programme and the circumstances in which the Contractor is entitled to extensions of the Time for Completion including, among other things, in the case of delays caused by public authorities. The Clause provides that the Engineer has the right to instruct the Contractor to expedite progress and to suspend the Work, and provides as well as for the Contractor's liability for Delay Damages should it fail to complete the Works within the Time for Completion, as extended. In addition, it requires each Party and the Engineer to provide advance warning to the others of any known or probable future event or circumstance which may adversely affect the execution of the Works.

--ooOOoo--

8.1 Commencement of Works

The Engineer shall give a Notice to the Contractor stating the Commencement Date, not less than 14 days before the Commencement Date. Unless otherwise stated in the Particular Conditions, the Commencement Date shall be within 42 days after the Contractor receives the Letter of Acceptance.

The Contractor shall commence the execution of the Works on, or as soon as is reasonably practicable after, the Commencement Date and shall then proceed with the Works with due expedition and without delay.

--ooOOoo--

8.2 Time for Completion

The Contractor shall complete the whole of the Works, and each Section (if any), within the Time for

Completion for the Works or Section (as the case may be), including completion of all work which is stated in the Contract as being required for the Works or Section to be considered to be completed for the purposes of taking over under Sub-Clause 10.1 [*Taking Over the Works and Sections*].

The Engineer must give a Notice to the Contractor of the Commencement Date within 42 days after the Contractor receives the Letter of Acceptance and not less than 14 days before the Commencement Date. The Contractor must then proceed with due expedition and without delay, and complete the Works and each Section (if any) within the Time for Completion for the Works or Section.

Commentary

(i) Main Changes from RB/99:

(1) According to new Sub-Clause 8.1, the Engineer must give the Contractor a Notice of the Commencement Date at least 14 days prior thereto, instead of 7 days as provided in RB/99.

(2) The Contractor is no longer expressly required by Sub-Clause 8.2 to achieve the passing of the Tests on Completion (as in Sub-Clause 8.2 of RB/99) as, for the Works to have been completed under RB/17, the Tests on Completion must have been passed.[1]

(ii) Related Clauses / Sub-Clauses: 1.3 [*Notices and Other Communications*], 1.6 [*Contract Agreement*], 4.3 [*Contractor's Representative*], 4.8 [*Health and Safety Obligations*], 4.9 [*Quality Management and Compliance Verification Systems*], 8.3 [*Programme*], 8.8 [*Delay Damages*], 10.1 [*Taking Over the Works and Sections*], 14.4 [*Schedule of Payments*], 15.2 [*Termination for Contractor's Default*], 16.2 [*Termination by Contractor*] and 17.1 [*Responsibility for Care of the Works*].

(iii) Analysis: As a practical matter, the Contractor cannot be expected to begin work until some weeks after the Contract has entered into effect. This is because the Contractor will need this time to, among other things, allocate and mobilise its resources (of labour, equipment, Plant and Materials), transport them to the Site, possibly in another country, provide a Performance Security, and arrange insurance. Similarly, the

1. *See* sub-para. (a) of Sub-Clause 10.1 [*Taking Over the Works and Sections*].

Employer will need time to arrange to give the Contractor right of access to, and possession of, the Site. For these and other reasons, Sub-Clause 8.1 provides for a 'Commencement Date' that is separate and distinct from the date of entry into the Contract, as described below.

(1) The Letter of Acceptance, Commencement Date and Time for Completion

Upon the Contractor's acknowledgement of receipt of the Letter of Acceptance from the Employer, if not earlier, the Parties are deemed to have entered into a binding Contract.[2] If there is no Letter of Acceptance, they will do so by the signing of a Contract Agreement.[3] The Parties have three important obligations linked to the Contractor's receipt of the Letter of Acceptance (or, absent one, the signing of the Contract Agreement):

(1) the Employer must give the Contractor right of access to, and possession of, all or part of the Site within the time (or times) stated in the Contract Data calculated from the Contractor's receipt of the Letter of Acceptance;[4]

(2) the Contractor must deliver the Performance Security to the Employer, with a copy to the Engineer, within 28 days after receiving the Letter of Acceptance;[5] and

(3) the Parties must jointly appoint the member(s) of the DAAB within the time stated in the Contract Data (if not stated, 28 days) after the date the Contractor receives the Letter of Acceptance.[6]

---

2. *See* the last paragraph of the form of the Letter of Acceptance in RB/17.
3. *See* Sub-Clause 1.1.50 **'Letter of Acceptance'** which provides that if there is no letter of acceptance, the expression 'Letter of Acceptance' in the Conditions means the Contract Agreement and the date of issuing or receiving the Letter of Acceptance means in the Conditions the date of signing of the Contract Agreement.
4. Sub-Clause 2.1 and form of Contract Data. By this time, the Employer should have provided the Contractor with such permits, permissions, licences and/or approvals, pursuant to sub-para. (a) of Sub-Clause 1.13 [*Compliance with Laws*], as required to enable it to commence work.
5. Sub-Clause 4.2.1.
6. Sub-Clause 21.1, first paragraph. *See also* **Figure 5 Sequence of Events Before the Commencement Date ('CD')** at the end of the commentary on Clause 4 above.

According to Sub-Clause 8.1, the Commencement Date must be within 42 days[7] after the Contractor receives the Letter of Acceptance unless otherwise stated in the Particular Conditions.[8] The Engineer (or the Employer) decides on that date, and the Engineer must give Notice of it to the Contractor not less than 14 days before the Commencement Date. If the Contractor does not receive Notice of the Commencement Date within 84 days after receiving the Letter of Acceptance, the Contractor is entitled to give the Employer a Notice of the Contractor's intention to terminate the Contract.[9]

The Contractor must commence the execution of the Works on, or as soon as reasonably practicable after, the Commencement Date.[10] In fact, the Contractor will already have agreed to do so by the Letter of Tender.[11] Once the Works are commenced, the Contractor must proceed with them 'with due expedition and without delay'[12] throughout the execution of the Works. The Contractor may not adjust its pace freely but must 'proceed in accordance with the Programme, subject to the Contractor's other obligations under the Contract'.[13] Should it fall behind the

7. A '**day**' is defined as a calendar day, *see* Sub-Clause 1.1.25.
8. The World Bank's COPA requires that Sub-Clause 8.1 be replaced by a provision providing, among other things, that the Engineer not issues the Notice of the Commencement Date until after five conditions (signature of the Contract Agreement, delivery of reasonable evidence of the Employer's financial arrangements, effective access to and possession of the Site, receipt by the Contractor of the Advance Payment and constitution of the DAAB) have been fulfilled. This seems like a useful provision.
9. *See* Sub-Clause 16.2.1(f). The Contractor may also be able to claim an adjustment of its rates and prices in the Tender.
10. Sub-Clause 8.1, second paragraph.
11. *See* the form of the Letter of Tender in RB/17 which provides that if:

> this offer is accepted, we will provide the specified Performance Security, commence the Works as soon as is reasonably practicable after the Commencement Date, and complete the Works … within the Time for Completion.

12. Sub-Clause 8.1, second paragraph.
13. *See* Sub-Clause 8.3, fourth paragraph. This assumes that the Contractor has submitted a detailed time programme to which the Engineer has given (or is deemed to have given) a Notice of No-objection under Sub-Clause 8.3. *See* Sub-Clause 1.1.66 '**Programme**'. The Contractor's obligation to proceed in accordance with the Programme is also important because the Employer's Personnel are entitled to rely on the Programme when planning their activities. *See* Sub-Clause 8.3, fourth paragraph. The Contractor's 'other

Programme, the Engineer may instruct it to take corrective measures so as to get back on schedule.[14]

The Contractor must complete the whole of the Works and each Section (if any) within the Time for Completion for the Works or Section,[15] as the case may be,[16] calculated from the Commencement Date[17] and as it may be extended.[18]

(2) Significance of the Commencement Date

The Commencement Date is of critical importance for many reasons. Not only is the Time for Completion calculated from that date but the Contractor takes full responsibility for the Works, Goods and Contractor's Documents (as they may then exist) as from that date.[19] From that date until the issue of the Performance Certificate, the Contractor must provide all necessary superintendence of the execution of the Works.[20]

In addition, the Contractor has the following specific obligations which are linked to the Commencement Date:[21]

---

obligations under the Contract' might include its obligation to accelerate under Sub-Clause 8.7 [*Rate of Progress*] or to comply with an instruction to suspend under Sub-Clause 8.9 [*Employer's Suspension*].

14. Sub-Clause 8.7 [*Rate of Progress*]. It has been stated that the obligation to 'proceed with the Works with due expedition and without delay' is 'not directed to every task on the contractor's to-do list. It is principally directed to activities which are or may become critical'. *Obrascon Huarte Lain SA v HM Attorney General for Gibraltar* [2015] EWCA Civ 712; [2015] BLR 521, 542 [para. 132] citing to *Sabic UK Petrochemicals Ltd v Punj Lloyd Ltd* [2013] EWHC 2916 (TCC); [2014] BLR 43 in particular para. 166. In *Obrascon*, the contract was based on YB/99.
15. The Time for Completion for any Section should be specified in the Contract Data form.
16. Sub-Clause 8.2 [*Time for Completion*].
17. Sub-Clause 1.1.84 **'Time for Completion'**.
18. Sub-Clause 8.5 [*Extension of Time for Completion*].
19. Sub-Clause 17.1 [*Responsibility for Care of the Works*].
20. Sub-Clause 6.8 [*Contractor's Superintendence*].
21. *See* **Figure 5 Sequence of Events Before the Commencement Date ('CD')** at the end of the commentary on Clause 4 above and **Figure 7 Sequence of Initial Events After the Commencement Date ('CD')** at the end of this commentary on Sub-Clauses 8.1 and 8.2 below.

(1) Unless the Contractor's Representative is named in the Contract, the Contractor must, before the Commencement Date, submit to the Engineer for consent the name and particulars of the person the Contractor proposes to appoint as Contractor's Representative.[22]

(2) If the Contractor finds an error in any items of reference, it must give a Notice to the Engineer describing it within the period stated in the Contract Data (if not stated, 28 days) calculated from the Commencement Date, if the items of reference are specified on the Drawings and/or in the Specification.[23]

(3) Within 21 days of the Commencement Date and before commencing any construction on the Site, the Contractor must submit to the Engineer for information a health and safety manual which has been specifically prepared for the Works, the Site and other places (if any) where the Contractor intends to execute the Works.[24]

(4) Within 28 days of the Commencement Date, the Contractor must submit to the Engineer the QM System which the Contractor is required to prepare specifically for the Works.[25]

(5) The Contractor must submit to the Engineer a first monthly progress report covering the period up to the end of the first month following the Commencement Date.[26]

(6) The Contractor must submit an initial programme for the execution of the Works to the Engineer within 28 days after receiving a Notice from the Engineer, pursuant to Sub-Clause 8.1, stating the Commencement Date.[27]

(7) Unless otherwise stated in the Particular Conditions, the Contractor must submit to the Engineer, within 28 days after the Commencement Date, a proposed breakdown of each lump sum price (if any) in the Schedules.[28]

---

22. Sub-Clause 4.3 [*Contractor's Representative*].
23. Sub-Clause 4.7.2 [*Setting Out – Errors*]. Presumably this refers to Drawings included in the Contract. *See* the commentary on Sub-Clause 4.7 [*Setting Out*] above.
24. Sub-Clause 4.8 [*Health and Safety Obligations*].
25. Sub-Clause 4.9.1 [*Quality Management and Compliance Verification Systems – Quality Management System*].
26. Sub-Clause 4.20 [*Progress Reports*]. It must be submitted within seven days of that month.
27. Sub-Clause 8.3 [*Programme*].
28. Sub-Clause 14.1 [*The Contract Price*].

(8) If the Contract does not include a Schedule of Payments, the Contractor must submit non-binding estimates of the payments which the Contractor expects to become due during each successive period of 3 months; the first estimate must be submitted within 42 days after the Commencement Date.[29]

(9) The Contractor must insure the Works, Contractor's Documents, Materials and Plant for incorporation in the Works from the Commencement Date until the date of the issue of the Taking-Over Certificate for the Works.[30]

(iv) Related law: A construction contract will almost always stipulate a time for completion, generally measured in days, rather than simply a specified completion date as in other commercial contracts. In the case of FIDIC contracts, such as RB/17, this is because the starting date, called the 'Commencement Date', is not a fixed date but may vary within certain limits[31] making it impossible to specify a fixed completion date in the contract.[32]

However, occasionally a construction contract will not stipulate a time for completion, or any such time that might have been stipulated may have ceased to apply. In that case, the Contractor is not generally entitled to complete at any time. Instead, as provided, for example, by the UNIDROIT Principles, it must do so 'within a reasonable time after the conclusion of the contract'.[33] While English and French law are to the same effect,[34] the situation may be different in other countries, as 'some civil law countries order the obligor [the Contractor] to perform immediately',[35] whatever that may mean in a construction contract context.

29. Sub-Clause 14.4 [*Schedule of Payments*].
30. Sub-Clause 19.2.1 [*Insurance to Be Provided by the Contractor – The Works*].
31. For the reasons given in the first paragraph under **(iii) Analysis** above of this commentary on Sub-Clauses 8.1 and 8.2.
32. *See* Sub-Clause 1.1.7 '**Commencement Date**'.
33. Art. 6.1.1(c) (*Time of performance*) of the UNIDROIT Principles.
34. Julian Bailey, *Construction Law* (3rd edn, London Publishing, UK, 2020) vol 2, 966-967 (para. 11.14) and Philippe Malinvaud (ed in chief), *Droit de la Construction* (7th edn, Dalloz Action, Paris, 2018) 1136 (para. 402.91). *See* the discussion under **(iv) Related Law** in the commentary on Sub-Clause 8.5 below.
35. Stefan Vogenauer (ed), *Commentary on the UNIDROIT Principles of International Commercial Contracts (PICC)* (2nd edn, OUP, Oxford, 2015) 722

(v) Improvements: When giving the Contractor Notice of the Commencement Date, the Engineer should require the Contractor to submit the insurance policies required by Sub-Clause 19.2 unless the Contractor would have submitted these previously. RB/17 does not specify the time for their submission.

--ooOOoo--

(para. 17). This work refers to provisions of the German, Swiss, Dutch and Italian civil codes to this effect.

Figure 7 Sequence of Initial Events after the Commencement Date ('CD')[1]

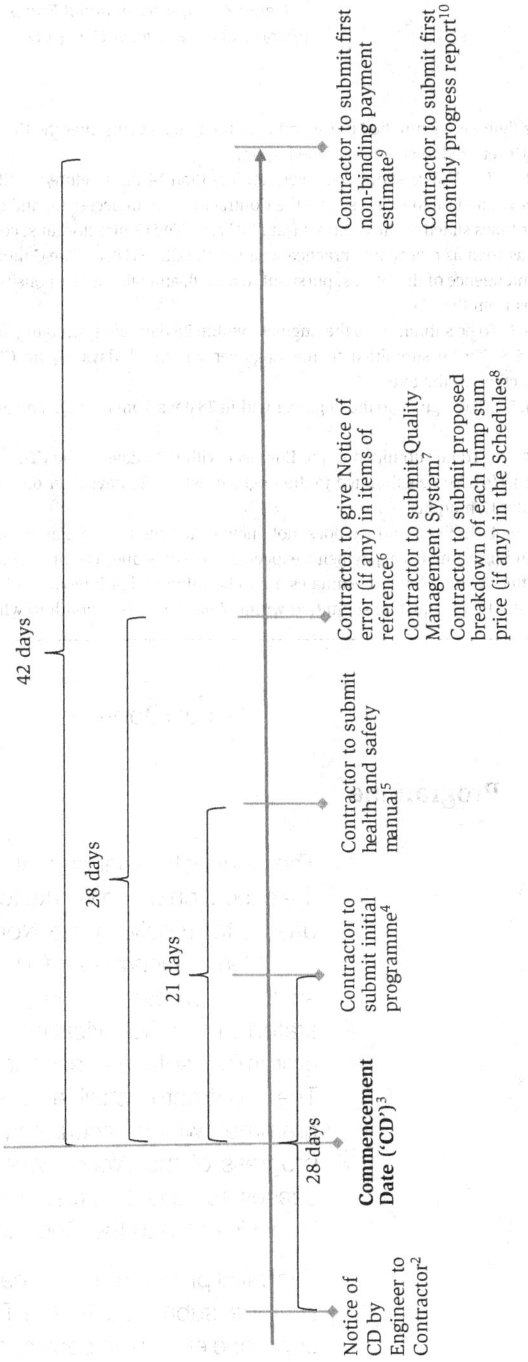

42 days

28 days

21 days

28 days

Notice of CD by Engineer to Contractor[2]

Commencement Date ('CD')[3]

Contractor to submit initial programme[4]

Contractor to submit health and safety manual[5]

Contractor to give Notice of error (if any) in items of reference[6]

Contractor to submit Quality Management System[7]

Contractor to submit proposed breakdown of each lump sum price (if any) in the Schedules[8]

Contractor to submit first non-binding payment estimate[9]

Contractor to submit first monthly progress report[10]

Source: Author's own work.

Figure 7 Sequence of Initial Events after the Commencement Date ('CD')

Notes SC = Sub-Clause

1. This figure is a simplified presentation of the initial events after the CD. Only the text of the Sub-Clauses ('SC(s)') referred to should be relied upon.
2. SC 8.1. The Notice should be given not less than 14 days before the CD.
3. SC 8.1. The Employer must give the Contractor right of access to, and possession of, the Site within the time or times stated in the Contract Data (SC 2.1). The Contractor must commence execution of the Works on, or as soon as reasonably practicable after, the CD (SC 8.1). The Contractor must provide all necessary superintendence of the Works, pursuant to SC 6.8, and take full responsibility for their care pursuant to SC 17.1, as from the CD.
4. SC 8.3. To be submitted to the Engineer within 28 days after receiving the Notice of the CD under SC 8.1.
5. SC 4.8. To be submitted to the Engineer within 21 days of the CD and before commencing any construction on the Site.
6. SC 4.7.2. To be given to the Engineer within 28 days from the CD, if no other period stated in the Contract Data.
7. SC 4.9.1. To be submitted to the Engineer within 28 days of the CD.
8. SC 14.1(d). To be submitted to the Engineer within 28 days after the CD unless otherwise stated in the Particular Conditions.
9. SC 14.4. If the Contract does not include a Schedule of Payments, the Contractor must submit non-binding estimates of payments expected to become due. The first estimate is to be submitted within 42 days after the CD. Revised estimates are to be submitted at intervals of 3 months thereafter.
10. SC 4.20. This must be submitted within 7 days after the month to which it relates.

--ooOOoo--

8.3 Programme

The Contractor shall submit an initial programme for the execution of the Works to the Engineer within 28 days after receiving the Notice under Sub-Clause 8.1 [*Commencement of Works*]. This programme shall be prepared using programming software stated in the Specification (if not stated, the programming software acceptable to the Engineer). The Contractor shall also submit a revised programme which accurately reflects the actual progress of the Works, whenever any programme ceases to reflect actual progress or is otherwise inconsistent with the Contractor's obligations.

The initial programme and each revised programme shall be submitted to the Engineer in one paper copy, one electronic copy and additional paper copies (if any) as stated in the Contract Data, and shall include:

(a) the Commencement Date and the Time for Completion, of the Works and of each Section (if any);
(b) the date right of access to and possession of (each part of) the Site is to be given to the Contractor in accordance with the time (or times) stated in the Contract Data. If not so stated, the dates the Contractor requires the Employer to give right of access to and possession of (each part of) the Site;
(c) the order in which the Contractor intends to carry out the Works, including the anticipated timing of each stage of design (if any), preparation and submission of Contractor's Documents, procurement, manufacture, inspection, delivery to Site, construction, erection, installation, work to be undertaken by any nominated Subcontractor (as defined in Sub-Clause 5.2 [*Nominated Subcontractors*]) and testing;
(d) the Review periods for any submissions stated in the Specification or required under these Conditions;
(e) the sequence and timing of inspections and tests specified in, or required by, the Contract;
(f) for a revised programme: the sequence and timing of the remedial work (if any) to which the Engineer has given a Notice of No-objection under Sub-Clause 7.5 [*Defects and Rejection*] and/or the remedial work (if any) instructed under Sub-Clause 7.6 [*Remedial Work*];
(g) all activities (to the level of detail stated in the Specification), logically linked and showing the earliest and latest start and finish dates for each activity, the float (if any), and the critical path(s);
(h) the dates of all locally recognised days of rest and holiday periods (if any);
(i) all key delivery dates of Plant and Materials;
(j) for a revised programme and for each activity: the actual progress to date, any delay to such progress and the effects of such delay on other activities (if any); and
(k) a supporting report which includes:
    (i) a description of all the major stages of the execution of the Works;

(ii) a general description of the methods which the Contractor intends to adopt in the execution of the Works;
(iii) details showing the Contractor's reasonable estimate of the number of each class of Contractor's Personnel, and of each type of Contractor's Equipment, required on the Site, for each major stage of the execution of the Works;
(iv) if a revised programme, identification of any significant change(s) to the previous programme submitted by the Contractor; and
(v) the Contractor's proposals to overcome the effects of any delay(s) on progress of the Works.

The Engineer shall Review the initial programme and each revised programme submitted by the Contractor and may give a Notice to the Contractor stating the extent to which it does not comply with the Contract or ceases to reflect actual progress or is otherwise inconsistent with the Contractor's obligations. If the Engineer gives no such Notice:

- within 21 days after receiving the initial programme; or
- within 14 days after receiving a revised programme

the Engineer shall be deemed to have given a Notice of No-objection and the initial programme or revised programme (as the case may be) shall be the Programme.

The Contractor shall proceed in accordance with the Programme, subject to the Contractor's other obligations under the Contract. The Employer's Personnel shall be entitled to rely on the Programme when planning their activities.

Nothing in any programme, the Programme or any supporting report shall be taken as, or relieve the Contractor of any obligation to give, a Notice under the Contract.

If, at any time, the Engineer gives a Notice to the Contractor that any programme fails (to the extent stated) to comply with the Contract or ceases to reflect actual progress or is otherwise inconsistent with the Contractor's obligations, the Contractor shall within 14 days after receiving this Notice submit a revised programme to the Engineer in accordance with this Sub-Clause.

The Contractor shall submit an initial programme for the Works to the Engineer within 28 days after receiving the Notice under Sub-Clause 8.1. The Contractor must also submit a revised programme whenever any programme ceases to reflect actual progress or is otherwise inconsistent with the Contractor's obligations. The initial programme and each revised programme must include the information specified in sub-paragraphs (a) to (k). The Engineer must Review the initial programme and each revised programme and each must be the subject of a Notice (or deemed Notice) of No-objection from the Engineer, after which it becomes the Programme. Thereafter, the Contractor must proceed in accordance with the Programme, subject to the Contractor's other obligations, and the Employer's Personnel are entitled to rely on it. If, at any time, the Engineer gives a Notice to the Contractor that any programme ceases to reflect actual progress or is otherwise inconsistent with the Contractor's obligations, the Contractor must within 14 days submit a revised programme to the Engineer for Review.

Commentary

(i) Main Changes from RB/99:

(1) Unlike Sub-Clause 8.3 of RB/99, the new Sub-Clause provides in the first paragraph that the programme to be submitted by the Contractor must be prepared using programming software stated in the Specification or otherwise acceptable to the Engineer.

(2) Compared to RB/99, the required contents of the programme are set out in much greater detail (in sub-paragraphs (a) through (k) of the second paragraph), and are much more specific and require, among other things, that all activities, to the level of detail specified, are 'logically linked and showing the earliest

and latest start and finish dates for each activity, the float (if any), and the critical path(s)'.[36]

(3) Whereas previously it was implicit that the Engineer review the programme, now Review (as defined) by the Engineer of the initial programme and each revised programme is explicitly required and the procedure for Review is described.

(4) A new penultimate paragraph provides that nothing in any programme, the Programme (as defined) or any supporting report shall be taken as, or relieve the Contractor of any obligation to give, a Notice under the Contract.[37]

(5) The penultimate paragraph of Sub-Clause 8.3 of RB/99 requiring the Contractor to give advance warning of probable future adverse events is the subject of a new – and separate – Sub-Clause 8.4 [*Advance Warning*] in RB/17.

(ii) Related Clauses / Sub-Clauses: 1.3 [*Notice and Other Communications*], 1.9 [*Delayed Drawings or Instructions*], 2.1 [*Right of Access to Site*], 4.20 [*Progress Report*], 5.2 [*Nominated Subcontractors*], 6.10 [*Contractor's Records*], 7.5 [*Defects and Rejection*], 7.6 [*Remedial Work*], 8 [*Commencement, Delays and Suspension*] and 13.3 [*Variation Procedure*].

(iii) Analysis:

(1) The importance of the Contractor's Programme

The Contractor's Programme is a key management tool as it sets out how, in what sequence and with what resources (in terms of labour, Contractor's Equipment, Plant and Materials) and methods, the Contractor proposes to execute the Works during the Time for Completion. The Programme shows how the Contractor plans to organise its work, permits the Engineer to satisfy itself as to the Programme's feasibility and to monitor the Contractor's progress, and enables the Employer's Personnel to plan their activities.[38]

36. Sub-paragraph (g) of Sub-Clause 8.3.

37. The Programme, with a capital 'P', is defined as a detailed time programme submitted by the Contractor to which the Engineer has given, or is deemed to have given, a Notice of No-objection under Sub-Clause 8.3 [*Programme*]. Sub-Clause 1.1.66 **'Programme'**.

38. The Contractor is free to plan and schedule the execution of the Works as it pleases within the Time for Completion and subject to the constraints in the Contract.

The Contractor must keep the Programme continuously up-to-date. Whenever any programme ceases to reflect actual progress (whether such progress is behind or ahead of the programme) or is otherwise inconsistent with the Contractor's obligations, the Contractor must submit a revised programme which reflects the actual progress of the Works.[39] Unless the Programme is up-to-date, it serves no purpose.[40]

However, the Contractor's Programme is not, nor does it become, part of the Contract.[41] Instead, it is a separate document which the Contractor prepares and submits to the Engineer for Review and a Notice of No-objection, and which the Contractor updates pursuant to the Contract.

(2) The Engineer's Review of the Contractor's Programme

The Contractor must submit an initial programme for the execution of the Works to the Engineer within 28 days after receiving the Engineer's Notice of the Commencement Date.[42] Similarly, the Contractor must submit each revised or updated programme, reflecting the actual progress of the Works, to the Engineer.

The Engineer neither approves nor disapproves of the Contractor's programmes.[43] Instead, it is required to Review (as defined) the initial programme and each revised programme and either give a Notice stating the extent to which it is deficient (e.g., does not comply with the Contract), or a Notice of No-objection. If the Engineer gives no Notice

39. Sub-Clause 8.3, first paragraph.
40. The revised programmes should have the same content and be in the same format (e.g., have the same structure of activities) as the original programme so that the original and updated programmes can be readily compared. Where the content and/or format of programmes is allowed to change, this can substantially reduce their utility.
41. It is not unusual for the Employer to include a general or high-level time programme 'showing the work sequence, phases and completion dates' in the tender dossier (notably, in the Specification) and for this later to become part of the Contract. *See FIDIC Procurement Procedures Guide* (FIDIC, 2011), 119. However, such a programme is to be distinguished from, and will be superseded by, the more detailed initial and revised programmes which the Contractor prepares and submits under Sub-Clause 8.3.
42. Sub-Clause 8.3, first paragraph.
43. By contrast, prior to RB/99, the Engineer was required to either 'approve' (Clause 14, RB/77) or 'consent' to (Clause 14, RB/87) the Contractor's programme.

within specified time periods (21 days or 14 days), it is deemed to have given a Notice of No-objection and the Contractor's programme is then deemed to be the 'Programme', as defined.[44] This manner of proceeding is designed to limit the Engineer's responsibility for the Contractor's programmes.[45]

(3) The contents of the Contractor's Programme(s)

The new and much more detailed requirements for the contents of the Contractor's programmes reflect the important developments in the programming field since the publication of RB/99. Whereas experienced contractors would have been preparing most, if not all, of the programming information provided for by this Sub-Clause for their internal purposes anyway, the Contractor is now required to disclose that information in the programmes to be submitted to the Engineer for its Notice of No-objection,[46] allowing the Engineer to monitor the Contractor's work more closely.

Among other things:

(1) the programming software to be used must be agreed between the Parties or be acceptable to the Engineer;[47]
(2) each programme must state the date that the Employer is to provide right of access to and possession of each part of the Site to the Contractor in accordance with the time (or times) stated in the Contract Data;[48] and
(3) all activities (to the level of detail stated in the Specification) must be logically linked and show the earliest and latest start and finish dates for each activity, the float (if any) and the critical path(s).[49]

44. Sub-Clause 8.3, third paragraph. The Employer's Personnel are now entitled to rely on it. Sub-Clause 8.3, fourth paragraph.
45. This is reinforced by the last paragraph of Sub-Clause 3.2 [*Engineer's Duties and Authority*] providing that no 'Notice', 'No-objection', 'Review' or 'absence of any such act' by the Engineer shall relieve the Contractor of any obligation under the Contract.
46. *See* the new definition of '**Programme**', Sub-Clause 1.1.66.
47. Sub-Clause 8.3, first paragraph.
48. Sub-Clause 8.3(b).
49. Sub-Clause 8.3(g).

The requirements of the Contractor's programme may be especially relevant to the Contractor's claims. Thus, the requirement in sub-paragraph (c) that the programme includes 'the order in which the Contractor intends to carry out the Works' may be relevant, for example, to a claim that the Engineer has been late in issuing drawings, pursuant to Sub-Clause 1.9. Similarly, the requirement in sub-paragraph (i) that the programme includes 'all key delivery dates of Plant and Materials' may be relevant to a claim, pursuant to Sub-Clause 8.11, for payment of the value of Plant and Materials whose delivery to the Site has been prevented by a suspension instructed by the Engineer.

In general, the requirements for programmes follow quite closely the recommendations contained in the *Delay and Disruption Protocol* (the '*D&D Protocol*')[50] of the UK Society of Construction Law ('SCL') which is often used as 'guidance'[51] in construction projects around the world. Indeed, the *D&D Protocol* usefully complements the provisions of Clause 8.[52]

50. 2nd edition, February 2017. However, one point not dealt with in RB/17 which the Protocol recommends that parties address in their contracts (*see* para. 8.2 on p. 28) is who owns the 'float' (defined in the *D&D Protocol*, as '[t]he time available for an activity in addition to its planned duration', 64).

51. The *D&D Protocol* provides that:

> The object of the Protocol is to provide useful guidance on some of the common delay and disruption issues that arise on construction projects, where one party wishes to recover from the other an extension of time (EOT) and/or compensation for the additional time spent and the resources used to complete the project. 1 (Introduction para. A).

While it 'aims to be consistent with good practice' it 'is not put forward as the benchmark of good practice [...]', even in the United Kingdom, *D&D Protocol*, 1 (Introduction para. E). Like other documents derived from domestic law or practice, the *D&D Protocol* is of value internationally to the extent that its contents are recognised internationally as sensible.

52. Other helpful guides used in the United States for programming include the American Society of Civil Engineers, ASCE Standard 67-17 Schedule Delay Analysis (2017) and Association for the Advancement of Cost Engineering-AACE International Recommended Practice no 29R-03 Forensic Schedule Analysis (2011).

(4) Other provisions

As provided in RB/99, under RB/17, the Employer's Personnel are expressly entitled to rely on the Programme when planning their activities.[53] For example, the Employer's Personnel:

> may [...] need to arrange for certain personnel to be available when particular parts of the Works are being executed, or when particular Contractor's Documents are to be submitted for Review. It is also usually the case that more of the Employer's Personnel will need to be on the Site during periods when the rate of progress of the Works is at its peak, especially if the Contractor's Personnel will be working multiple shifts (perhaps, including night-work).[54]

The penultimate paragraph of Sub-Clause 8.3 disclaiming that any programme, the Programme or any supporting report may be taken as, or relieve the Contractor from, giving a Notice under the Contract is new and important. It means, for example, that the Contractor is denied the right to rely on anything in a programme (or Programme) or its supporting report as being a Notice of Claim under Sub-Clause 20.2.1 for additional payment and/or an EOT. This is consistent with the more formal and rigorous requirements for a Notice and for Claims under RB/17.[55]

(iv) Related Law: In general, detailed guidance (by way of, e.g., published judicial decisions) concerning programmes is much more readily available in common law systems than civil law systems.[56] In France,

53. Sub-Clause 8.3, fourth paragraph.
54. *The FIDIC Contracts Guide* (2nd edn, FIDIC, 2022), 277.
55. *See* Sub-Clauses 1.1.56 '**Notice**' and 1.3 [*Notices and Other Communications*] and Clause 20 [*Employer's and Contractor's Claims*].
56. United States law is the most developed on this subject. *See*, e.g., Philip Bruner and Patrick O'Connor, *Bruner and O'Connor on Construction Law* (Thomson Reuters, St Paul, MN, 2016) vol 5, Chapter 15 *Risks of Construction Time: Delay, Suspension, Acceleration and Disruption*. For English law, *see*, for example, Julian Bailey, *Construction Law* (3rd edn, London Publishing, UK, 2020) vol 2, 985-988 (paras 11.54-11.58). The 'typical' approach in civil law countries has been described as follows:

> From a jurisprudential view, both the VOB/B [a German standard form of construction contract] and the BGB [German Civil Code] follow an approach which is typical for civil law countries with a Civil Code, and particularly typical for German law. Instead of providing a large number of judicial precedents or contractual clauses which cover different situations (e.g. de-

courts usually refer construction disputes, including issues of delay, to a court-appointed technical expert (i.e., a non-lawyer) for a report. The court will usually accept the expert's recommendations, though it is not bound to do so. Consequently, there is not in France the rigorous and detailed analysis of the facts, causes and consequences of delay issues from a legal (as well as a technical, as in France) perspective by a court, as in common law jurisdictions, leading to instructive case law. On the other hand, the greater rigour and involvement of lawyers in common law construction litigation comes at a price. French civil proceedings tend to be substantially less expensive than common law ones.

--ooOOoo--

8.4 Advance Warning

Each Party shall advise the other and the Engineer, and the Engineer shall advise the Parties, in advance of any known or probable future events or circumstances which may:

(a) adversely affect the work of the Contractor's Personnel;
(b) adversely affect the performance of the Works when completed;
(c) increase the Contract Price; and/or
(d) delay the execution of the Works or a Section (if any).

The Engineer may request the Contractor to submit a proposal under Sub-Clause 13.3.2 [*Variation by Request for Proposal*] to avoid or minimise the effects of such event(s) or circumstance(s).

---

layed delivery of plans, antiquities in the ground, changes of the law etc.) the VOB/B and the BGB provide only a few rules with rather abstract words such as 'hindrance' (§6(2) no 1 of the VOB/B) or 'necessary act by employer' (§642 of the BGB) under which all the potential situations (of EOT and compensation claims) can be dealt with. Under this approach practising lawyers use deductive logic when deciding whether the particular situation falls under the legal rule.

Christopher Ennis and Dr Wolfgang Breyer, 'Claims for Extensions of Time and Compensation under the FIDIC Red Book: Civil Law and Common Law Approaches Compared', SCL, paper D162, October 2013, 8.

Each party must advise the other – and the Engineer must advise the Parties – of any known or probable future events or circumstances which may: adversely affect the work of the Contractor's Personnel or the performance of the Works; increase the Contract Price; and/or delay execution of the Works. The Engineer may request a proposal for a Variation to minimise the effects of such event(s) or circumstance(s).

Commentary

(i) Main Changes from RB/99: This is a new Sub-Clause in RB/17[57] highlighting the increased emphasis on better project management. However, the content of this Sub-Clause is not entirely new as the Contractor, though not the Employer or the Engineer, already had a duty to give notice to the Engineer of probable future adverse events under the third paragraph of Sub-Clause 8.3 of RB/99.

(ii) Related Clauses / Sub-Clauses: 1.3 [*Notices and Other Communications*], 1.5 [*Priority of Documents*], 1.8 [*Care and Supply of Documents*], 1.9 [*Delayed Drawings or Instructions*], 3.5 [*Engineer's Instructions*], 3.8 [*Meetings*], 4.6 [*Co-operation*], 4.20 [*Progress Reports*], 13.3.2 [*Variation Procedure – Variation by Request for Proposal*] and 20.2 [*Claims for Payment and/or EOT*].

(iii) Analysis:

(1) Need for advance warning

As has been well noted:

> Construction is a complex process. Even if a supervising engineer is based full time on site, it is impossible for an individual to observe, for example, that each and every electrical cable is terminated properly; piping is welded to specification; bolt is tightened to the required torque; or brick has received sufficient mortar. Likewise, it is impossible for a designer to confirm that there is no typing or drafting error in hundreds of drawings or specification pages prepared for the project.[58]

57. There was such a Sub-Clause in GB/08, *see* Sub-Clause 8.4 [*Advance Warning*] of GB/08.
58. Muhammad Imran Chaudhary '"Duty to Warn" in Construction Contracts' (2020) 36(3) Const L J, 183.

The same author further correctly notes:

> Construction by its very nature can be a dangerous occupation. Professionals involved in a construction project are not mere bystanders or strangers to the project and [...] they must raise concerns or doubts with their client over the dangerous nature of something they knew instead of relying on strict interpretation of the contractual obligation.[59]

This is recognised by RB/17: the Parties and the Engineer are required to cooperate with one another[60] and under Sub-Clause 8.4 each must advise the others in advance of known or probable future adverse events or circumstances, thereby permitting their effects to be mitigated or avoided.

(2) Advance warning in RB/99

While the Contractor already had an 'early warning' duty under RB/99,[61] neither the Employer nor the Engineer had a reciprocal obligation to warn the Contractor of probable future adverse events although it should always have been in the Employer's interest that they do so.[62]

(3) Advance warning in RB/17

While this Sub-Clause is contained in Clause 8 [*Commencement, Delays and Suspension*], which otherwise deals exclusively with the issue of time, the wording of sub-paragraphs (a) to (d) is broad so that the Sub-Clause covers virtually any matter that could in future negatively affect the execution of the Works, whether to increase the Contract Price and/or delay the Works.[63] These matters could encompass, among other

59. *Ibid.*, 184.
60. Sub-Clause 4.6 [*Co-operation*].
61. *See* third paragraph of Sub-Clause 8.3 of RB/99.
62. The reason given for this lack of reciprocity was that an inadvertent failure by the Employer's Personnel to give an early warning 'might then be construed as excusing delayed completion'. *The FIDIC Contracts Guide* (1st edn, FIDIC, 2000) 172.
63. Indeed, there is some overlap in this respect with, notably, Sub-Clauses 1.5 [*Priority of Documents*], last paragraph, 1.8 [*Care and Supply of Documents*], last paragraph, and 1.9 [*Delay Drawings or Instructions*], first paragraph, all of which require that a Notice (not merely advice, as under Sub-Clause 8.4) be given of a probable future or actual adverse fact or event. *See also*, Sub-Clause 4.20 [*Progress Reports*] requiring adverse events or circumstances to be reported monthly.

things, Unforeseeable conditions of any kind, including health and safety issues (sub-paragraph (a)), defects in the Works of any kind, whatever their possible cause (sub-paragraph (b)), and anything which is likely to increase the cost of the execution of the Works (sub-paragraph (c)) or delay it (sub-paragraph (d)), essentially, in other words, *known or probable future Claims for money or time.*

The level of warning to be given should be commensurate with the gravity of the danger or risk perceived.[64] Although focused, specifically on safety issues, this may be illustrated by Figure 8.

Figure 8 Level of Danger and Level of Warning[1]

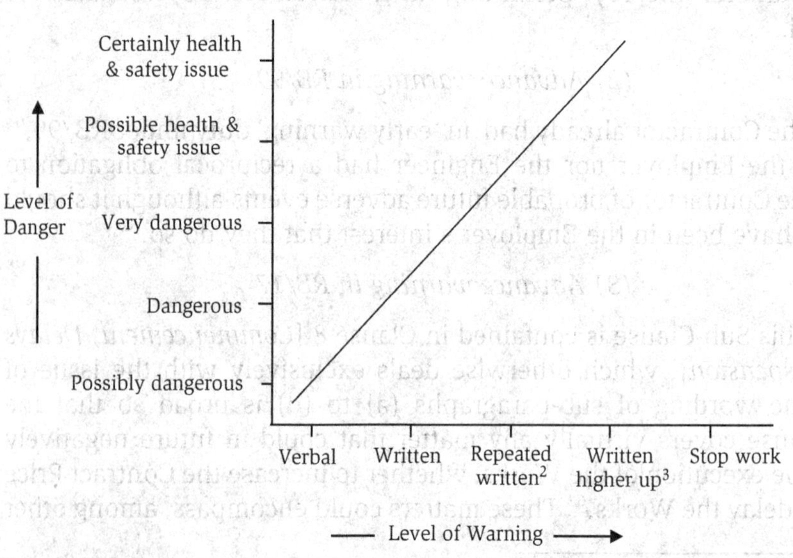

Notes:

1. Source: Muhammad Imran Chaudhary, '"Duty to Warn" in Construction Contracts' (2020), 36 Const L J, Issue 3, 183, 195.
2. This refers to repeated written warnings.
3. This refers to written warnings to higher authority.

64. Any 'advice' pursuant to this Sub-Clause must be given in writing and be in conformity with Sub-Clause 1.3 [*Notices and Other Communications*]. Such 'advice' would be a 'communication' under Sub-Clause 1.3, which must include therefore a reference to the provision(s) of the Contract under which it is issued (Sub-Clause 8.4).

Advice under this Sub-Clause is to be distinguished from a Notice of Claim under Sub-Clause 20.2.1 as it is required to be given 'in advance' of any known or probable future event or circumstances which may have adverse effects. On the other hand, a Notice of Claim may only be given once a Party 'is entitled' to additional payment or time,[65] which will usually be later in time.

(4) Sanction for failure to warn

While no formal sanction is stated for failing to comply with this Sub-Clause, a Party or the Engineer ignores it at its peril. Quite apart from a duty to warn that a Party may have as a matter of law (as to which *see* **(iv) Related law** below), a Party (or the Engineer) may be prejudiced if it has failed to warn of adverse events of which it has knowledge that could affect the time, cost or performance of the Contract.

If, for example, a Party has failed to advise of a particular probable future adverse event or circumstance of which it was aware (e.g., an epidemic or planned riot or rebellion) and subsequently asserts a Claim for its consequences, the EOT and/or additional payment claimed may be reduced or denied to the extent the delay and/or cost could have been minimised or avoided had the advance warning required by this Sub-Clause been given (e.g., by allowing necessary safety or protective measures to be taken).[66] *Every Claim is therefore susceptible of being screened under this Sub-Clause to ascertain whether an advance warning could have been given and, if so, could have reduced or prevented the damage suffered.*

(iv) Related law: Under civil law and common law systems, a contractor or the engineer (or other contract administrator) may have, as a matter of law, a duty to warn an employer or the engineer, or the engineer may have a duty to warn the contractor, of defects or other problems with their design, instructions or work.[67] Under English law, the duty of a

65. Sub-Clause 20.2 [*Claims for Payment and/or EOT*].
66. *See* last paragraph of Sub-Clause 20.2.7 [*Claims for Payment and/or EOT – General Requirements*].
67. For English law, *see* the description of *Plant Construction Ltd v Clive Adams Associates* under **(iv) Related Law** of the commentary on Sub-Clause 3.5 [*Engineer's Instructions*] above and Julian Bailey, *Construction Law* (3rd edn, London Publishing, UK, 2020) vol 2, 1283-1291 (paras 14.17-14.31). For French law (*le devoir de conseil*), *see* Albert Caston et al, *Traité des Marchés Privés de Travaux* (6th edn, Eds Le Moniteur, Paris, 2016) 533-537 and Marc Frilet and Laurent Karila, 'Contractors', Engineers' and Architects' Duty to

construction professional to perform a contract with skill and care carries with it a duty to warn his client, which arises when:

(a) there is an obvious danger either to life or to property or a clear defect in the design or a document; and
(b) the construction professional knows of the danger or defect.[68]

Under French law, the duty to warn (*le devoir de conseil*) is even more developed and far-reaching. For example, a contractor has a duty to warn not only the employer – the contractor has the burden of proof to show that it has done so – but also the contract administrator (e.g., the contractor must verify the drawings and instructions of the contract administrator and draw its attention to any failure to respect construction norms) as well as other contractors of the employer (e.g., where the proper execution of work by one contractor may depend upon advice that might be given by another).[69]

(v) Improvements: It could be useful to provide more clearly (than under sub-paragraph (h) of Sub-Clause 4.20) that the monthly progress reports submitted by the Contractor under Sub-Clause 4.20 include any early warnings provided pursuant to Sub-Clause 8.4 in the previous month.

--ooOOoo--

Advise and Decennial Liability in Civil Law Countries: Highlights of Some Prevailing Principles' (2012) 7(2) C L Int 21.

68. Muhammad Imran Chaudhary '"Duty to Warn" in Construction Contracts' (2020) 36 Const L J, Issue 3, 183, 191 and *Plant Construction Plc v Clive Adams Associates* [2000] BLR, 137, 147-148.

69. Philippe Malinvaud (ed in chief), *Droit de la Construction* (7th edn, Dalloz Action, Paris, 2018) 1133-1135 (paras 402.51-402.71). For example, a contractor specialised in installing pipes for heating was held liable to warn a general contractor subsequently on the site of the risks that the pouring of concrete could have for the heating pipes. Cass. 3e civ. 16 October 1985, 84-12.958, P cited in Albert Caston et al, *Traité des Marchés Privés de Travaux* (6th edn, Eds Le Moniteur, Paris, 2016) 544-545. *See also* sub-para. (b) of Sub-Clause 3.5 [*Engineer's Instructions*], which identifies certain cases where the Contractor may be excused from having to comply with an Engineer's instruction.

8.5 Extension of Time for Completion

The Contractor shall be entitled subject to Sub-Clause 20.2 [*Claims for Payment and/or EOT*] to Extension of Time if and to the extent that completion for the purposes of Sub-Clause 10.1 [*Taking Over the Works and Sections*] is or will be delayed by any of the following causes:

(a) a Variation (except that there shall be no requirement to comply with Sub-Clause 20.2 [*Claims for Payment and/or EOT*]);
(b) a cause of delay giving an entitlement to EOT under a Sub-Clause of these Conditions;
(c) exceptionally adverse climatic conditions, which for the purpose of these Conditions shall mean adverse climatic conditions at the Site which are Unforeseeable having regard to climatic data made available by the Employer under Sub-Clause 2.5 [*Site Data and Items of Reference*] and/or climatic data published in the Country for the geographical location of the Site;
(d) Unforeseeable shortages in the availability of personnel or Goods (or Employer-Supplied Materials, if any) caused by epidemic or governmental actions; or
(e) any delay, impediment or prevention caused by or attributable to the Employer, the Employer's Personnel, or the Employer's other contractors on the Site.

The Contractor shall be entitled subject to Sub-Clause 20.2 [*Claims for Payment and/or EOT*] to EOT if the measured quantity of any item of work in accordance with Clause 12 [*Measurement and Valuation*] is greater than the estimated quantity of this item in the Bill of Quantities or other Schedule by more than ten per cent (10%) and such increase in quantities causes a delay to completion for the purposes of Sub-Clause 10.1 [*Taking Over the Works and Sections*]. The agreement or determination of any such Claim, under Sub-Clause 20.2.5 [*Agreement or determination of the Claim*], may include a review by the Engineer of measured quantities of other items of work which are significantly less (by more than 10%) than the corresponding estimated quantities in the Bill of Quantities or other Schedule. To the extent that there are such lesser measured quantities, the Engineer may take account of any favourable effect on the critical path of the Programme. However, the net effect of all such consideration shall not result in a net reduction in the Time for Completion.

When agreeing or determining each EOT, the Engineer shall review previous agreements and determinations of EOT under Sub-Clause 3.7 [*Agreement or Determination*] and may increase, but shall not decrease, the total EOT.

If a delay caused by a matter which is the Employer's responsibility is concurrent with a delay caused by a matter which is the Contractor's responsibility, the Contractor's entitlement to EOT shall be assessed in accordance with the rules and procedures stated in the Special Provisions (if not stated, as appropriate taking due regard of all relevant circumstances).

The Contractor shall be entitled to EOT, subject to Sub-Clause 20.2, if and to the extent that completion is or will be delayed by any of the causes listed in sub-paragraphs (a) through (e).

The Contractor shall be entitled subject to Sub-Clause 20.2 to EOT if the measured quantity of any item of work is greater than its estimated quantity in the Bill of Quantities by more than 10% and such increase causes a delay to completion. However, when calculating such entitlement, the Engineer may take account of any favourable effect on the critical path of measured quantities of any other items which are significantly less (by more than 10%), than the corresponding estimated quantities, but the net effect shall not result in a net reduction in the Time for Completion.

If a delay which is the Employer's responsibility is concurrent with a delay which is the Contractor's responsibility, the Contractor's entitlement to EOT shall be assessed in accordance with the Special Provisions.

Commentary

(i) Main Changes from RB/99:

(1) Unlike Sub-Clause 8.4 of RB/99, sub-paragraph (a) of the new Sub-Clause states that, in the case of a Variation, there will be no requirement for the Contractor to comply with Sub-Clause 20.2 [*Claims for Payment and/or EOT*] (Sub-Clause 20.1 of RB/99).

(2) The provision in sub-paragraph (a) of Sub-Clause 8.4 of RB/99 for an EOT in the case of 'other substantial change in the quantity of an item of work included in the Contract' has now been made much more precise and detailed in the second paragraph of Sub-Clause 8.5.[70]

(3) In sub-paragraph (c) of the new Sub-Clause, exceptionally adverse climatic conditions is now defined for the first time as adverse climatic conditions at the Site which are Unforeseeable having regard to climatic data made available by the Employer under Sub-Clause 2.5 [*Site Data and Items of Reference*] and/or climatic data published in the Country for the location of the Site.

(4) In sub-paragraph (d), Unforeseeable shortages now expressly include those in Employer-Supplied Materials.

(5) The last paragraph of the new Sub-Clause provides for specific rules (to be stated in the Special Provisions) where a delay for which the Employer is responsible is concurrent with a delay for which the Contractor is responsible.

(ii) Related Clauses / Sub-Clauses: 1.3 [*Notices and Other Communications*]; 2.5 [*Site Data and Items of Reference*], 3.7 [*Agreement or Determination*], 10.1 [*Taking Over the Works and Sections*], 12 [*Measurement*

70. The Contractor is entitled to an EOT if the measured quantity of any item of work is greater than the estimated quantity in the Bill of Quantities (or other Schedule) by more than 10%, and causes a delay to completion, after taking account of any favourable effect on the critical path of any measured quantities that are significantly less (by more than 10%) than the estimated quantities. Thus, it requires the Engineer to perform a similar calculation exercise to that provided for in Sub-Clause 4.12.5 in the case of a Claim on account of Unforeseeable adverse physical conditions.

and Valuation], 13 [*Variations and Adjustments*], 18 [*Exceptional Events*], 20.2 [*Claims for Payment and/or EOT*] and Sub-Clauses entitling the Contractor to an EOT.[71]

(iii) Analysis:

(1) Benefits of an EOT

Provisions for extension of time benefit both Parties to the Contract. The Employer benefits as, if the Contractor is critically[72] delayed or prevented from performing its work by the Employer, or a matter for which the Employer is responsible, the Contractor will be entitled to an EOT, thereby establishing a new Date of Completion and preserving the Employer's right to Delay Damages under Sub-Clause 8.8. On the other hand, if the Contractor is critically delayed by any of the causes listed in Sub-Clause 8.5, the Contractor will benefit as it will be entitled to an EOT, and will thereby be relieved of liability for Delay Damages for that delay.

(2) Grounds for claiming an EOT

The five grounds for claiming an extension of time in Sub-Clause 8.5 are broadly the same as in RB/99, and refer to events outside of the Contractor's control. However, 'exceptionally adverse weather conditions' is now more specifically defined, as they are limited to conditions at the Site which are Unforeseeable (as defined) having regard to climatic data made available by the Employer and/or that are publicly available. The frequency, duration and intensity of the 'Unforeseeable' weather conditions should be compared with the typical weather ordinarily encountered at the location of the Site at the particular time the Works are being executed, as shown by the climatic data.

The *Guidance* provides that an exceptional degree of adversity might be regarded 'as one which has a probability of occurrence of once every four or five times the Time for Completion of the Works (for example, once every eight to ten years for a two-year contract)'.[73]

71. These are listed in **Table 4 Grounds Entitling a Contractor to an EOT,** under **(iii) Analysis** below.
72. That is, if the delay will cause a delay to completion.
73. *Guidance for the Preparation of Particular Conditions*, 34. As another example, the American Institute of Architects Document A201 *General Conditions of the Contract for Construction*, 2017, s 8.3.1, defines Force Majeure (entitling the Contractor to an EOT) as, among other things, 'unusually severe adverse weather conditions not common to the area where the Project

Probably the most important of the grounds for claiming an EOT is likely to be the one referred to in sub-paragraph (b), which refers to a cause of delay giving an entitlement to an EOT under a Sub-Clause of the Conditions, as there are more than 20 such grounds in the Conditions. These grounds, which may also in some cases entitle the Contractor to Cost or Cost Plus Profit, are provided in Table 4.

Table 4 Grounds Entitling a Contractor to an EOT

	Sub-Clause	*Contractor's Entitlement*
(1)	1.9 [*Delayed Drawings or Instructions*]	Contractor may claim an EOT and/or Cost Plus Profit if Engineer fails to issue a notified drawing or instruction within a reasonable time.
(2)	1.13 [*Compliance with Laws*]	Contractor may claim an EOT and/or Cost Plus Profit if Employer delays or fails to obtain any permit, permission, licence or approval.
(3)	2.1 [*Right of Access to the Site*]	Contractor may claim an EOT and/or Cost Plus Profit if Employer fails to give right of access to Site within the time stated in the Contract.
(4)	4.6 [*Co-operation*]	Contractor may claim an EOT and/or Cost Plus Profit if Engineer instructs cooperation that was Unforeseeable.
(5)	4.7 [*Setting Out*]	Contractor may claim an EOT and/or Cost Plus Profit for errors in the items of reference an experienced contractor would not have discovered.
(6)	4.12 [*Unforeseeable Physical Conditions*]	Contractor may claim an EOT and/or Cost if it encounters adverse physical conditions which are Unforeseeable.

is located (as determined on the basis of the past ten (10) year weather records collected by the National Oceanic and Atmospheric Administration)'.

	Sub-Clause	Contractor's Entitlement
(7)	4.15 [*Access Route*]	Contractor may claim EOT and/or Cost if an access route becomes non-suitable or non-available due to Employer or third party.
(8)	4.23 [*Archeological and Geological Findings*]	Contractor may claim an EOT and/or Cost attributable to complying with an Engineer's instruction to deal with a geological or archaeological finding.
(9)	7.4 [*Testing by the Contractor*]	Contractor may claim an EOT and/or Cost Plus Profit if testing is delayed and the Employer is responsible.
(10)	7.6 [*Remedial Work*]	Contractor may claim an EOT and/or Cost Plus Profit if remedial work is attributable to the Employer or the Employer's Personnel.
(11)	8.5 [*Extension of Time for Completion*]	Contractor may claim an EOT for a Variation, a Sub-Clause giving an entitlement to an EOT, exceptionally adverse climatic conditions (as defined), certain Unforeseeable shortages of personnel or Goods, any delay attributable to the Employer or its contractors and if a defined increase in quantities delays completion.
(12)	8.6 [*Delays Caused by Authorities*]	Contractor may claim an EOT if the Country's public authorities or private utilities cause Unforeseeable delay or disruption.
(13)	8.10 [*Consequences of Employer's Suspension*]	Contractor may claim an EOT and/or Cost Plus Profit if Engineer instructs a suspension of progress under Sub-Clause 8.9.
(14)	8.12 [*Prolonged Suspension*]	Parties may agree to an EOT and/or Cost Plus Profit and/or payment for suspended Plant and/or Materials in the case of a prolonged suspension.

	Sub-Clause	*Contractor's Entitlement*
(15)	10.3 [*Interference with Tests on Completion*]	Contractor may claim an EOT and/or Cost Plus Profit if Employer prevents Tests on Completion.
(16)	13.3 [*Variation Procedure*]	The Engineer may agree to or determine an EOT and an adjustment of the Contract Price as a result of a Variation.
(17)	13.6 [*Adjustments for Changes in Laws*]	Contractor may claim an EOT and/or Cost attributable to a change in Laws of the Country and certain other matters.
(18)	16.1 [*Suspension by Contractor*]	Contractor may claim an EOT and/or Cost Plus Profit if the Contractor suspends work (or reduces the rate of work) under this Sub-Clause.
(19)	16.2 [*Termination by Contractor*]	Contractor may claim an EOT and/or Cost Plus Profit if, in certain circumstances, Contractor terminates under this Sub-Clause.
(20)	17.2 [*Liability for Care of Works*]	Contractor may claim an EOT and/or Cost Plus Profit (in some cases) if Works, Goods or Contractor's Documents are damaged by events for which Employer is responsible.
(21)	18.4 [*Consequences of an Exceptional Event*]	Contractor may claim an EOT and (in some cases) Cost if an Exceptional Event prevents it from performing any of its obligations.

Source: Author's own work.

For the Contractor to be entitled to an EOT on a ground listed in Sub-Clause 8.5,[74] the Contractor must demonstrate that completion of the Works (or a Section) 'is or will be delayed' by the relevant event; i.e., the delay is on the critical path of the Contractor's Programme. The words 'will be delayed' make it clear that the relevant event need not already have begun to affect the Contractor's progress with the Works (or for the effect to have ended) for the Contractor to be able to claim, and for the Engineer to grant, an EOT. The Contractor is entitled to an EOT if such event 'will' affect the Contractor's progress so as to delay comple-

74. In US terminology, an 'excusable delay'.

tion.[75] This emphasises that the Engineer is to address delays currently, during the course of the Works, including on a forecast basis, rather than leaving them to the end of the project to be addressed retrospectively.

To be entitled to an EOT, the Contractor must give a Notice of Claim and otherwise comply with the Claims procedure in Sub-Clause 20.2. The Engineer appears to have no right to grant an EOT on its own initiative, but only if, and when, it is claimed by the Contractor under Sub-Clause 20.2.[76]

It is a common misperception that if the Contractor is entitled to an EOT, then it should automatically be entitled to be compensated for the extended time. However, entitlement to an EOT and compensation for the extended time are distinct issues, and the Contractor will not be entitled to compensation except where this is expressly stated in the Conditions or otherwise allowed under applicable law.

(3) Engineer's review of previous determinations

The penultimate paragraph provides that when agreeing or determining each EOT, the Engineer shall review previous agreements and determinations of EOT under Sub-Clause 3.7 and may increase, but shall not

75. The particular wording of the first sentence of Sub-Clause 8.5 as well as the fact that the Contractor's programme must disclose the Contractor's float (*see* Sub-Clause 8.3(g)) imply that the Contractor's total float must be used up before an EOT will be due. As the *Delay and Disruption Protocol* (2nd edn, SCL, UK, 2017) *('D&D Protocol')* states:

> Where the wording of the EOT clause in a contract is such that an EOT is only to be granted if the Employer Delay [defined as a 'delay caused by an Employer Risk Event', that is, an event or cause which is at the risk or responsibility of the Employer] delays completion beyond the contract completion date, *then the likely effect of that wording is that total float has to be used up before an EOT will be due.* If the wording of the EOT clause is such that an EOT will be due whenever the Employer Delay makes the Contractor's planned completion date later than it would have been if it were not for that delay, then total float will probably not be available for the benefit of the Employer in the event of Employer Delay. (Emphasis added) *D&D Protocol*, 28 (para. 8.2).

76. By contrast, under RB/87, if the Contractor was 'fairly' entitled to an EOT, the Engineer was entitled – even expected – to make that determination on its own initiative 'after due consultation with the Employer and the Contractor'. *See* Sub-Clause 44.1 of RB/87.

decrease, the total EOT.[77] A reason that the Engineer and, it is suggested, the DAAB or an arbitral tribunal after the Engineer may not decrease an EOT previously agreed or granted is that the Contractor can be expected to have relied on the EOT when scheduling its work.

(4) Right to EOT where concurrent delay

This Sub-Clause now provides in its last paragraph that concurrent delay be assessed in accordance with rules and procedures stated in the Special Provisions, which is understandable as the subject is complicated.

While how concurrent delay is defined will depend on the terms of the Contract and the governing law,[78] the solutions provided by the *D&D Protocol* may be briefly mentioned. The *D&D Protocol* defines 'true' concurrent delay as:

> the occurrence of two or more delay events at the same time, one an Employer Risk Event [that is, a delay at the risk of the Employer], the other a Contractor Risk Event [that is, a delay at the risk of the Contractor], and the effects of which are felt at the same time.[79]

However, the *D&D Protocol* recognises that this will rarely occur as it is unlikely that two delay events will span the exact same time period (or dates).[80] Accordingly, the *D&D Protocol* provides that, more commonly, 'concurrent delay' is where 'two or more delay events arise at different times, but the effects of them are felt at the same time'.[81] In both cases, the D&D Protocol states that the effect of the delay events must cause delay to completion of the works, that is, impact the critical path.[82]

Under the first edition of the *D&D Protocol* published in 2002, if completion was delayed by an event for which the Contractor was responsible concurrently with an event which delayed completion for which the Employer was responsible, the Contractor was nevertheless entitled to an

77. A similar provision is contained in art. 36.10 of the *ICC Model Turnkey Contract for Major Projects* (ICC Publication no 659 E 2007) but not in the 2020 edition of this form (ICC Publication 797E).
78. *See* Sub-Clause 1.4 [*Law and Language*]. For a discussion of concurrent delay in comparative law, *see* Kim Rosenberg, 'Concurrent Delay: What Is All the Fuss About?' (2018) 34(1) Const L J, 3.
79. *D&D Protocol*, 30 (para. 10.3).
80. *Ibid.*
81. *D&D Protocol*, 30 (para. 10.4).
82. *D&D Protocol*, 30 (para. 10.5).

extension of time for the event for which the Employer was responsible.[83] While this position is generally maintained,[84] the new edition provides for another solution where the delay event for which the Employer is responsible occurs simultaneously with, but commences after and finishes before, an event for which the Contractor is responsible.[85] The new solution has been described succinctly, as follows:

> where an owner/employer delay occurs concurrently with, but is engulfed by, a contractor delay, the owner/employer delay is not seen as 'causing Delay to Completion (and therefore there is no concurrency).' That is, the owner/employer's instruction/change would not result in entitlement to EOT and therefore would not reduce the delay caused by the contractor event (i.e. no reduction of exposure to liquidated damages).[86]

While this solution is 'consistent' with 'recent lower level English court decisions',[87] the author is not alone in finding it unpersuasive.[88]

(5) Right to compensation where concurrent delay

The new edition of the *D&D Protocol* also deals with prolongation compensation in the case of concurrent delay. It provides that where a delay to completion has been caused by the Employer which is concurrent with a delay to completion caused by the Contractor and as a result of that delay the Contractor incurs additional costs, then the Contractor should only recover compensation if it is able to separate the additional costs caused by the Employer's delay from those caused by the Contrac-

83. *Delay and Disruption Protocol* (1st edn, SCL, UK, 2002) 7, Core Principle 9.
84. *D&D Protocol*, 6, Core Principle 10.
85. *D&D Protocol*, 30-31 (paras 10.7-10.11).
86. Christopher M Burke and others, 'Time Is On (Their) Side: The United Kingdom's Society of Construction Law's Delay and Disruption Protocol. 2.0' (2017) 37(4) Const L, ABA for Const L, 15, 22. *See also* Julian Bailey, *Construction Law* (3rd edn, London Publishing, UK, 2020) vol 2, 997 (para. 11.75).
87. *D&D Protocol*, 31 (para. 10.9).
88. *See* Gabriel Mulero Clas, 'SCL's New Take on the Delay and Disruption Protocol', published by Corbett & Co. www.Corbett.co.uk, http://corbett.co.uk/wp-content/uploads/SCL%E2%80%99s-New-Take-on-the-Delay-and-Disruption-Protocol-KH-article.pdf accessed 10 November 2022. Some apportionment of responsibility between the parties would seem to be fairer than a complete denial of an extension of time as otherwise, as this author correctly notes, the Employer would enjoy a windfall.

tor's delay. If the Contractor would have incurred the additional costs in any event as a result of its own delay, the Contractor will not be entitled to recover those additional costs, according to the *D&D Protocol*.[89] In most cases, according to the *D&D Protocol*, this will mean that the Contractor will be entitled to compensation only for any period by which the Employer's delay exceeds the duration of the Contractor's delay.[90]

It should be stressed that the *D&D Protocol* merely presents one set of solutions to concurrent delay. Its proposals do not purport to represent the position under English or any other law[91] and are subject to the terms of each contract. Thus, the Parties are free to agree upon and include other rules in the Special Provisions.[92]

(6) Definitions in D&D Protocol

The *D&D Protocol* also contains an appendix[93] with useful definitions of such technical terms as 'activity', 'critical path' and 'float' (which are used in this Sub-Clause) as follows:

- '**Activity**: An operation or process consuming time and possibly other resources. An individual or work team can manage an activity. It is a measurable element of the total project programme.'
- '**critical path**: The longest sequence of activities through a project network from start to finish, the sum of whose durations determines the overall project duration. There may be more than one critical path depending on workflow logic. A delay to progress of any activity on the critical path will, without acceleration or re-sequencing, cause the overall project duration to be extended, and is therefore referred to as a "critical delay"'.
- '**float**: The time available for an activity in addition to its planned duration […]'.

89. *D&D Protocol*, 7, Core Principle 14.
90. *D&D Protocol*, 39 (para. 14.3). *See* final award, ICC case 12654 (2005), ICC Int'l Ct Arb Bull, vol 23, no 2, 2012, 77-79 (paras 135-156) (commentary 38-39), which takes the same position.
91. *D&D Protocol*, 1, Introduction (para. B) ('nor does [the Protocol] purport to […] be a statement of the law').
92. For example, a contract might exclude the contractor's right to an EOT where the cause of the contractor's delay was concurrent with a delay for which the contractor was itself responsible, as in *North Midland Building Ltd v Cyden Homes Ltd* [2018] EWCA Civ 1744.
93. *D&D Protocol*, Appendix A, Definitions and glossary.

The definition of 'logic links' (also referred to in this Sub-Clause) in the *D&D Protocol* is too detailed to set forth in full here.[94]

(7) Disruption

Sub-Clause 8.5 does not refer explicitly to disruption ('a disturbance, hindrance or interruption to a Contractor's normal working methods, resulting in lower efficiency'[95]) as distinct from delay, although a Claim for disruption will frequently accompany a Claim for delay. However, two other Sub-Clauses recognise that disruption may occur, namely Sub-Clause 1.9 [*Delayed Drawings or Instructions*] and Sub-Clause 8.6 [*Delays Caused by Authorities*].

(8) Post-completion delay

In addition, Sub-Clause 8.5 appears to have no application where delay occurs after the Date of Completion should execution of the Works still be ongoing then.

(iv) Related law:

(1) Absent an extension of time clause, such as Sub-Clause 8.5, an action by the Employer or the Employer's Personnel delaying or impeding the Contractor (such as is referred to in Sub-Clause 8.5(e)) would, under common law systems in accordance with the so-called prevention principle, be likely to release the Contractor from its obligation to complete the Works by the Time for Completion. Under common law systems, the Contractor's obligation to do so would become inoperative or 'at large' and the original obligation to complete the Works by the Time for Completion would be replaced by an implied obligation to complete within a reasonable time.[96]

94. Logic links effectively describe the construction logic relationship between activities, such as how one activity can only start when a prior activity has been completed (known as a 'finish-to-start' logic link). They are fundamental for a programme to work properly, and must reflect the reality of the activity relationship if the programme is going to reflect that reality.
95. *D&D Protocol*, 43 (para. 18.1).
96. *Multiplex Constructions (UK) Ltd v Honeywell Control Systems Ltd* (no 2) [2007] BLR 195 [paras 47-48] and Stephen Furst and Vivian Ramsey, *Keating on Construction Contracts* (11th edn, Sweet & Maxwell, London, 2021) 256-257 (para. 8-013–8-014).

The counterpart of Sub-Clause 8.5(e) (or the 'prevention principle') in the UNIDROIT Principles is Article 7.1.2 (*Interference by the other party*) providing:

> A party may not rely on the non-performance of the other party to the extent that such non-performance was caused by the first party's act or omission or by another event for which the first party bears the risk.

In other words, an Employer or Engineer may not – to deny an EOT – rely on the non-performance of the Contractor, such as delay to completion, to the extent that such non-performance was caused by an act or omission of the Employer (e.g., a delay in supplying drawings[97]) or another event for which the Employer bears the risk (e.g., delay caused by public authorities or utilities).[98]

(2) What about if the Employer had been responsible for delaying the Contractor on its critical path and the Contractor had neglected to request an EOT in compliance with Sub-Clause 8.5(e) – doing so only after the 28-day time bar provided for in Sub-Clause 20.2.1 – will the Employer be entitled to claim Delay Damages on account of the Contractor's delay in completion? While acknowledging 'conceptual difficulties' with the Employer recovering Delay Damages in this situation, as it would be benefiting from its own act of prevention, English authorities indicate that the Employer should be able to recover them.[99] However, by virtue of the doctrine of good faith,[100] the Employer may well be denied them under civil law.[101]

(3) While providing useful, practical guidance, the *D&D Protocol* has no special weight before common law courts. Thus, while the

97. *See* Sub-Clause 1.9 [*Delayed Drawings or Instructions*].
98. *See* Sub-Clause 8.6 [*Delays Caused by Authorities*].
99. Stephen Furst and Vivian Ramsey, *Keating on Construction Contracts* (11th edn, Sweet & Maxwell, London, 2021) 264-265 (para. 8-033); and Atkin Chambers, *Hudson's Building and Engineering Contracts* (14th edn, Sweet & Maxwell, 2020) 739-742 (para. 6-033). For a more detail, *see* Ngo-Martins Okonmah, 'The Prevention Principle and the Risk of Employer-Caused Delay under the 2017 FIDIC Suite of Contracts' [2021] ICLR 240.
100. *See* **Section 4 Common Law and Civil Law Compared – 4.3.1 Duty of Good Faith** in **Chapter II Applicable Law** above.
101. *See* under (*3*) *Doctrines used to overcome time bars* under **(iv) Related Law** of the commentary on Sub-Clause 20.2.1 [Notice of Claim] below.

D&D Protocol enumerates six different methods of delay analysis,[102] an Australian judge refused to apply either of the two used by the parties before him, stating that:

> for the purpose of any particular case, the fact that a method appears in the [D&D Protocol] does not give it any standing, and the fact that a method, which is otherwise logical or rational, but does not appear in the [*D&D Protocol*], does not deny it standing.[103]

(v) Improvements: A provision could be usefully inserted requiring the Contractor to use reasonable endeavours to minimise any delay to which it might be subjected, similar to that contained in the first paragraph of Sub-Clause 18.3 [*Duty to Minimise Delay*], which applies in the case of an Exceptional Event.

--ooOOoo--

8.6 Delays Caused by Authorities

> If:
>
> (a) the Contractor has diligently followed the procedures laid down by the relevant legally constituted public authorities or private utility entities in the Country;
> (b) these authorities or entities delay or disrupt the Contractor's work; and
> (c) the delay or disruption was Unforeseeable,
>
> then this delay or disruption will be considered as a cause of delay under sub-paragraph (b) of Sub-Clause 8.5 [*Extension of Time for Completion*].

If the Contractor has diligently followed the procedures of public authorities or private utilities in the Country, but these authorities or entities delay or disrupt its work and this was Unforeseeable, this will be considered a cause of delay under Sub-Clause 8.5(b).

---

102. *D&D Protocol*, 32 (para. 11.4).
103. *White Constructions Pty Ltd v PBS Holdings Pty Ltd* [2019] NSWSC 1166 [para. 191].

Commentary:

(i) Main Changes from RB/99: This Sub-Clause is unchanged from Sub-Clause 8.5 [*Delays Caused by Authorities*] in RB/99, except that it now allows for relief where the delay or disruption results from 'private utility entities' in the Country, and not just public authorities.

(ii) Related Clauses / Sub-Clauses: 1.13 [*Compliance with Laws*], 8.5 [*Extension of Time for Completion*], 13.6 [*Adjustments for Changes in Laws*] and 18 [*Exceptional Events*].

(iii) Analysis: This Sub-Clause is especially relevant in cases where the Contractor is required to apply to public authorities of the Country for permits, permissions, licences and/or approvals in relation to the execution of the Works.[104] It entitles the Contractor to an EOT if, despite having acted diligently, the Contractor's work is delayed or disrupted[105] in an Unforeseeable way by public authorities or private utilities in the Country, so that completion for the purposes of Sub-Clause 10.1 is or will be delayed.[106] The Contractor is not entitled to financial compensation nor to relief for disruption other than an EOT.[107] However, if the Employer and the public authorities concerned are part of the same legal person under applicable law, and delay or disrupt the Contractor in an Unfore-

104. Pursuant to sub-para. (b) of Sub-Clause 1.13 [*Compliance with Laws*].
105. 'Disruption' has been defined as follows:

> Dirsuption (as distinct from delay) is a disturbance, hindrance or interruption to a Contractor's normal working methods, resulting in lower efficiency. Disruption claims relate to loss of productivity in the execution of particular work activities. Because of the disruption, these work activities are not able to be carried out as efficiently as reasonably planned (or as possible). *D&D Protocol*, 43 (para. 18.1).

106. This 'Unforeseeability' test may not always be satisfactory as, in some countries, it may be perfectly foreseeable that public authorities or private utilities will be slow to act, causing delay or disruption, despite the Contractor's diligence in following required procedures. In those cases, it may not be the fact of delay or disruption which is Unforeseeable but its amount or extent. In those cases it might be appropriate to stipulate in the Particular Conditions at what point the amount or extent of delay or disruption should be considered to be Unforeseeable.
107. Assuming a claim for disruption can be separated from a claim for delay to completion, which was rejected in an English case, *McGee Group Ltd v Galliford Try Building Ltd* [2017] EWHC 87 (TCC) [paras 46-49].

seeable way, then the Contractor may be able to claim for the financial consequences on the basis of breach of contract or applicable law.[108]

(iv) Related law: In certain civil law countries, somewhat similar relief, including financial relief, in the case of delays by public authorities might be provided by mandatory law in the case of an administrative or public law contract under the legal doctrines of act of the prince (*fait du prince)* and hardship (*imprévision*).[109]

--ooOOoo--

8.7 Rate of Progress

> If, at any time:
>
> (a) actual progress is too slow to complete the Works or a Section (if any) within the relevant Time for Completion; and/or
>
> (b) progress has fallen (or will fall) behind the Programme (or the initial programme if it has not yet become the Programme) under Sub-Clause 8.3 [*Programme*],
>
> other than as a result of a cause listed in Sub-Clause 8.5 [*Extension of Time for Completion*], then the Engineer may instruct the Contractor to submit, under Sub-Clause 8.3 [*Programme*], a revised programme describing the revised methods which the Contractor proposes to adopt in order to expedite progress and complete the Works or a Section (if any) within the relevant Time for Completion.
>
> Unless the Engineer gives a Notice to the Contractor stating otherwise, the Contractor shall adopt these

108. *See* under **(iv) Related Law** immediately below. There may be some overlap between this Sub-Clause and Clause 18 [*Exceptional Events*] as a delay or disruption that might entitle the Contractor to relief under this Sub-Clause could fall within the definition of an 'Exceptional Event' in Sub-Clause 18.1. However, this should usually not matter as in each case the relief to which the Contractor is entitled is likely to be solely an EOT.
109. *See* **Section 4 Common Law and Civil Law Compared – 4.6.2 Hardship (*Imprévision*)** and, above all, **4.6.3 Act of the Prince *(Fait Du Prince)***, which entitles the Contractor to cost and possibly profit, of **Chapter II Applicable Law** above.

revised methods, which may require increases in the working hours and/or in the numbers of Contractor's Personnel and/or the Goods, at the Contractor's risk and cost. If these revised methods cause the Employer to incur additional costs, the Employer shall be entitled subject to Sub-Clause 20.2 [*Claims for Payment and/or EOT*] to payment of these costs by the Contractor, in addition to Delay Damages (if any).

Sub-Clause 13.3.1 [*Variation by Instruction*] shall apply to revised methods, including acceleration measures, instructed by the Engineer to reduce delays resulting from causes listed under Sub-Clause 8.5 [*Extension of Time for Completion*].

If actual progress is too slow to complete the Works or a Section within the Time for Completion and/or progress has fallen or will fall behind the Programme, other than as a result of a cause listed in Sub-Clause 8.5, the Engineer may instruct the Contractor to submit a revised programme describing the revised methods which the Contractor proposes to adopt to complete the Works or a Section within the relevant Time for Completion. Unless the Engineer gives a Notice otherwise, the Contractor shall adopt these revised methods at its risk and cost. If they cause the Employer additional costs, the Employer shall be entitled, subject to Sub-Clause 20.2, to their payment in addition to Delay Damages, if any. Sub-Clause 13.3.1 shall apply to revised methods of working instructed by the Engineer to reduce delays resulting from the causes listed in Sub-Clause 8.5.

Commentary:

(i) Main Changes from RB/99:

(1) The first paragraph has been revised to include references to Sections, as well as to Works, and to refer to the initial programme as well as the Programme, consistent with the new terminology in RB/17.

(2) The third paragraph, providing that Sub-Clause 13.3.1 [*Variation by Instruction*] shall apply to revised methods instructed by the Engineer to reduce delays resulting from causes listed in Sub-Clause 8.5, is new.[110]

(ii) Related Clauses / Sub-Clauses: 1.3 [*Notices and Other Communications*], 3.5 [*Engineer's Instructions*], 8.3 [*Programme*], 8.5 [*Extension of Time for Completion*], 13.3.1 [*Variation Procedure – Variation by Instruction*] and 20.2 [*Claims for Payment and/or EOT*].

(iii) Analysis: The first two paragraphs of this Sub-Clause assume that the Contractor's progress is slow, or that it has fallen behind its Programme, for reasons for which it is responsible. In this case, by entitling the Engineer to instruct the Contractor to submit a revised programme describing how it proposes to expedite progress, and requiring it to comply with that programme, the Engineer is enforcing the Contractor's obligation[111] to proceed with the Works 'with due expedition and without delay'.[112]

The Contractor must then accelerate in accordance with its new programme, 'which may require increases in the working hours and/or in the numbers of Contractor's Personnel and/or Goods',[113] at the Contractor's risk and cost. At the same time, if the revised methods adopted by the Contractor cause additional cost to the Employer, then, as the Contractor's conduct has made them necessary, the Employer is entitled, subject to Sub-Clause 20.2, to recover such costs from the Contractor, in addition to Delay Damages, if any.[114]

The third paragraph of this Sub-Clause assumes that the Contractor is in delay for causes which entitle the Contractor to an EOT under Sub-Clause 8.5. Yet, even in this case, it is implied that the Engineer is authorised to instruct revised methods, including acceleration measures, as they will

110. However, a somewhat similar provision according compensation ('[a]dditional costs' only) to the Contractor was contained in the last paragraph of Sub-Clause 8.6 [*Rate of Progress*] of the Pink Book issued in 2010.
111. Under Sub-Clause 8.1 [*Commencement of Works*], second paragraph.
112. Under Sub-Clause 3.5 [*Engineer's Instructions*], the Contractor must generally comply with the Engineer's instructions.
113. Sub-Clause 8.7, second paragraph.
114. *Ibid.*

be treated as a Variation under Sub-Clause 13.3.1.[115] Thus, the Engineer may instruct the Contractor to accelerate its work in order to make up for the delay for which the Employer is responsible instead of granting an EOT.[116] However, the Engineer may instruct the Contractor only 'to reduce delays resulting from causes listed' in Sub-Clause 8.5 and not to complete earlier than the Date of Completion.[117]

Time for Completion is defined to include extensions of time under Sub-Clause 8.5.[118] If the Engineer should fail to determine extensions of time in accordance with Sub-Clauses 8.5 and 20.2, this could result in there being no valid Time for Completion with the result that Sub-Clause 8.7 may be inapplicable.[119]

(iv) Related law: The last paragraph of this Sub-Clause refers to where the Contractor is required to accelerate pursuant to an instruction from the Engineer. If there is a disagreement about whether it involves a Variation, then this matter must be resolved under Sub-Clause 3.5 and, if necessary, Clauses 20 (including Sub-Clause 3.7) and 21. This may be compared to the US law concept of 'constructive acceleration' which may arise following an Engineer's unjustified refusal to grant a Contractor's request for an EOT. Under US law, to establish constructive acceleration, a Contractor must prove five elements:

(1) the contractor experienced an excusable delay and is entitled to an extension;
(2) the contractor properly requests a time extension;
(3) the owner denies the time extension;
(4) the owner demands completion by the original completion date; and

115. Although, as mentioned in the commentary on the definition of '**Variation**' in Sub-Clause 1.1.86, Sub-Clause 8.7 does not seem consistent with it. In Sub-Clause 1.1.86, a Variation is defined as 'any change to the Works, which is instructed as a Variation under Clause 13'. This definition, taken alone, does not appear sufficient to cover revised work methods.
116. In RB/99 there was no express power authorising the Engineer to do so. As a Variation is involved, the Contractor should still be entitled to object to any such instruction by a Notice, with detailed supporting particulars, on any of the grounds in sub-paras (a), (b) and (c) of Sub-Clause 13.1.
117. Sub-Clause 8.7, last paragraph.
118. Sub-Clause 1.1.84 '**Time for Completion**'.
119. *The FIDIC Contracts Guide* (1st edn, FIDIC, 2000) 176.

(5) the contractor incurs reasonable increased costs caused by its actual acceleration.[120]

If, pursuant to Sub-Clauses 3.5 and 3.7, the Engineer were to refuse to accept that its instruction involved a Variation, and if US law applied, the Contractor would have a potential claim for constructive acceleration.

The justification for such a claim is that where a contractor is denied a time extension to which it is entitled, the contractor is effectively being expected to meet the completion date required by the owner (rather than by the contract) and, hence, should be entitled to recover its additional costs in having to do so.[121]

--ooOOoo--

8.8 Delay Damages

> If the Contractor fails to comply with Sub-Clause 8.2 [*Time for Completion*], the Employer shall be entitled subject to Sub-Clause 20.2 [*Claims for Payment and/or EOT*] to payment of Delay Damages by the Contractor for this default. Delay Damages shall be the amount stated in the Contract Data, which shall be paid for every day which shall elapse between the relevant Time for Completion and the relevant Date of Completion of the Works or Section. The total amount due under this Sub-Clause shall not exceed the maximum amount of Delay Damages (if any) stated in the Contract Data.
>
> These Delay Damages shall be the only damages due from the Contractor for the Contractor's failure to comply with Sub-Clause 8.2 [*Time for Completion*], other than in the event of termination under Sub-Clause 15.2 [*Termination for Contractor's Default*] before completion of the Works. These Delay Damages shall not relieve the Contractor from the obligation to complete the Works, or from any other

120. Justin Sweet and others, *Construction Law for Design Professionals, Construction Managers, and Contractors* (Cengage Learning, Stamford, CT, 2015) 404.
121. *Ibid.*

duties, obligations or responsibilities which the Contractor may have under or in connection with the Contract.

This Sub-Clause shall not limit the Contractor's liability for Delay Damages in any case of fraud, gross negligence, deliberate default or reckless misconduct by the Contractor.

If the Contractor fails to comply with Sub-Clause 8.2, the Employer is entitled, subject to Sub-Clause 20.2, to payment of Delay Damages in the amount stated in the Contract Data for every day of delay. The total amount shall not exceed the maximum Delay Damages stated in the Contract Data. Delay Damages shall be the only damages due for the Contractor's delay, other than in the event of termination under Sub-Clause 15.2. Delay Damages shall not relieve the Contractor from any obligation under the Contract.

Commentary:

(i) Main Changes from RB/99:

(1) This Sub-Clause has been reworded to conform to RB/17 terminology, including the new defined term of 'Delay Damages',[122] as well as to refer to completion of a Section (not just the Works) for which Delay Damages may be due.
(2) The last paragraph, which is new, is to be found in other Sub-Clauses limiting a Party's liability.[123]

(ii) Related Clauses / Sub-Clauses: 1.15 [*Limitation of Liability*], 8.2 [*Time for Completion*], 8.5 [*Extension of Time for Completion*], 8.7 [*Rate of Progress*], 10.2 [*Taking Over Parts*], 14.15 [*Currencies of Payment*], 15.2 [*Termination for Contractor's Default*], 15.4 [*Payment after Termination for Contractor's Default*] and 20.2 [*Claims for Payment and/or EOT*].

122. *See* Sub-Clause 1.1.28 **'Delay Damages'**.
123. *See* Sub-Clauses 1.15 [*Limitation of Liability*], 11.10 [*Unfulfilled Obligations*] and 14.14 [*Cessation of Employer's Liability*].

(iii) Analysis:

(1) Nature of Delay Damages

This Sub-Clause describes the compensation payable by the Contractor if the Works (or a Section, if any) are not completed by the Time for Completion, that is, the time for completion stated in the Contract Data as it may be extended under Sub-Clause 8.5.[124] This compensation is a sum per day of delay, which may be expressed as a percentage[125] of the Accepted Contract Amount or as a monetary amount (or amounts if the Delay Damages may be payable in different currencies). The usual percentage limit on the amount of Delay Damages varies between 5% and 15% of the Accepted Contract Amount.[126]

Delay Damages ('liquidated damages' for delay in common law systems) benefit both Parties. The Employer benefits as it can claim them on account of the Contractor's delay, whether or not the Employer has suffered, or can prove, any damages. The Contractor benefits as they limit the Contractor's liability for delay by their fixed daily and maximum amounts, regardless of the length of its delay.

The Contractor cannot avoid liability for Delay Damages merely by submitting Claims for an EOT unless and until they are ultimately agreed or determined in its favour.[127] However, the Employer may lose its entitlement to claim Delay Damages, if it prevents EOTs from being agreed or determined in accordance with Sub-Clause 20.2. Thus, if the Employer prevents the Engineer from complying with Sub-Clause 8.5, it may be unable to rely upon Sub-Clause 8.2 [*Time for Completion*] and thus Sub-Clause 8.8.[128]

---

124. Sub-Clause 1.1.84 '**Time for Completion**'. Accordingly, if the Contract is terminated before the relevant Time for Completion, there is no right to Delay Damages. *See also* Atkin Chambers, *Hudson's Building and Engineering Contracts* (14th edn, Sweet & Maxwell, London, 2020) 748-750 (para. 6-040).
125. *The FIDIC Contracts Guide* (2nd edn, FIDIC, 2022) 287.
126. *The FIDIC Contracts Guide* (2nd edn, FIDIC, 2022) 288. The World Bank's COPA provides that they should not 'normally' exceed 10% of the Accepted Contract Amount less the provisional sum for the DAAB. Sub-Clause 8.8, Contract Data, COPA.
127. *The FIDIC Contracts Guide* (2nd edn, FIDIC, 2022) 287.
128. *Ibid.*, and Sub-Clause 8.5(e).

(2) Claiming Delay Damages

If the Employer considers itself to be entitled to Delay Damages, it may not simply deduct them from amounts that may become due to the Contractor, as the Employer sometimes did before RB/99. Instead, it is required to give a Notice of Claim and particulars in accordance with Sub-Clause 20.2. The Employer may only claim against the Contractor or make a deduction from any amount due to the Contractor after complying with Sub-Clause 20.2.[129] The Employer may do this as from the end of the relevant Time for Completion and is not required to wait until the actual completion of the Works.[130]

(3) Delay Damages are the 'only' damages for delay

Delay Damages are expressly stated to be the 'only' damages due from the Contractor for the Contractor's failure to comply with Sub-Clause 8.2 other than in the event of termination of the Contract for the Contractor's default pursuant to Sub-Clause 15.2.[131] Thus, regardless of the actual losses which the Employer may suffer, if any, as a result of the Contractor's delay, the Employer may not recover more than Delay Damages on this account except under Sub-Clause 15.2 or in the case of fraud or other misconduct, as described in the last paragraph.[132]

This provision would not appear to preclude, in theory at least, a claim for disruption if it can be separated from a claim for delay to completion.[133]

129. Sub-Clause 20.2.7 [*Claims for Payment and/or EOT – General Requirements*], second paragraph.
130. Where EOTs should subsequently be granted for the past, there would be need for some sort of credit procedure so as to allow for any Delay Damages, previously deducted from interim payments, to be recovered.
131. Sub-Clause 8.8, second paragraph. In the case of termination of the Contract for the Contractor's default, the Contractor may become liable for additional damages as provided for in Sub-Clause 15.4 [*Payment after Termination for Contractor's Default*].
132. Sub-Clause 1.15 [*Limitation of Liability*], last paragraph, contains similar wording which is discussed in the commentary on that Sub-Clause above. *See also* the second paragraph of Sub-Clause 8.7 [*Rate of Progress*] which entitles the Employer to recover certain costs 'in addition to Delay Damages (if any)'.
133. However, an attempt to argue such a distinction was strongly rejected in an English case, *McGee Group Ltd v Galliford Try Building Ltd* [2017] EWHC 87 (TCC) [paras 46-49].

Contractors sometimes argue that if they pay Delay Damages[134] they should then be free to complete the Works at any time. To foreclose this argument, the second paragraph provides that Delay Damages will *not* relieve the Contractor from its obligation to complete the Works or any of its other obligations in connection with the Contract.[135]

While the General Conditions do not provide that the Contractor will be entitled to a bonus in the case of early completion, should the Parties agree otherwise, an example Sub-Clause on this subject is contained in the *Guidance*.[136]

(4) Exception to limitation on liability

The last paragraph means that the limits on the Contractor's liability for Delay Damages, represented by any daily and/or total maximums or 'caps' on such liability provided for in the Contract Data do not apply where the Contractor's delay is attributable to fraud, gross negligence, deliberate default or reckless misconduct.[137]

(iv) Related law:

(1) Common law and civil law compared

As indicated above, Delay Damages are referred to in common law systems as liquidated damages for delay, whereas in some civil law systems they are referred to as penalties (in French: *pénalités*). Under both systems, they are subject to regulation and, to be enforceable, the amount of these predefined damages must, as a practical matter, be a reasonable estimate of the anticipated or actual loss caused to the Employer by the delay. However, as explained more fully in an earlier

134. And especially if they have reached the maximum amount or 'cap' on Delay Damages though, in this case, the Employer should have the right to terminate the Contract under Sub-Clause 15.2.1 (c).
135. For example, the Contractor's obligation to 'proceed with the Works with due expedition and without delay' under Sub-Clause 8.1, second paragraph. However, *see* the comment on this provision in item (2) under **(v) Improvements** below.
136. *Guidance for the Preparation of Particular Conditions*, 34.
137. A similar provision is contained in other Sub-Clauses limiting a Party's liability: Sub-Clauses 1.15 [*Limitation of Liability*], 11.10 [*Unfulfilled Obligations*] and 14.14 [*Cessation of Employer's Liability*]. This provision is commented upon under *(4) Third paragraph: fraud, etc., exception* under **(iii) Analysis** of the commentary on Sub-Clause 1.15 [*Limitation of Liability*] above.

Chapter (comparing the common law system with French and other laws),[138] the common law and civil law systems differ notably in the following respects:

(1) under the common law, a court has no power to adjust the amount of the pre-agreed sum, whereas it may often have such power under the civil law;
(2) under the common law, if the pre-agreed sum is found to constitute a penalty, then the corresponding clause is unenforceable and of no effect, whereas under the civil law, if such sum is found to be objectionable, the amount may be adjusted to correspond to actual damages and the clause will be saved;
(3) under the common law, the assessment of whether the pre-agreed sum is a penalty, and therefore objectionable, is made as of the date of contract, whereas, under the civil law, the assessment of whether it is objectionable is made at the date of judgment or award, in light of the actual damages which have been suffered; and
(4) under the civil law, there may be a requirement of having to give notice requiring performance before being entitled to payment.[139]

(2) UNIDROIT Principles

The UNIDROIT Principles also require the pre-agreed sum to satisfy a reasonableness criterion:

> notwithstanding any agreement to the contrary the specified sum may be reduced to a reasonable amount where it is grossly excessive in relation to the harm resulting from the non-performance and to the other circumstances.[140]

Furthermore, they provide that a clause which limits or excludes a party's liability for non-performance 'may not be invoked if it would be grossly unfair to do so, having regard to the purpose of the contract'.[141]

138. *See* **Section 4 Common Law and Civil Law Compared – 4.4.5 Liquidated Damages and Penalties** of **Chapter II Applicable Law** above.
139. *Ibid.*
140. Art. 7.4.13 (*Agreed payment for non-performance*) of the UNIDROIT Principles.
141. Art. 7.1.6 (*Exemption clauses*) of the UNIDROIT Principles.

Just as Sub-Clause 8.8 provides that it may not be invoked in the case of fraud, among other things, so do Articles 3.1.4 (*Mandatory character of the provisions*) and 3.2.5 (*Fraud*) of the UNIDROIT Principles.

(v) Improvements:

(1) The last words of the second sentence of the first paragraph should be revised to read: 'which shall be paid for every day which shall elapse between *the expiry of* the relevant Time for Completion and the relevant Date of Completion of the Works or Section'. (Emphasis added)

(2) The last sentence of the second paragraph of Sub-Clause 8.8 stating that '[t]hese Delay Damages shall not relieve the Contractor from the obligation to complete the Works […]' should instead state that '[t]he Contractor's *payment* of Delay Damages shall not relieve the Contractor from the obligation to complete the Works […]', as it is the Contractor's payment of such damages (and not the provision for them in the Conditions) which may allow the Contractor to argue that, in exchange, it should be relieved of having to complete the Works by any particular time.

--ooOOoo--

8.9 Employer's Suspension

> The Engineer may at any time instruct the Contractor to suspend progress of part or all of the Works, which instruction shall state the date and cause of the suspension.
>
> During such suspension, the Contractor shall protect, store and secure such part or all of the Works (as the case may be) against any deterioration, loss or damage.
>
> To the extent that the cause of such suspension is the responsibility of the Contractor, Sub-Clauses 8.10 [*Consequences of Employer's Suspension*], 8.11 [*Payment for Plant and Materials after Employer's Suspension*] and 8.12 [*Prolonged Suspension*] shall not apply.

The Engineer may instruct the Contractor to suspend progress of part or all of the Works, which instruction shall state the date and cause of the suspension. During the suspension, the Contractor shall protect, store and secure the suspended Works.

Commentary:

(i) Main Changes from RB/99:

(1) The Engineer is now required to state the date and – more importantly – the cause of the suspension, whereas Sub-Clause 8.8 of RB/99 had provided only that the Engineer 'may' notify the cause for the suspension.[142]

(2) Whereas RB/99 had provided that, if and to the extent that the cause was notified to the Contractor by the Engineer and was the responsibility of the Contractor, the Sub-Clauses which immediately followed would not apply, the new Sub-Clause provides more simply that, '[t]o the extent that the cause of the suspension is the responsibility of the Contractor', the Sub-Clauses which immediately follow will not apply.

(ii) Related Clauses / Sub-Clauses: 1.2 [*Interpretation*], 1.3 [*Notices and Other Communications*], 3.5 [*Engineer's Instructions*], 8.10 [*Consequences of Employer's Suspension*], 8.11 [*Payment for Plant and Materials after Employer's Suspension*], 8.12 [*Prolonged Suspension*], 11.3 [*Extension of Defects Notification Period*] and 17.1 [*Responsibility for Care of the Works*].

(iii) Analysis: Sub-Clauses 8.9 through 8.13 deal with the right of the Engineer to instruct a suspension in the progress of part or all of the Works and the consequences of a suspension. The first of these Sub-Clauses is 8.9 [*Employer's Suspension*] discussed here.

142. Sub-Clause 8.8, second paragraph, of RB/99. However, Sub-Clause 9.7 [*Suspension of Work*], second paragraph, of GB/08 had required the Employer's Representative to notify the cause of a suspension to the Contractor.

(1) The Engineer's right to suspend

This Sub-Clause provides that the Engineer (not the Employer as indicated by the Sub-Clause's marginal heading[143]) 'may' instruct a suspension of progress of part or all of the Works. Therefore, the Engineer has the choice of whether to do so or not.[144] It has no duty to do so even if it is obvious that certain works must be suspended: for example, where execution of the Works is affected by the flood season.[145]

The Engineer by and on behalf of the Employer may wish to suspend the Works temporarily for a variety of reasons, such as to accommodate unexpected or changing circumstances, including new budgetary constraints, or to change the Specification so as to comply with any new building standards, or on account of local political or economic conditions, or natural events such as flooding, or of some failure or shortcoming of either the Employer (e.g., failure or delay in obtaining a licence or permit for which it is responsible[146]) or the Contractor (e.g., a failure to protect and care for the Works),[147] although if the Contractor is responsible the consequences are different.[148]

(2) The Engineer's instruction

The Engineer has the right to instruct a suspension at any time, but it must state in the instruction the date and cause of the suspension.[149] The Engineer must give the cause so that the Contractor will know if the cause is its responsibility, in which case it must take the necessary corrective action. In this case, Sub-Clauses 8.10 to 8.12 inclusive, which otherwise

143. And the marginal headings of Sub-Clauses 8.10 and 8.11. Marginal headings are not to be taken into consideration in the interpretation of the Conditions. *See* the last paragraph of Sub-Clause 1.2 [*Interpretation*].
144. Sub-paragraph (e) of Sub-Clause 1.2 [*Interpretation*]. However, the phrase 'at the sole discretion of' is not used, whereas it is used sometimes in the case of a Party or the DAAB. *See* item (1) under **(v) Improvements** of the commentary in Sub-Clause 1.2 [*Interpretation*] above. But this is probably not intended to be significant.
145. *The FIDIC Contracts Guide* (2nd edn, FIDIC, 2022), 289. In these cases, it is the Contractor who is said to be at risk if it persists in executing work which should obviously be suspended.
146. *See* Sub-Clause 1.13(a).
147. *See* Sub-Clause 17.1.
148. *See* the third paragraph of Sub-Clause 8.9.
149. Sub-Clause 8.9, first paragraph.

would apply to Employer's suspensions, would not apply and the Contractor would bear the consequences of the suspension.[150]

Once the Engineer has instructed a suspension, then, as the Contractor is responsible for the care of the Works,[151] it is required to protect, store and secure such part or all of the Works (as the case may be) as are suspended against any deterioration, loss or damage.[152] The Contractor will not be excused for damage suffered by the Works[153] by claiming that the damage had occurred despite its best efforts to protect them.[154]

(3) The Contractor has generally no right to suspend

While the Engineer may suspend the Works under this Sub-Clause, the Contractor has no right unilaterally to suspend or reduce the rate of its work except under Sub-Clause 16.1 (e.g., if it is not being paid), but must instead, as previously indicated, proceed 'with due expedition and without delay'.[155]

--ooOOoo--

8.10 Consequences of Employer's Suspension

If the Contractor suffers delay and/or incurs Cost from complying with an Engineer's instruction under Sub-Clause 8.9 [*Employer's Suspension*] and/or from resuming the work under Sub-Clause 8.13 [*Resumption of Work*], the Contractor shall be en-

150. If the Engineer's instruction does not state the cause, then the Contractor may assume that the suspension is not its responsibility and so Sub-Clauses 8.10 to 8.12 inclusive will apply.
151. Under Sub-Clause 17.1 [*Responsibility for Care of the Works*].
152. Sub-Clause 8.9, second paragraph.
153. Subject to Sub-Clause 17.2 [*Liability for Care of the Works*].
154. Sub-paragraph (b) of Sub-Clause 8.10 [*Consequences of Employer's Suspension*]. The Engineer's instruction to the Contractor under this Sub-Clause to suspend also has no effect on the Employer's obligations. The Employer must, among other things, continue to pay the Contractor under Sub-Clause 14.7 as before.
155. *See* Sub-Clause 8.1 [*Commencement of Works*]. But *see* **Section 4 Common Law and Civil Law Compared – 4.3.3 Defence of Non-Performance (*Exceptio Non Adimpleti Contractus*)** in **Chapter II Applicable Law** above.

titled subject to Sub-Clause 20.2 [*Claims for Payment and/or EOT*] to EOT and/or payment of such Cost Plus Profit.

The Contractor shall not be entitled to EOT, or to payment of the Cost incurred, in making good:

(a) the consequences of the Contractor's faulty or defective (design, if any) workmanship, Plant or Materials; and/or

(b) any deterioration, loss or damage caused by the Contractor's failure to protect, store or secure in accordance with Sub-Clause 8.9 [*Employer's Suspension*].

If the Contractor suffers delay and/or incurs Cost from complying with an Engineer's instruction under Sub-Clause 8.9 and/or from resuming work under Sub-Clause 8.13, the Contractor shall be entitled, subject to Sub-Clause 20.2, to EOT and/or payment of such Cost plus Profit provided the Contractor was not at fault in its work or in violation of Sub-Clause 8.9.

Commentary:

(i) Main Changes from RB/99:

(1) Just as Sub-Clause 8.9 [*Consequences of Suspension*] of RB/99 had required the Contractor to comply with the claims' procedure in Sub-Clause 20.1 of RB/99, under the new Sub-Clause the Contractor is required to comply with the Claims' procedure in Sub-Clause 20.2 of RB/17.

(2) The Contractor is now entitled to Cost Plus Profit and not just Cost as under RB/99 on account of the suspension.[156]

(3) The references to 'Plant' in sub-paragraph (a), and to the words 'deterioration, loss or damage caused by' in sub-paragraph (b), were not contained in the last paragraph of Sub-Clause 8.9 of RB/99 and are new.

156. '**Cost Plus Profit**' is defined in Sub-Clause 1.1.20 to mean Cost (as defined in Sub-Clause 1.1.19) plus the applicable percentage for profit stated in the Contract Data (if not stated, 5%).

(ii) Related Clauses / Sub-Clauses: 8.9 [*Employer's Suspension*], 8.11 [*Payment for Plant and Materials after Employer's Suspension*], 8.12 [*Prolonged Suspension*], 8.13 [*Resumption of Work*] and 20.2 [*Claims for Payment and/or EOT*].

(iii) Analysis: The Sub-Clause sets out the procedure which is to apply where a suspension has been instructed by the Engineer under Sub-Clause 8.9 for which the Contractor is not (or not wholly) responsible and where it has suffered delay and/or incurred Cost. Essentially, the standard claims' procedure provided for in Sub-Clause 20.2 applies (including its time bar provisions). A significant change compared to Sub-Clause 8.9 of RB/99 is that the Contractor is now entitled to Profit, as well as Cost, during the suspension period. This is normal where the suspension has been caused by the Employer, as the Contractor is generally entitled to profit where the Employer is blameworthy.[157]

--ooOOoo--

8.11 Payment for Plant and Materials after Employer's Suspension

The Contractor shall be entitled to payment of the value (as at the date of suspension instructed under Sub-Clause 8.9 [*Employer's Suspension*]) of Plant and/or Materials which have not been delivered to Site, if:

(a) the work on Plant, or delivery of Plant and/or Materials, has been suspended for more than 28 days and

(i) the Plant and/or Materials were scheduled, in accordance with the Programme, to have been completed and ready for delivery to the Site during the suspension period; and

(ii) the Contractor provides the Engineer with reasonable evidence that the Plant and/or Materials comply with the Contract; and

157. *See* the commentary on Sub-Clause 1.1.20 **'Cost Plus Profit'** above. While the Employer is not required to take over Plant or Materials, if the suspension exceeds 28 days, it may wish to do so, if they would otherwise have been delivered to the Site, since it is required to pay for them under Sub-Clause 8.11.

(b) the Contractor has marked the Plant and/or Materials as the Employer's property in accordance with the Engineer's instructions.

The Contractor is entitled to payment of the value of Plant and/or Materials which have not been delivered to the Site, if: the work on, or delivery of, Plant and/or Materials has been suspended for more than 28 days; they were scheduled for delivery during the suspension period; they comply with the Contract; and the Contractor has marked them as the Employer's property.

Commentary:

(i) Main Changes from RB/99: The new Sub-Clause is similar to the corresponding Sub-Clause (Sub-Clause 8.10) in RB/99 except that sub-paragraph (a) has been supplemented by item (i) providing expressly that the Plant and/or Materials were scheduled to have been ready for delivery during the suspension period (in RB/99 this requirement may have been implied), and item (ii) providing that the Contractor provides reasonable evidence that they comply with the Contract.

(ii) Related Clauses / Sub-Clauses: 7.7 [*Ownership of Plant and Materials*], 8.3 [*Programme*], 8.9 [*Employer's Suspension*] and 14 [*Contract Price and Payment*].

(iii) Analysis: To the extent that the suspension was not the responsibility of the Contractor and lasts for more than 28 days, the Contractor will be entitled to payment of the value of Plant and/or Materials which, but for the suspension, would have been delivered to the Site[158] and which the Contractor can show comply with the Contract.[159] The Contractor must also mark them as the Employer's property in accordance with the Engineer's instructions. In this case, under Sub-Clause 7.7(b), once the Contractor is paid the value of Plant and Materials, they will become the Employer's property, subject to any applicable mandatory law to the contrary.

158. Sub-paragraph (i) of Sub-Clause 8.3 [*Programme*] provides that the Contractor's programmes shall include 'all key delivery dates of Plant and Materials'.
159. Apparently, payment would be made in the ordinary way pursuant to Clause 14 and Sub-Clause 20.2 would not apply.

Similarly, for a provision entitling the Contractor to advance payment(s) for Plant and/or Materials subject to various conditions, *see* Sub-Clause 14.5 [*Plant and Materials Intended for the Works*].

--ooOOoo--

8.12 Prolonged Suspension

If the suspension under Sub-Clause 8.9 [*Employer's Suspension*] has continued for more than 84 days, the Contractor may give a Notice to the Engineer requesting permission to proceed.

If the Engineer does not give a Notice under Sub-Clause 8.13 [*Resumption of Work*] within 28 days after receiving the Contractor's Notice under this Sub-Clause, the Contractor may either:

(a) agree to a further suspension, in which case the Parties may agree the EOT and/or Cost Plus Profit (if the Contractor incurs Cost), and/or payment for suspended Plant and/or Materials, arising from the total period of suspension;

or (and if the Parties fail to reach agreement under this sub-paragraph (a))

(b) after giving a (second) Notice to the Engineer, treat the suspension as an omission of the affected part of the Works (as if it had been instructed under Sub-Clause 13.3.1 [*Variation by Instruction*]) with immediate effect including release from any further obligation to protect, store and secure under Sub-Clause 8.9 [*Employer's Suspension*]. If the suspension affects the whole of the Works, the Contractor may give a Notice of termination under Sub-Clause 16.2 [*Termination by Contractor*].

If the Employer's suspension has continued for more than 84 days, the Contractor may give a Notice to the Engineer requesting permission to proceed. If the Engineer does not do so within 28 days, the Contractor may: (a) agree to a further suspension, in which case the Parties may agree the EOT and/or other payments to the Contractor for the total period of suspension or, failing any such agreement; (b) after giving

a (second) Notice to the Engineer, treat the suspension as an omission of the affected part of the Works (as if it were a Variation) or, if it affects the whole of the Works, give a Notice of termination under Sub-Clause 16.2.

Commentary:

(i) Main Changes from RB/99: The Sub-Clause is essentially the same as Sub-Clause 8.11 in RB/99, except that, after a suspension has continued for more than 84 days and the Contractor has given a Notice requesting permission to proceed, the Contractor is now given the option of:

(1) under sub-paragraph (a), agreeing to a further suspension on terms to be agreed with the Employer (and not having the sole option, as under RB/1999, to treat the suspension as a Variation of omission), or failing agreement;
(2) under sub-paragraph (b), after giving a (second) Notice, treating the suspension as a Variation of omission or, if the suspension affects the whole of the Works, as a ground for terminating the Contract under Sub-Clause 16.2.

(ii) Related Clauses / Sub-Clauses: 1.3 [*Notices and Other Communications*], 8.9 [*Employer's Suspension*], 8.13 [*Resumption of Work*], 12.4 [*Omissions*], 13.3.1 [*Variation by Instruction*], 16.2 [*Termination by Contractor*] and 18.5 [*Optional Termination*].

(iii) Analysis: While (by virtue of a significant change in Sub-Clause 8.10 of RB/17 compared to Sub-Clause 8.9 of RB/99) the Contractor is now fully compensated during the period of suspension,[160] the Contractor is not required to remain on the Site indefinitely, assuming the cause of the suspension is not the Contractor's responsibility. Under this Sub-Clause, if the suspension has continued for more than 84 days, the Contractor may give a Notice to the Engineer requesting permission to proceed. If the Engineer does not give a Notice to proceed (under Sub-Clause 8.13) within 28 days thereafter to enable the Contractor to resume work, the Contractor has the option either: (a) to agree with the Employer on a further suspension, assuming they can do so; or (b) after giving a second Notice to the Engineer, to treat the suspended work as a Variation of

160. By an EOT and/or payment of Cost Plus Profit under Sub-Clause 8.10.

omission or, if the suspension affects the whole of the Works, to give a 'Notice of termination' under Sub-Clause 16.2 [*Termination by Contractor*].[161]

The new option, after 84 days, for the Parties to agree to a further suspension is a useful addition as it recognises what often happens in practice. The Employer might need the Works to be suspended for more than 84 days (e.g., if there are disturbances at or near the Site which extend beyond 84 days, but which the Employer is confident will eventually cease) yet not want to lose the resources, or the benefit of the prices, of the Contractor who is already mobilised on the Site. On the other hand, the Contractor may have no objection to continuing to remain on standby so long as it is given an EOT and adequate compensation.

It has been suggested that the corresponding Sub-Clause in RB/99 (Sub-Clause 8.11) was open to abuse by the Engineer, as there was nothing to prevent it from instructing multiple, possibly consecutive, suspensions of up to 84 days.[162] The potential for abuse is much reduced under the new Sub-Clause, as the Employer is liable to pay the Contractor's Profit during the suspension period[163] and not just the Contractor's Cost as under RB/99.[164]

(iv) Improvements: This Sub-Clause assumes a single continuous period of suspension lasting more than 84 days and fails to address the not uncommon situation of multiple suspensions each of less than 84 days but which in the aggregate might far exceed 84 days. This subject is addressed in another international form of contract – where the permitted period of suspension is not 84 days but 120 days – in the following terms:

> If suspension [...] has lasted for a continuous period of more than one hundred and twenty (120) Days or, if the period is not continuous, for a total of more than one hundred and eighty (180) Days in the aggregate and the suspension is not due primarily to a cause attribut-

---

161. The relevant provision is Sub-Clause 16.2.1(h) giving the Contractor the right to terminate the Contract immediately. The Contractor's remedy in this case is as provided for in Sub-Clause 16.4 [*Payment after Termination by Contractor*].
162. Ellis Baker and others, *FIDIC Contracts: Law and Practice* (Informa, London, 2009) 237 (para. 5.86).
163. *See* Sub-Clause 8.10.
164. *See* Sub-Clause 8.9, RB/99.

able to the Contractor, the Contractor may by Notice to the Employer require agreement to proceed [...].[165]

--ooOOoo--

8.13 Resumption of Work

> The Contractor shall resume work as soon as practicable after receiving a Notice from the Engineer to proceed with the suspended work.
>
> At the time stated in this Notice (if not stated, immediately after the Contractor receives this Notice), the Contractor and the Engineer shall jointly examine the Works and the Plant and Materials affected by the suspension. The Engineer shall record any deterioration, loss, damage or defect in the Works or Plant or Materials which has occurred during the suspension and shall provide this record to the Contractor. The Contractor shall promptly make good all such deterioration, loss, damage or defect so that the Works, when completed, shall comply with the Contract.

The Contractor shall resume work as soon as practicable after receiving a Notice from the Engineer to proceed. At the time stated in the Notice, the Contractor and the Engineer shall jointly examine the Works affected by the suspension. The Engineer shall record any deterioration, damage or defect in the Works and the Contractor shall make good the same.

Commentary:

(i) Main Changes from RB/99:

(1) The first paragraph provides that '[t]he Contractor shall resume work as soon as practicable after receiving a Notice from the Engineer to proceed', which is new.

165. The *ICC Model Turnkey Contract for Major Projects* (ICC Publication no 797 E 2020) art. 55.4.

(2) Also new is the provision in the second paragraph that at the time stated in the Notice (if not stated, immediately after the Contractor receives it) the Contractor and the Engineer shall jointly examine the Works, Plant and Materials affected by the suspension (although a joint examination was provided for in Sub-Clause 8.12 of RB/99).

(3) The requirement that the Engineer records any deterioration, loss, damage or defect in the Works or Plant or Materials during the suspension and provides this record to the Contractor is also new.[166]

(ii) Related Clauses / Sub-Clauses: 1.3 [*Notices and Other Communications*], 8.9 [*Employer's Suspension*], 8.10 [*Consequences of Employer's Suspension*], 8.11 [*Payment for Plant and Materials after Employer's Suspension*] 8.12 [*Prolonged Suspension*] and 17.1 [*Responsibility for Care of the Works*].

(iii) Analysis: This Sub-Clause provides that the Contractor shall resume work as soon as practicable after receiving a Notice to proceed from the Engineer. This may be given by the Engineer on its own initiative or, if the suspension has continued for more than 84 days, in response to the Contractor's request to proceed under the first paragraph of Sub-Clause 8.12.

Upon the instruction of a suspension by the Engineer under Sub-Clause 8.9 [*Employer's Suspension*], the Contractor is required to protect, store and secure the Works that are suspended against 'any deterioration, loss or damage' during the suspension (which is already ordinarily the Contractor's duty under Sub-Clause 17.1). Accordingly, after a suspension ends, the second paragraph of Sub-Clause 8.13 provides for a joint examination of the Works, Plant and Materials affected by the suspension, and for the Engineer to prepare a record of 'any deterioration, loss, damage or defect' in those Works, Plant and Materials, and for the Contractor to make good the same.[167]

Unless the cause of the suspension was the responsibility of the Contractor,[168] if the Contractor suffers delay and/or Cost from the suspension (such as the Cost of protection against 'any deterioration, loss or damage'

166. It is derived from Sub-Clause 9.11 [*Resumption of Work*] in GB/08.

167. This record must comply with Sub-Clause 1.3 [*Notices and Other Communications*].

168. Sub-Clause 8.9, third paragraph.

during the suspension) and/or resuming work, the Contractor is entitled, subject to Sub-Clause 20.2, to an EOT and/or payment of Cost plus Profit on this account.[169]

--ooOOoo--

9 Tests on Completion

This Clause sets out the Contractor's obligations to carry out the Tests on Completion of the Works or a Section. These obligations include: the submission of a detailed test programme to the Engineer for Review, for purposes of obtaining its Notice of No-objection thereto so as to permit the commencement of the tests; and, following the tests, the submission of a certified report of their results to the Engineer for Review. It also describes the consequences where tests have been unduly delayed whether by the Employer or the Contractor. Finally, the Clause deals with the procedure for retesting and describes the Employer's remedies if the Works or a Section should fail repeatedly to pass the Tests on Completion.

--ooOOoo--

9.1 Contractor's Obligations

The Contractor shall carry out the Tests on Completion in accordance with this Clause and Sub-Clause 7.4 [*Testing by the Contractor*], after submitting the documents under Sub-Clause 4.4.2 [*As-Built Records*] (if applicable) and Sub-Clause 4.4.3 [*Operation and Maintenance Manuals*] (if applicable).

The Contractor shall submit to the Engineer, not less than 42 days before the date the Contractor intends to commence the Tests on Completion, a detailed test programme showing the intended timing and resources required for these tests.

The Engineer may Review the proposed test programme and may give a Notice to the Contractor stating the extent to which it does not comply with the Contract. Within 14 days after receiving this Notice, the Contractor shall revise the test pro-

169. Sub-Clause 8.10, first paragraph.

gramme to rectify such non-compliance. If the Engineer gives no such Notice within 14 days after receiving the test programme (or revised test programme), the Engineer shall be deemed to have given a Notice of No-objection. The Contractor shall not commence the Tests on Completion until a Notice of No-objection is given (or is deemed to have been given) by the Engineer.

In addition to any date(s) shown in the test programme, the Contractor shall give a Notice to the Engineer, of not less than 21 days, of the date after which the Contractor will be ready to carry out each of the Tests on Completion. The Contractor shall commence the Tests on Completion within 14 days after this date, or on such day or days as the Engineer shall instruct, and shall proceed in accordance with the Contractor's test programme to which the Engineer has given (or is deemed to have given) a Notice of No-objection.

As soon as the Works or Section have, in the Contractor's opinion, passed the Tests on Completion, the Contractor shall submit a certified report of the results of these tests to the Engineer. The Engineer shall Review such a report and may give a Notice to the Contractor stating the extent to which the results of the tests do not comply with the Contract. If the Engineer does not give such a Notice within 14 days after receiving the results of the tests, the Engineer shall be deemed to have given a Notice of No-objection.

In considering the results of the Tests on Completion, the Engineer shall make allowances for the effect of any use of (any part of) the Works by the Employer on the performance or other characteristics of the Works.

The Contractor must carry out the Tests on Completion in accordance with this Clause and Sub-Clause 7.4, after submitting as-built records under Sub-Clause 4.4.2 and operation and maintenance manuals under Sub-Clause 4.4.3, if applicable.

The Contractor must submit a proposed detailed test programme to the Engineer for Review not less than 42 days before the Contractor

intends to commence the Tests on Completion. The Engineer may give a Notice stating the extent to which the programme does not comply with the Contract. Within 14 days after receiving this Notice, the Contractor must rectify any non-compliance. If the Engineer gives no Notice within 14 days after receiving the programme (or a revised programme), the Engineer is deemed to have given a Notice of No-objection. The Contractor may not commence the Tests on Completion until a Notice of No-objection is, or is deemed to have been, given by the Engineer.

The Contractor must give 21 days' Notice to the Engineer of the date after which it will be ready to carry out each of the Tests on Completion, and must commence the tests within 14 days after this date or on such day or days as the Engineer instructs.

As soon as the Works or a Section has, in the Contractor's opinion, passed the Tests on Completion, the Contractor shall submit a certified report of the results to the Engineer for Review, who may give a Notice stating the extent to which they do not comply with the Contract. If the Engineer gives no such Notice within 14 days, the Engineer will be deemed to have given a Notice of No-objection.

Commentary

(i) Main Changes from RB/99:

(1) Whereas the first paragraph of Sub-Clause 9.1 of RB/99 had required the Contractor to provide documents in accordance with sub-paragraph (d) of Sub-Clause 4.1, the first paragraph in the new Sub-Clause provides for their submission by express reference to Sub-Clause 4.4.2 [*As-Built Records*] and Sub-Clause 4.4.3 [*Operation and Maintenance Manuals*], if applicable.

(2) The second and third paragraphs of the new Sub-Clause, dealing with the Contractor's obligation to submit a detailed (and possibly revised) test programme to the Engineer for Review, are new.

(3) In Sub-Clause 9.1 of RB/99, the Contractor had to give the Engineer not less than 21 days' notice of the date after which the Contractor would be ready to carry out the Tests on Completion and, unless otherwise agreed, such tests had to be 'carried out' (i.e., not only commenced but completed) within 14 days after this date, on such day or days as instructed by the Engineer. In the new Sub-Clause, and following not less than 21 days' Notice

from the Contractor (as in RB/99), the Tests on Completion must be 'commence[d] [...] within 14 after this date, *or* on such day or days as the Engineer shall instruct' (emphasis added).[1] Thereafter, the Contractor must proceed in accordance with its test programme to which the Engineer has given a Notice of No-objection.

(4) Whereas RB/99 simply provided that the Contractor submit a certified report of the test results to the Engineer as soon as the Works or a Section had passed any Tests on Completion, the new Sub-Clause adds that the Engineer must Review such report and may give a Notice to the Contractor stating the extent to which the test results do not comply with the Contract.

(5) The new Sub-Clause also states that the Engineer will be deemed to have given a Notice of No-objection to such report if it does not give a Notice of non-compliance with the Contract within 14 days after receiving the test results.

(ii) Related Clauses / Sub-Clauses: 1.3 [*Notices and Other Communications*], 4.4.2 [*Contractor's Documents – As-Built Records*], 4.4.3 [*Contractor's Documents – Operation and Maintenance Manuals*], 4.9.2 [*Quality Management etc. – Compliance Verification System*], 4.20 [*Progress Reports*], 7.1 [*Manner of Execution*], 7.4 [*Testing by the Contractor*], 8.3 [*Programme*], 9 [*Tests on Completion*], 10.1 [*Taking Over the Works and Sections*], 10.2 [*Taking Over Parts*], 10.3 [*Interference with Tests on Completion*], 11.5 [*Remedying of Defective Work Off Site*], 11.6 [*Further Tests after Remedying Defects*], 11.9 [*Performance Certificate*] and 13.1 [*Right to Vary*].

(iii) Analysis: The Tests on Completion must normally be carried out by the Contractor before the taking over of the Works (or a Section, if applicable),[2] as they determine whether the Works (or Section) are ready for takeover by the Employer.[3]

1. Sub-Clause 9.1, fourth paragraph.
2. Sub-Clause 10.1(a). However, *see* Sub-Clause 10.2 that allows for the carrying out of the Tests on Completion after the taking over of Part of the Works in cases where the Employer uses such Part of the Works before a Taking-Over Certificate is issued. Similarly, Sub-Clause 10.3 envisages that the Tests on Completion be carried out after the issue of the Taking-Over Certificate where the Contractor had been prevented from carrying out those tests by a cause for which the Employer is responsible.
3. *See* **Figure 9 Steps in Tests on Completion** immediately following this commentary on Sub-Clause 9.1.

(1) General requirements for Tests on Completion

The Tests on Completion are defined as tests 'which are specified in the Contract or agreed by both Parties or instructed as a Variation'.[4] The types of tests expected to be required should be described in detail in the Specification.[5] Tests on Completion may vary widely in kind depending on the type and complexity of the Works concerned. Thus, for building works they are likely to be less sophisticated than those for an industrial plant.

Sub-Clause 9.1 must be read together with Sub-Clause 7.4, which applies to all tests to be carried out by the Contractor until Completion.[6] Among other things, Sub-Clause 7.4 requires the Contractor to provide all apparatus, facilities and qualified staff necessary to carry out tests.[7]

(2) As-built records and/or operation and maintenance manuals

If the Contractor is required by the Specification[8] to submit as-built records and/or operation and maintenance manuals to the Engineer for Review, it should do so before carrying out the Tests on Completion. There is, however, no explicit requirement that the Engineer will have (or be deemed to have) given a Notice of No-objection with regard to these documents before the Contractor carries out the Tests on Completion. While such a Notice of No-objection is a precondition to the taking over

---

4. *See* Sub-Clause 1.1.83 '**Tests on Completion**'. A common problem with the description of tests in a Contract (or, more often, in the Specification or annex to the Contract) is that they are written by specialist technicians without being vetted by lawyers, which may prove unfortunate if the tests subsequently become the subject of dispute. In an arbitration, the arbitrators who will, more often than not, be lawyers will need to understand the tests. Therefore they need to be written in a way that a lawyer (assisted by a technical expert) can understand. Accordingly, descriptions of important tests, at least, should be vetted by a qualified lawyer to ensure that they will be understandable to a lay tribunal.
5. *FIDIC Procurement Procedures Guide* (FIDIC 2011), 119-120, and the *Guidance for the Preparation of Particular Conditions*, 35.
6. *See* the commentary on Sub-Clause 7.4 above. On the other hand, Tests after Completion, if any, are carried out by the Employer. *See*, e.g., Clause 12 [*Tests after Completion*] of YB/17 and SB/17.
7. Sub-Clause 7.4, second paragraph.
8. *See* Sub-Clauses 4.4.2 [*As-Built Records*] and 4.4.3 [*Operation and Maintenance Manuals*] which refer to the Specification.

of the Works or a Section under Sub-Clause 10.1,[9] such a Notice may apparently be given after the carrying out of the Tests on Completion.

(3) The requirement of a detailed test programme

Not less than 42 days before the date on which the Contractor intends to commence the Tests on Completion, the Contractor must submit to the Engineer a proposed 'detailed test programme' showing the 'intended timing and resources' required for the tests.[10]

The Engineer 'may'[11] Review[12] the submitted detailed test programme and may, within 14 days, give a Notice to the Contractor stating the extent to which it does not comply with the Contract. If the Engineer gives such a Notice of non-compliance, the Contractor must revise the test programme within 14 days and resubmit it to the Engineer. If the Engineer gives no such Notice within 14 days after receiving the test programme, whether the initial or a revised one, the Engineer is deemed to have given a Notice of No-objection to it. The Contractor may not commence the Tests on Completion until a Notice of No-objection with regard to the test programme is (or is deemed to have been) given by the Engineer.[13]

Thus, if the Contractor's initial submission is refused, the Contractor must submit a revised test programme or programmes until a Notice of No-objection is (or is deemed to have been) given by the Engineer.

(4) Timing of tests

The Contractor must give not less than 21 days' Notice to the Engineer of the date after which the Contractor will be ready to carry out the Tests on Completion.[14] This advance notice is necessary to allow time to the Engineer to arrange for the Employer and any specialists to attend (e.g., the Employer may require that its staff who will be in charge of operating

9. Sub-Clause 4.4.2, third paragraph, Sub-Clause 4.4.3, third paragraph, and Sub-Clause 10.1(b) and (c).
10. This new obligation is in addition to the Contractor's obligation under Sub-Clause 8.3 [*Programme*] to submit, in its time programmes, information concerning tests specified in, or required by, the Contract. *See* Sub-Clause 8.3 [*Programme*], sub-para. (e).
11. Sub-Clause 9.1, third paragraph. The Engineer is not obliged to Review the detailed test programme. Sub-Clause 1.2(e).
12. As defined in Sub-Clause 1.1.70 '**Review**'.
13. Sub-Clause 9.1, third paragraph.
14. Sub-Clause 9.1, fourth paragraph.

and/or maintaining the Works be present).[15] Thereafter, the Contractor is required to commence the Tests on Completion 'within 14 days after this date, or on such day or days as the Engineer shall instruct'. Unlike RB/99, which had provided that the Tests on Completion be 'carried out' (i.e., not only commenced but completed) within such 14-day period, there is no similar requirement in the new Sub-Clause. Moreover, the Engineer is given discretion to decide whether the Tests on Completion are commenced within or beyond such 14-day period, although the timing should be compatible with the test programme to which the Engineer has given a Notice of No-objection, as well as with the Programme.

(5) Certified report of test results

The Contractor is required to submit to the Engineer a certified report[16] of the test results signed by the Contractor's Representative[17] as soon as the Works or a Section has, in the Contractor's opinion, passed the Tests on Completion.[18] The Engineer must Review the report and give a Notice to the Contractor if the test results do not satisfy contractual standards. In that case, the Notice must state 'the extent to which the results of the tests do not comply with the Contract'. If the Engineer fails to give such a Notice within 14 days after receiving the test results, the Engineer is deemed to have given a Notice of No-objection.[19] If the Engineer accepts

15. Brian Barr and Leo Grutters, *FIDIC Users' Guide* (3rd edn, ICE Publishing, London, 2014) 180.
16. The term 'certified report' of the results of the tests is not defined. However, both a 'certificate' and a 'report' must comply with Sub-Clause 1.3 [*Notices and Other Communications*]. Moreover, more generally, a certificate has been defined as:

    > the expression in a definite form of the exercise of the opinion of the certifier in relation to some matter provided for by the terms of the contract.

    Atkin Chambers, *Hudson's Building and Engineering Contracts* (14th edn, Sweet & Maxwell, London, 2020) 484 (para. 4-001). Thus, one would expect the Contractor to have to attest, in a document entitled 'Certificate', to the truth or accuracy of the report containing the test results.
17. Sub-paragraph (a)(i) of Sub-Clause 1.3 [*Notices and Other Communications*].
18. Sub-Clause 9.1, fifth paragraph.
19. In this connection, Sub-Clause 4.9.2 contains a general requirement that the Compliance Verification System, which the Contractor is required to prepare and implement, includes a method for reporting the results of all tests carried out by the Contractor.

that the tests have been passed,[20] the Engineer must endorse the Contractor's test certificate or issue a test certificate to the Contractor to that effect.[21]

The Contractor's Programme is required to include the sequence and timing of tests specified in, or required by, the Contract.[22] In each monthly progress report under Sub-Clause 4.20 [*Progress Reports*], the Contractor is required to include a detailed description of progress in testing, including the Tests on Completion, as well as the actual or expected date of tests of each main item of Plant and Materials.[23]

--ooOOoo--

20. Which the Engineer is not stated to be required to confirm by a Notice.
21. Sub-Clause 7.4, seventh paragraph.
22. Sub-Clause 8.3(e).
23. Sub-Clause 4.20(a) and (c)(iii).

Figure 9 Steps in Tests on Completion[1]

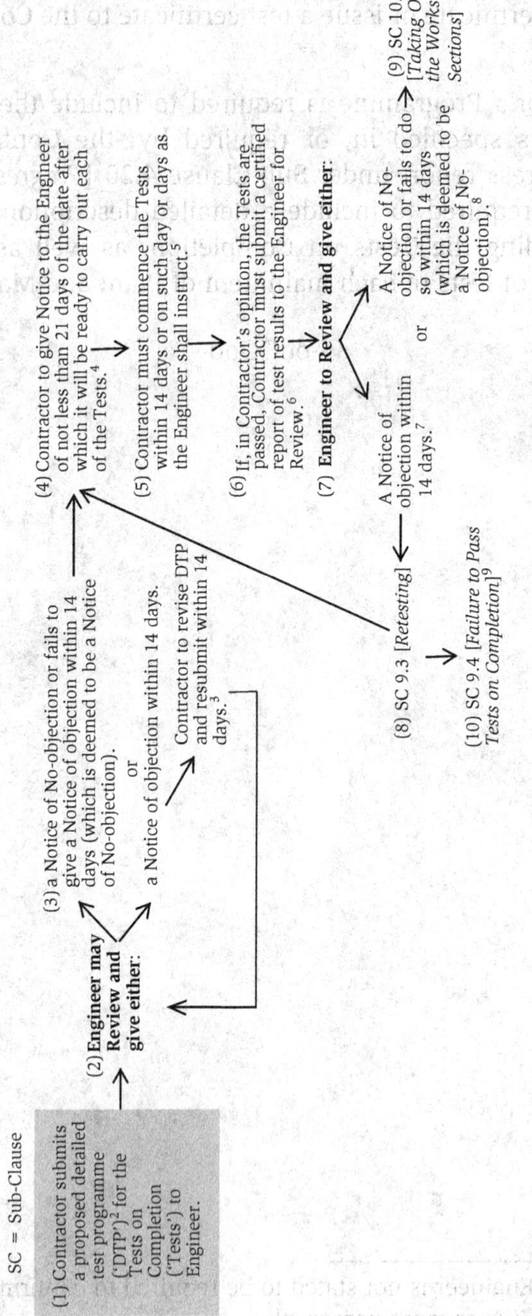

SC = Sub-Clause
(1) Contractor submits a proposed detailed test programme ('DTP')[2] for the Tests on Completion ('Tests') to Engineer.
(2) Engineer may Review and give either:
(3) a Notice of No-objection or fails to give a Notice of objection within 14 days (which is deemed to be a Notice of No-objection).
or
a Notice of objection within 14 days.
Contractor to revise DTP and resubmit within 14 days.[3]
(4) Contractor to give Notice to the Engineer of not less than 21 days of the date after which it will be ready to carry out each of the Tests.[4]
(5) Contractor must commence the Tests within 14 days or on such day or days as the Engineer shall instruct.[5]
(6) If, in Contractor's opinion, the Tests are passed, Contractor must submit a certified report of test results to the Engineer for Review.[6]
(7) Engineer to Review and give either:
A Notice of objection within 14 days.[7]
or
A Notice of No-objection or fails to do so within 14 days (which is deemed to be a Notice of No-objection).[8]
(8) SC 9.3 [Retesting]
(9) SC 10.1 [Taking Over the Works and Sections]
(10) SC 9.4 [Failure to Pass Tests on Completion][9]

Source: Author's own work.

Figure 9 Steps in Tests on Completion

Notes

1. This figure is a simplified presentation of the procedure for Tests in Clause 9 [*Tests on Completion*] for illustrative purposes. Only the actual text of that Clause should be relied upon. Note that SC 7.4 is also relevant but its requirements are not depicted in this figure.
2. The DTP must be submitted not less than 42 days before the date on which the Contractor intends to commence the Tests (SC 9.1, second paragraph).
3. This process is to be repeated until the Contractor has received a Notice of No-objection or the Engineer fails to give a Notice of objection within 14 days (SC 9.1, third paragraph).
4. SC 9.1, fourth paragraph. Before carrying out the Tests on Completion and if required by the Specification, the Contractor must submit as-built records and/or operation and maintenance manuals to the Engineer for Review. SC 9.1, first paragraph.
5. *Ibid.*
6. SC 9.1, fifth paragraph.
7. *Ibid.*
8. *Ibid.*
9. If the Works or Section fails to pass the Tests repeated under SC 9.3, the Engineer has the remedies provided for in SC 9.4 (namely: (a) further repetition of testing, (b) and (c) rejection of the Works or Section, or (d) issue of a Taking-Over Certificate and payment by the Contractor or reduction in the Contract Price).

--ooOOoo--

9.2 Delayed Tests

If the Contractor has given a Notice under Sub-Clause 9.1 [*Contractor's Obligations*] that the Works or Section (as the case may be) are ready for Tests on Completion, and these tests are unduly delayed by the Employer's Personnel or by a cause for which the Employer is responsible, Sub-Clause 10.3 [*Interference with Tests on Completion*] shall apply.

If the Tests on Completion are unduly delayed by the Contractor, the Engineer may by giving a Notice to the Contractor require the Contractor to carry out the tests within 21 days after receiving the Notice. The Contractor shall carry out the tests on such day or days within this period of 21 days as the Contractor may fix, for which the Contractor shall give a prior Notice to the Engineer of not less than 7 days.

If the Contractor fails to carry out the Tests on Completion within this period of 21 days:

(a) after a second Notice is given by the Engineer to the Contractor, the Employer's Personnel may proceed with the tests;
(b) the Contractor may attend and witness these tests;
(c) within 28 days of these tests being completed, the Engineer shall send a copy of the test results to the Contractor; and
(d) if the Employer incurs additional costs as a result of such testing, the Employer shall be entitled subject to Sub-Clause 20.2 [*Claims for Payment and/or EOT*] to payment by the Contractor of the costs reasonably incurred.

Whether or not the Contractor attends, these Tests on Completion shall be deemed to have been carried out in the presence of the Contractor and the results of these tests shall be accepted as accurate.

If the Contractor has given a Notice under Sub-Clause 9.1 that the Works or a Section is ready for Tests on Completion and these tests are unduly delayed by the Employer's Personnel, or a cause for which the Employer is responsible, Sub-Clause 10.3 will apply.

If the Tests on Completion are unduly delayed by the Contractor, the Engineer may, by a Notice, require the Contractor to carry out the tests within 21 days. The Contractor must then do so on such day(s) within the 21 days as the Contractor may fix, for which the Contractor must give a prior Notice to the Engineer of not less than 7 days.

If the Contractor fails to carry out the tests within the 21 days then, after a second Notice by the Engineer to the Contractor, the Employer's Personnel may proceed with the tests, which the Contractor may attend, and within 28 days of these tests being completed, the results must be sent to the Contractor. Subject to Sub-Clause 20.2, the Employer may claim payment of any additional costs incurred. Such Tests on Completion will be deemed to have been carried out in the presence of the Contractor and the results must be accepted as accurate.

Commentary

(i) Main Changes from RB/99:

(1) The first paragraph of Sub-Clause 9.2 of RB/99 had provided that Sub-Clause 7.4 [*Testing*], fifth paragraph, and/or Sub-Clause 10.3 [*Interference with Tests on Completion*] would apply if the Tests on Completion had been unduly delayed by the Employer; in the first paragraph of this new Sub-Clause, the reference to Sub-Clause 7.4 has been removed and it has been clarified that, if the Contractor has given a Notice under Sub-Clause 9.1 that the Works or Section are ready for Tests on Completion and these tests are unduly delayed by the Employer's Personnel or a cause for which the Employer is responsible, Sub-Clause 10.3 will apply.

(2) Unlike RB/99, the first paragraph of the new Sub-Clause refers to delays by the Employer's Personnel, as well as delays by a cause for which the Employer is responsible.

(3) Both RB/99 and RB/17 provide that, where the Tests on Completion are unduly delayed by the Contractor, the Engineer may by a Notice/notice[24] require the Contractor to carry out the Tests within 21 days; however, RB/99 provided that the Contractor had to give a notice to the Engineer of simply the day or days (within the 21 days required by the Engineer) on which the Contractor would carry out the Tests on Completion, whereas the second paragraph of the new Sub-Clause provides that the Contractor must give a prior Notice of not less than 7 days (within the 21 days required by the Engineer) of such day or days.

(4) The third paragraph of the new Sub-Clause is more detailed as regards the consequences of the Contractor's failure to carry out the Tests on Completion within the 21-day period required by the Engineer: whereas RB/99 simply stated that in this case the Employer's Personnel may proceed with the Tests of Completion 'at the risk and cost of the Contractor', the new Sub-Clause provides that the Employer's Personnel may proceed with the

24. '**Notice**', with an initial capital letter, is a defined term in RB/17 but not in RB/99.

tests after a second Notice has been given to the Contractor and the Employer may recover the additional costs it has incurred as a result of such testing.

(5) The new Sub-Clause contains details concerning the Contractor's right to attend and witness tests carried out by the Employer's Personnel and the Engineer's obligation to send copies of the test results to the Contractor, which are new.

(ii) Related Clauses / Sub-Clauses: 1.3 [*Notices and Other Communications*], 4.4.2 [*Contractor's Documents – As-Built Records*], 4.4.3 [*Contractor's Documents – Operation and Maintenance Manuals*], 7.4 [*Testing by the Contractor*], 9.1 [*Contractor's Obligations*], 9.3 [*Retesting*] 10.3 [*Interference with Tests on Completion*] and 20.2 [*Claims for Payment and/or EOT*].

(iii) Analysis: This Sub-Clause deals with delays by either the Employer or the Employer's Personnel (first paragraph) or the Contractor (second to fourth paragraphs) in carrying out the Tests on Completion.

(1) Tests delayed by Employer or Employer's Personnel

The first paragraph provides that if:

(1) the Contractor has given a Notice under Sub-Clause 9.1 to the Engineer that the Works or a Section 'are ready'[25] for Tests on Completion, and
(2) these tests are 'unduly delayed' by the Employer's Personnel or a cause for which the Employer is responsible,[26]

25. Contrary to what this Sub-Clause literally provides, the Contractor does not give a Notice under Sub-Clause 9.1 that the Works 'are ready' for Tests on Completion but, instead, gives a Notice to the Engineer of not less than 21 days of the date after which the Contractor will be ready to carry out such tests. Accordingly, to make sense of this provision, it appears necessary to disregard the 'are ready' language and to interpret those words as referring to readiness to carry out the tests as from the date (not less than 21 days after the Notice) indicated in the Notice of the Contractor.

26. It is not clear what delay 'by the Employer's Personnel or by a cause for which the Employer is responsible' (which are to be found in Sub-Clauses 9.2, first paragraph, and 10.3, first paragraph) is referring to. Under the common law legal doctrine of *respondeat superior* ('holding an employer [...] liable for an employee's or agent's wrongful acts committed within the scope of the employment or agency', Bryan A Garner (ed in chief), *Black's*

Sub-Clause 10.3 [*Interference with Tests on Completion*] shall apply.

Sub-Clause 10.3 envisages, among other things, that if the Contractor is prevented for more than 14 days (either a continuous period or multiple periods which total more than 14 days) from carrying out the Tests on Completion for the Works or a Section, the Contractor is to give a Notice to the Engineer describing the prevention. The Employer will then be deemed to have taken over the Works or Section on the date when the Tests on Completion would otherwise have been completed, and the Engineer must immediately issue a Taking-Over Certificate for the Works or a Section. Pursuant to Sub-Clause 10.3, second paragraph, the Tests on Completion should then be carried out as soon as practicable (and before expiry of the DNP) and, if the Contractor has suffered delay and/or incurred Costs as the result of the prevention, the Contractor will be entitled, subject to Sub-Clause 20.2, to an EOT and/or payment of Cost Plus Profit.[27]

However, it is unclear when the 14 days of prevention referred to in the first paragraph of Sub-Clause 10.3 are to begin. They might begin:

(1) when either the Employer's Personnel or the Employer has prevented their commencement *within the 14 days* mentioned in the fourth paragraph of Sub-Clause 9.1 (assuming the Engineer has not already under that paragraph instructed that the tests proceed at a later date), or
(2) *on the 14th day* mentioned in the fourth paragraph of Sub-Clause 9.1 (on the same assumption as in (1)).

Law Dictionary (11th edn, Thomson Reuters, St Paul, MN, 2019)), there should be no reason to distinguish the Employer from the Employer's Personnel, or at least any of the Employer's Personnel who are employees or agents, as the Employer would normally be responsible for them as a matter of law. But what then is 'a cause for which the Employer is responsible'? This could be referring to the five 'causes' listed in sub-paras (a) through (e) of Sub-Clause 8.5 [*Extension of Time for Completion*] or the six 'events' described in sub-paras (a) through (f) of Sub-Clause 17.2 [*Liability for Care of the Works*] for which the Employer is liable. Alternatively, it could be referring to some combination of the foregoing and/or other things for which the Employer may have some responsibility.

27. *See* the commentary on Sub-Clause 10.3 [*Interference with Tests on Completion*] below.

If, under the fourth paragraph[28] of Sub-Clause 9.1, the Engineer has instructed that the tests shall be commenced on a later day or days (than the 14 days) and the Employer's Personnel or the Employer prevents their commencement on that day or days, *presumably the 14 days of prevention referred to in the first paragraph of Sub-Clause 10.3 would commence on that day or days,* but the situation is unclear.

Although the first paragraph of Sub-Clause 9.2 no longer contains an explicit reference to Sub-Clause 7.4 [*Testing by the Contractor*] (as was the case in RB/99) as applicable to delays to the Tests on Completion caused by the Employer, the fifth paragraph of Sub-Clause 7.4, which entitles the Contractor to claim an EOT and/or payment of Cost Plus Profit, may still apply in the case of such delays, especially if Sub-Clause 10.3 cannot be applied for some reason.[29] Delays of the Employer for which the Contractor might claim include failure by the Employer to adhere to the Contractor's detailed test programme for which a Notice of No-objection has been (or is deemed to have been) given.

(2) Tests delayed by the Contractor and carried out by the Employer's Personnel

The second, third and fourth paragraphs of Sub-Clause 9.2 address the procedure to be followed where the Tests on Completion are 'unduly' delayed *by the Contractor*.[30] When are tests 'unduly' delayed by the Contractor? Presumably, this may occur, among other things, if the Contractor:

28. Beginning 'In addition to [...].'
29. Sub-Clause 10.3 envisages that the Contractor has been prevented from carrying out the Tests on Completion for more than 14 days by either the Employer's Personnel or a cause for which the Employer is responsible. Thus, if the Contractor has been prevented from carrying them out for 14 days or less, Sub-Clause 10.3 is inapplicable. In such a case, the Contractor may be able to rely on the fifth paragraph of Sub-Clause 7.4 to claim an EOT and/or payment of Cost Plus Profit as pertaining to the delay. Sub-Clause 9.1 states that the Contractor shall carry out the Tests on Completion in accordance with Sub-Clause 7.4 and Sub-Clause 7.4 states that it applies to 'all tests specified in the Contract', other than Tests *after* Completion.
30. 'Unduly' delayed here may also be defined by reference to 14 days' delay referred to in Sub-Clause 10.3 – a delay is undue if it is of more than 14 days duration, but again, if so, it is unclear when the 14 days begin. Does this delay also include where Tests on Completion have been delayed by a 'cause' for which the Contractor is responsible? *See* the third paragraph of Sub-Clause 8.9 [*Employer's Suspension*] which refers to this type of delay

(1) fails to submit on time either the documents required under Sub-Clauses 4.4.2 [*As-Built Records*] or 4.4.3 [*Operation and Maintenance Manuals*] or a compliant (revised, if necessary) detailed test programme;[31] or

(2) submits a detailed test programme, but fails to give not less than 21 days' Notice of the date after which it will be ready to carry out the Tests on Completion, or fails to commence the Tests within 14 days after this date or on such other day or days as the Engineer shall instruct;[32] or

(3) fails to comply with a detailed test programme for which a Notice of No-objection is (or deemed to have been) given by the Engineer.

Where Tests are unduly delayed by the Contractor, the Engineer must first, by giving a Notice to the Contractor, require the Contractor to carry out the tests within 21 days after receiving such a Notice. The Contractor is then obliged to do so on a day or days within this 21-day period. The Contractor must give a prior Notice to the Engineer of not less than 7 days of the day or days when it is going to carry out the Tests on Completion.[33] These 7 days allow the Engineer time to make necessary arrangements for the appropriate people to attend.

If the Contractor fails to carry out the tests within the above-mentioned 21-day period, the Engineer is required to give a second Notice to the Contractor after which the Employer's Personnel may proceed themselves with the tests.[34] While it is stated that the Contractor may attend and witness these tests, it is not indicated how the Contractor will know about them unless this information is in this second Notice. The Engineer must send a copy of the test results[35] to the Contractor within 28 days

---

and Jakob B Sørensen, *FIDIC Red Book: A Companion to the 2017 Construction Contract* (1st edn, ICE Publishing, London, 2019) 112. While this is unclear, the author suggests that it should do so.

31. Sub-Clause 9.1, first, second and third paragraphs.
32. Sub-Clause 9.1, fourth paragraph.
33. Sub-Clause 9.2, second paragraph.
34. Sub-Clause 9.2, third paragraph.
35. Unlike the Contractor who is required to submit a 'certified report' of the results of tests which it undertakes, pursuant to Sub-Clause 9.1, the Engineer is not bound to observe this formality.

after completion of the tests.[36] The Employer is entitled, subject to Sub-Clause 20.2, to payment of the costs reasonably incurred as a result of the carrying out of these tests.[37]

Whether or not the Contractor attends these Tests on Completion, their results are deemed to be accepted as accurate, presumably especially by the Contractor,[38] whether the Contractor is shown to have passed them or not.[39] If it has failed them, Sub-Clause 9.3 will apply.

(iv) Improvements:

(1) The description in the first paragraph of a Notice under Sub-Clause 9.1 as stating when the Works or Section 'are ready' for Tests on Completion needs to be corrected as that Notice (*see* the fourth paragraph of Sub-Clause 9.1) does not so provide but, instead, refers to a future date (of not less than 21 days) after which the Contractor would be ready to carry out the Tests on Completion.

(2) In the third paragraph of Sub-Clause 9.2, the following words which begin sub-paragraph (a), namely, 'after a second Notice is given by the Engineer to the Contractor' might be better removed from sub-paragraph (a) and be placed in the immediately preceding text, after the words '21 days' and before the colon (the comma in sub-paragraph (a) should be removed). In the same paragraph, it should also be clarified how the Contractor will be informed of tests to be carried out by the Employer's Personnel.

--ooOOoo--

36. Sub-Clause 1.3 [*Notices and Other Communications*] will almost certainly apply as they are likely to be in the form of a 'report' (as is true of the test results under Sub-Clause 9.1) or 'similar type of communication' under that Sub-Clause.
37. Sub-Clause 9.2, sub-para. (d).
38. Sub-Clause 9.2, last paragraph. Pursuant to Sub-Clause 3.2, last paragraph, acceptance by the Engineer would not relieve the Contractor of any contractual obligation.
39. But this should not prevent the Contractor from asserting a Claim under Sub-Clause 20.1 if it has reason to challenge them.

9.3 Retesting

> If the Works, or a Section, fail to pass the Tests on Completion, Sub-Clause 7.5 [*Defects and Rejection*] shall apply. The Engineer or the Contractor may require these failed tests, and the Tests on Completion on any related work, to be repeated under the same terms and conditions. Such repeated tests shall be treated as Tests on Completion for the purposes of this Clause.

If the Works, or a Section, fail to pass the Tests on Completion, Sub-Clause 7.5 shall apply. The Engineer or the Contractor may require these failed tests, and the Tests on Completion on any related work, to be repeated. Such repeated tests shall be treated as Tests on Completion for the purposes of Clause 9.

<u>Commentary</u>

(i) Main Changes from RB/99: The only significant difference from Sub-Clause 9.3 of RB/99 is the addition of the last sentence providing that the repeated tests shall be treated as Tests on Completion for the purposes of Clause 9.

(ii) Related Clauses / Sub-Clauses: 7.4 [*Testing by the Contractor*], 7.5 [*Defects and Rejection*] and 9 [*Tests on Completion*].

(iii) Analysis: This Sub-Clause provides that Sub-Clause 7.5 [*Defects and Rejection*] will apply if the Works or a Section fails to pass the Tests on Completion. Sub-Clause 7.5 provides that if, as a result of testing, any Plant, Materials, Contractor's design or workmanship is found to be not in accordance with the Contract, the Engineer shall give a Notice to the Contractor describing the defect, and the Contractor shall then promptly prepare and submit a proposal for necessary remedial work.[40] The Engineer may Review the proposal and may give (or be deemed to have given) a Notice of No-objection to it, after which the Contractor may proceed with the proposal.[41]

Sub-Clause 7.5 also deals with, among other things, the consequences of the Contractor's failure to submit such a proposal or to carry out proposed remedial work to which the Engineer has not objected. In such

40. Sub-Clause 7.5, first paragraph.
41. Sub-Clause 7.5, second paragraph.

a case, the Engineer may instruct the Contractor either to repair or remedy, or remove from the Site and replace or re-execute, any work not in accordance with the Contract,[42] or, finally, to reject the defective work, in which case the Employer may carry out the work itself or have it carried out by others.[43]

The last sentence of Sub-Clause 9.3 states that the repeated tests will be treated as Tests on Completion for the purposes of Clause 9. This means that if the Works or Section passes such repeated tests, the Tests on Completion will have been passed for the purposes of the taking over of the Works or a Section under Sub-Clause 10.1.

--ooOOoo--

9.4 Failure to Pass Tests on Completion

If the Works, or a Section, fail to pass the Tests on Completion repeated under Sub-Clause 9.3 [*Retesting*], the Engineer shall be entitled to:

(a) instruct further repetition of Tests on Completion under Sub-Clause 9.3 [*Retesting*];
(b) reject the Works if the effect of the failure is to deprive the Employer of substantially the whole benefit of the Works in which event the Employer shall have the same remedies as are provided in sub-paragraph (d) of Sub-Clause 11.4 [*Failure to Remedy Defects*];
(c) reject the Section if the effect of the failure is that the Section cannot be used for its intended purpose(s) under the Contract, in which event the Employer shall have the same remedy as is provided in sub-paragraph (c) of Sub-Clause 11.4 [*Failure to Remedy Defects*]; or
(d) issue a Taking-Over Certificate, if the Employer so requests.

In the event of sub-paragraph (d) above, the Contractor shall then proceed in accordance with all other obligations under the Contract, and the

42. Sub-Clause 7.5(a) which refers to Sub-Clause 7.6(a) and/or (b).
43. Sub-Clause 7.5(b) which refers to Sub-Clause 11.4(a). For more details concerning Sub-Clause 7.5, *see* the commentary on this Sub-Clause above.

Employer shall be entitled subject to Sub-Clause 20.2 [*Claims for Payment and/or EOT*] to payment by the Contractor or a reduction in the Contract Price as described under sub-paragraph (b) of Sub-Clause 11.4 [*Failure to Remedy Defects*], respectively. This entitlement shall be without prejudice to any other rights the Employer may have, under the Contract or otherwise.

If the Works or a Section fails to pass the Tests on Completion repeated under Sub-Clause 9.3, the Engineer will be entitled to:

(a) instruct further repetition of the tests under Sub-Clause 9.3;
(b) reject the Works if the effect of the failure is to deprive the Employer of substantially the whole benefit of the Works, in which event the Employer has the remedies in Sub-Clause 11.4(d);
(c) reject the Section if it cannot be used for its intended purpose(s) in which event the Employer has the remedy in Sub-Clause 11.4(c); or
(d) issue a Taking-Over Certificate, if the Employer so requests.

In the event of sub-paragraph (d), the Contractor must proceed under the Contract and the Employer will be entitled, subject to Sub-Clause 20.2 and without prejudice, to payment by the Contractor or a reduction in the Contract Price as described in Sub-Clause 11.4(b).

Commentary

(i) Main Changes from RB/99:

(1) Whereas Sub-Clause 9.4 of RB/99 provided for three potential remedies in case of the Contractor's failure to pass repeated Tests on Completion, the new Sub-Clause provides for four: sub-paragraph (b) of Sub-Clause 9.4 of RB/99, which dealt with cases where the failure deprived the Employer of substantially the whole benefit of the Works or a Section, has now been split into sub-paragraphs (b) and (c) in Sub-Clause 9.4 of RB/17.[44]

44. Sub-paragraph (c) of Sub-Clause 9.4 of RB/99 has become sub-para. (d) of RB/17.

(2) New sub-paragraph (b), which deals with where the effect of the failure is to deprive the Employer of substantially the whole benefit of the Works, entitles the Employer to terminate the Contract pursuant to Sub-Clause 11.4(d) (which is the same solution as in RB/99), whereas new sub-paragraph (c), which deals with where its effect is that a Section cannot be used for its intended purpose(s), entitles the Engineer to treat the Section as an omission instructed under Sub-Clause 13.3.1[45] (which is a new solution in RB/17).

(3) Under the last paragraph, there is a difference in the Employer's remedy where, at the Employer's request, the Engineer issues a Taking-Over Certificate:
  (a) in RB/99, the Employer was entitled to a reduction in the Contract Price and (unless the reduction was provided for in the Contract) could require the reduction to be either (i) agreed by both Parties (in full satisfaction of this failure only) and paid before the issue of the Taking-Over Certificate (in which case compliance with the Employer's claims' procedure would not be required) or (ii) determined and paid in accordance with the claims' procedure for Employer's claims;[46] and
  (b) in the new Sub-Clause, the Employer is entitled to either payment by the Contractor or a reduction in the Contract Price as described in Sub-Clause 11.4(b); in both cases, compliance with the claims' procedure under Sub-Clause 20.2 is required and the Employer's entitlement is without prejudice to the Employer's other rights.

(ii) Related Clauses / Sub-Clauses: 1.3 [*Notices and Other Communications*], 9 [*Tests on Completion*], 10.1 [*Taking Over the Works and Sections*], 11.4 [*Failure to Remedy Defects*], 13.3.1 [*Variation Procedure – Variation by Instruction*] and 20.2 [*Claims for Payment and/or EOT*].

(iii) Analysis: This Sub-Clause addresses the potentially serious case of a failure of the Works or a Section to pass the Tests on Completion which have been repeated under Sub-Clause 9.3 [*Retesting*].

45. *See* Sub-Clause 9.4(c) which refers to Sub-Clause 11.4(c) which refers in turn to Sub-Clause 13.3.1.

46. *See* Sub-Clause 9.4, second paragraph, which refers in turn to Sub-Clauses 2.5 and 3.5 of RB/99.

(1) Repetition of tests (sub-paragraph (a))

Under sub-paragraph (a), the Engineer may instruct further repetition of the Tests on Completion. According to FIDIC, there is 'no limit on the number of repetitions [...] which may be' instructed as it may appear after testing 'that only minor remedial work will be required' to overcome the apparent reasons for the failure to pass the tests.[47]

(2) Rejection of Works (sub-paragraph (b))

Under sub-paragraph (b), the Engineer may reject the Works if the effect of the failure is to deprive the Employer of 'substantially the whole benefit of the Works'. In this case, the Employer may, pursuant to Sub-Clause 11.4(d), terminate the Contract as a whole with immediate effect, in which case Sub-Clause 15.2 [*Termination for Contractor's Default*] will not apply and the Employer may recover from the Contractor, subject to Sub-Clause 20.2, all sums paid for the Works, plus financing charges and any costs incurred in dismantling the same, clearing the Site, and returning the Plant and Materials to the Contractor,[48] without prejudice to the Employer's other rights (as discussed below). *The Parties are basically restored to where they were before entry into the Contract*. This is a most drastic remedy,[49] which should only be resorted to in the most extreme case.

(3) Rejection of Section (sub-paragraph (c))

If the effect of the failure is that a Section cannot be used for its intended purpose(s) under the Contract,[50] the Engineer may reject the Section under sub-paragraph (c). In this case, no Taking-Over Certificate will be issued for that Section and the Employer may, pursuant to Sub-Clause 11.4(c), require the Engineer to treat that Section as an omission, as if such omission had been instructed under Sub-Clause 13.3.1 [*Variation of Instruction*]. However, unlike the ordinary case of a Variation comprising

47. *The FIDIC Contracts Guide* (2nd edn, FIDIC, 2022) 303. This appears to mean that there may be some minor tests that may need to be repeated multiple times. As they are minor this should not, according to FIDIC, be objectionable to the Contractor. Multiple tests also are justified where there is reasonable hope that the problem can be overcome.
48. *See* the commentary on sub-para. (d) of Sub-Clause 11.4 [*Failure to Remedy Defects*] below.
49. It corresponds to the common law remedy of restitution.
50. *See (3) Fitness for purpose obligations* under **(iii) Analysis** of the commentary on Sub-Clause 4.1 [*Contractor's General Obligations*] above.

the omission of work, no agreement of the Parties is required with regard to such an omission under Sub-Clauses 9.4(c) and 11.4(c) if the omitted work is to be carried out by the Employer or others.[51] In the case of sub-paragraph (c) of Sub-Clause 9.4, the Contractor should not be paid for the omitted work and such work may be carried out by the Employer or by others.

(4) Issue of Taking-Over Certificate (sub-paragraph (d))

Under sub-paragraph (d), the Engineer may issue a Taking-Over Certificate for the Works or a Section, as the case may be, if the Employer so requests, in which case the Employer may claim, subject to Sub-Clause 20.2, 'payment by the Contractor'[52] or a reduction in the Contract Price. Such reduction:

> shall be in full satisfaction of this failure only and shall be in the amount as shall be appropriate to cover the reduced value to the Employer

as a result of the Contractor's failure to pass the Tests on Completion.[53]

It has been suggested that the phrase 'reduced value to the Employer' might be intended to take into account not only the reduced value of the Works or a Section as physical structures but also the value of these as revenue – or profit – generating assets.[54] Such an argument does not sit easily with Sub-Clause 1.15 [*Limitation of Liability*],[55] which excludes

51. *See* Sub-Clause 9.4(c) which refers to Sub-Clause 11.4 (c) which refers in turn to the instruction of a Variation of omission under Sub-Clause 13.3.1. The second paragraph of Sub-Clause 13.1 provides that '[o]ther than as stated under Sub-Clause 11.4' a Variation shall not comprise the omission of work which is to be carried out by the Employer or others unless agreed by the Parties. The inference is that an agreement of the Parties is unnecessary in the case of omitted work under Sub-Clause 9.4 (c) which is to be carried out by the Employer or others.
52. These words, which are also in Sub-Clause 9.4 of YB/17 and SB/17, where they refer to the Contractor's possible liability for Performance Damages, may have been included in error in RB/17 as, unlike YB/17 and SB/17, it contains no provision for the payment of Performance Damages.
53. Sub-Clause 11.4(b) which is referred to in the last paragraph of Sub-Clause 9.4.
54. Ellis Baker and others, *FIDIC Contracts: Law and Practice* (Informa, London, 2009) 421 (para. 8.92).
55. Sub-Clause 17.6 [*Limitation of Liability*] of RB/99.

liability for 'loss of use of any Works' and/or for 'loss of profit'. Consequently, the phrase should be construed as referring simply to the reduced value of the Works or a Section to the Employer, the reduction corresponding to the portion of the Contract Price fairly allocable (e.g., by reference to values in the Bill of Quantities) to the damaged or defective work.

The Employer's remedy in Sub-Clause 9.4(d) is stated to be without prejudice[56] to any other rights the Employer may have under the Contract or otherwise, such as the right to Delay Damages[57] or other damages as a result of the Contractor's failure to complete the Works or a Section in accordance with the Contract.[58]

--ooOOoo--

10 Employer's Taking Over

This Clause describes the conditions for the taking over (or deemed taking over) of the Works or a Section by the Employer. It describes how, if the Employer uses any part of the Works, other than as a permitted temporary measure, before a Taking-Over Certificate for the part has been issued, the Employer may be deemed to have taken over this part. In addition, if the Contractor is prevented from carrying out the Tests on Completion for the Works or a Section by a cause for which the Employer is responsible, the Employer may be deemed to have taken over the Works or Section, as the case may be, on the date when the Tests on Completion would otherwise have been completed. In that case, the Engineer must issue a Taking-Over Certificate for the corresponding Works or Section.

--ooOOoo--

56. The Employer's remedies in Sub-Clause 9.4 (b) and (c) are also without prejudice to the Employer's other rights as they refer to the remedies in Sub-Clause 11.4 (d) and (c), respectively, which are stated in the last paragraph of Sub-Clause 11.4 to be without prejudice to the Employer's other rights.
57. Under Sub-Clause 8.8 [*Delay Damages*].
58. Subject to the limitation in Sub-Clause 1.15 [*Limitation of Liability*].

10.1 Taking Over the Works and Sections

Except as stated in Sub-Clause 9.4 [*Failure to Pass Tests on Completion*], Sub-Clause 10.2 [*Taking Over Parts*] and Sub-Clause 10.3 [*Interference with Tests on Completion*], the Works shall be taken over by the Employer when:

(a) the Works have been completed in accordance with the Contract, including the passing of the Tests on Completion and except as allowed in sub-paragraph (i) below;
(b) if applicable, the Engineer has given (or is deemed to have given) a Notice of No-objection to the as-built records submitted under Sub-Clause 4.4.2 [*As-Built Records*];
(c) if applicable, the Engineer has given (or is deemed to have given) a Notice of No-objection to the operation and maintenance manuals under Sub-Clause 4.4.3 [*Operation and Maintenance Manuals*];
(d) if applicable, the Contractor has carried out the training as described under Sub-Clause 4.5 [*Training*]; and
(e) a Taking-Over Certificate for the Works has been issued, or is deemed to have been issued in accordance with this Sub-Clause.

The Contractor may apply for a Taking-Over Certificate by giving a Notice to the Engineer not more than 14 days before the Works will, in the Contractor's opinion, be complete and ready for taking over. If the Works are divided into Sections, the Contractor may similarly apply for a Taking-Over Certificate for each Section.

If any Part is taken over or is deemed to have been taken over under Sub-Clause 10.2 [*Taking Over Parts*], the remaining Works or Section shall not be taken over until the conditions described in sub-paragraphs (a) to (e) above (where applicable) have been fulfilled.

The Engineer shall, within 28 days after receiving the Contractor's Notice, either:

(i) issue the Taking-Over Certificate to the Contractor, stating the date on which the Works or Section were completed in accordance with the Contract, except for any minor outstanding work and defects (as listed in the Taking-Over Certificate) which will not substantially affect the safe use of the Works or Section for their intended purpose (either until or while this work is completed and these defects are remedied); or

(ii) reject the application by giving a Notice to the Contractor, with reasons. This Notice shall specify the work required to be done, the defects required to be remedied and/or the documents required to be submitted by the Contractor to enable the Taking-Over Certificate to be issued. The Contractor shall then complete this work, remedy such defects and/or submit such documents before giving a further Notice under this Sub-Clause.

If the Engineer does not issue the Taking-Over Certificate or reject the Contractor's application within this period of 28 days, and if the conditions described in sub-paragraphs (a) to (d) above (where applicable) have been fulfilled, the Works or Section shall be deemed to have been completed in accordance with the Contract on the fourteenth day after the Engineer receives the Contractor's Notice of application and the Taking-Over Certificate shall be deemed to have been issued.

Except as stated in Sub-Clauses 9.4, 10.2 and 10.3, the Works shall be taken over by the Employer when the conditions in sub-paragraphs (a) to (e) of this Sub-Clause have been fulfilled. These include, among others, the completion of the Works except for minor outstanding work and defects (as listed in the Taking-Over Certificate), including the passing of the Tests on Completion and the issue (or deemed issue) of a Taking-Over Certificate.

The Contractor may apply for a Taking-Over Certificate by giving a Notice to the Engineer not more than 14 days before the Works will, in the Contractor's opinion, be complete. If the Works are divided into Sections, the Contractor may similarly apply for a Taking-Over Certificate for each Section. Within 28 days of receiving the Contractor's

Notice, the Engineer must either issue the Taking-Over Certificate or reject the application by giving a Notice with reasons, specifying the work required to be done. The Contractor must then complete this work before giving a further Notice under the Sub-Clause.

If, within such 28 days, the Engineer neither issues a Taking-Over Certificate nor rejects the Contractor's application and if the conditions in sub-paragraphs (a) to (d) have been fulfilled, the Works or Section shall be deemed to have been completed on the fourteenth day after the Engineer receives the Contractor's application and the Taking-Over Certificate shall be deemed to have been issued.

Commentary

(i) Main Changes from RB/99:

(1) Whereas Sub-Clause 10.1 of RB/99 referred – in its first paragraph – to Sub-Clause 9.4 [*Failure to Pass Tests on Completion*] as the only exception to the conditions for the taking over of the Works, the new Sub-Clause refers to two more exceptions: Sub-Clauses 10.2 [*Taking Over Parts*] and 10.3 [*Interference with Tests on Completion*].

(2) Unlike Sub-Clause 10.1 of RB/99, the new Sub-Clause stipulates in sub-paragraphs (b) to (d) that, if applicable, the provision of as-built records and operation and maintenance manuals with regard to which the Engineer has given a Notice of No-objection, and the training of the Employer's employees, are conditions to the taking over of the Works.[1]

(3) The third paragraph of the new Sub-Clause stating that, upon the taking over, or deemed taking over, of a Part under Sub-Clause 10.2 [*Taking Over Parts*], the remaining Works or Section shall

1. Even though the submission of as-built documents and operation and maintenance manuals was not explicitly addressed in Sub-Clause 10.1 of RB/99, the provision of these documents (if due) was a condition for taking over of the Works under RB/99 as well. Sub-Clause 4.1(d) of RB/99 stated that if the Contractor was to design any part of the Permanent Works, then unless otherwise stated in the Particular Conditions, such part would not be considered completed for the purposes of taking over under Sub-Clause 10.1 until these documents and manuals were submitted to the Engineer. There was, however, no requirement in RB/99 that the Engineer should have given a notice of no-objection to these documents.

not be taken over until the fulfilment of the conditions in sub-paragraphs (a) to (e) of the Sub-Clause, is new.

(4) In the fourth paragraph, there is a new requirement that any minor outstanding work and defects should be 'listed in the Taking-Over Certificate' and must not substantially affect the 'safe' use of the Works or Section for their intended purpose.

(5) In the last paragraph, there is a change in the consequences of the Engineer's failure to reply within the period of 28 days to a Contractor's application for a Taking-Over Certificate: whereas RB/99 stated that if the Works or Section 'are substantially in accordance with the Contract', the Taking-Over Certificate would be deemed to have been issued on the last day of that period, the new Sub-Clause provides, instead, that if the conditions in sub-paragraphs (a) to (d) of the Sub-Clause (where applicable) have been fulfilled, the Works or Section shall be deemed to have been completed in accordance with the Contract on the fourteenth day after the Engineer receives the Contractor's Notice of application and the Taking-Over Certificate shall be deemed to have been issued.

(ii) Related Clauses / Sub-Clauses: 1.3 [*Notices and Other Communications*], 4.4.2 [*Contractor's Documents – As-Built Records*], 4.4.3 [*Contractor's Documents – Operation and Maintenance Manuals*], 4.5 [*Training*], 4.20 [*Progress Reports*], 4.22 [*Contractor's Operations on Site*], 7.6 [*Remedial Work*], 8.2 [*Time for Completion*], 8.5 [*Extension of Time for Completion*], 8.8 [*Delay Damages*], 9.4 [*Failure to Pass Tests on Completion*], 10 [*Employer's Taking Over*], 11.1 [*Completion of Outstanding Work*], 13.1 [*Right to Vary*], 14.2.3 [*Repayment of Advance Payment*], 14.9 [*Release of Retention Money*] 15.4 [*Payment after Termination for Contractor's Default*], 17.1 [*Responsibility for Care of the Works*], 17.2 [*Liability for Care of the Works*], 19.2.1 [*The Works*] and 19.2.6 [*Other Insurances Required by Laws and by Local Practice*].

(iii) Analysis:

(1) The significance and types of taking over

The issuance of the Taking-Over Certificate for the Works is a major milestone for the Contractor, as it demonstrates that it has substantially completed the Works in accordance with the Contract. It is no less significant for the Employer, as it evidences that it will have received essentially what it had bargained for when it entered into the Contract.

Although traditionally (in common law systems) construction contracts identified a single date for the completion of the works, it is now common that, like RB/17, they also provide for the possibility of sectional completion.[2] Sections may be determined by reference, for example, to different physical parts of the project or different stages of physical completion.[3] Under RB/17, the division of the Works into Sections allows the Employer (or the Parties) to allocate to each: (1) a separate percentage of retention money, (2) a Time for Completion and a Defects Notification Period ('DNP'), and (3) a separate amount of Delay Damages, should this be desired.[4]

This Sub-Clause describes the conditions for the taking over or deemed taking over of the Works or a Section by the Employer and the issuance of a Taking-Over Certificate for the Works or a Section to the Contractor. As regards the degree of completion of the Works that may be required, a construction contract differs from a contract for the manufacture and sale of goods, as the same degree of completion cannot be achieved in the case of a construction contract:

> [t]he size of the project, site conditions, use of many materials and employment of various types of operatives make it virtually impossible to achieve the same degree of perfection as can a manufacturer. It must be a rare new building in which every screw and every brush of paint is absolutely correct.[5]

(2) Conditions to taking over

The Employer is *required* to take over the Works, or a Section, if any, when they are completed in accordance with Sub-Clause 10.1. The first

2. Provision may also be made for separate treatment of a part of the Works or part of a Section. *See* Sub-Clauses 1.1.58 '**Part**' and 10.2 [*Taking Over Parts*] and the third paragraph of this Sub-Clause 10.1
3. Atkin Chambers, *Hudson's Building and Engineering Contracts* (14th edn, Sweet & Maxwell, London, 2020) 697 (para. 6-010).
4. *See* the form of Contract Data included in RB/17 which provides on the last page spaces for the definition of Sections, if any, and the allocation of certain matters per Section.
5. *Emson Eastern Limited (in receivership) v E.M.E. Developments Limited* [1991] 55 BLR 114, 121.

paragraph of this Sub-Clause sets out the conditions under which the Employer must do so, except in the limited cases described in Sub-Clauses 9.4, 10.2 and/or 10.3.[6]

To initiate a taking over, the Contractor must, by a Notice,[7] apply to the Engineer for a Taking-Over Certificate for the Works or a Section (as the case may be). The Contractor must do so no more than 14 days before the Works or Section will, in the Contractor's opinion, be complete and ready for taking over. For the Works or Section to be ready for taking over, three conditions need to be fulfilled:

(i) the Works or Section must have been completed in accordance with the Contract, including the passing of the Tests on Completion, except for certain minor outstanding work and defects;
(ii) the Engineer must have given (or be deemed to have given) a Notice of No-objection in respect of the as-built drawings and operation and maintenance manuals (if the Specification had required the Contractor to submit them); and
(iii) the training of the Employer's employees under Sub-Clause 4.5 [*Training*] (if the Specification had required such training) must have been carried out.

As indicated by point (i) above, a Taking-Over Certificate may be issued notwithstanding:

> any minor outstanding work and defects (as listed in the Taking-Over Certificate) which will not substantially affect the safe use of the Works or Section for their intended purpose (either until or whilst this work is completed and these defects are remedied)[...].[8]

---

6. Thus, Sub-Clause 9.4 applies where the Contractor has failed to pass the Tests on Completion, Sub-Clause 10.2 where the Employer uses any part of the Works before a Taking-Over Certificate has been issued and Sub-Clause 10.3 where the Employer is responsible for preventing the Contractor from carrying out the Tests on Completion for more than 14 days. *See* the commentaries on these respective Sub-Clauses herein.
7. The Notice must comply with Sub-Clause 1.3 [*Notices and Other Communications*].
8. Sub-paragraph (i) of Sub-Clause 10.1. Such minor outstanding Works and defects are typically the subject of a so-called punch list or snagging list. Regarding the fitness of the Works or a Section for their purpose, *see* the commentary on Sub-Clause 4.1(e) above.

To what extent such outstanding work and defects are minor and will not 'substantially affect' the safe use of the Works or a Section will be a question of fact for the Engineer to decide in the first instance. For example, in the case of a contract to build a house, the Contractor's failure to construct a porch over the front door should not prevent the issue of a Taking-Over Certificate for the house if it is otherwise complete and habitable (as this 'will not substantially affect the safe use of the Works [...] for their intended purpose').[9] On the other hand, the Contractor's failure to construct the handrails on the staircase or, if the house is a luxurious personal residence in a high crime area, to instal an alarm system, would probably substantially affect the safe use of the house for its intended purpose, and could therefore serve as a ground for a rejection of the Contractor's application.

The requirement for the Contractor to give 14 days' Notice is to allow time for the Employer's Personnel to effect insurance, if necessary, and to make arrangements to effect the Employer's taking over.[10] Often there will be a joint inspection of the Works or a Section when it appears to be complete, attended by representatives of the Parties and the Engineer.[11] This inspection is intended, among other things, to allow them to ascertain whether the Works are substantially complete, and to identify what further work, if any, must be done before taking over, and what 'minor outstanding work and defects'[12] need to be included in a punch or snagging list for completion after taking over.

(3) Issue of a Taking-Over Certificate

Within 28 days after receiving the Contractor's Notice of application, the Engineer must either issue the Taking-Over Certificate or reject it with reasons.[13] If the Engineer issues a Taking-Over Certificate, the Certificate should state the date on which the Works or Section has been completed

9. *Menolly Investments 3 SARL v Cerep SARL* [2009] EWHC 516 (Ch) at [paras 91-92] cited in Julian Bailey, *Construction Law* (3rd edn, London Publishing, UK, 2020) vol 1, 396 (para. 5.117).
10. *The FIDIC Contracts Guide* (2nd edn, FIDIC, 2022) 306.
11. *Ibid.*
12. Sub-Clause 10.1(i).
13. When doing so, it is suggested that the Engineer must act neutrally and fairly for the reasons given in *(2) When exercising discretion the Engineer must act fairly* under **(iii) Analysis** of the commentary on Sub-Clause 3.2 [*Engineer's Duties and Authority*] above.

in accordance with the Contract,[14] and list any outstanding work (which is expected to be minor) or defects which are to be remedied after the issue of the Taking-Over Certificate.[15] The list might include a time(s) for the completion of any such minor outstanding work or defects.[16] In case of a rejection, the Engineer must give a Notice to the Contractor, with reasons, specifying the work required to be done, the defects required to be remedied and/or the documents required to be submitted before the Contractor may apply again for a Taking-Over Certificate.[17]

(4) Deemed issue of a Taking-Over Certificate

If the Engineer does not reply at all within 28 days after receiving the Contractor's application, then provided that the conditions for taking over in the Sub-Clause listed under (2) *Conditions to taking over* above have, where applicable, been satisfied, the Works or a Section, as the case may be, will be deemed to have been completed in accordance with the Contract and a Taking-Over Certificate will be deemed to be issued for

14. This date is the Date of Completion which has important contractual consequences, *see* the commentary on Sub-Clause 1.1.24 '**Date of Completion**' above.
15. *The FIDIC Contracts Guide* contains sample forms of Taking-Over Certificates for the Works and a Section. Thus, the sample form of a letter for the Works provides as follows:

    Having received your notice under Sub-Clause 10.1 of the Conditions of Contract, I hereby certify that the whole of the Works was completed in accordance with the Contract on [...] [date], except for minor outstanding work and defects including those listed in the attached 'Snagging List for the Works', and which should not substantially affect the safe use of the Works for their intended purpose. You are required to complete all such outstanding work and remedy all such defects no later than _______ [date].

    The FIDIC Contracts Guide (2nd edn, FIDIC, 2022) 308.

16. *See* Sub-Clause 11.1(a).
17. Sub-Clause 10.1(ii). Any disagreement as to whether the Works or a Section has been completed to the extent required by the Contract may give rise to a Claim under sub-para. (c) of Sub-Clause 20.1 [*Claims*] which a Party may refer to the Engineer for an agreement or determination under Sub-Clause 3.7 [*Agreement or Determination*]. If this Claim escalates into a Dispute, it may be referred to the DAAB under Sub-Clause 21.4 [*Obtaining DAAB's Decision*] and ultimately to arbitration under Sub-Clause 21.6 [*Arbitration*].

the Works or Section. Completion is deemed to have occurred on the fourteenth day after the Engineer had received the Contractor's application.[18]

(5) Consequences of Taking Over the Works

At the Date of Completion of the Works (defined as the date stated in the Taking-Over Certificate or when the Works are deemed to have been completed or taken over),[19] or issue of the Taking-Over Certificate for the Works,[20] the following are the principal consequences:

- the Works are considered practically or functionally complete except for any minor outstanding work and defects as permitted by Sub-Clause 10.1(i);
- the Contractor is required to leave the Site and Works to which the Taking-Over Certificate refers, subject to its obligations under Clause 11 [*Defects after Taking Over*];[21]
- the Employer takes over responsibility for the care of the Works, except for work which is outstanding on the Date of Completion or any loss or damage to the Works, Goods or Contractor's Documents during the period when the Contractor was responsible for their care and which the Contractor is responsible for rectifying;[22]
- the Contractor's liability to Delay Damages for failure to meet the Time for Completion for the Works ends;[23]

18. As already mentioned, the Contractor may apply for a Taking-Over Certificate not more than 14 days before the Works or a Section is, in the Contractor's opinion, ready for taking over. *See* the second paragraph of Sub-Clause 10.1. Thus, the date of the deemed issue of the Taking-Over Certificate corresponds to the expiry of this 14-day period, which is when, in the Contractor's opinion, the Works or a Section would be complete and ready for taking over.
19. Sub-Clause 1.1.24 '**Date of Completion**'.
20. Which of the two dates mentioned applies will depend on what the relevant Sub-Clause provides. The Date of Completion may also apply to a Section or Part (*see* Sub-Clauses 1.1.24 '**Date of Completion**' and 10.2).
21. *See* Sub-Clause 4.22, last paragraph. If the Taking-Over Certificate relates to a Section or Part of the Works, then the Contractor is required to leave the relevant Section or Part of the Site and Works.
22. Sub-Clauses 17.1 and 17.2. This may apply also for a Section or Part (*see* Sub-Clauses 10.2(b) and 17.1).
23. Sub-Clause 8.8. This may apply also for a Section and, in the case of the taking over of a Part (*see* Sub-Clause 10.2, last paragraph), may reduce

- the DNP for the Works begins during which the Contractor must complete any outstanding work and remedy any defects or damage of which Notice is given to the Contractor by (or on behalf of) the Employer;[24]
- the Contractor's obligation to provide monthly progress reports ends except that, in the case of outstanding work listed in the Taking-Over Certificate, the reporting of it ends when such work is completed;[25]
- the Engineer's right to instruct repair or remedial work ends;[26]
- the Engineer's right to initiate Variations under Sub-Clause 13.3 [*Variation Procedure*] ends;[27]
- if the advance payment, if any, has not been repaid by the Contractor, the whole of the balance then outstanding is immediately due and payable;[28]
- the Contractor's obligation, if any, to submit non-binding estimates of payments, which the Contractor expects to become due every 3 months, ends;[29]
- the Contractor is entitled to apply for payment of the first half of the Retention Money;[30]
- the Contractor's obligation to insure, in the joint names of the Contractor and the Employer, the Works and Contractor's Documents, together with Materials and Plant for incorporation in the Works, ends, with certain exceptions;[31] and

---

proportionately the Delay Damages which might otherwise be due for the remainder of the Works or a Section in which this Part is included.

24. Sub-Clauses 1.1.27 '**Defects Notification Period**' or '**DNP**' and 11.1. The DNP may apply also for a Section or Part (*see* Sub-Clauses 1.1.27 and 10.2).
25. Sub-Clause 4.20.
26. Sub-Clause 7.6. But subject to Sub-Clause 11.1 [*Defects after Taking Over*] which provides for the possible application of Sub-Clause 7.5 which, in turn, provides for the possible application of Sub-Clause 7.6. These cross-references mean that Sub-Clauses 7.5 and 7.6 may apply during the DNP.
27. Sub-Clause 13.1, first paragraph. But Sub-Clause 13.3.1 may still apply by analogy, *see* Sub-Clauses 11.2, last paragraph, and 11.4(c).
28. Sub-Clause 14.2.3, last paragraph.
29. Sub-Clause 14.4, last paragraph.
30. Sub-Clause 14.9, first paragraph. A percentage of the first half of the retention money may also apply for a Section.
31. Sub-Clause 19.2.1. However, the Contractor's obligation to insure against injury to persons and damage to property (Sub-Clause 19.2.4) and (probably) against injury to employees (Sub-Clause 19.2.5.) continues until the

- the Engineer's ability to withhold an IPC for less than a minimum amount ceases to apply.[32]

Within 84 days after the Date of Completion of the Works, the Contractor must submit to the Engineer a Statement at completion with supporting documents.[33]

(iv) Related Law: The extent of completion required for the purposes of taking over of the Works under this Sub-Clause corresponds to 'practical completion' or 'substantial completion' in common law jurisdictions.[34] Indeed, all of the RB editions until RB/99 used the terms 'substantially completed' or 'substantial completion'[35] when referring to what was required for the issuance of a Certificate of Completion of Works[36] or Taking-Over Certificate,[37] and there is no indication that a significantly different degree of completion was required by RB/99 or is required by RB/17.

In common law jurisdictions, construction contracts (like RB/17) are said often to provide that the contractor's works are ready for taking over:

issue of the Performance Certificate. The Contractor's obligation to maintain professional indemnity insurance continues for the period specified in the Contract Data (Sub-Clause 19.2.3). Moreover, the Parties' respective indemnities to each other under Sub-Clauses 17.3 [*Intellectual and Industrial Property Rights*] through 17.6 [*Shared Indemnities*] remain alive through the DNP and, it appears, thereafter.

32. Sub-Clause 14.6.2, first paragraph.
33. Sub-Clause 14.10 [*Statement at Completion*].
34. For discussion of practical completion under the common law, *see* Julian Bailey, *Construction Law* (3rd edn, London Publishing, UK, 2020) vol 1, 394-402 (paras 5.115-5.126) and Atkin Chambers, *Hudson's Building and Engineering Contracts* (14th edn, Sweet & Maxwell, London, 2020) 579-581 (paras 4-085-088). As regards the position in the US, *see* Justin Sweet and Marc M Schneier, *Construction Law for Design Professionals, Construction Managers, and Contractors* (Cengage Learning, Stamford, CT, 2015) 350-353 ('[s]ubstantial completion is the point at which the project may be occupied and used for its intended purpose' 350), and John M Mastin and others (eds), *Smith, Currie & Hancock's Common Sense Construction Law: A Guide for the Construction Professional* (6th edn, Wiley, Hoboken, NJ, 2020) 308-309, 352-353.
35. *See* Clause 48 of RB/57, RB/69, RB/77 and RB/87, and Sub-Clause 10.1 of RB/99 ('substantially in accordance with the Contract').
36. RB/57, RB/69, RB/77.
37. RB/87.

> where the works are physically complete, or certified as complete, save for minor omissions or defects, and the works are otherwise reasonably capable of their intended use. If there are patent defects in the works that are not de minimis, practical completion will not have been achieved. [...] Similarly, the fact that the owners of the property have moved into it does not necessarily mean it is practically complete, at least where significant works are incomplete or defective.[38]

The principal US standard form for private works defines 'Substantial Completion' as follows:

> Substantial Completion is the stage in the progress of the Work when the Work or designated portion thereof is sufficiently complete in accordance with the Contract Documents so that the Owner can occupy or utilize the Work for its intended use.[39]

In certain civil law countries, notably, as from the Date of Completion (also referred to as 'handing over' or 'provisional acceptance' ('*réception provisoire*' in French)), a statutory warranty regime may, as a matter of public policy, apply to the liability of the Contractor (and others, like an Engineer or architect, who have contracted with the Employer) to the Employer for latent defects in the works.[40] For example, under French law, the Date of Completion will be the commencement date of the decennial (ten-year) warranty[41] or liability.[42] Under French law, the Contractor (and others liable) must take out insurance to cover their decennial warranty obligations.[43] Many other civil law countries have a statutory warranty regime, of varying duration, that is based on French

38. Julian Bailey, *Construction Law* (3rd edn, London Publishing, UK, 2020) vol 1, 395-396 (para. 5.117).
39. S 9.8.1 of American Institute of Architects (AIA) Document A201 - 2017 *General Conditions of the Contract for Construction*.
40. That is, defects which were not visible at taking over.
41. For a discussion on this subject, *see* Amaury Teillard, 'The Start Date for Post Contractual Liability in French Law in the FIDIC Red and Yellow Books' [2014] ICLR 269-280.
42. *See* **Section 4 Common Law and Civil Law Compared - 4.4.4 Decennial Liability** in **Chapter II Applicable Law** above.
43. *See* the commentary on Sub-Clause 19.2.6 [*Other Insurances Required by Laws and by Local Practice*] below.

law and which, as under French law, is mandatory and may therefore complement Clauses 10 and 11 and the DNP.[44]

A statutory warranty regime, as it applies in France, provides that the Contractor (and others) is (are) absolutely liable to the Employer for defects which impair the stability of a work and which appear within 10 years after completion. It is to be distinguished from a period of limitation which, under the common law, establishes a time limit for the bringing of litigation or arbitration, and under French law, provides for the extinction of rights by the lapse of time.[45] Moreover, a statutory warranty regime and a limitation period will not necessarily be coterminous.

In Germany, it is likely that acceptance (*Abnahme*) of the Works 'would not take place until after the Engineer has issued a Performance Certificate, which states that the Contractor has fulfilled its obligations under the Contract'.[46] The German Civil Code stipulates a warranty period of five years following acceptance (*Abnahme*) for buildings with regards to any defects.[47] Thus, assuming a DNP of two years, the Contractor could possibly be held responsible for defects in buildings in Germany for seven years after the Date of Completion.[48]

(v) Improvements:

(1) As stated under **(iii) Improvements** of the commentary on Sub-Clause 1.1 [*Definitions*] above, given its considerable practical importance, there should be a definition of the term 'completion'. This is particularly necessary given the different way completion or acceptance is defined under different national laws, e.g., German law (as discussed under **(iv) Related Law** above) compared to English and French law.

(2) Unlike Sub-Clauses 3.7 and 14.6, Sub-Clause 10.1 does not explicitly require the Engineer to act 'fairly' between the Parties when issuing the Taking-Over Certificate. However, for reasons

44. Other civil law countries providing for a system of liability similar to French law are identified in fn. 176 in **Section 4 Common Law and Civil Law Compared – 4.4.4 Decennial Liability** in **Chapter II Applicable Law** above.
45. *See* **Section 4 Common Law and Civil Law Compared – 4.5.3 Limitation Periods** of **Chapter II Applicable Law** above.
46. Wolfgang Breyer and others 'What Do the Words Mean: Different Approaches to the Interpretation of Contracts' [2019] ICLR 172, 191.
47. *Ibid.*
48. *Ibid.*

explained previously,[49] the Engineer must act 'fairly' when issuing the Taking-Over Certificate – if its action is not to be overturned by the Engineer under Sub-Clause 3.7 or the DAAB or in arbitration – and Sub-Clause 10.1 should so provide.[50]

--ooOOoo--

10.2 Taking Over Parts

The Engineer may, at the sole discretion of the Employer, issue a Taking-Over Certificate for any part of the Permanent Works.

The Employer shall not use any part of the Works (other than as a temporary measure, which is either stated in the Specification or with the prior agreement of the Contractor) unless and until the Engineer has issued a Taking-Over Certificate for this part. However, if the Employer does use any part of the Works before the Taking-Over Certificate is issued the Contractor shall give a Notice to the Engineer identifying such part and describing such use, and:

(a) that Part shall be deemed to have been taken over by the Employer as from the date on which it is used;
(b) the Contractor shall cease to be liable for the care of such Part as from this date, when responsibility shall pass to the Employer; and
(c) the Engineer shall immediately issue a Taking-Over Certificate for this Part, and any outstanding work to be completed (including Tests on Completion) and/or defects to be remedied shall be listed in this certificate.

49. *See* under *(2) When exercising discretion the Engineer must act fairly* under **(iii) Analysis** of the commentary on Sub-Clause 3.2 [*Engineer's Duties and Authority*] above.
50. Moreover, in common law jurisdictions, the Engineer is required to act fairly when issuing a final certificate even absent specific wording in that respect. Julian Bailey, *Construction Law* (3rd edn, London Publishing, UK, 2020) vol 1, 409 (para. 5.142).

After a Part has been taken over or is deemed to have been taken over, the Contractor shall be given the earliest opportunity to take such steps as may be necessary to carry out the outstanding work (including Tests on Completion) and/or remedial work for any defects listed in the certificate. The Contractor shall carry out these works as soon as practicable and, in any case, before the expiry date of the relevant DNP.

If the Contractor incurs Cost as a result of the taking over or deemed taking over of a Part, the Contractor shall be entitled subject to Sub-Clause 20.2 [*Claims for Payment and/or EOT*] to payment of such Cost Plus Profit.

For any period of delay after the date that a Part has been taken over or is deemed to have been taken over, the Delay Damages for completion of the Works or the Section (as the case may be) in which this Part is included shall be reduced. This reduction shall be calculated as the proportion which the value of the Part (except the value of any outstanding works and/or defects to be remedied) bears to the value of the Works or Section (as the case may be) as a whole. The Engineer shall proceed under Sub-Clause 3.7 [*Agreement or Determination*] to agree or determine this reduction (and, for the purpose of Sub-Clause 3.7.3 [*Time limits*], the date the Engineer issues the Taking-Over Certificate under the first paragraph of, or receives the Contractor's Notice under the second paragraph of, this Sub-Clause (as the case may be) shall be the date of commencement of the time limit for agreement under Sub-Clause 3.7.3). The provisions of this paragraph shall only apply to the daily rate of Delay Damages, and shall not affect the maximum amount of these damages.

The Engineer may, at the sole discretion of the Employer, issue a Taking-Over Certificate for any part of the Permanent Works.

The Employer shall not use any part of the Works (other than as a temporary measure agreed with the Contractor) until the Engineer has issued a Taking-Over Certificate for it. However, if the Employer

does so, the Contractor shall give a Notice to the Engineer identifying such part, and it will be deemed to have been taken over as from the date used, the Contractor shall cease to be liable for it, and the Engineer must immediately issue a Taking-Over Certificate for it listing any outstanding work and/or defects.

After a Part has been taken over or is deemed to have been taken over, the Contractor shall be given the earliest opportunity to carry out the listed outstanding work and/or remedial work for any defects, which it shall do before the expiry of the relevant DNP. If the Contractor incurs Cost as a result of the taking over or deemed taking over of a Part, it is entitled, subject to Sub-Clause 20.2, to payment of such Cost Plus Profit.

For any period of delay after the taking over or deemed taking over of a Part, the Delay Damages for completion of the remainder of the Works or Section including such Part shall be proportionately reduced, as agreed or determined by the Engineer under Sub-Clause 3.7.

Commentary

(i) Main Changes from RB/99:

(1) Unlike Sub-Clause 10.2 of RB/99, the second paragraph explicitly states that if the Employer uses a part of the Works (other than as an agreed temporary measure) before issue of the Taking-Over Certificate, the Contractor shall give a Notice to the Engineer identifying the part and describing such use.

(2) Whereas RB/99 provided that the Engineer must issue a Taking-Over Certificate for the part that the Employer had used, if requested by the Contractor, the second paragraph of the new Sub-Clause provides that, after the Contractor has given a Notice to the Engineer describing the Employer's use of a part, then, among other things, the Engineer must immediately issue a Taking-Over Certificate for it which must list any outstanding work to be completed (including Tests on Completion) and/or defects to be remedied.

(3) Whereas Sub-Clause 10.2 of RB/99, third paragraph, stated that after the issue of the Taking-Over Certificate for a part, the Contractor had to be given the earliest opportunity to carry out any outstanding Tests on Completion, the third paragraph of the new Sub-Clause refers in addition to the Contractor having to

carry out the outstanding and/or remedial work for any defects listed in the Taking-Over Certificate, which must be done as soon as practicable and before expiry of the relevant DNP.

(4) In RB/99, the Contractor's entitlement to Cost and profit was excluded in cases where the Employer's use of a part was specified in the Contract or agreed by the Contractor, but there is no such exclusion in the new Sub-Clause.

(5) The last paragraph of the new Sub-Clause, dealing with the reduction of the amount of Delay Damages upon the taking over of part of the Works, takes into account not only cases where a Taking-Over Certificate for this Part has been issued (as in RB/99) but also cases where the Employer is deemed to have taken over this Part.

(6) It is now also specified for the first time that the value of any outstanding work and/or defects to be remedied should be taken into account in determining the value of the Part when calculating the proportionate reduction in the amount of Delay Damages.

(ii) Related Clauses / Sub-Clauses: 1.3 [*Notices and Other Communications*], 3.7 [*Agreement or Determination*], 8.5 [*Extension of Time for Completion*], 8.8 [*Delay Damages*], 9 [*Tests on Completion*], 10 [*Employer's Taking Over*], 11.1 [*Completion of Outstanding Work and Remedying Defects*], 17.1 [*Responsibility for Care of the Works*], 17.2 [*Liability for Care of the Works*] and 20.2 [*Claims for Payment and/or EOT*].

(iii) Analysis:

(1) Scope of Sub-Clause

A Contract may provide either for the Works to be completed by the Contractor and taken over by the Employer as a whole within a single Time for Completion and with a single Taking-Over Certificate or for the division of the Works into Sections, as described in the Contract Data,[51] each with its own Time for Completion and Taking-Over Certificate.[52]

51. *See* the last page of the form of Contract Data in RB/17, which provides spaces for the definition of Sections, if any.

52. The Employer may wish to have certain parts of the Works completed within certain times but without taking them over when completed (as the Employer would have to do in the case of Sections). In this case, such parts should be clearly described in the Specification as 'Milestones' and certain

However, before the Works or a Section is taken over – and although not provided for by the Contract – it is not unusual for the Employer to want to take over or use a part[53] of the Works that has not been designated as a Section and this is addressed in Sub-Clause 10.2. This Sub-Clause provides that:

(1) the Engineer may, at the sole discretion of the Employer,[54] issue a Taking-Over Certificate for any part of the Permanent Works which is not a Section;[55] and
(2) if the Employer does use any part of the Works before a Taking-Over Certificate for it is issued (other than as a temporary measure, as discussed below), then, following a Notice by the Contractor to the Engineer, that Part of the Works shall be deemed to have been taken over and become the subject of a Taking-Over Certificate,[56] as described below.

(2) Taking-Over Certificate for a Part at Employer's discretion

The first sentence of the Sub-Clause provides that the Engineer may 'at the sole discretion of the Employer' issue a Taking-Over Certificate for any part of the Permanent Works. This appears to mean that the Employer is entirely free to decide whether or not such a Certificate for a part shall be issued.[57]

The Employer has, apparently, unlimited – and possibly excessive – freedom to select a part for takeover.[58]

additions should be made to the Contract Data and to the Conditions. *See* the *Guidance for the Preparation of the Particular Conditions*, 26-27.

53. This Sub-Clause, when referring to part of the Works as distinct from a Section of the Works, uses both the term 'part' and the term 'Part'. The explanation for this is that a part of the Works (or of a Section) does not become a '**Part**', as defined, unless it is taken over by the Employer under the first paragraph of Sub-Clause 10.2 or 'used by the Employer and deemed to have been taken over under' the second paragraph of Sub-Clause 10.2. *See* the definition of '**Part**' in Sub-Clause 1.1.58 and the commentary on it above.
54. The meaning of which is discussed below.
55. Sub-Clause 10.2, first paragraph.
56. Sub-Clause 10.2, second paragraph.
57. *See* the author's comments on this subject under **(v) Improvements** in the commentary on Sub-Clause 1.2 [*Interpretation*] above.
58. For example, it might instead have been stipulated that, to be eligible for taking over, the part would have to be an autonomous, separately

(3) Employer's use of a part before the issue of a Taking-Over Certificate

As a general rule, the Employer is prohibited from using any part of the Works, unless and until the Engineer has issued a Taking-Over Certificate for this part.[59] As an exception, the Employer is allowed to do so as a temporary measure, which is either stated in the Specification or agreed to by the Contractor.[60] A temporary measure stated in the Specification should identify the part concerned, describe the temporary measure, the period of time over which this measure applies and the consequences of the Employer's use (if any).[61]

If the Employer does use any part of the Works (other than as a temporary measure), the Contractor is required to give a Notice to the Engineer identifying the part and describing the Employer's use, with the following consequences:

(a) the Part is deemed to have been taken over as from the date on which it is used;
(b) the Contractor will cease to be liable for the care of this Part as from this date, and the responsibility for it will pass to the Employer; and

functioning and usable part of the Works. However, this is not the case. It might also have been required that the Employer's takeover of the part not interfere significantly with the Contractor's remaining work, but this also is not specified (although, if the Employer's takeover does interfere, the Contractor should be able to claim pursuant to the fourth paragraph of this Sub-Clause and/or Sub-Clause 8.5 (e)). *See* John M Mastin and others (eds), *Smith, Currie & Hancock's Common Sense Construction Law: A Practical Guide for the Construction Professional* (6th edn, Wiley, Hoboken, NJ, 2020) 349-350.

59. Sub-Clause 10.2, second paragraph.
60. The Contractor's agreement must comply with the requirements in Sub-Clause 1.3 [*Notices and Other Communications*]. *See* the commentary on this Sub-Clause above.
61. For example, if the Employer wants the Contractor to rehabilitate a road, it may require that, as a temporary measure, the Contractor does this in such a way so as not to prevent its continuous use. *See* partial award, ICC case 23397 (2019) (unreported so far).

(c) the Engineer must immediately issue a Taking-Over Certificate for this Part, listing any outstanding work to be completed, including Tests on Completion and/or defects to be remedied.[62]

The Employer must indemnify the Contractor against third-party claims, damages, losses and expenses arising from the Employer's use or occupation of the part of the Works, pursuant to Sub-Clause 17.5(b).[63]

(4) Carrying out of outstanding work after the Taking-Over Certificate

After a Part has been taken over or is deemed to have been taken over, the Employer will be in possession of the Part, which would ordinarily deprive the Contractor of access to it.[64] To address this issue, the Sub-Clause provides that the Contractor shall be given [by the Employer] 'the earliest opportunity' to carry out any outstanding work, including Tests on Completion, and/or remedial work.[65] Such work must be carried out as soon as practicable and, in any case, before the expiry of the relevant DNP.[66]

---

62. Sub-Clause 10.2, second paragraph. *The FIDIC Contracts Guide* contains a sample form of a Taking-Over Certificate for a Part of the Works which provides as follows:

> *I hereby certify in accordance with Sub-Clause 10.2 of the Conditions of Contract that the following Part was taken-over by the Employer in accordance with the Contract on the date stated below:*
> *[name and description of the Part __________]*
> *[the completion date __________]*
> *except for outstanding work and defects including those listed in the attached Snagging List for Part ________. You are required to complete all such outstanding work and remedy all such defects no later than ________[date].*

The FIDIC Contracts Guide (2nd edn, FIDIC, 2022) 312. The Employer's use of the Works in this way may constitute 'constructive acceptance' in US practice. John M Mastin and others (eds), *Smith, Currie & Hancock's Common Sense Construction Law: A Practical Guide for the Construction Professional* (6th edn, Wiley, Hoboken, NJ, 2020) 349-350.

63. *See* Sub-Clauses 17.5(b) and 17.2(b). The Employer may also have liability under Sub-Clause 17.5 (a).
64. *See* Sub-Clause 4.22, last paragraph.
65. Sub-Clause 10.2, third paragraph.
66. *Ibid.*

(5) Contractor's Claims

The penultimate paragraph entitles the Contractor to claim, subject to Sub-Clause 20.2, Cost Plus Profit if the Contractor incurs Cost as a result of the Employer's taking over or deemed taking over of a Part. Unlike RB/99, the Contractor is not expressly excluded from claiming Cost Plus Profit in cases where the Employer's use is specified in the Contract or agreed by the Contractor (e.g., in the case of a temporary measure under the second paragraph of this Sub-Clause). The Contractor may also be able to claim an EOT under Sub-Clause 8.5(e) if the Employer's use or occupation has delayed the Contractor in completing the Works or a Section within the relevant Time for Completion.[67]

(6) Proportionate reduction in the amount of Delay Damages

The last paragraph providing that the amount of Delay Damages for the Works or a Section will be reduced in proportion to the value of a Part (less the value of any outstanding work or defects) which has been, or is deemed to have been, taken over, is self-explanatory.

(iv) Related Law:[68] An English case has briefly discussed an Employer's possible right to use part of the Works 'as a temporary measure', as provided for in the second paragraph of Sub-Clause 10.2 of a 1999 FIDIC form of contract (which is similar to Sub-Clause 10.2 of RB/17). The case concerned a contract for the manufacture and supply of two boilers for a power plant in Brazil. The contractor had applied to an English court for an interim injunction to restrain the calling of performance security in the form of demand guarantees by the employer on the ground that the taking-over certificates for the boilers should already have been issued, which would have resulted in the expiry of the demand guarantees. The

67. According to FIDIC's discussion of Sub-Clause 10.2 of RB/99:

> No mention is made of any entitlement to extension of the Time for Completion for the Works or any Section, because it is covered by Sub-Clause 8.4(e).
>
> *The FIDIC Contracts Guide* (1st edn, FIDIC 2000) 192. Sub-Clause 8.4(e) of RB/99 is the predecessor of Sub-Clause 8.5(e) of RB/17.

68. Under the laws of some unidentified countries, the taking over of parts of the Works by the Employer may prejudice the Employer's entire entitlement to Delay Damages as the amount of such damages has to have been determined solely by the Parties and may not (as under Sub-Clause 10.2) be subject to assessment by someone appointed by the payee (i.e., by the Engineer under Sub-Clause 3.7, as provided for in the last paragraph). *See The FIDIC Contracts Guide* (1st edn, FIDIC 2000) 192.

employer argued that it had only been using the two boilers 'as a temporary measure' and so it was entitled to withhold issuance of the taking-over certificates, and thus, the demand guarantees had not expired. The court rejected the employer's argument that its use of the boilers was a temporary measure because, among other things, their commercial operation had been publicly announced to have been authorised, and they had exported 7,500 hours of power to the local grid.[69]

--ooOOoo--

10.3 Interference with Tests on Completion

If the Contractor is prevented, for more than 14 days (either a continuous period, or multiple periods which total more than 14 days), from carrying out the Tests on Completion by the Employer's Personnel or by a cause for which the Employer is responsible:

(a) the Contractor shall give a Notice to the Engineer describing such prevention;
(b) the Employer shall be deemed to have taken over the Works or Section (as the case may be) on the date when the Tests on Completion would otherwise have been completed; and
(c) the Engineer shall immediately issue a Taking-Over Certificate for the Works or Section (as the case may be).

After the Engineer has issued this Taking-Over Certificate, the Contractor shall carry out the Tests on Completion as soon as practicable and, in any case, before the expiry date of the DNP. The Engineer shall give a Notice to the Contractor, of not less than 14 days, of the date after which the Contractor may carry out each of the Tests on Completion. Thereafter, Sub-Clause 9.1 [*Contractor's Obligations*] shall apply.

If the Contractor suffers delay and/or incurs Cost as a result of being prevented from carrying out the Tests on Completion, the Contractor shall be entitled

69. *Doosan Babcock Ltd v Comercializadora de Equipos y Materiales Mabe Limitada* [2013] EWHC 3010 (TCC), 2014 BLR 33.

subject to Sub-Clause 20.2 [*Claims for Payment and/or EOT*] to EOT and/or payment of such Cost Plus Profit.

If the Contractor is prevented, for more than 14 days, from carrying out the Tests on Completion by the Employer's Personnel or a cause for which the Employer is responsible: the Contractor shall give a Notice to the Engineer, the Employer shall be deemed to have taken over the Works or Section (as the case may be) on the date when the Tests on Completion would otherwise have been completed and the Engineer shall immediately issue a Taking-Over Certificate.

Thereafter, the Contractor shall carry out the Tests on Completion as soon as practicable and before expiry of the DNP. The Engineer shall give not less than 14 days' Notice to the Contractor of the date after which the Contractor may carry out the tests. If the Contractor suffers delay and/or Cost as a result of the Employer's prevention, the Contractor is entitled, subject to Sub-Clause 20.2, to an EOT and/or payment of Cost Plus Profit.

Commentary

(i) Main Changes from RB/99:

(1) Whereas Sub-Clause 10.3 of RB/99 referred simply to a prevention of more than 14 days, the first paragraph adds that this period may constitute either a continuous period or multiple periods which total more than 14 days.
(2) The first paragraph refers not only to where the prevention is by a cause for which the Employer is responsible (as in RB/99) but also to where it is caused by the Employer's Personnel.
(3) The requirement in sub-paragraph (a) of the first paragraph, that the Contractor must give a Notice to the Engineer describing the prevention, is new.
(4) The requirement in sub-paragraph (c) of the first paragraph, that the Engineer must 'immediately' issue a Taking-Over Certificate after receiving Notice of the prevention, is new.
(5) Unlike RB/99, the second paragraph states that Sub-Clause 9.1 [*Contractor's Obligations*] applies with regard to the carrying out of the Tests on Completion.

(ii) Related Clauses / Sub-Clauses: 1.3 [*Notices and Other Communications*], 2.3 [*Employer's Personnel and Other Contractors*], 7.4 [*Testing by the Contractor*], 9.1 [*Contractor's Obligations*], 9.2 [*Delayed Tests*], 10.1 [*Taking Over the Works and Sections*], 17.1 [*Responsibility for Care of the Works*] and 20.2 [*Claims for Payment and/or EOT*].

(iii) Analysis:

(1) Purpose of Sub-Clause

As discussed in relation to Sub-Clause 10.1 above,[70] the Employer is required to take over the Works, or a Section, if any, when they are completed in accordance with the Contract. A condition to the Employer's obligation to do so is that they have passed the Tests on Completion.[71] Sub-Clause 10.3 deals with where either the Employer's Personnel, which includes the Engineer,[72] or a cause for which the Employer is responsible, which could include one attributable to another contractor of the Employer, prevents the Contractor from carrying out the Tests on Completion.[73]

70. *See* the commentary on Sub-Clause 10.1 above.
71. Sub-paragraph (a) of Sub-Clause 10.1.
72. For example, by an instruction of the Engineer pursuant to Sub-Clause 9.1, fourth paragraph.
73. It is not entirely clear what the words which describe a delay 'by the Employer's Personnel or by a cause for which the Employer is responsible' (which are also to be found in Sub-Clause 9.2) are referring to. Under the common law legal doctrine of *respondeat superior* ('holding an employer [...] liable for an employee's or agent's wrongful acts committed within the scope of the employment or agency', Bryan A Garner (ed in chief), *Black's Law Dictionary* (11th edn, Thomson Reuters, St Paul, MN, 2019)), there should be no reason to distinguish the Employer from the Employer's Personnel, or at least any of the Employer's Personnel who are employees or agents, as the Employer would be responsible for them as a matter of law. But what then is 'a cause for which the Employer is responsible'? This could be referring to the five 'causes' listed in sub-paras (a) through (e) of Sub-Clause 8.5 [*Extension of Time for Completion*] or the five 'events' described in sub-paras (a) through (f) of Sub-Clause 17.2 [*Liability for Care of the Works*] for which the Employer is liable. Alternatively – and this seems most reasonable – it refers to any of the foregoing as well as any other thing for which the Employer is responsible.

Obviously, the Employer and the Employer's Personnel should not ordinarily be preventing the Contractor from carrying out such tests.[74] But the Employer may, for example, be experiencing financial difficulty and wish to delay taking over the Works, or the Engineer may be inexperienced or unprepared and/or lack the qualified staff to attend the Tests on Completion.[75]

(2) The Employer's prevention

For this Sub-Clause to apply, the Contractor must have been prevented from carrying out the Tests on Completion for a continuous period of, or multiple periods totalling, more than 14 days. It is unclear when such 14 days begin, as previously explained.[76] If the Contractor has been prevented from carrying out the Tests of Completion for a period of 14 days or less (under Sub-Clause 10.3), it cannot invoke this Sub-Clause, but may be entitled to claim an EOT and/or Cost Plus Profit under Sub-Clause 7.4 [*Testing by the Contractor*][77] and/or Sub-Clause 8.5(e).

Sub-paragraph (a) of this Sub-Clause contains a new requirement that the Contractor must give a Notice to the Engineer of the prevention. This clarifies when, at least in the Contractor's view, the prevention will have lasted for more than 14 days. If the prevention has continued for more than 14 days, then, according to sub-paragraph (b), the Works or a Section will be deemed to have been taken over 'on the date when the Tests on Completion would otherwise have been completed', which appears to mean 'had there been no prevention at all'.[78]

Even if the prevented tests are limited to those which should have been carried out on a Section, they may result in a deemed taking over of the Works as a whole, if all other Sections have been completed and the Contractor is prevented from carrying out the Tests on Completion on the last Section of the Works.[79]

74. This could be contrary to the Employer's obligation under Sub-Clause 2.3 [*Employer's Personnel and Other Contractors*] to ensure that Employer's Personnel cooperate with the Contractor.
75. This Sub-Clause complements Sub-Clause 9.2, first paragraph, which refers to where the Contractor is unduly delayed in carrying out Tests on Completion by the Employer's Personnel or the Employer.
76. *See (1) Tests delayed by Employer or Employer's Personnel* under **(iii) Analysis** of the commentary on Sub-Clause 9.2 [*Delayed Tests*] above.
77. *See* Sub-Clause 7.4, fifth paragraph, and the commentary on it.
78. *The FIDIC Contracts Guide* (2nd edn, FIDIC, 2022) 313.
79. *Ibid*.

Sub-paragraph (c) then provides that the Engineer must immediately issue a Taking-Over Certificate. After its issue, the Contractor must carry out the Tests on Completion 'as soon as practicable' (i.e., as soon as the Employer gives it the necessary access to the Site and allows it to do so[80]) and before the expiry of the relevant DNP.

(3) After the prevention ceases

After the issue of the Taking-Over Certificate – and assuming the cause of prevention has ceased (or is ceasing) – the second paragraph provides that the Engineer must give a Notice to the Contractor of not less than 14 days of the date after which the Contractor may carry out the tests. The Contractor must then carry them out as soon as practicable and, in any case, before the expiry of the DNP. When doing so, the Contractor must comply with Sub-Clause 9.1 [*Contractor's Obligations*].[81]

(4) Resolution of disagreements

A disagreement as to whether the interference with the Tests on Completion is attributable to the Employer's Personnel, or a cause for which the Employer is responsible, may give rise to a Claim under Sub-Clause 20.1(c) which the claiming Party may refer to the Engineer for an agreement or determination under Sub-Clause 3.7. If the Contractor has suffered delay and/or incurred Costs, as a result of being prevented from carrying out the tests, the Contractor would be entitled, subject to Sub-Clause 20.2, to an EOT and/or payment of Cost Plus Profit.[82]

80. Somewhat anomalously, Sub-Clause 10.3 does not provide, as does Sub-Clause 10.2, third paragraph, that the Contractor 'shall be given the earliest opportunity' (by the Employer and/or the Engineer) to carry out the Tests on Completion.
81. This requires, among other things, compliance with Sub-Clause 7.4 [*Testing by the Contractor*] and that not less than 42 days before the date the Contractor intends to commence the Tests on Completion the Contractor will submit its proposed detailed test programme for Review by the Engineer. *See* the commentaries on Sub-Clauses 7.4 and 9.1 above and **Figure 9 Steps in Tests on Completion** which follows the commentary on Sub-Clause 9.1 above.
82. Sub-Clause 10.3, last paragraph. *Note that under Sub-Clause 20.2 failure to give a Notice of Claim within 28 days may time bar the claim.*

(iv) Related Law: Whether under the common law[83] or the civil law,[84] a party to a contract (e.g., the Employer) cannot insist upon the performance of an obligation – here, the carrying out of the Tests on Completion – which it has prevented the other party from performing. Similarly, Article 7.1.2 (*Interference by the other party*) of the UNIDROIT Principles provides that:

> [a] party [the Employer] may not rely on the non-performance of the other party [the Contractor] to the extent that such non-performance was caused by the first party's act or omission or by another event for which the first party bears the risk.

Applying this article, and consistent with Sub-Clause 10.3, the Employer may not rely on the Contractor's failure to carry out the Tests on Completion so as to deny the Contractor the Taking-Over Certificate if either the Employer's Personnel or a cause for which the Employer is responsible prevented the Contractor from carrying out those tests.

(v) Improvements: As explained under *(1) Tests delayed by Employer or Employer's Personnel* under **(iii) Analysis** of the commentary on Sub-Clause 9.2 [*Delayed Tests*] above, it needs to be clarified when the 14-day period provided for in the first paragraph of Sub-Clause 10.3 begins.

--ooOOoo--

10.4 Surfaces Requiring Reinstatement

> Except as otherwise stated in the Taking-Over Certificate, a certificate for a Section or Part shall not be deemed to certify completion of any ground or other surfaces requiring reinstatement.

Except as stated in the Taking-Over Certificate, a certificate for a Section or Part is not deemed to certify completion of any ground requiring reinstatement.

83. Called the 'prevention principle'. *Multiplex Constructions (UK) Ltd v Honeywell Control Systems Ltd (no 2)* [2007] BLR 195 [para. 47]. *See* under **(iv) Related Law** of the commentary on Sub-Clause 8.5 above.
84. This would be a violation of the obligation to perform a contract in good faith under art. 1104 of the French Civil Code. *See* **Section 4 Common Law and Civil Law Compared – 4.3.1 Duty of Good Faith** in **Chapter II Applicable Law** above.

Commentary

(i) Main Changes from RB/99: No significant change.

(ii) Related Clauses / Sub-Clauses: 10 [*Employer's Taking Over*], 11.1 [*Completion of Outstanding Work and Remedying Defects*] and 11.11 [*Clearance of the Site*].

(iii) Analysis: As the Contractor is required, pursuant to Sub-Clause 11.1, to complete any outstanding work and remedy any defects during the DNP, the Contractor may need, following that work and during the DNP, to reinstate ground or other surfaces. Consequently, this Sub-Clause provides that a Taking-Over Certificate for a Section or Part of the Works will not be deemed to certify completion of any ground or other surfaces which require reinstatement, unless stated otherwise in the Taking-Over Certificate.[85]

It is puzzling why there is not a similar provision that, except as stated in the Taking-Over Certificate for the whole of the Works, such certificate shall not be deemed to certify completion of any ground or other surfaces requiring reinstatement. The same qualification as applies to a Taking-Over Certificate for a Section or Part of the Works should apply to a Taking-Over Certificate for the whole of the Works.

What is clear is that, after the issue of the Performance Certificate (following expiry of the DNP), the Contractor will be obliged (according to new language in RB/17) to 'reinstate all parts of the Site which were affected by the Contractor's activities during the execution of the Works and are not occupied by the Permanent Works'.[86]

(iv) Improvements: As indicated above, it is unclear why this provision should not also apply to a Taking-Over Certificate for the whole of the Works, instead of just a certificate for a Section or Part of the Works. This apparent anomaly should be remedied.

--ooOOoo--

85. The outstanding work needs to be 'minor' and such as 'will not substantially affect the safe use of the Works or Section for their intended purpose', as provided in Sub-Clause 10.1(i).
86. Sub-paragraph (b) of Sub-Clause 11.11 [*Clearance of Site*].

11 Defects after Taking Over

This Clause sets out the Contractor's obligations during the Defects Notification Period ('DNP') to complete any outstanding work and remedy any defects or damage in the Works and Contractor's Documents. It deals with the allocation of costs for the remedying of defects or damage during, and the possible extension of, the DNP. It also deals with: the Employer's remedies upon the Contractor's failure to rectify defects or damage, the possibility of off-Site remedial work, retesting, the Contractor's right of access to the Works during the DNP and the Contractor's responsibility to search for the cause of any defect. The Clause also provides for the issue of the Performance Certificate after expiry of the DNP and, following this, for each Party's continuing liability for unperformed obligations, including the Contractor's obligation to clear the Site.

--ooOOoo--

11.1 Completion of Outstanding Work and Remedying Defects

In order that the Works and Contractor's Documents, and each Section and/or Part, shall be in the condition required by the Contract (fair wear and tear excepted) by the expiry date of the relevant Defects Notification Period or as soon as practicable thereafter, the Contractor shall:

(a) complete any work which is outstanding on the relevant Date of Completion, within the time(s) stated in the Taking-Over Certificate or such other reasonable time as is instructed by the Engineer; and

(b) execute all work required to remedy defects or damage, of which a Notice is given to the Contractor by (or on behalf of) the Employer on or before the expiry date of the DNP for the Works or Section or Part (as the case may be).

If a defect appears (including if the Works fail to pass the Tests after Completion, if any) or damage occurs during the relevant DNP, a Notice shall be given to the Contractor accordingly, by (or on behalf of) the Employer. Promptly thereafter:

(i) the Contractor and the Employer's Personnel shall jointly inspect the defect or damage;
(ii) the Contractor shall then prepare and submit a proposal for necessary remedial work; and
(iii) the second, third and fourth paragraphs of Sub-Clause 7.5 [*Defects and Rejection*] shall apply.

In order that the Works and Contractor's Documents, and each Section and/or Part, shall be in the condition required by the Contract by the expiry date of the relevant DNP or as soon as practicable thereafter, the Contractor shall: (a) complete any outstanding work within the time(s) stated in the Taking-Over Certificate or such other reasonable time as instructed by the Engineer; and (b) execute all remedial work of which a Notice is given to the Contractor by the expiry of the relevant DNP.

If a defect appears or damage occurs during the relevant DNP, a Notice shall be given to the Contractor by the Employer. Promptly thereafter, the Contractor and the Employer's Personnel shall jointly inspect it, the Contractor shall submit a proposal for necessary remedial work, and the second, third and fourth paragraphs of Sub-Clause 7.5 will apply.

Commentary

(i) Main Changes from RB/99:

(1) Whereas Sub-Clause 11.1 of RB/99 referred to the Works and a Section, the new Sub-Clause also refers, in the first paragraph, to a Part.
(2) Whereas Sub-Clause 11.1(a) of RB/99 referred to completing work which is outstanding on the date stated in the relevant Taking-Over Certificate, the new Sub-Clause refers to work outstanding on the relevant Date of Completion.
(3) Unlike Sub-Clause 11.1(a) of RB/99 that stated that any outstanding work must be completed by the Contractor 'within such reasonable time as is instructed by the Engineer', the new Sub-Clause 11(a) states that this work must be completed 'within the time(s) stated in the Taking-Over Certificate or such other reasonable time as is instructed by the Engineer'.

(4) The second paragraph of the new Sub-Clause, dealing with the Parties' obligations following the giving by the Employer of a Notice to the Contractor of a defect appearing or a damage occurring during the DNP, is almost entirely new.

(ii) Related Clauses / Sub-Clauses: 1.3 [*Notices and Other Communications*], 7.5 [*Defects and Rejection*], 7.6 [*Remedial Work*], 10.1 [*Taking Over the Works and Sections*], 10.2 [*Taking Over Parts*] and 11 [*Defects after Taking Over*].

(iii) Analysis:

(1) Purpose of Sub-Clause

This Sub-Clause provides for the obligations of the Contractor during the DNP and for the action which must be taken if a defect appears or damage occurs during this period.

(2) Status of Parties at Date of Completion

At the Date of Completion, which is defined as being, among other things, the date stated in the Taking-Over Certificate issued by the Engineer,[1] the DNP begins, which is defined as:

> the period for notifying defects and/or damage in the Works or a Section or a Part (as the case may be) under Sub-Clause 11.1 [*Completion of Outstanding Work and Remedying Defects*], as stated in the Contract Data (if not stated, one year) and as may be extended under Sub-Clause 11.3 [*Extension of Defects Notification Period*]. This period is calculated from the Date of Completion of the Works or Section or Part.[2]

Thus, the DNP will be one year unless otherwise stated in the Contract Data.

At the outset of the DNP for the Works, the general position of the Parties is, as follows:

1. Sub-Clause 1.1.24 **'Date of Completion'**.
2. Sub-Clause 1.1.27 and *see* the commentary above on this Sub-Clause.

(1) while the Contractor has the obligation to complete outstanding work and remedy defects or damage during the DNP, the Employer, not the Contractor, is now in possession of the Site and may be using the Works;[3]

(2) the Employer continues to hold at least the second half of the Contractor's Retention Money[4] as well as its Performance Security;[5] and

(3) while the Contractor will have been paid for work done based on the IPCs, it will not yet have submitted its Final Statement,[6] and, until after the expiry of the DNP:

   (a) the Contractor will not be entitled to the return of the second half of the Retention Money nor to receive the Performance Certificate[7] nor to return of the Performance Security; and

   (b) the Employer will not be entitled to the Contractor's discharge,[8] releasing the Employer from liability to the Contractor.

Sub-Clause 11.1 sets out the regime that applies during the DNP so that the Works and the Contractor's Documents, which are not part of the Works, will be in the condition required by the Contract, 'fair wear and tear excepted', by the expiry of the DNP 'or as soon as practicable thereafter'.[9] As the Employer will be occupying and/or using the Works during this period, routine maintenance and 'fair wear and tear' from such occupation, use and passage of time is the responsibility of the Employer.[10]

---

3. Sub-Clause 4.22, last paragraph.
4. According to Sub-Clause 14.9, first paragraph, the Contractor may include the first half of the Retention Money in a Statement after issue of the Taking-Over Certificate for the Works.
5. Sub-Clause 4.2.1, second paragraph.
6. Sub-Clause 14.11.
7. Sub-Clause 11.9. The Performance Certificate establishes that the Contractor had fulfilled its obligations under the Contract.
8. Sub-Clause 14.12.
9. The phrase 'as soon as practicable thereafter' covers situations where a defect has been notified to the Contractor shortly before the expiry of the DNP, which would require the carrying out of remedial works that extend beyond the DNP.
10. With respect to 'wear and tear':

(3) The Contractor's obligation to complete outstanding work

Sub-Clause 11.1(a) requires the Contractor to 'complete any work which is outstanding on the relevant Date of Completion'. By referring to the 'Date of Completion', it requires the Contractor to complete work which remains to be done on that date, even if no Taking-Over Certificate was issued for the relevant Works, Section or Part.[11] In this case, the outstanding work could comprise, among other things, any of the matters referred to in Sub-Clause 10.1(a) to (d).[12]

The reference to 'outstanding' work in Sub-Clause 11.1 should be read together with Sub-Clause 10.1(i) that allows for 'minor outstanding work and defects' at the time of taking over:

> which will not substantially affect the safe use of the Works or Section for their intended purpose (either until or while this work is completed and these defects are remedied).

The Taking-Over Certificate, if any, must list this outstanding work, and may state the time(s) within which it must be completed.[13] Otherwise, it must be completed within such reasonable time as is instructed by the Engineer.[14] What is reasonable would depend on the type of work and the time that is normally required, under the specific circumstances, to complete the work.[15]

'wear' is concerned with the results of usage and 'tear' is concerned with the impact of ordinary natural causes, such as weather upon a thing (*JSM Management Pty Ltd v QBE Insurance (Aust) Ltd* [2011] VSC 339 at [25]). Together, the meaning that the words convey is 'deterioration caused by ordinary use' (*Black's Law Dictionary*, Bryan A Garner (ed in chief), 8th edn, 2006).

Paul Reed, *Construction All Risks Insurance* (2nd edn, Sweet & Maxwell, London, 2016) 405 (para. 15-014).

11. *See* the commentary on Sub-Clause 1.1.24 '**Date of Completion**' above.
12. That is, completion of Tests on Completion, submission of as-built records and operation and maintenance manuals, to which the Engineer has given a Notice of No-objection and completion of training.
13. Sub-Clause 10.1 (i) and Sub-Clause 11.1(a).
14. Sub-Clause 11.1(a). While what is a reasonable time is not defined in the Conditions, for a definition of 'reasonableness' *see* fn. 263 in the commentary on **Clause 1** above of **Chapter IV**.
15. The Engineer's instruction must comply with the requirements set out in Sub-Clause 1.3 [*Notices and Other Communications*].

(4) The Contractor's obligation to remedy defects during the DNP

Under Sub-Clause 11.1(b), the Contractor is required to remedy defects or damage of which a Notice has been given to it by (or on behalf) the Employer during the DNP.[16] While the Conditions do not define the term 'defect', defective work is usually taken to mean work which 'fails to comply with the requirements of the contract and so is a breach of contract'.[17] Thus, if the Works or Contractor's Documents fail to comply with the Drawings or Specification or with local building or similar standards which are incorporated into the Contract, they would be regarded as defective. On the other hand, 'damage' appears to refer to loss, harm or injury to the Works or Contractor's Documents whether caused by either Party, a third party or external events.

The Employer's Notice must describe the defect and/or damage, but does not need to specify either the cause, or how it should be remedied.[18] The Contractor must execute all work required to remedy the defect or damage 'on or before the expiry date of the DNP', whatever may be the cause of it. *Thus, even if the defect and/or damage were caused by the Employer or the Employer's Personnel, or resulted from events beyond the control of either Party (e.g., an Exceptional Event),*[19] *the Contractor must remedy it if notified to do so.*[20] This is because it is likely to be more

16. The Notice is given by, or on behalf of, the Employer as the Employer is in possession of the Site and may be using the Works and, thus, is most likely to be aware of any defects arising during the DNP. The Engineer, as the Employer's agent, may also give this Notice on behalf of the Employer.
17. Atkin Chambers, *Hudson's Building and Engineering Contracts* (14th edn, Sweet & Maxwell, London, 2020) 572 (para. 4-075). As the Conditions do not define the term 'defect', its meaning might vary according to applicable law.
18. As the remedial work is the responsibility of the Contractor. *The FIDIC Contracts Guide* (2nd edn, FIDIC, 2022) 317.
19. *See* Sub-Clause 1.1.37 '**Exceptional Event**' and Sub-Clause 18.1 [*Exceptional Events*].
20. Some other standard forms have adopted a different approach. For example, pursuant to GC 27.5 of the *ENAA Model Form – International Contract for Process Plant Construction* (3rd edn, 2010), the contractor's obligations to make good a defect during the 'Defects Liability Period' do not apply to non-conformance which is attributable to, among other things, the improper handling, operation or maintenance of the plant by the owner or any design specifications, data, equipment, materials or other supplies of the owner. A similar approach is adopted in arts 49.1-2 of the *ICC Model Turnkey Contract for Major Projects* (ICC Publication no 797 E 2020) which also relieves the contractor from having to correct defects attributable to third parties.

efficient for the Contractor – who is already familiar with the Works and will still have Goods at the Site[21] – to do this than another contractor. However, the cause of the defect and/or damage will determine which Party will bear the costs of the remedial work.[22]

Unlike Sub-Clause 11.1(a), there is no explicit requirement in sub-paragraph (b) as to the time within which the Contractor must remedy notified defects or damage other than that it must be done on or before the expiry date of the relevant DNP. However, the Contractor may not delay such work unduly as otherwise the Engineer may withhold from an IPC amounts otherwise due,[23] and the Employer may exercise the remedies in Sub-Clause 11.4 [*Failure to Remedy Defects*], as discussed below.

(5) Notification of a defect and Parties' related obligations

Under the second paragraph, if a defect 'appears' or damage occurs during the relevant DNP,[24] the Employer is not entitled to rectify the defect or damage itself. Instead, the Employer (or the Engineer, on the Employer's behalf) must give a Notice of it to the Contractor, who is then required – and entitled[25] in lieu of the Employer or another contractor of the Employer – to remedy it. This is sensible because (as mentioned above) the Contractor will normally be able to do so more efficiently than the Employer or another contractor.

The Contractor and the Employer's Personnel must then 'promptly' jointly inspect the defect or damage, after which (as in the case under Sub-Clause 7.5 of a defect found before taking over) the Contractor must submit a proposal for necessary remedial work. Where there are several remedial options, the Contractor is normally entitled to decide which one to use, provided it will rectify the defect in conformity with the Contract.[26]

21. Sub-Clause 4.22, last paragraph.
22. *See* Sub-Clause 11.2.
23. Pursuant to Sub-Clause 14.6.2 (a) and/or (b).
24. A defect which 'appears' *after* the DNP would not be within the ambit of the clause under English law, Atkin Chambers, *Hudson's Building and Engineering Contracts* (14th edn, Sweet & Maxwell, London, 2020) 587 (para. 4-095).
25. This right is recognised in English contract practice. *See* Julian Bailey, *Construction Law* (3rd edn, London Publishing, UK, 2020) vol 2,1331 (para. 14.121) and Stephen Furst and Vivian Ramsey, *Keating on Construction Contracts* (11th edn, Sweet & Maxwell, London, 2021) 359 (para. 11-032).
26. Julian Bailey, *Construction Law* (3rd edn, London Publishing, UK, 2020) vol 2, 1333 (para. 14.124).

The paragraph then stipulates that the last three paragraphs of Sub-Clause 7.5 [*Defects and Rejection*] will apply. It follows from this cross-reference that the Engineer may Review[27] the Contractor's proposal and either give a Notice of No-objection or a Notice stating the extent to which, if carried out, it would not result in the Works complying with the Contract. If the Contractor should fail promptly to submit a proposal (or revised proposal), or to carry out proposed remedial work to which the Engineer has given (or is deemed to have given) a Notice of No-objection, the Engineer may either:

(a) instruct the Contractor to repair or remedy, or remove and replace, or remove and re-execute, the defective or damaged work under sub-paragraphs (a) and/or (b) of Sub-Clause 7.6 [*Remedial Work*]; or

(b) reject the Plant, Materials, Contractor's Design or workmanship by a Notice, with reasons, in which case the Employer may carry out the remedial work itself or have others do so, at the Contractor's cost pursuant to Sub-Clause 11.4(a).[28]

The Engineer may also require retesting, at the Contractor's risk and cost, after remedying the defects.[29]

(6) Difficulties with Sub-Clause 11.1

There are two difficulties with the cross-reference to Sub-Clause 7.5 in Sub-Clause 11.1(iii).

First, Sub-Clause 7.5 provides that if the Contractor fails, among other things, to submit a proposal for remedial work, the Engineer may instruct the Contractor under sub-paragraphs (a) and (b) of Sub-Clause 7.6 [*Remedial Works*]. However, Sub-Clause 7.6 only applies 'at any time before the issue of the Taking-Over Certificate for the Works'[30] which is inconsistent with having it apply after taking over.

Second, one of the Employer's remedies under Sub-Clause 7.5 is, under sub-paragraph (b), to reject the defective work and carry it out at the Contractor's cost under Sub-Clause 11.4(a). However, under Sub-Clause 11.4, the conditions under which this remedy may be exercised are

27. *See* Sub-Clause 1.1.70 '**Review**'.
28. For further details, *see* the commentary on Sub-Clause 7.5 above.
29. Sub-Clause 7.5, last paragraph.
30. Sub-Clause 7.6, first paragraph.

different. The remedy under sub-paragraph (a) of Sub-Clause 11.4 may only be relied upon, according to the Sub-Clause's first paragraph, if the Contractor has failed to remedy a defect or damage within a reasonable time fixed in a Notice given by (or on behalf of) the Employer after the Contractor has unduly delayed the carrying out of the remedial work. It is unclear whether this Notice requirement is to apply in the context of Sub-Clause 11.1(iii).

(7) Contractor's right to perform remedial work

Assuming that the Contractor has submitted a proposal under Sub-Clause 11.1(ii) to which the Engineer (or Employer) has given a Notice of No-objection, the Contractor must be given an opportunity to remedy the defect, including being allowed right of access to the Works under Sub-Clause 11.7 [*Right of Access after Taking Over*]. Only if the Contractor fails to submit a proposal or to carry out the proposed remedial work to which the Engineer (or Employer) has given a Notice of No-objection, may the Employer, at some point (possibly after a further Notice to the Contractor which goes unremedied), carry out the work itself or have it carried out by others under Sub-Clause 11.4. Similarly, as stated above, the Employer may not, without breaching the Contract, refrain from notifying a defect or damage to the Contractor because the Employer should prefer to remedy it on its own.

(iv) Related Law: On the other hand, there may be exceptional circumstances where the Contractor's original performance has been so unsatisfactory and/or the Contractor so unwilling to do the work correctly, that the Employer loses confidence, with good reason, in the Contractor's ability and willingness to execute work to the requisite standard. In such an exceptional case, the Employer may be justified – subject to the governing law – either to perform the work itself or to engage another contractor to do so and recover the cost of rectification from the Contractor.[31]

As from the Date of Completion, the Contractor may also have an obligation to rectify defects under applicable law and not just under the Contract. For example, under French law and the law of civil law

31. *See* Atkin Chambers, *Hudson's Building and Engineering Contracts* (14th edn, Sweet & Maxwell, London, 2020) 591-592 (paras 4-101 to 4-102).

countries influenced by French law the Contractor and the Engineer may be subject to mandatory decennial or similar liability.[32]

(v) Improvements:

(1) Consideration should be given to: (1) as stated in the commentary on Sub-Clause 1.1 [*Definitions*] above, providing a definition of the term 'defect';[33] (2) addressing the question of how Sub-Clause 7.6 is to apply after taking over when it expressly provides that it only applies 'before the issue of the Taking-Over Certificate for the Works'; and (3) clarifying under what conditions the remedy under sub-paragraph (a) of Sub-Clause 11.4 may be invoked (as provided in Sub-Clause 7.5, which is referred to in Sub-Clause 11.1 (iii)) given that compliance with the first paragraph of Sub-Clause 11.4 is ordinarily a condition to its application.

(2) The term 'Defects Limitation Period' should be replaced by the simpler expression 'Correction Period', as the Contractor is required (and entitled) to correct or rectify the Works during this period and this expression is shorter.

--ooOOoo--

11.2 Cost of Remedying Defects

All work under sub-paragraph (b) of Sub-Clause 11.1 [*Completion of Outstanding Work and Remedying Defects*] shall be executed at the risk and cost of the Contractor, if and to the extent that the work is attributable to:

(a) design (if any) of the Works for which the Contractor is responsible;
(b) Plant, Materials or workmanship not being in accordance with the Contract;
(c) improper operation or maintenance which was attributable to matters for which the Contractor

32. *See* **Section 4 Common Law and Civil Law Compared – 4.4.4 Decennial Liability** of **Chapter II Applicable Law** above where a number of countries providing for decennial or similar liability are listed.

33. *See* under **(iii) Improvements** in the commentary on Sub-Clause 1.1 [*Definitions*] above.

is responsible (under Sub-Clauses 4.4.2 [*As-Built Records*], Sub-Clause 4.4.3 [*Operation and Maintenance Manuals*] and/or Sub-Clause 4.5 [*Training*] (where applicable) or otherwise); or

(d) failure by the Contractor to comply with any other obligation under the Contract.

If the Contractor considers that the work is attributable to any other cause, the Contractor shall promptly give a Notice to the Engineer and the Engineer shall proceed under Sub-Clause 3.7 [*Agreement or Determination*] to agree or determine the cause (and, for the purpose of Sub-Clause 3.7.3 [*Time limits*], the date of this Notice shall be the date of commencement of the time limit for agreement under Sub-Clause 3.7.3). If it is agreed or determined that the work is attributable to a cause other than those listed above, Sub-Clause 13.3.1 [*Variation by Instruction*] shall apply as if such work had been instructed by the Engineer.

All remedial work under Sub-Clause 11.1(b) shall be executed at the Contractor's risk and cost if the work is attributable to the causes listed in sub-paragraphs (a) to (d) of Sub-Clause 11.2.

If the Contractor considers that the work is attributable to any other cause, it shall promptly give a Notice to the Engineer, who shall proceed under Sub-Clause 3.7 to agree or determine the cause. If it is agreed or determined that the work is attributable to such other cause, Sub-Clause 13.3.1 shall apply.

Commentary

(i) Main Changes from RB/99:

(1) Sub-paragraph (c), referring to improper operation or maintenance attributable to matters for which the Contractor is responsible, is new.[34]

(2) Whereas Sub-Clause 11.2 of RB/99 had provided that remedial work attributable to a cause that is not the Contractor's responsibility must be notified by (or on behalf of) the Employer to the

34. However, a similar paragraph was contained in Sub-Clause 11.2 of YB/99 and SB/99.

Contractor, the new Sub-Clause envisages instead that, where the Contractor considers that the work (to remedy defects or damage) 'is attributable to any other cause', the Contractor must promptly give a Notice to the Engineer who must then agree or determine the cause under Sub-Clause 3.7; as in the case of RB/99, where the work is attributable to such other cause, Sub-Clause 13.3 [*Variation Procedure*] will then apply.

(ii) Related Clauses / Sub-Clauses: 1.3 [*Notices and Other Communications*], 3.7 [*Agreement or Determination*], 4.4.2 [*As-Built Records*], 4.4.3 [*Operation and Maintenance Manuals*], 4.5 [*Training*], 11 [*Defects after Taking Over*] and 13.3 [*Variation Procedure*].

(iii) Analysis*:* Whereas Sub-Clause 11.1 requires the Contractor to remedy defects or damage during the DNP regardless of which Party is responsible, this Sub-Clause deals with the question of which Party should bear the risk and cost of doing so. The Contractor will bear the risk and cost 'if and to the extent'[35] that the remedial work is attributable to the causes listed in sub-paragraphs (a) to (d) of Sub-Clause 11.2 (all being matters for which the Contractor is manifestly responsible).[36]

On the other hand, if the Contractor considers that the work is attributable to 'any other cause', it must promptly give a Notice to the Engineer, who must then proceed under Sub-Clause 3.7 to agree or determine the cause.[37] The Notice should identify the defective/damaged part of the Works, set out the facts regarding the cause of the defects/damage and explain why the Contractor is not responsible.

If the Contractor 'unduly' delays in carrying out remedial work then, pursuant to Sub-Clause 11.4, the Employer may by a Notice fix a final date – allowing the Contractor 'reasonable time' – by which the Contractor is to remedy the defect or damage. If the Contractor still does not do

35. Recognising that responsibility may be shared between the Parties.
36. The 'improper operation or maintenance' referred to in sub-para. (c) may be by the Employer's Personnel but result from misinformation provided by the Contractor pursuant to the Sub-Clauses referred to in that sub-paragraph.
37. *See* the commentary on Sub-Clause 3.7 above. This is an improvement on Sub-Clause 11.2 of RB/99 which had provided that the Employer – who would have little incentive to do so – should notify the Contractor if the necessity for remedial work was not attributable to the Contractor.

so and the remedial work was to be done at the Contractor's Cost, the Employer may, among other things, have the work carried out by others at the Contractor's cost.

Pursuant to the last sentence of Sub-Clause 11.2, if it is agreed or determined under Sub-Clause 3.7 that the work is attributable to a cause other than those listed in sub-paragraphs (a) to (d), the remedial work will be treated 'as if' it had been instructed by the Engineer as a Variation under Sub-Clause 13.3.1.[38] In this case, the Contractor may be entitled to an EOT and/or adjustment of the Contract Price without the need to comply with the claims procedure under Sub-Clause 20.2 [*Claims for Payment and/or EOT*].[39]

(iv) Related Law: *See* the reference to decennial liability in the last paragraph under **(iv) Related Law** of the commentary on Sub-Clause 11.1 above.

--ooOOoo--

11.3 Extension of Defects Notification Period

> The Employer shall be entitled to an extension of the DNP for the Works, or a Section or a Part:
>
> (a) if and to the extent that the Works, Section, Part or a major item of Plant (as the case may be, and after taking over) cannot be used for the intended purpose(s) by reason of a defect or damage which is attributable to any of the causes under sub-paragraphs (a) to (d) of Sub-Clause 11.2 [*Cost of Remedying Defects*]; and
>
> (b) subject to Sub-Clause 20.2 [*Claims for Payment and/or EOT*].

38. It can only be treated 'as if' it were a Variation (i.e., as a hypothetical Variation) as an actual Variation may only be initiated 'before the issue of the Taking-Over Certificate for the Works' according to Sub-Clause 13.1.
39. *See* the commentary on Sub-Clause 13.3.1 below. If the Engineer determines that the remedial works are attributable to a cause that is the responsibility of the Contractor and the Contractor disagrees and gives a NOD under Sub-Clause 3.7.5, this matter may be referred by either Party under Sub-Clause 21.4 [*Obtaining DAAB's Decision*].

However, a DNP shall not be extended by more than a period of two years after the expiry of the DNP stated in the Contract Data.

If delivery and/or erection of Plant and/or Materials was suspended under Sub-Clause 8.9 [*Employer's Suspension*] (other than where the cause of such suspension is the responsibility of the Contractor) or Sub-Clause 16.1 [*Suspension by Contractor*], the Contractor's obligations under this Clause shall not apply to any defects or damage occurring more than two years after the DNP for the Works, of which the Plant and/or Materials form part, would otherwise have expired.

The Employer shall be entitled, subject to Sub-Clause 20.2, to an extension of the DNP for the Works or a Section or a Part if the relevant Works, Section, Part or a major item of Plant cannot be used for the intended purpose(s) by reason of a defect or damage attributable to the causes in Sub-Clause 11.2(a)-(d). A DNP may not be extended by more than a period of two years.

If delivery and/or erection of Plant and/or Materials was suspended under Sub-Clause 8.9 (other than for a cause that is the Contractor's responsibility) or Sub-Clause 16.1, the Contractor's obligations under Clause 11 will not apply to defects or damage occurring more than two years after the DNP for the Works, of which such Plant and/or Materials form part, would otherwise have expired.

Commentary

(i) Main Changes from RB/99:

(1) Whereas Sub-Clause 11.3 of RB/99 referred to an extension of the DNP for the Works or Section, the new Sub-Clause refers to an extension of the DNP for a Part as well.

(2) Whereas RB/99 had provided that the Employer would be entitled to an extension of the DNP if the relevant works could not be used for their intended purpose due to a defect or damage, regardless apparently of the cause, the new Sub-Clause stipulates (in sub-paragraph (a)) that such defect or damage must be attributable to a cause for which the Contractor is responsible under Sub-Clause 11.2(a)-(d).

(3) Whereas Sub-Clause 11.3 stipulated that a DNP 'shall not be extended by more than two years', the second paragraph of the new Sub-Clause clarifies that the DNP 'shall not be extended by more than a period of two years after the expiry of the DNP stated in the Contract Data'.

(4) It is stated in the last paragraph of the new Sub-Clause for the first time that the limitation on the Contractor's liability in time in the last paragraph (two years after certain matters) will not apply to a suspension under Sub-Clause 8.9 (Sub-Clause 8.8 in RB/99) where 'the cause of such suspension is the responsibility of the Contractor'.

(ii) Related Clauses / Sub-Clauses: 8.9 [*Employer's Suspension*], 11.1 [*Completion of Outstanding Work and Remedying Defects*], 11.2 [*Cost of Remedying Defects*], 16.1 [*Suspension by Contractor*] and 20.2 [*Claims for Payment and/or EOT*].

(iii) Analysis:

(1) Purpose of Sub-Clause

This Sub-Clause provides that the Employer may be entitled to an extension of the DNP for the Works, Section or a Part, if and to the extent that any one of these, or a major item of Plant, cannot be used for its purpose by reason of a defect or damage attributable to the Contractor.

(2) Conditions for an extension of the DNP

To assert a Claim under this Sub-Clause, the Employer must:

(i) give a Notice of a defect or damage to the Contractor pursuant to Sub-Clause 11.1(b);

(ii) establish that the Works, Section, Part or a major item of Plant, as the case may be, cannot be used for its respective intended purpose(s)[40] after taking over by reason of a defect or damage attributable to a cause referred to in Sub-Clause 11.2(a)-(d);[41] and

(iii) comply with the claims procedure in Sub-Clause 20.2 [*Claims for Payment and/or EOT*].

40. Ideally, the Contract should describe the intended purpose of each Section or Part, if any, and each major item of Plant.

41. The period of time when equipment is not available or power supply or other service cannot be used is sometimes referred to as an 'outage'.

Consequently, the Employer may only request an extension of the DNP for any defect or damage for which the Contractor is responsible that is so material that it prevents the Works, a Section, Part or major item of Plant from being used for its intended purpose(s) after taking over. The defect or damage need not have occurred after taking over. It may have occurred before then, though it may have only appeared afterwards.[42]

The length of extension of the relevant DNP will be the number of days during which the Works, Section, Part or a major item of Plant could not have been used for their intended purpose(s).

(3) Maximum extension of the DNP

The second paragraph introduces a long-stop date for an extension of the DNP. The DNP may not be extended 'by more than a period of two years after the expiry of the DNP stated in the Contract Data'. This wording clarifies that the two-year period should be calculated from the expiry of the initial DNP, as stated in the Contract Data, and not from the expiry of a DNP that has already been extended.[43]

(4) Defects liability for Plant and/or Materials upon suspension

The last paragraph addresses where delivery and/or erection of Plant and/or Materials was suspended under Sub-Clauses 8.9 [*Employer's Suspension*] (other than for a cause for which the Contractor was responsible) or 16.1 [*Suspension by Contractor*] which would also not be the Contractor's responsibility. Such a suspension would postpone the commencement of the relevant DNP. In these circumstances, it would be unjustified, where the cause of a suspension was not the Contractor's responsibility, for the Contractor to be liable for a defect and/or damage related to the Works containing such Plant and/or Materials for a period longer than the maximum period of extension of the initial DNP (i.e., the DNP that would have started to run had no suspension occurred). Therefore, the Contractor's obligations under Clause 11 will not apply to 'any defects or damage occurring more than two years after the DNP for the Works, of which the Plant and/or Materials form part, would otherwise have expired'.

42. *See The FIDIC Contracts Guide* (1st edn, FIDIC, 2000), 197.

43. The position was unclear in RB/99. Sub-Clause 11.3 of RB/99 simply stated that 'a Defects Notification Period shall not be extended by more than two years'. The definition of a Defects Notification Period in Sub-Clause 1.1.3.7 of RB/99 had also included Defects Notification Period(s) that had already been extended.

It is not clear when, for the purposes of this Sub-Clause, the two-year extension of the DNP would commence in a case where the Plant and/or Materials are included in a Section or Part which is the subject of a separate Taking-Over Certificate, and a separate DNP, from the Taking-Over Certificate and DNP for the Works as a whole. There appear to be two possibilities: (i) from the expiration of the DNP for the Works as a whole (i.e., from the taking over or deemed taking over of the Works as a whole); or (ii) from the expiration of the DNP for a Section or Part in which the Plant and/or Materials are included (i.e., from the taking over or deemed taking over of that Section or Part).[44]

(iv) Related Law: The expiry of the DNP for the Works only brings the Contractor's obligations (and rights) during the DNP to an end. The Contractor is not considered to have completed its contractual obligations until issuance of the Performance Certificate,[45] and will in any event remain liable for defects at law until expiry of the applicable limitation period.[46] In addition, in France and other civil law jurisdictions, as a matter of mandatory law (i.e., from which Parties may not deviate), a contractor will be absolutely liable (i.e., liable without proof of fault) for defects impairing the stability of a work which appear within some period of years (ten in France) after completion.[47]

(v) Improvements: As mentioned under **(iii) Analysis** above, where:

(1) the delivery and/or erection of Plant and/or Materials have been suspended, other than for a cause which is the responsibility of the Contractor; and

44. The wording refers to a 'DNP for the Works' and therefore seems to give preference to the first option. On the other hand, if this were FIDIC's intention the phrase 'of which the Plant and/or Materials form part' would become redundant, as Plant and/or Materials would in all cases form part of the Works. *See* the definitions of Plant and Materials in Sub-Clauses 1.1.65 **'Plant'** and 1.1.53 **'Materials'**. The second option appears to be most reasonable and the one intended.
45. Under Sub-Clause 11.9 [*Performance Certificate*].
46. *See* the commentary on Sub-Clause 11.10 [*Unfulfilled Obligations*] below. *See also* **Section 4 Common Law and Civil Law Compared – 4.5.3 Limitation Periods** in **Chapter II Applicable Law**.
47. *See* **Section 4 Common Law and Civil Law Compared – 4.4.4 Decennial Liability** in **Chapter II Applicable Law** above. *See also* the commentary on Sub-Clause 11.10 [*Unfulfilled Obligations*] below.

(2) they are included in a Section or Part of the Works for which a Taking-Over Certificate has been issued (or is deemed to have been issued);

it should be clarified when the two-year extension of the DNP starts to run, whether upon expiration of the DNP for the Works as a whole or upon expiration of the DNP for the Section or Part in which the Plant and/or Materials may be included.[48]

--ooOOoo--

11.4 Failure to Remedy Defects

If the remedying of any defect or damage under Sub-Clause 11.1 [*Completion of Outstanding Works and Remedying Defects*] is unduly delayed by the Contractor, a date may be fixed by (or on behalf of) the Employer, on or by which the defect or damage is to be remedied. A Notice of this fixed date shall be given to the Contractor by (or on behalf of) the Employer, which Notice shall allow the Contractor reasonable time (taking due regard of all relevant circumstances) to remedy the defect or damage.

If the Contractor fails to remedy the defect or damage by the date stated in this Notice and this remedial work was to be executed at the cost of the Contractor under Sub-Clause 11.2 [*Cost of Remedying Defects*], the Employer may (at the Employer's sole discretion):

(a) carry out the work or have the work carried out by others (including any retesting), in the manner required under the Contract and at the Contractor's cost, but the Contractor shall have no responsibility for this work. The Employer shall be entitled subject to Sub-Clause 20.2 [*Claims for*

48. Sub-Clause 11.3 of RB/99 referred to 'the Defects Notification Period for the Plant and/or Materials'. This wording was also imprecise as there was no separate DNP for the Plant and/or the Materials (*see* Sub-Clause 1.1.3.7 of RB/99). Presumably, this wording covered both the DNP for the Works and the DNP for a Section in which such Plant and/or Materials were included.

Payment and/or EOT] to payment by the Contractor of the costs reasonably incurred by the Employer in remedying the defect or damage;

(b) accept the damaged or defective work, in which case the Employer shall be entitled subject to Sub-Clause 20.2 [*Claims for Payment and/or EOT*] to a reduction in the Contract Price. The reduction shall be in full satisfaction of this failure only and shall be in the amount as shall be appropriate to cover the reduced value to the Employer as a result of this failure;

(c) require the Engineer to treat any part of the Works which cannot be used for its intended purpose(s) under the Contract by reason of this failure as an omission, as if such omission had been instructed under Sub-Clause 13.3.1 [*Variation by Instruction*]; or

(d) terminate the Contract as a whole with immediate effect (and Sub-Clause 15.2 [*Termination for Contractor's Default*] shall not apply) if the defect or damage deprives the Employer of substantially the whole benefit of the Works. The Employer shall then be entitled subject to Sub-Clause 20.2 [*Claims for Payment and/or EOT*] to recover from the Contractor all sums paid for the Works, plus financing charges and any costs incurred in dismantling the same, clearing the Site and returning Plant and Materials to the Contractor.

The exercise of discretion by the Employer under sub-paragraph (c) or (d) above shall be without prejudice to any other rights the Employer may have, under the Contract or otherwise.

If the remedying of a defect or damage is unduly delayed by the Contractor, a date may be fixed by the Employer in a Notice of the time by which it should be remedied, which must allow the Contractor reasonable time to do so.

If the Contractor fails to remedy the defect or damage by this date, and the remedial work was to be executed at the cost of the Contractor under Sub-Clause 11.2, the Employer may:

(a) carry out the work or have it carried out by others (but the Contractor shall have no responsibility for it), and recover, subject to Sub-Clause 20.2, any costs reasonably incurred;
(b) accept the damaged or defective work, and claim, subject to Sub-Clause 20.2, a reduction in the Contract Price;
(c) require the Engineer to treat any part of the Works which cannot be used for its intended purpose as an omission, as if it had been instructed under Sub-Clause 13.3.1; or
(d) terminate the Contract with immediate effect (without Sub-Clause 15.2 applying) if the defect or damage deprives the Employer of substantially the whole benefit of the Works, and recover, subject to Sub-Clause 20.2, all sums paid for the Works, financing charges and costs incurred in dismantling the same, clearing the Site and returning Plant and Materials to the Contractor.

The exercise of sub-paragraph (c) or (d) above shall be without prejudice to the Employer's rights.

Commentary

(i) Main Changes from RB/99:

(1) Unlike Sub-Clause 11.4 of RB/99, the new Sub-Clause clarifies that the defect or damage referred to in the opening sentence of the Sub-Clause, which the Contractor has delayed in remedying, is a defect or damage 'under Sub-Clause 11.1'.
(2) Unlike RB/99, the first paragraph provides that a Notice of a fixed date by which the defect or damage is to be remedied must be given by (or on behalf of) the Employer and that it must allow the Contractor reasonable time (taking due regard of all relevant circumstances) to carry out the remedial work.
(3) Unlike RB/99 which, in sub-paragraph (a), entitled the Employer to 'carry out the work himself or by others, in a reasonable manner', the new Sub-Clause provides, in the same sub-paragraph, that the Employer carry out the work or have it carried out by others '(including any retesting), in the manner required under the Contract'.
(4) Whereas sub-paragraph (b) of RB/99 had required the Engineer to agree or determine a reasonable reduction in the Contract Price under Sub-Clause 3.5, the new sub-paragraph (b) provides

that the reduction in the Contract Price is subject to Sub-Clause 20.2 and will be in full satisfaction of the Contractor's failure only and provides criteria for calculation of its amount.

(5) Sub-paragraph (c) of the new Sub-Clause, providing for an Employer's remedy in the form of a deemed omission of the Works under Sub-Clause 13.3.1, is new.

(6) Unlike sub-paragraph (c) of RB/99, the Employer may no longer terminate the Contract 'in respect of such major part [of the Works] which cannot be put to the intended use'.

(7) Pursuant to sub-paragraph (d) of the new Sub-Clause, the Contract may be terminated as a whole only 'if the defect or damage deprives the Employer of substantially the whole benefit of the Works' and, unlike RB/99, the new Sub-Clause provides that termination will be with immediate effect and that Sub-Clause 15.2 shall not apply.

(ii) Related Clauses / Sub-Clauses: 1.3 [*Notices and Other Communications*], 1.5 [*Limitation of Liability*], 1.16 [*Contract Termination*], 7.5 [*Defects and Rejection*], 9.4 [*Failure to Pass Tests on Completion*], 11 [*Defects after Taking Over*], 12.4 [*Omissions*], 13.1 [*Right to Vary*], 13.3.1 [*Variation by Instruction*], 14.9 [*Release of Retention Money*], 15.2 [*Termination for Contractor's Default*] and 20.2 [*Claims for Payment and/or EOT*].

(iii) Analysis:

(1) Purpose of Sub-Clause

Where the Contractor has unduly delayed in remedying a defect or damage under Sub-Clause 11.1, this Sub-Clause provides the Employer with specific remedies.

(2) Employer's Notice of date by which remedial work to be done

In any such case, whether or not the defect or damage was the Contractor's responsibility,[49] the Employer may, by a Notice, fix a date by which the Contractor must carry out the necessary remedial work. This provision applies specifically to the obligation of the Contractor under sub-paragraph (b) of Sub-Clause 11.1, as well as the last paragraph of that Sub-Clause, to execute all work required to remedy defects or damage of which a Notice has been given by the Employer to the Contractor.

49. As this is irrelevant.

The purpose of the Employer's further Notice under Sub-Clause 11.4 is to provide the Contractor with an additional – and final – period of time in which to carry out the remedial work. If the remedial work is to be executed at the cost of the Contractor (as determined under Sub-Clause 11.2), this Notice also serves as a warning that the Employer may exercise the more drastic remedies provided for in Sub-Clause 11.4 should the Contractor fail to carry out the work by the fixed date.

The Sub-Clause 11.4 Notice must allow the Contractor reasonable time to remedy the defect 'taking due regard of all relevant circumstances'. Such circumstances may include the proximity of the Site to the Contractor's Equipment and Contractor's Personnel (who may have left the Country), the delivery periods for replacement Plant as well as the operational status of the Works.[50] Other factors that may be relevant are the nature of the defect or damage, the need to consult technical experts and the time that is normally required in the circumstances to rectify the same. The Employer should be careful to respect the above Notice requirements, as any failure to do so would endanger the Employer's rights to the remedies under the Sub-Clause.

(3) Employer's remedies upon Contractor's failure to carry out the remedial work

The second paragraph lists the remedies available to the Employer if the Contractor 'fails'[51] to carry out the remedial work by the date stated in the Notice and if, in addition, it was to be executed at the cost of the Contractor under Sub-Clause 11.2. Consequently, the Employer may not exercise these remedies if, for example, the defect or damage was caused by the Employer's Personnel or matters for which the Contractor was not responsible.[52]

50. *The FIDIC Contracts Guide* (2nd edn, FIDIC, 2022), 323.

51. This Sub-Clause only applies if the Contractor 'fails' to carry out the remedial work, and therefore does not apply if and to the extent that the Contractor has been prevented from doing so by the Employer's failure to grant right of access to the Site under Sub-Clause 11.7. *The FIDIC Contracts Guide* (2nd edn, FIDIC, 2022), 325.

52. However, this does not mean that the Employer would be without remedies if the remedial work was not to be executed at the Contractor's cost. The Contractor's failure to carry out the remedial work would be a breach of Sub-Clause 11.1. Consequently, the Employer could recover from the Contractor the difference (if any) between the amount to which the Contractor

Under the second paragraph, the Employer has four remedies, as follows:

(1) to carry out the remedial work itself or have it done by others at the Contractor's cost;
(2) to reduce the Contract Price;
(3) to treat any part of the Works as an omission; and
(4) termination of the Contract.

These remedies can be exercised 'at the Employer's sole discretion', which appears to mean, in this context, that the Employer has the complete freedom to decide which remedy, if any, to exercise.[53]

(a) Carrying out of the work by the Employer or others at the Contractor's cost (Sub-Clause 11.4(a))

If the Employer carries out the Work itself or has it done by others, the Contractor is stated to have no responsibility for the rectification work, which is understandable as it is not carrying it out. For this reason, it will remain in the Employer's best interest to persuade the Contractor, where possible, to undertake this work itself in order to avoid a dispute as to whether any subsequent underperformance of the Works is due to a defect in the Contractor's original work or in the Employer's rectification work.[54] Furthermore, the Employer's election to carry out the work itself or to have it done by others at the Contractor's Cost may preclude any other remedy in respect of the defective work.[55] In the case of this remedy, if there is any retesting required, such retesting would also be carried out at the Contractor's cost.

would have been entitled for performing such work and the reasonable cost incurred by the Employer when carrying out the work itself or having it performed by others.

53. However, for possible limits on this discretion *see* under **(iv) Related Law** of the commentary on this Sub-Clause below. *See also* item (1) under **(v) Improvements** of the commentary on Sub-Clause 1.2 [*Interpretation*] above.
54. *The FIDIC Contracts Guide* (2nd edn, FIDIC, 2022), 324. The Sub-Clause 11.4(a) remedy is similar to the sanction of *mise en régie* (literally, placed under state supervision) under French administrative or public law (*see* **Section 4.2.2 Public and Private Contracts** of **Chapter II Applicable Law** above) Philippe Malinvaud (ed in chief) *Droit de la Construction* 7th edn Dalloz Action, Paris, 2018) 1355 (para 417.612).
55. This is implied by the last paragraph of Sub-Clause 11.4 which states that the exercise of the Employer's discretion under sub-para. (c) or (d) will be

The costs that the Employer may recover, subject to Sub-Clause 20.2, are limited to those 'reasonably incurred' in remedying the defect or damage.[56]

(b) Reduction in the Contract Price (Sub-Clause 11.4(b))

The Employer may decide to accept the damaged or defective work and claim, subject to Sub-Clause 20.2, a reduction in the Contract Price, in an amount 'appropriate to cover the reduced value to the Employer as a result of this failure'. The reduction is stated to be 'in full satisfaction of this failure only'. This text presumably means that the Employer's exercise of its rights under sub-paragraph (b) will preclude exercise of any other rights which the Employer may have in respect of the defective work, most obviously the right to require that the defect be remedied by the Contractor,[57] but possibly not rights in respect of work that is different from the defective work but is somehow affected by the defect.

(c) Treating part of the work as an omission (Sub-Clause 11.4(c))

The third remedy allows the Employer to treat any part of the Works which cannot, by reason of the defect, be used for its intended purpose[58] as an omission, as if such omission had been instructed under Sub-Clause 13.3.1 [*Variation by Instruction*].[59] Unlike the ordinary case of a Variation comprising the omission of work, no agreement of the Parties is required for the omitted Work to be carried out by the Employer or by others.[60]

---

without prejudice to any other rights that the Employer may have under the Contract or otherwise. This last paragraph does not refer to sub-paras (a) and (b).

56. As noted in the commentary on Sub-Clause 7.5 above, Sub-Clause 7.5(b) refers to, and incorporates by reference, sub-para. (a) of Sub-Clause 11.4 in such a way that it may be construed to provide the Employer with a shortcut to reject the work and carry it out at the Contractor's cost without having to give the Notice provided for by the first paragraph of Sub-Clause 11.4.
57. As in the case of sub-para. (a), the last paragraph of Sub-Clause 11.4 does not refer to sub-para. (b).
58. Even though this is not explicitly stated in the Sub-Clause, the intended purpose would be the one stated in the Contract or, if no purpose is stated there, the ordinary purpose (*see* Sub-Clause 4.1(e)).
59. As a consequence, Sub-Clause 20.2 [*Claims for Payment and/or EOT*] will not apply. *See* Sub-Clause 13.3.1, last paragraph.
60. This is the inference from Sub-Clause 13.1, second paragraph.

(d) Terminating the Contract (Sub-Clause 11.4(d))

The last remedy allows the Employer to terminate the Contract as a whole with immediate effect if the defect or damage deprives the Employer of substantially the whole benefit of the Works. This has been described as occurring 'where the defect/damage is so serious (and, presumably, irremediable) that the Employer cannot use and benefit from the [...] Works'.[61] It constitutes a material breach of contract[62] which '[i]t is common to make [...] a ground for termination (of a contract)'.[63]

If the defective construction can still be used and/or has some substantial benefit to the Employer, the Employer may be unable to elect this ground. For example, in the case of a bridge intended for the passage of vehicles, the Employer might not be able to terminate if the load capacity would be below the contract requirements but still permitted the safe passage of vehicles. On the other hand, it most probably could do so if the load capacity would be insufficient for the passage of vehicles, limiting the bridge's use to pedestrians.

Under Sub-Clause 11.4(d), the consequences are more drastic than under a normal contract termination provision.[64] *The Employer's right to terminate under Sub-Clause 11.4(d) is designed to put the Employer in the same position that it would have been had the Contract never been entered into.*[65] The Employer will be entitled, subject to Sub-Clause 20.2, to recover all sums paid for the Works, financing charges (on the sums

61. *The FIDIC Contracts Guide* (2nd edn, FIDIC, 2022) 324.
62. Material breach of contract is discussed and defined under **(iii) Analysis** of the commentary on Sub-Clause 15.2 [*Termination for Contractor's Default*] below.
63. *See* Atkin Chambers, *Hudson's Building and Engineering Contracts* (14th edn, Sweet & Maxwell, London, 2020) 959 (para. 8-057) US law is to the same effect, *see* Justin Sweet and Marc M Schneier, *Legal Aspects of Architecture, Engineering and the Construction Process* (9th edn, Cengage Learning, Stamford, CT, 2013) 685. *See* the commentary on Sub-Clause 15.2 [*Termination for Contractor's Default*] below for a discussion of material breach of contract.
64. Such as Sub-Clause 15.2 [*Termination for Contractor's Default*].
65. In connection with any Contract termination, *see* Sub-Clause 1.16 [*Contract Termination*] and the commentary thereon above.

paid) as well as all costs in dismantling the Works, clearing the Site and returning the Plant and Materials to the Contractor.[66]

Sub-Clause 15.2 [*Termination for Contractor's Default*] is stated not to apply, as its effect is more limited. Under that Sub-Clause, the Employer retains the work which has been performed, the Contractor is paid for work done and the Contract is terminated only for the future. On the other hand, under sub-paragraph (d) Sub-Clause 11.4, the Contract is effectively extinguished for the past as well as the future, given that the Employer is entitled to recover all sums paid for the Works, financial charges and costs and the Contractor must dismantle the Works and clear the Site.[67]

Given the severity of the remedy provided for in Sub-Clause 11.4(d), it should only be exercised in the most extreme circumstances.

--ooOOoo--

The last paragraph of Sub-Clause 11.4 provides that the last two remedies discussed above[68] are without prejudice to any other rights the Employer

66. A disagreement as to whether the Employer is deprived of substantially the whole benefit of the Works may give rise to a Claim under Sub-Clause 20.1(c) which may escalate into a Dispute which can be referred to a DAAB, and ultimately to arbitration, under Clause 21.
67. While the remedy in sub-para. (d) of Sub-Clause 11.4 may be appropriate where the Works consist mainly of Plant, as in the YB and SB, it may be less appropriate in the RB. In the case of a contract for civil works, like the RB, such as for a road, bridge or dam, the Employer will usually want to retain such work as has been done and terminate the contract for the future only, as provided for in Sub-Clause 15.2. Accordingly, if an Employer under RB/17 wishes to terminate the contract, it may prefer to do so under Sub-Clause 15.2. The Sub-Clause 11.4(d) remedy was introduced into the RB in 1999, when the RB was published as part of the Rainbow Suite in that year. The same remedy had been provided for in a design-build and turnkey form, the Orange Book (Sub-Clause 12.4) published in 1995, and was derived from Sub-Clause 30.5 [*Failure to Remedy Defects*] of YB/87, relating to electrical and mechanical works. By the Rainbow Suite, FIDIC had sought, for the first time, to harmonise as much as possible the clauses in the RB and YB, as well as with the SB which was being published for the first time (as was stated by the chief draftsman of the Rainbow Suite, Peter Booen, '[w]henever possible, similar wording is used in all three new Books in the equivalent sub-clauses'. Peter Booen, 'The Three Major New FIDIC Books' [2000] ICLR 24, 29). But sometimes this led to over-harmonisation.
68. In sub-paras (c) and (d) of Sub-Clause 11.4.

may have, under the Contract or otherwise. Such other rights might comprise the right to Delay Damages under Sub-Clause 8.8 or other damages at law resulting from breach of contract and the Contractor's failure to complete the remedial work but subject to Sub-Clause 1.15 [*Limitation of Liability*].

(iv) Related Law: Under the common law, the remedy provided for in sub-paragraph (a) (requiring that the work be carried out in the manner required under the Contract, also referred to as the 'cost to cure' or the 'cost to repair') is the normal starting position in a claim for damages arising from the Contractor's defective or incomplete work.[69] It satisfies the Employer's 'expectation interest' as it puts the Employer in the position which it would have been in had the Contractor properly performed the Contract. However, this remedy of damages will not be appropriate in all cases (e.g., where the cost of replacement would be wholly disproportionate to the advantages of replacement and constitute 'economic waste').[70] Consequently, the remedy provided for in sub-paragraph (b) (reduced value of the completed work due to the breach of contract) is also frequently used.[71] Proof of diminution in value is

69. Philip Bruner and Patrick O'Connor, *Bruner and O'Connor on Construction Law* (Thomson Reuters, St Paul, MN, 2016) vol 6, 375-379 (s 19:80) and Atkin Chambers, *Hudson's Building and Engineering Contracts* (14th edn, Sweet & Maxwell, London, 2020) 828, para. 7-008.

70. *See Jacob & Youngs v Kent* 230 NY 239 (1921), *per* Cardozo J. In that case it was discovered after completion of a house that the contractor had inadvertently substituted a different brand of pipe from the one specified. Finding that the pipe substituted was of equal quality to that specified, the court concluded that the owner was not entitled to 'the cost of replacement, which would be great [as it would have involved demolition of 'substantial parts' of the house], but the difference in value, which would be either nominal or nothing'. The court found that the owner is entitled to the cost of replacement:

> unless the cost of completion is grossly and unfairly out of proportion to the good to be attained. When that is true, the measure is the difference in value.

English law appears to be to the same effect. *See Ruxley Electronics and Construction Ltd v Forsyth* [1996] A.C. 344 which cites *Jacob & Youngs* with approval (while providing a further possible basis of damages, loss of amenity) and Atkin Chambers, *Hudson's Building and Engineering Contracts* (14th edn, Sweet & Maxwell, London, 2020) 828-831 (paras 7-008 to 7-011).

71. Philip Bruner and Patrick O'Connor, *Bruner and O'Connor on Construction Law* (Thomson Reuters, St Paul, MN, 2016) vol 6, 380-381 (s 19:81) and

ordinarily provided for by the opinions of independent appraisers or experts as to the extent to which the value of the Works is impacted by the defective items or matters.[72]

The UNIDROIT Principles are to similar effect. Whereas a party in the position of the Employer would ordinarily be entitled, upon a breach of contract by the Contractor, to require the Contractor to perform the Contract (i.e., rectify the defect of damage), it could not require the Contractor to do so where performance would be 'unreasonably burdensome or expensive'.[73] A commentary on the Principles has stated:

> the major factor which should be taken into account is the **proportionality** between the expenses which the non-performing party [the Contractor] has now to incur in order to render performance, and the actual value of the contract. Thus, when the cost of performance to the non-performing party is out of proportion to the benefit which performance will confer on the aggrieved party [the Employer], an order to perform [...] will be denied.[74] (Emphasis in the original)

Accordingly, while Sub-Clause 11.4 does not establish a hierarchy of remedies but leaves the choice from among them to the sole discretion of the Employer, the position may be different under applicable law.[75]

(v) Improvements: As indicated under **(iv) Related Law** above, to avoid the objection of 'economic waste', it might be provided that, where the cost of performance under sub-paragraph (a) is out of proportion to the benefit which performance will confer on the Employer, another remedy, such as sub-paragraph (b), should be the preferred and apply.

--ooOOoo--

Atkin Chambers, *Hudson's Building and Engineering Contracts* (14th edn, Sweet & Maxwell, London, 2020) 828 (para. 7-008).

72. Philip Bruner and Patrick O'Connor, *Bruner and O'Connor on Construction Law* (Thomson Reuters, St Paul, MN, 2016) vol 6, 383 (s 19:81).
73. Art. 7.2.2 (*Performance of non-monetary obligation)* of the UNIDROIT Principles.
74. Stefan Vogenauer (ed), *Commentary on the UNIDROIT Principles of International Commercial Contracts (PICC)* (2nd edn, OUP, Oxford, 2015) 894 (para. 27).
75. While Sub-Clause 11.4(a) entitles the Employer only to costs 'reasonably incurred by the Employer in remedying the defect', this relates solely to costs incurred in exercising the remedy under sub-para. (a) and not in deciding which of the remedies (whether sub-paras (a) to (d)) to exercise.

11.5 Remedying of Defective Work off Site

If, during the DNP, the Contractor considers that any defect or damage in any Plant cannot be remedied expeditiously on the Site the Contractor shall give a Notice, with reasons, to the Employer requesting consent to remove the defective or damaged Plant off the Site for the purposes of repair. This Notice shall clearly identify each item of defective or damaged Plant, and shall give details of:

(a) the defect or damage to be repaired;
(b) the place to which defective or damaged Plant is to be taken for repair;
(c) the transportation to be used (and insurance cover for such transportation);
(d) the proposed inspections and testing off the Site;
(e) the planned duration required before the repaired Plant shall be returned to the Site; and
(f) the planned duration for reinstallation and retesting of the repaired Plant (under Sub-Clause 7.4 [*Testing by the Contractor*] and/or Clause 9 [*Tests on Completion*] if applicable).

The Contractor shall also provide any further details that the Employer may reasonably require.

When the Employer gives consent (which consent shall not relieve the Contractor from any obligation or responsibility under this Clause), the Contractor may remove from the Site such items of Plant as are defective or damaged. As a condition of this consent, the Employer may require the Contractor to increase the amount of the Performance Security by the full replacement cost of the defective or damaged Plant.

If, during the DNP, the Contractor considers that a defect or damage in any Plant cannot be remedied expeditiously on the Site, the Contractor may request, by a Notice, with reasons, the Employer's consent to remove the Plant off the Site for repair. The Notice must identify the defective Plant and contain the details described in sub-paragraphs (a) to (f). The Contractor must also provide any further details reasonably required by the Employer.

The Contractor may remove the defective Plant from the Site after the Employer gives consent, who in turn may require the Contractor to increase the Performance Security.

<u>Commentary</u>

(i) Main Changes from RB/99:

(1) Unlike Sub-Clause 11.5 of RB/99, the new Sub-Clause provides that if, during the DNP, the Contractor considers that any defect or damage in Plant cannot be remedied on the Site, it must give a Notice to the Employer, with reasons, requesting consent to remove the Plant concerned and containing the detailed information listed in sub-paragraphs (a) to (f).

(2) Unlike RB/99, the new Sub-Clause authorises the Employer to require further details.

(3) Unlike RB/99 under which the Employer could, as a condition to granting consent, require the Contractor to either increase the amount of the Performance Security or provide other appropriate security, the new Sub-Clause entitles the Employer to require an increase of the amount of the Performance Security only.

(4) Unlike RB/99, the new Sub-Clause provides that the Employer's consent will not relieve the Contractor from any obligation or responsibility under this Clause.

(ii) Related Clauses / Sub-Clauses: 1.3 [*Notices and Other Communications*], 4.2.2 [*Performance Security – Claims under the Performance Security*], 7.4 [*Testing by the Contractor*], 7.7 [*Ownership of Plant and Materials*], 9 [*Tests on Completion*] and 11 [*Defects after Taking Over*].

(iii) Analysis:

(1) Purpose of Sub-Clause

This Sub-Clause establishes the procedure to enable the Contractor to remove any Plant from the Site during the DNP when the Contractor considers this necessary to remedy any defect or damage in the Plant which cannot be remedied expeditiously on the Site.[76] In the case of more

76. As Plant is more important in the Yellow and Silver Book contracts than a Red Book contract, this Sub-Clause, which also appears in those contracts, is likely to have less application in RB/17.

sophisticated Plant (e.g., gas turbines or electrical transformers), this is understandable as the Contractor may not have the necessary resources to remedy it on the Site.

(2) Contractor's Notice

If the Contractor considers that a defect or damage in any Plant cannot be remedied expeditiously on the Site, it must give a Notice to the Employer, with reasons, requesting the Employer's consent to the removal of the Plant, and identifying each item of the defective or damaged Plant. Such consent is required as, among other things, the Plant is likely now to be Employer's property.[77] The Notice must set out the details described in sub-paragraphs (a) to (f),[78] and the Employer may reasonably require further details.

(3) Employer's consent

As a condition to its consent, the Employer may require the Contractor to increase the amount of the Performance Security by the full replacement cost of the defective or damaged Plant, as a security against further damage to the Plant that may occur during its removal, transportation, repair, retesting and/or reinstallation on the Site.[79] However, the Employer's consent cannot be unreasonably withheld or delayed.[80]

The Employer may refuse to give its consent if it has reasonable grounds to believe that the remedial work may be carried out expeditiously on the Site. Any disagreement between the Parties on this subject may develop into a Claim under Sub-Clause 20.1(c), which the Engineer must agree or determine under Sub-Clause 3.7 [*Agreement or Determination*].

--ooOOoo--

77. *See* Sub-Clause 7.7 [*Ownership of Plant and Materials*].
78. And comply with Sub-Clause 1.3 [*Notices and Other Communications*].
79. The Employer's consent will not relieve the Contractor from any of its obligations under Clause 11 (under Sub-Clause 11.5, third paragraph), just as under Sub-Clauses 3.2 [*Engineer's Duties and Authority*] actions of the Engineer do not relieve the Contractor of its contractual obligations. *See* the last paragraph of Sub-Clause 3.2 [*Engineer's Duties and Authority*].
80. As 'consent' is 'another type of communication' under Sub-Clause 1.3 [*Notices and Other Communications*], it must also otherwise comply with that Sub-Clause.

11.6 Further Tests after Remedying Defects

Within 7 days of completion of the work of remedying of any defect or damage, the Contractor shall give a Notice to the Engineer describing the remedied Works, Section, Part and/or Plant and the proposed repeated tests (under Clause 9 [*Tests on Completion*]). Within 7 days after receiving this Notice, the Engineer shall give a Notice to the Contractor either:

(a) agreeing with such proposed testing; or
(b) instructing the repeated tests that are necessary to demonstrate that the remedied Works, Section, Part and/or Plant comply with the Contract.

If the Contractor fails to give such a Notice within the 7 days, the Engineer may give a Notice to the Contractor, within 14 days after the defect or damage is remedied, instructing the repeated tests that are necessary to demonstrate that the remedied Works, Section, Part and/or Plant comply with the Contract.

All repeated tests under this Sub-Clause shall be carried out in accordance with the terms applicable to the previous tests, except that they shall be carried out at the risk and cost of the Party liable, under Sub-Clause 11.2 [*Cost of Remedying Defects*], for the cost of the remedial work.

Within 7 days of completion of any remedial work, the Contractor shall give a Notice to the Engineer describing the remedied Works and the proposed repeated Tests on Completion. Within a further 7 days, the Engineer shall, by a Notice, either agree with the proposed testing or instruct the repeated tests necessary to demonstrate compliance with the Contract.

If the Contractor fails to give such Notice, the Engineer may give a Notice to the Contractor within 14 days after the defect or damage is remedied, instructing the repeated tests that are necessary. All repeated tests shall be carried out in accordance with the previous tests at the risk and cost of the Party liable, under Sub-Clause 11.2, for the cost of the remedial work.

Commentary

(i) Main Changes from RB/99:

(1) Under Sub-Clause 11.6 of RB/99, '[i]f the work of remedying of any defect or damage may affect the performance of the Works', the Engineer has the discretion to decide whether to require the repetition of any tests described in the Contract. On the other hand, under the new Sub-Clause, within 7 days of completion of *any* remedial work, the Contractor must give a Notice to the Engineer describing the remedied Works, Section, Part and/or Plant and repeated tests (under Clause 9) which it proposes. Within 7 days thereafter, the Engineer must give a Notice to the Contractor either agreeing with such proposed testing or instructing the repeated tests which it considers necessary.

(2) Whereas Sub-Clause 11.6 of RB/99 referred to the repetition of 'any of the tests described in the Contract', the new Sub-Clause in its first paragraph refers to repetition of Tests on Completion.

(3) Although RB/99 had provided for a notice from the Engineer (within 28 days after the remedied work), the provisions requiring the giving of Notice(s) by the Engineer in the first and second paragraphs are new.

(ii) Related Clauses / Sub-Clauses: 1.3 [*Notices and Other Communications*], 7.4 [*Testing by the Contractor*], 7.5 [*Defects and Rejection*], 9 [*Tests on Completion*] and 11 [*Defects after Taking Over*].

(iii) Analysis:

(1) Purpose of Sub-Clause

This Sub-Clause sets out the procedure for the repetition of Tests on Completion by the Contractor after any defect or damage in the Works, Section, Part or Plant has been repaired. It applies regardless of which Party has to bear the risk and cost of repair under Sub-Clause 11.2.

(2) Sub-Clause procedure

Within 7 days of completion of any work of remedying any defect or damage (at least of which the Employer had given the Contractor Notice under Sub-Clause 11.1), the Contractor is required to give a Notice to the Engineer describing such work and 'the proposed repeated tests (under

Clause 9 [*Tests on Completion*])'.[81] Within 7 days after receiving the Contractor's Notice, the Engineer must respond by either agreeing with the Contractor's proposal or instructing 'the repeated tests' (i.e., Tests on Completion) which, in the view of the Engineer, are 'necessary to demonstrate that the [remedied works] comply with the Contract'.

If the Contractor has failed to give such a Notice within 7 days of completion of remedial work, the Engineer may give a Notice to the Contractor, within 14 days after the defect or damage is remedied, instructing 'the repeated tests' which, in the Engineer's view, are necessary to demonstrate compliance with the Contract. *However, it is not clear how the Engineer can be sure to meet this 14-day deadline if the Contractor has failed to give a Notice of the completion of remedial work.* It is assumed that the Engineer will necessarily know when remedial work has been completed, but will it?

All repeated Tests on Completion must be carried out in accordance with the terms applicable to the previous tests,[82] except that this should be done at the risk and cost of the Party liable, pursuant to Sub-Clause 11.2, for the cost of the remedial work. If the Contractor considers that none of the sub-paragraphs of Sub-Clause 11.2 applies and that it is entitled to be paid for the repeated tests, it should comply with the Engineer's instruction and assert a Claim under Sub-Clause 20.1(b) or (c), as may be appropriate.

Completion of all tests, including the remedying of any defects, is an express condition to issuance of the Performance Certificate under Sub-Clause 11.9.

(iv) Improvements:

(1) While this Sub-Clause appears to relate exclusively to Tests on Completion (*see* the first and last paragraphs), if this is correct, its exact scope could be made clearer by an explicit statement to this effect.

81. *See* George Rosenberg, Clause 11: Defects After Taking Over, 5, at http://corbett.co.uk/wp-content/uploads/Clause-11-Defects-After-Taking-Over.pdf accessed 10 November 2022. In an example given by that author, if there has been physical damage to a structure repaired during the DNP, there is unlikely to be a Test on Completion but there might be other tests specified elsewhere in the Contract.

82. This should ordinarily mean those specified in the Contract, agreed by the Parties or instructed as a Variation, *see* Sub-Clause 1.1.83 '**Tests on Completion**'.

(2) Where the Contractor has failed to give a Notice within 7 days after any defect or damage has been remedied, it needs to be clarified how the Engineer can be sure to know when a defect or damage has been remedied so that it can give a Notice within the required 14 days instructing the repeated tests which it considers are necessary.

--ooOOoo--

11.7 Right of Access after Taking Over

Until the date 28 days after issue of the Performance Certificate, the Contractor shall have the right of access to the Works as is reasonably required in order to comply with this Clause, except as may be inconsistent with the Employer's reasonable security restrictions.

Whenever the Contractor intends to access any part of the Works during the relevant DNP:

(a) the Contractor shall request access by giving a Notice to the Employer, describing the parts of the Works to be accessed, the reasons for such access, and the Contractor's preferred date for access. This Notice shall be given in reasonable time in advance of the preferred date for access, taking due regard of all relevant circumstances including the Employer's security restrictions; and

(b) within 7 days after receiving the Contractor's Notice, the Employer shall give a Notice to the Contractor either:

    (i) stating the Employer's consent to the Contractor's request; or

    (ii) proposing reasonable alternative date(s), with reasons. If the Employer fails to give this Notice within the 7 days, the Employer shall be deemed to have given consent to the Contractor's access on the preferred date stated in the Contractor's Notice.

If the Contractor incurs additional Cost as a result of any unreasonable delay by the Employer in permitting access to the Works by the Contractor, the Contractor shall be entitled subject to Sub-Clause 20.2 [*Claims for Payment and/or EOT*] to payment of any such Cost Plus Profit.

Until 28 days after issue of the Performance Certificate, the Contractor will have right of access to the Works to comply with Clause 11, except as inconsistent with the Employer's security restrictions.

The Contractor must give a Notice to the Employer whenever it intends to access the Works, describing, among other things, its preferred date for access with reasons. Within 7 days the Employer must by a Notice either consent or propose alternative date(s) with reasons. If the Employer fails to give such Notice, it will be deemed to have consented to the access requested by the Contractor.

If the Contractor incurs Cost as a result of any unreasonable delay by the Employer in permitting access, it will be entitled, subject to Sub-Clause 20.2, to Cost Plus Profit.

<u>**Commentary**</u>

(i) Main Changes from RB/99:

(1) Unlike Sub-Clause 11.7 of RB/99 which envisaged that the Contractor would be entitled to access the Works only until the issue of the Performance Certificate, the new Sub-Clause extends this right to 28 days after issue of the Performance Certificate.
(2) The second and third paragraphs of the Sub-Clause are new.

(ii) Related Clauses / Sub-Clauses: 1.3 [*Notices and Other Communications*], 1.13 [*Compliance with Laws*], 4.21 [*Security of the Site*], 4.22 [*Contractor's Operations on Site*], 10.2 [*Taking Over Parts*], 11 [*Defects after Taking Over*] and 20.2 [*Claims for Payment and/or EOT*].

(iii) Analysis:

(1) Purpose of Sub-Clause

After the issue of a Taking-Over Certificate, the Contractor is expected to leave the part of the Site and Works to which the Taking-Over Certificate relates.[83] However, as the Contractor will need access to fulfil its Clause 11 obligations (e.g., completing any outstanding work and remedying defects or damage), this Sub-Clause provides for the Contractor's right to such access.[84]

Under the first paragraph, the Contractor has a right of access to the Works until 28 days after the issue of the Performance Certificate. This ensures that the Contractor has the time to fulfil, among other things, its obligations under Sub-Clause 11.11 [*Clearance of Site*] which are to be fulfilled after issue of the Performance Certificate.

The Employer is only required to provide access to the extent that is 'reasonably required' by the Contractor to comply with Clause 11 and is consistent with 'the Employer's reasonable security restrictions'. What is reasonable will depend on, among other things, the security situation at the Site (as may be described in the Specification) and the nature of the Employer's occupation, use and/or operation of the Works.

(2) Procedure for access and Cost

The second paragraph sets out the procedure for giving access.[85] The Contractor is required to give a Notice to the Employer in reasonable time in advance with reasons, describing the parts of the Works to be accessed and the preferred date for access. Within 7 days, the Employer must respond by a Notice either giving the Employer's consent or proposing reasonable alternative date(s), with reasons.[86] The Employer is not authorised to respond in any other way. The Employer's failure to respond within 7 days will result in the Employer's deemed consent to the requested access on the preferred date(s) stated in the Contractor's Notice.

83. Third paragraph of Sub-Clause 4.22 [*Contractor's Operations on Site*].
84. If the Employer should not provide such access, it may lose the ability to sanction the Contractor, pursuant to Sub-Clause 11.4, for failing to perform remedial work and, instead, may be exposed to a Claim from the Contractor under Sub-Clause 20.2. *The FIDIC Contracts Guide* (2nd edn, FIDIC, 2022) 330.
85. The World Bank's COPA, correctly, provides that the beginning of the second paragraph should be replaced by: 'Whenever, until the date 28 days after issue of the Performance Certificate, the Contractor intends to access any part of the Works': this makes it consistent with the first paragraph.
86. Both Notices as well as the Employer's consent must comply with the requirements set out in Sub-Clause 1.3 [*Notices and Other Communications*].

Under the last paragraph, the Contractor is entitled – for the first time explicitly in RB/17 and subject to Sub-Clause 20.2 – to Cost Plus Profit if it has incurred Cost as a result of 'unreasonable delay' by the Employer in permitting access to the Works. What is unreasonable delay is a matter of fact. For example, the Employer's refusal to give access on the preferred date requested by the Contractor without valid reason may result in unreasonable delay.

(iv) Related Law: Construction projects under the Red Book are often located in dangerous and/or unstable regions of the world and/or may be of national or strategic importance, e.g., airports, dams, hydroelectric or nuclear projects. Consequently, obtaining access to them may not be a straightforward matter. Therefore, in addition to obtaining the Employer's consent to access and to respecting the Employer's security restrictions, there may be national laws and regulations relating to security or other matters which would have to be complied for access to the Works, including permitted means of access, e.g., whether by air, road, sea or otherwise.[87]

--ooOOoo--

11.8 Contractor to Search

The Contractor shall, if instructed by the Engineer, search for the cause of any defect, under the direction of the Engineer. The Contractor shall carry out the search on the date(s) stated in the Engineer's instruction or other date(s) agreed with the Engineer.

Unless the defect is to be remedied at the cost of the Contractor under Sub-Clause 11.2 [*Cost of Remedying Defects*], the Contractor shall be entitled subject to Sub-Clause 20.2 [*Claims for Payment and/or EOT*] to payment of the Cost Plus Profit of the search.

If the Contractor fails to carry out the search in accordance with this Sub-Clause, the search may be carried out by the Employer's Personnel. The Contractor shall be given a Notice of the date when such a search will be carried out and the Contractor may attend at the Contractor's own cost. If the

87. *See* Sub-Clause 1.13 [*Compliance with Laws*].

> defect is to be remedied at the cost of the Contractor under Sub-Clause 11.2 [*Cost of Remedying Defects*], the Employer shall be entitled subject to Sub-Clause 20.2 [*Claims for Payment and/or EOT*] to payment by the Contractor of the costs of the search reasonably incurred by the Employer.

The Contractor shall, if instructed by the Engineer, search for the cause of any defect under the Engineer's direction and on the date(s) stated in the Engineer's instruction or other date(s) agreed with the Engineer. The Contractor is entitled, subject to Sub-Clause 20.2, to the Cost Plus Profit of the search, unless the defect is to be remedied at the Contractor's cost under Sub-Clause 11.2.

If the Contractor fails to carry out the search, the Employer's Personnel may do so. If the defect is to be remedied at the Contractor's cost under Sub-Clause 11.2, the Employer will be entitled, subject to Sub-Clause 20.2, to recover its reasonable costs of the search.

Commentary

(i) Main Changes from RB/99:

(1) Unlike under Sub-Clause 11.8 of RB/99, under the new Sub-Clause the Engineer must 'instruct' the search and the Contractor must carry it out on the date(s) stated in the Engineer's instruction or other date(s) agreed with the Engineer.

(2) Whereas, under RB/99, unless the defect was to be remedied at the cost of the Contractor under Sub-Clause 11.2, the Cost of the search plus reasonable profit was to be agreed or determined by the Engineer under Sub-Clause 3.5 and included in the Contract Price,[88] the new Sub-Clause provides that in such cases the Contractor is entitled, subject to Sub-Clause 20.2, to the Cost Plus Profit of the search.

(3) The last paragraph of the new Sub-Clause is new.

88. It was unclear under Sub-Clause 11.8 of RB/99 whether the claims procedure in Sub-Clause 20.1 had to be complied with as a condition to entitling the Contractor to payment under that Sub-Clause.

(ii) Related Clauses / Sub-Clauses: 1.3 [*Notices and Other Communications*], 3.5 [*Engineer's Instructions*], 11 [*Defects after Taking Over*] and 20.2 [*Claims for Payment and/or EOT*].

(iii) Analysis: This Sub-Clause applies where the Engineer has identified a 'defect' (or what it considers to be one)[89] whose apparent cause is unknown, as it often may be. The Engineer is authorised to instruct the Contractor to search for the cause under the Engineer's direction and on date(s) instructed by or agreed with the Engineer.[90] Establishing the cause will help to determine who is liable for the defect and the remedial measures which may be appropriate. As the Contractor will have executed (and may partly have designed) the Works, no one is likely to be in a better position to identify the cause than the Contractor.

Whether the Contractor agrees or not that there is a defect, it must comply with the Engineer's instruction.[91] While carrying out a search may be costly and/or time-consuming, the Contractor cannot claim merely on this account, as it has the contractual obligation to search, whatever the cause of a defect may be.

The search will be carried out at the Contractor's cost if the defect is attributable to the matters listed in the first paragraph of Sub-Clause 11.2. Accordingly, so long as there is a reasonable possibility that the defect may be attributable to the Contractor under such paragraph, the Contractor should be allowed to choose – or at least be consulted by the Engineer about – the search methods to be used for finding the cause.[92] Alternatively, if the Contractor clearly is not responsible for the defect, the Contractor should not necessarily have the right to choose the method, and in this case, the Contractor will be entitled, subject to Sub-Clause 20.2, to Cost Plus Profit for searching for the defect.

If the Contractor fails to carry out the search (e.g., because it denies that there is a defect and therefore believes, incorrectly, that it is not required to do so), the Employer's Personnel is authorised to do so, although they may be, without specialist support, less qualified to do so than the Contractor. The Employer will be entitled, also subject to Sub-Clause

89. No reference is made (as in the previous Sub-Clauses of Clause 11 of RB/17) to 'damage', possibly because identifying the cause of damage is less likely to require the special knowledge and resources of the Contractor.
90. The Engineer's instruction must comply with Sub-Clause 1.3 [*Notices and Other Communications*].
91. Sub-Clause 3.5, second paragraph.
92. *See The FIDIC Contracts Guide* (2nd edn, FIDIC, 2022) 331.

20.2, to the costs reasonably incurred if the defect is to be remedied at the Contractor's cost under Sub-Clause 11.2. If the defect is to be remedied at the Employer's cost, it will bear the costs of the search.

--ooOOoo--

11.9 Performance Certificate

> Performance of the Contractor's obligations under the Contract shall not be considered to have been completed until the Engineer has issued the Performance Certificate to the Contractor, stating the date on which the Contractor fulfilled the Contractor's obligations under the Contract.
>
> The Engineer shall issue the Performance Certificate to the Contractor (with a copy to the Employer and to the DAAB) within 28 days after the latest of the expiry dates of the Defects Notification Periods, or as soon thereafter as the Contractor has:
>
> (a) supplied all the Contractor's Documents; and
> (b) completed and tested all the Works (including remedying any defects) in accordance with the Contract.
>
> If the Engineer fails to issue the Performance Certificate within this period of 28 days, the Performance Certificate shall be deemed to have been issued on the date 28 days after the date on which it should have been issued, as required by this Sub-Clause.
>
> Only the Performance Certificate shall be deemed to constitute acceptance of the Works.

Performance of the Contractor's obligations shall not be considered complete until the Engineer has issued the Performance Certificate. The Engineer shall do so within 28 days after the latest of the expiry dates of the DNPs, or as soon thereafter as the Contractor has supplied all the Contractor's Documents and completed and tested all the Works (including remedying defects). If the Engineer fails to do so, the Certificate will be deemed to have been issued on the date 28 days after the date on which it should have been issued.

Only the Performance Certificate shall be deemed to constitute acceptance of the Works.

Commentary

(i) Main Changes from RB/99:

(1) Unlike Sub-Clause 11.9 of RB/99, the new Sub-Clause envisages that a copy of the Performance Certificate must also be given to the DAAB.
(2) The second paragraph has been broken down to include two sub-paragraphs, (a) and (b), and the words 'in accordance with the Contract' have been added at the end of sub-paragraph (b).
(3) The third paragraph of the Sub-Clause, providing for the deemed issue of the Performance Certificate, is new.

(ii) Related Clauses / Sub-Clauses: 1.3 [*Notices and Other Communications*], 3.2 [*Engineer's Duty and Authority*], 4.2.1 [*Contractor's Obligations*], 4.2.3 [*Return of the Performance Security*], 4.4 [*Contractor's Documents*], 6.8 [*Contractor's Superintendence*], 11 [*Defects after Taking Over*], 14.9 [*Release of Retention Money*], 14.11.1 [*Draft Final Statement*], 19.2.1 [*The Works*] and 19.2.4 [*Injury to Persons and Damage to Property*]

(iii) Analysis:

(1) Nature of a Performance Certificate

The Performance Certificate is the document issued (or deemed to be issued) by the Engineer[93] which confirms that the Engineer: (i) considers that the Contractor has performed its obligations under the Contract[94] and (ii) accepts the Works.[95] It must state the date on which the Contractor fulfilled its obligations under the Contract.[96]

93. While not stated in this Sub-Clause, when issuing the Performance Certificate, the Engineer should act neutrally and fairly, for the reasons given in (2) *When exercising discretion the Engineer must act fairly* under **(iii) Analysis** of the commentary on Sub-Clause 3.2 [*Engineer's Duties and Authority*] above.
94. Sub-Clause 11.9, first paragraph.
95. Sub-Clause 11.9, last paragraph.
96. Sub-Clause 11.9, first paragraph. *The FIDIC Contracts Guide* (2nd edn, FIDIC, 2022) 334 contains a form of Performance Certificate.

However, like any document issued by the Engineer, it does not relieve the Contractor from any duty, obligation or responsibility under the Contract[97] and may be revised later on by the DAAB[98] or in arbitration.[99] Therefore, if the Contractor should, in fact, have failed to perform a duty under the Contract, it cannot take refuge in the Performance Certificate.

(2) Procedure for the issue of a Performance Certificate

The Engineer must issue the Performance Certificate to the Contractor[100] within 28 days after 'the latest' of the expiry dates (i.e., the last and final expiry date) of the DNPs for all the Works,[101] or 'as soon thereafter' (i.e., after the period of 28 days) as the Contractor has supplied all Contractor's Documents[102] and completed and tested all Works, including remedying of defects, in accordance with the Contract.[103] The Engineer may withhold the Performance Certificate if any of the above conditions has not been fulfilled.

---

97. Sub-Clause 3.2 [*Engineer's Duties and Authority*], last paragraph.
98. Rule 5.1(k) of the DAAB Rules annexed to the General Conditions of DAAB Agreement in RB/17.
99. *See* Sub-Clause 21.6, second paragraph, providing that the arbitrator(s) shall have full power to open up, review and revise 'any certificate [...] of the Engineer [...] relevant to the Dispute'.
100. With a copy to the Employer and the DAAB. Sub-Clause 11.9, second paragraph.
101. This takes account of the effect of Sub-Clause 11.3 [*Extension of Defects Notification Period*] on different DNPs. *The FIDIC Contracts Guide* (2nd edn, FIDIC, 2022) 333.
102. *See* the commentaries on Sub-Clauses 1.1.15 '**Contractor's Documents**' and 4.4 [*Contractor's Documents*] above. While the Contractor is required to have supplied all of the Contractor's Documents, they are not necessarily all required to have been subject of a Notice of No-objection from the Engineer. However, under Sub-Clause 10.1, the Engineer's Notice of No-objection with regard to the as-built records and operation and maintenance manuals is required as a precondition to taking over of the Works (assuming that they are required by the Specification to be submitted by the Contractor).
103. A DNP may relate to the Works as a whole, a Section or Part, as may be extended under Sub-Clause 11.3. *See* Sub-Clause 1.1.27 '**Defects Notification Period**' or '**DNP**'. The period of 28 days is said to allow time for a joint inspection of the Works and for the Contractor to complete any outstanding work. *See* Brian Barr and Leo Grutters, *FIDIC Users' Guide: A Practical Guide to the Red, Yellow, MDB Harmonised and Subcontract Books* (3rd edn, ICE Publishing, London, 2014) 194.

On the other hand, if the required conditions have been fulfilled, the Engineer is obliged to issue the Performance Certificate at the prescribed time without the Contractor having to apply for it.

(3) Deemed issue of a Performance Certificate

If the Engineer fails to issue the Performance Certificate within 28 days after the latest of the expiry dates of the DNPs although the Contractor has completed all its obligations, it is provided that the Performance Certificate shall be deemed to have been issued on the date 28 days after the date on which 'it should have been issued'. However, as the Engineer is required to issue the Performance Certificate 'within' 28 days after the latest of the expiry dates of the DNPs, it is not clear on what day the Performance Certificate 'should have been issued'[104] and, consequently, on what date it should be deemed to have been issued, as it is deemed to have been issued 'on the date 28 days after the date on which it should have been issued'.

Where the Engineer has not issued the Performance Certificate within 28 days after the latest of the expiry dates of the DNPs because the Contractor has not supplied all the Contractor's Documents or completed tests of all the Works, the Engineer is required to issue the Performance Certificate 'as soon thereafter as the Contractor' has supplied such documents and completed such tests. If the Engineer should fail to do so, it would appear that the Performance Certificate would be deemed to have been issued in that case 'on the date 28 days after the date' on which the Contractor has supplied all such documents and completed such tests.

(4) Consequences of the issue of the Performance Certificate

The last paragraph states that '[o]nly' the Performance Certificate will be deemed to constitute acceptance of the Works. It is common for the Works to be taken over in Sections or parts, each giving rise to a separate Taking-Over Certificate and, consequently, to a separate DNP.[105] However, this Sub-Clause makes it clear that only the Performance Certificate which is issued after the expiration of the last DNP to occur under the

---

104. As it could have been issued at any time within those 28 days.
105. *See* the commentaries on Sub-Clauses 10.1 [*Taking Over the Works and Sections*] and 10.2 [*Taking Over Parts*] above.

Contract establishes – provisionally at least, as indicated above – that the Contractor has fulfilled its contractual obligations.[106]

The following are the other principal consequences of the issue of the Performance Certificate:

- The Contractor has no longer to maintain the validity of the Performance Security, and the Employer must return it within 21 days, provided that the Contractor has complied with its obligations under Sub-Clause 11.11 [*Clearance of Site*].[107]
- The Contractor has no longer to provide superintendence of the Works.[108]
- The Contractor's right of access to the Works will cease after 28 days.[109]
- Each Party remains liable for the fulfilment of any unperformed obligation.[110]
- The Contractor must clear the Site within 28 days.[111]
- The Contractor may apply for the release of the second half of the Retention Money.[112]
- The insurance cover for the Works to be provided by the Contractor may be allowed to lapse.[113]
- Third-party liability insurance to be provided by the Contractor may be allowed to lapse.[114]

106. Subject to what is stated in the second paragraph under *(1) Nature of a Performance Certificate* above of this commentary on Sub-Clause 11.9. *See also Guide to the Use of FIDIC Conditions of Contract for Works of Civil Engineering Construction, fourth edition*, FIDIC, 1989, 142, commenting on Sub-Clause 61.1 of RB/87 (dealing with the Defects Liability Certificate, the precursor of the Performance Certificate, and which had the same consequence).
107. Sub-Clause 4.2.3 [*Performance Security – Return of the Performance Security*].
108. Sub-Clause 6.8 [*Contractor's Superintendence*].
109. Sub-Clause 11.7 [*Right of Access after Taking Over*].
110. Sub-Clause 11.10 [*Unfulfilled Obligations*].
111. Sub-Clause 11.11 [*Clearance of Site*].
112. If not already applied for. Sub-Clause 14.9 [*Release of Retention Money*].
113. Sub-Clause 19.2.1 [*Insurance to Be Provided by the Contractor – The Works*].
114. Sub-Clause 19.2.4 [*Insurance to Be Provided by the Contractor – Injury to Persons and Damage to Property*].

- The Contractor must submit a draft final Statement to the Engineer within 56 days.[115]

(iv) Related Law:

Notwithstanding the issue of the Performance Certificate, the Contractor will remain liable at law for defects in the Works for the duration of whatever limitation period may apply.[116] In addition, in France and certain other civil law jurisdictions, as a matter of mandatory law, a Contractor will be absolutely liable (i.e., liable without proof of fault) for defects impairing the stability of the work for a period of 10 years after its completion.[117]

(v) Improvements:

(1) As explained under heading *(3) Deemed issue of a Performance Certificate* of **(iii) Analysis** above, in relation to the third paragraph, it needs to be clarified on what date the Performance Certificate is deemed to have been issued.

(2) For the same reason that the Engineer should be expected to act 'fairly' when issuing a Taking-Over Certificate (as explained in item (2) under **(v) Improvements** of the commentary on Sub-Clause 10.1 [*Taking Over the Works and Sections*]), the Engineer should do so when issuing the Performance Certificate - and Sub-Clause 11.9 should so provide.

--ooOOoo--

11.10 Unfulfilled Obligations

> After the issue of the Performance Certificate, each Party shall remain liable for the fulfilment of any obligation which remains unperformed at that time. For the purposes of determining the nature and

115. Sub-Clause 14.11.1 [*Final Statement - Draft Final Statement*].
116. *See* **Section 4 Common Law and Civil Law Compared – 4.5.3 Limitation Periods** in **Chapter II Applicable Law** above.
117. *See* **Section 4 Common Law and Civil Law Compared – 4.4.4 Decennial Liability** in **Chapter II Applicable Law** above. *See also* the commentary on Sub-Clause 11.10 [*Unfulfilled Obligations*] below.

extent of unperformed obligations, the Contract shall be deemed to remain in force.

However in relation to Plant, the Contractor shall not be liable for any defects or damage occurring more than two years after expiry of the DNP for the Plant except if prohibited by law or in any case of fraud, gross negligence, deliberate default or reckless misconduct.

After the issue of the Performance Certificate, each Party shall remain liable for the fulfilment of any unperformed obligations except that the Contractor will not be liable for any defects or damage to Plant occurring more than two years after the expiry of the DNP for the Plant.

Commentary

(i) Main Changes from RB/99: The second paragraph is new.

(ii) Related Clauses / Sub-Clauses: 1.13 [*Compliance with Laws*], 1.15 [*Limitation of Liability*], 11 [*Defects after Taking Over*], 14.14 [*Cessation of Employer's Liability*] and Clause 21 [*Disputes and Arbitration*].

(iii) Analysis*:*

(1) Liability for unperformed obligations

As provided for in Sub-Clause 11.9, the Employer is deemed to have accepted the Works upon issuance of the Performance Certificate. However, Sub-Clause 11.10 provides that thereafter each Party remains liable for the fulfilment of any unperformed obligations and for these purposes the Contract is deemed to remain in force. Unperformed obligations may arise under the Contract or at law, as described below:

a) Under the Contract

Thus, for example, the Employer must return the Performance Security to the Contractor within 21 days after issue of the Performance Certificate and after the Contractor has complied with its obligations to clear the Site under Sub-Clause 11.11.[118]

On the other hand, the Contractor must: (i) submit to the Engineer a draft final Statement under Sub-Clause 14.11.1 within 56 days after the issue of

118. Sub-Clause 4.2.3 [*Performance Security – Return of the Performance Security*].

the Performance Certificate; (ii) thereafter submit either a Final Statement or Partially Agreed Final Statement to the Engineer under Sub-Clause 14.11.2, together with a discharge under Sub-Clause 14.12; and (iii) as mentioned above, clear the Site under Sub-Clause 11.11.

The Engineer must then, pursuant to Sub-Clause 14.13, issue an FPC or an IPC and the Employer must then, under Sub-Clause 14.7, pay the amount certified, and each Party must thereafter pay any sum which may become due in respect of any Dispute submitted to a DAAB proceeding, or resolved by amicable settlement or arbitration under Clause 21.

Thereafter, subject to the exceptions stated in Sub-Clause 14.14, the Employer's liability to the Contractor in connection with the Contract or the execution of the Works is said to cease. *No similar provision in the Conditions – other than in respect of Plant*[119] *– provides, however, for the cessation of the Contractor's liability to the Employer.*

b) At law

(i) Limitation period

Subject to the Contract, each Party remains liable to the other for any legal obligations which it may have (e.g., such as a right to claim damages for breach of contract) until the expiration of the applicable limitation period fixed by law.[120] In this connection, the DNP should not be confused with a limitation period. Whereas a DNP is a *contractual period*, normally of one or two years, within which the Contractor must complete outstanding work and – and is entitled to – rectify any damage or defect of which it has been notified,[121] a limitation period is a *period established by law* either: (1) within which a right must be asserted before a tribunal, after which it becomes invalid or unenforceable (common law) or (2) that provides for the extinction of a right by the lapse of time or 'extinctive prescription' (French law). Thus, one Party's liability to the other (e.g., the Contractor's liability to the Employer) may extend for a number of years after the DNP until the expiration of the applicable limitation period, unless it has been validly limited by contract.[122]

119. As to Plant, *see (2) Liability limit for Plant* below of this commentary on Sub-Clause 11.10.

120. *See* **Section 4 Common Law and Civil Law Compared – 4.5.3 Limitation Periods** of **Chapter II Applicable Law** above.

121. Sub-Clauses 11.1 and 1.1.27 **'Defects Notification Period'** or **'DNP'**.

122. *See* the discussion under heading *(2) Liability limit for Plant* below.

Thus, if a latent defect[123] is discovered in the Works after the issuance of the Performance Certificate but before the expiration of the applicable limitation period which the Contractor refuses to remedy, the Employer may justifiably commence arbitration[124] against the Contractor in respect of that defect. However, the Employer will be in a much less favourable position to obtain relief then,[125] compared to during the DNP, as the Contractor (if foreign) may have left the Country and the Employer will no longer hold the Contractor's Performance Security and Retention Money.[126]

While the duration of national limitation periods varies widely, from 6 months to 30 years,[127] the UNIDROIT Principles provides for a 'general limitation period' of 3 years and a 'maximum limitation period' of 10 years.[128] This period begins 'on the day after the day the [person] knows or ought to know the facts as a result of which the [person's] right can be exercised'.[129]

As explained earlier,[130] a limitation period is a matter of procedural law under the common law, whereas under civil law it is a matter of substantive law and, under a FIDIC contract, this can cause uncertainty in some cases as to which country's limitation period may apply.

(ii) 'Decennial' liability

Quite apart and separate from a period of limitation, in France and in certain other civil law countries, the Contractor, the Engineer and others in contract with the Employer may, by mandatory law, have some type of 'decennial' liability to the Employer for a fixed number of years, usually ten, after completion. Under this kind of liability, the Contractor, the Engineer and others employed in the construction of a work, who have

123. That is, a defect which is hidden or not visible.
124. Assuming the DAAB's appointment has expired and Sub-Clause 21.8 [*No DAAB in Place*] therefore applies.
125. For example, by enforcing an arbitral award.
126. As they must both be released at or about the time the Performance Security is issued, *see* the commentary on Sub-Clause 11.9 [*Performance Certificate*] above.
127. UNIDROIT Principles, art. 10.2 (*Limitation periods*), official comment 1.
128. UNIDROIT Principles, art. 10.2 (*Limitation periods*).
129. *Ibid.*
130. *See* **Section 4 Common Law and Civil Law Compared – 4.5.3 Limitation Periods** in **Chapter II Applicable Law** above.

had a contract with the Employer, will be absolutely liable (i.e., liable without proof of fault) for certain defects in the Works.[131]

(2) Liability limit for Plant

Unlike RB/99, the second paragraph introduces a cut-off date in respect of the Contractor's liability for Plant:[132] two years after the expiry of the DNP, as it may be extended, for the Plant. This limitation applies unless prohibited by law or in the case of fraud, gross negligence, deliberate default or reckless misconduct.[133] Even though this is not explicitly stated,[134] the reference to law should be construed to mean mandatory law.

This new paragraph, which applies only to defects in Plant, is a welcome addition. While after the expiry of the DNP, the Contractor's liability for civil works is left to applicable law (as discussed under heading *(1)* b) At law above), its liability for Plant is treated differently, as Plant (e.g., a revolving turbine or electrical generator) is likely to have a much shorter working life than civil works (e.g., a road, dam or canal). As FIDIC noted in 2000:

> If the Works include major items of Plant, it is usually appropriate for the Contract to limit the duration of the Contractor's liability for such Plant; for example, to a stated number of years after the completion date stated in the Taking-Over Certificate. After a few years' operation, it becomes increasingly difficult to establish whether any alleged defects are attributable to the Plant's design, manufacture, manuals, operation, maintenance, or a combination of these and/or other matters.[135]

131. This type of liability is discussed in **Section 4 Common Law and Civil Law Compared – 4.4.4 Decennial Liability** in **Chapter II Applicable Law** above.
132. That is, 'apparatus, equipment, machinery and vehicles (including any components) [...] intended to form or forming part of the Permanent Works', Sub-Clause 1.1.65 '**Plant**'. Plant is to be distinguished from Materials, as defined. *See* Sub-Clause 1.1.53 '**Materials**'.
133. For a discussion of the exception for fraud, gross negligence, deliberate default or reckless misconduct *see* under *(4) Third paragraph: fraud, etc., exception* under **(iii) Analysis** of the commentary on Sub-Clause 1.15 [*Limitation of Liability*] above where similar words are used. The same expression is also in Sub-Clauses 8.8 [*Delay Damages*] and 14.14 [*Cessation of Employer's Liability*].
134. Though implied by 'prohibited'.
135. *The FIDIC Contracts Guide* (1st edn, FIDIC, 2000), 279.

In practice, Parties may often want to vary the two-year cut-off date for Plant so as to adapt it to the nature of the different types of Plant being provided. Thus, in the case of a complex project, such as hydroelectric plant, there may be separate cut-off dates for the turbines, gates and electrical transformer, respectively, depending upon the expected or agreed working life of each.

(iv) Related Law: The *Guidance* warns that it may be necessary to review the effect of this Sub-Clause, and in particular the second paragraph, in relation to the period of liability imposed by applicable law.[136] For example, the laws of some countries may provide for a longer defects liability than two years after expiry of the DNP for Plant, which are of a mandatory nature.[137]

Civil law and common law approaches to post-contractual liability for defects differ significantly. While in France and certain civil law jurisdictions the doctrine of decennial liability (as indicated above) applies,[138] in common law jurisdictions, there is no defects liability regime similar to decennial liability. Instead, the Contractor's liability for defects will continue for the period of the relevant limitation period.[139]

(v) Improvements:

(1) As users often confuse the DNP with a limitation period, it would be useful to specify in the Conditions that the DNP, which provides for a contractual time period during which the Contractor must rectify defects or damage, has no relation to any limitation period which may apply, that is, to the legal time period within which proceedings must be brought (common

136. *Guidance for the Preparation of Particular Conditions*, 35.
137. Pursuant to art. 20(4), para. 5, of Ordinance no 2 of 31 July 2003 for Commissioning of Constructions in the Republic of Bulgaria, and Minimum Warranty Periods for Executed Construction and Mounting Works and Equipment, the mandatory minimum warranty period for machines and equipment is five years from commissioning.
138. *See* **Section 4 Common Law and Civil Law Compared – 4.4.4 Decennial Liability** in **Chapter II Applicable Law** above.
139. For a detailed discussion of post-completion defects liability in common law jurisdictions, *see* Julian Bailey, *Construction Law* (3rd edn, London Publishing, UK, 2020) vol 2, 1303-1316 (paras 14.58-90). For the position specifically in the US, *see* Justin Sweet and others, *Construction Law for Design Professionals, Construction Managers, and Contractors* (Cengage Learning, Stamford, CT, 2015) 252-253, 335-336.

law) or providing for the extinction of rights by the lapse of time (French law). Some standard forms of construction contract state explicitly, for the benefit of users, that a DNP (or similar contractual period) is to be clearly distinguished from a limitation period.[140]

(2) Instead of providing for the Parties to be liable to each other for the duration of any limitation period which might by law apply, in the interest of greater certainty, it would be appropriate to establish some maximum time limit by the Contract, even for latent defects. Thus, the principal form of contract for private works in the United States provides that no claim may be asserted against a party more than 10 years after the date of Substantial Completion (as defined).[141] A maximum limitation period of 10 years, beginning on the day after the right can be exercised, is also provided for by the UNIDROIT Principles.[142]

---

140. *See*, for example, s 12.2.5 of AIA Document A201-2017, 2017, *General Conditions of the Contract for Construction*, and ss 3.9.4 and 3.9.6 of *ConsensusDocs 200 – Standard Agreement and General Conditions Between Owner and Constructor (Lump Sum Price)* – 2011, Revised 2014. Thus s 12.2.5 of the AIA form provides:

> § 12.2.5 Nothing contained in this Section 12.2 [entitled 'Correction of Work'] shall be construed to establish a period of limitation with respect to other obligations the Contractor has under the Contract Documents. Establishment of the one-year period for correction of Work as described in Section 12.2.2 relates only to the specific obligation of the Contractor to correct the Work, and has no relationship to the time within which the obligation to comply with the Contract Documents may be sought to be enforced, nor to the time within which proceedings may be commenced to establish the Contractor's liability with respect to the Contractor's obligations other than specifically to correct the Work.

141. S 15.1.2 of American Institute of Architects (AIA) Document A201-2017 *General Conditions of the Contract for Construction*. A further reason for a contractual limitation period is that national limitation periods can be anachronistic and unusually long. Thus, for example, the Austrian Civil Code (Section 1489, second sentence) provides for a 30-year limitation period for claims for damages in certain cases (as did the French Civil Code until relatively recently). On the other hand, the Austrian Code does not prohibit shortening a limitation period (Section 1502). The author is grateful to Prof. Andreas Reiner in Vienna for this information.
142. Art. 10.2 (*Limitation periods*).

The Conditions could provide for such a contractual limit, subject to applicable mandatory law.

--ooOOoo--

11.11 Clearance of Site

Promptly after the issue of the Performance Certificate, the Contractor shall:

(a) remove any remaining Contractor's Equipment, surplus material, wreckage, rubbish and Temporary Works from the Site;
(b) reinstate all parts of the Site which were affected by the Contractor's activities during the execution of the Works and are not occupied by the Permanent Works; and
(c) leave the Site and the Works in the condition stated in the Specification (if not stated, in a clean and safe condition).

If the Contractor fails to comply with sub-paragraphs (a), (b) and/or (c) above within 28 days after the issue of the Performance Certificate, the Employer may sell (to the extent permitted by applicable Laws) or otherwise dispose of any remaining items and/or may reinstate and clean the Site (as may be necessary) at the Contractor's cost.

The Employer shall be entitled subject to Sub-Clause 20.2 [*Claims for Payment and/or EOT*] to payment by the Contractor of the costs reasonably incurred in connection with, or attributable to, such sale or disposal and reinstating and/or cleaning the Site, less an amount equal to the moneys from the sale (if any).

Promptly after the issue of the Performance Certificate, the Contractor must reinstate and clear the Site as stated in sub-paragraphs (a) to (c). If it fails to do so within 28 days after issue of the Performance Certificate, the Employer may sell, if permitted by applicable Laws, or otherwise dispose of any remaining items and/or reinstate and clean

the Site at the Contractor's cost. The Employer will be entitled, subject to Sub-Clause 20.2, to payment of the costs incurred, less moneys from the sale.

Commentary

(i) Main Changes from RB/99:

(1) Whereas under Sub-Clause 11.11 of RB/99 the Contractor's obligations to clear the Site arose '[u]pon receiving the Performance Certificate', under the new Sub-Clause the Contractor must undertake the activities specified thereunder '[p]romptly after the issue of the Performance Certificate'.

(2) Sub-paragraphs (b) and (c), regarding reinstatement of parts of the Site affected by the Contractor's activities and leaving the Site clean, are new.

(3) Whereas in RB/99 the Employer's remedies in the second paragraph could be invoked if the Contractor had not cleared the Site within 28 days after the Employer's receipt of a copy of the Performance Certificate, under the new Sub-Clause these remedies are available upon the Contractor's failure to comply with sub-paragraphs (a), (b) and/or (c) within 28 days after the issue of the Performance Certificate.

(4) The Employer's remedies in the second paragraph have been expanded and include not only the Employer's right to sell or otherwise dispose of the remaining items (as in RB/99) but also the right to reinstate and clean the Site at the Contractor's cost; furthermore, the Contractor's right to sell is qualified in the new Sub-Clause by the phrase '(to the extent permitted by applicable Laws)'.

(5) Unlike RB/99, the last paragraph of the Sub-Clause explicitly states that the Employer's entitlement to reimbursement of the costs reasonably incurred is subject to the claims procedure (Sub-Clause 20.2 in RB/17).

(6) Unlike RB/99, the new Sub-Clause does not explicitly state that any balance of the money from the sale must be paid to the Contractor (if higher than the costs the Employer may recover).

(ii) Related Clauses / Sub-Clauses: 4.2.1 [*Performance Security – Contractor's Obligations*], 4.2.3 [*Performance Security – Return of the Performance Security*], 4.17 [*Contractor's Equipment*], 4.18 [*Protection of the*

Environment], 4.22 [*Contractor's Operations on Site*], 10.4 [*Surfaces Requiring Reinstatement*], 11.9 [*Performance Certificate*], 11.10 [*Unfulfilled Obligations*], 15.4 [*Payment after Termination for Contractor's Default*] and Sub-Clause 20.2 [*Claims for Payment and/or EOT*].

(iii) Analysis: After the taking over of the Works, when the Employer recovers possession of the Site, some of the Contractor's Equipment and other Goods may remain there to enable the Contractor to perform its DNP obligations.[143] Under this Sub-Clause, promptly upon issue of the Performance Certificate, the Contractor must clear and reinstate the Site within 28 days; otherwise the Employer may invoke the remedies in the last two paragraphs.

Clearance and reinstatement activities include the removal of the Contractor's Equipment, surplus material, wreckage, rubbish and Temporary Works, the reinstatement of all parts of the Site affected by the Contractor's activities that are not occupied by the Permanent Works[144] and leaving the Site and the Works in the condition stated in the Specification. If no condition is stated in the Specification, the Site and the Works must be left 'in a clean and safe condition'.[145] The above concerns the *final* clearance of the Site.[146]

The Contractor must maintain the validity of the Performance Security until compliance with its obligations under Sub-Clause 11.11,[147] and the Employer has ordinarily no obligation to return it before then.[148]

If the Contractor fails to comply with its obligations under sub-paragraphs (a) to (c), the Employer may invoke the remedies in the second paragraph, which include the right to sell (to the extent permitted by applicable Laws) or otherwise dispose of any remaining items on the

143. *See* Sub-Clause 4.22 [*Contractor's Operations on Site*], last paragraph.
144. On this point, *see also* the commentary on Sub-Clause 10.4 [*Surfaces Requiring Reinstatement*] above.
145. Sub-Clause 11.11(c).
146. The Contractor has an obligation throughout the execution of the Works, as well as after the issue of a Taking-Over Certificate, to remove from the Site any wreckage, rubbish, Contractor's Equipment and Temporary Works which are no longer required. *See* Sub-Clause 4.22 [*Contractor's Operations on Site*], second paragraph.
147. *See* Sub-Clause 4.2.1 [*Performance Security – Contractor's Obligations*], second paragraph.
148. *See* Sub-Clause 4.2.3 [*Performance Security – Return of the Performance Security*].

Site and/or reinstate or clean the Site at the Contractor's cost. Thereafter, the Employer is entitled to recover, subject to Sub-Clause 20.2, any reasonably incurred costs less the amount from the sale.

(iv) Related Law: Applicable Laws may contain provisions of a mandatory nature (i.e., which may not be deviated from) that regulate the disposal of waste[149] and the environment[150] which may apply. Furthermore, applicable Laws may introduce limitations on the Employer's right to sell or otherwise dispose of the remaining items on the Site especially when they are not owned by the Contractor[151] and/or are encumbered with liens.

(v) Improvements:

(1) The parenthetical phrase '(to the extent permitted under applicable Laws)' in the second paragraph should qualify the Contractor's right not only to sell the remaining items on the Site but also to dispose of such items in other ways as this may also be subject to mandatory legal regulation.

(2) Consideration should be given to reinserting the RB/99 wording that the Employer must pay the Contractor the balance of the money from the sale of the remaining items on the Site, where the proceeds from the sale exceed the costs which the Employer may recover under the Sub-Clause.

--ooOOoo--

12 Measurement and Valuation

This Clause provides that the Contract Price is to be calculated based on measurement of the quantities of work executed, and their valuation at the rates and prices in the Bill of Quantities (or other Schedule), subject to such adjustments as are provided for by the Contract. It also provides a procedure for ensuring that any cost which the Contractor might incur in relation to omitted work, which is not otherwise compensated, is taken into account by the Engineer in its valuation of that work.

149. *See*, for examples, Julian Bailey, *Construction Law* (3rd edn, London Publishing, UK, 2020) vol 2, 708-709 (para. 8.33).

150. *See* Sub-Clause 4.18 [*Protection of the Environment*] and the commentary thereon above.

151. For example, are owned by a Subcontractor.

12.1 Works to Be Measured

The Works shall be measured, and valued for payment, in accordance with this Clause.

Whenever the Engineer requires any part of the Works to be measured on Site, he/she shall give a Notice to the Contractor of not less than 7 days, of the part to be measured and the date on which and place on Site at which the measurement will be made. Unless otherwise agreed with the Contractor, the measurement on Site shall be made on this date and the Contractor's Representative shall:

(a) either attend or send another qualified representative to assist the Engineer and to endeavour to reach agreement of the measurement, and

(b) supply any particulars requested by the Engineer.

If the Contractor fails to attend or send a representative at the time and place stated in the Engineer's Notice (or otherwise agreed with the Contractor), the measurement made by (or on behalf of) the Engineer shall be deemed to have been made in the Contractor's presence and the Contractor shall be deemed to have accepted the measurement as accurate.

Any part of the Permanent Works that is to be measured from records shall be identified in the Specification and, except as otherwise stated in the Contract, such records shall be prepared by the Engineer. Whenever the Engineer has prepared the records for such a part, he/she shall give a Notice to the Contractor of not less than 7 days, stating the date on which and place at which the Contractor's Representative shall attend to examine and agree the records with the Engineer. If the Contractor fails to attend or send a representative at the time and place stated in the Engineer's Notice (or otherwise agreed with the Contractor), the Contractor shall be deemed to have accepted the records as accurate.

If, for any part of the Works, the Contractor attends the measurement on Site or examines the measurement records (as the case may be) but the Engineer and the Contractor are unable to agree the measurement, then the Contractor shall give a Notice to the Engineer setting out the reasons why the Contractor considers the measurement on Site or records are inaccurate. If the Contractor does not give such a Notice to the Engineer within 14 days after attending the measurement on Site or examining the measurement records, the Contractor shall be deemed to have accepted the measurement as accurate.

After receiving a Contractor's Notice under this Sub-Clause, unless at that time such measurement is already subject to the last paragraph of Sub-Clause 13.3.1 [*Variation by Instruction*], the Engineer shall:

(i) proceed under Sub-Clause 3.7 [*Agreement or Determination*] to agree or determine the measurement; and

(ii) for the purpose of Sub-Clause 3.7.3 [*Time limits*], the date on which the Engineer receives the Contractor's Notice shall be the date of commencement of the time limit for agreement under Sub-Clause 3.7.3.

Until such time as the measurement is agreed or determined, the Engineer shall assess a provisional measurement for the purposes of Interim Payment Certificates.

The Works shall be measured and valued for payment. Whenever the Engineer requires any Works to be measured on Site, it must give a Notice to the Contractor of not less than 7 days of the part to be measured and of when and where this will be done. If the Contractor fails to attend, the measurement made by the Engineer shall be deemed to have been accepted.

Any part of the Permanent Works that is required to be measured from records shall be identified in the Specification. Whenever the Engineer has prepared the records for such a part, it must give a Notice to the Contractor of not less than 7 days stating where and when the Contractor's Representative should attend to agree the records with the Engineer. If the Contractor fails to attend, then it is deemed to have accepted the records.

If the Engineer and Contractor are unable to agree upon any measurement, then the Contractor must give a Notice to the Engineer of the reasons for its disagreement. If the Contractor fails to do so within 14 days, it will be deemed to have accepted the measurement (of the Engineer). After receiving a Contractor's Notice then, unless the measurement is already subject to the last paragraph of Sub-Clause 13.3.1, the Engineer shall proceed under Sub-Clause 3.7 to agree or determine the measurement. Until then, the Engineer shall assess a provisional measurement for the purposes of IPCs.

12.2 Method of Measurement

The method of measurement shall be as stated in the Contract Data or, if not so stated, that which shall be in accordance with the Bill of Quantities or other applicable Schedule(s).

Except as otherwise stated in the Contract, measurement shall be made of the net actual quantity of each item of the Permanent Works and no allowance shall be made for bulking, shrinkage or waste.

The method of measurement shall be as stated in the Contract Data or, if not stated, in accordance with the Bill of Quantities or other applicable Schedule(s). Except if the Contract states otherwise, measurement shall be made of the net actual quantity of each item of the Permanent Works.

<u>**Commentary**</u>

(i) Main Changes from RB/99:

(1) The provisions in the second paragraph of Sub-Clause 12.1 that, if the Engineer requires any part of the Works to be measured, the Engineer must give not less than 7 days' Notice of the part to be measured and the date and place on Site at which the measurement will be made and, unless otherwise agreed, the measurement will be made on that date, are more detailed and precise.

(2) The provision in sub-paragraph (a) of Sub-Clause 12.1 that the Engineer and the Contractor shall endeavour to reach agreement on the measurement is new.

(3) The provisions in the fourth paragraph of Sub-Clause 12.1 dealing with measurement from records and providing for the Contractor's Representative to agree with (or be deemed to have accepted) the records prepared by the Engineer for measuring any part of the Permanent Works are expanded, providing more precise information about how such agreement (or deemed agreement) shall be arrived at.

(4) The sixth and seventh paragraphs of Sub-Clause 12.1 are entirely new: the sixth paragraph provides that, if the Contractor has given the Engineer a Notice (under the fifth paragraph) disagreeing with a measurement, the Engineer shall proceed under Sub-Clause 3.7 to agree or determine the measurement; and the seventh paragraph provides that until the measurement is agreed or determined, the Engineer shall assess a provisional measurement for the purposes of IPCs.

(5) Whereas Sub-Clause 12.2 of RB/99 had provided that the method of measurement would, '[e]xcept as otherwise stated in the Contract and notwithstanding local practice', be the one in accordance with the Bill of Quantities or other applicable Schedules, in new Sub-Clause 12.2 it is provided that it will be as stated in the Contract Data or, if not so stated, in accordance with the Bill of Quantities or other applicable Schedule(s), it being added that 'no allowance shall be made for bulking, shrinkage or waste'.

(ii) Related Clauses / Sub-Clauses: 1.3 [*Notices and Other Communications*], 3.2 [*Engineer's Duties and Authority*], 3.7 [*Agreement or Determination*], 4.3 [*Contractor's Representative*], 7.3 [*Inspection*], 7.5 [*Defects and Rejection*], 7.6 [*Remedial Work*], 8.5 [*Extension of Time for Completion*], 12.3 [*Valuation of the Works*], 13.3 [*Variation Procedure*] and 14.1 [*The Contract Price*].

(iii) Analysis*:*

(1) Clause 12 and Sub-Clause 14.1 to be read together

Clause 12 and Sub-Clause 14.1 [*The Contract Price*] together determine the Contract Price and therefore need to be read together. Sub-paragraph (a) of Sub-Clause 14.1 provides that the Contract Price shall be 'the value of the Works in accordance with Sub-Clause 12.3 [*Valuation of the*

Works]' subject to various adjustments provided for in the Contract.[1] Sub-Clause 12.3 provides for the valuation of each item of work by reference to the measurement agreed or determined for such item and the appropriate rate or price for it in the Bill of Quantities (or other Schedule(s)) included in the Contract.[2] It follows under Clauses 12 and 14 that the Contractor is to be paid based on the value of the actual or *measured* quantities of the Works executed subject to adjustments provided for in the Contract.

(2) Measurement procedures

Sub-Clause 12.1 describes the two procedures that the Engineer and the Contractor may follow when measuring quantities of the executed Permanent Works: measurement on Site and measurement from records. Whenever the Engineer requires any part of the Works to be measured on Site, the Engineer must give a Notice to the Contractor so that the Contractor's Representative can attend, and so that the two of them can endeavour to reach agreement on the quantities of work that have been executed. If the Contractor should fail to attend, it is deemed to have accepted the Engineer's measurement.[3]

If a part of the Permanent Works is to be measured according to records of its construction then this part should be identified, and the particular records to be prepared by the Engineer stated in the Specification.[4] If the Contractor is to prepare the records instead of the Engineer, then the Contract should so specify.[5]

If the Engineer and the Contractor are unable to agree on any measurement, then the Contractor must give a Notice to the Engineer of its reasons, as provided in the Sub-Clause; otherwise, it is deemed to have accepted the Engineer's measurement.[6] After receiving the Contractor's Notice, the Engineer must then proceed to agree or determine the measurement pursuant to Sub-Clause 3.7 and, until then, the Engineer must make a provisional measurement for the purposes of IPCs.[7]

1. Under otherwise stated in the Particular Conditions.
2. Or as otherwise provided in Sub-Clause 12.3.
3. Sub-Clause 12.1, third paragraph.
4. *Guidance for the Preparation of Particular Conditions*, 36.
5. *Ibid.*
6. Sub-Clause 12.1, fifth paragraph.
7. Sub-Clause 12.1, sixth and seventh paragraphs. FIDIC acknowledges (in relation to Sub-Clause 14.1 [*The Contract Price*]) that a 'positive cash-flow is clearly of benefit to the Contractor'. *Guidance for the Preparation of the Particular Conditions*, 37.

(3) Method of measurement

The method of measurement referred to in Sub-Clause 12.2 relates primarily to what quantities are to be applicable to the evaluation, rather than to the measuring techniques (although they may also be described).[8] The method of measurement may comprise: (1) principles for measurement which are specified in a preamble to the Bill of Quantities; (2) principles of measurement, specified in (to take one example) *The Civil Engineering Standard Method of Measurement* ('CESMM')[9] which may be incorporated by reference into the Contract Data; and/or (3) for a contract which does not contain many or complex items of work, principles included in each of the item descriptions in the Bill of Quantities.[10]

(iv) Improvements: Sub-Clause 12.1 provides for measurement to be initiated by the Engineer but does not state when, or with what frequency, measurements of the Works are to take place.[11] It would be most useful if this could be provided for in the Conditions. Moreover,

8. *The FIDIC Contracts Guide* (2nd edn, FIDIC, 2022) 341.
9. 4th edn, 2012 ('CESMM4'), published by the UK Institution of Civil Engineers ('ICE'). It is understood that earlier versions of CESMM are often used with the Red Book in developing markets.
10. *The FIDIC Contracts Guide* (2nd edn, FIDIC, 2022) 341. The wording 'net actual quantity of each item of the Permanent Works' means, as to earthworks, for example: the volume as built in the Permanent Works and not either the quantity placed by the Contractor before compaction or the extra material required to be placed for operational safety reasons (typically in connection with safe slope gradients) which will eventually be removed before completion of the Permanent Works. The wording 'no allowance shall be made for bulking, shrinkage or waste' is typically expressly stated in standard methods of measurement.
11. Sub-Clause 14.3 [*Application for Interim Payment*] requires the Contractor to submit a Statement for payment to the Engineer 'after the end of the period of payment stated in the Contract Data (if not stated, after the end of each month)'. The same Sub-Clause provides that the Statement is to include 'the estimated contract value of the Works executed', sub-para. (i) of Sub-Clause 14.3. The inference may therefore be that the Engineer makes the measurement monthly so as to enable the Contractor to include the estimated contract value of the executed Works in its monthly Statement. However, this practice (if it be one) is reflected neither in the Conditions nor in any FIDIC publication.

consideration should be given to according to the Contractor the right, in some circumstances, to request the Engineer to initiate the measurement procedure.[12]

12.3 Valuation of the Works

Except as otherwise stated in the Contract, the Engineer shall value each item of work by applying the measurement agreed or determined in accordance with Sub-Clauses 12.1 [*Works to be Measured*] and 12.2 [*Method of Measurement*], and the appropriate rate or price for the item.

For each item of work, the appropriate rate or price for the item shall be the rate or price specified for such item in the Bill of Quantities or other Schedule or, if there is no such an item, specified for similar work.

Any item of work which is identified in the Bill of Quantities or other Schedule, but for which no rate or price is specified, shall be deemed to be included in other rates and prices in the Bill of Quantities or other Schedule(s).

A new rate or price shall be appropriate for an item of work if:

(a) the item is not identified in, and no rate or price for this item is specified in, the Bill of Quantities or other Schedule and no specified rate or price is appropriate because the item of work is not of similar character, or is not executed under similar conditions, as any item in the Contract;

(b) (i) the measured quantity of the item is changed by more than 10% from the quantity of this item in the Bill of Quantities or other Schedule,

(ii) this change in quantity multiplied by the rate or price specified in the Bill of Quantities or other Schedule for this item exceeds 0.01% of the Accepted Contract Amount,

12. Jakob B Sørensen, *FIDIC Red Book: A Companion to the 2017 Construction Contract* (1st edn, ICE Publishing, London, 2019) 131.

(iii) this change in quantity directly changes the Cost per unit quantity of this item by more than 1%, and
(iv) this item is not specified in the Bill of Quantities or other Schedule as a "fixed rate item", "fixed charge" or similar term referring to a rate or price which is not subject to adjustment for any change in quantity; and/or

(c) the work is instructed under Clause 13 [*Variations and Adjustments*] and sub-paragraph (a) or (b) above applies.

Each new rate or price shall be derived from any relevant rates or prices specified in the Bill of Quantities or other Schedule, with reasonable adjustments to take account of the matters described in sub-paragraph (a), (b) and/or (c), as applicable. If no specified rates or prices are relevant for the derivation of a new rate or price, it shall be derived from the reasonable Cost of executing the work, together with the applicable percentage for profit stated in the Contract Data (if not stated, five percent (5%)), taking account of any other relevant matters.

If, for any item of work, the Engineer and the Contractor are unable to agree the appropriate rate or price, then the Contractor shall give a Notice to the Engineer setting out the reasons why the Contractor disagrees. After receiving a Contractor's Notice under this Sub-Clause, unless at that time such rate or price is already subject to the last paragraph of Sub-Clause 13.3.1 [*Variation by Instruction*], the Engineer shall:

- proceed under Sub-Clause 3.7 [*Agreement or Determination*] to agree or determine the appropriate rate or price; and
- for the purpose of Sub-Clause 3.7.3 [*Time limits*], the date on which the Engineer receives the Contractor's Notice shall be the date of commencement of the time limit for agreement under Sub-Clause 3.7.3.

Until such time as an appropriate rate or price is agreed or determined, the Engineer shall assess a provisional rate or price for the purposes of Interim Payment Certificates.

Except as otherwise stated in the Contract, the Engineer shall value each item of work by applying the measurement agreed or determined in accordance with Sub-Clauses 12.1 and 12.2, and the rate or price for the item specified in the Bill of Quantities. If an item of work has not been identified in the Bill of Quantities, then that item must be valued by applying the rate or price specified for similar work. Any identified item of work for which no rate or price is specified shall be deemed included in other rates or prices in the Bill of Quantities. A new rate or price is appropriate for an item if the conditions of sub-paragraphs (a), (b) and/or (c) are satisfied.

Each new rate or price shall be derived from any relevant rates or prices in the Bill of Quantities, with reasonable adjustments made for the matters described in sub-paragraphs (a), (b) and/or (c) above as applicable. If the Contractor and Engineer are unable to agree upon the appropriate rate or price for any item, then the Contractor must give a Notice to the Engineer with reasons. Unless the rate or price is already subject to the last paragraph of Sub-Clause 13.3.1, the Engineer must proceed under Sub-Clause 3.7 to agree or determine the appropriate rate or price. Until then, the Engineer shall assess a provisional rate or price for the purposes of IPCs.

Commentary

(i) Main Changes from RB/99:

(1) The reference in the first paragraph of Sub-Clause 12.3 of RB/99 to Sub-Clause 3.5 (equivalent to Sub-Clause 3.7 in RB/17) has been deleted in the new Sub-Clause (and the requirement for the Engineer to proceed in accordance with Sub-Clause 3.7, where the Engineer and the Contractor are unable to agree on a new rate or price, appears in the sixth paragraph).
(2) The third paragraph, dealing with when no rate or price is specified in the Bill of Quantities or other Schedule, is new.
(3) In the fourth paragraph providing in sub-paragraphs (a), (b) and (c) a formula for fixing a new rate or price:

- sub-paragraph (a) is new;
- sub-paragraph (b) (iv) is an expanded version of sub-paragraph (a)(iv) in Sub-Clause 12.3 of RB/99; and
- sub-paragraph (c) is an expanded version of sub-paragraph (b)(i) in Sub-Clause 12.3 of RB/99.

(4) In the fifth paragraph, the reference to 5% profit is new.

(5) In the sixth paragraph, the requirement for the Engineer to proceed under Sub-Clause 3.7 (replacing Sub-Clause 3.5 in RB/99) if the Engineer and the Contractor are unable to agree is new.

(ii) Related Clauses / Sub-Clauses: 1.2 [*Interpretation*], 1.3 [*Notices and Other Communications*], 3.2 [*Engineer's Duties and Authority*], 3.7 [*Agreement or Determination*], 8.5 [*Extension of Time for Completion*], 12 [*Management and Valuation*], 13 [*Variations and Adjustments*], 14.1 [*The Contract Price*], 14.3 [*Application for Interim Payment*], 20.1 [*Claims*] and 21.6 [*Arbitration*] and Rule 5.1(k) of the DAAB Rules.

(iii) Analysis:

(1) Purpose of the Sub-Clause

This Sub-Clause describes the means of calculating the Contract Price before adjustments, additions and/or deductions in accordance with the Contract.[13]

(2) Valuation of the Works

The valuation of the Permanent Works by the Engineer is a two-step process: (1) the Engineer ascertains or 'measures' the quantities of the items of work performed by the Contractor in accordance with Sub-Clauses 12.1 and 12.2, and, then;[14] (2) values those items of work by applying 'the appropriate rate or price' – namely, the rate or price for each such item in the Bill of Quantities (or other Schedule) or, if there is no such item, specified for similar work. Any item of work identified in the Bill of Quantities or other Schedule for which no rate or price is specified is deemed included in other rates and prices in the Bill of

13. 'Unless otherwise stated in the Particular Conditions', *see* Sub-Clause 14.1 [*The Contract Price*] as re-emphasised by the exception at the beginning of Sub-Clause 12.3.
14. 'Except as otherwise stated in the Contract', *see* Sub-Clause 12.3, first paragraph.

Quantities or other Schedule(s).[15] A new rate or price is appropriate in the circumstances where sub-paragraphs (a), (b) and/or (c) apply.

The final Contract Price is thus the valuation of the complete Works, as described above, subject to such adjustments, additions and/or deductions as are provided for in the Contract.

The Contractor applies for each interim payment by submitting a Statement including 'the estimated contract value of the Works executed, and the Contractor's Documents produced, up to the end of the period of payment',[16] the 'estimated contract value' being the amount determined pursuant to Sub-Clause 12.3. After receiving the Statement, the Engineer issues an IPC stating the amount which the Engineer fairly considers to be due.[17]

(3) Fixing of a new rate or price

The term 'rate' refers to a rate or price for a unit of work, such as a cubic metre of concrete, and is sometimes referred to as a 'unit price'. The term 'price' refers to a lump sum price for an item of work which is not to be measured – for example, US $ 75,000 for mobilisation to the Site.

The Sub-Clause sets out in sub-paragraphs (a) and (b) the two circumstances, respectively, in which a new rate or price for an item of work may be fixed without, necessarily, any need for the instruction of a Variation. According to sub-paragraph (a), this may occur where there is no rate or price specified for an item and no specified rate or price is appropriate because the item of work 'is not of similar character' (e.g., a rate for the excavation of soft ground is inappropriate for granite) or 'is not executed under similar conditions' (e.g., on a site in Northern Europe, a rate for work to be done in the summer is inappropriate for work done in the winter). Alternatively, according to sub-paragraph (b), this may occur where four conditions cumulatively have been met: (i) the measured quantity of an item has changed by more than 10% (from the estimated quantity in the Bill of Quantities), (ii) the change in quantity multiplied by the rate or price specified in such Bill exceeds 0.01% of the Accepted Contract Amount, (iii) the change in quantity directly changes

15. Sub-Clause 12.3, third paragraph.
16. Sub-Clause 14.3 [*Application for Interim Payment*], sub-para. (i). The Statement is to be accompanied by supporting documents.
17. Sub-Clause 14.6.1 [*Issue of IPC – The IPC*]. The Engineer may still modify or correct this amount pursuant to Sub-Clause 14.6.3 [*Issue of IPC – Correction or modification*].

the Cost[18] per unit quantity of the item by more than 1%, and (iv) the item is not specified as a 'fixed rate' or 'fixed charge' item (or similar) in the Bill of Quantities. Sub-paragraph (c) then recognises that the new rate or price for an item fixed pursuant to sub-paragraph (a) or (b) may have resulted from the instruction of a Variation pursuant to Clause 13.

Each new rate or price is to be derived from any relevant rates or prices specified in the Bill of Quantities or other Schedule 'with reasonable adjustments to take account of' the matters described in sub-paragraphs (a), (b) and/or (c), as applicable.[19] The logic behind this provision, which is unchanged from RB/99, is that any new rates or prices should be based on the commercial bargain reflected in the Bill of Quantities or other Schedule included in the Contract.

If no specified rates or prices are relevant, the new rate or price is to be derived from the 'reasonable Cost' of executing the work, together with the applicable percentage for profit stated in the Contract Data (if not stated, 5%), taking account of any other relevant matters.[20] The 'reasonable Cost' is to be determined in the first instance by the Engineer and thereafter, if disputed, by the DAAB and, if necessary, international arbitration.

(4) Disagreement about a new rate or price

If the Engineer and the Contractor are unable to agree on the appropriate rate or price for any item of work, the Contractor must give a Notice to the Engineer setting out the reasons why the Contractor disagrees. Then, unless at that time such rate or price is already subject to the last paragraph of Sub-Clause 13.3.1, the Engineer must proceed under Sub-Clause 3.7 to agree or determine the matter.[21] Until an appropriate rate or price is agreed or determined, the Engineer must assess a provisional rate or price for the purposes of IPCs.[22]

18. *See* Sub-Clause 1.1.19 '**Cost**'. While the Engineer will not ordinarily have a breakdown of the Contractor's rates and prices (e.g., in the Bill of Quantities or other Schedule, containing the estimated quantities provided by the Employer), the Contractor will have an incentive to disclose its Cost when applying for a new rate or price.
19. Sub-Clause 12.3, fifth paragraph.
20. *Ibid.*
21. Sub-Clause 12.3, sixth paragraph Sub-Clause 20.2 [*Claims for Payment and/or EOT*] does not apply. *The FIDIC Contracts Guide* (2nd edn, FIDIC, 2022) 500.
22. To ease the Contractor's cash flow. *Guidance for the Preparation of the Particular Conditions*, 37.

Any valuation of the Engineer may ultimately be opened up, reviewed and revised by the DAAB and, if necessary, in international arbitration.[23]

(iv) Related law: Under English law, it has been held, in relation to an English domestic form of contract containing somewhat similar provisions regarding the valuation of variations,[24] that the valuation provisions should be followed strictly as they are written, and that no account should be taken of an error or mistake in a rate or price that rendered it 'not reasonable'.[25] However, in another, more recent, Hong Kong case, the contractor had included in a rate an element of fixed cost which was unrelated directly to the work covered by the rate. In that case, it was held that an increase in quantities had rendered the rate unreasonable because, if the original rate were applied, the contractor would receive an element of fixed cost that had not increased proportionally with the volume of work undertaken. It would have produced 'a pure windfall for the contractor' and, consequently, a rerating was justified.[26]

--ooOOoo--

12.4 Omissions

Whenever the omission of any work forms part (or all) of a Variation;

(a) the value of which has not otherwise been agreed;
(b) the Contractor will incur (or has incurred) cost which, if the work had not been omitted, would have been deemed to be covered by a sum forming part of the Accepted Contract Amount;
(c) the omission of the work will result (or has resulted) in this sum not forming part of the Contract Price; and

23. *See* Rule 5.1(k) of the DAAB Rules annexed to the General Conditions of DAAB Agreement and Sub-Clause 21.6 [*Arbitration*] and the commentary on both these provisions below.
24. ICE Conditions (6th edn) Clauses 52, 55, 56 and 57.
25. *Henry Boot Construction Ltd v Alstom Combined Cycles Ltd* [1999] BLR 123 (TCC) and [2000] BLR 247 (CA). However, this decision has been questioned, *see* Atkin Chambers, *Hudson's Building and Engineering Contracts* (14th edn, Sweet & Maxwell, London, 2020) 608 (para. 5-012).
26. *Maeda Corporation v HKSAR* [2014] BLR 22, 31 (paras 55-59).

(d) this cost is not deemed to be included in the valuation of any substituted work;

then the Contractor shall, in the Contractor's proposal under sub-paragraph (c) of Sub-Clause 13.3.1 [*Variation by Instruction*], give details to the Engineer accordingly, with detailed supporting particulars.

Whenever the omission of any work forms part or all of a Variation and sub-paragraphs (a) through (d) apply, the Contractor shall, in its proposal under sub-paragraph (c) of Sub-Clause 13.3.1, give details to the Engineer accordingly.

Commentary

(i) Main Changes from RB/99: This Sub-Clause is essentially unchanged except that, instead of the Contractor being required to give a notice to the Engineer and for the Engineer to proceed under Sub-Clause 3.5 (of RB/99), the new Sub-Clause provides that the Contractor shall include information about the omission in its proposal for adjustment of the Contract Price under sub-paragraph (c) of Sub-Clause 13.3.1 [*Variation by Instruction*].

(ii) Related Clauses / Sub-Clauses: 8.12 [*Prolonged Suspension*], 11.4 [*Failure to Remedy Defects*], 13.1 [*Right to Vary*] and 13.3 [*Variation Procedure*].

(iii) Analysis: If work is omitted (by the Engineer), this will usually necessitate a reduction in the Contract Price. However, the value of the omitted work may not be agreed upon and the Engineer may not have the information to hand to calculate the amount of the reduction. As a consequence, if the Engineer were simply to apply the *apparently* relevant rates in the Contract to the calculation of the value of the omitted work, the Contractor might not recover the cost it would unavoidably incur for items of expenditure[27] not included in those rates. Accordingly, this Sub-Clause enables the Contractor to apply for reimbursement of such 'cost' in its proposal under Sub-Clause 13.3.1(c) to the Engineer,

27. For example, a corresponding portion of the cost of insurance premiums or other item of overhead cost.

accompanied by 'detailed supporting particulars'.[28] Sub-Clause 12.4 refers to cost 'in its usual usage' rather than 'Cost' as defined in Sub-Clause 1.1.19.[29]

--ooOOoo--

13 Variations and Adjustments

This Clause authorises the Engineer to vary the Works, whether directly by an instruction or following a proposal requested from the Contractor, and entitles the Contractor to make a value engineering proposal to the Engineer. The Clause also provides for the Engineer to instruct the use of Provisional Sums and for a Variation to be executed on a daywork basis. Finally, it provides for an adjustment of the Contract Price and/or Time for Completion for changes in Laws as well as an adjustment of the Contract Price for changes in Cost.

--ooOOoo--

13.1 Right to Vary

Variations may be initiated by the Engineer under Sub-Clause 13.3 [*Variation Procedure*] at any time before the issue of the Taking-Over Certificate for the Works.

Other than as stated under Sub-Clause 11.4 [*Failure to Remedy Defects*], a Variation shall not comprise the omission of any work which is to be carried out by the Employer or by others unless otherwise agreed by the Parties.

The Contractor shall be bound by each Variation instructed under Sub-Clause 13.3.1 [*Variation by Instruction*], and shall execute the Variation with due expedition and without delay, unless the Contractor promptly gives a Notice to the Engineer stating (with detailed supporting particulars) that:

28. *See* one of the example provisions for a lump sum contract dealing with this issue in the *Guidance for Preparation of Particular Conditions*, 38-39.
29. *The FIDIC Contracts Guide* (2nd edn, FIDIC, 2022) 347.

(a) the varied work was Unforeseeable having regard to the scope and nature of the Works described in the Specification;
(b) the Contractor cannot readily obtain the Goods required for the Variation; or
(c) it will adversely affect the Contractor's ability to comply with Sub-Clause 4.8 [*Health and Safety Obligations*] and/or Sub-Clause 4.18 [*Protection of the Environment*].

Promptly after receiving this Notice, the Engineer shall respond by giving a Notice to the Contractor cancelling, confirming or varying the instruction. Any instruction so confirmed or varied shall be taken as an instruction under Sub-Clause 13.3.1 [*Variation by instruction*].

Each Variation may include:

(i) changes to the quantities of any item of work included in the Contract (however, such changes do not necessarily constitute a Variation);
(ii) changes to the quality and other characteristics of any item of work;
(iii) changes to the levels, positions and/or dimensions of any part of the Works;
(iv) the omission of any work, unless it is to be carried out by others without the agreement of the Parties;
(v) any additional work, Plant, Materials or services necessary for the Permanent Works, including any associated Tests on Completion, boreholes and other testing and exploratory work; or
(vi) changes to the sequence or timing of the execution of the Works.

The Contractor shall not make any alteration to and/or modification of the Permanent Works, unless and until the Engineer instructs a Variation under Sub-Clause 13.3.1 [*Variation by Instruction*].

Variations may be initiated by the Engineer under Sub-Clause 13.3 before the issue of the Taking-Over Certificate for the Works. Other

than under Sub-Clause 11.4, a Variation shall not comprise the omission of any work to be carried out by the Employer or others unless otherwise agreed.

The Contractor shall be bound by each Variation instructed under Sub-Clause 13.3.1, and shall execute it with due expedition and without delay, unless the Contractor gives a Notice that: (i) the varied work was Unforeseeable having regard to the Specification; (ii) the Contractor cannot readily obtain the Goods required; or (iii) it will adversely affect the Contractor's ability to comply with Sub-Clause 4.8 and/or Sub-Clause 4.18. The Engineer must respond by cancelling, confirming or varying the instruction. Any instruction so confirmed or varied will be taken as an instruction under Sub-Clause 13.3.1.

Each Variation may include the matters listed in items (i) to (vi) of this Sub-Clause. The Contractor must not alter the Permanent Works unless the Engineer instructs a Variation under Sub-Clause 13.3.1.

Commentary

(i) Main Changes from RB/99:

(1) Whereas sub-paragraph (d) of Sub-Clause 13.1 of RB/99 had provided that a Variation might include the 'omission of any work unless it is to be carried out by others', the new Sub-Clause, while also acknowledging (in item (iv)) that a Variation may include the omission of any work, provides (in the second paragraph) that, other than as stated under Sub-Clause 11.4, a Variation shall not 'comprise the omission of any work which is to be carried out by the Employer[1] or by others unless otherwise agreed by the Parties'.

(2) The Sub-Clause requires the Contractor, in the third paragraph, to execute a Variation 'with due expedition and without delay', which is new.[2]

(3) The Sub-Clause provides that the Contractor may object to a Variation where '(a) the varied work was Unforeseeable having

1. Although item (iv) of the fifth paragraph of Sub-Clause 13.1 of RB/17 contains a similar provision, somewhat anomalously, it makes no mention of the Employer.
2. Although the same words are in Sub-Clause 8.1 [*Commencement of Works*], second paragraph, of RB/99 and RB/17.

regard to the scope and nature of the Works described in the Specification' and where '(c) it will adversely affect the Contractor's ability to comply with' Sub-Clauses 4.8 and/or 4.18, both of which provisions are also new.

(4) Also largely new is the provision in the fourth paragraph that any Notice from the Engineer cancelling, confirming or varying an earlier instruction to which the Contractor had objected is to be taken as an instruction under Sub-Clause 13.3.1.

(ii) Related Clauses / Sub-Clauses: 1.2 [*Interpretation*], 1.3 [*Notices and Other Communications*], 2.4 [*Employer's Financial Arrangements*], 3.2 [*Engineer's Duties and Authority*], 3.5 [*Engineer's Instructions*], 4.2 [*Performance Security*], 4.7 [*Setting Out*], 4.8 [*Health and Safety Obligations*], 4.12 [*Unforseeable Physical Conditions*], 4.18 [*Protection of the Environment*], 4.20 [*Progress Reports*], 11.4 [*Failure to Remedy Defects*], 12.4 [*Omissions*] and 13 [*Variations and Adjustments*].[3]

(iii) Analysis:

(1) Purpose of a Variations clause

Changes in the Works may become necessary or desirable for many reasons including: changes of mind by the Employer about what it wants executed or changes in its financial condition; errors in the Drawings or Specification; Goods that may no longer be available or affordable; Unforeseeable adverse geological, weather or other natural conditions; changes in Laws, building or other technical standards; and changes in the political, economic or social situation (due to war, political disturbances, inflation, fluctuations in commodity prices, currency movements or strikes) in the Country making execution of the Works more difficult, costly, or protracted.

Consequently, Clause 13 authorises the Engineer, on behalf of the Employer, to instruct changes to the Works (called 'Variations') unilaterally,[4] within certain limits, and provides for the Contractor, where appropriate, to be compensated. Without such a Clause, the right of the Engineer to change the Works would have to be agreed upon by the Parties in each case, in circumstances where the Contractor – being mobilised on the Site – could hold out for an exorbitant price, with the

3. As many Clauses or Sub-Clauses relate to Variations, this is only a selection of those provisions.

4. That is, without the Contractor's further consent.

attendant consequences, e.g., possible delay and/or disruption or even no agreement. To avoid such a prospect, Clause 13, like other common law forms of construction contract, authorises the Engineer to instruct Variations to the Works (not amendments to the Contract),[5] within certain limits, with which the Contractor must ordinarily comply, as discussed below.[6]

(2) Types of Variations: Sub-Clauses 13.1, 13.2 and 13.3 and Sub-Clause 3.5

Whereas Sub-Clause 13.1 provides that the Engineer may initiate Variations and sets certain limits on that right, as discussed below, Sub-Clauses 13.2 and 13.3, discussed thereafter, describe the three *formal* ways in which Variations may arise under the Contract. These are as follows:

(1) A request of the Engineer for a proposal from the Contractor to which proposal the Engineer consents;[7]
(2) An instruction of the Engineer to the Contractor;[8] and
(3) A value engineering proposal from the Contractor to the Engineer to which the Engineer consents.[9]

In addition, there is – as FIDIC has acknowledged for the first time in its 2017 RB, YB and SB contracts – an *informal* way that a Variation may arise. This may occur under Sub-Clause 3.5 [*Engineer's Instructions*], commented on earlier, if the Contractor receives an instruction from the Engineer which is not stated to be a Variation but which the Contractor considers to be one. In this case, according to that Sub-Clause, the Contractor must immediately, before commencing any work related to the instruction, give a Notice to the Engineer that a Variation is justified (in the Contractor's view) with reasons. Thereafter, unless the instruc-

5. While Variations change the content of the contract, notably the Works, they do not entail an amendment to the contract in a legal sense. *See* Sub-Clause 3.2 second paragraph: '[t]he Engineer shall have no authority to amend the Contract'. For an article, treating the subject of unilateral Variations from a civil lawyer's perspective, *see* Christophe Fischer, 'Unilateral Variations in Construction Contracts' (2013) 29 Const. L J 211.
6. *See* '*(5) Contractor's right to object to Variations*' in the commentary on this Sub-Clause below.
7. Sub-Clause 13.3.2.
8. Sub-Clause 13.3.1.
9. Sub-Clause 13.2.

tion is revoked by the Engineer or deemed to be revoked, it may become a Variation if either the Engineer acknowledges it to be one (in which case Sub-Clause 13.3.1 will apply) or, should the Engineer not do so, and the Contractor asserts a Claim on this account, if it is determined finally to be a Variation by the Engineer under Sub-Clause 3.7 or, failing this, by the DAAB or in international arbitration.[10]

(3) The Engineer's power to instruct Variations

As indicated above, under Sub-Clause 13.1, the Engineer may, as the agent of the Employer, initiate Variations. While the Engineer has the general authority to do so,[11] nevertheless, if, pursuant to Sub-Clause 3.2, the Engineer's power has been limited by the Particular Conditions, the Engineer may need to obtain the Employer's prior consent in particular instances.[12] On the other hand, pursuant to the same Sub-Clause, whenever the Engineer instructs a Variation, the Contractor has no obligation to verify whether the Engineer had obtained the Employer's consent, as such consent is deemed to have been given.[13]

Variations may be initiated by the Engineer at any time before the issue of the Taking-Over Certificate 'for the Works'.[14] Once this Taking-Over Certificate is issued, the Contractor is required to demobilise, retaining on the Site only such Goods as are required to enable it to comply with its obligations during the DNP.[15] Therefore, if a need for additional work arises after the Taking-Over Certificate for the Works, then, understandably, such additional works would need to be the subject of a separate agreement between the Parties.[16]

---

10. Clause 21 [*Disputes and Arbitration*].
11. Pursuant to Sub-Clauses 3.2, 13.1 and 13.3.
12. Sub-Clause 3.2 [*Engineer's Duties and Authorities*], third paragraph.
13. Sub-Clause 3.2, fourth paragraph.
14. Sub-Clause 13.1, first sentence. Therefore, even if a Section or a Part has been taken over, the Employer will still have the right to initiate Variations in respect of that Section or Part until the Taking-Over Certificate is issued for the Works overall.
15. *See* Sub-Clause 4.22, last paragraph.
16. On the other hand, the Contractor will be required to comply with a Variation instruction issued before the Taking-Over Certificate for the Works, even if the effect of the instruction is to prevent the Contractor from completing the Works by the foreseen completion date. *See* Sub-Clause 13.1, first paragraph ('any time'), and Sub-Clause 8.5 (a) which may entitle the Contractor to an EOT. *See also* Julian Bailey, *Construction Law* (3rd edn, London Publishing, UK, 2020) vol 2, 676 (para. 7.38).

Under the last paragraph, the Contractor may not make any alteration or modification of the Permanent Works unless the Engineer instructs a Variation under Sub-Clause 13.3.1 [*Variation by Instruction*].[17] It follows from that paragraph and from Sub-Clause 3.5 providing that '[t]he Contractor shall *only* take instructions from the Engineer' (emphasis added), that only the Engineer (or its delegate) is empowered to instruct a Variation. Accordingly, the Employer may not do so directly but only through the Engineer (or its delegate).

(4) The scope of Variations

A Variation is defined in Sub-Clause 1.1.86 as 'any change to the Works, which is instructed as a variation under Clause 13 [*Variations and Adjustments*]'. The 'Works' are in turn defined to mean the 'Permanent Works and the Temporary Works, or either of them as appropriate'.[18] Therefore, a Variation may comprise a change in the Permanent Works and/or the Temporary Works.

But this definition is too narrow.[19] For it to be sufficiently broad and workable, it needs to be read together with Sub-Clause 13.1, which contains a non-exhaustive[20] list of matters (sub-paragraphs (i) to (vi)) which a Variation may include.[21] Sub-paragraph (i) states that a Variation may include changes to the quantities of any item of work included in the Contract, but such changes do not necessarily constitute a Variation.[22] The work carried out will be measured under Clause 12, and the

17. Unauthorised alterations of the Permanent Works, far from entitling the Contractor to extra payment, will usually be a breach of contract for which damages would in principle be recoverable. Atkin Chambers, *Hudson's Building and Engineering Contracts* (14th edn, Sweet & Maxwell, London, 2020) 615 (para. 5-018).
18. *See* Sub-Clause 1.1.87 '**Works**'.
19. *See* the commentary on Sub-Clause 1.1.86 '**Variation**' above.
20. The fifth paragraph of Sub-Clause 13.1 states what each Variation 'may include' and Sub-Clause 1.2(h) provides that 'include' is not to be interpreted as being limitative.
21. As an illustration of the breadth of the term 'Variation' – in addition to what is provided in sub-paras (i) to (vi) – an adjustment of the Contract Price to take account of any increase or decrease in Cost resulting from a change in Laws, or in the requirements for a permit or licence to be obtained by the Contractor, is treated under Sub-Clause 13.6 as a Variation.
22. Instead, together with the satisfaction of other criteria, they may justify a new rate or price under sub-para. (b) of Sub-Clause 12.3 [*Valuation of the Works*].

Contractor will be paid for the actual quantities of work done, which will normally differ from the estimated quantities in the Bill of Quantities included in the Contract. Hence, a change to the quantities stipulated in the Bill of Quantities will not necessarily amount to a Variation.[23]

While sub-paragraphs (ii) and (iii)[24] are self-explanatory, sub-paragraph (iv) provides that a Variation may include the omission of work 'unless it is to be carried out by others without the agreement of the Parties'. Thus, a Variation may comprise an omission of work if this work is not going to be carried out at all. Unlike RB/99, a Variation may also comprise an omission of work which is to be carried out by others[25] on condition that the Contractor agrees, as the Contractor would be deprived of profit on the omitted work. To induce the Contractor to agree, Sub-Clause 13.3.1(c) provides that the Contractor may include in its proposal for adjustment to the Contract Price the amount of any loss of profit and other losses and damages that it may suffer as a result.[26]

Sub-paragraph (v) provides that a Variation may include any additional work, Plant, Materials or services necessary for the Permanent Works, subject however to the Contractor's right to object if, among other things,

23. *The FIDIC Contracts Guide* (2nd edn, FIDIC, 2022) 359, states: 'For example, the final volume of general excavation is typically not exactly identical to the estimated quantity in the Bill of Quantities for this work, without there having been any Variation.'
24. With regard to (iii), *see* Sub-Clause 4.7 [*Setting Out*].
25. Unlike the second paragraph of Sub-Clause 13.1, anomalously, sub-para. (iv) and sub-para. (c) of Sub-Clause 13.3.1 do not contemplate that omitted Work may be carried out by the Employer. However, if the Employer wishes to carry out the omitted Work itself, nothing prevents the Parties from agreeing that it may do so.
26. *See also* the commentary on Sub-Clause 12.4 [*Omissions*]. The treatment of Variations of omission is consistent with Sub-Clauses 15.5 to 15.7 relating to termination of the Contract for the Employer's convenience. Like Sub-Clauses 13.1 and 13.3, Sub-Clause 15.6(b) allows the Contractor to recover profit on the anticipated work it will no longer perform as well as other losses and damages suffered. In addition, where the Contractor has failed to remedy a defect or damage of which it has been given Notice under Sub-Clause 11.4 and the remedial work was to be executed at the cost of the Contractor under Sub-Clause 11.2, the Employer may require the Engineer to omit the part of the Works affected pursuant to Sub-Clause 11.4 (c) 'as if such omission had been instructed under Sub-Clause 13.3.1'. In such case, no agreement of the Parties is required.

the work was 'Unforeseeable having regard to the scope and nature of the Works described in the Specification'.[27]

Sub-paragraph (vi) provides that a Variation may change the sequence or timing of the execution of the Works, these being matters which are ordinarily for the Contractor to decide in its programme.[28] This ground would not entitle the Engineer to instruct the Contractor to complete any or all of the Works or a Section before the relevant Time for Completion expires.[29] On the other hand, the Engineer may instruct the Contractor to complete the Works which are delayed within the Time for Completion under Sub-Clause 8.7 [*Rate of Progress*].[30] An Engineer's instruction to the Contractor to undertake such measures to reduce the delays resulting from events for which the Contractor is entitled to claim an EOT under Sub-Clause 8.5 [*Extension of Time for Completion*] will constitute a Variation.[31]

To determine whether an instruction will amount to a Variation involves 'a comparison between what [the Contractor] was required to do (and how it was required or permitted to go about doing it)' under the Contract, and 'what it is being instructed [by the Engineer] to do'.[32] Thus, the essential feature of a Variation is that 'it requires [the Contractor] to do something different to what it is otherwise required to do by the relevant contract'.[33]

Thus, a clarification by the Engineer of a document forming the Contract, pursuant to Sub-Clause 1.5 [*Priority of Documents*], will not ordinarily constitute a Variation, nor will an instruction by the Engineer under Sub-Clause 3.5 [*Engineer's Instructions*], if it is just to carry out work already provided for in the Contract.

(5) Contractor's right to object to Variations

Under Sub-Clause 13.1, the Contractor is bound to comply with each Variation as instructed, and to execute it 'with due expedition and

27. Sub-paragraph (a) of Sub-Clause 13.1 which applies to all instructed Variations.
28. *See* Sub-Clause 8.3 [*Programme*].
29. *The FIDIC Contracts Guide* (2nd edn, FIDIC, 2022) 359.
30. *See* the commentary on Sub-Clause 8.7 above.
31. *See* Sub-Clause 8.7, third paragraph.
32. Julian Bailey, *Construction Law* (3rd edn, London Publishing, UK, 2020) vol 2, 661 (para. 7.03).
33. *Ibid.*

without delay'[34] unless the Contractor promptly gives a Notice to the Engineer stating '(with detailed supporting particulars)' any of three grounds, listed in sub-paragraphs (a), (b) and (c).[35] If the Contractor has given such Notice, it is relieved provisionally – until at least the Engineer responds – from having to execute the Variation.

Ground (a) represents FIDIC's first attempt to recognise and prescribe, in one of its forms of contract, overall limits or parameters on the scope of the Engineer's power to instruct Variations. It provides that the Contractor may object to a Variation if 'the varied work was Unforeseeable having regard to the scope and nature of the Works described in the Specification'. 'Unforeseeable' is defined as 'not reasonably foreseeable by an experienced contractor by the Base Date'.[36] If a proposed Variation goes beyond what the Contractor could have reasonably expected or anticipated from the Specification when preparing its tender, the Contractor may object to it.

It is commendable that the Conditions explicitly recognise limits on the Engineer's power to instruct a Variation. However, ground (a) would be better expressed if, instead of referring to varied work that was 'Unforeseeable' having regard to the scope or nature of the Works described in the Specification, it referred to varied work which 'falls outside' the scope and nature of the Works described in the Specification. This is better as ground (a) is really concerned with what are the parameters of the Contract – something of which both Parties should be fully aware – and not with what was reasonably foreseeable by one Party (or a hypothetical experienced contractor) at the Base Date.[37]

34. Sub-Clause 13.1, third paragraph, reaffirming how the Contractor is bound to proceed under Sub-Clause 8.1, second paragraph.
35. Under Sub-Clause 3.5 [*Engineer's Instructions*], the Contractor may also resist an instruction if it 'does not comply with applicable Laws or will reduce the safety of the Works or is technically impossible'.
36. Sub-Clause 1.1.85 '**Unforeseeable**'.
37. While Sub-Clause 13.1 does not define when varied work is Unforeseeable, other Sub-Clauses recognise that Variations may be of a certain magnitude. Thus, Sub-Clause 2.4 [*Employer's Financial Arrangements*] recognises that the Contractor might receive an instruction to execute a Variation with a price greater than 10% of the Accepted Contract Amount or an accumulated total of Variations exceeding 30% of the Accepted Contract Amount. In these cases, the Contractor may request the Employer to provide reasonable evidence that financial arrangements have been made and are being maintained to enable the Employer to pay the Contract Price remaining to be paid.

Under ground (b), the Contractor may object to a Variation if it cannot readily obtain the Goods (i.e., the Contractor's Equipment, Materials, Plant and/or Temporary Works[38]) required for the Variation.[39] This might be the case if the varied work should require specialised equipment (e.g., large tower cranes or specified tunnel boring machines) that is not readily available or, if the Site is in a remote area, the Materials, Plant and/ or Temporary Works are scarce or, due to transportation difficulties, available only at exorbitant cost.[40] '[R]eadily obtain' would appear to mean being able to obtain consistent with the Programme.

Under ground (c), the Contractor may also object to a Variation if it will adversely affect the Contractor's compliance with Sub-Clause 4.8 [*Health and Safety Obligations*] and/or Sub-Clause 4.18 [*Protection of the Environment*], the latter of which requires the Contractor to 'take all necessary measures' to protect the environment.[41]

Promptly after receiving a Notice of a Contractor's objection to a Variation, the Engineer must respond by giving a Notice cancelling, confirming or varying the instruction. A confirmed or varied instruction is to be taken as the instruction of a Variation under Sub-Clause 13.3.1. But what if the Engineer has rejected the Contractor's objection and confirmed its instruction, yet the Contractor maintains its objection? How should the Contractor proceed?

It appears that, notwithstanding that the Contractor may continue to object, the Contractor must execute the Variation[42] (except, in the case of grounds (a) or (b), if performance is impossible[43] and except, in the case of grounds (a) or (c), if a violation of law could be involved)[44] but may at the same time, by a Notice with details to the Engineer, assert a Claim

38. *See* the definition of '**Goods**' in Sub-Clause 1.1.44.
39. A similar ground had existed in RB/99 (*see* second paragraph of Sub-Clause 13.1 of RB/99).
40. Sub-Clause 18.6 [*Release from Performance under the Law*] might become relevant if certain Goods become impossible to obtain. *See also* sub-para. (d) of Sub-Clause 8.5 [*Extension of Time for Completion*].
41. *See* the commentaries on Sub-Clauses 4.8 and 4.18 above.
42. This follows from Sub-Clauses 3.5, second paragraph, and 13.3.1, second paragraph, which require the Contractor to proceed with the execution of a Variation instructed by the Engineer.
43. *See* Sub-Clause 18.6 [*Release from Performance under the Law*]. *See also* Sub-Clause 3.5, sub-para. (b).
44. *See* Sub-Clause 1.13 [*Compliance with Laws*], which applies to both Parties, and sub-para. (b) of Sub-Clause 3.5 [*Engineer's Instructions*].

under Sub-Clause 20.1(c) as the Contractor's right to object to a Variation may be considered as giving rise to 'another entitlement or relief' under that provision. The Engineer is then required to proceed, acting 'fair[ly]' and 'neutrally', to agree or determine the Claim under Sub-Clause 3.7 [*Agreement or Determination*] and, if the Contractor is dissatisfied with any determination, it may refer the ensuing Dispute to the DAAB and, if necessary, to international arbitration.[45]

(6) Potential consequences of Variations

Where Variations and/or other adjustments under Clause 13 should result in significant changes to the Contract Price, the amount of the Performance Security may need to be changed[46] and the Contractor may be entitled to request further assurance that the Employer can meet its payment obligations.[47]

(iv) Related Law:

(1) When is a Variation 'Unforeseeable'?

Under Sub-Clause 13.1(a), the Contractor may object to the instruction of a Variation where the varied work is Unforeseeable having regard to the scope and nature of the Works described in the Specification.

Similarly, under English law, a variation clause is said to be 'subject to an implied limitation of reasonableness' so that:

> the power to order extras, although apparently unlimited, must in fact be limited to ordering extras of a certain value and type. Additional work outside these limits will no longer be governed by the terms of the contract, [...] not least because the word 'variation' [...] has a restricted meaning, and like words such as 'alteration' will not be appropriate to something wholly different from the original work or project. The project as a whole and, if necessary, the pre-contract correspondence, must be looked at [...] and a commonsense view taken of the variations ordered. Thus in the case of an ordinary contract for a single dwelling-house, an order for a small outbuilding or garage might be acceptable, but not for, say, a further identical

45. *See* the commentary on Clause 21 [*Disputes and Arbitration*] below.
46. Sub-Clause 4.2.1 [*Performance Security – Contractor's Obligations*], third paragraph.
47. Sub-Clause 2.4 [*Employer's Financial Arrangements*], third paragraph.

> dwelling-house. On the other hand, a contract for 300 dwelling-houses for a local authority might not be 'vitiated' by an order for a further 10 or 20 houses on the same site.[48]

It is, in effect, this implied limitation of reasonableness which FIDIC has sought, by ground (a) of Sub-Clause 13.1, to reflect explicitly in the Conditions.

(2) Consequences of an 'Unforeseeable' Variation

If the Engineer rejects the Contractor's objection, and the Contractor performs the extra-contractual work under protest, and the Contractor's objection is later upheld, the Contractor will normally be entitled under the common law to be paid for such work on a *quantum meruit* basis,[49] that is, the reasonable value of its services.[50] On the other hand, if the Contractor's objection is unjustified, the Contract pricing and rates will apply.

---

48. Atkin Chambers, *Hudson's Building and Engineering Contracts* (14th edn, Sweet & Maxwell, London, 2020) 632 (para. 5-032). Under US law, the criterion for determining whether changes are permitted by the contract and compensable is whether they are within the 'general scope' of the contract:

> [t]he 'scope' of a contract refers to the work, responsibilities and risks assumed by the contractor in consideration for the contract price. Changes 'within the scope' of the undertaking [the contract] are presumed to be covered by the contract price and are non-compensable. *Changes outside the 'scope' but within the 'general scope' of the contract are compensable under the administrative adjustment provisions of the contract.* Changes 'beyond the general scope' of the contract constitute material breaches of contract remediable under common law damage principles.

Philip Bruner and Patrick O'Connor, *Bruner and O'Connor on Construction Law* (Thomson Reuters, St Paul, MN, 2016) vol 1A, 319-20 (s 4.10). Under US federal contracting law, work 'beyond the general scope' of the contract, which is a material breach of contract, is called a 'cardinal' change. Philip Bruner and Patrick O'Connor, *Bruner and O'Connor on Construction Law* (Thomson Reuters, St Paul, MN, 2016) vol 1A, 328-329 (s 4.13).

49. Julian Bailey, *Construction Law* (3rd edn, London Publishing, UK, 2020) vol 2, 683 (para. 7.50) and Atkin Chambers, *Hudson's Building and Engineering Contracts* (14th edn, Sweet & Maxwell, London, 2020) 627-629 (para. 5-029). Similar to quantum meruit, French law has a doctrine of unjustified enrichment (*l'enrichissement injustifiée*), *see* art. 1303 of the French Civil Code.

50. *Quantum meruit* is the Latin for 'as much as he has deserved'. Bryan A Garner (ed in chief), *Black's Law Dictionary* (11th edn, Thomson Reuters, St Paul, MN, 2019).

Quantum meruit will apply to the varied part of the work only. On the other hand, in some exceptional cases, revaluation of the whole work may be justified:

> if a man contracts to work by a certain plan, and that plan is so entirely abandoned that it is impossible to trace the contract, and say to what part of it the work shall be applied, in such case the workman shall be permitted to charge for the whole work done by measure and value, as if no contract at all had ever been made [...].[51]

As to this case, an English authority states that:

> whenever it is possible to trace and identify the work which has been ordered outside the scope of a variation clause, together with its consequential effects [...], it is only the work outside the scope of the contract which may be separately valued, as a matter of law, on a cost or reasonable price basis. Even in such a case, the original contract prices will at least be evidence of what is a reasonable price until the contrary is proved.[52]

(3) Multiple Variation instructions

Sub-Clause 13.1 envisages the possibility of an individual Variation instruction requiring varied work that is Unforeseeable, referred to in US law as a 'cardinal' change. However, there may also be multiple Variation instructions – hundreds or even thousands in some cases – each of which is not Unforeseeable, but whose cumulative effect is Unforeseeable. This situation is recognised under US law also to be a cardinal change (and also under US (but not English) law as a material breach of contract),[53] which the Contractor may object to and refuse to perform. Although this is not plainly recognised by this Sub-Clause, perhaps it should be.

Finally, there may be cases where the Contractor may argue that the number, character and impact of the Variations instructed have been so significant that the whole contract should be repriced. While such a claim

51. *Pepper v Burland* [1792] 1 Peake N.P. 139, 140.
52. Atkin Chambers, *Hudson's Building and Engineering Contracts* (14th edn, Sweet & Maxwell, London, 2020) 631 (para. 5-031).
53. Philip Bruner and Patrick O'Connor, *Bruner and O'Connor on Construction Law* (Thomson Reuters, St Paul, MN, 2016) vol 1A, 333 (s 4.14).

does not appear to have succeeded in England or the Commonwealth,[54] there may be judicial support for it in the United States.[55]

(4) Civil law

A somewhat similar doctrine exists under French law in the case of a lump sum contract. This is known as *le bouleversement de l'économie du contrat*, which may be translated as the upsetting of the economy or economic balance of the contract. This may apply when the 'economic balance' of a lump sum contract has been totally disrupted by exceptionally large changes required by the employer, or its representative, in the volume and/or nature of the work which had originally been agreed upon.[56]

(5) Variation for the benefit of the Contractor

Finally, under the common law at least, there may be exceptional circumstances where the Engineer is *required* to issue a Variation instruction. For example, in a case:

> where a contractor is unable to perform its works, or it is technically able to perform its works but they will be disproportionately expensive and time consuming, unless a variation order is given so as to permit the contractor to overcome the particular hindrance.[57]

---

54. Atkin Chambers, *Hudson's Building and Engineering Contracts* (14th edn, Sweet & Maxwell, London, 2020) 628, para. 5-029, citing to *McAlpine Humberoak Ltd v McDemott International Inc* (no 1) [1992] 58 B.L.R.I.
55. *See* Philip Bruner and Patrick O'Connor, *Bruner and O'Connor on Construction Law* (Thomson Reuters, St Paul, MN, 2016) vol 1A, 333 (s 4:14, fn. 5), and *Dillingham-Ray Wilson v City of Los Angeles*, 182 Cal App 4th 1396, 106 Cal Reptr 3rd 691 (2nd Dist 2010) and *Edward R. Marden Corp. v US* 194 Ct Cl 799, 442 F 2nd 364 [1971], being cases cited in that fn. 5.
56. Christophe Sizaire, 'Marché à forfait et bouleversement de l'économie du contrat', note under Cass. Civ. 3rd, Construction-Urbanisme, no 3 (March 2017) comm. 39; Albert Caston *Traité des marchés privés de travaux* (6th edn, Le Moniteur, Paris) 258-261; and Jane Jenkins and Dominique Ryder, 'In Search of the Holy Grail (or How to Escape a Lump Sum Price: an Analysis of English and French Law)' [1995] ICLR 240, 253. *See* **Section 4 Common Law and Civil Law Compared – 4.4.2 Lump Sum Contracts** in **Chapter II Applicable Law** above.
57. Julian Bailey, *Construction Law* (3rd edn, London Publishing, UK, 2020) vol 2, 668 (para. 7.19).

In such circumstances, the Employer may, as an incident of its obligation to cooperate with the Contractor, pursuant to Sub-Clause 2.3 [*Employer's Personnel and Other Contractors*] and perhaps implied by law as well, be required to issue a Variation instruction to permit the Contractor to perform the Works.[58] Thus, a Variation instruction may be required to be issued to protect the Contractor.

(v) Improvements:

(1) The reference to 'the Taking-Over Certificate for the Works' in the first paragraph of the Sub-Clause should be replaced by 'the Date of Completion of the Works' in order to cover situations where the Works are deemed to have been completed in accordance with the Contract, even though no Taking-Over Certificate for the Works was issued.

(2) As explained under **(iii) Analysis** above, it would be better if Sub-Clause 13.1(a) referred to varied work 'which falls outside the scope and nature of the Works described in the Specification' instead of to whether it is Unforeseeable having regard to the Works described in the Specification.

(3) If the Contractor objects to a Variation on grounds (a), (b) or (c) and the Engineer confirms its instruction, but the Contractor maintains its objection then – given the possibly 'Unforeseeable', impossible, dangerous and/or illegal situation which may be involved – it would be sensible (the Engineer having already considered the matter twice) to allow the Contractor to refer the matter directly to the DAAB for a decision instead of having to go back to the Engineer under Sub-Clause 3.7 by way of Sub-Clause 20.1, as presently envisaged.

(4) The last two paragraphs of Sub-Clause 3.5 [*Engineer's Instructions*] relating to whether or not an instruction constitutes a Variation, suitably modified, might be better placed in this Sub-Clause dealing with Variations than in Sub-Clause 3.5.

--ooOOoo--

58. *Ibid.*

13.2 Value Engineering

The Contractor may, at any time, submit to the Engineer a written proposal which (in the Contractor's opinion) will, if adopted:

(a) accelerate completion;
(b) reduce the cost to the Employer of executing, maintaining or operating the Works;
(c) improve the efficiency or value to the Employer of the completed Works; or
(d) otherwise be of benefit to the Employer.

The proposal shall be prepared at the cost of the Contractor and shall include the details as stated in sub-paragraphs (a) to (c) of Sub-Clause 13.3.1 [*Variation by Instruction*].

The Engineer shall, as soon as practicable after receiving such a proposal, respond by giving a Notice to the Contractor stating his/her consent or otherwise. The Engineer's consent or otherwise shall be at the sole discretion of the Employer. The Contractor shall not delay any work while awaiting a response.

If the Engineer gives his/her consent to the proposal, with or without comments, the Engineer shall then instruct a Variation. Thereafter, the Contractor shall submit any further particulars that the Engineer may reasonably require, and the last paragraph of Sub-Clause 13.3.1 [*Variation by Instruction*] shall apply which shall include consideration by the Engineer of the sharing (if any) of the benefit, costs and/or delay between the Parties stated in the Particular Conditions.

If a proposal under this Sub-Clause, to which the Engineer gives his/her consent, includes a change in the design of part of the Permanent Works, then unless otherwise agreed by both Parties:

(i) the Contractor shall design this part at his/her cost; and
(ii) sub-paragraphs (a) to (h) of Sub-Clause 4.1 [*Contractor's General Obligations*] shall apply.

The Contractor may, at any time, submit a written proposal to the Engineer, which will: (a) accelerate completion; (b) reduce the Employer's costs of executing, maintaining or operating the Works; (c) improve the efficiency or value to the Employer of the completed Works; or (d) otherwise benefit the Employer. The proposal must be prepared at the Contractor's cost and include the details in sub-paragraphs (a) to (c) of Sub-Clause 13.3.1. The Engineer must respond with its consent or otherwise at the sole discretion of the Employer.

If the Engineer consents it must instruct a Variation. Thereafter, the Contractor must submit any further particulars that the Engineer may require and the Engineer must proceed under Sub-Clause 3.7 to agree or determine the EOT, if any, and/or adjustment of the Contract Price including consideration by the Engineer of the sharing, if any, of the benefit, costs and/or delay between the Parties as stated in the Particular Conditions.

If the proposal consented to includes a change in the design of the Permanent Works, then unless the Parties agree otherwise, the Contractor shall design this part at its cost and sub-paragraphs (a) to (h) of Sub-Clause 4.1 shall apply.

Commentary

(i) Main Changes from RB/99: A value engineering provision was first introduced into FIDIC's forms by Sub-Clause 13.2 in the 1999 Rainbow Suite.[59] The present Sub-Clause is similar to its predecessor but with the following major differences:

(1) According to the second paragraph, the Contractor's proposal must include the more elaborate details described in sub-paragraphs (a) to (c) of Sub-Clause 13.3.1 [*Variation by Instruction*] as compared to the list in Sub-Clause 13.3 of RB/99.[60]

(2) The third paragraph provides that the Engineer shall respond as soon as practicable, with its consent or otherwise (previously, Sub-Clause 13.2, third paragraph, like Sub-Clause 13.3, second paragraph, of RB/99, had referred to the Engineer's 'approval').

59. However, it was less detailed in YB/99 and SB/99 than in RB/99, as is the case also with YB/17 and SB/17 compared to RB/17.

60. Provided for in Sub-Clause 13.2, second paragraph, of RB/99.

(3) The third paragraph also provides that the Engineer's consent or otherwise shall be 'at the sole discretion' of the Employer, which is new.
(4) The fourth paragraph, providing that if the Engineer gives its consent the Engineer shall instruct a Variation, is also entirely new.
(5) The last paragraph provides that if a proposal to which the Engineer consents includes a change in the design of part of the Permanent Works, then, unless otherwise agreed by the Parties, the Contractor shall design this part at its cost, which had not been stated previously, and that the somewhat different provisions of Sub-Clause 4.1 (from those in RB/99) shall apply.

(ii) Related Clauses / Sub-Clauses: 1.2 [*Interpretation*], 1.3 [*Notices and Other Communications*], 3.5 [*Engineer's Instructions*], 3.7 [*Agreement or Determination*], 4.1 [*Contractor's General Obligations*], 13 [*Variations and Adjustments*] and 14.15 [*Currencies of Payment*].

(iii) Analysis:

(1) Why a value engineering clause?

The Contractor, especially one having significant design capacity in-house, may recognise a way in which the Works can be executed more efficiently and/or at less cost to the Employer, or in which the completed Works can be improved, as compared to what is envisaged by the Drawings and Specification. But the Contractor will normally have no incentive to propose an innovation, as not only will it take time and expense to do so, for which it has no assurance of being compensated, the innovation may reduce the Contract Price and, thus, the Contractor's profit.[61] On the other hand, the Employer has an obvious interest to motivate the Contractor to propose innovations that could benefit the Employer.

The concept of value engineering reflects an effort, originating in US Federal Government defence contracts in the second half of the 20th century, to incentivise a contractor to propose design and other solutions that will reduce construction costs by permitting the contractor to share with the owner or employer in the resulting cost savings. Currently, a value engineering clause is required by the US *Federal Acquisition*

61. It may also imply criticism of the work of the designer, who may be the Engineer.

Regulation ('*FAR*') in all US Federal Government contracts above a certain financial threshold.[62] That clause begins '[t]he contractor is encouraged to develop, prepare and submit value engineering change proposals (VECPs) voluntarily' and is designed to save public money. Such clauses are being used increasingly on public and private construction projects in the United States.[63]

(2) Comparison of FIDIC's value engineering clause with the US FAR clause from which it originated

While the *FAR* provision invites proposals that will reduce the contract price or estimated cost of a project, Sub-Clause 13.2 of RB/17 invites proposals that may generate a wider range of benefits, including, among other things, accelerating completion and improving the efficiency or value to the Employer of the completed Works. Such a proposal may be made 'at any time' implying it might even be made after the issue of the Taking-Over Certificate for the Works. As in the case of the *FAR* provision, the proposal must be prepared at the cost of the Contractor, and otherwise contain the details stated in sub-paragraphs (a) to (c) of Sub-Clause 13.3.1 [*Variation by Instruction*].

The Sub-Clause then provides that the Engineer shall respond to the Contractor's proposal as soon as practicable by giving a Notice stating its 'consent' or otherwise, and that such consent shall be at the sole discretion of the Employer.[64] Where the proposal is rejected, no reasons are required to be given and the Contractor must not delay any work while awaiting a response from the Engineer. If the Engineer consents, it must then instruct a Variation.

On the other hand, the *FAR* clause provides that the government must notify the contractor of the status of its proposal within 45 calendar days

62. This clause is to be found in US *Federal Acquisition Regulation* ('*FAR*') s 52.248 - 3 Value Engineering - Construction, Title 48, Code of Federal Regulations ('C.F.R.'), U.S.A. The link to the FAR document is: https://www.govinfo.gov/content/pkg/CFR-2011-title48-vol2/pdf/CFR-2011-title48-vol2-sec52-248-3.pdf accessed 10 November 2022. The threshold is reported to be generally USD 100,000 for contracts performed in the United States, Smith, Currie and Hancock's *Federal Government Construction Contracts* (Thomas J Kelleher, Jr and others eds) (Wiley, Hoboken, NJ, 2010) 309.
63. Philip Bruner and Patrick O'Connor, *Bruner and O'Connor on Construction Law* (Thomson Reuters, St Paul, MN, 2016) vol 1A, 363 (s 4:24, fn. 5).
64. For the apparent meaning of this expression *see* under **(v) Improvements** of the commentary on Sub-Clause 1.2 [*Interpretation*] above.

after receiving it, and that the decision whether to accept or reject it is (as under Sub-Clause 13.2) at the sole discretion of the US Government (the Employer).[65] Under the *FAR* provision, if the contractor's proposal is not accepted, the Contracting Officer must 'notify the Contractor in writing, explaining the reasons for rejection'. Given that the contractor will have gone to the effort and expense of preparing, on its own initiative, the value engineering change proposal in the first place, and that the US Government can reject it at its discretion, it is only reasonable that the US Government is required to explain the reasons for the rejection, especially as the proposal is alleged to save public money.

The biggest difference between the *FAR* provision and Sub-Clause 13.2 relates to the benefit which the contractor may receive if its proposal is consented to or accepted. The *FAR* provision provides for a formula enabling a contractor to calculate the US dollar amount it can expect to receive.[66] In light of this formula, a contractor is able to make a cost/benefit analysis of whether it has a financial incentive to make a proposal.

Unfortunately, Sub-Clause 13.2 of RB/17 does not provide the Contractor with this kind of information. Instead, it provides for the application of the last paragraph of Sub-Clause 13.3.1, which in turn provides that the Engineer shall proceed under Sub-Clause 3.7 to agree or determine what is due to the Contractor 'which shall include *consideration by the Engineer* of *the sharing (if any) of the benefit, costs and/or delay between the Parties stated* in the Particular Conditions'. (Emphasis added) *Thus, given the wide discretion conferred upon the Engineer, the Contractor is unable to make a cost/benefit analysis to determine whether it is justified in making a proposal or not.*

65. *FAR* s 52.248-3 Value Engineering – Construction, paragraph (e) 3. The link to the *FAR* document is: https://acquisition.gov/sites/default/files/current/far/pdf/FAR.pdf accessed 10 November 2022.
66. The contractor is entitled to receive: (1) a percentage (approximately 55%) of the estimated reduction in the contractor's cost of performance resulting from the proposal, less the cost of the development and implementation of the proposal; and (2) approximately 20% of the savings in the Government's cost of operations, maintenance, logistical support, or Government furnished property, in a typical year of use but capped at USD 100,000 per year. *FAR* s 52.248-3 Value Engineering – Construction, paragraphs (f) and (g).

The prior Sub-Clause in RB/99 had at least provided a formula for the calculation of a fee payable to the Contractor which might apply,[67] but this has been removed. The new Sub-Clause simply refers users to the Particular Conditions, without providing in the *Guidance*[68] solutions or illustrative provisions which might be resorted to.

A US authority has stated:

> Contractual formalization of the concept of value engineering is crucial to: (1) give contractors an incentive to make suggestions; (2) enhance contractor's confidence that their suggestions will not be misappropriated; and (3) *define clearly the cost sharing arrangement.*[69] (Emphasis added)

Unfortunately, Sub-Clause 13.2 does not accomplish any of these objectives, which is truly a lost opportunity, especially for Employers.

(3) Advice to Contractors

In the present situation, if the Contractor believes it has a value engineering proposal to make, then, before going to the effort and expense of doing so, it would be well advised to explore with the Employer and the Engineer whether its proposal might be of interest to them in principle, and if so, the terms upon which it might be made. Unless the Contractor is able to negotiate in advance clearly defined compensation, as well as protection against the misappropriation of its ideas, it is unlikely to have an incentive to make a proposal under this Sub-Clause.[70]

(iv) Related Law: In 1984, the concept of value engineering was incorporated into *FAR* which, as mentioned above, applies to US Federal

---

67. Where a change in the design of the Permanent Works was involved.
68. *Guidance for the Preparation of Particular Conditions.*
69. Philip Bruner and Patrick O'Connor, *Bruner and O'Connor on Construction Law* (Thomson Reuters, St Paul, MN, 2016) vol 1A, 365 (s 4:24).
70. Indeed, in relation to the Sub-Clause in RB/99, FIDIC had suggested that if the Contractor considers that the cost of preparing a fully detailed proposal may be excessive:

> he may initially describe the general concept of the changes proposed, together with financial proposals which may include suggestions regarding compensation for reimbursement of his Costs of performing the next stage: more detailed design, possibly.

The FIDIC Contracts Guide (1st edn, FIDIC, 2000) 220.

Government procurement.[71] As there has been a lot of US experience with this concept, US legal materials contain valuable information about it, which can be consulted.

In 2017, when the *NEC 4 Engineering and Construction Contract* ('NEC 4') was published, it included a value engineering provision among its Main Option Clauses[72] for the first time. This provision is better than Sub-Clause 13.2 as it provides for a formula designed to enable the Contractor to share equally[73] with the Employer in the benefit resulting from a value engineering 'compensation event', allowing the Contractor to *see* exactly what it can expect to receive.

(v) Improvements: *As mentioned under* ***(iii) Analysis*** *above, Sub-Clause 13.2 (unlike Sub-Clause 13.2 of RB/99) fails to provide an incentive to the Contractor to make a value engineering proposal, rendering it most probably inoperative*. Accordingly, future editions of the RB should, like *FAR* and NEC 4, provide a clear formula for the Contractor's compensation, so that the Contractor will have an incentive to make a value engineering proposal, in both the Employer's and the Contractor's interest.

--ooOOoo--

13.3 Variation Procedure

Subject to Sub-Clause 13.1 [*Right to Vary*], Variations shall be initiated by the Engineer in accordance with either of the following procedures:

13.3.1 Variation by Instruction

The Engineer may instruct a Variation by giving a Notice (describing the required change and stating any requirements for the recording of Costs) to the Contractor in accordance with Sub-Clause 3.5 [*Engineer's Instructions*].

71. Philip Bruner and Patrick O'Connor, *Bruner and O'Connor on Construction Law* (Thomson Reuters, St Paul, MN, 2016) vol 1A, 362 (s 4:24).
72. *See* Clause 63.12 in Option A: Priced Contract with Activity Schedule and Clause 63.12 in Option B: Priced Contract with Bill of Quantities of *NEC 4 Engineering and Construction Contract*.
73. Unless the parties agree otherwise.

The Contractor shall proceed with execution of the Variation and shall within 28 days (or other period proposed by the Contractor and agreed by the Engineer) of receiving the Engineer's instruction, submit to the Engineer detailed particulars including:

(a) a description of the varied work performed or to be performed, including details of the resources and methods adopted or to be adopted by the Contractor;

(b) a programme for its execution and the Contractor's proposal for any necessary modifications (if any) to the Programme according to Sub-Clause 8.3 [*Programme*] and to the Time for Completion; and

(c) the Contractor's proposal for adjustment to the Contract Price by valuing the Variation in accordance with Clause 12 [*Measurement and Valuation*], with supporting particulars (which shall include identification of any estimated quantities and, if the Contractor incurs or will incur Cost as a result of any necessary modification to the Time for Completion, shall show the additional payment (if any) to which the Contractor considers that the Contractor is entitled). If the Parties have agreed to the omission of any work which is to be carried out by others, the Contractor's proposal may also include the amount of any loss of profit and other losses and damages suffered (or to be suffered) by the Contractor as a result of the omission.

Thereafter, the Contractor shall submit any further particulars that the Engineer may reasonably require.

The Engineer shall then proceed under Sub-Clause 3.7 [*Agreement or Determination*] to agree or determine:

(i) EOT, if any; and/or

(ii) the adjustment to the Contract Price (including valuation of the Variation in accordance with Clause 12 [*Measurement and Valuation*] using measured quantities of the varied work) (and, for the purpose of Sub-Clause 3.7.3 [*Time limits*], the date the Engineer receives the Contractor's submission (including any requested further particulars) shall be the date of commencement of the time limit for agreement under Sub-Clause 3.7.3). The Contractor shall be entitled to such EOT and/or adjustment to the Contract Price, without any requirement to comply with Sub-Clause 20.2 [*Claims for Payment and/or EOT*].

13.3.2 Variation by Request for Proposal

The Engineer may request a proposal, before instructing a Variation, by giving a Notice (describing the proposed change) to the Contractor.

The Contractor shall respond to this Notice as soon as practicable, by either:

(a) submitting a proposal, which shall include the matters as described in sub-paragraphs (a) to (c) of Sub-Clause 13.3.1 [*Variation by Instruction*]; or
(b) giving reasons why the Contractor cannot comply (if this is the case), by reference to the matters described in sub-paragraphs (a) to (c) of Sub-Clause 13.1 [*Right to Vary*].

If the Contractor submits a proposal, the Engineer shall, as soon as practicable after receiving it, respond by giving a Notice to the Contractor stating his/her consent or otherwise. The Contractor shall not delay any work while awaiting a response.

If the Engineer gives consent to the proposal, with or without comments, the Engineer shall then instruct the Variation. Thereafter, the Contractor shall submit any further particulars that the Engineer may reasonably require and the last paragraph of Sub-Clause 13.3.1 [*Variation by Instruction*] shall apply.

If the Engineer does not give consent to the proposal, with or without comments, and if the Contractor has incurred Cost as a result of submitting it, the Contractor shall be entitled subject to Sub-Clause 20.2 [*Claims for Payment and/or EOT*] to payment of such Cost.

Subject to Sub-Clause 13.1, Variations must be initiated by the Engineer.

13.3.1 Variation by Instruction

The Engineer may instruct a Variation by a Notice to the Contractor in accordance with Sub-Clause 3.5. The Contractor must proceed with the Variation, and within 28 days (or other period agreed by the Engineer) submit to the Engineer detailed particulars, including: (a) a description of the varied work with details of the resources and methods; (b) a programme for its execution and the Contractor's proposal for any modifications to the Programme and the Time for Completion; and (c) a proposal for adjustment of the Contract Price. If the Parties have agreed to the omission of any work which is to be carried out by others, the proposal may include the amount of any losses as a result of the omission.

The Engineer must then proceed under Sub-Clause 3.7, without the Contractor being required to comply with Sub-Clause 20.2.

13.3.2 Variation by Request for Proposal

The Engineer may request a proposal before instructing a Variation by giving a Notice to the Contractor. The Contractor must respond by either: (a) submitting a proposal, which includes the matters in sub-paragraphs (a) to (c) of Sub-Clause 13.3.1; or (b) giving reasons why it cannot comply by reference to the matters in sub-paragraphs (a) to (c) of Sub-Clause 13.1.

If the Contractor submits a proposal, the Engineer must respond by giving a Notice stating its consent or otherwise. If the Engineer consents, it shall instruct the Variation and then proceed under Sub-Clause 3.7, without the Contractor being required to comply with Sub-Clause 20.2.

If the Contractor has incurred Cost as a result of submitting a proposal to which the Engineer has not consented, the Contractor will be entitled to payment of such Cost subject to Sub-Clause 20.2.

Commentary

(i) Main Changes from RB/99: The new Sub-Clause provides a better-structured description of the procedure for the initiation of Variations, distinguishing clearly between a 'Variation by Instruction' and a 'Variation by Request for Proposal'.[74] The main changes are as follows:

(1) Whereas, under Sub-Clause 13.3 of RB/99, the Contractor was explicitly required to submit certain information[75] only in the case of the Engineer's request for a proposal before instructing a Variation, under the new Sub-Clause 13.3.1, second paragraph, similar (albeit more detailed) information must be submitted also in the case of a Variation by instruction.
(2) Whether the Variation results from an instruction or a request for proposal, if it comprises the omission of work to be carried out by others, the Contractor is required, under new Sub-Clauses 13.3.1 and 13.3.2, to include in its proposal the amount of any loss of profit and other losses or damages suffered (or to be suffered) as a result of the omission, which is new.
(3) The new Sub-Clauses 13.3.1 and 13.3.2 require the Engineer to proceed under Sub-Clause 3.7 to agree or determine the EOT, if any, and adjustment of the Contract Price resulting from the Variation, whereas there was no such explicit requirement to proceed under the corresponding Sub-Clause (Sub-Clause 3.5) in RB/99.
(4) The new Sub-Clause stipulates that the Contractor will be entitled to such EOT and/or adjustment of the Contract Price without having to comply with the claims procedure under Sub-Clause 20.2, whereas RB/99 had required, at least arguably,[76] compliance with the corresponding claims procedure under that form.[77]

---

74. Sub-Clause 13.3 of RB/99 was not that clear as, whereas the first two paragraphs dealt with Variations by a request for a proposal, the last two paragraphs of the same Sub-Clause appeared to apply to both a Variation by instruction and a Variation following a request for a proposal, though this was not explicitly stated.
75. Such as a description of the proposed work to be performed, a programme for its execution, the Contractor's proposal for modifications to the programme according to Sub-Clause 8.3 and to the Time for Completion and for evaluation of the Variation.
76. Given the broad wording of the first sentence of Sub-Clause 20.1 of RB/99.
77. Unless, as regards an EOT, an adjustment to the Time for Completion had been agreed. *See* Sub-Clause 8.4(a) of RB/99.

(5) No longer does the Engineer 'approve' the Contractor's proposal under Sub-Clause 13.3.2, as in Sub-Clause 13.3 of RB/99, but instead gives 'consent' to it.[78]

(6) The Contractor is entitled, subject to Sub-Clause 20.2, to payment of the Cost of submitting a proposal for a Variation requested by the Engineer to which the Engineer does not consent, whereas the Contractor had no similar right in RB/99.

(ii) Related Clauses / Sub-Clauses: 1.2 [*Interpretation*], 1.3 [*Notices and Other Communications*], 1.15 [*Limitation of Liability*], 2.4 [*Employer's Financial Arrangements*], 3.5 [*Engineer's Instructions*], 3.7 [*Agreement or Determination*], 4.7.3 [*Setting Out-Agreement or Determination of rectification measures, delay and/or Cost*], 4.20 [*Progress Reports*], 8.3 [*Programme*], 8.7 [*Rate of Progress*], 8.12 [*Prolonged Suspension*], 12 [*Measurement and Valuation*], 13 [*Variations and Adjustments*], 17.2 [*Liability for Care of the Works*] and 20.2 [*Claims for Payment and/or EOT*].[79]

(iii) Analysis: Pursuant to the opening sentence of Sub-Clause 13.3, a Variation may be initiated by the Engineer in accordance with the procedure either for a 'Variation by Instruction' under Sub-Clause 13.3.1 or for a 'Variation by Request for Proposal' under Sub-Clause 13.3.2 (in addition to a Variation resulting from a value engineering proposal by the Contractor pursuant to Sub-Clause 13.2).[80]

---

78. The intention by this word change being to minimise the Engineer's responsibility for the Contractor's proposal. *See* sub-para. (g) of Sub-Clause 1.2 [*Interpretation*] and the last paragraph of Sub-Clause 3.2 [*Engineer's Duties and Authority*].
79. This is a listing of some of the most important related Clauses or Sub-Clauses. However, many other Sub-Clauses refer to Sub-Clause 13.3.1 and it is therefore impracticable to list them all here.
80. However, as mentioned earlier (*see* the commentaries on Sub-Clauses 3.5 [*Engineer's Instructions*] and 13.1 [*Right to Vary*] above), there is also an *informal* way in which a Variation may arise. If the Engineer should issue an instruction which the Engineer does not state to be a Variation but which the Contractor considers to be one then, pursuant to Sub-Clause 3.5, and following a Notice from the Contractor to the Engineer, with reasons, the Engineer may then confirm, reverse or vary the instruction (*see* the commentary on Sub-Clause 3.5 above). This could lead the Engineer to re-qualify its instruction as a Variation.

(1) Variation by instruction

While Sub-Clause 13.3.1 is entitled 'Variation by Instruction', it is something of a misnomer as all Variations under the Conditions are instructed by the Engineer. What the title of Sub-Clause 13.3.1 is referring to is a Variation instructed *directly* by the Engineer, as distinguished from one preceded by either an unsolicited proposal from the Contractor under Sub-Clause 13.2 [*Value Engineering*] or a request for a proposal from the Engineer (and a subsequent response from the Contractor) under Sub-Clause 13.3.2. However, once the Engineer consents to a proposal under Sub-Clause either 13.2 or 13.3.2 (or, pursuant to Sub-Clause 3.5, acknowledges a previous instruction to be a Variation), Sub-Clause 13.3.1 will generally apply to the instruction of the Variation.

The Engineer is required to instruct a Variation by way of a Notice, which must comply with Sub-Clause 1.3 [*Notices and Other Communications*]; that is, it must be in writing and identified as a Notice.[81] The Engineer's Notice must describe the required change, and state any requirements for the recording of Costs.[82]

After receiving the Engineer's Notice instructing a Variation, the Contractor must proceed with the execution of the Variation – with due expedition and without delay[83] – and submit, within 28 days (or another period proposed by the Contractor and agreed by the Engineer), detailed particulars regarding the matters listed in sub-paragraphs (a) to (c) of Sub-Clause 13.3.1,[84] including 'any necessary modifications (if any) to

81. An Employer (or the Engineer on its behalf) cannot avoid the characterisation of work as a Variation simply by refusing to issue a written instruction. Thus, in an Australian case, the employer had insisted that the contractor perform certain work, maintaining that it was included in the contract. The contractor claimed that the work was outside the contract. At the same time, the employer refused to issue an order in writing for the work to be done. In these circumstances, the English Privy Council, finding that the work was outside the contract, held that the contractor could recover the cost of the work it had been required to do upon the basis that the employer had, by its conduct, impliedly promised to pay for it. *Molloy v Liebe* [1910] 102 L.T.616 PC. *See also* under **(iv) Related Law** below.
82. Sub-Clause 13.3.1, first paragraph.
83. Sub-Clause 13.1, third paragraph.
84. The World Bank's COPA requires the description of the varied work in sub-para. (a) to include sufficient Environmental and Social ('ES') information to enable an evaluation of the ES risks and impacts. Sub-Clause 13.3.1, COPA.

the Programme [...] and to the Time for Completion', and 'the additional payment (if any) to which the Contractor considers that the Contractor is entitled'.[85] The Contractor may not delay execution of the instruction on the ground that it has not yet submitted the particulars.

After the Contractor submits such particulars, it must submit any further particulars that the Engineer 'may reasonably require', such as any the Contractor may have overlooked or which are otherwise relevant to the execution of the Variation.

Under the last paragraph of Sub-Clause 13.3.1, the Engineer is then required to proceed under Sub-Clause 3.7 to agree or determine the EOT, if any, and/or the adjustment of the Contract Price. The Contractor will be entitled to such EOT and/or adjustment without having to comply with the claims procedure under Sub-Clause 20.2 (such as the requirement to submit a Notice of Claim within 28 days, maintain contemporary records and submit a fully detailed Claim).[86] The 42-day 'time limit for agreement' provided for in Sub-Clause 3.7.3 for the Engineer to give a Notice of agreement will commence on the date when the Engineer receives the Contractor's submission (including any requested further particulars) under Sub-Clause 13.3.1. Thus, this time limit will not commence to run until the Engineer has been provided with all particulars that it may reasonably have required.

(2) Variation by request for proposal

The Employer or the Engineer, acting on its behalf, may want information from the Contractor about a Variation they are contemplating before the Engineer instructs one. With such information, the Engineer may be able better to anticipate the consequences of the additional or changed work, its time and cost impact. Accordingly, instead of directly instruct-

85. Sub-Clause 13.3.1, second paragraph. No sanction is specified if this 28-day period is not complied with. The Contractor's valuation of the Variation must be done in accordance with Clause 12 [*Measurement and Valuation*] by using estimated quantities of the varied work.

86. However, the claims procedure in Clause 20 will apply if the Engineer issues an instruction under Sub-Clause 3.5 which is not stated to be a Variation but which the Contractor maintains – under Sub-Clause 3.5, last paragraph – is one notwithstanding the Engineer's Notice under that paragraph to the contrary.

ing a Variation, the Engineer may instead, by a Notice to the Contractor, request a proposal from the Contractor for the Variation.[87]

This manner of proceeding enables the Parties to reach an agreement regarding the consequences of the possible Variation in advance, limiting the risk of disputes. Therefore, a Variation by request for a proposal may often be a better method of instructing varied work than by way of a direct instruction, unless a Variation needs to be instructed urgently and there is no time to request and consider a proposal from the Contractor.

The Contractor must respond to the Engineer's request 'as soon as practicable' by either submitting a proposal including the matters described in Sub-Clause 13.3.1(a) to (c), or by giving reasons why it cannot comply with the request by reference to the matters described in Sub-Clause 13.1(a) to (c).[88] Assuming the Contractor submits a proposal, the Engineer must respond 'as soon as practicable' by giving a Notice to the Contractor stating its 'consent' or otherwise. The Contractor may not delay any work while waiting for the Engineer's response.

If the Engineer consents to the Contractor's proposal, with or without comments, the Engineer must instruct the Variation. The Contractor must not undertake any work pertaining to a proposed Variation until it has received such instruction.[89]

After the Engineer instructs the Variation, it may require the Contractor to submit any further particulars that the Engineer may 'reasonably require'[90] and the last paragraph of Sub-Clause 13.3.1 applies, which means that the Sub-Clause 3.7 procedure discussed above with regard to a 'Variation by Instruction' applies, but there is no obligation to comply with the claims procedure in Sub-Clause 20.2.

The last paragraph of Sub-Clause 13.3.2 contains a new provision which entitles the Contractor to recover the Cost of 'submitting' a proposal not consented to by the Engineer. While the wording could be improved ('preparing and submitting' would be clearer),[91] the principle of compen-

87. Sub-Clause 13.3.2 [*Variation by Request for Proposal*]. The Notice must comply with Sub-Clause 1.3 [*Notices and Other Communications*].
88. *See* the commentary on Sub-Clause 13.1 above.
89. *See* Sub-Clause 13.1, last paragraph.
90. Sub-Clause 13.3.2, fourth paragraph.
91. As noted in Jakob B Sørensen, *FIDIC Red Book: A Companion to the 2017 Construction Contract* (ICE Publishing, London, 2017) 138-139.

sating the Contractor is a welcome addition. The Contractor is obliged in this case to comply with the claims procedure under Sub-Clause 20.2 to recover such Cost.[92]

(iv) Related Law:[93]

(1) As discussed above, a Variation instruction must satisfy a number of requirements, as provided for in Sub-Clauses 1.3, 3.5 and 13.3.1, including that it be given in writing. May an instruction of the Engineer ever be considered a Variation instruction without satisfying these requirements?

This question is similar to that raised by the effectiveness of 'no oral modification' clauses ('NOM clauses'), that is, the practice of parties to insert in a written agreement a specific provision precluding its oral modification. Are there circumstances in which such an agreement may be modified orally notwithstanding the existence of such a provision?

Traditionally, the common law courts had reasoned that any prior agreement, including the NOM clause itself, could be modified by a later agreement.[94] But this view has changed as reflected by a decision of the UK Supreme Court.[95] In this case, the relevant clause had provided '[a]ll variations to this Licence must be agreed, set out in writing and signed on behalf of both parties before they take effect'. The licensee was late in paying licence fees and proposed a revised schedule of payments to

92. Sub-Clause 13.3.2, last paragraph. Numerous Sub-Clauses require the Variation procedure in Sub-Clause 13.3 to be followed including, but not limited to: Sub-Clauses 3.5 [*Engineer's Instructions*], 4.2.1 [*Performance Security – Contractor's Obligations*], 4.7.3 [*Setting-Out – Agreement or Determination of Rectification Measures, Delay and/or Cost*], 8.7 [*Rate of Progress*], 8.12 [*Prolonged Suspension*], 13.6 [*Adjustment for Changes in Laws*] and 17.2 [*Liability for Care of the Works*].

93. *See also* under **(iv) Related Law** of the commentary on Sub-Clause 13.1 above.

94. E Allan Farnsworth, *Contracts* (4th edn, Aspen Publishers, NY, 2004) 436 (para. 7.6). The courts said: '[t]hose who make a contract may unmake it. The clause which forbids a change, may be changed like any other. The prohibition of oral waiver, may itself be waived'. *Beatty v Guggenheim Exploration Co.*, 225 NY 380, 387 [1919].

95. *Rock Advertising Ltd v MWB Business Exchange Centres Ltd* [2018] UKSC 24 ('*Rock Advertising*') *per* Lord Sumption.

which the other party had orally agreed. Did the oral agreement to vary the payments also amount to an agreement to dispense with the NOM clause?

The UK Supreme Court said 'no' and gave effect to the NOM clause. It noted that: (1) such clauses prevent attempts to undermine written agreements by informal means; (2) in circumstances where oral discussions can easily give rise to misunderstandings and crossed purposes, it avoids disputes not just about whether a variation was intended but also about its exact terms; and (3) formality in recording variations makes it easier for corporations to police internal rules restricting the authority to agree to them.[96]

On the other hand, although the issue was not before it, the UK Supreme Court appeared to recognise that a party might be precluded by its conduct from asserting such a provision to the extent that the other party has relied on that conduct.[97] This exception may be illustrated by the following statement from a US case:

> when an owner requests a builder to do extra work, promises to pay for it and watches it performed knowing that it is not authorised in writing, he cannot refuse to pay on the ground that there was no written change order.[98]

Thus, as a general rule in common law countries, the Parties (including the Engineer) can be expected to have to comply with Sub-Clauses 1.3, 3.5 and 13.3.1 in relation to the formalities for Variation instructions, except possibly where the Employer is precluded by its conduct from invoking such provi-

96. *Rock Advertising*, para. 12.
97. The court cited to art. 2.1.18 (*Modification in a particular form*) of the UNIDROIT Principles providing that:

> A contract in writing which contains a clause requiring any modification or termination by agreement to be in a particular form may not be otherwise modified or terminated. *However, a party may be precluded by its conduct from asserting such a clause to the extent that the other party has reasonably acted in reliance on that conduct.* (Emphasis added)
>
> *Rock Advertising*, para. 13.

98. *Universal Builders v Moon Motor Lodge*, 244 A. 2d 10, 16 (Pa 1968). A similar illustration (illustration no 2) is contained in the official comment to art. 2.1.18 of the UNIDROIT Principles.

sions to the extent that the Contractor has reasonably acted in reliance on that conduct. The Employer might be precluded from doing so on the basis of the legal doctrine of estoppel in common law countries, and the legal doctrines of good faith or abuse of rights in civil law countries.[99]

(2) In addition to the Engineer's right to vary the Works as provided for in Sub-Clause 13.3, in those civil law countries where, in the case of contracts with the State or other public bodies, the doctrine of the administrative contract applies,[100] the State or public body concerned may – by mandatory law and independent of the contract's terms – have 'exceptional powers' to modify, suspend or terminate a contract in the public interest regardless of what the contract provides.[101]

(v) Improvements:

(1) As a Variation may involve a significant change, the RB should make clear that the Notice by which the Engineer either instructs a Variation, or requests a proposal from the Contractor with a view to a possible Variation, must refer to the Sub-Clause pursuant to which such Notice is given. Arguably this is already the case, as it appears to be necessary under Sub-Clause 1.3(b) for any 'instruction', 'request' or 'proposal' to include a reference to the provision of the Contract under which it was issued. On the other hand, it may equally be argued that, as the instruction of a Variation must be given by a Notice and as a Notice does not, under Sub-Clause 1.3(b), need to include a reference to the provision of the Contract under which it is issued, this requirement does not apply. Thus, this matter needs to be clarified.

(2) In circumstances where the Engineer has requested a proposal from the Contractor pursuant to Sub-Clause 13.3.2, the Contrac-

99. *Rock Advertising*, para. 16. For further information about the position in civil law countries, *see* Marcel Fontaine and Filip De Ly, *Drafting International Contracts: An Analysis of Contract Clauses* (Martinus Nijhoff, Leiden, the Netherlands, 2009) 159-163.

100. *See* **Section 4 Common Law and Civil Law Compared – 4.2.2 Public and Private Contracts** of **Chapter II Applicable Law** above.

101. *See* **Section 4 Common Law and Civil Law Compared – 4.6 Civil Law: Special Public Law Theories** of **Chapter II Applicable Law** above.

tor incurs Cost in preparing and submitting the proposal, and then the Engineer does not consent to it, it may be excessive to require the Contractor to claim for this Cost pursuant to Sub-Clause 20.2. The Cost has been incurred at the Engineer's request and, if it is reasonable in amount, it should be reimbursed directly.[102]

(3) As noted under **(iii) Analysis** above, in the interest of clarity, the last paragraph of Sub-Clause 13.3.2 should refer to the Cost of 'preparing and submitting' a proposal and not just to 'submitting' a proposal.

--ooOOoo--

13.4 Provisional Sums

> Each Provisional Sum shall only be used, in whole or in part, in accordance with the Engineer's instructions, and the Contract Price shall be adjusted accordingly. The total sum paid to the Contractor shall include only such amounts for the work, supplies or services to which the Provisional Sum relates, as the Engineer shall have instructed.
>
> For each Provisional Sum, the Engineer may instruct:
>
> (a) work to be executed (including Plant, Materials or services to be supplied) by the Contractor, and for which adjustments to the Contract Price shall be agreed or determined under Sub-Clause 13.3.1 [*Variation by Instruction*]; and/or
>
> (b) Plant, Materials, works or services to be purchased by the Contractor from a nominated Subcontractor (as defined in Sub-Clause 5.2

102. By way of comparison, the Employer is not required to proceed under Sub-Clause 20.2 to recover an amount due by the Contractor for its use of utilities provided by the Employer under Sub-Clause 4.19 [*Temporary Utilities*]. Instead, according to item (ix) of Sub-Clause 14.3 [*Application for Interim Payment*], this amount may be deducted from the Contractor's Statement of the amount due.

[*Nominated Subcontractors*]) or otherwise; and for which there shall be included in the Contract Price:

(i) the actual amounts paid (or due to be paid) by the Contractor; and
(ii) a sum for overhead charges and profit, calculated as a percentage of these actual amounts by applying the relevant percentage rate (if any) stated in the applicable Schedule. If there is no such rate, the percentage rate stated in the Contract Data shall be applied.

If the Engineer instructs the Contractor under sub-paragraph (a) and/or (b) above, this instruction may include a requirement for the Contractor to submit quotations from the Contractor's suppliers and/or subcontractors for all (or some) of the items of the work to be executed or Plant, Materials, works or services to be purchased. Thereafter, the Engineer may respond by giving a Notice either instructing the Contractor to accept one of these quotations (but such an instruction shall not be taken as an instruction under Sub-Clause 5.2 [*Nominated Subcontractors*]) or revoking the instruction. If the Engineer does not so respond within 7 days of receiving the quotations, the Contractor shall be entitled to accept any of these quotations at the Contractor's discretion.

Each Statement that includes a Provisional Sum shall also include all applicable invoices, vouchers and accounts or receipts in substantiation of the Provisional Sum.

Each Provisional Sum must only be used in accordance with Engineer's instructions, and the Contract Price must be adjusted accordingly. The total sum paid to the Contractor must only include such amounts for work to which the Provisional Sum relates, as the Engineer shall have instructed.

For each Provisional Sum, the Engineer may instruct: (a) work to be executed (including Plant, Materials or services) by the Contractor and for adjustments to the Contract Price to be made under Sub-Clause 13.3.1, and/or (b) Plant, Materials, works or services to be

purchased by the Contractor from a nominated Subcontractor or otherwise and for the amounts paid to be included in the Contract Price.

The Engineer may require the Contractor to submit quotations for the work to be executed which, by a Notice, the Engineer may instruct the Contractor to accept or not. If the Engineer fails to respond within 7 days of receiving the quotations, the Contractor may accept any of them. Each Statement that includes a Provisional Sum must include all applicable invoices.

Commentary

(i) Main Changes from RB/99:

(1) Whereas Sub-Clause 13.5 of RB/99 had provided that work done for a Provisional Sum was to be valued under Sub-Clause 13.3 [*Variation Procedure*],[103] the new Sub-Clause requires that adjustments to the Contract Price for work done at a Provisional Sum (under sub-paragraph (a)) be agreed or determined under Sub-Clause 13.3.1 which requires, among other things, that the Engineer proceeds under Sub-Clause 3.7 [*Agreement or Determination*].

(2) The third paragraph, which provides that the Engineer's instruction may include a requirement for the Contractor to submit quotations from suppliers and/or subcontractors, allowing the Engineer to decide which one to accept, is much more detailed than the corresponding provision (the last paragraph) in RB/99.

(3) Whereas Sub-Clause 13.5 of RB/99 had required the Contractor to produce quotations, invoices, vouchers and accounts or receipts only when required by the Engineer, the last paragraph of the new Sub-Clause requires that each Statement includes all applicable invoices, vouchers and accounts or receipts in substantiation of the Provisional Sum.[104]

(ii) Related Clauses / Sub-Clauses: 1.2 [*Interpretation*]; 1.3 [*Notices and Other Communications*], 5.2 [*Nominated Subcontractors*], 13.3.1 [*Varia-*

103. Sub-Clause 13.5(a) and Sub-Clauses 13.3, last paragraph, of RB/99.
104. *See also* item (vii) and sub-para. (c) of Sub-Clause 14.3 [*Application for Interim Payment*] of RB/17.

tion Procedure-Variation by Instruction], 14.2.3 [*Advance Payment-Repayment of Advance Payment*], 14.3 [*Application for Interim Payment*] and 14.15 [*Currencies of Payment*].

(iii) Analysis:

(1) The nature of Provisional Sums

A Provisional Sum is defined in the Conditions as:

> a sum (if any) which is specified in the Contract by the Employer as a provisional sum, for the execution of any part of the Works or for the supply of Plant, Materials or services under Sub-Clause 13.4 [*Provisional Sums*].[105]

Thus, it is a sum of money provided for by the Employer, normally in the Specification,[106] for the execution of additional work, or the provision of additional services or the purchase of particular equipment or Materials to be selected by the Engineer. Among other things, it may be for any uncertain parts of the Works, such as underground conditions,[107] or for Plant, Materials, works or services to be purchased from a nominated Subcontractor.[108] Whatever its specified purpose, a Provisional Sum may only be used for that purpose.

FIDIC recommends that the Employer prepares, for inclusion in the Contract, a separate Schedule listing and defining the scope of each Provisional Sum.[109] It might also be necessary to clarify the timing of any relevant instructions related to the work covered by a Provisions Sum.[110]

A Provisional Sum may only be used, whether in whole or in part, if instructed by the Engineer.[111] As Provisional Sums are defined as sums

105. Sub-Clause 1.1.67 '**Provisional Sum**'.
106. *FIDIC Procurement Procedures Guide* (FIDIC, 2011) 120. The amount is included in the Bill of Quantities.
107. *FIDIC DBO Guide* (FIDIC, 2011) 17 and *The FIDIC Contracts Guide* (1st edn, FIDIC, 2000) 225.
108. *See* sub-para. (b) of Sub-Clause 13.4.
109. *Guidance for the Preparation of Particular Conditions*, 36.
110. *The FIDIC Contracts Guide* (1st edn, FIDIC, 2000) 225.
111. Sub-Clause 13.4, first sentence. The World Bank's COPA provides that a Provisional Sum shall be used to cover the Employer's share of the DAAB Members' fees and expenses and no prior instruction of the Engineer shall be required with respect to the work of the DAAB. Sub-Clause 13.4, COPA. This seems like a useful addition.

'specified in the Contract', neither the Engineer nor the Employer may add new Provisional Sums, whether by a Variation or otherwise.[112] The amount of the Provisional Sum specified should represent the Employer's realistic estimate of the amount to be expended. However, the Contractor will not be bound or limited by the amount of the Provisional Sum if the value of its work should exceed it.[113]

(2) The Engineer's instruction

The Engineer's instruction for the use of a Provisional Sum may take one of two forms. It may either be a Variation for the carrying out of additional work instructed under Sub-Clause 13.3.1 or an instruction for the purchase of Plant, Materials, works or services from a nominated Subcontractor or other supplier. In the first case, the adjustment of the Contract Price as a result of the use of the Provisional Sum must be 'agreed or determined under Sub-Clause 13.3.1', which requires that the Engineer proceed under Sub-Clause 3.7 [*Agreement or Determination*]. In the second case, the amount to be included in the Contract Price must include the actual amounts paid (or due to be paid) by the Contractor as well as a percentage of these amounts for the Contractor's overhead charges and profit.[114] This percentage should be specified by the Parties in the applicable Schedule or the Contract Data.[115]

The third paragraph of Sub-Clause 13.4 entitles the Engineer to require that the Contractor submit quotations from the Contractor's suppliers and/or subcontractors for the work to be executed or the Plant, Materials, works or services to be purchased. After receiving these quotations, the Engineer may respond by a Notice either instructing the Contractor to accept one of these quotations or, where the Engineer is dissatisfied with the quotations received, 'revoking the instruction'. If the Engineer does not respond within 7 days of receiving the quotations, the Contractor is entitled to accept any of them.

---

112. *The FIDIC Contracts Guide* (1st edn, FIDIC, 2000) 225.
113. *Ibid.*
114. Sub-Clause 13.4(b)(i) and (ii).
115. Sub-Clause 13.4(b)(ii) provides that if no rate is stated in an applicable Schedule 'the percentage rate stated in the Contract Data shall be applied'. In this connection, it has been correctly noted that the rate in Sub-Clause 1.1.20 '**Cost Plus Profit**' (5%) does not apply as the Sub-Clause 1.1.20 rate is to cover profit and *not* 'overheads or similar changes', *see* Sub-Clause 1.1.19 '**Cost**', Jakob Sørensen, *FIDIC Red Book: A Companion to the 2017 Construction Contract* (ICE Publishing, London, 2019) 139.

The Contractor must include in each Statement that includes a Provisional Sum all applicable invoices, vouchers and accounts or receipts in substantiation of its use.[116]

(iv) Related Law: The concept of provisional sums originated in England and is closely related to the figure of the nominated subcontractor.[117] Since the end of the 19th century, English construction contracts have contained provisions that enable employers to select particular subcontractors to carry out particular parts of the main contract work.[118] These subcontractors, often referred to as nominated subcontractors, entered into direct contractual relations with the main contractor. For historical reasons, the work that was to be carried out by these subcontractors was indicated in the specifications or the bills of quantities as 'Provisional Sums' items of work.[119]

--ooOOoo--

13.5 Daywork

If a Daywork Schedule is not included in the Contract, this Sub-Clause shall not apply.

For work of a minor or incidental nature, the Engineer may instruct that a Variation shall be executed on a daywork basis. The work shall then be valued in accordance with the Daywork Schedule, and the following procedure shall apply.

Before ordering Goods for such work (other than any Goods priced in the Daywork Schedule), the Contractor shall submit one or more quotations from the Contractor's suppliers and/or subcontractors to

116. *See* the last paragraph of Sub-Clause 13.4 and Sub-Clause 14.3 (vii). If the Engineer does not instruct the use of a particular Provisional Sum, then that money will remain unused and the Contractor has no right or claim on it.
117. For the definition of 'nominated Subcontractor' *see* Sub-Clause 5.2.1.
118. I N Duncan Wallace, *The International Civil Engineering Contract, A Commentary on the FIDIC International Standard Form of Civil Engineering and Building Contract* (Sweet & Maxwell, London, 1974) 120.
119. *Ibid.*, 120, 123. The late Mr Duncan Wallace had also noted that the word 'provisional' probably arose originally as a corruption of the words '*provide* the sums' or '*provisions*' in early contracts and not from its usual English language sense of 'contingent' work, 123.

the Engineer. Thereafter, the Engineer may instruct the Contractor to accept one of these quotations (but such an instruction shall not be taken as an instruction under Sub-Clause 5.2 [*Nominated Subcontractors*]). If the Engineer does not so instruct the Contractor within 7 days of receiving the quotations, the Contractor shall be entitled to accept any of these quotations at the Contractor's discretion.

Except for any items for which the Daywork Schedule specifies that payment is not due, the Contractor shall deliver each day to the Engineer accurate statements in duplicate (and one electronic copy), which shall include records (as described under Sub-Clause 6.10 [*Contractor's Records*]) of the resources used in executing the previous day's work.

One copy of each statement shall, if correct and agreed, be signed by the Engineer and promptly returned to the Contractor. If not correct or agreed, the Engineer shall proceed under Sub-Clause 3.7 [*Agreement or Determination*] to agree or determine the resources (and for the purpose of Sub-Clause 3.7.3 [*Time limits*], the date the works which are the subject of the Variation under this Sub-Clause are completed by the Contractor shall be the date of commencement of the time limit for agreement under Sub-Clause 3.7.3).

In the next Statement, the Contractor shall then submit priced statements of the agreed or determined resources to the Engineer, together with all applicable invoices, vouchers and accounts or receipts in substantiation of any Goods used in the daywork (other than Goods priced in the Daywork Schedule).

Unless otherwise stated in the Daywork Schedule, the rates and prices in the Daywork Schedule shall be deemed to include taxes, overheads and profit.

This Sub-Clause only applies if a Daywork Schedule is included in the Contract.

For work of minor or incidental nature, the Engineer may instruct that a Variation be executed on a daywork basis and valued in

accordance with the Daywork Schedule. Before ordering Goods for such work (unless they are priced in the Daywork Schedule), the Contractor must submit quotations from its suppliers and/or subcontractors, and the Engineer may instruct the Contractor to accept one of these quotations. If the Engineer does not do so within 7 days, the Contractor may accept any of them.

The Contractor must deliver each day statements, including records (as described in Sub-Clause 6.10) of the resources used in executing the previous day's work. If correct and agreed, a copy must be signed by the Engineer and returned to the Contractor. If not correct or agreed, the Engineer must proceed under Sub-Clause 3.7.

In the next Statement, the Contractor must submit priced statements of the agreed or determined resources together with invoices in substantiation of the Goods used in the daywork (unless priced in the Daywork Schedule). The rates and prices in the Daywork Schedule are deemed to include taxes, overheads and profits.

Commentary

(i) Main Changes from RB/99:

(1) Whereas by Sub-Clause 13.6, second paragraph, of RB/99 the Contractor was required simply to submit quotations to the Engineer before ordering Goods, the new Sub-Clause adds, in its third paragraph, that the Engineer may instruct the Contractor to accept one of these quotations and that, if the Engineer does not do so within 7 days, the Contractor may accept any of them.

(2) The new Sub-Clause provides, in the fourth paragraph, that each statement of the resources used the previous day must include the records listed in Sub-Clause 6.10 [*Contractor's Records*], whereas RB/99 had not required so much information.

(3) RB/99, third paragraph, provided that, except for items in the Daywork Schedule for which payment was not due, the Contractor had to deliver each day to the Engineer accurate statements of the resources used in executing the previous day's work, and the Engineer would sign a copy of each such statement 'if correct, or when agreed' and then return it to the Contractor. RB/99 did not deal with where the submitted statements were incorrect or not agreed. On the other hand, the new Sub-Clause provides, in its fifth paragraph, that if a statement was not

correct and agreed, the Engineer must proceed under Sub-Clause 3.7 to agree or determine the resources.

(4) The new Sub-Clause explicitly provides (in its last paragraph), unlike RB/99, that the rates and prices in the Daywork Schedule (unless otherwise stated therein) are deemed to include taxes, overheads and profit.

(ii) Related Clauses / Sub-Clauses: 1.3 [*Notices and Other Communications*], 3.7 [*Agreement or Determination*], 5.2 [*Nominated Subcontractors*], 6.10 [*Contractor's Records*] and 13.3.1 [*Variation Procedure – Variation by Instruction*].

(iii) Analysis:

(1) When daywork rates apply

Sub-Clause 13.5 only applies if there is a Daywork Schedule[120] included in the Contract. If such a Schedule is included, then this Sub-Clause authorises the Engineer, for 'work of a minor or incidental nature', to instruct that it be carried out as a Variation on the basis of the daywork rates in the Daywork Schedule.[121] Typically, daywork rates are favourable to the Contractor. Thus, unless minor or incidental work is involved and daywork has been instructed by the Engineer, there is no justification for using daywork rates.

(2) The Daywork Schedule

The Daywork Schedule should define:

(a) a time charge rate for each category of labour (for example, US$ - / pipelayer/hour),
(b) a time charge rate for each category of Contractor's Equipment (for example, US$ - /30 ton excavator/hour), and
(c) the payment due for each category of Materials. This can be on a Cost-plus basis or a rate per unit quantity basis.[122]

120. A Daywork Schedule is defined as a document entitled 'daywork schedule' and showing 'the amounts and manner of payments to be made to the Contractor for labour, materials and equipment used for daywork under Sub-Clause 13.5 [*Daywork*]'. Sub-Clause 1.1.26 '**Daywork Schedule**'.

121. The Engineer's instruction must comply with Sub-Clause 13.3.1 [*Variation by Instruction*] and Sub-Clause 1.3 [*Notices and Other Communications*].

122. *The FIDIC Contracts Guide* (2nd edn, FIDIC, 2022) 22.

The last paragraph of Sub-Clause 13.5 provides that the rates and prices in the Daywork Schedule are deemed to include taxes, overheads and profit, unless otherwise stated in the Daywork Schedule.

Before ordering any Goods for such work, which are not priced in the Daywork Schedule, the Contractor must submit to the Engineer one or more quotations from its suppliers and/or subcontractors.[123] The Engineer is then authorised to instruct the Contractor to accept one of them. The Contractor may accept any quotation at its discretion in case the Engineer does not issue such an instruction within seven days of receiving the quotations.

(3) Payment for daywork

The Contractor is required to deliver to the Engineer each day accurate statements that include records of the resources used in executing the previous day's work.[124] Such records must include (unless the Contractor and Engineer otherwise agree) the information listed in sub-paragraphs (a) to (e) of Sub-Clause 6.10 [*Contractor's Records*] for each activity shown in the Programme, at each location, and for each day of work.[125]

If a statement is 'correct and agreed', the Engineer is required to sign a copy of it and return it promptly to the Contractor. If not correct and agreed, the Engineer must proceed under Sub-Clause 3.7 and agree or determine the resources used in executing the daily work.[126]

The Contractor should claim payment for daywork in its next interim Statement under Sub-Clause 14.3 by submitting to the Engineer 'priced statements of the agreed or determined resources' together with documents in substantiation of the Goods used in the daywork, such as invoices, vouchers and accounts or receipts. Consequently, the Contractor is paid for daywork only if the priced statements of the resources have been accepted or agreed or determined by the Engineer.

--ooOOoo--

123. Sub-Clause 13.5, third paragraph.
124. Except for any items for which the Daywork Schedule specifies that payment is not due. Sub-Clause 13.5, fourth paragraph.
125. Sub-Clause 13.5, fourth paragraph, and Sub-Clause 6.10.
126. Sub-Clause 13.5, fifth paragraph.

13.6 Adjustments for Changes in Laws

Subject to the following provisions of this Sub-Clause, the Contract Price shall be adjusted to take account of any increase or decrease in Cost resulting from a change in:

(a) the Laws of the Country (including the introduction of new Laws and the repeal or modification of existing Laws);
(b) the judicial or official governmental interpretation or implementation of the Laws referred to in sub-paragraph (a) above;
(c) any permit, permission, licence or approval obtained by the Employer or the Contractor under sub-paragraph (a) or (b), respectively, of Sub-Clause 1.13 [*Compliance with Laws*]; or
(d) the requirements for any permit, permission, licence and/or approval to be obtained by the Contractor under sub-paragraph (b) of Sub-Clause 1.13 [*Compliance with Laws*],

made and/or officially published after the Base Date, which affect the Contractor in the performance of obligations under the Contract. In this Sub-Clause "change in Laws" means any of the changes under sub-paragraphs (a), (b), (c) and/or (d) above.

If the Contractor suffers delay and/or incurs an increase in Cost as a result of any change in Laws, the Contractor shall be entitled subject to Sub-Clause 20.2 [*Claims for Payment and/or EOT*] to EOT and/or payment of such Cost.

If there is a decrease in Cost as a result of any change in Laws, the Employer shall be entitled subject to Sub-Clause 20.2 [*Claims for Payment and/or EOT*] to a reduction in the Contract Price.

If any adjustment to the execution of the Works becomes necessary as a result of any change in Laws:

(i) the Contractor shall promptly give a Notice to the Engineer, or
(ii) the Engineer shall promptly give a Notice to the Contractor

(with detailed supporting particulars).

Thereafter, the Engineer shall either instruct a Variation under Sub-Clause 13.3.1 [*Variation by Instruction*] or request a proposal under Sub-Clause 13.3.2 [*Variation by Request for Proposal*].

Subject to this Sub-Clause, the Contract Price must be adjusted to take account of any increase or decrease in Cost resulting from a 'change in Laws' after the Base Date, which affects the Contractor in the performance of obligations under the Contract. A 'change in Laws' is a change in: (a) the Laws of the Country; (b) the judicial or official governmental interpretation or implementation of these Laws; (c) any permit, permission, licence or approval obtained by either Party under Sub-Clause 1.13; or (d) the requirements for any permit, permission, licence or approval to be obtained by the Contractor under Sub-Clause 1.13.

If the Contractor suffers delay and/or incurs an increase in Cost as a result of any change in Laws, the Contractor is entitled, subject to Sub-Clause 20.2, to EOT and/or payment of such Cost. If the change in Laws results in a Cost decrease, the Employer is entitled, subject to Sub-Clause 20.2, to a reduction in the Contract Price.

If any adjustment to the execution of the Works becomes necessary as a result of any change in Laws, the Contractor must give a Notice to the Engineer or the Engineer must give a Notice to the Contractor. Thereafter, the Engineer must instruct, or request a proposal for, a Variation under Sub-Clause 13.3.

Commentary

(i) Main Changes from RB/99:

(1) A 'change in Laws' has been expanded to comprise, among other matters, a change in the 'implementation' (not just the 'judicial or official governmental interpretation') of the Laws of the Country, a change in 'any permit, permission, licence or approval' obtained by either Party under Sub-Clause 1.13 [*Compliance with Laws*] as well as a change in 'the requirements for any permit, permission, licence and/or approval' to be obtained by the Contractor under that Sub-Clause.

(2) The Contractor's entitlement to claim an EOT and/or additional payment has been narrowed down: under Sub-Clause 13.7 of

RB/99, the Contractor had a right to claim additional time and Cost if it 'suffers (or will suffer) delay and/or incurs (or will incur) additional Cost'. Under the new Sub-Clause, the Contractor is only entitled to claim an EOT and/or payment of additional Cost if it *actually* 'suffers delay and/or incurs an increase in Cost' as a result of the change in Laws.

(3) Whereas Sub-Clause 13.7 of RB/99 had envisaged that the Contract Price be adjusted in case of any 'decrease in Cost' resulting from a change in Laws of the Country, it did not refer to the claims procedure with which the Employer might have to comply;[127] however, the third paragraph of the new Sub-Clause stipulates that, in the case of a decrease in Cost, the Employer will be entitled to a reduction of the Contract Price subject to compliance with Sub-Clause 20.2.

(4) The provision in the last two paragraphs, dealing with any necessary adjustment to the execution of the Works as a result of a change in Laws and the instruction of a Variation, is new and has no analogue in RB/99.

(5) The definition of 'Laws' has been expanded and now explicitly includes, among other things, treaties and international law.[128]

(ii) Related Clauses / Sub-Clauses: 1.3 [*Notices and Other Communications*], 1.13 [*Compliance with Laws*], 4.6 [*Co-operation*], 6.4 [*Labour Laws*], 13.3.1 [*Variation by Instruction*], 13.3.2 [*Variation by Request for Proposal*], 14.1 [*The Contract Price*], 14.3 [*Application for Interim Period*], 14.15 [*Currencies of Payments*] and 20.2 [*Claims for Payment and/or EOT*].[129]

---

127. However, Sub-Clause 2.5 of RB/99, concerning Employer's claims, applied in all cases where the Employer considered itself 'to be entitled to any payment under any Clause of these Conditions'. Consequently, even though compliance with the claims procedure was not explicitly mentioned in Sub-Clause 13.7, such compliance was necessary because of the wording of Sub-Clause 2.5. *See also The FIDIC Contracts Guide* (1st edn, FIDIC, 2000) 228.

128. *See* the commentary on Sub-Clause 1.1.49 **'Laws'** above. The title of Sub-Clause 13.6 (13.7 in RB/99) has changed from 'Adjustments for Changes in Legislation' in 1999 to the broader expression to 'Adjustments for Changes in Laws' in the new Sub-Clause.

129. Numerous other Sub-Clauses refer to Laws. This is a selection of those which appear most relevant.

(iii) Analysis:

(1) Purpose of the Sub-Clause

In the case of an RB Contract, a Contractor from one country will typically be performing work in another country. The Contract will often be performed over a period of years during which the Contractor is required by the Contract to comply with the laws of, among others, the Country, that is, the country in which the Site (or most of it) is located.[130] During that time, changes in the laws of the Country may occur which increase (or, much more rarely, reduce) the Contractor's Cost of performing the Works. In the absence of any provision for relief in the Contract, the Contractor would have to bear these increases in Cost (and the Employer would not benefit – in the much less likely case – of any reduction in the Contractor's Cost) as the result of changes in the law of the Country.

To address this situation, the RB has, since RB/77, contained a Sub-Clause providing for adjustment of the Contract Price where a change in the Laws of the Country causes additional or reduced cost to the Contractor in the execution of the Works.[131]

(2) Elements of Claim

The new Sub-Clause is much more detailed than the corresponding provision, Sub-Clause 13.7, in RB/99 and it is important to identify what the Contractor or the Employer must do in order to obtain relief. In order to do so, the Contractor needs to establish the following *six elements*:

(1) There has been *an increase in Cost*, which is defined as an increase in 'expenditure reasonably incurred (or to be incurred) by the Contractor in performing the Contract, whether on or off the Site, including taxes, overheads and similar charges, but does not include profit'.[132]
Thus, the increase (or, if the Employer is claiming, a decrease) must be in relation to expenditure incurred by the Contractor only. The Employer's costs are irrelevant and of no

130. *See* Sub-Clause 1.13 [*Compliance with Laws*] which requires both Parties to comply with 'all applicable Laws' and not just the Laws of the Country.
131. In RB/77 this was Clause 70 (2) entitled 'Subsequent Legislation'.
132. Sub-Clause 1.1.19 '**Cost**'.

consequence.[133] The main types of costs concerned are likely to be taxes, customs duties and other governmental charges, changes in rates of wages or changes in labour conditions or building or environmental regulations as a result of changes in Law, all of which may affect Cost.

(2) The increase (or decrease) in Cost *must result from a 'change in Laws'*, as defined in sub-paragraphs (a), (b), (c) or (d). These refer to a change in any of the following four matters: (a) the Laws of the Country, defined as where the Site is located;[134] (b) the judicial or official governmental interpretation or implementation of the Laws of the Country;[135] (c) any permit, permission, licence or approval obtained *in any country* by either Party under Sub-Clause 1.13 [*Compliance with Laws*];[136] or (d) the requirements for any permit, permission, licence and/or approval to be obtained *in any country* by the Contractor under Sub-Clause 1.13. Thus, changes of the kind referred to in sub-paragraphs (c) and (d) may involve changes in the Laws of the Contractor's country.

'Laws' are defined very broadly as comprising 'all national (or state or provincial) legislation, statutes, acts, decrees, rules, ordinances, orders, treaties, international law and other laws, and regulations and by-laws of any legally constituted public authority'.[137] Thus, they include a wide variety of legal norms. But the definition of 'Laws' is not without limit. Thus, it does not encompass government actions generally or changes in govern-

133. Obviously, therefore, it will be easier for the Contractor, as it will be referring to its own records, to identify and demonstrate an increase in Cost than for the Employer to identify and demonstrate a decrease in the Contractor's Cost.
134. For the full definition, *see* Sub-Clause 1.1.21 '**Country**'.
135. While a clause providing relief in the case of changes in the judicial or official interpretations of laws may not be that common in international constructions contracts, it is common in, for example, illegality clauses in international loan agreements. *See* Philip Wood, *Law and Practice of International Finance* (1st edn, Sweet & Maxwell, London, 1980) 143 (para. 5.2(5)).
136. It is unclear how any change in 'any permit, permission, license or approval obtained by the Employer' in sub-para. (c) would result in a change in Cost, as defined, that is, the Contractor's cost.
137. Sub-Clause 1.1.49 '**Laws**'.

ment or central bank policy.[138] By contrast, a change in the permitted speeds on, or hours of use of, roads, if it resulted from an ordinance or other law or regulation, that increase the Contractor's Cost, would be sufficient to justify application of the Sub-Clause.

Only the Laws of the Country are relevant, as regards sub-paragraphs (a) and (b).[139]

(3) The 'change in Laws' must be *made and/or officially published*[140] *after the Base Date*, which is defined as the date 28 days before the latest date for submission of the Tender.[141]

Thus, it is irrelevant whether the 'change in Laws' was foreseeable or known to one or both of the Parties at the Base Date or the date of the Letter of Acceptance or Contract Agreement.[142]

(4) The 'change in Laws' must *'affect the Contractor in the performance of obligations under the Contract'*. In view of element 1) above and element 5) below, it is evident that the change in Laws will 'affect' the Contractor in the performance of the Contract. Accordingly, element 4) (which was also in Sub-Clause 13.7 of RB/99) appears to be superfluous.

---

138. For example, it would not include where a central bank reverses a policy of supporting the national currency, causing a drastic fall in its value, upsetting international transactions in that currency, e.g., the decision of the Egyptian central bank in November 2016 to allow the Egyptian pound to float, halving the value of the pound against the US dollar overnight. *See* 'Cairo Attracts as Currency Falls', *The Financial Times*, 23 March 2017.
139. This is important to note as the Contractor may be impacted by changes in the Laws of other countries as well, such as its home country and any countries from which Goods may be procured, Contractor's Personnel may be engaged or through which either may transit. Changes in their tax, customs, immigration and other laws which increase Cost are not compensated under this Sub-Clause.
140. It is commonplace for a law or regulation to be put into effect by its official publication, also referred to as 'promulgation'. Bryan A Garner (ed in chief) *Black's Law Dictionary* (11th edn, Thomson Reuters, St Paul MN, 2019).
141. Sub-Clause 1.1.4 '**Base Date**'.
142. There would certainly be a case for saying that the Contractor should not be entitled to recover for an increase in Costs on account of a 'change in Laws' which it could reasonably have foreseen at the Base Date and priced for or which it knew about when signing the Contract Agreement. But this is not the position taken in the General Conditions.

(5) The Contractor *suffers delay and/or incurs an increase in Cost as a result of any change in Laws*. This item is self-explanatory and requires no comment.
(6) The Contractor must give a Notice of Claim to the Engineer within 28 days – *or be time barred*, as provided for in Sub-Clause 20.2.1, and otherwise comply with Sub-Clause 20.2.

If the Contractor can establish all *six elements* – it has the burden to prove or establish them – it is entitled (subject to Sub-Clause 20.2) to an EOT and a payment of such Cost.

On the other hand, for the Employer to establish an entitlement to a reduction in the Contract Price, it needs to establish only *the first four elements above (the first one being, however, a decrease, rather than an increase, in the Contractor's Cost*[143]) *and the last, sixth element*. If it can do so, then it is entitled (subject to Sub-Clause 20.2) to a reduction in the Contract Price.

(3) Change in Laws affecting Works

A change in Laws may have the effect of restricting or even prohibiting the execution of some part of the Works, e.g., in the case of a change in environmental or zoning legislation limiting or prohibiting the Works that may be constructed, or local acts of terrorism which result in Laws requiring that work be changed (e.g., a road be diverted) or suspended for security reasons.[144] To address this kind of situation, the two last paragraphs of the Sub-Clause authorise the Engineer[145] to instruct a Variation or request a proposal for one from the Contractor.

(iv) Related Law: Absent a provision such as Sub-Clause 13.6, in civil law countries following the French administrative law tradition, a Contractor having a contract with a public body, which is affected by a

143. This is likely to necessitate the Contractor's cooperation. *See* Sub-Clause 4.6 [*Co-operation*].
144. If execution of the Works is prohibited entirely, Sub-Clause 18.6 [*Release from Performance under the Law*] may apply.
145. Subject to the giving of a prompt Notice from the Contractor to the Engineer or the Engineer to the Contractor, as the case may be.

change in Laws, might be able to seek relief on the basis of the 'act of the prince' (*fait du prince*) or hardship (*imprévision*) doctrines described earlier.[146]

(v) Improvements:

(1) Consideration might be given to providing, as an alternative (though the present Sub-Clause is perfectly satisfactory), that the change in Laws must be Unforeseeable at the Base Date, and/or to exclude from operation of the Sub-Clause changes in Laws which are anticipated at the Base Date *and are listed in a Schedule or the Contract Data.* This list might include, for example, draft laws or regulations that were under consideration by the legislature or a regulatory body at the Base Date.
(2) Instead of requiring that a change in Laws 'affect the Contractor in the Performance of obligations under the Contract' (element (4) under the heading *(2) Elements of Claim* under **(iii) Analysis** above), it might be sufficient to require that the increase or decrease in Cost has been incurred by the Contractor 'in relation to the execution of the Works'.
(3) There should be a provision protecting against the Contractor enjoying a double recovery under both this Sub-Clause and Sub-Clause 8.5 [*Extension of Time for Completion*] and/or 13.7 [*Adjustments for Changes in Cost*].[147]

--ooOOoo--

13.7 Adjustments for Changes in Cost

If Schedule(s) of cost indexation are not included in the Contract, this Sub-Clause shall not apply.

The amounts payable to the Contractor shall be adjusted for rises or falls in the cost of labour, Goods and other inputs to the Works, by the addition or

146. *See* **Section 4 Common Law and Civil Law Compared – 4.6.2 Hardship (*Imprévision*)** and **4.6.3 Act of the Prince (*Fait Du Prince*)**, in **Chapter II Applicable Law** above.
147. The World Bank's COPA contains a provision to this effect in relation to Sub-Clause 13.6.

deduction of the amounts calculated in accordance with the Schedule(s) of cost indexation.

To the extent that full compensation for any rise or fall in Costs is not covered by this Sub-Clause or other Clauses of these Conditions, the Accepted Contract Amount shall be deemed to have included amounts to cover the contingency of other rises and falls in costs.

The adjustment to be applied to the amount otherwise payable to the Contractor, as certified in Payment Certificates, shall be calculated for each of the currencies in which the Contract Price is payable. No adjustment shall be applied to work valued on the basis of Cost or current prices.

Until such time as each current cost index is available, the Engineer shall use a provisional index for the issue of Interim Payment Certificates. When a current cost index is available, the adjustment shall be recalculated accordingly.

If the Contractor fails to complete the Works within the Time for Completion, adjustment of prices thereafter shall be made using either:

(a) each index or price applicable on the date 49 days before the expiry of the Time for Completion of the Works; or
(b) the current index or price

whichever is more favourable to the Employer.

This Sub-Clause only applies if a Schedule(s) of cost indexation is included in the Contract.

The amounts payable to the Contractor must be adjusted for rises or falls in the cost of labour, Goods and other inputs to the Works, by the addition or deduction of the amounts calculated in accordance with the Schedule(s) of cost indexation. If full compensation for any rise or fall in Costs is not covered by these Conditions, the Accepted Contract Amount shall be deemed to cover it.

The adjustment must be calculated for each of the currencies in which the Contract Price is payable. Until such time as each current cost index is available, the Engineer must use a provisional index for the issue of IPCs.

If the Contractor fails to complete the Works within the Time for Completion, price adjustments thereafter must be made by using the index specified in either sub-paragraph (a) or (b), whichever is more favourable to the Employer.

Commentary

(i) Main Changes from RB/99:

(1) The price adjustment formula (called 'Schedule(s) of cost indexation' and in RB/99 called 'table of adjustment data') has been transferred from the General Conditions in RB/99 to the Special Provisions in the Particular Conditions of RB/17.[148]

(2) The last paragraph of Sub-Clause 13.8 in RB/99 providing that the weightings (coefficients) for each factor of cost may be adjusted if rendered unreasonable, unbalanced or inapplicable by Variations has also been moved to the Particular Conditions as it only applies if a formula uses weightings/coefficients.

(ii) Related Clauses / Sub-Clauses: 4.11 [*Sufficiency of the Accepted Contract Amount*], 13.6 [*Adjustments for Changes in Laws*], 14.3 [*Application for Interim Payment*] and 14.6 [*Issue of IPC*].

(iii) Analysis:

(1) Price adjustment is an option

Like Sub-Clause 13.6 [*Adjustments for Changes in Laws*], Sub-Clause 13.7 may often be appropriate in a long-term construction contract, as it is designed to neutralise the risk of changes in the cost of labour, Goods and other inputs to the Works which can occur over such a contract's duration.[149] However, unlike Sub-Clause 13.6, Sub-Clause 13.7 is op-

148. *Guidance for the Preparation of Particular Conditions*, 36-37.

149. The World Bank's regulations provide that:

> [p]rice adjustment provisions are usually not necessary in simple contracts involving [...] completion of Works [...] within eighteen (18) months, but are included in contracts that extend beyond eighteen (18) months.

tional and will only apply if a price adjustment formula (referred to as 'Schedule(s) of cost indexation') is included in the Contract.

If none is included, or if the Schedule(s) of cost indexation does not fully compensate for any rise or fall in Costs, a Party will have no further right to recovery, as the Accepted Contract Amount is deemed to cover all contingencies[150] and, pursuant to Sub-Clause 4.11 [*Sufficiency of the Accepted Contract Amount*], the Contractor is deemed to have satisfied itself as to the sufficiency of the Accepted Contract Amount.[151]

(2) Nature of price adjustment

Whereas Sub-Clause 13.6 provides that, where there has been a change in Laws, as defined, the Contract Price may be adjusted to take account of any resulting increase or decrease in Cost that the Contractor may incur, Sub-Clause 13.7 provides that the amounts otherwise payable to the Contractor shall be adjusted for rises or falls in the cost of labour, Goods and other inputs to the Works by reference to a particular adjustment formula: the Schedule(s) of cost indexation.[152]

Thus, while Sub-Clause 13.6 provides for adjustment of the Contract Price based on changes in *actual* Cost of the Contractor (as the result of changes in Laws), Sub-Clause 13.7 provides for adjustment of the Contract Price based on a formula which, while designed to reflect relevant inflation (or deflation), *may or may not reflect the actual rises or falls in the cost of labour, Goods or other items* of the Contractor.[153]

Where it does not do so, each Party bears the corresponding risk as Sub-Clause 13.7 provides that:

> [t]o the extent that full compensation for any rise or fall in Costs is not covered by this Sub-Clause or other Clauses of these Conditions, the

S 2.18 of Annex IX Contract Conditions in International Competitive Procurement of *The World Bank Procurement Regulations for IPF Borrowers – Procurement in Investment Project Financing – Goods, Works, Non-Consulting and Consulting Services* (4th edn, November 2020).

150. Sub-Clause 13.7, third paragraph.
151. Sub-Clause 4.11(a). But *see* **(iv) Related Law** below.
152. Sub-Clause 13.7, second paragraph.
153. The accuracy of the formula may be improved by allowing different indices to apply to different stages or Sections of the Works since not all indices will be relevant to all stages or Sections and/or all the time. *European International Contractors Guide to the FIDIC Conditions of Contract for Plant and Design-Build* (2nd edition 2017) EIC, Berlin, 2020, 40.

> Accepted Contract Amount *shall be deemed to have included amounts to cover the contingency of other rises and falls in costs.*[154] (Emphasis added)

Similarly, during the performance of the Contract, the Contractor may find that it is able to engage labour or find Goods or other inputs at a lower cost than the cost of those items reflected by an index in the formula. If so, the Contractor is not prevented from taking advantage of these more favourable inputs while being paid, nevertheless, based upon the formula in the Contract. This is because the Parties have agreed that, instead of being paid based on rises or falls in the *actual* cost of labour, Goods and other inputs, the Contractor should be compensated for rises or falls in the cost of labour, Goods and other inputs to the Works *based on the formula* in the Contract (the Schedule(s) of cost indexation). The Parties have agreed that the formula should apply to the exclusion of any other criterion.

The adjustment is 'to be applied to the amount otherwise payable to the Contractor, as certified in Payment Certificates'.[155] Thus, calculation of the adjustment is made by the Contractor in the first instance and included in its Statement for the period in question pursuant to Sub-Clause 14.3(ii). The Engineer decides the final adjustment in a Payment Certificate, pursuant to Clause 14. Sub-Clause 20.2 [*Claims for Payment and/or EOT*] does not apply.

(3) Effect of delay in completion

Where the Contractor fails to complete the Works within the Time for Completion, it is understandable that, pursuant to the last paragraph of this Sub-Clause, the adjustment of price mechanism should then cease to operate. Instead, the last paragraph of Sub-Clause 13.7 provides that, in that case, adjustment of prices shall be made using either each index or price applicable just before the expiry of the Time for Completion of the Works or the current index or price, whichever is more favourable to the Employer. Application of the first option will, in effect, freeze prices for the purposes of Sub-Clause 13.7 during the period of the Contractor's delay, whereas application of the second will allow the Employer to benefit should prices fall over the same period.

154. Sub-Clause 13.7, third paragraph.
155. Sub-Clause 13.7, fourth paragraph.

(4) Common problems

In addition to the possibility that the formula may fail to reflect economic reality during the execution of the Works, a common problem in some less-developed countries is that there are no published official cost indices (e.g., for labour) to which reference may be made or they are untrustworthy. In these circumstances, it may be necessary for the Parties to create an index of costs by reference to some reliable local standard or measure of costs, e.g., in the case of a contract for the construction of a road in a Middle Eastern country, the salary rate in a designated city for drivers of 5-ton trucks and lorries was used. Another common problem is that, while the Works are being executed, a published or official cost index is modified, suspended or discontinued.[156] To protect against this contingency, suitable fallback indices should be provided in the Contract.

--ooOOoo--

The Employer should seek advice from a qualified professional when preparing the content(s) of the Schedule(s) of cost indexation.[157]

(iv) Related Law:

(1) Absent a provision such as Sub-Clause 13.7, in civil law countries in the French administrative law tradition, a contractor having a contract with a public body, when faced with unforeseeable circumstances that 'upset the economy of the Contract'[158] causing the contractor substantial loss, might be entitled to relief under the doctrine of *imprévision* (hardship), described in **Chapter II** above.[159] The existence of a price adjustment clause like Sub-Clause 13.7 in a contract should make the need for resort to such doctrine much less likely. However, *the existence of such a clause would not necessarily preclude the application of this doctrine*, as it has been held to apply where a price adjustment clause did not function as it was intended to or

156. *See*, e.g., final award, ICC case 25333 (2021) (so far unpublished) relating to the Pink Book where the steel index price referred to in the relevant contract ceased to be published.

157. *Guidance for the Preparation of Particular Conditions*, 36.

158. In French: *bouleversement économique du contrat*.

159. *See* **Section 4 Common Law and Civil Law Compared – 4.6.2 Hardship (*Imprévision*)** of **Chapter II Applicable Law** above.

when its application was insufficient to correct the effects of the upsetting of the economy of the contract.[160]

(2) A price adjustment clause can sometimes give rise to an aberrational result. An apparently small error or miscalculation in such a clause can lead to a dramatic change in the contract price.[161] Nonetheless, English law tends to interpret and enforce such clauses strictly[162] and, in this context, to be unforgiving.[163] On the other hand, under French administrative law, it is well established that if a price adjustment clause gives rise to a result which the parties could not reasonably have intended, then, under the theory of *imprévision*, a court is empowered to adjust the result that would be obtained from a literal application of the clause to a result which the parties could reasonably have intended.[164]

160. *See* André de Laubadère and others, *Traité des contrats administratifs* (LGDJ, Paris, 1984) vol II, 600-601 (para. 1365).
161. For an example, *see* Christopher R Seppälä, 'The Development of a Case Law in Construction Disputes Relating to FIDIC Contracts' in Emmanuel Gaillard (gen ed) *Precedent in International Arbitration* (Juris Publishing, Huntington, NY, 2008) 67, 79-80 (third example).
162. *See Henry Boot v LCC* [1959] I W.L.R. 1069 where an index for 'the rate of wages payable for any labour employed in the execution of the Works' was held not to include holiday payments or credits.
163. *See* the remarks of Lord Neuberger: 'The mere fact that a contractual arrangement, if interpreted according to its natural language, has worked out badly, or even disastrously, for one of the parties is not a reason for departing from the natural language.' *Arnold v Britton* [2015] UKSC 36; [2015] 2 W. L. R. 1593, para. 19.
164. This theory is known as the '*théorie du jeu imparfait de la formule de révision*' (literally, 'the theory of the imperfect operation of a price revision clause'). It has been applied in at least two decisions of the French Council of State (France's highest administrative court) of 5 November 1937 (*Département des Côtes-du-Nord* no 49.958, Rec Lebon, 900 and *Sieur Ducos et Fils* no 49.113, Rec Lebon 902) and was referred to in a decision of 19 February 1992 (*SA Dragages et Travaux Publics*, no 47.265, Rec. Lebon 1108). *See also* André de Laubadère and others, *Traité des contrats administratifs* (LGDJ, Paris, 1984) vol II, 600-601 (para. 1365) and **Section 4 Common Law and Civil Law Compared – 4.6.2 Hardship (*Imprévision*)** of **Chapter II Applicable Law** above.

Also, in an appropriate case, the doctrine of hardship may be invoked pursuant to Articles 6.2.1 to 6.2.3 of the UNIDROIT Principles.[165]

(v) Improvements:

(1) The Sub-Clause should state explicitly (as did Sub-Clause 13.8 of RB/99) that the provisional index referred to in the fifth paragraph of the Sub-Clause is to be determined by the Engineer.
(2) The Sub-Clause should state explicitly that, in the case of this Sub-Clause (as in the case of Variations), the claims procedure in Sub-Clause 20.2 does not apply.

--ooOOoo--

14 Contract Price and Payment

This Clause provides for the Contract Price and its payment to the Contractor by way of an advance payment, interim payments and a final payment, including the possibility for the payment of an advance for Plant and Materials which have been shipped or delivered to the Site. It also provides for the release of Retention Money, the Contractor's submission of a Statement at Completion and Final Statement ('FS') or a Partially Agreed Final Statement ('PAFS') and, after submission by the Contractor of a discharge, the Final Payment Certificate ('FPC') and the cessation of the Employer's liability to the Contractor. Finally, it deals with how the Contract Price is to be paid when it is payable in more than one currency.

--ooOOoo--

14.1 The Contract Price

Unless otherwise stated in the Particular Conditions:

(a) the Contract Price shall be the value of the Works in accordance with Sub-Clause 12.3 [*Valuation of the Works*] and be subject to adjustments,

165. Art. 6.2.2. of the UNIDROIT Principles, which contains the definition of hardship, is cited in fn. 90 in the commentary on Clause 18 below of **Chapter IV**. *See also* the discussion of the UNIDROIT Principles in **Section 7 International Legal Principles** of **Chapter II Applicable Law** above.

additions (including Cost or Cost Plus Profit to which the Contractor is entitled under these Conditions) and/or deductions in accordance with the Contract;

(b) the Contractor shall pay all taxes, duties and fees required to be paid by the Contractor under the Contract, and the Contract Price shall not be adjusted for any of these costs except as stated in Sub-Clause 13.6 [*Adjustments for Changes in Laws*];

(c) any quantities which may be set out in the Bill of Quantities or other Schedule(s) are estimated quantities and are not to be taken as the actual and correct quantities:

(i) of the Works which the Contractor is required to execute, or

(ii) for the purposes of Clause 12 [*Measurement and Valuation*]; and

(d) the Contractor shall submit to the Engineer, within 28 days after the Commencement Date, a proposed breakdown of each lump sum price (if any) in the Schedules. The Engineer may take account of the breakdown when preparing Payment Certificates, but shall not be bound by it.

Unless otherwise stated in the Particular Conditions: (a) the Contract Price shall be the value of the Works in accordance with Sub-Clause 12.3, subject to adjustments in accordance with the Contract; (b) the Contractor shall pay all taxes, duties and fees required to be paid by it under the Contract; (c) any quantities in the Bill of Quantities or other Schedules are estimated quantities of the Works; and (d) within 28 days after the Commencement Date, the Contractor shall submit to the Engineer a proposed breakdown of each lump sum price, if any, in the Schedules.

Commentary

(i) Main Changes from RB/99: Compared to Sub-Clause 14.1 of RB/99, the wording of sub-paragraph (a) has been changed to provide that:

(1) the Contract Price 'shall be the value of the Works in accordance with Sub-Clause 12.3', in place of the previous wording that it 'shall be agreed or determined under Sub-Clause 12.3'; and
(2) the Contract Price shall be 'subject to adjustments, additions (including Cost or Cost plus Profit to which the Contractor is entitled under these Conditions) and/or deductions' in accordance with the Contract, in place of the previous wording referring simply to 'subject to adjustments in accordance with the Contract'.

(ii) Related Clauses / Sub-Clauses: 1.3 [*Notices and Other Communications*], 1.13 [*Compliance with Laws*], 2.4 [*Employer's Financial Arrangements*], 4.2 [*Performance Security*], 8.4 [*Advance Warning*], 12 [*Measurement and Valuation*], 13.6 [*Adjustment for Changes in Laws*] and 14 [*Contract Price and Payment*].[1]

(iii) Analysis:

(1) Contract Price (Sub-Clause 14.1(a))

As it describes the Contract Price, Sub-Clause 14.1(a) is an important provision. Sub-Clause 14.1(a) provides that, subject to the Particular Conditions, the Contract Price shall be 'the value of the Works in accordance with Sub-Clause 12.3', that is, the value of the actual quantities of each item of work executed, determined on the basis of the rates and prices included in the Bill of Quantities (or other Schedule) or (in the case of a new rate or price) determined pursuant to Sub-Clause 12.3. This value is, in turn, subject to adjustments, additions and/or deductions in accordance with the Contract.[2] Thus, unlike the Accepted Contract Amount, which is a fixed sum which the Parties agreed to when they entered into the Contract (it being set out in the Letter of Acceptance),[3] the Contract Price is determined by the valuation of the Works executed, and by such adjustments as are made pursuant to the Contract.

1. Many other Clauses and Sub-Clauses refer to the Contract Price. It is not practicable to list them all here.
2. For lists of certain of these adjustments *see* **Table 5 Employer's Claims for Time and/or Money** and **Table 6 Contractor's Claims for Time and/or Money** at the end of the commentary on Sub-Clause 20.2 [*Claims for Payment and/or EOT*] below.
3. *See* the commentary on Sub-Clause 1.1.1 '**Accepted Contract Amount**' above.

The final Contract Price will therefore be determined by the 'as-built' quantities of work ultimately carried out, priced in accordance with the Bill of Quantities for different items or units of work, subject to adjustments provided for in the Contract. However, the Particular Conditions may qualify this provision. For example, they may provide instead that a portion of the work be executed and priced based upon a lump sum (e.g., where the drawings and Specification define the work sufficiently to enable the Contractor to price the work in this way) and/or on a cost plus price basis (e.g., where the nature and quantity of the work may be difficult to define, as in the case of underground work). The balance of the work would then be executed and priced by reference to a Bill of Quantities.

Indeed, the *Guidance* describes two alternative pricing methods, in addition to unit pricing as provided for in Sub-Clause 14.1.[4] Pricing may be based on a lump sum or, alternatively, on a cost plus basis although this is described as 'unusual' and risky for the Employer.[5]

(2) Liability for taxes and duties (Sub-Clause 14.1(b))

Sub-Clause 14.1(b) provides that, subject to the Particular Conditions, the Contractor shall pay all taxes, duties and fees required to be paid by the Contractor[6] and that the Contract Price shall not be adjusted for these except as stated in Sub-Clause 13.6 [*Adjustments for Changes in Laws*]. On the other hand, once again, the *Guidance* contains example clauses for where Goods of the Contractor are exempted from customs and other import duties or its expatriate staff are exempted from having to pay local income tax.[7] However, no example clause is provided for where the Contractor is itself exempted from all taxes, duties or other governmental charges or impositions of the Country, as may sometimes be the case for contracts with States or other public bodies.

4. *Guidance for the Preparation of Particular Conditions*, 37-39.
5. The *Guidance*, 38-39, includes an example provision for a lump sum contract price and the General Conditions of both YB/17 and SB/17 provide for lump sum prices.
6. Notably in compliance with Sub-Clause 1.13 [*Compliance with Laws*], sub-para. (b).
7. *Guidance for the Preparation of Particular Conditions*, 39-40. The World Bank's COPA contains additional alternative provisions for exemption from taxes. Sub-Clause 14.1, COPA.

(3) Bill of Quantities and lump sums (Sub-Clauses 14.1(c) and (d))

Sub-Clauses 14.1(a) and (c) establish that, subject to the Particular Conditions, this is a 'remeasurement' contract, that is, a contract where the Contract Price is determined based on the actual quantities of work executed. As indicated in the commentary on Clause 12 [*Measurement and Valuation*] above, Clause 12 and Clause 14 must be read together.

Sub-Clause 14.1(d) provides that, subject to the Particular Conditions, the Contractor must submit to the Engineer shortly after the Commencement Date a proposed breakdown of each lump sum price, if any, in the Schedules, which includes the Bill of Quantities. Among other things, this can be of assistance to the Engineer in valuing Variations, but the Engineer is not bound by this breakdown.[8]

Some have argued that the successful tenderer should supply a detailed breakdown not just of each lump sum price but of all its rates and prices, as between labour, plant, materials and possibly subcontractors, and to do so before final acceptance of the tender.[9] However, FIDIC has never gone so far.

(iv) Related law: The use of a measurement contract or 'measure and value', as it is sometimes called, based on unit prices, like RB/17, is known in the common law countries as the traditional approach or method for much civil engineering and building work.[10] It is also generally accepted and used in civil law countries.[11] It is one of the three common forms of contracting, the other two being: (1) lump sum (also, in the United States, called 'fixed-price') contracts, where the contractor takes the risk of changes in the quantities of work executed; and (2) cost plus or reimbursement contracts, where the contractor is paid its cost of

8. As the Contractor's breakdown may be 'front-end loaded', that is, provide for more money to be payable early in the project, or otherwise be self-serving.
9. I N Duncan Wallace, *Construction Contracts: Principles and Policies in Tort and Contract* (Sweet & Maxwell, London, 1996) vol 2, 516.
10. *FIDIC Procurement Procedures Guide* (FIDIC, 2011) 39.
11. It is provided for by the main standard forms of conditions of contract (*Cahier des Clauses Administratives Générales* or 'CCAG') for private works in France [French norm (AFNOR) NF P 03-001, 2016 (building works) and NF P 03-002, 2014 (civil engineering works)].

performing the work plus an amount or fee which is usually a percentage of the cost to cover its overheads and profit.[12]

--ooOOoo--

14.2 Advance Payment

If no amount of advance payment is stated in the Contract Data, this Sub-Clause shall not apply.

After receiving the Advance Payment Certificate, the Employer shall make an advance payment, as an interest-free loan for mobilisation (and design, if any). The amount of the advance payment and the currencies in which it is to be paid shall be as stated in the Contract Data.

14.2.1 Advance Payment Guarantee

The Contractor shall obtain (at the Contractor's cost) an Advance Payment Guarantee in amounts and currencies equal to the advance payment, and shall submit it to the Employer with a copy to the Engineer. This guarantee shall be issued by an entity and from within a country (or other jurisdiction) to which the Employer gives consent, and shall be in the form annexed to the Particular Conditions or on another form agreed by the Employer (but such consent and/or agreement shall not relieve the Contractor from any obligation under this Sub-Clause).

The Contractor shall ensure that the Advance Payment Guarantee is valid and enforceable until the advance payment has been repaid, but its amount may be progressively reduced by the amount repaid by the Contractor as stated in the Payment Certificates.

If the terms of the Advance Payment Guarantee specify its expiry date, and the advance payment has not been repaid by the date 28 days before the expiry date:

12. *FIDIC Procurement Procedures Guide* (FIDIC 2011) 39-40; and Julian Bailey, *Construction Law* (3rd edn, London Publishing, UK, 2020) vol 2, 441-446 (paras 6.04-6.13).

(a) the Contractor shall extend the validity of this guarantee until the advance payment has been repaid;
(b) the Contractor shall immediately submit evidence of this extension to the Employer, with a copy to the Engineer; and
(c) if the Employer does not receive this evidence 7 days before the expiry date of this guarantee, the Employer shall be entitled to claim under the guarantee the amount of advance payment which has not been repaid.

When submitting the Advance Payment Guarantee, the Contractor shall include an application (in the form of a Statement) for the advance payment.

14.2.2 Advance Payment Certificate

The Engineer shall issue an Advance Payment Certificate for the advance payment within 14 days after:

(a) the Employer has received both the Performance Security and the Advance Payment Guarantee, in the form and issued by an entity in accordance with Sub-Clause 4.2.1 [*Contractor's obligations*] and Sub-Clause 14.2.1 [*Advance Payment Guarantee*] respectively; and
(b) the Engineer has received a copy of the Contractor's application for the advance payment under Sub-Clause 14.2.1 [*Advance Payment Guarantee*].

14.2.3 Repayment of Advance Payment

The advance payment shall be repaid through percentage deductions in Payment Certificates. Unless other percentages are stated in the Contract Data:

(a) deductions shall commence in the IPC in which the total of all certified interim payments in the same currency as the advance payment (excluding the advance payment and deductions and release of retention moneys) exceeds ten percent (10%) of the portion of the Accepted Contract Amount payable in that currency less Provisional Sums; and

(b) deductions shall be made at the amortisation rate of one quarter (25%) of the amount of each IPC (excluding the advance payment and deductions and release of retention moneys) in the currencies and proportions of the advance payment, until such time as the advance payment has been repaid.

If the advance payment has not been repaid before the issue of the Taking-Over Certificate for the Works, or before termination under Clause 15 [*Termination by Employer*], Clause 16 [*Suspension and Termination by Contractor*] or Clause 18 [*Exceptional Events*] (as the case may be), the whole of the balance then outstanding shall immediately become due and payable by the Contractor to the Employer.

This Sub-Clause only applies if an amount of advance payment is stated in the Contract Data.

After receiving the Advance Payment Certificate, the Employer shall make an advance payment, the amount and currencies of which shall be as stated in the Contract Data.

The Contractor shall submit an Advance Payment Guarantee in amounts and currencies equal to the advance payment, together with an application for the advance payment, to the Employer with a copy to the Engineer. The guarantee, which shall be issued by an entity and from within a country consented to by the Employer and be on a form agreed by the Employer, shall be valid until the advance payment has been repaid, but may be progressively reduced by the amount repaid. If the guarantee specifies an expiry date, and the advance payment has not been repaid by 28 days before this date, the guarantee's validity must be extended until the advance payment has been repaid.

The Engineer shall issue an Advance Payment Certificate for the advance payment within 14 days after: (a) the Employer has received both the Performance Security and the Advance Payment Guarantee, and (b) the Engineer has received the Contractor's application for the advance payment.

The advance payment shall be repaid through percentage deductions in Payment Certificates. If it has not been repaid before the issue of the

Taking-Over Certificate for the Works, or earlier termination of the Contract, the outstanding balance shall become immediately due and payable to the Employer.

Commentary

(i) Main Changes from RB/99:

(1) The entire Sub-Clause has been restructured under three separate headings: 14.2.1 Advance Payment Guarantee, 14.2.2 Advance Payment Certificate and 14.2.3 Repayment of Advance Payment, which is new.
(2) As compared to Sub-Clause 14.2 of RB/99, the first two paragraphs are worded differently, and assume that the advance payment will be made as a single payment without the possibility of instalments as in RB/99.
(3) In Sub-Clause 14.2.1, the first paragraph is new, as are sub-paragraphs (b) and (c) of the penultimate paragraph, entitling the Employer possibly to claim under the guarantee, and the last paragraph.
(4) Sub-Clause 14.2.2 is partly new, notably the provision for an Advance Payment Certificate.[13]

(ii) Related Clauses / Sub-Clauses: 1.2 [*Interpretation*], 1.3 [*Notices and Other Communications*], 4.2 [*Performance Security*], 14.3 [*Application for Interim Payment*], 14.5 [*Plant and Materials Intended for the Works*], 14.7 [*Payment*], 14.8 [*Delayed Payment*], 15 [*Termination by Employer*], 16 [*Suspension and Termination by Contractor*] and 18 [*Exceptional Events*].

13. Surprisingly, although the use of an advance payment has long been standard practice in international construction, the RB did not provide for it in its General Conditions until 1999. Even today, it is still only an option and some of the leading English construction law texts hardly discuss the subject. Atkin Chambers, *Hudson's Building and Engineering Contracts* (14th edn, Sweet & Maxwell, London, 2020) does not refer to it at all and Stephen Furst and Vivian Ramsey, *Keating on Construction Contracts* (11th edn, Sweet & Maxwell, London, 2021) only mentions it on p. 851 in relation to Clause 4.7 in the English JCT form of contract. However, an exception is Julian Bailey, *Construction Law* (3rd edn, London Publishing, UK, 2020) vol 2, 451-452 (para. 6.24).

(iii) Analysis:

(1) Purpose of an advance payment

Given that an advance payment has long been standard in international construction, it is surprising that, as indicated by the first paragraph of this Sub-Clause, it should still be treated as an option.[14] FIDIC should accept its common usage.

The advance payment, which typically represents 10% to 20% of the Accepted Contract Amount,[15] is an interest-free loan 'for mobilization (and design, if any)'.[16] It provides the Contractor with funds to purchase equipment, Plant, Materials and other items needed for the Works; make advances to subcontractors; help mobilise staff, labour, equipment and Materials to the Site,[17] often in a foreign country; and, generally, provides cash to cover design costs, if any, and other costs at the outset of a project when otherwise the Contractor might have to engage in borrowing (which it may have to do anyway).[18]

The Contractor will not be entitled to receive its first interim payment under the Contract until about three months after it has begun work and submitted its first Statement.[19] In the meantime, in addition to the

14. The use of an advance payment is not discussed at all in *FIDIC's Procurement Procedures Guide* published in 2011.
15. Wendy Kennedy et al (eds.) *International Construction Law: A Guide for Cross-Border Transactions and Legal Disputes* (ABA Publishing, Chicago, IL, 2009) 174. Sub-Clause 14.2 assumes the advance payment will be less than 22% of the Accepted Contract Amount. *See Guidance for the Preparation of the Particular Conditions*, 40.
16. Sub-Clause 14.2, second paragraph.
17. The World Bank's regulations provide that:

> [a]ny advance payment for mobilization and similar expenses, made upon signature of a contract for [...] Works [...] shall be related to the estimated amount of these expenses and be specified in the request for bids/request for proposals document.

S 2.15 of Annex IX Contract Conditions in International Competitive Procurement of *The World Bank Procurement Regulations for IPF Borrowers – Procurement in Investment Project Financing – Goods, Works, Non-Consulting and Consulting Services* (4th edn, November 2020).
18. If Sub-Clause 14.5 [*Plant and Materials Intended for the Works*] applies, it may also assist the Contractor in relation to the financing of Plant and/or Materials.
19. *See* Sub-Clauses 14.3 through 14.7 below.

mobilisation costs described above, the Contractor will have had to put up Performance Security[20] equal to perhaps 10% or more of the Contract Price and procure insurance.[21] Financing these costs will obviously be alleviated by an advance payment.

(2) Steps in relation to the advance payment

The new Sub-Clause is clearer, more detailed and better structured than its predecessor. It sets out how the Contractor is to apply for the advance payment,[22] when the Engineer is to certify that the advance payment is due and, therefore, to be made and, finally, how and when the advance payment is to be repaid by the Contractor.[23]

Essentially, the Conditions provide for the following *six steps* in making and repaying the advance payment:

(1) Promptly after receiving the Letter of Acceptance, the Contractor should obtain, at its cost, an Advance Payment Guarantee in the amounts and currencies equal to the advance payment and otherwise in a form, issued by an entity and from within a country, agreed or consented to by the Employer.[24]

20. As others have noted, *see* Leo Grutters and Brian Barr, *FIDIC, Red, Yellow and Silver Books: A Practical Guide to the 2017 Editions* (Sweet & Maxwell, London, 2018) 218-219. These authors are equally surprised that FIDIC has not accepted an advance payment as standard in its contracts.
21. As required by Clause 19 [*Insurance*].
22. While the Sub-Clause envisages that the advance payment will be made by way of a single payment, the *Guidance for the Preparation of Particular Conditions*, 40-41, contains suggested changes to the Sub-Clause and the Contract Data should the Employer wish to pay the advance payment in instalments instead (as the General Conditions of RB/99 had envisaged). In addition, by referring to 'each' Advance Payment Certificate, Sub-Clause 14.7(a) appears to envisage payment of the advance payment by instalments and is inconsistent with Sub-Clause 14.2 providing for an advance payment to be a single payment (as noted in under **(iv) Improvements** of the commentary on Sub-Clause 14.7 below).
23. Sub-Clause 14.2 is not the sole sub-clause which may entitle the Contractor to an advance payment. Sub-Clause 14.5 [*Plant and Materials Intended for the Works*] may entitle the Contractor to advance payments for Plant and Materials.
24. *See* Sub-Clause 14.2.1. Such agreement or consent may not be unreasonably withheld or delayed. *See* Sub-Clause 1.3.

(2) Within 28 days after receiving the Letter of Acceptance, the Contractor should deliver both the Performance Security[25] and (if possible) the Advance Payment Guarantee[26] to the Employer with a copy of each to the Engineer and, at the same time, deliver to the Engineer a copy of the Contractor's application for the advance payment.[27]

(3) Within 14 days after the Employer and/or the Engineer has received the three documents in (2) above, the Engineer is required to issue to the Employer an Advance Payment Certificate for the advance payment.[28]

(4) Pursuant to Sub-Clause 14.7, the Employer must pay the amount certified in the Advance Payment Certificate within the time stated in the Contract Data or, if not stated, 21 days.[29] If payment is delayed, then Sub-Clause 14.8 [*Delayed Payment*] would apply.[30]

(5) The advance payment is to be repaid through percentage deductions in Payment Certificates, until it has been fully repaid.[31]

(6) If the advance payment has not been repaid before either the issue of the Taking-Over Certificate for the Works or the termination of the Contract under Clauses 15, 16 or 18, the outstanding balance of the advance payment becomes due and payable.[32]

---

25. *See* Sub-Clause 4.2.1 regarding the time for delivery of the Performance Security to the Employer.
26. The exact date for the delivery of the Advance Payment Guarantee is not specified. But *see* Sub-Clause 14.2.2(a).
27. *See* Sub-Clause 14.2.1, last paragraph, according to which the application should be in the form of a Statement.
28. Sub-Clause 14.2.2, which does not state whether the Contractor is to receive a copy of the Advance Payment Certificate as it does in the case of an IPC under Sub-Clause 14.6.1. However, Sub-Clause 1.3, last paragraph, indicates that the Contractor should receive a copy.
29. Sub-paragraph (a) of Sub-Clause 14.7 [*Payment*].
30. For where a contractor was awarded damages for late payment (by 202 days) of an advance payment under a FIDIC contract (RB/69), *see* the final award, ICC case 5948 (1993), ICC Int'l Ct Arb Bull vol 9, no 1, May 1998, 80, and (for commentary) vol 9, no 2, November 1998, 44-45.
31. Sub-Clause 14.2.3.
32. Sub-Clause 14.2.3, last paragraph. There is no requirement for the Employer to make a Claim for this payment. It can deduct the full amount of the outstanding balance from the very next payment to the Contractor.

(3) Form of Advance Payment Guarantee

As indicated above, the Advance Payment Guarantee must be based on a form agreed by the Employer. As a practical matter, as the Guarantee is being provided to secure the repayment of an advance in cash, the Employer will require that the Guarantee be in the form of a guarantee payable on demand issued by a bank. Accordingly, the commentary on Sub-Clause 4.2 [*Performance Security*] above in relation to a Performance Security in the form of a guarantee payable on demand is directly relevant here and will not be repeated.[33] Among other things, the Employer will likely require that the bank (or branch of, perhaps, an international bank) which issues the guarantee is not only acceptable to the Employer but also located in the Employer's country so as to facilitate suit against it by the Employer should this be necessary.

Attached as Annex E to the Conditions is an example form of demand guarantee which can be provided as an Advance Payment Guarantee. As in the case of the form of Performance Security attached as Annex C to the Conditions, this form is based upon, and incorporates by reference, the *Uniform Rules for Demand Guarantees*, 2010 revision ('URDG').[34] Like the form of Performance Security, the Annex E example form provides for an expiry date. If the advance payment has not been repaid by 28 days before the expiry date, and the Employer has not received evidence of the extension of the guarantee by 7 days before the expiry date, the Employer may be entitled to claim under the guarantee for the amount of the advance payment which has not been repaid.[35]

As explained in the commentary on Sub-Clause 14.4 [*Schedule of Payments*] below, where a Schedule of Payments is used instead of a Bill of

33. However, unlike Sub-Clause 4.2.2 [Claims under the Performance Security], Sub-Clause 14.2.1 does not explicitly address the consequences of an unjustified drawdown of an advance payment guarantee. But in ICC case 22481 (2021) (unpublished so far), it was held (in relation to a contract based on SB/99) that the obligation of the Employer under Sub-Clause 4.2 (of SB/99, which is similar to Sub-Clause 4.2 of RB/17) to indemnify the Contractor for its damages in the case of an unjustified drawdown of a Performance Security should apply by analogy to an unjustified drawdown by the Employer of an advance payment guarantee, which seems a sensible result.
34. ICC Publication no 758. The URDG are discussed under **(iii) Analysis** of the commentary on Sub-Clause 4.2 [*Performance Security*] above.
35. *See* the penultimate paragraph of Sub-Clause 14.2.1 and the commentary on Sub-Clause 4.2 [*Performance Security*] above.

Quantities, payments to the Contractor can be calculated and scheduled in such a way as to eliminate the need for an advance payment.

(iv) Related Law:[36] As an indication of how usual an advance payment is, the main form of construction contract for civil engineering (private) works in France provides for an advance of 10% of the contract price unless the parties agree otherwise.[37] The *NEC4 Engineering and Construction Contract* in the UK also provides for the possibility of an advance payment, though in an unspecified amount.[38]

(v) Improvements: An advance payment should no longer be treated as an option but instead be recognised for what it is, namely, a standard practice in international construction. Also, Sub-Clauses 14.2.2 and 14.7 need to be reconciled so as to make it clear whether there is to be a single disbursement of an advance payment (if that is FIDIC's current position) or multiple disbursements in instalments as under RB/99, or whether both options are to be available.

--ooOOoo--

14.3 Application for Interim Payment

The Contractor shall submit a Statement to the Engineer after the end of the period of payment stated in the Contract Data (if not stated, after the end of each month). Each Statement shall:

(a) be in a form acceptable to the Engineer;
(b) be submitted in one paper-original, one electronic copy and additional paper copies (if any) as stated in the Contract Data; and
(c) show in detail the amounts to which the Contractor considers that the Contractor is entitled, with supporting documents which shall include sufficient detail for the Engineer to investigate

36. *See also* under **(iv) Related Law** in the commentary on Sub-Clause 4.2 [*Performance Security*] above.
37. *See* art. 20.2 of French norm *(AFNOR) NF P 03-002*, 2014 (civil engineering works), the main standard form applicable to such private (non-public) works in France.
38. Option X14: Advanced payment to the Contractor, *NEC4 Engineering and Construction Contract*, Institution of Civil Engineers, 2017.

these amounts together with the relevant report on progress in accordance with Sub-Clause 4.20 [*Progress Reports*].

The Statement shall include the following items, as applicable, which shall be expressed in the various currencies in which the Contract Price is payable, in the sequence listed:

(i) the estimated contract value of the Works executed, and the Contractor's Documents produced, up to the end of the period of payment (including Variations but excluding items described in sub-paragraphs (ii) to (x) below);
(ii) any amounts to be added and/or deducted for changes in Laws under Sub-Clause 13.6 [*Adjustments for Changes in Laws*], and for changes in Cost under Sub-Clause 13.7 [*Adjustments for Changes in Cost*];
(iii) any amount to be deducted for retention, calculated by applying the percentage of retention stated in the Contract Data to the total of the amounts under sub-paragraphs (i), (ii) and (vi) of this Sub-Clause, until the amount so retained by the Employer reaches the limit of Retention Money (if any) stated in the Contract Data;
(iv) any amounts to be added and/or deducted for the advance payment and repayments under Sub-Clause 14.2 [*Advance Payment*];
(v) any amounts to be added and/or deducted for Plant and Materials under Sub-Clause 14.5 [*Plant and Materials intended for the Works*];
(vi) any other additions and/or deductions which have become due under the Contract or otherwise, including those under Sub-Clause 3.7 [*Agreement or Determination*];
(vii) any amounts to be added for Provisional Sums under Sub-Clause 13.4 [*Provisional Sums*];
(viii) any amount to be added for release of Retention Money under Sub-Clause 14.9 [*Release of Retention Money*];
(ix) any amount to be deducted for the Contractor's use of utilities provided by the Employer under Sub-Clause 4.19 [*Temporary Utilities*]; and

(x) the deduction of amounts certified in all previous Payment Certificates.

The Contractor shall submit a Statement to the Engineer after the end of the period of payment stated in the Contract Data (if not stated, after the end of each month), complying with sub-paragraphs (a), (b) and (c) of the first paragraph.

The Statement shall include, as applicable, the items listed in (i) through (x) of the second paragraph, expressed in the various currencies in which the Contract Price is payable.

Commentary

(i) Main Changes from RB/99:

(1) In the first paragraph, sub-paragraph (b), requiring that each Statement be submitted in one paper-original, one electronic copy and additional copies (if any) as stated in the Contract Data, is new.

(2) In the first paragraph, sub-paragraph (c), the description of the supporting documents for each Statement ('which shall include sufficient detail for the Engineer to investigate these amounts'), is new.

(3) In the second paragraph, item (vi), the words 'including those under Sub-Clause 3.7 [*Agreement on Determination*]' have replaced 'including those under Clause 20 [*Claims, Disputes and Arbitration*]' in sub-paragraph (f) of Sub-Clause 14.3 of RB/99.

(4) In the second paragraph, items (vii) relating to Provisional Sums, (viii) relating to release of Retention Money and (ix) relating to the Contractor's use of the Employer's utilities, are all new.

(ii) Related Clauses / Sub-Clauses: 1.3 [*Notices and Other Communications*], 3.7 [*Agreement on Determination*], 4.9 [*Release of Retention Money*], 4.19 [*Temporary Utilities*], 4.20 [*Progress Reports*], 12.1 [*Works to be Measured*], 12.3 [*Valuation of the Works*], 13.4 [*Provisional Sums*], 13.6 [*Adjustments for Changes in Laws*], 13.7 [*Adjustments for Changes in Costs*] and 14 [*Contract Price and Payment*].

(iii) Analysis:

(1) Contract payment system

In a long-term construction contract like the RB, it is normal for the Contractor to be paid principally by way of interim payments. They provide the Contractor with regular cash flow, relieving it of having to finance execution of the Works from its own resources.[39] Sub-Clause 14.3 is the first of a series of Sub-Clauses (through to Sub-Clause 14.8) providing for the Contractor to apply to the Engineer to certify, and for the Employer to pay, interim payments, including financing charges for delayed payments, if any, as the Works progress and until their completion.

This Sub-Clause provides that the Contractor shall apply for interim payments for work done by submitting a 'Statement'[40] to the Engineer. After issue of the Performance Certificate, the Contractor applies for a final payment by the submission of a draft 'Final Statement'[41] to the Engineer.

(2) Form of Statement

An application for interim payment is required to be made after the end of the period of payment stated in the Contract Data, but will usually be made after the end of each month,[42] and this is the default position under this Sub-Clause.

The Contractor's Statement must be in a form 'acceptable to the Engineer', which means that the Contractor would be well advised to clear the form with the Engineer in advance at the beginning of the Contract. The Statement must be submitted in the number and kinds of copies indicated in the first paragraph. It must show 'in detail' the amounts to which the Contractor considers that it is 'entitled', together with supporting documents 'which shall include sufficient detail for the Engineer to investigate these amounts', together with the relevant monthly progress report to be provided pursuant to Sub-Clause 4.20 which provides, among other

39. *See* Julian Bailey, *Construction Law* (3rd edn, London Publishing, UK, 2020) vol 2, 466-467 (para. 6.57).
40. *See* the definition in Sub-Clause 1.1.77 '**Statement**'.
41. *See* the definition in Sub-Clause 1.1.41 '**Final Statement**'.
42. Defined as a calendar month (according to the Gregorian calendar). Sub-Clause 1.1.54. The same procedure applies to an application for the advance payment.

things, for 'comparisons of actual and planned progress, with details of any events or circumstances which may adversely affect the completion of the Works'.[43]

The Statement must comply with Sub-Clause 1.3 [*Notices and Other Communications*] which means, among other things, that the paper-original must be signed by the Contractor's Representative.

(3) Contents of Statement

While the second paragraph lists 10 different items which, if applicable, are to be included in a Statement, the largest single item by far is likely to be item (i) presenting the 'estimated contract value' of the Works executed in the preceding period of payment including Variations but excluding the subsequently listed items. The contract value is 'estimated' because, as stated in the last paragraph of Sub-Clause 12.1, until measurement of the Works (or part thereof) is agreed or determined, 'the Engineer shall assess a provisional measurement for the purposes of Interim Payment Certificates'.

The other items listed are all for amounts to be added to, or deducted from, the amount to be paid to the Contractor under various provisions of the Contract. Of particular note is item (iii) relating to the deduction for Retention Money calculated by applying the percentage of retention stated in the Contract Data (usually 5% or 10% of the Accepted Contract Amount[44]) to certain amounts due to the Contractor until the limit of Retention Money (if any) stated in the Contract Data is reached.[45] Finally, item (x) provides for the deduction of amounts certified in all previous Payment Certificates. Thus, the balance shown as due to the Contractor by the Statement will represent a sum calculated after deduction of all amounts previously certified by the Engineer (and presumed to have been paid or be payable by the Employer).

In addition to amounts payable to the Contractor pursuant to items (i) through (v), the Contractor may apply for payment of any amount which has 'become due under the Contract or otherwise' (item (vi)), that is, an amount which has been certified by the Engineer or agreed with the

43. Sub-Clause 4.20, item (h).
44. The World Bank's COPA provides that retention should normally be 5% and not exceed 10% of the Accepted Contract Amount. Sub-Clause 14.3 (iii), Contract Data, COPA.
45. The release of Retention Money is provided for in Sub-Clause 14.9. and in item (viii) of Sub-Clause 14.3.

assistance of the Engineer or determined by the Engineer pursuant to Sub-Clause 20.2 and/or Sub-Clause 3.7. The term 'or otherwise' refers to matters which have, in the Contractor's view, become due otherwise than under the Contract, such as pursuant to applicable law.[46]

Thus, the Contractor should not be including its Claims in a Statement under this Sub-Clause until they have been agreed with the Employer or determined by the Engineer pursuant to Sub-Clause 3.7. When this is the case, the Contractor is entitled to the amounts which have been agreed or determined. On the other hand, amounts due pursuant to a DAAB's decision or arbitral award are payable directly and do not require certification.[47] Similarly, financing charges payable for delayed payments do not require certification.[48]

(4) Engineer's certification and the Employer's payment

Within 28 days after receiving the Statement and supporting documents of the Contractor, the Engineer is required, assuming the Employer has received the Performance Security and the Contractor's Representative has been appointed,[49] to issue an IPC to the Employer for the amount which the Engineer 'fairly' considers to be due.[50] Thereafter the Employer is required[51] to pay the Contractor the amount certified by the Engineer within the period stated in the Contract Data or, if no period is

46. *Guide to the Use of FIDIC Conditions of Contract for Works of Civil Engineering Construction, Fourth Edition* (FIDIC 1989) 119 (commenting on Sub-Clause 53.1 [*Notice of Claim*] in RB/87).
47. This is clear from the General Conditions (Sub-Clause 21.4.3(i) providing that a DAAB's decision is 'immediately due and payable without any certification or Notice') and the ICC Rules of Arbitration (art. 35(6) of the ICC Rules of Arbitration providing that an award is binding on the parties who must 'carry out any award without delay'). The position had been unclear under Sub-Clause 14.3 of RB/99 as item (f) of that Sub-Clause had referred to amounts 'under Clause 20' as being due by way of IPCs.
48. *See* Sub-Clause 14.8 [*Delayed Payment*], last paragraph.
49. *See* Sub-Clause 14.6 [*Issue of IPC*]. The requirement that the Contractor's Representative has been appointed is redundant because, as previously mentioned, pursuant to Sub-Clause 1.3, the paper-original of a Statement must be signed by the Contractor's Representative.
50. Sub-Clause 14.6.1. For a discussion of 'fairly', which is also used in Sub-Clause 3.7 [*Agreement or Determination*], *see* item (2) under **(i) Main Changes from RB/99** of the commentary on that Sub-Clause above.
51. Pursuant to Sub-Clause 14.7 [*Payment*].

stated, *within 56 days (eight weeks) after the Engineer receives the Statement and supporting documents*.[52]

(iv) Related law: While it is customary in common law countries for the Engineer or other contract administrator to 'certify' applications for interim payment of the Contractor, and to require the Employer to pay the Contractor on the basis of such certificates, this is not normal practice in civil law countries. In civil law countries, while the contract administrator may advise and assist the Employer in relation to payments to the Contractor, it is for the Employer to decide whether and what to pay the Contractor.[53]

--ooOOoo--

14.4 Schedule of Payments

If the Contract includes a Schedule of Payments specifying the instalments in which the Contract Price will be paid then, unless otherwise stated in this Schedule:

(a) the instalments quoted in the Schedule of Payments shall be treated as the estimated contract values for the purposes of sub-paragraph (i) of Sub-Clause 14.3 [*Application for Interim Payment*];

(b) Sub-Clause 14.5 [*Plant and Materials intended for the Works*] shall not apply; and

(c) if:

   (i) these instalments are not defined by reference to the actual progress achieved in the execution of the Works; and

   (ii) actual progress is found by the Engineer to differ from that on which the Schedule of Payments was based,

52. *See* the commentaries on Sub-Clauses 14.6 and 14.7 below.
53. *See*, for example, arts 19 and 20 of French norm *(AFNOR) CCAG applicable aux travaux de génie civil faisant l'objet de marchés privés NF P 03-002*, AFNOR, Paris 2014, the main standard form applicable to private (non-public) civil engineering works in France. *See also* **Section 4 Common Law and Civil Law Compared – 4.4.1 Contract Administrator (*Maître D'Oeuvre*) *v* Engineer** of **Chapter II Applicable Law** above.

then the Engineer may proceed under Sub-Clause 3.7 [*Agreement or Determination*] to agree or determine revised instalments (and for the purpose of Sub-Clause 3.7.3 [*Time limits*] the date when the difference under sub-paragraph (ii) above was found by the Engineer shall be the date of commencement of the time limit for agreement under Sub-Clause 3.7.3). Such revised instalments shall take account of the extent to which progress differs from that on which the Schedule of Payments was based.

If the Contract does not include a Schedule of Payments, the Contractor shall submit non-binding estimates of the payments which the Contractor expects to become due during each period of 3 months. The first estimate shall be submitted within 42 days after the Commencement Date. Revised estimates shall be submitted at intervals of 3 months, until the issue of the Taking-Over Certificate for the Works.

If the Contract includes a Schedule of Payments, then unless otherwise stated, the instalments in this Schedule are to be used to determine the estimated contract values in Sub-Clause 14.3(i) and Sub-Clause 14.5 shall not apply. If these instalments are not defined by reference to actual progress achieved, and the actual progress is found by the Engineer to differ from that on which the Schedule was based, the Engineer may proceed under Sub-Clause 3.7 to agree or determine revised instalments. If the Contract includes no Schedule of Payments, the Contractor shall submit non-binding estimates of the payments it expects to become due during each period of 3 months.

Commentary

(i) Main Changes from RB/99:

(1) The Schedule of Payments (formerly 'schedule of payments') is now a defined term.

(2) The Engineer may proceed to agree or determine revised instalments where progress is less or more (not merely less as in Sub-Clause 14.4 of RB/99) than that on which the instalments were based.

(3) The reference to Sub-Clause 3.5 in RB/99 has been replaced by reference to Sub-Clause 3.7 in RB/17.

(ii) Related Clauses / Sub-Clauses: 1.3 [*Notices and Other Communications*], 3.7 [*Agreement or Determination*], 14.3 [*Application for Interim Payment*] and 14.5 [*Plant and Materials Intended for the Works*].

(iii) Analysis: If interim payments are not based upon a monthly or other periodic measurement of quantities of work executed, applying the rates and prices in the Bill of Quantities,[54] they are likely to be based upon what the Conditions refer to as a 'Schedule of Payments'.[55] Under such a schedule, the Contractor is entitled to payment of a designated amount after each month or other period of time or, alternatively, after achieving a defined milestone of progress.[56]

Where the Contractor is to be paid an amount after each month or other period of time then, if progress falls behind, or is ahead of, the time programme on which the schedule was based, this Sub-Clause provides that, pursuant to Sub-Clause 3.7, the Engineer may amend it to 'take account of the extent to which progress differs from that on which the Schedule of Payments was based'.[57]

Where a Schedule of Payments is used, there may be less need for an advance payment or payments, pursuant to Sub-Clauses 14.2 and 14.5 (which is already excluded), as instalments under the Schedule can be calculated to be in such amounts, and to be paid at such times, as to replace advance payment(s).

If the Contract does not include a Schedule of Payments, the last paragraph requires the Contractor to submit to the Engineer non-binding estimates of the payments which it expects to become due during each period of three months.

(iv) Improvements: As this Sub-Clause is entitled and deals with a Schedule of Payments, it would be preferable if the last paragraph, *which expressly applies when there is no Schedule of Payments (which will usually be the case)*, were placed in, for example, Sub-Clause 14.3

54. As provided for in Sub-Clause 12.3 [*Valuation of the Works*].
55. *See* Sub-Clause 1.1.72 '**Schedule of Payments**'.
56. If payments to the Contractor are to be made on completion of milestones of progress, then these milestones should be carefully defined in the Schedule of Payments and Sub-Clause 14.4 should be amended to refer to milestone payments. *See Guidance for the Preparation of Particular Conditions*, 26-27 (example provisions for milestones) and 41 (discussion of Schedule of Payments).
57. Sub-Clause 14.4, last sentence of first paragraph.

[*Application for Interim Payment*]. Otherwise, where a Contract includes no Schedule of Payments, a Party could consider there to be no reason to examine this Sub-Clause and, consequently, overlook its last paragraph.

--ooOOoo--

14.5 Plant and Materials Intended for the Works

If no Plant and/or Materials are listed in the Contract Data for payment when shipped and/or payment when delivered, this Sub-Clause shall not apply.

The Contractor shall include, under sub-paragraph (v) of Sub-Clause 14.3 [*Application for Interim Payment*]:

- an amount to be added for Plant and Materials which have been shipped or delivered (as the case may be) to the Site for incorporation in the Permanent Works; and
- an amount to be deducted when the contract value of such Plant and Materials is included as part of the Permanent Works under sub-paragraph (i) of Sub-Clause 14.3 [*Application for Interim Payment*].

The Engineer shall proceed under Sub-Clause 3.7 [*Agreement or Determination*] to agree or determine each amount to be added for Plant and Materials if the following conditions are fulfilled (and for the purpose of Sub-Clause 3.7.3 [*Time limits*] the date these conditions are fulfilled shall be the date of commencement of the time limit for agreement under Sub-Clause 3.7.3):

(a) the Contractor has:

(i) kept satisfactory records (including the orders, receipts, Costs and use of Plant and Materials) which are available for inspection by the Engineer;

(ii) submitted evidence demonstrating that the Plant and Materials comply with the Contract (which may include test certificates under Sub-Clause 7.4 [*Testing by the Contractor*] and/or compliance verification documentation under Sub-Clause 4.9.2 [*Compliance Verification System*]) to the Engineer; and

(iii) submitted a statement of the Cost of acquiring and shipping or delivering (as the case may be) the Plant and Materials to the Site, supported by satisfactory evidence;

and either:

(b) the relevant Plant and Materials:

(i) are those listed in the Contract Data for payment when shipped;

(ii) have been shipped to the Country, en route to the Site, in accordance with the Contract; and

(iii) are described in a clean shipped bill of lading or other evidence of shipment, which has been submitted to the Engineer together with:

- evidence of payment of freight and insurance;
- any other documents reasonably required by the Engineer; and
- a written undertaking by the Contractor that the Contractor will deliver to the Employer (prior to submitting the next Statement) a bank guarantee in a form and issued by an entity to which the Employer gives consent (but such consent shall not relieve the Contractor from any obligation in the following provisions of this sub-paragraph), in amounts and currencies equal to the amount due under this Sub-Clause. This guarantee shall be in a similar form to the form described in Sub-Clause 14.2.1 [*Advance Payment Guarantee*] and shall be valid until the Plant and Materials are properly stored on Site and protected against loss, damage or deterioration;

or

(c) the relevant Plant and Materials:

(i) are those listed in the Contract Data for payment when delivered to the Site, and

(ii) have been delivered to and are properly stored on the Site, are protected against loss, damage or deterioration, and appear to be in accordance with the Contract.

The amount so agreed or determined shall take account of the evidence and documents required under this Sub-Clause and of the contract value of the Plant and Materials. If sub-paragraph (b) above applies, the Engineer shall have no obligation to certify any payment under this Sub-Clause until the Employer has received the bank guarantee in accordance with sub-paragraph (b)(iii) above. The sum to be certified by the Engineer in an IPC shall be the equivalent of eighty percent (80%) of this agreed or determined amount. The currencies for this certified sum shall be the same as those in which payment will become due when the contract value is included under sub-paragraph (i) of Sub-Clause 14.3 [*Application for Interim Payment*]. At that time, the Payment Certificate shall include the applicable amount to be deducted which shall be equivalent to, and in the same currencies and proportions as, this additional amount for the relevant Plant and Materials.

If no Plant and/or Materials are listed in the Contract Data for payment pursuant to this Sub-Clause, it shall not apply.

The Contractor may, subject to having satisfied the conditions described in sub-paragraphs (a) and either (b) or (c), include in an application for interim payment, pursuant to Sub-Clause 14.3 (v):

- **an addition for Plant and Materials which have been shipped or delivered to the Site for incorporation in the Permanent Works; and**
- **a deduction when such Plant and Materials are included as part of the Permanent Works under Sub-Clause 14.3(i).**

The Engineer is required to proceed under Sub-Clause 3.7 to agree or determine each amount to be added for Plant and Materials if the relevant conditions are fulfilled. The sum to be certified by the Engineer in an IPC shall be the equivalent of 80% of the agreed or determined amount. The currencies for this certified sum shall be the

same as those in which payment will become due when the contract value is included under Sub-Clause 14.3(i).

<u>Commentary</u>

(i) Main Changes from RB/99:

(1) Before the Contractor may include an addition for Plant and Materials in an application for interim payment, a new step has been introduced (compared to Sub-Clause 14.5 of RB/99): the Engineer must have proceeded under Sub-Clause 3.7 to agree or determine such amount, which it can only do if satisfied that the Contractor has complied with the conditions described in sub-paragraphs (a) and either (b) or (c).

(2) Sub-paragraph (a) (ii), which requires submission of evidence demonstrating, among other things, that the Plant and Materials comply with the Contract, is new.

(3) Sub-paragraph (b) (iii), third bullet point, which requires the Contractor to submit a written undertaking that it will deliver to the Employer the bank guarantee provided for by the Sub-Clause, is new (in RB/99, the same sub-paragraph had instead required that the Contractor submit the bank guarantee itself instead of, initially, a written undertaking); this has in turn necessitated changes in the language of the last paragraph.

(ii) Related Clauses / Sub-Clauses: 1.3 [*Notices and Other Communications*], 3.7 [*Agreement or Determination*], 4.9.2 [*Compliance Verification System*], 7.4 [*Testing by the Contractor*], 7.7 [*Ownership of Plant and Materials*], 8.3 [*Programme*], 8.11 [*Payment for Plant and Materials after Employer's Suspension*], 14.2 [*Advance Payment*], 14.3 [*Application for Interim Payment*], 14.4 [*Schedule of Payments*] and 14.9 [*Release of Retention Money*].

(iii) Analysis:

(1) Purpose of Sub-Clause 14.5: Advances for Plant and Materials

The Contractor may normally only apply to be paid for the value of the Works which it has *already* executed and the Contractor's Documents which it has *already* produced.[58] On the other hand, like Sub-Clause 14.2 [*Advance Payment*], Sub-Clause 14.5, if adopted (the Sub-Clause is also

58. *See* Sub-Clause 14.3(i).

optional), provides for advances to the Contractor against Plant and Materials before their incorporation in the Works, which may be of special importance in the case of high-value items.

Sub-Clause 14.5 applies if Plant and/or Materials are listed in the Contract Data as being for payment when shipped and/or for payment when delivered to the Site.[59] The Sub-Clause enables the Contractor to include in its applications for interim payment, subject to certain conditions, 80% of the value of such listed Plant and Materials (together with shipping, freight and insurance costs, if any)[60] already at the moment when they either are shipped, whether from abroad or elsewhere (sub-paragraph (b)), or, alternatively, when they are delivered to, and stored on, the Site (sub-paragraph (c)), before they are due to be incorporated in the Permanent Works. The conditions which the Contractor must satisfy relate, among other things, to demonstrating that the Plant and Materials comply with the Contract, their Cost of acquisition and shipment or delivery, and their protection against loss or damage.[61]

(2) Lengthier procedures

Under the previous Sub-Clause, the Engineer could determine and certify each addition for Plant and Materials directly if the conditions in sub-paragraphs (a) and either (b) or (c) of Sub-Clause 14.5 (of RB/99) were satisfied. However, under the new Sub-Clause, before the Engineer may make any certification, the Engineer is required to proceed under Sub-Clause 3.7, which involves more formalities and is likely to take more time.

It will be recalled that Sub-Clause 3.7 allows the Parties, in consultation with the Engineer, 42 days to reach agreement; should the Parties fail to do so, the Engineer has a further 42 days to make a determination. Thus, in the case of an issue between the Parties (e.g., over the Contractor's record-keeping or over whether any document submitted by the Contractor is satisfactory), 84 days (42 days + 42 days) may have to elapse before the Contractor is entitled to add an amount for Plant and Materials

59. However, Sub-Clause 14.5 will not apply if the Contract includes a Schedule of Payments, unless otherwise stated in the Schedule. *See* Sub-Clause 14.4(b).

60. *See* Sub-Clause 14.5(a)(iii) and (b)(iii).

61. Pursuant to Sub-Clause 8.11, the Contractor may also be entitled to payment for Plant and/or Materials even before they have been delivered to the Site in the case of a suspension of the Works by the Employer for more than 28 days.

to an application for an interim payment. The Engineer will then have 28 days after receiving the Contractor's Statement to certify payment,[62] and the Employer possibly 56 days after the Engineer receives the Statement to make payment.[63] Thus, it may take 140 days (84 + 56 days) or even longer[64] from when the Contractor initiates the procedure under Sub-Clause 3.7 before it receives payment. Consequently, a Contractor should initiate the procedure for doing so at the earliest practicable time.

--ooOOoo--

14.6 Issue of IPC

No amount will be certified or paid to the Contractor until:

(a) the Employer has received the Performance Security in the form, and issued by an entity, in accordance with Sub-Clause 4.2.1 [*Contractor's obligations*]; and
(b) the Contractor has appointed the Contractor's Representative in accordance with Sub-Clause 4.3 [*Contractor's Representative*].

14.6.1 The IPC

The Engineer shall, within 28 days after receiving a Statement and supporting documents, issue an IPC to the Employer, with a copy to the Contractor:

(a) stating the amount which the Engineer fairly considers to be due; and
(b) including any additions and/or deductions which have become due under Sub-Clause 3.7 [*Agreement or Determination*] or under the Contract or otherwise,

with detailed supporting particulars (which shall identify any difference between a certified amount

62. Pursuant to Sub-Clause 14.6.
63. Pursuant to Sub-Clause 14.7.
64. The 42 days for agreement and the 42 days for a determination may each be extended if such extension is proposed by the Engineer and agreed by the Parties. *See* Sub-Clause 3.7.3.

and the corresponding amount in the Statement and give the reasons for such difference).

14.6.2 Withholding (amounts in) an IPC

Before the issue of the Taking-Over Certificate for the Works, the Engineer may withhold an IPC in an amount which would (after retention and other deductions) be less than the minimum amount of the IPC (if any) stated in the Contract Data. In this event, the Engineer shall promptly give a Notice to the Contractor accordingly.

An IPC shall not be withheld for any other reason, although:

(a) if any thing supplied or work done by the Contractor is not in accordance with the Contract, the estimated cost of rectification or replacement may be withheld until rectification or replacement has been completed;
(b) if the Contractor was or is failing to perform any work, service or obligation in accordance with the Contract, the value of this work or obligation may be withheld until the work or obligation has been performed. In this event, the Engineer shall promptly give a Notice to the Contractor describing the failure and with detailed supporting particulars of the value withheld; and/or
(c) if the Engineer finds any significant error or discrepancy in the Statement or supporting documents, the amount of the IPC may take account of the extent to which this error or discrepancy has prevented or prejudiced proper investigation of the amounts in the Statement until such error or discrepancy is corrected in a subsequent Statement.

For each amount so withheld, in the supporting particulars for the IPC the Engineer shall detail his/her calculation of the amount and state the reasons for it being withheld.

14.6.3 Correction or modification

The Engineer may in any Payment Certificate make any correction or modification that should properly be made to any previous Payment Certificate. A

Payment Certificate shall not be deemed to indicate the Engineer's acceptance, approval, consent or Notice of No-objection to any Contractor's Document or to (any part of) the Works.

If the Contractor considers that an IPC does not include any amounts to which the Contractor is entitled, these amounts shall be identified in the next Statement (the "identified amounts" in this paragraph). The Engineer shall then make any correction or modification that should properly be made in the next Payment Certificate. Thereafter, to the extent that:

(a) the Contractor is not satisfied that this next Payment Certificate includes the identified amounts; and
(b) the identified amounts do not concern a matter for which the Engineer is already carrying out his/her duties under Sub-Clause 3.7 [*Agreement or Determination*]

the Contractor may, by giving a Notice, refer this matter to the Engineer and Sub-Clause 3.7 [*Agreement or Determination*] shall apply (and, for the purpose of Sub-Clause 3.7.3 [*Time limits*], the date the Engineer receives this Notice shall be the date of commencement of the time limit for agreement under Sub-Clause 3.7.3).

No amount shall be certified or paid to the Contractor until the Employer has received the Performance Security, and the Contractor has appointed the Contractor's Representative.

Within 28 days after receiving a Statement and supporting documents, the Engineer shall issue an IPC to the Employer, with a copy to the Contractor, stating the amount the Engineer fairly considers to be due, including any additions and/or deductions under Sub-Clause 3.7. Before the Taking-Over Certificate for the Works, the Engineer may withhold an IPC in an amount which would be less than the minimum amount of the IPC (if any) stated in the Contract Data. Otherwise, an IPC shall not be withheld, although: (a) if anything done by the Contractor is not in accordance with the Contract, the estimated cost of rectification may be withheld; (b) if the Contractor is failing to perform any work, service or obligation, its value may be

withheld; and/or (c) if the Engineer finds any significant error in the Statement, the amount of the IPC may take account of this. The Engineer must state its calculation of, and reasons for, any withholding.

The Engineer may correct or modify any previous Payment Certificate. If the Contractor considers that an IPC does not include any amounts to which it is entitled, these amounts shall be identified in the next Statement. Thereafter, to the extent the Contractor is not satisfied that the next Payment Certificate includes the identified amounts, the Contractor may refer this matter to the Engineer and Sub-Clause 3.7 shall apply.

Commentary

(i) Main Changes from RB/99: The new Sub-Clause is much longer, clearer and better structured than Sub-Clause 14.6 of RB/99. The main changes are:

(1) in the first paragraph, sub-paragraph (b) is new;
(2) the rest of the Sub-Clause is broken down into three parts: 14.6.1 The IPC, 14.6.2 Withholding (amounts in) an IPC and 14.6.3 Correction or modification, which is new;
(3) in 14.6.1, the requirement that the Engineer provides a copy of the IPC to the Contractor is new;[65]
(4) in 14.6.1, sub-paragraph (b) is new as is, mostly, the text following sub-paragraph (b);
(5) in 14.6.2, sub-paragraph (b) is partly new and sub-paragraph (c) is new as is the last sentence of 14.6.2; and
(6) in 14.6.3, the entire last paragraph is new.

(ii) Related Clauses / Sub-Clauses: 1.3 [*Notices and Other Communications*], 3.2 [*Engineer's Duties and Authority*], 3.7 [*Agreement or Determination*] 4.2 [*Performance Security*], 4.3 [*Contractor's Representative*], 12.1 [*Works to be measured*], 12.3 [*Valuation of the Works*], 13.7 [*Adjustments for Changes in Cost*], 14.3 [*Application for Interim Payment*], 14.7 [*Payment*], 16.1 [*Suspension by Contractor*], 16.2 [*Termination by Contractor*] and 22.1 [*Failure to Appoint DAAB Member(s)*].

65. But this was provided for by Sub-Clause 1.3 [*Communications*] of RB/99.

(iii) Analysis:

(1) Engineer to certify payments to the Contractor fairly[66]

During the execution of the Works, the Contractor is normally paid pursuant to IPCs issued by the Engineer. This Sub-Clause provides for how they are to be issued.

As indicated by Sub-Clause 14.6.1, after receiving a Statement and supporting documents from the Contractor under Sub-Clause 14.3, the Engineer has 28 days 'within'[67] which to examine it and issue an IPC to the Employer with a copy to the Contractor.[68] In the IPC, the Engineer must state the amount which it 'fairly' considers to be due to the Contractor.[69]

Both Parties are free to make representations to and communicate with the Engineer on the subject of the Engineer's proposed certification decision.[70] However, the Employer must not attempt to interfere with the independence of the Engineer or apply pressure on the Engineer in connection with this decision.[71] On the contrary, as the Engineer has been engaged and is employed by the Employer, the Employer will

66. For a discussion of 'fairly', which is also used in Sub-Clause 3.7 [*Agreement or Determination*], *see* item (2) under **(i) Main Changes from RB/99** of the commentary on that Sub-Clause above including accompanying fns 95 and 96.
67. *See* item (2) under **(v) Improvements** of the commentary on Sub-Clause 1.2 [*Interpretation*] above.
68. If the Engineer should fail to certify within 28 days and, if the failure constitutes a material breach of the Employer's obligations, the Contractor may, after giving not less than 21 days' Notice to the Employer, have a right to suspend or reduce the rate of work under Sub-Clause 16.1 [*Suspension by Contractor*].
69. This is one of three places in the General Conditions in which they state that the Engineer is to act 'fairly' between the Parties. The others being Sub-Clause 14.13, when the Engineer issues an FPC, and Sub-Clause 3.7.2, which requires the Engineer to make a 'fair' determination between the Parties. Sub-Clause 3.7 also requires the Engineer to 'act neutrally between the Parties'.
70. Atkin Chambers, *Hudson's Building and Engineering Contracts* (14th edn, Sweet & Maxwell, London, 2020) 559 (para. 4-063).
71. Julian Bailey, *Construction Law* (3rd edn, London Publishing, UK, 2020) vol 1, 380-381 (para. 5.84) and Atkin Chambers, *Hudson's Building and Engineering Contracts* (14th edn, Sweet & Maxwell, London, 2020) 557-559 (paras 4-061 to 4-062).

usually be subject to a positive obligation to ensure, or at least take all possible action to try to ensure, that the Engineer carries out its functions in accordance with the Contract.[72] The Employer may therefore be responsible if, for example, the Engineer fails to issue an IPC within the time prescribed for its issue.[73]

The IPC must include any additions and/or deductions which have become due under Sub-Clause 3.7 or under the Contract[74] 'or otherwise',[75] with supporting particulars. As previously indicated, those quoted words refer to a Claim, agreed with the Employer or determined as due by the Engineer, that is based in law rather than one that is based on wording in the Contract.[76]

An excellent new addition in Sub-Clause 14.6.1 is the requirement that the Engineer must identify any difference between a certified amount and the corresponding amount in a Statement and give the reasons for such difference. In this way, the Contractor – and later the DAAB and arbitrator(s) – can be informed why the Engineer denied a requested payment.

(2) Permitted withholdings

The Engineer may not generally decline to issue an IPC.[77] The Engineer may also not withhold amounts in an IPC[78] except for the three reasons, and for the respective amounts, specified in Sub-Clause 14.6.2(a), (b) and (c), respectively.[79]

---

72. Julian Bailey, *Construction Law* (3rd edn, London Publishing, UK, 2020) vol 1, 381 (para. 5.86).
73. *Ibid. See also* Sub-Clause 16.1 [*Suspension by Contractor*]. What if the Engineer acts unfairly without the Employer's interference? According to English law, 'if a certifier [the Engineer] behaves unfairly without interference by the Employer, the [c]ertifier's own unfairness may be enough to invalidate the certificate'. Atkin Chambers, *Hudson's Building and Engineering Contracts* (14th edn, Sweet & Maxwell, London, 2020) 567 (para. 4-067). If the Engineer should have acted unfairly to the Contractor, the Contractor's remedy would be under Sub-Clause 16.1 and/or to assert a Claim under Sub-Clause 20.1 (b) or (c), as may be appropriate.
74. For example, *see* items (i) through (ix) of Sub-Clause 14.3 [*Application for Interim Payment*].
75. *See* Sub-Clause 14.3(vi).
76. *Guide to the Use of FIDIC Conditions of Contract for Works of Civil Engineering Construction, Fourth Edition* (FIDIC 1989) 119 (commenting on Sub-Clause 53.1 [*Notice of Claim*] in RB/87). The terms 'or otherwise' are also

These reasons are, first, if anything supplied or work done is defective or 'not in accordance with the Contract'; second, if the Contractor fails to perform any contractual obligation;[80] and, third, if the Engineer finds a significant error or discrepancy in the Statement or supporting documents. The first two reasons can have a very wide application and are not required to relate to the Statement that the Contractor has most recently submitted.[81]

These provisions need to be read with the rest of the Conditions,[82] and for each of the amounts withheld the Engineer must, in the supporting particulars for the IPC, detail its calculation of the amount and 'state the reasons for it being withheld'.[83] As a practical matter, this right to

---

used in, among other places, Sub-Clause 20.2, first paragraph, relating to Claims and in the definition of '**Claim**' in Sub-Clause 1.1.6.

77. Assuming the Employer has received the Performance Security and the Contractor has appointed the Contractor's Representative and unless it would be for an amount which would be less than the minimum amount of an IPC stated in the Contract Data. In the latter case, it must give a prompt Notice of this to the Contractor. *See* Sub-Clause 14.6.2, first paragraph.
78. The second paragraph of Sub-Clause 14.6.2 refers to withholding an IPC ['[a]n IPC shall not be withheld'], whereas it should refer to withholding amounts in an IPC, as indicated by the content of Sub-Clause 14.6.2 and its title.
79. The Engineer may also withhold certification of the estimated cost of uncompleted work from Retention Money under Sub-Clause 14.9, third paragraph. In the case of an unjustified failure to certify by the Engineer, the Contractor has the remedies provided for in Sub-Clauses 16.1 [*Suspension by Contractor*] and 16.2 [*Termination by Contractor*].
80. In this case, the Engineer must give a Notice to the Contractor of the failure with detailed supporting particulars.
81. Whatever the reason may be, the Engineer must act fairly in deciding whether and what to withhold. This follows from Sub-Clause 14.6.1(a) which requires the Engineer, in relation to any Statement, to state what it 'fairly' considers to be due.
82. Thus, for example, if the Contractor should fail to complete the Works by the Time for Completion, Sub-Clause 14.6.2 (b) ('failing to perform [...] in accordance with the Contract') may not immediately apply since, among other things, the Engineer may not withhold Delay Damages that may be due under Sub-Clause 8.8 [*Delay Damages*] unless the Employer has first proceeded under Sub-Clause 20.2 and become entitled to them (*see* Sub-Clause 8.8, first paragraph, and Sub-Clause 20.2.7, second paragraph) under the Conditions.
83. Sub-Clause 14.6.2, last paragraph.

withhold of the Engineer (Employer), although limited in scope, may be more important to the Employer than any claim right it may have against the Contractor.[84]

While each IPC is provisional in the sense that the Engineer may correct or modify it in a later Payment Certificate, pursuant to Sub-Clause 14.6.3,[85] the Employer is bound to pay it within the period stated in the Contract Data (if not stated, 56 days) after the Engineer receives the Statement and supporting documents.[86] Such a certificate is stated under the common law to create 'a debt due'[87] and possess 'temporary finality'.[88]

(3) Correction of certificates

Sub-Clause 14.6.3, first paragraph, clarifies that the Engineer may correct 'any Payment Certificate' (not just an IPC) and that the Contractor may not rely on a Payment Certificate as evidence of 'acceptance', 'approval' or a Notice of No-objection to any Contractor's Document or any part of

84. As a former Chairman of the FIDIC Contracts Committee stated, presumably of practice prior to the 1999 Rainbow Suite and its Sub-Clause 2.5:

> if [the Contractor] fails, e.g. if the quality of any of the work is not up to the required standard or if an item of equipment is missing, then the Employer, theoretically speaking, has a claim against the Contractor. What normally happens, however, is that the Employer just does not pay the full contract amount for that piece of work. If that piece of work has been approved and actually paid for, and later is revealed to be defective or below standard, the usual procedure is for the Employer (or the Engineer) to simply deduct the relevant amount from the next payment certificate [...] This procedure is normal and fully acceptable provided that the deductions or withholding of payment are fair and proper.
>
> Christopher Wade, 'Presentation Notes on: Claims of the Employer' 1, ICC–FIDIC conference Paris, 29-30 April 2004: Resolution of Disputes: International Construction Contracts.

85. An Engineer's certificate may also be reviewed, revised and opened up by the Dispute Avoidance/Adjudication Bond ('DAAB') pursuant to Rule 5.1 (k) of the DAAB Rules and later in arbitration pursuant to Sub-Clause 21.6, second paragraph. *See also* the last paragraph of Sub-Clause 3.2 [*Engineer's Duties and Authority*].
86. Sub-Clause 14.7 [*Payment*], sub-para. (b).
87. Stephen Furst and Vivian Ramsey, *Keating on Construction Contracts* (11th edn, Sweet & Maxwell, London, 2021) 133 (para. 5-019).
88. Julian Bailey, *Construction Law* (3rd edn, London Publishing, UK, 2020) vol 2, 540-541 (para. 6.206).

the Works.[89] The Sub-Clause also requires the Contractor to identify, and draw to the Engineer's attention in a Statement, any amounts which the Contractor considers the Engineer had failed to include in an earlier IPC so that the Engineer may – once more, acting 'fairly', as it must do under this Sub-Clause – make any correction or modification which may be appropriate. Thereafter, if the Contractor is still dissatisfied with the next Payment Certificate, it may, by giving a Notice (and bypassing Clause 20 [*Employer's and Contractor's Claims*] which would otherwise apply), refer this matter to the Engineer and Sub-Clause 3.7 will apply.[90]

(iv) Related law:

(1) The procedure whereby a contractor is paid based upon a payment certificate of a third party, such as an engineer (as under the FIDIC forms) or other contract administrator, is standard practice in the common law, though not civil law, world.[91] Under RB/17, the Engineer issues not only Payment Certificates (of various kinds) but also a Taking-Over Certificate and a Performance Certificate. In this context, a certificate is defined by an English legal authority as:

> the expression in a definite form of the exercise of the opinion of the certifier in relation to some matter provided for by the terms of the contract.[92]

Under English law, 'the purpose and effect of any certificate is ultimately a question of construction and depends on the terms of the individual contract'.[93]

89. *See also* the last paragraph of Sub-Clause 3.2 [*Engineer's Duties and Authority*].
90. Sub-Clause 14.6.3, last paragraph. If the Contractor is dissatisfied with any determination of the Engineer under Sub-Clause 3.7 then, after giving a NOD with the Engineer's determination under Sub-Clause 3.7.5, the Contractor may refer the Dispute to the DAAB pursuant to Sub-Clause 21.4.1.
91. *See* **Section 4.4.1 Contract Administrator (*Maître D'Oeuvre*) *v* Engineer** in **Chapter II Applicable Law** above.
92. Atkin Chambers, *Hudson's Building and Engineering Contracts* (14th edn, Sweet & Maxwell, London, 2020) 484 (para. 4-001).
93. *Ibid.*, 487 (para. 4-008).

(2) For discussion of the Engineer's potential liability to the Employer or the Contractor in relation to its certificates, *see* under **(iv) Related Law** of the commentary on Sub-Clause 3.7 [*Agreement or Determination*] above.

--ooOOoo--

14.7 Payment

The Employer shall pay to the Contractor:

(a) the amount certified in each Advance Payment Certificate within the period stated in the Contract Data (if not stated, 21 days) after the Employer receives the Advance Payment Certificate;

(b) the amount certified in each IPC issued under:

(i) Sub-Clause 14.6 [*Issue of IPC*], within the period stated in the Contract Data (if not stated, 56 days) after the Engineer receives the Statement and supporting documents; or

(ii) Sub-Clause 14.13 [*Issue of FPC*], within the period stated in the Contract Data (if not stated, 28 days) after the Employer receives the IPC; and

(c) the amount certified in the FPC within the period stated in the Contract Data (if not stated, 56 days) after the Employer receives the FPC.

Payment of the amount due in each currency shall be made into the bank account, nominated by the Contractor, in the payment country (for this currency) specified in the Contract.

The Employer shall pay the Contractor: the amount certified in each Advance Payment Certificate, the amount certified in each IPC issued under Sub-Clause 14.6 or 14.13 and the amount certified in the FPC, within the respective periods stated in the Contract Data or (if not stated) within the default periods indicated. Payment of the amount due in each currency shall be made to the Contractor's bank in the payment country (for this currency) specified in the Contract.

Commentary

(i) Main Changes from RB/99:

(1) In the new Sub-Clause, sub-paragraph (a) replaces the same sub-paragraph in Sub-Clause 14.7 of RB/99, and provides that payment of the advance payment is to be made within a specified time period after the Employer receives each Advance Payment Certificate.

(2) Sub-paragraph (b) (ii) is entirely new and had no counterpart in RB/99.

(3) All time periods for payment now refer to periods stated in the Contract Data or, if none is stated, to a default time period (whether of 21, 28 or 56 days), both of which are to some extent new.

(4) The wording of sub-paragraphs (a), (b) and (c) has been revised to take account, among other things, of other changes introduced by RB/17, such as the provision for Advance Payment Certificate(s).

(ii) Related Clauses / Sub-Clauses: 1.3 [*Notices and Other Communications*], 2.4 [*Employer's Financial Arrangements*], 14 [*Contract Price and Payment*], 16.1 [*Suspension by Contractor*] and 16.2 [*Termination by Contractor*].

(iii) Analysis: This Sub-Clause makes it a contractual obligation of the Employer to pay ('[t]he Employer shall pay') the Contractor, 'within'[94] the periods of days stated in the Contract Data or the default periods indicated, the amounts certified in different Payment Certificates issued by the Engineer. In the case of an IPC issued under Sub-Clause 14.6 [*Issue of IPC*], payment must be made within a time period (if not stated in the Contract Data, 56 days) 'after the Engineer receives the Statement and supporting documents' from the Contractor, *not after the date of issue of the IPC by the Engineer to the Employer with a copy to the Contractor*. Moreover, receipt by the Employer of a copy of a Statement and supporting documents submitted to the Engineer[95] is not a condition to the obligation of the Employer to pay an IPC.

94. *See* item (2) under **(v) Improvements** of the commentary on Sub-Clause 1.2 [*Interpretation*] above.

95. Pursuant to the last paragraph of Sub-Clause 1.3 [*Notices and Other Communications*].

The Employer must make payment *in full*, regardless of any entitlement to compensation arising from any Claim which the Employer may have against the Contractor.[96] If the Employer considers that it has a Claim against the Contractor (e.g., for Delay Damages), then it must comply with the procedure for Claims provided for in Clause 20 [*Employer's and Contractor's Claims*].[97] The Employer has no right to act unilaterally and set off or make any deduction from any amount certified as due to the Contractor.

The *Guidance* sensibly provides in relation to this Sub-Clause that '[p]eriods for payment should be long enough for the Employer to meet, but not so long as to prejudice the Contractor's positive cash-flow'.[98] If the Employer fails to make payments within the periods indicated, the Contractor may be entitled to financing charges, pursuant to Sub-Clause 14.8 [*Delayed Payment*], possibly to suspend, or reduce the rate of, work, pursuant to sub-paragraph (c) of Sub-Clause 16.1 [*Suspension by Contractor*], and ultimately to terminate the Contract, pursuant to Sub-Clause 16.2 [*Termination by Contractor*].[99]

Payment of the amount due in each currency of the Contract is to be made into the bank account (and in the country) nominated by the Contractor and specified in the Contract.[100]

(iv) Improvements: As Sub-Clause 14.2.2 of RB/17 provides for a single Advance Payment Certificate, Sub-Clause 14.7(a) needs to be corrected

96. *See The FIDIC Contracts Guide* (2nd edn, FIDIC, 2022) 409.
97. The Claim is then agreed or determined under Sub-Clause 3.7, and if so agreed or determined, may result in a deduction in a Statement of the Contractor under Sub-Clause 14.3(vi).
98. *Guidance for the Preparation of the Particular Conditions*, 41.
99. After giving a Notice of intention to terminate which goes unremedied and without prejudice to any other rights which the Contractor may have. Sub-Clause 16.2 first sentence.
100. As a practical matter, payments in Local Currency (i.e., the currency of the Country), which are usually intended to cover the Contractor's local expenses, are likely to be made to an account in the Country, whereas Foreign Currency payments will often be made to a bank account or accounts in the Contractor's country or (if the Contractor is a joint venture) possibly in different countries.

to remove the reference to 'each' Advance Payment Certificate so as to make it consistent with Sub-Clause 14.2.2.[101]

--ooOOoo--

14.8 Delayed Payment

If the Contractor does not receive payment in accordance with Sub-Clause 14.7 [*Payment*], the Contractor shall be entitled to receive financing charges compounded monthly on the amount unpaid during the period of delay. This period shall be deemed to commence on the expiry of the time for payment specified in Sub-Clause 14.7 [*Payment*], irrespective (in the case of sub-paragraph (b) of Sub-Clause 14.7) of the date on which any IPC is issued.

Unless otherwise stated in the Contract Data, these financing charges shall be calculated at the annual rate of three percent (3%) above:

(a) the average bank short-term lending rate to prime borrowers prevailing for the currency of payment at the place of payment; or
(b) where no such rate exists at that place, the same rate in the country of the currency of payment; or
(c) in the absence of such a rate at either place, the appropriate rate fixed by the law of the country of the currency of payment.

The Contractor shall by request be entitled to payment of these financing charges by the Employer, without:

(i) the need for the Contractor to submit a Statement or any formal Notice (including any requirement to comply with Sub-Clause 20.2 [*Claims for Payment and/or EOT*]) or certification; and
(ii) prejudice to any other right or remedy.

101. However, if payment of the advance payment by instalments is desired, the *Guidance* proposes how Sub-Clause 14.2 and the Contract Data may be amended to allow for this. *See* the *Guidance for the Preparation of the Particular Conditions*, 40-41.

If the Contractor does not receive payment in accordance with Sub-Clause 14.7, the Contractor is entitled to financing charges compounded monthly on the amount unpaid. Unless otherwise stated in the Contract Data, these financing charges are at the annual rate of three percent above the average bank short-term lending rate to prime borrowers for the currency of payment at the place of payment. The Contractor shall, by request, be entitled to payment of these charges without having to comply with Sub-Clause 20.2.

Commentary

(i) Main Changes from RB/99:

(1) In the second paragraph, instead of financing charges being 'at the annual rate of three percentage points above the discount rate of the central bank in the country of the currency of payment' (as was the case in Sub-Clause 14.8 of RB/99), they are now at the annual rate of 3% above the rate provided for by sub-paragraphs (a), (b) or (c).

(2) The third paragraph is new – notably, the provision for a 'request' by the Contractor without the need for a Statement (or compliance with Sub-Clause 20.2) – and replaces the previous third paragraph.

(ii) Related Clauses / Sub-Clauses: 1.3 [*Notices and Other Communications*], 11.4 [*Failure to Remedy Defects*], 14.7 [*Payment*], 16.1 [*Suspension by Contractor*] and 16.2 [*Termination by Contractor*].[102]

(iii) Analysis:

(1) Purpose of Sub-Clause

This Sub-Clause entitles the Contractor to receive financing charges[103] on any amount unpaid, calculated from when it should have been paid

102. *See also* Sub-Clause 9.6 of the General Conditions of DAAB Agreement and Rule 5.1 (i) of the DAAB Rules.

103. As a number of countries do not allow the payment of interest (*see* under **(iv) Related Law** below), FIDIC uses the term 'financing charges' instead of interest.

under Sub-Clause 14.7 *and irrespective of whether an IPC had in fact been issued.*[104]

(2) The rate of financing charges

The rate of financing charges on delayed payments is stipulated to be a particular annual market rate plus a 3% uplift (on account of the Employer's delay). The particular annual market rate is stated in sub-paragraph (a) to be the average bank short-term lending rate to prime borrowers prevailing for the currency of payment at the place of payment.[105]

Sub-paragraph (b) of this Sub-Clause provides that if no such rate exists at the place of payment, then the rate will be the same rate in the country of the currency of payment. The UNIDROIT Principles (from which this provision is derived) give an example: 'if a loan is made in pounds sterling payable in country X and there is no rate for loans in pounds on country X financial market, reference will be made to the rate in the United Kingdom'.[106] Sub-paragraph (c) provides that in the absence of such rate at either place, the rate shall be 'the appropriate rate fixed by the law of the country of the currency of payment'. The UNIDROIT Principles provide that:

> [i]n most cases [the 'appropriate rate'] will be the legal rate of interest and, as there may be more than one, that most appropriate for

104. *The FIDIC Contracts Guide* (2nd edn, FIDIC, 2022) 411. However, if no IPC had been issued, it could be difficult to establish the amount to which the financing charges applied. *Ibid.*
105. This rate is derived from paragraph (2) of art. 7.4.9 [*Interest for failure to pay money*] of the UNIDROIT Principles. As to this rate, UNIDROIT says:

> This solution seems to be that best suited to the needs of international trade and most appropriate to ensure an adequate compensation of the harm sustained. The rate in question is the rate at which the aggrieved party [the Contractor] will normally borrow the money which it has not received from the non-performing party [the Employer]. That normal rate is the average bank short-term lending rate to prime borrowers prevailing at the place for payment for the currency of payment.

UNIDROIT Principles, art. 7.4.9 [*Interest for failure to pay money*], official comment 2. Rate of interest. For a useful commentary on art. 7.4.9, *see* Stefan Vogenauer (ed), *Commentary on the UNIDROIT Principles of International Commercial Contracts (PICC)* (2nd edn, OUP, Oxford, 2015) 1012-1017 (paras 1-18).
106. UNIDROIT Principles, art. 7.4.9, official comment 2. Rate of Interest.

international transactions. If there is no legal rate of interest, the rate will be the most appropriate bank rate.[107]

The Sub-Clause expressly provides that the Contractor's right to financing charges is without prejudice to the Contractor's other rights or remedies, which is also consistent with the UNIDROIT Principles.[108]

Thus, if the Contractor can prove that the delay in payment has caused damages in addition to interest (e.g., if the Contractor's borrowing costs to obtain replacement funds were higher than these financing charges), the Contractor is entitled to recover such higher amount. In addition, in the case of delayed payments, the Contractor may have the right to suspend work under Sub-Clause 16.1 or to terminate the Contract under Sub-Clause 16.2. These rights are unaffected by the Contractor's right to financing charges under this Sub-Clause.

(3) The need for a request

The last paragraph of this Sub-Clause provides that the Contractor shall 'by request' be entitled to payment of these financing charges.[109] Such a 'request' should be made by issuing an invoice to the Employer for the calculated amount of these financing charges,[110] which should otherwise comply with Sub-Clause 1.3 [*Notices and Other Communications*].

---

107. *Ibid.*
108. UNIDROIT Principles, art. 7.4.9 (3) [*Interest for failure to pay money*]. This may be contrasted with Delay Damages under Sub-Clause 8.8 which are stated to be the 'only' damages due for the Contractor's delay, other than in the event of termination under Sub-Clause 15.2 before completion of the Works (or 'fraud, gross negligence, deliberate default or reckless misconduct').
109. This paragraph has apparently been added to alert the Employer and the Engineer contemporaneously to the Employer's liability for financing charges (as there have been cases where the Contractor has first claimed financing charges at a much later stage, retroactively and to the surprise of the Employer). Such a 'request' corresponds, approximately, to a notice of default (*mise en demeure*), the giving of which is usually a condition to liability for interest in civil law countries. *See* **Section 4 Common Law and Civil Law Compared – 4.3.4 Notice of Default (*Mise En Demeure*)** in **Chapter II Applicable Law** above.
110. Compliance with Sub-Clause 20.2 is not required. A failure to receive payment within 28 days of a request gives rise to a deemed Dispute under Sub-Clause 21.4 (b), permitting its direct referral to the DAAB.

The 'request' should not be a condition to entitlement to financing charges, but only to their payment. The Contractor becomes entitled to financing charges if it 'does not receive payment in accordance with Sub-Clause 14.7 [*Payment*]'.[111] Financing charges accrue from that point. But a request is necessary to 'be entitled to payment of these financing charges'.[112]

(iv) Related law:

(1) Validity of interest (financing charges)[113]

Under the laws of most countries, where a debtor (here the Employer) fails to pay an amount that is due, it may validly be required – in some countries, after a notice of default[114] – to pay interest on that amount.[115]

A number of countries do not allow the payment of interest. Most of these countries are in the Middle East and Africa and have a legal system based on *Sharia* (Islamic law).[116] On the other hand, while Saudi Arabia, for

---

111. Sub-Clause 14.8, first paragraph. This is consistent with the position in common law countries:

> in England, interest typically accrues from the time payment was due or should have been made.
>
> John Y Gotanda, 'A Study of Interest' in Filip de Ly and Laurent Lévy (eds), *Interest, Auxiliary and Alternative Remedies in International Arbitration* (ICC Publication no 684, ICC Services, Paris 2008) 169, 175.

112. Sub-Clause 14.8, third paragraph. While this paragraph also provides that the Contractor is not required to submit a Statement to be entitled to financing charges, the Contractor may want to do so anyway as, if it is certified by the Engineer, it may reinforce the Contractor's right to financing charges and help to quantify their amount.
113. *See also* **Section 4 Common Law and Civil Law Compared – 4.5.1 Interest on Monies Due** in **Chapter II Applicable Law** above.
114. *See* **Section 4 Common Law and Civil Law Compared – 4.3.4 Notice of Default (*Mise en Demeure*)** in **Chapter II Applicable Law** above.
115. John Y Gotanda, 'A Study in Interest,' in Filip De Ly and Laurent Lévy (eds), *Interest, Auxiliary and Alternative Remedies in International Arbitration* (ICC Publication no 684, 2008) 169, 171.
116. Whether describing interest as 'financing charges', as Sub-Clause 14.8 does, will improve the legal position in those countries may be an open question. Professor Klaus Peter Berger notes that a claim for interest may be qualified 'as a damage claim [and thus not as just "illegal" interest] because the creditor has to borrow the money he does not receive from his debtor elsewhere and has to pay interest for this money which constitutes his

example, generally prohibits interest, the civil and commercial codes of a number of Arab countries, such as Egypt, Iraq, Kuwait, Lebanon, Libya, Oman, Syria and the United Arab Emirates, have for a long time allowed for the payment of interest.[117]

(2) Rate of interest

Any provision for the payment of interest must comply with applicable law relating to usury,[118] meaning that the rate of interest may not exceed some maximum rate fixed by law. Subject to this consideration, in civil law countries, as in common law countries, parties are generally free to fix by contract the rate of interest which is to apply in the case of delay in the payment of money. In civil law countries at least, if no rate of interest is provided for in a contract, then the civil code will often fix, directly or indirectly, the rate of interest (referred to as 'moratory interest') which is to apply.[119]

For example, failing agreement of the parties on the amount of interest, Article 226 of the Egyptian Civil Code provides that in civil matters interest will be 4% per annum and in commercial matters 5% per

---

damage'. Professor Klaus Peter Berger, 'General Principles of Law in International Commercial Arbitration: How to Find Them – How to Apply Them' (2011) 5(2) World Arb & Med Rev, 97, 130-31. In this article, Professor Berger notes that, among others, the Iran-US Claims Tribunal, which has been concerned with Islamic law issues, has upheld claims for interest on this basis. *See* pages 131-33.

117. Tarek Riad, 'The Issue of Interest in Middle East Laws and Islamic Law' in (Filip De Ly and Laurent Lévy eds) *Interest, Auxiliary and Alternative Remedies in International Arbitration* (ICC Publication no 684, 2008) 203, 204.
118. Usury refers to the 'charging of an illegal rate of interest as a condition to lending money'. Bryan A Garner (ed in chief), *Black's Law Dictionary* (11th edn, Thomson Reuters, St Paul, MN, 2019).
119. Thus, where the parties have not themselves agreed upon a rate, as provided in art. 1231-5 of the French Civil Code, art. 1231-6 of the same code provides:

> Damages due on the ground of delay in satisfaction of a monetary obligation consist of interest at the rate set by legislation, starting from the time of notice to perform (*mise en demeure*).
>
> These damages are due without the creditor having to establish any loss.

See also art. 1344 -1 of the same Code regarding the notice to be given to the debtor.

annum. Article 227(1) of the same Civil Code allows the parties to agree to an interest rate of no more than 7%. Other Arab civil codes, such as those of Syria and Libya, contain similar provisions.[120]

The maximum rate of interest permitted by law will vary from country to country. According to the UNIDROIT Principles, an agreement to pay interest for non-performance of a contract is valid (and a party is entitled to the sum irrespective of its actual harm) so long as the rate is not 'grossly excessive in relation to the harm resulting from the non-performance and to the other circumstances'.[121]

(3) Compounding interest[122]

Compounding interest (as provided for in the first paragraph of Sub-Clause 14.8) may be illegal in some countries. Thus, under French law, overdue interest must have been due for at least a full year in order for it validly to generate interest.[123] Article 232 of the Egyptian Civil Code provides that, subject to any commercial rules or practice to the contrary, interest does not run on outstanding interest, and in no case shall the total interest that the creditor may collect exceed the amount of the capital.

The UNIDROIT Principles take no position on compound interest, noting that compound interest 'in some national laws is subject to rules of public policy limiting compound interest with a view to protecting the

120. Tarek Riad, 'The Issue of Interest in Middle East Laws and Islamic Law' in Filip De Ly and Laurent Lévy (eds), *Interest, Auxiliary and Alternative Remedies in International Arbitration* (ICC Publication no 684, 2008) 203, 205.

121. Art. 7.4.13 (*Agreed payment for non-performance*) of the UNIDROIT Principles. *See also* the UK Supreme Court case *Cavendish Square Holding BV v Makdessi* [2015] UKSC 67, [2016] AC 1172 where the Court discusses the issue of the validity of a provision for interest at a higher rate during a period of default in comparative law at paras 26-39, 146-153 and 265.

122. Compounding interest, as referred to in Sub-Clause 14.8, refers to calculating interest on both the principal and the previously accumulated interest. *See* Bryan A Garner (ed in chief), *Black's Law Dictionary* (11th edn, Thomson Reuters, St Paul, MN, 2019).

123. Art. 1343-2 of the French Civil Code which is mandatory law in France. Philippe Malaurie and others, *Droit des Obligations* (11th edn, LGDJ, Issy-les-Moulineaux, 2020) 556 (para. 610).

non-performing party'.[124] Consequently, whether and to what extent compound interest is valid and may apply is left to applicable law.

--ooOOoo--

14.9 Release of Retention Money

After the issue of the Taking-Over Certificate for:

(a) the Works, the Contractor shall include the first half of the Retention Money in a Statement; or

(b) a Section, the Contractor shall include the relevant percentage of the first half of the Retention Money in a Statement.

After the latest of the expiry dates of the Defects Notification Periods, the Contractor shall include the second half of the Retention Money in a Statement promptly after such latest date. If a Taking-Over Certificate was (or was deemed to have been) issued for a Section, the Contractor shall include the relevant percentage of the second half of the Retention Money in a Statement promptly after the expiry date of the DNP for the Section.

In the next IPC, or the FPC (as the case may be), after the Engineer receives any such Statement, the Engineer shall certify the release of the corresponding amount of Retention Money. However, when certifying any release of Retention Money under Sub-Clause 14.6 [*Issue of IPC*], if any work remains to be executed under Clause 11 [*Defects after Taking Over*], the Engineer shall be entitled to withhold certification of the estimated cost of this work until it has been executed.

The relevant percentage for each Section shall be the percentage value of the Section as stated in the Contract Data. If the percentage value of a Section is not stated in the Contract Data, no percentage of either half of the Retention Money shall be released under this Sub-Clause in respect of such Section.

124. UNIDROIT Principles, art. 7.4.10 [*Interest on damages*], official comment.

After the issue of the Taking-Over Certificate for the Works, the Contractor shall include the first half of the Retention Money in a Statement or, in the case of such a certificate for a Section, the relevant percentage of the first half of the Retention Money. After the latest of the expiry dates of the DNPs, the Contractor shall include the second half of the Retention Money in a Statement or, for a Section, the relevant percentage of the second half of the Retention Money. In the next IPC or FPC (as the case may be) after any such Statement, the Engineer shall certify the release of the corresponding amount of Retention Money, but may withhold certification for unexecuted work under Clause 11. The relevant percentage for each Section shall be the percentage value stated in the Contract Data.

<u>Commentary</u>

(i) Main Changes from RB/99:

(1) As compared to Sub-Clause 14.9 of RB/99, the Sub-Clause has been restructured so that the first and second paragraphs deal with the action which the Contractor must take, the third paragraph deals with the action which the Engineer must take and the last paragraph describes the relevant percentage of the Retention Money, if any, to be released for each Section.

(2) Unlike Sub-Clause 14.9 of RB/99, the Contractor must include its application for release of each half of the Retention Money in a Statement submitted under Sub-Clause 14.3.

(3) For the purposes of the release of each half of the Retention Money for a Section taken over, the new Sub-Clause provides that the amount to be released shall be calculated by reference to the percentage value of the Section, if any, stated in the Contract Data, instead of the proportionate amount (40%) of a particular proportion provided for in Sub-Clause 14.9 of RB/99.

(4) If no percentage value of a Section is stated in the Contract Data, then, under the new Sub-Clause, no percentage of either half of the Retention Money should be released in respect of the Section, which is new.

(5) The new Sub-Clause no longer provides (as did Sub-Clause 14.9 of RB/99) that no account shall be taken of adjustments under Sub-Clauses '13.7 and 13.8' (Sub-Clauses 13.6 and 13.7 in RB/17).

(iii) Related Clauses / Sub-Clauses: 1.3 [*Notices and Other Communications*], 11 [*Defects after Taking Over*], 14.2 [*Advance Payment*], 14.3 [*Application for Interim Payment*] and 14.6 [*Issue of IPC*].

(iv) Analysis: In addition to the provision of Performance Security, pursuant to Sub-Clause 4.2, the Contractor is required to provide the Employer with security in the form of Retention Money. In order to do so, the Contractor is required by Sub-Clause 14.3(iii) to include in each periodic Statement an amount to be deducted for 'retention' – from what would otherwise be paid to the Contractor – calculated by applying the percentage of retention stated in the Contract Data[125] until the limit of Retention Money, if any, stated in the Contract Data has been reached. This limit is expressed in the Contract Data form as a percentage of the Accepted Contract Amount.

Typical retention amounts are 5% or 10% of the Accepted Contract Amount.[126] On the other hand, another authority puts the typical amount at 3% to 5% of the value of the work performed by the Contractor.[127] Although the Sub-Clause entitles the Engineer to withhold certifying release of Retention Money for incomplete or defective work, and although the aim of retention is often said to be to provide the Employer with security against defects,[128] the Employer is not restricted by the General Conditions in the use of Retention Money, or required to keep it in a separate account from its own funds. Accordingly, Retention Money appears to be available to the Employer generally as security against any breaches or other failures of the Contractor.

Retention Money will negatively affect the Contractor's cash flow. Accordingly, to limit this impact, an Employer will often accept an

125. According to Sub-Clause 14.3(iii), the percentage of retention should be applied to the total of the amounts under sub-paras (i), (ii) and (vi) of Sub-Clause 14.3.
126. This is the author's experience internationally and also the percentage given by Philip Bruner and Patrick O'Connor, *Bruner and O'Connor on Construction Law* (Thomson Reuters, St Paul, MN, 2016) vol 3, 40 (s 8:18).
127. Julian Bailey, *Construction Law* (3rd edn, London Publishing, UK, 2020) vol 2, 1058 (para. 12.03). This lower percentage may reflect UK and Commonwealth practice.
128. The example form of Retention Money guarantee included as Annex F to RB/17 provides for its payment where the Contractor has failed 'to rectify the following defects [...]'.

appropriate guarantee instead of a retention in cash.[129] Annex F of the Conditions contains an example form of Retention Money Guarantee for this purpose. Like the forms of Performance Security and Advance Payment Guarantee attached as Annexes C and E, respectively, of the Conditions, this Guarantee is in the form of a demand guarantee based on the URDG.[130]

This Sub-Clause provides for the release of Retention Money to the Contractor in stages. After the issue of the Taking-Over Certificate, the Contractor may include the first half of the Retention Money for release in a Statement and then, later, after the latest of the expiry dates of the DNPs, the Contractor may include the second half of the Retention Money for release in a Statement. This is the usual practice. But the Sub-Clause also provides for the possibility of relating the release to the completion of a Section (or Sections) rather than to the completion of the Works as a whole.

(iv) Related law: The amount and the terms of Retention Money may be regulated by mandatory local law. This is, for example, the case in France where retention money is limited to 5% of progress payments, and must normally be released upon completion.[131] The contractor is entitled to substitute a bank guarantee in lieu of having this money retained.[132]

--ooOOoo--

129. The World Bank's COPA provides that, when the Taking-Over Certificate has been issued for the Works and the first half of the Retention Money has been certified for payment, the Contractor is entitled to substitute a guarantee issued by a reputable bank or financial institution selected by the Contractor for the second half of the Retention Money. Moreover, if the Performance Security and, if applicable, an ES (Environmental and Social) Performance Security, which together are not normally (according to The World Bank) to exceed 10% of the Accepted Contract Amount, are in the form of demand guarantees and the amount guaranteed under them when the Taking-Over Certificate is issued is more than half of the Retention Money, then the Retention Money guarantee will not be required. Sub-Clauses 4.2 and 14.9, COPA.

130. For a discussion of demand guarantees based on the *Uniform Rules for Demand Guarantees* ('URDG'), *see* under **(iii) Analysis** of the commentary on Sub-Clause 4.2 [*Performance Security*] above.

131. French Law no 71-584 of 16 July 1971, as amended by Law no 96-609 of 5 July 1996, art. 1.

132. *Ibid.*

14.10 Statement at Completion

Within 84 days after the Date of Completion of the Works, the Contractor shall submit to the Engineer a Statement at completion with supporting documents, in accordance with Sub-Clause 14.3 [*Application for Interim Payment*], showing:

(a) the value of all work done in accordance with the Contract up to the Date of Completion of the Works;

(b) any further sums which the Contractor considers to be due at the Date of Completion of the Works; and

(c) an estimate of any other amounts which the Contractor considers have or will become due after the Date of Completion of the Works under the Contract or otherwise. These estimated amounts shall be shown separately (to those of sub-paragraphs (a) and (b) above) and shall include estimated amounts for:

  (i) Claims for which the Contractor has submitted a Notice under Sub-Clause 20.2 [*Claims for Payment and/or EOT*];

  (ii) any matter referred to the DAAB under Sub-Clause 21.4 [*Obtaining DAAB's Decision*]; and

  (iii) any matter for which a NOD has been given under Sub-Clause 21.4 [*Obtaining DAAB's Decision*].

The Engineer shall then issue an IPC in accordance with Sub-Clause 14.6 [*Issue of IPC*].

Within 84 days after the Date of Completion of the Works, the Contractor shall submit to the Engineer a Statement at completion with supporting documents, in accordance with Sub-Clause 14.3, showing the information listed in sub-paragraphs (a), (b) and (c). The Engineer shall then issue an IPC in accordance with Sub-Clause 14.6.

Commentary

(i) Main Changes from RB/99:

(1) The reference to '[w]ithin 84 days after receiving the Taking-Over Certificate of the Works' in the first line of Sub-Clause 14.10 of RB/99 has been changed to '[w]ithin 84 days after the Date of Completion of the Works' in the first line of the Sub-Clause in RB/17.

(2) Whereas sub-paragraph (c) in RB/99 had referred to an estimate of any other amounts which the Contractor considers 'will become due to him under the Contract', sub-paragraph (c) now refers to an estimate of amounts which the Contractor considers 'have or will become due after the Date of Completion of the Works under the Contract or otherwise'.

(3) Sub-paragraph (c) requires – which is new – that estimated amounts be broken down and shown separately for: (i) Claims for which the Contactor has submitted a Notice under Sub-Clause 20.2, (ii) any matter referred to the DAAB under Sub-Clause 21.4, and (iii) any matter for which a NOD has been given under Sub-Clause 21.4.

(ii) Related Clauses / Sub-Clauses: 1.3 [*Notices and Other Communications*], 14.3 [*Application for Interim Payment*], 14.6 [*Issue of IPC*], 14.11 [*Final Statement*], 14.14 [*Cessation of Employer's Liability*] 20.2 [*Claims for Payment and/or EOT*] and 21.4 [*Obtaining DAAB's Decision*].

(iii) Analysis:

(1) Scope of Sub-Clauses 14.10 through 14.14

Sub-Clauses 14.10 through 14.14 [*Cessation of Employer's Liability*] need to be read together. They deal, first, with the Statement at completion which the Contractor must submit to the Engineer after the Date of Completion of the Works. They then deal with the Final Statement or Partially Agreed Final Statement, together with a discharge, which the Contractor is required to submit to the Engineer much later in time – following the DNP(s) – and after issue of the Performance Certificate. They finally provide for the Engineer to issue an FPC or, where the Contractor has submitted (or is deemed to have submitted) a Partially Agreed Final Statement, an IPC, and the cessation of the Employer's liability to the Contractor, subject to some exceptions.

(2) The Statement at completion

Within 84 days or 12 weeks after the Date of Completion of the Works, which includes where they are deemed to have been completed or taken over,[133] the Contractor should normally be in a position to estimate the overall price for the Works. Accordingly, Sub-Clause 14.10 requires the Contractor by this time to submit a 'Statement at completion' with supporting documents which is required to be in the form of its Statement for interim payment under Sub-Clause 14.3. The Statement at completion must show:

(a) the value of all work done in accordance with the Contract up to the Date of Completion of the Works;
(b) any further sums which the Contractor considers to be due at the Date of Completion (which could include, e.g., the return of the first half of the Retention Money); and
(c) an estimate of any other amounts which the Contractor considers have or will become due to it 'under the Contract or otherwise'.[134]

The Contractor's estimate in sub-paragraph (c) must be broken down into three categories, each corresponding to a different stage in the Claims/Disputes process:

(i) Claims for which the Contractor has submitted a Notice under Sub-Clause 20.2 [*Claims for Payment and/or EOT*];
(ii) any matter referred to the DAAB under Sub-Clause 21.4 [*Obtaining DAAB's Decision*]; and
(iii) any matter for which a NOD has been given under Sub-Clause 21.4 [*Obtaining DAAB's Decision*].[135]

---

133. Pursuant to Sub-Clauses 10.1, 10.2 and 10.3, *see* Sub-Clause 1.1.24 '**Date of Completion**'.

134. '[o]r otherwise' refers to under the governing law. *Guide to the Use of FIDIC Conditions of Contract for Works of Civil Engineering Construction, Fourth Edition* (FIDIC 1989) 119 (commenting on Sub-Clause 53.1 [*Notice of Claim*] in RB/87).

135. It is not entirely clear whether, when Sub-Clause 14.10 refers to a 'matter' in items (ii) and (iii), it is using that word in its generic sense (according to the dictionary) or in the more limited sense of the matters listed in **Table 3, Matters to be Agreed or Determined by the Engineer**, in the commentary on Clause 1 above. It appears to be using the term in its generic sense.

No indication is given of how the estimates should be calculated. However, the Contractor would be well advised not to underestimate them as it is likely to be less contentious later to reduce, than to increase, them.

The Statement at completion represents the Contractor's final account or invoice as of roughly the Date of Completion, but before the Contractor has performed all of its obligations during the DNP. It is a sort of draft final account or draft Final Statement *as of the Date of Completion*, although the Contract does not use these terms or expressions.

(3) The Statement must include all Claims

Before submitting its Statement at completion, the Contractor will want to ensure that it has given at least a Notice of Claim, pursuant to Sub-Clause 20.2, for all Claims of which it was then aware.[136] Having done this, the Contractor should then list these Claims in its Statement at completion together with their amounts or estimated amounts, where possible. This is very important as Sub-Clause 14.14 [*Cessation of Employer's Liability*] expressly provides that *the Employer shall have no liability for any matter or thing arising until the issue of the Taking-Over Certificate for the Works 'except to the extent that [...] an amount expressly for it' was included in the Statement at completion under Sub-Clause 14.10*. It needs to be appreciated that the procedure in Sub-Clauses 14.11 through 14.14 is designed, beginning with the Statement at completion, to close progressively the accounts for the project, and ultimately to bar the Contractor from asserting previously undisclosed Claims, if any.[137]

(4) The Engineer's IPC

Having received the Statement at completion with supporting documents, the Engineer is required to issue an IPC within 28 days, in accordance with Sub-Clause 14.6.1, stating 'fairly'[138] what it considers to

136. And for which it has kept or is keeping contemporary records under Sub-Clause 20.2.3 and, where appropriate, submitted a fully detailed Claim pursuant to Sub-Clause 20.2.4.

137. *See* Sub-Clause 14.14 [*Cessation of Employer's Liability*]. On the other hand, there is no time bar in Sub-Clause 14.14 for matters or things which arise after the Taking-Over Certificate.

138. *See* for a discussion of 'fairly', which is also used in Sub-Clause 3.7 [*Agreement or Determination*], in item (2) under **(i) Main Changes from RB/99** of the commentary on that Sub-Clause above including the accompanying fns 95 and 96.

be due, thereby enabling the Contractor to be paid whatever the Engineer considers to be owing at the Date of Completion of the Works. As required by that Sub-Clause, the IPC should identify any difference between a certified amount and any corresponding amount in the Statement which the Contractor considers to be due, giving the reasons for such difference.

In this connection, *see* **Figure 10 Sequence of Final Payment Events**.

--ooOOoo--

Figure 10 Sequence of Final Payment Events[1]

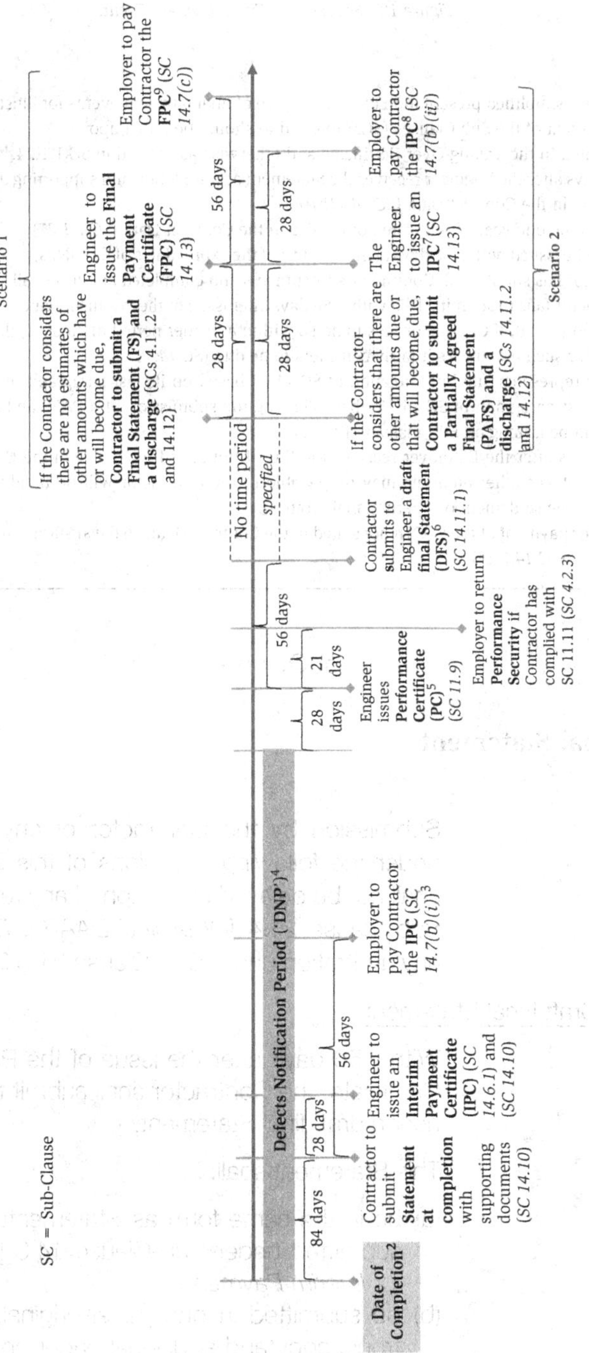

Source: Author's own work.

Figure 10 Sequence of Final Payment Events

Notes

1. This figure is a simplified presentation of the sequence of final payment events for illustrative purposes. Only the actual text of the Sub-Clauses (SCs) referred to should be relied upon.
2. The date stated in the Taking-Over Certificate and otherwise as defined in SC 1.1.24.
3. Within 56 days after the Engineer receives the Statement at completion and supporting documents, if not stated otherwise in the Contract Data (*SC 14.7(b)(i)*).
4. The DNP will be one year, if not stated otherwise in the Contract Data (*SC 1.1.27*).
5. The PC must be issued within 28 days after the latest of the expiry dates of the DNPs, or as soon thereafter as the Contractor has supplied all Contractor's Documents and completed and tested all Works (*SC 11.9*).
6. If the Contractor fails to submit a DFS within 56 days after issue of the PC, the Engineer shall request the Contractor to do so and, if Contractor fails to do so within a further period of 28 days, the Engineer shall issue the FPC for such amount as it fairly considers to be due (*SC 14.13*).
7. This merely represents one interpretation of SC 14.13 based on its last paragraph. It may be argued, based on the first paragraph of SC 14.13, that following the submission of a PAFS and a discharge, the Engineer should be issuing an FPC instead of an IPC.
8. Within 28 days after the Employer receives the IPC, if not stated otherwise in the Contract Data (*SC 14.7(b)(ii)*).Whatever other amounts may be payable to the Contractor will be finally decided by the DAAB, an amicable settlement or international arbitration.
9. The period for payment of the FPC (if not stated in the Contract Data, 56 days) starts when the Employer receives the FPC (*SC 14.7(c)*).

--ooOOoo--

14.11 Final Statement

Submission by the Contractor of any Statement under the following provisions of this Sub-Clause shall not be delayed by reason of any referral under Sub-Clause 21.4 [*Obtaining DAAB's Decision*] or any arbitration under Sub-Clause 21.6 [*Arbitration*].

14.11.1 Draft Final Statement

Within 56 days after the issue of the Performance Certificate, the Contractor shall submit to the Engineer a draft final Statement.

This Statement shall:

(a) be in the same form as Statements previously submitted under Sub-Clause 14.3 [*Application for Interim Payment*];
(b) be submitted in one paper-original, one electronic copy and additional paper copies (if any) as stated in the Contract Data; and
(c) show in detail, with supporting documents:

(i) the value of all work done in accordance with the Contract;
(ii) any further sums which the Contractor considers to be due at the date of the issue of the Performance Certificate, under the Contract or otherwise; and
(iii) an estimate of any other amounts which the Contractor considers have or will become due after the issue of the Performance Certificate, under the Contract or otherwise, including estimated amounts, by reference to the matters described in sub-paragraphs (c) (i) to (iii) of Sub-Clause 14.10 [*Statement at Completion*]. These estimated amounts shall be shown separately (to those of sub-paragraphs (i) and (ii) above).

Except for any amount under sub-paragraph (iii) above, if the Engineer disagrees with or cannot verify any part of the draft final Statement, the Engineer shall promptly give a Notice to the Contractor. The Contractor shall then submit such further information as the Engineer may reasonably require within the time stated in this Notice, and shall make such changes in the draft as may be agreed between them.

14.11.2 Agreed Final Statement

If there are no amounts under sub-paragraph (iii) of Sub-Clause 14.11.1 [*Draft Final Statement*], the Contractor shall then prepare and submit to the Engineer the final Statement as agreed (the "Final Statement" in these Conditions).

However if:

(a) there are amounts under sub-paragraph (iii) of Sub-Clause 14.11.1 [*Draft Final Statement*]; and/or
(b) following discussions between the Engineer and the Contractor, it becomes evident that they cannot agree any amount(s) in the draft final Statement,

the Contractor shall then prepare and submit to the Engineer a Statement, identifying separately: the agreed amounts, the estimated amounts and the disagreed amount(s) (the "Partially Agreed Final Statement" in these Conditions).

Within 56 days after the issue of the Performance Certificate, the Contractor shall submit to the Engineer a draft final Statement in a form and comprising the matters described in sub-paragraphs (a), (b) and (c) of Sub-Clause 14.11.1. If the Engineer disagrees with or cannot verify any part of the draft final Statement (other than amounts estimated in sub-paragraph (c) (iii)), the Engineer must give a Notice to the Contractor, who must submit such further information as the Engineer may require and make such changes in the draft as they may agree upon.

If there are no estimated amounts under sub-paragraph (c) (iii), the Contractor shall submit the final statement as agreed (the 'Final Statement'). However, if there are such estimated amounts or other amounts that the Engineer and the Contractor cannot agree upon, the Contractor shall submit a Statement identifying separately: the agreed, the estimated and the disagreed amounts, respectively (the 'Partially Agreed Final Statement').

Commentary

(i) Main Changes from RB/99:

(1) The heading or title of Sub-Clause 14.11 has been changed from 'Application for Final Payment Certificate' in RB/99 to 'Final Statement' in RB/17.
(2) The first paragraph regarding no delays on account of referrals under Sub-Clause 21.4 or 21.6 is new.
(3) The restructuring of the Sub-Clause under two headings, Sub-Clauses 14.11.1 Draft Final Statement and 14.11.2 Agreed Final Statement, is new.
(4) Sub-paragraphs (a), (b) and (c)(iii) of Sub-Clause 14.11.1 are almost entirely new.
(5) The further references to sub-paragraph (c)(iii) in Sub-Clauses 14.11.1 and 14.11.2 are new.
(6) The final paragraph of Sub-Clause 14.11.2 Agreed Final Statement is almost entirely new (replacing the final paragraph in

RB/99) and includes reference to an entirely new document, the Partially Agreed Final Statement.

(ii) Related Clauses / Sub-Clauses: 1.3 [*Notices and Other Communications*], 11.9 [*Performance Certificate*], 14.3 [*Application for Interim Payment*], 14.10 [*Statement at Completion*], 14.12 [*Discharge*], 14.13 [*Issue of FPC*], 14.14 [*Cessation of Employer's Liability*], 21.4 [*Obtaining DAAB's Decision*] and 21.6 [*Arbitration*].

(iii) Analysis:

(1) Issuance of Performance Certificate

Within 28 days after the expiry date of the DNP,[139] which will normally be one year (or more) in length after the Date of Completion,[140] and assuming the Contractor has satisfied its obligations during that period, the Engineer is required to issue the Performance Certificate to the Contractor, with a copy to the Employer and the DAAB.[141]

The Performance Certificate is the Engineer's written statement that the Contractor has performed its obligations under the Contract.[142] Furthermore, '[o]nly the Performance Certificate shall be deemed to constitute acceptance of the Works'.[143]

(2) Draft final Statement

As the Works are now deemed to have been accepted, the Contractor is entitled to submit a draft of its final account or invoice (called 'draft final Statement'), to the Engineer, which it must do within 56 days after the issue of the Performance Certificate.[144]

The draft final Statement is required to be in the same form as Statements submitted under Sub-Clause 14.3, and show 'in detail, with supporting

139. If there are multiple DNPs, then the latest expiry date of such periods.
140. Sub-Clause 1.1.27 '**Defects Notification Period**' or '**DNP**'.
141. Sub-Clause 11.9.
142. Sub-Clause 11.9 provides that 'the Contractor's obligations under the Contract shall not be considered to have been completed until the Engineer has issued the Performance Certificate to the Contractor [...]'.
143. Sub-Clause 11.9, last paragraph.
144. Sub-Clause 14.11.1. If the Contractor fails to comply with this time limit, the Engineer may ultimately issue the FPC for such amount as it fairly considers to be due. Sub-Clause 14.13, second paragraph.

documents', the same information as is contained in the Statement at completion pursuant to Sub-Clause 14.10, except that it should be updated through until at least the date of the issue of the Performance Certificate. The submission of the final Statement in the form of a draft enables the Engineer and the Contractor to discuss and, if possible, agree on what will be in the Final Statement.

The Engineer is required promptly to give a Notice to the Contractor if it disagrees with or cannot verify any part of the draft final Statement, other than the Contractor's estimates of:

> any other amounts which the Contractor considers have [since the Performance Certificate] or will become due after the issue of the Performance Certificate [...].[145]

The Contractor must then submit such further information as the Engineer may reasonably require, and make such changes in the draft as the Contractor and the Engineer may agree upon.

The emphasis in this Sub-Clause is on trying to get the Contractor and the Engineer to agree, if possible, about all amounts which the Contractor considers are due and to limit the risk of costly and time-consuming Disputes.

(3) Final Statement and Partially Agreed Final Statement

If the draft final Statement contains no estimates of other amounts which the Contractor considers have or will become due after the issue of the Performance Certificate, the Contractor is required to prepare and submit to the Engineer a final statement as agreed, called a 'Final Statement' ('FS'), together with a discharge.[146] The FS represents, in effect, the Contractor's final account or invoice as provisionally agreed by the Engineer.

However, if the draft final Statement contains estimates of amounts which the Contractor considers have or will become due, and/or there are other amounts which the Engineer and the Contractor cannot agree upon, the Contractor is required to prepare and submit to the Engineer a Statement identifying separately:

145. Sub-Clause 14.11.1(c)(iii).
146. As provided for in Sub-Clause 14.12 [*Discharge*].

(a) the agreed amounts;
(b) the estimated amounts; and
(c) the disagreed amounts.[147]

This Statement is called a 'Partially Agreed Final Statement' ('PAFS') and is also to be accompanied by a discharge.[148] The PAFS contains not only amounts agreed upon by the Engineer but also other amounts with which the Engineer has not agreed. Amounts that are not agreed upon with the Engineer may, subject to Sub-Clause 20.2, ultimately have to be referred for settlement to the DAAB (assuming this has not already occurred) and, if necessary, to arbitration.[149]

The content of the FS and PAFS is extremely important as the Employer may not be liable except to the extent that the Contractor has included 'an amount expressly' in them.[150]

(4) Separate Disputes procedures

The first paragraph of the Sub-Clause emphasises that, as stated elsewhere,[151] referrals to the DAAB or to arbitration do not excuse the Contractor from having to perform the Contract, including submitting Statements under Sub-Clause 14.11.

--ooOOoo--

14.12 Discharge

When submitting the Final Statement or the Partially Agreed Final Statement (as the case may be), the Contractor shall submit a discharge which confirms that the total of such Statement represents full and final settlement of all moneys due to the Contractor under or in connection with the Contract. This discharge may state that the total of the Statement is subject to any payment that may become due in respect of any Dispute for which a DAAB proceeding or arbitration is in progress under Clause 21 [*Dis-*

147. Sub-Clause 14.11.2, last paragraph.
148. As provided for in Sub-Clause 14.12 [*Discharge*].
149. Arbitration might also already have begun. *See* the commentary on Clause 21 [*Disputes and Arbitration*] below.
150. Sub-Clause 14.14(a) [*Cessation of Employer's Liability*].
151. Sub-Clauses 21.4.2, second paragraph, and 21.6, penultimate paragraph.

putes and Arbitration] and/or that it becomes effective after the Contractor has received:

(a) full payment of the amount certified in the FPC; and

(b) the Performance Security.

If the Contractor fails to submit this discharge, the discharge shall be deemed to have been submitted and to have become effective when the conditions of sub-paragraphs (a) and (b) have been fulfilled.

A discharge under this Sub-Clause shall not affect either Party's liability or entitlement in respect of any Dispute for which a DAAB proceeding or arbitration is in progress under Clause 21 [*Disputes and Arbitration*].

When submitting the Final Statement or Partially Agreed Final Statement, the Contractor shall submit a discharge confirming that the total amount of such Statement represents full and final settlement of all moneys due to the Contractor. This discharge may state that the total of the Statement is subject to any payment that may be due in respect of a DAAB proceeding or arbitration in progress and/or that it becomes effective after the Contractor's receipt of (a) full payment of the amount certified in the FPC, and (b) the Performance Security.

A discharge shall not affect either Party's liability or entitlement in respect of any DAAB proceeding or arbitration in progress under Clause 21.

Commentary

(i) Main Changes from RB/99: RB/99 had not provided for a Partially Agreed Final Statement ('PAFS') and, although it had provided in Sub-Clause 14.12 for a discharge, it had not provided for one that could be qualified as envisaged by Sub-Clause 14.12 of RB/17. Instead, RB/99 had stated that, in a case where a dispute existed as to any amounts in a draft final statement, the Engineer should deliver an IPC for the agreed parts in that draft[152] and that thereafter, if the dispute was finally resolved pursuant to the disputes procedures in the Conditions, the

152. Sub-Clause 14.11 [*Application for Final Payment Certificate*], last paragraph, of RB/99.

Contractor would submit a Final Statement ('FS').[153] The FS would be accompanied by a written discharge confirming that the total of the FS represents full and final settlement of all moneys due to the Contractor, and might state that, once it was paid and the Performance Security returned, the discharge would become effective.[154]

A shortcoming of this procedure was that, as international construction arbitrations typically take years to conclude, it could take several years or more before an FS could be submitted and the Contractor's discharge could become effective. In the interim, although the Employer might have paid the Contractor all undisputed amounts, there would have been no reduction in the Employer's potential liability to the Contractor.

The new procedure under RB/17 seeks to address this issue by providing that, when submitting an FS or PAFS, the Contractor must submit a discharge which, among other things, 'may state' that the total amount due to the Contractor is subject to the outcome of a DAAB proceeding or arbitration under Clause 21 and/or that it becomes effective after the Contractor has received full payment of the amount certified in the FPC and return of the Performance Security.[155] The Sub-Clause also provides for the case of where the Contractor has failed to submit a discharge by providing for the existence of a possible deemed discharge in that situation.

(ii) Related Clauses / Sub-Clauses: 1.3 [*Notices and Other Communications*], 11.9 [*Performance Security*], 14.11 [*Final Statement*], 14.13 [*Issue of FPC*], 14.14 [*Cessation of Employer's Liability*] and 21 [*Disputes and Arbitration*].

(iii) Analysis:

(1) Problems with Sub-Clause 14.12

This Sub-Clause presents issues which need to be cleared up in the Particular Conditions:

153. *Ibid.*
154. Sub-Clauses 14.11 and 14.12 [*Discharge*] of RB/99. *The FIDIC Contracts Guide* (2nd edn, FIDIC, 2022) 422 contains a sample form of discharge, which may be in the form of a letter.
155. As provided in Sub-Clause 21.1, ninth paragraph, unless the Parties agree otherwise, on the date the discharge becomes, or is deemed to have become, effective the term of the DAAB expires, if it has not expired earlier.

(a) The first sentence of Sub-Clause 14.12 states that, when submitting the FS or the PAFS, as the case may be, the Contractor shall submit a discharge which confirms that 'the total of such Statement' represents full and final settlement of all moneys due to the Contractor. This is clear enough as regards the FS as, by definition,[156] the FS contains no estimated amounts, that is, the amounts provided for by Sub-Clause 14.11.1(c)(iii). Thus, the Contractor can confirm that the total of the FS represents full and final settlement of all monies due. But how can this be true of a PAFS, which by definition[157] contains estimated amounts and/or amounts upon which the Engineer and the Contractor cannot agree? The Contractor cannot confirm that the total of a PAFS represents full and final settlement of all moneys due to it, as it includes estimates and/or disagreed amounts.

A practical solution would be for the Contractor to submit a discharge which confirms that the amounts agreed with the Engineer represent full and final settlement of all that may be due to the Contractor *except in respect of a list of items (or Claims) for which the Contractor has given estimates and/or the amounts of which are disagreed*. Such a discharge would provide the Employer with protection against further Claims by the Contractor except in respect of the listed items (or Claims). The Employer's further exposure would then be limited strictly to the items (or Claims) on that list.

(b) A similar difficulty arises in connection with the second sentence of Sub-Clause 14.12. The first part of the second sentence provides that the discharge 'may state' that 'the total of the Statement' is subject to any payment that may become due in respect of any Dispute under Clause 21 and/or that it becomes effective after certain specified events. While this 'may state' clause may be appropriate for the estimated and/or disagreed amounts, the amounts agreed with the Engineer should be unqualified and be accepted by both Parties as final. Thus, the 'may state' clause should be made to qualify the estimated and/or disagreed amounts only, and not (as it does now) the amounts so agreed.

(c) The second paragraph of Sub-Clause 14.12 provides that if the Contractor fails to submit the discharge, it shall be deemed to

156. *See* Sub-Clause 14.11.2, first paragraph.
157. Sub-Clause 14.11.2, second paragraph.

have been submitted and to become effective when the conditions of sub-paragraphs (a) and (b) of that sub-clause have been fulfilled. However, the condition in sub-paragraph (a), requiring full payment of the amount certified in the FPC, cannot be fulfilled without the Contractor having submitted an FS or PAFS 'and the discharge', as required by the first sentence of Sub-Clause 14.13.[158] Consequently, the discharge cannot be deemed to have been submitted and to have become effective pursuant to the second paragraph of Sub-Clause 14.12 as, pursuant to Sub-Clause 14.13, it would require an already-existing discharge to have been submitted to the Engineer under that Sub-Clause.[159]

(2) The Contractor should be required to describe its 'Reserved Claims' (estimated and/or disagreed amounts) in detail in any discharge

As provided in Sub-Clause 14.11.2, if there are amounts under sub-paragraph (c) (iii) of Sub-Clause 14.11.1 and/or other amounts the Engineer and the Contractor cannot agree upon, the Contractor must submit a PAFS identifying separately: the agreed amounts, the estimated amounts and the disagreed amounts (the estimated amounts and disagreed amounts are herein referred to for convenience as 'Reserved Claim(s)'). *However, neither Sub-Clause 14.11, nor 14.12 relating to the Contractor's discharge which is to be submitted together with a PAFS, deals with the important question of how a Reserved Claim(s) is (are) to be detailed or described. Yet, if the Contractor is left free to describe in the PAFS its Reserved Claims in a generalised way – as it will ordinarily have every incentive to do so as to 'keep the door open'– this would enable it to present further Claims under the guise of such generalised descriptions, undermining the purpose of Sub-Clauses 14.11 and 14.12 to finalise the accounts under the Contract.*

For a Reserved Claim to be included in a PAFS, pursuant to Sub-Clause 14.11.2, and to be excluded from the discharge to be provided by the Contractor, pursuant to Sub-Clause 14.12, the Contractor should be required by the Particular Conditions to describe, at a minimum, the

158. The second paragraph of Sub-Clause 14.13 providing for issue of an FPC is inapplicable as it would only apply '[i]f the Contractor has not submitted a draft final Statement', which would not be the case under Sub-Clause 14.12.

159. This problem and others with the Sub-Clause have been well highlighted by Leo Grutters & Brian Barr, *FIDIC Red, Yellow and Silver Books: A Practical Guide to the 2017 Editions* (Sweet & Maxwell, London, 2018) 234-236.

substance of the Reserved Claim (i.e., the relevant facts, at least in summary form, and the contractual or other legal basis of the Reserved Claim) and to state its amount or, if the amount is not yet ascertainable, an estimate of the amount.[160] Generalised statements referring to a claim for 'overhead', 'breach of contract' or 'Delay Damages', or of an intention to file a further Reserved Claim or Claims, should be unacceptable. Instead, the Contractor should be required to state the substance of its contention,[161] as well as its amount or estimated amount, as otherwise the Employer will be unable to assess its potential liability and, instead, be exposed to potentially unlimited liability.[162]

(3) When the discharge should become effective

When the discharge is submitted together with a PAFS, the discharge should provide that it becomes effective after the Contractor has received:

(a) full payment of the amount certified in the FPC, other than the Reserved Claim(s); and
(b) the Performance Security.

Pursuant to Sub-Clause 14.13, first paragraph, the Engineer is required to issue the FPC within 28 days after receiving the FS or the PAFS, as the case may be, and the Contractor's discharge under Sub-Clause 14.12. Assuming that the Contractor is paid the full amount certified in the FPC (other than the Reserved Claim(s)) and receives the Performance Security, the Contractor's discharge should then become effective. The dis-

160. In short, the Contractor should be required, to the extent possible, to provide – but in summary form and without contemporary records or detailed supporting particulars – the main elements of a fully detailed Claim, as defined in Sub-Clause 20.2.4.
161. For example, 'delayed access to the entire Site from 1 to 15 June 2021'.
162. Sub-Clause 21.6 provides for the final resolution of Disputes pursuant to the ICC Arbitration Rules. To initiate arbitration under those Rules, a Request for Arbitration must be filed with the ICC which must contain essentially the same details about a Party's Claims. Art. 4.3 of the Rules requires that the Request contains, among other things, the following:

> (c) a description of the nature and circumstances of the dispute giving rise to the claims and of the basis upon which the claims are made;
> (d) a statement of the relief sought, together with the amounts of any quantified claims and, to the extent possible, an estimate of the monetary value of any other claims.

charge should become effective by this point – that is, possibly some 140 to 168 days[163] or about five months after the DNP – as by then the Employer should be entitled to know that it is protected against Claims of the Contractor other than defined Reserved Claim(s).

Once the FPC, excluding the Reserved Claim(s), has been paid and the Performance Security returned to the Contractor, the discharge would have become effective pro tanto, or to that extent. The Reserved Claim(s) should then be left to be finally settled, subject to Sub-Clause 20.2, by the DAAB or an amicable settlement or by way of an international arbitration award.[164] The Employer would then know that it would have no further liability to the Contractor except possibly for the Reserved Claims.

(iv) Related law: 'Discharge' is a legal term which refers to a document releasing a debtor – the Employer here – from liability, meaning here further liability under or in connection with the Contract.[165] It should be drafted with care and be prepared or reviewed by a qualified lawyer.

(v) Improvements: This Sub-Clause should be amended to address the three problems (1)(a), (b) and (c) raised under **(iii) Analysis** above. Among other things, any discharge accompanying a PAFS should be required to set forth the Reserved Claims with specificity. In particular, there should be stated for each Reserved Claim the relevant facts, at least in summary form, and the contractual or other legal basis of the Claim

163. The Engineer is required to issue the Performance Certificate within 28 days after the latest DNP (Sub-Clause 11.9). The Contractor is required to submit a draft FS to the Engineer within 56 days after the issue of the Performance Certificate (Sub-Clause 14.11.1). There is no timescale for when an FS or PAFS has to be submitted (Sub-Clause 14.11.2). However, the Engineer is required to certify the FS or PAFS and issue the FPC or IPC within 28 days after receiving the FS or PAFS and the discharge (Sub-Clause 14.13) and the Employer is required to pay within 56 days (FPC) or 28 days (IPC), if not stated otherwise (Sub-Clause 14.7). 28 days + 56 days + 28 days + 28 days or 56 days = 140 to 168 days. *See* **Figure 10 Sequence of Final Payment Events** following the commentary on Sub-Clause 14.10 [*Statement at Completion*] above.
164. No further action under the Contract for their payment should be required.
165. Discharge is defined in a law dictionary as: '[a]ny method by which a legal duty is extinguished; esp., the payment of a debt or satisfaction of some other obligation'. Bryan A Garner (ed in chief), *Black's Law Dictionary* (11th edn, Thomson Reuters, St Paul, MN, 2019).

together with its amount or an estimate of its amount.[166] If this is not done with precision, the Employer may continue to be exposed to new Claims from the Contractor.

--ooOOoo--

14.13 Issue of FPC

Within 28 days after receiving the Final Statement or the Partially Agreed Final Statement (as the case may be), and the discharge under Sub-Clause 14.12 [*Discharge*], the Engineer shall issue to the Employer (with a copy to the Contractor), the Final Payment Certificate which shall state:

(a) the amount which the Engineer fairly considers is finally due, including any additions and/or deductions which have become due under Sub-Clause 3.7 [*Agreement or Determination*] or under the Contract or otherwise; and

(b) after giving credit to the Employer for all amounts previously paid by the Employer and for all sums to which the Employer is entitled, and after giving credit to the Contractor for all amounts (if any) previously paid by the Contractor and/or received by the Employer under the Performance Security, the balance (if any) due from the Employer to the Contractor or from the Contractor to the Employer, as the case may be.

If the Contractor has not submitted a draft final Statement within the time specified under Sub-Clause 14.11.1 [*Draft Final Statement*], the Engineer shall request the Contractor to do so. Thereafter, if the Contractor fails to submit a draft final Statement within a period of 28 days, the Engineer

166. Under US government contract practice, a discharge or release 'must, at a minimum describe the substance of the claim and the amount demanded'. John Cibinic and others, *Administration of Government Contracts* (4th edn, CCH Incorporated, Chicago, IL, 2006) 1205, which cites to a number of US cases. *See also* the United States *Federal Acquisition Regulation* ('*FAR*'), s 52.232-5, Payments under Fixed-Price Construction Contracts, *(h) Final payment*.

shall issue the FPC for such an amount as the Engineer fairly considers to be due.

If the Contractor has not submitted a discharge under Sub-Clause 14.12 [*Discharge*] but has either:

(i) submitted a Partially Agreed Final Statement under Sub-Clause 14.11.2 [*Agreed Final Statement*]; or
(ii) not done so but, to the extent that a draft final Statement submitted by the Contractor is deemed by the Engineer to be a Partially Agreed Final Statement,

the Engineer shall proceed in accordance with Sub-Clause 14.6 [*Issue of IPC*] to issue an IPC.

Within 28 days after receiving the Final Statement ('FS') or Partially Agreed Final Statement ('PAFS'), and the discharge, the Engineer shall issue to the Employer, with a copy to the Contractor, the FPC stating the amount which the Engineer fairly considers is due to the Contractor. If the Contractor has failed to submit a draft final Statement, the Engineer shall request the Contractor to do so. If it fails to do so within 28 days, the Engineer shall issue the FPC for such amount as the Engineer fairly considers to be due. If the Contractor has not submitted a discharge but has submitted, or is deemed to have submitted, a PAFS, the Engineer shall proceed under Sub-Clause 14.6 to issue an IPC.

Commentary

(i) Main Changes from RB/99:

(1) Unlike Sub-Clause 14.13 of RB/99 which only referred to an FS and written discharge, the first paragraph of the new Sub-Clause refers to a PAFS, a new document in RB/17, as well as to the FS and discharge.
(2) Unlike RB/99, sub-paragraph (a) refers to what is 'fairly' due (not 'finally' due as under RB/99) and to the inclusion of any additions and/or deductions which have become due under Sub-Clause 3.7 or under the Contract or otherwise.

(3) Unlike RB/99, sub-paragraph (b) provides for the giving of credit to the Contractor for all amounts (if any) it has previously paid and/or amounts the Employer has received under the Performance Security.

(4) The last paragraph of this Sub-Clause is entirely new.

(ii) Related Clauses / Sub-Clauses: 1.3 [*Notices and Other Communications*], 3.7 [*Agreement or Determination*], 4.2.2 [*Performance Security – Claims under the Performance Security*], 14.6 [*Issue of IPC*], 14.11 [*Final Statement*] and 14.12 [*Discharge*].

(iii) Analysis:

(1) Issuance of FPC

The first paragraph provides that within 28 days after receiving the FS or the PAFS of the Contractor, and the related discharge,[167] the Engineer shall issue to the Employer, with a copy to the Contractor, the FPC, which shall state the amount which the Engineer fairly considers is finally due after taking account of all entitlements, whether of the Contractor or the Employer, under the Contract or otherwise.

(2) Consequences of Contractor's failure to submit a draft FS

The second paragraph provides that, if the Contractor has not submitted a draft FS within the time specified under Sub-Clause 14.11.1, the Engineer shall request the Contractor to do so. If the Contractor then does so, the procedures in Sub-Clauses 14.11 through 14.13 should presumably be complied with. If the Contractor fails to do so within 28 days, the Engineer is required to issue the FPC for such amount as the Engineer fairly considers to be due based, presumably, on the Statement at completion (assuming this has been submitted) and such other information as may be available to it. While, in this case, the Contractor will likely not have submitted a discharge, nevertheless, when the Contractor has received both full payment of the amount certified in the FPC and the Performance Security, a discharge (as described in Sub-Clause 14.12) is deemed then to have been submitted and to have become effective.[168]

---

167. *See* the problems with that document discussed under **(iii) Analysis** in the commentary on Sub-Clause 14.12 above.
168. Pursuant to the second paragraph of Sub-Clause 14.12.

An obvious difficulty here is that, as the Contractor will not have submitted a draft FS, there may be estimated amounts[169] and/or other amounts which the Engineer and the Contractor are not agreed upon. Moreover, the Contractor will likely have provided no discharge (other than a deemed discharge of uncertain scope). Consequently, while the Engineer may have issued, and the Employer paid, an FPC, the final accounting under the Contract will remain unsettled.[170]

In this scenario, occurring after the expiration of the DNP, there would seem little point in requiring the Contractor to proceed under Sub-Clauses 20.2 and 3.7, especially as the Engineer may no longer be in office.[171] As the term of the DAAB would have expired on the date the discharge would be deemed to have become effective,[172] the Contractor should be able to refer a Claim directly to arbitration, pursuant to Sub-Clause 21.8.

(3) Engineer's power to issue an IPC

The third paragraph assumes that the Contractor has not submitted a discharge but has submitted, or is deemed by the Engineer to have submitted, a PAFS.[173] In this case, the Engineer will issue an IPC for such amount as the Engineer considers to be due, and not an FPC.[174] As the Engineer will only issue an IPC, the provision in Sub-Clause 14.12 for a

169. As described in Sub-Clause 14.11.1(c)(iii).
170. Accordingly, it will remain to be settled by way of a decision of the DAAB, an amicable settlement or international arbitration.
171. The FIDIC White Book foresees that it would end when the engineering consultant has completed the Services (as defined in Appendix 1). Sub-Clause 4.2.1 of the White Book. RB/17 does not specify what services, if any, that the Engineer is to perform after issue of the Performance Certificate.
172. Sub-Clause 21.1 [*Constitution of the DAAB*], ninth paragraph.
173. This may arise because the Engineer may find that it cannot agree with some amounts in a draft FS which the Contractor has submitted pursuant to Sub-Clause 14.11.1.
174. It has been suggested that it is impossible for the Engineer to issue an IPC at this time because this would be contrary to Sub-Clause 14.6(a) (providing that no amount be certified until the Employer has received the Performance Security) as the 'Employer no longer holds the Performance Security'. Leo Grutters and Brian Barr, *FIDIC, Red, Yellow and Silver Books: A Practical Guide to the 2017 Editions* (Sweet & Maxwell, London, 2018) 238. However, this should not be an obstacle. Sub-Clause 14.6(a) only requires that 'the Employer has received the Performance Security', which

deemed discharge cannot apply (as a condition for it to apply is the full payment of an FPC, not an IPC). Consequently, the final accounting under the Contract, again, remains unsettled.[175]

In this scenario, occurring after the expiration of the DNP, there would seem little point in requiring the Contractor to refer the matter back to the Engineer under Sub-Clauses 20.2 and 3.7, especially because (as previously mentioned) the Engineer may no longer be in office. Instead, the Contractor should be able to refer any Claim, as a Dispute, directly to the DAAB for a decision (which, as there would have been no discharge, should still be in office)[176] and any payment ordered by the DAAB would be made outside the provisions of Clause 14.[177]

--ooOOoo--

14.14 Cessation of Employer's Liability

> The Employer shall not be liable to the Contractor for any matter or thing under or in connection with the Contract or execution of the Works, except to the extent that the Contractor shall have included an amount expressly for it in:
>
> (a) the Final Statement or Partially Agreed Final Statement; and
>
> (b) (except for matters or things arising after the issue of the Taking-Over Certificate for the Works) the Statement under Sub-Clause 14.10 [*Statement at Completion*].
>
> Unless the Contractor makes or has made a Claim under Sub-Clause 20.2 [*Claims for Payment and/or EOT*] in respect of an amount or amounts under the

will have been the case, not that the Employer holds the Performance Security at the time that an IPC is issued.

175. It will remain to be settled by way of a decision of the DAAB, an amicable settlement or international arbitration.

176. As recommended by Leo Grutters and Brian Barr, *FIDIC, Red, Yellow and Silver Books: A Practical Guide to the 2017 Editions* (Sweet & Maxwell, London, 2018) 238.

177. As provided for by item (i) of Sub-Clause 21.4.3 (the amount of a DAAB decision 'shall be immediately due and payable without any certification or Notice').

FPC within 56 days of receiving a copy of the FPC the Contractor shall be deemed to have accepted the amounts so certified. The Employer shall then have no further liability to the Contractor, other than to pay the amount due under the FPC and return the Performance Security to the Contractor.

However, this Sub-Clause shall not limit the Employer's liability under the Employer's indemnification obligations, or the Employer's liability in any case of fraud, gross negligence, deliberate default or reckless misconduct by the Employer.

The Employer shall not be liable to the Contractor for any matter or thing under or in connection with the Contract except to the extent that the Contractor has included an amount for it in the Final Statement ('FS') or Partially Agreed Final Statement ('PAFS') and (except for matters arising after the Taking-Over Certificate), the Statement at completion under Sub-Clause 14.10. Unless the Contractor makes a Claim under Sub-Clause 20.2 in respect of amount(s) under the FPC within 56 days of receiving it, the Contractor shall be deemed to have accepted the FPC.

Commentary

(i) Main Changes from RB/99:

(1) Compared to Sub-Clause 14.14(a) of RB/99, the reference to a PAFS in sub-paragraph (a) is new.
(2) Compared to RB/99, the entire second paragraph is new.
(3) The reference in the third paragraph to 'gross negligence' is new.

(ii) Related Clauses / Sub-Clauses: 1.3 [*Notices and Other Communications*], 1.15 [*Limitation of Liability*], 11.10 [*Unfulfilled Obligations*], 14.10 [*Statement at Completion*], 14.11 [*Final Statements*], 14.12 [*Discharge*], 14.13 [*Issue of FPC*], 17 [*Care of the Works and Indemnities*], 20.2 [*Claims for Payment and/or EOT*].

(iii) Analysis: As its title indicates, the purpose of this Sub-Clause is to limit as much as possible the liability of the Employer after it has paid an FPC. This Sub-Clause limits the potential liability of the Employer to the Contractor mainly to:

(1) an amount expressly stated in the FS or PAFS;
(2) except for matters or things that arose *after* the issue of the Taking-Over Certificate for the Works, an amount expressly included in the Statement at completion under Sub-Clause 14.10; and
(3) an amount or amounts under the FPC in respect of which the Contractor makes a Claim under Sub-Clause 20.2 'within'[178] 56 days of receiving a copy of the FPC.[179]

Pursuant to this Sub-Clause, and except as above, after paying the amount due under the FPC and returning the Performance Security to the Contractor,[180] the Employer has no further liability to the Contractor other than (1) the Employer's continuing liability under its indemnification obligations[181] and (2), as in the case of other provisions of the Conditions limiting a Party's liability,[182] fraud and other serious misconduct as described in the last paragraph of this Sub-Clause. Accordingly, *if the Contractor makes any other Claim it will, in principle, be time barred from doing so under this Sub-Clause.*

However, this Sub-Clause does not necessarily exclude the Employer's liability for matters of which the Contractor was not aware, or at least

178. *See* item (2) under **(v) Improvements** of the commentary on Sub-Clause 1.2 [*Interpretation*] above.
179. This would typically be the case where the Contractor does not agree with an amount in the FPC.
180. Sub-Clause 4.2.3 [*Performance Security – Return of the Performance Security*] envisages that the Employer would ordinarily return the Performance Security to the Contractor 'within 21 days after issue of the Performance Certificate and the Contractor has complied with Sub-Clause 11.11 [*Clearance of Site*]'.
181. Sub-Clause 14.14, third paragraph. The Employer has or may have indemnification obligations under Sub-Clauses 1.13, 4.2.2, 5.2.2, 17.3, 17.5, 17.6, 19.1 of the Conditions and Sub-Clause 8 of the General Conditions of DAAB Agreement.
182. Such as Sub-Clauses 1.15 [*Limitation of Liability*] and 8.8 [*Delay Damages*]. *See* under **(iii) Analysis** of the above commentary on Sub-Clause 1.15 for a discussion of the meaning of fraud, gross negligence, deliberate default and reckless misconduct.

could not have been aware, at the relevant time. No clear words purport to exclude the Employer's liability for a Contractor's Claim in this case.[183]

(iv) Related law: While this Sub-Clause provides, subject to certain exceptions, for the cessation of the Employer's liability under or in connection with the Contract or execution of the Works, each Party will otherwise remain liable to the other at law (e.g., the Employer will remain liable for matters not excluded by this Sub-Clause) until expiration of the applicable limitation period.[184]

--ooOOoo--

14.15 Currencies of Payment

The Contract Price shall be paid in the currency or currencies named in the Contract Data. If more than one currency is so named, payments shall be made as follows:

(a) if the Accepted Contract Amount was expressed in Local Currency only or in Foreign Currency only:

(i) the proportions or amounts of the Local and Foreign Currencies, and the fixed rates of exchange to be used for calculating the payments, shall be as stated in the Contract Data, except as otherwise agreed by both Parties;

(ii) payments and deductions under Sub-Clause 13.4 [*Provisional Sums*] and Sub-Clause 13.6 [*Adjustments for Changes in Laws*] shall be made in the applicable currencies and proportions; and

(iii) other payments and deductions under sub-paragraphs (i) to (iv) of Sub-Clause 14.3 [*Application for Interim Payment*] shall be made

183. As has been noted by Jeremy Glover & Simon Hughes, *Understanding the FIDIC Red and Yellow Books* (3rd edn, Sweet & Maxwell, London, 2018) 411.

184. For further discussion of limitation periods *see* under **(iii) Analysis** of the commentary on Sub-Clause 11.10 [*Unfulfilled Obligations*] and **Section 4 Common Law and Civil Law Compared – 4.5.3 Limitation Periods** in **Chapter II Applicable Law** above.

in the currencies and proportions specified in sub-paragraph (a)(i) above;

(b) whenever an adjustment is agreed or determined under Sub-Clause 13.2 [*Value Engineering*] or Sub-Clause 13.3 [*Variation Procedure*], the amount payable in each of the applicable currencies shall be specified. For this purpose, reference shall be made to the actual or expected currency proportions of the Cost of the varied work, and to the proportions of various currencies specified in sub-paragraph (a)(i) above;

(c) payment of Delay Damages shall be made in the currencies and proportions specified in the Contract Data;

(d) other payments to the Employer by the Contractor shall be made in the currency in which the sum was expended by the Employer, or in such currency as may be agreed by both Parties;

(e) if any amount payable by the Contractor to the Employer in a particular currency exceeds the sum payable by the Employer to the Contractor in that currency, the Employer may recover the balance of this amount from the sums otherwise payable to the Contractor in other currencies; and

(f) if no rates of exchange are stated in the Contract Data, they shall be those prevailing on the Base Date and published by the central bank of the Country.

The Contract Price shall be paid in the currency or currencies named in the Contract Data. If more than one currency is so named, payments shall be made as described in sub-paragraphs (a) through (f). In particular, if the Accepted Contract Amount was expressed in Local Currency only or in Foreign Currency only sub-paragraphs (a) (i), (ii) and (iii) apply.

Commentary

(i) Main Changes from RB/99:

(1) Sub-paragraph (a) now refers to where the Accepted Contract Amount was expressed in Local Currency only or in Foreign Currency only, whereas in Sub-Clause 14.15 of RB/99 it referred to where it was expressed in Local Currency only.
(2) Sub-paragraph (b), dealing with the currency(ies) in which Variations (including for value engineering) are payable, is entirely new.
(3) Sub-paragraph (c), dealing with payment of Delay Damages, replaces former sub-paragraph (b), dealing with 'payment of the damages specified in the Appendix to Tender' (which was 'delay damages' in RB/99).

(ii) Related Clauses / Sub-Clauses: 2.6 [*Employer-Supplied Materials and Employer's Equipment*] 4.2 [*Performance Security*], 4.19 [*Temporary Utilities*], 8.8 [*Delay Damages*], 13.2 [*Value Engineering*], 13.3 [*Variation Procedure*], 13.4 [*Provisional Sums*], 13.6 [*Adjustments for Changes in Laws*], 13.7 [*Adjustments for Changes in Cost*], 14.2 [*Advance Payment*], 14.3 [*Application for Interim Payment*], 14.5 [*Plant and Materials Intended for the Works*], 14.7 [*Payment*] and 14.8 [*Delayed Payment*].

(iii) Analysis: Where the Contract Price is to be paid – according to the Contract Data – in more than one currency, this Sub-Clause provides for how payments are to be made. If the Contract Price is to be paid in a single currency, the Sub-Clause does not apply.[185]

(1) Accepted Contract Amount and currencies of payment

At the tender stage, the instructions to tenderers will normally contain information concerning the currency or currencies to be used in the preparation of tenders and the currency or currencies in which payments

185. The *Guidance for the Preparation of Particular Conditions*, 42, contains an example Sub-Clause for the case where all payments are to be made in Local Currency. The example Sub-Clause would replace the present Sub-Clause.

under any future contract will be made. In the interests of receiving consistent tenders, they will also often define the exchange rates to be used.[186]

When entering into the Contract, the situation which is perhaps most common is for the Employer to require that the Accepted Contract Amount be expressed in Local Currency (the currency of the Country) only[187] but for payments to be made partly in Foreign Currency, often the currency of the Contractor's country (or United States dollars), and partly in Local Currency. The proportion of Local Currency to be paid will normally be calculated so as to cover the Contractor's estimated expenses to be incurred in Local Currency in the Country.[188]

Sub-Clause 14.15 provides that, where the Accepted Contract Amount is expressed in Local Currency (or Foreign Currency) only, 'the proportions or amounts of the Local and Foreign Currencies, and the fixed rates of exchange to be used for calculating the payments, shall be as stated in the Contract Data', except as otherwise agreed by both Parties.[189]

(2) Proportions and currencies for payments

With regard to payments and deductions under sub-paragraph (a), the vast majority are likely to be made under sub-paragraphs (i) to (iv) of Sub-Clause 14.3 [*Application for Interim Payment*] and in the currencies and proportions specified in Sub-Clause 14.15(a)(i) and (iii) and in the Contract Data.

If payments or deductions become due under Sub-Clause 13.4 [*Provisional Sums*], the relevant Provisional Sum in the Contract should indicate the currency or currencies and proportions which will apply.[190] If they become due under Sub-Clause 13.6 [*Adjustments for Changes in*

186. FIDIC suggests that these rates should be the selling prices quoted by the local central bank in the Country, and the rates should be those quoted at the time of closing on the Base Date. *See FIDIC Procurement Procedures Guide* (FIDIC, 2011) 117.
187. *Ibid.*
188. The other situation dealt with by sub-para. (a), namely, where the Accepted Contract Amount is expressed only in a Foreign Currency, is less usual.
189. Sub-Clause 14.15 (a) (i).
190. Sub-Clause 14.15 (a)(ii).

Laws], the currency or currencies and proportions, if any, in which the Cost was incurred should indicate the appropriate currency(ies) and any proportions.[191]

Sub-paragraph (b) is a new and useful addition to RB/17 as it recognises that the proportions of currencies in which the Contract Price is payable may be inapplicable to varied work under Sub-Clauses 13.2 and 13.3. For example, the Contract might provide for the payment of the Contract Price in a Foreign Currency and Local Currency in the proportions of 70:30, but the Contractor might perform certain varied work entirely in the Country with the consequence that 100% of the Cost is incurred in Local Currency. In this case, it may be inappropriate for the varied work to be paid for in the proportions of currencies in which the Contract Price is payable. Accordingly, the amount payable in each of the applicable currencies is to be specified in the agreement or determination under Sub-Clause 3.7 of the Engineer.[192]

As Delay Damages are payable to the Employer, the currencies and proportions in which the Contract Price is payable are not necessarily relevant. Consequently, payment of them is made in the currencies and proportions specified in the Contract Data.[193] Other payments to the Employer are to be made in the currency in which the sum was expended by the Employer, unless otherwise agreed.[194] Examples include payments for Employer-Supplied Materials and Employer's Equipment, pursuant to Sub-Clause 2.6, and temporary utilities, pursuant to Sub-Clause 4.19.

(iv) Related law: The issues to which a clause such as Sub-Clause 14.15 may give rise are well illustrated by a 2005 English case.[195] In that case, the Contractor, a consortium of European contractors, and the Employer, an entity of the African State of Lesotho, in 1991 entered into a construction contract based upon RB/87 and governed by the law of Lesotho. The contract provided, based on example clauses in the particular conditions of RB/87, that the currency of account[196] was to be Maloti, the currency

191. *Ibid.*
192. Both Sub-Clauses 13.2 and 13.3 require the Engineer to proceed under Sub-Clause 3.7 to determine the Contractor's entitlement.
193. Sub-Clause 14.15 (c).
194. Sub-Clause 14.15 (d).
195. *Lesotho Highlands Development Authority v Impregilio SpA* [2005] BLR 351.
196. The 'currency of account' refers to the currency in which a contractual obligation is expressed and provides the measure of the obligation, whereas

of Lesotho, and that payments to the Contractor were to be made 58% in Maloti and 42% in specified European currencies of the respective contractors comprising the consortium. For the purposes of payment, conversion between Maloti and the various European currencies was – as in RB/17 – to be at fixed rates of exchange calculated as of a date before the submission of tenders.

Between 1996 and 1997, while the works were ongoing, the Contractor claimed various amounts under the contract which the Employer failed to pay. If these claims had been paid when they should have been, the Employer would have paid them in the contractual currencies of payment, the majority (58%) being, as noted, in Maloti. Between 1997, when the last of the payments should have been made, and the date of the arbitration award in January 2002, Maloti fell heavily in value in relation to other currencies.

As the Employer had failed to pay the Contractor's claims, in 1997 the Contractor submitted them to ICC arbitration in London. When doing so, it argued that it no longer had any use for Maloti as the works had been completed. The Contractor further argued that, as it had funded the shortfall in payments from the Employer with the Contractor's hard European currencies, in order to remedy the Employer's failure to make payments when they were due, the tribunal should make their award entirely in such currencies, converted from Maloti at the rates of exchange prescribed by the contract, which preceded Maloti's collapse.[197]

If the arbitral tribunal had expressed an award mainly in Maloti (as the contract envisaged), then, in light of Maloti's collapse, this would have been comparatively beneficial to the Employer as the paying party but disadvantageous to the Contractor. On the other hand, an award entirely in European currencies, converted at the fixed exchange rates in the

---

the 'currency of payment' refers to the currency for performing the obligation which has been so defined and measured. Charles Proctor and others, *Mann on the Legal Aspect of Money* (7th edn, OUP, Oxford, 2012) 125-128 (paras 5.01-5.09) and 211-217 (paras 7.64-7.74). In RB/17, the currency denomination of the Accepted Contract Amount will likely constitute the currency of account of the Contract.

197. Antonio Crivellaro, 'All's Well That Ends Well: London Remains A Suitable Venue for International Arbitration – But Only Thanks To The House Of Lords' [2005] ICLR 480, 489-490.

contract, as the Contractor requested, would be greatly beneficial to the Contractor and correspondingly disadvantageous to the Employer.[198]

The arbitral tribunal,[199] which was seated in London, considered that the question of the currency in which sums should be awarded was a matter of procedural law. It noted that, according to Section 48(4) of the English Arbitration Act, '[u]nless otherwise agreed by the parties', an arbitral tribunal may order the payment of a sum of money in any currency. While recognising that the contract provided for the currencies in which payments under the contract were to be made, the arbitral tribunal found that 'the contract is silent as to the currency in which any arbitral award is to be given'.[200] Therefore it concluded that Section 48(4) was available and that it had the power to order payment in any currency. On this basis, it ordered the Employer to make payment of the amount of its award in favour of the Contractor entirely in the Contractor's own European currencies, applying the fixed exchange rates provided for in the contract, which preceded Maloti's collapse.

Although a majority of the judges in the House of Lords found that the arbitrators had been in error in applying Section 48(4), which gave a result different from the currency of payment provisions of the contract, the majority found that the error was not sufficient to justify setting the award aside[201] and, thus it survived.[202]

---

198. Ellis Baker and Anthony Lavers, 'Lessons from Lesotho: Arbitrators' Powers Reviewed' [2004] ICLR 140, 144. As the House of Lords later put it: 'the complaint of the employer against the award relates not to the currencies in which the award is expressed but rather against the rate at which Maloti had been converted into those hard currencies' [2005] BLR 351, 355 (para. 12).
199. '[T]hree experienced ICC arbitrators', according to the House of Lords' judgment, para. 2.
200. Paragraph 13.17 of the award cited in the judgment of the Court of Appeal [2003] BLR 347, 352 [para. 20].
201. On the basis of 'serious irregularity' under s 68(2)(b) of the Arbitration Act 1996.
202. In a subsequent article, counsel for the Contractor in the arbitration noted, among other things, that art. 7.4.12 (*Currency in which to assess damages*) of the UNIDROIT Principles provides that, unless otherwise agreed, damages are to be assessed 'either in the currency in which the monetary obligation was expressed or in the currency in which the harm was suffered, *whichever is more appropriate*' (emphasis added). Antonio Criv-

This case illustrates, among other things, the importance of currency risk and highlights the uncertainty of whether the provisions in the RB dealing with payment of the Contract Price necessarily also apply to payment of an arbitral award.[203]

(v) Improvements: As discussed in the commentary on Sub-Clause 21.6 [*Arbitration*] below,[204] consideration should be given to addressing in that Sub-Clause – or inviting the Parties to address in the Particular Conditions – the issue of whether the rules relating to currencies of payment in Sub-Clause 14.15 should apply to an arbitration award. Given the different views of the arbitrators and judges on this subject in the case described under **(iv) Related law** above, it should be clarified in the Contract whether they are intended to apply or not.

--ooOOoo--

15 TERMINATION BY EMPLOYER

This Clause provides that if the Contractor fails to carry out a contractual obligation, the Engineer may give the Contractor a Notice to Correct (as defined). Thereafter, if the Contractor fails to comply with a Notice to Correct, or if the Contractor commits other specified defaults, the Employer has two possible remedies:

(1) in some cases, after giving the Contractor a *Notice of the Employer's intention to terminate the Contract*, the Employer may, if the default remains unremedied, terminate the Contract by a *Notice of termination*; or
(2) in other cases, the Employer may give the Contractor a *Notice of termination* immediately terminating the Contract.

---

ellaro, 'All's Well That Ends Well: London Remains A Suitable Venue for International Arbitration – But Only Thanks To The House Of Lords' [2005] ICLR 480, 490.

203. This had already been a disputed issue under FIDIC contracts, *see*, e.g., partial award, ICC case 3790 (1983), Sigvard Jarvin and others, *Coll of ICC Arbitral Awards (1986 – 1990)* (ICC, Paris /Kluwer, the Netherlands, 1994) 3,11 and second partial award, ICC case 12048 (2004), ICC Int'l Ct Arb Bull, vol 23, no 2 (2012) (commentary 27-29) (relevant extracts of the award were not published).

204. And on page 52 of the *Guidance for the Preparation of Particular Conditions*.

The Clause also provides for the Employer's right to terminate the Contract for its convenience.

--ooOOoo--

15.1 Notice to Correct

If the Contractor fails to carry out any obligation under the Contract the Engineer may, by giving a Notice to the Contractor, require the Contractor to make good the failure and to remedy it within a specified time ("Notice to Correct" in these Conditions).

The Notice to Correct shall:

(a) describe the Contractor's failure;
(b) state the Sub-Clause and/or provisions of the Contract under which the Contractor has the obligation; and
(c) specify the time within which the Contractor shall remedy the failure, which shall be reasonable, taking due regard of the nature of the failure and the work and/or other action required to remedy it.

After receiving a Notice to Correct the Contractor shall immediately respond by giving a Notice to the Engineer describing the measures the Contractor will take to remedy the failure, and stating the date on which such measures will be commenced in order to comply with the time specified in the Notice to Correct.

The time specified in the Notice to Correct shall not imply any extension of the Time for Completion.

If the Contractor fails to carry out any contractual obligation, the Engineer may, by giving a Notice to Correct containing prescribed information, require the Contractor to remedy it within a specified time. After receiving this Notice, the Contractor shall respond immediately by giving a Notice to the Engineer describing the measures it will take to remedy the failure and the date they will be commenced.

Commentary

(i) Main Changes from RB/99: In RB/99, this Sub-Clause was just one sentence long and similar to the first sentence in the new Sub-Clause. Thus, the entire Sub-Clause is new apart from the first sentence.

(ii) Related Clauses / Sub-Clauses: 1.3 [*Notices and Other Communications*], 3.4 [*Delegation by the Engineer*], 4.2.2 [*Performance Security – Claims under the Performance Security*] and 15.2 [*Termination for Contractor's Default*].

(iii) Analysis:

(1) Engineer's Notice to Correct

If the Contractor has failed to perform a particular obligation under the Contract, this Sub-Clause 'is designed to give the Contractor an opportunity and a right to put right its previous and identified contractual failure'.[1] The Sub-Clause authorises the Engineer to give the Contractor a Notice to Correct which must:

(a) describe the Contractor's failure;
(b) state the Sub-Clause and/or provisions of the Contract under which the Contractor has the obligation; and
(c) specify the time within which the Contractor must remedy the failure, which must be reasonable 'taking due regard of the nature of the failure and the work and/or other action required to remedy it'.[2]

The Notice may, but is not required to, specify the rectification or remedial steps to be taken. As regards what may be a reasonable time:

> [It] must be reasonable in all the circumstances prevailing at the time of the notice. Thus, if 90 per cent of the workforce had gone down with cholera at that time, the period given for compliance would need reasonably to take that into account, even if that problem was the

1. Statement made in relation to Sub-Clause 15.1 of YB/99 [identical to Sub-Clause 15.1 of RB/99] in *Obrascon Huarte Lain SA v Attorney General for Gibraltar* [2014] BLR 484, 516 [para. 318].
2. Sub-Clause 15.1, sub-para. (c). The World Bank's COPA requires that the Notice to Correct also 'specify the time within which the Contractor shall respond to the Notice to Correct' and requires the Contractor to respond within that time. Sub-Clause 15.1, COPA. This seems like a useful addition.

> Contractor's risk. It may well be relevant to take into account whether the clause 15.1 [of YB/99] notice is coming out of the blue or if the subject matter has been raised before and the Contractor has chosen to ignore what it has been told. What is reasonable is fact sensitive.[3]

The Notice to Correct procedure is the normal way to bring to the Contractor's attention any substantial default in its performance. Given that a Notice alleging a default is always a serious matter, a Notice to Correct must be issued by the Engineer itself[4] and care should be taken to ensure the requirements for Notices in Sub-Clause 1.3 are complied with.[5]

(2) Contractor's response

After receiving a Notice to Correct,[6] the Contractor is required to respond 'immediately' by a Notice describing the remedial measures it will take, and the date on which they will be commenced, in order to comply with the time by which they must be remedied stated in the Engineer's Notice to Correct. If the Contractor should fail to remedy the default within 42 days or such other time as is stated in the Notice to Correct, the Employer is entitled to make a claim under the Performance Security.[7] In addition, if the Contractor's failure to comply with a Notice to Correct should constitute a 'material breach'[8] of the Contract, the Employer is entitled to give a Notice to the Contractor under sub-paragraph (a) of Sub-Clause 15.2.1 (which must state that it is given under that Sub-Clause) of the Employer's intention to terminate the Contract. While a failure to comply with a Notice to Correct in the case of a minor (i.e., non-material) breach will not suffice by itself to constitute a material breach, it may become one if it is repeated or is continuing and is not remedied.

3. *Obrascon Huarte Lain SA v Attorney General for Gibraltar* [2014] BLR 484, 516 [para. 318].
4. Sub-Clause 3.4 [*Delegation by the Engineer*] prohibits the Engineer to delegate the authority to issue a Notice to Correct.
5. As the Contractor will generally remedy the default promptly, the Notice to Correct procedure is arguably misplaced in a Clause entitled 'Termination by Employer'.
6. *See* Sub-Clause 1.3 as regards when a Notice is received or deemed to have been received.
7. Sub-Clause 4.2.2(c).
8. For the meaning of 'material breach' *see* under **(iii) Analysis** of the commentary on Sub-Clause 15.2 below.

(3) Notice to Correct not always required but often advisable

There is generally[9] no formal obligation for the Contractor to have been given a Notice to Correct by the Engineer before the Employer is entitled to give, pursuant to Sub-Clause 15.2.1, a Notice to the Contractor of the Employer's intention to terminate the Contract or a Notice of termination. The Employer may, in theory at least, give a Notice under Sub-Clause 15.2.1 on numerous grounds without the Contractor having first been given a Notice to Correct.

However, the Employer has few more drastic remedies than under Sub-Clause 15.2. If the Employer's Notice of its intention to terminate the Contract is contested, as it usually will be, the Employer will want to demonstrate that it had acted reasonably in the circumstances. Thus, if the default was one which the Contractor could have remedied within a reasonable time, it would be normal and expected for the Engineer to have first given the Contractor a Notice to Correct so as to allow it to do so before the Employer would issue a Notice of intention to terminate under Sub-Clause 15.2.1. *Therefore, before invoking Sub-Clause 15.2, a prudent Employer should ascertain whether – where the Contractor's default is one that could be remedied within a reasonable time – the Engineer had given the Contractor a Notice to Correct.* If not, then the Employer should require the Engineer to do so, as otherwise the Employer could be seen as having acted precipitously and/or unreasonably, exposing it to the risk that it be found to have terminated the Contract wrongfully.[10]

(iv) Related Law: In relation to interpretation of the corresponding, but rather different, provisions of YB/99, relating to contract termination (Sub-Clauses 15.1 and 15.2),[11] an English court has said that 'a commer-

9. Other than under Sub-Clause 15.2.1(a).

10. On the other hand, a Contractor cannot rely on the absence of a Notice to Correct as persuasive evidence that the Contractor had been performing correctly, as such absence does not relieve the Contractor from any duty or obligation under the Contract. *See* the last paragraph of Sub-Clause 3.2 [*Engineer's Duties and Authority*].

11. Sub-Clauses 15.1 and 15.2 of YB/99 (like RB/99) referred to various 'failures' of the Contractor to comply with the Contract without distinguishing between trivial failures and material ones.

cially sensible construction is required. The parties cannot sensibly have thought (objectively) that a trivial contractual failure in itself could lead to contractual termination'.[12]

Under the civil law, a party is generally required to give a notice of default (*mise en demeure* in French) to the other party as a condition to being able to claim damages (and interest) for breach of contract and/or to terminate the Contract.[13] The Notice to Correct corresponds, approximately, to such a notice of default under civil law.

(v) Improvements:

(1) The last paragraph of this Sub-Clause may be deleted as the last paragraph of Sub-Clause 3.2 already provides that any Notice by the Engineer shall not relieve the Contractor of any obligation under the Contract.
(2) The term 'Notice to Correct', which is referred to elsewhere than in Clause 15 (e.g., in Sub-Clause 3.4), should be included among the definitions in Clause 1 and might also, for convenience, be referred to by the abbreviation 'NTC'.

--ooOOoo--

15.2 Termination for Contractor's Default

Termination of the Contract under this Clause shall not prejudice any other rights of the Employer under the Contract or otherwise.

15.2.1 Notice

The Employer shall be entitled to give a Notice (which shall state that it is given under this Sub-Clause 15.2.1) to the Contractor of the Employer's intention to terminate the Contract or, in the case of sub-paragraph (f), (g) or (h) below a Notice of termination, if the Contractor:

12. *Obrascon Huarte Lain SA v Attorney General for Gibraltar* [2014] BLR 484, 517 [para. 321].
13. *See* **Section 4 Common Law and Civil Law Compared – 4.3.4 Notice of Default (*Mise En Demeure*)** of **Chapter II Applicable Law** above. Consistent with Sub-Clause 15.1, arts 7.1.4 (*Cure by non-performing party*) and 7.1.5 (*Additional period for performance*) of the UNIDROIT Principles

(a) fails to comply with:

(i) a Notice to Correct;

(ii) a binding agreement, or final and binding determination, under Sub-Clause 3.7 [*Agreement or Determination*]; or

(iii) a decision of the DAAB under 21.4 [*Obtaining DAAB's Decision*] (whether binding or final and binding)

and such failure constitutes a material breach of the Contractor's obligations under the Contract;

(b) abandons the Works or otherwise plainly demonstrates an intention not to continue performance of the Contractor's obligations under the Contract;

(c) without reasonable excuse fails to proceed with the Works in accordance with Clause 8 [*Commencement, Delays and Suspension*] or, if there is a maximum amount of Delay Damages stated in the Contract Data, the Contractor's failure to comply with Sub-Clause 8.2 [*Time for Completion*] is such that the Employer would be entitled to Delay Damages that exceed this maximum amount;

(d) without reasonable excuse fails to comply with a Notice of rejection given by the Engineer under Sub-Clause 7.5 [*Defects and Rejection*] or an Engineer's instruction under Sub-Clause 7.6 [*Remedial Work*], within 28 days after receiving it;

(e) fails to comply with Sub-Clause 4.2 [*Performance Security*];

(f) subcontracts the whole, or any part of, the Works in breach of Sub-Clause 5.1 [*Subcontractors*], or assigns the Contract without the required agreement under Sub-Clause 1.7 [*Assignment*];

(g) becomes bankrupt or insolvent; goes into liquidation, administration, reorganisation, winding-up or dissolution; becomes subject to

provide that a non-performing party may, at its own expense and subject to certain conditions, cure any non-performance and may be allowed time to do so.

the appointment of a liquidator, receiver, administrator, manager or trustee; enters into a composition or arrangement with the Contractor's creditors; or any act is done or any event occurs which is analogous to or has a similar effect to any of these acts or events under applicable Laws;

or if the Contractor is a JV:

(i) any of these matters apply to a member of the JV, and

(ii) the other member(s) do not promptly confirm to the Employer that, in accordance with Sub-Clause 1.14(a) [*Joint and Several Liability*], such member's obligations under the Contract shall be fulfilled in accordance with the Contract; or

(h) is found, based on reasonable evidence, to have engaged in corrupt, fraudulent, collusive or coercive practice at any time in relation to the Works or to the Contract.

15.2.2 Termination

Unless the Contractor remedies the matter described in a Notice given under Sub-Clause 15.2.1 [*Notice*] within 14 days of receiving the Notice, the Employer may by giving a second Notice to the Contractor immediately terminate the Contract. The date of termination shall be the date the Contractor receives this second Notice.

However, in the case of sub-paragraph (f), (g) or (h) of Sub-Clause 15.2.1 [*Notice*], the Employer may by giving a Notice under Sub-Clause 15.2.1 immediately terminate the Contract and the date of termination shall be the date the Contractor receives this Notice.

15.2.3 After termination

After termination of the Contract under Sub-Clause 15.2.2 [*Termination*], the Contractor shall:

(a) comply immediately with any reasonable instructions included in a Notice given by the Employer under Sub-Clause 15.2.2 [*Termination*]:

(i) for the assignment of any subcontract; and
(ii) for the protection of life or property or for the safety of the Works;

(b) deliver to the Engineer:

(i) any Goods required by the Employer,
(ii) all Contractor's Documents, and
(iii) all other design documents made by or for the Contractor to the extent, if any, that the Contractor is responsible for the design of part of the Permanent Works under Sub-Clause 4.1 [*Contractor's General Obligations*]; and

(c) leave the Site and, if the Contractor does not do so, the Employer shall have the right to expel the Contractor from the Site.

15.2.4 Completion of the Works

After termination under this Sub-Clause, the Employer may complete the Works and/or arrange for any other entities to do so. The Employer and/or these entities may then use any Goods and Contractor's Documents (and other design documents, if any) made by or on behalf of the Contractor to complete the Works.

After such completion of the Works, the Employer shall give another Notice to the Contractor that the Contractor's Equipment and Temporary Works will be released to the Contractor at or near the Site. The Contractor shall then promptly arrange their removal, at the risk and cost of the Contractor. However, if by this time the Contractor has failed to make a payment due to the Employer, these items may be sold (to the extent permitted by applicable Laws) by the Employer in order to recover this payment. Any balance of the proceeds shall then be paid to the Contractor.

The Employer is entitled to give a Notice (which states it is given under this Sub-Clause) to the Contractor of the Employer's intention to terminate the Contract in the five cases listed in sub-paragraphs (a), (b), (c), (d), and (e) of Sub-Clause 15.2.1. Unless the Contractor

remedies the matter within 14 days of receiving the Notice, the Employer may, by a second Notice to the Contractor and without prejudice to the Employer's rights, immediately terminate the Contract. The Employer is also entitled to give a Notice of termination, terminating the Contract immediately, in the three cases listed in sub-paragraphs (f), (g) and (h) of Sub-Clause 15.2.1.

After termination, the Contractor must: (a) comply immediately with any reasonable instructions for the assignment of any subcontract and protection of life or property; (b) deliver to the Engineer any Goods, all Contractor's Documents and all other design documents made by the Contractor; and (c) leave the Site. After termination, the Employer may complete the Works and/or arrange for any other entities to do so, using any Goods and Contractor's Documents.

After completion, the Employer shall give a Notice to the Contractor that the Contractor's Equipment and Temporary Works will be released to it. However, if the Contractor has failed to make any payment due, these items may be sold to recover this payment.

Commentary

(i) Main Changes from RB/99:

(1) Whereas Sub-Clause 15.2 of RB/99 had provided that, if the Contractor committed any of the defaults listed in it, the Employer could, upon giving 14 days' notice to the Contractor, terminate the Contract, the new Sub-Clause, which has been divided into four parts (Sub-Clauses 15.2.1 through 15.2.4), provides for both:

(a) a *Notice of the Employer's intention to terminate the Contract* applicable in the case of sub-paragraphs (a) through (e) which, if the matter is not remedied within 14 days, may entitle the Employer to give a second Notice terminating the Contract immediately; and

(b) a *Notice terminating the Contract immediately* applicable in the case of sub-paragraphs (f), (g) or (h).

(2) Certain grounds for termination are also new, specifically:

(a) sub-paragraph (a) (ii) and (iii), including the requirement that such a failure to comply with the Contract constitute a material breach of the Contract;

(b) sub-paragraph (c) as regards when any maximum amount of Delay Damages stated in the Contract Data would be exceeded;

(c) sub-paragraph (f) (sub-paragraph (d) in RB/99) as regards subcontracting 'any part of' the Works in breach of Sub-Clause 5.1;

(d) sub-paragraph (g) (sub-paragraph (e) in RB/99) as regards the more detailed description of bankruptcy events including the provision relating to if the Contractor is a JV; and

(e) sub-paragraph (h) (sub-paragraph (f) in RB/99) as regards the description of corrupt practices.

(3) Sub-paragraph (f) (sub-paragraph (d) in RB/99) relating to subcontracting the Works, or assigning the Contract, in breach of Contract has become a ground for immediate termination of the Contract.

(4) The description of the situation after termination contained in Sub-Clauses 15.2.3 [*After Termination*] is more elaborate and detailed than in Sub-Clause 15.2 of RB/99.

(ii) Related Clauses / Sub-Clauses: 1.3 [*Notices and Other Communications*], 1.7 [*Assignment*], 1.10 [*Employer's Use of Contractor's Documents*], 1.12 [*Confidentiality*], 1.14 [*Joint and Several Liability*], 1.16 [*Contract Termination*], 3.7 [*Agreement or Determination*], 4.2.2 [*Performance Security – Claims under the Performance Security*], 5.1 [*Subcontractors*], 8 [*Commencement, Delays and Suspension*], 8.2 [*Time for Completion*], 8.8 [*Delay Damages*], 11.4 [*Failure to Remedy Defects*], 15.3 [*Valuation after Termination for Contractor's Default*], 15.4 [*Payment after Termination for Contractor's Default*], 17.1 [*Responsibility for Care of the Works*] and 21.4 [*Obtaining DAAB's Decision*].

(iii) Analysis:

(1) General

As terminating a Contract for the Contractor's default is one of the most serious steps that the Employer can take, it should only be done as a last resort and after taking legal advice. When considering whether to terminate, the Employer needs to ascertain not only that its termination (or stated intention to terminate) is justified under a contractual ground for termination, that is, any of sub-paragraphs (a) through (h), but also that, in implementing the termination, it respects meticulously the procedural steps in Sub-Clauses 15.2.1, where appropriate, and 15.2.2. If the Employer is unable to justify termination under its chosen ground (or grounds), and/or fails to respect the procedure for termination, it may find itself to have breached the Contract[14] and, if the Contract terminates, to be responsible in damages (including lost anticipated profits) to the Contractor for having wrongfully terminated the Contract.[15]

(2) Notice of intention to terminate (Sub-Clause 15.2.1) and/or to terminate (Sub-Clause 15.2.2)

The procedure for termination of the Contract by the Employer for the Contractor's default has been clarified in RB/17, and several additional grounds for termination (or for giving a Notice of intention to terminate, as discussed below) have been added.[16]

The Employer must now give a *Notice of intention to terminate the Contract* – *not* a Notice to terminate the Contract as under RB/99 – to the Contractor on one (or more) of the grounds described in sub-paragraphs (a) to (e), which are all cases of default which the Contractor is still entitled to remedy. *This Notice must state that it is given under Sub-Clause 15.2.1.*

This Notice of intention operates, in effect, like a second Notice to Correct[17] as, if the Contractor remedies the matter described in the Notice 'within 14 days of receiving the Notice',[18] the Employer will be disen-

---

14. *See* final award, ICC case 10892 (2002), ICC Int'l Ct Arb Bull, vol 19, no 2, 2008, 91, 94-95 (failure of the Employer to respect 14-day time period for terminating the Contractor was a breach of contract) (commentary 57, 59-60).
15. *See* Atkin Chambers, *Hudson's Building and Engineering Contracts* (14th edn, Sweet & Maxwell, London, 2020) 969-974 (paras 8-068-073) and Justin Sweet and others, *Construction Law for Design Professionals, Construction Managers, and Contractors* (Cengage Learning, Stamford, CT, 2015) 64-66 for the common law position.
16. Sub-Clause 15.2 of RB/99 had provided that in the case of certain specific defaults the Employer could, upon giving 14 days' notice to the Contractor, terminate the Contract. It was unclear under that Sub-Clause whether the Contractor would be entitled to cure the default within the 14 days in which event no termination would occur or whether the notice was merely to inform the Contractor that termination would occur inevitably after 14 days. The new Sub-Clause resolves this issue.
17. Assuming that the Employer had already given a Notice to Correct under Sub-Clause 15.1.
18. '**day**' means a calendar day, Sub-Clause 1.1.25. *See also* Sub-Clause 1.3 describing when a Notice is received or deemed to have been received as

titled to give a further Notice terminating the Contract and the Contract will be preserved. However, if the Contractor fails to remedy the matter within 14 days, the Employer may, by giving a second Notice, immediately terminate the Contract, pursuant to Sub-Clause 15.2.2.

On the other hand, the grounds for termination described in sub-paragraphs (f), (g), and (h) are generally cases of default which cannot be remedied easily or, indeed, at all.[19] Accordingly, in those cases, the termination procedure is different: the Employer is entitled, under Sub-Clause 15.2.2, to give a *Notice of immediate termination of the Contract, which must also state that it is given under Sub-Clause 15.2.1.*[20]

Pursuant to Sub-Clause 1.3(b), any Notice should be identified as a Notice.[21] In the case of any Notice terminating the Contract immediately, the date of termination is the date the Contractor receives this Notice.[22]

(3) Grounds for Notice of intention to terminate or of termination (Sub-Clause 15.2.1)

(a) Contractor's failure to comply (sub-paragraph (a))

As previously noted,[23] the ground for termination in sub-paragraph (a) has been expanded, beyond a failure to comply with a Notice to Correct (as in RB/99), to include a failure to comply with a binding agreement (of the Parties), or a final and binding determination, under Sub-Clause 3.7, as well as a failure to comply with a DAAB decision under Sub-Clause 21.4, whether binding or final and binding. These grounds are qualified by the provision that any such failure must constitute a 'material breach' of the Contractor's obligations under the Contract, implying that a failure to comply with a Notice to Correct, binding agreement or final and

well as the possible need to send a copy to the Engineer. As regards the inherent ambiguity of 'within' a period of time, *see* point (2) under **(v) Improvements** in the commentary on Sub-Clause 1.2 [*Interpretation*] above.

19. Arguably, it may be going too far to allow the Employer to terminate the Contract immediately if the Contractor has subcontracted only a 'part' of the Works in breach of Sub-Clause 5.1, but this is what sub-para. (f) of Sub-Clause 15.2.1 provides for.
20. This follows from the fact that it is described as being given under Sub-Clause 15.2.1, *see* Sub-Clause 15.2.2, second paragraph.
21. *See* Sub-Clause 1.3 [*Notices and Other Communications*] for other details.
22. By exercising the procedure for termination, the Employer does not forego any of its other rights against the Contractor. *See* the first sentence of Sub-Clause 15.2.
23. *See* under **(i) Main Changes from RB/99** above of this commentary on Sub-Clause 15.2.

binding determination or DAAB decision will not, alone, be sufficient to justify a Notice of intention to terminate the Contract.

There is nothing unusual in the further requirement for a 'material breach' in this context as '[i]t is common to make a "material breach" [...] a ground for termination (of a contract)'.[24] Whether such a breach has occurred, however, is often not a simple matter and requires a legal analysis which:

> is to be addressed by looking at *objective* facts and circumstances [...] The objective materiality of a breach of contract may be determined having regard to the consequences of the breach: the more serious the consequences the more material the breach.[25]

The events listed in sub-paragraphs (b) through (h) of Sub-Clause 15.2.1 are helpful in this analysis as they indicate the degree of gravity expected for a breach to be considered material.

---

24. *See* Atkin Chambers, *Hudson's Building and Engineering Contracts* (14th edn, Sweet & Maxwell, London, 2020) 959 (para. 8-057) US law is to the same effect, *see* Justin Sweet and Marc M Schneier, *Legal Aspects of Architecture, Engineering and the Construction Process* (9th edn, Cengage Learning, Stamford, CT, 2013) 685. Similarly, under French law, the non-performance must be 'sufficiently serious' (*suffisamment grave*), art. 1224, French Civil Code, in order to justify termination.
25. *See* Julian Bailey, *Construction Law* (3rd edn, London Publishing, UK, 2020) vol 2, 805-806 (para. 9.67). The circumstances which have been regarded as significant in determining whether a material breach of any contract has occurred have been described by a US authority as follows:

    (a) the extent to which the injured party [the Employer] will be deprived of the benefit which he reasonably expected;
    (b) the extent to which the injured party can be adequately compensated for the part of that benefit of which he will be deprived;
    (c) the extent to which the party failing to perform or to offer to perform [the Contractor] will suffer forfeiture;
    (d) the likelihood that the party failing to perform or to offer to perform will cure this failure, taking account of all the circumstances including any reasonable assurances;
    (e) the extent to which the behavior of the party failing to perform or to offer to perform comports with standards of good faith and fair dealing.

    US Restatement (Second) of Contracts, s 241, Circumstances Significant in Determining Whether a Failure Is Material (ALI, Philadelphia, PA, 1981). Sub-paragraph (e) might be disregarded where the governing law is that of a country which does not require that a contract should be performed in good faith.

(b) Abandonment of works (sub-paragraph (b))

Sub-paragraph (b) refers to where the Contractor abandons the Works, which should normally be relatively easy to demonstrate (as the Contractor will leave the Site), or 'plainly demonstrates an intention not to continue performance' of the Contract. Sub-Clause 63.1(a) [*Default of Contractor*] of RB/87 had referred to where the Contractor 'has repudiated the Contract', repudiation being a common law concept. In 1999, as FIDIC had sought to avoid using the vocabulary of any one legal system, FIDIC replaced 'repudiated' by 'plainly demonstrates the intention not to continue performance' of the Contract,[26] and the same expression has been carried through to sub-paragraph (b).[27]

In relation to the language in sub-paragraph (b) ('plainly demonstrate[d] the intention not to continue performance of his obligations under the Contract') and sub-paragraph (c) ('without reasonable excuse fail[ed] [...] to proceed with the works in accordance with Clause 8') of Sub-Clause 15.2 of YB/99, which is very similar to the same sub-paragraphs in Sub-Clause 15.2.1, the court in *Obrascon* stated the following 'basic points of principle':

> (a) The test must be an objective one in relation to the grounds in both sub-paragraphs. Thus, if [the contractor] privately intended to stop work permanently but continued openly and assiduously to work hard at the site, this would, without more, objectively not give rise to a plain 'demonstration' of intention not to continue performance. Similarly, the fact that [the contractor] was and had for many months been doing no work of any relevance without contractual excuse could, without more, objectively judged, give rise to a conclusion that it had failed to proceed in accordance with clause 8.
>
> (b) [...] these grounds for termination must relate to significant and more than minor defaults on the part of [the contractor] on the grounds that it cannot mutually have been intended that a (relatively) Draconian clause such as a termination provision should be capable of being exercised for insignificant or insubstantial defaults. Thus, a few days delay in the context of a

26. *See* Sub-Clause 15.2(b) of RB/99.
27. However, 'the intention' in RB/99 has become 'an intention' in RB/17. In *Obrascon*, the judge acknowledged that this terminology (in YB/99 as in RB/99) 'is not unlike the test for English common law repudiation'. *Obrascon Huarte Lain SA v Attorney General for Gibraltar* [2014] BLR 484, 517 [para. 323].

two-year Contract would not justify termination on the clause 8 ground and an unwillingness or even refusal to perform relatively minor obligations would not justify termination on the 'intention not to continue' ground.[28]

(c) Failure to proceed/long delay (sub-paragraph (c))

'[W]ithout reasonable excuse' failing to proceed with the Works in accordance with Clause 8 refers to without such excuse failing to proceed 'with due expedition and without delay', as required by Sub-Clause 8.1, second paragraph.[29]

As a new ground for termination, sub-paragraph (c) refers to where the Employer would be entitled to Delay Damages that exceed any maximum amount stated in the Contract Data.[30] Given that, after the maximum is reached, the Employer may be continuing to suffer damage on account of the Contractor's delay for which it may no longer be compensated,[31] it is reasonable that the Employer should have a right to terminate in these circumstances and, if it elects to do so, engage another contractor and/or take other steps to minimise its damage.

---

28. *Obrascon Huarte Lain SA v Attorney General for Gibraltar* [2014] BLR 484, 524 [para. 356]. Sub-Clause 15.2 of YB/99 had provided (like Sub-Clause 15.2 of RB/99 described under **(i) Main Changes from RB/99** above) that, in the case of certain defaults, the Employer could, upon giving 14 days' notice to the Contractor, terminate the Contract, it being unclear whether the 14-day period was a cure period or whether termination would inevitably take place after 14 days.
29. *See* the commentary on Sub-Clause 8.1 above.
30. This is usually between 5% and 15% of the Accepted Contract Amount. *The FIDIC Contracts Guide* (2nd edn, FIDIC, 2022) 288. Such a ground for termination is quite usual in common law countries. *See* Atkin Chambers, *Hudson's Building and Engineering Contracts* (14th edn, Sweet & Maxwell, London, 2020) 718 (fn. 149) (para. 6-022). An Employer in one case has been held entitled to the maximum of liquidated damages for delay under a Pink Book contract even where it was terminated before the date for completion where, at termination, the Contractor's expected liability for liquidated damages already far exceeded the maximum. Final award, ICC case 24093 (2022) (unpublished).
31. As, according to Sub-Clause 8.8, second paragraph, Delay Damages are the 'only' damages due for delay other than Sub-Clause 15.2 [*Termination for Contractor's Default*].

(d) Failure to comply with Engineer's Notice of rejection or instruction (sub-paragraph (d))

This sub-paragraph refers to where, without reasonable excuse, the Contractor fails to comply with a Notice of rejection of the Engineer under Sub-Clause 7.5, or an instruction of the Engineer under Sub-Clause 7.6, within 28 days after receiving it. However, for reasons given in the commentary on Sub-Clause 7.5 above,[32] an Employer may be better off relying on a failure by the Contractor to comply with an Engineer's instruction under Sub-Clause 7.6, than a Notice of rejection of the Engineer under Sub-Clause 7.5.

(e) Failure to comply with Sub-Clause 4.2 (sub-paragraph (e))

As the Contractor must deliver the Performance Security to the Employer within 28 days of receiving the Letter of Acceptance,[33] and as no amount may be certified or paid to the Contractor until then,[34] the failure referred to here is unlikely to be a failure to provide the Performance Security in the first place. Instead, it is likely to relate to a failure of the Contractor to either extend or increase the amount of the Performance Security when required to do so pursuant to Sub-Clause 4.2.1.

(f) Unauthorised subcontracting or assignment (sub-paragraph (f))

If the Contractor should subcontract the whole or part of the Works in breach of Sub-Clause 5.1, or assign the Contract without the Employer's agreement, the rights of a third party (a subcontractor or assignee) would be implicated. Accordingly, it might be difficult for the Contractor to withdraw from the subcontract or the assignment if required to do so by the Employer. Consequently, pursuant to Sub-Clause 15.2.2, the Employer is given the right to terminate the Contract immediately in this case by giving the Contractor a Notice of termination.

(g) Bankruptcy or insolvency (sub-paragraph (g))

This sub-paragraph covers not just where the Contractor may have filed for bankruptcy or reorganisation with a court in any jurisdiction, apparently, but also where the Contractor is simply insolvent. Insolvency is defined as: '[t]he condition of being unable to pay debts as they fall due

32. *See* under *(4) Remedies upon Contractor's failure* under **(iii) Analysis**, as well as under **(v) Improvements**, of the commentary on Sub-Clause 7.5 [*Defects and Rejection*] above.
33. Sub-Clause 4.2.1.
34. Sub-Clause 14.6.

or in the usual course of business' or simply as '[t]he inability to pay debts as they mature'.[35] As the Contractor is likely no longer than to have the resources to perform the Contract, the Employer is given the right, pursuant to Sub-Clause 15.2.2, to terminate the Contract immediately by a Notice of termination.

The sub-paragraph provides that, where the Contractor is a JV,[36] the sub-paragraph should be interpreted as applying to each member of the JV. Where the act of bankruptcy or insolvency affects any one member and if the other members do not promptly confirm that they will fulfil the defaulting member's obligations,[37] then this will be a ground for terminating the Contract with the Contractor immediately, pursuant to Sub-Clause 15.2.2.

However, the right of the Employer to terminate the Contract in the case of bankruptcy or insolvency will be subject to applicable bankruptcy laws. Thus, for example, under French law, a bankruptcy trustee may require the Parties to continue with the Contract and the US *Bankruptcy Code* 'prohibits termination of a contract solely because of the debtor's insolvency or bankruptcy of the debtor'.[38]

(h) Corrupt practices (sub-paragraph (h))

The new wording of sub-paragraph (h) dealing with illicit practices of various kinds is taken from Sub-Clause 15.6 [*Corrupt or Fraudulent Practices*] of the Pink Book.[39] FIDIC had considered Sub-Clause 15.2(f) of RB/99 unsatisfactory as it only dealt with bribery and not, like Sub-Clause 15.6 of the Pink Book, with corrupt, fraudulent, collusive or coercive practice generally. Accordingly, it now does so. However,

35. Bryan A Garner (ed in chief), *Black's Law Dictionary* (11th edn, Thomson Reuters, St Paul, MN, 2019).
36. Defined as an 'unincorporated grouping of two or more persons'. *See* Sub-Clause 1.1.46.
37. As they should be prepared to do, pursuant to Sub-Clause 1.14(a) [*Joint and Several Liability*].
38. *See* **Section 4 Common Law and Civil Law Compared – 4.5.2 Bankruptcy** of **Chapter II Applicable Law**, above and John M Mastin and others (eds), *Smith, Currie, and Hancock's Common Sense Construction Law: A Practical Guide for the Construction Professional* (6th edn, Wiley, Hoboken, NJ, 2020) 607 citing to 11 United States Code, s 365(e)(i)(A)-(C) and related case law.
39. Conditions of Contract for Construction, MDB (Multilateral Development Bank) Harmonised Edition, for Building and Engineering Works Designed by the Employer, 2010.

whereas 'corrupt practice', 'fraudulent practice', 'collusive practice' and 'coercive practice' are all helpfully defined in the Pink Book[40] and in other forms of construction contract,[41] these terms have, unfortunately, been left undefined in sub-paragraph (h).[42]

Any termination is likely to be contentious. It may be even more so where the meaning of such terms is unclear. Accordingly – especially given the importance of the issue of corruption[43] – the practices referred to in sub-paragraph (h) ('corrupt, fraudulent, collusive or coercive practice') should be defined in the Particular Conditions.

40. The Pink Book contains six different versions of the relevant provision, Sub-Clause 15.6 [*Corrupt or Fraudulent Practices*], as the MDBs apparently could not agree on a common version in this respect. FIDIC also has its own definitions of 'Bribery', 'Fraud', 'Coercion' and 'Collusion' in Appendix C of FIDIC's *Guidelines for Integrity Management in the Consulting Industry Part 1 – Policies and Principles* (1st edn, 2011) *and Part II – Firms Procedures* (1st edn, 2015). *See also* Part C–Bank's Policy–Corrupt and Fraudulent Practices of The World Bank's COPA which defines these terms as well as the further term 'obstructive practice' which is defined to include, among other things, deliberately destroying or falsifying evidence, or intentionally impeding the exercise of The World Bank's inspection and audit rights. The COPA also provides for a new Sub-Clause 15.8 requiring compliance with the Bank's Anti-Corruption Guidelines.
41. *See*, for example, art. 8.5 of the *Form of Agreement between Owner and Design-Builder on the Basis of a Stipulated Price* prepared by the US Engineer's Joint Contract Documents Committee, US National Society of Professional Engineers (2016).
42. FIDIC expands on its intentions somewhat in the *Guidance for the Preparation of Particular Conditions*, 44, where it states that sub-para. (h) is intended:

    > to include situations, where the Contractor or any of the Contractor's employees, agents, Subcontractors or Contractor's Personnel gives or offer to give (directly or indirectly) to any person any bribe, gift, gratuity, commission or other thing value, as an inducement or reward for showing or forbearing to show favour or disfavour to any person in relation to the Contract. However, this is not intended to include lawful inducements and rewards by the Contractor to the Contractor's Personnel.

43. According to FIDIC's former President Bill Howard, the global cost of corruption is up to USD 4 trillion a year. Speech at webinar entitled 'Recovery with integrity' to mark the UN's International Anti-Corruption Day on 9 December 2020.

It is also unclear in sub-paragraph (h) what is meant by 'is found, based on reasonable evidence'.[44] In this connection, because of the inherent difficulties of proving corruption, arbitrators and some courts are relying upon a 'red flags' methodology to determine whether such activity exists. This methodology refers to the practice of relying upon circumstantial evidence – in the form of recognised indicators of corruption or 'red flags' – to establish corruption. If a certain number of these indicators is present in a case, this may satisfy a tribunal of the existence of corruption.[45] Arguably, therefore, today, such circumstantial evidence or 'red flags' should be sufficient to satisfy the 'reasonable evidence' test in sub-paragraph (h).

Given the evident gravity of illicit practices, pursuant to Sub-Clause 15.2.2, the Employer is given the right to terminate the Contract immediately.

(4) Notice of termination (Sub-Clause 15.2.2)

As stated above, except in the case of the grounds for termination in sub-paragraphs (f), (g) and (h) (all providing for immediate termination), if the Contractor fails to remedy a ground for termination within 14 days, the Employer may, by giving a second Notice, immediately terminate the Contract, pursuant to Sub-Clause 15.2.2.[46] Termination is without prejudice to the Employer's other rights, e.g., to claim

44. Who is to do the finding? The other Party? The Engineer? The DAAB? The Arbitrator(s)? A national court? This is not explained.
45. For an example of the use of such 'red flags' methodology, *see* Ct of App Paris (1st Ch), 17 November 2020, no 18/02568, and Cass 1re civ, 14 September 2022, no 20-22.119 (*State of Libya v SORELEC*) where the French courts found that the circumstantial evidence of corruption was strong enough to warrant the setting aside of two ICC awards. For information about 'red flags' indicators generally, *see* the 2016 OECD booklet entitled '*Preventing Corruption in Public Procurement*' www.oecd.org/gov/ethics/corruption-public-procurement-brochure.pdf 10 November 2022 and the 2019 Basel Institute on Governance publication entitled '*Corruption and Money Laundering in International Arbitration: A Toolkit for Arbitrators*' http://www.baselgovernance.org/publications/corruption-and-money-laundering-international-arbitration-toolkit-arbitrators accessed 10 November 2022. *See also* Emmanuel Gaillard, 'The Emergence of Transnational Responses to Corruption in International Arbitration' (2019) 35, Arb Int'l, 1-19.
46. This Notice must comply with Sub-Clause 1.3 [*Notices and Other Communications*]. A Notice of intention to terminate and a Notice to terminate may each give rise to a deemed Dispute under Sub-Clause 21.4 (c), permitting its direct referral to the DAAB.

damages.[47] The date of termination will be the date the Contractor receives this second Notice.[48]

(5) After termination (Sub-Clause 15.2.3)

After termination, the Contractor must, pursuant to Sub-Clause 15.2.3, comply 'immediately' with any reasonable instructions of the Employer in a Notice under Sub-Clause 15.2.2 to assign any subcontract and as the Contractor has ceased to be responsible for the care of the Works[49] to safeguard persons, property and the Works. However, to achieve this goal, Sub-Clause 5.1 [*Subcontractors*] needs to be modified to entitle the Employer to require that all subcontracts be assigned to the Employer pursuant to Sub-Clause 15.2.3(a) (as at present, in its relationship with the Contractor, the Employer does not have this entitlement).[50]

The Contractor must also deliver to the Engineer any Goods required by the Employer, all Contractor's Documents and all other design documents made by or for the Contractor to the extent the Contractor was responsible for design work.[51] These will enable the Employer to continue – should it wish to do so – with the execution of the Works expeditiously either itself or by engaging another contractor.[52] However, no time period is specified for such delivery. The Contractor must also leave the Site. While, again, no time period is specified, should the Contractor not do so,[53] the Employer has the express right to expel it from the Site.[54]

47. Sub-Clause 15.2.
48. Sub-Clause 15.2.2, first paragraph.
49. *See* Sub-Clause 17.1, second paragraph.
50. A sample provision on this subject is contained in the *Guidance*, 28. *See* under **(v) Improvements** of the commentary on Sub-Clause 5.1 [*Subcontractors*] above.
51. Pursuant to Sub-Clause 1.10 (d)(i), the Employer will have the right 'to copy, use and communicate' the Contractor's Documents and other design documents, if any, made by or for the Contractor.
52. The Contractor should also deliver to the Engineer any Employer-Supplied Materials and/or Employer's Equipment made available to the Contractor, pursuant to Sub-Clause 2.6. *See* the *Guidance for the Preparation of Particular Conditions*, 44, for an example provision on this subject.
53. Sometimes a terminated Contractor will seek improperly to retain possession of the Site and try to use its possession as a bargaining chip in negotiating a settlement with the Employer.
54. The Employer may seek an interim or provisional measure from a local court (or from the DAAB under 5.1(j) of the DAAB Rules or an Emergency Arbitrator under art. 29 of the ICC Rules of Arbitration) expelling the Contractor from the Site. *See* art. 28 of the ICC Rules of Arbitration (referred

(6) Completion of the Works (Sub-Clause 15.2.4)

After completion of the Works, the Employer must give Notice to the Contractor and release the Contractor's Equipment and Temporary Works to it at or near the Site. But, if the Contractor has failed to make a payment due to the Employer, these items may be sold ('to the extent permitted by applicable Laws'),[55] subject to the rights of third parties (e.g., the Contractor's Equipment may belong to a subcontractor or be leased or purchased under a conditional sales contract), to enable the Employer to recover any payment that is due to it.

(iv) Related Law:

(1) Manner of termination

It will usually be more advantageous for the Employer to terminate the Contract by reference to a sub-paragraph in Sub-Clause 15.2.1 than under applicable law as, if the relevant conditions are met, the Employer will have the clear right to do so,[56] whereas it might not enjoy such a clear right of termination under the law governing the Contract. However, as the first sentence of the Sub-Clause provides, termination of the Contract under Sub-Clause 15.2 'shall not prejudice' the right of the Employer to terminate the Contract on another ground, such as under the governing law.[57] Accordingly, when giving a Notice of intention to terminate and/or a Notice to terminate under Sub-Clause 15.2, the Employer may wish to reaffirm that its Notice is without prejudice to its other rights under the Contract or at law.

If the Employer had erroneously relied on one contractual ground for termination, but it had another contractual ground available to it which it did not rely upon, at least under the common law, it may subsequently

to in Sub-Clause 21.6 [*Arbitration*]) which recognises a party's right to apply to 'any competent judicial authority' for such a remedy. *See also* the commentary on Clause 21 [*Disputes and Arbitration*] below.

55. At least in Brazil, the enforceability of this provision would be 'highly questionable', as the taking of property belonging to another in that country would appear to require a judicial decision. Alexandre Salles and Francisco Ferreira, 'Construction Law in South America: Key Tendencies and Points for Consideration' (2018) ICLR, 299, 305.
56. Subject, however, as regards sub-para. (g), to the application of local bankruptcy laws, as stated above.
57. Thus, the Employer might do so on the basis of repudiation under the common law or a material (serious) breach of contract under either the common or civil law.

be able to rely upon that other ground so as to justify the termination of the Contract.[58] However, its ability to do so may be constrained by Sub-Clause 15.2 if the new ground was one capable of remedy (i.e., it was one of the grounds in sub-paragraphs (a) to (e)) and if the Employer (through the Engineer) had failed to give the Contractor an opportunity to remedy it before termination as provided for by Sub-Clause 15.2.[59] To what extent it will be constrained is likely to be a matter of contract interpretation.[60]

Whether under the civil or common law, a party generally has the right to terminate a contract in the case of material breach, or fundamental non-performance, of the contract by the other party.[61]

(2) UNIDROIT Principles

Similarly, under the UNIDROIT Principles, termination is available if the other party's non-performance amounts to a 'fundamental non-

58. *See* Julian Bailey, *Construction Law* (3rd edn, London Publishing, UK, 2020) vol 2, 826-827 (para. 9.107).
59. *Ibid.*
60. In the case of US Federal Government contracts, the US courts allow what are referred to as 'post hoc justifications of a default termination', which are to the effect that, where the government's original ground for termination was not sustainable then, if there was another existing ground for default termination which was justified by the circumstances at the time of termination, regardless of whether that ground was known to the government official concerned at the time of the termination, default termination on this ground will be upheld. It has been stated that:

    > [a]lthough some commentators strongly criticize this post hoc principle because it 'overlooks the long-standing practical common law justification for cure notices to encourage contractors to cure their curable deficiencies in lieu of termination,' the courts and boards remain unmoved.

    Steven Feldman 'The Rhetoric and Reality of Termination for Default', *The Procurement Lawyer*, Section of Public Contract Law, (Spring 2018) 53(3) A.B.A., 5, 7-8 and Philip Bruner and Patrick O'Connor, *Bruner and O'Connor on Construction Law* (Thomson Reuters, St Paul, MN, 2017) vol 5, 991-995 (s 18.37).
61. Atkin Chambers, *Hudson's Building and Engineering Contracts* (14th edn, Sweet & Maxwell, London, 2020) 902-904 (para. 8-004) (English law); Justin Sweet and Marc M Schneier, *Legal Aspects of Architecture, Engineering and the Construction Process* (9th edn, Cengage Learning, Stamford, CT, 2013) 685 (US law); under French law, the non-performance must be 'sufficiently serious' (*suffisamment grave*), art. 1224, French Civil Code, in order to justify termination.

performance' (Article 7.3.1) which the Principles equate to 'material' non-performance.[62] In determining whether a failure to perform an obligation amounts to a fundamental (material) non-performance, regard is to be had, in particular, to five factors.[63] Under the Principles, the right to terminate a contract is, as under Sub-Clause 15.2, exercised by a notice to the other party (Article 7.3.2).

(3) Civil law countries influenced by French law

As stated earlier[64] and in relation to Sub-Clause 15.2.2 under **(iii) Analysis** above, it remains the case in many civil law countries that a party must obtain an order from a court (or an arbitral award) to be able to terminate a contract. In such countries, termination of a contract without a court order will only be possible where a contract contains a clause that effectively excludes the need for a court order.[65] As stated in relation to the commentary on Sub-Clause 1.16 [*Contract Termination*] above, it remains to be seen whether that Sub-Clause will be sufficient to permit termination without a court order in those countries.

---

62. Official comment 2 to art. 7.3.1 (*Right to terminate the contract*) of the UNIDROIT Principles.
63. According to art. 7.3.1 (*Right to terminate the contract*) (2) of the UNIDROIT Principles regard should be had, in particular, to whether:
    (a) the non-performance substantially deprives the aggrieved party of what it was entitled to expect under the contract unless the other party did not foresee and could not reasonably have foreseen such result;
    (b) strict compliance with the obligation which has not been performed is of essence under the contract;
    (c) the non-performance is intentional or reckless;
    (d) the non-performance gives the aggrieved party reason to believe that it cannot rely on the other party's future performance;
    (e) the non-performing party will suffer disproportionate loss as a result of the preparation or performance if the contract is terminated.

    See also art. 7.3.2 (*Notice of termination*) of the Principles.
64. **Section 4 Common Law and Civil Law Compared – 4.3.5 Contract Termination** of **Chapter II Applicable Law** above.
65. For example, art. 158 of the Egyptian Civil Code provides for such a dispensation:

    > The parties may agree that in case of non-performance of the obligations flowing from the contract, the contract will be deemed to have been rescinded '*ipso facto*' without a Court order [...].

(v) Improvements:

(1) In relation to the discussion of Sub-Clause 15.2.1(d) in **(iii) Analysis** above, *see* under **(v) Improvements** in the commentary on Sub-Clause 7.5 [*Defects and Rejection*] above.

(2) As discussed in **(iii) Analysis** above, it is assumed (*see* Sub-Clause 15.2.3(a)(i)), but is not expressly provided for in Sub-Clause 5.1 (as it should be), that the Employer is entitled to require that all subcontracts be assigned to it if Sub-Clause 15.2 applies. The Employer will normally want the subcontracts of subcontractors who have been performing well to be assigned to it. Accordingly, provision should be made for this in Sub-Clause 5.1.[66]

(3) Sub-Clause 15.2 could usefully provide that both Parties shall mitigate (minimise) their costs, losses, damages and expenses in the event of any termination.

(4) As discussed in **(iii) Analysis** above, the terms used in Sub-Clause 15.2.1(h) ('corrupt, fraudulent, collusive or coercive practice') need to be defined and the provision needs generally to be clarified.[67]

(5) Given the increasing length and complexity of the RB, it would be useful to add a Clause or Sub-Clause which lists all the Clauses or Sub-Clauses of the Conditions which are to survive the termination of the Contract, whether termination follows the complete execution of the Works, issuance of the Performance Certificate and return of the Performance Security or results from earlier termination under Clauses 15, 16, 18 or otherwise under applicable law. Those Clauses and Sub-Clauses that survive would deal with such matters as governing law, limitation of liability, the Employer's use of Contractor's Documents, liability for defects, patents and protected rights, indemnities, confidentiality, disputes and arbitration.[68]

--ooOOoo--

66. *See* under **(v) Improvements** of the commentary on Sub-Clause 5.1 [*Subcontractors*] above.
67. In addition, the Employer could require in the tender dossier that tenderers have in place ISO 37001 anti-bribery management systems and that they are certified under that standard. *See* www.iso.org/iso/iso37001 accessed 10 November 2022.
68. *See* for examples of this, Sub-Clause 44.13 of the *Form of Contract – Lump Sum Contract – The Red Book* (5th edn, IChemE 2013), and art. 55.18 of the

15.3 Valuation after Termination for Contractor's Default

After termination of the Contract under Sub-Clause 15.2 [*Termination for Contractor's Default*], the Engineer shall proceed under Sub-Clause 3.7 [*Agreement or Determination*] to agree or determine the value of the Permanent Works, Goods and Contractor's Documents, and any other sums due to the Contractor for work executed in accordance with the Contract (and, for the purpose of Sub-Clause 3.7.3 [*Time limits*], the date of termination shall be the date of commencement of the time limit for agreement under Sub-Clause 3.7.3).

This valuation shall include any additions and/or deductions, and the balance due (if any), by reference to the matters described in sub-paragraphs (a) and (b) of Sub-Clause 14.13 [*Issue of FPC*].

This valuation shall not include the value of any Contractor's Documents, Materials, Plant and Permanent Works to the extent that they do not comply with the Contract.

After termination of the Contract, the Engineer shall proceed under Sub-Clause 3.7 to agree or determine the value of the Permanent Works, Goods and Contractor's Documents and any other sums due to the Contractor. The valuation shall include the balance due by reference to the matters in Sub-Clause 14.13(a) and (b).

Commentary

(i) Main Changes from RB/99:

(1) The first paragraph has been changed to take account of the new procedure for agreeing or determining claims in Sub-Clause 3.7 and to refer to a date of termination.

(2) The second and third paragraphs dealing with valuation are entirely new.

ICC Model Turnkey Contract for Major Projects (ICC Publication no 797 E 2020).

(ii) Related Clauses/Sub-Clauses: 3.7 [*Agreement or Determination*], 14.2.3 [*Advance Payment – Repayment of Advance Payment*], 14.13 [*Issue of FPC*], 15.2 [*Termination for Contractor's Default*] and 15.4 [*Payment after Termination for Contractor's Default*].

(iii) Analysis: After termination under Sub-Clause 15.2 and before determining what may be due to be paid by the Employer to the Contractor (or vice versa), which is addressed in Sub- Clause 15.4, it is first necessary to value the work done by the Contractor and this is the purpose of Sub-Clause 15.3. It is in both Parties' interests that the Engineer promptly undertakes to value the work done pursuant to Sub-Clause 3.7,[69] as this will form the basis of the final payment to be made to the Contractor under the Contract. If the advance payment has not been repaid before termination, then, pursuant to Sub-Clause 14.2.3, the outstanding balance becomes immediately due and payable to the Employer and, if not promptly paid, the Employer may call the Contractor's Advance Payment Guarantee.

--ooOOoo--

15.4 Payment after Termination for Contractor's Default

The Employer may withhold payment to the Contractor of the amounts agreed or determined under Sub-Clause 15.3 [*Valuation after Termination for Contractor's Default*] until all the costs, losses and damages (if any) described in the following provisions of this Sub-Clause have been established.

After termination of the Contract under Sub-Clause 15.2 [*Termination for Contractor's Default*], the Employer shall be entitled subject to Sub-Clause 20.2 [*Claims for Payment and/or EOT*] to payment by the Contractor of:

(a) the additional costs of execution of the Works, and all other costs reasonably incurred by the Employer (including costs incurred in clearing, cleaning and reinstating the Site as described under Sub-Clause 11.11 [*Clearance of Site*]), after allowing for any sum due to the Contractor

69. This would be 'a matter to be agreed or determined' by the Engineer pursuant to sub-paragraph (a) of Sub-Clause 3.7.

under Sub-Clause 15.3 [*Valuation after Termination for Contractor's Default*];

(b) any losses and damages suffered by the Employer in completing the Works; and

(c) Delay Damages, if the Works or a Section have not been taken over under Sub-Clause 10.1 [*Taking Over the Works and Sections*] and if the date of termination under Sub-Clause 15.2 [*Termination for Contractor's Default*] occurs after the date corresponding to the Time for Completion of the Works or Section (as the case may be). Such Delay Damages shall be paid for every day that has elapsed between these two dates.

After termination of the Contract, the Employer may withhold payment to the Contractor of amounts due under Sub-Clause 15.3 until all costs and damages (if any) of the Employer have been established. The Employer shall be then entitled subject to Sub-Clause 20.2 to: (a) the additional costs of execution of the Works and all other costs reasonably incurred by the Employer, (b) any losses and damages in completing the Works, and (c) Delay Damages, if the Works or a Section have not been taken over under Sub-Clause 10.1 and if the date of termination under Sub-Clause 15.2 occurs after the date corresponding to the Time for Completion of the Works or Section.

Commentary

(i) Main Changes from RB/99:

(1) The first paragraph essentially replaces sub-paragraph (b) in Sub-Clause 15.4 of RB/99.

(2) The second paragraph begins by referring to the procedure for Claims in Sub-Clause 20.2 instead of to Sub-Clause 2.5 as in sub-paragraph (a) in RB/99.

(3) Sub-paragraphs (a) and (b) correspond roughly to sub-paragraph (c) in RB/99 but refer now to costs 'reasonably' incurred by Employer, including costs in clearing, cleaning and reinstating the Site under Sub-Clause 11.11.

(4) Sub-paragraph (c), providing for the recovery of Delay Damages if the Works or a Section have not been taken over by the date of termination under Sub-Clause 15.2 and if that date occurs after the date corresponding to the Time for Completion of the Works or Section, is new.

(ii) Related Clauses / Sub-Clauses: 1.15 [*Limitation of Liability*], 4.2.2 [*Performance Security-Claims under the Performance Security*], 8.8 [*Delay Damages*], 10.1 [*Taking Over the Works and Sections*], 11.11 [*Clearance of Site*], 15.2 [*Termination for Contractor's Default*], 15.3 [*Valuation after Termination for Contractor's* Default] and 20.2 [*Claims for Payment and/or EOT*].

(iii) Analysis:

(1) Recoverable damages

This Sub-Clause provides essentially that, after the Contract has been terminated for the Contractor's default, the Contractor may recover nothing unless and until the Employer's damages have been established. As a practical matter, this may mean that the Contractor will be entitled to no payment, if any, until after the Works have been completed by the Employer, or by a new contractor on the Employer's behalf, *which may often be years later*.

The damages which the Employer may recover, subject to Sub-Clause 20.2, include: (a) the 'additional costs' of execution of the Works (e.g., the cost of engaging a new Contractor), and all other costs reasonably incurred by the Employer, after allowing for any sum due to the Contractor under Sub-Clause 15.3; (b) any losses and damages suffered by the Employer in completing the Works;[70] and (c) Delay Damages, if the Works or a Section has not been taken over under Sub-Clause 10.1 and if the date of termination under Sub-Clause 15.2 occurs after the date corresponding to the Time for Completion of the Works or Section. Thus, Delay Damages will run only until the date of termination and not, as under some contracts, continue thereafter, e.g., until completion of the Works by the Employer or a new Contractor.[71]

70. However, these are limited by Sub-Clause 1.15 [*Limitation of Liability*], i.e., loss of use of any Works, loss of profit, loss of any contract and indirect or consequential damages are excluded except in the case of fraud, gross negligence, deliberate default or reckless misconduct. In addition, Sub-Clause 1.15 places a cap on the Contractor's total liability subject to the same exception.
71. In this connection, *see* Julian Bailey, *Construction Law* (3rd edn, London Publishing, UK, 2020) vol 2, 843 (para. 9.138). For a discussion of alternative approaches to liquidated damages for delay under a contract completed by another party, *see* David Inns and Kevin Touhey, 'Liquidated Damages for Delay after Termination: Until Completion Do Us Part?' (2019) 35(4) Const L J, 221.

The Employer's right to damages is subject to Sub-Clause 20.2, requiring it to give a Notice of Claim within 28 days[72] and to comply with the other procedures in that Sub-Clause.

Given the limitations on the Contractor's liability under both Sub-Clauses 1.15 [*Limitation of Liability*] and 8.8 [*Delay Damages*], where the Contractor is in substantial delay, the Employer may have an incentive to terminate the Contract, pursuant to Sub-Clause 15.2.1(c), once any maximum amount of Delay Damages stated in the Contract Data is reached.[73]

(2) The decision to terminate requires a careful weighing of pros and cons

As a practical matter, if the Contract is terminated for the Contractor's default, when substantial work remains to be done, and the Employer decides to replace the Contractor by another contractor, the time and cost of doing so may be considerable given the likely need for new pre-qualification and invitation to tender procedures to identify and engage a new Contractor and the possibility of litigation and/or arbitration with the terminated Contractor. Apart from the loss of time, this cost, together with other damages, may far exceed whatever amount may have been due to the Contractor at the termination date. Among the difficult issues to which termination may give rise (and whose cost will need to be quantified) is who will take responsibility for the Contractor's uncompleted work – a new contractor may be unwilling to do so without full indemnification from the Employer. Even if there are amounts withheld from the original Contractor under the first paragraph of this Sub-Clause, it may be years before a new Contractor is engaged and can complete the Works and the additional costs, losses and damages of having the Works completed can be established. Consequently, an Employer will want to weigh very carefully the advantages of termination (including the availability of the Performance Security, Retention Money and other funds of the Contractor which it may be holding, if any) against the disadvantages, risks, costs and uncertainties, before making the decision to terminate the Contractor.

72. *Subject to a time bar.*

73. Unless the Employer can demonstrate that the Contractor has committed fraud, gross negligence, deliberate default or reckless misconduct, as provided for in Sub-Clause 1.15, enabling it to claim its full actual damages, assuming they are higher.

(iv) Improvements: As part of any settlement under this Sub-Clause, the Employer should require the Contractor to provide an appropriately worded discharge, just as the Contractor is obliged to provide a discharge – but in another form – under Sub-Clause 14.12 [*Discharge*].[74]

15.5 Termination for Employer's Convenience

The Employer shall be entitled to terminate the Contract at any time for the Employer's convenience, by giving a Notice of such termination to the Contractor (which Notice shall state that it is given under this Sub-Clause 15.5).

After giving a Notice to terminate under this Sub-Clause, the Employer shall immediately:

(a) have no right to further use any of the Contractor's Documents, which shall be returned to the Contractor, except those for which the Contractor has received payment or for which payment is due under a Payment Certificate;
(b) if Sub-Clause 4.6 [*Co-operation*] applies, have no right to allow the continued use (if any) of any Contractor's Equipment, Temporary Works, access arrangements and/or other of the Contractor's facilities or services; and
(c) make arrangements to return the Performance Security to the Contractor.

Termination under this Sub-Clause shall take effect 28 days after the later of the dates on which the Contractor receives this Notice or the Employer returns the Performance Security. Unless and until the Contractor has received payment of the amount due under Sub-Clause 15.6 [*Valuation after Termination for Employer's Convenience*], the Employer shall not execute (any part of) the Works or arrange for (any part of) the Works to be executed by any other entities.

After this termination, the Contractor shall proceed in accordance with Sub-Clause 16.3 [*Contractor's Obligations After Termination*].

74. *See* the commentary on Sub-Clause 14.12 [*Discharge*] above.

The Employer may terminate the Contract at any time for its convenience by giving a Notice to the Contractor stating it is given under Sub-Clause 15.5. Thereafter, the Employer shall immediately: (a) cease use of, and return, the Contractor's Documents, except those for which the Contractor has been paid or for which payment is due under a Payment Certificate; (b) cease use of any Contractor's Equipment, Temporary Works, access arrangements and/or other facilities; and (c) return the Performance Security. Termination takes effect 28 days after the later of the dates on which the Contractor receives this Notice or the Employer returns the Performance Security.

Commentary

(i) Main Changes from RB/99: Before RB/99, the Employer had no right to terminate the contract for its convenience. Thus, this was a new provision in RB/99.[75] The main changes from Sub-Clause 15.5 of RB/99 are as follows:

(1) The Employer's Notice of termination must now state that it is given under Sub-Clause 15.5.
(2) The second paragraph, including sub-paragraphs (a), (b) and (c), is new.
(3) Whereas the former Sub-Clause had provided that the Employer could not terminate the Contract for its convenience in order to execute the Works itself or arrange for another contractor to do so, the new Sub-Clause contains no such prohibition but provides that unless and until the Contractor has received payment under Sub-Clause 15.6,[76] the Employer shall not execute or arrange for any part of the Works to be executed by other entities.

75. Although the relevant Sub-Clause in RB/99, Sub-Clause 15.5, did not use the expression 'termination for convenience'. The concept (and expression) of 'termination for convenience' appears to have originated in the context of Federal Government procurement in the United States. One of the first cases was *United States v Corliss Steam-Engine Company* 91 US (1 Otto) 321 (1875). In that case, the US Department of the Navy cancelled contracts for the supply of equipment for warships as their completion had become unnecessary following the end of the US civil war (1861-1865). The current US Federal Government provision on this subject is *FAR* s 52.249-2.
76. Sub-Clause 15.6 is a new Sub-Clause in RB/17.

(4) Under Sub-Clause 15.6, the Contractor is entitled to loss of profit on the anticipated work which will no longer be performed, whereas it was not so entitled under RB/99.

(ii) Related Clauses / Sub-Clauses: 1.3 [*Notices and Other Communications*], 1.10 [*Employer's Use of Contractor's Documents*], 1.15 [*Limitation of Liability*], 1.16 [*Contract Termination*], 4.2.3 [*Performance Security-Return of the Performance Security*], 4.6 [*Co-operation*], 15.6 [*Valuation after Termination for Employer's Convenience*] and 16.3 [*Contractor's Obligations after Termination*].

(iii) Analysis:

(1) Employer's right to terminate for convenience

This Sub-Clause entitles the Employer to terminate the Contract 'at any time for the Employer's convenience', giving the Employer broad freedom to do so by a Notice at its discretion.[77] The Employer does not have to give any reason for doing so.[78]

(2) Employer would only invoke for a compelling reason

Some of the reasons why an Employer may wish to terminate a Contract for its convenience include that:

> the project in question has become economically unviable, or if the initial purpose of the project has been rendered obsolete, or, […] if a critical planning application has been refused, thus rendering the project works impossible.[79]

Absent some such compelling need to terminate a project, the Employer is unlikely to invoke this Sub-Clause as, pursuant to Sub-Clause 15.7, the Employer will have to pay the Contractor for not only the value of the work done *but also the Contractor's loss of profit on the anticipated work*

77. However, this Notice must state that it is given under Sub-Clause 15.5 and comply with Sub-Clause 1.3.
78. In contrast to Sub-Clause 8.9 [*Employer's Suspension*] which provides that if the Engineer instructs the Contractor to suspend progress of the Works the instruction must state the 'cause of the suspension', although this was not an obligation (only an option) under Sub-Clause 8.8 [*Suspension of Work*] in RB/99.
79. *See* Julian Bailey, *Construction Law* (3rd edn, London Publishing, UK, 2020) vol 2, 809 (para. 9.74).

which will no longer be performed.[80] The Contractor will recover essentially what it would have recovered under Sub-Clause 16.4 had it terminated the Contract for the Employer's default.[81] The Employer will be entitled to copy, use and communicate the Contractor's Documents for the purposes of completing the Works (if it wishes to do so) for which the Contractor has received payment.[82]

The solution provided by RB/17 is justifiable, at least in the case of a contract between private parties. A contract is an item of property, and if the Employer wishes to terminate it prematurely (a right, incidentally, that the Contractor does not enjoy), then the Employer should ordinarily be required to compensate the Contractor for its damages, which would include the profit it might otherwise have earned under the Contract. Otherwise, the Contractor will not have been made whole for having been deprived of the Contract.

(3) After termination for convenience, the Employer is free to engage others

Another notable difference with the corresponding Sub-Clause in RB/99 is that, provided that the Contractor has been paid the amount due to it under Sub-Clause 15.6,[83] the Employer is entirely free to execute the remainder of the Works itself or arrange for them to be executed by other entities.[84] Thus, if the Employer finds a less expensive or more efficient way for having the work done, then, provided that it pays off the

80. *See* notably sub-para. (b) of Sub-Clause 15.6 to which Sub-Clause 15.7 refers.
81. The situation in this respect under RB/17 is to be contrasted with that under RB/99. Under Sub-Clause 15.5 [*Employer's Entitlement to Termination*] of RB/99, the Contractor was to be paid in accordance with Sub-Clause 19.6 [*Optional Termination, Payment and Release*] which provided that the Contractor was to be paid the same amount as if the Contract had been terminated on account of Force Majeure (referred to as 'Exceptional Events' under RB/17). That is, the value of work done but not the loss of profit on the anticipated work which would no longer be performed. In short, the Contractor would ordinarily be the clear loser in the case of termination for convenience under RB/99, whereas it will be a clear winner in the same case under RB/17 – assuming the Contract was to be profitable for the Contractor.
82. Sub-Clause 1.10 (d) (ii).
83. Promptly after termination, the Employer must also return the Performance Security to the Contractor. Sub-paragraph (b) of Sub-Clause 4.2.3 [*Performance Security – Return of the Performance Security*].
84. Sub-Clause 15.5, third paragraph.

Contractor fully, as described above, the Employer is free to proceed with the new solution.[85] As the Contractor will have been fully compensated for being deprived of the Contract, it is logical that the Employer should thereafter have a free hand as well.

(iv) Related law: In many countries, in the case of public contracts, the public party has the right, either by law or by contract, to terminate such a contract for its convenience.[86] However, the conditions under which it may do so vary. Thus, in Chile,[87] France[88] and the United States,[89] for example, the public party may only do so if termination is in the government's or the public interest or, in Chile, national security demands it.[90] In France, the private party will be able to recover not merely its damages and costs at the date of termination but also its anticipated profit, if any[91] (as under Sub-Clause 15.6), with the result, apparently, that the remedy is rarely used,[92] whereas in England and Wales[93] and the United States[94] it will not recover its anticipated profit, if any.

---

85. This is consistent with Sub-Clause 13.1 [*Right to Vary*], second paragraph, providing that 'a Variation shall not comprise the omission of any work which is to be carried out by the Employer or by others unless otherwise agreed by the Parties'.
86. Paul Craig, 'Specific Powers of Public Contractors' in (Rozen Noguellou and Ulrich Stelkens eds) *Comparative Law on Public Contracts* (Bruylant, Brussels, 2010) 173, 175 (s 2).
87. Claudio Moraga Klenner in 'Chile' in (Rozen Noguellou and Ulrich Stelkens eds) *Comparative Law on Public Contracts* (Bruylant, Brussels, 2010) 465, 478 (s 4.4).
88. *See* **Section 4 Common Law and Civil Law Compared – 4.6.6 Termination for Convenience** of **Chapter II Applicable Law** above.
89. *FAR* s 52.249.2 (a).
90. Claudio Moraga Klenner in 'Chile' in (Rozen Noguellou and Ulrich Stelkens eds) *Comparative Law on Public Contracts* (Bruylant, Brussels, 2010) 465, 478 (s 4.4).
91. *See* **Section 4 Common Law and Civil Law Compared – 4.6.6 Termination for Convenience** of **Chapter II Applicable Law** above.
92. Rozen Noguellou in 'France' in (Rozen Noguellou and Ulrich Stelkens eds) *Comparative Law on Public Contracts* (Bruylant, Brussels, 2010) 675, 690 (s 4.1.2).
93. Paul Craig and Martin Trybus, 'England and Wales' in (Rozen Noguellou and Ulrich Stelkens eds) *Comparative Law on Public Contracts* (Bruylant, Brussels, 2010) 339, 352 (s 4.3).
94. Joshua Schwartz, 'United States of America' in (Rozen Noguellou and Ulrich Stelkens eds) *Comparative Law on Public Contracts* (Bruylant, Brussels,

In France[95] and the United States,[96] at least, the public party may terminate the contract for its convenience whether this is provided for in the contract or not.

As the Contractor is fully indemnified under Sub-Clause 15.6 for its losses, including loss of profit on the anticipated work it will no longer perform, none of the restrictions which may apply to termination for convenience clauses which do not provide for full indemnification of the Contractor (e.g., the need for the Employer to demonstrate a change of circumstances or that it is terminating in good faith)[97] is relevant here.

15.6 Valuation after Termination for Employer's Convenience

> After termination under Sub-Clause 15.5 [*Termination for Employer's Convenience*] the Contractor shall, as soon as practicable, submit detailed supporting particulars (as reasonably required by the Engineer) of:
>
> (a) the value of work done, which shall include:

2010) 613, 641 (s 4.3). United States government contract law also recognises as valid a clause which permits the government to convert what would otherwise be a wrongful termination of contract into an after-the-fact exercise of the termination for convenience clause, enabling an arguably wrongful termination to be transformed into a contractually permissible termination for convenience. Carl J Circo, *Contract Law in the Construction Industry Context* (Routledge, Abingdon, Oxon, 2020), 105-106 and Philip Bruner and Patrick O'Connor, *Bruner & O'Connor on Construction Law* (Thomson Reuters, St Paul, MN, 2016) vol 5, 985-987 (s 18.37).

95. *See* **Section 4 Common Law and Civil Law Compared – 4.6.6 Termination for Convenience** of **Chapter II Applicable Law**, above.
96. According to the *Christian Doctrine* derived from the US Court of Claims case, *G.L. Christian & Associates v United States* 312 F.2d 418 rehearing denied 320 F.2d 345 (Ct Cl 1963) cited in John M Mastin and others (eds), *Smith, Currie and Hancock's Common Sense Construction Law: A Practical Guide for the Construction Professional* (6th edn, Wiley, Hoboken, NJ, 2020) 655.
97. For a description of such restrictions *see*, for example, Bronwyn Lincoln and Katherine Aistrope, 'Current Issues in the Termination of Construction Contracts', [2002] ICLR 488; Martin Hirst, 'Termination for Convenience Clauses-A Shield or a Sword in Times of Economic Downturn', [2010] ICLR 419 and Franco Mastrandrea, 'Termination for Convenience: Recovering the Expectancy', [2015] ICLR 286.

(i) the matters described in sub-paragraphs (a) to (e) of Sub-Clause 18.5 [*Optional Termination*], and

(ii) any additions and/or deductions, and the balance due (if any), by reference to the matters described in sub-paragraphs (a) and (b) of Sub-Clause 14.13 [*Issue of FPC*]; and

(b) the amount of any loss of profit or other losses and damages suffered by the Contractor as a result of this termination.

The Engineer shall then proceed under Sub-Clause 3.7 [*Agreement or Determination*] to agree or determine the matters described in sub-paragraphs (a) and (b) above (and, for the purpose of Sub-Clause 3.7.3 [*Time limits*], the date the Engineer receives the Contractor's particulars under this Sub-Clause shall be the date of commencement of the time limit for agreement under Sub-Clause 3.7.3).

The Engineer shall issue a Payment Certificate for the amount so agreed or determined, without the need for the Contractor to submit a Statement.

After termination under Sub-Clause 15.5, the Contractor shall, as soon as practicable, submit detailed supporting particulars of: (a) the value of work done and (b) the amount of any loss of profit or other losses and damages suffered by the Contractor. The Engineer shall then proceed under Sub-Clause 3.7 to agree or determine these matters. The Engineer shall then issue a Payment Certificate for the amount so agreed or determined without the need for the Contractor to submit a Statement.

Commentary

(i) Main Changes from RB/99: This Sub-Clause is entirely new. Sub-Clause 15.5 [*Employer's Entitlement to Termination*] of RB/99 had provided that in the case of a termination for the Employer's convenience, the Contractor would be paid in accordance with Sub-Clause 19.6 [*Optional Termination, Payment and Release*].

(ii) Related Clauses / Sub-Clauses: 1.15 [*Limitation of Liability*], 3.7 [*Agreement or Determination*] 14.13 [*Issue of FPC*], 15.5 [*Termination for*

Employer's Convenience], 15.7 [*Payment after Termination for Employer's Convenience*] and 18.5 [*Optional Termination*].

(iii) Analysis: After termination of the Contractor for default pursuant to Sub-Clause 15.2, as discussed above, the Engineer should proceed to value the work it has done pursuant to Sub-Clause 15.3 for the purposes of determining what may be due to the Contractor. However, in the case of a termination for convenience, as the Contractor is being prevented from completing the Works at the Employer's request, the procedure for the valuation of the Contractor's work is reversed. In this case, as provided for in Sub-Clause 15.6, the Contractor's valuation of the work done is the 'starting point' for determining what monies may be due, not the Engineer's valuation as in the case of a termination for the Contractor's default. Accordingly, under Sub-Clause 15.6, the Engineer is required to proceed under Sub-Clause 3.7 on the basis of the Contractor's financial particulars as described in sub-paragraphs (a) and (b) of Sub-Clause 15.6.

Under sub-paragraph (a)(i), the value of work done which the Contractor is entitled to recover includes the matters described in Sub-Clause 18.5(a) to (e). These include, among other things, 'any other Cost or liability [...] reasonably incurred by the Contractor in the expectation of completing the Works',[98] the Cost of removal of Temporary Works and Contractor's Equipment and their return to the Contractor's country, as well as the Cost of the repatriation of the Contractor's staff and labour.[99] Under paragraph (a) (ii), the Contractor is entitled to any amounts that are due or have become due under the Contract or otherwise (after crediting any amounts due to the Employer),[100] thereby making clear that they are unaffected by the Employer's decision to terminate.

As noted in relation to Sub-Clause 15.5 above, under sub-paragraph (b) of the present Sub-Clause, the Contractor is entitled, most significantly (and unlike under RB/99), to 'the amount of any loss of profit' or other losses and damages that it might suffer as a result of this termination. *Thus, the Contractor is entitled to recover the profit it might otherwise have earned under the Contract.*[101]

98. Sub-Clause 18.5(c).
99. Sub-Clause 18.5(d) and (e).
100. Sub-Clause 14.13(a) and (b).
101. The Contractor will have the burden of proving the level of profit, if any, that it could have been expected to earn had it completed the Contract. The Contractor's right to loss of profit under Sub-Clause 15.6 is expressly

(iv) Related Law: *See* the discussion under **(iv) Related Law** in the commentary on Sub-Clause 15.5 above.

(v) Improvements: In the case of the termination of a contract by an employer for its convenience, some forms of contract, instead of entitling the contractor to profit on the unperformed balance of the work, provide for the payment to the contractor of a predetermined termination fee.[102] The amount of this fee reduces progressively, the greater the amount of work which had been executed (and hence profit potentially earned by the Contractor) by the date of termination. Payment of such a fee 'strike[s] a balance between the owner's need for the flexibility to terminate the agreement for its convenience and the contractor's right to be compensated for at least a portion of the financial benefit it bargained for'.[103]

--ooOOoo--

15.7 Payment after Termination for Employer's Convenience

> The Employer shall pay the Contractor the amount certified in the Payment Certificate under Sub-Clause 15.6 [*Valuation after Termination for Employer's Convenience*] within 112 days after the Engineer receives the Contractor's submission under that Sub-Clause.

excluded by sub-para. (c) from the limitation of liability provided for by the first paragraph of Sub-Clause 1.15 (although Sub-Clause 1.15 mistakenly refers to Sub-Clause 15.7 instead of 15.6). However, what if the Contract was a 'losing contract', that is, one where the Contractor would suffer a loss on completion? In this case, not only would there be no profit for the Contractor to recover but the Employer would, by terminating the Contract, be rescuing the Contractor from further losses for which, in theory at least, the Employer might claim compensation. Nevertheless, the Engineer is accorded no right by this Sub-Clause to reduce what is owed to the Contractor on account of a projected loss on the Contract.

102. *See* e.g. Sub-Clause 10.4.1(c) of FIDIC's *Short Form of Contract* ('Green Book'), second edition, 2021 and s 14.4.3 of the American Institute of Architects ('AIA') Document A201- 2017 *General Conditions of the Contract for Construction*.

103. Peter W Hahn and others (eds), The *2017 A201 Deskbook* (ABA For Const L, Chicago, IL, 2017), 237.

The Employer shall pay the amount of the Payment Certificate under Sub-Clause 15.6 within 112 days after the Engineer receives the Contractor's submission.

Commentary

(i) Main Changes from RB/99: This Sub-Clause is entirely new. Sub-Clause 15.5 of RB/99 had merely provided that the Contractor shall be paid in accordance with Sub-Clause 19.6 [*Optional Termination, Payment and Release*].

(ii) Related Clauses / Sub-Clauses: 1.3 [*Notices and Other Communications*], 1.15 [*Limitation of Liability*], 4.2.2 [*Performance Security – Claims under the Performance Security*], 14 [*Contract Price and Payment*], 15.5 [*Termination for Employer's Convenience*] and 15.6 [*Valuation after Termination for Employer's Convenience*].

(iii) Analysis: FIDIC has calculated the 112 days after the Engineer receives the Contractor's submission[104] on the basis that there would be a maximum of 84 days for an agreement or determination by the Engineer under Sub-Clause 3.7[105] plus 28 days for both certification of the amount due by the Engineer and payment by the Employer of the amount certified (84 + 28 = 112). This accelerated certification and payment schedule by comparison to that provided for by Clause 14 is justified, in FIDIC's view, by the fact that the Employer is benefitting as it is terminating the Contract for its convenience.

(iv) Improvements: As part of any settlement under this Sub-Clause, the Employer should require the Contractor to provide an appropriately worded discharge, just as the Contractor is obliged to provide a discharge – but in another form – under Sub-Clause 14.12 [*Discharge*] when the Contract is not terminated prematurely.[106]

--ooOOoo--

104. The submission must comply with Sub-Clause 1.3 [*Notices and Other Communications*].
105. 42 days for an agreement and, failing that, 42 days for a determination.
106. *See* the commentary on Sub-Clause 14.12 [*Discharge*] above.

16 Suspension and Termination by Contractor

This Clause provides that if the Engineer fails to certify payment to the Contractor, or if the Employer commits certain specified defaults, the Contractor may, after 21 days' Notice, suspend work or reduce the rate of work unless and until the Employer remedies the default. Thereafter, if the Engineer continues to fail to certify payment to the Contractor, or if the other default or defaults for which the Employer is responsible continue, then: (1) in some cases, after a *Notice of the Contractor's intention to terminate the Contract*, the Contractor may terminate the Contract by a *Notice of termination*; and (2) in other cases, the Contractor may terminate the Contract immediately by a *Notice of termination*.

--ooOOoo--

16.1 Suspension by Contractor

If:

(a) the Engineer fails to certify in accordance with Sub-Clause 14.6 [*Issue of IPC*];

(b) the Employer fails to provide reasonable evidence in accordance with Sub-Clause 2.4 [*Employer's Financial Arrangements*];

(c) the Employer fails to comply with Sub-Clause 14.7 [*Payment*]; or

(d) the Employer fails to comply with:

(i) a binding agreement, or final and binding determination under Sub-Clause 3.7 [*Agreement or Determination*]; or

(ii) a decision of the DAAB under 21.4 [*Obtaining DAAB's Decision*] (whether binding or final and binding)

and such failure constitutes a material breach of the Employer's obligations under the Contract,

the Contractor may, not less than 21 days after giving a Notice to the Employer (which Notice shall state that it is given under this Sub-Clause 16.1), suspend work (or reduce the rate of work) unless and until the Employer has remedied such a default.

> This action shall not prejudice the Contractor's entitlements to financing charges under Sub-Clause 14.8 [*Delayed Payment*] and to termination under Sub-Clause 16.2 [*Termination by Contractor*].
>
> If the Employer subsequently remedies the default as described in the above Notice before the Contractor gives a Notice of termination under Sub-Clause 16.2 [*Termination by Contractor*], the Contractor shall resume normal working as soon as is reasonably practicable.
>
> If the Contractor suffers delay and/or incurs Cost as a result of suspending work (or reducing the rate of work) in accordance with this Sub-Clause, the Contractor shall be entitled subject to Sub-Clause 20.2 [*Claims for Payment and/or EOT*] to EOT and/or payment of such Cost Plus Profit.

If: (a) the Engineer fails to certify payment under Sub-Clause 14.6; (b) the Employer fails to provide reasonable evidence under Sub-Clause 2.4; (c) the Employer fails to comply with Sub-Clause 14.7; or (d) the Employer fails to comply with a binding agreement or a final and binding determination under Sub-Clause 3.7, or any decision of the DAAB under Sub-Clause 21.4, and such failure constitutes a material breach of the Contract, the Contractor may, after 21 days' Notice and without prejudice to its other rights, suspend (or reduce the rate of) work unless and until the default is remedied. If the Employer subsequently remedies the default before the Contractor gives a Notice of termination under Sub-Clause 16.2, the Contractor shall resume normal working. If the Contractor suffers delay and/or incurs Cost, the Contractor shall be entitled subject to Sub-Clause 20.2 to EOT and/or such Cost plus Profit.

Commentary

(i) Main Changes from RB/99: The right of the Contractor to suspend (or reduce the rate of) work was introduced into the RB by Sub-Clause 69.4 of RB/87 where it had simply applied if the Employer had failed to pay the amount due under any certificate of the Engineer. By Sub-Clause 16.1 of RB/99, the right of the Contractor was broadened to include other failures by the Employer or the Engineer. In Sub-Clause 16.1 of RB/17, there are two further changes compared to Sub-Clause 16.1 in RB/99:

(1) sub-paragraph (d) provides for an additional right for the Contractor to suspend, in case of the Employer's failure to comply with a binding agreement or a final and binding determination under Sub-Clause 3.7 or any decision of the DAAB under Sub-Clause 21.4, which constitutes a material breach of the Contract; and

(2) the requirement in the first paragraph that the Contractor's Notice expressly state that it is given under Sub-Clause 16.1 is also new.

(ii) Related Clauses / Sub-Clauses: 1.3 [*Notices and Other Communications*], 2.4 [*Employer's Financial Arrangements*], 3.7 [*Agreement or Determination*], 11.3 [*Extension of Defects Notification Period*], 14.6 [*Issue of IPC*], 14.7 [*Payment*], 14.8 [*Delayed Payment*], 16.2 [*Termination by Contractor*], 20.2 [*Claims for Payment and/or EOT*] and 21.4 [*Obtaining DAAB's Decision*].

(iii) Analysis:

(1) Purpose of Sub-Clause

As a counterpart, among other things, for the Contractor's obligation to execute the Works and proceed 'with due expedition and without delay',[1] the Contractor is entitled to regular interim payments from the Employer.[2] Therefore, it is logical that, if the Contractor should not be receiving interim payments (because the Engineer has failed to certify under Sub-Clause 14.6 or the Employer to pay under Sub-Clause 14.7) or may not be likely to do so (because the Employer is unable to comply with Sub-Clause 2.4, or other material obligations), the Contractor should be able – as this Sub-Clause provides – after not less than 21 days' Notice to the Employer, to suspend work or reduce the rate of work unless and until the Employer has remedied its default.

This Sub-Clause – which is the only provision in the Conditions entitling the Contractor to suspend work – (1) enables the Contractor to pressure the Employer to comply (and/or cause the Engineer to comply[3]) with the Contract, without terminating the Contract, and (2) relieves the

1. Sub-Clause 8.1, second paragraph.
2. Pursuant to Sub-Clauses 14.3, 14.6 and 14.7.
3. The Notice must be copied to the Engineer, *see* Sub-Clause 1.3, last paragraph.

Contractor from continuing to perform work for which it is not, or may not in future, be paid, mitigating the Contractor's damages.

(2) Grounds for suspension

Sub-paragraph (a) refers to a failure of the Engineer to certify 'in accordance with Sub-Clause 14.6'. In this connection, the Engineer has the express power under that Sub-Clause to withhold certain amounts in an IPC.[4] Thus, if the Engineer were properly to exercise that authority, the Contractor would not be entitled to give a Notice of its intention to suspend work as the Engineer would simply be exercising a right under that Sub-Clause.[5]

Sub-paragraph (b) is significant as it indicates that the Contractor is entitled not only to be paid currently but also not to be deprived of reasonable evidence that the Employer will have the means to do so. This is important as the execution of a construction contract may extend over several years during which the financial circumstances of the Employer might change. It clarifies that, if the Employer does not provide reasonable evidence of the necessary financial arrangements (pursuant to Sub-Clause 2.4), the Contractor is not required to continue working.

Sub-paragraph (c) calls for no special comment. Sub-paragraph (d) provides for where the Employer fails to comply with a binding agreement or a final and binding determination of the Engineer or any decision of the DAAB, and such failure constitutes a 'material breach'[6] of the Contract. The events listed in sub-paragraphs (f) through (j) of Sub-Clause 16.2.1 indicate the gravity required for a breach to be considered material.

(3) Notice

Assuming a ground for suspension exists, the Contractor may – not less than 21 days after giving a Notice to the Employer, *which must state that it is given under Sub-Clause 16.1 and be copied to the Engineer*[7] – suspend work or reduce the rate of work unless and until the Employer has remedied this default. Given the importance of such a Notice, the Contractor will want to take special care to comply with the formal requirements of both Sub-Clause 1.3 and Sub-Clause 16.1.

4. Sub-Clause 14.6.2, second paragraph.
5. And hence there would be no 'fail[ure] to certify' under Sub-Clause 14.6.
6. For the meaning of 'material breach', *see* under **(iii) Analysis** of the commentary on Sub-Clause 15.2 above.
7. *See* Sub-Clause 1.3 [*Notices and Other Communications*].

(4) Consequences of suspension

If, in compliance with this Sub-Clause, the Contractor suspends work or reduces the rate of work, with the result that completion may be delayed, the Contractor will normally be entitled to an EOT and/or payment of Cost plus Profit, subject to complying with the claims procedure provided for in Sub-Clause 20.2.[8]

The suspension or reduction in the rate of work does not prejudice the Contractor's entitlement to financing charges on delayed payments under Sub-Clause 14.8 or to termination of the Contract under Sub-Clause 16.2.[9] Indeed, the Contractor's decision to suspend may merely be a prelude to the giving of a Notice of intention to terminate under Sub-Clause 16.2.1.

(iv) Related law:

(1) Common law and civil law

As indicated in item **(i) Main Changes from RB/99** above, the early editions of the RB gave the Contractor no right to suspend if the Employer was in breach of contract, almost certainly because the Contractor had no such right under English common law.[10] However, as discussed earlier, the opposite is generally true in civil law countries except (often) in the case of public or administrative contracts.[11] Under French and other civil laws, the Contractor enjoys the defence of non-performance,[12] pursuant to which if the Employer does not perform a substantial contractual duty, such as paying amounts certified by the Engineer, the Contractor may use this as an excuse not to perform a correlative duty, such as by suspending work. Thus, Sub-Clause 16.1 gives effect to a legal principle that

8. Sub-Clause 16.1, last paragraph.
9. Sub-Clause 16.1, second paragraph.
10. As stated by one authority, 'in England and the Commonwealth there is no common law right to suspend work [...] upon a breach by the other party' and to do so would therefore be 'extremely perilous'. Atkin Chambers, *Hudson's Building and Engineering Contracts* (14th edn, Sweet & Maxwell, London, 2020) 916 (para. 8-016). To the same effect *see* Julian Bailey, *Construction Law* (3rd edn, London Publishing, UK, 2020) vol 2, 651 (para. 6.423).
11. *See* **Section 4 Common Law and Civil Law Compared – 4.3.3 Defence of Non-Performance** (*Exceptio Non Adimpleti Contractus*) of **Chapter II Applicable Law** above.
12. *Exceptio non adimpleti contractus* or in French *l'exception d'inexécution*.

generally exists under the civil law which is not available under English and Commonwealth common law, unless provided for by statute.[13]

(2) UNIDROIT Principles

Article 7.1.3 (*Withholding performance*) of the UNIDROIT Principles provides for the defence of non-performance, as follows:

(1) Where the parties are to perform simultaneously, either party may withhold performance until the other party tenders its performance.
(2) Where the parties are to perform consecutively, the party that is to perform later may withhold its performance until the first party has performed.[14]

--ooOOoo--

16.2 Termination by Contractor

Termination of the Contract under this Clause shall not prejudice any other rights of the Contractor, under the Contract or otherwise.

16.2.1 Notice

The Contractor shall be entitled to give a Notice (which shall state that it is given under this Sub-Clause 16.2.1) to the Employer of the Contractor's intention to terminate the Contract or, in the case of sub-paragraph (g)(ii), (h), (i) or (j) below a Notice of termination, if:

(a) the Contractor does not receive the reasonable evidence within 42 days after giving a Notice under Sub-Clause 16.1 [*Suspension by Contractor*] in respect of a failure to comply with Sub-Clause 2.4 [*Employer's Financial Arrangements*];
(b) the Engineer fails, within 56 days after receiving a Statement and supporting documents, to issue the relevant Payment Certificate;

13. This right has been made available to a contractor by statute in the UK by s 112 of the HGCRA.
14. This art. needs to be read together with art. 6.1.4 (*Order of performance*) of the UNIDROIT Principles.

(c) the Contractor does not receive the amount due under any Payment Certificate within 42 days after the expiry of the time stated in Sub-Clause 14.7 [*Payment*];

(d) the Employer fails to comply with:

 (i) a binding agreement, or final and binding determination under Sub-Clause 3.7 [*Agreement or Determination*]; or

 (ii) a decision of the DAAB under 21.4 [*Obtaining DAAB's Decision*] (whether binding or final and binding)

 and such failure constitutes a material breach of the Employer's obligations under the Contract;

(e) the Employer substantially fails to perform, and such failure constitutes a material breach of, the Employer's obligations under the Contract;

(f) the Contractor does not receive a Notice of the Commencement Date under Sub-Clause 8.1 [*Commencement of Works*] within 84 days after receiving the Letter of Acceptance;

(g) the Employer:

 (i) fails to comply with Sub-Clause 1.6 [*Contract Agreement*], or

 (ii) assigns the Contract without the required agreement under Sub-Clause 1.7 [*Assignment*];

(h) a prolonged suspension affects the whole of the Works as described in sub-paragraph (b) of Sub-Clause 8.12 [*Prolonged Suspension*];

(i) the Employer becomes bankrupt or insolvent; goes into liquidation, administration, reorganisation, winding-up or dissolution; becomes subject to the appointment of a liquidator, receiver, administrator, manager or trustee; enters into a composition or arrangement with the Employer's creditors; or any act is done or any event occurs which is analogous to or has a similar effect to any of these acts or events under applicable Laws; or

(j) the Employer is found, based on reasonable evidence, to have engaged in corrupt, fraudulent, collusive or coercive practice at any time in relation to the Works or to the Contract.

16.2.2 Termination

Unless the Employer remedies the matter described in a Notice given under Sub-Clause 16.2.1 [*Notice*] within 14 days of receiving the Notice, the Contractor may by giving a second Notice to the Employer immediately terminate the Contract. The date of termination shall then be the date the Employer receives this second Notice.

However, in the case of sub-paragraph (g)(ii), (h), (i) or (j) of Sub-Clause 16.2.1 [*Notice*], by giving a Notice under Sub-Clause 16.2.1 the Contractor may terminate the Contract immediately and the date of termination shall be the date the Employer receives this Notice.

If the Contractor suffers delay and/or incurs Cost during the above period of 14 days, the Contractor shall be entitled subject to Sub-Clause 20.2 [*Claims for Payment and/or EOT*] to EOT and/or payment of such Cost Plus Profit.

The Contractor is entitled to give a Notice (which states it is given under this Sub-Clause) to the Employer of the Contractor's intention to terminate the Contract in the seven cases listed in sub-paragraphs (a), (b), (c), (d), (e), (f) and (g)(i). Unless the Employer remedies the matter within 14 days of receiving the Notice, the Contractor may, by a second Notice to the Employer and without prejudice to the Contractor's rights, immediately terminate the Contract. The Contractor is also entitled to give a Notice of termination, terminating the Contract immediately, in the four cases listed in sub-paragraphs g (ii), (h), (i) and (j). If the Contractor suffers delay and/or incurs Cost during the 14 days, it is entitled subject to Sub-Clause 20.2 to EOT and/or payment of such Cost plus Profit.

Commentary

(i) Main Changes from RB/99:

(1) Whereas Sub-Clause 16.2 of RB/99 had provided that, if the Employer committed any of the defaults listed in it, the

Contractor could terminate the Contract upon giving 14 days' notice to the Employer, the new Sub-Clause, which has been broken down into two parts (16.2.1 and 16.2.2), provides for the Contractor to give either or both:

(a) a *Notice of intention to terminate the Contract* applicable in the case of seven grounds for termination (sub-paragraphs (a) through (g)(i)) which, if not remedied within 14 days, may entitle the Contractor to give a second Notice terminating the Contract immediately; and

(b) a *Notice terminating the Contract immediately* applicable in the case of four grounds for termination (sub-paragraphs (g)(ii) through (j)).

(2) Certain grounds for termination are new, specifically:

(a) sub-paragraph (d) in the case of the Employer's failure to comply with a binding agreement or final and binding determination under Sub-Clause 3.7 or any decision of the DAAB, if such failure constitutes a material breach of the Contract;

(b) sub-paragraph (f) if the Contractor does not receive Notice of the Commencement Date within 84 days after receiving the Letter of Acceptance; and

(c) sub-paragraph (j) where the Employer has engaged in corrupt practices.

(3) The wording of sub-paragraph (e) has been changed (from the corresponding sub-paragraph in RB/99, sub-paragraph (d)) by requiring that the Employer's substantial failure to perform its obligations constitutes a material breach of the Contract.

(4) If the Contractor suffers delay and/or incurs Costs during the relevant 14-day period, it is entitled, subject to Sub-Clause 20.2, to an EOT and/or payment of such Cost plus Profit,[15] which is new.

(ii) Related Clauses / Sub-Clauses: 1.3 [*Notices and Other Communications*], 1.6 [*Contract Agreement*], 1.7 [*Assignment*], 1.10 [*Employer's Use of Contractor's Documents*], 1.16 [*Contract Termination*], 2.4 [*Employer's Financial Arrangements*], 3.7 [*Agreement or Determination*], 4.2.3 [*Performance Security – Return of the Performance Security*], 8.1 [*Commencement of Works*], 8.12 [*Prolonged Suspension*], 14.7 [*Payment*], 16.1 [*Suspension by Contractor*], 16.3 [*Contractor's Obligation after Termina-*

15. Sub-Clause 16.2.2, last paragraph.

tion], 16.4 [*Payment after Termination by Contractor*], 17.1 [*Responsibility for Care of the Works*], 20.2 [*Claims for Payment and/or EOT*] and 21.4 [*Obtaining DAAB's Decision*].

(iii) Analysis:

(1) General

As terminating a Contract for the Employer's default is one of the most serious steps that the Contractor can take, it should only be done as a last resort, after taking legal advice. When considering whether to do so, the Contractor needs to ascertain, not only that its termination (or, stated intention to terminate) is justified under a contractual ground for termination, that is, any of sub-paragraphs (a) to (j) of Sub-Clause 16.2.1, but also that, in implementing termination, it respects meticulously the procedural steps in Sub-Clauses 16.2.1, where appropriate, and 16.2.2. If the Contractor is unable to justify termination under its chosen ground (or grounds) and/or fails to respect the procedure for termination, it may find itself to have breached the Contract and, if the Contract terminates, to be responsible in damages to the Employer for having wrongfully terminated the Contract.[16]

(2) Notice of intention to terminate (Sub-Clause 16.2.1) and/or to terminate (Sub-Clause 16.2.2)

The procedure for termination of the Contract by the Contractor for the Employer's default has (like the procedure for terminating the Contractor for its default under Clause 15) been clarified in RB/17, and several additional grounds for termination (or for giving a Notice of intention to terminate, as discussed below) have been added.

The Contractor must now give a *Notice of intention to terminate the Contract* – *not* a Notice to terminate the Contract – to the Employer on one (or more) of the grounds described in sub-paragraphs (a) through (g)(i), which are all cases of default which the Employer is still entitled to remedy. *This Notice must state that it is given under Sub-Clause 16.2.1.* If the Employer fails to remedy the matter 'within 14 days of receiving the

16. *See* Atkin Chambers, *Hudson's Building and Engineering Contracts* (14th edn, Sweet & Maxwell, London, 2020) 969-974 (para. 8-068-073) and Justin Sweet and others, *Construction Law for Design Professionals, Construction Managers, and Contractors* (Cengage Learning, Stamford, CT, 2015) 59-64, for the common law position.

Notice',[17] the Contractor may, by a second Notice, immediately terminate the Contract, pursuant to Sub-Clause 16.2.2, without prejudice to the Contractor's other rights, e.g., to claim damages.[18]

On the other hand, the grounds for termination described in sub-paragraphs (g)(ii) through (j) are generally cases of default which cannot be remedied easily or at all. Accordingly, in those cases, the termination procedure is different: the Contractor is entitled under Sub-Clause 16.2.1 to give a *Notice of immediate termination of the Contract, which must also state that it is given under Sub-Clause 16.2.1.*[19]

Pursuant to Sub-Clause 1.3(b), any Notice should be identified as a Notice.[20] In the case of any Notice terminating the Contract immediately, the date of termination is the date the Employer receives this Notice.[21]

(3) Grounds for Notice of intention to terminate or of termination (Sub-Clause 16.2.1)

(a) Employer's failure to provide reasonable evidence, or to pay, and failure of Engineer to certify (sub-paragraphs (a), (b) and (c))

Sub-paragraphs (a), (b) and (c) presuppose that the Employer continues to be in default for specified time periods on similar grounds as had entitled the Contractor to suspend or reduce the rate of work pursuant to Sub-Clause 16.1 [*Suspension by the Contractor*]. However, only in the case of sub-paragraph (a) (prolonged failure of the Contractor to receive reasonable evidence in accordance with Sub-Clause 2.4) is the Contractor required to have given a prior Notice of its default to the Employer under

17. '**day**' means a calendar day. Sub-Clause 1.1.25. *See also* Sub-Clause 1.3 describing when a Notice is received or deemed to have been received as well as the possible need to send a copy to the Engineer. As regards the inherent ambiguity of 'within' a period of time, *see* point (2) under **(v) Improvements** in the commentary on Sub-Clause 1.2 [*Interpretation*] above.
18. Sub-Clause 16.2.
19. *See* Sub-Clause 16.2.2, second paragraph.
20. *See* Sub-Clause 1.3 [*Notices and Other Communications*] for other relevant details.
21. As regards the receipt of Notices, *see* Sub-Clause 1.3 [*Notices and Other Communications*]. By exercising the procedure for termination, the Contractor does not forego any of its other rights against the Employer. *See* the first sentence of Sub-Clause 16.2.

Sub-Clause 16.1, which has gone unremedied, before giving a Notice of intention to terminate under Sub-Clause 16.2.1.[22]

(b) Failure of Employer to comply (sub-paragraph (d))

As for the ground for termination in sub-paragraph (d), *see* the commentary on the similar provision contained in sub-paragraph (a) of Sub-Clause 15.2.1 above.

(c) Employer's material breach (sub-paragraph (e))

Sub-paragraph (e) refers to where the Employer has committed a 'material breach'[23] of the Contract and the text could simply have been drafted in this way.

(d) No Notice of Commencement Date (sub-paragraph (f))

Under Sub-Clause 8.1, the Engineer must give a Notice of the Commencement Date to the Contractor within 42 days after the Contractor receives the Letter of Acceptance. Thus, if another 42 days would pass, making for a total of 84 days, without the Contractor having received such Notice, the Contractor is entitled by this provision to give a Notice of intention to terminate the Contract.[24]

(e) Employer's failure to comply, assignment, prolonged suspension, bankruptcy or insolvency (sub-paragraphs (g), (h) and (i))

Sub-paragraphs (g), (h) and (i) are essentially unchanged from RB/99 except that assignment of the Contract without the agreement of the Contractor (sub-paragraph (g)(ii)) has now become a ground for immediate termination under Sub-Clause 16.2.2. The right of the Contractor to terminate the Contract immediately in the case of bankruptcy or insolvency of the Employer will be subject to applicable bankruptcy laws, as described in the commentary on Sub-Clause 15.2.1(g) above in the case of termination of the Contract in the case of the Contractor's bankruptcy or insolvency.

22. A failure under sub-paragraph (b) and a non-payment under sub-paragraph (c) each also gives rise to a deemed Dispute under Sub-Clause 21.4 (a), permitting its direct referral to the DAAB.
23. For a definition of 'material breach', *see* under **(iii) Analysis** of the commentary on Sub-Clause 15.2 above.
24. The World Bank's COPA has changed this provision to 'within 180 days [instead of 84 days] after receiving the Letter of Acceptance, for reasons not attributable to the Contractor'. Sub-Clause 16.2.1(f), COPA.

(f) Corrupt practices (sub-paragraph (j))

The ground for immediate termination in sub-paragraph (j) is expressed in the same terms as the ground for termination in Sub-Clause 15.2.1(h) except that sub-paragraph (j) refers to a finding, based on reasonable evidence, that the Employer has engaged in a corrupt or illicit practice whereas Sub-Clause 15.2.1(h) refers to a finding, based on reasonable evidence, that the Contractor has engaged in a corrupt or illicit practice. Accordingly, all the comments made in relation to Sub-Clause 15.2.1(h) above as regards the Contractor are directly relevant here as regards the Employer.

--ooOOoo--

If the Contractor suffers delay and/or incurs Cost during the 14 days after it has given a Notice of intention to terminate the Contract, the Contractor is now entitled, subject to Sub-Clause 20.2, to an EOT and/or payment of such Cost plus Profit.[25] The assumption is that, as the Contractor has been impelled to give such a Notice by a breach of contract of the Employer, the Employer should be bearing the consequences of that breach from the date that the Notice is given. However, if this assumption proves incorrect – as there has, in fact, been no breach – the Contractor should not be entitled to such relief.

(iv) Related Law:

(1) General

As regards Sub-Clause 16.2.1(a) (entitling the Contractor to give a Notice of intention to terminate if the Employer fails to provide reasonable evidence in accordance with Sub-Clause 2.4), the UNIDROIT Principles provide for a somewhat analogous situation:

> A party who reasonably believes that there will be a fundamental non-performance [of contract] by the other party may demand adequate assurance of due performance [...] Where this assurance is not provided within a reasonable time the party demanding it may terminate the contract.[26]

Otherwise, *see* under item **(iv) Related Law** of the commentary on Sub-Clause 15.2 above. The same considerations apply to termination of the Contract by the Contractor as they apply to termination of the

25. Sub-Clause 16.2.2, last paragraph.
26. Art. 7.3.4 (*Adequate assurance of due performance*).

Contract by the Employer under that Sub-Clause, including the one which is repeated (for emphasis) in point (2) immediately below.

(2) Civil law countries influenced by French law

As stated earlier,[27] it remains the case in many civil law countries that a party must obtain an order from a court (or an arbitral award) in order to be able to terminate a contract. In such countries, termination of a contract without a court order will only be possible where a contract contains a clause that effectively excludes the need for a court order. As stated in relation to the commentary on Sub-Clause 1.16 [*Contract Termination*] above, it remains to be seen whether that Sub-Clause will be sufficient to permit termination without a court order in those countries.

(v) Improvements:

(1) Sub-paragraph (e) of Sub-Clause 16.2.1 can be simplified to read as follows: 'the Employer has committed a material breach of the Contract'.

(2) Comment numbers (3) (relating to mitigation of damages), (4) (relating to the need to define corrupt and other improper practices) and (5) (relating to provisions that survive termination) under **(v) Improvements** of the commentary on Sub-Clause 15.2 are equally relevant here.

--ooOOoo--

16.3 Contractor's Obligations after Termination

After termination of the Contract under Sub-Clause 15.5 [*Termination for Employer's Convenience*], Sub-Clause 16.2 [*Termination by Contractor*] or Sub-Clause 18.5 [*Optional Termination*], the Contractor shall promptly:

(a) cease all further work, except for such work as may have been instructed by the Engineer for the protection of life or property or for the safety of the Works. If the Contractor incurs Cost as a

27. **Section 4 Common Law and Civil Law Compared – 4.3.5 Contract Termination** of **Chapter II Applicable Law** above.

result of carrying out such instructed work the Contractor shall be entitled subject to Sub-Clause 20.2 [*Claims for Payment and/or EOT*] to be paid such Cost Plus Profit;

(b) deliver to the Engineer all Contractor's Documents, Plant, Materials and other work for which the Contractor has received payment; and

(c) remove all other Goods from the Site, except as necessary for safety, and leave the Site.

After termination of the Contract under Sub-Clauses 15.5, 16.2 and 18.5, the Contractor shall: (a) cease all work except as instructed by the Engineer and, if the Contractor incurs Cost, the Contractor shall be entitled subject to Sub-Clause 20.2 to be paid such Cost plus Profit; (b) deliver to the Engineer all Contractor's Documents, Plant and Materials for which the Contractor has received payment, and (c) remove all other Goods from the Site.

Commentary

(i) Main Changes from RB/99: The main change is, in relation to sub-paragraph (a), that, if the Contractor incurs Cost as a result of carrying out instructions of the Engineer, the Contractor is now explicitly entitled, subject to Sub-Clause 20.2, to payment of such Cost plus Profit.

(ii) Related Clauses / Sub-Clauses: 1.10 [*Employer's Use of Contractor's Documents*], 15.5 [*Termination for Employer's Convenience*], 16.2 [*Termination by Contractor*], 18.5 [*Optional Termination*] and 20.2 [*Claims for Payment and/or EOT*].

(iii) Analysis: This Sub-Clause describes the obligations of the Contractor after termination pursuant to Sub-Clause 16.2 (and to other Sub-Clauses providing for termination except for the Contractor's default) and before it leaves the Site. Following termination, the Contractor is no longer responsible for the care of the Works.[28] Accordingly, as an exception to this general rule, this Sub-Clause requires the Contractor, to comply with any instruction of the Engineer for the protection of life or property or for the safety of the Works. As the Contractor is no longer

28. Sub-Clause 17.1, second paragraph.

responsible for the care of the Works, the Contractor is entitled, subject to Sub-Clause 20.2, to be paid Cost Plus Profit.[29]

--ooOOoo--

16.4 Payment after Termination by Contractor

After termination under Sub-Clause 16.2 [*Termination by Contractor*], the Employer shall promptly:

(a) pay the Contractor in accordance with Sub-Clause 18.5 [*Optional Termination*]; and

(b) subject to the Contractor's compliance with Sub-Clause 20.2 [*Claims for Payment and/or EOT*], pay the Contractor the amount of any loss of profit or other losses and damages suffered by the Contractor as a result of this termination.

After termination under Sub-Clause 16.2, the Employer shall: (a) pay the Contractor in accordance with Sub-Clause 18.5 and (b) subject to Sub-Clause 20.2, pay the Contractor the amount of any loss of profit or other losses and damages as a result of this termination.

Commentary

(i) Main Changes from RB/99: The only significant changes are: (1) that the Employer is no longer required to return the Performance Security under this Sub-Clause as its return is now provided for in Sub-Clause 4.2.3(b) and (2) the new requirement that in order for the Contractor to be paid, pursuant to Sub-Clause (b), it must comply with Sub-Clause 20.2.

(ii) Related Clauses / Sub-Clauses: 1.10 [*Employer's Use of Contractor's Documents*], 1.15 [*Limitation of Liability*], 4.2 [*Performance Security*], 16.2 [*Termination by Contractor*], 18.5 [*Optional Termination*] and 20.2 [*Claims for Payment and/or EOT*].

(iii) Analysis: As regards sub-paragraph (a) *see* the commentary on Sub-Clause 18.5 [*Optional Termination*] below. Sub-paragraph (b) is very important to the Contractor as it provides that, where the Contractor has terminated the Contract pursuant to Sub-Clause 16.2, the Contractor

29. After termination, the Employer will also be entitled 'to copy, use and communicate' the Contractor's Documents for the purposes of completing

will be entitled to be paid the profit, if any, that it would have earned had it been able to complete the Contract.[30] The Contractor will have the burden of proving the level of profit, if any.[31] However, the Contractor must comply with Sub-Clause 20.2 which will require it, among other things, to give a Notice of Claim within 28 days – *otherwise it will be time barred.*

--ooOOoo--

17 Care of the Works and Indemnities

This Clause provides that the Contractor is fully responsible, with certain exceptions, for the care of the Works, Goods and Contractor's Documents from the Commencement Date until issue of the Taking-Over Certificate for the Works. The Contractor may also be liable for loss or damage to them after issue of the Taking-Over Certificate in certain cases. It also provides for each Party to indemnify the other against third-party claims arising from the execution of the Works, including claims of alleged infringement of intellectual and industrial property rights, and provides for shared indemnities in certain cases.

--ooOOoo--

17.1 Responsibility for Care of the Works

> Unless the Contract is terminated in accordance with these Conditions or otherwise, subject to Sub-Clause 17.2 [*Liability for Care of the Works*] the Contractor shall take full responsibility for the care of

the Works (if it wishes to do so) for which the Contractor has received payment. Sub-Clause 1.10 (d) (ii). The *Guidance*, 45, and the World Bank's COPA contain special provisions in relation to Sub-Clause 16.3 and (in the case of COPA) Sub-Clause 17.1 regarding Employer-Supplied Materials and/or Employer's Equipment. Sub-Clauses 16.3 and 17.1, COPA.

30. Entitlement to loss of profit under this Sub-Clause is an explicit exclusion from the limitation on a Party's (the Employer's) liability in the first paragraph of Sub-Clause 1.15 [*Limitation of Liability*].
31. The one other case where the Contractor is entitled by the Conditions to recover this profit is where the Contract is terminated by the Employer for its convenience pursuant to Sub-Clause 15.6 [*Valuation after Termination for Employer's Convenience*]. *See* under **(iii) Analysis** of the commentary on that Sub-Clause above.

the Works, Goods and Contractor's Documents from the Commencement Date until the issue (or deemed issue) of the Taking-Over Certificate for the Works, when responsibility for the care of the Works shall pass to the Employer. If a Taking-Over Certificate is issued (or is deemed to be issued) for any Section or Part, responsibility for the care of the Section or Part shall then pass to the Employer.

If the Contract is terminated in accordance with these Conditions or otherwise, the Contractor shall cease to be responsible for the care of the Works from the date of termination.

After responsibility has accordingly passed to the Employer, the Contractor shall take responsibility for the care of any work which is outstanding on the Date of Completion, until this outstanding work has been completed.

If any loss or damage occurs to the Works, Goods or Contractor's Documents, during the period when the Contractor is responsible for their care, from any cause whatsoever except as stated in Sub-Clause 17.2 [*Liability for Care of the Works*], the Contractor shall rectify the loss or damage at the Contractor's risk and cost, so that the Works, Goods or Contractor's Documents (as the case may be) comply with the Contract.

Subject to Sub-Clause 17.2, the Contractor shall take full responsibility for the care of the Works, Goods and Contractor's Documents from the Commencement Date until the issue of the Taking-Over Certificate for the Works, when responsibility shall pass to the Employer. If a Taking-Over Certificate is issued for any Section or Part, responsibility for its care shall then pass to the Employer. The Contractor shall take responsibility for the care of any work which is outstanding on the Date of Completion.

If any loss or damage occurs to the Works, Goods or Contractor's Documents while the Contractor is responsible for them, from any cause except as stated in Sub-Clause 17.2, the Contractor shall rectify the same at its risk and cost.

Commentary

(i) Main Changes from RB/99: This Sub-Clause corresponds with minor wording changes to Sub-Clause 17.2 [*Contractor's Care of the Works*] of RB/99 except that:

(1) under the first paragraph, the Contractor is responsible for the care not only of the Works and Goods from the Commencement Date until the Taking-Over Certificate but also now for Contractor's Documents;
(2) the second paragraph of this Sub-Clause dealing with where the Contract is terminated is entirely new; and
(3) the last paragraph of Sub-Clause 17.2 of RB/99 has now, with minor wording changes, been moved down to become the first paragraph of Sub-Clause 17.2 of RB/17.

(ii) Related Clauses / Sub-Clauses: 1.8 [*Care and Supply of Documents*], 1.15 [*Limitation of Liability*], 7.7 [*Ownership of Plant and Materials*], 10.1 [*Taking Over the Works and Sections*], 11.1 [*Completion of Outstanding Work and Remedying Defects*], 15.2 [*Termination for Contractor's Default*], 16.2 [*Termination by Contractor*], 17.2 [*Liability for Care of the Works*], 17.6 [*Shared Indemnities*], 18.6 [*Release from Performance under the Law*] and 19.2 [*Insurance to Be Provided by the Contractor*].

(iii) Analysis:

(1) Responsibility for care of the Works

Sub-Clauses 17.1 and 17.2 need to be read together. The first sentence of Sub-Clause 17.1 provides that, subject to Sub-Clause 17.2 which contains certain exceptions, the Contractor has full responsibility for the care of the Works, Goods and Contractor's Documents from the Commencement Date until the 'issue (or deemed issue) of the Taking-Over Certificate' for the Works.[1] However, if before the issue of such Certificate, a Taking-Over Certificate is issued (or is deemed to be issued) for any Section or Part, responsibility for the care of that Section or Part would then pass to the Employer (the transfer of responsibility is not delayed, in that case,

1. However, Sub-Clause 1.8 [*Care and Supply of Documents*], second paragraph, provides that the Contractor is only responsible for the care of the Contractor's Documents 'unless and until submitted to the Engineer' and not until the 'issue of the Taking-Over Certificate'. *See* the commentary on Sub-Clause 1.8 above.

until a Taking-Over Certificate is issued for the Works as a whole).[2] Responsibility for the care of the Works also passes to the Employer if the Contract is terminated under the Conditions 'or otherwise'.[3]

After responsibility is passed to the Employer, the Contractor remains responsible to complete any work which is outstanding on the Date of Completion.[4]

(2) Liability for loss

It is understandable and normal that under this Sub-Clause the Contractor must rectify any loss or damage to the Works at its risk and cost, except as stated in Sub-Clause 17.2. The Contractor has possession of the Site and is executing the Works.[5] However, the full consequences of a risk allocation determined by reference to the Commencement Date may be less obvious in the case of Goods, that is, Contractor's Equipment, Materials, Plant and Temporary Works, as illustrated by the ICC case described under **(iv) Related Law** immediately below.[6]

(iv) Related law: In an ICC case, a Middle East-based Contractor, the claimant, had entered into a construction contract – based on RB/87 – with the Government of an Asian State, the Employer, for the performance of certain works in that State.

Immediately following the Commencement Date, while the Contractor was mobilising the Contractor's Equipment, Plant and materials in the

2. Responsibility for the care of the Works, Goods and Contractor's Documents is to be distinguished from ownership of Plant and Materials. The transfer of ownership of Plant and Materials to the Employer takes place according to Sub-Clause 7.7 [*Ownership of Plant and Materials*], as explained in the commentary on that Sub-Clause above, and may occur before responsibility for the care of the Works and other things is transferred.
3. Responsibility passes on the 'date of termination'. Sub-Clause 17.1, second paragraph. The expression 'or otherwise' in the Conditions refers to a legal ground for termination. *Guide to the Use of FIDIC Conditions of Contract for Works of Civil Engineering Construction, Fourth Edition* (FIDIC 1989) 119 (commenting on Sub-Clause 53.1 [*Notice of Claim*] in RB/87).
4. Sub-Clause 17.1, third paragraph.
5. The Contractor is required to secure its obligations under Sub-Clause 17.1 (and Sub-Clause 17.2) to the Employer and others by insurance pursuant to Sub-Clauses 19.2.1 and 19.2.2. Thus, the cost of rectification should be covered by insurance subject to permitted deductible limits in the Contract Data.
6. *See* Sub-Clause 1.1.44 **'Goods'**.

Contractor's country for shipment to the Asian State concerned, about one thousand miles away, the Contractor's country was invaded and war ensued. As a result of looting by the invaders, all of the Contractor's Equipment, Plant and materials to perform the works in the Asian State were lost. Under RB/87 (as under RB/17), as the Commencement Date had occurred, the Contractor had full responsibility for the care of the Contractor's Equipment, Plant and materials *except in the case of, among other things, war, hostilities and invasion* (which are, similarly, excluded from being the Contractor's risk by Sub-Clause 17.2 of RB/17).[7] Accordingly, the Contractor claimed for the value of the lost Contractor's Equipment, Plant and materials and, as the Employer denied the Contractor's claim, brought an ICC arbitration to recover for the same.

The tribunal found that, as the Commencement Date (defined in a manner similar to RB/17) had occurred, the Contractor had assumed responsibility for the Contractor's Equipment, Plant and materials to be incorporated in the works, *except in the case of loss or damage resulting from 'war' and 'invasion'*. Consequently, the Employer was held to be liable for the loss of the Contractor's Equipment, Plant and materials even though this had occurred as a result of the invasion of the Contractor's country, before their transportation to the Employer's country and before the Contractor had started work on the Site.[8] The case turned on the fact that the Commencement Date had occurred which, in turn, determined the allocation of risk for the Contractor's Equipment, Plant and materials. While decided in relation to RB/87, the principle of the case is equally applicable to Clause 17 of RB/17.

(v) Improvements: It should be clarified whether the Contractor is responsible for the care of Contractor's Documents until submitted to the Engineer, as indicated by Sub-Clause 1.8, second paragraph, or until the issue of the Taking-Over Certificate, as indicated by the first paragraph of this Sub-Clause.

--ooOOoo--

7. Sub-Clause 17.2(e) excludes Exceptional Events under Sub-Clause 18.1 which include in sub-para. (a) 'war, hostilities [...] invasion'.
8. Final award, ICC case 8677 (1997), ICC Int'l Ct Arb Bull, vol 19, no 2 – 2008, 71-76 (commentary 60-63).

17.2 Liability for Care of the Works

The Contractor shall be liable for any loss or damage caused by the Contractor to the Works, Goods or Contractor's Documents after the issue of a Taking-Over Certificate. The Contractor shall also be liable for any loss or damage, which occurs after the issue of a Taking-Over Certificate and which arose from an event which occurred before the issue of this Taking-Over Certificate, for which the Contractor was liable.

The Contractor shall have no liability whatsoever, whether by way of indemnity or otherwise, for loss or damage to the Works, Goods or Contractor's Documents caused by any of the following events (except to the extent that such Works, Goods or Contractor's Documents have been rejected by the Engineer under Sub-Clause 7.5 [*Defects and Rejection*] before the occurrence of any of the following events):

(a) interference, whether temporary or permanent, with any right of way, light, air, water or other easement (other than that resulting from the Contractor's method of construction) which is the unavoidable result of the execution of the Works in accordance with the Contract;

(b) use or occupation by the Employer of any part of the Permanent Works, except as may be specified in the Contract;

(c) fault, error, defect or omission in any element of the design of the Works by the Employer or which may be contained in the Specification and Drawings (and which an experienced contractor exercising due care would not have discovered when examining the Site and the Specification and Drawings before submitting the Tender), other than design carried out by the Contractor in accordance with the Contractor's obligations under the Contract;

(d) any operation of the forces of nature (other than those allocated to the Contractor in the Contract Data) which is Unforeseeable or against which an experienced contractor could not reasonably have been expected to have taken adequate preventative precautions;

(e) any Exceptional Event; and/or
(f) any act or default of the Employer, the Employer's Personnel or the Employer's other contractors.

If any of the events described in sub-paragraphs (a) to (f) above occurs and results in loss and/or damage to the Works, Goods or Contractor's Documents the Contractor shall promptly give a Notice to the Engineer. Thereafter, the Contractor shall rectify any such loss and/or damage that may arise to the extent instructed by the Engineer. Such instruction shall be deemed to have been given under Sub-Clause 13.3.1 [*Variation by Instruction*] and, in the case of sub-paragraph (e) above, shall be without prejudice to any other rights the Contractor may have under Sub-Clause 18.4 [*Consequences of an Exceptional Event*].

If the loss and/or damage to the Works or Goods or Contractor's Documents results from a combination of:

(i) any of the events described in sub-paragraphs (a) to (f) above, and
(ii) a cause for which the Contractor is liable,

and the Contractor suffers a delay and/or incurs Cost from rectifying the loss and/or damage, the Contractor shall subject to Sub-Clause 20.2 [*Claims for Payment and/or EOT*] be entitled to a proportion of EOT and/or Cost Plus Profit to the extent that any of the above events have contributed to such delay and/or Cost.

The Contractor shall be liable for any loss or damage it causes to the Works, Goods or Contractor's Documents after the issue of a Taking-Over Certificate, as well as for any loss or damage which occurs after the issue of such Certificate from an event which occurred before its issue for which the Contractor was liable. However, the Contractor shall have no liability for loss or damage caused by events listed in sub-paragraphs (a) through (f) (except where the Works, Goods or Contractor's Documents have been rejected by the Engineer under Sub-Clause 7.5).

Subject to Sub-Clause 18.4, if any of the listed events results in damage to the Works, Goods or Contractor's Documents, the Contractor shall give Notice to the Engineer and rectify the loss or damage to the extent instructed by the Engineer, which instruction shall be deemed given under Sub-Clause 13.3.1. If the loss or damage results from a combination of any such events and any cause for which the Contractor is liable, the Contractor may, subject to Sub-Clause 20.2, claim an EOT and/or Cost Plus Profit to the extent any of such events contributed to delays and/or Cost.

Commentary

(i) Main Changes from RB/99:

(1) The first paragraph corresponds, with minor changes, to the last paragraph of Sub-Clause 17.2 of RB/99.
(2) The second paragraph corresponds to Sub-Clause 17.3 of RB/99, with a number of changes in the listed events (sub-paragraphs (a), (c), (d), (e) and (f) are either new or partly new), including the elimination of 'Employer's Risks' in the marginal heading.
(3) The third paragraph corresponds to, though it is significantly longer than, the first paragraph of Sub-Clause 17.4 of RB/99.
(4) The last paragraph, dealing with where loss or damage results from a combination of a listed event and a cause for which the Contractor is liable, is entirely new.

(ii) Related Clauses / Sub-Clauses: 1.3 [*Notices and Other Communications*], 1.15 [*Limitation of Liability*], 4.10 [*Use of Site Data*], 7.5 [*Defects and Rejection*], 13.3.1 [*Variation by Instruction*], 17.1 [*Responsibility for Care of the Works*], 17.5 [*Indemnities by Employer*], 17.6 [*Shared Indemnities*], 18.1 [*Exceptional Events*], 18.4 [*Consequences of an Exceptional Event*], 19.2 [*Insurance to be provided by the Contractor*] and 20.2 [*Claims for Payment and/or EOT*].

(iii) Analysis:

(1) Effect of Sub-Clause

This Sub-Clause provides that the Contractor shall be liable for any loss or damage which it has caused to the Works, Goods or Contractor's

Documents after the issue of the Taking-Over Certificate.[9] The Contractor is also liable for any loss or damage which occurs after the issue of that certificate, which arose from an event for which the Contractor was liable before its issue. At the same time, the Sub-Clause provides that the Contractor shall have no liability for any of the six events listed in sub-paragraphs (a) through (f) (except to the extent the Works, Goods or Contractor's Documents had been rejected under Sub-Clause 7.5 before its occurrence).[10]

(2) Excluded events

The events listed in sub-paragraphs (a), (b), (c) and (f) are all events for which the Employer is responsible or considered responsible. Sub-paragraphs (a) and (b) are either comprehended by or complement the Employer's obligation to give the Contractor possession of the Site pursuant to Sub-Clause 2.1.

Sub-paragraph (c) provides that the Employer is responsible for errors in its design of the Works or contained in the Specification and Drawings 'which an experienced contractor exercising due care would not have discovered when examining the Site and the Specification and Drawings before submitting the Tender'. This is similar to the qualification to be found in Sub-Clause 4.7.3 dealing with the allocation of responsibility between the Parties for errors in the items of reference provided by the Engineer.[11]

Sub-paragraph (d) reflects the general philosophy of an RB (like a YB) contract (e.g., as reflected in Sub-Clause 4.12) that the Contractor does not bear the consequences of Unforeseeable adverse conditions, or other adverse conditions against which it could not reasonably have been

9. This should be understood to include the deemed issue of the Taking-Over Certificate, so as to be consistent with Sub-Clause 17.1.
10. The rejection must be done by a Notice to the Contractor with reasons. Sub-Clause 7.5(b).
11. However, the form of the Letter of Tender of RB/17 would make it clearer to a prospective Contractor that it was assuming this responsibility if it contained (which it does not) the following language contained in the form of the Letter of Tender of YB/17: '[w]e have examined, understood and checked these documents [the tender dossier] and have ascertained that they contain no errors or other defects'.

expected to provide, as the Contractor could not reasonably have allowed for them in its price at the tender stage.[12]

As regards, sub-paragraph (e), most, if not all, Exceptional Events are likely to be uninsurable[13] and, unless otherwise stated in the Contract Data, are not required to be insured against.[14] As they are standard exclusions in insurance policies, they have been the subject of interpretation and definition in English and other case law, which can usefully be looked to.[15]

(3) Consequences of an excluded event

If any event in sub-paragraphs (a) to (f) occurs and results in loss and/or damage to the Works, Goods or Contractor's Documents, the Contractor must promptly give a Notice to the Engineer (identifying the event and the resulting loss and/or damage) and, thereafter, must rectify the loss and/or damage if instructed to do so by the Engineer. *Thus, regardless of what may have been the cause of the event – whether it was one listed in sub-paragraphs (a) through (f), and therefore one for which the Contractor was not responsible, or not so listed – the Contractor must rectify the loss and/or damage if so instructed by the Engineer.*[16] However, if the cause was one of the events listed in those sub-paragraphs, then, in addition to any relief to which the Contractor may be entitled under any other Clause – Sub-Clause 18.4 [*Consequences of an Exceptional Event*] is specifically referred to, which may entitle the Contractor to recover Cost

12. As FIDIC has stated:

> the contractor takes all the risks associated with his business of contracting, while the employer takes the risks, inter alia, of the unforeseen and unexpected, i.e., items that are difficult or impossible to price accurately in advance. Consequently, the employer only pays the extra costs incurred when an unforeseeable event or circumstance actually occurs – he does not have to pay what the contractor would have allowed for in his price to cover himself for the risk of that event or circumstance eventuating.

FIDIC Procurement Procedures Guide (FIDIC, 2011) 35.

13. *See* Paul Reed, *Construction All Risks Insurance* (2nd edn, Sweet & Maxwell, London, 2016) 414-28 (paras 15-031-067).
14. Sub-Clause 19.2.1, item (iv) of the last paragraph.
15. *See* Paul Reed, *Construction All Risks Insurance* (2nd edn, Sweet & Maxwell, London, 2016) 414-28 (paras 15-031-067).
16. The cost of rectification should in most cases be covered by insurance pursuant to Sub-Clause 19.2 subject to permitted deductible limits in the Contract Data.

in addition to an EOT[17] – any instruction of the Engineer is deemed to be a Variation instruction under Sub-Clause 13.3.1.[18]

It follows that it will be important to ascertain whether or not an event listed in sub-paragraphs (a) to (f) has resulted in the loss or damage sustained, as this will determine who must bear the cost of rectification. This may call for a complex enquiry, not only into whether the event has occurred but also into whether it has resulted in the loss or damage claimed, as illustrated by, for example, 'war':[19]

> On one view, the consequences of war, for instance, are extremely wide-ranging. For example, it could be argued that, in a general sense, as a result of a state of war existing, trust between neighbours has broken down and a car is stolen. On a much narrower view, however, war itself does not cause any particular loss; instead the losses are caused by specific acts such as the firing of a torpedo that would not, taken in isolation, amount to war.
>
> The [English] courts resolve this issue pragmatically. A loss which arises from an act of war is proximately caused by the war. For example, if a shop is looted or set fire to during fighting, or a ship is sunk by a torpedo, and it occurs in the context of an excluded conflict situation, the loss will be held to have been caused by that conflict situation.
>
> By contrast, losses which are ancillary to the war (or conflict) itself are not caused by the war. For example, a ship which runs aground having altered its usual course in order to avoid enemy submarines will not be lost as a result of enemy peril.[20]

(4) 'Combined' events

If the loss or damage results from a combination of any of the events listed in sub-paragraphs (a) through (f) and a cause for which the

17. In this case, the Notice procedure in Sub-Clause 18.2 [*Notice of an Exceptional Event*] would have also to be respected.
18. As a consequence, the Contractor may be entitled to an EOT and/or adjustment of the Contract Price without having to comply with Sub-Clause 20.2. *See* the last paragraph of Sub-Clause 13.3.1.
19. Sub-Clause 18.1 (a) referred to in sub-para. (e).
20. Paul Reed, *Construction All Risks Insurance* (2nd edn, Sweet & Maxwell, London, 2016) 424-25 (para. 15-056) (case citations omitted).

Contractor is liable, then the responsibility and cost of them are to be shared between the Employer and the Contractor, as provided in the last paragraph of this Sub-Clause.[21]

(iv) Related Law: *See* under **(iv) Related Law** of the commentary on Sub-Clause 17.1 above.

(v) Improvements: As explained in footnote 11 under **(iii) Analysis** above, it would be desirable if the form of the Letter of Tender of RB/17 made it clear (as does the form of the Letter of Tender of YB/17) that a tenderer is responsible for examining the tender dossier and ascertaining that it contained no errors or other defects.

--ooOOoo--

17.3 Intellectual and Industrial Property Rights

In this Sub-Clause, "infringement" means an infringement (or alleged infringement) of any patent, registered design, copyright, trademark, trade name, trade secret or other intellectual or industrial property right relating to the Works; and "claim" means a third party claim (or proceedings pursuing a third party claim) alleging an infringement.

Whenever a Party receives a claim but fails to give a Notice to the other Party of the claim within 28 days of receiving it, the first Party shall be deemed to have waived any right to indemnity under this Sub-Clause.

The Employer shall indemnify and hold the Contractor harmless against and from any claim (including legal fees and expenses) alleging an infringement which is or was:

21. In this case, Sub-Clause 20.2 [*Claims for Payment and/or EOT*] will apply. The Contractor is required to secure its obligations under Clause 17 by insurance pursuant to Sub-Clauses 19.2.1 and 19.2.2. If the Contractor should be subject to third-party claims arising out of an event described in sub-paras (a) to (f) of Sub-Clause 17.2, the Contractor is entitled to be indemnified by the Employer pursuant to Sub-Clause 17.5 (b) commented on below.

(a) an unavoidable result of the Contractor's compliance with the Specification and Drawings and/or any Variation; or
(b) a result of any Works being used by the Employer:

(i) for a purpose other than that indicated by, or reasonably to be inferred from, the Contract, or
(ii) in conjunction with any thing not supplied by the Contractor, unless such use was disclosed to the Contractor before the Base Date or is stated in the Contract.

The Contractor shall indemnify and hold the Employer harmless against and from any other claim (including legal fees and expenses) alleging an infringement which arises out of or in relation to:

(i) the Contractor's execution of the Works; or
(ii) the use of Contractor's Equipment.

If a Party is entitled to be indemnified under this Sub-Clause, the indemnifying Party may (at the indemnifying Party's cost) assume overall responsibility for negotiating the settlement of the claim, and/or any litigation or arbitration which may arise from it. The other Party shall, at the request and cost of the indemnifying Party, assist in contesting the claim. This other Party (and the Contractor's Personnel or the Employer's Personnel, as the case may be) shall not make any admission which might be prejudicial to the indemnifying Party, unless the indemnifying Party failed to promptly assume overall responsibility for the conduct of any negotiations, litigation or arbitration after being requested to do so by the other Party.

Whenever a Party receives a third-party claim alleging an infringement of an intellectual or industrial property right relating to the Works, but fails to give a Notice to the other Party of it within 28 days, the first Party shall be deemed to have waived any right to indemnity under this Sub-Clause.

The Employer shall indemnify the Contractor against any such claim which is: (a) an unavoidable result of compliance with the Specification, Drawings and/or any Variation or (b) a result of any Works being used by the Employer either for a purpose other than that inferable from the Contract or in conjunction with any thing not supplied by the Contractor unless disclosed to the Contractor before the Base Date or stated in the Contract.

The Contractor shall indemnify the Employer against any such claim which arises in relation to the Contractor's execution of the Works or use of Contractor's Equipment.

The indemnifying Party may, at its cost, assume overall responsibility for negotiating the settlement of any claim, litigation or arbitration. The other Party shall, at the request and cost of the indemnifying Party, assist, but shall make no prejudicial admission unless the indemnifying Party should fail to assume overall responsibility for the matter after being requested to do so.

Commentary

(i) Main Changes from RB/99:

(1) In the first paragraph, a 'claim' is defined as a 'third party claim' rather than as a 'claim' as in Sub-Clause 17.5 of RB/99.
(2) In the third and fourth paragraphs, a claim is qualified as '(including legal fees and expenses)', which is new.
(3) In the third paragraph, the Employer must indemnify against any claim of an infringement which is or was an unavoidable result of the Contractor's compliance 'with the Specification and Drawings and/or any Variation' rather than 'with the Contract', as in RB/99.
(4) In the fourth paragraph, the Contractor must indemnify against any claim of infringement which arises in relation to 'the Contractor's execution of the Works' or 'the use of Contractor's Equipment' rather than arising in relation to '(i) the manufacture [...] of any Goods' or '(ii) any design for which the Contractor is responsible', as in RB/99.

(ii) Related Clauses / Sub-Clauses: 1.2 [*Interpretation*], 1.3 [*Notices and Other Communications*], 1.10 [*Employer's Use of Contractor's Docu-*

ments], 1.11 [*Contractor's Use of Employer's Documents*], 1.15 [*Limitation of Liability*], 17.6 [*Shared Indemnities*] and 20.2 [*Claims for Payment and/or EOT*].

(iii) Analysis:

(1) Use of the other Party's intellectual property rights

Each Party has the right to use – and will be using – proprietary documents of the other Party during the execution of the Works. Thus, while the Employer retains the copyright and other intellectual property[22] rights in the Specification, Drawings and other documents made by it or on its behalf, the Contractor has the right to use them for the purposes of the Contract.[23] On the other hand, while the Contractor retains the copyright and other intellectual property rights in the Contractor's Documents[24] (and other design documents made by it), it must give the Employer a licence to use those documents for the purposes of the Works.[25]

(2) Right to indemnity – time bar

Where one Party is using the other's proprietary documents, there is always the risk that a third party may claim either that the Employer's use of the Contractor's Documents infringes its rights or that the Contractor's use of the Employer's documents does so. If such a situation should arise, then, under Sub-Clause 17.3, the Party receiving a claim in relation to the other's documents must notify the other Party of the claim 'within'[26] 28 days.[27] If it does so, then it is entitled to be indemnified[28] against such a claim as provided for in this Sub-Clause and Sub-Clause 17.6 [*Shared*

22. Intellectual property comprises 'primarily trademark, copyright, and patent rights, but also includes trade-secret rights, publicity rights, moral rights and rights against unfair competition'. Bryan A Garner (ed in chief), *Black's Law Dictionary* (11th edn, Thomson Reuters, St Paul, MN, 2019).
23. Sub-Clause 1.11 [*Contractor's Use of Employer's Documents*].
24. As defined in Sub-Clause 1.1.15 '**Contractors Documents**'.
25. Sub-Clause 1.10 [*Employer's Use of Contractor's Documents*].
26. *See* item (2) of **(v) Improvements** in the commentary on Sub-Clause 1.2 [*Interpretation*] above.
27. Sub-Clause 17.3, second paragraph.
28. To indemnify means 'to reimburse (another) for a loss suffered because of a third party's or one's own act or default'. Bryan A Garner (ed in chief), *Black's Law Dictionary* (11th edn, Thomson Reuters, St Paul, MN, 2019).

Indemnities]. *If the Party fails to provide such notification, then it is deemed to have 'waived' (that is, given up) any right to an indemnity under this Sub-Clause.*[29]

This Sub-Clause does not exclude the need to comply with Sub-Clause 20.2. Consequently, as a matter of prudence, a Party seeking an indemnity should comply with it as well, *which requires, among other things, the giving of a Notice of Claim under Sub-Clause 20.2.1 within 28 days – or else be time barred.*[30]

(3) Nature of indemnity

Each Party's right to be indemnified is unlimited in amount.[31] This is normal as the Party to be indemnified will, in the usual case, have had no responsibility for the events giving rise to the claim. Each Party's right to be indemnified is also unlimited in time, subject to the applicable period of limitation provided for by law.[32]

However, the indemnifying Party also has the right, at its cost, to assume overall responsibility for negotiating the settlement of a claim and/or any litigation or arbitration which may arise from it.[33] This is normal and understandable as the rights at issue will be the property (or alleged property) of the indemnifying Party, who will therefore have a personal interest in protecting them. But this is an option of the indemnifying Party ('may'[34]) and not an obligation. Thus, the Party entitled to be indemnified cannot require the indemnifying Party to assume such overall responsibility.[35]

(iv) Related law: Each country is likely to have laws designed to protect intellectual and industrial property rights such as copyright, patents and

29. Sub-Clause 17.3, second paragraph.
30. *The FIDIC Contracts Guide* (2nd edn, FIDIC, 2022) 193 acknowledges that the same Notice may, if properly prepared and given, satisfy the requirements of different Sub-Clauses.
31. Sub-Clause 1.15 [*Limitation of Liability*] provides that neither the exclusion from liability (for 'loss of use of any Works', etc. [...]) nor the total liability limit of the Contractor, provided for by that Sub-Clause, shall apply.
32. *See* **Section 4 Common Law and Civil Law Compared – 4.5.3 Limitation Periods** in **Chapter II Applicable Law** above.
33. Sub-Clause 17.3, last paragraph.
34. *See* sub-para. (e) of Sub-Clause 1.2 [*Interpretation*].
35. Though if the indemnifying Party does not promptly assume overall responsibility after being requested to do so, it is not protected against prejudicial admissions by the indemnified Party.

confidential information. These may, in some cases, require local registration of the right concerned as a condition to protection. Such rights are also the subject of numerous international conventions.[36]

(v) Improvements:

(1) While providing for an indemnity, the Sub-Clause does not address what happens in the event that the indemnified Party's use of the intellectual property concerned is restricted or prohibited by reason of a third-party claim. Solutions might include a requirement for the indemnifying Party, at its cost to: (a) procure for the indemnified Party a licence to the relevant third party's rights, (b) replace the relevant item with a non-infringing alternative with the same functionality as the infringing item, or (c) modify the relevant infringing item so that it ceases to be infringing but has the same functionality.

(2) It should be clarified whether a Party seeking an indemnity must comply with Sub-Clause 20.2 [*Claims for Payment and/or EOT*].

(3) In relation to all the indemnities referred to in Clause 17, it should be specified that – as appears to be the intention[37] – they survive termination of the Contract for any reason. *See* point (5) under **(v) Improvements** in the commentary on Sub-Clause 15.2 [*Termination for Contractor's Default*] above.

--ooOOoo--

36. For example, the *Berne Convention for the Protection of Literary and Artistic Works* (1886) ('Berne Convention'), which has been ratified by more than 170 contracting parties and the *Universal Copyright Convention* (1952), which is relevant for States which have not ratified the Berne Convention. These are the two principal conventions protecting copyright. Also of special importance in relation to the protection of intellectual property generally is the *Agreement on Trade-Related Aspects of Intellectual Property Rights* (1994) ('TRIPS'), which is an agreement among the more than 160 members of the World Trade Organisation (WTO). TRIPS establishes minimum standards for the regulation by national governments of many forms of intellectual property and entitles a member country, whose nationals are injured by another member's failure to comply with TRIPS' standards, to file a complaint with a WTO panel which can lead to trade sanctions against the offending country.

37. *See*, e.g., the last paragraph of Sub-Clause 14.14 [*Cessation of the Employer's Liability*].

17.4 Indemnities by Contractor

The Contractor shall indemnify and hold harmless the Employer, the Employer's Personnel, and their respective agents, against and from all third party claims, damages, losses and expenses (including legal fees and expenses) in respect of:

(a) bodily injury, sickness, disease or death of any person whatsoever arising out of or in the course of or by reason of the Contractor's execution of the Works, unless attributable to any negligence, wilful act or breach of the Contract by the Employer, the Employer's Personnel, or any of their respective agents; and

(b) damage to or loss of any property, real or personal (other than the Works), to the extent that such damage or loss:

   (i) arises out of or in the course of or by reason of the Contractor's execution of the Works, and

   (ii) is attributable to any negligence, wilful act or breach of the Contract by the Contractor, the Contractor's Personnel, their respective agents, or anyone directly or indirectly employed by any of them.

To the extent, if any, that the Contractor is responsible for the design of part of the Permanent Works under Sub-Clause 4.1 [*Contractor's General Obligations*], and/or any other design under the Contract, the Contractor shall also indemnify and hold harmless the Employer against all acts, errors or omissions by the Contractor in carrying out the Contractor's design obligations that result in the Works (or Section or Part or major item of Plant, if any), when completed, not being fit for the purpose(s) for which they are intended under Sub-Clause 4.1 [*Contractor's General Obligations*].

The Contractor shall indemnify the Employer and related persons against all third-party claims in respect of: (a) bodily injury, sickness, disease or death of any person arising in the course of the Contractor's

execution of the Works, unless attributable to wrongful conduct of the Employer or related persons; and (b) damage or loss to any property, real or personal (other than the Works), arising in the course of the Contractor's execution of the Works and attributable to wrongful conduct of the Contractor and related persons.

To the extent that the Contractor is responsible for the design of the Permanent Works and/or other design under the Contract, the Contractor shall indemnify the Employer against any errors in its design that result in the Works (or Section or Part or major item of Plant), when completed, not being fit for their purpose(s) as intended by Sub-Clause 4.1.

Commentary

(i) Main Changes from RB/99:

(1) In the first paragraph of Sub-Clause 17.4, reference is made to 'third party claims' instead of 'claims' (as in Sub-Clause 17.1 of RB/99) and, in sub-paragraph (a), to 'execution of the Works'[38] instead of the 'execution and completion of the Works and the remedying of any defects'.

(2) The second paragraph, providing that if, and to the extent that, the Contractor is responsible for design, the Contractor shall indemnify the Employer against any errors in the design that result in the Works, when completed, not being fit for their intended purposes, is new.

(ii) Related Clauses / Sub-Clauses: 1.2 [*Interpretation*], 1.15 [*Limitation of Liability*], 4.1 [*Contractor's General Obligations*], 17.5 [*Indemnities by Employer*], 17.6 [*Shared Indemnities*] and 19.2 [*Insurance to be provided by the Contractor*].

(iii) Analysis:

(1) Purpose of Sub-Clauses 17.4, 17.5 and 17.6

In construction projects, the Contractor will be working on the Employer's site or land. Accordingly, the Employer may be the subject of claims of third parties (e.g., adjoining landowners or other contractors of the Employer) because of the alleged misconduct of the Contractor (e.g., negligent or reckless execution of the Works causing damage) and the

38. Now a defined term, *see* sub-para. (j) of Sub-Clause 1.2 [*Interpretation*].

Contractor may be the subject of claims of other third parties because of the Employer's alleged misconduct (e.g., lack of title to the Site or of a building permit). In cases such as these, Sub-Clauses 17.4, 17.5 and 17.6 apply and are designed to 'redistribute to the proper Party', be it the Employer or the Contractor, the ultimate liability for claims by third parties, should the latter choose to claim, sue or succeed in recovering judgment against the Party whom it has been agreed by the Contract shall not be responsible for the claim in question.[39]

(2) Contractor's general indemnity

Under the first paragraph, the Contractor must indemnify the Employer, the Employer's Personnel (who include the Engineer) and their agents against: third-party claims, damages and losses, including legal fees and expenses, in respect of: (a) bodily injury, sickness, disease or death arising out of or in the course of the Contractor's execution of the Works (unless attributable to wrongful conduct of the Employer or related persons); and (b) damage to or loss of any property, real or personal (other than the Works) arising out of or in the course of the Contractor's execution of the Works and attributable to the wrongful conduct of the Contractor or related persons.[40]

It is important to appreciate the breadth of the Contractor's indemnity. The Contractor must indemnify the Employer against 'third party claims', that is, claims of anyone other than the Contractor, the Contractor's Personnel, the Employer and the Employer's Personnel. The claims may be for damages and losses for 'bodily injury, sickness, disease or death', *regardless of whether or not the Contractor was negligent or at fault*. They need merely arise 'out of *or in the course of* or by reason of' (emphasis added) the Contractor's execution of the Works and must not be attributable to the negligence, wilful act or breach of the Contract by the Employer, the Employer's Personnel or their agents. Such a broad indemnity is said to be justified by the Contractor's overriding control over operations at the Site.

On the other hand, in the case of third-party claims for damages and losses in respect of 'property, real or personal (other than the Works)',

39. *See* I N Duncan Wallace, *The ICE Conditions of Contract Fifth Edition – A Commentary* (Sweet & Maxwell, London, 1978) 75-76.

40. The Contractor is required, pursuant to Sub-Clauses 19.2.4 and 19.2.5, to purchase insurance to secure its indemnities to the Employer under the first paragraph of this Sub-Clause.

the Contractor's obligation to indemnify only arises in the case of any negligence, wilful act or breach of the Contract by the Contractor or related persons.[41]

The Employer's right to be indemnified under the first paragraph is unlimited in amount.[42] This is normal as, except if the Employer has contributed to the damage, loss or injury (as to which *see* the commentary on Sub-Clause 17.6 below), the Employer will have had no responsibility for it. The Employer's right to be indemnified is also unlimited in time, at least by the Conditions.

(3) Contractor's 'fitness for purpose' indemnity

The second paragraph deals with where the Contractor is responsible for the design of part of the Permanent Works and/or other design under the Contract. To the extent, if any, that the Contractor is responsible for such design, the Contractor must indemnify the Employer against all acts, errors or omissions by the Contractor in carrying out the design that result in 'the Works (or Section or Part or major item of Plant, if any) when completed' not being fit for the purpose(s) for which they were intended under Sub-Clause 4.1.[43] *This indemnity is broader in scope than the Contractor's design obligation provided for in Sub-Clause 4.1(e).*

41. With reference to this limitation (first introduced in RB/99) on the Contractor's indemnity for property damage to cases of 'negligence, wilful act or breach of the Contract', Nael Bunni has noted that: 'to cover this gap [in insurance coverage to protect the Employer] a new policy is now needed, which is commonly referred to in the UK as the non-negligence insurance policy'. Nael Bunni, *The FIDIC Forms of Contract* (3rd edn, Blackwell Publishing, Oxford, 2005) 531-32. This limitation (to cases of negligence, wilful act or breach by the Contractor) on the Contractor's obligation to indemnify for 'property' damage is not in the Pink Book. *See* Sub-Clause 17.1 [*Indemnities*] of *Conditions of Contract for Construction MDB (Multilateral Development Bank) Harmonised Edition* for *Building and Engineering Works Designed by the Employer*, 2010 ('Pink Book').
42. Sub-Clause 1.15 [*Limitation of Liability*] expressly provides that neither the exclusion from liability (for 'loss of use of any Works', etc. [...]) nor the 'total liability' limit of the Contractor, provided for by that Sub-Clause, applies to the first paragraph of Sub-Clause 17.4.
43. For a discussion of this fitness for purpose obligation, *see* the commentary on Sub-Clause 4.1 [*Contractor's General Obligations*] above. The Contractor is required, pursuant to Sub-Clause 19.2.3, to purchase professional indemnity insurance to secure its indemnity under the second paragraph of Sub-Clause 17.4.

Under Sub-Clause 4.1(e), the Contractor has a fitness for purpose obligation for the part which it has designed only and not for the Works as a whole. Therefore, for consistency with that Sub-Clause, the Contractor should be indemnifying the Employer *only for acts errors or omissions which result in the part of the Works which the Contractor has designed* not being fit for the purposes for which it is intended. If that part is not fit for purpose, then the Contractor should not ordinarily have responsibility if the rest of the Works is not fit for purpose as this indemnity could otherwise imply.

The Contractor's liability is limited by the first paragraph of Sub-Clause 1.15 [*Limitation of Liability*], according to which the Contractor cannot be liable for any loss of use of any Works, loss of profit, loss of any contract or for any indirect or consequential loss or damage. Moreover, pursuant to the second paragraph of Sub-Clause 1.15, the 'total liability of the Contractor' under the second paragraph of Sub-Clause 17.4, together with other liabilities the Contractor may have, cannot exceed the sum stated in the Contract Data or, if no such sum is stated, the Accepted Contract Amount.[44] However, the Contractor's liability is not limited in time, subject to the applicable limitation period provided for by law.[45]

These limits on the amount of the Contractor's liability are justified by the difficulty for the Contractor to anticipate the magnitude of the losses for which it might become responsible if what it has designed was not fit for purpose and, thus, the difficulty of including an appropriate contingency allowance in its Tender.[46]

--ooOOoo--

As this Sub-Clause does not exclude the need to comply with Sub-Clause 20.2, as a matter of prudence, a Party seeking an indemnity should

---

44. Under Sub-Clause 1.15 [*Limitation of Liability*], the contractual limits on the Contractor's liability would not apply in the case of fraud, gross negligence, deliberate default or reckless misconduct. *See* the commentary on Sub-Clause 1.15 above.
45. *See* **Section 4 Common Law and Civil Law Compared – 4.5.3 Limitation Periods** of **Chapter II Applicable Law** above.
46. The *Guidance* further notes that where the Contractor's liability under the second paragraph of this Sub-Clause is covered by insurance under Sub-Clause 19.2.3 [*Insurance to be provided by the Contractor – Liability for breach of professional duty*], a statement to this effect should be included in the Contract Data. *Guidance for the Preparation of Particular Conditions*, 45.

comply with that Sub-Clause *including the need to give a Notice of Claim within 28 days – or else be time barred.*[47]

(iv) Improvements:

(1) Under the last paragraph of Sub-Clause 17.3 [*Intellectual and Industrial Property Rights*], the indemnifying Party, whether it be the Employer or the Contractor, may (at the indemnifying Party's cost) assume overall responsibility for negotiating the settlement of the third-party claim and/or any litigation or arbitration with the consequences provided for there. Consideration should be given to affording the Contractor, as the indemnifying Party, the same right under Sub-Clause 17.4.

(2) As explained under **(iii) Analysis** above, the indemnity of the Contractor in the second paragraph of Sub-Clause 17.4 needs to be aligned clearly with, and be limited to, the fitness for purpose obligation of the Contractor in Sub-Clause 4.1(e) (i.e., be limited to that part of the Works designed by the Contractor).

(3) Comments (2) and (3) under **(v) Improvements** of the commentary on Sub-Clause 17.3 above are equally relevant here.

--ooOOoo--

17.5 Indemnities by Employer

The Employer shall indemnify and hold harmless the Contractor, the Contractor's Personnel, and their respective agents, against and from all third party claims, damages, losses and expenses (including legal fees and expenses) in respect of:

(a) bodily injury, sickness, disease or death, or loss of or damage to any property other than the Works, which is attributable to any negligence, wilful act or breach of the Contract by the Employer, the Employer's Personnel, or any of their respective agents; and

(b) damage to or loss of any property, real or personal (other than the Works), to the extent that such damage or loss arises out of any event

47. Sub-Clause 20.2.1.

described under sub-paragraphs (a) to (f) of Sub-Clause 17.2 [*Liability for Care of the Works*].

The Employer shall indemnify the Contractor and related persons against all third-party claims in respect of: (a) bodily injury, sickness, disease or death or loss or damage to any property other than the Works, which is attributable to the wrongful conduct of the Employer or related persons; and (b) damage to any property other than the Works to the extent arising out of any event in sub-paragraphs (a) to (f) of Sub-Clause 17.2.

Commentary

(i) Main Changes from RB/99: Compared to the corresponding provision in RB/99 (the second paragraph of Sub-Clause 17.1), the main changes are:

(1) reference is made to 'third party claims' instead of 'claims' as before; and

(2) the indemnity from the Employer now covers: (a) loss of or damage to any property other than the Works (and not just bodily injury, sickness, disease or death as before) attributable to wrongful conduct of the Employer or related persons; and (b) damage to or loss of any property (other than the Works), to the extent arising from any event described in sub-paragraphs (a) to (f) of Sub-Clause 17.2 (instead of 'matters for which liability may be excluded from insurance cover, as described in sub-paragraphs (d) (i), (ii) and (iii) of Sub-Clause 18.3' of RB/99).

(ii) Related Clauses / Sub-Clauses: 1.15 [*Limitation of Liability*], 17.2 [*Liability for Care of the Works*], 17.4 [*Indemnities by Contractor*] and 17.6 [*Shared Indemnities*].

(iii) Analysis: Under this Sub-Clause, the Employer must indemnify the Contractor and related persons against third party claims, damages and losses, including legal fees and expenses, in respect of: (a) bodily injury, sickness, disease or death, or loss or damage to property other than the Works, attributable to any negligence, wilful act or breach of the Contract by the Employer, the Employer's Personnel or their agents; and (b) damage to or loss of property, real or personal (other than the Works) to the extent it arises out of any event described in sub-paragraphs (a) to (f) of Sub-Clause 17.2.

As discussed in the commentary on Sub-Clause 17.2 above, the events listed in sub-paragraphs (a), (b), (c) and (f) are all events for which the Employer is responsible or considered responsible. Sub-paragraph (d) reflects the general risk allocation philosophy of an RB contract. The remaining sub-paragraph (e) refers to Exceptional Events most if not all of which are uninsurable.[48]

Sub-Clause 1.15 [*Limitation of Liability*] expressly provides that the exclusion from liability provided for in the first sentence of that Sub-Clause (for 'loss of use of any Works', etc.) shall not apply to Sub-Clause 17.5. Consequently, the Employer's liability under this Sub-Clause for a claim by the Contractor for 'loss of profit, loss of any contract or for any indirect or consequential loss or damage' is unlimited in amount. The Employer's indemnity obligation under this Sub-Clause is also unlimited in time, at least by the General Conditions.

As in the case of Sub-Clauses 17.3 and 17.4, as discussed above, *Sub-Clause 20.2 may apply and consequently as a matter of prudence that Sub-Clause should be complied with.*

(iv) Improvements:

(1) Under the last paragraph of Sub-Clause 17.3 [*Intellectual and Industrial Property Rights*], the indemnifying Party, whether it be the Employer or the Contractor, may (at the indemnifying Party's cost) assume overall responsibility for negotiating the settlement of the third-party claim and/or any litigation or arbitration, with the consequences provided for there. Consideration should be given to affording the Employer, as the indemnifying Party, the same right under Sub-Clause 17.5.

(2) Comments (2) and (3) under **(v) Improvements** of the commentary on Sub-Clause 17.3 are equally relevant here.

--ooOOoo--

48. *See* under **(iii) Analysis** of the commentary on Sub-Clause 17.2 above.

17.6 Shared Indemnities

The Contractor's liability to indemnify the Employer, under Sub-Clause 17.4 [*Indemnities by Contractor*] and/or under Sub-Clause 17.3 [*Intellectual and Industrial Property Rights*], shall be reduced proportionately to the extent that any event described under sub-paragraphs (a) to (f) of Sub-Clause 17.2 [*Liability for Care of the Works*] may have contributed to the said damage, loss or injury.

Similarly, the Employer's liability to indemnify the Contractor, under Sub-Clause 17.5 [*Indemnities by Employer*], shall be reduced proportionately to the extent that any event for which the Contractor is responsible under Sub-Clause 17.1 [*Responsibility for Care of the Works*] and/or under Sub-Clause 17.3 [*Intellectual and Industrial Property Rights*] may have contributed to the said damage, loss or injury.

The Contractor's liability to indemnify the Employer under Sub-Clauses 17.4 and/or 17.3 shall be reduced proportionately to the extent any event in sub-paragraphs (a) to (f) of Sub-Clause 17.2 may have contributed.

Similarly, the Employer's liability to indemnify the Contractor under Sub-Clause 17.5 shall be reduced proportionately to the extent any event for which the Contractor is responsible under Sub-Clauses 17.1 and/or 17.3 may have contributed.

<u>**Commentary**</u>

(i) Main Changes from RB/99: This Sub-Clause is entirely new in the RB, and Sub-Clause 17.6 [*Limitation of Liability*] of RB/99 has now become Sub-Clause 1.15 [*Limitation of Liability*] of RB/17.[49]

(ii) Related Clauses / Sub-Clauses: 1.15 [*Limitation of Liability*] and 17 [*Care of the Works and Indemnities*].

49. However, GB/08 had included a similar shared indemnities sub-clause. *See* Sub-Clause 17.11 [*Shared Indemnities*] of GB/08 and the *FIDIC DBO Contract Guide* (FIDIC, 2011) 118.

(iii) Analysis: This new Sub-Clause recognises that the Employer and the Contractor may have shared responsibility for the events or circumstances giving rise to a third-party claim. In such instances, the Parties are permitted to set off their respective liabilities to indemnify each other, in proportion to their respective liabilities, thereby limiting the risk of multiple claims, arbitration and litigation.

Under the first paragraph, the Contractor's liability to indemnify the Employer under Sub-Clauses 17.4 and/or 17.3 must be reduced proportionately to the extent that any event described in sub-paragraphs (a) to (f) of Sub-Clause 17.2 – all being events for which the Contractor is expressly stated generally to have no liability[50] – may have contributed to the damage, loss or injury.

On the other hand, under the second paragraph, the Employer's liability to indemnify the Contractor under Sub-Clause 17.5[51] must be reduced proportionately to the extent that any event for which the Contractor is responsible under Sub-Clauses 17.1 and/or 17.3 may have contributed to the damage, loss or injury.[52]

(v) Improvements:

Comments (2) and (3) under **(v) Improvements** of the commentary on Sub-Clause 17.3 are equally relevant here.

--ooOOoo--

18 Exceptional Events

This Clause defines an 'Exceptional Event' as an exceptional event or circumstance beyond a Party's control, against which it could not reasonably have provided and which, having arisen, the Party could not reasonably have avoided or overcome and which is not substantially attributable to the other Party. After providing a non-exhaustive list of examples of such events or circumstances, the Clause describes what a

50. *See* the second paragraph of Sub-Clause 17.2 [*Liability for Care of the Works*].
51. It is unclear why the Employer's liability to indemnify the Contractor under Sub-Clause 17.3 is not reduced proportionately as well, as is the case of the Contractor's liability to indemnify the Employer under that Sub-Clause.
52. The World Bank's COPA provides, in addition, for a new Sub-Clause 17.7 requiring the Contractor to take responsibility for the care of any Employer-provided accommodation and facilities.

Party must do if prevented by an Exceptional Event from performing any contractual obligation and the relief to which it may thereafter be entitled. Finally, the Clause provides that, in certain extreme circumstances, the Parties may be discharged from further performing the Contract.

--ooOOoo--

18.1 Exceptional Events

"Exceptional Event" means an exceptional event or circumstance which:

(i) is beyond a Party's control;
(ii) the Party could not reasonably have provided against before entering into the Contract;
(iii) having arisen, such Party could not reasonably have avoided or overcome; and
(iv) is not substantially attributable to the other Party.

An Exceptional Event may comprise but is not limited to any of the following events or circumstances provided that conditions (i) to (iv) above are satisfied:

(a) war, hostilities (whether war be declared or not), invasion, act of foreign enemies;
(b) rebellion, terrorism, revolution, insurrection, military or usurped power, or civil war;
(c) riot, commotion or disorder by persons other than the Contractor's Personnel and other employees of the Contractor and Subcontractors;
(d) strike or lockout not solely involving the Contractor's Personnel and other employees of the Contractor and Subcontractors;
(e) encountering munitions of war, explosive materials, ionising radiation or contamination by radio-activity, except as may be attributable to the Contractor's use of such munitions, explosives, radiation or radio-activity; or
(f) natural catastrophes such as earthquake, tsunami, volcanic activity, hurricane or typhoon.

'Exceptional Event' means an exceptional event or circumstance: (i) beyond a Party's control; (ii) which it could not reasonably have provided against; (iii) which, having arisen, it could not reasonably have avoided or overcome; and (iv) is not substantially attributable to the other Party. The Sub-Clause provides in sub-paragraphs (a) to (f) for a non-exhaustive list of such events or circumstances.

Commentary

(i) Main Changes from RB/99:

(1) Clause 18 replaces Clause 19 entitled 'Force Majeure' in RB/99 and the term 'Exceptional Event(s)' replaces the term 'Force Majeure' in RB/99 (as it had done already in GB/08).[1]
(2) The list of events and circumstances in what was sub-paragraph (iii) of Clause 19 of RB/99 has been broken into two separate items: sub-paragraph (c) dealing with 'riot, commotion or disorder [...]'; and sub-paragraph (d) dealing with 'strike or lockout [...]'.[2]
(3) A 'tsunami' has been added in sub-paragraph (f).

Prior to RB/99, the RB had contained no Force Majeure clause but instead a clause entitled 'Special Risks'.[3] However, a Force Majeure clause had been contained in YB/87[4] and in FIDIC's Conditions of Contract for Design-Build and Turnkey 1995 (the 'Orange Book').[5]

(ii) Related Clauses / Sub-Clauses: 4.12 [*Unforeseeable Physical Conditions*], 6.11 [*Disorderly Conduct*], 7.6 [*Remedial Work*], 14.2 [*Advance*

1. *See* Sub-Clause 1.1.37 and Clause 18 of GB/08, although Clause 18 of that form referred somewhat confusingly both to 'Exceptional Risks' and to an 'Exceptional Event'. 'Force Majeure' was eliminated essentially because engineers and some lawyers found it difficult to understand this French legal term and its use.
2. A purpose of doing so appears to have been to clarify that a strike or lockout involving the Contractor's Personnel and other employees of the Contractor and Subcontractors may, contrary to RB/99, qualify as an Exceptional Event (or Force Majeure in RB/99), if the strike or lockout does not *solely* involve the Contractor's Personnel and other employees of the Contractor and Subcontractors.
3. Clause 65 entitled 'Special Risks' was contained in RB/57 through RB/87.
4. Clause 44 of YB/87.
5. Clause 19 of the Orange Book.

Payment – Repayment of Advance Payment], 17.2 [*Liability for Care of the Works*], and 19.2 [*Insurance to be provided by the Contractor*].

(iii) Analysis: While commented upon separately below, Sub-Clauses 18.1 through 18.4 need to be read together. Essentially, they provide for the circumstances in which a Party may be relieved temporarily from performing any obligations under the Contract if prevented from doing so by an Exceptional Event (as defined), and the further relief to which it may be entitled.

(1) Purpose of Clause 18

Under both the common law and the civil law systems, a Party may be excused and/or relieved from having to perform its contractual obligations by law in only a very narrow range of events or circumstances. Consequently, in keeping with common practice in international contracts, this Clause – like other *force majeure*-type clauses – broadens the range of events or circumstances in which a Party may be excused from having to perform the Contract, temporarily or permanently, beyond those commonly provided for by law.[6] In the case of certain events or circumstances, it even allows the Contractor (where it is the affected Party) to recover Cost.[7]

For an event or circumstance to qualify it must, as an 'Exceptional Event', be 'exceptional' and satisfy the four conditions in the first paragraph: (i) is beyond a Party's control; (ii) which the Party could not reasonably have provided against before entering into the Contract; (iii) having arisen, could not reasonably have been avoided or overcome; and (iv) is not substantially attributable to the other Party.[8] The second paragraph then provides that the Exceptional Event may comprise 'but is not limited to' any of the events or circumstances which are listed in sub-paragraphs (a) to (f) provided that they satisfy conditions (i) to (iv).

---

6. For example, under the doctrines of frustration and impracticability under the common law or of *force majeure* and hardship (*imprévision*) in many civil law countries. *See* **Section 4 Common Law and Civil Law Compared – 4.4.7 *Force Majeure* and Hardship,** in the case of a private or civil contract, and **4.6.2 Hardship (*Imprévision*) and 4.6.5 *Force Majeure*** in the case of a contract for public works (administrative contract), of **Chapter II Applicable Law** above.
7. Sub-Clause 18.4.
8. Sub-Clause 18.1, first paragraph. For a discussion of these conditions, *see The FIDIC Contracts Guide* (2nd edn, FIDIC, 2022) 475.

(2) Scope of Sub-Clause 18.1

While the list of events and circumstances in the second paragraph is not exhaustive,[9] it is nevertheless indicative of the range of the events or circumstances which may constitute an Exceptional Event. They should be of comparable gravity and character to – or share the same qualities as[10] – those described in sub-paragraphs (a) to (f).[11] It is not sufficient merely to satisfy the four conditions in the first paragraph for a matter to qualify as an Exceptional Event. In addition, the matter or event must be 'exceptional', as Sub-Clause 18.1 and the definition of 'Exceptional Event' in Sub-Clause 1.1.37 require.[12]

9. Many of these events or circumstances (notably, most of those listed in sub-paras (a) through (c)) derive from standard exclusions in insurance policies and have been referred to regularly in the Red Book, though for other purposes, since RB/57. These events or circumstances (as listed in this Sub-Clause) have come to serve multiple purposes in RB/99 and RB/17. Thus, in RB/17 not only may their occurrence excuse performance under Sub-Clause 18.1 but also it may relieve the Contractor from liability for loss or damage to the Works, Goods or Contractor's Documents under Sub-Clause 17.2 (*see* Sub-Clause 17.2 (e)) and, unless otherwise stated in the Contract Data, from having to insure against the risks arising from them pursuant to Sub-Clause 19.2.1 (*see* Sub-Clause 19.2.1 (iv)). Indeed, most, if not all of the risk arising from them is uninsurable. Paul Reed, *Construction All Risks Insurance* (2nd edn, Sweet & Maxwell, London, 2016) 414-28 (paras 15-031-067).
10. *See* Klaus Peter Berger and Daniel Behn 'Force Majeure and Hardship in the Age of Corona: A Historical and Comparative Study' (2019-2020) 6(4) McGill J Disp Resol, 78, 114-115, which discusses this distinction between exhaustive and non-exhaustive lists in *force majeure* clauses with multiple references.
11. With reference to 'explosive materials' in sub-para. (e), *see* the award in ICC case 2763 (1980) relating to a FIDIC contract where, although the presence of explosives was found to be a foreseeable circumstance, the importance and quantity of the explosives found justified their having a *force majeure* character. Sigvard Jarvin and Yves Derains (eds), *Coll of ICC Arbitral Awards (1974-1985)* (ICC, Paris / Kluwer, the Netherlands, 1998), 157.
12. In relation to sub-para. (c) ('riot, commotion or disorder'), it has been held in relation to Clause 65 of RB/77 that 'peaceful protests of [...] native landowners' did not amount to 'riot' or 'commotion'. ICC case 11499 (2002) (Issue 2), ICC Int'l Ct Arb Bull, vol 19, no 2, 2008, 97, 101-102 (commentary 51-52). In relation to sub-paras (c) and (d), *see* Sub-Clause 6.11 [*Disorderly Conduct*].

The *Guidance* provides that 'exceptionally adverse climatic conditions' (as referred to in sub-paragraph (c) of Sub-Clause 8.5 [*Extension of Time for Completion*]) will not constitute an Exceptional Event unless the conditions stated in sub-paragraphs (ii) and (iii) of Sub-Clause 18.1 are fulfilled. On the other hand, if they have the effect of delaying completion of the Works or a Section, the Contractor would be entitled to an EOT under Sub-Clause 8.5 (c).[13]

(iv) Related Law: Under the principle of freedom of contract recognised by practically all legal systems,[14] parties are generally at liberty to expand the events or circumstances, beyond those provided for by national law, which may relieve them (or one of them) from having to perform contractual obligations, e.g., under such doctrines as *force majeure* or hardship (*imprévision*) in civil law countries and frustration or impracticability in common law countries.[15] Thus, Clause 18 should normally be a valid clause under applicable law.

Article 7.1.7 (*Force majeure*) of the UNIDROIT Principles contains a provision similar to Clause 18.[16] Moreover, any relevant limitation period may be suspended as a result of *force majeure* under the Principles.[17]

(v) Improvements:

It would be helpful – in the interests of clarity – for the second paragraph to be expanded to include additional illustrative events (even though they may already implicitly be included, as they appear to be comparable to those listed) such as:

(a) in the case of sub-paragraph (a), 'the serious threat of' the events listed in that sub-paragraph ('war [...]', etc.) should be in-

13. *Guidance for the Preparation of Particular Conditions*, 46.
14. *See* **Section 2 Universal Principles** of **Chapter II Applicable Law** above and the discussion of the doctrines of frustration and impracticability under **(iv) Related Law** in the commentary on Sub-Clause 18.6 below.
15. *See* **Section 4 Common Law and Civil Law Compared – 4.4.7 *Force Majeure* and Hardship** in the case of an ordinary private or civil contract, and **4.6.2 Hardship (*Imprévision*) and 4.6.5 *Force Majeure*** in the case of a contract for public works (administrative contract), of **Chapter II Applicable Law** above.
16. In addition, arts 6.2.2-6.2.3 of the UNIDROIT Principles provide for the doctrine of hardship, which is to be distinguished from *force majeure*. *See* under **(iv) Related Law** in the commentary on Sub-Clause 18.6 below.
17. Art. 10.8 (*Suspension in case of force majeure, death or incapacity*).

serted[18] and the following events could be added, 'blockade, cyber attack, military embargo, extensive military mobilization and economic sanction';

(b) in the case of sub-paragraph (b), 'sabotage'[19] and 'piracy' might be added;

(c) a new sub-paragraph dealing with such things as 'plague', 'epidemic' and 'pandemic' should be added;[20]

(d) a new sub-paragraph dealing with such things as 'explosion', 'fire' and 'prolonged breakdown of telecommunication or information system' not attributable to the Contractor should be added;[21] and

(e) to the list of natural catastrophes in sub-paragraph (f), 'blizzard', 'tidal wave' and 'tornado' might usefully be added.

A more detailed listing of examples of Exceptional Events would delineate more clearly the scope of the Clause.[22]

--ooOOoo--

18.2 Notice of an Exceptional Event

> If a Party is or will be prevented from performing any obligations under the Contract due to an Exceptional Event (the "affected Party" in this Clause), then

18. This would allow for explicit recognition of cases such as ICC case 5195 (1986) and *The Kronprinzessin Cecilie* which are referred to under **(iv) Related Law** in the commentary on Sub-Clause 18.2 below.
19. The World Bank's COPA requires that 'sabotage' be added to sub-para. (c). Sub-Clause 18.1, COPA.
20. Among other things, this would arguably take account of the SARS virus outbreak of 2003 and of COVID-19 in 2019. *See* the Note of the UNIDROIT Secretariat on the UNIDROIT Principles of International Commercial Contracts and the COVID-19 Health Crisis, UNIDROIT, Rome, 2020, https://www.unidroit.org/english/news/2020/200721-principles-covid19-note/note-e.pdf accessed 10 November 2022. Sub-Clause 8.5 (d) already provides for an EOT in the case of certain Unforeseeable shortages caused by 'epidemic' or governmental actions.
21. The examples suggested are all included in the ICC Force Majeure Clause (Long Form) published by the International Chamber of Commerce, *ICC Force Majeure + Hardship Clauses* 2020.
22. An additional way to delineate the scope of the Clause would be to list also the type of events which should *not* be considered Exceptional Events.

the affected Party shall give a Notice to the other Party of such an Exceptional Event, and shall specify the obligations, the performance of which is or will be prevented (the "prevented obligations" in this Clause).

This Notice shall be given within 14 days after the affected Party became aware, or should have become aware, of the Exceptional Event, and the affected Party shall then be excused performance of the prevented obligations from the date such performance is prevented by the Exceptional Event. If this Notice is received by the other Party after this period of 14 days, the affected Party shall be excused performance of the prevented obligations only from the date on which this Notice is received by the other Party.

Thereafter, the affected Party shall be excused performance of the prevented obligations for so long as such Exceptional Event prevents the affected Party from performing them. Other than performance of the prevented obligations, the affected Party shall not be excused performance of all other obligations under the Contract.

However, the obligations of either Party to make payments due to the other Party under the Contract shall not be excused by an Exceptional Event.

If a Party is prevented from performing any obligations under the Contract due to an Exceptional Event, it must give a Notice of it to the other Party specifying the obligations which it is prevented from performing. The Notice must be given within 14 days after the affected Party became aware, or should have become aware, of the Exceptional Event in which case the Party is excused from performing the prevented obligations so long as performance is prevented. However, the obligations of each Party to make payments to the other under the Contract are not excused by an Exceptional Event.

Commentary:

(i) Main Changes from RB/99: While the new Sub-Clause provides, like its predecessor (Sub-Clause 19.2 of RB/99), that Notice ('notice' under RB/99) must be given within 14 days after the affected Party became aware, or should have become aware, of the alleged Exceptional Event, it also deals, helpfully, with what the situation is if, as often occurs in practice, no Notice has been given within 14 days. Under Sub-Clause 19.2 of RB/99, it was unclear whether the affected Party could validly claim relief for 'Force Majeure' if it had failed to give a Notice within 14 days as Sub-Clause 19.4 had indicated that relief was only available if a Party had given a notice 'under Sub-Clause 19.2', that is, within 14 days.[23] The new Sub-Clause resolves this issue by recognising that if the other Party should receive a Notice *after* 14 days, the affected Party is excused from performing the obligations affected only from the date on which the Notice is received by the other Party.

(ii) Related Clauses / Sub-Clauses: 1.2 [*Interpretation*], 1.3 [*Notices and Other Communications*], 8.4 [*Adverse Warning*], 14.7 [*Payment*] and 18.1 [*Exceptional Events*].

(iii) Analysis:

(1) Requirement of 'prevention'

A Party must, or must anticipate that it will, be 'prevented' from performing 'any obligations' under the Contract due to an Exceptional Event in order to be able to seek relief under this Clause. 'Prevent' does not require that it is impossible to perform. The dictionary defines the verb 'prevent' as meaning: 'keep from happening or arising' and 'make unable to do something'.[24] Thus, it may be sufficient if a Party is impeded somehow, whether physically, legally or psychologically (e.g., a justified apprehension of danger may suffice),[25] from performing the Contract. Moreover, the Sub-Clause will apply if a Party is prevented from performing just one obligation under the Contract – it does not need to have been impeded from performing most or all of the Contract. Thus, activities at the Site may be prevented by riot or disorder and therefore justify relief under this Clause while, on the other hand, design or programming activities at the head office, which are not so affected, would be expected to continue.

23. *See* Sub-Clause 19.4 of RB/99.
24. *Concise Oxford English Dictionary* (10th edn, rev'd, OUP, Oxford, 2002).
25. *See* under **(iv) Related Law** below. Where an Exceptional Event (as defined in Sub-Clause 18.1) affects a subcontractor of the Contractor, this would normally be interpreted as affecting the Contractor as well, *see* I N Duncan Wallace, *Construction Contracts: Principles and Policies in Tort and Contract*, vol 2 (Sweet & Maxwell, London, 1996) 425-429.

As others have suggested,[26] the term 'prevent' needs to be construed in relation to other provisions of Clause 18. Thus, item (iii) of Sub-Clause 18.1 implies that 'prevent' is referring to a matter which 'could not reasonably have [been] avoided or overcome' and, as Sub-Clause 18.6 [*Release from Performance under the Law*] provides a remedy for impossibility, 'prevent' in Sub-Clause 18.2 must be referring to something less than the impossible.

(2) Requirement of a Notice

If a Party is prevented from performing one or more obligations under the Contract by an Exceptional Event, it must give a Notice to the other Party with a copy to the Engineer[27] 'within 14 days'[28] after it became aware, or should have become aware, of the Exceptional Event. The Notice must 'specify the obligations, the performance of which is or will be prevented'.[29] The affected Party will then, subject to Sub-Clause 20.2 which requires the submission of a further Notice *subject to a 28-day time bar,*[30] be excused from performing the prevented obligation(s) from the date that the prevention began.

If this Notice 'is received by the other Party' after 14 days, the affected Party will be excused from performing the prevented obligation(s) only

26. Jakob B Sørensen, *FIDIC Red Book: A Companion to the 2017 Construction Contract* (ICE Publishing, London, 2019) 176.
27. *See* Sub-Clause 1.3, last paragraph.
28. '**day**' means a calendar day. Sub-Clause 1.1.25. *See also* Sub-Clause 1.3 describing when a Notice is received or deemed to have been received. As regards the inherent ambiguity of 'within' a period of time, *see* item (2) under **(v) Improvements** in the commentary on Sub-Clause 1.2 [*Interpretation*] above.
29. While not expressly stated, the affected Party must be prepared to provide evidence that its performance has been prevented by an Exceptional Event. Marcel Fontaine and Filip De Ly, *Drafting International Contracts: An Analysis of Contract Clauses* (Martinus Nijhoff, Leiden, the Netherlands, 2009), 421 ('[t]he party invoking *force majeure* must provide *evidence* of it'). It has the burden of proof. *See* Klaus Peter Berger and Daniel Behn 'Force Majeure and Hardship in the Age of Corona: A Historical and Comparative Study' (2019-2020) 6(4) McGill J Disp Resol, 78 (citing, among other things, at page 112 (fn. 185) to *Sylvania Technical Systems v Iran*, IUSCT case no 64 (1985) at para. 52).
30. Sub-Clause 18.4. *The FIDIC Contracts Guide* (2nd edn, FIDIC, 2022) 193 acknowledges that the same Notice may, if properly prepared and given, satisfy the requirements of different Sub-Clauses.

as from the date on which the Notice was received by the other Party.[31] However, as is commonplace in such clauses, neither Party may be excused from making payments due to the other on account of an Exceptional Event, as it is nearly always possible to make a payment, if not in one jurisdiction then in another, to an account at a bank or financial institution of another person.[32]

It is reasonable that a Party is not prevented from claiming under this Clause merely because it has failed to give a Notice within 14 days; an Exceptional Event is, by definition, the responsibility of neither Party and therefore denying relief entirely on this ground (as Sub-Clause 19.4 of RB/99 possibly did) would be too harsh. On the other hand, it is also justified that, where the affected Party has been late in giving a Notice, it should only be entitled to relief as from the date on which the other Party is notified of the affected Party's inability to perform, as this Sub-Clause provides.

(iv) Related Law: Under this Sub-Clause, a Party must be 'prevented' from performing one or more contractual obligations. As mentioned above, prevention can take many forms: physical,[33] legal (i.e., in the case of illegality[34]) or psychological: *a justified apprehension of physical danger may suffice*. Thus, in one case a contractor working on an airport project in a developing country was held to be entitled to abandon work on that project when a canal project some 300 kilometres away in the same country on which it was working was the subject of violent attacks by a rebel group, killing 12 of the Contractor's staff. The ICC tribunal found that a justified apprehension of danger was enough to frustrate the contract:[35]

31. Sub-Clause 18.2, second paragraph.
32. 'In principle, [...] the payment of a sum of money is never rendered impossible by the occurrence of *force majeure*.' Marcel Fontaine and Filip De Ly, *Drafting International Contracts: An Analysis of Contract Clauses* (Martinius Nijhoff, Leiden, the Netherlands, 2009) 436. Art. 7.2.1 (*Performance of monetary obligation*) of the UNIDROIT Principles is to the same effect. However, where payment is delayed by such an event, the issue of liability for interest could, in theory, be discussed.
33. *See* under **(iii) Analysis** of the commentary on Sub-Clause 18.6 below for an example (*Union of India v A.S. Chopra et al*).
34. *See* under **(iii) Analysis** of the commentary on Sub-Clause 18.6 below for an example (*Metropolitan Water Board v Dick, Kerr & Co Ltd*).
35. While this was a case of common law frustration, the same result should apply to events of prevention generally.

events which go beyond merely increasing the financial burden on the party performing, and which reach a point where they render performance unacceptably hazardous to the lives and safety of those performing, are in a different category altogether. If such events intervene, and if the risk which they create is unlikely to be removed within a reasonable time, under many legal systems further performance will be excused. Whether it is will usually depend on such matters as the foreseeability, character, and expected duration of the risk, as they would have appeared to an objective, informed observer.[36]

--ooOOoo--

18.3 Duty to Minimise Delay

Each Party shall at all times use all reasonable endeavours to minimise any delay in the performance of the Contract as a result of an Exceptional Event.

If the Exceptional Event has a continuing effect, the affected Party shall give further Notices describing the effect every 28 days after giving the first Notice under Sub-Clause 18.2 [*Notice of an Exceptional Event*].

The affected Party shall immediately give a Notice to the other Party when the affected Party ceases to be affected by the Exceptional Event. If the affected Party fails to do so, the other Party may give a Notice to the affected Party stating that the other Party considers that the affected Party's performance is no longer prevented by the Exceptional Event, with reasons.

36. Partial award, ICC case 5195 (1986), YB Comm Arb, vol XIII – 1988, 69,75 (construction contract discharged for frustration under common law). The tribunal comprised Robert A McCrindle, QC (UK), Chairman, Prof. Berthold Goldman (France) and Prof. Henry Lesguillons (France). The substantive law was the law of country X 'which originates from English law', 69. *See also The Kronprinzessin Cecilie* 244 US 12 (1917) (per Justice Holmes) (peril of capture by a belligerent on the eve of war justifies refusal to proceed with sea voyage).

Each Party must use all reasonable endeavours to minimise any delay as a result of an Exceptional Event. If it has a continuing effect, the affected Party must give further Notices every 28 days and must immediately give a Notice to the other Party when it ceases to be affected by the Exceptional Event. If the affected Party fails to do so, the other Party may give a Notice to the affected Party if it considers that the affected Party is no longer prevented from performing by the Exceptional Event, with reasons.

Commentary

(i) Main Changes from RB/99:

(1) The addition of the second paragraph, requiring the giving of a Notice every 28 days where an Exceptional Event has a continuing effect, is new.
(2) The addition of the last sentence of the third paragraph, providing that if the affected Party fails to give a Notice that its performance is no longer prevented by an Exceptional Event, then the other Party may do so, is also new.

(ii) Related Clauses / Sub-Clauses: 1.3 [*Notices and Other Communications*], 3.7.3 [*Agreement or Determination – Time Limits*], 18 [*Exceptional Events*] and 20.2.6 [*Claims for Payment and/or EOT – Claims of Continuing Effect*].

(iii) Analysis: The changes from Sub-Clause 19.3 of RB/99, described above, make the Sub-Clause clearer and more comprehensive. The treatment of an Exceptional Event having a continuing effect is similar to the treatment of Claims of continuing effect in Sub-Clause 20.2.6.

(iv) Related Law:

(1) Duty to minimise damages

The first and third paragraphs reflect the duty on the affected Party to mitigate (or minimise) its damages, which it is likely to have, at least, under the common law.[37] In the first paragraph, the Party is required to

37. Under the common law, 'a party is only entitled to recover for losses which could not have been avoided by taking reasonable steps'. Atkin Chambers, *Hudson's Building and Engineering Contracts* (14th edn, Sweet & Maxwell, London, 2020) 836 (para. 7-016). For the civil law position, *see* under *(3) Civil law and UNIDROIT Principles* in the main text below.

use 'all reasonable endeavours' to minimise delay in performance of the Contract. Linguistically at least, this is a lesser obligation than a requirement to use 'best efforts' or 'best endeavours'.[38] Nevertheless, it requires the Party affected to use reasonable effort to reduce the delay which may, depending on the circumstances, require the expenditure of money or other resources.[39]

(2) Recent English case

Thus, in an English case, the holder of two offshore oil concessions ('Tullow') had contracted with the owner of an oil rig ('Seadrill') to hire it to drill for oil from the concessions. The contract contained a *force majeure* clause providing that the parties would use 'reasonable endeavours' and 'all reasonable endeavours' to overcome the circumstances of *force majeure* should it arise.[40] Tullow claimed it was prevented by *force majeure* – specifically, a government moratorium on drilling – from using the rig in the areas within the concessions where it had planned to do so, and therefore terminated the contract. While the court held on the particular facts that Tullow was not entitled to claim *force majeure*, it nevertheless considered in detail whether Tullow had used 'reasonable endeavours' to mitigate the alleged *force majeure* occurrence. Although Tullow was prevented from providing Seadrill with drilling instructions in the areas where Tullow had planned for drilling to take place, and although it was more expensive for Tullow to provide such instructions for other areas within the concessions, the court stated that 'greater expense or a greater risk of an unprofitable outcome is not a matter which enables Tullow to say that it has exercised its reasonable endeavours'.[41] While Tullow was entitled to consider its own interests and, in particular, whether there was a business case for drilling at another well:

> Tullow was also bound to consider the interests of Seadrill. It was not entitled to ignore the interest of Seadrill in receiving instructions […] to drill at a well not affected by the moratorium [the claimed force majeure].[42]

---

38. Julian Bailey, *Construction Law* (3rd edn, London Publishing, UK, 2020) vol 1, 186 (para. 3.96).
39. *Ibid.*, 187 (para. 3.97).
40. According to the court, the second quoted expression ('all' reasonable endeavours) 'does not appear to add anything' to the first. *Seadrill Ghana Operations Ltd v Tullow Ghana Ltd [2018] EWHC 1640 (Comm)*, [2019] BLR 61 [para. 30].
41. *Ibid.* [para. 89].
42. *Ibid.* [para. 96].

The court found, in the circumstances, that Tullow had not taken into account Seadrill's interest, as well as its own, to avoid or circumvent the moratorium, and consequently had not exercised reasonable endeavours to mitigate *force majeure*.[43]

(3) Civil law and UNIDROIT Principles

Under the civil law, the affected Party is likely to have a similar duty of mitigation by virtue of a party's obligation, among other things, to perform a contract in good faith.[44] The duty to mitigate damages is also to be found in Article 7.4.8 (*Mitigation of harm*) of the UNIDROIT Principles. While this article assumes that one party has not performed the contract (instead of there having been, as under Clause 18, an Exceptional Event), the principle should be the same:

> (1) The non-performing party is not liable for harm suffered by the aggrieved party [i.e. the affected party] *to the extent that the harm could have been reduced by the latter party's taking reasonable steps.*
> (2) The aggrieved party is entitled to recover any expenses reasonably incurred in attempting to reduce the harm. (Emphasis added)

The rule reflected in Article 7.4.8 is 'recognized in most legal systems in the world'.[45]

--ooOOoo--

43. *Ibid.*
44. Although French law does not formally recognise a duty to mitigate, it arrives at much the same result indirectly through, among other things, the duty under art. 1104 of the French Civil Code to perform a contract in good faith. Philippe Malaurie and others, *Droit des Obligations* (11th edn, LGDJ, Issy-les-Moulineaux, 2020) 561-562 (para. 615). On good faith, *see* **Section 4 Common Law and Civil Law Compared – 4.3.1 Duty of Good Faith** of **Chapter II Applicable Law** above.
45. Stefan Vogenauer (ed), *Commentary on the UNIDROIT Principles of International Commercial Contracts (PICC)* (2nd edn, OUP, Oxford, 2015) 1008 (para. 2).

18.4 Consequences of an Exceptional Event

If the Contractor is the affected Party and suffers delay and/or incurs Cost by reason of the Exceptional Event of which he/she gave a Notice under Sub-Clause 18.2 [*Notice of an Exceptional Event*], the Contractor shall be entitled subject to Sub-Clause 20.2 [*Claims for Payment and/or EOT*] to:

(a) EOT; and/or

(b) if the Exceptional Event is of the kind described in sub-paragraphs (a) to (e) of Sub-Clause 18.1 [*Exceptional Events*] and, in the case of sub-paragraphs (b) to (e) of that Sub-Clause, occurs in the Country, payment of such Cost.

If the Contractor is the affected Party and suffers delay and/or incurs Cost by reason of an Exceptional Event of which it has given Notice, the Contractor is entitled, subject to Sub-Clause 20.2, to an EOT, and/or – if the Exceptional Event is of the kind described in sub-paragraphs (a) to (e) of Sub-Clause 18.1 and in the case of sub-paragraphs (b) to (e) occurs in the Country – payment of such Cost.

Commentary:

(i) Main Changes from RB/99: While the wording of this Sub-Clause is quite different from Sub-Clause 19.4 of RB/99 due, among other things, to the new claims procedure in RB/17 (notably, Sub-Clause 20.2), there has been no change in substance.[46]

(ii) Related Clauses / Sub-Clauses: 7.6 [*Remedial Work*], 8.5 [*Extension of Time for Completion*], 13.6 [*Adjustments for Changes in Laws*], 17.2 [*Liability for Care of the Works*], 18 [*Exceptional Events*] and 20.2 [*Claims for Payment and/or EOT*].

46. Sub-Clause 19.5 [*Force Majeure Affecting Subcontractor*] of RB/99, which had provided that if a Subcontractor were entitled to relief from *force majeure* under its subcontract on terms broader than those specified in Clause 19, such broader terms would not excuse the Contractor under Clause 19, has been eliminated. Such elimination is justified as, self-evidently, the terms of a subcontract do not prevail over those of a (main) construction contract.

(iii) Analysis: While Clause 18 does not describe the consequences where an Exceptional Event affects the Employer (other than when saying that a Party must continue to make payments due[47] and other than under Sub-Clauses 18.5 and 18.6), it does describe them in Sub-Clause 18.4 where an Exceptional Event affects the Contractor.

(1) Right to EOT

The normal effect of an Exceptional Event or of *force majeure* (in a *force majeure*-type clause) on the Contractor is that it will cause some or all of its work to stop or be delayed either once temporarily or, in some cases, multiple times for relatively brief periods. Most often, *force majeure*-type clauses will, like this one, excuse the Contractor's performance, that is, relieve it from having to perform the Contract (or one or more obligations under it), including liability for Delay Damages, for as long as the event of *force majeure* continues.[48] Thus, this Sub-Clause expressly entitles the Contractor, where it suffers critical delay, to an EOT subject to Sub-Clause 20.2.

(2) Right to Cost

What is less usual in such a clause is for the Contractor to be compensated for the additional Cost it may have incurred on account of such an event, as Sub-Clause 18.4 does in the cases indicated.

But, since the first edition of the RB in 1957, the RB has provided that the Contractor should be compensated for additional costs it incurred on account of a similar list of events to those described in sub-paragraphs (a) to (e) of Sub-Clause 18.1 in RB/17.[49] Specifically, Sub-Clause 19.4 of RB/99 provided that if the Contractor was prevented from performing by war and related 'man-made' events,[50] including strikes or lockouts not involving the Contractor's Personnel, it could recover Cost (as defined).[51] As in the case of Sub-Clause 19.4 of RB/99, under the new Sub-Clause,

47. As provided for in the last paragraph of Sub-Clause 18.2.
48. Marcel Fontaine and Filip De Ly, *Drafting International Contracts: An Analysis of Contract Clauses* (Martinus Nijhoff, Leiden, the Netherlands, 2009) 425.
49. *See* Clause 65 dealing with 'Special Risks' of RB/57 through RB/87. For an example of costs being recovered under that clause, *see* second interim award, ICC case 5277 (1987), Sigvard Jarvin and others (eds), *Coll of ICC Arb Awards (1986 – 1990)* (ICC, Paris / Kluwer, the Netherlands, 1994) 112.
50. As distinct from 'natural' events, such as hurricanes or typhoons.
51. *See* Sub-Clauses 19.1 (i) to (iv) and 19.4(b). In the case of Sub-Clause 19.1 (ii) to (iv), they had to occur in the Country.

the Contractor is entitled to recover Cost if it is prevented from performing by the man-made events listed in sub-paragraph (a), namely, 'war, hostilities (whether war be declared or not), invasion, act of foreign enemies' wherever in the world they might occur and not just in the country of the Contractor or of the Site (i.e., the Country, as defined). The breadth of this right of recovery is important for an international contractor who may be procuring equipment, materials and/or labour from numerous different countries.

On the other hand, the Contractor's right to recover Cost, if prevented from performing by the man-made events listed in sub-paragraphs (b) to (e) of Sub-Clause 18.1, is limited to those which occur within the Country.[52]

When recovery of Cost is not available under this Sub-Clause but the Exceptional Event has given rise to a change in Laws,[53] the Contractor may be able to recover Cost under Sub-Clause 13.6 [*Adjustments for Changes in Laws*].

52. While Sub-Clause 19.4 of RB/99 had added 'natural catastrophes' of various kinds to the list of 'Force Majeure' events (and they are listed as an Exceptional Event in Sub-Clause 18.1(f) of RB 17), the Contractor is not entitled to Cost on this account as most natural hazards, unlike man-made events, would be insured through a CAR insurance policy and therefore the Contractor and the Employer would (or should) be jointly covered for such risks by that policy. *See* the commentary on Sub-Clause 19.2.1 [*Insurance to be provided by the Contractor – The Works*] below (I am grateful to Dr Nael Bunni for this information). The World Bank's COPA provides expressly that Cost under Sub-Clause 18.4 would include the costs of rectifying or replacing the Works and/or Goods damaged or destroyed, to the extent that they are not indemnified through the insurance policy referred to in Sub-Clause 19.2. Sub-Clause 18.4, COPA.
53. Thus, the COVID-19 pandemic, which began in 2019, has given rise to changes in laws relevant to construction in numerous countries. *See*, for example, French Ordinance no 2020-319 of 25 March 2020 relating to public works projects and contracts affected by COVID-19 and, in the Kingdom of Saudi Arabia, its Supreme Court's General Assembly Decision no 45/M dated 08/05/1442 AH containing provisions dealing specifically with the impact of the pandemic on construction contracts.

(iv) Related Law: For a case where the Contractor recovered costs on account of war under a predecessor of Clause 18 (Clause 65 of RB/87), *see* the final award, ICC case 12654 (2005).[54]

--ooOOoo--

18.5 Optional Termination

If the execution of substantially all the Works in progress is prevented for a continuous period of 84 days by reason of an Exceptional Event of which Notice has been given under Sub-Clause 18.2 [*Notice of an Exceptional Event*], or for multiple periods which total more than 140 days due to the same Exceptional Event, then either Party may give to the other Party a Notice of termination of the Contract.

In this event, the date of termination shall be the date 7 days after the Notice is received by the other Party, and the Contractor shall proceed in accordance with Sub-Clause 16.3 [*Contractor's Obligations After Termination*].

After the date of termination the Contractor shall, as soon as practicable, submit detailed supporting particulars (as reasonably required by the Engineer) of the value of the work done, which shall include:

(a) the amounts payable for any work carried out for which a price is stated in the Contract;

(b) the Cost of Plant and Materials ordered for the Works which have been delivered to the Contractor, or of which the Contractor is liable to accept delivery. This Plant and Materials shall become the property of (and be at the risk of) the Employer when paid for by the Employer, and the Contractor shall place the same at the Employer's disposal;

54. ICC Int'l Ct Arb Bull, vol 23, no 2, 2012, 77, 79-82 (paras 273-305) (commentary 38, 39-40). *See also* the partial award in ICC case 5195 (1986) referred to under **(iv) Related Law** in the commentary on Sub-Clause 18.2 above.

(c) any other Cost or liability which in the circumstances was reasonably incurred by the Contractor in the expectation of completing the Works;

(d) the Cost of removal of Temporary Works and Contractor's Equipment from the Site and the return of these items to the Contractor's place of business in the Contractor's country (or to any other destination(s) at no greater cost); and

(e) the Cost of repatriation of the Contractor's staff and labour employed wholly in connection with the Works at the date of termination.

The Engineer shall then proceed under Sub-Clause 3.7 [*Agreement or Determination*] to agree or determine the value of work done (and, for the purpose of Sub-Clause 3.7.3 [*Time limits*], the date the Engineer receives the Contractor's particulars under this Sub-Clause shall be the date of commencement of the time limit for agreement under Sub-Clause 3.7.3).

The Engineer shall issue a Payment Certificate, under Sub-Clause 14.6 [*Issue of IPC*], for the amount so agreed or determined, without the need for the Contractor to submit a Statement.

If execution of substantially all of the Works in progress is prevented by an Exceptional Event (of which Notice has been given) for a continuous period of 84 days, or for multiple periods which total more than 140 days due to the same Exceptional Event, either Party may give the other a Notice of termination of the Contract. If so, the date of termination is 7 days after the Notice is received by the other Party and the Contractor must proceed as provided in Sub-Clause 16.3. After termination, the Contractor must submit particulars of the value of the work done, including the items listed in sub-paragraphs (a) to (e). The Engineer must then under Sub-Clause 3.7 agree or determine the value of such work and issue an IPC for the agreed or determined amount.

Commentary

(i) Main Changes from RB/99:

(1) The Sub-Clause is similar to Sub-Clause 19.6 [*Optional Termination, Payment and Release*] in RB/99 except for the second to last paragraph which has been added to take account of the new claims procedure provided for in Sub-Clause 3.7 [*Agreement or Determination*] of RB/17.
(2) The third paragraph expressly requires the Contractor, as soon as practicable, to submit detailed supporting particulars of the value of the work done, whereas under the second paragraph of Sub-Clause 19.6 of RB/99 the Engineer determined such value.
(3) While the last paragraph now provides expressly that the Engineer shall issue an IPC without the need for the Contractor to submit a Statement, this was, arguably, already implied by the second paragraph of Sub-Clause 19.6 of RB/99.

(ii) Related Clauses / Sub-Clauses: 1.3 [*Notices and Other Communications*], 1.10 [*Employer's Use of Contractor's Documents*], 1.16 [*Contract Termination*], 4.2.2 [*Performance Security – Claims under the Performance Security*], 4.2.3 [*Performance Security – Return of the Performance Security*], 8.9 [*Employer's Suspension*], 13.7 [*Agreement or Determination*], 14.2.3 [*Contract Price and Payment – Repayment of Advance Payment*], 14.6 [*Issue of IPC*], 15.6 [*Valuation after Termination for Employer's Convenience*], 16.3 [*Contractor's Obligations after Termination*], 16.4 [*Payment after Termination by Contractor*] and 18 [*Exceptional Events*].

(iii) Analysis:

(1) Purpose of Sub-Clause

When the Contractor is prevented from executing the Works by an Exceptional Event, then one or – more likely – both Parties will begin to suffer damage, though not necessarily in equal measure. The Employer will be damaged because completion may be delayed, and it may have to bear the Contractor's running Costs in the meantime in the cases indicated in Sub-Clause 18.4 (b). The Contractor will be damaged as, while it will be reimbursed for its running Costs in certain cases, it will not be reimbursed where, for example, the event or circumstance in the case of sub-paragraphs (b) to (e) of Sub-Clause 18.1 occurs outside the

Country.[55] Moreover, in no case will the Contractor be recovering profit,[56] whereas it would (presumably) be doing so if its work was not prevented or, if prevented, its resources were deployed under another contract. Thus, neither Party may want to continue with the Contract if the duration of the Exceptional Event is prolonged.[57]

Accordingly, if execution of substantially all of the Works in progress[58] is prevented either for a continuous period of 84 days[59] or for multiple periods which total more than 140 days due to the same Exceptional Event, each Party is given the right to terminate the Contract after giving a Notice of termination to the other.

(2) Multiple interruptions

It is easy to see how the violent political events, labour disputes and natural catastrophes described in Sub-Clause 18.1(a) to (f) can prevent performance temporarily on a construction site. But they can also do so repeatedly, for example, if the Works are being executed in a politically insecure region and/or are regularly disturbed by shootings, kidnappings and/or other sporadic acts of violence affecting the safety of those employed on the Works and their families. This explains the need to address the situation of where performance of the Works is interrupted for multiple time periods which, if they total more than 140 days and are due to the same Exceptional Event, give each Party the right to terminate the Contract.

(3) Termination procedure

If either Party elects to terminate under this Sub-Clause then it must give to the other Party and the Engineer[60] a Notice of termination, and the date

55. Sub-Clause 18.4 [*Consequences of an Exceptional Event*], sub-para. (b).
56. *See* the definition of '**Cost**' in Sub-Clause 1.1.19.
57. However, if work is prevented but the Employer would still like the Contract to continue, the Engineer could suspend the Works for at least another 84 days pursuant to Sub-Clause 8.9 [*Employer's Suspension*]. But then, in addition to an EOT, the Employer would be liable for the Contractor's Cost Plus Profit during the suspension period. Sub-Clause 8.10 [*Consequences of Employer's Suspension*].
58. According to FIDIC, '[i]n other words, [the Contractor] has been unable to progress the execution other than to an insubstantial extent'. *The FIDIC Contracts Guide* (1st edn, FIDIC, 2000) 297.
59. '**day**' means a calendar day. *See* Sub-Clause 1.1.25.
60. Sub-Clause 1.3, last paragraph. In connection with any termination, *see* Sub-Clause 1.16 [*Contract Termination*] and the commentary thereon above.

of termination will be 7 days after the Notice is received by the other Party. The Contractor must then cease further work and otherwise proceed in accordance with Sub-Clause 16.3 [*Contractor's Obligations After Termination*].[61]

The Contractor is paid for all the work which it has done, including the Cost of the return of the Contractor's Equipment and Temporary Works to the Contractor's country and the repatriation of its staff and labour, but is not entitled to profit on the balance of the work which it will have been prevented from doing.[62] If the advance payment has not already been repaid, then the remaining balance would be immediately due and payable to the Employer.[63]

If the Employer still wishes to complete the Works, perhaps with another contractor, it would be entitled to copy, use and communicate the Contractor's Documents for which the Contractor has received payment.[64]

(4) Amendment to Contract

As a practical matter, given the investment which each Party may already have made in the project, neither may wish to terminate the Contract. In that case, they would need to negotiate and agree on an amendment to the Contract setting out the terms under which the Contractor would agree to remain available to execute the Works beyond the relevant 84- or 140-day period.[65]

--ooOOoo--

61. Promptly after the date of termination, the Employer must return the Performance Security to the Contractor. *See* Sub-Clause 4.2.3.
62. Sub-Clause 18.5, third paragraph. If the Employer should be late in paying the Engineer's IPC then, as it would be issued under Sub-Clause 14.6, Sub-Clause 14.8 providing for the payment of financial charges should apply.
63. Sub-Clause 14.2.3. In this case, the advance payment guarantee should be reduced to zero and be returned to the Contractor.
64. Sub-Clause 1.10(d)(ii).
65. Resort to an amendment to permit continued performance of the Contract is referred to in Sub-Clause 18.6 [*Release from Performance under the Law*] below. Sub-Clauses 8.9 to 8.13 relating to an Employer's suspension may be helpful as a guide to the terms of such an amendment.

18.6 Release from Performance under the Law

In addition to any other provision of this Clause, if any event arises outside the control of the Parties (including, but not limited to, an Exceptional Event) which:

(a) makes it impossible or unlawful for either Party or both Parties to fulfil their contractual obligations; or

(b) under the law governing the Contract, entitles the Parties to be released from further performance of the Contract,

and if the Parties are unable to agree on an amendment to the Contract that would permit the continued performance of the Contract, then after either Party gives a Notice to the other Party of such event:

(i) the Parties shall be discharged from further performance, and without prejudice to the rights of either Party in respect of any previous breach of the Contract; and

(ii) the amount payable by the Employer to the Contractor shall be the same as would have been payable under Sub-Clause 18.5 [*Optional Termination*], and such amount shall be certified by the Engineer, as if the Contract had been terminated under that Sub-Clause.

If any event arises outside the control of the Parties, including an Exceptional Event, which: (a) makes it impossible or unlawful for either or both Parties to perform the Contract or (b) entitles the Parties to be released from the Contract under the law governing the Contract, and if the Parties are unable to agree to continued performance of the Contract then, after either Party gives a Notice to the other of such event, the Parties will be discharged from further performance of the Contract, and the Employer shall pay the Contractor as provided in Sub-Clause 18.5.

Commentary

(i) Main Changes from RB/99: The only significant change[66] is to provide that, if any 'event'[67] described in (a) or (b) of the new Sub-Clause occurs and (the following are the new words) 'if the Parties are unable to agree on an amendment to the Contract that would permit the continued performance of the Contract', then after either Party gives a Notice to the other of such event, they are discharged from further performance (although the Contract may have terminated as a matter of law already if it had become impossible or illegal to perform). The new language recognises that, depending on the circumstances, the Parties might be able, by amending the Contract, to enable it to continue.

(ii) Related Clauses / Sub-Clauses: 1.3 [*Notices and Other Communications*], 1.4 [*Law and Language*], 1.13 [*Compliance with Laws*], 1.16 [*Contract Termination*], 4.2.2 [*Performance Security – Claims under the Performance Security*], 4.2.3 [*Performance Security – Return of the Performance Security*] and 18.5 [*Optional Termination*].

(iii) Analysis: This Sub-Clause provides for more extreme – and less common – situations than those provided for in Sub-Clauses 18.1 to 18.5. It envisages three types of events, as follows:

(1) where the Contract becomes *impossible to perform* (e.g., the construction site is washed away in a flood, rendering performance of the contract impossible,[68] or construction is prevented by a rebellious army[69]);

(2) where the Contract has become *unlawful to perform* (e.g., due to wartime restrictions, a government ministry orders construction work to cease[70]); and

66. In addition, at the beginning of the Sub-Clause the words '[n]otwithstanding any other provision' (Sub-Clause 19.7 of RB/99) have been replaced by '[i]n addition to any other provision' (Sub-Clause 18.6 of RB/17).
67. The corresponding Sub-Clause 19.7 of RB/99 had referred to an 'event or circumstance'.
68. *See*, e.g., *Union of India v A.S. Chopra et al*, Ind. L.R. (Bombay Series) 1974, 26.
69. *See*, e.g., Second interim award in ICC case 5277 (1987), Sigvard Jarvin and others, *Coll of ICC Arb Awards (1986 – 1990)* (ICC, Paris / Kluwer, the Netherlands, 1994) 112.
70. *See*, e.g., *Metropolitan Water Board v Dick Kerr & Co.* [1918] A.C. 119.

(3) where, *under the law governing the Contract, the Parties are entitled to be released from further performance*,[71] which may, among other things, also be the situation in the case of events (1) and (2) above.[72]

Although one of these three obstacles to performance may have occurred, in some cases it may still be possible for the Parties to amend the Contract in such a way as to overcome or avoid it and thus allow the Contract to continue to be performed and completed. Accordingly, the Sub-Clause provides for this possibility. However, if such an amendment is not possible or cannot be agreed upon, then either Party may give a Notice to the other Party of such an impasse, and thereupon the Parties will be discharged from the Contract without prejudice to their respective rights, and Sub-Clause 18.5 [*Optional Termination*] will apply as regards the amount payable by the Employer to the Contractor.[73] This is a reasonable financial result as the event will have been beyond the Parties' control.[74]

(iv) Related Law: As stated above,[75] under both common law and civil law, a Party may be excused and/or relieved from its contractual obligations in only a very narrow range of events and circumstances. Under the civil law, the relevant legal doctrines include, but are not limited to, *force majeure*, as commonly provided for, or recognised, in the civil code or other law of a civil law country,[76] and hardship (or

71. *See* the legal doctrines described under **(iv) Related Law** below.
72. For example, partial award, ICC case 5195 (1986), YB Comm Arb, vol XIII – 1988, 69, 75-6 (construction contract discharged for frustration under common law). This case is described under **(iv) Related Law** in the commentary on Sub-Clause 18.2 above.
73. Promptly after the date of termination, the Employer must return the Performance Security to the Contractor, *see* Sub-Clause 4.2.3. If the Employer should be late in making payment, then the Contractor should be entitled to financing charges pursuant to Sub-Clause 14.8, for the same reason that it is so entitled under Sub-Clause 18.5.
74. In connection with any termination, *see* Sub-Clause 1.16 [*Contract Termination*] and the commentary thereon above.
75. *See* under **(iii) Analysis** of the commentary on Sub-Clause 18.1 above.
76. *Force majeure* as it may be provided for in the civil code or other law of a civil law country is to be clearly distinguished from *force majeure* as it may be provided for in a *force majeure* clause drafted for inclusion in a given contract which is effectively what Clause 18 [*Exceptional Events*] is. *Force*

imprévision), both of which have been described in an earlier Chapter.[77] Accordingly, discussion here is limited to the common law and the UNIDROIT Principles.

(1) English law: doctrine of frustration

Under English law, the main relevant doctrine is frustration[78] which will only 'very rarely'[79] apply. It has been described as a basis to discharge a contract when something occurs which renders:

> it physically or commercially impossible to fulfil the contract or transforms the obligation to perform into a radically different obligation from that undertaken at the moment of entry into the contract.[80]

---

majeure as provided for in the law of a civil law country will invariably be narrower in scope than *force majeure* as defined in a *force majeure* clause in a contract. *See* **Section 4 Common Law and Civil Law Compared – 4.4.7 *Force Majeure* and Hardship** of **Chapter II Applicable Law** above.

77. In the case of a contract for public works (an administrative contract), these doctrines are discussed in **Section 4 Common Law and Civil Law Compared – 4.6.2 Hardship (*Imprévision*)** and **4.6.5 *Force Majeure*** and, in the case of private or civil contracts, in **Section 4.4.7 *Force Majeure* and Hardship** of **Chapter II Applicable Law** above.
78. A related doctrine is common mistake, which 'is concerned with a common misapprehension which was present at the date of entry into the contract, whereas frustration is solely concerned with events which occur *after* the date of formation of the contract'. *Chitty on Contracts* (33rd edn, vol I, Sweet & Maxwell, London, 2018) 1669-1670 (para. 23-002).
79. Stephen Furst and Vivian Ramsey, *Keating on Construction Contracts* (11th edn, Sweet & Maxwell, London, 2021) 174 (para. 6-058). For frustration under a FIDIC contract (RB/69), *see*, e.g., second interim award, ICC case 5277 (1987), Sigvard Jarvin and others, *Coll of ICC Arb Awards (1986 – 1990)* (ICC, Paris / Kluwer, the Netherlands, 1994), 112.
80. *Chitty on Contracts* (33rd edn, vol I, Sweet & Maxwell, London, 2018) 1669 (para. 23-001). The frustration doctrine first appeared in the English case of *Taylor v Caldwell* (1863), where the court decided that a party is freed from its contractual obligation and from liability for damages if performance of the contract required the continued existence of a particular thing, and this thing was accidentally destroyed before the time of performance. The case involved a contract under which Taylor was to have the use of Caldwell's music hall for performances on four days but the music hall was accidentally destroyed by fire before the first performance. Taylor then sued Caldwell for breach of contract, claiming as damages the expenses he had incurred in preparing for the performances. However, the court held that Caldwell was excused, finding that the parties contracted on the basis of the continued

In *Davis Contractors Ltd. v Fareham Urban District Council* (1956), the contractor had to build 78 houses for a fixed price in 8 months, but due to unexpected circumstances (the unavailability of adequate supplies of labour), it actually took 22 months to finish the work. The English House of Lords, denying that frustration had been established, described it as occurring:

> whenever the law recognizes that without default of either party a contractual obligation has become incapable of being performed because the circumstances in which performance is called for would render it a thing radically different from that which was undertaken by the contract [...] It was not this I promised to do.[81]

Similarly, in the *British Movietonews, Ltd. v London & District Cinemas, Ltd.* case (1952), the English court held that an unanticipated 'wholly abnormal rise or fall in prices' would not be grounds for frustration.[82]

As another English court has stated:

> Frustration is a doctrine only too often invoked by a party to a contract which finds performance difficult or unprofitable, but it is very rarely relied on with success. It is in fact a kind of last ditch.[83]

As a practical matter, under English law, almost no increase in price or other change in economic circumstances of whatever magnitude or unforeseeability can lead to frustration. There has to have been an

existence of the music hall. The court stated that the 'principle seems to us to be that, in contracts in which the performance depends on the continued existence of a given person or thing, a condition is implied that the impossibility of performance arising from the perishing of the person or thing shall excuse the performance'. *Taylor v Caldwell* (1863) 3 B&S 826.

81. Per Lord Radcliffe, *Davis Contractors Ltd v Fareham Urban District Council* (1956) A.C. 696, 729. However, for construction cases where frustration was found *see* the partial award in ICC case 5195 (1986) referred to under **(iv) Related Law** of the commentary on Sub-Clause 18.2 above and *Union of India v A.S. Chopra et al* referred to in fn 68 under **(iii) Analysis** immediately above.
82. *British Movietonews Ltd v London & District Cinemas Ltd* (1952) A.C. 166, 185.
83. Harman L.J. in *Tsakiroglou & Co., Ltd v Noblee Thorl GmbH* (1960) 2 Q.B. at 370, CA; aff'd (1962) A.C. 93, HL; cited in Stephen Furst and Vivian Ramsey, *Keating on Construction Contracts* (11th edn, Sweet & Maxwell, London, 2021) 174 (para. 6-058) fn. 160.

economic catastrophe, which can rarely be established. The effect of frustration is, as stated above, automatically to discharge the parties from future performance of the contract and no compensation is payable.[84]

(2) US law: doctrine of impracticability

Under US law, the relevant doctrine which excuses a party's failure to perform a contract is impracticability.[85] The doctrine has four requirements, as follows: (i) the frustrating event must have made 'performance as agreed […] impracticable'; (ii) the non-occurrence of the supervening event (that caused the impracticability) must have been 'a basic assumption on which the contract was made'; (iii) the impracticability must have resulted without the fault of the party seeking to be excused; and (iv) that party must not have assumed a greater obligation than the law imposes.[86]

Unlike in England, relief is available for unforeseeable cost increases in extreme cases. For example, in *Mineral Park Land Co. v Howard* (1916),

84. *See* the English *Law Reform (Frustrated Contracts) Act 1943* for the financial consequences. Frustration may apply notwithstanding a clause like Clause 18 (a *force majeure*-type clause), e.g.:

(1) Although a six-year construction contract entered into in 1914 provided that the contractor would be entitled to a time extension for *'any difficulties, impediments, obstructions […] whatsoever and howsoever occasioned'*, when in 1916 (during World War I) the UK Government ordered the contractor to cease work, the contract was held to be frustrated; *Metropolitan Water Board v Dick Kerr and Company, Limited* (1918) A.C. 119.

(2) A contract for a sale of flats to be built provided that the vendor could rescind *'should any unforeseen circumstances beyond the Vendor's control arise'* to prevent the sale. When part of the hillside above the site slipped away obliterating the building works, the contract was held to have been frustrated; *Wong Lai Ying v Chinachem Investment Co. Ltd* [1980] HKLR 1 (1979) 13 BLR 81.

85. However, US law also recognises the doctrines of frustration and what it refers to as frustration of purpose. The latter doctrine applies where a supervening event has frustrated the purpose of a contract; e.g., a contractor was excused under a contract with a subcontractor that was to provide median barriers when the highway department decided not to instal barriers. *Chase Precast Corp v John J. Paonessa Co.*, 566 N.E. 2d 603 (Mass 1991) cited in E Allan Farnsworth, *Contracts* (4th edn Aspen, NY, 2004) 634 (para. 9.7, fn. 5).

86. *Ibid.*, 625 (para. 9.6).

the defendant – a contractor – had agreed by contract to take a quantity of gravel from the claimant's land at a certain price. When about half of the gravel was taken, the defendant refused to continue because the remainder was below water level and therefore it would have incurred great expense to do so. Although performance was not materially impossible, the court rejected the claimant's – the employer's – claim for damages for breach of contract, finding that it would have cost the defendant 10 to 12 times the usual cost to take the remaining gravel, declaring that:

> [a] thing is impossible in legal contemplation when it is not practicable; and a thing is impracticable when it can only be done at an excessive and unreasonable cost.[87]

The US courts have also addressed the issue in, among others, *Northern Corporation v Chugach Electric Association* (1974), where an Alaska dam contract required the contractor to transport rock across a frozen lake by truck. On several occasions, the contractor's trucks broke through the ice and two people working for the contractor were killed. While the court discharged the contract on the grounds of impossibility, rather than impracticability, the court added that a contract is discharged 'if the cost of performance would be so disproportionate to that reasonably contemplated by the parties as to make the contract totally impractical in a commercial sense'.[88]

The effect of impracticability is to discharge the parties from further performance of the contract, temporarily, partially or wholly depending on the circumstances. As in the case of frustration under English law, there is no recovery for any additional cost or damage that may have been suffered.

The rarity of the situations in which the common law – or even the civil law[89] – can be invoked so as to enable a party to be relieved from a Contract help explains the practical importance of Clause 18 [*Exceptional Events*].

87. *Mineral Park Land Co. v Howard* 156 P. 458, 460 (para. 4) (1916).

88. *Northern Corporation v Chugach Electric Association* 518 P. 2d 76 (1974) modified on rehearing 523 P. 2d 1243 (1974).

89. *See* **Section 4 Common Law and Civil Law Compared – 4.4.7 *Force Majeure* and Hardship** of **Chapter II Applicable Law** above.

(3) UNIDROIT Principles

Under the UNIDROIT Principles, a contract may be brought to an end in the case of illegality (Article 3.3.1 and 3.3.2), where a public permission is not granted or is refused (Article 6.1.16 and 6.1.17), hardship, as defined (Article 6.2.1-6.2.3),[90] and *force majeure*, as defined (Article 7.1.7).[91] The hardship and *force majeure* provisions are not very different from Clause 18. *Force majeure* may result, under the Principles, in the suspension of any limitation period (Article 10.8).

--ooOOoo--

90. Art. 6.2.2 defines hardship as follows:

> There is hardship where the occurrence of events fundamentally alters the equilibrium of the contract either because the cost of a party's performance has increased or because the value of the performance a party receives has diminished, and
> (a) the events occur or become known to the disadvantaged party after the conclusion of the contract;
> (b) the events could not reasonably have been taken into account by the disadvantaged party at the time of the conclusion of the contract;
> (c) the events are beyond the control of the disadvantaged party; and
> (d) the risk of the events was not assumed by the disadvantaged party.

91. Art. 7.1.7 provides for *force majeure* as follows:

> (1) Non-performance by a party is excused if that party proves that the non-performance was due to an impediment beyond its control and that it could not reasonably be expected to have taken the impediment into account at the time of the conclusion of the contract or to have avoided or overcome it or its consequences.
> (2) When the impediment is only temporary, the excuse shall have effect for such period as is reasonable having regard to the effect of the impediment on the performance of the contract.
> (3) The party who fails to perform must give notice to the other party of the impediment and its effect on its ability to perform. If the notice is not received by the other party within a reasonable time after the party who fails to perform knew or ought to have known of the impediment, it is liable for damages resulting from such non-receipt.
> (4) Nothing in this Article prevents a party from exercising a right to terminate the contract or to withhold performance or request interest on due money.

19 INSURANCE

This Clause requires the Contractor to effect and maintain insurances. Without limiting either Party's obligations under the Contract, Sub-Clause 19.1 sets out general requirements relating to the insurances which the Contractor is to obtain. Sub-Clause 19.2 then requires the Contractor to effect and maintain six different types of insurances beginning with insurances of the Works and Goods (Sub-Clause 19.2.1).

--ooOOoo--

19.1 General Requirements

Without limiting either Party's obligations or responsibilities under the Contract, the Contractor shall effect and maintain all insurances for which the Contractor is responsible with insurers and in terms, both of which shall be subject to consent by the Employer. These terms shall be consistent with terms (if any) agreed by both Parties before the date of the Letter of Acceptance.

The insurances required to be provided under this Clause are the minimum required by the Employer, and the Contractor may, at the Contractor's own cost, add such other insurances that the Contractor may deem prudent.

Whenever required by the Employer, the Contractor shall produce the insurance policies which the Contractor is required to effect under the Contract. As each premium is paid, the Contractor shall promptly submit either a copy of each receipt of payment to the Employer (with a copy to the Engineer), or confirmation from the insurers that the premium has been paid.

If the Contractor fails to effect and keep in force any of the insurances required under Sub-Clause 19.2 [*Insurance to be provided by the Contractor*] then, and in any such case, the Employer may effect and keep in force such insurances and pay any premium as may be necessary and recover the same from the Contractor from time to time by deducting the amount(s) so paid from any moneys due to the

Contractor or otherwise recover the same as a debt from the Contractor. The provisions of Clause 20 [*Employer's and Contractor's Claims*] shall not apply to this Sub-Clause.

If either the Contractor or the Employer fails to comply with any condition of the insurances effected under the Contract, the Party so failing to comply shall indemnify the other Party against all direct losses and claims (including legal fees and expenses) arising from such failure.

The Contractor shall also be responsible for the following:

(a) notifying the insurers of any changes in the nature, extent or programme for the execution of the Works; and
(b) the adequacy and validity of the insurances in accordance with the Contract at all times during the performance of the Contract.

The permitted deductible limits allowed in any policy shall not exceed the amounts stated in the Contract Data (if not stated, the amounts agreed with the Employer).

Where there is a shared liability the loss shall be borne by each Party in proportion to each Party's liability, provided the non-recovery from insurers has not been caused by a breach of this Clause by the Contractor or the Employer. In the event that non-recovery from insurers has been caused by such a breach, the defaulting Party shall bear the loss suffered.

Without limiting either Party's contractual obligations, the Contractor shall maintain insurances for which it is responsible with both insurers and in terms consented to by the Employer. The terms shall be consistent with those agreed by the Parties before the date of the Letter of Acceptance.

The insurances required by this Clause are the minimum required by the Employer. The Contractor may add other insurances at its cost. Whenever required by the Employer, the Contractor shall produce the insurance policies which the Contractor is required to effect under

the Contract. If the Contractor fails to maintain the insurances required by Sub-Clause 19.2, the Employer may effect such insurances and recover the premiums paid from the Contractor. Clause 20 shall not apply.

If either Party fails to comply with any condition of the insurances, it shall indemnify the other for any resulting direct losses.

The Contractor is responsible for notifying the insurers of changes in the Works as well for the adequacy and validity of the insurances under the Contract. The permitted deductibles must not exceed the amounts in the Contract Data or agreed with the Employer. Where there is a shared liability, each Party shall be liable in proportion to its liability. However, if a Party breaches this Clause causing a non-recovery from the insurers, then it shall bear the loss.

Commentary

(i) Main Changes from RB/99: Clause 19 of RB/17 is an almost complete revision of the corresponding Clause in RB/99, Clause 18:

(1) Sub-Clauses 19.1 and 19.2 of RB/17 are based closely on Sub-Clauses 19.1 and 19.2 of GB/08, which prescribe the insurances to be provided by the Contractor during the 'Design-Build Period' under that form of contract.[1]

(2) While Clause 18 of RB/99 had envisaged that insurances would be effected and maintained by an 'insuring Party', which could be either the Employer or the Contractor, Sub-Clauses 19.1 and 19.2 of RB/17, like Sub-Clauses 19.1 and 19.2 of GB/08, assume that the Contractor will generally effect and maintain all insurances.

(ii) Related Clauses / Sub-Clauses: 1.2 [*Interpretation*], 1.3 [*Notices and Other Communications*], 11.5 [*Remedying of Defective Work Off Site*], 14.5 [*Plant and Materials Intended for the Works*], 17.4 [*Indemnities by Contractor*], 19.2 [*Insurances to be provided by the Contractor*] and 20 [*Employer's and Contractor's Claims*].

1. Clause 19 of RB/17, like Clause 19 of GB/08, have been much influenced by comments made by Dr Nael G Bunni on Clauses 17 to 19 of the 1999 FIDIC suite of contracts, *see* Nael G Bunni, 'FIDIC's New Suite of Contracts – Clauses 17 to 19' [2001] ICLR 523 and Nael G. Bunni and Lydia B. Bunni, *Risk and Insurance in Construction* (3rd edn, Routledge, London, 2022).

(iii) Analysis:

(1) Purposes of Sub-Clauses 19.1 and 19.2

Civil engineering projects are subject to a wide range of risks which may cause loss to the Contractor, the Employer and/or to others. There is a correspondingly wide range of types of insurance available to cover the losses from their incidence.[2] While Sub-Clause 19.1 prescribes general rules applicable to insurances required by the Conditions, Sub-Clause 19.2 – commented upon separately below – provides for six different types of insurance which the Contractor is required to effect and maintain.

(2) Contractor's general insurance obligations

Sub-Clause 19.1 begins with the following important words that qualify the entirety of Clause 19:

> [w]ithout limiting either Party's obligations or responsibilities under the Contract, the Contractor shall effect and maintain all insurances for which the Contractor is responsible [...].

This provision makes clear that Clause 19 does not limit or replace the Parties' respective obligations under the Contract. Thus, by this provision, the Contractor is denied the right to argue – as contractors have done in similar situations[3] – that because it has provided the insurance policies prescribed in Sub-Clause 19.2 that they somehow modify or replace the Contractor's obligations under the Contract.

As mentioned above, this Clause assumes that the Contractor, and not the Employer, will be required to effect insurances.[4] However, in the *Guidance*, FIDIC recognises that the Employer may wish to provide some of the insurance cover under the Employer's own policies, and makes

2. Julian Bailey, *Construction Law* (3rd edn, London Publishing, UK, 2020) vol 3, 1401 (para. 17.02).
3. *See* the Scottish case of *SSE Generation Ltd v Hochtief* [2015] CSOH 92 where the contractor had argued – unsuccessfully – that the contractor's 'all risk' policy (CAR) provided for by the construction contract took the place of the parties' liabilities under the contract in respect of loss covered by that policy.
4. As FIDIC has explained: '[t]ypically, insurances are obtained by the Contractor, often from insurers with whom he maintains a continuous commercial relationship and who therefore may be able to offer competitive terms'. *The FIDIC Contracts Guide* (1st edn, FIDIC, 2000) 280.

certain recommendations in this regard.[5] Specifically, FIDIC strongly recommends that the tender documents include details of such insurances as an annex to the Special Provisions (which constitute Part B of the Particular Conditions) so that tenderers can estimate what other insurances they may wish to have for their own protection. FIDIC also recommends that the Employer be advised by a construction insurance specialist when preparing the wording of the revised sub-clauses.[6]

Assuming that the Contractor will be obtaining insurances, the General Conditions envisage that the Employer will state its particular requirements regarding insurance in the Particular Conditions, notably in the Contract Data,[7] included in the tender dossier. The instructions to tenderers may then request tenderers to submit details of the insurer(s) and insurances which they propose to provide in response, including conditions, limits, exclusions and deductibles/excesses.[8] The Parties would then discuss and agree to the main operative terms before the date of the Letter of Acceptance (or, if there is none, the Contract Agreement).[9] The terms agreed upon might then be contained in a memorandum annexed to the Letter of Acceptance.[10] However, as has been mentioned by others,[11] the prospect of the Employer and a tenderer having direct talks before the award of a contract may be regulated, or prohibited, by applicable procurement regulations.[12]

5. *Guidance for the Preparation of Particular Conditions*, 46.
6. *Ibid.*
7. *See* the numerous blank spaces in relation to Clause 19 [*Insurance*] in the Contract Data to be completed, at least initially, with details of the insurance required by the Employer.
8. *The FIDIC Contracts Guide* (1st edn, FIDIC, 2000) 280.
9. *See* Sub-Clause 19.1, first paragraph, and Sub-Clause 1.1.50 '**Letter of Acceptance**'.
10. *See* the definition of the '**Letter of Acceptance**', Sub-Clause 1.1.50, which refers to it as including 'annexed memoranda comprising agreements between and signed by both Parties'.
11. Leo Grutters and Brian Barr, *FIDIC Red, Yellow and Silver Books, A Practical Guide to the 2017 Editions* (Sweet & Maxwell, London, 2018), 275.
12. Thus, the *UNCITRAL Model Law on Public Procurement* (2011) provides:

    > No negotiations shall take place between the procuring entity and a supplier or contractor with respect to a tender presented by the supplier or contractor (art. 44).

    The World Bank's regulations require that, following competitive bidding, negotiations before final contract award may only take place in the presence of a 'Probity

Thereafter, pursuant to the first paragraph of this Sub-Clause, the actual insurance policies which the Contractor obtains must, as regards the insurers and their terms, be consented to by the Employer (assuming the Employer has not already done so before the Letter of Acceptance).[13] Pursuant to the same paragraph, the terms of the insurance must be consistent with the terms agreed by the Parties before the date of the Letter of Acceptance.

The insurances required to be provided under this Clause are stated to be the minimum required by the Employer and therefore the Contractor may, at its own cost, add such other insurances as it might deem prudent.[14] Thus, if Goods need to be transported by sea, the Contractor will likely want to buy marine insurance to cover this risk if such insurance is not required already by the Contract.

(3) Contractor's failure to keep insurances and notifications of changes

If the Contractor fails to keep any of the insurances required by Sub-Clause 19.2, then the Employer may effect such insurances, pay the premiums and recover the same from the Contractor by deductions from amounts due to it or otherwise as a debt due from the Contractor.[15] Exceptionally, it is provided that Clause 20 [*Employer's and Contractor's Claims*] will not apply to this Sub-Clause.[16]

The Contractor is responsible for notifying insurers of any changes in the nature, extent or programme for the execution of the Works, as well as for the adequacy and validity of the insurances in accordance with the Contract and during its performance.[17] Surprisingly, however, there is no requirement that the Contractor sends a copy of this notification to the Engineer or the Employer unless Sub-Clause 1.3 [*Notices and Other Communications*] is interpreted as requiring it to do so.[18]

Assurance Provider' agreed to by the Bank (*Procurement Regulations for Investment Project Financing ('IPF') Borrowers – Goods, Works, Non-Consulting and Consulting Services* (4th edn, November 2020, (S 6.35)).

13. Pursuant to Sub-Clause 1.3 [*Notices and Other Communications*], such consent must not be unreasonably withheld or delayed. *See also* Sub-Clause 1.2 (g) regarding 'consent'.
14. Sub-Clause 19.1, second paragraph.
15. Sub-Clause 19.1, fourth paragraph.
16. *Ibid.*
17. Sub-Clause 19.1, sixth paragraph.
18. *See* Sub-Clause 1.3, last paragraph, especially '[a]ll other communications …'.

(iv) Related Law: As stated in relation to Sub-Clause 19.2 below, various insurances may be required to be procured by the mandatory Laws of the countries where the Works are being carried out.

(v) Improvements:

(1) Under Sub-Clause 4.2.1, the Contractor must deliver the Performance Security to the Employer, with a copy to the Engineer, within 28 days after receiving the Letter of Acceptance. Under Sub-Clause 8.1, unless otherwise stated in the Particular Conditions, the Commencement Date shall be within 42 days after the Contractor receives the Letter of Acceptance. Thus, the intention is that the Employer receives the Performance Security before the Commencement Date. Similarly, it should be expressly provided that the Employer receives the insurances required by Clause 19 before the Commencement Date as at least the insurance required by Sub-Clause 19.2.1 [*The Works*] must be effective as from the Commencement Date. Indeed, the Employer's receipt of both the Performance Security and the insurances required by Clause 19 should be conditions to the Commencement Date.[19]

(2) As indicated under **(iii) Analysis** above, it could be made clearer that the Contractor should send to the Engineer or the Employer a copy of any notification to the insurers of changes in the nature, extent or programme for the Works and other matters. Indeed, it may be appropriate to require the Contractor to clear any such notification in advance with the Engineer or the Employer and to seek the Employer's prior consent to any such changes which may affect the Employer's rights or interests.[20]

--ooOOoo--

19. This suggestion is no more than a reflection of what is stated in the *FIDIC Procurement Procedures Guide* (FIDIC, 2011) 36 ('The insurances are to be in place before the contractor commences work at the site').
20. *See*, for example, art. 56.16 of the *ICC Model Turnkey Contract for Major Works*, ICC Services, Paris (ICC Publication no 797E), 2020, which provides for a similar solution.

19.2 Insurance to Be provided by the Contractor

As Sub-Clause 19.2 is long and divided into six parts (19.2.1. to 19.2.6), instead of proceeding in the usual way by a quotation of the text of the Sub-Clause (and its parts) followed by a summary of its content **in bold text**, the Commentary on this Sub-Clause is, exceptionally, organised as follows:

(i) **Main Changes from RB/99**;
(ii) **Related Clauses/Sub-Clauses**;
(iii) **to (ix) Analysis** of each of the six parts (of Sub-Clause 19.2) following a quotation of such part and a summary of its content **in bold text**; and
(x) **Related Law**.

Commentary

(i) Main Changes from RB/99: As indicated above in relation to Sub-Clause 19.1 (*see* **(i) Main Changes from RB/99**), Clause 19 of RB/17 is an almost total revision of the corresponding Clause in RB/99, Clause 18:

(1) Sub-Clauses 19.1 and 19.2 are based closely on Sub-Clauses 19.1 and 19.2 of GB/08; and
(2) the new Sub-Clause 19.2, like Sub-Clause 19.2 of GB/08, sets out the kinds of insurances that the 'Contractor' (no longer the 'insuring Party' as in RB/99) is required to obtain under six headings corresponding to the six matters to be insured, as follows:
   (a) Sub-Clauses 19.2.1 [The Works] and 19.2.2 [Goods], which correspond roughly to Sub-Clause 18.2 [*Insurance for Works and Contractor's Equipment*] in RB/99;
   (b) Sub-Clause 19.2.3 [Liability for breach of professional duty], which is provided for in GB/08 but which has no counterpart in RB/99;
   (c) Sub-Clause 19.2.4 [Injury to persons and damage to property], which corresponds roughly to Sub-Clause 18.3 [*Insurance Against Injury to Persons and Damage to Property*] in RB/99;
   (d) Sub-Clause 19.2.5 [Injury to employees], which corresponds roughly to Sub-Clause 18.4 [*Insurance for Contractor's Personnel*] in RB/99; and

(e) Sub-Clause 19.2.6 [Other insurances required by Laws and by local practice], which is provided for in GB/08 but which has no counterpart in RB/99.

(ii) Related Clauses / Sub-Clauses: 1.13 [*Compliance with Laws*], 1.15 [*Limitation of Liability*], 4.1 [*Contractor's General Obligations*], 4.8 [*Health and Safety Obligations*], 6.4 [*Labour Laws*], 10 [*Employer's Taking Over*], 11 [*Defects after Taking Over*], 17 [*Care of the Works and Indemnities*], 18 [*Exceptional Events*] and 19.1 [*Insurance - General Requirements*].

(iii) Analysis:

The Contractor shall provide the following insurances:

19.2.1 The Works

The Contractor shall insure and keep insured in the joint names of the Contractor and the Employer from the Commencement Date until the date of the issue of the Taking-Over Certificate for the Works:

(a) the Works and Contractor's Documents, together with Materials and Plant for incorporation in the Works, for their full replacement value. The insurance cover shall extend to include loss and damage of any part of the Works as a consequence of failure of elements defectively designed or constructed with defective material or workmanship; and

(b) an additional amount of fifteen percent (15%) of such replacement value (or such other amount as may be specified in the Contract Data) to cover any additional costs incidental to the rectification of loss or damage, including professional fees and the cost of demolition and removal of debris.

The insurance cover shall cover the Employer and the Contractor against all loss or damage from whatever cause arising until the issue of the Taking-Over Certificate for the Works. Thereafter, the insurance shall continue until the date of the issue of the Performance Certificate in respect of any incomplete work for loss or damage arising from any cause occurring before the date of the issue of the Taking-Over Certificate for the Works, and for any loss or damage occasioned by the Contractor in the course of any operation carried out by the Contractor for the purpose of complying with the Contractor's obligations under Clause 11 [*Defects after Taking Over*].

However, the insurance cover provided by the Contractor for the Works may exclude any of the following:

(i) the cost of making good any part of the Works which is defective (including defective material and workmanship) or otherwise does not comply with the Contract, provided that it does not exclude the cost of making good any loss or damage to any other part of the Works attributable to such defect or non-compliance;
(ii) indirect or consequential loss or damage including any reductions in the Contract Price for delay;
(iii) wear and tear, shortages and pilferages; and
(iv) unless otherwise stated in the Contract Data, the risks arising from Exceptional Events.

The Contractor shall insure in the joint names of the Contractor and the Employer from the Commencement Date until the Taking-Over Certificate for the Works:

(a) the Works and Contractor's Documents, together with Materials and Plant for incorporation in the Works, for their full replacement value; the insurance shall cover loss and damage of any part of the Works as a consequence of failure of elements defectively designed or constructed with defective material or workmanship; and
(b) an additional amount of 15% of such replacement value (or other amount in the Contract Data) to cover incidental costs.

The insurance shall cover the Employer and the Contractor against all loss or damage from whatever cause arising until the issue of the

Taking-Over Certificate for the Works and, thereafter, until the issue of the Performance Certificate in respect of any incomplete work for loss or damage arising from any cause before issue of the Taking-Over Certificate for the Works, and for any loss or damage occasioned by the Contractor in complying with its obligations under Clause 11.

However, the insurance may exclude:

- **(i) the cost of making good any part of the Works which is defective or otherwise does not comply with the Contract, other than making good any part attributable to such defect or non-compliance;**
- **(ii) indirect or consequential loss or damage, including any reductions in the Contract Price for delay;**
- **(iii) wear and tear, shortages and pilferages; and**
- **(iv) unless otherwise stated in the Contract Data, risks from Exceptional Events.**

(iv) Analysis:

(a) Purpose

The purpose of the insurance provisions in Sub-Clauses 19.2.1 [The Works] and 19.2.2 [Goods] is to ensure that the Contractor and, if necessary, the Employer have the financial resources available to execute the Works irrespective of whether they suffer fortuitous loss or damage.[21] Requiring the Contractor to purchase such insurances will inevitably have the effect, from the Employer's point of view, of increasing the Contract Price by the amount of the premiums which the Contractor will have to pay. But an Employer will ordinarily be ready to bear this cost so as:

> to safeguard the Employer against the heavy losses and liabilities to which the Employer might be exposed if the Contractor's financial resources were to prove inadequate to meet its contractual liability to indemnify the Employer against them.[22]

Whatever be the cause of the unexpected loss or damage to the Works and/or Goods, whether it be fire, flood, carelessness or other accident,

21. *The FIDIC Contracts Guide* (2nd edn, FIDIC, 2022) 486.
22. Atkin Chambers, *Hudson's Building and Engineering Contracts* (14th edn, Sweet & Maxwell, London, 2020), 1076-77 (para. 10-002).

and whatever be the resources of the Contractor (or perhaps the Employer), insurance can provide the funds necessary to have them rebuilt or repaired.[23]

(b) Insurance Particulars

It will be recalled that, under Sub-Clause 17.1 [*Responsibility for Care of the Works*], the Contractor is responsible for the care of the Works, Goods and Contractor's Documents from the Commencement Date until the issue of the Taking-Over Certificate for the Works and, with certain exceptions, must rectify any loss or damage to the same at its risk and cost. Under Sub-Clause 17.2 [*Liability for Care of the Works*], the Contractor is also liable for any loss or damage caused by it to such items after the issue of a Taking-Over Certificate, as well as for any loss or damage to them which arose from an event which occurred before issue of the Taking-Over Certificate, for which the Contractor was liable.

To secure these obligations, Sub-Clause 19.2.1 requires the Contractor to insure the Works and Contractor's Documents, together with Materials and Plant for incorporation in the Works, in the joint names of the Contractor and the Employer from the Commencement Date until the Taking-Over Certificate for the Works and thereafter, to the extent of the Contractor's obligations under Sub-Clause 17.2.[24] Insurance is to be for

23. This type of insurance is commonly referred to in the UK as contract works insurance or 'Contractor's All-Risk' (CAR) insurance, although the latter expression is a misnomer as this type of insurance does not, in fact, protect against all risks to which the Works and Goods might be exposed. In the US, this type of insurance is commonly referred to as 'builders' risk insurance'. Brook B Roberts and John M Wilson, 'Insurance for International Projects', Chapter 8 in Wendy Kennedy Venoit and others (eds), *International Construction Law: A Guide for Cross-border Transactions and Legal Disputes* (ABA For Const L, Chicago, IL, 2009), 201-2.
24. In the fourth and fifth lines of the second paragraph of Sub-Clause 19.2.1 of RB/17, the words 'incomplete work for' in the phrase 'in respect of any incomplete work for loss or damage arising from any cause occurring before the date of the issue of the Taking-Over Certificate for the Works' may be confusing. The explanation appears to be that they refer to work 'for which a Contractor remains liable'; *see* the words in the corresponding indemnity in SC 17.2, first paragraph, which refer to work 'for which the Contractor was liable' in the phrase 'for any loss or damage, which occurs after the issue of a Taking-Over Certificate and which arose from an event which occurred before the issue of this Taking-Over Certificate, for which the Contractor was liable'. The issue is important as the Contractor is not liable for loss or

their full 'replacement value' plus an additional 15% to cover additional incidental costs. The 'replacement value' should be the *current* replacement value because:

> [o]n a contract stretching over several years, the replacement value of a destroyed facility may be considerably larger than the original construction price. The insured value should also include the costs of demolition, removal of debris, professional fees and profit.[25]

The requirement that the insurance be in the 'joint names' of the Contractor and the Employer means that either Party may claim under the policy but, at the same time, the insurer is usually prevented from being 'subrogated' to the rights of whichever Party it pays.[26] 'Subrogation' refers here to the right of an insurer to step in and exercise the rights of a Party which it has paid against another Party. Take the example of where the Contractor has negligently caused a fire and the insurer pays the Employer for the damage. The insurer will not be able to pursue the Contractor for causing the fire because, as the insurance is in the joint names of the Contractor and the Employer, the insurer will usually be considered to have waived its rights of subrogation against the Contractor. Instead, the insurer will bear the entire loss.[27]

Typically when an insurance policy indemnifies joint insured parties:

> they are jointly entitled to receive payment from the insurer in respect of an insurance claim and so [...] the insurer should [...] make

damage occurring after the issue of the Taking-Over Certificate which arose from just *any* event which occurred before the issue of the Taking-Over Certificate (e.g., the Contractor is not liable for the events described in Sub-Clause 17.2 (a) through (f)) *but only for loss and damage which arose from an event for which the Contractor was then (that is, before the issue of the Taking-Over Certificate) liable.*

25. *FIDIC Procurement Procedures Guide* (FIDIC, 2011), 36.
26. Paul Reed, *Construction All Risks Insurance* (2nd edn, Sweet & Maxwell, London, 2016) 26 (para. 2-020-021) and Atkin Chambers, *Hudson's Building and Engineering Contracts* (14th edn, Sweet & Maxwell, London, 2020), 1108-1109 (para. 10-038). Such risk allocation is often fortified by the inclusion of a 'waiver of subrogation' clause in the insurance policy. Julian Bailey, *Construction Law* (3rd edn, London Publishing, UK, 2020) vol 3, 1412 (para. 17.26).
27. Justin Sweet, Marc M Schneier, *Legal Aspects of Architecture Engineering and the Construction Process* (9th edn, Cengage Learning, Stamford, CT, 2013) 717.

> payment to both of them [...], [and] leave them to determine their respective entitlements under the policy. The insurer will then have no obligation to monitor how the payment is held or allocated between them, or how it is used to rectify the consequences of the insured circumstances.[28]

There are four exclusions from liability, listed as (i), (ii), (iii) and (iv) in Sub-Clause 19.2.1, which are quite standard under contract works or Contractor's All-Risks ('CAR') insurance. With respect to (i), the exclusion for defective or non-compliant work other than the cost of making good another part of the Works attributable to such defect or non-compliance is normal.[29] With respect to (ii), the Contractor's liability for indirect or consequential loss or damage is already generally excluded under Sub-Clause 1.15.[30] Reductions in the Contract Price for delay are excluded as general business risks and are not covered by this kind of insurance.[31] With respect to (iii), wear and tear are standard exclusions,[32] and the Contractor should normally bear the risk of shortages

28. *The FIDIC Contracts Guide* (2nd edn, FIDIC, 2022) 507. When FIDIC states that the insurer should 'make payment to both', FIDIC appears to mean that the insurer pays for the loss just once (e.g., to a joint account of the Parties) leaving it to them to decide how that payment is allocated between them.
29. As stated by one author:

> The Contractor must take care to ensure that the policy will continue to cover damage to parts of the Works that are not themselves defective, where that damage was caused by defective workmanship or materials in relation to other parts of the Works. An example might be where a wall – itself not defective – is damaged by the collapse of a roof defective in its construction. In this situation, the Contractor would not expect to be covered for the damage to the roof but may not be covered for the wall either, depending on the way in which the exclusion clause has been drafted. Accordingly, the Contractor should check the general exclusion and should seek to modify it to ensure that damage to non-defective parts of the Works is still covered. Paul Reed, *Construction All Risks Insurance* (2nd edn, Sweet & Maxwell, London, 2016) 37 (para. 2-077).

30. Except in the case of 'fraud, gross negligence, deliberate default or reckless misconduct'.
31. Brook B Roberts and John M Wilson, 'Insurance for International Projects' Chapter 8 in Wendy Kennedy Venoit and others (eds), *International Construction Law: A Guide for Cross-border Transactions and Legal Disputes* (ABA For Const L, Chicago, IL, 2009) 203.
32. Paul Reed, *Construction All Risks Insurance* (2nd edn, Sweet & Maxwell, London, 2016) 37 (para. 2-078).

and pilferages itself.[33] With respect to (iv), it is also common to exclude, unless otherwise stated, risks such as those constituting Exceptional Events.[34]

The onus of proving that a policy exclusion applies is on the insurer.[35]

19.2.2 Goods

> The Contractor shall insure, in the joint names of the Contractor and the Employer, the Goods and other things brought to Site by the Contractor to the extent specified and/or amount stated in the Contract Data (if not specified or stated, for their full replacement value including delivery to Site).
>
> The Contractor shall maintain this insurance from the time the Goods are delivered to the Site until they are no longer required for the Works.

The Contractor shall insure, in the joint names of the Contractor and the Employer, the Goods and other things brought to Site by the Contractor to the extent stated in the Contract Data and until they are no longer required for the Works.

(v) Analysis:

The purpose of this insurance has been described above in relation to 19.2.1 [The Works].

To further secure the Contractor's obligations under Sub-Clauses 17.1 and 17.2, the Contractor must insure, in the joint names of the Contractor and the Employer, the Goods and other things brought to Site by the Contractor to the extent specified and/or amount stated in the Contract Data (if not specified or stated for their full replacement value 'including delivery to Site').

The Contractor is required to maintain this insurance from the time the Goods 'are delivered to the Site' until they are no longer required for the

33. As to pilferages, *see* Sub-Clause 17.1 [*Responsibility for Care of the Works*] and 4.21 [*Security of the Site*].
34. Paul Reed, *Construction All Risks Insurance* (2nd edn, Sweet & Maxwell, London, 2016) 36 (para. 2-072-073).
35. Julian Bailey, *Construction Law* (3rd edn, London Publishing, UK, 2020) vol 3, 1419 (para. 17.42).

Works. As Goods are only required to be insured as from their 'delivery to the Site', their transportation to the Site does not apparently have to be insured under this provision. If so – and if Goods are of high value (such as turbines for a hydroelectric plant) – it might be appropriate to require the Contractor (who is responsible for the Goods as from the Commencement Date[36]) to obtain marine insurance, for example, to cover this type of risk.[37]

19.2.3 Liability for breach of professional duty

> To the extent, if any, that the Contractor is responsible for the design of part of the Permanent Works under Sub-Clause 4.1 [*Contractor's General Obligations*], and/or any other design under the Contract, and consistent with the indemnities specified in Clause 17 [*Care of the Works and Indemnities*]:
>
> (a) the Contractor shall effect and maintain professional indemnity insurance against liability arising out of any act, error or omission by the Contractor in carrying out the Contractor's design obligations in an amount not less than that stated in the Contract Data (if not stated, the amount agreed with the Employer); and
>
> (b) if stated in the Contract Data, such professional indemnity insurance shall also indemnify the Contractor against liability arising out of any act, error or omission by the Contractor in carrying out the Contractor's design obligations under the Contract that results in the Works (or Section or Part or major item of Plant, if any), when completed, not being fit for the purpose(s) for which they are intended under Sub-Clause 4.1 [*Contractor's General Obligations*].
>
> The Contractor shall maintain this insurance for the period specified in the Contract Data.

If the Contractor is responsible for the design of part of the Permanent Works and/or other design under the Contract:

36. *See* Sub-Clause 17.1.
37. The author is grateful to Dr Nael G Bunni for this suggestion.

(a) **the Contractor must maintain professional indemnity insurance against liability arising out of its design obligations in an amount not less than stated in the Contract Data; and**
(b) **if stated in the Contract Data, such professional indemnity insurance must also indemnify the Contractor against liability arising out of design that results in the Works, when completed, not being fit for purpose under Sub-Clause 4.1.**

(vi) Analysis:

RB/17 has more detailed provisions on the Contractor's role as designer of the Works than had RB/99.[38] As a result of this increased attention to the role of the Contractor as designer, the Contractor is required under the last paragraph of Sub-Clause 17.4 [*Indemnities by Contractor*] and to the extent the Contractor is responsible for design to indemnify the Employer should the Works (or Section, Part or major item of Plant), when completed, not be fit for the purposes for which they are intended.[39] To further secure the Contractor's indemnity obligations under Clause 17, the Contractor is required by Sub-Clause 19.2.3(a) to obtain professional indemnity insurance, which will ordinarily protect the Contractor against the risk of loss arising from professional negligence or a failure to exercise due skill and care.[40]

However, in addition, if stated in the Contract Data, to secure the Contractor's indemnification obligation to the Employer under the last paragraph of Sub-Clause 17.4,[41] the Contractor is required by Sub-Clause 19.2.3(b) to obtain professional indemnity insurance to indemnify the Contractor against its negligence in carrying out its design obligations

38. For example, compare the last paragraph of Sub-Clause 4.1 [*Contractor's General Obligations*] of RB/17 with the last paragraph of the same Sub-Clause in RB/99.
39. For a discussion of fitness for purpose, *see* under **(iii) Analysis** of the commentary on Sub-Clause 4.1 [*Contractor's General Obligations*] above as well as under **(iii) Analysis** of the commentary on Sub-Clause 17.4 [*Indemnities by Contractor*] above.
40. Julian Bailey, *Construction Law* (3rd edn, London Publishing, UK, 2020) vol 3, 1404 (para. 17.09).
41. Limited by Sub-Clause 1.15 [*Limitation of Liability*].

that result in the Works (or Section or Part or major item of Plant), when completed, not being fit for the purpose(s) for which they are intended under Sub-Clause 4.1.[42]

When preparing the tender dossier, the Employer should consider whether it requires the insurance required by Sub-Clause 19.2.3(b), taking account of the status of pre-qualified tenderers and their apparent ability to self-insure.[43]

19.2.4 Injury to persons and damage to property

> The Contractor shall insure, in the joint names of the Contractor and the Employer, against liabilities for death or injury to any person, or loss of or damage to any property (other than the Works) arising out of the performance of the Contract and occurring before the issue of the Performance Certificate, other than loss or damage caused by an Exceptional Event.
>
> The insurance policy shall include a cross liability clause such that the insurance shall apply to the Contractor and the Employer as separate insureds.
>
> Such insurance shall be effected before the Contractor begins any work on the Site and shall remain in force until the issue of the Performance Certificate and shall be for not less than the amount stated in the Contract Data (if not stated, the amount agreed with the Employer).

The Contractor shall insure, in the joint names of the Contractor and the Employer, against liabilities for death or injury to any person, or loss of or damage to any property (other than the Works) arising out of the performance of the Contract and occurring before the Performance Certificate, other than loss caused by an Exceptional Event.

42. However, as indicated under *(3) Contractor's 'fitness for purpose' indemnity* under **(iii) Analysis** of the commentary on Sub-Clause 17.4 [*Indemnities by Contractor*] above, the scope of the Contractor's indemnity under that Sub-Clause is broader than the Contractor's actual fitness for purpose obligation under Sub-Clause 4.1(e). Accordingly, the scope of that indemnity, and hence of the professional indemnity insurance to secure it, should be curtailed.
43. *The FIDIC Contracts Guide* (2nd edn, FIDIC, 2022) 494.

This insurance shall include a cross liability clause and be effected before work on Site begins, and remain in force until the Performance Certificate. It shall be for not less than the amount stated in the Contract Data (or as otherwise agreed with the Employer).

(vii) Analysis:

To secure the Contractor's obligation to indemnify the Employer against third party claims under the first paragraph of Sub-Clause 17.4, the Contractor must insure, in the joint names of the Contractor and the Employer, against liabilities for death or injury to any person, or damage to any property (other than the Works) arising out of the performance of the Contract, other than damage caused by an Exceptional Event. The insurance policy must include 'a cross liability clause' such that the insurance shall apply to the Contractor and the Employer as separate insureds. This allows each Party to bring suit against the other Party (and recover from the insurer) in respect of a third party claim even though the Parties are insured under the same policy.[44]

This insurance must be for no less than the amount stated in the Contract Data or as otherwise agreed with the Employer. In setting the amount of this insurance:

> it is useful to try to consider what the maximum damage to third parties that a catastrophic accident could cause. For example, if the contract is for work on an airfield, perhaps the maximum damage might occur if one of the contractor's trucks was crossing the runway and was hit by a landing aircraft.[45]

19.2.5 Injury to employees

The Contractor shall effect and maintain insurance against liability for claims, damages, losses and

44. Such a clause:

> allows insurers to indemnify each insured party against a third party claim, as if a separate policy had been issued to each party; but they will only do so to the extent that the total liability of the insurer does not exceed the defined limit of indemnity as a result of one occurrence or series of occurrences.
>
> Paul Reed, *Construction All Risks Insurance* (2nd edn, Sweet & Maxwell, London, 2016) 521 (para. 18-051).

45. *FIDIC Procurement Procedures Guide* (FIDIC, 2011) 36.

> expenses (including legal fees and expenses) arising out of the execution of the Works in respect of injury, sickness, disease or death of any person employed by the Contractor or any of the Contractor's other personnel.
>
> The Employer and the Engineer shall also be indemnified under the policy of insurance, except that this insurance may exclude losses and claims to the extent that they arise from any act or neglect of the Employer or of the Employer's Personnel.
>
> The insurance shall be maintained in full force and effect during the whole time that the Contractor's Personnel are assisting in the execution of the Works. For any person employed by a Subcontractor, the insurance may be effected by the Subcontractor, but the Contractor shall be responsible for the Subcontractor's compliance with this Sub-Clause.

The Contractor shall, during the time that the Contractor's Personnel are assisting in the execution of the Works, maintain insurance against liability for claims of employees of the Contractor or its other personnel in respect of injury, sickness, disease or death arising out of such execution. The Employer and the Engineer must be indemnified under this insurance except for claims that arise from any act or neglect of the Employer or the Employer's Personnel. If the insurance is obtained by a Subcontractor, the Contractor is responsible for its compliance with this Sub-Clause.

(viii) Analysis:

The Contractor must obtain insurance against liability for claims arising out of the execution of the Works in respect of injury, sickness or death of any of the Contractor's employees or the Contractor's other personnel. The Employer and the Engineer must also be indemnified under this policy, although it may exclude claims arising out of the negligence of the Employer or the Employer's Personnel.

In many - but not all - countries, employers are required by mandatory law to take out insurance to protect their employees against harm, sickness or injury in the course of their employment, referred to in some countries as employers' liability or workmen's compensation insurance,[46] and such insurance may complement or replace the insurance required by this provision. A Contractor must naturally comply with such mandatory laws in the Country (and in its home country as well).[47]

19.2.6 Other insurances required by Laws and by local practice

> The Contractor shall provide all other insurances required by the Laws of the countries where (any part of) the Works are being carried out, at the Contractor's own cost.
>
> Other insurances required by local practice (if any) shall be detailed in the Contract Data and the Contractor shall provide such insurances in compliance with the details given, at the Contractor's own cost.

The Contractor shall provide all other insurances required by applicable Laws at its cost. Other insurances required by local practice shall be detailed in the Contract Data and be provided by the Contractor at its cost.

(ix) Analysis:

Consistent with Sub-Clauses 1.13 [*Compliance with Laws*] and 6.4 [*Labour Laws*], the Contractor must provide all other insurances required by the Laws of the countries where the Works are being carried out, at the Contractor's cost.[48] Motor vehicle liability insurance is an obvious example. In France and Egypt, at least, a contractor must take out insurance to cover its warranty obligations for decennial liability.[49]

46. *The FIDIC Contracts Guide* (2nd edn, FIDIC, 2022) 496 and Julian Bailey, *Construction Law* (3rd edn, London Publishing, UK, 2020) vol 3, 1406-1407 (para. 17.14).
47. *See* Sub-Clauses 1.13 [*Compliance with Laws*], 4.8 [*Health and Safety Obligations*], 6.4 [*Labour Laws*] and 6.7 [*Health and Safety of Personnel*].
48. The Contractor should have investigated such Laws and made due allowance for such other insurances at the tender stage. *See* sub-para. (d) of Sub-Clause 4.10 [*Use of Site Data*], second paragraph. If the Contractor has difficulties in obtaining copies of such Laws then, pursuant to Sub-Clause 2.2 [*Assistance*], the Employer is required, at the Contractor's request, to provide reasonable assistance to the Contractor to enable it to do so.
49. *See* **Section 4 Common Law and Civil Law Compared – 4.4.4 Decennial Liability** of **Chapter II Applicable Law**, above.

Other insurances required by local practice, if any, must be detailed in the Contract Data, and the Contractor must comply with those requirements at its cost. They should be identified in the Contract Data since tenderers may not be familiar with 'local practice'.[50]

(x) Related Law:

In some countries, mandatory law may require that insurances on construction projects in the Country, especially where the Employer is from the public sector, should be carried in whole or in part by a local insurance company. Unless at least the local insurance company reinsures in, for example, the London market or Switzerland (and reflects their standards), this can raise various issues for the Contractor such as: whether the local insurance terms are consistent with international standards; whether they are particularly disadvantageous to the insured; whether the local insurance companies concerned are sufficiently strong financially and whether they will be paying claims in local currency, and if so, whether such currency is freely convertible.[51] These issues should be considered with a qualified insurance expert.

--ooOOoo--

20 Employer's and Contractor's Claims

After describing in Sub-Clause 20.1 how a Claim may arise, this Clause describes in Sub-Clause 20.2 the procedure which:

(1) the Employer must follow if it considers it is entitled to any additional payment (or reduction in the Contract Price) and/or extension of the DNP; and
(2) the Contractor must follow if it considers it is entitled to any additional payment and/or an EOT.

This Clause also describes, more briefly in the last paragraph of Sub-Clause 20.1, the procedure which each Party must follow if it considers it is entitled to another entitlement or relief against the other Party. Clause 20 should be read in conjunction with Sub-Clause 3.7.

--ooOOoo--

50. *FIDIC DBO Contract Guide* (1st edn, FIDIC, 2011) 126.
51. *See* the *Guide Notes to the ENAA Model Form International Contract for Process Plant Construction*, ENAA, Japan, 2010, 41-42.

20.1 Claims

A Claim may arise:

(a) if the Employer considers that the Employer is entitled to any additional payment from the Contractor (or reduction in the Contract Price) and/or to an extension of the DNP;
(b) if the Contractor considers that the Contractor is entitled to any additional payment from the Employer and/or to EOT; or
(c) if either Party considers that he/she is entitled to another entitlement or relief against the other Party. Such other entitlement or relief may be of any kind whatsoever (including in connection with any certificate, instruction, Notice, opinion or valuation of the Engineer) except to the extent that it involves any entitlement referred to in sub-paragraphs (a) and/or (b) above.

In the case of a Claim under sub-paragraph (a) or (b) above, Sub-Clause 20.2 [*Claims for Payment and/or EOT*] shall apply.

In the case of a Claim under sub-paragraph (c) above, where the other Party or the Engineer has disagreed with the requested entitlement or relief (or is deemed to have disagreed if he/she does not respond within a reasonable time), a Dispute shall not be deemed to have arisen except if any of sub-paragraphs (a) to (c) of Sub-Clause 21.4 [*Obtaining DAAB's Decision*] applies. The claiming Party may, by giving a Notice refer the Claim to the Engineer and Sub-Clause 3.7 [*Agreement or Determination*] shall apply. This Notice shall be given as soon as practicable after the claiming Party becomes aware of the disagreement (or deemed disagreement) and shall include details of the claiming Party's case and the other Party's or the Engineer's disagreement (or deemed disagreement).

A Claim may arise where:

- **(a) the Employer considers it is entitled to any additional payment (or reduction in the Contract Price) and/or an extension of the DNP;**
- **(b) the Contractor considers it is entitled to any additional payment and/or an EOT; or**
- **(c) either Party considers that it is entitled to another entitlement or relief against the other Party.**

Claims under sub-paragraphs (a) or (b) above are subject to Sub-Clause 20.2.[1] Claims under sub-paragraph (c) are subject to the last paragraph of Sub-Clause 20.1, which provides that, where there has been a disagreement about such a Claim, a Dispute shall not be deemed to have arisen, except if sub-paragraphs (a) to (c) of Sub-Clause 21.4 applies, and the Claim may be referred – by a Notice – to the Engineer and Sub-Clause 3.7 shall apply. The Notice must be given as soon as practicable after the claiming Party becomes aware of the disagreement, and include details.

Commentary

(i) Main Changes from RB/99:

(1) Sub-Clause 20.1 is a new provision with no analogue in RB/99, except to a limited extent with Sub-Clause 20.1 of RB/99.
(2) The Sub-Clause refers to a 'Claim' which is a newly defined term in RB/17.[2]
(3) Unlike RB/99, which dealt with Parties' claims for time and/or money in two separate Sub-Clauses (Sub-Clause 2.5 applicable to Employer's claims and Sub-Clause 20.1 applicable to Contractor's claims), Sub-Clause 20.1 of RB/17 addresses both Parties' Claims (as defined) together in a single provision.
(4) Whereas Sub-Clauses 2.5 and 20.1 of RB/99 dealt with claims for time and/or money only, Sub-Clause 20.1 of RB/17 addresses where either Party is also seeking 'another entitlement or relief'.

1. Sub-Clause 20.2 takes up almost the entirety of Clause 20.
2. *See* Sub-Clause 1.1.6 '**Claim**'.

(ii) Related Clauses / Sub-Clauses: 1.3 [*Notices and Other Communications*], 3.7 [*Agreement or Determination*], 8.4 [*Advance Warning*], 8.5 [*Extension of Time for Completion*], 11.3 [*Extension of Defects Notification Period*] and 20.2 [*Claims for Payment and/or EOT*].

(iii) Analysis:

(1) Purpose of Claims procedure

The purpose of a Claims procedure is to ensure the good and proper administration of a construction project:

> Claims should not be regarded as either inevitable or unpalatable, and making a Claim should not be regarded as being an aggressive act. Construction projects normally give rise to major risks, which have to be dealt with if they occur. While one or both of the Parties might prefer the price accepted just after the tender to remain unchanged, it will not be helpful to the project if the Parties instinctively seek to attribute blame where it transpires [...] that circumstances arise or events occur which give rise to an adjustment of the Contract Price. In these events, the procedures for making and dealing with Claims [...] are specified so as to provide the degree of structure and formality considered necessary for the proper contract administration of [a] construction project. By complying with these procedures, and by maintaining a co-operative approach to the determination of all adjustments, the Parties should enhance the likelihood of achieving a successful project.[3]

(2) Three types of Claim

Sub-Clause 20.1 describes three types of Claim – listed in sub-paragraphs (a), (b) and (c), respectively, of the Sub-Clause – which the Employer or the Contractor may have against the other in relation to the Contract. Sub-Clauses 20.1 and 20.2 then describe the procedure which is to apply to each of these types of Claims. A 'Claim' is broadly defined as:

> a request or assertion by one Party to the other Party (excluding a matter to be agreed or determined under sub-paragraph (a) of Sub-Clause 3.7 [*Agreement or Determination*]) for an entitlement or relief under any Clause of these Conditions or otherwise in connection with, or arising out of, the Contract or the execution of the Works.[4]

3. *The FIDIC Contracts Guide* (2nd edn, FIDIC, 2022) 20.
4. Sub-Clause 1.1.6..

The term 'execution of the Works' in turn means the 'construction and completion of the Works and the remedying of any defects (and shall be deemed to include design to the extent, if any, specified in the Contract)'.[5] Thus, the term 'Claim' has a broad, but not unlimited meaning as it expressly excludes a matter to be agreed or determined under Sub-Clause 3.7(a).[6]

The following subsections (3) and (4) discuss the three types of Claim provided for by Sub-Clause 20.1:

(3) Claims provided for by Sub-Clause 20.1(a) and (b)

The first two types of Claim concern, first, an Employer's Claim for an 'additional'[7] payment from the Contractor (or reduction in the Contract Price) and/or to an extension of the DNP (Sub-Clause 20.1(a)) and, second, a Contractor's Claim for an additional payment and/or an EOT (Sub-Clause 20.1(b)) from the Employer. The procedure applicable to these first two types of Claim is that provided for in Sub-Clause 20.2[8] and therefore will not be discussed here but in the commentary on that Sub-Clause below. The commentary here will discuss the third type of Claim.

(4) Claim provided for by Sub-Clause 20.1(c)

(a) Scope

The third type of Claim listed in the Sub-Clause concerns a Claim of a different nature, i.e., a request or assertion for an entitlement or relief other than an additional payment, extension of the DNP and/or an EOT. This Claim may be 'of any kind whatsoever (including in connection with

---

5. Sub-Clause 1.2 (j).
6. *See* the commentary on Sub-Clause 1.1.6 '**Claim**' above.
7. An 'additional' payment in Sub-Clause 20.1 (a) is to be distinguished from a payment normally due under the Contract, such as (in the case of a payment due by the Contractor) under Sub-Clause 4.19 [*Temporary Utilities*], or (in the case of a payment due by the Employer) based on the value of work in the Bill of Quantities pursuant to Sub-Clauses 12.3 and 14.1, before any adjustments. *See The FIDIC Contracts Guide* (2nd, FIDIC, 2022) 499.
8. With regard to Claims under sub-paragraphs (a) and (b) of Sub-Clause 20.1, the related Sub-Clauses are listed in **Table 5 Employer's Claims for Time and/or Money** and **Table 6 Contractor's Claims for Time and/or Money**, respectively, at the end of this commentary on Clause 20.

any certificate, instruction, Notice, opinion or valuation of the Engineer)'.[9] The *Guidance* provides that it may be for subjects such as:

- interpretation of a provision of the Contract;
- rectification of an ambiguity or discrepancy found in the Contract documents;
- a declaration in favour of the claiming Party;
- access to the Site or to places where the Works are being (or to be) carried out; and/or
- any other matter of entitlement under the Conditions of Contract or in connection with, or arising out of, the Contract, [that does not involve additional payment by one Party to the other Party and/or EOT and/or extension of the DNP[10]].

While this third type of Claim is described in an extremely broad way, it is to be clearly distinguished from, and not to be confused with, 'a matter to be agreed or determined by the Engineer', which is defined in sub-paragraph (a) of Sub-Clause 3.7. As provided in that sub-paragraph, there are 13 instances, neither more or less, of such 'matters' in the Conditions. They are listed in **Table 3 Matters to Be Agreed or Determined by the Engineer** included in the commentary on Sub-Clause 3.7 above.[11]

(b) Procedure

This third type of Claim presupposes the existence of a disagreement (or deemed disagreement) between the Parties or a Party and the Engineer. It assumes that certain relief (e.g., an interpretation of the Contract or a rectification of an ambiguity) has already been requested by one Party from the other Party or the Engineer, who has disagreed with it, either by way of rejecting it explicitly or by failing to respond within a reasonable time, which is described as amounting to a deemed disagreement.[12] The claiming Party is then required to give a Notice[13] referring the Claim to

9. Sub-Clause 20.1 (c).
10. *Guidance for the Preparation of Particular Conditions* to RB/17, 46-47.
11. The procedure applicable to each 'matter' is that contained in the Sub-Clause providing for the 'matter', in Sub-Clause 3.7, including item (ii) of the last paragraph of Sub-Clause 3.7.3, as well as in Sub-Clause 21.4.
12. For a definition of 'reasonableness' *see* fn. 263 in the commentary on **Clause 1** above of **Chapter IV**.
13. Like all Notices, it must comply with Sub-Clause 1.3 [*Notices and Other Communications*].

the Engineer, who must proceed under Sub-Clause 3.7 to consult with the Parties in an endeavour to reach agreement and, if no agreement is achieved, to make a 'fair' determination of the Claim.[14] The Notice to the Engineer must be given as soon as practicable after the claiming Party becomes aware of the disagreement (or deemed disagreement) and must include details of the claiming Party's case and the other Party's or the Engineer's disagreement (or deemed disagreement).

The provision states that 'a Dispute shall not be deemed to have arisen' (except in the cases provided for in sub-paragraphs (a) to (c) of Sub-Clause 21.4), which appears to be superfluous as a NOD would have to have been given (subject to those exceptions) for a Dispute (as defined)[15] to have been constituted and no NOD is stated to have been given.

The reference of a Claim to the Engineer under Sub-Clause 3.7 is a significant step. Once taken, it leads to the start of a series of time periods which may, as a practical matter, be unstoppable, and which, if they are not scrupulously respected, *may lead to denial of the right to pursue the Claim*.[16] In the normal case, these time periods are:

- 42 days to reach an agreement with the assistance of the Engineer;[17]
- if no agreement is reached, 42 days for an Engineer's determination (or absence of determination);[18]
- if a Party is dissatisfied with the determination (or absence of a determination), a further 28 days within which the Party must give a Notice of Dissatisfaction ('NOD');[19]
- if a NOD has been given, a further 42 days in which a Party must refer the resulting Dispute to the DAAB;[20]
- 84 days for the DAAB to give a decision and, if a Party is dissatisfied with it (or the DAAB's failure to decide), a further 28

---

14. *See* the commentary on Sub-Clause 3.7 above.
15. *See* the definition of **'Dispute'** in Sub-Clause 1.1.29.
16. For example, if there has been a failure to give a NOD within 28 days of receiving the Engineer's determination or the DAAB's decision.
17. Sub-Clauses 3.7.1 and 3.7.3 (b).
18. Sub-Clauses 3.7.1.,3.7.2 and 3.7.3.
19. Sub-Clause 3.7.5.
20. Sub-Clause 21.4.1(a).

days within which the Party must give a NOD with respect to it in order to be entitled to commence arbitration with respect to the Dispute;[21]

- having given a NOD with respect to the decision, the Parties are required to attempt amicable settlement for at least 28 days;[22] and
- whether they do so or not, arbitration of the Dispute may be commenced on or after the 28th day after the day on which the NOD was given.[23]

However, with respect to this last stage, a Party is not required actually to begin arbitration by any particular time or even at all.

This third type of Claim is subject to a more lenient procedure[24] than that which applies to a Claim for time or money. This more lenient procedure is summarised in **Figure 11 Procedure for Claims Unrelated to Time and/or Money.**

--ooOOoo--

21. Sub-Clauses 21.4.3 and 21.4.4.
22. Sub-Clause 21.5.
23. Sub-Clause 21.5. These time periods total 294 days (42 + 42 + 28 + 42 + 84 + 28 + 28) or nearly 10 months. This is merely the sum of the time periods provided for in the Conditions. It is neither the minimum nor the maximum number of days that may elapse between (1) a referral of a Claim under Sub-Clause 3.7, and (2) the commencement of arbitration. The actual number of days will depend upon the facts in each case.
24. Thus, the requirements to give a Notice of Claim (*see* Sub-Clause 20.2.1) to maintain contemporary records (Sub-Clause 20.2.3) and to submit a fully detailed Claim (Sub-Clause 20.2.4) do not apply to this third type of Claim. *See*, for comparison, the commentary on Sub-Clause 20.2 [*Claims for Payment and/or EOT*] below.

Figure 11 Procedure for Claims Unrelated to Time and/or Money

SC = Sub-Clause

Cumulative n° of days	Procedure[1]
N.A.[2]	1. The claiming Party must notify the other Party or the Engineer of a requested entitlement or relief resulting in a **Claim**[3] ↓
N.A.[4]	2. The other Party or the Engineer disagrees (or is deemed to have disagreed) ↓
N.A.[5]	3. The claiming Party must, by a Notice, refer the **Claim** to the Engineer under SC 3.7 'as soon as practicable', together with details of the claiming Party's case and the disagreement ↓
84	4. The Engineer must agree or determine the **Claim** under SC 3.7 within 84 days ↓
112	5. Assuming no agreement, either Party may give a NOD in respect of the Engineer's determination (or deemed determination) within 28 days, creating a **Dispute** – otherwise the determination is final and binding ↓
154	6. A **Dispute** must be referred to the DAAB within 42 days of giving or receiving a NOD – otherwise the NOD is invalid ↓
238	7. The **DAAB** has 84 days to give a decision ↓
266	8. Either Party may give a NOD in respect of the **DAAB**'s decision within 28 days after receiving it – otherwise the decision is final and binding ↓
294	9. Both Parties have to attempt amicable settlement for 28 days ↓
294 and thereafter	10. If the **Dispute** is not settled, either Party may refer it to arbitration

Source: Author's own work.

Notes

1. This figure contains a simplified version of steps in the Conditions. Only the actual text of the relevant Sub-Clauses should be relied upon. The 10 steps shown are not identified as such in the Conditions. For a related figure *see* Figure 4 'Agreement/Determination Procedure'.
2. Not applicable as no time is specified.
3. A Party may have been required to have previously advised the Engineer of this event or circumstance pursuant to Sub-Clause 8.4 [*Advance Warning*].
4. Not applicable as no time is specified.
5. *Ibid.*

(5) Claim based on law

While Sub-Clause 20.1 does not refer explicitly to a Claim based on some legal ground, as distinct from a Claim based on a provision in the Contract, the broad definition of the word 'Claim' quoted above (notably, the words 'or otherwise in connection with, or arising out of, the Contract or the execution of the Works') would cover not only Claims arising under a Sub-Clause but also requests or assertions arising under applicable law.[25] Accordingly, the procedures for Claims in this Clause 20 should apply to them, and the particular procedure to be applied would – it is suggested – depend upon the entitlement or relief being sought, e.g., a Claim by a Contractor for additional payment because Site conditions had been misrepresented under applicable law would fall under Sub-Clause 20.1(b), whereas a Claim by an Employer for simply a declaration that the Contract had terminated because the Contractor had abandoned the Works would fall under Sub-Clause 20.1(c).

Thus, the Engineer may have to consult the Parties and/or make determinations with regard to Claims based on legal grounds, in which case it should seek legal advice.

(iv) Improvements: It is not clear for how long the procedure for Claims provided for by Clause 20 is intended to apply. Accordingly, it could usefully be provided that it ceases to apply, for example, to any Claim arising from an event or circumstance occurring after the DNP or issuance of the FPC.

--ooOOoo--

20.2 Claims for Payment and/or EOT

Sub-Clause 20.2 sets out the procedure that is to apply equally to the Employer and the Contractor in the case of Claims for time and/or money.

As Sub-Clause 20.2 is long, important and divided, after an introductory paragraph, into seven parts (20.2.1 to 20.2.7), it will not be discussed in the usual way, that is, by quoting the entire Sub-Clause and summarising its essential content in bold text, followed by a commentary under the usual five headings.[26] Instead, the overall procedure provided for by this

25. *See Guide to the Use of FIDIC Conditions of Contract for Works of Civil Engineering Construction, Fourth Edition* (FIDIC 1989) 119 (commenting on Sub-Clause 53.1 [*Notice of Claim*] in RB/87). Examples of such Claims include Claims for 'misrepresentation' concerning Site conditions, for defamation, or for contract termination under the governing law. *See also*, for example, the public contract law theories available in civil law countries described in **Section 4 Common Law and Civil Law Compared – 4.6 Civil Law: Special Public Contract Theories** of **Chapter II Applicable Law** above.
26. *See* **Section 3 Organisation of Commentary** above of **Chapter IV Clause-by-Clause Commentary** for a description of these five headings.

Sub-Clause will be summarised here before examining its individual parts and paragraphs in detail under the usual five headings used in **Chapter IV**.

This Claim procedure provides, in summary, as follows:

(1) The claiming Party, who may be the Employer or the Contractor, must give a Notice to the Engineer describing the event or circumstance giving rise to the Claim no later than 28 days[27] after it became aware, or should have become aware, of the event or circumstance ('Notice of Claim');[28] *if the claiming Party does not do so, it will not be entitled to relief*.[29]
(2) The Engineer must give a Notice to the claiming Party (with reasons) 'within'[30] 14 days after receiving the Notice of Claim if it considers that the claiming Party has failed to give the Notice of Claim within the 28-day time period; if the Engineer does not do so, the Notice of Claim is deemed to be valid.[31]
(3) The claiming Party must keep such 'contemporary records' (as defined) as may be necessary to substantiate the Claim.[32]
(4) After receiving the Notice of Claim and until the Claim is agreed or determined under Sub-Clause 20.2.5, in each IPC the Engineer must include such amounts for any Claim as have been reasonably substantiated as due to the claiming Party.[33]
(5) The claiming Party must submit to the Engineer its 'fully detailed Claim' (as defined) '[w]ithin' either 84 days after the claiming Party became aware, or should have become aware, of the event or circumstance giving rise to the Claim, or such other period as may be proposed by the claiming Party and agreed by the Engineer. The fully detailed Claim must include,

27. A '**day**' is defined as a calendar day. Sub-Clause 1.1.25. According to Sub-Clause 1.3, a Notice has effect when it is received or deemed to have been received at the recipient's current address according to sub-paragraph (d) of that Sub-Clause. According to the same Sub-Clause, electronic communications are deemed to have been received *on the day after* transmission, provided no non-delivery notification was received by the sender.
28. Sub-Clause 20.2.1, first paragraph.
29. Sub-Clause 20.2.1, second paragraph.
30. *See* item (2) under **(v) Improvements** in the commentary on Sub-Clause 1.2 [*Interpretation*] above.
31. Sub-Clause 20.2.2, first two paragraphs.
32. Sub-Clause 20.2.3.
33. Sub-Clause 20.2.7, first paragraph.

among other things, 'a statement of the contractual and/or other legal basis of the Claim';[34] *if it does not include this basis, the Notice of Claim will be deemed no longer valid.*[35]

(6) The Engineer must give a Notice to the claiming Party 'within' 14 days from the expiry of the time limit under item (5) above if it considers that the claiming Party has failed to submit a statement of the contractual and/or other legal basis of its Claim within such time limit;[36] if the Engineer does not do so, the Notice of Claim is deemed to be valid.[37]

(7) After receiving the fully detailed Claim (or the interim or final fully detailed Claim if the event or circumstance giving rise to the Claim has continuing effect), the Engineer must proceed under Sub-Clause 3.7 to agree or determine the Claim.[38]

(8) If the Engineer has given a Notice to the claiming Party under items (2) and/or (6) above, the Claim must nevertheless be agreed or determined and the Engineer must consider whether or not the Notice of Claim must be treated as a valid one, taking into account, among other things, the details (if any) included in the fully detailed Claim.[39]

(9) The Engineer may require necessary additional particulars by promptly giving a Notice to the claiming Party describing the additional particulars and the reasons for requiring them,[40] in which case the claiming Party must submit them as soon as practicable.[41]

(10) The time limit for the Engineer to agree or determine the Claim under Sub-Clause 3.7.3 commences on the date when the Engineer receives the additional particulars,[42] but the Engineer must nevertheless give its response on the contractual and/or other legal basis of the Claim by giving a Notice to the claiming Party within the 42-day time limit for agreement under Sub-Clause 3.7.3 (calculated from the date of receiving the fully

34. Sub-Clause 20.2.4 (b), first paragraph.
35. Sub-Clause 20.2.4, third paragraph.
36. *Ibid.*
37. Sub-Clause 20.2.4, fourth paragraph.
38. Sub-Clause 20.2.5, first paragraph.
39. Sub-Clause 20.2.5, second paragraph.
40. Sub-Clause 20.2.5, third paragraph, item (i).
41. Sub-Clause 20.2.5, third paragraph, item (iii).
42. Sub-Clause 20.2.5, third paragraph item (iv).

detailed Claim or, in case of a Claim of continuing effect, an interim or final fully detailed claim, as the case may be).[43]

Special rules apply to Claims of continuing effect and these are addressed below in the commentary on Sub-Clause 20.2.6. A more detailed summary of the content of Sub-Clauses 20.2.1 to 20.2.7 is given in the commentary on those individual Sub-Clauses below.

It is now appropriate to examine the first paragraph of Sub-Clause 20.2 and then the subsequent seven parts of Sub-Clause 20.2 (Sub-Clauses 20.2.1 to 20.2.7) in detail.

20.2 Claims for Payment and/or EOT

If either Party considers that he/she is entitled to any additional payment by the other Party (or, in the case of the Employer, a reduction in the Contract Price) and/or to EOT (in the case of the Contractor) or an extension of the DNP (in the case of the Employer) under any Clause of these Conditions or otherwise in connection with the Contract, the following Claim procedure shall apply:

If either Party considers that it is entitled to any additional payment by the other Party and/or to EOT or an extension of the DNP, the following Claim procedure shall apply:

Commentary

(i) Main Changes from RB/99:

(1) Since RB/57, the RB has always contained provisions entitling the Contractor to claim additional money or time (or both) upon the occurrence of defined circumstances.[44] Under RB/99, Sub-

43. Sub-Clause 20.2.5, third paragraph, item (ii) and Sub-Clause 3.7.3, sub-paragraph (c).

44. For commentaries on Contractor's claims under RB/77, RB/87 and RB/99, *see* Christopher R Seppälä, 'Contractor's Claims under the FIDIC International Civil Engineering Contract' (1986) 14 Int'l Bus L (IBA), 179-187, 'Contractor's Claims under the FIDIC Civil Engineering Contract, Fourth (September 1987) Edition' (1991) 19 Int'l Bus L (IBA), 395-404, 457-460 and 'Contractor's Claims under the FIDIC Contracts for Major Works' (2005) 21 Const L J 278-290, respectively.

Clause 20.1 sets out the procedure for Contractor's claims and Sub-Clause 2.5 sets out the procedure for Employer's claims. On the other hand, under RB/17, the Employer's and Contractor's Claims are treated together in a single Clause, Clause 20, which provides for such radically different and more detailed procedures than those contained in RB/99 that no attempt will be made to identify them all here.

(2) To some extent, the changes in the procedures for claims reflected in Clause 20 of RB/17 are based on principles that were already in Clause 20 of GB/08, such as the principle that time bars could be disapplied in certain circumstances,[45] although GB/08 envisaged this would be done by the DAB (which was provided for in GB/08) whereas Sub-Clause 20.2.5 of RB/17 envisages that this would be done by the Engineer.

(ii) Related Clauses / Sub-Clauses: 1.3 [*Notices and Other Communications*], 1.8 [*Care and Supply of Documents*], 3.7 [*Agreement or Determination*], 4.20 [*Progress Reports*], 8.4 [*Advance Warning*], 8.5 [*Extension of Time for Completion*], 11.3 [*Extension of Defects Notification Period*], 14.10 [*Statement at Completion*] and 14.14 [*Cessation of Employer's Liability*].

(iii) Analysis: Sub-Clause 20.2, which is the longest Sub-Clause in the General Conditions, sets out the procedure applicable to each Party's Claims for time and money. The three subsections below of (1), (2) and (3) deal with the scope of application of Sub-Clause 20.2.

(1) Claims explicitly subject to Sub-Clause 20.2

Pursuant to the opening sentence of Sub-Clause 20.2, the procedure applies if either Party considers that it is entitled to:

> any additional payment by the other Party (or, in the case of the Employer, a reduction in the Contract Price) and/or to EOT (in the case of the Contractor) or an extension of the DNP (in the case of the Employer) under any Clause of these Conditions or otherwise in connection with the Contract, [...].

Sub-Clause 20.2 will, self-evidently, apply in the numerous cases where a Sub-Clause in the Conditions specifies that a Party's Claim under that

45. Sub-Clause 20.1 of GB/08.

Sub-Clause is 'subject to Sub-Clause 20.2'.[46] For example, Sub-Clause 4.12.4 provides, among other things, that if the Contractor suffers delay and/or incurs Cost due to Unforeseeable physical conditions (and having complied with Sub-Clauses 4.12.1 to 4.12.3) '[it] shall be entitled subject to Sub-Clause 20.2 [*Claims for Payment and/or EOT*] to EOT and/or payment of such Cost'. As another example, Contractor's Claims for EOT under Sub-Clause 8.5 [*Extension of Time for Completion*] are generally 'subject to Sub-Clause 20.2'.[47]

The particular entitlement that the claiming Party may seek under the Sub-Clauses of the Conditions is specified in the individual Sub-Clauses. Such entitlement may be, in the case of the Contractor, in the form of Cost, Cost Plus Profit and/or an EOT and, in the case of the Employer, a payment of some kind, reduction of the Contract Price and/or an extension of the DNP. The Contractor's entitlement to an EOT does not automatically give it a right to compensation for the extended time. For example, the occurrence of exceptionally adverse climatic conditions at the Site which are Unforeseeable may entitle the Contractor to claim an EOT if they will cause delay to completion,[48] but will not entitle the Contractor necessarily to claim additional payment. Whether the Contractor can obtain Cost or Cost Plus Profit will depend on the circumstances of the case. Generally speaking, the Contractor may be entitled to Cost upon the occurrence of exceptional circumstances for which the Employer is not blameworthy (e.g., in the case of Unforeseeable physical conditions under Sub-Clause 4.12). By contrast, if the Employer is

46. For lists of the Sub-Clauses in the Conditions subject to Sub-Clause 20.2, *see* **Tables 5 Employer's Claims for Time and/or Money** and **6 Contractor's Claims for Time and/or Money** at the end of this commentary on Clause 20. *See* **Figure 13 Procedure for Claims for Time and/or Money – Detailed**, also at the end of this commentary on Clause 20, containing a flow chart of the Claims procedure in Sub-Clause 20.2. For information about how claims should be accounted for in financial statements, whether by the claimant or the respondent, *see*, *in particular*, International Financial Reporting Standard ('IFRS') 15 Revenue from Contracts with Customers and International Accounting Standard ('IAS') 37 (Provisions, Contingent Liabilities and Contingent Assets), both published by the International Accounting Standards Board https://www.ifrs.org/groups/international-accounting-standards-board/ accessed 10 November 2022.
47. Except in the case of a Variation, *see* Sub-Clause 8.5(a) and Sub-Clause 13.3.1, last paragraph.
48. *See* Sub-Clause 8.5, sub-para. (c).

blameworthy, the Contractor can usually claim Cost Plus Profit.[49] For example, under Sub-Clause 2.1 [*Right of Access to the Site*], the Contractor may claim Cost Plus Profit if the Employer has failed to give the Contractor timely access to the Site.

Table 5 Employer's Claims for Time and/or Money and **Table 6 Contractor's Claims for Time and/or Money** at the end of this commentary on Clause 20 list all the Sub-Clauses which entitle the Employer and the Contractor, respectively, to claim relief related to time and/or money under the General Conditions, subject to Sub-Clause 20.2.

(2) Claims not necessarily subject to Sub-Clause 20.2

There are other cases where a Party is entitled to relief of time and/or money, which are not explicitly made 'subject to Sub-Clause 20.2'. For example, the Contractor may be entitled to an upward adjustment of the Contract Price and/or to an EOT in case of Variations instructed by the Engineer under Sub-Clause 13.3.1. Even though such an adjustment might be considered as an additional payment covered by the opening sentence of Sub-Clause 20.2, the last sentence of Sub-Clause 13.3.1 makes it clear that the Contractor shall be entitled to an EOT and/or adjustment of the Contract Price 'without any requirement to comply with Sub-Clause 20.2'.[50] Similarly, Sub-Clause 8.5, sub-paragraph (a), stipulates that there is no requirement to comply with Sub-Clause 20.2 with regard to an entitlement for an EOT arising out of a Variation.

There are also Sub-Clauses that entitle a Party to some relief, but which do not specify whether Sub-Clause 20.2 applies. Such Sub-Clauses include, for example, 4.14 [*Avoidance of Interference*], 17.3 [*Intellectual and Industrial Property Rights*], 17.4 [*Indemnities by Contractor*] and 17.5 [*Indemnities by Employer*]. *However, the lack of explicit reference to Sub-Clause 20.2 should not be construed as implying that compliance with Sub-Clause 20.2 is not mandatory*. If the claimed relief concerns an additional payment, an EOT or an extension of the DNP, then, pursuant

49. *See* the commentary on Sub-Clause 1.1.20 '**Cost Plus Profit**' above.

50. The provisions of Clause 20 also do not apply to deductions made by: (1) the Employer from amounts due to the Contractor on account of insurance premiums paid by the Employer because of the Contractor's failure to keep required insurances in force, pursuant to Sub-Clause 19.1, fourth paragraph; or (2) the Engineer of one-half of the amount paid to an appointing entity or official (for the appointment of DAAB members) if the Employer has paid its remuneration in full, pursuant to Sub-Clause 21.2, last paragraph.

to the opening sentence of Sub-Clause 20.2, Sub-Clause 20.2 will likely apply to the Claim even if the Sub-Clause giving rise to the Claim does not explicitly say so.

(3) Claims based on law

The Sub-Clause 20.2 procedure applies not just to Claims made under individual Sub-Clauses but also to Claims made outside of the Contract terms on some legal ground. This follows from the language of Sub-Clause 20.2 to the effect that it covers not just Claims made under any Clause of these Conditions but also Claims 'otherwise in connection with the Contract'.[51]

20.2.1 Notice of Claim

> The claiming Party shall give a Notice to the Engineer, describing the event or circumstance giving rise to the cost, loss, delay or extension of DNP for which the Claim is made as soon as practicable, and no later than 28 days after the claiming Party became aware, or should have become aware, of the event or circumstance (the "Notice of Claim" in these Conditions).
>
> If the claiming Party fails to give a Notice of Claim within this period of 28 days, the claiming Party shall not be entitled to any additional payment, the Contract Price shall not be reduced (in the case of the Employer as the claiming Party), the Time for Completion (in the case of the Contractor as the claiming Party) or the DNP (in the case of the Employer as the claiming Party) shall not be extended, and the other Party shall be discharged from any liability in connection with the event or circumstance giving rise to the Claim.

51. Sub-Clause 20.2, first paragraph, and *see Guide to the Use of FIDIC Conditions of Contract for Works of Civil Engineering Construction, Fourth Edition* (FIDIC 1989) 119 (commenting on Sub-Clause 53.1 [*Notice of Claim*] in RB/87).

The claiming Party must give a Notice to the Engineer describing the event or circumstance giving rise to the Claim no later than 28 days after it became aware, or should have become aware, of the event or circumstance ('Notice of Claim'). If the claiming Party does not do so, it is denied relief, and the other Party is discharged from liability.

(i) Main Changes from RB/99:

(1) Under Sub-Clause 20.1 of RB/99, as under RB/17, the Contractor is required to give a notice of a claim within 28 days after it became aware, or should have become aware, of an event or circumstance giving rise to a claim.[52] On the other hand, under RB/99 and unlike RB/17, the Employer is merely required to give a notice of its claim 'as soon as practicable after the Employer became aware of the event or circumstances giving rise to the claim'.[53] Under Sub-Clause 20.2.1 of RB/17 both Parties are subject to the same 28-day Notice of Claim procedure.

(2) RB/99 contained no provision allowing for the 28-day time limit – commonly referred to as a time bar – applicable to notices of claim from the Contractor to be disapplied.[54] As will be seen,[55] RB/17 empowers the Engineer to disapply the time bar and stipulates criteria for it to use when exercising this power.

(ii) Related Clauses / Sub-Clauses: 1.3 [*Notices and Other Communications*], 4.20 [*Progress Reports*], 8.4 [*Advance Warning*], 8.5 [*Extension of*

52. In FIDIC's view, 28 days appeared to be a reasonable period as international contractors tend to be fairly large companies, or consortia of companies, that employ a staff that is experienced in claims and therefore is fully capable of recognising a claim situation when it arises. Christopher R Seppälä, 'Contractor's Claims under the FIDIC Contracts for Major Works' (2005) Const L J, 278, 287.

53. Sub-Clause 2.5, second paragraph, of RB/99.

54. However, GB/08 entitled a Contractor, if it considered that there were circumstances which justified the late submission of a Notice of a claim, to refer the matter to the DAB which was authorised to 'overrule the relevant 28-day limit' if it considered 'in all the circumstances, it is fair and reasonable that the late submission be accepted'. Sub-Clause 20.1, sub-para. (a), GB/08. But, no guidance was given as to how the DAB, and, later, if necessary, an arbitral tribunal, was to assess what was 'fair and reasonable'.

55. *See* the commentary on Sub-Clause 20.2.5 below.

Time for Completion], 11.3 [*Extension of Defects Notification Period*], and 20.2 [*Claims for Payment and/or EOT*].

(iii) Analysis:

(1) Notice of Claim

The first step in the claims' procedure is the giving of a Notice of Claim (as defined) to the Engineer, which should describe the event or circumstance giving rise to the Claim.[56] It gives a warning to the other Party that the claiming Party (who may be the Contractor or the Employer) believes it is entitled to more time and/or money on this account under the Contract. At this stage, the claiming Party is not required to set out the details of its Claim or provide supporting particulars.

A separate Notice must be given for each "event or circumstance" giving rise to a claim for additional time or money, reflecting the fact that 'each event or circumstance has its own delay or cost consequence and requirement for action'.[57]

The Notice of Claim must be given:

> as soon as practicable, and no later than 28 days after the claiming Party became aware, or should have become aware, of the event or circumstance [...].[58]

A Party's failure to give a Notice of Claim 'within'[59] *this period will, under the second paragraph, deprive it of its entitlement to relief, as the giving of it is a condition precedent to the pursuit of the Claim.* But, as will be seen

56. If the relevant event or circumstance was already known or probable – and one of which a Party was aware – the Notice of Claim should have been preceded by advice by that Party to the other Party and the Engineer under Sub-Clause 8.4 [*Advance Warning*].
57. Final award, ICC case 23432 (2022) (so far unpublished) commenting on Clause 20.1.1 of a contract based on the 2005 edition of the Pink Book.
58. Sub-Clause 20.2.1, first paragraph. A '**day**' is defined as a calendar day. Sub-Clause 1.1.25. According to Sub-Clause 1.3, a Notice has effect when it is received or deemed to have been received at the recipient's correct address according to the second paragraph of that Sub-Clause. According to the same paragraph, electronic communications are deemed to have been received *on the day after* transmission, provided no non-delivery notification was received by the sender.
59. *See* item (2) under **(v) Improvements** of the commentary on Sub-Clause 1.2 [*Interpretation*] above.

below,[60] the Engineer (and therefore later, if necessary, the DAAB and arbitrators) has discretion to disapply this time bar in certain circumstances.

Time bars are standard features of both international and domestic standard forms of construction contract. In the case of Claims, they are intended to induce a Party to notify and substantiate them promptly so that the other Party and the Engineer are alerted to them and their potential consequences as soon as practicable. This enables evidence to be investigated when it is fresh and allows the other Party to take remedial measures or withdraw instructions (where it is the Employer) before additional cost or delay is incurred. Thus, they have a salutary purpose.[61]

(2) Form of Notice of Claim

Under Sub-Clause 20.1 of RB/99, a bare notice was sufficient to qualify as a notice of claim.[62] No particular form was required, so long as it was in writing to the Engineer, was intended to notify a claim, described the event or circumstance giving rise to it and was recognisable as a (notice of) claim for more time and/or money.[63] GB/08, which for the first time (in a FIDIC form) defined a 'Notice', required a Notice of a claim to be identified as a Notice and to be otherwise issued in accordance with Sub-Clause 1.3 of GB/08.[64] There is now a similar requirement in RB/17.[65] Therefore, a Party's failure to identify a Notice under Sub-

60. *See* Sub-Clause 20.2.5.

61. The same Notice may, if properly prepared and given, satisfy the requirements of different Sub-Clauses. *The FIDIC Contracts Guide* (2nd edn, FIDIC, 2022) 193. A separate Notice is not necessary for each Sub-Clause requiring a Notice so long as the single Notice document satisfies the Notice requirements of each relevant Sub-Clause.

62. Christopher R Seppälä, 'Contractor's Claims under the FIDIC Contracts for Major Works' (2005) 21 Const L J 278, 285.

63. *Obrascon Huarte Lain SA v Attorney General for Gibraltar* [2014] BLR 484, 515 [para. 313]. Hence, the Contractor's progress report blandly stating: 'The adverse weather conditions (rain) have [sic] affected the works' was, according to the Court, 'clearly nowhere near a notice under [Sub-Clause] 20.1' [Para. 315].

64. *See* Sub-Clause 1.1.53 and Sub-Clause 1.3, sub-para. (a) of GB/08.

65. *See* Sub-Clause 1.1.56 **'Notice'** and Sub-Clause 1.3 [*Notices and Other Communications*] of RB/17.

Clause 20.2.1 as a Notice and to issue it in conformity with Sub-Clause 1.3 of RB/17 may result in an argument about whether a valid Notice of Claim has been given.[66]

Sub-Clause 1.3 states that any Notice must be in writing and in the form of a paper-original, an electronic original or both. If it is to be given in the form of a paper-original, the Notice of Claim should be signed by the Contractor's Representative (in case of Contractor's Claims) or by the authorised representative of the Employer (in case of Employer's Claims).[67] It must be delivered, sent or transmitted in accordance with Sub-Clause 1.3 which contains other important requirements.[68]

(3) When does the 28-day time limit start?

The period for giving the Notice of Claim commences to run after the claiming Party 'became aware, or should have become aware' of the event or circumstance giving rise to the Claim. The expression 'became aware' introduces a subjective element, as it requires actual knowledge of the event or circumstance by the claiming Party. The second expression 'should have become aware' introduces an objective standard which is not dependent on any actual knowledge but upon when the claiming Party could reasonably have been expected to have become aware of the event or circumstance concerned. This second expression is there 'to prevent a claiming Party arguing that he/she was not aware of the event/circumstance when everyone knows that he/she was, or at the very least should have been [aware of it]'.[69]

---

66. There is however a difference between GB/08 and RB/17 as to whether a Notice of Claim must state that it is given under Clause 20. Whereas GB/08 explicitly required that such Notices state that they are given under Sub-Clause 20.1 of that form (Sub-Clause 20.1(a) and Sub-Clause 1.3(a) of GB/08), there is no similar requirement in RB/17. Sub-Clause 1.3 of RB/17 only requires communications other than Notices to refer to the provision(s) of the Contract under which they are issued. Nevertheless, it would be good practice for any Notice of Claim to state that it is given under Sub-Clause 20.2.1. *See* the commentary on Sub-Clause 1.3 [*Notices and Other Communications*] above.
67. Sub-paragraph (a), item (i) of Sub-Clause 1.3 [*Notices and Other Communications*].
68. The Contractor's monthly progress reports under Sub-Clause 4.20 should include a list of all Notices of Claims given under Sub-Clause 20.2.1. Sub-Clause 4.20, sub-para. (f).
69. *The FIDIC Contracts Guide* (2nd edn, FIDIC, 2022) 505. Consistent with this, in an ICC case relating to Sub-Clause 20.1 of YB/99, the tribunal observed

A question may arise as to what is the event or circumstance giving rise to the cost, loss, delay or extension of the DNP for which the Claim is made. An 'event', it is suggested, is an incident or occurrence or something that happens, such as a flash of lightning, a volcanic eruption or an invasion of a country;[70] whereas a 'circumstance' refers to a condition or something which may accompany or be the consequence of an event, such as a state of affairs of some kind, like flooding, prolonged rainfall, lack of site access or wartime.[71] A 'circumstance' suggests something of longer duration than an 'event'.

The event or circumstance may have been caused by the other Party (e.g., a Claim by the Contractor under Sub-Clause 2.1 for the Employer's delay in granting right of access to, and possession of, the Site). Whatever may have been the cause, whether it results from natural or man-made events on circumstances, a Notice of Claim is required as, although the other Party might know of the event or circumstance concerned, it could not necessarily know that it would be the subject of a Claim by the affected Party.

The Notice of Claim needs only to be given when the event or circumstance is actually 'giving rise to the cost, loss, delay or extension of DNP for which the Claim is made'.[72] Where a Party merely anticipates that a known or probable future event or circumstance may give rise to a Claim, it should not give a Notice of Claim, but instead consider advising the other Party and the Engineer of the same, pursuant to Sub-Clause 8.4 [*Advance Warning*]. But once a Party knows that cost, loss or delay is occurring, it must give a Notice of Claim within 28 days, as *otherwise it may be forfeiting the right to Claim*, as explained above.

---

that this Sub-Clause 'was drafted [...] to avoid any [purely] subjective interpretation of' the date on which the 28 days should start running. It does this by providing that the date is 'the day the Claimant became or should have become aware of the event or circumstance giving rise to the claim'. Final award, ICC case 16765 (2013), ICC Disp Resol Bull 2015 – Issue 1, 101, 104 (para. 167) (commentary 26-27).

70. An 'event' is defined in the dictionary as 'anything that happens or takes place', *Concise Oxford English Dictionary* (10th edn, rev'd, OUP, Oxford, 2002).

71. A 'circumstance' is defined in the dictionary as 'a fact or condition connected with or relevant to an event or action', *Concise Oxford English Dictionary* (10th edn, rev'd, OUP, Oxford, 2002). *See also The FIDIC Contracts Guide* (2nd edn, FIDIC, 2022) 503.

72. Sub-Clause 20.2.1, first paragraph.

(4) Possible response of recipient to a Notice of Claim

Although the recipient of a Notice of Claim should, ideally, draw attention to any factual errors in the Notice of Claim, it is not required to respond and the mere absence of a rebuttal should not be taken as agreement to the contents of a Notice of Claim.

(iv) Related Law:

(1) Time bars in common law countries

In common law jurisdictions, the courts have traditionally construed time bar clauses strictly.[73] Under English law, a notice provision will be construed as a condition precedent to making a claim if such provision states a precise time limit within which the notice should be given and makes plain by express language that a failure to serve the notice on time will result in the claiming party losing its right under that provision.[74] Sub-Clause 20.2.1 satisfies these requirements for a condition precedent. Similarly, in an English case, Sub-Clause 20.1 of YB/99 (which is identical to Sub-Clause 20.1 of RB/99) was found to be 'a condition precedent' to a claim under that form of contract.[75]

In this case, the judge made a number of other findings that are relevant to Sub-Clause 20.2.1 of RB/17. As regards Sub-Clause 20.1, he stated:

> The 'event or circumstance' described in the first paragraph of Clause 20.1 in the appropriate context can mean either the incident (variation, exceptional weather or one of the other specified grounds for extension) or the delay which results or will inevitably result from the incident in question.[76]

---

73. For a general discussion of time bar provisions under common law, *see* Julian Bailey, *Construction Law* (3rd edn, London Publishing, UK, 2020) vol 2, 600-606 (paras 6.326-6.335).
74. *Bremer Handelsgesellschaft v Vanden Avenne-Izegem* (1978) 2 Lloyd's Rep 109, 128 (Lord Salmon).
75. *Obrascon Huarte Lain SA v Attorney General for Gibraltar* [2014] BLR 484, 514 [para. 311]. The decision of the Technology and Construction Court in this case was appealed to the Court of Appeal and upheld without comment on the lower court's discussion of the time bar under Sub-Clause 20.1 [2015] EWCA Civ 712.
76. *Obrascon Huarte Lain SA v Attorney General for Gibraltar* [2014] BLR 484, 515 [para. 312].

The judge found that the 28-day period in Sub-Clause 20.1 started from when there was 'either awareness by the Contractor or the means of knowledge or awareness of that event or circumstance', so that the test was objective.[77] However, he also found that the phrase 'event or circumstance giving rise to the claim' in Sub-Clause 20.1 should not be read strictly against the Contractor, but should instead be 'construed reasonably broadly'. He found that, where the Contractor was claiming an extension of time, Sub-Clause 20.1 had to be read together with Sub-Clause 8.4 of YB/99[78] which provided that an extension of time was available to the extent that completion 'is or will be delayed'.[79] He concluded that the 28-day notice period under Sub-Clause 20.1 can run from either when it is clear there will be delay (a prospective delay) or when the delay has at least started to be incurred (a retrospective delay).[80] He gave an example of where a Variation was instructed in June, but it did not become obvious until October that this Variation would cause a delay in completion, and then the actual delay began in November. He concluded that the Contractor did not need to give notice until November, although it was free to do so from October onwards.[81] However, as a matter of prudence, Parties are advised to give their notices as soon as possible after they became aware, or should have become aware, for example, that an event will delay the completion of the works, i.e., in October in the above example.[82]

In the US, time bar provisions are also strictly enforced subject to well-established exceptions. The three main exceptions in US Federal Government contracting are: (1) the non-claiming party already knew the circumstances that were the basis of the claim; (2) the contract administrator (being the equivalent of the Engineer under RB/17) actually considered the merits of the claim without raising the lack of notice;

77. *Ibid.*
78. Corresponding to Sub-Clause 8.5 [*Extension of Time for Completion*] of RB/17.
79. The same words are in Sub-Clause 8.5 of RB/17.
80. *Obrascon Huarte Lain SA v Attorney General for Gibraltar* [2014] BLR 484, 514-515 [para. 312].
81. *Ibid.*
82. Lack of notice may bar a claim even where the employer 'had a reasonable inkling' that a claim from the contractor was coming, as the fact that an employer 'may anticipate a claim in the future does not equate to notification of an actual compensation event'. *Glen Water Ltd v Northern Ireland Water Ltd* [2017] N.I.Q.B. 20 [59].

and (3) the lack of a timely notice of the claim did not cause any prejudice to the non-claiming party.[83] The scenario in item (2) above will result in a waiver[84] and could apply equally under English law, at least if the contract administrator were expressly authorised to waive the employer's rights.[85]

(2) Time bars in civil law countries

In civil law countries, time bar provisions, such as Sub-Clause 20.2.1, may be strictly enforced. In France, for example, contractual time bar clauses are to be found in standard forms of construction contract for both public and private works. Indeed, both the standard general conditions incorporated into public works contracts[86] and the standard general conditions for private works contracts[87] contain several time bar provisions.[88] Based on Article 1103 of the French Civil Code, which provides

83. *See* Douglas S Oles, 'Lack of Claim Notice as a Defense to Construction Claims' (2012) 32(1) Const L, ABA for Const L, 6, 8.
84. 'Waiver' is a legal term meaning '(t)he voluntary relinquishment or abandonment – express or implied – of a legal right or advantage'. Bryan A Garner (ed in chief), *Black's Law Dictionary* (11th edn, Thomson Reuters, St Paul, MN, 2019).
85. Julian Bailey, *Construction Law* (3rd edn, London Publishing, UK, 2020) vol 2, 605-606 (para. 6.334). Under RB/17, the Engineer is denied authority to waive the Employer's rights. *See* Sub-Clause 3.2, last paragraph.
86. *Cahier des Clauses Administratives Générales Applicables aux Marchés Publics de Travaux*, 2014.
87. *Cahier des Clauses Administratives Générales (CCAG) applicables aux travaux de génie civil faisant l'objet de marchés privés* – NF P03-002, AFNOR, 3 October 2014.
88. *See*, for example, for claims relating to the final account, Clause 50.3 of the French public works form (*Cahier des Clauses Administratives Générales Applicables aux Marchés Publics de Travaux, 2014*): this provides that the contractor must file a complaint before the administrative court, limited to the claims in the contractor's statement of claim which had previously been communicated to the employer, within a time limit of six months as from either: (i) the employer's response to the contractor's previous statement of claim or (ii) failing the employer's response, the employer's deemed rejection ('*décision implicite de rejet*') of the contractor's claims. Otherwise, the contractor is time-barred. *See also* Clause 19.5 of the French private works form (CCAG – NF P03-002, AFNOR 3 October 2014): this provides that if the employer fails to notify its comments on the draft final account to the contractor within 30 days (or within the extended period of four months) of the receipt by the contract administrator (*maître d'oeuvre*) of the contractor's

that '[c]ontracts which are lawfully formed have the binding force of legislation for those who have made them', French judicial courts consistently uphold contractual time bars.[89] In Germany, however, time bar provisions might be unenforceable if found to be disproportionately prejudicial to the claiming Party.[90]

In some civil law countries, time bar clauses are erroneously considered as invalid on the ground that they contradict statutory limitation periods, which are of a mandatory nature and thus cannot be modified by the Parties.[91] This view is also shared in some countries in Central Europe and elsewhere.[92]

---

draft final account, the employer is deemed to have accepted the draft final account communicated by the contractor to the contract administrator, which then becomes final.

89. *See*, for example, Court of Cassation, 6 July 2011, no 10-10694: in this case, a French form of contract provided that when the contractor receives the final account from the employer, it must challenge it within 30 days. Otherwise, its objection is time barred. When the employer sent the final account on 1 December, and the contractor failed to challenge it until the following 6 January, the Court of Cassation (France's highest court for civil matters) held that the contractor was time barred. Time bar provisions are also upheld by French administrative courts. *See*, for example, the Council of State or *Conseil d'Etat* (France's highest administrative court), 18 September 2015, no 384523. After the employer dismissed the contractor's claims in the final account, the contractor filed a complaint before the lower administrative court but did so after the expiry of the six-month time limit under art. 50.32 of the relevant public works contract *(Cahier des Clauses Administratives Générales – Travaux)*. The lower court rejected the contractor's claim on the basis that the contractor was time barred. The Council of State, to which the contractor appealed, upheld the contractual time bar provision and thus confirmed that the contractor was time barred from filing a complaint before the administrative courts.

90. Dr Alexander Kus and others, 'FIDIC's New 'Silver Book' Under the German Form Contracts Act' [1999] ICLR 533, 547-549. According to this article, the general conditions of a FIDIC form will be considered as general conditions under German law and, pursuant to such law, general conditions considered to be 'disproportionately prejudicial' to one of the parties may be declared ineffective.

91. *See*, e.g., Michael Grose, *Construction Law in the United Arab Emirates and the Gulf* (Wiley Blackwell, Oxford, 2016) 226-228 and Marwan Sakr, 'Turnkey Contracting under the ICC Model Contract for Major Projects: A Middle Eastern Law Perspective' [2009] ICLR 146, 147-149.

92. *See*, e.g., Lukas Klee, *International Construction Contract Law* (2nd edn, Wiley Blackwell, Oxford, 2018) 379-81, 383-85.

However, there is a difference between a statutory limitation period and contractual time bar. A statutory limitation period provides for a period of time within which a right or a claim must be asserted before a court or arbitral tribunal if it is not to be lost. This period of time may range from six months to 30 years.[93] On the other hand, a contractual time bar refers to a right that must be claimed during usually a short period of time (such as 28 days under Sub-Clause 20.2.1) in order for it to be acquired or not lost. A contractual time bar results in the forfeiture of a right, which parties are free to regulate by contract, as distinct from a limitation of a right provided for by law by a limitation period. All legal systems recognise the forfeiture of rights as distinct from the limitation of rights provided for by statutory limitation periods.[94] The UNIDROIT Principles expressly exclude the forfeiture of rights from their provisions dealing with limitation periods.[95]

Therefore a contractual time bar should not be contrary to a mandatory limitation period laid down by law.[96]

---

93. Piero Bernardini 'Limitation Periods' UNIDROIT Principles: New Developments and Applications – 2005, Spec Supp ICC Int'l Ct Arb Bull 43.
94. *Ibid.*, 43, 46. For French law, *see* Sébastien Ribac and Erwan Robert, 'Validity of Time Bar Clauses in International Construction Contracts under French Law' (2019) (2) Cahiers de l'arbitrage, 255.
95. Art. 10.1(2) of the UNIDROIT Principles, contained in the chapter dealing with limitation periods, provides:

    > this [c]hapter ['Limitation Periods'] does not govern the time within which one party is required under the Principles, as a condition for the acquisition or exercise of its right, to give notice to the other party to perform any act other than the institution of legal proceedings.

    The main commentary on the UNIDROIT Principles notes that, while the exclusion 'provided for by art 10.1(2) only applies to notice requirements "under the Principles", it should be extended by analogy to **notice requirements contractually agreed upon**'. (Emphasis in the original) Stefan Vogenauer (ed), *Commentary on the UNIDROIT Principles of International Commercial Contracts (PICC)* (2nd edn, OUP, Oxford, 2015) 1157 [para. 8].
96. Thus, Egyptian law recognises the validity of forfeiture clauses, even where the person whose contractual right is forfeited generally benefits from strengthened legal protection (as is the case of an insured party under an insurance contract). According to art. 750(2) of the Egyptian Civil Code, a clause in a policy of insurance providing for the forfeiture of the rights of the insured on account of its delay in notifying the authorities of the occurrence of the insured risk or in producing documents is void, if it appears from the circumstances that there was a reasonable excuse for the delay. It follows

(3) Doctrines used to overcome time bars

Depending on applicable law and the relevant facts, there are various legal arguments a Party may advance to overcome a time bar:[97]

(1) The obligation to give a timely notice of a claim may be waived[98] (or relinquished) under both civil law[99] and – as indicated above – common law. Thus, for example, if the Employer or the Engineer has been settling Contractor's claims without any regard to the provisions for notices, conditions or other formalities applicable to these claims under the Contract, then, at some point, the Employer may be precluded from insisting that the Contractor should have complied with those provisions.[100]

(2) The application of the principle of good faith may sometimes be used in civil law countries to prevent a claim from being time barred. The example given under item (1) above may also be seen as concrete application of the principle of good faith, as it would be unfair for a party (e.g., the Employer) to rely on a time

---

from this legal provision that a clause providing for the forfeiture of the insured's right is perfectly valid when there exists no reasonable excuse for the delay by the insured in notifying the authorities of the insured risk or in producing the required documents. If the insured is negligent in this way, it suffers the full consequences of the contractual clause providing for forfeiture of its right, as the insurer is seen as having a vital interest in being notified of such risk and in receiving such documents without delay. If, as a matter of principle, forfeiture clauses are valid even when they work against the weaker party in a contract of adhesion, such as an insurance contract, forfeiture clauses are, *a fortiori*, perfectly valid in a normal contract of works, such as a construction contract. Legal opinion of the late Dr Aktham El Kholy, Professor and former Vice-Dean, Faculty of Law, Cairo University, 23 September 1991 (in the author's possession).

97. For a broad overview of these theories, *see* Rupert Choat, 'Time bar provisions – the devil in the contract', IBA 5th Biennial Construction Projects from Conception to Completion Conference, Brussels, 6-7 September 2013.

98. For the definition of the legal term 'waiver' *see* fn. 84 earlier in this commentary on Clause 20.

99. Thus, under French law waiver is known as *renonciation*. *See*, e.g., art. 2251 of the French Civil Code dealing with the express or tacit waiver of a limitation period.

100. However, in the case of the Engineer, the Engineer's Representative, or any assistant, waiver may not apply because of Sub-Clause 3.2, last paragraph, of RB/17.

bar clause to defeat a Contractor's claim if the Employer or its agent, the Engineer, had consistently not previously required compliance with it and the Contractor had reasonably come to rely on the Employer's or Engineer's behaviour in this respect.[101] The principle of good faith may trump the strict application of a time bar clause also in cases where an Employer who had delayed the Contractor's work on the critical path denies a Contractor's claim for an extension of time (on account of the Employer's delay) because such claim was notified late.[102] If the Employer were allowed to enforce the time bar clause in such a case, it may be argued that the Employer would be taking advantage of its own wrong by having delayed the Contractor in the first place.[103] An Employer may also be found not to act in good faith if it were to raise an objection that a Notice of Claim was given late – even if this were true – in a case where it had prior knowledge of the event or circumstance giving rise to the claim.[104]

---

101. A similar outcome is indicated by art. 1.8 (*Inconsistent behaviour*) of the UNIDROIT Principles, according to which '[a] party cannot act inconsistently with an understanding it has caused the other party to have and upon which that other party reasonably has acted in reliance to its detriment'.
102. In a final award in ICC case 23229 (2020) (so far unpublished), a majority of the tribunal held under a contract based on RB/99 that, in cases where the contractor had delayed completion of the Works and had failed to give notices requesting extension of time under Sub-Clause 20.1, it was liable for delay damages. However, the majority also held that, in cases where the contractor had been delayed by events for which the employer was responsible (such as delays caused by other contractors of the employer), under the doctrine of good faith provided for by the law of the civil law system that applied and notwithstanding the contractor's failure to give notices under Sub-Clause 20.1, the employer was not entitled to delay damages (the dissenting arbitrator, however, stated that employer should be entitled to delay damages in that case).
103. Rupert Choat, 'Time Bar Provisions: The Devil in the Contract', IBA 5th Biennal Construction Projects from Conception to Completion Conference, Brussels, 6-7 September 2013, 4.
104. For a well-reasoned award on this subject, where Egyptian substantive law, which is close to French law, was applied, *see J.V. of American and EU Dredging Companies v. Red Sea Public Authority (RSPA), final award, CRCICA case No. 281/2002, 28 June 2004* in Mohie-Eldin Alam-Eldin (ed.), *Arbitral Awards of the Cairo Regional Centre for International Commercial Arbitration IV* (Kluwer L. Int'l, the Netherlands, 2014) 185, especially 217,232 and 238. This award relied on the principle of good faith and the

(3) In some common law jurisdictions (e.g., Australia), the 'prevention principle' may be used to defeat a time bar provision. According to this principle, liquidated damages for delay are not recoverable by an Employer where a Contractor failed to complete the Works by the contract completion day on account of some conduct on the part of the Employer that prevented the Contractor from doing so (e.g., failing to give access to the Site on time).[105] The prevention principle is based on the universally recognised proposition that a party to a contract cannot benefit from its own breach.[106] As seen in item (2) above, a similar outcome may be reached in civil law countries by applying the principle of good faith. On the other hand, if, as is true of RB/17, a contract contains an extension of time clause (Sub-Clause 8.5 in RB/17) and the Contractor fails to avail itself of its right to an extension of time thereunder on account of a delay caused by the Employer, then the Contractor might not be able to rely on the prevention principle to relieve it of liability for liquidated damages for delay (Delay Damages under RB/17).[107]

(4) In Australia, it has been argued that time bar clauses may under certain circumstances be considered as penalties and thus unenforceable according to the penalty doctrine under the common law.[108]

---

common intention of the parties to determine whether a time bar should apply. Other doctrines available to overcome a time bar are 'abuse of right' under the civil law and estoppel. *See* Emmanuel Gaillard & John Savage (eds.), *Fouchard Gaillard and Goldman on International Commercial Arbitration* (Kluwer L. Int'l, the Netherlands, 1999), 818-820 (paras. 1459-1462) and the UNIDROIT Principles, arts. 1.7 (*Good faith and fair dealing*) and 1.8 (*Inconsistent behaviour*).

105. For a discussion of the prevention principle in common law, *see* Julian Bailey, *Construction Law* (3rd edn, London Publishing, UK, 2020) vol 2, 1215-1224 (para 13.151-13.168).

106. *See*, for example, art. 7.1.2 (*Interference by the other party*) of the UNIDROIT Principles which provides for the prevention principle. This art is quoted under **(iv) Related Law** in the commentary on Sub-Clause 8.5 above.

107. Julian Bailey, *Construction Law* (3rd edn, London Publishing, UK, 2020) vol 2, 1219-1220 (para. 13.158). In this connection, *see* ICC case 23229 (2020) referred to in fn. 102 above of this commentary on Clause 20.

108. *See* Andrew Downie, 'Time Bars as Penalties after Andrews v ANZ' (2014) 9(2) CLI 28-33. *See also* **Section 4 Common Law and Civil Law Compared – 4.4.5 Liquidated Damages and Penalties** of **Chapter II Applicable Law** above.

In practice, when dealing with time bars, dispute board members and arbitrators will usually want to look at all of the facts on the merits of a claim before deciding what to do. Depending on the facts, they may be hesitant to deny an otherwise valid claim on the basis of a time bar.[109]

While there may be arguments to overcome a time bar, a Party should always assume that it will be strictly enforced and comply with provisions for the notification of Claims, their required form, content and mode of delivery or transmission.

(v) Improvements: There is no explicit requirement that a Notice of Claim under Sub-Clause 20.2.1 should refer to the Sub-Clause under which it is given. As it is important that a Notice of Claim be recognised for what it is, given its time bar feature, future editions of RB/17 should provide for this, as was the case in GB/08. But a failure to comply with this requirement should not necessarily invalidate the Notice of Claim.[110]

20.2.2 <u>Engineer's initial response</u>

> If the Engineer considers that the claiming Party has failed to give the Notice of Claim within the period of 28 days under Sub-Clause 20.2.1 [*Notice of Claim*] the Engineer shall, within 14 days after receiving the Notice of Claim, give a Notice to the claiming Party accordingly (with reasons).
>
> If the Engineer does not give such a Notice within this period of 14 days, the Notice of Claim shall be

109. Thus, in an ICC case based on YB/99 applying civil law, the tribunal, noting that Sub-Clause 3.5 required the Engineer to make a 'fair determination in accordance with the Contract, taking due regard of all relevant circumstances' and finding that (1) the Employer had known in detail and for some time of the Contractor's grounds for claiming an extension of time and (2) the employees of both Parties had jointly been trying to resolve the issues causing the delays concerned, refused to apply the 28-day time limit in Sub-Clause 20.1 of that form to bar the Contractor's otherwise justified extension of time request (Final award, ICC case 24862 (2021) (so far unpublished)). *Compare* with the common law case of *Glen Water Ltd v Northern Ireland Water Ltd* [2017] N.I.Q.B. 20 referred to in fn 82 immediately above.
110. *See* item (2) under **(v) Improvements** of the commentary on Sub-Clause 1.3 [*Notices and Other Communications*] above.

deemed to be a valid Notice. If the other Party disagrees with such deemed valid Notice of Claim the other Party shall give a Notice to the Engineer which shall include details of the disagreement. Thereafter, the agreement or determination of the Claim under Sub-Clause 20.2.5 [*Agreement or determination of the Claim*] shall include a review by the Engineer of such disagreement.

If the claiming Party receives a Notice from the Engineer under this Sub-Clause and disagrees with the Engineer or considers there are circumstances which justify late submission of the Notice of Claim, the claiming Party shall include in its fully detailed Claim under Sub-Clause 20.2.4 [*Fully detailed Claim*] details of such disagreement or why such late submission is justified (as the case may be).

The Engineer must give a Notice to the claiming Party (with reasons) within 14 days after receiving the Notice of Claim if it considers that the claiming Party has failed to give the Notice of Claim within the relevant 28-day time period. If the Engineer does not do so, the Notice of Claim is deemed to be a valid Notice.

If the other Party disagrees with such deemed valid Notice, it must give a Notice to the Engineer with details. Thereafter, the agreement or determination of the Claim under Sub-Clause 20.2.5 must include review by the Engineer of such disagreement.

If the claiming Party receives a Notice from the Engineer under this Sub-Clause and considers there are circumstances which justify late submission of the Notice of Claim, it must include details about this in its fully detailed Claim.

Commentary

(i) Main Changes from RB/99: This is a new provision which has no analogue in RB/99.

(ii) Related Clauses / Sub-Clauses: 1.3 [*Notices and Other Communications*], 3.7 [*Agreement or Determination*] and 20.2 [*Claims for Payment and/or EOT*].

(iii) Analysis:

(1) Engineer's Notice of objection

Under this Sub-Clause, the Engineer must, 'within'[111] 14 days after receiving a Notice of Claim, give a Notice to the claiming Party, with reasons, if it considers that the claiming Party has failed to give the Notice of Claim within the period of 28 days under Sub-Clause 20.2.1.[112] While there is no explicit requirement for the Engineer's Notice to include a reference to Sub-Clause 20.2.2, given the Notice's importance, it is advisable that it does so. If the Engineer does not give such a Notice, the Notice of Claim is deemed – provisionally – to be a valid Notice of Claim.

If the other Party disagrees with the deemed provisional validity of the Notice of Claim, it must give a Notice to the Engineer which includes details of the disagreement. Thereafter, resolution of the Claim under Sub-Clause 20.2.5 must include a review by the Engineer of such disagreement.[113]

(2) Disagreement with Engineer's Notice of objection

If the claiming Party disagrees with a Notice from the Engineer under this Sub-Clause, or considers there are circumstances which justify its late submission, the claiming Party is required to include details of such disagreement or justification, as the case may be, in its fully detailed Claim under Sub-Clause 20.2.4.[114] These circumstances may comprise, among others, two of the mitigating circumstances listed in Sub-Clause 20.2.5:

(1) whether or to what extent the non-claiming Party would be prejudiced by acceptance of the late submission; and
(2) any evidence of the non-claiming Party's prior knowledge of the event or circumstance giving rise to the Claim.[115]

However, there may be other circumstances which the claimant may want to include in its fully detailed Claim, for example, the claimant's view about the date on which the 28-day period commenced to run (e.g.,

---

111. *See* item (2) under **(v) Improvements** in the commentary on Sub-Clause 1.2 [*Interpretation*] above.
112. Sub-Clause 20.2.2, first paragraph.
113. Sub-Clause 20.2.2, second paragraph.
114. Sub-Clause 20.2.2, third paragraph.
115. Sub-Clause 20.2.5, second paragraph.

when the Contractor 'became aware or should have become aware' of 'exceptionally' adverse weather conditions entitling the Contractor to an EOT under Sub-Clause 8.5), where there was a significant lapse of time between the actual event or circumstance giving rise to the Claim and when the claimant 'became aware or should have become aware' that it would have, or was having, a time and/or cost impact.[116]

The Engineer is expressly authorised to decide whether the Notice of Claim shall be treated as a valid Notice or not, pursuant to Sub-Clause 20.2.5.[117] If the Engineer rejects the Notice of Claim and the matter escalates into a Dispute, the relevant facts and circumstances may later be referred to the DAAB and, if necessary, to arbitrators. If there are no justifying facts and circumstances, the claiming Party may eventually drop the Claim.

(3) Disagreement with the absence of Engineer's Notice of objection

If the Engineer gives no Notice within the above period of 14 days, the Notice of Claim is deemed – provisionally – to be a valid Notice.[118] The validity of the Notice of Claim is only provisional, as the non-claiming Party is entitled to object to it and have the Notice of Claim invalidated. For example, if the Employer had given a late Notice of Claim and the Engineer had failed to give a Notice objecting to it within 14 days, the Employer's Notice of Claim would be provisionally valid, but the Contractor could object to it by giving a Notice to the Engineer with details of its disagreement, which could result in invalidation of the Notice of Claim.[119] If the Contractor has given such a Notice to the Engineer, the agreement or determination of the Claim by the Engineer under Sub-Clause 20.2.5 should include a review by it of such disagreement and could result in invalidation of the Notice of Claim.[120] If the Contractor were dissatisfied with the results of this review, it could give a NOD with respect to the Engineer's determination, and refer the resulting Dispute to the DAAB[121] and, if necessary, thereafter to arbitration.[122]

116. *See* the discussion of the *Obrascon* case under *(1) Time bars in common law countries* under **(iv) Related Law** of the commentary on Sub-Clause 20.2.1 above.
117. Sub-Clause 20.2.5, second paragraph.
118. *Ibid.*
119. *Ibid.*
120. *Ibid.*
121. Sub-Clause 3.7.5.
122. Sub-Clauses 21.4.4, 21.5 and 21.6.

(4) Conclusion

Sub-Clause 20.2.2 is an excellent innovation as it requires the Engineer and the Parties to address the often vexing issue of whether there has been non-compliance with the time bar in Sub-Clause 20.2.1 promptly while the relevant evidence is likely to be fresh and available. If the Sub-Clause 20.2.2 procedure has not been invoked, when it should be, by the Engineer or, failing the Engineer, the non-claiming Party, it will be more difficult for the non-claiming Party to question the validity of a Notice of Claim later, as it would need then to justify its failure to have invoked Sub-Clause 20.2.2.

(iv) Improvements: There is no explicit requirement that the Engineer's Notice of objection should refer to the Sub-Clause under which it is given. Given the importance of such Notice, this should be required.

20.2.3 Contemporary records

> In this Sub-Clause 20.2, "contemporary records" means records that are prepared or generated at the same time, or immediately after, the event or circumstance giving rise to the Claim.
>
> The claiming Party shall keep such contemporary records as may be necessary to substantiate the Claim.
>
> Without admitting the Employer's liability, the Engineer may monitor the Contractor's contemporary records and/or instruct the Contractor to keep additional contemporary records. The Contractor shall permit the Engineer to inspect all these records during normal working hours (or at other times agreed by the Contractor), and shall if instructed submit copies to the Engineer. Such monitoring, inspection or instruction (if any) by the Engineer shall not imply acceptance of the accuracy or completeness of the Contractor's contemporary records.

'Contemporary records' are records that are prepared or generated at the same time, or immediately after, the event or circumstance giving rise to the Claim. The claiming Party must keep contemporary records as may be necessary to substantiate the Claim. The Engineer

may monitor these records and/or instruct the Contractor to keep additional records. The Contractor shall permit the Engineer to inspect these records and shall, if instructed, submit copies to the Engineer.

Commentary

(i) Main Changes from RB/99: The requirement for the Contractor to keep and allow the Engineer to inspect contemporary records was first introduced in RB/87.[123] Under RB/87 and RB/99,[124] only the Contractor had an obligation to keep and allow the Engineer to inspect contemporary records.[125] Under the new Sub-Clause:

(1) 'contemporary records' are defined for the first time;
(2) the Employer (if it is the 'claiming Party') must now also keep contemporary records; and
(3) the provision that the Engineer may inspect such records 'during normal business hours', or other hours agreed, is new.

(ii) Related Clauses / Sub-Clauses: 1.8 [*Care and Supply of Documents*], 3.5 [*Engineer's Instructions*], 4.4 [*Contractor's Documents*], 4.9 [*Quality Management and Compliance Verification Systems*], 4.20 [*Progress Reports*], 6.5 [*Working Hours*], 6.10 [*Contractor's Records*], 7.3 [*Inspection*], 13.5 [*Daywork*], 14.5 [*Plant and Materials Intended for the Works*], and 20.2 [*Claims for Payment and EOT*].

(iii) Analysis:

(1) Purpose and definition of contemporary records

This Sub-Clause requires each Party to keep contemporary records in order to be able to substantiate a Claim.

123. *See* Sub-Clause 53.2, RB/87.
124. *See* Sub-Clause 20.1, fourth paragraph, RB/99.
125. FIDIC had stated that:

> The extent of recording is the responsibility of the Contractor, who should not assume that recording requirements will be specified by others, because they may not be able fully to anticipate what substantiation will be appropriate. However, [the] Engineer may be able to specify the form of records which he wishes to monitor on a routine basis.
>
> *The FIDIC Contracts Guide* (1st edn, FIDIC, 2000) 302.

Contemporary records are defined as 'records that are prepared or generated at the same time, or immediately after, the event or circumstance giving rise to the Claim'.[126] They may comprise, among other things, weather reports, programmes, progress reports, Site diaries, records of used resources and/or expenditure, photographs (ideally, dated) or videos, records relating to specific work activities (e.g., concrete pour records) and minutes of meetings.[127]

(2) Obligation to keep contemporary records

Unlike RB/99, Sub-Clause 20.2.3 of RB/17 specifies that the 'claiming Party' – and not just the Contractor – has an obligation to keep 'such contemporary records as may be necessary to substantiate [its] Claim'.

---

126. This definition is similar to the one given in *Attorney General for the Falkland Islands v Gordon Forbes Construction (Falklands) Ltd* (discussed under **(iv) Related Law** below) and therefore the observations in that case are relevant to the new definition.
127. *See* Sub-Clause 6.10, which describes records the Contractor must regularly keep. *See also* Nael G Bunni, *The FIDIC Forms of Contract* (3rd edn Blackwell Publishing, Oxford, 2005) 332, which provides the following list of 'contemporary records' for the purposes of Sub-Clause 53.2 of RB/87, which corresponds to Sub-Clause 20.2.3 of RB/17:
    - Clause 14 programme setting out what the contractor had intended for the order, sequence and timing of the various activities at the time of tender.
    - An estimate of resources and anticipated expenditure in units of time, which are required to achieve the Clause 14 programme.
    - Any update and revision programmes in accordance with events which may occur during the progress of the works, as required in Sub-Clause 14.2.
    - Progress programmes setting out the progress of the various activities against the Clause 14 programme.
    - Records of actual resources and actual expenditure based on progress.
    - Records of any resources which were standing or uneconomically employed.
    - Records of overtime worked, and the cost thereof.
    - Progress photographs and/or videos.
    - Drawings register (with details of amendments and updates, if any).
    - Site Diaries.
    - Approved minutes of meetings.
    - Labour allocation sheets.
    - Plant allocation sheets.

They should allow the claiming Party to substantiate not only the event or circumstance giving rise to the Claim but also its quantum.[128]

(3) How contemporary records are to be kept and monitored by the Engineer

Sub-Clause 20.2.3 does not stipulate how such contemporary records should be maintained. But well-known international standards provide guidance in this respect. ISO 15-489:1-2016(E), for example, establishes 'core concepts and principles for the creation, capture and management of records' and is perhaps the key ISO standard regarding good practice in this field.[129]

Under the last paragraph of Sub-Clause 20.2.3, the Engineer is authorised to monitor the Contractor's contemporary records and/or instruct the Contractor to keep additional contemporary records. The Contractor must keep a copy of contemporary records on the Site at all times.[130] The Contractor must permit the Engineer to inspect these records during normal working hours or at other times agreed by the Contractor,[131] and to submit copies to the Engineer if instructed by it. Any such monitoring, inspection and/or instruction by the Engineer is stated not to imply acceptance of the accuracy or completeness of such records.[132]

128. *FIDIC DBO Contract Guide* (FIDIC, 2011) 129.
129. International Standard ISO 15489-1:2016 (*Information and documentation – Records management – Part 1: Concepts and Principles*), Second Edition dated 15 April 2016. The standard can be obtained from: https://www.iso.org/standard/62542.html accessed 10 November 2022. This is in addition to the requirements of any applicable laws, e.g., in relation to the keeping of company and accounting records.
130. Sub-Clause 1.8 [*Care and Supply of Documents*], sub-para. (b).
131. The Employer's Personnel have a similar right of inspection. Sub-Clause 1.8.
132. Sub-Clause 20.2.3, third paragraph. With regard to the similar authority of the Employer's Representative [who corresponds to the Engineer under RB/17] under GB/08, FIDIC has stated:

> Very often, having been given Notice [of a claim], the Employer's Representative will keep his own records of events so that he can check the application from the Contractor, but this will not relieve the Contractor of the requirement to keep his own records [...]. [The] Employer's Representative may require the Contractor to keep specific additional records or [...] ask the Contractor to compile the records in a specific manner to simplify subsequent checking and analysis.
>
> *FIDIC DBO Contract Guide* (FIDIC, 2011) 129.

(4) Sanction

The claiming Party has the burden of proving the facts to support a Claim,[133] which it will ordinarily need to do primarily by reference to written records, and the more contemporaneous they are the better. If the claimant is unable to justify a Claim by records, then, as it has the burden of proof, its Claim may be rejected or its amount substantially reduced.

Under Sub-Clause 20.2.7, if it fails to keep contemporary records which it should have kept pursuant to any Sub-Clause of the Conditions, or which the Engineer had instructed it to keep, any claimed additional payment, EOT and/or extension of DNP:

> shall take account of the extent (if any) to which the failure [to comply with Sub-Clause 20.2 or any other Sub-Clause] has prevented or prejudiced proper investigation of the Claim by the Engineer.

In other words, if a Party has failed to comply with its contemporary record-keeping obligations, it can expect to bear the consequences.

(iv) Related Law: In an English case, it was stated that contemporary records in the context of RB/87 meant 'original or primary documents, or copies thereof, produced or prepared at or about the time giving rise to the claim, whether by or for the contractor or the employer'.[134] As the word 'contemporary' suggested, these were documents that recorded the events or circumstances giving rise to the Claim which were produced at or around the same time as the time when such events or circumstances occurred. Therefore, witness statements produced after such event or circumstance could not be classified as contemporary records.[135]

(v) Improvements: As RB/17 has now introduced a single claim procedure applicable to both Parties, it would appear justified that the Engineer be given the same explicit authority in relation to the contemporary records of the Employer as it has in relation to those of the Contractor. It

133. Gary Born, *International Commercial Arbitration* (3rd edn, Kluwer L Int'l, the Netherlands, 2021) vol II, 2487-2489 (s 15. 09 [B]) and W Laurence Craig and others, *International Chamber of Commerce Arbitration* (3rd edn, Oceana publications, USA 2000) 646.

134. *Attorney General for the Falkland Islands v Gordon Forbes Construction (Falklands) Ltd* [2003] BLR 280 (Falklands Islands Supreme Court), 285 [para. 33].

135. *Ibid*. A witness statement may be relied upon to identify or to clarify extant contemporary records. *Ibid*.

may have been presumed that, as the Engineer is employed by the Employer, it will necessarily have this authority[136] but, for the Contractor's information, it would be better if this were stated expressly.

20.2.4 Fully detailed Claim

In this Sub-Clause 20.2, "fully detailed Claim" means a submission which includes:

(a) a detailed description of the event or circumstance giving rise to the Claim;
(b) a statement of the contractual and/or other legal basis of the Claim;
(c) all contemporary records on which the claiming Party relies; and
(d) detailed supporting particulars of the amount of additional payment claimed (or amount of reduction of the Contract Price in the case of the Employer as the claiming Party), and/or EOT claimed (in the case of the Contractor) or extension of the DNP claimed (in the case of the Employer).

Within either:

(i) 84 days after the claiming Party became aware, or should have become aware, of the event or circumstance giving rise to the Claim; or
(ii) such other period (if any) as may be proposed by the claiming Party and agreed by the Engineer,

the claiming Party shall submit to the Engineer a fully detailed Claim.

If within this time limit the claiming Party fails to submit the statement under sub-paragraph (b) above, the Notice of Claim shall be deemed to have lapsed, it shall no longer be considered as a valid

136. The Engineer may also itself be preparing and/or generating and keeping the Employer's contemporary records.

Notice, and the Engineer shall, within 14 days after this time limit has expired, give a Notice to the claiming Party accordingly.

If the Engineer does not give such a Notice within this period of 14 days, the Notice of Claim shall be deemed to be a valid Notice. If the other Party disagrees with such deemed valid Notice of Claim the other Party shall give a Notice to the Engineer which shall include details of the disagreement. Thereafter, the agreement or determination of the Claim under Sub-Clause 20.2.5 [*Agreement or determination of the Claim*] shall include a review by the Engineer of such disagreement.

If the claiming Party receives a Notice from the Engineer under this Sub-Clause 20.2.4 and if the claiming Party disagrees with such Notice or considers there are circumstances which justify late submission of the statement under sub-paragraph (b) above, the fully detailed Claim shall be supplemented with details of the claiming Party's disagreement or why such late submission is justified (as the case may be).

If the event or circumstance giving rise to the Claim has a continuing effect, Sub-Clause 20.2.6 [*Claims of continuing effect*] shall apply.

The claiming Party must submit a fully detailed Claim within either: (i) 84 days after it became aware, or should have become aware, of the event or circumstance giving rise to the Claim; or (ii) such other period (if any) as may be agreed by the Engineer. The 'fully detailed Claim' should include a detailed description of the event or circumstance giving rise to the Claim, a statement of the contractual and/or other legal basis of the Claim, all contemporary records on which the claiming Party relies, and detailed supporting particulars.

If the claiming Party fails to submit a statement of the contractual and/or other legal basis of the Claim within this time limit, the Notice of Claim shall be deemed to have lapsed and the Engineer shall, within 14 days after expiry of the above time limit, give a Notice to the claiming Party accordingly.

If the Engineer does not give such Notice, the Notice of Claim shall be deemed to be valid. If the other Party disagrees, it shall give a Notice

to the Engineer with details of its disagreement. Thereafter, the agreement or determination of the Claim under Sub-Clause 20.2.5 must include a review by the Engineer of such disagreement.

If the claiming Party receives a Notice from the Engineer under the second paragraph above, and disagrees with it or considers that there are circumstances that justify its late submission, the fully detailed Claim shall include details of such disagreement or why such late submission is justified.

In the case of Claims of continuing effect, Sub-Clause 20.2.6 shall apply.

Commentary

(i) Main Changes from RB/99:

(1) The new Sub-Clause describes the fully detailed Claim in more detail than Sub-Clause 20.1 of RB/99 which had provided that the Contractor had to submit a fully detailed claim within 42 days (not 84 days as under the new Sub-Clause) after it became aware (or should have become aware) of the event or circumstance giving rise to the claim.[137]

(2) Whereas the new Sub-Clause applies to Employer's Claims, Sub-Clause 2.5 of RB/99, which dealt with Employer's claims, did not require a fully detailed claim, but only that the Employer or Engineer submit 'particulars' of the claim to the Contractor. There was, moreover, no explicit time period within which they were to be submitted.[138]

(3) Under the new Sub-Clause, if the Contractor fails to submit a statement of the 'contractual or other basis' of the claim within an 84-day time limit, its Notice of Claim will be deemed to have lapsed and no longer be valid. However, RB/17 empowers the Engineer to disapply the 84-day time bar[139] and provides criteria for it to use when exercising this power.[140]

137. Sub-Clause 20.1, fifth paragraph, RB/99.

138. FIDIC justified this difference (in the treatment of Employer's claims compared to Contractor's claims) by saying that '[Contractors] may be more familiar with preparing claims than many Employers.' *The FIDIC Contracts Guide* (1st edn, FIDIC, 2000) 80.

139. *See* the commentary on Sub-Clause 20.2.5 below.

140. *Ibid.*

(ii) Related Clauses / Sub-Clauses: 1.3 [*Notices and Other Communications*], 3.7 [*Agreement or Determination*], 4.12 [*Unforeseeable Physical Conditions*] and 20.2 [*Claims for Payment and/or EOT*].

(iii) Analysis: This Sub-Clause specifies the content of a fully detailed Claim, provides the time frame within which such a Claim must be submitted and the consequences of a failure to submit the contractual and/or other legal basis of the Claim within that time.

(1) The fully detailed Claim

As stated above,[141] it is up to the claiming Party to prove its case. For this purpose, Sub-Clause 20.2.4 requires that it must submit a fully detailed Claim which must include:

(a) a detailed description of the event or circumstance giving rise to the Claim;
(b) a statement of the contractual and/or other legal basis of the Claim;
(c) all contemporary records on which the claiming Party relies; and
(d) detailed supporting particulars concerning the amount claimed and/or the EOT claimed and/or the extension of the DNP claimed, as the case may be.[142]

Thus, a fully detailed Claim should, as a minimum, include a detailed description of the relevant facts (including technical issues, if any) and a statement of the contractual and/or other legal basis of the Claim accompanied by all contemporary records and particulars of the amount and/or time claimed. A failure to supply any of these elements might lead to an issue over whether a 'fully detailed Claim' has been submitted and, accordingly, whether the 84-day time limit for its submission has been complied with and the time limit for agreement, pursuant to Sub-Clause 3.7.3, has commenced.[143] Consequently, *a Party should take great care to submit a fully detailed Claim that satisfies the definition in the first paragraph of Sub-Clause 20.2.4.*

141. *See* under *(4) Sanction* under **(iii) Analysis** of the commentary on Sub-Clause 20.2.3 above.
142. Sub-Clause 20.2.4, first paragraph. *See also The FIDIC Contracts Guide* (2nd edn, FIDIC, 2022) 510.
143. *See* Sub-Clauses 20.2.4, 20.2.5 and Sub-Clause 3.7.3, sub-para. (c), among others, of RB/17.

The statement of the contractual and/or other legal basis of the Claim should include reference to the Clause(s) or Sub-Clause(s), if any, on the basis of which the Claim is made.[144]

(2) Time limit for submission

The fully detailed Claim has to be submitted to the Engineer '[w]ithin either 84 days'[145] after the claiming Party became aware, or should have become aware, of the event or circumstance giving rise to the Claim, or other period as may be proposed by the claiming Party and agreed by the Engineer. *It should be emphasised that the above-mentioned period starts to run from the Party's awareness (or deemed awareness) of the event or circumstance giving rise to the Claim*[146] and not from the date of the Notice of Claim. The 84-day period is longer than the corresponding 42-day period under RB/99[147] as it is believed that otherwise the Contractor might have insufficient time in which to prepare and submit a fully detailed Claim.[148] On the other hand, unlike the Contractor's failure to comply with the 42-day period, failure to comply in a specified particular way with the 84-day period may result in severe sanction as discussed next below.

(3) Consequences of failure to submit basis within time limit

Under the third paragraph of Sub-Clause 20.2.4, the claiming Party's failure to submit the statement in sub-paragraph (b) above (i.e., the statement of the contractual and/or other legal basis of the Claim) within the time period for submission of the fully detailed Claim (84 days) will invalidate the previously given Notice of Claim and, accordingly, result in

144. If the Claim is made under any applicable Laws, the statement should identify the particular provision or principle of law of a particular jurisdiction that is invoked.
145. A '**day**' is defined as a calendar day. Sub-Clause 1.1.25. Note also that the term 'within' is ambiguous as explained in item (2) under **(v) Improvements** in the commentary on Sub-Clause 1.2 [*Interpretation*] above.
146. As to this language, *see* under *(3) When does the 28-day time limit start?* under **(iii) Analysis** of the commentary on Sub-Clause 20.2.1 above.
147. Sub-Clause 20.1, fifth paragraph, RB/99.
148. For example, if a Contractor had for some reason given its Notice of Claim on the 28th day after becoming aware of the event or circumstance giving rise to its Claim and if the 42-day period had been retained, the Contractor would have had only an additional 14 days to prepare and submit its fully detailed Claim.

the forfeiture of the claiming Party's right to assert the Claim.[149] *Thus, Sub-Clause 20.2.4 introduces a second time bar in addition to the one in Sub-Clause 20.2.1 [Notice of Claim].*

If the Engineer considers that a Party has failed to submit the statement in sub-paragraph (b) within the required time period, the Engineer must, within 14 days after the expiry of the time period for submission of the fully detailed Claim, give a Notice to the claiming Party.[150] If the Engineer does not do so, the Notice of Claim 'shall be deemed to be a valid Notice'.[151] However, as in the case of the Engineer's initial response under Sub-Clause 20.2.2, such validity is only provisional as the non-claiming Party is entitled to object to such deemed valid Notice by giving a Notice to the Engineer with details of its disagreement and to have the Notice of Claim invalidated.[152] Thereafter, the agreement or determination of the Claim under Sub-Clause 20.2.5 must include a review by the Engineer of such disagreement.[153] If the disagreeing Party is dissatisfied with the result of the Engineer's review, it may serve a NOD against the Engineer's determination and refer the resulting Dispute to the DAAB.[154]

If the Engineer gives a Notice to the claiming Party that it has failed to submit the statement under sub-paragraph (b) on time, and if the claiming Party disagrees with such Notice or considers that there are circumstances that justify late submission of such statement, then 'the fully detailed Claim shall be supplemented with details of the claiming

149. If the claiming Party has a bona fide Claim, the assumption is that it should be able to identify a contractual and/or other legal basis for it within 84 days. Under Sub-Clause 20.2.7, first paragraph, having received the Notice of Claim, the Engineer is obliged to include in a Payment Certificate 'such amounts for any Claim as have been reasonably substantiated as due to the claiming Party'. If the Engineer has been informed of the contractual/legal basis of the Claim, it will be readily able to decide what is 'reasonably substantiated' and so this provision can apply, whereas otherwise the Engineer might not be able to do so. The claiming Party is not irrevocably committed to the particular contractual and/or other legal basis of the Claim that it has specified, as explained under **(iv) Related Law** below.
150. Sub-Clause 20.2.4, third paragraph. This must be copied to the other Party and the Engineer. Sub-Clause 1.3.
151. Sub-Clause 20.2.4, fourth paragraph.
152. *Ibid.*
153. *Ibid.*
154. Sub-Clauses 3.7.5 and 21.4. If necessary, it can refer the Dispute later to arbitration. Sub-Clauses 21.4.4, 21.5 and 21.6.

Party's disagreement or why such late submission is justified (as the case may be)'.[155] These circumstances may include, but are not limited to, those described in Sub-Clause 20.2.5, second paragraph.[156] The Engineer is then expressly authorised to decide whether the Notice of Claim shall be treated as a valid Notice or not, pursuant to Sub-Clause 20.2.5.[157]

Sub-Clause 20.2.6 will apply with regard to Claims of continuing effect.

(iv) Related Law:

(1) Contrary to the position taken by the Hong Kong courts, in relation to a requirement to state "the contractual basis" of a claim in a notice under another form of construction contract (than FIDIC), that a contractor is bound by the contractual basis which it has selected,[158] under RB/17 the claiming Party is not so bound. RB/17 does not state that the claiming Party is bound and other provisions of the Conditions are consistent with the notion that a Party may change the contractual and/or legal basis of a Claim during the Claims and Disputes process.[159] Moreover, it would be unrealistic to expect a claimant to have finalized its legal case within the 84-day period provided for in Sub-Clause 20.2.4, especially as it is not expected to have sought legal advice when preparing its Claims.

(2) *See*, in relation to the time bar in Sub-Clause 20.2.4, **(iv) Related Law** in the commentary on Sub-Clause 20.2.1 above as the same comments apply.

155. Sub-Clause 20.2.4, fifth paragraph.
156. *See (2) Disagreement with Engineer's Notice of objection* under **(iii) Analysis** in the commentary on Sub-Clause 20.2.2 [*Engineer's initial response*] above.
157. Sub-Clause 20.2.5, second paragraph.
158. *Maeda Corporation v Bauer Hong Kong Ltd* [2020] HKCA 830 (overturning unjustifiably in the author's opinion, the award of an experienced arbitrator, Sir Vivian Ramsey).
159. *See* DAAB Rules, Art 5.1 (k) and Sub-Clause 21.6, second paragraph, as well as Sub-Clause 21.6, fourth paragraph, providing that a Party is not limited to the reasons for dissatisfaction given in an NOD under Sub-Clause 21.4.

20.2.5 Agreement or determination of the Claim

After receiving a fully detailed Claim either under Sub-Clause 20.2.4 [*Fully detailed Claim*], or an interim or final fully detailed Claim (as the case may be) under Sub-Clause 20.2.6 [*Claims of continuing effect*], the Engineer shall proceed under Sub-Clause 3.7 [*Agreement or Determination*] to agree or determine:

(a) the additional payment (if any) to which the claiming Party is entitled or the reduction of the Contract Price (in the case of the Employer as the claiming Party); and/or
(b) the extension (if any) of the Time for Completion (before or after its expiry) under Sub-Clause 8.5 [*Extension of Time for Completion*] (in the case of the Contractor as the claiming Party), or the extension (if any) of the DNP (before its expiry) under Sub-Clause 11.3 [*Extension of Defects Notification Period*] (in the case of the Employer as the claiming Party),

to which the claiming Party is entitled under the Contract.

If the Engineer has given a Notice under Sub-Clause 20.2.2 [*Engineer's initial response*] and/or under Sub-Clause 20.2.4 [*Fully detailed Claim*], the Claim shall nevertheless be agreed or determined in accordance with this Sub-Clause 20.2.5. The agreement or determination of the Claim shall include whether or not the Notice of Claim shall be treated as a valid Notice taking account of the details (if any) included in the fully detailed Claim of the claiming Party's disagreement with such Notice(s) or why late submission is justified (as the case may be). The circumstances which may be taken into account (but shall not be binding) may include:

- whether or to what extent the other Party would be prejudiced by acceptance of the late submission;

- in the case of the time limit under Sub-Clause 20.2.1 [*Notice of Claim*], any evidence of the other Party's prior knowledge of the event or circumstance giving rise to the Claim, which the claiming Party may include in its supporting particulars; and/or
- in the case of the time limit under Sub-Clause 20.2.4 [*Fully detailed Claim*], any evidence of the other Party's prior knowledge of the contractual and/or other legal basis of the Claim, which the claiming Party may include in its supporting particulars.

If, having received the fully detailed Claim under Sub-Clause 20.2.4 [*Fully detailed Claim*], or in the case of a Claim under Sub-Clause 20.2.6 [*Claims of continuing effect*] an interim or final fully detailed Claim (as the case may be), the Engineer requires necessary additional particulars:

(i) he/she shall promptly give a Notice to the claiming Party, describing the additional particulars and the reasons for requiring them;

(ii) he/she shall nevertheless give his/her response on the contractual or other legal basis of the Claim, by giving a Notice to the claiming Party, within the time limit for agreement under Sub-Clause 3.7.3 [*Time limits*];

(iii) as soon as practicable after receiving the Notice under sub-paragraph (i) above, the claiming Party shall submit the additional particulars; and

(iv) the Engineer shall then proceed under Sub-Clause 3.7 [*Agreement or Determination*] to agree or determine the matters under sub-paragraphs (a) and/or (b) above (and, for the purpose of Sub-Clause 3.7.3 [*Time limits*], the date the Engineer receives the additional particulars from the claiming Party shall be the date of commencement of the time limit for agreement under Sub-Clause 3.7.3).

After receiving a fully detailed Claim (or an interim or final fully detailed Claim in the case of Claims of continuing effect), the Engineer shall proceed under Sub-Clause 3.7 to agree or determine the Claim.

If the Engineer has given a Notice under Sub-Clause 20.2.2, and/or under Sub-Clause 20.2.4, the Claim shall nevertheless be agreed or determined by the Engineer under Sub-Clause 20.2.5. Such agreement or determination shall include consideration of whether or not the Notice of Claim shall be treated as valid, taking account of the details included in the fully detailed Claim and other circumstances, including those listed in three bullet points.

If, after having received the fully detailed Claim (or an interim or final fully detailed Claim in the case of Claims of continuing effect), the Engineer requires necessary additional particulars, the Engineer shall:

(a) promptly give a Notice with reasons to the claiming Party, which shall submit the particulars as soon as practicable;
(b) nevertheless give its response on the contractual or other legal basis of the Claim by a Notice within the time limit for agreement under Sub-Clause 3.7.3; and
(c) agree or determine the Claim under Sub-Clause 3.7, and the date the Engineer receives the necessary additional particulars shall be the date of commencement of the time limit for agreement under Sub-Clause 3.7.3.

Commentary

(i) Main Changes from RB/99:

(1) Unlike the strict time limits in the new Sub-Clause and in Sub-Clause 3.7, Sub-Clause 20.1 of RB/99 had merely provided that within 42 days after receiving the fully detailed claim or any further particulars supporting a previous claim, the Engineer was required to 'respond with approval, or with disapproval and detailed comments',[160] and to give its response on the 'principles of the claim'.[161]

160. Sub-Clause 20.1, sixth paragraph, RB/99.
161. *Ibid*. There was no time limit for the Engineer's determination under Clause 20 of RB/99.

(2) Whereas under RB/99 the Engineer was required to agree or determine the claim under Sub-Clause 3.5[162] without being bound by any time limit, Sub-Clause 3.7 of the new Sub-Clause provides strict time limits for doing so.
(3) Unlike the second paragraph of Sub-Clause 20.2.5, under RB/99, the Engineer was not authorised to disapply any time bar.
(4) The Engineer's right, in the third paragraph of Sub-Clause 20.2.5, to require additional particulars from the Contractor is much more detailed than in Sub-Clause 20.1 of RB/99.

(ii) Related Clauses / Sub-Clauses: 1.3 [*Notices and Other Communications*], 3.7 [*Agreement or Determination*], 8.5 [*Extension of Time for Completion*], 11.3 [*Extension of Defects Notification Period*] and 20.2 [*Claims for Payment and/or EOT*].

(iii) Analysis:

(1) Agreement or determination by the Engineer

The first paragraph of Sub-Clause 20.2.5 deals with the procedure for agreement or determination of Claims for additional payment, an EOT (in the case of the Contractor) and/or an extension of the DNP (in the case of the Employer). After receiving a fully detailed Claim (or an interim or final fully detailed Claim in the case of Claims of continuing effect), under Sub-Clause 3.7, the Engineer should first consult with the Parties in an endeavour to reach an agreement on the Claim.[163] The time limit for the Parties' agreement is 42 days, or such other time limit as is proposed by the Engineer and agreed by the Parties, and commences on the date when the Engineer receives the fully detailed Claim (or the interim or final fully detailed Claim in the case of a Claim of continuing effect).[164]

If no agreement is achieved within this time limit, or if both Parties advise the Engineer that no agreement can be reached within it, whichever is earlier, the Engineer must give a Notice to the Parties accordingly and proceed to make a fair determination of the Claim, in accordance with the Contract, taking due regard of all relevant circumstances.[165] The Engineer must give its Notice of determination within 42 days, or such other

162. Sub-Clause 20.1, eighth paragraph, RB/99.
163. Sub-Clause 3.7.1.
164. Sub-Clause 3.7.3, sub-para. (c).
165. Sub-Clauses 3.7.1 and 3.7.2.

limit as may be proposed by the Engineer and agreed by the Parties after the date corresponding to its obligation to proceed to make a determination.[166]

(2) Time bar issues

The second paragraph of Sub-Clause 20.2.5 outlines the Engineer's duties in cases where the Engineer has given a Notice that the claiming Party has failed, within the relevant time period, to:

(1) give a Notice of Claim under Sub-Clause 20.2.1; and/or
(2) submit a statement of the contractual and/or other legal basis of the Claim under Sub-Clause 20.2.4.[167]

As provided for in Sub-Clauses 20.2.2 and 20.2.4, if the claiming Party disagrees with the Engineer, and/or considers that there are circumstances that justify late submission of the Notice of Claim or the statement of the contractual and/or other legal basis of the Claim, as the case may be, the claiming Party must include in its fully detailed Claim details of such disagreement or why a late submission is justified. If the claiming Party does not do so, it is likely to be found to have acquiesced in the Engineer's position that its Notice of Claim is invalid and/or has lapsed, with the consequences described in the second paragraph of Sub-Clause 20.2.1 (namely, discharge from liability of the other Party).

While not expressly mentioned in the second paragraph of Sub-Clause 20.2.5, where the Engineer has given no Notice within 14 days under Sub-Clause 20.2.2 or 20.2.4 with the result that the Notice of Claim is provisionally deemed valid but the other Party has given a Notice of disagreement with such deemed validity with details, the Engineer's consideration under Sub-Clause 3.7 should also include a review of such

166. Sub-Clause 3.7.3, second paragraph. For a more detailed commentary on the procedure for agreement or determination, *see* the commentary on Sub-Clause 3.7 above.

167. The provision requires that the Engineer is nevertheless obliged to agree or determine the Claim under Sub-Clause 3.7. This provision assumes – as it does not state – that the claiming Party disagrees with such Notice or considers there are circumstances which justify its late submission as it would make no sense for the Engineer to proceed under Sub-Clause 3.7 unless the claiming Party had previously expressed disagreement with the Engineer's Notice or maintains that there are justifying circumstances.

disagreement.[168] Having considered each Party's submissions, the Engineer is entitled to disapply the time bars in Sub-Clauses 20.2.1 and 20.2.4.[169]

(3) Disapplying time bars

Sub-Clause 20.2.5 identifies three circumstances that 'may be taken into account' by the Engineer when deciding whether to disapply time bar provisions, as follows:

(1) whether or to what extent the non-claiming Party would be prejudiced by acceptance of the late submission;
(2) where a Notice of Claim was submitted late, any evidence of the non-claiming Party's prior knowledge of the event or circumstance giving rise to the Claim, which the claiming Party may include in its supporting particulars; and/or
(3) where a statement of the contractual or other legal basis was submitted late, any evidence of the non-claiming Party's prior knowledge of such basis of the Claim, which the claiming Party may include in its supporting particulars.[170]

These three circumstances correspond to the general exceptions to the enforcement of time bars in the case of US Federal Government construction contracts,[171] and each may constitute a compelling reason to disapply the relevant time bar. The first circumstance refers to the prejudice which the non-claiming Party may suffer as a result of the late submission, recognising its legitimate interest to receive prompt notice of Claims, as they may have serious time-related or financial consequences. A late notice of a Claim might, for example, deprive the non-claiming Party of the opportunity to examine evidence when it is still fresh, and to

168. As stated in Sub-Clause 20.2.2, second paragraph, and Sub-Clause 20.2.4, fourth paragraph.
169. Sub-Clause 20.2.5, second paragraph. There is no provision for disapplying other time bars under the General Conditions, such as in the case of a failure to give a timely NOD with respect to either an Engineer's determination under Sub-Clause 3.7.5 or a DAAB's decision under Sub-Clause 21.4.4, or a failure to refer a Dispute to the DAAB within 42 days as required by Sub-Clause 21.4.
170. *Ibid.*
171. *See* under *(1) Time bars in common law countries* under **(iv) Related Law** in the commentary on Sub-Clause 20.2.1 above.

take remedial measures or withdraw instructions (in the case of the Employer) before additional costs and/or delays are incurred.

The second and third criteria deal with where the non-claiming Party may already have known of the event or circumstance that gave rise to the Claim and/or of the contractual and/or other legal basis of the Claim. If it already had such knowledge, it might not have been damaged by the late submission and therefore strict enforcement of the time bar might be unfair. On the other hand, it might not be unfair if, although the non-claiming Party had known of such event or circumstance, it could not reasonably have anticipated that the claiming Party would assert a Claim for it or could not reasonably have had knowledge of its contractual and/or other legal basis.

The above-mentioned three circumstances are not binding on the Parties or the Engineer.[172] Moreover, this list is not exhaustive. The Engineer may take into account other circumstances.[173]

(4) Engineer's request for additional particulars

The last paragraph of Sub-Clause 20.2.5 deals with 'necessary additional particulars' that the Engineer may request after having received the fully detailed Claim or, in the case of a Claim of continuing effect, the interim or final fully detailed Claim. Under this paragraph, the Engineer may only require 'necessary' additional particulars, i.e., particulars that are additional to those supplied pursuant to Sub-Clause 20.2.4(d) and that are required for the agreement or determination of the Claim under Sub-Clause 3.7. To do so, the Engineer must 'promptly' give a Notice to the claiming Party, describing the additional particulars and the reasons for requiring them, and the claiming Party must submit the requested details 'as soon as practicable' after having received such a Notice. The Engineer must then proceed to agree or determine the Claim under Sub-Clause 3.7, in which case the 42-day time limit for agreement will commence on the date when the Engineer has received the requested additional particulars.[174]

However, the Engineer is required by a Notice to give its response on the contractual or other legal basis of the Claim within the initial time period

172. Sub-Clause 20.2.5, second paragraph.
173. However, the Contractor may not rely on any act or failure to act of the Engineer, the Engineer's Representative or any assistant to relieve it (the Contractor) of a time bar. *See* Sub-Clause 3.2, last paragraph.
174. Sub-Clause 20.2.5 (iv).

for agreement under Sub-Clause 3.7.3, that is, the 42-day time limit calculated from the date of receiving the fully detailed Claim or, in the case of a Claim of continuing effect, the interim or final fully detailed Claim (as the case may be).[175]

The entire procedure is designed so that any necessary additional particulars required by the Engineer are requested promptly after the Engineer receives the final fully detailed Claim and are supplied promptly ('as soon as practicable'[176]) by the claiming Party, so as to allow an agreement or determination to be made without unnecessary delay.

(iv) Improvements: As indicated in footnote 167 under **(iii) Analysis** above, the second paragraph of Sub-Clause 20.2.5 should be amended so as to make it clear that the Engineer shall have no obligation to proceed to agree and/or determine a Claim under Sub-Clause 3.7 in cases where the claiming Party has not expressed disagreement with the Engineer's Notice under Sub-Clause 20.2.2 and/or Sub-Clause 20.2.4, as in those cases the Notice of Claim is deemed invalid or to have lapsed.

--ooOOoo--

Figure 12 Procedure for Claims for Time and/or Money summarises in 12 steps the procedure applicable to Claims provided for by Sub-Clause 20.1(a) or (b), including the steps involved if the Claim later becomes a Dispute.[177] In the figure, the 'claiming Party' may be either the Employer or the Contractor. For a more detailed figure treating the same subject, *see* **Figure 13 Procedure for Claims for Time and/or Money – Detailed** at the end of this commentary on Clause 20.

--ooOOoo--

175. Sub-Clauses 20.2.5 (ii) and 3.7.3(c).
176. Sub-Clause 20.2.5 (iii).
177. *See* the commentary on Clause 21 [*Disputes and Arbitration*] below.

Figure 12 Procedure for Claims for Time[1] and/or Money

SC = Sub-Clause

Cumulative n° of days	Procedure[2]
0	1. An 'event or circumstance' giving rise to a **Claim** occurs[3]
28	2. The claiming Party must: (1) give a **Notice of Claim** to the Engineer within 28 days after it became aware/should have become aware of the 'event or circumstance' (otherwise the **Notice of Claim** is invalid) and (2) keep contemporary records
42	3. The Engineer must give any Notice of objection to the validity of **Notice of Claim** within 14 days after receiving it – otherwise Notice of Claim is deemed provisionally valid
84	4. The claiming Party must submit a **fully detailed Claim** within 84 days after it became aware/should have become aware of the 'event or circumstance' (if the contractual/legal basis of the **Claim** is not submitted, the **Notice of Claim** is invalid)
98	5. The Engineer must give any Notice of objection within 14 days after the expiry of the above 84-day period if the claiming Party has failed to submit the contractual/legal basis of the **Claim** – otherwise the **Notice of Claim** is deemed provisionally valid
168	6. The Engineer must agree or determine the **Claim** under SC 3.7 including validity of **Notice of Claim,** within 84 days after receiving a **fully detailed Claim**
196	7. Assuming no agreement, either Party may give a NOD in respect of the Engineer's determination within 28 days of receiving it, creating a **Dispute** – otherwise the determination is final and binding
238	8. A **Dispute** must be referred to the DAAB within 42 days of the giving or receiving of a NOD – otherwise the NOD is invalid
322	9. The **DAAB** has 84 days to give a decision
350	10. Either Party may give a NOD in respect of the **DAAB**'s decision within 28 days after receiving it – otherwise the decision is final and binding
378	11. Both Parties have to attempt amicable settlement for 28 days
378 and thereafter	12. Either Party may refer the Dispute to **arbitration**

Source: Author's own work.

Notes

1. In the case of the Contractor, 'Time' refers to a Claim for an EOT whereas, in the case of the Employer, 'Time' refers to a Claim for an extension of the DNP.
2. This figure contains a simplified version of steps in the Conditions. Only the actual text of the relevant Sub-Clauses should be relied upon. The 12 steps shown are not identified as such in the Conditions. For a related figure *see* Figure 4 'Agreement/Determination Procedure'.
3. A Party may have been required to have previously advised the Engineer of this event or circumstance pursuant to SC 8.4 [*Advance Warning*].

20.2.6 Claims of continuing effect

If the event or circumstance giving rise to a Claim under this Sub-Clause 20.2 has a continuing effect:

(a) the fully detailed Claim submitted under Sub-Clause 20.2.4 [*Fully detailed Claim*] shall be considered as interim;
(b) in respect of this first interim fully detailed Claim, the Engineer shall give his/her response on the contractual or other legal basis of the Claim, by giving a Notice to the claiming Party, within the time limit for agreement under Sub-Clause 3.7.3 [*Time limits*];
(c) after submitting the first interim fully detailed Claim the claiming Party shall submit further interim fully detailed Claims at monthly intervals, giving the accumulated amount of additional payment claimed (or the reduction of the Contract Price, in the case of the Employer as the claiming Party), and/or extension of time claimed (in the case of the Contractor as the claiming Party) or extension of the DNP (in the case of the Employer as the claiming Party); and
(d) the claiming Party shall submit a final fully detailed Claim within 28 days after the end of the effects resulting from the event or circumstance, or within such other period as may be proposed by the claiming Party and agreed by the Engineer. This final fully detailed Claim shall give the total amount of additional payment claimed (or the reduction of the Contract Price, in the case of the Employer as the claiming Party), and/or extension of time claimed (in the case of the Contractor as the claiming Party) or extension of the DNP (in the case of the Employer as the claiming Party).

If the event or circumstance giving rise to the Claim has a continuing effect:

- **(a) the fully detailed Claim submitted under Sub-Clause 20.2.4 shall be considered as interim;**
- **(b) in respect of this first interim fully detailed Claim, the Engineer shall give its response on the contractual or other legal basis of the Claim, by a Notice to the claiming Party within the time limit for agreement under Sub-Clause 3.7.3;**
- **(c) the claiming Party shall submit further interim fully detailed Claims at monthly intervals; and**
- **(d) the claiming Party shall submit a final fully detailed Claim giving the total amount claimed and/or EOT claimed, or the extension of the DNP (as the case may be), within 28 days after the end of the effects resulting from the event or circumstance, or within such other period as may be agreed by the Engineer.**

Commentary

(i) Main Changes from RB/99: Compared to the corresponding provision in RB/99, which applied to the Contractor's claims only,[178] the discussion of Claims having continuing effect has been significantly expanded and, like Sub-Clause 20.2 generally, now deals with Claims of both Parties.

(ii) Related Clauses / Sub-Clauses: 1.3 [*Notices and Other Communications*], 3.7 [*Agreement or Determination*], 8.5 [*Extension of Time for Completion*], 11.3 [*Extension of Defects Notification Period*] and 20.2 [*Claims for Payment and/or EOT*].

(iii) Analysis: This Sub-Clause sets out the procedure that deals with Claims arising out of events or circumstances that have a continuing effect. Examples are certain natural conditions (e.g., continuous rainfalls, prolonged flooding or continued volcanic activity) or certain political events (e.g., continuous riots, disturbances or local incidents of violence endangering the Contractor's staff) that go on in the area or region of the Site or otherwise affect the execution of the Works, virtually without interruption, for weeks, months if not years.

178. Sub-Clause 20.1, fifth paragraph, RB/99.

In the case of events or circumstances that have a continuing effect, the claiming Party's fully detailed Claim under Sub-Clause 20.2.4 is considered to be interim.[179] Thereafter, the claiming Party should submit further interim fully detailed Claims at monthly intervals and a final fully detailed Claim within 28 days after the end of the effects resulting from the event or circumstance giving rise to the Claim, or within such other period as may be proposed by the claiming Party and agreed by the Engineer.[180] The submission of such interim fully detailed Claims permits the Engineer to include such amounts as have been 'reasonably substantiated' in IPCs.[181]

Sub-Clause 20.2.6 now explicitly provides that the Engineer should give its response on the contractual or other legal basis of the Claim following receipt of the first interim fully detailed Claim.[182] This will allow the claiming Party to know the Engineer's position on this crucial matter at an early stage. The Engineer must give its response by a Notice to the claiming Party within the time limit for agreement under Sub-Clause 3.7.3, that is, within 42 days or within such other time limit as may be proposed by the Engineer and agreed by the Parties after the Engineer receives the first interim fully detailed Claim.[183]

It is 'only after the claiming Party has submitted the final fully detailed Claim that the Engineer [...] becomes obliged to proceed' to agree or determine the Claim under Sub-Clause 3.7.[184]

20.2.7 General requirements

> After receiving the Notice of Claim, and until the Claim is agreed or determined under Sub-Clause 20.2.5 [*Agreement or determination of the Claim*], in each Payment Certificate the Engineer shall include such amounts for any Claim as have been reasonably substantiated as due to the claiming Party under the relevant provision of the Contract.

179. Sub-Clause 20.2.6, sub-para. (a).
180. Sub-Clause 20.2.6, sub-paras (c) and (d).
181. Sub-Clause 20.2.7, first paragraph.
182. Sub-Clause 20.2.6, sub-para. (b).
183. Sub-Clause 20.2.6 in relation to Sub-Clause 3.7.3, sub-para. (c)(ii).
184. *The FIDIC Contracts Guide* (2nd edn, 2022) 517.

> The Employer shall only be entitled to claim any payment from the Contractor and/or to extend the DNP, or set off against or make any deduction from any amount due to the Contractor, by complying with this Sub-Clause 20.2.
>
> The requirements of this Sub-Clause 20.2 are in addition to those of any other Sub-Clause which may apply to the Claim. If the claiming Party fails to comply with this or any other Sub-Clause in relation to the Claim, any additional payment and/or any EOT (in the case of the Contractor as the claiming Party) or extension of the DNP (in the case of the Employer as the claiming Party), shall take account of the extent (if any) to which the failure has prevented or prejudiced proper investigation of the Claim by the Engineer.

After receiving a Notice of Claim and until the Claim is agreed or determined, the Engineer shall include in each Payment Certificate such amounts for it as have been reasonably substantiated as due.

The Employer shall only be entitled to claim payment from the Contractor and/or an extension of the DNP, or to set off or make any deduction from any amount due to the Contractor, by complying with Sub-Clause 20.2.

The requirements of Sub-Clause 20.2 are in addition to those of any other Sub-Clause which may apply to a Claim. If the claiming Party fails to comply with Sub-Clause 20.2 or any other Sub-Clause in relation to the Claim, any additional payment and/or EOT or extension of the DNP shall take account of the extent to which the failure has prevented or prejudiced proper investigation of the Claim by the Engineer.

Commentary

(i) Main Changes from RB/99:

(1) Provisions corresponding, roughly, to the first and third paragraphs of Sub-Clause 20.2.7 are to be found in the seventh and ninth paragraphs of Sub-Clause 20.1 of RB/99.

(2) The second paragraph of Sub-Clause 20.2.7 corresponds approximately to the second sentence of the last paragraph of Sub-Clause 2.5 of RB/99.

(3) Unlike Sub-Clause 20.1 of RB/99, Sub-Clause 20.2.7 applies to the Employer's Claims as well as the Contractor's Claims.

(ii) Related Clauses / Sub-Clauses: 1.3 [*Notices and Other Communications*], 3.7 [*Agreement or Determination*], 6.10 [*Contractor's Records*], 8.5 [*Extension of Time for Completion*], 11.3 [*Extension of Defects Notification Period*], 14.3 [*Application for Interim Payment*] and 14.6 [*Issue of IPC*].

(iii) Analysis: This Sub-Clause introduces some important general requirements with regard to Claims under Sub-Clause 20.2.

(1) Payment by way of Payment Certificates

After receiving a Notice of Claim, and before the Claim is agreed or determined under Sub-Clause 20.2.5, the Engineer is required to include in each Payment Certificate such amounts for any Claim as, in the Engineer's view, have been reasonably substantiated (in terms of entitlement and quantum) as due to the claiming Party. If the Contractor is the claiming Party, it should include such amounts as additions in its applications for interim payment under Sub-Clause 14.3, sub-paragraph (vi). If the Contractor has provided sufficient evidence to substantiate these amounts, they should be included by the Engineer in the next IPC and certification should not wait until the agreement or determination of the Claim under Sub-Clause 3.7.[185] If the Employer is the claiming Party, the Engineer may include these amounts as deductions in the next IPC under Sub-Clause 14.6.1.

(2) Employer's Claims

The second paragraph of Sub-Clause 20.2.7 provides that the Employer shall only be entitled to claim any payment from the Contractor and/or to extend the DNP, or to set off against or make any deduction from any amount due to the Contractor, by complying with the procedure set out in Sub-Clause 20.2. Thus, for example, if an IPC has been issued by the Engineer, the Employer must pay the amount certified,[186] and may not make unilateral deductions from such amount, such as by exercising a right of set-off in respect of amounts that the Employer may assert are due

185. Where the Engineer is considering including an amount for a Claim in an IPC, the Engineer should not 'attempt to minimize that amount' unless the Claim 'has little or no validity'. *The FIDIC Contracts Guide* (2nd edn, FIDIC, 2022) 518.

186. *See* Sub-Clause 14.7: '[t]he Employer *shall* pay [...]' (emphasis added).

by the Contractor, e.g., Delay Damages.[187] Indeed, Sub-Clause 8.8 [*Delay Damages*] explicitly states that the Employer's Claim for Delay Damages is subject to Sub-Clause 20.2. Thus, if the Employer considers itself to be entitled to any payment from the Contractor, it must submit a Claim and follow the procedure under Sub-Clause 20.2, and is not generally entitled to engage in self-help by, for example, withholding or deducting amounts while awaiting the outcome of that procedure.[188]

(3) Sub-Clause 20.2 complements other Claims' Sub-Clauses

The last paragraph states that the requirements of Sub-Clause 20.2 are in addition to those under any other Sub-Clause which may apply to the Claim. What this statement means is that Sub-Clause 20.2 provides *only for the procedure to be followed* in respect of Claims for time and money and that the claiming Party *must first have complied with the require-*

187. *See The FIDIC Contracts Guide* (2nd edn, FIDIC, 2022) 519. As one authority has stated:

> where the parties have agreed to deploy a comprehensive scheme for the certification of interim payments [...], with either party having the right to refer any dispute over the certification to arbitration, or some other adversarial forum, the scheme of the contract may be construed *as one whereunder the obligation of the owner is to pay the amount certified, with any issues concerning overpayment or underpayment being left to resolution by a further adversarial process, or by correction in a later certificate.* (Emphasis added)

Julian Bailey, *Construction Law* (3rd edn, London Publishing, UK, 2020) vol 2, 591 (para. 6.306).

188. However, while this is what this Sub-Clause literally provides, there are at least three provisions of the Conditions which permit deductions to be made from the Contractor's Statements without any need to pass through Sub-Clause 20.2: (1) item (ix) of Sub-Clause 14.3 [*Application for Interim Payment*] in the case of the Contractor's use of utilities provided by the Employer under Sub-Clause 4.19 [*Temporary Utilities*]; (2) Sub-Clause 19.1 [*Insurance – General Requirements*], fourth paragraph, entitling the Employer to deduct the amounts of insurance premiums which it may have paid where the Contractor has failed to keep in force the insurances required under Sub-Clause 19.2 (the provisions of Clause 20 are expressly stated not to apply in this situation); and (3) Sub-Clause 21.2 [*Failure to Appoint DAAB Member(s)*], third paragraph, entitling the Engineer to deduct one-half of the amount of the remuneration of an appointing entity or official for the appointment of the DAAB pursuant to Sub-Clause 14.6.1 (b) where the Contractor has failed to pay such amount.

ments of the Sub-Clause which has given it the substantive right to claim.[189] For example, the Contractor has substantive claim rights under:

(1) Sub-Clause 1.9, if the Works are likely to be delayed or disrupted if any necessary drawing or instruction is not issued to the Contractor within a particular time, and
(2) Sub-Clause 4.12, if the Contractor should encounter Unforeseeable adverse physical conditions.

In each of these cases, if the Contractor has been delayed, disrupted and/or incurred additional Cost, it is required to give a Notice having a prescribed content and, in the case of Sub-Clause 4.12, to comply with the Engineer's instructions. In such cases the Contractor will, subject to Sub-Clause 20.2, have the *substantive right* to claim an EOT and/or Cost or Cost Plus Profit.

Sub-Clause 20.2.7 adds that the requirements of Sub-Clause 20.2, which are all of a procedural nature, are 'in addition' to those providing the Contractor with substantive rights to claim, such as those in Sub-Clauses 1.9 and 4.12. Thus, both the Clauses or Sub-Clauses providing a Party with the substantive right to claim, and Sub-Clause 20.2 providing for the giving of a Notice of Claim and observance of other procedures, must be satisfied in order for relief to be granted.[190]

(4) Sanction for not complying with Claims' procedure

The last sentence of Sub-Clause 20.2.7 provides that if a claiming Party fails to comply with this Sub-Clause or any other Sub-Clause in relation to a Claim, then the assessment of that Party's entitlement (whether in the form of an additional payment, an EOT and/or an extension of the DNP) 'shall take account of the extent (if any) to which such failure has prevented or prejudiced proper investigation of the Claim by the Engineer'. In such a case, the amount of a requested entitlement may, depending on the facts, be reduced or the Claim denied entirely if the

189. The position was the same under RB/99, *see* Christopher R Seppälä, 'Contractor's Claims under the FIDIC Contracts for Major Works' (2005) Const L J, 278, 287.

190. *The FIDIC Contracts Guide* (2nd edn, FIDIC, 2022) 193 acknowledges that it may be possible for one Notice to satisfy the requirements of different Sub-Clauses. But to achieve this, a Party needs to make it clear in that communication that it constitutes both Notices and ensure that the specific requirements for each Notice are complied with in that communication.

Engineer was not given a proper opportunity to investigate the Claim. A failure to comply with a Sub-Clause in relation to a Claim may comprise, for example, a Party's failure:

(i) in the case of the Contractor, to give a Notice, or a timely Notice, under Sub-Clause 4.12.1 relating to Unforeseeable adverse physical conditions;
(ii) in the case of the Employer, to give a Notice, or a timely Notice, under Sub-Clause 11.4 relating to the Contractor's failure to remedy a defect during the DNP; or
(iii) in the case of either Party, to keep contemporary records under Sub-Clause 20.2.3, or submit detailed supporting particulars of its fully detailed Claim as required under Sub-Clause 20.2.4(d);

(iv) Improvements: In order to remove any doubt, the Sub-Clause should be revised to provide explicitly (or it should be provided elsewhere explicitly) that the Employer shall not be entitled, on its own initiative, to withhold or deduct any amounts by way of set-off, abatement, claim or counterclaim from any payment to the Contractor, or extend the DNP, except in specified cases,[191] but must instead proceed under Clause 20.[192] RB/99 was clearer in this respect.[193]

For a figure containing a flow chart of the procedure in Sub-Clause 20.2 for Claims for payment and/or EOT, *see* **Figure 13 Procedure for Claims *for* Time and/or Money – Detailed**. This is followed by **Table 5 Employer's Claims for Time and/or Money** and **Table 6 Contractor's Claims for Time and/or Money**.

--ooOOoo--

191. *See* the deductions referred to in fn. 188 above of this commentary on **Clause 20**.
192. *See*, for example, the prohibition on the Employer's withholdings in art. 42.8 of the *ICC Model Turnkey Contract for Major Projects*, ICC Services, Paris (ICC Publication no 797 E 2020).
193. *See* Sub-Clause 2.5 [*Employer's Claims*] of RB/99.

Figure 13[1] *Procedure for Claims for Time and/or Money*[2] *– Detailed*

SC = Sub-Clause

Event or circumstance giving rise to a Claim[3]

A Party becomes aware or should have become aware of the event or circumstance (SC 20.2.1)

28 days

Notice of Claim (SC 20.2.1)

Claiming Party keeps contemporary records (SC 20.2.3)

If Engineer considers Notice of Claim is submitted late (SC 20.2.2)

Within 14 days after receiving the Notice of Claim

Engineer gives a Notice (SC 20.2.2)

If the claiming Party disagrees or considers there are circumstances justifying late submission, it should include details in its fully detailed Claim (SC 20.2.2)

Engineer fails to give a Notice → a deemed provisionally valid Notice of Claim (SC 20.2.2)

If the other Party disagrees with such deemed provisionally valid Notice of Claim, it should give a Notice to the Engineer with details. Thereafter, the Engineer should review such disagreement in its agreement/determination under SC 20.2.5 (SC 20.2.2)

84 days or other period proposed by the claiming Party and agreed by the engineer

Claiming Party submits a fully detailed Claim,[2] including statement of contractual/other legal basis of the Claim (SC 20.2.4)

Engineer considers if contractual/other legal basis of Claim is submitted late (SC 20.2.4)

Within 14 days after expiry of the time period for submission of a fully detailed Claim

Engineer gives Notice → Notice of Claim deemed provisionally to have lapsed (SC 20.2.4)

If claiming Party disagrees or considers there are circumstances justifying late submission, it should include details in its fully detailed Claim (SC 20.2.4)

Engineer fails to give a Notice → Notice of Claim deemed provisionally valid (SC 20.2.4)

If the other Party disagrees with such deemed valid Notice of Claim, it should give a Notice to the Engineer with details. Thereafter, the Engineer should review such disagreement in its agreement/ determination under SC 20.2.5 (SC 20.2.4)

Engineer requires necessary additional particulars (SC 20.2.5)

42 days

Engineer should give response on the contractual/other legal basis of Claim (SC 20.2.5)

Claiming Party provides requested particulars (SC 20.2.5)

Engineer does not require necessary additional particulars (SC 20.2.5)

Engineer should proceed under SC 3.7 to agree or determine the Claim (SC 20.2.5). *See* Figure 3 on SC 3.7

A Party gives a NOD in respect of Engineer's determination (SC 3.7.5). *See* Figure 3 on SC 3.7

A Dispute arises which may be referred to a DAAB (SC 21.4)[4]

Source: Author's own work.

Figure 13 Procedure for Claims for Time and/or Money – Detailed

Notes

1. This figure presents a simplified version of SC 20.2 for illustrative purposes. Only the actual text of SC 20.2 should be relied upon.
2. Claims of continuing effect (SC 20.2.6) are not considered.
3. Depending on the circumstances, a Party may have been required to have previously advised the other Party and the Engineer of this event or circumstance pursuant to SC 8.4 [*Advance Warning*].
4. Pursuant to SC 21.4.1(a), with certain exceptions, reference of a Dispute to the DAAB must be made within 42 days of giving or receiving (as the case may be) a NOD under SC 3.7.5. Otherwise, such NOD is deemed to have lapsed and no longer be valid.

Table 5 Employer's Claims for Time[1] and/or Money[2]

This table lists, in summary form, the Sub-Clauses under which the Employer may claim its costs, an indemnity, an extension of the Defects Notification Period ('DNP') or certain other relief under the Conditions indicating, in the case of each Sub-Clause, the Employer's entitlement.[3]

No	*Sub-Clause/ paragraph*	*Event*	*Entitlement*
1.	1.9 [*Delayed Drawings or Instructions*], third paragraph	Engineer's failure to issue a notified drawing or instruction because of error or delay by Contractor	Contractor bears responsibility for the delay and/or Cost
2.	1.13 [*Compliance with Laws*], last paragraph.	Contractor's failure to: (i) pay all taxes, duties and fees and to obtain all other permits, permissions, licences and/or approvals; (ii) provide assistance and documentation so as to allow Employer to obtain any permit, permission, licence or approval; (iii) comply with permits, permissions, licences and/or approvals obtained by Employer	Employer's costs in case of (i), (ii) and (iii) provided, in case of (i) and (iii), Employer has complied with Sub-Clause 2.2

No	*Sub-Clause/ paragraph*	*Event*	*Entitlement*
3.	2.6 [*Employer-Supplied Materials and Employer's Equipment*], first paragraph.	If Employer-Supplied Materials and/or Employer's Equipment listed in the Specification made available for the Contractor's use in the execution of the Works	Rates and prices stated in the Specification
4.	4.2.2 [*Claims under the Performance Security*], first paragraph.	Occurrence of any event listed in sub-paragraphs (a), (b), (c), (d) and (e)	Claim under the Performance Security for amounts to which the Employer is entitled under the Contract
5.	4.7.3 [*Agreement or Determination of rectification measures, delay and/or Cost*], first paragraph.	If determined that an experienced contractor should have identified error in terms of reference	Contractor bears responsibility for the delay and/or Cost
6.	4.12.5 [*Agreement or Determination of Delay and/or Cost*], second paragraph.	Physical conditions are more favourable than could reasonably have been foreseen	Reductions in Cost to be taken account of in calculating the additional Cost due to the Contractor[4]
7.	4.14 [*Avoidance of Interference*], second paragraph.	Damages resulting from Contractor's unnecessary or improper interference with the convenience of the public or access to and use and occupation of roads and footpaths	Contractor's indemnity
8.	4.15 [*Access Route*], second paragraph.	Contractor's responsibility for suitability and availability of access routes	Costs due to non-suitability or non-availability of access routes[5]

No	*Sub-Clause/ paragraph*	*Event*	*Entitlement*
9.	4.16 [*Transport of Goods*], sub-paragraph (d).	Damages resulting from the import, transport and handling of Goods, including settlement of related third-party claims	Contractor'sindemnity
10.	4.19 [*Temporary Utilities*], second paragraph.	Payment for temporary utilities provided by Employer for Contractor's use	Prices in Specification
11.	5.2.4 [*Evidence of Payments*], second paragraph.	Payment of any amount directly by the Employer to a nominated Subcontractor	Amount Employer paid nominated Subcontractor
12.	7.4 [*Testing by the Contractor*], sixth paragraph.	Delays caused by Contractor to specified tests (including varied or additional tests)	Employer's costs
13.	7.5 [*Defects and Rejection*], last paragraph.	Engineer's rejection and Contractor's retesting of defective Plant, Materials, design (if any) or workmanship	Employer's costs
14.	7.6 [*Remedial Work*], last paragraph.	Contractor's failure to comply with Engineer's instruction to carry out remedial work provided that the Contractor would not have been entitled to payment under the Sub-Clause	Employer's costs
15.	8.7 [*Rate of Progress*], second paragraph.	Revised methods which Contractor adopts in order to expedite progress (following an instruction from the Engineer) and which cause the Employer to incur additional costs	Employer's costs

No	*Sub-Clause/ paragraph*	*Event*	*Entitlement*
16.	8.8 [*Delay Damages*], first paragraph.	Contractor's failure to complete the Works or a Section within Time for Completion	Delay Damages
17.	8.9 [*Employer's Suspension*], third paragraph.	Employer's suspension caused by the Contractor	Contractor bears responsibility for the delay and/or Cost including of resuming work
18.	8.10 [*Consequences of Employer's Suspension*], second paragraph.	Contractor's faulty or defective work, or deterioration, loss or damage to the Works as the result of Contractor's failure to protect the Works	Contractor bears responsibility for the delay and/or Cost
19.	8.12 [*Prolonged Suspension*], sub-paragraph (b).	If suspension lasts for more than 84 days and the Contractor elects to treat the suspension as an omission of the affected part of the Works	Reduction in the Contract Price as the result of an omission under Sub-Clause 13.3.1
20.	9.2 [*Delayed Tests*], third paragraph, sub-paragraph (d).	Contractor's failure to carry out the Tests on Completion within 21 days after being required to do so by the Engineer and the tests are carried out by the Employer's Personnel	Employer's costs
21.	9.4 [*Failure to Pass Tests on Completion*], last paragraph.	Contractor's failure to pass repeated Tests on Completion and Employer requests the Engineer to issue a Taking-Over Certificate	'[P]ayment by the Contractor' or a reduction in Contract Price

No	*Sub-Clause/ paragraph*	*Event*	*Entitlement*
22.	11.1 [*Completion of Outstanding Work and Remedying Defects*], second paragraph and Sub-Clause 7.5	Contractor's failure to submit a proposal for remedial work or to carry out proposed remedial work during the DNP, in accordance with second, third and fourth paragraphs of Sub-Clause 7.5.	Employer's costs and other relief
23.	11.3 [*Extension of Defects Notification Period*], first paragraph.	Defect or damage for which Contractor responsible that prevents the Works, Section, Part or a major item of Plant from being used for their intended purpose(s)	Extension of the DNP up to 2 years after expiry of the DNP stated in the Contract Data
24.	11.4 [*Failure to Remedy Defects*],	Contractor's failure to remedy a damage or defect by a date fixed by the Employer:	
	sub-paragraph (a)	- Employer carries out the remedial work or has it carried out by others; or	Employer's costs
	sub-paragraph (b)	- Employer accepts the damaged or defective work; or	Reduction in Contract Price
	sub-paragraph (c)	- the Engineer treats any part of the Works that are unusable for their purpose as an omission under Sub-Clause 13.3.1; or	Variation of omission under Sub-Clause 13.3.1

No	*Sub-Clause/ paragraph*	*Event*	*Entitlement*
	sub-paragraph (d)	- Employer terminates the Contract as a whole with immediate effect because the defect or damage deprives the Employer of substantially the whole benefit of the Works	(i) Termination of Contract as a whole with immediate effect; and (ii) Recovery of all sums paid for the Works, plus financing charges and any costs incurred in dismantling the Works, clearing the Site and returning Plant and Materials to the Contractor
25.	11.8 [*Contractor to Search*], last paragraph.	Contractor's failure to carry out an instruction of the Engineer to search for the cause of any defect which is to be remedied at Contractor's cost and this search is carried out by the Employer's Personnel	Employer's costs
26.	11.11 [*Clearance of Site*], last paragraph.	Contractor's failure to clear the Site	Employer's costs of sale or disposal of items remaining on Site and of reinstating and/or cleaning Site (less any amount received from sale of any such items)
27.	12.3 [*Valuation of the Works*], fourth, fifth and sixth paragraphs.	An item of work is unidentified in the Bill of Quantities or other Schedule or whose measured quantity has changed in a certain respect and subject to other conditions	New rate or price
28.	13.2 [*Value Engineering*], fourth paragraph.	Variation resulting from Value Engineering proposal consented to by the Engineer	Employer may share with the Contractor in any benefit, costs and/or delay

No	*Sub-Clause/ paragraph*	*Event*	*Entitlement*
29.	13.3.1 [*Variation by Instruction*], second and fourth paragraphs.	Variation by instruction	Reduction in Contract Price
30.	13.6 [*Adjustments for Changes in Laws*], third paragraph.	Decrease in Contractor's Cost due to change in Laws (as defined)	Reduction in Contract Price
31.	13.7 [*Adjustments for Changes in Cost*], second, fourth and fifth paragraphs.	Fall in the cost of labour, Goods and other inputs to the Works according to the Schedule(s) of cost indexation in the Contract	Reduction in Contract Price corresponding to deemed decrease in Contractor's Cost
32.	14.2.1 [*Advance Payment Guarantee*], third paragraph (sub-paragraph (c))	Advance Payment Guarantee has not been repaid by 28 days before its expiry date and Employer does not receive evidence of its extension 7 days before the expiry date	Claim under the Advance Payment Guarantee
33.	14.4 [*Schedule of Payments*], first paragraph (sub-paragraph (c))	If the Contract includes a Schedule of Payments, and interim payment instalments are not defined by reference to actual progress and actual progress is slower than that on which the Schedule of Payments was based	Revision of instalments of payment of Contract Price by the Engineer

No	*Sub-Clause/ paragraph*	*Event*	*Entitlement*
34.	15.4 [*Payment after Termination for Contractor's Default*], second paragraph (sub-paragraphs (a), (b) and (c))	Termination of Contract for Contractor's default	(a) Additional costs of execution of Works and all other costs reasonably incurred by Employer, including for clearing the Site under Sub-Clause 11.11, after allowing for any sum due to Contractor under Sub-Clause 15.3 (b) Losses and damages suffered by Employer in completing the Works (c) Delay Damages, if the Works or a Section has not been taken over under Sub-Clause 10.1 and if the date of termination under Sub-Clause 15.2 occurs after the date corresponding to the Time for Completion
35.	17.2 [*Liability for Care of the Works*], first paragraph.	Loss or damage caused by Contractor to the Works, Goods or Contractor's Documents after the Taking-Over Certificate, or which occurs after the issue of such Certificate and arose from an event that occurred before issue of the Taking-Over Certificate for which Contractor was liable	Loss or damage caused

No	*Sub-Clause/ paragraph*	*Event*	*Entitlement*
36.	17.3 [*Intellectual and Industrial Property Rights*], fourth paragraph.	Any third-party claim for infringement of intellectual property rights in relation to either the Contractor's execution of the Works or use of Contractor's Equipment	Contractor's indemnity
37.	17.4 [*Indemnities by Contractor*], first and second paragraphs.	(a) Any third-party claim in respect of matters listed in sub-paragraphs (a) and (b) of this Sub-Clause	Contractor's indemnity
		(b) Errors in the Contractor's design, which result in the Works (Section or Part or major item of Plant) not being fit for their intended purpose under Sub-Clause 4.1	Contractor's indemnity
38.	18.6 [*Release from Performance under the Law*], sub-paragraph (i)	Contract becomes impossible or unlawful to perform and the Parties are unable to agree on continued performance	Discharge from the Contract
39.	19.1 [*General Requirements*], fourth and fifth paragraphs.	(a) Employer pays for maintaining insurances that the Contractor has failed to keep in force as required under Sub-Clause 19.2;	Amounts paid may be deducted by Employer from moneys due to the Contractor or recovered as a debt
		(b) Contractor's failure to comply with any condition of the insurances effected under the Contract	Contractor's indemnity
40.	21.2 [*Failure to Appoint DAAB Member(s)*], last paragraph.	If Employer pays full amount of remuneration of DAAB appointing official	One-half of such amount may be deducted by the Engineer in an IPC

Source: Author's own work.

Notes

[1] 'Time' refers to extension of the 'Defects Notification Period' as defined in Sub-Clause 1.1.27.
[2] These Claims are generally, but not always, subject to Sub-Clause 20.2 [*Claims for Payment and/or EOT*].
[3] Although not providing the Employer with a formal right to claim, Sub-Clause 14.6.2 entitles the Engineer, acting 'fairly', to withhold an amount from an IPC if: (a) any thing supplied or work done by the Contractor is not in accordance with the Contract, (b) the Contractor is failing to perform any contractual obligation, or (c) the Engineer finds any significant error or discrepancy in a Statement or supporting documents of the Contractor.
[4] However, this may not result in a net reduction of the Contract Price. Sub-Clause 4.12.5, second paragraph.
[5] Except as a result of changes by the Employer or a third party after the Base Date. Sub-Clause 4.15, third paragraph.

--ooOOoo--

Table 6 Contractor's Claims for Time[1] *and/or Money*[2]

This table lists, in summary form, the Sub-Clauses under which the Contractor may claim an Extension of Time ('EOT'), Cost, Cost Plus Profit, an indemnity, or certain other relief under the Conditions indicating, in the case of each Sub-Clause, the Contractor's entitlement.

No	*Sub-Clause/ Paragraph*	*Event*	*EOT*[3]	*Cost*[4]	*Profit*[5]	*Others*
1.	1.9 [*Delayed Drawings or Instructions*], second paragraph.	Engineer's failure to issue a notified drawing or instruction on time	Yes	Yes	Yes	–
2.	1.13 [*Compliance with Laws*], first paragraph (sub-paragraph (a)) and second paragraph.	Employer's delay or failure in obtaining permits, permissions, licences and/or approvals (the Contractor having complied with sub-paragraph (c))	Yes	Yes	Yes	–
3.	2.1 [*Right of Access to the Site*], third paragraph.	Employer's failure to give right of access to and possession of the Site on time	Yes	Yes	Yes	–
4.	4.2.2 [*Claims under the Performance Security*], second paragraph.	Damages resulting from an unjustified claim under the Performance Security	No	No	No	Employer's indemnity

No	*Sub-Clause/ Paragraph*	*Event*	*EOT*[3]	*Cost*[4]	*Profit*[5]	*Others*
5.	4.6 [*Co-operation*], third paragraph.	Engineer's instruction to Contractor to cooperate with others was Unforeseeable having regard to the Specification	Yes	Yes	Yes	–
6.	4.7.3 [*Agreement or Determination of rectification measures, delay and/or Cost*], second paragraph.	Error in the items of reference which an experienced contractor exercising due care would not have discovered	Yes	Yes	Yes	Variation
7.	4.12.4 [*Delay and/or Cost*]	Unforeseeable adverse physical conditions	Yes	Yes	No	–
8.	4.15 [*Access Route*], third paragraph.	Non-suitability or non-availability of access route arising from changes by the Employer or a third party after the Base Date	Yes	Yes	No	–
9.	4.23 [*Archaeological and Geological Findings*], third paragraph.	Compliance with Engineer's instructions concerning archaeological and/or geological findings	Yes	Yes	No	–

No	*Sub-Clause/ Paragraph*	*Event*	*EOT*[3]	*Cost*[4]	*Profit*[5]	*Others*
10.	7.4 [*Testing by the Contractor*], fifth paragraph.	Compliance with Engineer's instructions concerning testing or delay (in testing) for which the Employer is responsible	Yes	Yes	Yes	–
11.	7.6 [*Remedial Work*], third paragraph.	Urgent remedial work required for safety and attributable to any act by the Employer or the Employer's Personnel or an Exceptional Event in which case Sub-Clause 18.4 applies	Yes	Yes, except possibly if an Exceptional Event	Yes, except if an Exceptional Event	–
12.	8.5 [*Extension of Time for Completion*].	A cause listed or described in the Sub-Clause that is delaying or will delay the completion of the Works	Yes	No	No	–

No	*Sub-Clause/ Paragraph*	*Event*	*EOT*[3]	*Cost*[4]	*Profit*[5]	*Others*
13.	8.6 [*Delays Caused by Authorities*]	Completion is or will be delayed by an Unforeseeable delay or disruption caused by a public authority or private utility entity in the Country	Yes	No	No	–
14.	8.7 [*Rate of Progress*], third paragraph.	Adoption of revised methods to accelerate progress pursuant to Engineer's instruction where cause of delay is listed in Sub-Clause 8.5	*See* under 'Others'	*See* under 'Others'	*See* under 'Others'	Variation
15.	8.10 [*Consequences of Employer's Suspension*], first paragraph.	Engineer's instruction for suspension of part or all of the Works and/or resumption of work	Yes	Yes	Yes	–
16.	8.11 [*Payment for Plant and Materials after Employer's Suspension*]	Plant and/or Materials are not delivered to Site due to a suspension which has lasted more than 28 days and if other conditions are satisfied	No	No	No	Value of Plant and/or Materials undelivered to Site

No	*Sub-Clause/ Paragraph*	*Event*	*EOT*[3]	*Cost*[4]	*Profit*[5]	*Others*
17.	8.12 [*Prolonged Suspension*], second paragraph (sub-paragraphs (a) and (b))	Engineer does not give a Notice to resume work within 28 days after receiving Contractor's Notice requesting permission to proceed	Yes	Yes	Yes	Alternative: variation of omission (if suspension affects part of the Works) or Termination (if suspension affects the whole of the Works)
18.	10.2 [*Taking Over Parts*], fourth paragraph	Employer takes over and/or uses a Part of the Works before issue of Taking-Over Certificate	No	Yes	Yes	–
19.	10.3 [*Interference with Tests on Completion*], last paragraph.	Contractor is prevented from carrying out the Tests on Completion by the Employer's Personnel or by a cause for which the Employer is responsible	Yes	Yes	Yes	–

No	*Sub-Clause/ Paragraph*	*Event*	*EOT*[3]	*Cost*[4]	*Profit*[5]	*Others*
20.	11.2 [*Cost of Remedying Defects*], last paragraph.	Remedying defects or damage, not attributable to Contractor, during the DNP	*See* under 'Others'	*See* under 'Others'	*See* under 'Others'	Variation
21.	11.7 [*Right of Access after Taking Over*], last paragraph.	Unreasonable delay by the Employer in permitting access to the Works by the Contractor during the DNP	No	Yes	Yes	–
22.	11.8 [*Contractor to Search*], second paragraph.	Instruction of the Engineer to search for the cause of a defect which is not to be remedied at Contractor's cost	No	Yes	Yes	–
23.	12.3 [*Valuation of the Works*], fourth, fifth and sixth paragraphs	An item of work is unidentified in the Bill of Quantities or other Schedule or whose measured quantity has changed in a certain respect and subject to other conditions	No	No	No	New rate or price

No	*Sub-Clause/ Paragraph*	*Event*	*EOT*[3]	*Cost*[4]	*Profit*[5]	*Others*
24.	12.4 [*Omissions*]	No reimbursement for cost covered under the Accepted Contract Amount but which, because work has been omitted by a Variation, the Contractor is not recovering	No	Yes	No	–
25.	13.2 [*Value Engineering*], fourth paragraph.	Variation resulting from Value Engineering proposal consented to by Engineer	No	No	No	Contractor may share with the Employer in any benefit, costs and/or delay
26.	13.3.1 [*Variation by Instruction*], second, third and fourth paragraphs	Variation by instruction	Yes	*See* under 'Others'	*See* under 'Others'	Increase of Contract Price
27.	13.3.2 [*Variation by Request for Proposal*], last paragraph.	Engineer's failure to consent to a proposal for a Variation requested by the Engineer	No	Yes (of proposal)	No	–

No	*Sub-Clause/ Paragraph*	*Event*	*EOT*[3]	*Cost*[4]	*Profit*[5]	*Others*
28.	13.4 [*Provisional Sums*], second paragraph.	Use of a Provisional Sum instructed by the Engineer	No	*See* under 'Others'	*See* under 'Others'	Increase of Contract Price
29.	13.5 [*Daywork*], fifth and sixth paragraphs	Execution of a Variation on a daywork basis, for work of a minor or incidental nature, instructed by the Engineer	No	*See* under 'Others'	*See* under 'Others'	Payment based on Daywork Schedule
30.	13.6 [*Adjustments for Changes in Laws*], second and fifth paragraphs	(a) Delay and/or increase of Cost due to change in Laws of the Country	Yes	Yes	No	–
		(b) Adjustment to execution of the Works as a result of a change in Laws of the Country	*See* under 'Others'	*See* under 'Others'	*See* under 'Others'	Variation
31.	13.7 [*Adjustments for Changes in Cost*], second, fourth and fifth paragraphs	Rise in the cost of labour, Goods and other inputs to the Works according to any Schedule(s) of cost indexation in the Contract	No	Yes[6]	No	–

No	*Sub-Clause/ Paragraph*	*Event*	*EOT*[3]	*Cost*[4]	*Profit*[5]	*Others*
32.	14.4 [*Schedule of Payments*], first paragraph (sub-paragraph (c))	If the Contract includes a Schedule of Payments, interim payment instalments are not defined by reference to actual progress and actual progress is faster than that on which the Schedule of Payments is based	No	No	No	Revision of instalments of payment of Contract Price by the Engineer
33.	14.6.3 [*Correction or Modification*], second paragraph.	Contractor considers an IPC does not include any amounts to which it is entitled	No	No	No	Correction or modification by the Engineer directly or (if necessary) pursuant to Sub-Clause 3.7
34.	14.8 [*Delayed Payment*].	Contractor does not receive payment in accordance with Sub-Clause 14.7 and requests financing charges	No	No	No	Financing charges at a specified annual rate on the unpaid amount

No	*Sub-Clause/ Paragraph*	*Event*	*EOT*[3]	*Cost*[4]	*Profit*[5]	*Others*
35.	14.14 [*Cessation of Employer's Liability*]	Contractor's Claim in respect of Final Payment Certificate	Yes	Yes	Yes	-
36.	16.1 [*Suspension by Contractor*], last paragraph.	Suspension of work (or reduction in the rate of work) due to a specified default of the Employer (including the Engineer)	Yes	Yes	Yes	–
37.	16.2.2 [*Termination*], last paragraph.	Contractor suffers delay and/or incurs Cost during 14 days allowed to Employer to remedy a default	Yes	Yes	Yes	–
38.	16.3 [*Contractor's Obligations after Termination*], sub-paragraph (a)	After the Contract has been terminated under Sub-Clause 15.5, 16.2 or 18.5, the Contractor's carrying out of work instructed by the Engineer for the protection of life, property or for the safety of the Works	No	Yes	Yes	–

No	*Sub-Clause/ Paragraph*	*Event*	*EOT*[3]	*Cost*[4]	*Profit*[5]	*Others*
39.	16.4 [*Payment after Termination by Contractor*]	Termination of Contract by Contractor for Employer's default	No	Yes (under Sub-Clause 18.5)	Yes (*see* under 'Others')	The Contractor is paid as under Sub-Clause 18.5 and 'the amount of any loss of profit or other losses and damages suffered […] as a result of this termination'
40.	17.2 [*Liability for Care of the Works*], last paragraph.	Rectifying loss or damage to Works or Goods or Contractor's Documents that result from a combination of events for which the Contractor is not liable (those listed in items (a) to (f)) and a cause for which the Contractor is liable	Yes (proportionate share)	Yes (proportionate share)	Yes (proportionate share)	–

No	*Sub-Clause/ Paragraph*	*Event*	*EOT*[3]	*Cost*[4]	*Profit*[5]	*Others*
41.	17.3 [*Intellectual and Industrial Property Rights*], third paragraph.	Any third-party claim for infringement of intellectual property rights which is or was: (a) an unavoidable result of the Contractor's compliance with the Specification and Drawings and/or any Variation; or (b) a result of any Work being used by the Employer for certain purposes	No	No	No	Employer's indemnity
42.	17.5 [*Indemnities by Employer*]	Any third-party claim in respect of matters listed in sub-paragraphs (a) and (b), attributable to the Employer, or for which it is liable	No	No	No	Employer's indemnity

No	*Sub-Clause/ Paragraph*	*Event*	*EOT*[3]	*Cost*[4]	*Profit*[5]	*Others*
43.	18.4 [*Consequences of an Exceptional Event*]	Occurrence of Exceptional Event preventing Contractor from performing any contractual obligations	Yes	Yes[7]	No	–
44.	18.5 [*Optional Termination*], fourth and fifth paragraphs	Execution of the Works is prevented for 84 days by an Exceptional Event or in certain other circumstances and Contractor gives a Notice of termination	No	Yes (*see* under 'Others')	No	Contractor paid the value of work done and certain other Costs
45.	18.6 [*Release from Performance under the Law*], sub-paragraphs (i) and (ii)	Contract becomes impossible or unlawful to perform Contract and the Parties are unable to agree on continued performance	No	Yes (under Sub-Clause 18.5)	No	Discharge from the Contract and payment as under Sub-Clause 18.5
46.	19.1 [*General Requirements*], fifth paragraph.	Employer's failure to comply with any condition of insurances effected under the Contract	No	No	No	Employer's indemnity

No	*Sub-Clause/ Paragraph*	*Event*	*EOT*[3]	*Cost*[4]	*Profit*[5]	*Others*
47.	21.2 [*Failure to Appoint DAAB Member(s)*], last paragraph.	If Contractor pays full amount of remuneration of DAAB appointing entity or official	No	No	No	One-half of such amount may be included in a Statement

Source: Author's own work.

Notes

[1]'Time' refers to 'Extension of Time' or 'EOT' as defined in Sub-Clause 1.1.38.
[2]These Claims are generally, but not always, subject to Sub-Clause 20.2 [*Claims for Payment and/or EOT*].
[3]EOT under Sub-Clause 8.5.
[4]As defined in Sub-Clause 1.1.19 'Cost'.
[5]As profit is defined in Sub-Clause 1.1.20 'Cost Plus Profit'.
[6]As determined by any Schedule(s) of cost indexation included in the Contract.
[7]The Contractor is entitled to Cost only if the Exceptional Event is of the kind described in sub-paras (a) to (e) of Sub-Clause 18.1, and, in the case of sub-paras (b) to (e) of that Sub-Clause, occurs in the Country.

--ooOOoo--

21 Disputes and Arbitration

This is a new Clause dealing with the procedure for settling Disputes and arbitration, whereas in RB/99 these were dealt with in Sub-Clauses 20.2 to 20.8. This new Clause provides for the constitution of a 'standing DAAB'[1] comprising one or three persons who are independent of the Parties and who are available to assist the Parties to resolve any issue between them if the Parties jointly request the DAAB to do so. The DAAB is also to be available, if requested by a Party, to make a decision on a Dispute. If thereafter either Party is dissatisfied with the DAAB's decision and, if the Dispute is not settled by the Parties during a subsequent amicable settlement period of 28 days, either may refer it for final settlement to arbitration under the Rules of the International Chamber of Commerce ('ICC Arbitration Rules').[2]

--ooOOoo--

21.1 Constitution of the DAAB

Disputes shall be decided by a DAAB in accordance with Sub-Clause 21.4 [*Obtaining DAAB's Decision*]. The Parties shall jointly appoint the member(s) of the DAAB within the time stated in the Contract Data (if not stated, 28 days) after the date the Contractor receives the Letter of Acceptance.

The DAAB shall comprise, as stated in the Contract Data, either one suitably qualified member (the "sole member") or three suitably qualified members (the

1. A 'standing DAAB' is one that is appointed at the start of the Contract and remains in place for its duration. It is required to become and remain familiar with the project, to visit the Site on a regular basis and to assist the Parties to resolve issues or Disputes between them.
2. For commentary on the documents which make up the DAAB Agreement, namely: (1) a two-page document entitled 'DAAB Agreement', (2) the appended General Conditions of DAAB Agreement ('GCs' or 'DAAB GCs'), and (3) DAAB Procedural Rules ('DAAB Rules'), which are annexed to such appended General Conditions, *see* **Chapter V Commentary on Other Documents**, which follows this commentary on Clause 21. These three documents describe the DAAB, its powers and duties.

"members"). If the number is not so stated, and the Parties do not agree otherwise, the DAAB shall comprise three members.

The sole member or three members (as the case may be) shall be selected from those named in the list in the Contract Data, other than anyone who is unable or unwilling to accept appointment to the DAAB.

If the DAAB is to comprise three members, each Party shall select one member for the agreement of the other Party. The Parties shall consult both these members and shall agree the third member, who shall be appointed to act as chairperson.

The DAAB shall be deemed to be constituted on the date that the Parties and the sole member or the three members (as the case may be) of the DAAB have all signed a DAAB Agreement.

The terms of the remuneration of either the sole member or each of the three members, including the remuneration of any expert whom the DAAB consults, shall be mutually agreed by the Parties when agreeing the terms of the DAAB Agreement. Each Party shall be responsible for paying one-half of this remuneration.

If at any time the Parties so agree, they may appoint a suitably qualified person or persons to replace any one or more members of the DAAB. Unless the Parties agree otherwise, a replacement DAAB member shall be appointed if a member declines to act or is unable to act as a result of death, illness, disability, resignation or termination of appointment. The replacement member shall be appointed in the same manner as the replaced member was required to have been selected or agreed, as described in this Sub-Clause.

The appointment of any member may be terminated by mutual agreement of both Parties, but not by the Employer or the Contractor acting alone.

Unless otherwise agreed by both Parties, the term of the DAAB (including the appointment of each member) shall expire either:

(a) on the date the discharge shall have become, or deemed to have become, effective under Sub-Clause 14.12 [*Discharge*]; or

(b) 28 days after the DAAB has given its decision on all Disputes, referred to it under Sub-Clause 21.4 [*Obtaining DAAB's Decision*] before such discharge has become effective,

whichever is later.

However, if the Contract is terminated under any Sub-Clause of these Conditions or otherwise, the term of the DAAB (including the appointment of each member) shall expire 28 days after:

(i) the DAAB has given its decision on all Disputes, which were referred to it (under Sub-Clause 21.4 [*Obtaining DAAB's Decision*]) within 224 days after the date of termination; or

(ii) the date that the Parties reach a final agreement on all matters (including payment) in connection with the termination

whichever is earlier.

The Parties must constitute a DAAB within the time stated in the Contract Data and, if no time is stated, within 28 days after the Contractor receives the Letter of Acceptance. The DAAB must decide Disputes in accordance with Sub-Clause 21.4.

The DAAB must comprise one or three qualified members, as stated in the Contract Data or, if no number is stated, three members. They must be selected from those listed in the Contract Data. If the DAAB is to comprise three members, each Party shall select one for the agreement of the other Party. The Parties must consult both such members and agree on a third member to serve as chairperson.

The DAAB is constituted on the date that the Parties and the DAAB member(s) sign the DAAB Agreement. The Parties must agree to the remuneration of the DAAB member(s), and any expert whom the DAAB consults, when agreeing to the DAAB Agreement. Each Party is responsible for paying one-half of this remuneration.

A replacement member may be appointed where a member declines to act or is otherwise unable to do so. A member's appointment may only be terminated by the Parties' mutual agreement.

The DAAB's term expires on the date the discharge under Sub-Clause 14.12 becomes effective or 28 days after the DAAB has given its decision on all Disputes referred to it before the discharge becomes effective, whichever is later. However, if the Contract is terminated earlier, its term expires 28 days after: (i) the DAAB has given its decision on all Disputes referred to it within 224 days after the date of termination or (ii) the date the Parties finally agree on all matters connected with the termination, whichever is earlier (the decision or the final agreement).

<u>Commentary</u>

(i) Main Changes from RB/99:

(1) There is a slight change in terminology as the 'DAB' is now referred to as the 'DAAB' and the 'Appendix to Tender' is now referred to as 'Contract Data' in RB/17.

(2) Whereas Sub-Clause 20.2 of RB/99 merely provided for the appointment of the DAB 'by the date stated in the Appendix to Tender', the new Sub-Clause provides for appointment 'within the time stated in the Contract Data (if not stated, 28 days) after the date the Contractor receives the Letter of Acceptance'.

(3) Whereas RB/99 had provided for the selection of DAB members from a list as an option, the new Sub-Clause provides that the DAAB members are to be selected from a list in the Contract Data.

(4) Whereas RB/99 had provided that each Party was to nominate one member for the 'approval' of the other Party (in the case of a three-member DAB), the new Sub-Clause requires 'agreement' of the other Party.

(5) While Sub-Clause 20.2 of RB/99 had provided that the agreement between the Parties and the DAB member(s) shall incorporate by reference the General Conditions of Dispute Adjudication Agreement contained in the Appendix to the Conditions, in RB/17 the form of DAAB Agreement instead itself expressly

incorporates the General Conditions of DAAB Agreement ('DAAB GCs' or 'GCs') into them by reference.[3]

(6) Unlike RB/99, the new Sub-Clause provides that the DAAB is deemed to be constituted on the date that the Parties and the sole member or the three members of the DAAB have signed a DAAB Agreement.

(7) While Sub-Clause 20.2 of RB/99 had provided that if at any time the Parties so agree, they may jointly refer a matter to the DAB for it to give its opinion, the essence of this provision has now been transferred to a new Sub-Clause 21.3 [*Avoidance of Disputes*] in RB/17.

(8) The new Sub-Clause adds 'illness' to the grounds on which a DAAB Member may be replaced, in addition to those provided for in RB/99.

(9) Whereas RB/99 had provided for a single date on which the term of the DAB would expire – the date of the effectiveness of the discharge – the new Sub-Clause provides for two possible expiry dates – whichever is later:
   (a) effectiveness of the discharge under Sub-Clause 14.12 [*Discharge*]; or
   (b) 28 days after the DAAB had given its decision on all Disputes referred to it under Sub-Clause 21.4 [*Obtaining DAAB's Decision*] before such discharge has become effective.

(10) The new Sub-Clause clarifies the effect of any earlier termination of the Contract on the term of the DAAB by providing that such term shall expire 28 days after:
   (a) the DAAB has given a decision on all Disputes referred to it under Sub-Clause 21.4 within 224 days after the date of termination; or
   (b) the date on which the Parties reach a final agreement on all matters in connection with the termination, whichever is earlier.

(ii) Related Clauses / Sub-Clauses: 1.3 [*Notices and Other Communications*], 14.12 [*Discharge*], 15 [*Termination by Employer*], 16 [*Suspension and Termination by Contractor*], 18 [*Exceptional Events*], and 21 [*Disputes and Arbitration*].[4]

---

3. *See* Sub-Clause 1(b) of the form of DAAB Agreement.
4. *See also* the DAAB GCs and DAAB Rules.

(iii) Analysis:

(1) Reference to DAAB is mandatory

Under the Conditions, a Dispute[5] arises where a Party has made a Claim, or asserted a matter, which has been rejected by the Engineer under Sub-Clause 3.7, and the Party decides to pursue that Claim or matter by giving a NOD under Sub-Clause 3.7.5 with respect to the Engineer's determination.

The first sentence of Sub-Clause 21.1 is important as it provides that 'Disputes' must be referred to a DAAB for decision: 'Disputes *shall be decided* by a DAAB [...]' (emphasis added). This is the first indication – confirmed later[6] – that the referral of a Dispute, as defined, to the DAAB for decision is a *condition precedent* to further steps under Clause 21, including arbitration. This *condition precedent applies to Claims or matters of either Party which have arisen and given rise to Disputes*. The fact, for example, that one Party has referred a Dispute to arbitration does not relieve the other Party from having to satisfy this same condition as regards Claims or matters that it may want to pursue. Thus, if the other Party has a Claim or matter that has been rejected by the Engineer and in relation to which it had given a NOD, then it still has to refer it as a Dispute to the DAAB as a condition to referring it to arbitration.

For example, in one case, when after a Contractor had initiated arbitration – following a referral to a DAB under the YB/99 – the Employer asserted a counterclaim in the arbitration which it had not previously referred as a dispute to the DAB, the counterclaim was held to be

5. A '**Dispute**' is defined in Sub-Clause 1.1.29 which is quoted in full in the commentary on Clause 1 above.
6. This is confirmed by (1) Sub-Clause 21.4.4 providing that, with certain exceptions, 'neither Party shall be entitled to commence arbitration of a Dispute unless a NOD [with the DAAB's decision] in respect of that Dispute has been given' and (2) the first sentence of Sub-Clause 21.6 ('[u]nless settled amicably, [...], any Dispute in respect of which the DAAB's decision (if any) has not become final and binding shall be finally settled by international arbitration [...]') – the reference to '(if any)' being to where the DAAB fails to give a Decision, *see* Sub-Clause 21.4.4, second paragraph. The only clear exceptions to the requirement of a prior referral to the DAAB as a condition to arbitration are those listed under **(iii) Analysis** – *(6) Direct Arbitration* in the commentary on Sub-Clause 21.6 [*Arbitration*] below. *See also* **Figure 16 Paths to ICC Arbitration** contained in the commentary on Sub-Clause 21.6 below.

inadmissible in that proceeding.[7] On the other hand, if the counterclaim was encompassed by, or been within the scope of, a dispute which had previously been referred to a DAB, it might have been admitted to arbitration.[8]

(2) Emphasis on dispute avoidance

The most important change in the provisions for a DAAB[9] since the 1999 Rainbow Suite is the greater emphasis on having the DAAB help avoid Disputes and not just decide them. As FIDIC states:

> construction projects depend for their success on *the avoidance of Disputes* [...] and, if Disputes arise [their timely resolution].
>
> Therefore, the Contract should include [...] Clause 21 which, while not discouraging the Parties from reaching their own agreement on Disputes as the Works proceed, allow them to bring contentious matters to an independent and impartial dispute avoidance/ adjudication board (DAAB) for resolution.[10] (Emphasis added)

---

7. *See* first partial award, ICC case 12048 (2003) (Issue 4), in relation to RB/87, ICC Int'l Ct Arb Bull, vol 23, no 2, 2012 (commentary 25, 27 - relevant extract from award unfortunately not published), final award, ICC case 16765 (2013), in relation to YB/99, ICC Disp Resol Bull, 2015, Issue 1, 101 (paras 123-129) (commentary, 21, 25) and final award, ICC case 21488 (2018) (unpublished).
8. For example, an earlier Dispute (a dispute under RB/99) about whether the Contractor had been wrongfully denied an extension of time by the Engineer, which had properly been referred to arbitration, might be considered to encompass the Employer's claim for Delay Damages for the same period. Therefore, the Employer should not have to (although it may) submit such claim, as a Dispute, to the DAAB or to mandatory amicable settlement in order to be able to assert it as a counterclaim in the arbitration. *See* C. Seppälä, 'The Arbitration Clause in FIDIC Contracts for Major Works' [2005] ICLR 4, 7-9 and final award, ICC case 19346 (2014), ICC Disp Resol Bull, 2015, Issue 1, 142, 143-147 (commentary, 21, 33-34).
9. Called the 'DAB' in RB/99.
10. *Guidance for the Preparation of Particular Conditions*, 47. The DAAB (formerly, the DAB) is the successor of the Engineer who had decided disputes before arbitration under the first (1957) through fourth (1987) editions of the Red Book and prior to the 1999 edition which had introduced the DAB. For this history, and references to related materials, *see* **Section 3.1 Origin and History** in **Chapter I General Introduction** above and Christopher R Seppälä, 'The New FIDIC Provision for a Dispute Adjudication Board', [1997] ICLR 443.

As a result, FIDIC 'strongly recommends' the appointment of a 'standing DAAB' (that is, one which is appointed at the start of the Contract and which is available to assist the Parties on a continuous basis both to avoid Disputes and – when necessary – to decide them),[11] as compared to an '*ad hoc* DAB' (that is, one which is appointed only if and when a Dispute arises, only decides that Dispute and terminates once that Dispute is decided). *This is because only a standing DAAB,* which is in place throughout the life of a Contract, *is available permanently to perform a Dispute avoidance function.* As a consequence, whereas under the 1999 Rainbow Suite, only the Red Book had provided for a standing board, under the 2017 Rainbow Suite, all three Books (Red, Yellow, and Silver) provide for such a DAAB.[12]

However, FIDIC recognises that Parties may still sometimes prefer an '*ad hoc* DAB', and therefore RB/17 includes proposed amendments to the Conditions of Contract to enable Parties to implement this alternative.[13]

(3) Qualifications of DAAB members

The DAAB is to comprise, as stated in the Contract Data, one or three 'suitably qualified' members.[14] If the number is not stated in the Contract

11. *Guidance for the Preparation of Particular Conditions*, 47.
12. In 1999 – before FIDIC's present emphasis on dispute avoidance – FIDIC had felt that in the case of the Yellow and Silver Books:

> [i]t would be more appropriate (and probably, less expensive for the parties) to provide in the General Conditions for an *ad hoc* DAB, that is, a DAB which would only need to be constituted if and when a dispute or disputes arise(s) and which would normally cease to operate once a decision on such dispute or disputes had been issued. The main reason for a standing DAB is to deal with disputes on or related to the construction site. But, when the contract provides mainly for the design and manufacture of electrical or mechanical equipment in a factory rather than construction work on the site (as is true of many projects for which the [Yellow and Silver Books] would be used), the incidence of disputes should be much less and, hence, it is much more difficult to justify the time and expense of maintaining a standing DAB in such a case. Accordingly, FIDIC has opted for an *ad hoc* DAB in the General Conditions for these types of contracts.
>
> Christopher R Seppälä, 'FIDIC's New Standard Forms of Contract – Force Majeure, Claims, Disputes and Other Clauses' [2000] ICLR 235, 249.

13. *See Guidance for the Preparation of Particular Conditions*, 49.
14. Sub-Clause 21.1, second paragraph. While not expressly stated in the Sub-Clause, the *Guidance for the Preparation of Particular Conditions*, 47, foresees that a DAAB Member will be a 'natural person' and not a legal entity of any kind.

Data and the Parties do not agree otherwise, the DAAB must comprise three members.[15] The appropriate number may depend on the size and duration of the project, its complexity, estimated value and the fields of expertise involved.[16]

'Suitably qualified' means, first of all, that they have no financial interest in the Contract or the project of which they are a part, and are impartial and independent of the Employer, the Contractor, the Employer's Personnel and the Contractor's Personnel.[17] In addition, a DAAB member must represent, among other things, that the member is:

(a) experienced and/or knowledgeable in the type of work which the Contractor is to carry out under the Contract;
(b) experienced in the interpretation of construction and/or engineering contract documentation; and
(c) fluent in the language for communications stated in the Contract Data (or the language as agreed between the Parties and the DAAB).[18]

FIDIC maintains a list of approved adjudicators: The President's List of Approved Dispute Adjudicators.[19] In general, DAAB members are likely to be engineers or other construction professionals. However, they may include lawyers experienced in international construction contracts and dispute resolution.[20]

15. Sub-Clause 21.1, second paragraph.
16. *See Guidance for the Preparation of Particular Conditions*, 47. The World Bank's COPA provides that, for a Contract estimated to cost above USD 50 million, the DAAB shall comprise three members, for a Contract estimated to cost between USD 20 million and USD 50 million, the DAAB may comprise three members or a sole member and for a Contract estimated to cost less than USD 20 million, a sole member is recommended. Sub-Clause 21.1, Contract Data, COPA.
17. Except as disclosed. Sub-Clause 4.1, DAAB GCs.
18. Sub-Clause 3.3, DAAB GCs. The World Bank's COPA provides for a more rigorous set of representations which a DAAB Member is required to make including having a bachelor's degree in a relevant discipline, 10 years of experience in contract administration/management and dispute resolution and formal training as an adjudicator by an internationally recognised organisation. Sub-Clause 3.3, Appendix – DAAB GCs, COPA.
19. This is available to access online on the FIDIC website at https://fidic.org/president-list, accessed 21 November 2022.
20. Thus, it may be appropriate that the chairperson be a lawyer, as a lawyer will be better able to deal with legal issues, such as disputes over the DAAB's jurisdiction or contract interpretation.

(4) Appointment of DAAB members

DAAB members are to be selected from those listed in the Contract Data. The form of Contract Data envisages that, at the tender stage, the Employer and the Contractor would each propose three candidates as members of the DAAB, i.e., a total of six potential DAAB members. The Employer would normally have proposed three persons in the Contract Data sent out with the tender dossier, leaving each tenderer to propose an additional three persons in the spaces in the Contract Data form which it returns with its tender. If the Employer or a tenderer should disagree with one or more of the names put forward by the other, then the best time to voice this disagreement and agree upon alternatives is before the Contract is signed.[21]

This list procedure is designed to prevent DAAB members from being 'imposed' by either Party – most obviously, the Employer – on the other and to ensure that both Parties will have equal opportunity to propose potential DAAB members.[22]

Where a DAAB is to comprise three members, each Party has to select one member for the agreement of the other Party. The Parties must then consult both these members and agree from the list upon the third member, who shall act as chairperson.[23] The requirement for the Parties to agree on all three members is designed to foster their confidence in the DAAB selected, which is important to the success of the DAAB procedure.[24]

While the new Sub-Clause provides that the DAAB members shall be appointed by the time stated in the Contract Data or, if not stated there, within 28 days after the Contractor's receipt of the Letter of Acceptance,

21. On the other hand, if there is no discussion before the Contract is signed (the applicable procurement procedure may prohibit such discussion), the discussion may have to take place later, at the time of the appointment of the DAAB, and, if no agreement as to actual DAAB member(s) can be reached, then Sub-Clause 21.2 referred to below will apply.
22. *Guidance for the Preparation of Particular Conditions*, 48.
23. Sub-Clause 21.1, fourth paragraph. Unlike the position of arbitrators in an ICC arbitration, the chairperson is not more important than the other two members.
24. *Guidance for the Preparation of Particular Conditions*, 48. *See also* Sub-Clause 6.2 of the DAAB GCs which requires the Parties to cooperate with each other in constituting the DAAB. If a Party fails to do so, the arbitrator(s) may take account of this in any award dealing with the costs of the arbitration. Sub-Clause 21.6, third paragraph.

it is preferable for them to be appointed even sooner, i.e., before receipt of the Letter of Acceptance.[25] Once the Letter of Acceptance is received, the Contract will enter into legal effect[26] and, where possible, it is preferable that – like all other issues between the Parties – the members of the DAAB have been agreed upon before then.

(5) Remuneration of DAAB members

The remuneration of members is to be stipulated in the DAAB Agreement. A DAAB member is paid a monthly fee for remaining available to assist, as well as a daily fee for attending meetings and hearings as well as for travel time.[27] In addition, the DAAB member is entitled to reimbursement of all reasonable expenses, including necessary travel expenses, as well as of taxes levied in the Country on payments to the DAAB member (unless a national or resident of the Country).[28]

There is no generally accepted standard for the amount of fees payable to members of dispute boards, nor of whether it comprises a monthly fee plus a daily fee plus expenses (as under RB/17) or otherwise. This is a matter for negotiation in each case taking account, among other things, of the qualifications and experience of candidates. Daily fees (in addition to, or in lieu of, a monthly retainer) may range from Euros 700-800 per day for a dispute board member in certain developing countries (such as India or in Eastern Europe) to Euros 6,000 per day, depending upon the candidate's qualifications. The reality is that, with the increasing worldwide demand for construction professionals and lawyers to serve on dispute boards, the fees of members are escalating, eroding to some extent the cost advantage that dispute boards have had over international arbitration.

25. *Guidance for the Preparation of Particular Conditions*, 47. The default period of 28 days for the appointment of the DAAB might have to be reconsidered and lengthened if the Contract Data does not list the potential DAAB Members' names. *Guidance for the Preparation of Particular Conditions*, 48.
26. *See* the last paragraph of the form of Letter of Acceptance included in RB/17.
27. Sub-Clause 9.1, DAAB GCs. The World Bank's COPA provides that a Provisional Sum, pursuant to Sub-Clause 13.4, shall be used to cover the Employer's share of the DAAB Members' fees and expenses. Sub-Clause 13.4, COPA. No prior instruction of the Engineer shall be required, according to COPA, with respect to the work of the DAAB.
28. Sub-Clause 9.1, DAAB GCs.

The manner in which members are to be paid is described in the DAAB GCs.[29] Each Party is responsible for paying one-half of the members' remuneration.[30] DAAB members must be paid regularly. If, by the time the DAAB is to give a decision, the invoice of a DAAB member is overdue for payment, the DAAB may refuse to give its decision until the invoice has been fully paid.[31]

(6) Replacement of a DAAB member

The DAAB is deemed to be constituted on the date when the Parties and all the members have signed the DAAB Agreement.[32] A member may be replaced if it declines to act, or is unable to act as a result of death, illness, disability, resignation or termination of appointment.[33] The Parties may also agree together to replace one or more members of the DAAB.[34] Any replacement member is to be appointed by the same process as applied to the appointment of the replaced member.[35] When a member is replaced, the Parties and the other members are obliged to disclose the details of the Contract, provide necessary documents and update the new member about the DAAB's Activities (as defined[36]) and decisions, in order to enable the new member to discharge its functions effectively.[37]

The Parties may jointly terminate the appointment of a member at any time, by giving a Notification[38] of not less than 42 days to the member.[39]

(7) Termination of the DAAB

The term of the DAAB expires either on the date the discharge (or deemed discharge) is effective under Sub-Clause 14.12 [*Discharge*] or 28 days after the DAAB has given its decision on all Disputes referred to it under Sub-Clause 21.4 [*Obtaining DAAB's Decision*] before the discharge becomes effective, whichever is later.[40] However, if the Contract is termi-

29. *See* Clause 9, DAAB GCs.
30. Sub-Clause 21.1, sixth paragraph.
31. *See* Sub-Clause 21.4.3, second paragraph.
32. Sub-Clause 21.1, fifth paragraph.
33. Sub-Clause 21.1, seven paragraph.
34. *Ibid.*
35. *Ibid.*
36. Sub-Clause 1.4, DAAB GCs.
37. Sub-Clause 7.4, DAAB GCs.
38. As defined in Sub-Clause 1.8, DAAB GCs.
39. Sub-Clause 10.3, DAAB GCs. Other relevant provisions of Clause 10 of the DAAB GCs also apply to such termination.
40. Sub-Clause 21.1, second to last paragraph.

nated earlier for any reason, then the term of the DAAB expires 28 days after the DAAB has given its decision on all Disputes referred to it within 224 days[41] after the date of termination, or the Parties have reached a final agreement on all matters in connection with the termination, whichever is earlier.[42] In the case of an early termination,[43] the clear intention is that all Disputes related to the termination must first be referred to the DAAB.

(iv) Related Law:

(1) In the common law world, the DAAB (or DAB) will be regarded as a species of expert determination.[44] Thus, published works on expert determination in the common law world may be of assistance in understanding the nature of the DAAB. Analogous systems are recognised in countries around the world.[45] There is also a growing literature about dispute boards in international construction contracts.[46] An increasing number of countries,

41. The explanation for this 224-day period is given in the *Guidance for the Preparation of the Particular Conditions*, 48-49.
42. Sub-Clause 21.1, last paragraph.
43. For example, under Clauses 15, 16 or Sub-Clause 18.6.
44. Clive Freedman and James Farrell, *Kendall on Expert Determination* (5th edn, Sweet & Maxwell, London, 2015) 97 (para. 5.2-1). Sub-Clause 21.4.3, last paragraph, confirms that a DAAB proceeding 'shall not be deemed to be an arbitration and the DAAB shall not act as arbitrator(s)'. A DAAB proceeding differs from arbitration in multiple ways. Whereas arbitration is usually provided for by a statute law, a DAAB proceeding will normally be regulated exclusively by contract. While a DAAB proceeding is an expedited and relatively informal procedure, an arbitration is not subject to strict time limits, entails a thorough examination of the evidence and, in the construction field, commonly takes at least a year or more to complete.
45. *See* Chapter 18 'Expert Determination in Other Countries' in Clive Freedman and James Farrell, *Kendall on Expert Determination* (5th edn, Sweet & Maxwell, London, 2015) and Filip De Ly and Paul-A Gelinas (eds), *Dispute Prevention and Settlement Through Expert Determination and Dispute Boards*, ICC, Paris (ICC Publication no 792E) 2017.
46. Perhaps the first study of dispute boards, which originated in the United States in the 1960s and 1970s, is Robert M Matyas and others, *Construction Dispute Review Board Manual* (McGraw-Hill, New York, 1995). A more recent study emphasising international construction projects is Cyril Chern, *Chern in Dispute Boards Practice and Procedure* (4th edn, Informa Law, London, 2020). *See also* Christopher R Seppälä, 'Recent Case Law on Dispute

such as Brazil, Honduras, Italy and Peru, are reported to have laws regulating dispute boards.[47]

(2) While not directly relevant to the dispute board, which is generally solely a creature of contract, the numerous reported cases in the UK and elsewhere dealing with statutory adjudication may in some cases provide, by analogy, guidance in relation to dispute boards.

(3) Although the form of DAAB Agreement in RB/17 contains a governing law provision, in the absence of any such provision specifically applicable to the DAAB provisions in the Conditions,[48] there can be an issue about what law governs them. In theory, this could be the law governing the contract or (if different) the law governing the arbitration clause itself or (if different) the law of the country of the construction site.[49]

Boards' constituting Chapter 12 of Filip de Ly and Paul-A Gelinas (eds), *Dispute Prevention and Settlement through Expert Determination and Dispute Boards*, ICC, Paris (ICC Publication no 792E) 2017. The mere existence of a dispute board has been described as persuading parties amicably to settle:

> the existence of the [dispute board] seems to have a dampening effect on controversies by, in effect, giving the parties an incentive to resolve disputes among themselves rather that suffer the inconvenience, disruption, and possible embarrassment of having to call in the [dispute board].

Wendy Kennedy Venoit and others (eds), *International Construction Law: A Guideline for Cross-Border Transactions and Legal Disputes* (ABA For Const L, Chicago, IL, 2009) 254.

47. As regards Brazil *see* Victor Filho and Gabriel Simões, 'Brazil: City of São Paulo Kick-Starts Regulation of Dispute Boards in State Contracts', ICC Disp Resol Bull (2018, no 2) discussing São Paulo Municipal Law 16,873/2018 of 23 February 2018 and, as regards Honduras and Peru, *see* 'Dispute Boards in Latin America: Experiences and Challenges in a Promising Market' by Roberto Hernández Garcia, a Mexican lawyer, published in the electronic newsletter of the Dispute Board Federation, http://www.comad.com.mx/pdf/solucion_controversias/201406dsiputeboardsexperoenciasyretos.pdf accessed 10 November 2022, Geneva, October 2014. As regards Italy, *see* Giuseppe Giancarlo Franco 'The New Framework of the Italian Dispute Board' DLA Piper Publications, 24 July 2020 referring to an Italian Decree no 76 of 16 July 2020 (so-called law decree *Semplificazioni*) art. 6.
48. Sub-Clauses 21.1 to 21.4.
49. Compare the position taken in Swiss Federal Court decision 4A_124/2014, 7 July 2014, ASA Bull 4/2014, 826 and interim award, ICC case 16083 (2010)

(v) Improvements: As stated above, if a DAAB is to comprise three members, each Party is expected to propose three names for the DAAB in the Contract Data. It is also expected that the chairperson be selected from these names. However, this may be unrealistic, as neither Party may wish to agree to a person who has been proposed by the other Party to act as the chairperson. It might therefore be better to provide that the chairperson be selected by the Parties from any candidate, whether or not listed in the Contract Data, proposed by the two Party-appointed members. A specific time limit might be set for this process, upon the expiry of which – without a resolution – the appointment would be made by the appointing official (or entity) named in the Contract Data, pursuant to Sub-Clause 21.2.

--ooOOoo--

21.2 Failure to Appoint DAAB Member(s)

If any of the following conditions apply, namely:

(a) if the DAAB is to comprise a sole member, the Parties fail to agree the appointment of this member by the date stated in the first paragraph of Sub-Clause 21.1 [*Constitution of the DAAB*]; or

(b) if the DAAB is to comprise three persons, and if by the date stated in the first paragraph of Sub-Clause 21.1 [*Constitution of the DAAB*]:

(i) either Party fails to select a member (for agreement by the other Party);

ICC Disp Resol Bull 2015, Issue 1, 57 (commentary, 28) (both applying the law governing the arbitration clause, being found in these cases to be the law of the place of arbitration) with ICC case 20118 (a so far unpublished partial award) (2015) (applying the law governing the contract to the DAB appointment process). French law would appear to recognise, at least for the purposes of contract termination, the autonomous nature of a dispute board clause as new art. 1230 of the French Civil Code provides that (translation):

> Termination [of a contract] affects neither *clauses relating to the resolution of disputes, nor* [...] clauses relating to confidentiality and non-competition. [Emphasis added]
>
> [*La résolution n'affecte ni les clauses relatives au règlement des différends, ni* [...] *les clauses de confidentialité et de non-concurrence.*] [Emphasis added]

(ii) either Party fails to agree a member selected by the other Party; and/or
(iii) the Parties fail to agree the appointment of the third member (to act as chairperson) of the DAAB;

(c) the Parties fail to agree the appointment of a replacement within 42 days after the date on which the sole member or one of the three members declines to act or is unable to act as a result of death, illness, disability, resignation, or termination of appointment; or
(d) if, after the Parties have agreed the appointment of the member(s) or replacement, such appointment cannot be effected because one Party refuses or fails to sign a DAAB Agreement with any such member or replacement (as the case may be) within 14 days of the other Party's request to do so, or because the terms of the DAAB Agreement (including the amount of the monthly fee or the daily fee) cannot be agreed with the member or replacement within 14 days after he/she has been advised by the Parties that they have agreed to his/her appointment,

then, unless otherwise agreed by the Parties, either or both Parties may apply to the President of FIDIC or a person appointed by the President, who shall be the appointing official under the Contract. The appointing official shall, after due consultation with both Parties and after consulting the prospective member(s) or replacement:

- appoint the member(s) of the DAAB or the replacement; and
- set the terms of the appointment, including the amounts of the monthly fee and the daily fee for each member or replacement.

Selection of the member(s) or replacement to be so appointed shall not be limited to those persons named in the list in the Contract Data or, in the case of sub-paragraph (d) above, to the member(s) or replacement agreed by the Parties.

This appointment and its terms shall be final and conclusive.

Thereafter, the Parties and the member(s) so appointed shall be deemed to have signed and be bound by a DAAB Agreement under which:

(i) the monthly services fee and daily fee shall be as stated in the terms of the appointment; and
(ii) the law governing the DAAB Agreement shall be the governing law of the Contract defined in Sub-Clause 1.4 [*Law and Language*].

Each Party shall be responsible for paying one-half of the remuneration of the appointing official. If the Contractor pays the remuneration in full, the Contractor shall include one-half of the amount of such remuneration in a Statement and the Employer shall then pay the Contractor in accordance with the Contract. If the Employer pays the remuneration in full, the Engineer shall include one-half of the amount of such remuneration as a deduction under sub-paragraph (b) of Sub-Clause 14.6.1 [*The IPC*].

If there is a failure to appoint DAAB member(s) under any of sub-paragraphs (a) to (d) of this Sub-Clause then, unless otherwise agreed by the Parties, either or both Parties may apply to the President of FIDIC to make the necessary appointment and set its terms. This appointment shall be final and conclusive. The Parties and the member(s) so appointed shall be deemed bound by the DAAB Agreement. The monthly services and daily fee of the member(s) will be as stated in the terms of appointment and the law governing the DAAB Agreement will be the governing law of the Contract.

Each Party must pay one-half of the remuneration of the appointing official. If the Contractor pays the remuneration in full, then it may recover the Employer's share by including it in a Statement. If the Employer pays the remuneration in full, then the Engineer may include one-half of such amount as a deduction under Sub-Clause 14.6.1(b).

Commentary

(i) Main Changes from RB/99:

(1) Compared to Sub-Clause 20.3 of RB/99, the new Sub-Clause (as amended in 2022) adds two grounds entitling the Parties, or either of them, to call on an appointing official (unless otherwise agreed, the President of FIDIC or the President's appointee) to appoint a DAAB member, namely, (i) where the DAAB is to comprise three persons and either Party fails to agree to a member selected by the other Party (sub-paragraph (b)(ii)) and (ii) where (*see* (2) below for more detail), after the Parties have agreed the appointment of the member(s) or a replacement, such appointment cannot be effected for specified reasons (sub-paragraph (d)).

(2) The new Sub-Clause provides in sub-paragraph (d) for a situation where, after agreeing to the appointment of the DAAB member(s) or their replacement, a Party refuses or fails to sign a DAAB Agreement within 14 days of the other Party's request to do so, or the DAAB Agreement cannot be agreed with the member or replacement within 14 days after the Parties' agreement on his/her appointment. In this case, unless otherwise agreed, either or both Parties may apply to the President of FIDIC or the President's appointee to make the appointment and set its terms.

(3) The new Sub-Clause contains a 'deeming' provision whereby, once the appointing official appoints the DAAB member(s), the Parties and the member(s) so appointed are deemed to have signed and be bound by a DAAB Agreement including the member(s)' remuneration and the law to govern the DAAB Agreement.

(4) The new Sub-Clause provides a remedy to an Employer or a Contractor to enforce the provision that each Party must pay one-half of the remuneration due to an appointing official. If the Contractor pays the amount in full, it may claim half of it from the Employer by including it within a Statement. Similarly, if the Employer pays the amount in full, the Engineer may include one-half of such amount as a deduction from an IPC under Sub-Clause 14.6.1(b) [*The IPC*].

(ii) Related Clauses / Sub-Clauses: 1.3 [*Notices and Other Communications*], 1.4 [*Law and Language*], 14.6.1 [*IPC*] and 21 [*Disputes and Arbitration*].[50]

(iii) Analysis:

(1) Enforcing a DAAB Agreement

A major practical difficulty with the provision for a DAB in RB/99 was that a recalcitrant party had several ways to delay or prevent the constitution of a DAB. Thus, in the case of a three-person DAB, it could refuse to approve the member proposed by the other Party – RB/99 had provided no solution in this situation. Even if the appointing entity or official appointed a member, the recalcitrant Party could refuse to sign a DAB agreement with that member or that member could refuse to sign the DAB agreement – RB/99 had also provided no solution in these situations.

These difficulties appear now to have been overcome by:

(i) a provision making a failure to agree to a member selected by the other Party a ground for applying to an appointing official to make the appointment;[51]

(ii) a provision authorising reference to an appointing official in case a Party refuses or fails to sign a DAAB Agreement or because the terms of the DAAB Agreement cannot be agreed with a prospective member or replacement; in such case, selection of the member or replacement is not limited to those listed in the Contract Data or, in the case of sub-paragraph (d), to those whom the Parties may have agreed upon;[52] and

(iii) a provision that where members have been appointed by an appointing official, the Parties and member(s) shall be deemed to have signed and to be bound by a DAAB Agreement.[53]

50. *See also* the DAAB GCs and DAAB Rules.
51. *See* Sub-Clause 21.2(b)(ii). RB/17 no longer refers, as did RB/99, to an appointing entity, though there is no reason an entity could not appoint also.
52. *See* Sub-Clause 21.2(d).
53. Sub-Clause 21.2, penultimate paragraph. This change is also reflected in the DAAB GCs, which provide that the DAAB Agreement shall take effect, among other things, when it is 'deemed' to have been signed by the relevant persons. Sub-Clause 2.1, DAAB GCs.

To further induce Parties to cooperate in a DAAB's constitution,[54] an arbitral tribunal is empowered under Sub-Clause 21.6 [*Arbitration*] to take into account a Party's failure to cooperate in constituting a DAAB, when apportioning between the Parties the costs of an arbitration proceeding.[55]

(2) Appointing official

Unless otherwise agreed, the appointing official will be the President of FIDIC or the President's appointee.[56] Accordingly, if the Parties would prefer another appointing official they would need to agree upon one. In this connection, before designating another appointing official, they should ascertain that it:

- is willing and able to make an independent appointment of DAAB member(s);
- is familiar with the qualifications and competence required of a DAAB member;
- has experience in appointing DAAB members or similar experts; and
- is willing and able to set 'the monthly services fee and daily fee' of each appointee as stated in sub-paragraph (i) in the penultimate paragraph of this Sub-Clause.

The appointing official selected is required to duly consult with both Parties when making appointment(s) (as well as consult the prospective member(s) or replacement).[57] 'Due consultation' in this context means 'consultation with both parties to the extent required by the nature of the difficulty encountered'.[58] However, the appointing official need not inform the Parties of the person it is considering appointing.[59] Once made, any such appointment and its terms are 'final and conclusive'.[60]

54. Under Sub-Clause 6.2 of the DAAB GCs, the Parties agree to cooperate in constituting the DAAB 'without delay'.
55. Sub-Clause 21.6, third paragraph.
56. Sub- Clause 21.2, first paragraph.
57. Sub-Clause 21.2, first paragraph.
58. Nael Bunni, *The FIDIC Forms of Contract* (3rd edn, Blackwell Publishing, Oxford, 2005) 617.
59. Partial award, ICC case 16262 (2010), ICC Disp Resol Bull, 2015, Issue 1, 75, 81-83 (commentary, 21, 30-31).
60. Sub-Clause 21.2, second paragraph.

(3) President of FIDIC as appointing official

The President of FIDIC is the default appointing official.[61] However, the President may not agree to serve as the appointing official in cases where the Contract, while purportedly based on a FIDIC form, contains major departures from it. For understandable reasons, FIDIC will need to be satisfied that the Contract remains faithful to its principles.[62]

A request to the President of FIDIC to appoint a DAAB member must follow the relevant process provided for on the FIDIC website.[63]

(4) Importance of promptly constituting the DAAB

Under RB/17, it is particularly important that the Parties constitute the DAAB at the outset of the Contract as the Claims and Disputes procedures provided for in the Conditions assume that a DAAB is in place. If the Parties should delay in constituting a DAAB, then the Parties will be unable to request its assistance pursuant to Sub-Clause 21.3 [*Avoidance of Disputes*], neither Party will be able to refer a Dispute to it within the required 42-day time period provided for by Sub-Clause 21.4.1(a) and Sub-Clause 21.8 [*No DAAB in Place*] may apply.

--ooOOoo--

61. Or the President's appointee.
62. For example, its 'Golden Principles', *see* **Sub-Clause 4.4.3 FIDIC's 'Golden Principles'** of **Chapter I General Introduction** above.
63. It must be submitted to the FIDIC Secretariat in Geneva, Switzerland, in the English language, along with the prescribed fee and include details such as the extent to which members have been agreed, copies of certified contract documents and a brief description of the Works, http://fidic.org/node/2552 accessed 10 November 2022.

Figure 14 illustrates the DAAB's two functions: Dispute avoidance and Dispute resolution.

Figure 14 The DAAB's Two Functions[1]

Clause 21 provides for two functions of the DAAB which, in *simple* terms, are as follows:

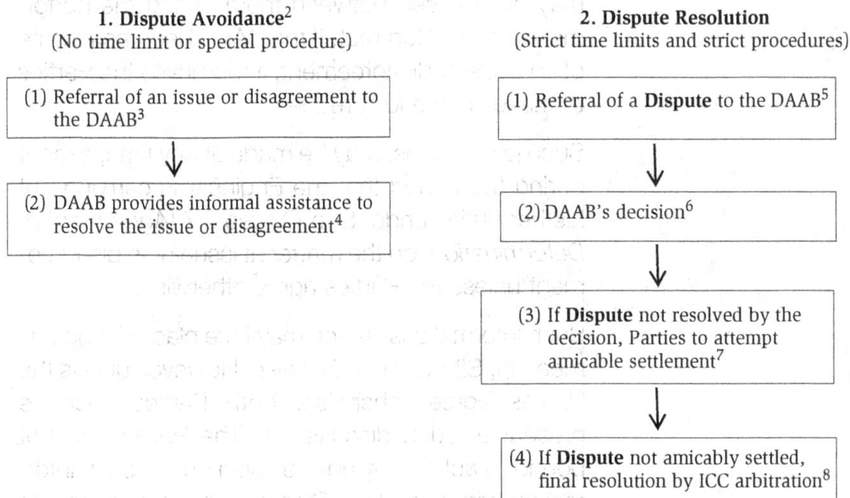
1. Dispute Avoidance[2]
(No time limit or special procedure)
(1) Referral of an issue or disagreement to the DAAB[3]
(2) DAAB provides informal assistance to resolve the issue or disagreement[4]
2. Dispute Resolution
(Strict time limits and strict procedures)
(1) Referral of a Dispute to the DAAB[5]
(2) DAAB's decision[6]
(3) If Dispute not resolved by the decision, Parties to attempt amicable settlement[7]
(4) If Dispute not amicably settled, final resolution by ICC arbitration[8]

Source: Author's own work.

Notes SC = Sub-Clause

1. This figure is a simplified presentation of the DAAB's two functions. Only the actual text of the General Conditions should be relied upon.
See also Figures 15 Timeline for Claims for Time and/or Money and 16 Paths to ICC Arbitration in the commentary on SC 21.6 below.
2. SC 21.3.
3. Pursuant to SC 21.3, the Parties may jointly request the DAAB to provide assistance and the DAAB may invite the Parties to make such a referral if it becomes aware of any issue or disagreement.
4. An issue/disagreement may give rise to a Dispute (as defined in SC 1.1.29), in which case it may be referred to the DAAB. *See* the 'Dispute Resolution' column in the figure.
5. SC 21.4.
6. *Ibid.*
7. SC 21.5.
8. SC 21.6.

--ooOOoo--

21.3 Avoidance of Disputes

If the Parties so agree, they may jointly request (in writing, with a copy to the Engineer) the DAAB to provide assistance and/or informally discuss and attempt to resolve any issue or disagreement that may have arisen between them during the performance of the Contract. If the DAAB becomes aware of an issue or disagreement, it may invite the Parties to make such a joint request.

Such joint request may be made at any time, except during the period that the Engineer is carrying out his/her duties under Sub-Clause 3.7 [*Agreement or Determination*] on the matter at issue or in disagreement unless the Parties agree otherwise.

Such informal assistance may take place during any meeting, Site visit or otherwise. However, unless the Parties agree otherwise, both Parties shall be present at such discussions. The Parties are not bound to act on any advice given during such informal meetings, and the DAAB shall not be bound in any future Dispute resolution process or decision by any views or advice given during the informal assistance process, whether provided orally or in writing.

The Parties may jointly request, in writing with a copy to the Engineer, the DAAB to assist the Parties informally in resolving any issue between them. Such request may not be made when the Engineer is considering the issue under Sub-Clause 3.7, unless the Parties agree otherwise. The DAAB may also invite the Parties to make such a joint request. Both Parties need to be present at discussions with the DAAB, unless otherwise agreed. The Parties are not bound to act on any advice given by the DAAB, nor is the DAAB bound by it.

Commentary

(i) Main Changes from RB/99:

(1) This Sub-Clause, which had no counterpart in RB/99, is based on, and similar to, Sub-Clause 20.5 [*Avoidance of Disputes*] of GB/08.

(2) Sub-Clause 20.2, seventh paragraph, of RB/99 had merely provided that if the Parties so agreed they could jointly refer a matter to the DAB for an opinion.

(ii) Related Clauses / Sub-Clauses: 1.3 [*Notices and Other Communications*], 3.7 [*Agreement or Determination*], 20 [*Employer's and Contractor's Claims*] and 21 [*Disputes and Arbitration*].

(iii) Analysis:

(1) Purpose of Sub-Clause

In keeping with the adage 'prevention is better than cure', this new Sub-Clause endows the DAAB with the role to assist the Parties to resolve any issue or disagreement between them.[64] Once the DAAB is constituted,[65] the Parties may call upon it for informal assistance, as referred to in this Sub-Clause, without the need for there to have been a prior referral of a Dispute to the DAAB and, indeed, preferably before the existence of any Dispute.[66] In this respect the activity of the DAAB may precede activity of the Engineer under Sub-Clause 3.7 [*Agreement or Determination*].

(2) How may the DAAB be called upon for informal assistance?

The informal assistance of the DAAB may be invoked in two ways.

First, the Parties may themselves jointly request the DAAB 'in writing, with a copy to the Engineer', to assist in resolving any disagreement that may arise. The request must be made by both Parties and the scope of the assistance is 'wide and flexible'.[67] The assistance may take place 'during any meeting, Site visit or otherwise'.[68] While the Parties may request informal assistance 'at any time', whether before or after a Dispute has been referred to the DAAB, they may not do so when the same issue is

64. *FIDIC DBO Contract Guide* (FIDIC, 2011) 135.
65. *See* Sub-Clause 21.1, fifth paragraph.
66. This may be inferred from the second paragraph of Sub-Clause 21.3 ('at any time') and the first sentence of Sub-Clause 21.4, notably the parenthetical in that sentence: '(whether or not any informal discussions have been held under Sub-Clause 21.3 [*Avoidance of Disputes*])'. The forms which informal assistance of a dispute board can take are described in *The FIDIC Contracts Guide* (2nd edn, FIDIC, 2022) 529 and art. 17 (2) of the ICC Dispute Board Rules, 2015.
67. *FIDIC DBO Contract Guide* (FIDIC, 2011) 135.
68. Sub-Clause 21.3, third paragraph.

pending before the Engineer under Sub-Clause 3.7 [*Agreement or Determination*], unless the Parties agree otherwise.[69] Normally, the Parties should not agree otherwise as, once an issue has been submitted to the Engineer under that Sub-Clause, both should benefit from allowing the Engineer to perform its functions in getting the matter resolved, whether by an agreement or a determination.

Second – and this is not contained in the corresponding provision of GB/08[70] – if the DAAB becomes aware of an issue or disagreement between the Parties, the DAAB may, on its own initiative, invite the Parties to make a joint request for the DAAB's assistance.[71] Thus, the DAAB need not wait passively until called upon by the Parties, but may – and should instead – actively and assertively assist the Parties to resolve issues or disagreements between them.[72]

(3) Effect of the DAAB's informal assistance

While no view or advice expressed by the DAAB is binding on either the Parties or the DAAB, it may nevertheless indicate how the issue would eventually be resolved by the DAAB if it were formally referred to it as a Dispute. Knowing in advance how an issue is likely to be resolved may cause a Party to re-evaluate its position, which in turn may contribute to enabling the issue to be amicably resolved.

Informal assistance offers the Parties a 'face-saving' procedure. If a Party refers a Dispute to the DAAB for a decision, there will most likely be a winner and a loser. On the other hand, if the Parties merely refer an issue or disagreement to the DAAB for its non-binding opinion, they will have the benefit of its informal views without there being such a clear winner and loser.

(iv) Related Law: Members of a DAAB have to be careful when providing informal assistance. In an English statutory adjudication case, an adjudicator (who is similar to a DAAB member) accepted to act also as a mediator and, during the mediation, had held meetings with each party separately and confidentially. When the case was referred to a court, the judge found that as a result of meeting and having discussions with each

69. Sub-Clause 21.3, second paragraph.
70. Sub-Clause 20.5 of GB/08.
71. Sub-Clause 21.3, first paragraph.
72. The assistance which the DAAB may provide under this Sub-Clause is defined as 'Informal Assistance' in Sub-Clause 1.6 of the DAAB GCs (an Appendix to the Conditions of Contract).

party separately, the adjudicator's impartiality was compromised, as he could have become aware of information during a meeting with one party alone which was prejudicial to the other party[73] and, thus, to his later determination.[74]

(v) Improvements

(1) As the avoidance of Disputes should be encouraged, why should the Parties have to make a 'joint' request to the DAAB for assistance? Each Party should be entitled to do so.

(2) The requirement in Sub-Clause 21.4.1 that a Dispute be referred to the DAAB within 42 days of the giving or receiving of a NOD may discourage dispute avoidance provided for by Sub-Clause 21.3. In many cases, Parties will be requesting informal assistance of the DAAB only after an Engineer's determination under Sub-Clause 3.7. If so, there will be limited time for the provision of such assistance given the time limit, subject to a time bar, for referral of a Dispute to the DAAB.[75]

--ooOOoo--

21.4 Obtaining DAAB's Decision

If a Dispute arises between the Parties then either Party may refer the Dispute to the DAAB for its

73. As the other party, not being present at the meeting, might have been denied the opportunity to rebut it.
74. *Glencot Development and Design Co Ltd v Ben Barrett & Son (Contractors) Ltd.* [2001] BLR 207. The judge described the case as one of apparent, not actual, bias. The test of whether the adjudicator was biased was, according to the judge, whether the 'circumstances would lead a fair-minded and informed observer to conclude that there was a real possibility or a real danger [...] that the tribunal was biased'. The judge concluded that they would. 219. The same result could obtain under French law by virtue of the principle according to which each party is entitled to respond to the case of the other party (*principe du contradictoire*).
75. The author is grateful to Mr James Perry, PS Consulting, Paris for this point. To limit inhibiting dispute avoidance, it would be better if the 42-day time limit were expressed to be flexible by providing that it applies unless otherwise agreed by the Parties.

decision (whether or not any informal discussions have been held under Sub-Clause 21.3 [*Avoidance of Disputes*]).

In addition to the situation described in the definition of Dispute under Sub-Clause 1.1.29 above, a Dispute shall be deemed to have arisen if:

(a) there is a failure as referred to under sub-paragraph (b), or a non-payment as referred to under sub-paragraph (c), of Sub-Clause 16.2.1 [*Notice*];
(b) the Contractor is entitled to receive financing charges under Sub-Clause 14.8 [*Delayed Payment*] but does not receive payment thereof from the Employer within 28 days after his request for such payment; or
(c) a Party has given:
   (i) a Notice of intention to terminate the Contract under Sub-Clause 15.2.1 [*Notice*] or Sub-Clause 16.2.1 [*Notice*] (as the case may be); or
   (ii) a Notice of termination under Sub-Clause 15.2.2 [*Termination*], Sub-Clause 16.2.2 [*Termination*], 18.5 [*Optional Termination*] or Sub-Clause 18.6 [*Release from Performance under the Law*] (as the case may be);

and the other Party has disagreed with the first Party's entitlement to give such Notice;

which Dispute may be referred by either Party under this Sub-Clause 21.4 without the need for a NOD (and Sub-Clause 3.7 [*Agreement or Determination*] and sub-paragraph (a) of Sub-Clause 21.4.1 [*Reference of a Dispute to the DAAB*] shall not apply).

Where a Dispute is to be referred to the DAAB for its decision, the following provisions shall apply.

21.4.1 Reference of a Dispute to the DAAB

The reference of a Dispute to the DAAB (the "reference" in this Sub-Clause 21.4) shall:

(a) subject to sub-paragraph (ii) of Sub-Clause 3.7.3 [*Time limits*] and the provisions of the second paragraph of Sub-Clause 21.4 [*Obtaining*

DAAB's Decision], be made within 42 days of giving or receiving (as the case may be) a NOD under Sub-Clause 3.7.5 [*Dissatisfaction with Engineer's determination*]. If the Dispute is not referred to the DAAB within this period of 42 days, such NOD shall be deemed to have lapsed and no longer be valid;

(b) state that it is given under this Sub-Clause;
(c) set out the referring Party's case relating to the Dispute;
(d) be in writing, with copies to the other Party and the Engineer; and
(e) for a DAAB of three persons, be deemed to have been received by the DAAB on the date it is received by the chairperson of the DAAB.

The reference of a Dispute to the DAAB under this Sub-Clause shall, unless prohibited by law, be deemed to interrupt the running of any applicable statute of limitation or prescription period.

21.4.2 The Parties' obligations after the reference

Both Parties shall promptly make available to the DAAB all information, access to the Site, and appropriate facilities, as the DAAB may require for the purposes of making a decision on the Dispute.

Unless the Contract has already been abandoned or terminated, the Parties shall continue to perform their obligations in accordance with the Contract.

21.4.3 The DAAB's decision

The DAAB shall complete and give its decision within:

(a) 84 days after receiving the reference; or
(b) such period as may be proposed by the DAAB and agreed by both Parties.

However, if at the end of this period, the due date(s) for payment of any DAAB member's invoice(s) has passed but such invoice(s) remains unpaid, the DAAB shall not be obliged to give its decision until such outstanding invoice(s) have been paid in full, in which case the DAAB shall give its decision as soon as practicable after payment has been received.

The decision shall be given in writing to both Parties with a copy to the Engineer, shall be reasoned, and shall state that it is given under this Sub-Clause.

The decision shall be binding on both Parties, who shall promptly comply with it whether or not a Party gives a NOD with respect to such decision under this Sub-Clause. The Employer shall be responsible for the Engineer's compliance with the DAAB decision.

If the decision of the DAAB requires a payment of an amount by one Party to the other Party:

(i) subject to sub-paragraph (ii) below, this amount shall be immediately due and payable without any certification or Notice; and
(ii) the DAAB may (as part of the decision), at the request of a Party but only if there are reasonable grounds for the DAAB to believe that the payee will be unable to repay such amount in the event that the decision is reversed under Sub-Clause 21.6 [*Arbitration*], require the payee to provide an appropriate security (at the DAAB's sole discretion) in respect of such amount.

The DAAB proceeding shall not be deemed to be an arbitration and the DAAB shall not act as arbitrator(s).

21.4.4 Dissatisfaction with DAAB's decision

If either Party is dissatisfied with the DAAB's decision:

(a) such Party may give a NOD to the other Party, with a copy to the DAAB and to the Engineer;
(b) this NOD shall state that it is a "Notice of Dissatisfaction with the DAAB's Decision" and shall set out the matter in Dispute and the reason(s) for dissatisfaction; and
(c) this NOD shall be given within 28 days after receiving the DAAB's decision.

If the DAAB fails to give its decision within the period stated in Sub-Clause 21.4.3 [*The DAAB's decision*], then either Party may, within 28 days after this period has expired, give a NOD to the other Party in accordance with sub-paragraphs (a) and (b) above.

Except as stated in the last paragraph of Sub-Clause 3.7.5 [*Dissatisfaction with Engineer's determination*], in Sub-Clause 21.7 [*Failure to Comply with DAAB's Decision*] and in Sub-Clause 21.8 [*No DAAB In Place*], neither Party shall be entitled to commence arbitration of a Dispute unless a NOD in respect of that Dispute has been given in accordance with this Sub-Clause 21.4.4.

If the DAAB has given its decision as to a matter in Dispute to both Parties, and no NOD under this Sub-Clause 21.4.4 has been given by either Party within 28 days after receiving the DAAB's decision, then the decision shall become final and binding on both Parties.

If the dissatisfied Party is dissatisfied with only part(s) of the DAAB's decision:

(i) this part(s) shall be clearly identified in the NOD;
(ii) this part(s), and any other parts of the decision that are affected by such part(s) or rely on such part(s) for completeness, shall be deemed to be severable from the remainder of the decision; and
(iii) the remainder of the decision shall become final and binding on both Parties as if the NOD had not been given.

Either Party may refer a Dispute to the DAAB for its decision, regardless of whether any informal discussions have been held under Sub-Clause 21.3.

In addition to the situation specified in the definition of Dispute in Sub-Clause 1.1.29, a Dispute is deemed to arise in three other specific situations in which case it may be referred under Sub-Clause 21.4 without the need for a NOD and Sub-Clauses 3.7 and 21.4.1 (a) shall not apply.

21.4.1 Reference of a Dispute to the DAAB

Subject to sub-paragraph (ii) of Sub-Clause 3.7.3 and the second paragraph of Sub-Clause 21.4, the reference of a Dispute to the DAAB must be made within 42 days of giving or receiving a NOD under Sub-Clause 3.7.5, failing which the NOD is deemed no longer to be valid. Unless prohibited by law, a reference under this Sub-Clause interrupts any applicable limitation period.

21.4.2 The Parties' obligations after the reference

The Parties must make available to the DAAB all information, access to the Site and facilities, as the DAAB may require to make its decision.

21.4.3 The DAAB's decision

The DAAB must give its decision within 84 days of receiving the reference, or within such period as proposed by the DAAB and agreed to by the Parties. However, if at the end of this period, any invoice(s) of a DAAB member is overdue and unpaid, then the DAAB may withhold its decision until it is fully paid. The decision must be given in writing to both Parties, with a copy to the Engineer, must be reasoned and state that it is given under this Sub-Clause. The decision is binding on the Parties, who must promptly comply with it, whether or not a Party has given a NOD with respect to it. The Employer is responsible for compliance by the Engineer. If the decision requires the payment of money, the amount is immediately due and payable, and the DAAB may, if there are reasonable grounds to do so, require the payee to provide security.

21.4.4 Dissatisfaction with DAAB's decision

If either Party is dissatisfied with the DAAB's decision, then it may give a NOD to the other Party, with reasons, within 28 days after receiving the decision. The NOD must state that it is a 'Notice of Dissatisfaction with the DAAB's Decision', and be copied to the DAAB and the Engineer. If the DAAB fails to give a decision within the time period in Sub-Clause 21.4.3, then either Party may, within 28 days after this time period expires, give a NOD under this Sub-Clause.

Except as stated in Sub-Clause 3.7.5, 21.7 and 21.8, neither Party may commence arbitration of a Dispute unless a NOD in respect of it has been given under Sub-Clause 21.4.4. If neither Party has given a NOD

within 28 days after receiving the decision, the decision becomes final and binding on the Parties. If a Party is dissatisfied with only part(s) of the DAAB's decision, then it must identify the part(s) in the NOD, and those parts and any part(s) affected by, or which rely upon, such part(s) shall be severable from the decision and the remainder shall become final and binding.

Commentary

(i) Main Changes from RB/99:

(1) Compared to Sub-Clause 20.4 of RB/99, the new Sub-Clause is greatly expanded and structured under four separate headings: 21.4.1, 21.4.2, 21.4.3 and 21.4.4.
(2) In the first paragraph, the reference to '(whether or not any informal discussions have been held under Sub-Clause 21.3 [*Avoidance of Disputes*])' is new as are the second and third paragraphs (resulting from amendments in 2022).
(3) Sub-Clause 21.4.1 is almost entirely new (the principle of a time limit for the referral of a Dispute to the DAAB derives from Sub-Clause 20.6 of the Gold Book).
(4) In Sub-Clause 21.4.3, the second, fourth and fifth paragraphs are largely or entirely new.
(5) In Sub-Clause 21.4.4, the requirement in sub-paragraph (a) that a copy of the NOD be given to the DAAB and the Engineer and certain of the requirements in sub-paragraph (b) are new.
(6) In Sub-Clause 21.4.4, the reference in the third paragraph to the last paragraph of Sub-Clause 3.7.5 is new.
(7) The last paragraph of Sub-Clause 21.4.4 dealing with where a Party is dissatisfied with only part(s) of the DAAB's decision is new.

(ii) Related Clauses / Sub-Clauses: 1.3 [*Notices and Other Communications*], 3.7 [*Agreement or Determination*], 4.2.2 [*Performance Security – Claims under the Performance Security*], 14.10 [*Statement at Completion*], 14.11 [*Final Statement*], 15.2 [*Termination for Contractor's Default*], 16.1 [*Suspension by Contractor*], 16.2 [*Termination by Contractor*], 20 [*Employer's and Contractor's Claims*] and 21 [*Disputes and Arbitration*].

(iii) Analysis:

(1) Steps in Dispute resolution

Pursuant to Sub-Clause 3.7, the Engineer is required to agree or determine any matter or Claim referred to it by a Party. Assuming that the matter or Claim is not agreed to by the Parties, and that the Engineer therefore has to make a determination, then one of two separate procedures applies depending upon whether or not the Engineer makes a determination on the matter or Claim within the 42-day time limit for determination under Sub-Clause 3.7.3.[76]

(a) The Engineer makes a determination within the 42-day time limit

Assuming the Engineer makes a determination within the 'time limit for determination'[77] and that either Party is dissatisfied with that determination, then that Party may (*and must*, if it wishes to pursue the matter or Claim) give a NOD to the other Party (with a copy to the Engineer) in respect of the Engineer's determination (or corrected determination, if applicable[78]) within 28 days after receiving Notice of it,[79] thereby creating a Dispute (as defined).[80] *Otherwise, the determination will become final and binding on the Parties.*[81]

If a Party is dissatisfied with only part(s) of the Engineer's determination, then it must clearly identify the part(s) in the NOD, and those part(s) and any other part(s) affected by, or which rely upon, such part(s) for completeness will be deemed severable from the remainder of the determination. Those severable parts will then become the subject of a Dispute, while the remainder will then become final and binding.[82]

The only exceptions to the procedure described in the preceding two paragraphs are the cases of a deemed Dispute described in the second paragraph of Sub-Clause 21.4 (namely, failure of the Engineer to issue, or of the Employer to pay, a Payment Certificate; failure of the Contractor to receive financing charges when due; and in cases involving possible or

76. Or, within such other time limit as may be proposed by the Engineer and agreed by both Parties. Sub-Clause 3.7.3 [*Agreement or Determination – Time Limits*].
77. Sub-Clause 3.7.3, second paragraph.
78. Sub-Clause 3.7.4, third and fourth paragraphs.
79. Sub-Clause 3.7.5, first paragraph.
80. *See* the commentary on Sub-Clause 1.1.29 '**Dispute**'.
81. Sub-Clause 3.7.5, second paragraph.
82. Sub-Clause 3.7.5, third paragraph.

actual termination of the Contract). In each of these cases FIDIC considered it to be unjustified, as excessively and/or unnecessarily burdensome, to require the Party concerned to have to assert a matter or Claim to the Engineer under Sub-Clause 3.7 and, if dissatisfied with the Engineer's determination, to have to give a NOD and refer the resulting Dispute to the DAAB within 42 days (of the NOD). Consequently, in these cases a Dispute is deemed to have arisen.

If a Party wishes to pursue the Dispute, it must – except in the case of a deemed Dispute as described below – comply with the procedure in Sub-Clauses 21.4 [*Obtaining DAAB's Decision*] through 21.8 [*No DAAB in Place*]. In summary, this procedure requires observance of five steps, as follows:

(1) Except in the case of a deemed Dispute, the Party must refer the Dispute to the DAAB within 42 days of giving or receiving a NOD under Sub-Clause 3.7.5. *Otherwise, the NOD will become invalid.*[83]
(2) The DAAB must then give a decision on the Dispute within 84 days of a reference, or such other period as may be proposed by the DAAB and agreed by the Parties.[84]
(3) If either Party is dissatisfied with the decision of the DAAB, then it must give a NOD in respect of the decision within 28 days after receiving it.[85] *Otherwise, the DAAB's decision will become final and binding.*[86]
(4) Thereafter, assuming a NOD has been given, the Parties are required to attempt amicable settlement of the Dispute for 28 days.[87]
(5) Whether or not the Parties have attempted amicable settlement during the 28-day period, if the Dispute has not been amicably settled, then, unless the Parties agree otherwise, either Party may thereafter commence arbitration with respect to the Dispute.[88]

83. Sub-Clause 21.4.1, first paragraph.
84. Sub-Clause 21.4.3, first paragraph.
85. Sub-Clause 21.4.4, first paragraph.
86. Sub-Clause 21.4.4, fourth paragraph.
87. Sub-Clause 21.5 [*Amicable Settlement*].
88. *Ibid.* A failure by a Party to comply with these conditions to arbitration is likely to mean under the laws of numerous countries (e.g., England, France, Germany, Singapore and the United States) that its claim is 'inadmissible' (in

Steps (1), (2) and (3) will be examined after subsection (b) immediately below, *see (2) Reference to the DAAB* below. Step (4) will be examined in the commentary on Sub-Clause 21.5 [*Amicable Settlement*] and step (5) in the commentary on Sub-Clause 21.6 [*Arbitration*] below.

(b) The Engineer fails to make a determination within the 42-day time limit

If the Engineer fails to make a determination of a *Claim* within the time limit for determination, the Engineer is deemed to have given a determination rejecting it.[89] Assuming a Party is dissatisfied with the rejection, the Party may (*and must*, if it wishes to pursue the Claim) give a NOD in respect of the deemed determination of rejection within 28 days after the

French: *irrecevable*) in arbitration. Admissibility has been distinguished from jurisdiction as follows: (1) '[J]urisdiction is the power of the tribunal to hear the case; admissibility is whether the case itself is defective – whether it is appropriate for the tribunal to hear it', dissenting opinion of Keith Highet in *Waste Management, Inc v United Mexican States*, ICSID Case ARB(AF)/98/2, 265 (para. 58) (2000); and (2) inadmissibility, as distinct from lack of arbitral jurisdiction, refers to 'alleged impediment[s] to consideration of the merits of the dispute which [do] not put into question the investiture of the tribunal as such'. Jan Paulsson, 'Jurisdiction and Admissibility' in *Global Reflections on International Law, Commerce and Dispute Resolution, Liber Amicorum in honour of Robert Briner* (ICC Publishing, 2005) (ICC Publication 693), 601, 617. The distinction is important as a determination as to the admissibility of a claim is – or should be – made *finally* by an arbitral tribunal and not a national court, whereas a decision as to jurisdiction is made *finally* by a national court. *Ibid.*, 601. For English law, *see The Republic of Sierra Leone and SL Mining Ltd* [2021] EWHC 286 (Comm); for French law, *see* Charles Jarrosson, ' Observations on *Poiré v Tripler*' (2003) 19(3) Arb Int'l, 363 and *Aktor et autres v Administration Routière Albanaise*, Ct of App Paris (18th Ch), 31 May 2022, no. 58/2022 (dealing with RB/99); for U S law, *see BG Group plc v Argentina*, 572 U.S.25 (2014); and for comparative (including German) law *see* Milivoje Mitrovic, 'Dealing with the Consequences of Non-compliance with Mandatory Pre-arbitral Requirements in Multi-Tiered Dispute Resolution Clauses: The Swiss Approach and a Look Across the Border' (2019) 37(3) ASA Bull, 559. *See* generally Gary Born, *International Commercial Arbitration* (3rd edn, Kluwer L Int'l, the Netherlands, 2021) vol I, 997-1007 (s 5.08 [C]). *See also* **Figures 11 Procedure for Claims Unrelated to Time and/or Money** and **13 Procedure for Claims for Time and/or Money – Detailed** at the end of the commentary on Clause 20 above.

89. Sub-Clause 3.7.3, last paragraph, sub-para. (i).

time limit for determination under Sub-Clause 3.7.3 has expired[90] and thereafter steps (1) to (5) listed in subsection (a) above will apply. *Otherwise, the deemed determination of rejection will become final and binding on the Parties.*[91]

On the other hand, if the Engineer has failed to determine a *matter* (not a Claim) within the time limit for determination, then the matter is deemed to be a Dispute which may be referred by either Party directly to the DAAB for its decision under Sub-Clause 21.4 without the need for a NOD or being bound by a particular time period, and sub-paragraph (a) of Sub-Clause 21.4.1 will not apply.[92] In this case, only steps (2) to (5) listed in subsection (a) above will apply.

(2) Reference to the DAAB

Sub-Clause 3.7.5 provides that if a Party is dissatisfied with a determination (or, in the case of a Claim,[93] a deemed determination) of the Engineer (or part(s) of one), it must – if it wishes to pursue the issue – give a NOD with respect to the determination (or part(s)) within 28 days after receiving the Engineer's Notice of the determination (or, in the case of a deemed determination rejecting a Claim, within 28 days after the time limit for determination has expired), and otherwise comply with this Sub-Clause.[94]

Thereafter, except in the cases of a deemed Dispute described earlier,[95] 'either Party may' (*and must* if it wishes to pursue the issue) within 42 days of 'giving or receiving (as the case may be) a NOD' under Sub-Clause 3.7.5 refer the issue – which is now a 'Dispute' – to the DAAB (such reference is referred to in Sub-Clause 21.4.1 as the 'reference').[96] *If the Dispute is not referred to the DAAB within this period of 42 days, the*

90. Sub-Clause 3.7.5, first paragraph, sub-para. (c).
91. Sub-Clause 3.7.5, second paragraph.
92. Sub-Clause 3.7.3, last paragraph, sub-para. (ii).
93. Neither Sub-Clause 3.7.5 nor Sub-Clause 21.4.1(a) applies to a deemed determination of a matter, *see* sub-paragraph (ii) of Sub-Clause 3.7.3.
94. *See* the commentary on Sub-Clause 3.7 [*Agreement or Determination*] above.
95. Under sub-paragraph (ii) of Sub-Clause 3.7.3 or Sub-Clause 21.4, second paragraph.
96. Sub-Clause 21.4. It does not have to be the claiming Party which refers the Dispute to the DAAB – where one Party has given a NOD within time, either Party may refer the Dispute to the DAAB. *See also* Sub-Clause 3.7.5(d).

NOD is deemed 'no longer [...] valid',[97] *meaning that that Dispute may no longer be referred to the DAAB. Thus, this is a further time bar.*[98]

Sub-Clause 21.4.1 contains precise details as to the content and form of the required 'reference' to the DAAB and, where the DAAB consists of three persons, of when the reference is deemed to have been received by the DAAB. Careful attention to these details[99] is important as failure to comply with them may render the NOD invalid.

An excellent addition is the provision that the reference of a Dispute to the DAAB shall, unless prohibited by law, be deemed to interrupt any applicable period of limitation.[100] This is important because, given the relatively lengthy claims and DAAB procedures with which a Party must comply before it may begin arbitration,[101] the applicable period of limitation might expire in the meantime.[102]

(3) Importance of the Dispute

When the Dispute is referred to the DAAB, the DAAB gives a decision *on that Dispute* and, thereafter, if a Party is dissatisfied with the decision, the Party gives a NOD with the decision on that *same Dispute*. Whatever other Disputes there may be between the Parties, no Dispute may be referred to arbitration pursuant to Sub-Clause 21.6 unless the *Dispute* has first been referred to the DAAB and otherwise gone through the channels in Sub-Clause 21. This can clearly be seen from the italicised text, which is not in square brackets, in the first sentence of Sub-Clause 21.6:

97. Sub-Clause 21.4.1(a).
98. There is no provision for disapplying this time bar, as is the case under Sub-Clause 20.2.5 [Agreement or determination of the Claim].
99. And to Sub-Clause 1.3 [*Notices and Other Communications*].
100. Sub-Clause 21.4.1, last paragraph. *See* **Section 4 Common Law and Civil Law Compared – 4.5.3 Limitation Periods** in **Chapter II Applicable Law** above.
101. It may take more than a year from the time a Notice of Claim is given until arbitration may begin. *See* **Figure 15 Timeline for Claims for Time and/or Money** in the commentary on Sub-Clause 21.6 below.
102. This provision is also consistent with modern practice (*see* under **(iv) Related Law** below). Sub-Clause 21.4.2 makes clear that the mere fact that a Party has referred a Dispute to the DAAB does not relieve it from having to continue to perform the Contract. However time-consuming or burdensome pursuing a Dispute before the DAAB may be, each Party must continue to perform its contractual obligations exactly as before.

> Unless settled amicably, and subject to Sub-Clause 3.7.5 [*Dissatisfaction with Engineer's determination*], Sub-Clause 21.4.4 [*Dissatisfaction with DAAB's decision*], Sub-Clause 21.7 [*Failure to Comply with DAAB's Decision*] and Sub-Clause 21.8 [*No DAAB In Place*], *any Dispute in respect of which the DAAB's decision (if any)*[103] *has not become final and binding shall be finally settled by arbitration* (italicised text not in square brackets added).

It follows from this sentence that *the only matter that may be submitted to arbitration is a Dispute* which has:

(1) been referred to the DAAB for decision pursuant to Sub-Clause 21.4; and
(2) not become the subject of a final and binding decision of the DAAB because, as will be explained in detail below, a Party has given a NOD with respect to the decision (or deemed decision) on that Dispute within 28 days.

The 'subject to' provisions in the above quotation are discussed in the commentary on Sub-Clause 21.6 below.

(4) DAAB's decision

The DAAB has broad authority to adopt a procedure that is suitable to the Dispute while 'avoiding unnecessary delay and/or expense'.[104] The DAAB must act 'fairly and impartially' between the Parties and, having regard to the time period provided for giving its decision – normally 84 days – and other relevant circumstances, give each Party a 'reasonable opportunity (consistent with the expedited nature of the DAAB proceeding)' of putting its case and responding to the other Party's case.[105]

---

103. This refers to the possibility that the DAAB has failed to make a decision after being requested to do so, *see* Sub-Clause 21.4.4, second paragraph.
104. Rule 6.2(b), DAAB Rules.
105. Rule 6.2(a), DAAB Rules. The right to a fair trial is enshrined in, among other places, art. 6 of The European Convention on Human Rights which provides, among other things, that:

> In the determination of his civil rights and obligations [...], everyone is entitled to a fair and public hearing within a reasonable time by an independent and impartial tribunal established by law.

The DAAB's powers include, among other things, to:

> [o]pen up, review and revise any certificate, decision, determination, instruction, opinion or valuation of (or acceptance, agreement, approval, consent, disapproval, No-objection, permission, or similar act by) the Engineer that is relevant to the Dispute; [...].[106]

In the case of a three-member DAAB, the decision must be given either unanimously or by a majority of the DAAB members.[107] The decision must be given in writing to both Parties with a copy to the Engineer.[108] It must be reasoned[109] and, as the decision has important consequences, state that it is given under Sub-Clause 21.4.[110] It must be given 'within'[111] 84 days after the reference, or such other period as may be proposed by the DAAB and agreed by both Parties in writing.[112]

Where a Dispute is particularly complicated or fact intensive, it is not unusual for the DAAB to propose that the Parties agree to a longer period than 84 days for the DAAB's decision. If so, the Parties' agreement must not be 'unreasonably withheld or delayed'.[113]

At the same time, a DAAB proceeding is to be 'expeditious, efficient and cost effective'[114] and the right to propose a time extension for making a

106. Rule 5.1(k), DAAB Rules. This should exclude a final and binding determination of the Engineer. *See*, for example, Sub-Clause 21.6, second paragraph. The DAAB's powers include to rule on its own jurisdiction. Rule 5.1(c), DAAB Rules.
107. Rule 8.2, DAAB Rules. *See also (6) New Procedures for the DAAB's decision* in **Section 2.3 DAAB Rules** of **Chapter V Commentary On Other Documents** below.
108. Sub-Clause 21.4.3, third paragraph.
109. *Ibid.* The better and more convincing the DAAB's reasons, the more likely the decision will be accepted by the Parties and further proceedings avoided. *The FIDIC Contracts Guide* (2nd Edn, FIDIC, 2022) 537.
110. Sub-Clause 21.4.3, third paragraph. There is no provision for the DAAB to award a Party the costs of a DAAB proceeding (apart from providing in Sub-Clause 21.1 for the sharing by the Parties of the costs of the DAAB).
111. *See* item (2) under **(v) Improvements** in commentary on Sub-Clause 1.2 [*Interpretation*] above.
112. Sub-Clause 21.4.3, first paragraph. An agreement in 'writing' is required by both Sub-Clause 1.3 of the Conditions and Rule 8.1, DAAB Rules.
113. Sub-Clause 1.3, third paragraph.
114. Rule 1(b), DAAB Rules.

decision must not be abused. A DAAB proceeding should not approach the length and/or procedural complexity of an arbitration.[115]

If the DAAB should fail to give its decision within 84 days or such other period agreed by the Parties, and instead do so after this time limit has elapsed, then it will not be a valid decision under Clause 21.[116]

Also, if at the end of the 84-day period the invoice of any DAAB member remains overdue for payment, the DAAB is not obliged to give its decision until the outstanding invoice has been paid in full.[117]

(5) Consequences of the DAAB's decision

The Sub-Clause states the effect of the decision as follows:

> The decision shall be binding on both Parties, who shall promptly comply with it whether or not a Party gives a NOD with respect to such decision [...].[118]

This makes it clear that each Party must comply with a decision whether it expresses dissatisfaction with it or not.[119] If the decision requires the

115. Unless the Parties and the DAAB agree otherwise.
116. A three-person ICC arbitral tribunal so ruled by an arbitration award dated 18 March 2019 in relation to a contract based upon a FIDIC form in *Todini Impregilo Kazakhdorstroy v The Road Committee of the Ministry of Industry of Kazakhstan*. The Paris-based tribunal found the decision of a DAB in favour of the contractor to be unenforceable as it was rendered outside the time limit provided for by FIDIC rules. *See* Cosmo Sanderson, *Kazakhstan Defeats ICC Claim over Road Project, 12 August 2019* published in the Global Arbitration Review on 20 August 2019, https://globalarbitrationreview.com/article/1196216/kazakhstan-defeats-icc-claim-over-road-project > and < http://www.adilet.gov.kz/en/news/international-court-arbitration-international-chamber-commerce-city-paris-made-decision-favor accessed 10 November 2022. *See also* the *Farmex* case, Paris Court of Appeal (Chamber 1), 4 November 2014, 13/22288 (DAB decision treated as arbitral award and set aside under art. 1520 of the French Code of Civil Procedure for having been rendered beyond the agreed time limit for arbitral awards). This is also the position in English statutory adjudication (Clive Freedman and James Farrell, *Kendall on Expert Determination* (5th edn, Sweet & Maxwell, London, 2015) 114-115 (para. 5.5-11)).
117. Sub-Clause 21.4.3, second paragraph.
118. Sub-Clause 21.4.3, fourth paragraph.
119. While courts and arbitral tribunals had earlier been divided on the issue of whether a Party had to comply with a decision of the DAB under RB/99

payment of money, then, subject to the possible need to provide security discussed below, the amount is 'immediately due and payable without any certification or Notice'.[120]

Where a decision requires the payment of money, the DAAB may:

> at the request of a Party but only if there are reasonable grounds for the DAAB to believe that the payee will be unable to repay such amount in the event that the decision is reversed under Sub-Clause 21.6 [*Arbitration*]

require the payee to provide an 'appropriate security (at the DAAB's sole discretion)' in respect of such amount.[121] Such security might, for example, take the form of a parent company guarantee or a demand guarantee issued by a bank.

In applying this provision, it is important to appreciate that the Contractor, who is bound to execute the Works without interruption,[122] is dependent on the Employer for funds to cover its ongoing costs and, hopefully, earn a profit. Consequently, if the Contractor should prevail in a request for a decision for money, then, whether or not the Employer expresses dissatisfaction with the DAAB's decision, the Contractor should normally, as the decision is binding and must 'immediately' be paid, receive that payment unconditionally.[123] It should be a rare case

---

with which the Party had expressed dissatisfaction, the Singapore Court of Appeal (Singapore's highest Court) correctly ruled, after the Singapore courts (among others) had thoroughly – in a series of four decisions – examined the issue, that such a decision had to be complied with whether a Party was dissatisfied with it or not. *See Perusahan Gas Negara (Persero) TBK v CRW Joint Operation* [2015] SGCA 30. Sub-Clause 21.4.3, fourth paragraph, confirms that solution as regards RB/17.

120. Sub-Clause 21.4.3, fifth paragraph.
121. *Ibid.*
122. '[w]ith due expedition and without delay' according to Sub-Clause 8.1, second paragraph.
123. *See* Sub-Clause 21.4.3, fourth and fifth paragraphs. On the other hand, if the Employer should prevail in the Dispute before the DAAB and the Contractor be denied payment, then, whether or not the Contractor expresses dissatisfaction with the DAAB's decision, the Contractor must nevertheless keep working without interruption. *See* Sub-Clause 8.1, second paragraph. Thus, each Party is expected to bear the risk of a possibly mistaken DAAB decision until the Dispute is finally resolved, whether by an amicable settlement or arbitration, often years later.

(e.g., where it is close to bankruptcy) in which a Contractor is required to provide security – which may negatively impact its credit – under this provision.

(6) Expressing dissatisfaction

If either Party is dissatisfied with the decision of a DAAB, it may (and *must*, if it wishes to challenge the decision), 'within'[124] 28 days of receiving it:

(1) give a NOD to the other Party, with a copy to the DAAB and the Engineer,
(2) which states that it is a 'Notice of Dissatisfaction with the DAAB's Decision' and sets out the matter in Dispute and the reason(s) for dissatisfaction.[125]

However, as mentioned earlier, giving a NOD will not relieve the Party from having to comply with the decision.[126] If the DAAB fails to give its decision within 84 days, or any agreed extension, then either Party may (and *must* if it wishes to pursue the subject) give a NOD to the other Party, in accordance with the preceding sentence, within 28 days after the period for decision has expired.[127]

124. *See* item (2) under **(v) Improvements** in the commentary on Sub-Clause 1.2 [*Interpretation*] above.
125. Sub-Clause 21.4.4, first paragraph. Under the 1999 Rainbow Suite, there have been conflicting decisions as to whether a failure to set out reasons in a NOD – reasons were required by Sub-Clause 20.4 – would invalidate it. In one ICC award it was held that this should invalidate the NOD. Final award, ICC case 14429 (2007), Jean-Jacques Arnaldez and others (eds), *Coll of ICC Arb Awards, 2012 – 2015* (ICC, Paris / Kluwer, the Netherlands, 2019) 673 (French translation of original English text). On the other hand, in another, better reasoned award, a failure to state reasons was held not to invalidate the NOD. Final award, ICC case 18320 (2013), ICC Disp Resol Bull, 2015, Issue 1, 132, 133-135 (commentary 21, 33).
126. Indeed, should it fail to comply with it, the other Party has the right under Sub-Clause 21.7 [*Failure to Comply with DAAB's Decision*] to refer the failure directly to arbitration under Sub-Clause 21.6 [*Arbitration*].
127. Sub-Clause 21.4.4, second paragraph. Where the DAAB has failed to issue a decision within the time period for it to do so and no NOD has been given within 28 days after the expiration of that time period, may the claimant later resubmit the same dispute to the DAAB? There are differing awards on this subject. One award (based on the Pink Book) found this would be

If either Party has given a NOD with respect to a DAAB's decision, if any, then either Party may later commence arbitration with respect to the Dispute concerned subject to compliance with Sub-Clause 21.5. The Party which commences the arbitration need not be the one which gave the NOD.[128]

Once again, it is critical that each Party complies carefully with the foregoing provisions as, if it should fail to do so, *the decision, if any, of the DAAB may become final and binding,*[129] *with the consequence that the merits of the Dispute may no longer be contested, whether in arbitration or elsewhere.* Moreover, if the DAAB has failed to give a decision, and if neither Party has given a NOD within 28 days of the expiry of the 84-day period, *then neither Party will thereafter be able to commence arbitration of the Dispute.*[130] *Each Party will have lost the right to commence arbitration or otherwise litigate the matter.*[131]

---

inconsistent with this provision's preclusive intent (final award, ICC case 22877 (2020), *see* Cosmo Sanderson, 'Kazakh road authority beats bulk of ICC claim' in Global Arbitration Review, 23 August 2021). On the other hand, another award (based, again, on the Pink Book) found that 'nothing' in Sub-Clause 20.4 precluded the claimant from 'starting again' by re-referring the dispute to the DAB (partial award, ICC case 25318 (2021) (unpublished so far)).

128. This has always been the case under the RB's disputes clause. *See*, e.g., final award, ICC case 10619 (2001), ICC Int'l Ct Arb Bull, vol 19, no 2, 2008, 85, 90, paras 17 and 18 (commentary 41, 52, 54-56).

129. Thus, under RB/69, where the Employer had failed to take the necessary action in time, eight decisions of the Engineer (a predecessor of the DAAB) were held to be final and binding on the Employer Partial award, ICC case 3790 (1983) Sigvard Jarvin and others (eds) *Coll of ICC Arb Awards 1986-1990* (ICC, Paris / Kluwer, the Netherlands, 1994) 3, 7-9. *See also* ICC case 2150 (1975) to the same effect, McNeill Stokes, *International Construction Contracts* (2nd edn, McGraw-Hill, 1980) 58, and, more recently, final award, ICC case 22724 (2020) (unpublished), where a failure to submit a notice of intention to commence arbitration within the time limit required by the relevant contract (28 days from the expiry of the 56-day period within which the Employer's Representative had to make a decision) resulted in the relevant claim being held inadmissible in arbitration.

130. Sub-Clause 21.4.4, third paragraph. Final award, ICC case 15282 (2010), ICC Int'l Ct Arb Bull, vol 24, no 2, 2013, 71, 74-76 (commentary 49, 53-54).

131. *See* Sub-Clause 21.4.4, third paragraph. When complying with the foregoing provisions, a Party will also want to take special care to observe the rules for communications in Sub-Clause 1.3 [*Notices and Other Communi-*

While the time within which to give a NOD is quite short – 28 days – a Party should not be overly concerned about the reasons for dissatisfaction which it gives in its NOD, as it will not be limited by them in any later arbitration.[132]

A decision of a DAAB may be quite lengthy and contain several different parts. In this case, a Party may express dissatisfaction with certain part(s) of a DAAB's decision only.[133] This new provision allows a Party to accept, and have the benefit of, any parts of the decision with which it is satisfied, and allow them to become final and binding.[134]

(iv) Related Law:

(1) Numerous cases have confirmed, under earlier editions of the RB, that the reference of a dispute to a dispute board[135] is a mandatory condition to arbitration.[136]

(2) Under the common law, '[t]he usual position is that decisions of a [dispute board] are enforceable as a term of contract'.[137] In analogous situations, the civil law (French) position is no different.[138]

---

cations]. There is no provision for disapplying this time bar, as is the case under Sub-Clause 20.2.5 [Agreement or determination of the Claim].

132. *See* Sub-Clause 21.6, fourth paragraph.
133. Sub-Clause 21.4.4, last paragraph.
134. Assuming the other Party does not give a NOD with respect to them.
135. Or to the Engineer under Clause 67 of RB/87 and earlier editions of the Red Book.
136. *Channel (Tunnel) Group v Balfour Beatty Ltd* [1993] AC 334; *Peterborough City Council v Enterprise Managed Services Ltd* [2014] EWHC 3193 (TCC); and Swiss Federal Court decision 4A_124/2014, 7 July 2014, ASA Bull 4/2014, 826 (although in this case the court found the dispute board procedure inapplicable for other reasons). *See also* interim award, ICC case 14431 (2008), interim award, ICC case 16155 (2010), partial award, ICC award 16262 (2010) and final award, ICC case 16765 (2013), ICC Disp Resol Bull, 2015, Issue 1, 35, 71, 75 and 101, respectively. For a commentary on these cases *see* 21, 28 to 30 of the same issue of the ICC Disp Resol Bull. However, where the amount concerned is so small as not to justify another arbitration and is not really in dispute, an exception may be made, *see* final award, ICC case 8677 (1997), ICC Int'l Ct Arb Bull, vol 19, no 2, 2008, 71-73 (commentary 60, 62-63).
137. Clive Freedman and James Farrell, *Kendall on Expert Determination* (5th edn, Sweet & Maxwell, London, 2015) 118 (para. 5.6-5).
138. Cass com no. 205, 6 June 1950 and Cass com no 333, 3 November 1952.

(3) In certain limited cases, the validity of a DAAB decision may be challenged (in addition to a challenge to the merits of the decision by arbitration). This might occur if, for example:
  (1) a DAAB fails to act 'fairly and impartially' and to ensure each Party has 'a reasonable opportunity' to present its case (consistent with the expedited nature of the DAAB proceeding),[139] that is, violates due process or natural justice;[140]
  (2) the DAAB lacks jurisdiction; e.g., there exists no 'Dispute'[141] or the DAAB has been improperly constituted;[142]
  (3) fraud or collusion has occurred;[143] or
  (4) there are any other grounds under applicable law.[144]
(4) With respect to the provision in Sub-Clause 21.4.1 that the reference of a Dispute to the DAAB shall, unless prohibited by law, interrupt any statute of limitation or prescription period,[145] the UNIDROIT Principles – though not addressing an identical

---

139. Rule 6.2 of the DAAB Rules. In this connection, *see* final award, ICC case 19581 (2014), ICC Disp Resol Bull, 2015 Issue 1, 147, 150-154 (commentary 30).
140. An example, drawn from statutory adjudication in England, would be where a DAAB makes a decision on the basis of arguments not put forward by either party and not referred by the DAAB to the parties:

> In essence, [...] the adjudicator has gone off 'on a frolic of his own' in using a method of assessment [of damages] which neither party argued and which he did not put to the parties. In some cases, this may not be sufficient to prevent enforcement of the decision where the 'frolic' makes no material difference to the outcome of the decision. Thus, an adjudicator who refers to a legal authority which neither party relied upon, may have his or her decision enforced nonetheless if the application of that the legal authority obviously makes no difference to the outcome. The breach of the rules of natural justice has to be material. Here, [...] the breach is material and has or has apparently led to a very substantial financial difference in favour of [the contractor] but necessarily against the interests of [the Employer].

As a result, the decision was not enforceable. *Herbosch-Kiere Marine Contractors Ltd v Dover Harbour Board* [2012] EWHC 84 (TCC) [para. 33].
141. *See* final award, ICC case 6535 (1992), ICC Int'l Ct Arb Bull, vol 9, no 2, November 1998, 60 (commentary 34).
142. *See* final award, ICC case 19581 (2014), ICC Disp Resol Bull, 2015, Issue 1, 147, 150-154 (commentary 30).
143. *See*, in England, *Campbell v Edwards* [1976] 1 WLR 403 at 407: 'Fraud or collusion unravels everything' per Lord Denning.
144. *See* under **(iv) Related Law** of the commentary on Sub-Clause 21.1 above.
145. In this connection:

situation – are to similar effect. They provide that a limitation period is suspended not just by arbitral proceedings[146] but also in the case of proceedings 'whereby the parties request a third person to assist them in their attempt to reach an amicable settlement of their dispute'.[147]

(v) Improvements:

(1) As shown in **Figure 15 Timeline for Claims for Time and/or Money**, it may take eight months from the time an 'event or circumstance' giving rise to a Claim occurs before it may be referred as a Dispute to the DAAB and another four months before it may be referred to ICC arbitration, making for a total of 12 months or one year. Such a lengthy pre-arbitral procedure may be suitable for the majority of Claims and for limiting the risk of international arbitration. But, whether due to their size, technical complexity or other reasons, some Claims – it may be recognised early on – cannot be resolved except by international arbitration. Yet under RB/17 all Claims, regardless of their nature or importance, are subject to a mandatory 12-month pre-arbitral procedure. This 'one size fits all' approach will be unreasonable in some cases. Accordingly, as the procedure for

---

> [t]here is a considerable divergence of views amongst legal systems as to the validity of agreements on limitation periods.

Stefan Vogenauer (ed), *Commentary on the UNIDROIT Principles of International Commercial Contracts (PICC)* (2nd edn, OUP, Oxford, 2015) 1165 (para. 2). Thus, modification of a limitation period by law is, for example, prohibited in Italy and Switzerland (Stefan Vogenauer (ed), *Commentary on the UNIDROIT Principles of International Commercial Contracts (PICC)* (2nd edn, OUP, Oxford, 2015) 1165 (para. 2)), note 56 (citing to art. 2936 of the Italian Civil Code and art. 129 of the Swiss Code of Obligations) while permitted without restriction in England (*ibid.*, note 57).

146. Art. 10.6 (*Suspension by arbitral proceeding*).
147. Art. 10.7 (*Alternative dispute resolution*). *See also* fn. 4 to art. 5 (Commencement of mediation proceedings) of the *UNCITRAL Model Law on International Commercial Mediation and International Settlement Agreements Resulting from Mediation*, 2018. National law may be to similar effect (reference of a dispute to a DAB under a FIDIC contract held to suspend the limitation period under the Romanian Civil Code, final award, ICC case 21488 (2018) (unpublished)).

the treatment of Claims by the Engineer has become lengthier and more detailed – and is, thus, expected to be more efficacious – under Sub-Clause 3.7 than under Sub-Clause 3.5 of RB/99, consideration could be given to providing that, where a Claim is unresolved after exhaustion of the Sub-Clause 3.7 procedure, a Party should have the option to bypass the DAAB and refer the corresponding Dispute directly to ICC arbitration (possibly, after compliance with the amicable settlement procedure). Resolution of a Dispute by a DAAB is unlikely to be effective unless each Party sees it to be in its interest. Accordingly, if after eight months a Party would prefer to refer a particular Dispute to arbitration rather than to a DAAB, it should be entitled to do so.

(2) In light of the conflicting ICC awards on the subject (discussed in footnote 127 under **(iii) Analysis** above), Sub-Clause 21.4 needs to be clarified to explain whether and, if so, under what circumstances, the same matter or Claim may be referred as a Dispute for a second time to the DAAB for decision, e.g., where the DAAB has failed to give a decision following the first referral and neither Party had given a NOD within 28 days after the expiration of the time period for that decision, may a Party refer the same matter or Claim to the DAAB again?

(3) As noted under item (2) of **(v) Improvements** under Sub-Clause 21.3 [*Avoidance of Disputes*], the requirement in Sub-Clause 21.4.1 that a Dispute be referred to the DAAB within 42 days of the giving or receiving of a NOD – which is new in RB/17 – may discourage dispute avoidance under Sub-Clause 21.3. To reduce the risk of inhibiting dispute avoidance, it would be better if the 42-day time limit were expressed to be flexible by providing that it applies unless otherwise agreed by the Parties.

(4) A difficulty with the Claims and Disputes procedure provided for by Sub-Clauses 3.7, 20.2 and 21.4 is that, because of its relative rigidity, it can result in 'over-loading' the DAAB with Disputes both large and small, regardless of the wishes of either Party or of the DAAB.[148] This is because once a Notice of Claim in relation to a matter has been given to the Engineer,[149] a series of fixed time periods begins to run with respect to that Claim, which – unless the Claim is abandoned or the other Party agrees – cannot

148. The author is grateful to Mr James Perry, PS-Consulting, Paris, for having drawn the author's attention to this potential problem.
149. Under Sub-Clause 20.2.1 [*Notice of Claim*].

be stopped and can lead ultimately to the referral of the Claim as a Dispute to the DAAB and a decision of the DAAB.[150] The Contractor may have multiple Claims arising within a fairly short time frame, in which case each of them will be subject to the same strict procedure, whether this suits the Parties or the DAAB or not. The claiming Party has limited control over the procedure once it has given a Notice of Claim.[151] Accordingly, more flexibility should be built into this procedure to permit the orderly and efficient resolution of Claims and Disputes.[152]

(5) Rule 5.1(k), DAAB Rules needs to be modified to exclude a final and binding determination of the Engineer. *See*, for example, Sub-Clause 21.6, second paragraph.

--ooOOoo--

21.5 Amicable Settlement

Where a NOD has been given under Sub-Clause 21.4 [*Obtaining DAAB's Decision*], both Parties shall attempt to settle the Dispute amicably before

150. *See* **Figure 15 Timeline for Claims for Time and/or Money** included in the commentary on Sub-Clause 21.6 below.
151. Thus, if the Contractor is dissatisfied with a determination of the Claim by the Engineer under Sub-Clause 3.7 and gives a NOD with respect to it, then, pursuant to Sub-Clause 21.4.1(a), the Contractor must submit the Dispute to the DAAB within 42 days; otherwise, the NOD is deemed to be invalid. Regardless of how many referrals the Contractor (or, indeed, the Employer) may recently have made to the DAAB or be planning to make, the same procedure must be followed with respect to each Claim/Dispute (unless it is abandoned), and the DAAB must in turn decide each referral within 84 days unless the DAAB proposes another period to which both Parties agree. Sub-Clause 21.4.3.
152. A possible solution would be to allow a Party, which refers a Dispute to the DAAB, to make a reasoned request to the DAAB to suspend action on it temporarily. The DAAB should then have the power, after hearing the Parties, to decide on the suspension by a decision binding on the Parties. If the DAAB rules in favour of a suspension, the 84-day time period in which the DAAB is normally required to make a decision would not run during the suspension period. As this issue has not been addressed in the General Conditions, any solution to it would need to be included in the Particular Conditions as well as possibly in the DAAB GCs including the DAAB Rules.

> the commencement of arbitration. However, unless both Parties agree otherwise, arbitration may be commenced on or after the twenty-eighth (28th) day after the day on which this NOD was given, even if no attempt at amicable settlement has been made.

Where a NOD has been given under Sub-Clause 21.4, the Parties must attempt to settle the Dispute amicably before commencing arbitration. Arbitration may be commenced on the 28th day after the day on which the NOD was given, even if no attempt at amicable settlement has been made.

Commentary

(i) Main Changes from RB/99: Under the new Sub-Clause, arbitration may begin 28 days after the day on which a NOD is given, whereas under Sub-Clause 20.5 of RB/99 it could only begin 56 days after the day on which a notice of dissatisfaction was given.

(ii) Related Clauses / Sub-Clauses: 1.3 [*Notices and Other Communications*], 1.12 [*Confidentiality*] and 21 [*Disputes and Arbitration*].

(iii) Analysis:

(1) Reason for this Sub-Clause

A time period for the Parties to attempt amicable settlement before arbitration was first introduced into the Red Book in the fourth edition published in 1987 ('RB/87'). The time period was 56 days. At that time, FIDIC explained that:

> in some countries […] if there is no reference to amicable settlement in the Contract then the individual responsible for administering the Contract may have no right to enter into negotiations for an amicable settlement. This Sub-Clause makes provision for this possibility but sets a time limit so that the settlement discussions will not be prolonged indefinitely. Whether or not an attempt at amicable settlement has been made within 56 days, the parties can thereafter proceed with arbitration.[153]

This statement probably remains true today – at least in the case of contracts with state parties – except that the time period is now 28 days

153. *Guide to the Use of FIDIC Conditions of Contract for Works of Civil Engineering Construction, fourth edition* (FIDIC 1989) 155.

after the day on which a NOD is given, whether or not an attempt at amicable settlement is made.[154] Thereafter, either Party may proceed to arbitration.

Since, under this Sub-Clause, initiating settlement discussions:

> *involves the discharge of a pre-existing contractual obligation*, it can allow the parties to participate in a process aimed at achieving a settlement without loss of face, and without the concern that participation may otherwise be perceived as a sign of weakness.[155] (Emphasis added)

Amicable settlement discussions will not relieve a Party from having to comply with the Contract. Thus, entry into such discussions following a DAAB's decision will not, absent a valid NOD, prevent a DAAB decision from becoming final and binding.[156]

(2) How to attempt amicable settlement

Parties are encouraged – indeed required – by this Sub-Clause to attempt to reach an amicable settlement by, for example: direct negotiation by senior executives from each of the Parties, who ideally should have had no prior involvement in the dispute; mediation; expert determination and any other form of alternative dispute resolution that is not as formal, time-consuming and costly as arbitration.[157] However, to allow time for any of these procedures to be implemented, the Parties are likely also to have to agree to extension of the 28-day time limit – a possibility recognised by this Sub-Clause.[158]

154. The 56-day period in RB/87 and in RB/99 was seen as too long because, if there were no genuine endeavours to pursue a settlement during this period, the Parties would simply mark time until they could proceed to arbitration. To address this criticism, FIDIC shortened the period to 28 days on the basis that, if real progress towards an amicable settlement is being made, the Parties could always agree to extend this period.
155. Dale S Brackin, 'Subclause 20.5 of the FIDIC Contracts and Amicable Dispute Resolution ("ADR")' [2006] ICLR 442, 443-444.
156. *See* final award, ICC case 14429 (2007) Jean-Jacques Arnaldez and others (eds), *Coll of ICC Arb Awards 2012 – 2015* (ICC, Paris / Kluwer, the Netherlands, 2019) 673.
157. *Guidance for the Preparation of Particular Conditions*, 50.
158. '[U]nless both Parties agree otherwise' in the second sentence of Sub-Clause 21.5.

(3) Use of a sealed or 'Calderbank' offer

Among other things, a Party may consider resorting to 'a sealed offer' procedure to settle a Dispute. In simple terms, a sealed offer is a type of settlement offer that is made by one party (the 'offeror') to the other (the 'recipient'). It is made in such a way that if it is rejected by the recipient, and if the recipient is less successful in the arbitration than the terms proposed in the offer, then the recipient should be liable for the arbitration costs (including legal fees and expenses)[159] which the offeror should incur going forward as from the date the offer is rejected. The rationale for this result is that, as the offeror would not have incurred those arbitration costs had the recipient accepted the offer, the recipient should be made to bear them.[160] The ICC has adopted procedures designed to facilitate this procedure and to protect the confidentiality of a sealed offer until after an arbitral tribunal has decided the merits of the case.[161]

(4) Keeping settlement negotiations confidential

A practical difficulty with attempts at amicable settlement, including settlement offers (though now much less so with the sealed offer),[162] is how to preserve their confidentiality.[163] The relevant law or rules (relat-

159. The allocation of the costs of an arbitration is in the discretion of the arbitral tribunal (art. 38(5) of the ICC Arbitration Rules), which is likely to give weight to a sealed offer.
160. The technique of the use of the sealed offer in ICC arbitration is explained in Christopher R Seppälä, Paul Brumpton and Mariele Coulet-Diaz, 'The New Assistance ICC Provides to Protect the Confidentiality of a Sealed Offer', which also includes an example form of such offer. ICC Disp Resol Bull, Issue 1, 2017, 84.
161. *ICC Note to Parties and Arbitral Tribunals on the Conduct of the Arbitration under the ICC Rules of Arbitration* dated 1 January 2021, paras 267 et seq. A sealed offer needs to be drafted with care. *See*, before issue of the ICC's Note on the subject, the final award in ICC case 11499 (2003), ICC Int'l Ct Arb Bull, vol 19, no 2, 2008, 103-104 (commentary 68-69).
162. In view of the ICC's procedures described under *(3) Use of a sealed or 'Calderbank' offer* above.
163. Although the Contractor may claim that its settlement offer, if marked 'confidential', constitutes 'information' under the third paragraph of Sub-Clause 1.12 [*Confidentiality*] and therefore should enjoy protection under that Sub-Clause.

ing to legal privilege and professional confidentiality) vary from country to country, and there are few international rules on this subject.[164]

In certain common law countries, exchanges between the Parties during the course of amicable settlement discussions are generally regarded as 'without prejudice' and confidential and, with some exceptions, are inadmissible in any arbitration.[165] This rule is founded on public policy grounds with a view to encouraging open negotiations towards a resolution of disputes.[166] Accordingly, in those countries, to ensure the benefit of this privilege, it is customary to mark correspondence as 'without prejudice' or 'without prejudice and confidential', with the consequence – in certain common law countries – that it may not be disclosed to an arbitral tribunal or a judge in court proceedings.

However, different rules prevail in civil law countries. For example, in France, only settlement correspondence directly between French lawyers (*avocats*) is protected by a legal rule of confidentiality.[167]

Given the disparate legal situation internationally, before embarking on amicable settlement negotiations, Parties may be well advised to enter into a written agreement to protect the confidentiality of their communications.[168] Even with such an agreement in place, they may still be better off – as an inadvertent disclosure cannot be undone – in avoiding *written* communications about settlement as much as possible.

(iv) Improvements: To address the issue of confidentiality discussed above, the following could be usefully be added to Sub-Clause 21.5:

> All communications during amicable settlement discussions are confidential and shall be treated as made in the course of compromise and settlement negotiations for purposes of applicable rules of evidence

164. *See* art. 22(3) of the ICC Arbitration Rules and arts 9.2(b), 9.2(e) (commercial confidentiality), 9.4 and 9.5 of the *IBA Rules on the Taking of Evidence in International Arbitration*, 2020.
165. Dale S Brackin, 'Subclause 20.5 of the FIDIC Contracts and Amicable Dispute Resolution ("ADR")' [2006] ICLR, 442, 446-47.
166. *Ibid.*
167. Art. 66-5 of French law no 71-1130 of 31 December 1971, relating to the reform of certain judicial and legal professions, as amended.
168. *See* **(iv) Improvements** below.

and any additional confidentiality and professional secrecy protections provided by applicable law.[169]

--ooOOoo--

21.6 Arbitration

Unless settled amicably, and subject to Sub-Clause 3.7.5 [*Dissatisfaction with Engineer's determination*], Sub-Clause 21.4.4 [*Dissatisfaction with DAAB's decision*], Sub-Clause 21.7 [*Failure to Comply with DAAB's Decision*] and Sub-Clause 21.8 [No DAAB In Place], any Dispute in respect of which the DAAB's decision (if any) has not become final and binding shall be finally settled by international arbitration. Unless otherwise agreed by both Parties:

(a) the Dispute shall be finally settled under the Rules of Arbitration of the International Chamber of Commerce;
(b) the Dispute shall be settled by one or three arbitrators appointed in accordance with these Rules; and
(c) the arbitration shall be conducted in the ruling language defined in Sub-Clause 1.4 [*Law and Language*].

The arbitrator(s) shall have full power to open up, review and revise any certificate, determination (other than a final and binding determination), instruction, opinion or valuation of the Engineer, and any decision of the DAAB (other than a final and binding decision) relevant to the Dispute. Nothing shall disqualify the Engineer from being called as a witness and giving evidence before the arbitrator(s) on any matter whatsoever relevant to the Dispute.

169. This provision is based upon a clause recommended in the *IBA Guidelines for Drafting International Arbitration Clauses*, 2010, 33 (para. 94). Any confidentiality provision added to Sub-Clause 21.5 should also be made consistent with Sub-Clause 1.12 [*Confidentiality*].

In any award dealing with costs of the arbitration, the arbitrator(s) may take account of the extent (if any) to which a Party failed to co-operate with the other Party in constituting a DAAB under Sub-Clause 21.1 [*Constitution of the DAAB*] and/or Sub-Clause 21.2 [*Failure to Appoint DAAB Member(s)*].

Neither Party shall be limited in the proceedings before the arbitrator(s) to the evidence or arguments previously put before the DAAB to obtain its decision, or to the reasons for dissatisfaction given in the Party's NOD under Sub-Clause 21.4 [*Obtaining DAAB's Decision*]. Any decision of the DAAB shall be admissible in evidence in the arbitration.

Arbitration may be commenced before or after completion of the Works. The obligations of the Parties, the Engineer and the DAAB shall not be altered by reason of any arbitration being conducted during the progress of the Works.

If an award requires a payment of an amount by one Party to the other Party, this amount shall be immediately due and payable without any further certification or Notice.

Subject to Sub-Clauses 3.7.5, 21.4.4, 21.7 and 21.8, any Dispute which has not been settled amicably and in respect of which the DAAB's decision (if any) has not become final and binding shall be finally settled by international arbitration. Unless otherwise agreed by the Parties, the rules of arbitration, number of arbitrators and the language of arbitration are as provided in sub-paragraphs (a) to (c) of this Sub-Clause.

The arbitrators have full power to open up, review and revise any certificate, determination or a final and binding decision of the Engineer or the DAAB (other than a final and binding determination or decision) that is relevant to the Dispute. The Engineer may be called as a witness before the arbitrator(s). The arbitrator(s) are also empowered to take into account the extent of a Party's failure to cooperate in constituting a DAAB under Sub-Clauses 21.1 and/or 21.2 in their award on costs of the arbitration. In the arbitration neither Party is limited by the evidence or arguments put before the DAAB, or the reasons for dissatisfaction given in a NOD under Sub-Clause 21.4. Any decision of the DAAB is admissible as evidence in the arbitration.

Arbitration may be commenced before or after the completion of the Works. The obligations of the Parties, the Engineer and the DAAB shall not be altered by any arbitration being conducted during the progress of the Works. Any payment due under an arbitral award is immediately due and payable without any further certification or Notice.

Commentary

(i) Main Changes from RB/99:

(1) Unlike Sub-Clause 20.6 of RB/99, the first paragraph is qualified by reference to Sub-Clauses 3.7.5, 21.4.4, 21.7 and 21.8.
(2) The first paragraph provides that the Dispute shall be settled by one or three arbitrators, whereas RB/99 had provided for three arbitrators.
(3) The second paragraph now excludes both a final and binding determination of the Engineer and a final and binding decision of the DAAB from being opened up and revised.
(4) The third paragraph concerning an award dealing with costs of the arbitration is new.
(5) The last paragraph dealing with an award requiring a payment of an amount to a Party is new.

(ii) Related Clauses / Sub-Clauses: 1.2 [*Interpretation*], 1.4 [*Law and Language*], 3.7 [*Agreement or Determination*], 4.2.2 [*Performance Security – Claims under the Performance Security*], 14.11 [*Final Statement*], 14.12 [*Discharge*], 14.14 [*Cessation of Employer's Liability*], 20 [*Employer's and Contractor's Claims*] and 21 [*Disputes and Arbitration*].

(iii) Analysis: While from its title Sub-Clause 21.6 [*Arbitration*] may look like the Parties' arbitration agreement, in fact the Parties' agreement to submit to arbitration in RB/17 is more complicated and requires consideration of numerous other sub-clauses. Accordingly, it is necessary to examine this subject in some detail.

(1) The reference to arbitration[170]

If one disregards the 'subject to' provisions in the first sentence of this Sub-Clause, the sentence reads as follows:

170. *See also* **Section 5.7 Effect of an International Arbitration Clause** in **Chapter III Contract Interpretation** above. While it is not unusual for

> Unless settled amicably [...], any Dispute in respect of which the DAAB's decision (if any) has not become final and binding shall be finally settled by international arbitration.

It follows from this sentence that, as a general rule, the only matter that may be 'finally settled by international arbitration' is a 'Dispute' which has not been 'settled amicably' and which has been the subject of a 'DAAB's decision (if any) [that] has not become final and binding'. Thus, the Dispute must have been referred to the DAAB for decision, and *either*:

(1) if the DAAB had rendered a decision within 84 days, such decision had been the subject of a NOD within 28 days of receipt of the decision;[171] *or*
(2) if the DAAB had rendered no decision, such failure to do so had been the subject of a NOD within 28 days after such 84-day period had expired,[172]

as otherwise the DAAB's decision (if any) will have become final and binding.[173]

---

parties to incorporate by reference the General Conditions of the Red Book into a contract, this can give rise to a question about whether the dispute resolution provisions and specifically the provision for arbitration have been knowingly agreed to by the parties and therefore have been validly incorporated *unless specific reference to their incorporation is made in the contract document which they sign*. While the better view is that, when incorporating standard terms or general conditions into a contract, specific reference to an arbitration clause is unnecessary (Gary Born, *International Commercial Arbitration* (3rd edn, Kluwer L Int'l, the Netherlands, 2021) vol I, 887-888 (s 5.05 [B][3]), some courts have held that incorporating the General Conditions of the Red Book by reference, without specifically referring to the arbitration clause, does not bind the parties to that clause. This was the reported ruling of the Dubai Court of Cassation, the highest court in Dubai, in 2021 in relation to a contract based upon RB/87, *see* 'Dubai Cassation Court rules FIDIC arbitration clause not enforceable', published by Wasel & Wasel, litigation lawyers, 23 March 2021 https://waselandwasel.com/articles/dubai-cassation-court-rules-fidic-arbitration-clause-not-enforceable accessed 10 November 2022.

171. Sub-Clause 21.4.4.
172. *Ibid.* This assumes that the DAAB and the Parties had not agreed to an extension of such 84-day period, *see* Sub-Clause 21.4.3(b).
173. Sub-Clause 21.4.4, second, third and fourth paragraphs.

It is necessary then to address the 'subject to' provisions or the exceptions to the general rule that a Dispute which has not become the subject of a final and binding decision of a DAAB may be finally settled by international arbitration. Sub-Clause 3.7.5 is an exception because it provides that, where a Party has failed to comply with an agreement of the Parties under Sub-Clause 3.7 or a final and binding determination of the Engineer, the other Party may refer the failure itself directly to arbitration under Sub-Clause 21.6.[174] Sub-Clause 21.4.4 is an exception because it envisages that a Party may give a NOD with respect to parts only of a DAAB's decision in which case only those parts shall not be final and binding and be eligible for arbitration (whereas the remainder of the decision shall become final binding).[175] Sub-Clause 21.7 is an exception because it provides that where a Party fails to comply with a decision of the DAAB, whether binding or final and binding, the other Party may refer the failure itself directly to arbitration under that Sub-Clause.[176] Sub-Clause 21.8 is an exception because it provides that if there is no DAAB in place, whether by reason of the expiry of its appointment or otherwise, the Dispute may be referred by either Party directly to arbitration.

(2) No time limit to begin arbitration

While numerous time limits or time bars apply to Claims and Disputes, there is no contractual time limit within which a Party must commence arbitration after the 28-day period for amicable settlement provided for in Sub-Clause 21.5 has expired.[177] This is reasonable as a Party may have numerous Disputes with the other Party, which it may refer to the DAAB over a period of months or years as the Works progress. As the Disputes are likely to be referred to the DAAB over time, they will, unless settled earlier, emerge from the Sub-Clause 21 procedures and become referable to arbitration under Sub-Clause 21.6 at different times. As it will generally be much more efficient for a Party – usually the Contractor – to bring a single arbitration in relation to all Disputes under a contract rather than separate ones, piecemeal, for individual Disputes, it will normally wish to

174. Sub-Clause 3.7.5, last paragraph.
175. Sub-Clause 21.4.4, second, third and last paragraphs.
176. Sub-Clause 21.7, first paragraph.
177. A special pre-release version of YB/17 had provided in Sub-Clause 21.4.4 that, if neither Party commenced arbitration of a Dispute within 182 days after giving or receiving a NOD, the NOD would be deemed to have lapsed and no longer be valid. However, this provision was not retained in the Rainbow Suite issued in 2017.

wait to see to what extent its Disputes have been resolved satisfactorily by the DAAB or by amicable settlement before deciding whether the remainder justifies the time and expense of arbitration. For these reasons, it is sensible that there is no time limit within which a Party must commence arbitration, other than the limitation period provided for by applicable law.[178]

Even without a time limit within which a Party must commence arbitration if the time periods in Sub-Clause 3.7 and Clauses 20 and 21 are added up, it *may still take 12 months* from the giving of a Notice of Claim under Sub-Clause 20.2.1 until international arbitration of the corresponding Dispute may be commenced. This is illustrated in **Figure 15 Timeline for Claims for Time and/or Money**.

--ooOOoo--

178. Which, as discussed above, may already have been suspended by a reference of the Dispute to the DAAB. *See* Sub-Clause 21.4.1, last paragraph, and the commentary on this Sub-Clause above.

Figure 15 Timeline for Claims for Time and/or Money[1]

SC = Sub-Clause

N° of days for each step	Procedural Step	Cumulative n° of days from the 'event or circumstance' giving rise to a Claim
0	An 'event or circumstance' giving rise to a Claim occurs (SC 20.2)	0
28[2]	Notice of Claim (SC 20.2)	28
14	Engineer's Notice of objection, if any (SC 20.2.2)	42
84[3]	Submission of a fully detailed Claim (SC 20.2.4)	84
14	Engineer's Notice of objection, if any (SC 20.2.4)	98
84[4]	Engineer's determination (SC 3.7.2)	168
28	NOD with Engineer's determination (SC 3.7.5)	196
42	Referral of Dispute to DAAB (SC 21.4.1)	238 (i.e., around 8 months)
84	DAAB decision (SC 21.4.3)	322
28	NOD with DAAB Decision (SC 21.4.4)	350
28	Attempt at amicable settlement (SC 21.5)	378 (i.e., around 12 months)
---	ICC arbitration (SC 21.6)	378 and thereafter

Source: Author's own work.

Notes

1. This figure presents a simplified version of steps in the Conditions. Only the actual text of the relevant SC should be relied upon. For a more detailed figure on this subject, *see* Figure 13 Procedure for Claims for Time and/or Money – Detailed at the end of the commentary on Clause 20 above.
2. This period runs from the date when the claiming Party became aware, or should have become aware, of the event or circumstance giving rise to the Claim. *See* SC 20.2.1.
3. SC 20.2.4.
4. This period runs from the date the Engineer receives a fully detailed Claim (SC 3.7.3(c)(i)) and assumes no agreement has been reached in consultation with the Engineer pursuant to SC 3.7.1.

(3) ICC Rules of Arbitration

Unless otherwise agreed by the Parties, any Dispute must finally be settled under the ICC Rules of Arbitration.[179] A Party[180] may begin an ICC

179. Since the first edition of the Red Book, RB/57, it has provided for arbitration under the ICC Rules of Arbitration. However, as indicated in the *Guidance for the Preparation of Particular Conditions*, 51-52, nothing prevents the Parties from selecting other rules of international arbitration should they be preferred. The ICC Rules of Arbitration have been referred to in the RB primarily for three reasons:

    (1) they have been and remain the best known and most widely used rules of international arbitration, and an ICC arbitration may take place any where in the world;
    (2) because international arbitration is a specialised field, FIDIC has felt it desirable that the Red Book provide parties with a good, ready-made arbitration solution rather than leaving the space for arbitration rules blank, as the Parties may not know enough about arbitration to fill in the blank appropriately; and
    (3) providing a solution, such as the ICC Rules of Arbitration, limits the risk that a national or domestic system of arbitration is inserted, which may often be inappropriate in an international construction contract. For a recent commentary on the ICC Rules, *see* Thomas H. Webster and Michael W. Bühler, *Handbook of ICC Arbitration* (5th edn, Sweet & Maxwell, London, 2021).

180. If the Party bringing the arbitration is the Contractor and the Contractor is a JV then, since the JV is by definition (*see* Sub-Clause 1.1.46 '**Joint Venture**' or '**JV**'), not a legal entity, the members of the JV normally need to bring the arbitration collectively unless they have authorised a JV leader (*see* Sub-Clause 1.14 [*Joint and Several Liability*]) to do so on their behalf. This is because, as the Contract is between the Employer and the Contractor, the Employer has only consented to arbitrate with the Contractor, that is, the members of the JV who collectively comprise the JV. *See*, e.g., Matthias Scherer and Joachim Knoll, 'Switzerland: Standing of Consortium Members in Consortium Disputes with Third Parties' (2007) 2(3) C L Int 39 (citing art. 544 of the Swiss Code of Obligations). However, in some cases, a single member of a JV constituting the contractor has been found to have standing to bring an arbitration either on its own behalf for its share in the JV and/or on behalf of the JV for the JV's claim, against an employer, e.g., in the latter case on the basis of 'active solidarity' under the French (*see* art. 1311) and other civil codes. *See*, e.g., interim award in ICC case 5029 (1986). YB Comm Arb, vol XII, 1987, 113 (contract was based on RB/77); partial award in ICC case 9691 (2000) (unpublished) described (pp.

arbitration by submitting a Request for Arbitration, containing specified information, to the Secretariat of the International Court of Arbitration of the ICC.[181] Within 30 days from the receipt of the Request from the Secretariat, the respondent Party is required to submit an Answer, containing specified information, which must be accompanied by any counterclaims that the respondent may wish to assert.[182] Thereafter the claimant may submit a reply to any counterclaims within 30 days from the date of their receipt from the Secretariat.[183]

While it is not the purpose here to summarise the ICC Arbitration Rules, it is necessary to emphasise that an ICC arbitration is not an open-ended proceeding. Instead, it has a defined scope as provided for by both the 'Terms of Reference' ('TOR')[184] and a time limit for the arbitration.[185] The TOR must summarise the Parties' respective claims and requests for relief, effectively limiting what the arbitral tribunal may decide. Thus, Article 23(4) of the Rules provides that:

> After the Terms of Reference have been signed [...] no party shall make new claims which fall outside the limits of the Terms of Reference unless it has been authorized to do so by the arbitral tribunal, which shall consider the nature of such new claims, the stage of the arbitration and other relevant circumstances.

Furthermore, an arbitral tribunal must render its final award within 6 months from the date of the signature of the TOR, though this time limit may be extended – and often is – by the ICC Court.[186]

As the scope of an ICC arbitration is limited (though with some flexibility), and as it is generally most efficient to submit all Disputes under a

---

110-112) in Horacio Grigera Naón, *Choice-of-Law and Procedural Issues* (Collected Courses of the Hague Academy of International Law, 289, 2001), 39-178; and Howard M Holtzmann, 'Disputes Concerning the Termination of Joint Ventures: Lessons from Awards of the Iran – US Claims Tribunal' (1993) 9(1) Arb Int'l, 103.

181. Art. 4 of the ICC Arbitration Rules. The date the Request of Arbitration is received by the ICC Court's Secretariat is deemed, according to this art, to be the date of the commencement of the arbitration.
182. Art. 5 of the ICC Arbitration Rules.
183. Art. 5(6) of the ICC Arbitration Rules.
184. The TOR, which must normally be signed by the Parties and the arbitrators, are provided for by art. 23 of the ICC Arbitration Rules.
185. Provided for by art. 31 of the ICC Rules of Arbitration.
186. Art. 31 of the ICC Arbitration Rules.

Contract to a single, rather than multiple, arbitration(s), a Party will not ordinarily wish to start an arbitration until all (or practically all) of its Disputes have become referable to arbitration. Consequently, as previously mentioned,[187] a Party may wish to wait until all or nearly all of its Disputes have passed through the Clause 21 channel before deciding whether and when to begin arbitration.

In addition, the following special rules appended to the ICC Arbitration Rules may apply depending on the facts of each case:

(a) ICC's Emergency Arbitration Rules

Assuming the Parties' contract was concluded on or after 1 January 2012, the Emergency Arbitrator ('EA') Rules attached as Appendix V to the ICC Rules of Arbitration will apply.[188] Under these provisions, a Party that needs an urgent interim or conservatory measure which cannot await the constitution of an arbitral tribunal may apply for such a measure to the Secretariat of the ICC Court.[189] Under the EA Rules, the President of the ICC Court shall 'within as short a time as possible'[190] appoint an EA who may issue interim or provisional orders which are binding upon the Parties.[191]

187. *See (2) No time limit to begin arbitration* above under this **(iii) Analysis** commenting on Sub-Clause 21.6.
188. *See* art. 29.6 of the ICC Arbitration Rules. Before the 2021 version of the ICC Arbitration Rules, the 2012 version had provided (in art. 29.6(c)) that the EA Rules would not apply if the parties had agreed to another pre-arbitral procedure that provides for the granting of conservatory, interim or similar measures. Thus, they would not apply to FIDIC contracts as they provide for a DAB (now a 'DAAB') with the power to grant such measures. However, this prohibition on resort to the EA Rules was rarely applied or enforced by the ICC in practice and, regardless of the date of conclusion of an arbitration agreement, it is unlikely that the availability of another pre-arbitral procedure would in future block the application of the EA provisions.
189. Art. 29 of the ICC Arbitration Rules.
190. Normally within two days from receipt of the application. Art. 2 of the EA Rules.
191. Arts 2 and 6 of the EA Rules. These orders may be enforced by state courts. *See* Maxime Chevalier, 'Enforcement of Emergency Arbitrator Decisions: Dream or Reality? The French Perspective', (2021) 38 (6), J. Int'l Arb. 835.

While a DAB (now called a 'DAAB') also has the power to issue an interim or conservatory measure,[192] an emergency arbitrator is likely to be more effective. DAABs are often composed of engineers or construction consultants who, unlike qualified lawyers, may have no experience in granting such measures. Compared to a DAAB, an EA is also likely to be more active as it will have been appointed by the ICC expressly for the purpose of deciding whether to grant such relief. Furthermore, the EA's order may have more weight before an ICC arbitral tribunal as the EA will almost certainly be a lawyer who will, like the arbitrators themselves, have been appointed or confirmed by the ICC Court.

A potential difficulty with the EA Rules is that a Request for Arbitration must normally have been received by the ICC Secretariat within 10 days of its receipt of any Application for Emergency Measures.[193] While there is a provision for extension of the time period,[194] the requirement to file a Request for Arbitration within this time limit needs to be reconciled with the times required to fulfil the several conditions to arbitration in Clause 21.[195]

(b) ICC's Expedited Procedure Rules

Assuming the Parties' arbitration agreement was concluded on or after 1 March 2017, if the amount in dispute does not exceed USD 2,000,000 (or, if the arbitration agreement was concluded on or after 1 January 2021, USD 3,000,000), or if the Parties so agree, the Expedited Procedure Rules provided for in Appendix VI to the ICC Arbitration Rules may apply.[196]

192. DAAB Rules, Rule 5.1(j). Parties are also not prevented from applying to a court for interim or provisional measures. Art. 28 of the ICC Rules of Arbitration. However, a practical difficulty which they have sometimes encountered is that, whether inadvertently or not, by doing so they waive their arbitration clause. *See*, e.g., *Uzineexportimport Romanian Co v Attock Cement Co.* 1995 Rev arb 107 and final award in ICC case 10904 (2002), Jean-Jacques Arnaldez and others, *Coll of ICC Arb Awards* 2001-2007 (ICC, Paris / Kluwer, the Netherlands) 2009, 363. Great care must therefore be taken to avoid such waiver.
193. Art. 1(6) of the EA Rules.
194. The President of the ICC Court may extend the time period if the EA determines that a longer period is necessary. Art. 1(6) of Appendix V – EA Rules.
195. Such as the requirement first to refer a Dispute to the DAAB (Sub-Clause 21.4) and to allow time for amicable settlement (Sub-Clause 21.5).
196. *See* art. 30(2) of the ICC Arbitration Rules and art. 1(2) of Appendix VI – Expedited Procedure Rules thereto.

The Expedited Procedure Rules provide for a simplified arbitration procedure which is intended to apply to smaller disputes. Under these Rules: notwithstanding any contrary provision in the Parties' agreement, the ICC Court may appoint a sole arbitrator; there is no requirement for the arbitral tribunal to prepare the TOR pursuant to Article 23 of the ICC Arbitration Rules; and the arbitral tribunal may, after consulting the parties, decide the dispute solely on the basis of the documents submitted by the Parties.[197]

(4) Number of arbitrators, place and language of arbitration

The new Sub-Clause 21.6 provides that, unless the Parties agree otherwise, a Dispute shall be settled by 'one or three' arbitrators, which provides flexibility. Flexibility is necessary as Disputes may be very large and/or complex, justifying three arbitrators, or very small or straightforward, justifying a sole arbitrator.

If the Parties are unable to agree on the number of arbitrators, whether one or three, then the decision will be made by the ICC Court.[198] While the ICC Court has no fixed rules for determining the number of arbitrators, in practice, it rarely departs from appointing a sole arbitrator where the amount in dispute is below USD 5 million and would most likely appoint three arbitrators if the amount in dispute is above USD 30 million.[199] The amount in dispute is, of course, only one criterion that the ICC Court considers and it will weigh other criteria, such as the complexity of the dispute, as well.[200]

The *Guidance* specifies that, for major projects tendered internationally, 'it is desirable that the place of arbitration be situated in a country other than that of the Employer or Contractor'.[201] In this connection, there is no need to specify the place of arbitration in the Contract as, where the Parties do not do so, the ICC Court, which has a fund of knowledge and experience about different places of arbitration, will select a suitable

197. *See* arts 2 and 3 of Appendix VI – Expedited Procedure Rules of the ICC Arbitration Rules.
198. Art. 12(2) of the ICC Arbitration Rules. As regards the selection of arbitrators, *see* Christopher R Seppälä, 'Obtaining the Right International Arbitral Tribunal: A Practitioner's View' [2008] ICLR 198.
199. *Construction Industry Arbitrations: Recommended Tools and Techniques for Effective Management, 2019 Update* (ICC Commission Report), ICC Disp Resol Bull, 2018, Issue 4, 88, 99 (para. 2.2).
200. *Ibid.*, 100 (para. 2.2).
201. *Guidance for the Preparation of Particular Conditions*, 52.

place which is neutral as between the Parties.[202] The place of arbitration should also be a country which has a modern, liberal arbitration law (such as one based on the UNCITRAL *Model Law on International Commercial Arbitration*, 1985, amended in 2006) and which has ratified a bilateral or multilateral convention (such as the 1958 *New York Convention on the Recognition and Enforcement of Foreign Arbitral Awards*), or both, that facilitates the enforcement of arbitral awards. When selecting a place for arbitration, the ICC Court will take these matters into account, as well as neutrality, the geographic convenience and accessibility of the place of arbitration to all Parties and their counsel, and suitable facilities for arbitration, such as reliable arbitration hearing rooms of hotels.[203]

As the new Sub-Clause provides, the language of the arbitration will normally be the language for communications defined in Sub-Clause 1.4. If there is uncertainty about the language, it will be determined by the arbitral tribunal.[204]

(5) Scope of the arbitration[205]

(a) 'The arbitrator(s) shall have full power to open up, review and revise any certificate, determination (other than a final and binding determination), instruction, opinion or valuation of the Engineer, and any decision of the DAAB (other than a final and binding decision) relevant to the Dispute.'

It follows from this language that the arbitrator(s) is (are) bound neither by any action or determination of the Engineer, other than a final and

202. Jason Fry and others, *The Secretariat's Guide to ICC Arbitration* (ICC, Paris, 2012) (ICC Publication 729E), 202-203 (paras 3-685-3-687). The World Bank's COPA expressly requires that, if the Contract is with foreign contractors, the place of arbitration shall normally be a neutral location. Sub-Clause 21.6, COPA.

203. Jason Fry and others, *The Secretariat's Guide to ICC Arbitration* (ICC, Paris, 2012) (ICC Publication no 729E), 202-203 (paras 3-685-3-687). For popular places of arbitration, *see (2) Places of arbitration* under **(iv) Related Law** below of this commentary on Sub-Clause 21.6.

204. Art. 20 of the ICC Arbitration Rules.

205. For how international arbitrators may interpret a FIDIC contract, *see* **Section 5.7 Effect of an International Arbitration Clause** in **Chapter III Contract Interpretation** above.

binding determination under Sub-Clause 3.7.5,[206] nor by any decision of the DAAB, other than a final and binding decision under Sub-Clause 21.4.4. On the other hand, the arbitrator(s) has (have) no power to open up an agreement of the Parties under Sub-Clause 3.7.

With these exceptions or qualifications, the arbitrator(s) is (are) at liberty to decide any Dispute as the arbitrator(s) sees (see) fit, de novo, that is, regardless of whatever the Engineer or the DAAB may have decided.[207]

(b) 'Nothing shall disqualify the Engineer from being called as a witness and giving evidence before the arbitrator(s) on any matter whatsoever relevant to the Dispute.'

In any arbitration, the Engineer may be an important witness, as the Engineer administers the Contract on the Employer's behalf so as to ensure that the Works are properly carried out.[208] Thus, the Engineer may be called upon to explain any instructions given under Sub-Clause 3.5 or determinations made under Sub-Clause 3.7.2.

---

206. Thus, to take some examples, any Taking-Over Certificate, IPC or Performance Certificate issued by the Engineer may be opened up, reviewed and revised by an arbitral tribunal.
207. However, the arbitrator(s) is (are) empowered solely to settle Disputes and not to alter the Parties' basic rights and obligations in the Contract. Indeed, the arbitrators are limited by what the Contract provides. Thus, for example, Sub-Clause 8.5 provides that, when determining each EOT, the Engineer shall review previous determinations under Sub-Clause 3.7 and may increase, but shall not decrease, the total EOT. Similarly, when reviewing the Engineer's determinations under that Sub-Clause, the arbitrators should have no more power than the Engineer. They may increase but may not decrease the total EOT. *See (3) Engineer's review of previous determinations* under **(iii) Analysis** of the commentary on Sub-Clause 8.5 [*Extension of Time for Completion*] above.
208. *FIDIC Procurement Procedures Guide* (FIDIC, 2011) 33-34. The Engineer may not normally be made a party to the arbitration as it has not agreed to arbitrate with the Employer and the Contractor. When, in a case involving RB/87, a Contractor had sought to bring the Engineer into an arbitration with the Employer, the ICC Court dismissed the case under art. 6(4) the ICC Arbitration Rules, finding no prima facie arbitration agreement among the three of them. ICC case 19426 described in Gustavo Scheffer da Silveira, *Les Modes de Règlement des Différends Dans Les Contrats Internationaux de Construction* (Bruylant, Brussels, 2019) 465-467 (para. 446).

On the other hand, members of the DAAB are prohibited from acting 'in any [...] arbitral capacity in relation to the Contract'.[209] Their primary role, in addition to dispute avoidance, is to decide Disputes referred to them and, unlike the Engineer, they are much less likely to have first-hand knowledge of the execution of the Works.

(c) 'In any award dealing with costs of the arbitration, the arbitrator(s) may take account of the extent (if any) to which a Party failed to cooperate with the other Party in constituting a DAAB [...].'

This new provision is designed to induce Parties to cooperate in the constitution of the DAAB,[210] as under RB/99 there had been numerous cases in which a Party had sought by various means to delay or prevent a DAAB from being formed.[211] However, the actual cost of DAAB proceedings is not recoverable as arbitration costs under the ICC Rules.[212]

(d) 'Neither Party shall be limited in the proceedings before the arbitrator(s) to the evidence or arguments previously put before the DAAB [...] or to the reasons for dissatisfaction given in the Party's NOD [...].'

The principle here is that in arbitration each Party is entirely free to present new arguments or evidence in relation to Disputes which have passed through the Contract's Claims and Disputes procedures. It is in no way limited by the evidence or contractual or legal arguments presented to the DAAB pursuant to Sub-Clause 21.4. *A fortiori*, it is in no way limited by what it may have said earlier to the Engineer under Sub-Clause 3.7 or in its NOD under Sub-Clause 3.7.5. In arbitration, the Parties will

209. DAAB GCs, Sub-Clause 4.1(d). Moreover, while Sub-Clause 21.6 provides that nothing shall disqualify the Engineer from being called as a witness in any arbitration, the same is not stated as regards a DAAB member, which may imply no right to call such a member as a witness in an arbitration.
210. The Parties are obliged by Sub-Clause 6.2 of the DAAB GCs to cooperate in the constitution of the DAAB 'without delay'.
211. *See*, for example, interim award, ICC case 16155 (2010), and final award, ICC case 18505 (2013), reported in ICC Disp Resol Bull 2015 – Issue 1, 71 and 137, respectively (commentary 21, 29). *See also* the Swiss Federal Court's decision 4A_124/2014 of 7 July 2014, ASA Bull 4/2014, 826.
212. In ICC case 20632 (2016), while awarding arbitration costs pursuant to the ICC Arbitration Rules, the arbitral tribunal by its final award (so far unpublished) denied the award of DAB-related costs, such as counsel fees, under a FIDIC contract finding no ground to conclude otherwise in the rules applicable to the DAB.

normally be represented by lawyers, while this may not have been so before the DAAB. Accordingly, contractual and/or legal arguments and evidence that may not have been presented earlier may be presented for the first time in arbitration.

A Party may also, at the arbitration stage, change the amount or quantum of a Claim, so long as the Dispute has not changed.[213]

(e) 'Any decision of the DAAB shall be admissible in evidence in the arbitration.'

As a DAAB will consist of construction professionals or lawyers who are independent of the Parties, who have been chosen with their consent, and who are familiar with the project, its decisions may well be instructive. Consequently, they are admissible in arbitration.[214]

(f) 'Arbitration may be commenced before or after completion of the Works. The obligations of the Parties, the Engineer and the DAAB shall not be altered by reason of any arbitration [...].'

Under early editions of the RB, the Contractor was not entitled to commence arbitration until after completion or alleged completion of the

213. As mentioned earlier (*see* in the commentary above on Sub-Clause 21.4 [*Obtaining DAAB's Decision*], **(iii) Analysis** *(3) Importance of the Dispute*, the jurisdiction of the arbitrators is limited to the Disputes which have been previously referred to the DAAB and otherwise satisfied the conditions in Clause 21.

214. It is sometimes argued that the Party who is dissatisfied with and challenges a DAAB decision has the burden of proof in arbitration to show that the decision is wrong. However, the two proceedings are not comparable. The DAAB provides relatively quick, rough and ready justice, whereas an arbitration is a thorough, often lengthy, legal proceeding, like a court action. The arbitrators have full power to open up, review and revise any decision of the DAAB and to decide the Dispute anew, just as if there had been no prior decision of the DAAB. Accordingly, while the DAAB decision is binding on the Parties until overturned, once it has been the subject of a NOD and been referred to arbitration, it should be entitled to no special deference nor affect allocation of the burden of proof. Final award, ICC case 24400 (2022) (so far unpublished) in relation to a modified version of RB/87 commenting that reversing the burden of proof 'would suggest that this arbitration is an appeal from the DRE's decision, but that is not the mechanism that was agreed between the Parties'.
This also appears to be the position in the case of an adjudicator's decision in the United Kingdom. *City Inn Ltd v Shepherd Construction Ltd 2002 S.L.T.* 781 [para. 59] (Lord MacFadyen).

Works except in very limited instances.[215] This restriction was lifted in RB/77 and, since then, either Party has been free to commence arbitration at any time once the conditions precedent to arbitration have been satisfied.[216]

At the same time, this Sub-Clause confirms that the obligations of the Parties, the Engineer and the DAAB shall not be altered by reason of any arbitration being conducted during the progress of the Works. All must perform their duties unaffected by the existence of an arbitration. This bears emphasising because it may be difficult for a Contractor and an Employer to engage in an arbitration while the Works are being executed as both activities are likely to require attention from the same management and supervisory personnel of the Parties. For this reason, among others, Contractors, who will usually be the claimants, tend to wait until near or after completion of the Works before beginning an arbitration.

> (g) *'If an award requires a payment […], this amount shall be immediately due and payable without any further certification or Notice.'*

This provision appears to have been included only for informational purposes as it is superfluous given the ICC Arbitration Rules.[217]

(6) Direct arbitration

In the normal case – which may be referred to here as case (1) – a Party will be expected to have referred any Dispute to the DAAB pursuant to Sub-Clause 21.4 and to have complied with Sub-Clause 21.5 [*Amicable Settlement*] before submitting it to arbitration under Sub-Clause 21.6 [*Arbitration*]. However, in four other cases, a Party may refer an issue or Dispute to arbitration directly without complying with those provisions. These additional cases are as follows:

---

215. *See* Clause 67 [*Settlement of Disputes – Arbitration*] of RB/57 and RB/69.
216. Christopher R Seppälä, 'The Arbitration Clause in FIDIC Contracts for Major Works' [2005] ICLR 4, 11-12.
217. Art. 35(6) of the ICC Arbitration Rules provides that:

> Every award shall be binding on the parties. By submitting the dispute to arbitration under the [ICC] Rules, the parties undertake to carry out any award without delay […].

(2) where a Party fails to comply with an agreement of the Parties under Sub-Clause 3.7.4, the other Party may, without prejudice to its rights, refer 'the failure itself' directly to arbitration;[218]
(3) where a Party fails to comply with a final and binding determination of the Engineer under Sub-Clause 3.7.5, the other Party may also, without prejudice to its rights, refer 'the failure itself' directly to arbitration;[219]
(4) where a Party fails to comply with any decision of the DAAB, whether binding or final and binding, then the other Party may, without prejudice to its rights, refer 'the failure itself' directly to arbitration;[220] and
(5) where there is no DAAB in place, or being constituted, whether by reason of the expiry of the DAAB's appointment or otherwise, then either Party may, without prejudice to its rights, refer a Dispute directly to arbitration.[221]

In cases (2), (3) and (4), the scope of the arbitration is, in principle, limited to addressing 'the failure' to comply with the agreement, final and binding determination of the Engineer or decision of the DAAB, whether binding or final and binding.[222] In these cases, the first and third paragraphs of Sub-Clause 21.7 will apply,[223] which generally provide that the arbitral tribunal shall have the power, by way of summary or other expedited procedure, to order the enforcement of the agreement, Engineer's determination, or decision of the DAAB,[224] and to award damages or other relief.[225]

218. Sub-Clause 3.7.5, last paragraph.
219. *Ibid.*
220. Sub-Clause 21.7, first paragraph. The second paragraph then provides that, in the case of a binding but not final decision of the DAAB, any interim or provisional measure or award is subject to the express reservation that the rights of the Parties as to the merits of the Dispute are reserved until they are resolved by an award.
221. Sub-Clause 21.8.
222. Nothing prevents the Parties, however, from broadening the arbitral tribunal's jurisdiction should they agree to do so.
223. *See* Sub-Clause 3.7.5, last paragraph, and Sub-Clause 21.7, first paragraph.
224. *See* under **(iii) Analysis** of the commentary on Sub-Clause 21.7 [*Failure to Comply with DAAB's Decision*] below.
225. In these cases, where the amount in dispute does not exceed the threshold (USD 2,000,000 or USD 3,000,000 depending on the case), resort to the ICC's Expedited Procedure Rules (*see under (3) ICC Rules of Arbitration –*

There is no limitation on the arbitral tribunal's jurisdiction in case (5), and the Dispute may be referred directly to arbitration and be addressed in an ordinary way by an ICC arbitral tribunal. *See* **Figure 16 Paths to ICC Arbitration.**

--ooOOoo--

Figure 16 Paths to ICC Arbitration[1]

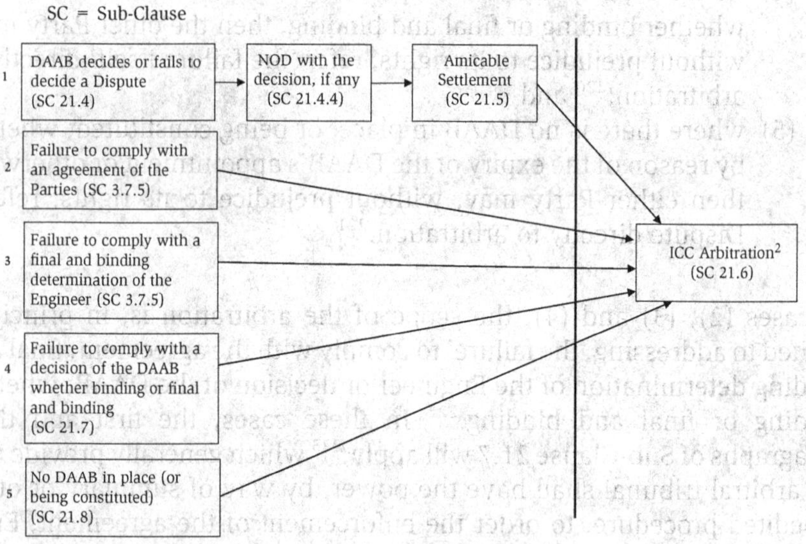

Source: Author's own work.

Notes

1. This figure is a simplified presentation of the paths to ICC Arbitration. Only the text of the Clauses of the General Conditions referred to should be relied upon. *See also* Figure 14 The DAAB's Two Functions in the commentary on SC 21.2 and Figure 15 Timeline for Claims for Time and/or Money above in this commentary on SC 21.6.
2. In addition, where one Party is a State, or a subdivision or agency of a State, there may be the possibility of an arbitration under the ICSID Convention, *see* under *(7) ICSID investment arbitration* immediately following this figure.

(7) ICSID investment arbitration

Where a construction contract is entered into between a State (or a constituent subdivision or agency of a State), which has ratified the 1965 *Convention on the Settlement of Investment Disputes Between States and*

(b) ICC's Expedited Procedure Rules under **(iii) Analysis** of this commentary on Sub-Clause 21.6 above) may be particularly appropriate.

Nationals of Other States (the 'ICSID Convention'),[226] and a Contractor from another State which has ratified the ICSID Convention, there may be a possibility for either Party to bring in arbitration under that treaty.[227] Such an arbitration may be possible where the State (or subdivision or agency) has consented to ICSID arbitration with the Contractor either by an arbitration clause or by national investment legislation or a multilateral or bilateral investment treaty.[228] A significant advantage of an ICSID arbitration, as compared to a non-ICSID international arbitration, is that an *ICSID award is more readily enforceable against a contracting State than other types of arbitration awards. This is because, under the ICSID Convention, each contracting State is required to recognise an award as binding, and to enforce it as if it were a final judgment of the State's highest court.*[229]

Thus, for example, a Contractor might bring an ICSID investment arbitration under national investment legislation or an investment treaty providing for ICSID investment arbitration if it could claim a violation of rights guaranteed under one of these instruments.[230] These rights commonly relate to matters such as: fair and equitable treatment, most favoured nation treatment, national treatment, full protection and security, compensation for expropriations and free transfer of payments and returns on investment.

It is not feasible here to comment further on ICSID investment arbitration. Instead, the purpose is merely to draw attention to the fact that, in special circumstances, ICSID investment arbitration may be available as an option for the resolution of disputes under a FIDIC Contract.

226. The ICSID Convention has been ratified by approximately 150 States. *See* https://icsid.worldbank.org/about/member-states/database-of-member-states (please consult the tab 'Contracting States Only') accessed 10 November 2022.
227. Both Parties are required by Sub-Clause 1.13 to comply with all applicable Laws and **'Laws'** are defined in Sub-Clause 1.1.49 to include treaties and international law.
228. These are more than 2,500 reported bilateral and multilateral investment treaties in force today.
229. Art. 54 of the ICSID Convention.
230. This right is in addition to the right to bring an ICC arbitration under Clause 21.

(8) Sovereign immunity

A State or a State entity may seek to rely on its immunity from jurisdiction[231] to challenge an arbitral tribunal's jurisdiction, or on its immunity from execution,[232] to oppose the enforcement of an award that has been rendered against it. However, under French laws and the laws of numerous other countries, a State, when it agrees to an arbitration clause in a contract, is deemed to have waived its immunity from jurisdiction and, therefore, may not rely on this immunity to challenge the arbitral tribunal's jurisdiction.[233] One way to prevent States and State entities from relying upon their sovereign immunities is to include a waiver of immunity clause in the Contract.[234]

(iv) Related Law: The law relating to the international arbitration of construction disputes is well beyond the scope of this book.[235] However, a few points may be noted.

(1) Arbitration law

Unlike a DAAB (or DAB) proceeding, an arbitration proceeding is usually carried out pursuant to a country's specific statute or law dealing with arbitration. This will normally be the statute or law of the country where the arbitration has its seat or place. This law will govern the arbitration proceedings[236] and determine the 'nationality' of any arbitration award, which may be important when, among other things, it comes to its

231. Based on the legal theory of sovereign community.
232. *Ibid.*
233. Christophe Seraglini and Jérôme Ortscheidt, *Droit de l'arbitrage interne et international* (2nd edn, LGDJ, Issy-les Moulineaux, 2019) 645-648 (para. 678). Immunity from execution is a separate issue and not so easily waived.
234. For example, ICSID proposes the following model clause: 'The Host State hereby waives any right of sovereign immunity as to it and its property in respect of the enforcement and execution of any award rendered by an Arbitral Tribunal constituted pursuant to this agreement', http://icsidfiles.worldbank.org/icsid/icsid/staticfiles/model-clauses-en/15.htm accessed 10 November 2022. The validity and scope of application of such a waiver will depend on applicable law.
235. For information on this subject *see* John W Hinchey and Troy L Harris, *International Construction Arbitration Handbook*, vols 1 and 2 (Thomson Reuters, 2021), for a US perspective, and Jane Jenkins, *International Construction Arbitration Law* (3rd revised edn, Kluwer L Int'l, the Netherlands, 2021), for an English perspective.
236. The mandatory rules and public policy requirements of the law of the place of arbitration will govern the proceedings. Nigel Blackaby and Constantine

enforcement.[237] This law is to be distinguished from the law which governs the Contract and which determines, among other things, how the Contract is to be interpreted.[238]

A useful indication of whether a country's arbitration law meets international standards is whether it is based on (or similar to) the UNCITRAL Model Law on International Commercial Arbitration 1985, as amended in 2006, a highly respected model law. The arbitration laws of some 80 States are based on (or similar to) the UNCITRAL Model Law.[239]

(2) Places of arbitration

The top five countries selected as places of arbitration according to the ICC's statistics are (in the order of their importance): Switzerland, France, United States, United Kingdom and Brazil.[240] Other popular places include the UAE and Singapore.

(3) International contract principles: damages

The UNIDROIT Principles, which may be relevant in various ways to a FIDIC Contract,[241] include in Chapter 7 (Non-Performance) a useful Section 4 on damages. Of relevance to construction contracts is the provision that compensation is only due for harm, including future harm, that 'is established with a reasonable degree of certainty',[242] and that, where the amount of damages cannot be established with a sufficient degree of certainty, 'the assessment is at the discretion of the court'.[243]

The UNIDROIT Principles further provide that damages are to be assessed 'either in the currency in which the monetary obligation was expressed, or in the currency in which the harm was suffered, whichever

Partasides, *Redfern and Hunter on International Arbitration* (6th edn, Kluwer L Int'l, the Netherlands, 2015) 353-354 (para. 6.02).

237. *See* art. V.1 of the *Convention on the Recognition and Enforcement of Foreign Arbitral Awards*, New York, 1958.
238. *See* the commentary on Sub-Clause 1.4 [*Law and Language*] above.
239. *See* United Nations Commission on International Trade Law http://www.uncitral.org/uncitral/en/uncitral_texts/arbitration/1985Model_arbitration_status.html accessed 10 November 2022.
240. ICC Disp Resol Bull, 2020, Statistics, 16.
241. *See* **Section 7 International Legal Principles – 7.4 Relevance to a FIDIC Contract** of **Chapter II Applicable Law** above.
242. Art. 7.4.3 (*Certainty of harm*) (1).
243. Art. 7.4.3 (*Certainty of harm*) (3).

is more appropriate'.[244] Thus, where a Party is claiming damages, the damages do not necessarily need to be expressed in the currencies for payment provided for by the Contract.[245]

(4) International arbitration procedure

In international arbitration, the procedure of the arbitration is frequently said to be 'guided' – though not necessarily governed – by the *IBA Rules on the Taking of Evidence in International Arbitration*.[246] Generally, arbitrator(s) no longer look to the procedural law of the place of arbitration except in the relatively rare cases – at least in the popular places for arbitration – where it contains mandatory provisions.[247] An alternative to the *IBA Rules* is the *Rules on the Efficient Conduct of Proceedings in International Arbitration* (the '*Prague Rules*') launched in Prague in 2018.

(5) International arbitration conventions

Two of the most important international conventions dealing with arbitration are the 1958 *New York Convention on the Recognition and Enforcement of Foreign Arbitral Awards* (the 'NY Convention') and, as mentioned above, the 1965 *Convention on the Settlement of Investment Disputes Between States and Nationals of Other States* (the 'ICSID Convention').

244. Art. 7.4.12 (*Currency in which to assess damages*). Assuming interest is payable, the rate of interest should normally be appropriate to the currency of the judgment or damages awarded. Michael Howard and others, *Foreign Currency Claims, Judgements and Damages* (Informa Law, Abingdon, Oxford, 2016) 270-271 (para. 12.31). This normal rule is reflected in art. 7.4.9(2) (*Interest for failure to pay money*) of the UNIDROIT Principles, which provides that the rate of interest shall be the one applicable to the 'currency of payment'. An exceptional case might be where the claimant was forced to borrow replacement funds in another currency from the currency of account of the contract, having another borrowing rate. Michael Howard and others (as above) 270 (para. 12.31) citing the English case *Helming Schiffahrts GMBH v Malta Drydocks Corporation* [1977] 2 Lloyds Reports 5.
245. *See* the commentary under Sub-Clause 14.15 [*Currencies of Payment*] above and especially the discussion of *Lesotho Highlands Development Authority v Impregilio SpA* [2005] BLR 351 under **(iv) Related law**.
246. The latest edition being 2020.
247. *See* art. 19 of the ICC Arbitration Rules which does not require reference to be made to the rules of procedure of any national law, whether of the place of arbitration or elsewhere.

The NY Convention is important both because it has been ratified by over 150 States including all major trading nations and because by it the contracting States must: (1) recognise and give effect to arbitration agreements (Article II) and (2) recognise and facilitate the enforcement of foreign arbitral awards (Articles III through VI).

(6) International arbitration practice

The ICC has published extracts of a number of awards relating to FIDIC contracts together with commentaries on them.[248] A source of practical information is an ICC Commission Report entitled '*Construction Industry Arbitrations: Recommended Tools and Techniques for Effective Management, 2019 Update*'.[249]

(v) Improvements:

(1) In the case of many arbitrations under FIDIC forms, an issue has been raised over whether, before arbitration, the Claimant had satisfied all the conditions precedent to arbitration provided for by the Conditions, e.g., whether there was a dispute (a 'Dispute' in RB/17) over the matter submitted to arbitration and, if so, whether it had been referred to the Engineer or DAB or DAAB

248. A first series of extracts from ICC awards dealing with construction contracts based on a FIDIC form was published in vol 2, no 1 of the ICC Int'l Ct Arb Bull in 1991. This was not accompanied by a commentary. A second series was published in vol 9, nos 1 and 2 in 1998, a third in vol 19, no 2 in 2008, a fourth in vol 23, no 2 in 2012, a fifth in vol 24, no 2 in 2013 (in each case of the ICC Int'l Ct Arb Bull) and a sixth (dealing with Dispute Adjudication Boards) in ICC Disp Resol Bull, 2015 – Issue 1, in most cases accompanied by a commentary of the present author. They can all be found in the ICC Dispute Resolution Library https://iccwbo.org/dispute-resolution-services/professional-development/icc-dispute-resolution-library/ accessed 10 November 2022. For other ICC awards dealing with the FIDIC contracts, *see*, e.g.: (i) *Coll of ICC Arb Awards, 1974-85* (vol I), *1986-90* (vol II), *1991-95* (vol III), *1996-2000* (vol IV), *2001-2007* (vol V), *2008-2011* (vol VI) and *2012-2015* (vol VII), prepared by different editors and co-published by the ICC, Paris and Kluwer Law, the Netherlands; (ii) The International Construction Law Review ('ICLR'), vols 1 to 3 (1983-86) and vol 6 (1989), published by Lloyds of London Press (now Informa UK Ltd); and (iii) the YB Comm Arb, published annually by ICCA/Kluwer, the Netherlands.

249. Published in the ICC Disp Resol Bull, 2018, Issue 4, 86. Among other things, this Report contains a list of considerations for dealing with the common question of whether to 'split a case', i.e., bifurcate the proceeding, *see* 91.

and, if so, whether the mandatory period for amicable settlement before arbitration had been respected.[250] This, in turn, has given rise to the question of what sanction should apply to a claimant in an arbitration who has failed to satisfy a condition precedent to arbitration and, in this connection, different ones have been imposed.[251] Accordingly, it could be helpful for Parties to indicate in the Conditions how this sort of question should be resolved.

---

250. *See* partial award, ICC cases 6238 (1989), and final award, ICC case 6535 (1992), ICC Int'l Ct Arb Bull, vol 9, no 2, November 1998, 48-49 and 60-61, respectively (commentary on the two cases 32, 34-35). *See also* partial award, ICC case 16262 (2010), ICC Disp Resol Bull 2015 – Issue 1, 75 (commentary 31).

251. *See*, e.g., Section II, *What Sanction for Failure to Refer to a DB?* in the author's 'Recent Case Law on Dispute Boards' constituting Chapter 12 of Filip De Ly and Paul-A Gelinas (eds), *Dispute Prevention and Settlement Through Expert Determination and Dispute Boards*, ICC, Paris (ICC Publication no 792E) 2017, 116, 118. At least three sanctions are possible: dismissal of the arbitration for lack of jurisdiction (or, more often today, as inadmissible – *see* fn. 88 of this commentary on Clause 21), suspension of the arbitration for a limited period to allow the condition precedent to be fulfilled and/or damages for breach of contract. For an interesting article discussing these sanctions or remedies, *see* Milivoje Mitrovic, 'Dealing with the Consequences of Non-compliance with Mandatory Pre-arbitral Requirements in Multi-Tiered Dispute Resolution Clauses: The Swiss Approach and a Look Across the Border' (2019) 37(3) ASA Bull, 559. Ordinarily, at least from a Swiss law perspective, the sanction should be dismissal, without prejudice, this author has explained as he:

> doubts whether a suspension of arbitral proceedings has a sufficient disciplinary effect on parties so as to fully satisfy the Swiss Federal Supreme Court's aspiration that 'non-compliance with prearbitral tiers should be sanctioned in one way or another'. *'If a party initiates arbitration before the completion of pre-arbitral steps, a stay of arbitral proceedings will only oblige it to comply with what it bound itself to in the first place.* Leaning on German and France jurisprudence, the admissibility approach should be favoured from this point of view as well despite the potential far-reaching consequences in terms of additional costs and prolongation of the proceedings. *If a party risks having its claim dismissed, an admissibility approach might deter parties more and avoid non-compliance with pre-arbitral tiers at the outset. Parties, thus, have more incentives to actively participate in the dispute resolution procedure they envisaged at the time of contract conclusion and which they deemed appropriate to resolve their issues.'* [Emphasis added]

(2) While the issue is referred to in the *Guidance for the Preparation of Particular Conditions*,[252] Parties should consider addressing in the Sub-Clause the issue of whether the rules relating to currencies of payment in Sub-Clause 14.15 should apply to an amount payable under an arbitration award, as discussed under **(iv) Related law** in relation to the *Lesotho* case in the commentary on that Sub-Clause.

--ooOOoo--

21.7 Failure to Comply with DAAB's Decision

In the event that a Party fails to comply with any decision of the DAAB, whether binding or final and binding, then the other Party may, without prejudice to any other rights it may have, refer the failure itself directly to arbitration under Sub-Clause 21.6 [*Arbitration*] in which case Sub-Clause 21.4 [*Obtaining DAAB's Decision*] and Sub-Clause 21.5 [*Amicable Settlement*] shall not apply to this reference. The arbitral tribunal (constituted under Sub-Clause 21.6 [*Arbitration*]) shall have the power, by way of summary or other expedited procedure, to order, whether by an interim or provisional measure or an award (as may be appropriate under applicable law or otherwise), the enforcement of that decision.

In the case of a binding but not final decision of the DAAB, such interim or provisional measure or award shall be subject to the express reservation that the rights of the Parties as to the merits of the Dispute are reserved until they are resolved by an award.

Any interim or provisional measure or award enforcing a decision of the DAAB which has not been

Milivoje Mitrovic, 'Dealing with the Consequences of Non-compliance with Mandatory Pre-arbitral Requirements in Multi-Tiered Dispute Resolution Clauses. The Swiss Approach and a Look Across the Border' (2019) 37(3) ASA Bull, 559, 577-578. For discussion of the admissibility approach, *see* fn. 88 above in this commentary on Clause 21.

252. On page 52.

complied with, whether such decision is binding or final and binding, may also include an order or award of damages or other relief.

A Party's failure to comply with any binding or final and binding decision of the DAAB may itself be referred directly to arbitration under Sub-Clause 21.6. Sub-Clauses 21.4 and 21.5 shall not apply to such reference. The arbitral tribunal may enforce such a decision by an interim or provisional measure or an award. If the decision is binding but not final, such enforcement shall be subject to the reservation that the rights of the Parties as to the merits are reserved. Any interim measure or award may order damages or other relief.

Commentary

(i) Main Changes from RB/99:

(1) Unlike Sub-Clause 20.7 of RB/99, it is now specified in the first paragraph that it applies to a decision of the DAAB[253] 'whether binding or final and binding'.
(2) In the first paragraph, the last sentence relating to the power of the arbitral tribunal is new.
(3) The second and third paragraphs are new.

(ii) Related Clauses / Sub-Clauses: 3.7.5 [*Agreement or Determination – Dissatisfaction with Engineer's Determination*] and 21 [*Disputes and Arbitration*].

(iii) Analysis: Sub-Clause 20.7 of RB/99 had only expressly addressed the situation of where a Party had failed to comply with a final and binding decision of the DAB, i.e., where neither Party had given a NOD with the DAB's decision. The Sub-Clause had provided that, in that case, the other Party might then, without prejudice to its rights, refer the failure itself directly to arbitration, without having to request a new decision from the DAB, pursuant to Sub-Clause 20.4, or attempt amicable settlement, pursuant to Sub-Clause 20.5. Sub-Clause 20.7 had not addressed expressly the situation where a Party had failed to comply with a binding but not final decision of the DAB, i.e., where a Party had given a NOD in

253. Instead of a DAB.

relation to it. Consequently, some authors[254] argued, and tribunals concluded, that there was no immediate means for an aggrieved Party to enforce a DAB decision that was merely binding and not final and binding.

While their view was understandable given the literal wording of Sub-Clause 20.7, the Sub-Clause was not intended to be interpreted in this way,[255] and the Singapore courts, among others, have recognised this.[256]

The new Sub-Clause has eliminated any difficulty in this respect, as it provides for the enforceability of any decision of the DAAB 'whether binding or final and binding'. It also empowers the arbitral tribunal to order enforcement 'by way of summary or other expedited procedure' and to do so by an interim or provisional measure or an award, as may be appropriate under applicable law or otherwise (e.g., under any rules applicable to the arbitration).[257] This gives an arbitral tribunal broad power to enforce – indeed, it should specifically enforce – decisions of the DAAB.[258]

---

254. Notably, Nael G Bunni, 'The Gap in Sub-Clause 20.7 of the 1999 FIDIC Contracts for Major Works' [2005] ICLR, 272.
255. *See* Christopher R Seppälä, 'Sub-Clause 20.7 of the FIDIC Red Book Does Not Justify Denying Enforcement of a "Binding" DAB Decision' (2011) 6(3) C L Int.
256. *PT Perusahaan Gas Negara (Persero) TBK v CRW Joint Operation* [2015] SGCA 30 and Christopher R Seppälä, 'An Excellent Decision from Singapore Which Should Enhance the Enforceability of Decisions of Dispute Adjudication Boards – the Second Persero Case Before the Court of Appeal' (2015) 31 *Const L J,* Issue 7, 367.
257. *See* paras 109-114 relating to 'Expeditious Determination of Manifestly Unmeritorious Claims or Defences' of the ICC's Note to Parties and Arbitral Tribunal's on the Conduct of the Arbitration effective as of 1 January 2021.
258. This was properly recognised already in the case of an Engineer's decision under Clause 67 of RB/87. *See* the interim award, ICC case 10619 (2001), ICC Int'l Ct Arb Bull, vol 19, no 2, 2008, 85 (commentary 52-54). For more recent cases, *see*, among others: partial award, ICC case 15846/GZ (2010), reported in Giovanni Di Folco and Mark Tiggeman, 'Enforcement of a DAB Decision through an ICC Final Partial Award', The Dispute Board Federation Bulletin, September 2010; the final award in ICC case 23652/MHM (2019) (unpublished); and the partial award in ICC case 23494/MHM (2020) (unpublished). While specific performance is not the primary remedy for breach of contract in common law countries, under civil law a claimant's 'primary recourse is in principle to have the contract performed'. Barry Nicholas, *The French Law of Contract* (2nd edn, OUP, Oxford, 1992)

In a sense, the second paragraph states the obvious, namely, that an interim or provisional measure or award enforcing a binding decision shall not prejudice the rights of the Parties as to the merits of the Dispute as, in the case of a binding decision, the merits are necessarily subject to review. The last paragraph recognises that a failure to comply with the decision of the DAAB is a breach of contract and thus, like any breach, may entitle the aggrieved Party to damages or other relief.

--ooOOoo--

21.8 No DAAB in Place

If a Dispute arises between the Parties in connection with, or arising out of, the Contract or the execution of the Works and there is no DAAB in place (or no DAAB is being constituted), whether by reason of the expiry of the DAAB's appointment or otherwise:

(a) Sub-Clause 21.4 [*Obtaining DAAB's Decision*] and Sub-Clause 21.5 [*Amicable Settlement*] shall not apply; and

211. What about arbitration? 'Why specific performance as a remedy in arbitration? The answer is simple: this is what the parties have agreed' (as in Sub-Clause 21.7). The same scholar (Michael Schneider) adds: 'there are numerous cases where parties seek as a remedy in the arbitration the performance of the contract which they have agreed and where arbitral tribunals award such a remedy'. Michael Schneider and Joachim Knoll (eds), *Performance as a Remedy: Non-monetary Belief in International Arbitration*, ASA Special Series No. 30 (Juris, Huntington, N.Y. 2011), 4-5 [*see* in this same work Chapter 2, 'A Comparative Overview on Performance as a Remedy: A Key to Divergent Approaches' by Christine Chappuis]. Decisions awarding performance of the contract as a remedy are upheld by state courts in common law countries. Julian Lew and others, *Comparative International Commercial Arbitration* (Kluwer L Int'l, the Netherlands, 2003) 650 (para 24-72). Both the CISG (art. 46) and the UNIDROIT Principles (arts 7.2.1 and 7.2.2), as well as the English *Arbitration Act 1996* (s 48 (5)(b)), provide for specific performance as a remedy for the enforcement of contracts. Under the UNIDROIT Principles, specific performance is *not* a discretionary remedy; a court or arbitral tribunal must order performance, unless an exception applies. In international arbitration, there should be no hesitancy to order specific performance of DAAB decisions.

(b) the Dispute may be referred by either Party directly to arbitration under Sub-Clause 21.6 [*Arbitration*] without prejudice to any other rights the Party may have.

When a Dispute arises between the Parties and no DAAB is in place for any reason, then either Party may refer the Dispute directly to arbitration without prejudice to its rights, and Sub-Clause 21.4 and 21.5 shall not apply.

Commentary

(i) Main Changes from RB/99:

(1) Compared to Sub-Clause 20.8 of RB/99, the parenthetical '(or no DAAB is being constituted)' has been added in the third line.
(2) In sub-paragraph (b), the words 'by either Party' and 'without prejudice to any other rights the Party may have' have been added.

(ii) Related Clauses / Sub-Clauses: 21 [*Disputes and Arbitration*].

(iii) Analysis: As noted above,[259] the Parties are required to constitute the DAAB within the time stated in the Contract Data or, if not stated, within 28 days after the Contractor receives the Letter of Acceptance. Constitution of the DAAB is deemed to be made when the Parties and the DAAB member(s) have signed a DAAB Agreement.[260] At this point, the DAAB may be considered to be 'in place' within the meaning of Sub-Clause 21.8.

Despite this obligation on the Parties, there may be circumstances where there is no DAAB in place. Most obviously, the term of the DAAB (including the appointment of each member) may have expired pursuant to Sub-Clause 21.1. Pursuant to that Sub-Clause, unless the Parties have agreed otherwise, the term of the DAAB expires either:

(a) on the date the discharge becomes effective under Sub-Clause 14.12; or

259. *See* Sub-Clause 21.1 [*Constitution of the DAAB*].
260. Sub-Clause 21.1, fifth paragraph.

(b) 28 days after the DAAB has given its decision on all Disputes referred to it before the discharge has become effective, whichever is later.[261]

Moreover, the Parties may have neglected to put a DAAB in place at the outset of the Contract when all was well (the 'honeymoon period') or one Party may have attempted to do so, but the other Party may, by obstructionist tactics, have made this impossible to achieve[262] (though this is now much less likely given, among other things, the new provisions to combat this in Sub-Clause 21.2). The DAAB may also have been improperly constituted[263] or otherwise be defective, with the result that there is no valid DAAB in place (though this too should be less of a problem given the new procedure for challenging and having a DAAB member replaced).[264]

In any of these circumstances (where the difficulty cannot be overcome under the DAAB's provisions), a Party may be entitled, under Sub-Clause 21.8, to proceed directly to arbitration and Sub-Clauses 21.4 [*Obtaining DAAB's Decision*] and 21.5 [*Amicable Settlement*] will not apply. The Party may do so without prejudice to its rights, e.g., to claim damages.

(iv) Related Law: In relation to the same Sub-Clause of the 1999 Rainbow Suite (notably, the Silver Book which, unlike the RB, provided for an ad hoc DAB), it was argued that this Sub-Clause entitled a Party to opt out of having to refer disputes to the DAB. But this argument was – quite properly – rejected by the English court concerned.[265]

--ooOOoo--

261. Sub-Clause 21.1, penultimate paragraph. However, if the Contract is terminated earlier, the DAAB's term expires 28 days after: (i) the DAAB has given its decision on all Disputes referred to it within 224 days after the date of termination or (ii) the date the Parties finally agree on all matters (including payment) in connection with the termination, whichever is earlier (the decision or the final agreement). Sub-Clause 21.1, last paragraph.
262. Interim award, ICC case 16155 (2010), and final award, ICC case 18505 (2013), ICC Disp Resol Bull, 2015 – Issue 1, 71 and 137, respectively (commentary 21, 29). *See also* Swiss Federal Court decision 4A_124/2014, 7 July 2014, ASA Bull 4/2014, 826.
263. Final award, ICC case 19581 (2014), ICC Disp Resol Bull, 2015, Issue 1, 147 (sole DAB member not impartial and independent) (commentary 21, 30).
264. Clause 11 of the DAAB GCs and Rules 10 and 11 of the DAAB Rules.
265. *Peterborough City Council v Enterprise Managed Services Ltd* [2014] EWHC 3193 (TCC).

Chapter V
Commentary on Other Documents

1 SCOPE OF CHAPTER

This chapter comments, first (in **Section 2** below), on the three documents which provide for the constitution of a Dispute Avoidance/ Adjudication Board ('DAAB') and, second (in **Section 3** below), on three additional documents, or sets of documents, which are contained within RB/17, namely: (1) an advisory note of FIDIC regarding building information modelling ('BIM') systems; (2) forms of securities, such as the forms of Performance Security and Advance Payment Guarantee; and (3) forms of Letter of Tender, Letter of Acceptance, Contract Agreement and Dispute Adjudication/Avoidance Agreement.

--ooOOoo--

2 DOCUMENTS PROVIDING FOR A DISPUTE AVOIDANCE/ADJUDICATION BOARD ('DAAB')

Clause 21 of the Conditions envisages that the Parties will enter into (or will already have entered into) a DAAB Agreement with a sole Member[1] or three Members of a DAAB. Indeed, Sub-Clauses 21.1 and 21.2 require the Parties to do so.

1. While Clause 21 of the Conditions refers to a 'member' (small initial 'm') of a DAAB, the DAAB Agreement and related documents refer to a 'Member' (big initial 'M') of a DAAB and this will be the usage followed here.

The DAAB Agreement comprises three documents:

(1) a two-page document entitled 'DAAB Agreement' which incorporates by reference Clause 21 [*Disputes and Arbitration*] of the Conditions, 'any other provisions of the Contract that are applicable to the DAAB's Activities'[2] and documents (2) and (3) below;
(2) the General Conditions of DAAB Agreement ('GCs' or 'DAAB GCs'); and
(3) DAAB Procedural Rules ('DAAB Rules') which are annexed to the GCs.

It is contemplated that a DAAB Agreement will be entered into by the Parties with a sole Member or, where (as stated in the Contract Data) there are to be three Members, a separate DAAB Agreement would be entered into by the Parties with each of the three Members.

The forms of the three documents are reproduced in **Appendix 4** of this book. Commentaries on these forms are set forth below. The commentary on each document follows the same structure as the clause-by-clause commentary above,[3] except that the forms themselves are omitted here and contained in **Appendix 4**. Thus, after setting forth in bold text the essential content of each document, there is a commentary on each under up to four headings (to the extent relevant) in bold text, as follows:

(i) Changes from RB/99
(ii) Related Clauses/Sub-Clauses of the Conditions of Contract
(iii) Analysis
(iv) Improvements.

2.1 DAAB Agreement[4]

The DAAB Agreement refers to the Contract, identifies the Employer, the Contractor and the DAAB Member and then contains recitals,

2. 'DAAB's Activities' is defined in Sub-Clause 1.4 of the General Conditions of DAAB Agreement ('GCs' or 'DAAB GCs').
3. *See* **Section 3 Organisation of Commentary** of **Chapter IV Clause-by-Clause Commentary** above.
4. **Section 2.1** discusses the 'umbrella' DAAB Agreement, that is, excluding the GCs, which are discussed in **Section 2.2** below, and excluding the DAAB Rules, which are discussed in **Section 2.3** below.

including a definition of the DAAB, a statement of the desire of the Employer and the Contractor to appoint the DAAB Member and the acceptance by the DAAB Member of his/her appointment. It incorporates into the DAAB Agreement: (a) Clause 21 of the Conditions and 'any other provisions of the Contract' applicable to the DAAB's Activities and (b) the GCs to which are annexed the DAAB Rules which form part of the GCs. It provides for the terms of payment of the DAAB Member by reference to the GCs and provides a space for the Parties to specify the currency of payment. It provides that the Employer and the Contractor are jointly and severally liable for the DAAB Member's fees and other payments to be made to the DAAB Member. It also provides for the law to govern the DAAB Agreement. In case it does not do so, the law governing the Contract under Sub-Clause 1.4 of the Conditions would apply.

Commentary

(i) Changes from RB/99: As noted in the commentary on Clause 21, the Dispute Adjudication Board ('DAB') in RB/99 has been replaced by a DAAB in RB/17. The Dispute Adjudication Agreement in RB/99 (the 'DAB Agreement') is now referred to as the 'DAAB Agreement' in RB/17. The principal changes from the DAB Agreement in RB/99 are as follows:

(1) In RB/99, there were two different forms of contract applicable to the DAB: one for signature with a sole Member DAB and another for signature with each Member of a three-Member DAB, respectively. The RB/17 now provides for a single form of contract, with provisions allowing it to be adapted to either a sole Member DAAB or a three-Member DAAB.

(2) The DAAB Agreement envisages the possibility of it being entered into even before the Contract is signed (as the result of the addition of '(or intend to enter)' in recital A), while in RB/99, the DAB Agreement assumed that the Employer and the Contractor had already entered into the Contract.

(3) Unlike the DAB Agreement, the DAAB Agreement no longer provides that words and expressions used in the Agreement have the same meanings as assigned to them in the GCs (this was perhaps felt to no longer be necessary in light of the more numerous definitions in the GCs and Sub-Clause 1.2 of the GCs).

(4) Unlike the DAB Agreement, the DAAB Agreement contains several recitals, including a definition of the DAAB, the desire of

the Parties to jointly appoint the DAAB Member and the acceptance by the DAAB Member of his/her appointment.

(5) Unlike the DAB Agreement, the DAAB Agreement states that it comprises: (a) Clause 21 [*Disputes and Arbitration*] of the Conditions of Contract as well as any other provisions of the Conditions of Contract that may be applicable to the DAAB's Activities and (b) the GCs to which are annexed the DAAB Rules which form part of the GCs.

(6) The DAAB Agreement also explicitly provides a space in which the Parties may specify the currency of payment of amounts due to the DAAB Member(s), which is new.

(7) The DAAB Agreement provides that the law governing the Contract under Sub-Clause 1.4 of the Conditions of Contract would apply if the Parties fail to choose the governing law, which is also new.

(ii) Related Clauses/Sub-Clauses of the Conditions of Contract: 1.4 [*Law and Language*], 3.7.5 [*Agreement or Determination – Dissatisfaction with Engineer's Determination*], 14.12 [*Discharge*], 14.15 [*Currencies of Payment*] and 21 [*Disputes and Arbitration*].

(iii) Analysis: The DAAB under RB/17 has the dual function of dispute avoidance (under Sub-Clause 21.3) and decision-making (under Sub-Clause 21.4). Unlike arbitration, which is generally provided for by a (national) arbitration law, a DAAB is purely a creature of contract.[5] As a DAAB does not, like arbitration, operate within the framework of a law, the DAAB Agreement, the GCs and the DAAB Rules need to be as comprehensive as possible so as to provide for all the issues that are likely to arise in a DAAB proceeding.

(1) Introduction

The DAAB Agreement (excluding documents incorporated by reference into it) is a two-page document which the Employer and the Contractor, together with a Member (if it is the sole Member DAAB) or with each Member (if it is a three-Member DAAB), sign. It describes the documents of which it is comprised, any amendments to the GCs, the remuneration

5. Only a few States, such as Brazil, Honduras, Italy and Peru, have laws dealing with dispute boards. *See* under **(iv) Related Law** of the commentary on Sub-Clause 21.1 [*Constitution of the DAAB*] above.

of DAAB Members and the undertaking of each Member to act as a DAAB Member in accordance with its terms.

However, while the DAAB Agreement contains detailed recitals – including a definition of the DAAB, together with the name(s) and contact details of DAAB Member(s), and the (each) DAAB Member's acceptance – *it does not (as it should) include a provision for the recitals to be binding on the Parties and for them to be an integral part of the Parties' agreement.*

(2) DAAB Members' fees and expenses

The DAAB Agreement provides the terms of payment of the DAAB Member by reference to the GCs and provides a space in which the Parties may specify the currency of payment. Clause 9 of the GCs provides that a DAAB Member shall be paid in the currency specified in the DAAB Agreement and that his/her fees shall consist of a fixed monthly fee and a daily fee for which spaces are provided.

If the Parties should have failed to designate a currency of payment, then it might have been provided that the DAAB Member(s) be paid in US dollars, due to its wide acceptability as a global currency. This is common in international dispute resolution, as both the International Centre for Settlement of Investment Disputes ('ICSID') and the International Chamber of Commerce ('ICC') provide for the payment of arbitrators in US dollars.[6]

If no monthly fee but a daily fee is specified in the DAAB Agreement, then, according to the GCs, the daily fee is deemed to cover the matters for which the monthly fee would be paid.[7]

The DAAB Agreement also provides that the Employer and the Contractor are jointly and severally liable for the DAAB Member's fees and other payments to be made to the DAAB Member, in accordance with the GCs. The manner of paying DAAB Members is provided for in Sub-Clause 9.5 of the GCs: the Contractor is to pay each of the DAAB Member's invoices in full within 28 days after receiving it, and then apply to the Employer

6. *See* ICSID, 'Memorandum on the Fees and Expenses' (*ICSID*, July 2022) https://icsid.worldbank.org/services/content/memorandum-fees-expenses/2022 and ICSID, 'Schedule of Fees' (ICSID, July 2022) https://icsid.worldbank.org/services/cost-of-proceedings/schedule-fees/2022 accessed 10 November 2022 (with effect from 1 July 2022). Both sections denominate the payments to arbitrators in US dollars. *See* Appendix III, art. 3.4 of the ICC Arbitration Rules.

7. *See* Sub-Clause 9.1 of the GCs.

(in Statements under the Contract) for reimbursement of one-half of these amounts. The Employer is then obliged to pay the Contractor in accordance with the Conditions, i.e., Clause 14 [*Contract Price and Payment*]. Clause 9.6 of the GCs sets out the procedure which is to apply should the Contractor fail to pay the DAAB Member within 28 days after receiving an invoice. Clause 9.7 of the GCs further sets out the procedure which is to apply if the DAAB Member does not receive payment of the amounts due within 56 days after submitting a valid invoice. These clauses are discussed in the commentary on the GCs below.

(iv) Improvements:

(1) As noted above, the recitals to the DAAB Agreement should expressly be made an integral part of it.
(2) The DAAB Agreement could usefully provide that, failing specification by the Parties of the currency of payment, amounts due to a DAAB Member should be paid in US dollars.

2.2 General Conditions of DAAB Agreement ('GCs')

The GCs provide a template of standard terms to be incorporated into the DAAB Agreement. These contain a set of definitions, a provision as to the date on which the DAAB Agreement comes into effect, a set of warranties by the DAAB Member as to his/her qualifications, provisions dealing with the independence and impartiality of the DAAB Member, the general obligations of the DAAB Member and the Parties, confidentiality and the manner in which the DAAB Member is to be paid. These also provide for the manner of resignation and termination of DAAB Members. Finally, they provide a procedure for the resolution of disputes arising under the DAAB Agreement.

Commentary

(i) Changes from RB/99:

(1) The GCs are more than twice as long as the General Conditions of Dispute Adjudication Agreement in RB/99 ('Old GCs'), specifically, 9 pages versus 4 pages. New defined terms have

been included in the GCs, namely 'DAAB's Activities',[8] 'DAAB Rules', 'Informal Assistance', 'Term of the DAAB' and 'Notification'.

(2) Clause 2.1 of the GCs provides for a simpler method to calculate the 'Effective Date', linking it to the date of the signing of the DAAB Agreement, as opposed to the more complex provision in the Old GCs regarding when the DAB Agreement took effect (Clause 2).

(3) A DAAB Member may resign under Sub-Clause 10.1 of the GCs upon not less than 28 days' notice (or other period agreed between the Parties), as opposed to a minimum notice period of 70 days under Clause 2 of the Old GCs.

(4) The provisions regarding warranties and the independence and impartiality of the DAAB Member have been greatly expanded:

  (a) Under Sub-Clause 3.1 of the GCs, a DAAB Member must be independent and impartial from the Employer's Personnel[9] and the Contractor's Personnel,[10] in addition to the Employer, Contractor and Engineer, as under Clause 3 of the Old GCs.

  (b) Sub-Clause 3.1 of the GCs clarifies that the requirement of independence and impartiality extends for the Term of the DAAB.[11]

  (c) Sub-Clause 3.2 of the GCs clarifies that the duty of disclosure of the DAAB Member is a continuing one. Any fact or circumstance after the signing of the DAAB Agreement that might compromise the independence or impartiality of the DAAB Member must be disclosed by him/her 'immediately' and 'in writing' to the Parties and the other DAAB Members (if any). This is a change from the requirement to make disclosure 'promptly' under Clause 3 of the Old GCs.

8. Note: In the initial printing of RB/17, the GCs had a typographical error in the numbering system with two clauses bearing the reference of Sub-Clause 1.3, i.e., 'DAAB Agreement' and 'DAAB's Activities'. This has been corrected in the 2022 reprint of RB/17.
9. '**Employer's Personnel**' is defined to include the Engineer, *see* Sub-Clause 1.1.33 of the Conditions.
10. *See* Sub-Clause 1.1.17 '**Contractor's Personnel**' of the Conditions.
11. The 'Term of the DAAB' is defined in Sub-Clause 1.7 of the GCs.

(d) In addition to no financial interest in the Contract (Clause 4(a) of the Old GCs), the GCs require that a DAAB Member have no financial interest in '[...] the project of which the Works are part', except for payment under the DAAB Agreement (Sub-Clause 4.1(a)).

(e) The DAAB Member, in the 5 years before signing the DAAB Agreement, must not have been employed as a consultant or otherwise by the Employer, the Contractor, the Employer's Personnel or the Contractor's Personnel except as disclosed to the Parties (Sub-Clause 4.1(c)). Under the Old GCs (Clause 4(b)), there was no time limit in the prohibition of prior employment.

(f) The DAAB Member must 'not previously have acted, and shall not act, in any judicial or arbitral capacity in relation to the Contract' (Sub-Clause 4.1(d)). This is a new prohibition.

(g) The DAAB Member must not have certain relationships or contacts with the Employer, the Contractor, the Employer's Personnel or Contractor's Personnel at all or, in some cases, must not have (or have had) relationships that are undisclosed (Sub-Clauses 4.1(e) and (f)). This is a new prohibition.

(h) Sub-Clause 4.1(g) introduces a new prohibition on the solicitation, acceptance or receipt (directly or indirectly) of any gift, gratuity, commission or 'other thing else of value'[12] by the DAAB Member from the Employer, Contractor, Employer's Personnel or Contractor's Personnel, except for payment under the DAAB Agreement.

(5) A DAAB Member is obliged under Sub-Clause 5.1(c) to ensure his/her availability for meetings (in addition to site visits and hearings under Clause 4(h) of the Old GCs) during the Term of the DAAB. The DAAB Member's non-availability may only be excused in 'exceptional circumstances' of which the DAAB Member has given a Notification[13] 'without delay'. There was no such provision in the Old GCs.

(6) Documents may now be maintained by the DAAB Member in electronic format (Sub-Clause 5.1(d)).

12. This effectively prohibits the solicitation, acceptance or receipt of any benefit from the other Party, other than payment under the DAAB Agreement.
13. As defined in Sub-Clause 1.8 of the GCs.

(7) 'Informal Assistance' requested jointly by the Parties is a defined duty of the DAAB under the GCs (Sub-Clause 1.6), replacing the giving of 'advice and opinions' at the request of the Parties subject to the agreement of the other Members (if any) under Clause 4(k) of the Old GCs.

(8) Sub-Clauses 6.2 and 6.3 of the GCs impose new duties upon the Parties to cooperate with each other in constituting the DAAB and to cooperate in good faith with the DAAB. Sub-Clause 6.6 clarifies that each Party has an obligation to provide documents and to ensure that DAAB Members are provided with the necessary information to enable the DAAB Members to be knowledgeable about the Contract and the progress of the Works.

(9) The confidentiality provisions under the GCs are much more detailed than in Clause 4(j) of the Old GCs, and are imposed upon not only the DAAB Members but also the Employer, the Contractor, the Employer's Personnel and the Contractor's Personnel (Sub-Clause 7.2), subject to certain limitations (Sub-Clause 7.3). They also provide for what disclosures are to be made to the replacement Member if a DAAB Member is replaced (Sub-Clause 7.4).

(10) The exceptions to the limitation of liability of a DAAB Member have been expanded from acts in bad faith (Clause 5(c) of the Old GCs) to include instances of 'fraud', 'gross negligence', 'deliberate default' or 'reckless misconduct' in Sub-Clause 8.1(c) of the GCs.

(11) The GCs contain more detailed provisions on fees and expenses (Clause 9), including the procedure which is to apply when a DAAB Member has been appointed by the appointing official named in the Contract Data (Sub-Clause 9.3) and a reduced time period for payment of fees by the Contractor (28 days from receipt of invoice (Sub-Clause 9.5), rather than 56 days in Clause 6 of the Old GCs).

(12) After resignation or termination, the DAAB Member remains bound by his/her confidentiality obligation and must return any originals of documents in its possession in connection with the DAAB's Activities (Sub-Clause 10.8), which is new.

(13) A procedure for challenge of a DAAB Member has been introduced (Clause 11), with no equivalent in the Old GCs.[14] This is provided for in more detail in the DAAB Rules (Rules 10 and 11).

(14) Any disputes arising out of the DAAB Agreement are to be resolved by reference to the ICC's Expedited Procedure Rules[15] (Clause 12 GCs), as opposed to normal ICC arbitration (Clause 9 Old GCs).

(ii) Related Clauses / Sub-Clauses of the Conditions of Contract: 1.4 [*Law and Language*], 1.12 [*Confidentiality*], 3.7.5 [*Agreement or Determination – Dissatisfaction with Engineer's Determination*], 14.12 [*Discharge*] and 21 [*Disputes and Arbitration*].

(iii) Analysis: The content of the GCs is largely self-explanatory and has been described, to some extent, in the commentary on Clause 21 [*Disputes and Arbitration*] of the Conditions above. Accordingly, the commentary below focuses on points not discussed in that commentary or which are problematic.

(1) New 'Notification' provision

Sub-Clause 1.8 of the GCs defines a 'Notification' as 'a notice in writing given under the GCs' which must satisfy various requirements which are similar, but not identical, to those contained in Sub-Clause 1.3 [*Notices and Other Communications*] of the Conditions, e.g., as regards when it shall have effect or whether it may be unreasonably withheld or delayed, both of which are dealt with in Sub-Clause 1.3 of the Conditions but not in Sub-Clause 1.8 of the GCs. As the DAAB Rules are an 'Annex' to the GCs, they may be deemed to be part of the GCs and, consequently, a 'Notification' given under the DAAB Rules would also have to comply with Sub-Clause 1.8 of the GCs.

(2) Independence and impartiality provisions expanded

As noted above, the requirement that a DAAB Member be independent and impartial is now, rightly, dealt with in much greater detail than

14. *See*, however, Clause 3, last paragraph of the General Conditions of Dispute Adjudication Agreement in GB/08 which had provided for a procedure – albeit probably ineffective – for the challenge of DAB members.

15. *See (3) ICC Rules of Arbitration – (b) ICC's Expedited Procedure Rules* under **(iii) Analysis** of the commentary on Sub-Clause 21.6 [*Arbitration*] above.

before given some of the cases which have arisen in the past.[16] For example, Sub-Clause 4.1 (c) now reasonably provides that in the 5 years before signing the DAAB Agreement, a DAAB Member shall not have been employed as a consultant or otherwise by either Party or its representatives except as disclosed by the DAAB Member. However, some provisions may be unnecessarily onerous. For example, Sub-Clause 4.1 provides that, among other things, the DAAB Members:

(a) have no financial interest in the Contract, or in the project of which the Works are part, except for payment under the DAAB Agreement;
(b) have no interest whatsoever (financial or otherwise) in the Employer, the Contractor, the Employer's Personnel or the Contractor's Personnel; and/or
(c) not previously have acted, and shall not act, in any judicial or arbitral capacity in relation to the Contract.

Instead of formulating each of the foregoing provisions as *an absolute prohibition* it would have been sufficient to have provided that each applies *except as otherwise disclosed by the DAAB Member*. If a prospective DAAB Member were to disclose facts or circumstances that are contrary to a prohibition, then this should not be an obstacle to the Member's appointment if neither Party objects. Each Party might waive an objection in this respect and it would have been desirable had the Sub-Clause recognised this. This difficulty can be overcome by making appropriate amendments to the GCs by way of the DAAB Agreement.[17]

16. In ICC case 19581 (2014), Mr X, the sole DAB member, had failed to disclose that his wife (or former wife, recently divorced) was a decision-maker and head of the claims and disputes unit in the Employer's organisation. The sole arbitrator found that, due to Mr X's violation of his disclosure obligations under the DAB Agreement and lack of impartiality and independence, there was no DAB in place for the purposes of Sub-Clause 20.8 (of the RB/99 contract concerned) when the dispute arose and, consequently, that the Contractor was entitled to refer the dispute directly to arbitration, pursuant to Sub-Clause 20.8. Final award, ICC case 19581 (2014), ICC Disp Resol Bull, 2015, Issue 1, 147 (commentary 21, 30).
17. *See* Clause 2 of the form of DAAB Agreement which expressly provides for possible amendments to the GCs.

(3) Obligations of the Parties expanded

Sub-Clause 6.1 obligates the Parties to comply with the GCs, the DAAB Rules and the Conditions of Contract relevant to the DAAB's Activities. It also makes the Employer and the Contractor responsible for causing their respective Personnel to comply with the foregoing. Sub-Clause 6.2 requires each Party to cooperate in constituting the DAAB under Sub-Clause 21.1 [*Constitution of the DAAB*] and if necessary, Sub-Clause 21.2 [*Failure to Appoint DAAB Member(s)*] of the Conditions, 'without delay'. As noted above,[18] in case a Party fails to fulfil this obligation of cooperation, any arbitral tribunal formed at a later stage may take into account this failure to cooperate, in dealing with any award of costs. Sub-Clause 6.3 introduces a new provision requiring each Party to cooperate in 'good faith' with the DAAB, as well as requiring each Party to fulfil its duties and exercise any right or entitlement in the manner necessary to achieve the objectives outlined under Rule 1 of the DAAB Rules. *It is unclear what the requirement to 'cooperate in good faith with the DAAB' may entail* – in arbitration, a Party is not normally said to have such a duty in relation to an arbitral tribunal. It would appear to mean that a Party must be open and honest and have no intention to deceive or mislead the DAAB.

The Parties' confidentiality obligations are much more detailed (Clause 7) but otherwise in normal form with standard exclusions. It is notable, however, that while the Parties are required to treat the DAAB's Activities as confidential, there is no such requirement applicable to arbitration in Sub-Clause 21.6, nor in the ICC Arbitration Rules. While an ICC arbitration is private,[19] it is not confidential unless applicable law should so provide.

(4) The more detailed provision for fees and expenses

Sub-Clause 9.1 provides that the DAAB Member will be paid, in the currency named in the DAAB Agreement, a monthly fee, a daily fee, all reasonable expenses and any taxes properly levied in the Country[20] on payments made to the DAAB Member.

Sub-Clause 9.2 provides that the amounts of a DAAB Member's monthly fee and daily fee shall be as specified in the DAAB Agreement. Sub-Clause 9.3 provides that, where the DAAB Member has been appointed by the

18. *See (5) Scope of the Arbitration* under **(iii) Analysis** of the commentary on Sub-Clause 21.6 [*Arbitration*] of the Conditions above.
19. Persons not involved in an ICC arbitration hearing will normally be refused admission. Art. 26.3 of the ICC Arbitration Rules.
20. For the definition of '**Country**', *see* Sub-Clause 1.1.21 of the Conditions.

appointing official named in the Contract Data, the Member's monthly fee and daily fee shall be as provided in Sub-Clause 21.2 [*Failure to Appoint DAAB Member(s)*].

Sub-Clause 9.4 provides for the manner in which a DAAB Member shall submit invoices. Sub-Clause 9.5 provides that the Contractor must pay the DAAB Member's invoices in full within 28 days of receipt of each invoice, and, thereafter apply to the Employer for reimbursement of half of that amount, under the payment procedure in the Contract. The Employer is obliged to pay the Contractor in accordance with the Contract. Should the Contractor fail to make this payment within 28 days of receipt of an invoice, the DAAB Member may inform the Employer, who must then make the payment 'promptly'. The Employer is entitled to payment from the Contractor of all sums paid in excess of half of these amounts, the reasonable costs of recovery and financing charges calculated according to Sub-Clause '14.9' [*Delayed Payment*][21] of the Conditions. This entitlement of the Employer does not require compliance with Sub-Clause 20.2 [*Claims for Payment and/or EOT*] of the Conditions.[22]

In case the DAAB Member does not receive payment of the amounts due to him/her within 56 days after submitting the invoice, the DAAB Member may suspend his/her services (on not less than 7 days' Notification to the Parties and the Other Member(s) if any) until the payment is received and/or, without prejudice to his/her rights, resign from the DAAB, in accordance with Sub-Clause 10.1.[23] There is no express provision for the DAAB Member to receive financing charges.[24]

(5) New resignation and termination clause

Clause 10 of the GCs addresses the resignation and termination of the DAAB Member(s). Sub-Clause 10.1 provides that *a DAAB Member may 'resign at any time for any reason' by giving a Notification of not less than 28 days*, or any other period agreed between the Parties. Unless amended

21. Sub-Clause 9.6 of the GCs. The correct Sub-Clause of the Conditions is Sub-Clause 14.8 [*Delayed Payment*].
22. Sub-Clause 9.6 of the GCs. Should both the Contractor and the Employer fail to pay the DAAB in accordance with this provision, it has been held, in relation to the 1999 Rainbow Suite, that the Contractor may proceed to arbitration directly as no DAAB would be 'in place' pursuant to Sub-Clause 20.8 (now Sub-Clause 21.8). Interim award, ICC case 24140 (2020) (so far unpublished).
23. Sub-Clause 9.7 of the GCs.
24. Compare Sub-Clause 14.8 [*Delayed Payment*] of the Conditions dealing with delayed payments to the Contractor.

by the Parties, this would be much less than the minimum 70 days' notice period provided for in Clause 2 of the Old GCs. *One may therefore question whether 28 days' notice allows the Parties enough time in which to find, appoint and sufficiently brief a replacement DAAB Member for a project which may, at least in theory, be anywhere in the world.* 56 days would seem to be more reasonable. Under the ICC's Dispute Board Rules (2015), for example, a 'DB Member' must give a minimum of three months' written notice to the Parties before it may terminate its 'DB Member Agreement'.[25]

(6) New objection and challenge procedures

As noted previously, one of the more significant innovations in the GCs is the procedure for challenging a DAAB Member. It highlights the importance attached to the independence and impartiality of DAAB Members, the requirements for which have been made more stringent. Sub-Clause 11.1 of the GCs provides that the Parties shall not raise an objection to a DAAB Member, except for an alleged lack of independence or impartiality or otherwise, in which case the procedures in Rules 10 and 11 of the DAAB Rules will apply. Rules 10 and 11 of the DAAB Rules are discussed in the section on those Rules below, but suffice to note here that challenges to a DAAB Member are decided by the ICC and administered by the ICC International Centre for ADR. Sub-Clause 11.2 provides that any decision rendered under Rule 11 of the DAAB Rules shall be final and conclusive. Should a DAAB Member resign at any time before the decision on his/her challenge is issued, the challenging Party must inform the ICC.[26] In such case, the termination takes place with immediate effect and not in accordance with Sub-Clause 10.2 (i.e., at the expiry of the period mentioned in Sub-Clause 10.1 of the GCs). Sub-Clause 11.4 requires the DAAB to continue with the DAAB's Activities until the decision on the challenge[27] is issued, unless the challenged DAAB Member resigns or his/her DAAB Agreement has been terminated pursuant to Sub-Clause 10.3.

If the challenge is successful, the appointment of the DAAB Member and his/her DAAB Agreement is deemed to have been terminated with immediate effect on the date of the notification of the decision on the

25. Art. 10.3 of the ICC Dispute Board Rules in force as of 1 October 2015 with Appendices in force as from 1 October 2018 (ICC Publication 873-5 ENG) ('ICC Dispute Board Rules').
26. Sub-Clause 11.3 of the GCs.
27. As defined in Sub-Clause 11.2 of the GCs.

challenge by the ICC.[28] From the date of notification of the decision on the challenge, the DAAB Member is no longer entitled to any fees or expenses.[29] Any decisions given by the DAAB under Sub-Clause 21.4.3 [*The DAAB's Decision*] of the Conditions after the challenge was raised,[30] and before the resignation, if any, of the challenged DAAB Member under Sub-Clause 11.3 or termination of his/her DAAB Agreement under Sub-Clause 11.5(a) or Sub-Clause 10.3, are void and ineffective.[31] For sole member DAABs, all other DAAB Activities during such period shall also become void and ineffective.[32] For three-member DAABs, all other activities of the DAAB shall be unaffected, except if the entire DAAB is successfully challenged.[33] The successfully challenged DAAB Member must be removed from the DAAB,[34] and the Parties are required to appoint a replacement DAAB Member in accordance with the Conditions.[35]

(7) New disputes procedure under the DAAB Agreement

Any dispute arising out of or in connection with the DAAB Agreement is to be finally settled under the ICC Arbitration Rules by a sole arbitrator, in accordance with the ICC's Expedited Procedure Rules.[36] This is an innovation, given that the Expedited Procedure was adopted by the ICC in 2017 and there is no equivalent in the Old GCs.

(iv) Improvements:

(1) The provisions of Sub-Clause 4.1(a), (b) and (d) should be modified to provide that each prohibition applies except where the relevant information has been disclosed by the DAAB Member. In the meantime, the Parties may want to make use of Clause 2 of the DAAB Agreement allowing for amendment of the GCs in this respect.

28. Sub-Clause 11.5(a) of the GCs.
29. Sub-Clause 11.5(b) of the GCs.
30. Under Rule 11 of the DAAB Rules.
31. Sub-Clause 11.5(c) of the GCs.
32. *Ibid.*
33. *Ibid.*
34. Sub-Clause 11.5(d) of the GCs.
35. Sub-Clause 11.5(e) of the GCs.
36. Appendix VI of the ICC Arbitration Rules. Clause 12 of the GCs. *See (3) ICC Rules of Arbitration – (b) ICC's Expedited Procedure Rules* under **(iii) Analysis** of the commentary on Sub-Clause 21.6 [*Arbitration*] above.

(2) The right of a DAAB Member to resign on 28 days' Notification (Clause 10.1) is too short. At least 56 days' Notification should be required.

2.3 DAAB Rules

The DAAB Rules, which are an Annex to the GCs, state their objectives at the outset to be the avoidance of Disputes and the achievement of the expeditious, efficient and cost-effective resolution of any Dispute that arises between the Parties (Rule 1). Thereafter, they provide for the carrying out of the avoidance of Disputes function (Rule 2), the regulation of meetings and Site Visits by the DAAB (Rule 3), and the rules governing communications and documentation exchanged with the DAAB (Rule 4). The DAAB Rules cover a range of issues in relation to DAAB proceedings: the powers of the DAAB (Rule 5), how Disputes are to be decided (Rule 6), how hearings are to be held (Rule 7), how decisions are to be rendered (Rule 8), the objection procedure (Rule 10) and the challenge procedure (Rule 11).

<u>Commentary</u>

(i) Changes from RB/99:

The DAAB Rules are much longer (6 ½ pages versus 1 ½ pages) and more detailed than the Procedural Rules in RB/99 ('Old Rules'). The major changes are as follows:

(1) The DAAB Rules state in Rule 1 that they have certain objectives, whereas there was no statement of objectives in the Old Rules. The objectives are:
  (a) to facilitate the avoidance of Disputes; and
  (b) to achieve the expeditious, efficient and cost-effective resolution of any Dispute that arises.

  The DAAB Rules state that they 'shall be interpreted' to achieve these objectives.

(2) Rule 2 relating to avoidance of Disputes is new.

(3) Rule 3.2 of the DAAB Rules mandates that '[a]s soon as practicable after the DAAB is appointed', the DAAB must convene an introductory meeting with the Parties, where it shall establish a schedule of planned meetings and Site visits in consultation with the Parties. This is new.

(4) Under the Old Rules, Site visits were to occur at intervals of not more than 140 Days, including times of critical construction events, unless otherwise agreed by the Employer and the Contractor.[37] Now, under Rule 3.3 of the DAAB Rules, the DAAB must hold meetings with the Parties and Site visits are to occur at 'regular intervals and/or at the written request of either Party'. Further, the frequency of meetings and/or Site visits must be sufficient to achieve the purpose set out in Rule 3.1,[38] and unless otherwise agreed by the Parties, be at intervals of not more than 140, and not less than 70, days. Each such meeting and Site visit is to be in-person unless the Parties and the DAAB agree that exceptional circumstances justify that it be carried out online.[39] This is all new.

(5) Rule 3.4 of the DAAB Rules provides that the DAAB may hold meetings with the Parties online (in addition to online or in-person meetings referred to in Rules 3.2 and 3.3). This is new.

(6) Although the term 'critical construction events' is not defined in either the Old Rules or the DAAB Rules, Rule 3.5 of the DAAB Rules clarifies that they 'may include suspension of the Works or termination of the Contract'.

(7) Rule 3.6 of the DAAB Rules provides that each Party may request an urgent meeting or Site visit by the DAAB. This is new.

(8) Rule 3.9 of the DAAB Rules assigns responsibility for coordinating Site visits to the Contractor (in cooperation with the Employer and the Engineer), as opposed to Rule 3 of the Old Rules, which put this responsibility on the Employer (in cooperation with the Contractor). This is possibly because the Contractor has possession of the Site. Rule 3.9 also makes the

37. Rule 1 of the Old Rules.

38. Rule 3.1 of the DAAB Rules provides that the purpose of the meetings and Site visits is to enable the DAAB to 'become and remain informed' about the matters described in Sub-Clause 5.1(d) of the GCs (i.e., the Parties' performance of the Contract, the Site and its surroundings, in addition to the progress of the Works and of any other parts of the project of which the Contract forms part), to become aware of, and remain informed about, actual or potential issues between the Parties and to give Informal Assistance if and when requested by the Parties jointly to do so.

39. Rule 3.3.

Contractor responsible for ensuring the provision of appropriate personal safety equipment and security controls, site transport and access to a virtual videoconference platform (in addition to conference facilities and copying and secretarial services).

(9) Rule 3.10 of the DAAB Rules sets out a different deadline for the DAAB to prepare a report on its activities during a Site visit (or meeting) from that under Rule 3 of the Old Rules. Such a report must now be prepared '[a]t the conclusion of each meeting and Site Visit and, if possible before leaving the venue of the face-to-face meeting or the Site (as the case may be) but in any event within 7 days', as opposed to '[a]t the conclusion of each site visit and before leaving the site' under Rule 3 of the Old Rules.

(10) Rule 4.1 of the DAAB Rules clarifies the language to be used in communications to and from the DAAB, in reports and decisions issued by the DAAB and during Site visits, meetings and hearings relating to the DAAB's Activities. It is to be the language of communications defined in Sub-Clause 1.4 of the Conditions unless otherwise agreed by the Parties and the DAAB. The Old Rules had not discussed this issue.

(11) Rule 4.3 of the DAAB Rules gives a more detailed list of the kinds of documents which the DAAB may request from the Parties than had Rule 4 of the Old Rules.

(12) Rule 5 of the DAAB Rules corresponds to Rule 8 of the Old Rules and specifies the powers of the DAAB. These are greater and now include the power to appoint one or more experts with the agreement of the Parties,[40] as well as to establish the procedure for Site visits and/or giving Informal Assistance. Rule 5.1 now explicitly clarifies that the powers of the DAAB set out in that Rule are '[i]n addition to' the powers already conferred upon the DAAB, pursuant to the Conditions, the GCs, and elsewhere in the DAAB Rules.

(13) Rule 7.1 of the DAAB Rules relating to hearings corresponds to Rules 6 and 7 of the Old Rules. However, it provides the DAAB with additional powers pertaining to hearings, such as the power to decide on the duration of the hearing (Rule 7.1(b)), to request the production of documents and/or oral submissions

40. The remuneration of any expert the DAAB appoints must be agreed to by the Parties, *see* Sub-Clause 21.1, sixth paragraph, of the Conditions.

by the Parties (Rule 7.1(e)), to request the attendance of persons at a hearing (Rule 7.1(f)), and to adjourn hearings (Rule 7.1(i)). Rule 7.3 clarifies whether, when and how the DAAB should step in to provide Informal Assistance, if requested to do so during a hearing.

(14) Rule 8.2(d) introduces the ground of 'exceptional circumstances, of which the Other Members and the Parties have received a Notification from the DAAB Member' as a situation where the Other Members may not proceed to make a decision in the absence of a DAAB Member. This is consistent with Sub-Clause 5.1(c) of the GCs which provides that a DAAB Member may be excused from making him/herself available during the term of the DAAB, in case of 'exceptional circumstances' of which the DAAB Member gives a Notification.

(15) Rules 8.3-8.7 of the DAAB Rules introduce new provisions to deal with the correction of typographical or other minor errors or ambiguities in DAAB decisions and the issuance of addenda to DAAB's decisions – these were not dealt with in the Old Rules.

(16) Rule 9 of the DAAB Rules provides for the situation where the DAAB Agreement is terminated and is entirely new.

(17) Rules 10 and 11 provide for procedures to object to and to challenge a DAAB Member and both are entirely new.

(ii) Related Clauses / Sub-Clauses of the Conditions of Contract: 1.4 [*Law and Language*], 3.7.5 [*Agreement or Determination – Dissatisfaction with Engineer's Determination*], 14.12 [*Discharge*] and 21 [*Disputes and Arbitration*].

(iii) Analysis: The content of the DAAB Rules is largely self-explanatory and has been described, to some extent, in the commentary on Clause 21 [*Disputes and Arbitration*] of the Conditions above. Accordingly, the discussion below focuses on certain provisions that may be of particular interest or which are problematic.

(1) New objectives

Rule 1.1 of the DAAB Rules lays down that their objectives are to facilitate the avoidance of Disputes between the Parties and to achieve the expeditious, efficient and cost-effective resolution of any Dispute. Rule 1.2 adds that these objectives should guide the manner in which the

DAAB Rules are to be interpreted, as well as how the DAAB carries out its Activities and uses its powers under the Contract and the DAAB Rules.

(2) New emphasis on Dispute avoidance

In keeping with the intent to promote the avoidance of Disputes, Rule 2 of the DAAB Rules states that the DAAB may provide Informal Assistance where Sub-Clause 21.3 [*Avoidance of Disputes*] of the Conditions applies. Such Informal Assistance may be provided during discussions at any meeting with the Parties (whether face-to-face or by telephone/videoconference) or at any Site visit or by 'an informal written note'[41] to the Parties. Rule 7.3 lays down the procedure for addressing the situation should Parties request Informal Assistance during a hearing. It provides that the DAAB must not ordinarily give Informal Assistance during a hearing but, if so requested, the DAAB must adjourn the hearing for the time that it takes for it to render Informal Assistance to the Parties.[42] In case the hearing is adjourned for more than 2 days, the period under Sub-Clause 21.4.3 [*The DAAB's Decision*] of the Conditions (i.e., the 84-day or other agreed period for giving a decision) is temporarily suspended until the date the hearing is resumed.[43] Hearings must resume 'promptly' after the DAAB has given Informal Assistance.[44]

(3) Greater powers of the DAAB

Rule 5 of the DAAB Rules sets out the powers of the DAAB, in addition to the ones set out in the Conditions,[45] the GCs and the other provisions of the DAAB Rules (notably Rules 3, 7 and 8). Unlike under the RB/99, the DAAB Rules explicitly empower the DAAB to appoint one or more experts (including technical and legal expert(s)) with the agreement of the Parties. Among other things, the Parties' agreement to the remuneration of such expert(s) will be required.[46] Of special note – and as already provided for in the Old Rules – the DAAB may decide on provisional relief

41. This note will be binding neither on the DAAB nor on the Parties, *see* Sub-Clause 21.3 [*Avoidance of Disputes*], last paragraph.
42. Rule 7.3(a), DAAB Rules.
43. Rule 7.3(b), DAAB Rules.
44. Rule 7.3(c), DAAB Rules.
45. *See* Sub-Clauses 21.1 [*Constitution of the DAAB*] – 21.4 [*Obtaining DAAB's Decision*] of the Conditions.
46. While an expert may provide an opinion to the DAAB upon which the DAAB may rely when giving its decision, the decision will be that of the DAAB and not of the expert and the DAAB will not be bound to accept the opinion of the expert. The DAAB can disregard an expert's opinion completely.

such as interim or conservatory measures (Rule 5.1(j)). Absent other established criteria for the granting of interim relief by DAABs, the common conditions for the granting of interim or conservatory measures in international arbitration practice (such as the establishment of a prima facie case on the merits, risk of irreparable harm and proportionality) ought to be relevant.

The DAAB may also (like arbitrator(s)[47]) open up, review and revise the certificates, decisions, determinations, instructions, opinions or valuations done by the Engineer, to the extent relevant to the Dispute referred to it.[48] *However, the DAAB Rules should also, as in the case of the arbitrator(s), have expressly excluded the power to open up, review and revise any final and binding determination of the Engineer under Sub-Clause 3.7.5 [Agreement or Determination – Dissatisfaction with Engineer's Determination] of the Conditions.*

The DAAB is also empowered to proceed with the DAAB's Activities in the absence of a Party who, after receiving Notification from the DAAB, fails to comply with Sub-Clause 6.3 of the GCs.[49] This provision prevents a Party from aborting the DAAB proceedings by absenting itself – similar to that in the ICC Arbitration Rules.[50]

(4) Disputes: balance between fairness and expedition

Under Rule 6.1, the DAAB is required to proceed in accordance with Sub-Clause 21.4 [*Obtaining DAAB's Decision*] of the Conditions and the DAAB Rules, or as otherwise agreed by the Parties in writing, once a Dispute has been referred to it.[51] The DAAB is required to act 'fairly and

47. *See* Sub-Clause 21.6 [*Arbitration*] of the Conditions, second paragraph.
48. Rule 5.1(k), DAAB Rules.
49. Rule 5.1(l), DAAB Rules. Sub-Clause 6.3 of the GCs provides that '(i)n connection with the DAAB's Activities, each Party shall:
    (a) cooperate in good faith with the DAAB; and
    (b) fulfill its duties, and exercise any right or entitlement, under the Contract, the GCs and the DAAB Rules and/or otherwise

    in the manner necessary to achieve the objectives under Rule 1 of the DAAB Rules'.
50. *See*, e.g., art. 26.2 of the ICC Arbitration Rules, pursuant to which the arbitral tribunal has the power to proceed with a hearing if one of the parties fails to appear without valid excuse after having been duly summoned by the tribunal. *See also* art. 21.4 of the ICC Dispute Board Rules, providing for a similar power for a dispute board.
51. *See* Sub-Clause 21.4.1 [*Reference of a Dispute to the DAAB*] of the Conditions.

impartially' between the Parties, give each Party a 'reasonable opportunity (consistent with the expedited nature of the DAAB proceedings) of putting forward its case', and 'adopt a procedure suitable to the Dispute', avoiding unnecessary delay and/or expense.[52] Thus, under Rule 6.2, the requirements of due process or natural justice need to be balanced with the stated objective of a DAAB proceeding to be 'expeditious, efficient and cost effective'.[53]

(5) Expanded hearings rules

Rule 7 governs the procedure for a hearing, should a hearing be deemed necessary. Except as otherwise may be agreed to in writing by the Parties, the DAAB may decide on the date and place for any hearing (in consultation with the Parties (Rule 7.1(a))) on the duration of the hearing (Rule 7.1(b)), request written documentation and arguments from the Parties (Rule 7.1(c)), request production of documents, and/or oral submissions by the Parties (Rule 7.1(e)) and request attendance of any persons at the hearing that the DAAB considers may assist it in ascertaining facts and matters for its decision (Rule 7.1(f)). Parties must, consistent with their duty to cooperate in good faith with the DAAB,[54] assist the DAAB by following its directions. The scope and breadth of document production must be reasonable and compatible with the expedited nature of the DAAB proceedings. The DAAB is also free to adopt an inquisitorial procedure during any hearing (Rule 7.1(d)).

Rule 7 is intended to give the DAAB maximum flexibility as to how to proceed in respect of a hearing. The DAAB may refuse admission to any hearing or audience at any hearing, to any persons, other than representatives of the Parties and the Engineer (Rule 7.1(g)), and may also adjourn proceedings when it considers that further investigation would benefit the resolution of the Dispute (Rule 7.1(i)). The DAAB is empowered to proceed in the absence of a Party that, to the DAAB's satisfaction received timely notice of the hearing (Rule 7.1(h)). The purpose of this

52. Rule 6.2, DAAB Rules. For English statutory adjudication cases on this subject (natural justice), *see Discain Project Services Ltd v Opecprime Development Ltd* [2001] BLR 285 and the statement of the court in *Herbosch-Kiere Marine Contractors Ltd v Dover Harbour Board* [2012] EWHC 84 (TCC), quoted in a fn. 140 under **(iv) Related Law** of the commentary on **Clause 21** above.
53. Rule 1.1(b), DAAB Rules.
54. Sub-Clause 6.3 of the GCs.

provision, as in arbitration (as mentioned earlier), is to prevent any party from derailing the proceedings by absenting itself.

Unlike arbitration proceedings, where an arbitral tribunal operates within the framework of an arbitration law and may seek assistance from the local courts in, for instance, the taking of evidence,[55] the DAAB cannot usually invoke any local court procedure and is confined to what it is empowered to do by the Parties' agreement.[56]

The prohibition of the DAAB under Rule 7.2 from expressing any opinions during any hearing regarding the merits of any arguments advanced by the Parties appears to be too strict. Arbitrators quite often comment at hearings on the strength or weaknesses of a Party's arguments and Parties often find this helpful, and it may induce them to settle earlier. It is not clear why a DAAB should be prevented from doing so. However, as discussed previously, the DAAB is not permitted normally to give any Informal Assistance during a hearing, and must proceed in accordance with Rule 7.3 should Parties request such assistance at a hearing.[57]

(6) New procedures for the DAAB's decision

Rule 8.1 refers to Sub-Clause 21.4.3 [*The DAAB's Decision*] of the Conditions which provides that the DAAB must give its decision within 84 days after receiving the reference, or within such period as may be proposed by the DAAB and agreed to by both Parties in writing.[58] Rule 8.2 provides that, for three-member DAABs, the members shall meet in private following the hearing (if any) for their discussions and to start preparing the decision (Rule 8.2(a)) and shall use all 'reasonable endeavours' to reach a unanimous decision (Rule 8.2(b)). If a unanimous decision is not possible, the decision shall be rendered by a majority of the DAAB Members, who may require the minority DAAB Member to prepare a separate written report (containing reasons and supporting particulars) which shall be provided to the Parties (Rule 8.2(c)).[59]

55. *See*, for example, art. 27 of the *UNCITRAL Model Law on International Commercial Arbitration*, 1985 (amended in 2006).
56. *See* under **(iv) Related Law** of the commentary on Sub-Clause 21.1 [*Constitution of the DAAB*] of the Conditions.
57. *See* under *(2) New emphasis on Dispute avoidance* above of this commentary on the DAAB Rules.
58. An agreement in 'writing' is required by both Sub-Clause 1.3 [*Notices and Other Communications*] of the Conditions and Rule 8.1, DAAB Rules.
59. If there is no majority, then there will have been a failure to decide within the meaning of Sub-Clause 21.4.4, second paragraph, in which case either Party

In case of a DAAB Member's failure to attend a hearing, or a DAAB Members' meeting, or to fulfil any required function (except for agreeing to a unanimous decision), the 'Other Members' shall proceed to make a decision (Rule 8.2(d)). There are three exceptions to this procedure:

(1) where such failure by a DAAB Member has been caused by exceptional circumstances, of which the Other Members and the Parties have received a Notification;
(2) the DAAB Member has suspended his/her services due to non-payment of amounts due to him/her within 56 days after submitting a valid invoice and after giving a Notification to the Parties and Other Members;[60] or
(3) where the Parties agree otherwise in writing.

(7) New procedures in case of termination of a DAAB Agreement

Rule 9 relates to the impact of the termination of a DAAB Member's DAAB Agreement. Rule 9.1 provides what happens if either a sole member or three-member DAAB is addressing a Dispute under Sub-Clause 21.4 [*Obtaining DAAB's Decision*] of the Conditions at the time of termination of a DAAB Member's DAAB Agreement due to his/her 'resignation or termination under Clause 10 of the GCs'. In that case, the period within which the DAAB must render a decision is temporarily suspended[61] and, when the replacement DAAB Member[62] is appointed, the full period within which the DAAB must render a decision begins afresh from the date of the replacement Member's appointment.[63] Rule 9.2 provides that, in the case of a three-member DAAB, on the resignation or termination of one of the Members in accordance with Clause 10 of the GCs, the 'Other Members' shall continue as members of the DAAB, but (whether or not the DAAB is addressing a Dispute at the time) they shall not conduct any hearing or make any decision prior to the replacement of the DAAB Member, unless otherwise agreed between the 'Other Members' and the Parties.

---

may, within 28 days after the period for giving a decision has expired, give a NOD to the other Party in accordance with Sub-Clause 21.4.4 (a) and (b).

60. Pursuant to Sub-Clause 9.7 of the GCs.
61. *See* Sub-Clause 21.4.3 [*The DAAB's Decision*] of the Conditions.
62. Appointed in accordance with Sub-Clause 21.1 [*Constitution of the DAAB*] of the Conditions.
63. *See* Sub-Clause 21.4.3 [*The DAAB's Decision*] of the Conditions and Rule 9.1 (b), DAAB Rules.

While Rule 9 addresses the situation of a 'resignation' of a Member, it does not address the other situations mentioned in Sub-Clause 21.1 [Constitution of the DAAB] of the Conditions where a 'member declines to act or is unable to act', namely, as a result of 'death, illness [or] disability'. It is suggested that it should be interpreted as applying to those situations as well.

(8) New objection and challenge procedures

As previously mentioned, Rules 10 and 11 are new and have no counterparts in the Old Rules. These DAAB Rules provide for how objections to a DAAB Member must be made, based on the Member's 'alleged lack of independence or impartiality or otherwise'.[64] Under DAAB Rule 10, the objecting Party must give a Notification to the DAAB Member to whom it objects (which must be simultaneously copied to the other Party and the Other Members), within 7 days of becoming aware of the facts and/or events giving rise to the objection. This Notification must state that it is given under Rule 10.1(a) and the reasons for the objection, substantiating the objection with relevant facts, a description of events and supporting particulars.

The expression 'alleged lack of independence or impartiality or otherwise' is practically identical to that in the challenge provision of the ICC Arbitration Rules (Article 14.1) and the ICC Dispute Board Rules (Article 8.4). Under the ICC Arbitration Rules, while the catch-all expression 'or otherwise' allows for challenges on widely diverse grounds, the vast majority of challenges are based on an alleged lack of independence or impartiality.[65] Challenges on the 'or otherwise' ground under ICC practice have been made *inter alia* because of the improper constitution of the arbitral tribunal (when not in compliance with the ICC Arbitration Rules or the parties' arbitration agreement), where the arbitrator was not authorised to act under the law of the place of arbitration (e.g., if the law required that anyone appointed as an arbitrator must be a registered legal practitioner in the country), and where the same tribunal was appointed for two closely related parallel arbitrations despite a Party's objection.[66]

64. Sub-Clause 11.1 of the GCs.
65. Andrea Carlevaris and Rocío Digón, 'Arbitrator Challenges under the ICC Rules and Practice' (2016) (1), ICC Disp Resol Bull (ICC Services, Paris) 23, 33.
66. Jason Fry and Simon Greenberg, 'The Arbitral Tribunal: Applications of Articles 7-12 of the ICC Rules in Recent Cases' (2009) 20(2) ICC Disp Resol Bull (ICC Services, Paris) 12.

By analogy, challenges to DAAB Members may be made on similar grounds and also in the case of serious misconduct or fraud on the part of a DAAB Member.

Rule 10.1(b) provides that 'the objected DAAB Member' shall respond to the objecting Party within 7 days after receiving the notice of objection and simultaneously copy such response to the other Party and the Other Members. If the DAAB Member does not respond within this time period, the DAAB Member is deemed to have given a response denying the matters raised in the objection. Rule 10.1(c) provides that the objecting Party may formally challenge the DAAB Member within the 7 days of receiving the objected DAAB Member's response or, if there is no response, after the expiry of the 7-day period stated in Rule 10.1(b). Rule 10.1(d) provides that, if a Party fails to formally challenge the objected DAAB Member within the period of 7 days in Rule 10.1(c), it is deemed to have agreed to the DAAB Member remaining on the DAAB and is precluded from objecting to and/or challenging him/her thereafter on the basis of the facts and/or evidence in the original notice of objection given under Rule 10.1(a).

Rule 11 of the DAAB Rules provides for the challenge of a DAAB Member. Rule 11.1 applies if and when the objecting Party challenges a DAAB Member, which such Party must do within 21 days of learning the facts forming the basis of the challenge. Such challenges are to be decided by the ICC and administered by the ICC International Centre for ADR.

Rule 11.2 states that the procedure for such challenge and information on the charges to be paid are to be set out on the FIDIC and the ICC websites. This procedure is set forth in Appendix III of the ICC Dispute Board Rules, 2015 (Appendices in force from 1 October 2018). It is envisaged to be supplemented by a Practice Note to the Parties that the ICC International Centre for ADR expects to release.

(iv) Improvements:

(1) No evident purpose appears to be served in having the DAAB Rules as a separate Annex to the GCs. Neither the ICC Dispute Board Rules nor the Dispute Board Rules of the Chartered Institute of Arbitrators in the UK provide for two sets of rules in this respect. The GCs relate to procedural matters like the DAAB Rules. It is suggested that, in the interests of simplicity, all three documents (the DAAB Agreement, the GCs and the DAAB Rules) be combined into a single one.

(2) The DAAB Rules could have provided more guidance to the Parties as to the submissions and other procedural conduct of the DAAB Proceedings as the ICC Dispute Board Rules and the Chartered Institute of Arbitrators' Rules do.

(3) Rule 5.1(k) needs to be changed to expressly exclude a final and binding determination of the Engineer.

(4) Rule 9 dealing with termination of a DAAB Agreement needs to be revised to make clear that it applies to the situations mentioned in Sub-Clause 21.1 of the Conditions other than resignation, namely, where a member declines to act or is unable to act as a result of death, illness or disability.

--ooOOoo--

3 MISCELLANEOUS DOCUMENTS

The *Guidance for the Preparation of Particular Conditions* also contains three additional sets of documents: (1) *Advisory Notes to Users of FIDIC Contracts Where the Project Uses Building Information Modelling Systems*; (2) as Annexes, seven forms of securities; and (3) forms of Letter of Tender, Letter of Acceptance, Contract Agreement and DAAB Agreement. Other than the DAAB Agreement (commented on at the beginning of this chapter), these are commented on in turn below:

(1) Advisory Notes on Building Information Modelling[67]

Building Information Modelling ('BIM') is familiar in the construction industry:

> as a system that creates a three dimensional digital model of a built facility, describing its physical and functional aspects and providing versatile design and cost data that can unlock inefficiencies and improvements throughout the facility's entire life-cycle.[68]

In the *Advisory Notes*, FIDIC provides brief guidance as to how BIM might be used in conjunction with the FIDIC forms of contract. FIDIC states that its contracts are 'suitable for use with projects featuring the use of BIM –

67. *Guidance for the Preparation of Particular Conditions*, 53.
68. David Mosey, 'BIM and Related Revolutions: A Review of the Cookham Wood Trial Project' (SCL, D171, 2014) 1.

providing that the parties recognise the difference in approach and use the contract appropriately'.[69] It notes that coordination of the goals and effort of project participants in a BIM project is essential and generally achieved by their entry into a BIM Protocol and a BIM Execution Plan (BEP). FIDIC emphasises that '[a]ll project participants need to understand and work to the Levels of Design (or Detail) (LOD) that will be spelled out in these documents to ensure that there is sufficient detail at each level to allow the works to progress efficiently and avoid unnecessary changes'.[70] FIDIC has identified the risks in working in a BIM environment as arising from:

- misunderstanding of the scope of services
- use of data for an inappropriate purpose and reliance on inappropriate data
- ineffective information, document or data management
- cyber security and responsibility for hosting information
- definition of deliverables, approval, and delivery.[71]

Finally, the *Advisory Notes* include a non-exhaustive list of Sub-Clauses of the General Conditions of RB/17 that should be thoroughly reviewed when drafting the Particular Conditions.[72]

(2) Annexes – forms of securities

The Annexes comprise seven forms of security that might be issued in connection with an RB/17 contract, as follows:

(1) Annex A example form of parent company guarantee;
(2) Annex B example form of tender security;
(3) Annex C example form of performance security – demand guarantee;
(4) Annex D example form of performance security – surety bond;
(5) Annex E example form of advance payment guarantee;
(6) Annex F example form of retention money guarantee; and
(7) Annex G example form of payment guarantee by employer.

69. *Guidance for the Preparation of Particular Conditions*, 53.
70. *Ibid.*
71. *Ibid.*, 54.
72. *Ibid.*, 55.

The forms in Annexes B, C, E, F, and G are all based upon the ICC's Uniform Rules for Demand Guarantees ('URDG'), 2010 Revision,[73] which has been discussed in the commentary on Sub-Clause 4.2 [*Performance Security*] above. On the other hand, Annex D is based on the ICC's somewhat older, but also excellent, Uniform Rules for Contract Bonds ('URCB'), 1994.[74] The URCB are also discussed in the commentary on Sub-Clause 4.2 [*Performance Security*] above.

(a) Form of parent company guarantee

Annex A, comprising the example form of parent company guarantee, is not based on any set of international rules. This document assumes that the Party entering an RB/17 contract as the Contractor will be a subsidiary company within a corporate group of companies. It constitutes a guarantee by a parent company that its subsidiary, the Contractor, will duly perform all its obligations and liabilities under the Contract towards the Employer. Obviously, before signature of the guarantee, the Employer should satisfy itself that the parent company selected to sign this guarantee will have, and is likely to continue to have, the financial resources necessary to meet its commitments.[75] Ideally, from the Employer's point of view, the parent company should be the highest company in the corporate group of companies of which the Contractor is a member.

Unlike the other forms of guarantee, the example form of guarantee in Annex A is merely illustrative of the kinds of things a parent company guarantee should contain and of how it should be worded. Such a form needs to be carefully reviewed, and almost certainly revised, to take account of the particular requirements of the law on guarantees of the law governing the guarantee.

This form provides that the law governing the guarantee would be the law which governs the Contract, which is one possibility. However, it is also not uncommon for such a guarantee to be governed by the law of the country of the parent company, which may be different. Whichever law is selected, as mentioned above, the content and wording of the guarantee need to take account of the law on guarantees of the law governing the guarantee.

73. ICC Publication no 758.
74. ICC Publication no 524.
75. For example, by the presentation of its latest consolidated financial statements, duly certified by reputable independent accountants.

Like the RB/17 Conditions, this form of guarantee provides for the final resolution of disputes between the guarantor and the Employer under the ICC Arbitration Rules. However, note that any arbitration under the guarantee is likely to be a separate proceeding from any arbitration under the Conditions, as the guarantee is a separate contract from the Contract incorporating the Conditions and, for this reason, may not ordinarily be consolidated with any arbitration under the Conditions, unless the parties should agree otherwise.

(b) Form of payment guarantee

In international contracting, it is unusual for an Employer to provide a payment guarantee from a third party, such as a bank, to the Contractor, although this is certainly appropriate where there may be concerns about the creditworthiness of the Employer. On the other hand, it is not unusual for such a form of guarantee to be required by domestic legislation in various countries. Thus, under French law, an employer under a construction contract may be required to provide to the contractor such a guarantee from a financial institution or bank.[76]

(3) Letter of Tender, Letter of Acceptance, Contract Agreement and Dispute Avoidance/Adjudication Agreement

(a) Letter of Tender

The Letter of Tender is a critically important document as it constitutes an offer by the tenderer – the signatory – to execute and complete the Works and remedy any defects for the amount stated therein. By this document, the tenderer agrees – and its agreement is normally accompanied by tender security[77] – to abide by its tender until a specified date, by which time it may have been accepted by the Employer and resulted in a binding contract between the tenderer (the Contractor) and the Employer.

76. Pursuant to art. 1799-1 of the French Civil Code and Decree no 99-658 of 30 July 1999, the employer for a private works contract exceeding EUR 12,000 (excluding taxes) in value must provide the contractor with a payment guarantee for the contract price from a specified financial institution. This obligation does not apply to a public works contract since the French legislature considers that a public body would necessarily be able to pay for the services provided.

77. *See*, as Annex B to the *Guidance for the Preparation of Particular Conditions*, the example form of tender security.

The form of Letter of Tender calls for no special comment, *except that it could include reference to the 'Contract Number' as well as the 'Name of Contract' (like the Letter of Acceptance), and the third paragraph could provide that – if the offer is accepted – the Contractor will provide not only the specified Performance Security before commencing the Works but also the insurances required to be provided by the Contractor before that time (see Sub-Clause 19.2 [Insurance to be provided by the Contractor] of the Conditions).*[78]

As mentioned above, *the actual Letter of Tender is usually accompanied by tender security. However, the form of the Letter of Tender does not refer to this security. It is suggested that it should do so.*

(b) Letter of Acceptance

The Letter of Acceptance is also critically important as by its express terms (and assuming that the Contractor's actual Letter of Tender conforms with the form of the Letter of Tender) it creates a binding contract between the Parties.[79]

(c) Contract Agreement

Although the Contract Agreement is the only contractual document which both Parties are expected to sign,[80] somewhat anomalously, the form of Contract Agreement says almost nothing itself about the terms of the Parties' Contract. The Parties' Contract can only be understood by reading the Contract Agreement together with the documents to which it refers such as the Letter of Acceptance, the Letter of Tender, the Conditions and the other documents listed in Article 2 the Contract Agreement. This is contrary to usual practice in other fields where the contract document which both parties sign contains the most important matters to which the parties agree. For this reason, sometimes the

---

78. *See* the commentary on Sub-Clauses 4.2 [*Performance Security*] and 19.2 [*Insurance to be provided by the Contractor*] of the Conditions above.
79. In practice, things may not be so simple. As stated by Keating:

> The contractor's offer to carry out the works is usually termed a tender. It may well happen that as a result of negotiation it is the employer who eventually makes the offer. In any event a statement, to amount to an offer, must be definite and unambiguous.
>
> Stephen Furst and Vivian Ramsey, *Keating on Construction Contracts* (11th edn, Sweet & Maxwell, London, 2021) 18 (para. 2-005).

80. *See* Sub-Clause 1.6 [*Contract Agreement*] of the Conditions.

Contract Agreement is revised so as to provide explicitly for, among other things, a description of the Works which are to be executed, the Contract Price which is to be paid and the agreed Time for Completion of the Works.

According to Sub-Clause 1.6 [Contract Agreement] of the Conditions, where the Contractor comprises a joint venture ('JV'), the authorised representative of each member of the JV must sign the Contract Agreement. This situation is not expressly recognised in the form of the Contract Agreement. Consequently, it is important to bear this in mind. Moreover, where the Employer comprises a JV, as can sometimes happen, it is suggested that the authorised representative of each member of the JV constituting the Employer should also sign the Contract Agreement.

--ooOOoo--

The DAAB Agreement has already been discussed in **Section 2** above of this **Chapter V**.

--ooOOoo--

Appendices[1]

Appendix 1	**Particular Conditions Part A: Contract Data**
Appendix 2	**Particular Conditions Part B: Special Provisions (omitting Notes on the Preparation of Special Provisions)**
Appendix 3	**Forms of Letter of Tender, Letter of Acceptance and Contract Agreement**
Appendix 4	**DAAB Agreement, General Conditions of DAAB Agreement and DAAB Procedural Rules**
Appendix 5	**Forms of Securities**

1. The Appendices reproduced here are (like the Conditions reproduced above) taken from the 2022 reprint with amendments of the Red Book 2017.

Appendix 1

Particular Conditions Part A: Contract Data

Particular Conditions Part A – Contract Data

INTRODUCTORY GUIDANCE NOTES

These Introductory Guidance Notes are for use in completing the Contract Data and shall not form part of the Contract Data.

Certain Sub-Clauses in the General Conditions require that specific information is provided in the Contract Data.

The Employer should amend as appropriate and complete all data and should insert 'Not Applicable' in the space next to any Sub-Clause which the Employer does not wish to use.

The Employer should insert 'Tenderer to Complete' in the space next to any Sub-Clause in the Contract Data which the Employer wishes the tenderers to complete. Except where indicated 'Tenderer to Complete' tenderers shall not amend the Contract Data as provided by the Employer.

All italicised text and any enclosing square brackets are for use in preparing the Contract Data and should be deleted from the final version of the Contract Data.

Failure by the Employer to provide the information and details required in the Contract Data could mean either that the documents forming the Contract are incomplete with vital information missing, or that the fall-back provisions to be found in some of the Sub-Clauses in the General Conditions will automatically take effect.

CONTRACT DATA

Sub-Clause	Data to be given	Data
1.1.20	where the Contract allows for Cost Plus Profit, percentage profit to be added to the Cost:	____________ %
1.1.27	Defects Notification Period (DNP):	__________ days
1.1.31	Employer's name and address:	____________ ____________ ____________
1.1.35	Engineer's name and address:	____________ ____________ ____________
1.1.84	Time for Completion:	__________ days
1.3 (a)(ii)	agreed methods of electronic transmission:	____________ ____________ ____________
1.3(d)	address of Employer for communications:	____________ ____________ ____________
1.3(d)	address of Engineer for communications:	____________ ____________ ____________
1.3(d)	address of Contractor for communications:	____________ ____________ ____________
1.4	Contract shall be governed by the law of:	____________
1.4	ruling language:	____________
1.4	language for communications:	____________
1.8	number of additional paper copies of Contractor's Documents	____________

Appendix 1

Sub-Clause	Data to be given	Data
1.15	total liability of the Contractor to the Employer under or in connection with the Contract:	___________ (*sum*)
2.1	after receiving the Letter of Acceptance, the Contractor shall be given right of access to, and possession of: (*tick the relevant box*)	
	❑ all of the Site	___________ days
	❑ parts of the Site as follows:	
	part:	___________ days
	part:	___________ days
	part:	___________ days
2.4	Employer's financial arrangements:	___________ ___________ ___________
4.2	Performance Security (as percentages of the Accepted Contract Amount in currencies):	
	percent:	___________ %
	currency:	___________
	percent:	___________ %
	currency:	___________
4.7.2	period for notification of errors in the items of reference:	___________ days
4.19	period of payment for temporary utilities:	___________ days
4.20	number of additional paper copies of progress reports:	___________
5.1(a)	maximum allowable accumulated value of work subcontracted (as a percentage of the Accepted Contract Amount):	___________ %
5.1(b)	parts of the Works for which subcontracting is not permitted:	___________ ___________ ___________
6.5	normal working hours on the Site:	___________
8.3	number of additional paper copies of programmes:	___________
8.8	Delay Damages payable for each day of delay:	___________
8.8	maximum amount of Delay Damages:	___________

Appendix 1

Sub-Clause	Data to be given	Data
12.2	method of measurement:	______________
12.3	percentage profit:	as stated under 1.1.20 above
13.4(b)(ii)	percentage rate to be applied to Provisional Sums for overhead charges and profit:	____________ %
14.2	total amount of Advance Payment (as a percentage of Accepted Contract Amount):	______________
14.2	currency or currencies of Advance Payment:	______________ ______________
14.2.3(a)	minimum amount of certified interim payments to commence repayment of the Advance Payment (as a percentage of the Accepted Contract Amount)	____________ %
14.2.3(b)	percentage deductions for the repayment of the Advance Payment:	____________ %
14.3	period of payment:	______________
14.3(b)	number of additional paper copies of Statements:	____________ %
14.3(iii)	percentage of retention:	______________
14.3(iii)	limit of Retention Money (as a percentage of Accepted Contract Amount):	____________ %
14.5(b)(i)	Plant and Materials for payment when shipped:	______________ ______________
14.5(c)(i)	Plant and Materials for payment when delivered to the Site:	______________ ______________
14.6.2	minimum amount of Interim Payment Certificate (IPC):	______________
14.7(a)	period for payment of Advance Payment to the Contractor:	___________ days

Sub-Clause	Data to be given	Data
14.7(b)(i)	period for the Employer to make interim payments to the Contractor under Sub-Clause 14.6 [*Interim Payment*]:	________ days
14.7(b)(ii)	period for the Employer to make interim payments to the Contractor under Sub-Clause 14.13 [*Final Payment*]:	________ days
14.7(c)	period for the Employer to make final payment to the Contractor:	________ days
14.8	financing charges for delayed payment (percentage points above the average bank short–term lending rate as referred to under sub-paragraph (a)):	________ %
14.11.1(b)	number of additional paper copies of draft final Statement:	________
14.15	currencies for payment of Contract Price:	________ ________ ________
14.15(a)(i)	proportions or amounts of Local and Foreign Currencies are: Local: .... Foreign:	 ________ ________
14.15(c)	currencies and proportions for payment of Delay Damages:	________ ________ ________
14.15(c)	rates of exchange:	________
17.2(d)	forces of nature, the risks of which are allocated to the Contractor:	________ ________ ________

Appendix 1

Sub-Clause	Data to be given	Data
19.1	permitted deductible limits:	
	insurance required for the Works:	______________
	insurance required for Goods:	______________
	insurance required for liability for breach of professional duty:	______________
	insurance required against liability for fitness for purpose (if any is required):	______________
	insurance required for injury to persons and damage to property:	______________
	insurance required for injury to employees:	______________
	other insurances required by Laws and by local practice:	
	______________	______________
	______________	______________
	______________	______________
19.2.1(b)	additional amount to be insured (as a percentage of the replacement value, if less or more than 15%):	______________ %
19.2.1(iv)	list of risks arising from Exceptional Events which shall not be excluded from the insurance cover for the Works:	______________ ______________ ______________
19.2.2	extent of insurance required for Goods:	______________
	amount of insurance required for Goods:	______________ ______________
19.2.3(a)	amount of insurance required for liability for breach of professional duty:	______________
19.2.3(b)	insurance required against liability for fitness for purpose:	yes/no (*delete as appropriate*)
19.2.3	period of insurance required for liability for breach of professional duty:	______________
19.2.4	amount of insurance required for injury to persons and damage to property:	______________
19.2.6	other insurances required by Laws and by local practice (give details):	______________

Sub-Clause	Data to be given	Data
21.1	time for appointment of DAAB:	__________
21.1	the DAAB shall comprise:	__________ members
21.1	list of proposed members of DAAB	
	– proposed by Employer:	1. __________
		2. __________
		3. __________
	– proposed by Contractor:	1. __________
		2. __________
		3. __________

Definition of Sections (if any):

Description of parts of the Works that shall be designated a Section for the purposes of the Contract (Sub-Clause 1.1.73)	Value: Percentage* of Accepted Contract Amount (Sub-Clause 14.9)	Time for Completion (Sub-Clause 1.1.84)	Delay Damages (Sub-Clause 8.8)

* These percentages shall also be applied to each half of the Retention Money under Sub-Clause 14.9.

--ooOOoo--

APPENDIX 2

Particular Conditions Part B: Special Provisions (Omitting Notes on the Preparation of Special Provisions)

Particular Conditions Part B – Special Provisions

INTRODUCTION

The terms of the Conditions of Contract for Construction have been prepared by the Fédération Internationale des Ingénieurs-Conseils (FIDIC) and are recommended for general use for the construction of building or engineering works, where tenders are invited on an international basis.

Modifications to the General Conditions may well be required to account for local legal requirements, particularly if they are to be used on domestic contracts.

Under the usual arrangements for this type of contract, the Contractor is responsible for the construction, in accordance with the design of the Employer, of building and/or engineering works. These Conditions allow for the possibility that the Contractor may be required to design a small proportion or a minor element of the Permanent Works, but they are not intended for use where significant design input by the Contractor is required or the Contractor is required to design a large proportion or any major elements of the Permanent Works. In this latter case, it is recommended that the Employer consider using FIDIC's Conditions of

Contract for Plant and Design-Build, Second Edition 2017 (or, alternatively and if suitable for the circumstances of the project, FIDIC's Conditions of Contract for EPC/Turnkey Projects, Second Edition 2017).

The guidance hereafter is intended to assist drafters of the Special Provisions (Particular Conditions-Part B) by giving options for various sub-clauses where appropriate. In some cases example wording is included between lines, while in other instances only an aide-memoire is given.

FIDIC strongly recommends that the Employer, the Contractor and all drafters of the Special Provisions take all due regard of the five FIDIC Golden Principles:

> **GP1: The duties, rights, obligations, roles and responsibilities of all the Contract Participants must be generally as implied in the General Conditions, and appropriate to the requirements of the project.**
> **GP2: The Particular Conditions must be drafted clearly and unambiguously.**
> **GP3: The Particular Conditions must not change the balance of risk/reward allocation provided for in the General Conditions.**
> **GP4: All time periods specified in the Contract for Contract Participants to perform their obligations must be of reasonable duration.**
> **GP5: Unless there is a conflict with the governing law of the Contract, all formal disputes must be referred to a Dispute Avoidance/Adjudication Board (or a Dispute Adjudication Board, if applicable) for a provisionally binding decision as a condition precedent to arbitration.**

These FIDIC golden principles are described and explained in the publication FIDIC's Golden Principles (http://fidic.org/books/fidic-golden-principles-2019 †), and are necessary to ensure that modifications to the General Conditions:

- **are limited to those necessary for the particular features of the Site and the project, and necessary to comply with the applicable law;**
- **do not change the essential fair and balanced character of a FIDIC contract; and**
- **the Contract remains recognisable as a FIDIC contract.**

Before incorporating any new or changed sub-clauses, the wording must be carefully checked to ensure that it is wholly suitable for the particular circumstances. Unless it is considered suitable, example wording should be amended before use.

Where any amendments or additions are made to the General Conditions, great care must be taken to ensure that the wording does not unintentionally alter the meaning of other clauses in the Conditions of Contract, does not inadvertently change the obligations assigned to the Parties or the balance of risks shared between them and/or does not create any ambiguity or misunderstanding in the rest of the Contract documents.

Each time period stated in the General Conditions is what FIDIC believes is reasonable, realistic and achievable in the context of the obligation to which it refers, and reflects the appropriate balance between the interests of the Party required to perform the obligation, and the interests of the other Party whose rights are dependent on the performance of that obligation. If consideration is given to changing any such stated time period in the Special Provisions (Particular Conditions – Part B), care should be taken to ensure that the amended time period remains reasonable, realistic and achievable in the particular circumstances.

There are a number of Sub-Clauses in the General Conditions which require data to be provided by the Employer and/or the Contractor and inserted into the Contract Data (Particular Conditions – Part A). However, there are no Sub-Clauses in the General Conditions which require data or information to be included in the Special Provisions (Particular Conditions – Part B).

Provisions found in the Contract documents under Special Provisions (Particular Conditions – Part B) indicate that the General Conditions have been amended or supplemented.

In describing the Conditions of Contract in the tender documents, the following text can be used:

> 'The Conditions of Contract comprise the 'General Conditions', which form part of the 'Conditions of Contract for Construction for Building and Engineering Works Designed by the Employer' Second Edition 2017, reprinted 2022 with amendments, published by the Fédération Internationale des Ingénieurs-Conseils (FIDIC), the Contract Data (Particular Conditions – Part A) and the following 'Special

> Provisions' (Particular Conditions – Part B), which include amendments and additions to such General Conditions.'

The provisions of the Special Provisions (Particular Conditions – Part B) will always over-rule and supersede the equivalent provisions in the General Conditions, and it is important that the changes are easily identifiable by using the same clause numbers and titles as appear in the General Conditions. Furthermore, it is necessary to add a statement in the tender documents for a contract that:

> 'The provisions to be found in the Special Provisions (Particular Conditions – Part B) take precedence over the equivalent provisions found under the same Sub-Clause number(s) in the General Conditions, and the provisions of the Contract Data (Particular Conditions–Part A) take precedence over the Special Provisions (Particular Conditions – Part B).'

† Please Note: all web links referred to in these guidance notes are up-to-date as of the date of this publication but it is recommended that users of these guidance notes check online, at the time that they wish to reference the relevant document, for the most up-to-date version of the document.

NOTES ON THE PREPARATION OF TENDER DOCUMENTS

When preparing the tender documents and planning the tender process, Employers should read the publication FIDIC Procurement Procedures Guide 1st edition 2011 (http://fidic.org/books/fidic-procurement-procedures-guide-1st-ed-2011) which presents a systematic approach to the procurement of engineering and building works for projects of all sizes and complexity, and gives invaluable help and advice on the contents of the tender documents, and the procedures for receiving and evaluating tenders. This publication provides internationally acceptable, comprehensive, best practice procedures designed to increase the probability of receiving responsive, clear and competitive tenders using FIDIC forms of contract. FIDIC intends to update the FIDIC Procurement Procedures Guide (planned for publication at a later date) to make specific reference to these Conditions of Contract for Construction, Second Edition 2017.

The tender documents should be prepared by suitably qualified engineers who are familiar with the technical aspects of the required works and the particular requirements and contractual provisions of a construction project. Furthermore, a review by suitably-qualified lawyers is advisable.

The tender documents issued to tenderers should normally include the following:

- Letter of invitation to tender
- Instructions to Tenderers (including advice on any matters which the Employer wishes tenderers to include in their Tenders but which do not form part of the Specification and/ or Drawings)
- Form of Letter of Tender and required appendices (if any)
- Conditions of Contract: General and Particular
- General information and data
- Technical information and data (including the data referred to in Sub-Clause 2.5 [*Site Data and Items of Reference*] of the General Conditions)
- the Specification
- the Drawings
- Schedules from the Employer
- details of schedules and other information required from tenderers
- required forms of agreement, securities and guarantees.

The publication FIDIC Procurement Procedures Guide referred to above provides useful guidance as to the content and format of each of the above.

For this type of contract where the Works are normally valued by measurement, the Bill of Quantities will usually be the most important Schedule. A Daywork Schedule may also be necessary to cover minor works to be executed at cost. In addition, each of the tenderers should receive the data referred to in Sub-Clause 2.5 [*Site Data and Items of Reference*], and the Instructions to Tenderers should advise them of any special matters which the Employer wishes them to take into account when pricing the Works but which are not to form part of the Contract.

When the Employer accepts the Letter of Tender, the Contract (which then comes into full force and effect) includes these completed Schedules.

The following Sub-Clauses make express reference to matters to be stated in the Specification and/ or Drawings. However, it may also be necessary under other Sub-Clauses for the Employer to give specific information in the Specification (for example, under Sub-Clause 7.2 [*Samples*]).

1.8 Care and Supply of Documents
1.13 Compliance with Laws
2.1 Right of Access to the Site
2.5 Site Data and Items of Reference
2.6 Employer-Supplied Materials and Employer's Equipment
4.1 Contractor's General Obligations
4.4 Contractor's Documents
4.5 Training
4.6 Co-operation
4.8 Health and Safety Obligations
4.9 Quality Management and Compliance Verification Systems
4.16 Transport of Goods
4.18 Protection of the Environment
4.19 Temporary Utilities
4.20 Progress Reports
5.2 Nominated Subcontractors
6.1 Engagement of Staff and Labour
6.6 Facilities for Staff and Labour
6.7 Health and Safety of Personnel
6.12 Key Personnel
7.3 Inspection
7.4 Testing by the Contractor
7.8 Royalties
8.3 Programme
9.1 Contractor's Obligations
10.2 Taking Over Parts
11.11 Clearance of Site.

Many Sub-Clauses in the General Conditions make reference to data being contained in the Contract Data (Particular Conditions – Part A). This data must be provided in the tender documents, and these Conditions of Contract assume that all such data will be provided by the Employer, except as expressly noted in the example form of Contract Data included in this publication. If the Employer requires tenderers to provide any of the other information required in the Contract Data, the tender documents must make this clear.

If the Employer requires tenderers to provide additional data or information, a convenient way of doing this is to provide a suitably worded questionnaire with the tender documents.

The Instructions to Tenderers may need to specify any constraints on the completion of the Contract Data and/or Schedules, and/or specify the extent of other information which each tenderer is to include with his/her Tender. If each tenderer is to produce a tender security and/or a parent company guarantee, these requirements should be included in the Instructions to Tenderers: example forms are included at the end of this publication.

The Instructions to Tenderers may require the tenderer to provide information on the matters referred to in some or all of the following Sub-Clauses:

4.3 Contractor's Representative
6.12 Key Personnel
19 Insurance

It is important for the Parties to understand which of the documents included in the tender dossier, and which of the documents submitted by tenderers, will form part of the Contract and therefore have continuing effect. For example, the Instructions to Tenderers are not, by definition, a part of the Contract. They are simply instructions and information on the preparation and submission of the tender, and they should not contain anything of a binding or contractual nature.

Finally, when planning the overall programme for the project, Employers must remember to allow a realistic time for:

- tenderers to prepare and submit a responsive Tender (avoiding time that is either too short which can reduce competition and result in inadequate submittals, or too long which can be wasteful to all parties involved); and
- the review and evaluation of tenders and the award of the Contract to the successful tenderer. This will be the minimum time which tenderers should be asked to hold their tenders valid and open to acceptance.

--ooOOoo--

If the Employer requires tenderers to provide additional data or information, a convenient way of doing this is to provide a suitably worded questionnaire with the tender documents.

The Instructions to Tenderers may need to specify any constraints on the compilation of the Contract Data and/or Schedules, and/or specify the extent of other information which each tenderer is to include with his/her Tender. If each tenderer is to produce a tender security and/or a parent company guarantee, these requirements should be included in the Instructions to Tenderers; example forms are included at the end of this publication.

The Instructions to Tenderers may require the tenderers to provide information on the matters referred to in some or all of the following Sub-Clauses:

4.3 Contractor's Representative
6.12 Key Personnel
19 Insurance

It is important for the Parties to understand which of the documents included in the tender dossier, and which of the documents submitted by tenderers, will form part of the Contract and therefore have contracting effect. For example, the Instructions to Tenderers are not, by definition, a part of the Contract. They are simply instructions and information on the preparation and submission of the tender, and they should not contain anything of a binding or contractual nature.

Finally, when planning the overall programme for the project, Employers must remember to allow a realistic time for:

- tenderers to prepare and submit a responsive Tender (avoiding time that is either too short which can reduce competition and result in inadequate submittals, or too long which can be wasteful to all parties involved); and
- the review and evaluation of tenders and the award of the Contract to the successful tenderer. This will be the minimum time which tenderers should be asked to hold their tenders valid and open to acceptance.

--ooOoo--

Appendix 3

Forms of Letter of Tender, Letter of Acceptance and Contract Agreement

LETTER OF TENDER

NAME OF CONTRACT:

TO:

We have examined the Conditions of Contract, Specification, Drawings, Schedules including the Bill of Quantities, the Contract Data and Addenda Nos ____________ for the above-named Contract and the words and expressions used herein shall have the meanings assigned to them in the Conditions of Contract. We offer to execute and complete the Works and remedy any defects therein, in conformity with this Tender which includes all these documents, for the sum of

____

[*currency and amount in figures*]

____

[*currency and amount in words*]

or such other amount as may be determined in accordance with the Contract.

We agree to abide by this Tender until ____________ [*date*] and it shall remain binding upon us and may be accepted at any time before that date.

If this offer is accepted, we will provide the specified Performance Security, commence the Works as soon as is reasonably practicable after the Commencement Date, and complete the Works in accordance with the above-named documents within the Time for Completion.

Unless and until a Contract Agreement is prepared and executed this Letter of Tender, together with your written acceptance thereof, shall constitute a binding contract between us.

We understand that you are not bound to accept the lowest or any tender you may receive.

Signature ____________ in the capacity of ____________ duly authorised to sign tenders for and on behalf of ________________

Address: ____________________

Date: ____________________

--ooOOoo--

LETTER OF ACCEPTANCE*

NAME OF CONTRACT: ______________________

CONTRACT NUMBER: ______________________

TO: ______________________

Date: ______________________

Your Reference: ______________________

Our Reference: ______________________

We thank you for your Tender dated ____________ for the execution and completion of the Works comprising the above-named Contract and remedying of defects therein, all in conformity with the terms and conditions contained in the Contract.

We have pleasure in accepting your Tender for the Accepted Contract Amount of:

____

[*currency and amount in figures*]

____

[*currency and amount in words*]

which amount includes the Provisional Sums (if any).

In consideration of you properly and truly performing the Contract, we agree to pay you the Accepted Contract Amount or such other sums to which you may become entitled under the terms of the Contract, at such times and as prescribed by the Contract.

We acknowledge that this Letter of Acceptance creates a binding Contract between us, and we undertake to fulfil all our obligations and duties in accordance with the terms of this Contract.

Signed by: ______________________ (signature)

For and behalf of: ______________________

Date: ______________________

- Memoranda (if any) to be annexed [*see Sub-Clause 1.1.50*]

CONTRACT AGREEMENT

This Agreement made the ____________ day of ____________ Between ____________ of ____________ (hereinafter called 'the Employer') of the one part, and ____________ of ____________ (hereinafter called 'the Contractor') of the other part

Whereas the Employer desires that the Works known as ________ [*name and number of the Contract*] should be executed by the Contractor, and has accepted a Tender by the Contractor for the execution and completion of these Works and the remedying of any defects therein.

The Employer and the Contractor agree as follows:

1. In this Agreement words and expressions shall have the same meanings as are respectively assigned to them in the Conditions of Contract hereinafter referred to.
2. The following documents shall be deemed to form and be read and construed as part of this Agreement:
   (a) The Letter of Acceptance dated ____________
   (b) The Letter of Tender dated ____________
   (c) The Addenda Nos ____________
   (d) The Conditions of Contract
   (e) The Specification
   (f) The Drawings
   (g) The Schedules and
   (h) The JV Undertaking.*
   * [*if the Contractor constitutes an unincorporated JV, otherwise delete*]
3. In consideration of the payments to be made by the Employer to the Contractor as hereinafter mentioned, the Contractor hereby covenants with the Employer to execute and complete the Works and remedy any defects therein, in conformity with the provisions of the Contract.
4. The Employer hereby covenants to pay the Contractor, in consideration of the execution and completion of the Works and the remedying of defects therein, the Contract Price at the times and in the manner prescribed by the Contract.

In Witness whereof the parties hereto have caused this Agreement to be executed the day and year first before written in accordance with their respective laws.

SIGNED by: ______________________
for and on behalf of the Employer in the presence of
Witness: ______________________
Name: ______________________
Address: ______________________
Date: ______________________

SIGNED by: ______________________
for and on behalf of the Contractor in the presence of
Witness: ______________________
Name: ______________________
Address: ______________________
Date: ______________________

--ooOOoo--

Appendix 4

DAAB Agreement, General Conditions of DAAB Agreement and DAAB Procedural Rules

DAAB AGREEMENT

[All italicised text and any text within square brackets (except sub-clause headings) in this form of agreement is for use in preparing the form and should be deleted from the final product].

Name and details of the Contract ________________________________

____

This Agreement made the ________ day of ________ *[month]*,________ *[year]*, between

Name and contact details of the Employer ________________________ *(name)*

________________________ *(address)*

________________________ *(telephone)*

________________ *(email/other contact details)*;

Name and contact details of the Contractor ________________________ *(name)*

________________________ *(address)*

________________________ *(telephone)*

________________ *(email/other contact details)*;

and

Name and contact details of the DAAB Member ________________________ *(name)*

________________________ *(address)*

________________________ *(telephone)*

________________ *(email/other contact details)*;

Appendix 4

('**DAAB Agreement**')

Whereas:

A. the Employer and the Contractor have entered (or intend to enter) into the Contract;

B. under the Contract, the '**DAAB**' or '**Dispute Avoidance/Adjudication Board**' means the sole member or three members (as stated in the Contract Data of the Contract) so named in the Contract, or appointed under Sub-Clause 21.1 [*Constitution of the DAAB*] or Sub-Clause 21.2 [*Failure to Appoint DAAB Members*] of the Conditions of Contract;

C. the Employer and the Contractor desire jointly to appoint the above-named DAAB Member to act on the DAAB as:

(a) the sole member of the DAAB, and where this is the case, all references to the 'Other Members' do not apply; or

(b) one of three members/chairperson [delete the one which is not applicable] of the DAAB and, where this is the case, the other two persons are:

____________ (*name*) ____________ (*address*) ____________ (*telephone*) ____________ (*email/ other contact details*)	____________ (*name*) ____________ (*address*) ____________ (*telephone*) ____________ (*email/ other contact details*)

the '**Other Members**'; and

D. the DAAB Member accepts this appointment.

The Employer, Contractor and DAAB Member jointly agree as follows:

1. The conditions of this DAAB Agreement comprise:

   (a) Clause 21 [*Disputes and Arbitration*] of the Conditions of Contract, and any other provisions of the Contract that are applicable to the DAAB's Activities; and

   (b) the 'General Conditions of DAAB Agreement', which is appended to the General Conditions of the 'Conditions of Contract for Construction' Second Edition 2017, reprinted in 2022 with amendments, published by FIDIC ('GCs'), as amended and/or added to by the following provisions.

2. [Details of amendments to the GCs, if any. For example:
   In the procedural rules annexed to the GCs, Rule _ is deleted and replaced by: ' … ']

3. The DAAB Member shall be paid in accordance with Clause 9 of the GCs. The currency of payment shall be ____________ .

   In respect of Sub-Clauses 9.1 and 9.2 of the GCs, the amounts of the DAAB Member's monthly fee and daily fee shall be:

   monthly fee ____________ per month, and

   daily fee of ____________ per day
   (or as otherwise set under Sub-Clause 9.3 of the GCs).

4. In consideration of the above fees, and other payments to be made to the DAAB Member in accordance with the GCs, the DAAB Member undertakes to act as DAAB Member in accordance with the terms of this DAAB Agreement.

5. The Employer and the Contractor shall be jointly and severally liable for the DAAB Member's fees and other payments to be made to the DAAB Member in accordance with the GCs.

6. This DAAB Agreement shall be governed by the law of ______________ (if not stated, the law that governs the Contract under Sub-Clause 1.4 of the Conditions of Contract).

SIGNED by: ______________	SIGNED by: ______________	SIGNED by: ______________
Print name: ______________	Print name: ______________	the DAAB Member
Title: ______________	Title: ______________	Title: ______________
for and on behalf of the Employer	for and on behalf of the Contractor	
in the presence of	in the presence of	in the presence of
Witness: ______________	Witness: ______________	Witness: ______________
Name: ______________	Name: ______________	Name: ______________
Address: ______________	Address: ______________	Address: ______________
______________	______________	______________
Date: ______________	Date: ______________	Date: ______________

--ooOOoo--

APPENDIX*

GENERAL CONDITIONS OF DAAB AGREEMENT

1 Definitions

1.1 ‘**General Conditions of DAAB Agreement**’ or ‘**GCs**’ means this document entitled ‘General Conditions of DAAB Agreement’, as published by FIDIC.

1.2 In the DAAB Agreement (as defined below) and in the GCs, words and expressions which are not otherwise defined shall have the meanings assigned to them in the Contract (as defined in the DAAB Agreement).

1.3 ‘**DAAB Agreement**’ is as defined under the Contract and is a tripartite agreement by and between:

(a) the Employer;
(b) the Contractor; and
(c) the DAAB Member who is defined in the DAAB Agreement as being either:
    (i) the sole member of the DAAB, or
    (ii) one of the three members (or the chairperson) of the DAAB.

1.4 ‘**DAAB’s Activities**’ means the activities carried out by the DAAB in accordance with the Contract and the GCs, including all Informal Assistance, meetings (including meetings and/or discussions between the DAAB members in the case of a three-member DAAB), Site visits, hearings and decisions.

1.5 ‘**DAAB Rules**’ means the document entitled ‘**DAAB Procedural Rules**’ published by FIDIC which are annexed to, and form part of, the GCs.

1.6 ‘**Informal Assistance**’ means the informal assistance given by the DAAB to the Parties when requested jointly by the Parties under Sub-Clause 21.3 [*Avoidance of Disputes*] of the Conditions of Contract.

* Note: This is an appendix to the General Conditions of RB/17.

1.7 **‘Term of the DAAB’** means the period starting on the Effective Date (as defined in Sub-Clause 2.1 below) and finishing on the date that the term of the DAAB expires in accordance with Sub-Clause 21.1 [*Constitution of the DAAB*] of the Conditions of Contract.

1.8 **‘Notification’** means a notice in writing given under the GCs, which shall be:

(a) (i) a paper-original signed by the DAAB Member or the authorised representative of the Contractor or of the Employer (as the case may be); or

(ii) an electronic original generated from the system of electronic transmission agreed between the Parties and the DAAB, which electronic original is transmitted by the electronic address uniquely assigned to the DAAB Member or each such authorised representative (as the case may be);

(b) delivered by hand (against receipt), or sent by mail or courier (against receipt), or transmitted using the system of electronic transmission under sub-paragraph (a)(ii) above; and

(c) delivered, sent or transmitted to the address for the recipient’s communications as stated in the DAAB Agreement. However, if the recipient gives a Notification of another address, all Notifications shall be delivered accordingly after the sender receives such Notification.

2 General Provisions

2.1 The DAAB Agreement shall take effect:

(a) in the case of a sole-member DAAB, on the date when the Employer, the Contractor and the DAAB Member have each signed (or, under the Contract, are deemed to have signed) the DAAB Agreement; or

(b) in the case of a three-member DAAB, on the date when the Employer, the Contractor, the DAAB Member and the Other Members have each signed (or under the Contract are deemed to have signed) a DAAB Agreement.

(the **‘Effective Date’** in the GCs).

2.2 Immediately after the Effective Date, either or both Parties shall give a Notification to the DAAB Member that the DAAB Agreement has come into effect. If the DAAB Member does not receive such a notice within 182 days after entering into the DAAB Agreement, it shall be void and ineffective.

	2.3	The employment of the DAAB Member is a personal appointment. No assignment of, or subcontracting or delegation of the DAAB Member's rights and/or obligations under the DAAB Agreement is permitted.
3 Warranties	3.1	The DAAB Member warrants and agrees that he/she is, and will remain at all times during the Term of the DAAB, impartial and independent of the Employer, the Contractor, the Employer's Personnel and the Contractor's Personnel (including in accordance with Sub-Clause 4.1 below).
	3.2	If, after signing the DAAB Agreement (or after he/she is deemed to have signed the DAAB Agreement under the Contract), the DAAB Member becomes aware of any fact or circumstance which might: (a) call into question his/her independence or impartiality; and/or (b) be, or appear to be, inconsistent with his/her warranty and agreement under Sub-Clause 3.1 above the DAAB Member warrants and agrees that he/she shall immediately disclose this in writing to the Parties and the Other Members (if any).
	3.3	When appointing the DAAB Member, each Party relies on the DAAB Member's representations that he/she is: (a) experienced and/or knowledgeable in the type of work which the Contractor is to carry out under the Contract; (b) experienced in the interpretation of construction and/or engineering contract documentation; and (c) fluent in the language for communications stated in the Contract Data (or the language as agreed between the Parties and the DAAB).

4 Independence and Impartiality	4.1	Further to Sub-Clauses 3.1 and 3.2 above, the DAAB Member shall: (a) have no financial interest in the Contract, or in the project of which the Works are part, except for payment under the DAAB Agreement; (b) have no interest whatsoever (financial or otherwise) in the Employer, the Contractor, the Employer's Personnel or the Contractor's Personnel; (c) in the 5 years before signing the DAAB Agreement, not have been employed as a consultant or otherwise by the Employer, the Contractor, the Employer's Personnel or the Contractor's Personnel, except in such circumstances as were disclosed in writing to the Employer and the Contractor before they signed the DAAB Agreement (or are deemed to have done so); (d) not previously have acted, and shall not act, in any judicial or arbitral capacity in relation to the Contract; (e) have disclosed in writing to the Employer, the Contractor and the Other Members (if any), before signing the DAAB Agreement (or before he/she is deemed to have signed the DAAB Agreement under the Contract) and to his/her best knowledge and recollection, any: (i) existing and/or past professional or personal relationships with any director, officer or employee of the Employer, the Contractor, the Employer's Personnel or the Contractor's Personnel (including as a dispute resolution practitioner on another project), (ii) facts or circumstances which might call into question his/her independence or impartiality, and (iii) previous involvement in the project of which the Contract forms part; (f) not, while a DAAB Member and for the Term of the DAAB: (i) be employed as a consultant or otherwise by, and/or (ii) enter into discussions or make any agreement regarding future employment with the Employer, the Contractor, the Employer's Personnel or the Contractor's Personnel, except as may be agreed by the Employer, the Contractor and the Other Members (if any); and/or

(g) not solicit, accept or receive (directly or indirectly) any gift, gratuity, commission or other thing of value from the Employer, the Contractor, the Employer's Personnel or the Contractor's Personnel, except for payment under the DAAB Agreement.

5 General Obligations of the DAAB Member

5.1 The DAAB Member shall:

(a) comply with the GCs, the DAAB Rules and the Conditions of Contract that are relevant to the DAAB's Activities;

(b) not give advice to the Employer, the Contractor, the Employer's Personnel or the Contractor's Personnel concerning the conduct of the Contract, except as required to carry out the DAAB's Activities;

(c) ensure his/her availability during the Term of the DAAB (except in exceptional circumstances, in which case the DAAB Member shall give a Notification without delay to the Parties and the Other Members (if any) detailing the exceptional circumstances) for all meetings, Site visits, hearings and as is necessary to comply with sub-paragraph (a) above;

(d) become, and shall remain for the duration of the Term of the DAAB, knowledgeable about the Contract and informed about:

(i) the Parties' performance of the Contract;
(ii) the Site and its surroundings; and
(iii) the progress of the Works (and of any other parts of the project of which the Contract forms part)

including by visiting the Site, meeting with the Parties and by studying all documents received from either Party under Rule 4.3 of the DAAB Rules (which shall be maintained in a current working file, in hard-copy or electronic format at the DAAB Member's discretion); and

(e) be available to give Informal Assistance when requested jointly by the Parties.

6 General Obligations of the Parties	6.1	Each Party shall comply with the GCs, the DAAB Rules and the Conditions of Contract that are relevant to the DAAB's Activities. The Employer and the Contractor shall be responsible for compliance with this provision by the Employer's Personnel and the Contractor's Personnel, respectively.
	6.2	Each Party shall co-operate with the other Party in constituting the DAAB, under Sub-Clause 21.1 [*Constitution of the DAAB*] and/or Sub-Clause 21.2 [*Failure to Appoint DAAB Member(s)*] of the Conditions of Contract, without delay.
	6.3	In connection with the DAAB's Activities, each Party shall: (a) co-operate in good faith with the DAAB; and (b) fulfil its duties, and exercise any right or entitlement, under the Contract, the GCs and the DAAB Rules and/or otherwise in the manner necessary to achieve the objectives under Rule 1 of the DAAB Rules.
	6.4	The Parties, the Employer's Personnel and the Contractor's Personnel shall not request advice from or consultation with the DAAB Member regarding the Contract, except as required for the DAAB Member to carry out the DAAB's Activities.
	6.5	At all times when interacting with the DAAB, each Party shall not compromise the DAAB's warranty of independence and impartiality under Sub-Clause 3.1 above.
	6.6	In addition to providing documents under Rule 4.3 of the DAAB Rules, each Party shall ensure that the DAAB Member remains informed as is necessary to enable him/her to comply with sub-paragraph (d) of Sub-Clause 5.1 above.
7 Confidentiality	7.1	Subject to Sub-Clause 7.4 below, the DAAB Member shall treat the details of the Contract, all the DAAB's Activities and the documents provided under Rule 4.3 of the DAAB Rules as private and confidential, and shall not publish or disclose them without the prior written consent of the Parties and the Other Members (if any).
	7.2	Subject to Sub-Clause 7.4 below, the Employer, the Contractor, the Employer's Personnel and the Contractor's Personnel shall treat the details of all the DAAB's Activities as private and confidential.

7.3 Each person's obligation of confidentiality under Sub-Clause 7.1 or Sub-Clause 7.2 above (as the case may be) shall not apply where the information:

(a) was already in that person's possession without an obligation of confidentiality before receipt under the DAAB Agreement;

(b) becomes generally available to the public through no breach of the GCs; or

(c) is lawfully obtained by the person from a third party which is not bound by an obligation of confidentiality.

7.4 If a DAAB Member is replaced under the Contract, the Parties and/or the Other Members (if any) shall disclose details of the Contract, the documents provided under Rule 4.3 of the DAAB Rules and previous DAAB's Activities (including decisions, if any) to the replacement DAAB Member as is necessary in order to:

(a) enable the replacement DAAB Member to comply with sub-paragraph (d) of Sub-Clause 5.1 above; and

(b) ensure consistency in the manner in which the DAAB's Activities are conducted following such replacement.

8 The Parties' Undertaking and Indemnity

8.1 The Employer and the Contractor undertake to each other and to the DAAB Member that the DAAB Member shall not:

(a) be appointed as an arbitrator in any arbitration under the Contract;

(b) be called as a witness to give evidence concerning any Dispute in any arbitration under the Contract; or

(c) be liable for any claims for anything done or omitted in the discharge or purported discharge of the DAAB Member's functions, except in any case of fraud, gross negligence, deliberate default or reckless misconduct by him/her.

8.2 The Employer and the Contractor hereby jointly and severally indemnify and hold the DAAB Member harmless against and from all damages, losses and expenses (including legal fees and expenses) resulting from any claim from which he/she is relieved from liability under Sub-Clause 8.1 above.

9 Fees and Expenses

9.1 The DAAB Member shall be paid as follows, in the currency named in the DAAB Agreement:

(a) a monthly fee, which shall be a fixed fee as payment in full for:

(i) being available on 28-days' notice for all meetings, Site visits and hearings under the DAAB Rules (and, in the event of a request under Rule 3.6 of the DAAB Rules, being available for an urgent meeting or Site visit);

(ii) becoming and remaining knowledgeable about the Contract, informed about the progress of the Works and maintaining a current working file of documents, in accordance with sub-paragraph (d) of Clause 5.1 above;

(iii) all office and overhead expenses including secretarial services, photocopying and office supplies incurred in connection with his/ her duties; and

(iv) all services performed hereunder except those referred to in sub-paragraphs (b) and (c) of this Clause.

This fee shall be paid monthly with effect from the last day of the month in which the Effective Date occurs until the end of the month in which the Term of the DAAB expires, or the DAAB Member declines to act or is unable to act as a result of death, illness, disability, resignation or termination of his/her DAAB Agreement.

If no monthly fee is stated in the DAAB Agreement, the matters described in sub-paragraphs (i) to (iv) above shall be deemed to be covered by the daily fee under sub-paragraph (b) below;

(b) a daily fee, which shall be considered as payment in full for each day:

(i) or part of a day, up to a maximum of two days' travel time in each direction, for the journey between the DAAB Member's home and the Site, or another location of a meeting with the Parties and/or the Other Members (if any);

(ii) spent on attending meetings and making Site visits in accordance with Rule 3 of the DAAB Rules, and writing reports in accordance with Rule 3.10 of the DAAB Rules;

(iii) spent on giving Informal Assistance;

(iv) spent on preparing and attending hearings (and, in case of a three-member DAAB, attending meeting(s) between the DAAB Members in accordance with sub-paragraph (a) of Rule 8.2 of the DAAB Rules, and communicating with the Other Members); and

(v) spent on preparing decisions, including studying written documentation and arguments from the Parties.

(c) all reasonable expenses, including necessary travel expenses (air fare in business class or equivalent, hotel and subsistence and other direct travel expenses, including visa charges) incurred in connection with the DAAB Member's duties, as well as the cost of internet access, courier charges and faxes. The DAAB Member shall provide the Parties with a receipt for each item of expenses;

(d) any taxes properly levied in the Country on payments made to the DAAB Member (unless a national or permanent resident of the Country) under this Sub-Clause 9.1.

9.2 Subject to Sub-Clause 9.3 below, the amounts of the DAAB Member's monthly fee and daily fee, under Sub-Clause 9.1 above, shall be as specified in the DAAB Agreement signed by the Parties and the DAAB Member.

9.3 If the DAAB Member has been appointed by the appointing official, the amounts of the DAAB Member's monthly fee and daily fee, under Sub-Clause 9.1 above, shall be as referred to under sub-paragraph (i) of Sub-Clause 21.2 [*Failure to Appoint DAAB Member(s)*] of the Conditions of Contract.

9.4 The DAAB Member shall submit invoices for payment of the monthly fee and air fares quarterly in advance. Invoices for other expenses and for daily fees shall be submitted following the conclusion of a meeting, Site visit or hearing; and following the giving of a decision or an informal written note (under Rule 2.1 of the DAAB Rules). All invoices shall be accompanied by a brief description of the DAAB's Activities performed during the relevant period and shall be addressed to the Contractor.

9.5 The Contractor shall pay each of the DAAB Member's invoices in full within 28 days after receiving each invoice. Thereafter, the Contractor shall apply to the Employer (in the Statements under the Contract) for reimbursement of one-half of the amounts of these invoices. The Employer shall then pay the Contractor in accordance with the Contract.

9.6 If the Contractor fails to pay to the DAAB Member the amount to which he/she is entitled under the DAAB Agreement within the period of 28 days stated at Sub-Clause 9.5 above, the DAAB Member shall inform the Employer who shall promptly pay the amount due to the DAAB Member and any other amount which may be required to maintain the function of the DAAB. Thereafter the Employer shall, by written request, be entitled to payment from the Contractor of:

(a) all sums paid in excess of one-half of these amounts;
(b) the reasonable costs of recovering these amounts from the Contractor; and
(c) financing charges calculated at the rate specified in Sub-Clause 14.9 [*Delayed Payment*] of the Conditions of Contract.

The Employer shall be entitled to such payment from the Contractor without any requirement to comply with Sub-Clause 20.2 [*Claims for Payment and/ or EOT*] of the Conditions of Contract, and without prejudice to any other right or remedy.

9.7 If the DAAB Member does not receive payment of the amount due within 56 days after submitting a valid invoice, the DAAB Member may:

(a) not less than 7 days after giving a Notification to the Parties and the Other Members (if any), suspend his/her services until the payment is received; and/or
(b) without prejudice to his/her other rights or remedies, resign his/her appointment by giving a Notification under Sub-Clause 10.1 below.

10 Resignation and Termination	10.1	The DAAB Member may resign at any time for any reason, by giving a Notification of not less than 28 days (or other period as may be agreed by the Parties) to the Parties and to the Other Members (if any). During this period the Parties shall take the necessary steps to appoint, without delay, a replacement DAAB Member in accordance with Sub-Clause 21.1 [*Constitution of the DAAB*] of the Conditions of Contract (and, if applicable, Sub-Clause 21.2 [*Failure to Appoint DAAB Member(s)*] of the Conditions of Contract).
	10.2	On expiry of the period stated in Sub-Clause 10.1 above, the resigning DAAB Member's DAAB Agreement shall terminate with immediate effect. However (except if the DAAB Member is unable to act as a result of illness or disability) if, on the date of the DAAB Member's Notification under Sub-Clause 10.1 above, the DAAB is dealing with any Dispute under Sub-Clause 21.4 [*Obtaining DAAB's Decision*] of the Conditions of Contract, the DAAB Member's resignation shall not take effect and his/her DAAB Agreement shall not terminate until after the DAAB has given all the corresponding decisions in accordance with the Contract.
	10.3	At any time the Parties may jointly terminate the DAAB Agreement by giving a Notification of not less than 42 days to the DAAB Member.
	10.4	If the DAAB Member fails, without justifiable excuse, to comply with Sub-Clause 5.1 above, the Parties may, without prejudice to their other rights or remedies, jointly terminate his/her DAAB Agreement by giving a Notification (by recorded delivery) to the DAAB Member. This notice shall take effect when it is received by the DAAB Member.
	10.5	If either Party fails, without justifiable excuse, to comply with Clause 6 above, the DAAB Member may, without prejudice to his/her other rights or remedies, terminate the DAAB Agreement by giving a Notification to the Parties. This notice shall take effect when received by both Parties.
	10.6	Any resignation or termination under this Clause shall be final and binding on the Parties and the DAAB Member. However, a notice given under Sub-Clause 10.3 or 10.4 above by either the Employer or the Contractor, but not by both, shall be of no effect.

	10.7	Subject to sub-paragraph (b) of Sub-Clause 11.5 below, in the event of resignation or termination under this Clause the DAAB Member shall nevertheless be entitled to payment of any fees and/or expenses under his/her DAAB Agreement that remain outstanding as of the date of termination of his/her DAAB Agreement.
	10.8	After resignation by the DAAB Member or termination of his/her DAAB Agreement under this Clause, the DAAB Member shall: (a) remain bound by his/her obligation of confidentiality under Sub-Clause 7.1 above; and (b) return the original of any document in his/her possession to the Party who submitted such document in connection with the DAAB's Activities, at that Party's written request and cost.
	10.9	Subject to any mandatory requirements under the governing law of the DAAB Agreement, termination of the DAAB Agreement under this Clause shall require no action of whatsoever kind by the Parties or the DAAB Member (as the case may be) other than as stated in this Clause.
11 **Challenge**	11.1	The Parties shall not object against the DAAB Member, except that either Party shall be entitled to do so for an alleged lack of independence or impartiality or otherwise in which case Rule 10 and Rule 11 of the DAAB Rules shall apply.
	11.2	The decision issued under Rule 11 of the DAAB Rules (the 'Decision on the Challenge' in the GCs) shall be final and conclusive.
	11.3	At any time before the Decision on the Challenge is issued, the challenged DAAB Member may resign under Sub-Clause 10.1 above and, in such case, the challenging Party shall inform the International Chamber of Commerce (ICC). However, Sub-Clause 10.2 shall not apply to such resignation and the resigning DAAB Member's DAAB Agreement shall terminate with immediate effect.
	11.4	Unless the challenged DAAB Member has resigned, or his/her DAAB Agreement has been terminated under Sub-Clause 10.3 above, the DAAB Member and the Other Members (if any) shall continue with the DAAB's Activities until the Decision on the Challenge is issued.

11.5. If the Decision on the Challenge is that the challenge is successful:

(a) the challenged DAAB Member's appointment, and his/her DAAB Agreement, shall be deemed to have been terminated with immediate effect on the date of the notification of the Decision on the Challenge by ICC;

(b) the challenged DAAB Member shall not be entitled to any fees or expenses under his/her DAAB Agreement from the date of the notification of the Decision on the Challenge by ICC;

(c) any decision under Sub-Clause 21.4.3 [*The DAAB's decision*] of the Conditions of Contract, given by the DAAB:

(i) after the challenge was referred under Rule 11 of the DAAB Rules, and

(ii) before the resignation (if any) of the challenged DAAB Member under Sub-Clause 11.3 above, or his/her DAAB Agreement is terminated under sub-paragraph (a) above or under Sub-Clause 10.3 above

shall become void and ineffective. In the case of a sole-member DAAB, all other DAAB's Activities during this period shall also become void and ineffective. In the case of a three-member DAAB, all other DAAB's Activities during this period shall remain unaffected by the Decision on the Challenge except if there has been a challenge to all three members of the DAAB and such challenge is successful;

(d) the successfully challenged DAAB Member shall be removed from the DAAB; and

(e) the Parties shall, without delay, appoint a replacement DAAB Member in accordance with Sub-Clause 21.1 [*Constitution of the DAAB*] of the Conditions of Contract.

12 Disputes under the DAAB Agreement Any dispute arising out of or in connection with the DAAB Agreement, or the breach, termination or invalidity thereof, shall be finally settled by arbitration under the Rules of Arbitration of the International Chamber of Commerce by one arbitrator appointed in accordance with these Rules of Arbitration, and the Expedited Procedure Rules of these Rules of Arbitration shall apply.

Annex[*]

DAAB PROCEDURAL RULES

Rule 1 Objectives	1.1	The objectives of these Rules are: (a) to facilitate the avoidance of Disputes that might otherwise arise between the Parties; and (b) to achieve the expeditious, efficient and cost effective resolution of any Dispute that arises between the Parties.
	1.2	These Rules shall be interpreted, the DAAB's Activities shall be conducted and the DAAB shall use its powers under the Contract and these Rules, in the manner necessary to achieve the above objectives.
Rule 2 Avoidance of Disputes	2.1	Where Sub-Clause 21.3 [*Avoidance of Disputes*] of the Conditions of Contract applies, the DAAB (in the case of a three-member DAAB, all three DAAB Members acting together) may give Informal Assistance during discussions at any meeting with the Parties (whether face-to-face or online) or at any Site visit or by an informal written note to the Parties.
Rule 3 Meetings and Site Visits	3.1	The purpose of meetings with the Parties and Site visits by the DAAB is to enable the DAAB to: (a) become and remain informed about the matters described in sub-paragraphs (d)(i) to (d)(iii) of Sub-Clause 5.1 of the GCs; (b) become aware of, and remain informed about, any actual or potential issue or disagreement between the Parties; and (c) give Informal Assistance if and when jointly requested by the Parties.

* Note: This is an annex to the General Conditions of the DAAB Agreement.

3.2 As soon as practicable after the DAAB is appointed, the DAAB shall convene an introductory meeting with the Parties. The date, time and type (online or in-person) of, and agenda for, the introductory meeting shall be set by the DAAB in consultation with the Parties. At this meeting, the DAAB shall establish a schedule of planned meetings and Site visits in consultation with the Parties, which schedule shall reflect the requirements of Rule 3.3 below and shall be subject to adjustment by the DAAB in consultation with the Parties.

3.3 The DAAB shall hold meetings with the Parties, and visit the Site, at regular intervals and/or at the written request of either Party. The frequency of such meetings and Site visits shall be:

(a) sufficient to achieve the purpose under Rule 3.1 above;

(b) at intervals of not more than 140 days unless otherwise agreed jointly by the Parties and the DAAB; and

(c) at intervals of not less than 70 days, subject to Rules 3.5 and 3.6 below and except as required to conduct a hearing as described under Rule 7 below, unless otherwise agreed jointly by the Parties and the DAAB.

Each such meeting shall be face-to-face and each Site visit shall be in-person, unless the Parties and the DAAB agree that exceptional circumstances mean that it would be prudent for the meeting and Site visit to be carried out online. The date, time and agenda for each such meeting and Site visit shall be set by the DAAB in consultation with the Parties.

3.4 In addition to the meetings referred to in Rules 3.2 and 3.3 above, the DAAB may also hold meetings with the Parties online.

3.5 At times of critical construction events (which may include suspension of the Works or termination of the Contract), the DAAB shall visit the Site at the written request of either Party. This request shall describe the critical construction event. If the DAAB becomes aware of an upcoming critical construction event, it may invite the Parties to make such a request.

3.6 Either Party may request an urgent meeting or Site visit by the DAAB. This shall be a written request and shall give reasons for the urgency of the meeting or Site visit. If the DAAB agrees that such a meeting or Site visit is urgent, the DAAB Members shall use all reasonable endeavours to:

(a) hold a meeting with the Parties online within 3 days after receiving the request; and

(b) if requested and (having given the other Party opportunity at this meeting to respond to or oppose this request) the DAAB agrees that an in-person Site visit is necessary, visit the Site within 14 days after the date of this meeting.

3.7 The time of, and agenda for, each meeting and Site visit shall be set by the DAAB in consultation with the Parties.

3.8 Each meeting and Site visit shall be attended by the Employer, the Contractor and the Engineer.

3.9 Each meeting and Site visit shall be co-ordinated by the Contractor in co-operation with the Employer and the Engineer. The Contractor shall ensure the provision of appropriate:

(a) personal safety equipment, security controls (if necessary) and site transport for each Site visit;

(b) meeting room/conference facilities and secretarial and copying services for each face-to-face meeting; and

(c) access to an online video conference platform for each online meeting and Site visit.

3.10 At the conclusion of each meeting and Site visit and, if possible before leaving the venue of the face-to-face meeting or the Site (as the case may be) but in any event within 7 days, the DAAB shall prepare a report on its activities during the meeting or Site visit and shall send copies of this report to the Parties and the Engineer.

Rule 4 Communications and Documentation

4.1 The language to be used:

(a) in all communications to and from the DAAB and the Parties (and, in the case of a three-member DAAB, between the DAAB Members);

(b) in all reports and decisions issued by the DAAB; and

(c) during all Site visits, meetings and hearings relating to the DAAB's Activities

shall be the language for communications defined in Sub-Clause 1.4 [*Law and Language*] of the Conditions of Contract, unless otherwise agreed jointly by the Parties and the DAAB.

4.2 All communications and/or documents sent between the DAAB and a Party shall simultaneously be copied to the other Party. In the case of a three-member DAAB, the sending Party shall send all communications and/or documents to the chairperson of the DAAB and simultaneously send copies of these communications and/or documents to the Other Members.

4.3 The Parties shall provide the DAAB with a copy of all documents which the DAAB may request, including:

(a) the documents forming the Contract;

(b) progress reports under Sub-Clause 4.20 [*Progress Reports*] of the Conditions of Contract;

(c) the initial programme and each revised programme under Sub-Clause 8.3 [*Programme*] of the Conditions of Contract;

(d) relevant instructions given by the Engineer, and Variations under Clause 13.3 [*Variation Procedure*] of the Conditions of Contract;

(e) Statements submitted by the Contractor, and all certificates issued by the Engineer under the Contract;

(f) relevant Notices;

(g) relevant communications between the Parties and between either Party and the Engineer

and any other document relevant to the performance of the Contract and/or necessary to enable the DAAB to become and remain informed about the matters described in sub-paragraphs (d)(i) to (d)(iii) of Sub-Clause 5.1 of the GCs.

Rule 5 Powers of the DAAB

5.1 In addition to the powers granted to the DAAB under the Conditions of Contract, the General Conditions of the DAAB Agreement and elsewhere in these Rules, the Parties empower the DAAB to:

(a) establish the procedure to be applied in making Site visits and/or giving Informal Assistance;
(b) establish the procedure to be applied in giving decisions under the Conditions of Contract;
(c) decide on the DAAB's own jurisdiction, and the scope of any Dispute referred to the DAAB;
(d) appoint one or more experts (including legal and technical expert(s)), with the agreement of the Parties;
(e) decide whether or not there shall be a hearing (or more than one hearing, if necessary) in respect of any Dispute referred to the DAAB;
(f) conduct any meeting with the Parties and/or any hearing as the DAAB thinks fit, not being bound by any rules or procedures for the hearing other than those contained in the Contract and in these Rules;
(g) take the initiative in ascertaining the facts and matters required for a DAAB decision;
(h) make use of a DAAB Member's own specialist knowledge, if any;
(i) decide on the payment of financing charges in accordance with the Contract;
(j) decide on any provisional relief such as interim or conservatory measures;
(k) open up, review and revise any certificate, decision, determination, instruction, opinion or valuation of (or acceptance, agreement, approval, consent, disapproval, No-objection, permission, or similar act by) the Engineer that is relevant to the Dispute; and
(l) proceed with the DAAB's Activities in the absence of a Party who, after receiving a Notification from the DAAB, fails to comply with Sub-Clause 6.3 of the GCs.

5.2 The DAAB shall have discretion to decide whether and to what extent any powers granted to the DAAB, under the Conditions of Contract, the GCs and these Rules, may be exercised.

Rule 6 Disputes

6.1 If any Dispute is referred to the DAAB in accordance with Sub-Clause 21.4.1 [*Reference of a Dispute to the DAAB*] of the Conditions of Contract, the DAAB shall proceed in accordance with Sub-Clause 21.4 [*Obtaining DAAB's Decision*] of the Conditions of Contract and these DAAB Rules, or as otherwise agreed by the Parties in writing.

6.2 The DAAB shall act fairly and impartially between the Parties and, taking due regard of the period under Sub-Clause 21.4.3 [*The DAAB's decision*] of the Conditions of Contract and other relevant circumstances, the DAAB shall:

(a) give each Party a reasonable opportunity (consistent with the expedited nature of the DAAB proceeding) of putting forward its case and responding to the other Party's case; and

(b) adopt a procedure in coming to its decision that is suitable to the Dispute, avoiding unnecessary delay and/or expense.

Rule 7 Hearings

7.1 In addition to the powers under Rule 5.1 above, and except as otherwise agreed in writing by the Parties, the DAAB shall have power to:

(a) decide on the date and place for any hearing, in consultation with the Parties;

(b) decide on the duration of any hearing;

(c) request that written documentation and arguments from the Parties be submitted to it prior to the hearing;

(d) adopt an inquisitorial procedure during any hearing:

(e) request the production of documents, and/or oral submissions by the Parties, at any hearing that the DAAB considers may assist in exercising the DAAB's power under sub-paragraph (g) of Rule 5.1 above;

(f) request the attendance of persons at any hearing that the DAAB considers may assist in exercising the DAAB's power under sub-paragraph (g) of Rule 5.1 above;

(g) refuse admission to any hearing, or audience at any hearing, to any persons other than representatives of the Employer, the Contractor and the Engineer;

(h) proceed in the absence of any party who the DAAB is satisfied received timely notice of the hearing;

(i) adjourn any hearing as and when the DAAB considers further investigation by one Party or both Parties would benefit resolution of the Dispute, for such time as the investigation is carried out, and resume the hearing promptly thereafter.

7.2 The DAAB shall not express any opinions during any hearing concerning the merits of any arguments advanced by either Party in respect of the Dispute.

7.3 The DAAB shall not give any Informal Assistance during a hearing, but if the Parties request Informal Assistance during any hearing:

(a) the hearing shall be adjourned for such time as the DAAB is giving Informal Assistance;

(b) if the hearing is so adjourned for longer than 2 days, the period under Sub-Clause 21.4.3 [*The DAAB's decision*] of the Conditions of Contract shall be temporarily suspended until the date that the hearing is resumed; and

(c) the hearing shall be resumed promptly after the DAAB has given such Informal Assistance.

Rule 8 The DAAB's Decision

8.1 The DAAB shall make and give its decision within the time allowed under Sub-Clause 21.4 [*Obtaining DAAB's Decision*] of the Conditions of Contract, or other time as may be proposed by the DAAB and agreed by the Parties in writing.

8.2 In the case of a three-member DAAB:

(a) it shall meet in private (after the hearing, if any) in order to have discussions and to start preparation of its decision;

(b) the DAAB Members shall use all reasonable endeavours to reach a unanimous decision;

(c) if it is not possible for the DAAB Members to reach a unanimous decision, the applicable decision shall be made by a majority of the DAAB Members, who may require the minority DAAB Member to prepare a separate written report (with reasons and supporting particulars) which shall be issued to the Parties; and

(d) if a DAAB Member fails to:

(i) attend a hearing (if any) or a DAAB Members' meeting; or

(ii) fulfil any required function (other than agreeing to a unanimous decision)

the Other Members shall nevertheless proceed to make a decision, unless:

- such failure has been caused by exceptional circumstances, of which the Other Members and the Parties have received a Notification from the DAAB Member;
- the DAAB Member has suspended his services under sub-paragraph (a) of Sub-Clause 9.7 of the GCs; or
- otherwise agreed by the Parties in writing.

8.3 If, after giving a decision, the DAAB finds (and, in the case of a three-member DAAB, they agree unanimously or by majority) that the decision contained any error:

(a) of a typographical or clerical nature; or
(b) of an arithmetical nature

the chairperson of the DAAB or the sole DAAB Member (as the case may be) shall, within 14 days after giving this decision, advise the Parties of the error and issue an addendum to its original decision in writing to the Parties.

8.4 If, within 14 days of receiving a decision from the DAAB, either Party finds a typographical, clerical or arithmetical error in the decision, that Party may request the DAAB to correct such error. This shall be a written request and shall clearly identify the error.

8.5 If, within 14 days of receiving a decision from the DAAB, either Party believes that such decision contains an ambiguity, that Party may request clarification from the DAAB. This shall be a written request and shall clearly identify the ambiguity.

8.6 The DAAB shall respond to a request under Rule 8.4 or Rule 8.5 above within 14 days of receiving the request. The DAAB may decline (at its sole discretion and with no requirement to give reasons) any request for clarification under Rule 8.5. If the DAAB agrees (in the case of a three-member DAAB they agree unanimously or by majority) that the decision did contain the error or ambiguity as described in the request, it may correct its decision by issuing an addendum to its original decision in writing to the Parties, in which case this addendum shall be issued together with the DAAB's response under this Rule.

8.7 If the DAAB issues an addendum to its original decision under Rule 8.3 or 8.6 above, such an addendum shall form part of the decision and the period stated in sub-paragraph (c) of Sub-Clause 21.4.4 [*Dissatisfaction with DAAB's decision*] of the Conditions of Contract shall be calculated from the date the Parties receive this addendum.

Rule 9 In the event of Termination of DAAB Agreement	9.1	If, on the date of termination of a DAAB Member's DAAB Agreement arising from resignation or termination under Clause 10 of the GCs, the DAAB is dealing with any Dispute under Sub-Clause 21.4 [*Obtaining DAAB's Decision*] of the Conditions of Contract: (a) the period under Sub-Clause 21.4.3 [*The DAAB's decision*] of the Conditions of Contract shall be temporarily suspended; and (b) when a replacement DAAB Member is appointed in accordance with Sub-Clause 21.1 [*Constitution of the DAAB*] of the Conditions of Contract, the full period under Sub-Clause 21.4.3 [*The DAAB's decision*] of the Conditions of Contract shall apply from the date of this replacement DAAB Member's appointment.
	9.2	In the case of a three-member DAAB and if one DAAB Member's DAAB Agreement is terminated as a result of resignation or termination under Clause 10 of the GCs, the Other Members shall continue as members of the DAAB except that they shall not conduct any hearing or make any decision prior to the replacement of the DAAB Member unless otherwise agreed jointly by the Parties and the Other Members.
Rule 10 Objection Procedure	10.1	The following procedure shall apply to any objection against a DAAB Member: (a) the objecting Party shall, within 7 days of becoming aware of the facts and/or events giving rise to the objection, give a Notification to the DAAB Member of its objection. This Notification shall: (i) state that it is given under this Rule; (ii) state the reason(s) for the objection; (iii) substantiate the objection by setting out the facts, and describing the events, on which the objection is based, with supporting particulars; and (iv) be simultaneously copied to the other Party and the Other Members; (b) within 7 days after receiving a notice under sub-paragraph (a) above, the objected DAAB Member shall respond to the objecting Party. This response shall be simultaneously copied to the other Party and the Other Members. If no response is given by the DAAB Member within this period of 7 days, the DAAB Member shall

be deemed to have given a response denying the matters on which the objection is based;

(c) within 7 days after receiving the objected DAAB Member's response under sub-paragraph (b) above (or, if there is no such response, after expiry of the period of 7 days stated in sub-paragraph (b) above) the objecting Party may formally challenge a DAAB member in accordance with Rule 11 below;

(d) if the challenge is not referred within the period of 7 days stated in sub-paragraph (c) above, the objecting Party shall be deemed to have agreed to the DAAB Member remaining on the DAAB and shall not be entitled to object and/or challenge him/her thereafter on the basis of any of the facts and/or evidence stated in the notice given under sub-paragraph (a) above;

Rule 11 Challenge Procedure

11.1 If and when the objecting Party challenges a DAAB Member, within 21 days of learning of the facts upon which the challenge is based, the provisions of this Rule shall apply. Any challenge is to be decided by the International Chamber of Commerce (ICC) and administered by the ICC International Centre for ADR.

11.2 The procedure for such challenge and information on associated charges to be paid are set out at http://fidic.org and http://iccwbo.org.

Appendix 5

Forms of Securities

Annexes FORMS OF SECURITIES

Acceptable form(s) of security should be included in the tender documents: for Annex A and/or B, in the Instructions to Tenderers; and for Annexes C to G, annexed to the Particular Conditions. The following example forms, which (except for Annex A) incorporate Uniform Rules published by the International Chamber of Commerce (the 'ICC', which is based at 33-43 Avenue du Président Wilson, 75116 Paris, France, www.iccwbo.org), need to be carefully reviewed against, and may have to be amended to comply with, applicable law. Although the ICC publishes guides to these Uniform Rules, legal advice should be taken before the securities are written. Note that the guaranteed amounts should be quoted in all the currencies, as specified in the Contract, in which the guarantor pays the beneficiary.

ANNEX A

Example Form of Parent Company Guarantee

Name of Contract/Contract No.: ______________ Name and address of Employer: ______________ (together with successors and assigns).

We have been informed that ______________ (hereinafter called the "Contractor") is submitting an offer for such Contract in response to your invitation, and that the conditions of your invitation require his/her offer to be supported by a parent company guarantee.

In consideration of you, the Employer, awarding the Contract to the Contractor, we (name of parent company) irrevocably and unconditionally guarantee to you, as a primary obligation, the due performance of all the Contractor's obligations and liabilities under the Contract, including the Contractor's compliance with all its terms and conditions according to their true intent and meaning.

If the Contractor fails to so perform his/her obligations and liabilities and comply with the Contract, we will indemnify the Employer against and from all damages, losses and expenses (including legal fees and expenses) which arise from any such failure for which the Contractor is liable to the Employer under the Contract.

This guarantee shall come into full force and effect when the Contract comes into full force and effect. If the Contract does not come into full force and effect within a year of the date of this guarantee, or if you demonstrate that you do not intend to enter into the Contract with the Contractor, this guarantee shall be void and ineffective. This guarantee shall continue in full force and effect until all the Contractor's obligations and liabilities under the Contract have been discharged, when this guarantee shall expire and shall be returned to us, and our liability hereunder shall be discharged absolutely.

This guarantee shall apply and be supplemental to the Contract as amended or varied by the Employer and the Contractor from time to time. We hereby authorise them to agree any such amendment or variation, the due performance of which and compliance with which by the Contractor are likewise guaranteed hereunder. Our obligations and liabilities under this guarantee shall not be discharged by any allowance of time or other indulgence whatsoever by the Employer to the Contractor, or by any variation or suspension of the works to be executed under the Contract, or by any amendments to the Contract or to the constitution of the Contractor or the Employer, or by any other matters, whether with or without our knowledge or consent.

This guarantee shall be governed by the law of the same country (or other jurisdiction) as that which governs the Contract and any dispute under this guarantee shall be finally settled under the Rules of Arbitration of the International Chamber of Commerce by one or more arbitrators appointed in accordance with such Rules. We confirm that the benefit of this guarantee may be assigned subject only to the provisions for assignment of the Contract.

SIGNED by: ____________________ SIGNED by[1]: ____________________

(signature) *(signature)*

____________________ ____________________

(name) *(name)*

____________________ ____________________

(position in the company) *(position in the company)*

Date: ____________________

[1]Whether one or more signatories for the parent company are required will depend on the parent company and/or applicable law.

Annex B

Example Form of Tender Security

Guarantee No.: ____________ [*insert guarantee reference number*]

The Guarantor: ____________ [*insert name and address of place of issue, unless indicated in the letterhead*]

Name of Contract/Contract No.: ____________ [*insert reference number or other information identifying the contract with regard to which the tender is submitted*]

The Beneficiary (the "Employer"): ____________ [*insert name and address of the Beneficiary*]

We have been informed that ____________ [*insert name and address of the Tenderer*] (hereinafter called the "Applicant") is submitting an offer for such Contract in response to your invitation, and that the conditions of your invitation (the "Conditions of Invitation", which are set out in a document entitled Instructions to Tenderers) require his/her offer to be supported by a tender security.

At the request of the Applicant, we ____________ [*insert name of Guarantor*] hereby irrevocably undertake to pay you, the Beneficiary/Employer, any sum or sums not exceeding in total the amount of ____________ [*insert in figures and words the maximum amount payable and the currency in which it is payable*] upon receipt by us of your demand in writing and your written statement (in the demand) that:

(a) the Applicant has, without your agreement, withdrawn his/her offer after the latest time specified for its submission and before the expiry of its period of validity, or
(b) the Applicant has refused to accept the correction of errors in his/her offer in accordance with such Conditions of Invitation, or
(c) you awarded the Contract to the Applicant and he/she has failed to comply with Sub-Clause 1.6 of the Conditions of Contract, or
(d) you awarded the Contract to the Applicant and he/she has failed to comply with Sub-Clause 4.2.1 of the Conditions of Contract.

Any demand for payment must contain your signature(s) which must be authenticated by your bankers or by a notary public. The authenticated demand and statement must be received by us at the following office [insert address of office] on or before __________________ [*insert the date 35 days after the expiry of the validity of the Letter of Tender*], when this guarantee shall expire.

The party liable for the payment of any charges: ____________ [*insert the name of the party*].

This guarantee shall be governed by the laws of ____________ [*insert the law governing the guarantee*], and shall be subject to the Uniform Rules for Demand Guarantees (URDG) 2010 Revision, ICC Publication No. 758.

SIGNED by: ________________ *(signature)* SIGNED by[1]: ________________ *(signature)*

________________ *(name)* ________________ *(name)*

Date: ________________

[1] Whether one or more signatories for the bank are required will depend on the bank and/or applicable law.

Annex C

Example Form of Performance Security – Demand Guarantee

Guarantee No.: ______________________ *[insert guarantee reference number]*

The Guarantor: ______________________ *[insert name and address of place of issue, unless indicated in the letterhead]*

Name of Contract/Contract No.: ______________________ *[insert reference number or other information identifying the contract between the Applicant and the Beneficiary on which the guarantee is based]*

The Beneficiary (the "Employer"): ______________________ *[insert name and address of the Beneficiary]*

We have been informed that ______________________ *[insert name and address of the Contractor]* (hereinafter called the "Applicant") is your Contractor under such Contract, which requires him/her to obtain a Performance Security.

At the request of the Applicant, we ______________________ *[insert name of Guarantor]* hereby irrevocably undertake to pay you, the Beneficiary/Employer, any sum or sums not exceeding in total the amount of ______________________ *[insert in figures and words the maximum amount payable and the currency in which it is payable]* (the "Guaranteed Amount") upon receipt by us of your demand in writing and your written statement indicating in what respect the Applicant is in breach of its obligations under the Contract.

[Following receipt by us of an authenticated copy of the Taking-Over Certificate for the whole of the Works under Clause 10 of the Conditions of Contract, the Guaranteed Amount shall be reduced by ________% and we shall promptly notify you that we have received such certificate and have reduced the Guaranteed Amount accordingly.][(1)]

Following receipt by us of an authenticated copy of a statement issued by ____________________ [*insert name and address of the Engineer under the Contract*] that, pursuant to Sub-Clause 4.2.1 of the Conditions of Contract, variations or adjustments under Clause 13 of the Conditions of Contract have resulted in an accumulative increase or decrease of the Contract Price by more than twenty percent (20%) of the Accepted Contract Amount, and that therefore the Guaranteed Amount should be adjusted by the percentage specified in the statement equal to the accumulative increase or decrease, respectively, we shall promptly inform you that we have received such statement and have adjusted the Guaranteed Amount accordingly. In the case of a request for a decrease of the amount of the Performance Security, the above statement shall be accompanied by your written consent to such decrease.

Any demand for payment must contain your signature(s) which must be authenticated by your bankers or by a notary public. The authenticated demand and statement must be received by us at the following office [insert address of office] on or before ____________________ (*insert the date 70 days after the expected expiry of the Defects Notification Period for the Works*) (the "Expiry Date"), when this guarantee shall expire.

The party liable for the payment of any charges: ____________ [*insert the name of the party*].

This guarantee shall be governed by the laws of [*insert the law governing the guarantee*], and shall be subject to the Uniform Rules for Demand Guarantees, (URDG) 2010 Revision, ICC Publication No. 758.

SIGNED by: ____________	SIGNED by[(2)]: ____________
(signature)	*(signature)*
____________	____________
(name)	*(name)*

Date: ____________________

[1] When drafting the tender documents, the writer should ascertain whether to include the optional text, shown in parentheses [ ].

[2] Whether one or more signatories for the bank are required will depend on the bank and/or applicable law.

--ooOOoo--

Annex D

Example Form of Performance Security – Surety Bond

Name of Contract/Contract No.: ____________________ Name and address of Beneficiary (the "Employer"): ____________________

We have been informed that ____________________ [*insert name of the Contractor*] (hereinafter called the "Principal") is your contractor under such Contract, which requires him/her to obtain a Performance Security.

By this Bond, ____________________ [*insert name and address of the Contractor*]

(who is your Contractor under such Contract) as Principal and: ______________ [*insert name and address of Guarantor*] as Guarantor are irrevocably held and firmly bound to the Beneficiary in the total amount of ____________________ [*insert in figures and words the maximum amount payable and the currency in which it is payable*] (the "Bond Amount") for the due performance of all such Principal's obligations and liabilities under the above named Contract.

[Such Bond Amount shall be reduced by ____________________ % upon the issue of the Taking-Over Certificate for the whole of the Works under Clause 10 of the Conditions of Contract.][(1)]

This Bond shall become effective on the Commencement Date defined in the Contract.

Upon Default by the Principal to perform any contractual obligation, or upon the occurrence of any of the events and circumstances listed in Sub-Clause 15.2.1 of the Conditions of Contract, the Guarantor shall satisfy and discharge the damages sustained by the Beneficiary due to such Default, event or circumstances.[2] However, the total liability of the Guarantor shall not exceed the Bond Amount.

The obligations and liabilities of the Guarantor shall not be discharged by any allowance of time or other indulgence whatsoever by the Beneficiary to the Principal, or by any variation or suspension of the Works to be executed under the Contract, or by any amendments to the Contract or to the constitution of the Principal or the Beneficiary, or by any other matters, whether with or without the knowledge or consent of the Guarantor.

Any claim under this Bond must be received by the Guarantor on or before __________________ [*insert the date six months after the expected expiry of the Defects Notification Period for the Works*] (the "Expiry Date"), when this Bond shall expire and shall be returned to the Guarantor.

The benefit of this Bond may be assigned subject to the provisions for assignment of the Contract, and subject to the receipt by the Guarantor of evidence of full compliance with such provisions.

This Bond shall be governed by the law of __________________ [*insert the law governing the bond*] being the same country (or other jurisdiction) as that which governs the Contract. This Bond incorporates and shall be subject to the Uniform Rules for Contract Bonds, published as number 524 by the International Chamber of Commerce, and words used in this Bond shall bear the meanings set out in such Rules.

Whereas this Bond has been issued by the Principal and the Guarantor on __________________ [*date*]

Signatures for and on behalf of the Principal[3]:

__________________	__________________
(signature)	*(signature)*
__________________	__________________
(name)	*(name)*

Signatures for and on behalf of the Guarantor[4]:

__________________	__________________
(signature)	*(signature)*

____________________ ____________________

(name) *(name)*

(1) When writing the tender documents, the writer should ascertain whether to include the optional text, shown in parentheses [ ].

(2) Insert: [and shall not be entitled to perform the Principal's obligations under the Contract.]
Or: [or at the option of the Guarantor (to be exercised in writing within 42 days of receiving the claim specifying such Default) perform the Principal's obligations under the Contract.]

(3) Whether one or more signatories for the Principal are required will depend on the Principal and/or applicable law.

(4) Whether one or more signatories for the Guarantor are required will depend on the Guarantor and/ or applicable law.

--ooOOoo--

ANNEX E

Example Form of Advance Payment Guarantee

Guarantee No.: ____________________ [*insert guarantee reference number*]

The Guarantor: ____________________ [*insert name and address of place of issue, unless indicated in the letterhead*]

Name of Contract/Contract No.: ____________________ [*insert reference number or other information identifying the contract between the Applicant and the Beneficiary on which the guarantee is based*]

The Beneficiary (the "Employer"): ____________________ [*insert name and address of the Beneficiary*]

We have been informed that ____________________ [*insert name and address of the Contractor*] (hereinafter called the "Applicant") is your Contractor under such Contract and wishes to receive an advance payment, for which the Contract requires him/her to obtain a guarantee.

At the request of the Applicant, we ____________________ [*insert name of Guarantor*] hereby irrevocably undertake to pay you, the Beneficiary/Employer, any sum or sums not exceeding in total the amount of ____________________ [*insert in figures and words the maximum amount payable and the currency in which it is payable*] (the "Guaranteed Amount") upon receipt by us of your demand in writing and your written statement that:

(a) the Applicant has failed to repay the advance payment in accordance with the Conditions of Contract, and

(b) the amount of the advance payment which the Applicant has failed to repay.

This guarantee shall become effective upon receipt [*of the first instalment*] of the advance payment by the Applicant. The Guaranteed Amount shall be reduced by the amounts of the advance payment repaid to you, as evidenced by interim payment certificates issued under Sub-Clause 14.6 of the Conditions of Contract. Following receipt of a copy of each interim payment certificate, we shall promptly notify you of the revised Guaranteed Amount accordingly.

Any demand for payment must contain your signature(s) which must be authenticated by your bankers or by a notary public. The authenticated demand and statement must be received by us at the following office [*insert address of office*] on or before ____________ [*insert the date 70 days after the expected expiry of the Time for Completion*] (the "Expiry Date"), when this guarantee shall expire.

The party liable for the payment of any charges: ____________ [*insert the name of the party*].

This guarantee shall be governed by the laws of ____________ [*insert the law governing the guarantee*], and shall be subject to the Uniform Rules for Demand Guarantees (URDG) 2010 Revision, ICC Publication No. 758.

SIGNED by: ____________	SIGNED by[1]: ____________
(signature)	*(signature)*
____________ *(name)*	____________ *(name)*

Date: ____________

[1] *Whether one or more signatories for the bank are required will depend on the bank and/or applicable law.*

--ooOOoo--

Annex F

Example Form of Retention Money Guarantee

Guarantee No.: ____________________ [*insert guarantee reference number*]

The Guarantor: ____________________ [*insert name and address of place of issue, unless indicated in the letterhead*]

Name of Contract/Contract No.: ____________________ [*insert reference number or other information identifying the contract between the Applicant and the Beneficiary on which the guarantee is based*]

The Beneficiary (the "Employer"): ____________________ [*insert name and address of the Beneficiary*]

We have been informed that ____________________ [*insert name and address of the Contractor*] (hereinafter called the "Applicant") is your Contractor under such Contract and wishes to receive an early payment of [*part of*] the retention money, for which the Contract requires him/her to obtain a guarantee.

At the request of the Applicant, we ____________________ [*insert name of Guarantor*] hereby irrevocably undertake to pay you, the Beneficiary/Employer, any sum or sums not exceeding in total the amount of ____________________ [*insert in figures and words the maximum amount payable and the currency in which it is payable*] (the "Guaranteed Amount") upon receipt by us of your demand in writing and your written statement that the Applicant has failed to carry out his/her obligation(s) to rectify the following defect(s) for which he/she is responsible under the Contract [*state the nature of the defect(s)*].

At any time, our liability under this guarantee shall not exceed the total amount of retention money released to the Applicant by you, as evidenced by Interim Payment Certificates issued under Sub-Clause 14.6 of the Conditions of Contract with a copy being submitted to us.

Any demand for payment must contain your signature(s) which must be authenticated by your bankers or by a notary public. The authenticated demand and statement must be received by us at the following office [*insert address of office*] on or before ________________ [*insert the date 70 days after the expected expiry of the Defects Notification Period for the Works*], (the "Expiry Date"), when this guarantee shall expire.

We have been informed that the Beneficiary may require the Applicant to extend this guarantee if the Performance Certificate under the Contract has not been issued by the date 28 days prior to such Expiry Date. We undertake to pay you the Guaranteed Amount upon receipt by us, within such period of 28 days, of your demand in writing and your written statement that the Performance Certificate has not been issued, for reasons attributable to the Applicant, and that this guarantee has not been extended.

The party liable for the payment of any charges: ____________ [*insert the name of the party*].

This guarantee shall be governed by the laws of ____________ [*insert the law governing the guarantee*] and shall be subject to the Uniform Rules for Demand Guarantees (URDG) 2010 Revision, ICC Publication No. 758.

SIGNED by: ____________ *(signature)* SIGNED by[(1)]: ____________ *(signature)*

____________ *(name)* ____________ *(name)*

Date: ____________

[(1)] Whether one or more signatories for the bank are required will depend on the bank and/or applicable law.

Annex G

Example Form of Payment Guarantee By Employer

Guarantee No.: ______________________ *[insert guarantee reference number]*

The Guarantor: ______________________ *[insert name and address of place of issue, unless indicated in the letterhead]*

Name of Contract/Contract No.: ______________________ *[insert reference number or other information identifying the contract between the Applicant and the Beneficiary on which the guarantee is based]*

The Beneficiary (the "Contractor"): ______________________ *[insert name and address of the Beneficiary]*

We have been informed that ______________________ *[insert name and address of the Employer]* (hereinafter called the "Applicant") is required to obtain a bank guarantee.

At the request of the Applicant, we ______________________ *[insert name of Guarantor]* hereby irrevocably undertake to pay you, the Beneficiary/Contractor, any sum or sums not exceeding in total the amount of ______________________ *[insert in figures and words the maximum amount payable and the currency in which it is payable]* upon receipt by us of your demand in writing and your written statement that:

(a) in respect of a payment due under the Contract, the Applicant has failed to make payment in full by the date fourteen days after the expiry of the period specified in the Contract as that within which such payment should have been made, and
(b) the amount(s) which the Applicant has failed to pay.

Any demand for payment must be accompanied by a copy of ____________________ [*insert list of documents evidencing entitlement to payment and the language in which these documents are to be submitted*], in respect of which the Applicant has failed to make payment in full.

Any demand for payment must contain your signature(s) which must be authenticated by your bankers or by a notary public. The authenticated demand and statement must be received by us at the following office [address of office] on or before ____________________ [*insert the date six months after the expected expiry of the Defects Notification Period for the Works*] when this guarantee shall expire.

The party liable for the payment of any charges: ____________________ [*insert the name of the party*].

This guarantee shall be governed by the laws of ____________________ [*insert the law governing the guarantee*] and shall be subject to the Uniform Rules for Demand Guarantees (URDG) 2010 Revision, ICC Publication No. 758.

SIGNED by: ____________________ (*signature*) SIGNED by[(1)]: ____________________ (*signature*)

____________________ (*name*) ____________________ (*name*)

Date: ____________________

[(1)] *Whether one or more signatories for the bank are required will depend on the bank and/or applicable law.*

--ooOOoo--

Index

Note: Page numbers in *italics* denote *Figures* and page numbers in **bold** denote **Tables**. Unless otherwise indicated, references are to page numbers